THE JOSEPH SMITH PAPERS

Ronald K. Esplin

Matthew J. Grow

Matthew C. Godfrey

GENERAL EDITORS

PREVIOUSLY PUBLISHED

THE JOSEPH SMITH PAPERS

DOCUMENTS
VOLUME 5: OCTOBER 1835–JANUARY 1838

Brent M. Rogers
Elizabeth A. Kuehn
Christian K. Heimburger
Max H Parkin
Alexander L. Baugh
Steven C. Harper
VOLUME EDITORS

THE CHURCH
HISTORIAN'S
PRESS

www.josephsmithpapers.org

The Joseph Smith Papers Project is endorsed by
the National Historical Publications and Records Commission.

Art direction: Richard Erickson.
Cover design: Scott Eggers. Interior design: Richard Erickson and Scott M. Mooy.
Typography: Carolyn Call.

Library of Congress Cataloging-in-Publication Data

Documents / Dean C. Jessee, Ronald K. Esplin, Richard Lyman Bushman, Matthew J. Grow, general editors.
volumes cm — (The Joseph Smith papers)
Planned publication in 12 volumes.
Includes bibliographical references and index.
ISBN 978-1-60907-577-4 (hardbound: alk. paper; v. 1)
ISBN 978-1-60907-598-9 (hardbound: alk. paper; v. 2)
ISBN 978-1-60907-987-1 (hardbound: alk. paper; v. 3)
ISBN 978-1-62972-174-3 (hardbound: alk. paper; v. 4)
ISBN 978-1-62972-312-9 (hardbound: alk. paper; v. 5)
1. Church of Jesus Christ of Latter-day Saints—History—19th century—Sources. 2. Mormon Church—
History—Sources. I. Jessee, Dean C., editor. II. Esplin, Ronald K., editor. III. Bushman, Richard L., editor.
IV. Grow, Matthew J., editor. V. Smith, Joseph, Jr., 1805–1844. VI. Series: Smith, Joseph, Jr., 1805–1844.
Joseph Smith papers.

BX8611.D63 2014   289.309'034—dc23   2013017521

Printed in the United States of America on acid-free paper.
10 9 8 7 6 5 4 3 2 1

The Joseph Smith Papers

Contents

Detailed Contents

Part 3: 12 February–28 March 1836

Part 4: 30 March–19 August 1836

PART 5: 5 OCTOBER 1836–10 APRIL 1837

PART 6: 20 APRIL–14 SEPTEMBER 1837

Part 7: 17 September 1837–21 January 1838

Appendix

Illustrations and Maps

Textual Illustrations

Contextual Illustrations

MAPS

OTHER VISUALS

Timeline of Joseph Smith's Life

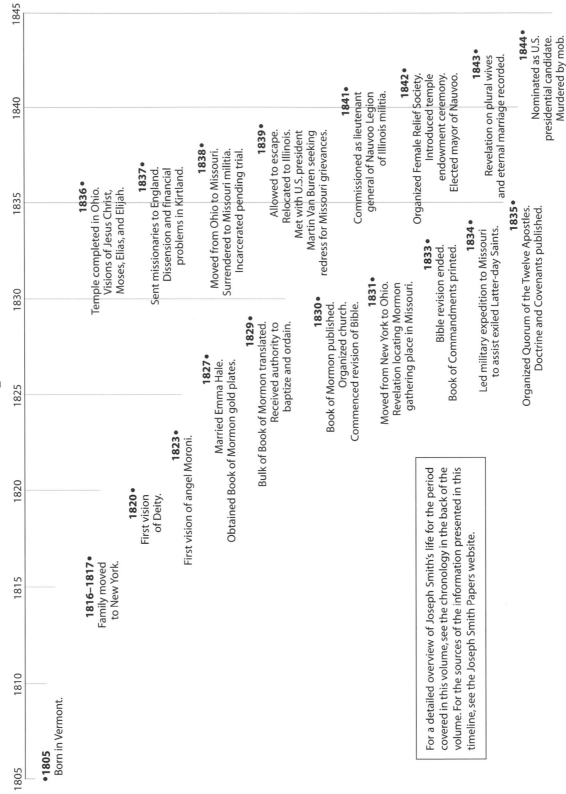

1805 1810 1815 1820 1825 1830 1835 1840 1845

1805
Born in Vermont.

1816–1817
Family moved to New York.

1820
First vision of Deity.

1823
First vision of angel Moroni.

1827
Married Emma Hale.
Obtained Book of Mormon gold plates.

1829
Bulk of Book of Mormon translated.
Received authority to baptize and ordain.

1830
Book of Mormon published.
Organized church.
Commenced revision of Bible.

1831
Moved from New York to Ohio.
Revelation locating Mormon gathering place in Missouri.

1833
Bible revision ended.
Book of Commandments printed.

1834
Led military expedition to Missouri to assist exiled Latter-day Saints.

1835
Organized Quorum of the Twelve Apostles.
Doctrine and Covenants published.

1836
Temple completed in Ohio.
Visions of Jesus Christ, Moses, Elias, and Elijah.

1837
Sent missionaries to England.
Dissension and financial problems in Kirtland.

1838
Moved from Ohio to Missouri.
Surrendered to Missouri militia.
Incarcerated pending trial.

1839
Allowed to escape.
Relocated to Illinois.
Met with U.S. president Martin Van Buren seeking redress for Missouri grievances.

1841
Commissioned as lieutenant general of Nauvoo Legion of Illinois militia.

1842
Organized Female Relief Society.
Introduced temple endowment ceremony.
Elected mayor of Nauvoo.

1843
Revelation on plural wives and eternal marriage recorded.

1844
Nominated as U.S. presidential candidate.
Murdered by mob.

For a detailed overview of Joseph Smith's life for the period covered in this volume, see the chronology in the back of the volume. For the sources of the information presented in this timeline, see the Joseph Smith Papers website.

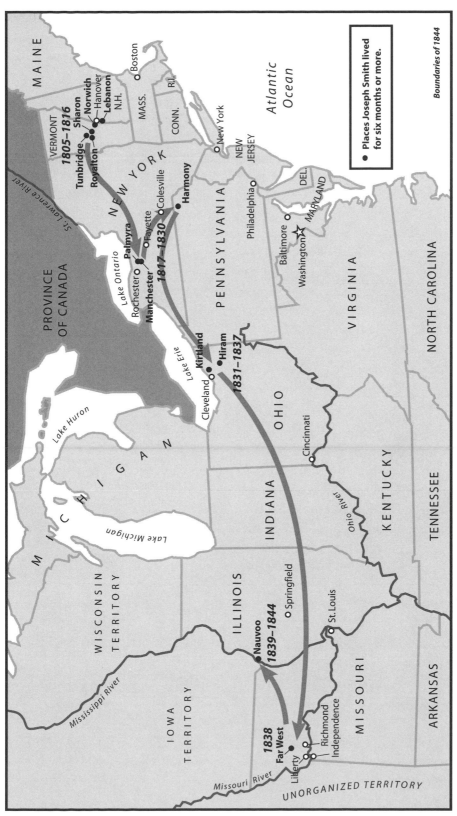

Joseph Smith's residences. Joseph Smith's major places of residence and the general direction of his migrations. Detailed maps relevant to the places mentioned in this volume appear on pages 549–557. (Design by John Hamer.)

About the Joseph Smith Papers Project

Joseph Smith was the founding prophet and first president of The Church of Jesus Christ of Latter-day Saints. The Joseph Smith Papers Project is an effort to gather together all extant Joseph Smith documents and to publish complete and accurate transcripts of those documents with both textual and contextual annotation. All such documents are being published electronically on the project website, josephsmithpapers.org, and a large number of the documents are being published in print. The print and electronic publications constitute an essential resource for scholars and students of the life and work of Joseph Smith, early Mormon history, and nineteenth-century American religion. For the first time, all of Joseph Smith's known surviving papers, which include many of the foundational documents of The Church of Jesus Christ of Latter-day Saints, will be easily accessible in one place.

The Joseph Smith Papers Project is not a "documentary history" project comprising all important documents relating to Joseph Smith. Instead, it is a "papers" project that is publishing, according to accepted documentary editing standards, documents created by Joseph Smith or by staff whose work he directed, including journals, revelations and translations, contemporary reports of discourses, minutes, business and legal records, editorials, and notices. The project also includes papers received and "owned" by Joseph Smith or his office, such as incoming correspondence.

The Joseph Smith Papers Project is a comprehensive edition, meaning it will include all known and available documents meeting the project's criteria as Joseph Smith documents. While selective editions may exclude some documents because they are of less interest or importance, comprehensive editions such as this one make no such exclusions. All Joseph Smith documents, even routine ones such as certificates, will be published.

The print and digital editions of the Joseph Smith Papers are divided into six series. The Documents series is the core of the edition, presenting, with the exception of some documents featured in other series, all of Joseph Smith's papers from July 1828 to June 1844. The other series will publish larger record books and standalone genres. The Journals series presents Joseph Smith's diaries from 1832 to 1844; the Histories series publishes Joseph Smith's many attempts to record his own story and the story of the church; the Revelations and Translations series provides textual studies of Smith's revelatory texts;

the Administrative Records series presents minute books, letterbooks, and records of organizations Smith was associated with, such as the Council of Fifty; and the Legal, Business, and Financial Records series presents the legal cases Smith was involved in as well as the documents related to his business and financial dealings.

Because the Joseph Smith Papers Project meets the requisite scholarly and documentary editing criteria, it has earned an endorsement by the National Historical Publications and Records Commission. To ensure accuracy of the texts, project editors undertake three independent levels of text verification for each manuscript, including a final verification against the original.

The project is staffed by scholars, archivists, and editors employed by the Church History Department of The Church of Jesus Christ of Latter-day Saints in Salt Lake City, Utah, and is funded by the church and by the Larry H. Miller and Gail Miller Family Foundation. Each print volume is submitted to peer review by a national board of scholars prior to publication. The publisher of the project's print and web publications is the Church Historian's Press, an imprint of the Church History Department.

Joseph Smith Documents from October 1835 through January 1838

The 118 documents found in this volume of *The Joseph Smith Papers* cover a period of Joseph Smith's life, October 1835–January 1838, that was punctuated both by moments of elation and moments of upheaval. The volume opens in the hopeful months leading up to the completion of the first Latter-day Saint temple, the House of the Lord in Kirtland, Ohio. Church members worked diligently and sacrificed much to complete the temple, and they were rewarded with spiritual outpourings in early 1836. Joseph Smith's journal for this period includes such exclamations as, "This has been one of the best days that I ever spent."[1]

The exuberance soon dissipated, however. Word reached Kirtland of renewed threats of violence in the church's settlements in Clay County, Missouri, forcing the Saints there to once again abandon their homes and find another place to settle. Church debts mounted in both Missouri and Ohio, and from late 1836 through the end of 1837, Joseph Smith was heavily involved in temporal and financial matters. Compounding his difficulties, the economic problems led many disaffected church members to challenge Smith's authority as a prophet. The volume closes with the Kirtland church in chaos and Smith facing legal and physical threats. At the command of revelation, he departed Kirtland and rode through the night, bound for Missouri. There he would resettle his family in Far West, a new gathering place for the Saints.[2]

The majority of documents found in this volume, as with previous volumes of the Documents series of *The Joseph Smith Papers,* are letters, minutes of meetings, and revelations. A wide range of other document types is also found here, including ecclesiastical charges, a conversation with an infamous visitor, a marriage license and a marriage certificate, rules and regulations for the temple, deeds, mortgages, promissory notes, an application for a federal land patent, and selections from the *Elders' Journal,* a church-run periodical with Joseph Smith as its founding editor. Two unusual documents warrant particular mention. Smith and several associates—notably William W. Phelps,

---

1. JS, Journal, 13 Jan. 1836, in *JSP,* J1:151.
2. Revelation, 12 Jan. 1838–C, pp. 500–502 herein; JS History, vol. B-1, 780.

Oliver Cowdery, Frederick G. Williams, and Warren Parrish—spent substantial time in the late summer and fall of 1835 studying recently acquired Egyptian papyri.[3] Their efforts produced several texts, two of which are presented in this volume: the first is a portion of what would later be referred to as the Book of Abraham; the second is a manuscript that was fashioned as an Egyptian alphabet.[4]

The first six months documented here emphasize the role Joseph Smith played, as president of the Church of the Latter Day Saints, in organizing the church and preparing its members for the dedication of the House of the Lord and the blessings they expected to receive there.[5] Smith is seen pursuing various endeavors, such as entertaining visitors to Kirtland, translating inspired texts, dictating revelations, studying Hebrew, and dealing with internal church business.[6] Several documents detail his efforts to maintain harmony among church leaders and his own family members, particularly his brother William. The Kirtland community also continued to develop as the population grew and church members built the physical landscape to match their ideal of a Zion community.[7] But it is the House of the Lord in Kirtland that most occupies Smith's documentary record in this period; more than a third of the documents created between October 1835 and April 1836 relate to his efforts to prepare the church and its members for the promised endowment of spiritual power that his revelations taught would occur in the completed temple.[8]

A January 1831 revelation had instructed church members to gather to Ohio and promised, "There you shall be endowed with power from on high."[9] Another revelation dictated by Joseph Smith in December 1832 called on church members to "establish, an house, even an house of prayer an house of fasting, an house of faith, an house of Learning, an house of glory, an house

---

3. On the acquisition of the Egyptian papyri by Smith and others, see Historical Introduction to Certificate from Michael Chandler, 6 July 1835, in *JSP*, D4:361–364.

4. See Introduction to Part 1: 2 Oct.–1 Dec. 1835, pp. 4–6 herein; see also Historical Introduction to Book of Abraham Manuscript, ca. Early July–ca. Nov. 1835–A [Abraham 1:4–2:6], pp. 71–77 herein; and Historical Introduction to Egyptian Alphabet, ca. Early July–ca. Nov. 1835–A, pp. 81–83 herein.

5. For more information on the name of the church at this time, see Minutes, 3 May 1834, in *JSP*, D4:42–44.

6. See, for example, Conversations with Robert Matthews, 9–11 Nov. 1835, pp. 39–47 herein; Book of Abraham Manuscript, ca. Early July–ca. Nov. 1835–A [Abraham 1:4–2:6], pp. 69–80 herein; and Certificate from Joshua Seixas, 30 Mar. 1836, pp. 214–216 herein.

7. Plat of Kirtland, OH, not before 2 Aug. 1833, in *JSP*, D3:208; Map of Kirtland City, between ca. 6 Apr. and 18 May 1837, pp. 377–382 herein.

8. Noting the significance of the work he was involved in, Newel Knight wrote in his journal that "it has been long since the Lord has had an house upon the Earth" and noted that in the House of the Lord the Saints would receive the endowment of power. (Knight, Autobiography and Journal, 24 May 1835.)

9. Revelation, 2 Jan. 1831, in *JSP*, D1:232 [D&C 38:32].

of order an house of God."[10] The initial building work began on 7 June 1833 but was halted in fall 1833 because builders lacked sufficient materials and because church leaders decided to focus on redeeming Zion—that is, helping the Saints regain the land in Jackson County, Missouri, from which they had been violently expelled.[11] Despite the shifted focus, Smith dictated a revelation instructing the elders of the church that they "should receive their endowment from on high" in the Kirtland House of the Lord.[12] Construction on the religious edifice resumed in spring 1834 and proceeded continuously, if slowly at times, until it was completed.[13] Many Saints contributed to the building of the temple, and Lucy Mack Smith perhaps best summed up the general sentiment of the Saints in 1835 and early 1836 when she wrote, "There was but one main spring to all our thoughts and that was building the Lords house."[14]

As construction on the temple neared completion, Joseph Smith's instruction and the revelations he dictated encouraged church members and leaders to unify themselves, repent, and live by the principles of equality and humility.[15] In January and February 1836, Smith oversaw a series of meetings intended to prepare men who held priesthood office to be endowed with power. Death and disciplinary removal had brought several changes in the church's administrative structure in the previous thirteen months, as had the creation of new offices such as the Quorum of the Twelve Apostles and Quorum of the Seventy.[16] On 13 January 1836 the church's "grand council," which consisted of the presidencies of Kirtland and Missouri, the Quorum of the Twelve, and the high councils and bishoprics of Kirtland and Missouri, met to organize the church's leadership structure. They set the quorums of the priesthood in order, ordained several men to priesthood offices, and established rules "for the regulation of the house of the Lord in times of worship."[17] Joseph Smith's

---

10. Revelation, 27–28 Dec. 1832, in *JSP*, D2:345 [D&C 88:119]; see also Revelation, 1 June 1833, in *JSP*, D3:106 [D&C 95:8].

11. Historical Introduction to Minutes, 6 June 1833, in *JSP*, D3:113–115; Revelation, 24 Feb. 1834, in *JSP*, D3:458–459, 460–463 [D&C 103:11–40].

12. Revelation, 22 June 1834, in *JSP*, D4:77 [D&C 105:33].

13. See Historical Introduction to Minutes and Discourses, 7–8 Mar. 1835, in *JSP*, D4:279–281; Johnson, "A Life Review," 11, 17–18; Johnson, Reminiscences and Journals, 18; Millet, Reminiscences, 3; JS, Journal, 15–17 Apr. 1834, in *JSP*, J1:40; and Ames, Autobiography, [10].

14. Lucy Mack Smith, History, 1844–1845, bk. 14, [3].

15. JS, Journal, 5 Oct. 1835, in *JSP*, J1:68; Revelation, 1 Nov. 1835, pp. 29–30 herein; Revelation, 3 Nov. 1835, pp. 32–36 herein; Historical Introduction to Revelation, 8 Nov. 1835, pp. 38–39 herein; Discourse, 12 Nov. 1835, pp. 47–51 herein; Letter from Orson Hyde, 15 Dec. 1835, pp. 104–109 herein.

16. Minutes, 28–29 Aug. 1834, in *JSP*, D4:123; Minutes, 24 Sept. 1834, in *JSP*, D4:174; Minutes, Discourse, and Blessings, 14–15 Feb. 1835, in *JSP*, D4:227–228; Minutes and Blessings, 28 Feb.–1 Mar. 1835, in *JSP*, D4:258–259; Minutes, 17 Feb. 1834, in *JSP*, D3:436–437.

17. Minutes, 13 Jan. 1836, pp. 139, 142 herein.

journal noted his optimism and joy following the meeting: "There has been an entire unison of feeling expressed in all our proceedings this day, and the Spirit of the God of Israel has rested upon us in mighty power, and it has been good for us to be here, in this heavenly place in Christ Jesus, and altho much fatiegued with the labours of the day, yet my spiritual reward has been verry great indeed."[18] The Saints believed they needed increased preparation and unity to receive the endowment of power, and Smith's journal indicates that in his estimation, they were approaching that state of readiness.[19]

Several church leaders gathered on 21 January 1836 to further prepare themselves. Drawing from Old Testament examples, Smith and others met that afternoon to perform a ritual of washing and perfuming their bodies, "preparatory to the annointing with the holy oil."[20] Later that day, several were "annointed with the same kind of oil and in the man[ner] that were Moses and Aaron, and those who stood before the Lord in ancient days," and were then blessed by the laying on of hands.[21] Joseph Smith was blessed by his father and then under the hands of "all of the presidency," after which the "heavens were opened." According to Smith's journal, he and others beheld "vissions and revelations," and "angels ministered unto them."[22] His account of those heavenly manifestations included a description of the celestial kingdom, supplementing an 1832 vision that depicted the separation of the afterlife into three kingdoms of heavenly glory: celestial, terrestrial, and telestial.[23] In his 1836 vision, Smith reported, he saw in the celestial kingdom both individuals then living—including the presidency and his parents—and deceased individuals such as his brother Alvin. Joseph Smith also described a series of visions involving members of the Twelve and the redemption of Zion.[24] In addition, Missouri bishop Edward Partridge recorded that a number of those present at the 21 January evening meeting "saw visions & others were blessed with the outpouring of the

---

18. JS, Journal, 13 Jan. 1836, in *JSP*, J1:151.

19. See Minutes, 13 Jan. 1836, pp. 138–143 herein; Minutes, 15 Jan. 1836, pp. 146–148 herein; and Minutes, 16 Jan. 1836, pp. 148–154 herein.

20. Cowdery, Diary, 21 Jan. 1836; see also Exodus 40:7–15, 30–32; and Ezekiel 16:9. Of this process, William W. Phelps wrote to his wife, Sally Waterman Phelps, "We are preparing to make ourselves clean, by first cleansing our hearts, forsaking our sins, forgiving every body, all we ever had against them; ano[in]ting washing the body; putting on clean decent clothes, by annointing our heads, and by keeping all the commandments." (William W. Phelps, Far West, MO, to Sally Waterman Phelps, Jan. 1836, William W. Phelps, Papers, BYU.)

21. Cowdery, Diary, 21 Jan. 1836; Whitmer, History, 83, in *JSP*, H2:91–92; JS, Journal, 21 Jan. 1836, in *JSP*, J1:166–170; see also Exodus 40:9–15, 30–32.

22. JS, Journal, 21 Jan. 1836, in *JSP*, J1:167.

23. Vision, 16 Feb. 1832, in *JSP*, D2:188–191 [D&C 76:50–113].

24. Visions, 21 Jan. 1836 [D&C 137], pp. 157–160 herein; JS, Journal, 21 Jan. 1836, in *JSP*, J1:167–170.

Holy Ghost."[25] Between 21 January and 6 February, Smith instructed men of the priesthood to anticipate more visions as they performed washings, anointings, and other blessings leading to the endowment of power.[26]

Then, on Sunday morning, 27 March 1836, a crowd of approximately one thousand men and women filled the completed temple to capacity for the dedicatory service. Joseph Smith's prayer of dedication, written out beforehand with the assistance of other members of the church presidency, echoed language from the December 1832 revelation that called on the Saints to build the temple, and it also spoke of the 1833 violence against the Latter-day Saints in Jackson County. The prayer asked that the House of the Lord be a place where the glory of God could rest upon his children.[27] Eliza R. Snow, who was in attendance, later stated, "The ceremonies of that dedication may be rehearsed, but no mortal language can describe the heavenly manifestations of that memorable day. Angels appeared to some, while a sense of divine presence was realized by all present, and each heart was filled with 'joy inexpressible and full of glory.'"[28]

Two days later, on the morning of 29 March, Joseph Smith and other church officials began two days and nights of meetings in the temple to receive instruction about Zion and to participate in the ordinance of foot washing. This purification ritual, described in the New Testament, was viewed by the participants as the culmination of the Saints' spiritual preparation and ceremonial order.[29] William W. Phelps called it "a solemn scene" to witness members of the church presidency, the Missouri presidency, and the two bishoprics of the church ceremoniously cleanse one another's feet.[30] They also partook of the Lord's Supper of bread and wine and then spent the night in the House of the Lord "prophesying

---

25. Partridge, Journal, 21 Jan. 1836.

26. JS, Journal, 22–23 and 28 Jan. 1836; 6 Feb. 1836, in *JSP*, J1:171–172, 174–175, 181–182; see also Letter from the Presidency of Elders, 29 Jan. 1836, pp. 162–163 herein; JS, Journal, 1 and 6 Feb. 1836, in *JSP*, J1:179, 181; Kirtland Elders Quorum, "Record," 11 Feb. 1836; Minutes, 12 Feb. 1836, pp. 170–173 herein; and Minutes, 3 Mar. 1836, pp. 180–185 herein.

27. Minutes and Prayer of Dedication, 27 Mar. 1836 [D&C 109], pp. 188–206 herein; Revelation, 27–28 Dec. 1832, in *JSP*, D2:336–346 [D&C 88:1–126].

28. Tullidge, *Women of Mormondom*, 95; see also 1 Peter 1:8. A second dedicatory event was held four days later, and as at the first dedication, "the spirit of God rested upon the congregation and great solemnity prevailed." (JS, Journal, 31 Mar. 1836, in *JSP*, J1:216.)

29. Minutes, 30 Mar. 1836, pp. 216–221 herein; Post, Journal, 30 Mar. 1836; see also John 13:4–17; and Discourse, 12 Nov. 1835, pp. 49–50 herein. While it was the final ceremony for the endowment of power at this time, foot washing had been instituted by the Latter-day Saints at the organization of the School of the Prophets in January 1833. (Minutes, 22–23 Jan. 1833, in *JSP*, D2:381–382; see also Doctrine and Covenants 7:45–46, 1835 ed. [D&C 88:138–141].)

30. William W. Phelps, [Kirtland, OH], to Sally Waterman Phelps, Liberty, MO, Apr. 1836, William W. Phelps, Papers, BYU; JS, Journal, 29 Mar. 1836, in *JSP*, J1:212.

and giving glory to God."[31] The next day, 30 March, three hundred men, including church officers and others ordained to the priesthood, met Smith inside the temple to participate in a solemn assembly during which they too received the foot-washing ordinance, the sacrament, and instruction. In the afternoon, church leaders including Joseph Smith "commenced prophesying." The "Spirit of prophecy was poured out upon the congregation," and the men in attendance gave "shouts of hosannas to God and the Lamb with amen and amen."[32] During the meeting, Smith stated that he "had now completed the organization of the church" and that the church officers and ordained men "had passed through all the necessary ceremonies" and had, therefore, received the long-awaited endowment of power from on high. The participants in this solemn assembly viewed themselves as armed with new knowledge and instruction from the prophet and as authorized "to go forth and build up the kingdom of God."[33] In the following weeks most of the ordained men left Kirtland to proselytize and to raise money for land in Missouri.[34]

The solemn assembly and endowment of power were not the end of the spiritual outpourings that accompanied the completion of the House of the Lord. Joseph Smith reported a manifestation he and Oliver Cowdery experienced one week after the dedication—a vision of immense theological and eschatological importance for the Latter-day Saint faith. According to Smith's journal, Jesus Christ, Moses, Elias, and Elijah appeared in succession to the two men in the temple and bestowed upon them "the Keys of this dispensation." These keys included the authority to gather "Israel from the four parts of the Eearth and the leading of the ten tribes from the Land of the North" and the authority "to turn the hearts of the Fathers to the children, and the children to the fathers," as had been prophesied in the Old Testament and the Book of Mormon.[35]

Believing that the long-promised endowment of spiritual power had now been bestowed, Joseph Smith turned to other unfinished business, the most important of which was redeeming Zion in Jackson County, Missouri. Following counsel given in a June 1834 revelation, he had encouraged Latter-day Saints to settle in Clay County as a step toward regaining Mormon lands in Jackson County.[36] However, just three months after the dedication of the House

---

31. JS, Journal, 29 Mar. 1836, in *JSP*, J1:212–213; Partridge, Journal, 29 Mar. 1836.

32. Minutes, 30 Mar. 1836, p. 218 herein; Post, Journal, 30 Mar. 1836; Partridge, Journal, 30 Mar. 1836.

33. Minutes, 30 Mar. 1836, pp. 220–221 herein.

34. William W. Phelps, [Kirtland, OH], to Sally Waterman Phelps, Liberty, MO, Apr. 1836, William W. Phelps, Papers, BYU.

35. Visions, 3 Apr. 1836, pp. 224–229 herein [D&C 110]; see also Malachi 4:5–6; and Book of Mormon, 1830 ed., 505 [3 Nephi 25:5–6].

36. See Revelation, 22 June 1834, in *JSP*, D4:75–76.

of the Lord in Kirtland, and unbeknownst to Smith at the time, the threat of displacement again loomed over church members in Missouri. As the Mormon population in Clay County swelled, other residents had grown increasingly uneasy. By spring 1836, hundreds of Latter-day Saint families lived in the county, where they owned approximately sixteen hundred acres of land,[37] and more than one hundred additional families arrived in the summer.[38] In addition, reports circulated among Missourians that Latter-day Saints planned to undertake a second Camp of Israel expedition, patterned after the 1834 expedition Smith led in an attempt to restore the Saints to their Jackson County lands.[39] The St. Louis *Daily Missouri Republican* reported that upwards of fifteen hundred Mormons, traveling in groups of between twenty and two hundred individuals, planned to come with arms to Clay County. In an article entitled "Another Mormon Invasion," the newspaper encapsulated the discontent of Clay County residents: "No doubt can remain but that the peace of this section is again to be disturbed by a military array of ragamuffins" under the command of Joseph Smith, whom the article called "the modern Mohamed."[40] As had occurred earlier in Jackson County, the tensions in Clay County between Mormons and other residents were fueled in part by fear that Mormons were opposed to slavery and would seek alliances with American Indians.[41] According to church member David Pettegrew, "The old feelings, and excitement of Jackson County now began to show itself in Clay."[42]

Violence erupted by late June. Anderson Wilson, a Clay County citizen who organized forces against the Saints, recounted that "there were Several outrages Committed on the night of the 28 [June 1836] Six of our party went to a mormon town Several mormons Cocked their guns & Swore they would Shoot them after Some Scrimiging two white men took a mormon out of Company & give him 100 lashes & it is thought he will Die of this Beating."[43] Missouri

---

37. Partridge, Journal, ca. May 1836.

38. Murdock, Journal, 27 July 1836.

39. For more on the Camp of Israel expedition of 1834, see "Joseph Smith Documents from April 1834 through September 1835," in *JSP*, D4:xviii–xxii. On plans for a second Camp of Israel expedition, see JS, Journal, 24 Sept. 1835, in *JSP*, J1:64; and Historical Introduction to Revelation, 18 Oct. 1835, p. 22 herein.

40. "Another Mormon Invasion," *Missouri Republican*, (St. Louis), 17 May 1836, [2].

41. See Letter to John Thornton and Others, 25 July 1836, pp. 263–264 herein. For more on the violence in and the expulsion of church members from Jackson County, Missouri, see "Joseph Smith Documents from February 1833 through March 1834," in *JSP*, D3:xvii, xxvii–xxx.

42. Pettegrew, "History of David Pettegrew," 26.

43. Anderson Wilson, Clay Co., MO, to Samuel Turrentine, Orange Co., NC, 4 July 1836, Wilson Family Papers, University of North Carolina Library, Chapel Hill; see also Parkin, "History of the Latter Day Saints in Clay County," 242–279.

Latter-day Saint Joseph Holbrook remembered that in the early summer of 1836, "it appeared that war was even at our doors."[44]

Local citizens and community leaders met in the town of Liberty to devise a resolution to the impending conflict.[45] On 29 June, Clay County citizens organized a "Committee of nine" to negotiate the departure of the Latter-day Saints from the county. Four of the committee members had previously assisted the Saints in their efforts to obtain redress and justice for their Jackson County exile.[46] The committee met the same day, drafted a set of resolutions calling for the removal of the Latter-day Saints from the county, and presented these resolutions to church officers.[47]

Under the guidance of William W. Phelps, the church leaders responded on 1 July. "For the sake of friendship," they said, "and to be in a covenant of peace with the citizens of Clay county," they acquiesced to the committee's request to leave.[48] This pacifist reaction likely prevented violence and bloodshed comparable to that experienced during the Jackson County episode nearly three years earlier, when church leaders did not immediately comply with demands for members to leave their homes and property. On 2 July 1836, church representatives met with the citizens' committee, which resolved to "assist the Mormons in selecting some abiding place for their people where they will be in a measure the only occupants and when [where] none will be anxious to molest them."[49] The Clay County committee suggested the church remove to Wisconsin Territory, where they would be the first white settlers and therefore able to exercise local self-determination under the federal government's supervision.[50] Instead, church leaders, who had been scouting new locations north and east of Clay County for a more permanent settlement place since at least May 1836, favored a "mill seat on Shoal creek" approximately thirty miles north of Liberty, Missouri.[51] That location would eventually be known as Far West. By the end of 1836, Alexander Doniphan and

---

44. Holbrook, Reminiscences, 41.

45. See Application for Land Patent, 22 June 1836, pp. 253–258 herein; and Letter to John Thornton and Others, 25 July 1836, pp. 258–268 herein.

46. The four community leaders were John Thornton (a former Ray County judge) and attorneys David R. Atchison, William T. Wood, and Alexander Doniphan. (See Historical Introduction to Letter to John Thornton and Others, 25 June 1834, in *JSP*, D4:85–86.)

47. "Public Meeting," *LDS Messenger and Advocate*, Aug. 1836, 2:353–355; Historical Introduction to Letter to John Thornton and Others, 25 July 1836, pp. 259–260 herein.

48. "Public Meeting," *LDS Messenger and Advocate*, Aug. 1836, 2:359–361; see also Letter to William W. Phelps and Others, 25 July 1836, pp. 268–271 herein.

49. "Public Meeting," *LDS Messenger and Advocate*, Aug. 1836, 2:361.

50. "Public Meeting," *LDS Messenger and Advocate*, Aug. 1836, 2:354.

51. Partridge, Journal, ca. May 1836; see also Historical Introduction to Application for Land Patent, 22 June 1836, pp. 253–256 herein.

other Clay County citizens introduced a bill in the Missouri state legislature that, when passed, designated the region around Far West as Caldwell County, a state-sanctioned haven for Mormon settlers.[52] Church members flooded into the area, and by July 1837 Far West included a population of fifteen hundred, almost all of whom were church members.[53]

Phelps and others in Clay County wrote to Joseph Smith and fellow church leaders in Kirtland on 1 July 1836 to inform them of the agreement they had made to vacate the county.[54] The church presidency replied in two letters dated 25 July, declaring the Missouri Saints innocent of wrongdoing in the conflict but indicating that it made good sense for them to leave the county peaceably.[55] That same day, Smith departed Kirtland for the eastern United States with his brother Hyrum, Sidney Rigdon, and Oliver Cowdery, likely seeking a solution to the church's financial troubles in Kirtland and Missouri.[56] They spent most of August in the Salem, Massachusetts, area, where they preached, raised funds, and reportedly searched for a buried treasure.[57]

His trip east being financially unsuccessful, Smith returned to Kirtland in September 1836 with a renewed focus on temporal, mercantile, and financial affairs. This focus is manifest in the documents created from October 1836 through spring 1837, which are devoted almost exclusively to pecuniary matters. In October 1836, on his own and in partnership with others, Smith purchased approximately 440 acres of land in Kirtland.[58] These acquisitions seem to have been motivated by a desire to make land available for church members newly arriving in Kirtland and, perhaps, to provide real estate backing for the establishment of a bank in Kirtland.[59]

---

52. An Act to Organize the Counties of Caldwell and Daviess [29 Dec. 1836], *Laws of the State of Missouri* [1836], 46–47; Alexander Doniphan, Jefferson City, MO, to William W. Phelps, Shoal Creek, MO, 8 Jan. 1837, William W. Phelps, Collection of Missouri Documents, CHL.

53. Letter from William W. Phelps, 7 July 1837, p. 402 herein.

54. See Letter to William W. Phelps and Others, 25 July 1836, pp. 269–270 herein; see also "Public Meeting," *LDS Messenger and Advocate,* Aug. 1836, 2:359–360.

55. See Letter to William W. Phelps and Others, 25 July 1836, pp. 268–271 herein.

56. See Historical Introduction to Revelation, 6 Aug. 1836 [D&C 111], pp. 271–272 herein.

57. Revelation, 6 Aug. 1836, pp. 271–278 herein [D&C 111].

58. This figure represents the acres of land documented in extant Geauga County deed records. There may have been additional land purchased by Smith and his associates. (See Historical Introduction to Mortgage to Peter French, 5 Oct. 1836, p. 295 herein.)

59. Many banks in the United States were backed to various degrees by real-estate investments. Traditionally, banks secured their loans by real estate and sold bonds to state governments and other investors based on the mortgages they held. In January 1837 Willard Richards wrote, in relation to the Kirtland Safety Society, that "private property is holden & Kirtland bills are as safe as Gold," expressing his confidence in the security of the society's notes backed by real estate. In a July 1837 editorial in the *Messenger and Advocate,* Warren A. Cowdery claimed that "the private property of the stockholders was holden in proportion to the amount of their subscription, for the redemption of the paper issued by the

Joseph Smith and other leaders of the church organized the Kirtland Safety Society Bank on 2 November 1836, and expectations were high. A bank, if successful, could provide considerable financial aid to the Latter-day Saints by supplying residents with a local currency and a source of credit, thereby establishing a stronger foundation for the local economy and a better means to provide liquidity for land purchases, construction, and mercantile activity.[60] When a bank was established in a frontier community, it was often eagerly supported by the local residents, but they often lacked the necessary capital. As a result, investors from the eastern United States frequently funded new banks.[61] Many frontier banks were operated by men who, like Joseph Smith and the Mormon leaders in Kirtland, had little or no banking experience and who came from diverse backgrounds.[62] Given such circumstances, bank closures and failures were a known risk in nineteenth-century America.[63]

Though the question of federal involvement in banking was a highly partisan and divisive issue in the 1830s, most financial transactions—particularly after the closure of the Second Bank of the United States in 1836—were managed by banks that were officially recognized and regulated at the state level.[64] Some states restricted banking services to a single bank operated by the state government, while other states, like Ohio, granted charters to private community banks. The Ohio legislature had granted a considerable number of bank charters in the early 1830s, but it began issuing fewer charters by the 1835–1836 legislative session. In the 1836–1837 session, when Orson Hyde was seeking state authorization for the Kirtland Safety Society, the legislature did not approve any bank charters.[65] By January 1837, uncertain whether they would be able to obtain a charter, Joseph Smith and his contemporaries decided to restructure their institution and rename it the Kirtland Safety Society

---

bank." (Bodenhorn, *History of Banking in Antebellum America*, 41, 124; Willard Richards, Kirtland, OH, to Hepzibah Richards, Hamilton, NY, 20 Jan. 1837, Levi Richards Family Correspondence, CHL; Warren A. Cowdery, Editorial, *LDS Messenger and Advocate*, July 1837, 3:535; see also Historical Introduction to Mortgage to Peter French, 5 Oct. 1836, p. 294 herein; Historical Introduction to Deed to Caroline Grant Smith, 11 Dec. 1836, pp. 317–318 herein; and Historical Introduction to Minutes, 22 Dec. 1836, pp. 321–322 herein.)

60. See Constitution of the Kirtland Safety Society Bank, 2 Nov. 1836, pp. 299–306 herein.

61. Golembe, *State Banks and the Economic Development of the West*, 222–223.

62. Stevens, "Bank Enterprisers in a Western Town," 150–156.

63. Rolnick and Weber, "Free Banking, Wildcat Banking, and Shinplasters," 16–19.

64. For more on the Bank War between Andrew Jackson and Nicholas Biddle, president of the Second Bank of the United States, see Hammond, *Banks and Politics in America*, 369–450; Howe, *What Hath God Wrought*, 375–386; and Sellers, *Market Revolution*, 321–326, 332–337.

65. Golembe, *State Banks and the Economic Development of the West*, 52, 251–255.

Anti-Banking Company.[66] The officers and stockholders drew up new articles of agreement to replace the original bank constitution on 2 January,[67] and in the days following the reorganization, the society opened and began conducting banking services in an unofficial capacity. The institution continued, unsuccessfully, to seek a bank charter from the state.[68]

By spring 1837 the optimism that came with the banking venture had all but ended. The Safety Society was heavily underfunded and barely had its doors open before it was putting an even greater strain on Joseph Smith's already precarious financial situation. Enemies of the church worked against the Safety Society, and church members themselves became divided over the institution and Smith's role in it.[69] Hoping to quiet critics, Smith spoke on the temporal affairs of the church at a 6 April 1837 meeting, while his brother Hyrum asked church members to support the Kirtland Safety Society.[70]

Notwithstanding such appeals, unrest among church members spread, while external opposition increased. Amid allegations made by a staunch opponent, Grandison Newell, Joseph Smith left Kirtland by 13 April, fearing for his life. His whereabouts for the next few weeks are largely unknown.[71] Emma Smith wrote two poignant letters to her husband during his absence, detailing the problems and anxieties she and her three young children faced. "I wish it could be possible for you to be at home," she wrote, encouraging him to return and asking that he remember his children, "for they all remember you." She continued, "I could hardly pacify Julia and Joseph when they found ou[t] you was not coming home soon." Still, she assured her husband, "I shall do the best I can in all things, and I hope that we shall be so humble and pure before God that he will set us at liberty to be our own masters in a few things at least."[72] Emma's letters featured in this volume provide some insight into the increasingly challenging conditions faced by church members in Ohio.

---

66. Warren A. Cowdery described the Society as a "bank, or monied institution," that was "considered a kind of joint stock association." (Warren A. Cowdery, Editorial, *LDS Messenger and Advocate,* July 1837, 3:535; see also Articles of Agreement for the Kirtland Safety Society Anti-Banking Company, 2 Jan. 1837, pp. 324–331 herein.)

67. Articles of Agreement for the Kirtland Safety Society Anti-Banking Company, 2 Jan. 1837, pp. 324–331 herein.

68. See Introduction to Part 5: 5 Oct. 1836–10 Apr. 1837, pp. 285–286, 293 herein; "About Matters in Kirtland," *Ohio Observer* (Hudson), 2 Mar. 1837, 198; and Articles of Agreement for the Kirtland Safety Society Anti-Banking Company, 2 Jan. 1837, pp. 324–331 herein.

69. See Introduction to Part 5: 5 Oct. 1836–10 Apr. 1837, p. 285–293 herein.

70. Discourse, 6 Apr. 1837, pp. 356–357 herein; Woodruff, Journal, 6 Apr. 1837.

71. See Historical Introduction to Letter from Newel K. Whitney, 20 Apr. 1837, pp. 367–368 herein; Letter from Emma Smith, 25 Apr. 1837, pp. 370–372 herein; and Letter from Emma Smith, 3 May 1837, pp. 372–376 herein.

72. Letter from Emma Smith, 3 May 1837, p. 376 herein.

At about the same time Joseph Smith was away from Kirtland, the national financial panic of 1837 reached its climax and began to adversely affect the Ohio economy. Important banking institutions in New Orleans and New York City failed in the spring of 1837, and the ramifications reverberated outward.[73] Prosperity in the 1830s had allowed investors, primarily from the eastern United States, to engage extensively in land speculation, purchasing land on the western frontier and then selling it to farmers or other investors at much higher rates.[74] In an effort to curb this practice and to reduce the use of banknotes and other paper currency, United States president Andrew Jackson issued an executive order in July 1836 known as the Specie Circular, which stipulated that government lands could be purchased only with specie—that is, gold or silver coin—and not with paper money. Specie shortages followed, and other government interventions left prominent banking houses unable to fulfill their financial obligations to investors, primarily those in Britain. Drained of their gold and silver, banks announced that they would no longer redeem notes with specie. These and other economic developments, such as a downturn in the international cotton trade, resulted in the financial panic of 1837 and a subsequent depression that continued into the 1840s. Fearing economic collapse, the public made runs on banks, and in response, financial institutions in New York suspended redemption of their banknotes for specie on 10 May 1837. Banks in other states quickly did likewise, severely curtailing people's access to specie. This in turn led creditors to prematurely demand repayment and left individuals throughout the country unable to meet the debts they had amassed under the assumption of continued economic success.[75]

Encouraged by the prosperity of 1836 and the availability of credit, many Kirtland church members, including Joseph Smith, had purchased land or begun new business ventures. In partnership with Sidney Rigdon, Smith opened a mercantile store in Chester, Ohio.[76] These investments and those of many other Kirtland church members—including investments in the Kirtland Safety Society—foundered in part because of the Panic of 1837, which caused devalued currency, inflation, declining land values, and a general downturn.[77]

---

73. Sellers, *Market Revolution*, 354–355.

74. Golembe, *State Banks and the Economic Development of the West*, 118–120, 150.

75. Lepler, *Many Panics of 1837*, 197–198, 209–210, 222–223; Rousseau, "Jacksonian Monetary Policy, Specie Flows, and the Panic of 1837," 457–488.

76. See Historical Introduction to Mortgage to Peter French, 5 Oct. 1836, pp. 294–295 herein; Letter from Emma Smith, 25 Apr. 1837, p. 371 herein; 373n52 herein; and Historical Introduction to Notes Receivable from Chester Store, 22 May 1837, pp. 382–384 herein.

77. Warren A. Cowdery, brother of Oliver Cowdery and then editor of the *Messenger and Advocate*, noted that these were calamities "common to our whole country" and that "causes of a similar nature

By summer 1837, the store in Chester had closed.[78] Saints throughout Kirtland were affected by the decline in the local economy and the difficulty they faced in finding work and feeding their families.[79] In a July 1837 letter to his son, John Smith noted the inability of several individuals in Kirtland to repay him, writing: "I have not Re[ceive]d money from any of those we held [promissory] notes against since you Left[.] Br. D Wood I fear will not be able to pay us very soon if at all."[80]

Joseph Smith and his financial partners faced frequent litigation in the summer and fall of 1837 regarding their outstanding debts.[81] The church president was involved in at least twenty-two different lawsuits between June 1837 and January 1838. These cases involved debts in the form of unpaid promissory notes for land, mercantile goods, loans, or other purchases made by Smith and his associates. Much of the litigation was brought against Smith in the June term of the Geauga County Court of Common Pleas, where he was a party to seven different cases.[82] To offset debts owed by their mercantile firms, Smith, Sidney Rigdon, Oliver Cowdery, Reynolds Cahoon, Jared Carter, and Hyrum Smith signed an agreement on 11 July 1837 mortgaging the Kirtland House of the Lord to the New York firm Mead, Stafford & Co.[83] Using their greatest asset—the object of the past four years of labor and the spiritual core of the Latter-day Saint community—as collateral demonstrated the desperate financial situation in which Joseph Smith and his associates found themselves. In order to avoid further litigation, the mercantile firms involving church leaders

---

have combined to produce nearly the same effect throughout our whole country." (Warren A. Cowdery, Editorial, *LDS Messenger and Advocate,* June 1837, 3:522.)

78. See Historical Introduction to Notes Receivable from Chester Store, 22 May 1837, pp. 383–384 herein.

79. Warren A. Cowdery, Editorial, *LDS Messenger and Advocate,* June 1837, 3:520–522; John and Clarissa Smith, Kirtland, OH, to George A. Smith, 1 Jan. 1838, George Albert Smith, Papers, CHL; Crosby, Reminiscences, 1836.

80. John and Clarissa Smith, Kirtland, OH, to George A. Smith, West Township, OH, 28 July 1837, George Albert Smith, Papers, CHL.

81. Transcript of Proceedings, 5 June 1837, Patterson & Patterson v. Cahoon et al. [Geauga Co. C.P. 1837], Record Book U, pp. 126–128; Transcript of Proceedings, 5 June 1837, Kelley v. Rigdon, JS, and Cowdery [Geauga Co. C.P. 1837], Record Book U, pp. 97–101; Transcript of Proceedings, 24 Oct. 1837, Seymour & Griffith v. Rigdon & JS [Geauga Co. C.P. 1837], Record Book U, p. 383; Transcript of Proceedings, 24 Oct. 1837, Newbould v. Rigdon, JS, and Cowdery [Geauga Co. C.P. 1837], Record Book U, pp. 351–353; Transcript of Proceedings, 24 Oct. 1837, Eaton v. JS & Cowdery [Geauga Co. C.P. 1837], Record Book U, pp. 277–278, Geauga County Archives and Records Center, Chardon, OH; Trial Record, 31 July–15 Sept. 1837, Rigdon, JS, and Cowdery for the use of JS v. Woodworth [J.P. Ct. 1837], Cowdery, Docket Book, 135.

82. Of the seven cases, only one was a criminal case, brought by Grandison Newell. (See Historical Introduction to Letter from Newel K. Whitney, 20 Apr. 1837, p. 367 herein; and Introduction to Part 5: 5 Oct. 1836–10 Apr. 1837, pp. 291–292 herein.)

83. See Historical Introduction to Mortgage to Mead, Stafford & Co., 11 July 1837, pp. 404–407 herein.

renegotiated their outstanding debts with several merchants in New York City and Buffalo, New York, during the month of September 1837.[84]

By the end of the turbulent year, the Safety Society had ceased its operations and financial hardships had befallen many of the Kirtland Saints.[85] Extant sources offer little credible documentation of monetary losses caused by the Kirtland Safety Society's closure, but it is clear that only a few individuals invested sizable funds in the institution.[86] Joseph Smith invested the most money, several thousand dollars, and no one lost more in the collapse of the Safety Society than he did.[87] The devaluation of society notes and the unwillingness of other banks to accept the notes as payment contributed to the financial hardships in Kirtland, but most individuals there were more adversely affected by the broader Panic of 1837, which caused the price of goods to increase and land values to decrease drastically.[88] Vilate Murray Kimball wrote to her husband, Heber C. Kimball, in January 1838 that "land will not sell for any thing."[89]

The spiritual exuberance that attended the dedication of the House of the Lord just eighteen months earlier seemed a distant memory. The debts, litigations, doubts, and accusations resulting from Joseph Smith's financial entanglements, including his role as an officer of the Kirtland Safety Society, further divided church members, with some remaining supportive and others unwilling to follow his direction. Many documents in this volume dating from May 1837 through January 1838 demonstrate the turmoil within the church and in Smith's life. In May 1837 he faced opposition from various church members, including Warren Parrish and Parley P. Pratt. Some had specific complaints related to the bank or land transactions, but dissenters also indicted him more broadly for his involvement as a religious leader in financial matters, challenging his authority over temporal affairs.[90] In June 1837 John F. Boynton, one of

---

84. See Introduction to Part 6: 20 Apr.–14 Sept. 1837, p. 365 herein; and Historical Introduction to Power of Attorney to Oliver Granger, 27 Sept. 1837, p. 459 herein.

85. Smith and Rigdon withdrew as officers of the Kirtland Safety Society by July 1837, and possibly in early June. (See Introduction to Part 6: 20 Apr.–14 Sept. 1837, p. 366 herein; JS History, B-1, 764; and Minutes, 3 Sept. 1837, p. 424 herein.)

86. See Daniel Allen, Reminiscences, ca. 1865, [1].

87. Joseph Smith personally invested at least $6,000 in the institution, none of which was withdrawn. He also took out $4,200 in loans from local banks, which he likely intended for the society. Smith and his family also suffered financial consequences due to the devaluation of notes. (Kirtland Safety Society, Stock Ledger, 13–14, 273–274; Introduction to Part 5: 5 Oct. 1836–10 Apr. 1837, pp. 290–291 herein.)

88. Warren A. Cowdery, Editorial, *LDS Messenger and Advocate,* July 1837, 3:535–536.

89. Vilate Murray Kimball, Kirtland, OH, to Heber C. Kimball, Preston, England, ca. 19–29 Jan. 1838, Heber C. Kimball, Collection, CHL; see also Stephen Burnett, Orange Township, OH, to Lyman Johnson, 15 Apr. 1838, in JS Letterbook 2, pp. 64–65.

90. Letter from Parley P. Pratt, 23 May 1837, pp. 386–391 herein; Warren Parrish, Kirtland, OH, 5 Feb. 1838, Letter to the Editor, *Painesville (OH) Republican,* 15 Feb. 1838, [3].

the Twelve Apostles, denounced Joseph Smith as a "fallen prophet."[91] By the end of July the dissent seemed to be lessening, particularly within the Quorum of the Twelve as Thomas B. Marsh worked to correct and reconcile several apostles who had challenged Smith's leadership. Boynton and others, meanwhile, continued to disagree with Smith.[92] In spite of the difficulties in this period, however, Smith organized an ambitious proselytizing endeavor. Led by Heber C. Kimball, missionaries departed for England in June 1837, and they became the first Latter-day Saints to preach overseas.[93]

In late summer 1837, the church president confronted the dissenters directly: he called the church together at a conference on 3 September to vote to support or disapprove its current leadership. The conference voted to sustain Smith as church president and supported the remainder of the presidency, but voted against Kirtland high council members John Johnson, Martin Harris, and Joseph Coe as well as apostles John F. Boynton, Lyman Johnson, and Luke Johnson, all of whom had been involved in dissent against Smith's leadership. The three dissenting high counselors were removed from office, but Boynton and Luke and Lyman Johnson all retained their positions in the Twelve after they made a public confession on 10 September 1837.[94]

The day after the conference, Smith sent word of the proceedings and changes in the church hierarchy to the Saints in Far West, Missouri.[95] Shortly after that, he traveled to Far West to oversee church business there, which included convening a conference similar to the 3 September gathering in Kirtland. This marked Smith's first visit to the new town. He presided over meetings wherein decisions were made about church officers, land, and plans for a new House of the Lord in Far West. These meetings brought direction and a sense of unity to the church's operations in Missouri, but Smith's visit was not without controversy. Even though Oliver Cowdery was the "second elder" of the church and a longtime friend of Smith's, the two men's relationship was deteriorating during fall 1837, and during Smith's stay in Far West, Cowdery aired grievances that had divided the two.[96]

---

91. Kimball, "History," 55; see also Warren Parrish, Kirtland, OH, 5 Feb. 1838, Letter to the Editor, *Painesville (OH) Republican,* 15 Feb. 1838, [3]; and Thomas B. Marsh, Independence, MO, to Wilford Woodruff, Scarborough, ME, ca. Apr. 1838, in *Elders' Journal,* July 1838, 36.

92. Historical Introduction to Revelation, 23 July 1837 [D&C 112], pp. 410–412 herein; Minutes, 3 Sept. 1837, pp. 420–425 herein.

93. See Recommendation for Heber C. Kimball, between 2 and 13 June 1837, pp. 397–401 herein.

94. Minutes, 3 Sept. 1837, pp. 420–425 herein; Minute Book 1, 10 Sept. 1837.

95. Letter to John Corrill and the Church in Missouri, 4 Sept. 1837, pp. 428–430 herein.

96. Minutes, 6 Nov. 1837, pp. 464–468 herein; Minutes, 7 Nov. 1837, pp. 468–472 herein; Minutes, 10 Nov. 1837, pp. 472–476 herein; see also Oliver Cowdery, Norton, OH, to William W. Phelps, 7 Sept. 1834, in *LDS Messenger and Advocate,* Oct. 1834, 14–16; and License for John Whitmer, 9 June 1830, in *JSP,* D1:146.

Joseph Smith returned to Kirtland in early December 1837 only to discover that in his absence, dissent had revived and become more threatening. Kirtland resident Hepzibah Richards wrote that the situation was a continuation of earlier events and that if the dissent had "appeared to be quelled it now appears that it was only preparing to operate with greater virulence."[97] John Smith wrote his son George A. Smith that the dissenters were "striving to Distroy" the church "with a great Deal more Zeal than they ever had to build [it] up," and that their "greatest enmity" was against those they had called friends.[98] By late December the Kirtland high council had excommunicated twenty-eight Saints, and by 1 January 1838 John Smith estimated that altogether church councils had "cut off Between 40 & 50 from the ch[urc]h."[99] Divisions in Kirtland became more pronounced in January 1838 as dissenters and other opponents threatened to kill Joseph Smith and other members of the First Presidency. Though Smith had long contemplated moving to Missouri, it was not until a 12 January 1838 revelation directed him and the First Presidency to leave Kirtland with their families that he ultimately left the place he and other Latter-day Saints had built with their precious resources.[100] Following this revelation and seeking to escape the threatened violence, Smith and Rigdon hastily departed Kirtland the evening of 12 January. Their families later met them in Norton, Ohio, and by 16 January they had begun their journey to Far West.[101] On 21 January, Oliver Cowdery penned a terse letter to Smith. The cold tone of Cowdery's letter, the last document featured in this volume, exposes the deep division and discontent that had emerged between the former friends and is indicative of continuing disunion in the church's leadership at the time Smith departed Kirtland for Far West.[102]

Violence in Kirtland escalated after Joseph Smith's departure. During the evening of 15 January, the printing office was set on fire and the building and its contents were destroyed.[103] Dissenters and non-Mormon opponents had

97. Hepzibah Richards, Kirtland, OH, to Willard Richards, Bedford, England, 18 Jan. 1838, Willard Richards, Papers, CHL.

98. John and Clarissa Smith, Kirtland, OH, to George A. Smith, Shinnston, VA, 15 Jan. 1838, George Albert Smith, Papers, CHL.

99. John and Clarissa Smith, Kirtland, OH, to George A. Smith, 1 Jan. 1838, George Albert Smith, Papers, CHL.

100. Revelation, 12 Jan. 1838–C, pp. 500–502 herein.

101. JS History, vol. B-1, 780. Joseph Smith, his family, and others who were traveling with them arrived in Far West on 14 March 1838. (JS, Journal, Mar.–Sept. 1838, 16, in *JSP,* J1:237.)

102. Letter from Oliver Cowdery, 21 Jan. 1838, pp. 504–505 herein; see also Oliver Cowdery, Far West, MO, to Warren A. Cowdery, Kirtland, OH, 21 Jan. 1838, in Cowdery, Letterbook, 80–83.

103. John and Clarissa Smith, Kirtland, OH, to George A. Smith, Shinnston, VA, 15 Jan. 1838, George Albert Smith, Papers, CHL; Hepzibah Richards, Kirtland, OH, to Willard Richards, Bedford,

organized and threatened church members with additional violence mere days after the church president left. Of the conditions in the city, Hepzibah Richards wrote her brother Willard, "We feel that we are in jeopardy every hour."[104] During spring and summer 1838, many Saints in Kirtland followed the church president west, including a company of more than five hundred known as the Kirtland Camp, which departed Kirtland on 6 July 1838.[105] Still, Kirtland was not wholly abandoned. A local church presidency was appointed, consisting of William Marks, John Smith, and Reynolds Cahoon, and agents remained to take care of the land and other church properties, settle debts, and oversee the preparation and facilitation of the migration of more Latter-day Saints to Missouri.[106]

The texts that document these critical years of Joseph Smith's life come from disparate places. Approximately half of the documents featured in this volume come from two sources: a record book kept by church scribes called Minute Book 1, and Joseph Smith's 1835–1836 journal. Minute Book 1 is the source for twenty-six of the documents, including minutes of meetings led by Smith and an assortment of documents dealing with organizational, administrative, and disciplinary matters. Twenty-six other texts come from Joseph Smith's journal, which was kept by various scribes including Warren Parrish, Sylvester Smith, and Warren A. Cowdery. The texts taken from the journal represent a variety of document types such as revelations, blessings, letters, minutes, and a discourse. Because they were copied into the journal, many of these documents were published in the Journals series of *The Joseph Smith Papers;* here in the Documents series, they are presented and contextualized as individual texts. Unfortunately, there is no extant journal for Joseph Smith from April 1836 to January 1838, a period that is one of the most poorly documented in the history of the early church. The remainder of the documents featured in this volume come from archival collections or from a range of other sources including periodicals, letterbooks, other Latter-day Saints' diaries, and county deed ledgers.[107] Given the paucity of extant sources, the documents

---

England, 18 Jan. 1838, Willard Richards, Papers, CHL; Vilate Murray Kimball, Kirtland, OH, to Heber C. Kimball, Preston, England, ca. 19–29 Jan. 1838, Heber C. Kimball, Collection, CHL.

104. Hepzibah Richards, Kirtland, OH, to Willard Richards, Bedford, England, 18 Jan. 1838, Willard Richards, Papers, CHL.

105. Kirtland Camp, Journal, 6 July 1838.

106. Hepzibah Richards, Kirtland, OH, to Willard Richards, Bedford, England, 18 Jan. 1838, Willard Richards, Papers, CHL; see also "Ecclesiastical Organizational Charts," in *JSP,* J1:458.

107. In addition to the 118 documents featured in this volume, the appendix at the end of the book presents four written blessings originally pronounced by Joseph Smith in 1833 but expanded when Oliver Cowdery copied them into a record book in October 1835. Smith's role in the expansion is unclear. (See Appendix, pp. 507–517 herein.)

presented here are among the best contemporary sources for researching and understanding this period of Mormon history.

The twenty-eight months covered by this volume of *The Joseph Smith Papers* reveal a tempestuous and unsettled time for Joseph Smith and the church he led. Smith and the Saints experienced spiritual elation surrounding the dedication of the Kirtland House of the Lord, followed by a series of intense trials. The church president struggled against major challenges to his leadership and left Kirtland for Missouri amid threats of violence. The documents presented in this volume provide greater details and insights into these and other events in Joseph Smith's life. This turbulent period can be better understood by studying these texts within their historical context, a task each document introduction undertakes. Although there is a scarcity of documents and other records, leaving important questions from this time period unanswered, the documents found in this volume and the discussion of their historical context illuminate the highs and lows of the period and shed light on the complex figure of Joseph Smith.

Editorial Method

The goal of the Joseph Smith Papers Project is to present verbatim transcripts of Joseph Smith's papers in their entirety, making available the most essential sources of Smith's life and work and preserving the content of aging manuscripts from damage or loss. The papers include documents that were created by Joseph Smith, whether written or dictated by him or created by others under his direction, or that were owned by Smith, that is, received by him and kept in his office (as with incoming correspondence). Under these criteria—authorship and ownership—the project intends to publish, either in letterpress volumes or electronic form, every extant Joseph Smith document to which its editors can obtain access. This fifth volume of the Documents series presents unaltered and unabridged transcripts of revelations, letters, minutes of meetings, and a variety of other Joseph Smith documents created between October 1835 and January 1838.

Document Selection

For many Joseph Smith documents, multiple versions were created during his lifetime. For example, a revelation originally recorded on loose paper might have been copied into a more permanent bound volume, and that version might then have been revised and published in one or more print editions. Individuals with access to the handwritten or printed versions might have made or obtained copies for personal use, or in some cases for unauthorized publication. For this volume, original documents are featured when they are extant; in cases when the original is not extant (as with most Joseph Smith revelations), the editors selected either the earliest extant version of the text or the version that in their judgment best represents the nonextant original. The source notes and historical introductions preceding the individual documents provide additional information about version selection. Editors compared the featured version against other early versions, and any significant differences are described in annotation. For the period covered in this volume, documents of certain types, including licenses, deeds, mortgages, and promissory notes, are so numerous that a comprehensive edition is impossible in print. Editors selected representative samples of these document types based on analysis of historical significance or uniqueness for the document type and period. For a comprehensive list of all documents in this period, consult the Calendar of Documents at josephsmithpapers.org.

Rules of Transcription

Because of aging and sometimes damaged texts and imprecise orthography and penmanship, not all handwriting is legible. Hurried writers often rendered words carelessly, and even the best writers and spellers left out letters on occasion or formed them imperfectly and incompletely. Even with rigorous methods, transcription and verification are not an exact science. Judgments about capitalization, for example, are informed not only by looking at the specific case at hand but by understanding the usual characteristics of each particular writer. The same is true for interpreting original spelling and punctuation. If a letter or other character is ambiguous, deference is given to the author's or scribe's usual spelling and punctuation. Where this is ambiguous, modern spelling and punctuation are favored. Even the best transcribers and verifiers will differ from one another in making such judgments. Interested readers may wish to compare the transcripts with images of the original documents at the Joseph Smith Papers website, josephsmithpapers.org, to better understand how our transcription rules have been applied to create these transcripts. Viewing the originals also provides other information that cannot be conveyed by typography.

To ensure accuracy in representing the texts, transcripts were verified three times, each time by a different set of eyes. The first two verifications were done using high-resolution scanned images. The first was a visual collation of the document images with the transcripts, while the second was an independent and double-blind image-to-transcript tandem proofreading. The third and final verification of the transcripts was a visual collation with the original document, when available. At this stage, the verifier employed magnification and ultraviolet light as needed to read badly faded text, recover heavily stricken material, untangle characters written over each other, and recover words canceled by messy "wipe erasures" made when the ink was still wet or removed by knife scraping after the ink had dried. The verified transcripts meet or exceed the transcription and verification requirements of the National Archives and Records Administration's National Historical Publications and Records Commission.

The approach to transcription employed in *The Joseph Smith Papers* is a conservative style of what is known as "expanded transcription." The transcripts render most words letter by letter as accurately as possible, preserving the exact spelling of the originals. This includes incomplete words, variant spellings of personal names, repeated words, and idiosyncratic grammatical constructions. The transcripts also preserve substantive revisions made by the original scribes. Canceled words are typographically rendered with the strikethrough bar, while inserted words are enclosed within angle brackets. Cancellations and insertions are also transcribed letter by letter when an original word was changed to a new word simply by canceling or inserting letters at the beginning or end of the word—such as "sparingly" or "attend⟨ed⟩". However, for cases in which an original word was changed to a new word by canceling or inserting letters in the middle of the word, to improve readability the original word is presented stricken in its entirety, followed by the revised word in its entirety. For example, when "falling" was revised to "failing" by canceling the first "l" and inserting an "i", the revision is transcribed as "falling ⟨failing⟩" instead of "fal⟨i⟩ling". Insubstantial cancellations and insertions—those used only to correct spelling and punctuation—are silently emended, and only the final spelling and punctuation are reproduced. For example, a manuscript reading "Joseph, Frederick, & and Oliver" will be rendered in the transcript as "Joseph, Frederick, and Oliver". And a manuscript reading "on Thirsday 31th⟨st⟩ arrived at Buffalo" will be rendered "on Thirsday 31st arrived at Buffalo".

The transcription of punctuation differs from the original in a few other respects. Single instances of periods, commas, apostrophes, and dashes are all faithfully rendered without regard to their grammatical correctness, except that periods are not reproduced when they appear immediately before a word, with no space between the period and the word. Also, in some cases of repetitive punctuation, only the final mark or final intention is transcribed while any other characters are silently omitted. Dashes of various lengths are standardized to a consistent pattern. The short vertical strokes commonly used in early American writing for abbreviation punctuation are transcribed as periods, except that abbreviation punctuation is not reproduced when an abbreviation is expanded in square brackets. Flourishes and other decorative inscriptions are not reproduced or noted. With the exception of the two documents titled "Selections from *Elders' Journal*," ellipsis marks appear in the featured text only where they occur in the original manuscript and are standardized to a consistent format; they do not represent an editorial abridgment. Punctuation is never added silently. When the original document sets off a quotation by using quotation marks at the beginning of each line that contains quoted matter, the quotation is formatted as a block quote, without the original quotation marks preserved.

Incorrect dates, place names, and other errors of fact are left to stand. The intrusive *sic,* sometimes used to affirm original misspelling, is never employed, although where words or phrases are especially difficult to understand, editorial clarifications or corrections are inserted in brackets. Correct and complete spellings of personal names are supplied in brackets the first time each incorrect or incomplete name appears in a document, unless the correct name cannot be determined. Place names that may be hard to identify are also clarified or corrected within brackets. When two or more words were inscribed or typeset together without any intervening space and the words were not a compound according to standard contemporary usage or the writer's or printer's consistent practice, the words are transcribed as separate words for readability.

Formatting is standardized. Original paragraphing is retained. All paragraphs are given in a standard format, with indention regularized and with empty lines between paragraphs omitted. Blank space of approximately five or more lines in the original is noted, as are lesser amounts of blank vertical space that appear significant. Extra space between words or sentences is not captured unless it appears the scribe left a blank space as a placeholder to be filled in later. Documents featured herein that are copies of nonextant original documents sometimes contain large blank spaces within a line of text, which seem to indicate where paragraph breaks appeared in the original documents. Where this occurs, the blank space is rendered as a paragraph break. Block quotations of letters, minutes, revelations, and other similar items within the texts are set apart with block indentions, even when such items are not set off in the original. Horizontal rules and other separating devices inscribed or printed in the original are not reproduced. Line ends are neither typographically reproduced nor symbolically represented. Because of the great number of words broken across a line at any point in the word, with or without a hyphen, end-of-line hyphens are not transcribed and there is no effort to note or keep a record of such words and hyphens. This leaves open the possibility that the hyphen of an ambiguously hyphenated compound escaped transcription or that a compound word correctly broken across a line ending without a hyphen is mistakenly transcribed as two words. As many end-of-line hyphens have been editorially introduced in the transcripts, a hyphen appearing at the end of a line may or may not be original to the document.

In transcripts of printed sources, typeface, type size, and spacing have been standardized. Characters set upside down are silently corrected. When the text could not be determined because of broken or worn type or damage to the page, the illegible text is supplied based on another copy of the printed text, if possible. Printers sometimes made changes to the text, such as to correct spelling mistakes or replace damaged type, after printing had already begun, meaning that the first copies to come off the press often differ from later copies in the same print run. No attempt has been made to analyze more than one copy of the printed texts transcribed here, aside from consulting another copy when the one used for transcription is indeterminable or ambiguous.

Within some of the documents, the ink color of the original text changes often, even in the middle of sentences. Such changes in ink color are not noted. In some cases, cancellations and insertions were made in a different color than the original inscription. Because these cancellations and insertions are already marked as revisions—with the horizontal strikethrough bar for cancellations and with a pair of angle brackets for insertions—the color of the ink used for the revision is not noted.

Clerical notations, such as signatures or posting endorsements, are often written on the back of a document or a document wrapper and are transcribed as insertions if they were made at the same time the document was created. Later clerical endorsements are transcribed in the source note. If contemporary or later notations are integral to the document's creation, as in the case of payment notations on a bond, they are transcribed as original text, not insertions. Redactions and other changes made to a document after the original production of the text are not transcribed, nor are labeling and other forms of archival marking. Source notes identify documents that include such redactions or labeling. Most handwritten documents in this volume were inscribed in black or brown ink using a quill pen. Exceptions are identified in source notes.

Transcription Symbols

The effort to render mistakes, canceled material, and later insertions sometimes complicates readability by putting Joseph Smith and his scribes behind the "barbed wire" of symbolic transcription. However, conveying such elements with transcription symbols can aid in understanding the text and the order and ways in which the words were inscribed. Typesetting can never effectively represent all the visual aspects of a document; it cannot fully capture such features as the formation of letters and other characters, spacing between words and between paragraphs, varying lengths of dashes and paragraph indentions, and varying methods of cancellation and the location of insertions. Despite its limitations, a conservative transcription method more faithfully represents the process by which the text was inscribed—especially cancellations and insertions—rather than just the final result.

The following symbols are used to transcribe and expand the text:

/ⁿ   In documents inscribed by more than one person, the slash mark indicates a change in handwriting. A footnote identifies the previous and commencing scribes.

[roman]   Brackets enclose editorial insertions that expand, correct, or clarify the text. This convention may be applied to the abbreviated or incorrect spelling of a personal name, such as Brigham Yo[u]ng, or of a place, such as Westleville [Wesleyville]. Obsolete or ambiguous abbreviations are expanded with br[acket]s. Bracketed editorial insertions also provide reasonable reconstructions of badly miss[p]elled worsd [words]. Missing or illegible words may be supplied within brackets when the supplied word is based on textual

or contextual evidence. Bracketed punctuation is added only when necessary to follow complex wording.

[roman?]   A question mark is added to conjectured editorial insertions, such as where an entire word was [accidentally?] omitted and where it is difficult to maintain the sense of a sentence without some editorial insertion.

[*italic*]   Significant descriptions of the writing medium—especially those inhibiting legibility—and of spacing within the text are italicized and enclosed in brackets: [*hole burned in paper*], [*leaf torn*], [*blank*], [*9 lines blank*], [*pages 99–102 blank*].

[*illegible*]   An illegible word is represented by the italicized word [*illegible*] enclosed in brackets.

◊   An illegible letter or other character within a partially legible word is rendered with a diamond. Repeated diamonds represent the approximate number of illegible characters (for example: sto◊◊◊◊s).

[p. x]   Bracketed editorial insertions indicate the end of an originally numbered page, regardless of the location of the page number on the original page. No page indicator is given for the last page of a document if the document was transcribed from a multiple-entry source (such as an article from a newspaper or a letter from a letterbook) and if there is text following the featured document on that same page.

[p. [x]]   Bracketing of the page number itself indicates that the page was not originally numbered and that the number of the page is editorially supplied.

underlined   Underlining is typographically reproduced, with multiple underlining typographically standardized to a single underline. Individually underlined words are distinguished from passages underlined with one continuous line. When underlining includes leading and trailing spaces , it indicates handwritten additions to preprinted forms.

superscript   Superscription is typographically reproduc^ed.

canceled   A single horizontal strikethrough bar is used to indicate any method of cancellation: strikethrough, cross-out, wipe erasure, knife erasure, overwriting, or other methods. Individually canceled words are distinguished from passages eliminated with a single cancellation. Characters individually canceled at the beginning or end of a word are distinguished from words canceled in their entirety.

⟨inserted⟩   Insertions in the text—whether interlinear, intralinear, or marginal—are enclosed in angle brackets. Letter⟨s⟩ and other characters individual⟨ly⟩ insert⟨ed⟩ at the beginning or end of a word are distinguished from ⟨words⟩ inserted in ⟨their⟩ entirety.

bold   Joseph Smith's handwriting is rendered in boldface type. Bracketed editorial insertions made within passages of **Smith's own h[and]writing** are also rendered in boldface type.

[roman]   Stylized brackets represent ⟦brackets⟧ used in the original text.

⊠   An envelope symbol signifies the beginning of a mailing address, postmark, or address panel on an original letter.

TEXT   The word TEXT begins textual footnotes describing significant details not comprehended by this scheme of symbolic transcription.

| A line break artificially imposed in an original document is rendered as a vertical line in source notes and textual footnotes.

✦   This symbol represents an Egyptian hieroglyph, hieratic character, or other unidentified character found in Egyptian-related documents. Where multiple characters were inscribed, it is not always possible to identify the exact number of characters intended.

Annotation Conventions

The Joseph Smith Papers do not present a unified narrative. Annotations—including historical introductions, editorial notes, and footnotes—supply background and context to help readers better understand and use the documents. The aim of the annotation is to serve scholars and students of early Mormon history and American religious history generally, whose familiarity with these fields may vary widely.

The *Papers* cite original sources where possible and practical. Secondary sources of sound scholarship are cited when they distill several primary sources or provide useful general context. Quotations from primary sources preserve original spelling but silently emend cancellations and insertions (unless judged highly significant).

Certain conventions simplify the presentation of the annotation. Joseph Smith is usually referred to by the initials JS. Most sources are referred to by a shortened citation form, with the complete citation given in the Works Cited. Some documents are referred to by editorial titles rather than by their original titles or the titles given in the catalogs of their current repositories. These editorial titles are in some cases similar to informal names by which the documents have come to be known. The editorial titles are listed in the Works Cited along with the complete citations by which the documents can be found in repositories. In cases in which two or more documents of the same genre bear the same date, a letter of the alphabet is appended to the date so that each document has a unique editorial title—for example, Revelation, 8 July 1838–A and Revelation, 8 July 1838–B. The most important sources used in annotation are discussed in the Essay on Sources preceding the Works Cited. Many of the documents featured in the Documents series have been extracted from letterbooks, minute books, or other records that contain multiple individual documents or entries. When more than one text in this volume came from the same record book, bibliographic and other information may be found in "Source Notes for Multiple-Entry Documents" in the back of the volume.

This volume uses a citation style that lists all source citations at the end of the footnote. Because of the complexity of some footnotes and the difficulty readers might have in determining which source citations document particular statements within such footnotes, superscript letters are sometimes used to key specific statements to their corresponding documentation. Though it goes beyond conventional citation style, this detailed approach may best serve researchers using this volume as a reference work.

Source citations in this volume identify revelations by their original date and by a citation of the version most relevant to the particular instance of annotation (usually the version published in the Documents series of *The Joseph Smith Papers*). For revelations that were later canonized by The Church of Jesus Christ of Latter-day Saints, revelation citations also include a bracketed "D&C" reference that provides the Doctrine and Covenants section and verse numbers that have been standard in the church since 1876. Bracketed D&C references are provided for the benefit of Latter-day Saints, who can easily access the revelations in their familiar canon of scriptural works, and other students of early Mormonism who may wish to access the most widely available editions of these revelations. A table titled Corresponding Section Numbers in Editions of the Doctrine and Covenants is provided following the Works Cited to help readers refer from the cited version of a canonized revelation to other published versions of the same revelation. For more information about revelation citations, see the aforementioned table and the introduction to the Works Cited.

Smith's revelations and revelatory translations published outside of the Doctrine and Covenants, such as the Book of Mormon, are referenced in *The Joseph Smith Papers* to an early published or manuscript version, with references to modern Latter-day Saint publications added in brackets. These books of Latter-day Saint scripture are described in more detail in the introduction to the Works Cited. When the Bible is used in annotation, the King James Version—the version read by Smith and his followers and contemporaries as well as by English-speaking Latter-day Saints today—is referenced.

In addition to the annotation in the main body of a volume, several supplementary resources in the back of each volume and at josephsmithpapers.org aid in understanding the text. As many of the places, people, organizations, and terms mentioned in the documents appear more than once, the reference material serves to remove duplicate footnotes and to otherwise systematically reduce the annotation in the main body. To minimize repetition and interruption, only rarely will annotation within the documents directly refer readers to the reference material in the back.

Many of the people whose names appear in the documents have been identified. Many of the first or last names supplied in square brackets in the transcripts presented in this volume have been inferred from the historical context of the document, without specific documentation. In most cases, information about people named in the documents appears in the Biographical Directory rather than in the notes. Some names have silently been left without identification either because resources did not permit research or because no information was found. Complete documentation for reference material in the back and for the timeline included earlier in the volume may be found at josephsmithpapers.org, as may other resources, including a complete calendar of Smith's papers, a glossary of Mormon terminology from Joseph Smith's time, and expanded versions of many of the reference resources.

DOCUMENTS
OCTOBER 1835–JANUARY 1838

PART 1: 2 OCTOBER–
1 DECEMBER 1835

In fall 1835, the township of Kirtland, Ohio, was bustling with activity. Already home to approximately one thousand church members, it continued to absorb migrants almost daily. Some were new converts seeking to gather with the Latter-day Saints, while others were elders assembling for the 1835–1836 session of the Elders School.[1] Work on the House of the Lord continued. With the central structure of the edifice largely completed by early fall, masons began applying plaster to the exterior and interior walls in early November.[2] Commercial activity was on the rise, facilitated by mercantile firms operated by church members. Having recently published the Doctrine and Covenants, the church's printing office continued to disseminate ecclesiastical instruction and church-related news in periodicals such as the *Latter Day Saints' Messenger and Advocate,* and the printers were preparing the church's first hymnbook for publication.[3]

As he oversaw these and many other efforts, JS continued to counsel church members and establish and explain doctrine through letters, sermons, and revelations. In a series of three letters printed in successive issues of the *Messenger and Advocate,* he expounded on doctrinal matters, provided specific instruction to missionaries, and responded to claims made by critics of the church.[4] In a 23 October prayer, JS and other church leaders pleaded for relief from financial debts and for assistance in redeeming Zion.[5] JS also continued to direct the church broadly and counsel or comfort its members individually through revelations, ten of which he dictated from mid-October to mid-November. A revelation dated 18 October prophesied that the sickness and distress experienced by Missouri church members would be mitigated; another, more personal revelation assured JS that his pregnant sister-in-law Mary Bailey Smith, who was "confined an[d] in a verry dangerous situation,"

---

1. Backman, *Heavens Resound,* 139–140; William W. Phelps, Kirtland, OH, to Sally Waterman Phelps, Liberty, MO, 27 Oct. and 14 Nov. 1835, in Historical Department, Journal History of the Church, 27 Oct. and 14 Nov. 1835.

2. JS, Journal, 12 Nov. 1835, in *JSP,* J1:96.

3. William W. Phelps, Kirtland, OH, to Sally Waterman Phelps, Liberty, MO, 20 July and 14 Nov. 1835, in Historical Department, Journal History of the Church, 20 July and 14 Nov. 1835; Crawley, *Descriptive Bibliography,* 1:47–52, 57–59.

4. Letter to the Elders of the Church, 2 Oct. 1835, pp. 6–15 herein; Letter to the Elders of the Church, 16 Nov. 1835, pp. 53–60 herein; Letter to the Elders of the Church, 30 Nov.–1 Dec. 1835, pp. 89–100 herein.

5. Prayer, 23 Oct. 1835, pp. 24–25 herein.

would deliver a healthy child.[6] Throughout this period, JS also received dozens of visitors. Many came to examine the Egyptian antiquities that JS and others had purchased from traveling exhibitor Michael Chandler in July, while others, such as Robert Matthews and Erastus Holmes, came to "enquire concerning the faith" of the Latter-day Saints, "having heard many reports."[7]

As church members worked to finish the House of the Lord, JS prepared members of the church's lay ministry to receive a promised endowment of power by urging sanctification and unity.[8] On 5 October, he advised the Quorum of the Twelve Apostles that it was the will of God that they attend the "solemn assembly of the first Elders for the organization of the School of the prophets, and attend to the ordinence of the washing of feet and to prepare their hearts in all humility for an endowment with power from on high."[9] Instruction sometimes included correction and chastisement.[10] A 3 November revelation reproved the Quorum of the Twelve and commanded them to "repent speedily and prepare their hearts for the solem assembly and for the great day which is to come."[11] Nine days later, JS urged the Twelve to prepare themselves for the ritual of foot washing, which he told them was "calculated to unite our hearts, that we may be one in feeling and sentiment and that our faith may be strong."[12] While organizing the Elders School in early November, he stressed the necessity of "our rightly improving our time and reigning up our minds to a sense of the great object that lies before us, viz, that glorious endowment that God has in store for the faithful."[13]

After purchasing Chandler's collection of mummies and papyri in early July, JS and several associates devoted time to two separate but related endeavors during the fall: the translation of what would later be referred to as the Book of Abraham, and a language-study effort that produced a number of Egyptian alphabet and grammar manuscripts.[14] Church leaders' interest in ancient languages developed during a period when intellectuals were trying to uncover the origins of human language; Christian scholars in particular

---

6. Revelation, 18 Oct. 1835, pp. 21–23 herein; Revelation, 27 Oct. 1835, pp. 25–26 herein; JS, Journal, 27 Oct. 1835, in *JSP*, J1:75.

7. JS, Journal, 15 and 17 Nov. 1835, in *JSP*, J1:100–101, 105; Conversations with Robert Matthews, 9–11 Nov. 1835, pp. 39–47 herein; JS, Journal, 4 Dec. 1835, in *JSP*, J1:115.

8. See Revelation, 22 June 1834, in *JSP*, D4:69 [D&C 105].

9. JS, Journal, 5 Oct. 1835, in *JSP*, J1:68.

10. Revelation, 1 Nov. 1835, pp. 29–30 herein; Revelation, 3 Nov. 1835, pp. 32–36 herein; Historical Introduction to Revelation, 8 Nov. 1835, pp. 38–39 herein.

11. Revelation, 3 Nov. 1835, p. 36 herein.

12. Discourse, 12 Nov. 1835, p. 50 herein.

13. JS, Journal, 3 Nov. 1835, in *JSP*, J1:84. The Elders School was just one of several "schools" established in Kirtland during this period, with other classes focused on English grammar, writing, history, and geography. (Revelation, 2 Nov. 1835, pp. 30–32 herein; William W. Phelps, Kirtland, OH, to Sally Waterman Phelps, Liberty, MO, 14 Nov. 1835, in Historical Department, Journal History of the Church, 14 Nov. 1835; William W. Phelps, Kirtland Mills, OH, to Sally Waterman Phelps, Liberty, MO, 18 Dec. 1835, in "Some Early Letters of William W. Phelps," *Utah Genealogical and Historical Magazine*, Jan. 1940, 30; Satterfield, "History of Adult Education in Kirtland," 102–104.)

14. Historical Introduction to Book of Abraham Manuscript, ca. Early July–ca. Nov. 1835–A [Abraham 1:4–2:6], pp. 71–77 herein; Historical Introduction to Egyptian Alphabet, ca. Early July–ca. Nov. 1835–A, pp. 81–83 herein.

were interested in reviving the study of biblical languages like Hebrew and Aramaic.[15] Though the arrival of the papyri in 1835 surely piqued JS's and others' interest in the Egyptian language, the translation of the ancient records and production of papyri-related texts—such as the Book of Abraham manuscript and the "Egyptian alphabet" that are featured in this section—were part of an abiding interest JS and his associates took in ancient languages and extra-biblical religious texts, an interest that extended back more than half a decade. JS reported that during the years 1828 and 1829, he translated the Book of Mormon from gold plates engraved in a language referred to as "reformed Egyptian."[16] While working on a revision of the Bible in 1830, JS added a passage to Genesis that referenced Adam passing down a "book of remembrance" so that his children could be taught in a language "which was pure & undefiled." Two years later, JS dictated a document that revealed and defined some words from the "pure language" of God.[17] Interest in ancient languages persisted into the mid-1830s;[18] in late May 1835, William W. Phelps penned a letter to his wife, Sally, that included six characters that he classified as "a specimen of some of the 'pure language.'"[19]

News of JS's translation of the papyri generated excitement and curiosity among many Latter-day Saints during the summer and fall of 1835.[20] Sometime in late 1835, Oliver Cowdery produced a document that featured several unknown characters paired with what appear to be translations; Frederick G. Williams later copied and identified them as "characters on the book of Mormon."[21] The existence of these character documents, along with Phelps's sample of the pure language, suggests that JS and his associates were experimenting with various kinds of language study during this period.[22] JS, Phelps, Cowdery, Williams, Warren Parrish, and others began working with Egyptian characters from the papyri in summer 1835, and later that year they also began to study and translate Hebrew as

---

15. Examples of such intellectuals include Stephen Sewall, Alexander Campbell, and Moses Stuart. (Goldman, *God's Sacred Tongue,* 45–50, 141–150; Brown, "Joseph [Smith] in Egypt," 36–40.)

16. JS History, vol. A-1, 13, in *JSP,* H1:276 (Draft 2); Book of Mormon, 1830 ed., 538 [Mormon 9:32]; see also Introduction to Part 1: July 1828–Mar. 1829, in *JSP,* D1:3–5.

17. Old Testament Revision 1, p. 11 [Moses 6:5–6]; Sample of Pure Language, between ca. 4 and ca. 20 Mar. 1832, in *JSP,* D2:213–215.

18. William W. Phelps, Oliver Cowdery, and Frederick G. Williams deciphered various characters related to what they believed was the "pure language," presumably the language used by Adam and Eve in the Garden of Eden, as well as characters reportedly copied from the gold plates. (William W. Phelps, [Kirtland, OH], to Sally Waterman Phelps, Liberty, MO, 26 May 1835, William W. Phelps, Papers, BYU; Characters Copied by Oliver Cowdery, ca. 1835–1836, in *JSP,* D1:361–365; Frederick G. Williams, Characters, Revelations Collection, CHL; see also in *JSP,* D1:363.)

19. William W. Phelps, [Kirtland, OH], to Sally Waterman Phelps, Liberty, MO, 26 May 1835, William W. Phelps, Papers, BYU.

20. William W. Phelps, Kirtland, OH, to Sally Waterman Phelps, Liberty, MO, 20 July 1835, in Historical Department, Journal History of the Church, 20 July 1835; Albert Brown to "Dear Parents," 1 Nov. 1835, Amos L. Underwood Correspondence, CHL; Oliver Cowdery, Kirtland, OH, to William Frye, Lebanon, IL, 22 Dec. 1835, in Cowdery, Letterbook, 71–74.

21. Characters Copied by Oliver Cowdery, ca. 1835–1836, in *JSP,* D1:361–365; Frederick G. Williams, Characters, Revelations Collection, CHL; see also in *JSP,* D1:363.

22. The same six characters that Phelps wrote later appeared in copies of the Egyptian alphabet. (Egyptian Alphabet, ca. Early July–ca. Nov. 1835–A, pp. 84–85 herein.)

a way to "understand his [the Lord's] word in the original language."[23] They commenced an informal study of Hebrew during the early fall, which later led to a more systematic study of the language under noted Hebraist Joshua Seixas.[24] The transcription, translation, and study of Egyptian characters undertaken by JS, Cowdery, Williams, Phelps, and Parrish likely overlapped with their informal study of Hebrew during the fall of 1835.[25]

———— ☙ ————

Letter to the Elders of the Church, 2 October 1835

Source Note

JS, Letter, [Kirtland Township, Geauga Co., OH], to "the elders of the church of Latter Day Saints," [2 Oct. 1835]. Featured version published in "To the Elders of the Church of Latter Day Saints," Latter Day Saints' Messenger and Advocate, *Sept. 1835, 1:179–182. For more information on* Latter Day Saints' Messenger and Advocate, *see Source Notes for Multiple-Entry Documents, p. 527 herein.*

Historical Introduction

This letter to the elders of the church was the first in a three-part series of open letters published in the September, November, and December 1835 issues of the church's newspaper, the *Latter Day Saints' Messenger and Advocate.* The letters instructed the church's increasingly large and sophisticated missionary force, which by that time included apostles and seventies. The three-part missive reminded them of essential doctrine, such as the establishment of Zion and the gathering of Israel, and provided specific direction to help them succeed in spreading the church's message. Instruction for traveling elders in the form of open letters such as this one appeared occasionally in the church's periodicals.[26]

In this letter, JS described the revelation that identified Independence, Jackson County, Missouri, as the central gathering place for a latter-day Zion. He acknowledged that this revelation had generated anxiety among Missourians and that the resulting migration of some 1,200 Mormons to western Missouri compounded the unease, culminating in the violent expulsion of Latter-day Saints from Jackson County in November 1833.[27] JS attempted to clarify the history of the Saints' settlement in Jackson County and contextualized the revelations and doctrines concerning Zion. He lamented that the Saints' intentions in

---

23. JS, Journal, 19 Jan. 1836, in *JSP,* J1:164; see also JS, Journal, 21 Nov. 1835 and 26 Jan. 1836, in *JSP,* J1:107–109, 173.

24. Historical Introduction to Letter to Henrietta Raphael Seixas, between 6 and 13 Feb. 1836, pp. 173–177 herein; see especially 173n22 herein.

25. See Historical Introduction to Letter to Henrietta Raphael Seixas, between 6 and 13 Feb. 1836, pp. 173–177 herein.

26. See, for example, Letter to the Church, not after 18 Dec. 1833, in *JSP,* D3:397; Letter to the Church, ca. Feb. 1834, in *JSP,* D3:412; and Letter to the Church, ca. Mar. 1834, in *JSP,* D3:472.

27. "The Elders Stationed in Zion to the Churches Abroad," *The Evening and the Morning Star,* July 1833, 110; John Corrill, Liberty, MO, to Oliver Cowdery, Kirtland, OH, Dec. 1833, *The Evening and the Morning Star,* Jan. 1834, 124–126; "Joseph Smith Documents from February 1833 through March 1834," in *JSP,* D3:xxvii–xxx.

settling Jackson County had been distorted by "designing and wicked men" and that the Saints' own outspoken zealousness regarding the doctrine of gathering had worsened relations in that county. The letter also referred to several New Testament passages to emphasize the duty the elders had to teach the church's basic doctrines—faith, repentance, remission of sins, and baptism.

JS wrote this first installment on 2 October and submitted it to editor John Whitmer, who published it shortly thereafter in the September issue of the *Messenger and Advocate,* which was then behind schedule.[28] The original letter is no longer extant. JS dictated the second letter of the series six weeks later, on 16 November 1835.[29]

Document Transcript

To the elders of the church of Latter Day Saints.

After so long a time, and after so many things having been said, I feel it my duty to drop a few hints, that, perhaps, the elders, traveling through the world to warn the inhabitants of the earth to flee the wrath to come,[30] and save themselves from this untoward generation, may be aided in a measure, in doctrine, and in the way of their duty. I have been laboring in this cause for eight years,[31] during which time I have traveled much, and have had much experience. I removed from Seneca county, N. Y. to Geauga county, Ohio, in February, 1831.

Having received, by an heavenly vision, a commandment, in June following, to take my journey to the western boundaries of the State of Missouri, and there designate the very spot, which was to be the central spot, for the commencement of the gathering together of those who embrace the fulness of the everlasting gospel[32]—I accordingly undertook the journey with certain ones of my brethren, and, after a long and tedious journey, suffering many

---

28. JS, Journal, 2 Oct. 1835, in *JSP,* J1:67. It appears that in late summer and fall 1835, issues of the *Messenger and Advocate* were being published about a month later than the dates found in the masthead. For instance, the August issue of the periodical was published sometime after 1 September, since it contained an obituary of Mary Hill stating that she died "on Tuesday, (the 1st of Sept.)" The September issue featured JS's 2 October letter. The October *Messenger and Advocate* contained letters dated 6 and 7 November 1835, indicating that issue was not published until after those dates. (Obituary for Mary Hill, *LDS Messenger and Advocate,* Aug. 1835, 1:176; L. T. Coons, 6 Nov. 1835, Letter to the Editor, and Noah Packard, 7 Nov. 1835, Letter to the Editor, *LDS Messenger and Advocate,* Oct. 1835, 2:207, 208.)

29. Letter to the Elders of the Church, 16 Nov. 1835, pp. 53–60 herein.

30. On warning the "inhabitants of the earth," see "Is the End Near?," *LDS Messenger and Advocate,* July 1835, 1:149–150; and Corrill, *Brief History,* 8, in *JSP,* H2:133.

31. JS here equated the beginning of "this cause" with the translation of the Book of Mormon. Elsewhere he stated that on 22 September 1827 he obtained a set of gold plates upon which was written an ancient record in an unknown language and that he began the work of translating that record, which would be known as the Book of Mormon, shortly thereafter. (See "Joseph Smith Documents Dating through June 1831," in *JSP,* D1:xxv.)

32. See Revelation, 6 June 1831, in *JSP,* D1:328 [D&C 52:2–3].

privations and hardships, I arrived in Jackson county Missouri;[33] and, after
viewing the country, seeking diligently at the hand of God, he manifested
himself unto me, and designated to me and others, the very spot upon which
he designed to commence the work of the gathering, and the upbuilding of an
holy city,[34] which should be called Zion:—Zion because it is to be a place of
righteousness, and all who build thereon, are to worship the true and living
God—and all believe in one doctrine even the doctrine of our Lord and Savior
Jesus Christ.[35] [p. 179]

"Thy watchmen shall lift up the voice; with the voice together shall
they sing: for they shall see eye to eye, when the Lord shall bring again
Zion."—Isaiah 52:8.

Here we pause for a moment, to make a few remarks upon the idea of
gathering to this place. It is well known that there were lands belonging to the
government, to be sold to individuals;[36] and it was understood by all, at least
we believed so, that we lived in a free country, a land of liberty and of laws,
guaranteeing to every man, or any company of men, the right of purchasing
lands, and settling, and living upon them: therefore we thought no harm in
advising the Latter Day Saints, or Mormons, as they are reproachfully called,
to gather to this place, inasmuch as it was their duty, (and it was well understood so to be,) to purchase, *with money*, lands, and live upon them—not
infringing upon the civil rights of any individual, or community of people:[37]

---

33. JS and others left Kirtland, Ohio, on 19 June 1831 and arrived at Independence, Jackson County,
Missouri, on 14 July 1831. (JS History, vol. A-1, 126; [William W. Phelps], "Extract of a Letter from the
Late Editor," *Ontario Phoenix* [Canandaigua, NY], 7 Sept. 1831, [2]; Gilbert, Notebook, [34]–[36].)

34. See Revelation, 20 July 1831, in *JSP*, D2:7–8 [D&C 57:1–3].

35. See Revelation, 9 Feb. 1831, in *JSP*, D1:250 [D&C 42:9]; Revelation, ca. 7 Mar. 1831, in *JSP*, D1:280
[D&C 45:65–67]; and Whitmer, History, 32, in *JSP*, H2:45; see also Revelation, 1 Aug. 1831, in *JSP*, D2:20
[D&C 58:57]; and Phelps, "Short History," [1].

36. In 1828 the U.S. government publicly announced that it would begin selling federal lands in
Missouri. Such lands were sold at auction for $1.25 per acre in tracts of at least eighty acres. Purchasers
paid the surveyors' fees up front, filed, and were required to complete payment within three years in order
to obtain title to the land. In 1831 the federal government offered for sale the lands it had reserved to
benefit public education, including the "Seminary Lands," which had been set aside to fund higher education in Missouri and which included much of the land in Jackson County. The seminary land was initially
offered for sale at $2.00 per acre. (An Act to Provide for the Sale of Seminary Lands [31 Dec. 1830],
Laws . . . of the State of Missouri, vol. 2, chap. 155, pp. 209–213.)

37. Revelations and instructions from church leaders directed church members to acquire lands in
Missouri by buying them, not by using violence. William W. Phelps, editor of *The Evening and the
Morning Star* at Independence, was aware of rumors that the Saints sought to acquire land violently, and
in 1833 he wrote: "To suppose that we can come up here and take possession of this land by the shedding
of blood, would be setting at nought the law of the glorious gospel, and also the word of our great
Redeemer: And to suppose that we can take possession of this country, without making regular purchases

always keeping in view the saying, "Do unto others as you would wish to have others do unto you."[38] Following also the good injunction: "Deal justly, love mercy, and walk humbly with thy God."[39]

These were our motives in teaching the people, or Latter Day Saints, to gather together, beginning at this place. And inasmuch as there are those who have had different views from this, we feel, that it is a cause of deep regret: For, be it known unto all men, that our principles concerning this thing, have not been such as have been represented by those who, we have every reason to believe, are designing and wicked men, that have said that this was our doctrine:—to infringe upon the rights of a people who inhabit our civil and free country: such as to drive the inhabitants of Jackson county from their lands, and take possession thereof unlawfully.[40] Far, yea, far be such a principle from our hearts: it never entered into our mind, and we only say, that God shall reward such in that day when he shall come to make up his jewels.

But to return to my subject: after having ascertained the very spot,[41] and having the happiness of seeing quite a number of the families of my brethren, comfortably situated upon the land, I took leave of them, and journeyed back to Ohio, and used every influence and argument, that lay in my power, to get those who believe in the everlasting covenant, whose circumstances would admit, and whose families were willing to remove to the place which I now designated to be the land of Zion: And thus the sound of the gathering, and of

---

of the same according to the laws of our nation, would be reproaching this great Republic." ("The Elders Stationed in Zion to the Churches Abroad, in Love," *The Evening and the Morning Star,* July 1833, 110; see also Revelation, 1 Aug. 1831, in *JSP,* D2:19–20 [D&C 58:51–53]; Revelation, 30 Aug. 1831, in *JSP,* D2:51 [D&C 63:29–31]; and Letter to Church Leaders in Jackson County, MO, 21 Apr. 1833, in *JSP,* D3:64.)

38. See Luke 6:31.

39. See Micah 6:8; and Revelation, May 1829–A, in *JSP,* D1:54 [D&C 11:12].

40. This may refer to some misrepresentations of the Saints' efforts to settle in Jackson County. In December 1833, Benton Pixley, a pastor in Jackson County, wrote that the Saints would use "blood and violence" to build up their kingdom and drive the non-Mormons away. In June 1834, Samuel C. Owens, Jackson County clerk and chairman of the committee that negotiated with the exiled Saints in summer 1834, was among those who expressed suspicions about Mormon land purchases in Jackson County. Even though an August 1831 revelation stated that church members were to obtain land only by legal purchase and were "forbidden to shed blood," Owens asserted that the revelation authorized church members to use violence to obtain land. Two months after Owens's letter and a year before the letter featured here, the church at Kirtland published "An Appeal" to the public to help dispel the rumors. It said that the Saints sought "only the peaceable possession of our rights and property." The appeal, signed by church leaders who had suffered in Jackson County, used the text of the August 1831 revelation as evidence. (B. Pixley, "The Mormonites in Missouri," *Christian Watchman* [Boston], 13 Dec. 1833, 2; *History of Jackson County, Missouri,* 256; "Propositions of the Mormons," *Painesville [OH] Telegraph,* 8 Aug. 1834, [3]; Declaration, 21 June 1834, in *JSP,* D4:59–69; Revelation, 30 Aug. 1831, in *JSP,* D2:51 [D&C 63:29–31]; "An Appeal," *The Evening and the Morning Star,* Aug. 1834, 183–184.)

41. See Revelation, 1 Aug. 1831, in *JSP,* D2:20 [D&C 58:57].

the doctrine, went abroad into the world; and many we have reason to fear, having a zeal not according to knowledge, not understanding the pure principles of the doctrine of the church, have no doubt, in the heat of enthusiasm, taught and said many things which are derogatory to the genuine character and principles of the church, and for these things we are heartily sorry, and would apologize if an apology would do any good.[42]

But we pause here and offer a remark upon the saying which we learn has gone abroad, and has been handled in a manner detrimental to the cause of truth, by saying, "that in preaching the doctrine of gathering, we break up families, and give license for men to leave their families; women their husbands; children their parents, and slaves their masters, thereby deranging the order, and breaking up the harmony and peace of society."[43] We shall here show our faith, and thereby, as we humbly trust, put an end to these faults, and wicked misrepresentations, which have caused, we have every reason to believe, thousands to think they were doing God's service, when they were persecuting the children of God: whereas, if they could have enjoyed the true light, and had a just understanding of our principles, they would have embraced them with all their hearts, and been rejoicing in the love of the truth.

And now to show our doctrine on this subject, we shall commence with the first principles of the gospel, which are repentance, and baptism for the remission of sins, and the gift of the Holy Ghost by the laying on of the hands.

---

42. David Whitmer, a church leader who resided in Jackson County in 1833, later said, "There were among us a few ignorant and simple-minded persons who were continually making boasts to the Jackson county people that they intended to possess the entire county, erect a temple, etc. This of course occasioned hard feelings and excited the bitter jealousy of the other religious denominations." On 12 October 1832, Benton Pixley wrote that the Saints were "most zealous and forward" in their cause. Isaac McCoy, a federal land surveyor and Baptist minister in Jackson County, wrote that the Mormons "have repeated, perhaps, hundreds of times, that this country was theirs, the Almighty had given it to them, and that they would assuredly have entire possession of it in a few years. . . . Such sayings, appeared to the people very near akin to many remarks which were common among them, and unfortunately for the Mormons, these reports were believed to be true, and the effect upon the public mind was accordingly." ("Mormonism," *Kansas City [MO] Daily Journal,* 5 June 1881, [1]; B. Pixley, "The Mormonites," *Independent Messenger* [Boston], 29 Nov. 1832; "The Disturbances in Jackson County," *Missouri Republican* [St. Louis], 20 Dec. 1833, 114; see also "To His Excellency, Daniel Dunklin," *The Evening and the Morning Star,* Dec. 1833, [2].)

43. Possibly in response to sentiments similar to the one quoted here by JS, church leaders issued a statement on marriage that first appeared in August 1835. It stated in part, "It is not right to persuade a woman to be baptized contrary to the will of her husband, neither is it lawful to influence her to leave her husband. All children are bound by law to obey their parents; and to influence them to embrace any religious faith, or be baptized, or leave their parents without their consent, is unlawful and unjust." Six months after writing this letter, JS wrote to Oliver Cowdery regarding the proselytizing then occurring in the southern United States. He counseled Cowdery and all members of the church that they were "not to preach at all to slaves, until after their masters are converted." (Statement on Marriage, ca. Aug. 1835, in *JSP,* D4:478; Letter to Oliver Cowdery, ca. 9 Apr. 1836, p. 242 herein.)

This we believe to be our duty, to teach to all mankind the doctrine of repentance, which we shall endeavor to show from the following quotations:

> "Then opened he their understanding, that they might understand the scriptures, and said unto them, thus it is written, and thus it behoved Christ to suffer, and to rise from the dead, the third day; and that repentance and remission of sins should be preached in his name among all nations, beginning at Jerusalem."—Luke 24:45, 46, 47.

By this we learn, that it behoved Christ to suffer, and to be crucified, and rise again on the third day, for the express purpose that repentance and [p. 180] remission of sins should be preached unto all nations.

> "Then Peter said unto them, repent, and be baptized every one of you, in the name of Jesus Christ, for the remission of sins, and ye shall receive the gift of the Holy Ghost. For the promise is unto you, and to your children, and to all that are afar off, even as many as the Lord our God shall call."—Acts 2:38, 39.

By this we learn, that the promise of the Holy Ghost, is unto as many as the doctrine of repentance was to be preached, which was unto all nations. And we discover also, that the promise was to extend by lineage: for Peter says, "not only unto you, but unto your children, and unto all that are afar off." From this we infer that it was to continue unto their children's children, and even unto as many generations as should come after, even as many as the Lord their God should call.— We discover here that we are blending two principles together, in these quotations. The first is the principle of repentance, and the second is the principle of remission of sins. And we learn from Peter, that remission of sins is obtained by baptism in the name of the Lord Jesus Christ; and the gift of the Holy Ghost follows inevitably: for, says Peter, "you shall receive the gift of the Holy Ghost." Therefore we believe in preaching the doctrine of repentance in all the world, both to old and young, rich and poor, bond and free, as we shall endeavor to show hereafter—how and in what manner, and how far it is binding upon the consciences of mankind, making proper distinctions between old and young men, women and children, and servants.

But we discover, in order to be benefitted by the doctrine of repentance, we must believe in obtaining the remission of sins. And in order to obtain the remission of sins, we must believe in the doctrine of baptism, in the name of the Lord Jesus Christ. And if we believe in baptism for the remission of sins, we may expect a fulfilment of the promise of the Holy Ghost: for the promise extends to all whom the Lord our God shall call. And hath he not surely said, as you will find in the last chapter of Revelations:

"And the Spirit and the bride say, Come. And let him that heareth, say, Come. And let him that is athirst, come. And whosoever will, let him take the water of life freely." Rev. 22:17.

Again the Savior says:

"Come unto me, all ye that labor, and are heavy laden, and I will give you rest. Take my yoke upon you, and learn of me; for I am meek and lowly in heart; and ye shall find rest unto your souls. For my yoke is easy, and my burden is light."—Math. 11:28, 29, 30.

Again Isaiah says:

"Look unto me, and be ye saved, all the ends of the earth: for I am God, and there is none else. I have sworn by myself, the word is gone out of my mouth in righteousness, and shall not return, that unto me every knee shall bow, every tongue shall swear. Surely, shall one say, in the Lord have I righteousness and strength: even to him shall men come; and all that are incensed against him shall be ashamed."—Isaiah 45:22, 23, 24.

And to show further connections in proof of the doctrine above named, we quote the following scriptures:

"Him hath God exalted with his right hand, to be a Prince and a Savior, for to give repentance to Israel, and forgiveness of sins. And we are his witnesses of these things; and so is also the Holy Ghost, whom God hath given to them that obey him."—Acts 5:31, 32.

"But when they believed Philip, preaching the things concerning the kingdom of God, and the name of Jesus Christ, they were baptized, both men and women. Then Simon himself believed also; and when he was baptized, he continued with Philip, and wondered, beholding the miracles and signs which were done. Now when the apostles, which were at Jerusalem, heard that Samaria had received the word of God, they sent unto them Peter and John; who, when they were come down, prayed for them, that they might receive the Holy Ghost. (For as yet he was fallen upon none of them: only they were baptized in the name of the Lord Jesus.)— Then laid they their hands on them, and they received the Holy Ghost. . . .[44] And as they went on their way, they came unto a certain water; and the eunuch said, See, here is water; what doth hinder me to be baptized?—And Philip said, If thou believest with all thine heart thou mayest. And he answered and said, I believe that Jesus Christ is the Son of God. And he commanded the chariot to stand still: and they went down both into the water, both Philip and the eunuch; and he baptized him. And, when they were come up out of the water, the Spirit of the Lord caught away Philip, that the eunuch saw him no more: and he went on his way rejoicing. But Philip was found at Azotus: and, passing through, he preached in all the cities, till he came to Cesarea."—Acts 8:12, 13, 14, 15, 16, 17,——36, to the end.

"While Peter yet spake these words, the Holy Ghost fell on all them which heard the word. And they of the circumcision, which believed, were astonished, as many as came with Peter, because that on the Gentiles also was poured out the gift of the Holy Ghost: for they heard them speak with tongues, and magnify God. Then answered Peter, Can any man forbid water, that these should not be baptized, which have received the Holy Ghost as well as we? And he commanded them to be baptized in the name of the Lord. Then prayed they him to tarry certain days."—Acts 10:44, 45, 46, 47, 48.

"And on the Sabbath, we went out of the city, by a river side, where prayer was wont to be made; and we sat down, and spake un[p. 181]to the women that resorted thither. And a certain woman, named Lydia, a seller of purple, of the city of Thyatira, which worshipped God, heard us: whose heart the Lord opened, that she attended unto the things which were spoken of Paul. And when she was baptized, and her household, she besought us, saying, If ye have judged me to be faithful to the Lord, come into my house, and abide there. And she constrained us. . . . .[45] And at midnight Paul and Silas prayed, and sang praises unto God: and the prisoners heard them. And suddenly there was a great earthquake, so that the foundations of the prison were shaken; and immediately all the doors were opened, and every one's bands were loosed. And the keeper of the prison awaking out of his sleep, and seeing the prison doors open, he drew out his sword, and would have killed himself, supposing that the prisoners had been fled. But Paul cried with a loud voice, saying, Do thyself no harm; for we are all here. Then he called for a light, and sprang in, and came trembling, and fell

---

44. TEXT: Ellipses in original.
45. TEXT: Ellipses in original.

down before Paul and Silas; and brought them out, and said, Sirs, what must I do to be saved? And they said believe on the Lord Jesus Christ, and thou shalt be saved and thy house. And they spake unto him the word of the Lord, and to all that were in his house. And he took them the same hour of the night, and washed their stripes, and was baptized, he and all his, staightway. And when he had brought them into his house, he set meat before them, and rejoiced, believing in God with all his house."—Acts 16:13, 14, 15.——25, to 35.

"And it came to pass, that, while Apollos was at Corinth, Paul, having passed through the upper coasts, came to Ephesus; and finding certain disciples, he said unto them, Have ye received the Holy Ghost since ye believed? And they said unto him, We have not so much as heard whether there be any Holy Ghost. And he said unto them, Unto what then were ye baptized? And they said, Unto John's baptism. Then said Paul, John verily baptized with the baptism of repentance, saying unto the people, that they should believe on him which should come after him, that is, on Christ Jesus. When they heard this, they were baptized in the name of the Lord Jesus. And, when Paul had laid his hands upon them, the Holy Ghost came on them; and they spake with tongues, and prophesied."—Acts 19:1, 2, 3, 4, 5, 6.

["]And one Ananias, a devout man, according to the law, having a good report of all the Jews which dwelt there, Came unto me, and stood, and said unto me, Brother Saul, receive thy sight. And the same hour I looked up upon him. And he said, the God of our fathers hath chosen thee, that thou shouldst know his will, and see that Just One, and shouldst hear the voice of his mouth. For thou shalt be his witness unto all men, of what thou hast seen and heard. And now why tarriest thou? arise, and be baptized, and wash away thy sins, calling on the name of the Lord."—Acts 22:12, 13, 14, 15, 16.

"For, when for the time ye ought to be teachers, ye have need that one teach you again which be the first principles of the oracles of God; and are become such as have need of milk, and not of strong meat. For every one that useth milk, is unskilful in the word of righteousness; for he is a babe. But strong meat belongeth to them that are of full age, even those who by reason of use, have their senses exercised to discern both good and evil."—Heb. 5:12, 13, 14.

"Therefore, leaving the principles of the doctrine of Christ, let us go on unto perfection; not laying again the foundation of repentance from dead works, and of faith towards God, of the doctrine of baptisms, and of laying on of hands, and of resurrection of the dead, and of eternal judgment. And this will we do, if God permit. For it is impossible for those who were once enlightened, and have tasted of the heavenly gift, and were made partakers of the Holy Ghost, and have tasted the good word of God, and the powers of the world to come, if they shall fall away, to renew them again unto repentance; seeing they crucify to themselves the Son of God afresh, and put him to an open shame.["]—Heb. 6:1, 2, 3, 4, 5, 6.

These quotations are so plain, in proving the doctrine of repentance and baptism for the remission of sins, I deem it unnecessary to enlarge this letter with comments upon them—but I shall continue the subject in my next.

In the bonds of the new and everlasting covenant,

JOSEPH SMITH, jr.

JOHN WHITMER, Esq.

———— ✑ ————

Charges against John Gould and Dean Gould Preferred to Joseph Smith, 2 October 1835

Editorial Note

For the full text of this letter, see Minutes, 3 October 1835, p. 17 herein.

———— ✑ ————

Minutes, 3 October 1835

Source Note

Kirtland high council, Minutes, Kirtland Township, Geauga Co., OH, 3 Oct. 1835. Featured version copied [between ca. 4 Apr. and ca. 16 May 1836] in Minute Book 1, p. 126; handwriting of Warren A. Cowdery; CHL. For more information on Minute Book 1, see Source Notes for Multiple-Entry Documents, p. 527 herein.

Historical Introduction

On 2 October 1835, Reynolds Cahoon, counselor to Bishop Newel K. Whitney in Kirtland, Ohio, preferred ecclesiastical charges against John Gould and Dean Gould (no apparent relation to each other). In the charges, which Cahoon sent to JS, he accused John Gould of "making expressions . . . calculated to do injury to the great cause which we have espoused" and demonstrating "strong dissatisfaction against the teachings of the Presidency of the church." Cahoon accused Dean Gould of "using wrong expressions and threatning the Elders of the Church." Both men were called before the Kirtland high council the following day. The minutes of that council, which include the text of Cahoon's charges, are presented here.

Formerly a Free Will Baptist minister, John Gould joined the church in western New York in 1832. He and his wife, Oliva, were baptized by Cahoon, who had joined the church in Ohio two years earlier.[46] Gould purchased forty-nine acres of property in Painesville, Ohio, sometime in fall 1833, but it appears that a steady stream of church assignments gave him little time to spend on the property in subsequent years.[47] In late August or early September 1833, JS dispatched Gould and Orson Hyde to Missouri with special instructions for the church members there, who, when confronted with mob violence, had signed an agreement to leave Jackson County by April of the next year.[48] By March 1834, Gould was in western New York, accompanying JS and Parley P. Pratt as they recruited men and raised money to reinstate the Saints to their land in Missouri.[49] During winter and spring 1835, he presided over congregations in western New York, including the areas around Freedom and Westfield.[50] By August 1835, Gould had returned to Kirtland, where on 10 August he participated in a disciplinary meeting at which Cahoon was accused of failing to correct and instruct his children.[51] A week later, Gould attended a conference in which the church accepted the Doctrine and Covenants as scripture. During the meeting, where he was listed as "President of the Elders," Gould declared that "he knew it was true and also the Book of Mormon, because he had received the testimony of the Spirit in favor of them."[52]

It is unclear when, where, or how Cahoon became aware of John Gould's alleged dissatisfaction with the teachings of the First Presidency. As presiding elder in the Freedom area, Gould appeared to be living—or at the least spending most of his time—in western New York during the winter and spring of 1835. Cahoon, meanwhile, lived in Kirtland, and there is no indication that he visited western New York during this time.[53] It is possible that Cahoon overheard comments Gould made during his stay in Kirtland in August.[54]

---

46. Stewart, *History of the Freewill Baptists,* 323–327, 475; Burgess and Ward, *Free Baptist Cyclopaedia,* 236, 473–474; Patten, Journal, [16] and 17 Dec. 1832; Obituary for Reynolds Cahoon, *Deseret News,* 1 May 1861, 72.

47. Geauga Co., OH, Deed Records, 1795–1921, vol. 17, p. 453, microfilm 20,237, U.S. and Canada Record Collection, FHL; see also Geauga Co., OH, Deed Records, 1795–1921, vol. 26, pp. 178–179, 185, microfilm 20,241, U.S. and Canada Record Collection, FHL.

48. Revelation, 12 Oct. 1833, in *JSP,* D3:320–325 [D&C 100]; see also Letter to Church Leaders in Jackson County, MO, 18 Aug. 1833, in *JSP,* D3:258–269.

49. JS, Journal, 4–6 Mar. 1834, in *JSP,* J1:31.

50. John Gould attended and chaired a regional church conference in Freedom, New York, on 24–25 January 1835; he was also listed as the presiding elder at a conference in Westfield the following May, though he did not in fact attend that conference. The *History of Cattaraugus County* confirms that he preached with JS, Sidney Rigdon, and Parley P. Pratt in the area around Fish Lake in about 1835, converting some thirty men and women. ("A Summary," *LDS Messenger and Advocate,* Feb. 1835, 75–77; Record of the Twelve, 4–9 May 1835; *History of Cattaraugus County, New York,* 398.)

51. Minutes, 10 Aug. 1835, in *JSP,* D4:380–382.

52. Minutes, 17 Aug. 1835, in *JSP,* D4:389, 395.

53. Whether John Gould spent much time in Kirtland in 1834 or 1835 is unclear. JS's journal entry for 3 March 1834 indicates that Gould was still living in western New York. While preaching in Westfield, New York, JS noted that "John Gould payed me on papers—$1.50." JS was likely referring to a subscription to *The Evening and the Morning Star,* which may indicate that Gould was not in Kirtland frequently enough to pay the subscription in person. (JS, Journal, 3 Mar. 1834, in *JSP,* J1:29–31.)

54. See *JSP,* D4:389n168.

Little is known about the other defendant, Dean Gould. Census records indicate that he was in his teens in 1835.[55] Though not a member of the church at the time he left, Dean Gould accompanied JS and others on the Camp of Israel expedition to Missouri; during the expedition he was baptized by Lyman Wight on 15 June 1834.[56]

The minutes of the 3 October disciplinary council indicate that, following discussions, the matters involving both John Gould and Dean Gould were amicably resolved. The original letter, in which Cahoon first presented the charges directly to JS, is no longer extant, but its contents were later copied into Minute Book 1.

Document Transcript

Minutes of a High Council met Oct 3d. 1835
Presiding Presidents, H[yrum] Smith & D[avid] Whitmer.
                                    Counsellors.

Sidney Rigdon	Joseph Smith Junr.
John Smith	Joseph Smith senior
William Smith	J[ohn] Johnson
J[ared] Carter	S[amuel] H. Smith
R[oger] Orton	Luke Johnson
Noah Packard	O[rson] Johnson

Opened as usual by Prayer.
Charges preferred against Elder John Gould & Dean Gould as follows.

Joseph Smith Junr. President of the church of the Latter Day Saints, Greeting

Sir, I prefer certain charges against Elder John Gould. (Viz.) of making expressions which is calculated to do injury to the great cause which we have espoused and manifesting a very strong dissatisfaction against the teachings of the Presidency of the church.[57]

Also Dean Gould for using wrong expressions and threatning the Elders of the Church.[58]

Yours &c.
R[eynolds] Cahoon

Kirtland Oct. 2d 1835

---

55. 1840 U.S. Census, Kirtland, Lake Co., OH, 93.

56. "Extracts from H. C. Kimball's Journal," *Times and Seasons,* 1 Feb. 1845, 6:789.

57. A 3 October 1835 entry in JS's journal specifies that John Gould was accused of "giving credence to false and slanderous reports instigated to Injure bro Sidney Rigdon." (JS, Journal, 3 Oct. 1835, in *JSP,* J1:67.)

58. JS's journal entry notes that Dean Gould had specifically threatened Sidney Rigdon as well as "others of the Elders." (JS, Journal, 3 Oct. 1835, in *JSP,* J1:67–68.)

After conversing on this subject, it was agreed by Complainant & Defendant, that the matter should be talked over, and no doubt entertained, but an amicable adjustment of this matter could be effected: After digesting this matter; all difference of feelings was allayed and the wound was healed, Charge preferred against Dean Gould. That he spoke unadvisedly against S. Rigdon. Dean Gould acknowledged his wrongs &, was forgiven.

Closed in prayer by John Whitmer Clerk

———— ℰ⅋ ————

Blessing to Newel K. Whitney, 7 October 1835

Source Note

JS, Blessing, to Newel K. Whitney, [Kirtland Township, Geauga Co., OH], 7 Oct. 1835. Featured version copied [ca. 7 Oct. 1835] in JS, Journal, 1835–1836, pp. 6–7; handwriting of Frederick G. Williams with additions in the handwriting of JS; JS Collection, CHL. For more information on JS, Journal, 1835–1836, see Source Notes for Multiple-Entry Documents, p. 524 herein.

Historical Introduction

On 7 October 1835, JS pronounced a blessing upon Newel K. Whitney, the bishop of the church in Kirtland, Ohio. The blessing addressed Whitney's role as a bishop, reminded him of his responsibility to the poor, counseled him about some shortcomings, and promised rich blessings. JS's journal suggests that the blessing was related to a business trip to Buffalo, New York, that Whitney and Hyrum Smith embarked on that day. In a 7 October entry, JS offered a prayer on behalf of the two men that "their lives may be spared and they have a safe Journey and no accident or sickness of the least kind befall them that they may return in health and in safety to the bosom of their families."[59] The entry then continues with the blessing featured here.

A successful merchant in Kirtland, Whitney joined the church in November 1830.[60] Within months of his conversion, he became a close associate of JS, and, over time, he also became an important financial benefactor to the church. Shortly after a July 1831 revelation identified Independence, Missouri, as "the place for the City of Zion," JS dictated another revelation in which Whitney was instructed to "impart all the money which he can impart to be sent up unto the land of Zion."[61] On 4 December 1831, Whitney was appointed as the bishop in Kirtland and, in conjunction with that calling, was directed "to keep the Lords storehouse," from which "the poor and needy" would be supplied with goods.[62] Whitney's

---

59. JS, Journal, 7 Oct. 1835, in *JSP*, J1:69.

60. [Elizabeth Ann Whitney], "A Leaf from an Autobiography," *Woman's Exponent,* 1 Sept. 1878, 7:51.

61. Revelation, 20 July 1831, in *JSP,* D2:8 [D&C 57:2]; Revelation, 30 Aug. 1831, in *JSP,* D2:53 [D&C 63:43].

62. Revelation, 4 Dec. 1831–A and 4 Dec. 1831–B, in *JSP,* D2:146–153 [D&C 72:1–23]. This instruction was similar to the directions given to Edward Partridge, who had been appointed bishop in Missouri on

mercantile business, N. K. Whitney & Co., was situated at the junction of Chillicothe and Chardon roads in Kirtland and likely operated as this storehouse.[63]

Whitney's financial ties to the church grew in April 1832 when a JS revelation appointed him and eight other men to direct the newly established United Firm, an organization that would manage the church's "Literary and Merchantile establishments."[64] On 26 April, N. K. Whitney & Co. was mentioned as one of two mercantile stores that would be included in the United Firm.[65] Whitney was also appointed, along with Sidney Gilbert, as agent "to act in the name of this Firm," and evidence suggests that Whitney's property and personal holdings made up a significant portion of the United Firm's assets by 1834.[66] A series of disastrous events in Missouri in 1833, including the destruction of the printing office and ransacking of Gilbert's merchandise and store, left the firm in serious financial distress, and by April 1834 the firm's members had decided to dissolve the organization.[67] Frederick G. Williams reported that shortly after this decision JS dictated a revelation requiring the members to "give up all notes & demands that they had against each other."[68] A 23 April revelation directed firm members to reorganize the firm and redistribute its assets among its individual members.[69] It appears that Whitney, and to a lesser extent Williams and John Johnson, absorbed most of the firm's debt.[70] Whitney struggled to pay his own personal debts following the collapse of the United Firm; by September, he was described as being in "embarrassed circumstances."[71]

Despite his financial struggles, Whitney relied on his reputation, business contacts, and good credit to help establish and stock other church-related mercantile businesses in 1835 and 1836.[72] Among these mercantile establishments was a "committee store," which marketed goods to Kirtland residents at large; the profits were directed toward the construction

4 February 1831. (Revelation, 4 Feb. 1831, in *JSP,* D1:244 [D&C 41:9]; Revelation, 9 Feb. 1831, in *JSP,* D1:251–252 [D&C 42:31–33].)

63. Revelation, 4 Dec. 1831–B, in *JSP,* D2:151 [D&C 72:9–23]; Revelation, 30 Aug. 1831, in *JSP,* D2:52–53 [D&C 63:42–45]; Revelation, between ca. 8 and ca. 24 Mar. 1832, in *JSP,* D2:220–221; Minutes, 26–27 Apr. 1832, in *JSP,* D2:233.

64. Revelation, 1 Mar. 1832, in *JSP,* D2:197–200 [D&C 78]; Revelation, 26 Apr. 1832, in *JSP,* D2:233–237 [D&C 82]. The publishing arm of the United Firm was called the Literary Firm. The other members of the United Firm (which included members of the Literary Firm) were JS, Oliver Cowdery, Edward Partridge, Sidney Rigdon, John Whitmer, William W. Phelps, and Martin Harris. Frederick G. Williams joined the United Firm on 15 March 1833; John Johnson became a member in June 1833. (Revelation, 26 Apr. 1832, in *JSP,* D2:233–237 [D&C 82]; Minute Book 1, 15 Mar. 1833; Minutes, 4 June 1833, in *JSP,* D3:108–110.)

65. The other store was Gilbert, Whitney & Co. in Independence, Missouri. (Revelation, 26 Apr. 1832, in *JSP,* D2:233–237 [D&C 82]; Minutes, 26–27 Apr. 1832, in *JSP,* D2:229–233.)

66. Minutes, 1 May 1832, in *JSP,* D2:245; Balance of Account, 23 Apr. 1834, in *JSP,* D4:31–33.

67. JS, Journal, 10 Apr. 1834, in *JSP,* J1:38; see also "From Missouri," *The Evening and the Morning Star,* Jan. 1834, 124–125.

68. Frederick G. Williams, Statement, no date, Frederick G. Williams, Papers, CHL.

69. Revelation, 23 Apr. 1834, in *JSP,* D4:19–31 [D&C 104].

70. Balance of Account, 23 Apr. 1834, in *JSP,* D4:31–33.

71. Minutes, 24 Sept. 1834, in *JSP,* D4:176.

72. William L. Perkins, Statement, 23 July 1867, in Franklin D. Richards, Liverpool, England, to Brigham Young, 27 Aug. 1867, Brigham Young Office Files, CHL.

of the House of the Lord.[73] The store's name referred to the committee to build the House of the Lord, which consisted of Jared Carter, Reynolds Cahoon, and Hyrum Smith, partners in a mercantile firm known as Cahoon, Carter & Co.[74] On the day of the blessing presented here, 7 October, Whitney and Hyrum Smith left Kirtland for New York to purchase goods for the committee store.[75] Whitney may have leveraged his business contacts in Buffalo and New York City to enable Hyrum Smith to purchase goods for the store.[76]

The text presented here, found in JS's journal, is in the handwriting of Frederick G. Williams and includes insertions in JS's handwriting. It is unclear whether this is the original manuscript or whether it was copied from another document that is no longer extant. At least three other versions of this document exist, though the featured text is the only one that contains corrections in JS's own hand. It is not known whether Newel K. Whitney was physically present when this blessing was dictated.[77] Several months later, Oliver Cowdery copied the text into Patriarchal Blessing Book 1 and included a preface noting that the blessing was given "through the Urim and Thummim."[78]

Document Transcript

Blessed of the lord is bro [Newel K.] Whitney even the bishop of the church of the latter day saints, for the bishoprick shall never be taken away from him while he liveth and the time cometh that he shall overcome all the narrow mindedness of his heart and all his covetous desires that so easily besetteth him and ⟨he⟩ shall ~~deliver~~ deal with a liberal hand to the poor

---

73. JS, Journal, 17 Dec. 1835, in *JSP*, J1:124; "Anniversary of the Church of Latter Day Saints," *LDS Messenger and Advocate,* Apr. 1837, 3:488; "Cahoon, Carter & Co." and "Kirtland, Ohio, June 13, 1835," *Northern Times,* 2 Oct. 1835, [4].

74. Minutes, 4 May 1833, in *JSP*, D3:81; Revelation, 2 Aug. 1833–B, in *JSP*, D3:203–207 [D&C 94].

75. JS's journal indicates that the purpose of the trip was to buy goods for the committee store; a receipt in JS's office papers seems to confirm this. (JS, Journal, 7 Oct. 1835, in *JSP*, J1:69; Gardner and Patterson, Invoice, 10 Oct. 1835, JS Office Papers, CHL.)

76. Several historical documents suggest that Whitney introduced church leaders to New York merchants in subsequent years. Entries in Whitney's account book demonstrate that he began purchasing goods from the New York City firm of Halsted, Haines & Co. as early as October 1833. An 1837 promissory note confirms that Hyrum Smith, Reynolds Cahoon, and Jared Carter purchased goods from the firm as early as 1836. An 1867 statement written by William Perkins suggests that Halsted issued credit to Cahoon, Carter & Co. based on his trust in Whitney. ("New York Account Book, Sept. 1834," 17 Oct. 1833, Newel K. Whitney, Papers, BYU; Hyrum Smith et al. to Halsted, Haines & Co., Promissory Note, 1 Sept. 1837, private possession, copy at CHL; William L. Perkins, Statement, 23 July 1867, in Franklin D. Richards, Liverpool, England, to Brigham Young, 27 Aug. 1867, Brigham Young Office Files, CHL.)

77. JS, Journal, 7 Oct. 1835, in *JSP*, J1:69; compare Blessing to David Whitmer, 22 Sept. 1835, in *JSP*, D4:428–430.

78. The complete preface reads: "The following blessing was given by president Joseph Smith, Jr. through the Urim and Thummim, according to the spirit of prophecy and revelation, on Wednesday, the 7th of October, 1835, and written by president Frederick G. Williams, who acted as clerk." (Patriarchal Blessings, 1:33–34.)

and the needy the sick and the afflicted the widow and the fatherless[79] and marviously [marvelously] and miraculously shall the Lord his God provid for him. even that he shall be blessed with a ⟨all the ~~the~~⟩ fullness of the good things of this earth and his seed after him from generation to generation and it shall come to pass that according to to the measure that he meeteth out with a liberal hand unto the poor so shall it be measured to him again by the hand of his God even an hundred fold Angels shall guard ⟨his⟩ house and shall guard the lives of his posterity, and they shall become very great and very numerous on the earth, whomsoever he blesseth they shall be blessed. whomsoever he curseth they shall be cursed. and when his enemies seek him unto his hurt and distruction let him rise up and curse and the hand of God shall be upon his enemies in Judgment [p. 6] they shall be utterly confounded and brought to dessolation, therefor he shall be preserved unto the utmost and his ⟨**life**⟩[80] ~~day~~ shall be precious in the sight of the Lord. he shall rise up and shake himself as a lion riseth out of his nest and roareth untill he shaketh the hills and as a lion goeth forth among the Lesser beasts, so shall the goings forth of him ⟨**be**⟩[81] whom the Lord hath anointed to exalt the poor and to humble the rich, therefor his name shall be on high and his rest among the sanctified.

———— ❧ ————

Revelation, 18 October 1835

Source Note

Revelation, Kirtland Township, Geauga Co., OH, 18 Oct. 1835. Featured version copied [ca. early 1838] in John Whitmer, History, 1831–ca. 1847, pp. 81–82; handwriting of John Whitmer; CCLA. For more information on John Whitmer, History, 1831–ca. 1847, see Source Notes for Multiple-Entry Documents, p. 522 herein.

---

79. This may have been a reminder of Whitney's responsibility as a bishop to assist the poor. In September 1832, JS dictated a revelation in which Whitney was exhorted to "travel round about and among all the churches searching after the poor to administer to ther wants by humbling the rich and the proud." There is evidence that Whitney acted on this admonition. During the second week of January 1836, he and his wife, Elizabeth Ann Smith Whitney, hosted a three-day "Feast for the Poor" at his Kirtland residence. Organized to feed the poor, "the lame, the halt, the deaf, the blind, the aged and infirm," the gathering was also where some of those present received patriarchal blessings. JS joined in the festivities on at least two separate occasions. (Revelation, 22–23 Sept. 1832, in *JSP,* D2:303 [D&C 84:112]; JS, Journal, 7 and 9 Jan. 1836, in *JSP,* J1:146–147; [Elizabeth Ann Smith Whitney], "A Leaf from an Autobiography," *Woman's Exponent,* 1 Oct. and 1 Nov. 1878, 7:71, 83.)

80. TEXT: Insertion in the handwriting of JS.

81. TEXT: Insertion in the handwriting of JS.

Historical Introduction

A group of church leaders gathered at the unfinished House of the Lord in Kirtland, Ohio, on 18 October 1835, where JS prophesied that the distress and sickness that had plagued the Saints in Missouri would dissipate. During the previous two years, church members in Missouri experienced great trauma and turmoil. After their expulsion from Jackson County during fall 1833, the Missouri Saints initially struggled to survive in Clay County, where most of the refugees settled.[82] Their continued attempts to regain their lands in Jackson County or receive compensation for confiscated property proved unsuccessful.

This revelation came at a time when church leaders renewed their plans to redeem Zion. In June 1834, JS dictated a revelation stating that Zion would be redeemed after men who held the priesthood obtained an endowment of power in the House of the Lord.[83] In a letter written in August, JS announced that 11 September 1836 was "the appointed time for the redemption of Zion."[84] In August 1835, JS and other church leaders wrote to church members in Missouri about the redemption of Zion. They encouraged church members to "cause as little excitement as posible and endure their afflictions patiently until the time appointed."[85] On 24 September 1835, less than a month before JS dictated this revelation, the high council met at JS's house in Kirtland and drew up an "Article of inrollment" to obtain volunteers to go to Missouri in spring 1836.[86]

John Whitmer, who served as church historian at the time, recorded the revelation. He likely copied it into his history in early 1838.[87]

Document Transcript

Oct 18, 1835. Sabbath

This day assembled in the house of the Lord as usual and the Spirit of the [p. 81] Lord decended upon J. Smith Jr[88]—the seer and he propheced: saying the L[or]d[89] has showd to me this day by the Spirit of Revelation that the

---

82. Letter from William W. Phelps, 14 Nov. 1833, in *JSP*, D3:342–343; Letter from Edward Partridge, between 14 and 19 Nov. 1833, in *JSP*, D3:344–351; Letter from William W. Phelps, 15 Dec. 1833, in *JSP*, D3:382–386.

83. Revelation, 22 June 1834, in *JSP*, D4:74 [D&C 105:9–11].

84. Letter to Lyman Wight and Others, 16 Aug. 1834, in *JSP*, D4:106.

85. Letter to Church Officers in Clay County, MO, 31 Aug. 1835, in *JSP*, D4:405.

86. JS, Journal, 24 Sept. 1835, in *JSP*, J1:64.

87. The entry in John Whitmer's history for 18 October 1835 also notes that several church leaders received blessings from JS that day and that those blessings were recorded in the "Patriarchal blessing Book." Many church leaders received blessings from JS in late September and early October 1835, but none received blessings on 18 October. It is likely that Whitmer, who did not have access to the Patriarchal Blessing Book when he made the 18 October 1835 entry in his history, mistakenly associated those September and October 1835 blessings with the date of the revelation featured here. (See JS, Journal, 22 Sept. 1835, in *JSP*, J1:61–62; and Patriarchal Blessings, 1:13–16; for further information about John Whitmer's history, see Historical Introduction to Whitmer, History, in *JSP*, H2:3–12.)

88. JS's journal does not mention this revelation but simply notes that he "attended meeting in the Chapel," or the House of the Lord, on 18 October 1835. (JS, Journal, 18 Oct. 1835, in *JSP*, J1:72.)

89. TEXT: "L[*hole in paper*]d".

distress, and sickness that has heretofore prevailed among the children of Zion[90] will be mitigated from this time forth.[91]

———— ☙ ————

Prayer, 23 October 1835

Source Note

JS, Oliver Cowdery, David Whitmer, Hyrum Smith, John Whitmer, Sidney Rigdon, Samuel Smith, Frederick G. Williams, and William W. Phelps, Prayer, [Kirtland Township, Geauga Co., OH], 23 Oct. 1835. Featured version copied [between 27 and 28 Nov. 1835] in JS, Journal, 1835–1836, pp. 50–51; handwriting of Warren Parrish; JS Collection, CHL. For more information on JS, Journal, 1835–1836, see Source Notes for Multiple-Entry Documents, p. 524 herein.

Historical Introduction

On 23 October 1835, the general church presidency and the Missouri presidency gathered in Kirtland, Ohio, and offered this prayer for deliverance from the difficulties associated with financial debt, as well as for the redemption of Zion, protection from mobs, and the means to purchase land in Missouri on which church members could settle. Also in attendance was JS's brother Samuel Smith, likely substituting for Joseph Smith Sr., an assistant church president, who was recovering from illness.[92]

Church leaders were saddled with debts they had incurred on behalf of the church since at least early 1833. At the date of this prayer, Kirtland bishop Newel K. Whitney still owed money for the purchase of land, including the Peter French farm (the land purchased in Kirtland for the House of the Lord), and for goods purchased on credit to stock his store.[93] Efforts to raise funds to pay these debts, to publish the Doctrine and

---

90. See Psalm 149:2; Joel 2:23; Revelation, 22–23 Sept. 1832, in *JSP*, D2:298 [D&C 84:56–58]; Revelation, 16–17 Dec. 1833, in *JSP*, D3:392, 395–396 [D&C 101:41, 81–85]; and Revelation, 24 Feb. 1834, in *JSP*, D3:462 [D&C 103:35].

91. Cholera broke out in June 1834 among members of the Camp of Israel, killing thirteen camp members and two other Saints in Clay County, but there is no other evidence of unusual or serious illness among church members in Clay County. JS's journal notes that he had recently attended to his father, Joseph Smith Sr., whose recovery from illness "caused us to marvel at the might power and condesension of our Heavenly Father in answering our prayers in his behalf." ("Joseph Smith Documents from April 1834 through September 1835," in *JSP*, D4:xxii; JS, Journal, 6–11, 13, and 18 Oct. 1835, in *JSP*, J1:68–71, 72–73; see also "Mormon War," *Painesville [OH] Telegraph*, 25 July 1834, [3]; Amasa Lyman, Journal, 1834; Smith, "History of George Albert Smith," 29–31; Bradley, *Zion's Camp 1834,* 207; and Burgess, Autobiography, 3.)

92. JS, Journal, 10–13 and 23 Oct. 1835, in *JSP*, J1:71–73.

93. In his role as bishop and in accordance with an early June 1833 revelation, Whitney managed the French farm property and was responsible for the outstanding payments on that mortgage. A $1,500 payment on the property mortgage was due in April 1834 but apparently remained delinquent at the time of this meeting, meaning that the second installment was likely not met in April 1835. In fall 1834, Whitney also owed over $2,000 to New York merchants for purchases made for the Kirtland store in October 1833. (Frederick G. Williams, Kirtland, OH, to "Dear Brethren," Independence, MO, 10 Oct. 1833, in

Covenants, and to construct the temple did not relieve the financial difficulties. In a June 1835 letter to his wife, Sally Waterman Phelps, William W. Phelps commented that church leaders in Kirtland "are considerably in debt, and are poor."[94]

Aside from finances, another concern weighed on church leaders at this time: the fate of Zion in Jackson County, Missouri. In fall 1835, JS and other church leaders renewed discussions regarding the gathering to and redemption of Zion, likely in preparation for restoring the Saints to their lands in 1836.[95] Accordingly, concern for the fate of the church in Missouri takes a prominent place in the 23 October prayer.

The prayer was copied onto pages 50–51 of JS's 1835–1836 journal. The page has the residue of two red wafers that apparently held a loose sheet with the original draft of the prayer. Warren Parrish presumably attached the sheet to the page as he recorded the prayer into the journal on 27 November 1835.[96]

Document Transcript

Copy of a prayer offered up. on the 23ᵈ day of Oct 1835, by the following individuals, at 4 oclock P.M. viz. Joseph Smith jn, Oliver Cowdery; David Whitmer, Hirum [Hyrum] Smith John Whitmer, Sidn[e]y Rigdon, Samuel H. Smith, Frederick G. Williams, and Wᵐ· W. Phelps, assembled and united in prayer, with one voice before the Lord,[97] for the following blessings:

That the Lord will give us means sufficient to deliver us from all our afflictions and difficulties, wherein we are placed by means of our debts; that he will open the way and deliver Zion in the app[p. 50]ointed time[98] and that without the shedding of blood; that he will hold our lives precious,[99] and grant that we

JS Letterbook 1, p. 58; Minutes, 23 Mar. 1833–A, in *JSP*, D3:46; Revelation, 4 June 1833, in *JSP*, D3:110; Geauga Co., OH, Deed Records, 1795–1921, vol. 17, pp. 360–361, 17 June 1833, microfilm 20,237, U.S. and Canada Record Collection, FHL; "New York Account Book, Sept. 1834," Oct. 1833, Newel K. Whitney, Papers, BYU; see also Minutes, 24 Sept. 1834, in *JSP*, D4:176; and Letter to Church Brethren, 15 June 1835, in *JSP*, D4:345–347.)

94. William W. Phelps to Sally Waterman Phelps and Children, 2 June 1835; Letters to John Burk, Sally Waterman Phelps, and Almira Mack Scobey, 1–2 June 1835, in *JSP*, D4:334.

95. See Revelation, 18 Oct. 1835, pp. 21–23 herein; see also JS, Journal, 24 Sept. 1835, in *JSP*, J1:64; Letter to the Elders of the Church, 2 Oct. 1835, pp. 6–15 herein; and Historical Introduction to Revelation, 18 Oct. 1835, p. 22 herein.

96. JS, Journal, 23 Oct. and 27 Nov. 1835, in *JSP*, J1:73, 111–112.

97. Numerous accounts in journals and minutes describe meetings where church members or leaders united in prayer. For example, the first two conferences of the church included "Prayer by all." Zebedee Coltrin remembered that during one of the meetings of the School of the Prophets in Kirtland in 1833, "a number joined in the circle, and prayed." (Minutes, 9 June 1830, in *JSP*, D1:142; Minutes, 26 Sept. 1830, in *JSP*, D1:192; School of the Prophets Salt Lake City Minutes, 11 Oct. 1883; see also, for example, JS, Journal, 11 Jan. 1834; 28 Jan. 1834; 7–9 Apr. 1834; 21 Aug. 1834; 29 Nov. 1834; 23 Sept. 1835, in *JSP*, J1:25, 27, 38, 45, 46, 62; and Minutes, Discourse, and Blessings, 14–15 Feb. 1835, in *JSP*, D4:228.)

98. In August 1834, JS declared that 11 September 1836 was the "appointed time for the redemption of Zion." (Letter to Lyman Wight and Others, 16 Aug. 1834, in *JSP*, D4:106.)

99. See 2 Kings 1:13–14.

may live to the common age of man, and never fall into the hands nor power of the mob in Missourie nor in any other place; that he will also preserve our posterity, that none of them fall even to the end of time; that he will give us the blessings of the earth sufficient to carry us to Zion, and that we may purchase inheritances in that land, even enough to carry on ⟨and accomplish⟩ the work unto which he has appointed us; and also that he will assist all others who desire, accordingly to his commandments, to go up and purchase inheritances;[100] and all this easily and without perplexity, and trouble; and finally, that in the end he will save us in his Celestial Kingdom.[101] Amen.

Oliver Cowdery <u>Clerk</u>

——— ℰↄ ———

Revelation, 27 October 1835

Source Note

Revelation, [Kirtland Township, Geauga Co., OH], 27 Oct. 1835. Featured version copied [ca. 27 Oct. 1835] in JS, Journal, 1835–1836, p. 10; handwriting of Warren Parrish; JS Collection, CHL. For more information on JS, Journal, 1835–1836, see Source Notes for Multiple-Entry Documents, p. 524 herein.

Historical Introduction

On 27 October 1835, Mary Bailey Smith, wife of Samuel Smith and sister-in-law to JS, gave birth to her first child, Susanna. Though the child would live a long life, Mary's labor and delivery had complications. JS's journal records that Mary was "confined an[d] in a verry dangerous situation," and the Smith family feared for Mary's life.[102] These circumstances prompted the family to dispatch Don Carlos Smith nine miles to Chardon, Ohio, to fetch Frederick G. Williams, a member of the First Presidency and a practicing physician.[103]

Following Don Carlos's departure, JS "went out into the field and bowed before the Lord and called upon him in mighty prayer in her [Mary's] behalf." As recorded in his journal, in response to his supplication JS received a revelation assuring him that Williams would come and that the baby and the mother would survive. Williams arrived at Samuel

---

100. For more on lands of inheritance, see Revelation, 20 July 1831, in *JSP,* D2:11 [D&C 57:5–7]; Revelation, 1 Aug. 1831, in *JSP,* D2:19 [D&C 58:44]; and Revelation, 24 Feb. 1834, in *JSP,* D3:460 [D&C 103:11].

101. See Vision, 16 Feb. 1832, in *JSP,* D2:189–190 [D&C 76:70–77, 87].

102. JS, Journal, 27 Oct. 1835, in *JSP,* J1:75.

103. Frederick G. Williams was considered a "botanic physician" and subscribed to the alternative medical philosophy and practices of Dr. Samuel Thomson, leader of the American botanical medical movement. Botanic or Thomsonian physicians used herbal remedies and heat treatments for healing patients, in contrast to the bloodletting, calomel purges, and other harsh methods employed by academically trained doctors. (Oliver Cowdery, Kirtland, OH, to Sampson Avard, 15 Dec. 1835, in Cowdery Letterbook, 67; Advertisement, *Northern Times,* 2 Oct. 1835, [3]; Haller, *People's Doctors,* 40; Whorton, *Nature Cures,* 28–31; Weinstock, "Samuel Thomson's Botanic System," 5–20.)

Smith's house about an hour later, and following another two hours of labor, Mary gave birth to Susanna.

After the delivery, JS recounted the experience to his scribe, Warren Parrish, who recorded the day's events, including the revelation, in JS's journal. Speaking of the revelation, the journal concluded, "Thus what God had manifested to me was fulfilled every whit."[104]

Document Transcript

the word of the Lord came unto me saying my Servant Fredrick [Frederick G. Williams] shall come and shall have wisdom given him to deal prudently and my handmaden shall be delivered of a living child & be spared

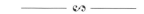

Minutes, 29 October 1835

Source Note

Kirtland high council, Minutes, Kirtland Township, Geauga Co., OH, 29 Oct. 1835. Featured version copied [between ca. 4 Apr. and ca. 16 May 1836] in Minute Book 1, pp. 127–129; handwriting of Warren A. Cowdery; CHL. For more information on Minute Book 1, see Source Notes for Multiple-Entry Documents, p. 527 herein.

Historical Introduction

In October 1835, the Kirtland high council met to discuss allegations that David Elliott, a member of the Quorum of the Seventy, and his wife, Mary Cahoon Elliott, had abused their teenage daughter by beating and whipping her.[105] According to one of the witnesses who testified at the meeting, the Elliott affair had provoked public discussion in the small village of Chagrin, Ohio.[106] On 29 October, the high council met to depose witnesses and determine if the Elliotts' actions merited official church discipline.

The complaint, instigated by William Smith, likely involved the couple's treatment of Lucena, David Elliott's eldest child from a previous marriage.[107] Elliott and William Smith

---

104. JS, Journal, 27 Oct. 1835, in *JSP*, J1:75–76.

105. David Elliott joined the church in upstate New York in early 1831 and married Mary Cahoon on 21 May 1831 in Kirtland, Ohio. The couple eventually settled in Chagrin, Ohio. Though Elliott was commanded to move to Jackson County, Missouri, in a 31 August 1831 revelation, he appears to have remained in Chagrin. (Revelation, 31 Aug. 1831, in *JSP*, D2:55; Letter from Oliver Cowdery, 28 Jan. 1832, in *JSP*, D2:177–178; Letter to Church Leaders in Jackson County, MO, 21 Apr. 1833, in *JSP*, D3:68, 69n78.)

106. Chagrin was officially renamed Willoughby sometime in late 1834 or early 1835, following the establishment of Willoughby Medical College. However, JS and other church members often referred to the town as Chagrin.

107. Little is known about the Elliott family. Family genealogical records suggest that Mary Cahoon was David Elliott's third wife. According to these records, he married Almira Holliday in 1821, and in the following year Almira gave birth to Lucena. He later married Margery Quick in 1823. Mary Cahoon was therefore Lucena's stepmother. ("History Written by David Elliott," attached to "David Elliott, 1799–1855," 27 Nov. 2014, FamilySearch; "Elliott, David," born 18 Nov. 1799, submitted by Alvin E. Morris, Church

had been acquainted for several years prior to the accusation. Both men marched to Missouri as part of the Camp of Israel in May 1834, and both were ordained as leaders in the church's governing bodies in February 1835.[108] No extant records indicate how William Smith became aware of the alleged abuse within the Elliott family.

The Elliott trial unfolded in two sessions. The opening session seems to have focused on William Smith's allegations against David Elliott. Five witnesses, including JS, were deposed during the first trial; JS testified in favor of the defendant. As the minutes indicate, the council ultimately ruled that although "the complaint was not without foundation," the charge of abuse "had not been fully sustained." The council reconvened later that evening to hear William Smith's charges against Mary Elliott. During this hearing, a "Sister Childs," who testified she lived in the Elliott household, was introduced as a witness. JS's journal indicates that in contrast to the first hearing, in which he was called to testify, JS was asked to "take a seat with the presidency and preside" over the second session.[109]

An account in JS's journal suggests that the second session was contentious. Six members of the council, rather than the usual four, were appointed to speak during the evening session, which according to established protocol meant that the case was deemed difficult.[110] During the meeting, JS and William Smith engaged in a heated exchange that opened up an unpleasant rift between the two brothers.[111] At the conclusion of the second session, both Mary and David Elliott confessed their wrongs before the council, pledged to correct their behavior, and were forgiven.

Document Transcript

Kirtland Oct. 29th 1835

This day a High Council was called at E[dmund] Bosley's for the purpose of trying certain cases.

Names of the counsellors present

David W. Patten	John Smith
Brigham Young	Wm. E. M[c.] Lellin
John F. Boynton	Orson Hyde
Joseph Coe	Simeon Carter
Lyman Sherman	Alpheus Cutler
James Emmitt [Emmett]	S[elah] J. Griffin

---

of Jesus Christ of Latter-day Saints, Family Group Records Collection; Archives Section, 1942–1969, microfilm 1,274,009, U.S. and Canada Record Collection, FHL.)

108. William Smith was chosen to be a member of the Quorum of the Twelve Apostles on 14 February 1835; Elliott was called as a member of the Quorum of the Seventy on 28 February 1835. (Minutes, Discourse, and Blessings, 14–15 Feb. 1835, in *JSP*, D4:228; Minutes and Blessings, 28 Feb.–1 Mar. 1835, in *JSP*, D4:259.)

109. JS, Journal, 29 Oct. 1835, in *JSP*, J1:77.

110. See Revised Minutes, 18–19 Feb. 1834, in *JSP*, D3:439 [D&C 102].

111. JS, Journal, 29 Oct. 1835, in *JSP*, J1:77–79.

After the council had taken their seats according to their respective numbers President O[liver] Cowdery opened the council by prayer.

A charge was read against David Elliott & wife preferred by Elder Wm. Smith for abusing their daughter by beating and whipping her. Two counsellors on each side were appointed to speak. (Viz.) David W. Patten and Brigham Young on one side and on the other John Smith & Wm. E. Mc Lellin. Witnesses on part of the complainent were Aaron C Lyon & his wife Roxana.

Aaron C. Lyon testified that said Elliott's girl came to his house and complained that her father had abused her, and whipped her & that some marks were found upon her arms, body &c. when she had been whipped. This circumstance took place about ten days since, The girl was about fifteen years old, and that she said she would, or had a mind to make away with herself, hang herself, or something of the kind to get rid of her trouble and affliction. The testimony of Roxana Lyons, that was that Mrs. Elliott threatned to take the broomstick and kill her, and also confirmed the testimony of her husband.

Sister Osgood testifies, that some three years since she (sister Osgood) lived at said Elliott's and that [p. 127] the girl told her that she was sorry that sister Osgood was going to leave her father, for said she I know how I shall fare when you leave I shall run away or destroy myself and went down into the well for the purpose of drowning herself but was prevented by sister Osgood,

Testimony of Erastus Babbit[t] was that the people of Chagrin where the circumstances took place, were much excited about the affair, and that it was a topic of public conversation.

The testimony of President Smith was that he was at their house in Chagrin and talked with the girl, and with her parints, and that he was satisfied that the girl was in the fault, and that the neighbors were trying to create a difficulty.

Testimony of Brother Elliott's father was that the girl was refractory and stubborn, and would sometimes vary from the truth and had never seen brother or Sister Elliot abuse her. After the Counsellors had made their observations, the accuser and the accused were heard. The Presidents then proceeded to give the following decision. That the complaint was not without foundation, yet the charge has not been fully sustained, but he has acted injudiciously and brought a disgrace upon himself, upon his daughter & upon this Church, because he ought to have trained his child in a way, that she should not have required the rod at the age of 15 years.

Council adjourned till candle light.

Council again convened and Hezekiah Fisk was appointed in the room of Alpheus Cutler, who was absent and Almon Babbit[t] in the place of Joseph Coe. After the council was organized, a charge was [p. 128] preferred against Mary Elliott for abusing said E.s daughter as referred to before, and also abusing the rest of her children, by Wm. Smith.[112]

Six were appointed to speak on this case.[113] Testimony of Sister Childs was that she lived in the house with Sister Elliot confessed her wrong and promised to do so no more consequently the council forgave her. Brother Elliott made his confession and was forgiven, and both he and his wife were restored to fellowship.

Council closed, by prayer by President [Sidney] Rigdon

Orson Hyde Clerk.

——————— ❧ ———————

Revelation, 1 November 1835

Source Note

Revelation, [Kirtland Township, Geauga Co., OH], 1 Nov. 1835. Featured version copied [ca. 1 Nov. 1835] in JS, Journal, 1835–1836, p. 16; handwriting of Warren Parrish; JS Collection, CHL. For more information on JS, Journal, 1835–1836, see Source Notes for Multiple-Entry Documents, p. 524 herein.

Historical Introduction

On 1 November 1835, JS dictated a revelation that chastised Reynolds Cahoon for "his iniquities[,] his covetous and dishonest principles in himself and family" and for failing to "set his house in order." At the time, Cahoon was serving as a counselor to Bishop Newel K. Whitney and as a member of the building committee for the House of the Lord in Kirtland, Ohio.[114] This was not the first time he had been accused of shirking his duties at home—on 10 August 1835, the Kirtland high council ruled that Cahoon had "failed to do his duty in correcting his children, and instructing them in the way of truth & righteousness,"

---

112. The couple may have had as many as eight children living with them, including five from David Elliott's previous marriages. ("Elliott, David," born 18 Nov. 1799, submitted by Alvin E. Morris, Church of Jesus Christ of Latter-day Saints, Family Group Records Collection; Archives Section, 1942–1969, microfilm 1,274,009, U.S. and Canada Record Collection, FHL.)

113. In addition to the six members of the high council who were appointed to speak (three for each side), several other people served as witnesses, including Lucy Mack Smith. Though there is no indication of what Lucy Mack Smith said during her deposition, it is likely that she testified against David Elliott. JS's journal recounts that when Lucy began to testify, JS objected on the grounds that her testimony concerned matters that had already been considered and settled in the earlier session. William took offense to his brother's unilateral action, insisting that he was "invalidating or doubting" their mother's testimony. The tension escalated. According to JS's journal, "I told him [William] that he was out of place & asked him to set down." When William demurred, JS ordered him to sit. Enraged, William told JS that he would not sit down unless JS "knocked him down." JS also became angry, and it was only after Joseph Smith Sr. intervened that order was restored. (JS, Journal, 29 Oct. 1835, in *JSP*, J1:76–79.)

114. Cahoon, Diary, 10 Feb. 1832; Minutes, 4 May 1833, in *JSP*, D3:81–82; Minutes, 6 June 1833, in *JSP*, D3:112–115.

a decision that Cahoon acknowledged as being justified.[115] The revelation presented here demonstrates that concerns relating to Cahoon's domestic affairs persisted after the high council's ruling.

JS's 1 November journal entry explains that he recorded this revelation during the morning and immediately sent for Cahoon; JS then "read what the Lord had said concerning him." Cahoon allegedly "acknowledged that it was verily so & expressed much humility."[116] Though it is not clear what actions Cahoon took in response to this revelation, he remained in his position in the bishopric and on the building committee.

The original text of the revelation is no longer extant, but a transcript was copied into JS's journal by his scribe, Warren Parrish.

Document Transcript

Verily thus Saith the Lord unto me, his servant Joseph Smith jun mine anger is kindle[d] against my servant Reynolds Cahoon because of his iniquities his covetous and dishonest principles in himself[117] and family and he doth not purge them away and set his house in order, therefore if he repent not chastisment awaiteth him even as it seemeth good in my sight therefore go and declare unto him ~~this~~ ⟨these⟩ word⟨s⟩

———— ☙ ————

Revelation, 2 November 1835

Source Note

Revelation, [Kirtland Township, Geauga Co., OH], 2 Nov. 1835. Featured version copied [ca. 2 Nov. 1835] in JS, Journal, 1835–1836, p. 17; handwriting of Warren Parrish; JS Collection, CHL. For more information on JS, Journal, 1835–1836, see Source Notes for Multiple-Entry Documents, p. 524 herein.

Historical Introduction

This revelation, dictated by JS on 2 November 1835, settled a disagreement among church leaders about who should travel to New York to purchase bookbinding equipment and texts for the new Hebrew School in Kirtland, Ohio. Apparently, Oliver Cowdery and Frederick G. Williams were the two candidates. The revelation featured here

---

115. Minutes, 10 Aug. 1835, in *JSP*, D4:382.

116. JS, Journal, 1 Nov. 1834, in *JSP*, J1:81.

117. It is not entirely clear what "iniquities" or "covetous and dishonest principles" were being referred to here. It is possible that Cahoon, when operating the building committee store, was reluctant to distribute goods to those who donated to or worked on the House of the Lord. In a 15 December letter to JS, Orson Hyde accused Cahoon of being stingy with committee store credit, when Hyde himself had given the committee "$275 in cash besides some more." Concerning Hyde's treatment at the committee store, JS's journal noted that "on the part of the committee [store], he [Hyde] was not treated, right in all thing[s]." (Letter from Orson Hyde, 15 Dec. 1835, p. 108 herein; JS, Journal, 17 Dec. 1835, in *JSP*, J1:128.)

directed Frederick G. Williams not to go to New York on church business and instead authorized him to travel to preach to his relatives. Oliver Cowdery was ultimately chosen to go to New York.

Earlier that day, several men—including JS, Sidney Rigdon, Cowdery, Williams, and Warren Parrish—had traveled to the nearby Willoughby Medical College to attend a medical lecture given by Dr. Daniel Peixotto.[118] Church leaders had been seeking an "accomplished" Hebrew scholar since at least mid-October, and shortly after the lecture, Cowdery and Parrish contracted Peixotto to teach Hebrew classes in Kirtland.[119] According to an account recorded in JS's journal, some of the men who went to Willoughby later discussed making a trip to New York to procure bookbinding equipment as well as materials for the Hebrew School in Kirtland; they then asked JS to decide who should make the trip.[120] Both Cowdery and Williams were intimately involved in the church's publishing efforts, and procuring the equipment and know-how to bind books may have been part of that endeavor.[121] Contemporary records confirm that Cowdery did in fact travel to New York City to "purchase a book-binding establishment," yet it is unclear whether or not he was successful in obtaining the necessary equipment; he did, however, return with "a quantity of Hebrew books."[122]

Though the revelation granted Williams permission to preach to his relatives, it is unclear to which family members the revelation refers. Williams's family had migrated to

---

118. JS, Journal, 2 Nov. 1835, in *JSP*, J1:82. A professor of the theory and practice of medicine, Daniel Peixotto had been a prominent physician in New York before accepting a position as professor at Willoughby Medical College, which was located in Willoughby, Ohio. Prior to his appointment at the college, he served as an editor of the *New York Medical and Physical Journal*, as cofounder and secretary of the Academy of Medicine of New York, and as president of the New York County Medical Society. (Hays, "Daniel L. M. Peixotto, M.D.," 221–227.)

119. Leaders initially corresponded with Lucius Parker, a cousin of Willard Richards, about teaching Hebrew in Kirtland. When Parker informed them that he was able to teach only the rudiments of Hebrew, Cowdery replied that his "services will not be wanted" because they "wished an accomplished scholar." Peixotto never fulfilled his contract, and Joshua Seixas was eventually selected to teach the Hebrew School in Kirtland. (Oliver Cowdery, Kirtland, OH, to Lucius Parker, Southborough, MA, 28 Oct. 1835, in Cowdery, Letterbook, 57; Oliver Cowdery, [Kirtland, OH], to John M. Henderson, Willoughby, OH, 2 Nov. 1835, in Cowdery, Letterbook, 62; see also Historical Introduction to Letter to Henrietta Raphael Seixas, between 6 and 13 Feb. 1836, pp. 173–177 herein.)

120. JS, Journal, 2 Nov. 1835, in *JSP*, J1:82. Though the account in JS's journal does not specifically mention Hebrew books, letters written by Oliver Cowdery and William W. Phelps a few weeks later suggest that the acquisition of Hebrew materials was another important aspect of the New York trip. (Oliver Cowdery, Kirtland, OH, to Warren A. Cowdery, [Freedom, NY], 22 Nov. 1835, in Cowdery, Letterbook, 63; William W. Phelps, [Kirtland, OH], to Sally Waterman Phelps, Liberty, MO, 14 Nov. 1835, in Historical Department, Journal History of the Church, 14 Nov. 1835.)

121. Less than a week before this revelation was dictated, William W. Phelps, the third partner in the publishing endeavor, informed his wife that "we are also establishing a bindery to bind our own books." (William W. Phelps, [Kirtland, OH], to Sally Waterman Phelps and the Saints, 27 Oct. 1835, William W. Phelps, Papers, BYU.)

122. JS, Journal, 20 Nov. 1835, in *JSP*, J1:107; Oliver Cowdery, Kirtland, OH, to Warren A. Cowdery, [Freedom, NY], 22 Nov. 1835, in Cowdery, Letterbook, 63. Contemporary sources make no mention of a bookbindery in Kirtland until January 1837, when an advertisement for one was placed in the local newspaper. ("Kirtland Printing Office and Bookbindery," *LDS Messenger and Advocate*, Jan. 1837, 3:448.)

the Connecticut Western Reserve from Suffield, Connecticut, in 1800, and he may have had extended family still living in New England.[123] Most of Williams's family, including his in-laws, were not members of the faith, and it appears that this fact weighed on Williams and his wife, Rebecca Swain Williams.[124] Seven weeks before the 2 November 1835 revelation was recorded, Frederick and Rebecca Williams were each blessed by Joseph Smith Sr. In his blessing, Frederick was granted "the power to call thy kindreds and friends into the church." Rebecca was told, "In conseq[u]ence of thy prayers and thy tears thou shalt yet prevail, and the Lord will give thee thy father's family, who are now far from the way of salvation. But the Lord will make bare his arm and show mercy unto them in making thy husband a savior unto them."[125] Contemporary records do not indicate whether or not Williams preached to his relatives as discussed in this revelation.

The original manuscript of this revelation is not extant. Warren Parrish later copied the text of the revelation into JS's journal, the source for the text featured here.

Document Transcript

thus came the word of the Lord unto me saying it is not my will that my servant Frederick [G. Williams] should go to New York, but inasmuch as he wishes to go and visit his relatives that he may warn them to flee the wrath to come let him go and see them, for that purpose and let that be his only business, and behold in this thing he shall be blessed with power ~~while~~ to overcome their prejudices, Verily thus saith the Lord Amen.

——— ☙ ———

Revelation, 3 November 1835

Source Note

Revelation, [Kirtland Township, Geauga Co., OH], 3 Nov. 1835. Featured version copied [ca. 3 Nov. 1835] in JS, Journal, 1835–1836, pp. 17–19; handwriting of Warren Parrish; JS Collection, CHL. For more information on JS, Journal, 1835–1836, see Source Notes for Multiple-Entry Documents, p. 524 herein.

Historical Introduction

This revelation, dictated by JS on 3 November 1835, reproved the members of the Quorum of the Twelve Apostles for exhibiting "covetous desires," making themselves unequal, and failing to be "sufficiently humble." The revelation counseled them to "repent

---

123. While Williams's distant relatives may have remained in Connecticut, his parents and siblings appear to have been living near Cleveland, Ohio. (JS, Journal, 18 Apr. 1834, in *JSP*, J1:40; Williams, *Life of Dr. Frederick G. Williams,* 32–37, 206.)

124. Williams, *Life of Dr. Frederick G. Williams,* 206.

125. Joseph Smith Sr. to Frederick G. Williams, Blessing, 14 Sept. 1835; Joseph Smith Sr. to Rebecca Swain Williams, Blessing, 14 Sept. 1835, in Patriarchal Blessings, 1:30–31.

speedily" and "prepare their hearts for the solem assembly and for the great day which is to come." In addition to receiving a collective chastisement, several members of the quorum—William Smith, David Patten, Orson Hyde, and William E. McLellin—were singled out for unspecified "sinful" behaviors. Several contentious episodes between members of the Twelve and the First Presidency during the previous four months provide important context for understanding this revelation.

After the Twelve Apostles were appointed on 14 February 1835, JS provided them "much instruction" pertaining to their office in the months that followed.[126] He advised the men that they were to serve as a "travelling high council to preside over all the churches of the saints . . . when there is no presidency established" and that they were to "travel and preach among the Gentiles."[127] In preparation for their initial mission, the Twelve met on 28 April 1835 and approved a motion to "forgive one another every wrong that has existed among us; and that from hence forth each one of the twelve love his brother as himself in temporal as well as in spiritual things; always enquiring into each others welfare."[128] Six days later, the twelve men departed Kirtland for a four-month mission to New York, Upper Canada, and New England.[129]

As the Twelve preached and conducted conferences in various branches of the church, JS and the presidency in Kirtland received troubling letters from the eastern United States; the issues raised by these communications may be at least partially responsible for the 3 November censure. Though the Twelve had been expected to solicit money for construction of the House of the Lord, Warren A. Cowdery, a branch president in Freedom, New York, informed the presidency that "the twelve, the Bishop, nor any others, clothed with authority have ever mentioned this subject to us, except incidently."[130] JS and the presidency also became aware of a letter sent by William E. McLellin to his wife, Emeline Miller McLellin, implying that McLellin and Orson Hyde disapproved of the way Sidney Rigdon was conducting his school back in Kirtland.[131] In addition to these two letters, JS and the presidency indicated that they had received other troubling correspondence about the Twelve's conduct.[132]

---

126. "History of Brigham Young," *Deseret News,* 10 Feb. 1858, 385; Minutes, Discourse, and Blessings, 14–15 Feb. 1835, in *JSP,* D4:219–234; see also Minutes, 26 Apr. 1835, in *JSP,* D4:293–295; Minutes and Discourse, 2 May 1835, in *JSP,* D4:299–308; and Instruction on Priesthood, between ca. 1 Mar. and ca. 4 May 1835, in *JSP,* D4:308–321 [D&C 107].

127. Minutes and Discourses, 27 Feb. 1835, in *JSP,* D4:252.

128. Record of the Twelve, 28 Apr. 1835.

129. Record of the Twelve, 4–9 May 1835; Orson Hyde and William E. McLellin, Kirtland, OH, Oct. 1835, Letter to the Editor, *LDS Messenger and Advocate,* Oct. 1835, 204–207.

130. Cowdery's letter was dated 29 July 1835. Though the letter is no longer extant, it is quoted in Letter to Quorum of the Twelve, 4 Aug. 1835, in *JSP,* D4:374–375.

131. Letter to Quorum of the Twelve, 4 Aug. 1835, in *JSP,* D4:375–376. In mid-June, JS asked Brigham Young, Orson Hyde, and William Smith to return temporarily to Kirtland to testify in court on his behalf. Hyde likely attended one of Rigdon's classes during this brief interlude and then shared his observations with McLellin, who had also taught in the school, upon his return to the East. ("History of Brigham Young," *LDS Millennial Star,* 18 July 1863, 25:456.)

132. This included a letter from Thomas B. Marsh that has not been located. (See Letter to Quorum of the Twelve, 4 Aug. 1835, in *JSP,* D4:376–377.)

The First Presidency took action. On 4 August, they and the Missouri presidency wrote a letter to the Twelve in which they rebuked and temporarily disfellowshipped McLellin and Hyde; the letter also chastised the quorum collectively for failing to support fund-raising efforts for the House of the Lord and for setting themselves up "as an independant counsel subject to no authority of the church."[133] When the Twelve returned to Kirtland in late September, they met with JS and the presidency to address the accusations. After some deliberation, the council dismissed Warren A. Cowdery's complaints, concluding that they "originated in the minds of persons whose minds were darkened." Hyde and McLellin were "found to be in the fault" for criticizing Rigdon's school, and they acknowledged their errors and were forgiven.[134] JS's journal indicates that "all things were settled satisfactorily."[135] Nonetheless, bad feelings caused by the 4 August letter continued to fester through winter 1835–1836 as other problems related to the Twelve's eastern mission surfaced.[136] For example, this 3 November revelation appears to refer to the eastern mission when it charged that the quorum had "not dealt equally with each other in the division of moneys which came into their hands."[137]

Though the Twelve's mission to the East had bearing on the 3 November revelation, another event that transpired after the Twelve returned to Kirtland contributed to the discord within the quorum. The rebuke directed at William Smith almost certainly related to his confrontation with JS five days earlier, when the two brothers engaged in a heated argument during a disciplinary hearing for David and Mary Elliott.[138] After the Kirtland high council proposed to censure William, he called on JS at his home. In the presence of Hyrum Smith and Warren Parrish, another heated dispute erupted, after which William "declared that he wanted no more to do" with JS or the church. The next day, William sent JS his ecclesiastical

---

133. Letter to Quorum of the Twelve, 4 Aug. 1835, in *JSP*, D4:376.

134. Minutes, 26 Sept. 1835, in *JSP*, D4:442.

135. JS, Journal, 26 Sept. 1835, in *JSP*, J1:66.

136. See Minutes, 28–29 Sept. 1835, in *JSP*, D4:446–455; JS, Journal, 16 Jan. 1836, in *JSP*, J1:156–160; and Minutes, 16 Jan. 1836, pp. 148–154 herein.

137. Though preachers and missionaries of the day often traveled without "purse or scrip," they occasionally received donations in the form of money or material goods from the patrons of their preaching. These donations were used for basic necessities, and, according to Orson Hyde, a portion of the income went to family support. William E. McLellin, for example, recorded the occasions when he received donations, ranging from sixty cents to five dollars, in his journal. When the Twelve gathered in Freedom, New York, in late May 1835, McLellin noted that "a public collection [was] taken up for the benefit of the twelve, which together with what we had all received since we had parted at the last conference amounted to $2.00 and a few cents each." Orson Hyde also mentioned contributions given to him during the eastern mission. In the Record of the Twelve, Hyde, serving as scribe, wrote that the church in Saco, Maine, "contributed money unto us to assist us in returning home to Ohio, to the amt of 70 or 80 Dollars." In a 15 December letter to JS, Hyde remarked that "we straind every nerve to obtain a little something for our familys and regularly divided the monies equally for ought that I know." Though it appears they divided the money equally on these occasions, it is possible that they failed to do so on others. (McLellin, Journal, 4 May–3 Sept. 1835; Record of the Twelve, 21–23 Aug. 1835; Letter from Orson Hyde, 15 Dec. 1835, p. 108 herein; see also License for Frederick G. Williams, 20 Mar. 1833, in *JSP*, D3:43–46.)

138. See Minutes, 29 Oct. 1835, pp. 26–29 herein; JS, Journal, 29 Oct. 1835, in *JSP*, J1:76–79; Letter from William Smith, 18 Dec. 1835, pp. 109–115 herein; and Letter to William Smith, ca. 18 Dec. 1835, pp. 115–121 herein.

license and began, according to JS's journal, to "spread the levavin [leaven] of iniquity among my brethren." Another brother, Samuel, was especially persuaded by William's denouncements.[139] Besides generating significant tension within the Smith family, this episode also undermined the unity that was expected to prevail among the Quorum of the Twelve.

It is unclear how knowledge of the revelation was disseminated, but Orson Hyde and William E. McLellin "came in and desired to hear the revelation concerning the Twelve" two days after its dictation. JS's journal notes that Warren Parrish read the revelation to the men, after which they "expressed some little dissatisfaction but after examining their own hearts, they acknowledged it to be the word of the Lord and they were satisfied." Brigham Young also heard the revelation read and according to JS, "appeared perfectly satisfied."[140] Despite the observation recorded in JS's journal that these three apostles were satisfied, some of the issues that precipitated the 3 November revelation lingered on.[141] It was not until after a lengthy meeting between JS, the presidency, and the Twelve on 16 January 1836 that these issues were more fully resolved.[142]

Document Transcript

Thus came the word of the Lord unto me ~~saying~~ concerning the, Twelve ⟨saying⟩

behold they are under condemnation, because they have not been sufficiently humble in my sight, and in consequence of their covetous desires, in that they have not dealt equally with each other in the division of the moneys which came into their hands, nevertheless some of them, dealt equally therefore they shall be rewarded, but Verily I say unto you they must all humble themselves before Me, before they will be accounted worthy to receive an endowment to go forth in my name unto all nations,[143] as for my Servant William [Smith] let the Eleven humble themselves in prayer and in faith [p. 17] and wait on me in patience and my servant William shall return, and I will yet make him a polished shaft in my quiver, in bringing down the wickedness and abominations of men and their shall be none mightier than he in his day and generation, nevertheless if he repent not spedily he shall be brought low and shall be chastened sorely for all his iniquities he has commited against me, nevertheless the sin

---

139. JS, Journal, 31 Oct. 1835, in *JSP*, J1:80. A license, such as the one William turned over to JS, certified a priesthood holder's ordination to a specific office, such as elder, and authorized him to preach the gospel.

140. JS, Journal, 5 Nov. 1835, in *JSP*, J1:84.

141. For instance, in mid-December, Orson Hyde raised concerns about unequal treatment of members of the Twelve at the committee store. (JS, Journal, 15–17 Dec. 1835, in *JSP*, J1:123–129; Letter from Orson Hyde, 15 Dec. 1835, pp. 107–109 herein.)

142. Minutes, 16 Jan. 1836, pp. 148–154 herein; see also Esplin, "Emergence of Brigham Young," 181–186.

143. See Revelation, 2 Jan. 1831, in *JSP*, D1:232; Revelation, 1 June 1833, in *JSP*, D3:104–108; and Minutes and Blessings, 21 Feb. 1835, in *JSP*, D4:237–247.

which he hath sin[n]ed against me is not even now more grevious than the sin with which my servant David W. Patten and my servant Orson Hyde and my servant Wm E. McLellen [McLellin] have sinded [sinned] against me, and the residue are not sufficiently humble before me, behold the parable which I spake concerning a man having twelve Sons, for what man amon[g] you having twelve Sons and is no respecter to them and they serve him obediantly and he saith unto the one be thou clothed in robes and sit thou here, and to the other be thou clothed in rages [rags] and sit thou there, and looketh upon his sons and saith I am just, ye will answer and say no man, and ye answer truly,[144] therefore Verily thus saith the Lord your God I appointed these twelve that they should be equal in their ministry and in their portion and in their evangelical rights, wherefore they have sined a verry grevious sin, in asmuch as they have made themselves unequal and have not hearkned unto my voice therfor let them repent speedily and prepare their hearts for the solem assembly [p. 18] and for the great day which is to come Verely thus saith the Lord Amen.

———— ⟨⟩ ————

Revelation, 7 November 1835

Source Note

Revelation, [Kirtland Township, Geauga Co., OH], 7 Nov. 1835. Featured version copied [ca. 7 Nov. 1835] in JS, Journal, 1835–1836, pp. 20–21; handwriting of Warren Parrish; JS Collection, CHL. For more information on JS, Journal, 1835–1836, see Source Notes for Multiple-Entry Documents, p. 524 herein.

Historical Introduction

JS dictated this revelation for Missouri bishop Edward Partridge and his counselor Isaac Morley on 7 November 1835. Partridge and Morley had recently arrived in Kirtland, Ohio, from a five-month proselytizing and fund-raising mission in the eastern United States.[145]

On 1 June 1835, JS had called for Partridge and Morley to "visit the churches in the east and obtain donations for the poor saints" and to provide counsel to church members

---

144. This parable was first referenced in a 2 January 1831 JS revelation. Among other things, that revelation admonished each church member to "esteem his brother as himself" and then related the same parable of the twelve sons. Following the parable in the 2 January 1831 revelation, the church was warned: "Behold I have given unto you a Parable & it is even as I am I say unto you, be one & if ye are not one ye are not mine." (Revelation, 2 Jan. 1831, in *JSP*, D1:232.)

145. The five-month journey was the second multiple-month mission for both Isaac Morley and Edward Partridge in 1835. Morley had proselytized while traveling from Missouri to Kirtland from 17 February to 29 April 1835, preaching mostly in Illinois and Indiana. Partridge traveled from late January through the end of April 1835 in similar regions, in company with Thomas B. Marsh. (Isaac Morley, Report, ca. 1835, Missionary Reports, 1831–1900, CHL; Edward Partridge, Report, 29 Apr. 1835, Missionary Reports, 1831–1900, CHL.)

generally.[146] On the following day, Partridge and Morley "started with a one horse waggon on a tour to visit the churches, in the eastern states, strengthning them; and instructing them concerning the gathering."[147] They began by visiting Partridge's family and preaching in western Pennsylvania. The bishop and his counselor then traveled approximately two thousand miles through Pennsylvania, New York, Massachusetts, Maine, Vermont, and Connecticut, visiting twenty-five branches of the church with a combined membership of seven hundred. During this time, they held some fifty meetings. According to Partridge, "I preached about thirty two sermons and spoke by the way of exhortation about half a dozen times. Elder Morley preached from fifteen to twenty times and spoke a number of times more. We baptized three. We spent most of our time and labours in the churches, and collected some donations for the poor. We found the churches doing as well as could reasonably be expected."[148] At some point, Partridge and Morley separated, but by 5 November, both men had returned to Kirtland, Ohio.[149]

The revelation featured here instructed Partridge and Morley to remain in Kirtland until the completion of the House of the Lord, and they did so.[150] JS dictated this revelation to Warren Parrish, who recorded it on 7 November 1835 in JS's journal.

Document Transcript

The word ⟨of the Lord⟩ came to me saying, behold I am well pleased with my servant Isaac Morley and my servant Edward Partridge, because of the integrity of their harts in laboring in my vinyard for the salvation of the souls of men, Verily I say unto you their sins are [p. 20] forgiven them, therefor say unto them in my name that it is my will that they should tarry for a little season and attend the school,[151] and also the solem assembly for a wise purpose in me,[152] even so amen

---

146. Partridge, Journal, 29 June 1835; Recommendation for Edward Partridge and Isaac Morley, 1 June 1835, in *JSP*, D4:322–325; see also Partridge, Genealogical Record, 24.

147. Partridge, Journal, 120.

148. Edward Partridge, Kirtland, OH, to Newel K. Whitney, Kirtland, OH, 31 Oct. 1835, Missionary Reports, 1831–1900, CHL.

149. Partridge returned on 29 October 1835, while Morley returned on 5 November 1835. (JS, Journal, 29 Oct. and 5 Nov. 1835, in *JSP*, J1:76, 84.)

150. Partridge, Journal, 9 Apr. 1836.

151. The Elders School in Kirtland. A notice in the September 1835 *Messenger and Advocate* declared that a school for the church's elders would begin on 2 November 1835. On 3 November 1835, just four days before dictating this revelation, JS "went to assist in organizing the Elders School called to order and I made some remarks upon the object of this School, and the great necessity there is of our rightly improving our time and reigning up our minds to a sense of the great object that lies before us, viz, that glorious endowment that God has in store for the faithful I then dedicated the School in the name of the Lord Jesus Christ." ("The Elders Abroad," *LDS Messenger and Advocate*, Sept. 1835, 1:191; JS, Journal, 3 Nov. 1835, in *JSP*, J1:84.)

152. Partridge and Morley were among a group of Missouri church leaders named in June 1834 to travel to Kirtland to receive the endowment of "power from on high" when the House of the Lord in

Revelation, 8 November 1835

Source Note

Revelation, [Kirtland Township, Geauga Co., OH], 8 Nov. 1835. Featured version copied [ca. 8 Nov. 1835] in JS, Journal, 1835–1836, p. 22; handwriting of Warren Parrish; JS Collection, CHL. For more information on JS, Journal, 1835–1836, see Source Notes for Multiple-Entry Documents, p. 524 herein.

Historical Introduction

In April 1835, William W. Phelps and John Whitmer—who, along with David Whitmer, made up the presidency of the church in Missouri—commenced a three-week journey from Clay County, Missouri, to Kirtland, Ohio. Phelps and Whitmer were among fifteen church leaders selected in a 23 June 1834 meeting to travel to Ohio to receive the long-awaited endowment of power in the House of the Lord.[153] During their nearly one-year stay in Kirtland, Phelps and Whitmer labored on the church's printing endeavors, including the *Latter Day Saints' Messenger and Advocate* and the church's first hymnal.[154] Phelps also acted as a scribe for JS during the late summer and early fall.[155]

On 8 November, JS dictated a revelation in which Phelps and Whitmer were chastised for their "iniquities." What precipitated the rebuke is unclear; it may have been related to the men's work in the printing office or to their roles as assistant presidents in the Missouri presidency. Blessings given by JS to both men on 22 September, while overwhelmingly positive, give some indication of concern: Phelps was warned that "the Lord will chasten him because he taketh honor to himself, and when his Soul is greatly humbled he will forsake the evil"; similarly, Whitmer was told that he "shall truly be chastened wherein he steps aside."[156]

Five days before he dictated the 8 November revelation, JS reminded the men in the Elders School of the necessity of "our rightly improving our time and reigning up our minds to a sense of the great object that lies before us, viz, that glorious endowment that

---

Kirtland was completed and the solemn assembly was held therein. (Minutes, 23 June 1834, in *JSP*, D4:80–84; see also Revelation, 22 June 1834, in *JSP*, D4:77 [D&C 105:33].)

153. See Whitmer, History, 79, in *JSP*, H2:79.

154. After they arrived in Kirtland, Whitmer was appointed editor of the *Messenger and Advocate*, presumably to allow Oliver Cowdery to focus on publishing the Doctrine and Covenants. Phelps assisted Cowdery in his work with the Doctrine and Covenants and helped Whitmer with the *Messenger and Advocate*, as well as the hymnbook. (William W. Phelps, Kirtland, OH, to Sally Waterman Phelps, Liberty, MO, 14 Nov. 1835, in Historical Department, Journal History of the Church, 14 Nov. 1835; "To the Patrons of the Latter Day Saints' Messenger and Advocate," *LDS Messenger and Advocate*, June 1835, 1:135–137; JS History, vol. B-1, 592.)

155. See Historical Introduction to Book of Abraham Manuscript, ca. Early July–ca. Nov. 1835–A [Abraham 1:4–2:6], pp. 73–74 herein.

156. Blessing to William W. Phelps, 22 Sept. 1835, in *JSP*, D4:435–436; Blessing to John Whitmer, 22 Sept. 1835, in *JSP*, D4:430–433.

God has in store for the faithful."[157] In this context, the revelation directed to Phelps and Whitmer can be seen as part of a larger effort by JS to correct what he saw as improper behavior and to prepare church members for the much-anticipated solemn assembly and endowment of power.

On the same day the revelation featured here was recorded, JS corrected several other church members. During the Sunday morning worship service, Isaac Hill arose and confessed to unspecified actions that had led to his excommunication. Apparently unsatisfied with Hill's confession, John Smith proposed that Hill "make a public confession of his crime." Following Smith's motion, Sidney Rigdon arose and "verry abruptly militated against the sentiment of Uncle John." JS was not pleased with any of these actions, believing that Hill's confession was "not satisfactory," that Smith had been "wrong" in his proposal, and that Rigdon's speech had "destroy[ed] his [John Smith's] influence, . . . misrepresented Mr. Hill's case and spread darkness rather than light upon the subject." Following the meeting, JS visited with John Smith and Rigdon separately to convince them of their errors.[158] Later that day, JS's journal indicates, he "took up a labour" with John Corrill for his failure to partake of the sacrament and chastised his wife Emma for leaving the Sunday meeting "before sacrament."[159]

Document Transcript

The word of the Lord came unto me saying that President [William W.] Phelps & President J[ohn] Whitmer are under condemnation before the Lord, for their iniquities[160]

———— ⁊ ————

Conversations with Robert Matthews, 9–11 November 1835

Source Note

JS, Conversations with Robert Matthews, [Kirtland Township, Geauga Co., OH], 9–11 Nov. 1835. Featured version copied [ca. 11 Nov. 1835] in JS, Journal, 1835–1836, pp. 22–29; handwriting of Warren Parrish; JS Collection, CHL. For more information on JS, Journal, 1835–1836, see Source Notes for Multiple-Entry Documents, p. 524 herein.

---

157. JS, Journal, 3 Nov. 1835, in *JSP,* J1:84.

158. JS, Journal, 8 Nov. 1835, in *JSP,* J1:85–86.

159. JS's journal records that Corrill "made his confession" and Emma "manifested contrition by weeping." (JS, Journal, 8 Nov. 1835, in *JSP,* J1:86.)

160. Sometime after the revelation was recorded in the journal, Phelps made some changes to the entry. Close inspection of the document suggests that Phelps knife-erased the word "iniquities" and wrote the word "errors." Following the word "errors," Phelps inserted the phrase "for which they made satisfaction the same day." It is not known precisely when he made these changes, though it was likely while he was helping to write JS's history, sometime after mid-1841. Phelps began his contribution to JS's history following the death of Robert B. Thompson on 27 August 1841; he assisted Willard Richards with the history until at least 1843. (See JS, Journal, 8 Nov. 1835, in *JSP,* J1:86; and Jessee, "Writing of Joseph Smith's History," 439, 441, 446.)

Historical Introduction

Robert Matthews, also known as Joshua the Jewish minister or the Prophet Matthias, visited Kirtland, Ohio, and conversed with JS from 9 to 11 November 1835.[161] In the early 1820s, Matthews proclaimed himself an Israelite, temporarily identified himself with the Zionist movement of Manuel Mordecai Noah, and came to reject Christianity.[162] In Albany, New York, in 1830 and in Rochester, New York, in 1831, Matthews launched his career as a religious figure, calling himself the Prophet Matthias, and sought to win over recent converts of Charles G. Finney's revivals. In 1832, Matthews gained a small following and converted Elijah Pierson, a man of wealth who in February 1830 had organized an independent Christian perfectionist church on Bowery Hill in New York City.[163] Pierson died from an apparent poisoning in early August 1834, and Matthews, who claimed ownership over Pierson's property following his death, was charged with murder. Matthews was acquitted of that charge, but immediately after the acquittal he was tried and sentenced to three months in jail for beating his adult daughter and obtaining money under false pretenses; thirty days were added to his sentence for contempt of court. Suffering from internal dissension, compounded by the public spectacle and press coverage of the trials and Matthews's four-month incarceration, his religious experiment in New York crumbled in 1835.[164]

Three months after his release from jail in New York in August 1835, Matthews was reported to be traveling in Ohio. The 5 November issue of the *Western Reserve Chronicle* detailed Matthews's travels in Ohio and noted that while in Warren, Ohio, Matthews "inquired the way to Geauga county, where, perhaps, he has gone to join the 'democratic' community of Mormons, at Kirtland."[165] Prior to Matthews's arrival in Kirtland, the *Painesville Telegraph* also notified the Geauga County community of his presence, publishing two articles that labeled him as a deluded religious fraud.[166]

On the morning of 9 November, Matthews, calling himself "Joshua the Jewish minister," arrived at the home of JS in Kirtland. JS did not initially recognize him as the notorious figure Matthias, and Matthews's visit prompted him to relate the "circumstances connected with the coming forth of the book of Mormon," including an account of his first vision of Deity. The narrative JS presented to Matthews, one of the few early written accounts of this vision, expands upon some of the details found in JS's circa summer 1832 history, which is the earliest extant account of JS's first vision. In his telling of the event to Matthews, JS included details such as the presence of "two personages" as well as "many

161. JS, Journal, 9–11 Nov. 1835, in *JSP,* J1:87–95.

162. Johnson and Wilentz, *Kingdom of Matthias,* 62–68, 94–95, 103–104.

163. Johnson and Wilentz, *Kingdom of Matthias,* 32, 79–100. The idea of Christian perfectionism derived from John Wesley's *A Plain Account of Christian Perfection,* which describes the journey of an individual to the state of perfection or sanctification through the purity of intention and dedication of one's life to God. (Wesley, *Plain Account,* 3–5, 172.)

164. Johnson and Wilentz, *Kingdom of Matthias,* 137–164.

165. "Matthias," *Western Reserve Chronicle* (Warren, OH), 5 Nov. 1835, [2]; Matthias, *Cleveland Whig,* 11 Nov. 1835, [3].

166. "Matthias, the Impostor," *Painesville (OH) Telegraph,* 8 May 1835, [2]; 24 July 1835, [2].

angels" in the "silent grove."[167] The narrative also provides an account of the visit he received in 1823 from an "Angel," later identified as Moroni, who described "a sacred record which was written on plates of gold," and it gives the timeline for JS's obtaining of the plates.[168]

JS hosted Matthews for the next two days and invited him to expound on his religious views, but he ultimately denounced his visitor and told him to leave.[169] Nevertheless, regional newspapers reported on the visit of Matthews and JS and claimed that the two were joining forces. The *Daily Cleveland Herald* stated, "The impostor who lately figured so conspicuously in the city of New York, has turned Mormon; and, as we learn from the *Chardon Spectator*, is now at Kirtland in that county, in high favor with the prophet *Joe Smith*."[170] The *Ohio Repository,* published in Canton, noted that "eastern papers state this impostor has taken up his abode among the Mormons, on the borders of the Lake, in this state—and that both himself and his doctrines are received with great favor by them."[171] More aligned with JS's journal account, the *Painesville Telegraph* reported a much less favorable interaction between JS and Matthews. In an article titled "Prophet Catch Prophet," the *Telegraph* stated, "The notorious impostor Matthias has performed a pilgrimage to the temple of the equally notorious Joe Smith, where he held forth his doctrines last week. It appears that the new pretender met with less encouragement than he anticipated from the Latter-Day-ites, and after a two days conference the *Prophets* parted, each declaring he had miraculously discerned a devil in the other!"[172] By the end of November 1835, the *New York Herald* informed its readers that "Matthias has not joined the Mormons" but added sarcastically that "if they have pretty women among them no doubt he will."[173] No interaction between JS and Matthews after 11 November 1835 is known, though a July 1837 report in the *Baltimore Gazette and Daily Advertiser* noted that Matthews was back in northeastern Ohio "to regulate the Mormonites, at Kirtland, and spread his new doctrines among the benighted of the west."[174]

Matthews's visit to JS was recorded in JS's journal by Warren Parrish. Residue from an adhesive wafer at the top of page 25 of JS's 1835–1836 journal—as well as some paper residue still stuck to the wafer residue—indicates that a loose leaf had been attached in the journal

---

167. Substantial differences between the two versions of JS's vision are noted in the footnotes to the text featured here; compare JS History, ca. Summer 1832, 1–6, in *JSP,* H1:11–16.

168. JS, Journal, 9–11 Nov. 1835, in *JSP,* J1:87; Historical Introduction to History, ca. Summer 1832, in *JSP,* H1:6; [JS], Editorial, *Elders' Journal,* July 1838, 42–44. For JS's other accounts of his first vision of Deity, visit from the angel, and finding of the gold plates, see JS History, vol. A-1, 1–34, in *JSP,* H1:212–214, 220–232, 236 (Draft 2); and JS, "Church History," *Times and Seasons,* 1 Mar. 1842, 3:706–707, in *JSP,* H1:492–494; see also Oliver Cowdery's letters published in the *LDS Messenger and Advocate,* Oct. 1834–July 1835, copied in JS History, 1834–1836, pp. 46–50, 62–65, 81–99, in *JSP,* H1:40–44, 57–60, 73–86.

169. Conversations with Robert Matthews, 9–11 Nov. 1835, pp. 44, 47 herein.

170. "The Notorious Matthias," *Daily Cleveland Herald,* 17 Nov. 1835, [2], italics in original.

171. "Mathias," *Ohio Repository* (Canton), 19 Nov. 1835, [3].

172. "Prophet Catch Prophet," *Painesville (OH) Telegraph,* 20 Nov. 1835, 3, italics in original.

173. "Matthias," *New York Herald,* 28 Nov. 1835, [2].

174. "Matthias, the Prophet," *Baltimore Gazette and Daily Advertiser,* 17 July 1837, [2].

and suggests that part of the entry for 9–11 November 1835 was probably copied into the journal from an earlier manuscript, which is no longer extant.[175]

Document Transcript

while setting in my house between the hours of ~~nine~~ ⟨ten⟩ & ~~10~~ 11 this morning[176] a man came in, and introduced himself to me, calling ⟨himself⟩ ~~self~~ ⟨by the name of⟩ Joshua the Jewish minister, his appearance was some ~~what~~ ⟨thing⟩ singular, having a beard about 3 inches in length which is quite grey, also his hair is long and considerably silvered with age [p. 22] I should think he is about 50 or 55 years old,[177] tall and strait slender built of thin visage blue eyes, and fair complexion, he wears a sea green frock coat, & pantaloons of the same, black fur hat with narrow brim, and while speaking frequently shuts his eyes, with a scowl on his countinance;[178] I made some enquiry after his name but received no definite answer; we soon commenced talking upon the subject of religion and after I had made some remarks concerning the bible I commenced giving him a relation of the circumstances connected with the coming forth of the book of Mormon, as follows— being wrought up in my mind, respecting the subject of religion and looking ~~upon~~ ⟨at⟩ the different systems taught the children of men, I knew not who was right or who was wrong and concidering it of the first importance that I should be right, in matters that involved eternal consequences; being thus perplexed in mind I retired to the silent grove and bowd down before the Lord, under a realising sense that he had said (if the bible be true) ask and you shall recieve knock and it shall be opened seek and you shall find and again, if any man lack wisdom let him ask of God who giveth to all men liberally and upbra[i]deth not;[179] information was what I most desired at this time, and with a fixed determination ~~I~~ to obtain it, I called upon the Lord for the first time, in the place above stated or in other words I made a fruitless attempt to pray, my toung seemed to be swolen in my mouth, so that I could not utter,[180] I heard a noise behind me like some person walking towards me, ⟨I⟩ strove again to

---

175. JS, Journal, 9–11 Nov. 1835, in *JSP*, J1:89.

176. Monday, 9 November 1835.

177. Matthews was closer to 47 years old. (Johnson and Wilentz, *Kingdom of Matthias,* 50.)

178. For more on Matthews's appearance, see "Matthias," *Western Reserve Chronicle* (Warren, OH), 5 Nov. 1835, [2]; and Johnson and Wilentz, *Kingdom of Matthias,* 106–108.

179. See Matthew 7:7; Luke 11:9; and James 1:5; compare the account of JS's early religious experience with JS History, ca. Summer 1832, 1–2; and JS, History, vol. A-1, 2, in *JSP*, H1:11–12, 208–212 (Draft 2).

180. JS later explained, "I was seized upon by some power which entirely overcame me and had such astonishing influence over me as to bind my tongue so that I could not speak. Thick darkness gathered around me and it seemed to me for a time as if I were doomed to sudden destruction." (JS History, vol. A-1, 3, in *JSP*, H1:212 [Draft 2].)

pray, but could not, the noise of walking seemed to draw nearer, I sprung
up on my feet, ~~and~~ [p. 23] and looked around, but saw no person or thing
that was calculated to produce the noise of walking, I kneeled again my
mouth was opened and my toung liberated, and I called on the Lord in
mighty prayer, a pillar of fire appeared above my head, it presently rested
down upon ~~my~~ ⟨me⟩ ~~head~~, and filled me with joy unspeakable, a personage
appeard in the midst, of this pillar of flame which was spread all around, and
yet nothing consumed, another personage soon appeard like unto the first,
he said unto me thy sins are forgiven thee, he testifyed unto me that Jesus
Christ is the son of God;[181] ⟨and I saw many angels in this vision⟩ I was about
14. years old when I recieved this first communication;[182] When I was about 17
years old I saw another vision of angels, in the night season after I had retired
to bed I had not been a sleep, ~~when~~ but was meditating upon my past life and
experiance, I was verry concious that I had not kept the commandments,
and I repented hartily for all my sins and transgression, and humbled myself
before Him; ⟨whose eyes are over all things⟩, all at once the room was ilumi-
nated above the brightness of the sun an angel appeared before me, his hands
and feet were naked pure and white, and he stood between the floors of the
room, clothed ⟨with⟩ ~~in~~ purity inexpressible,[183] he said unto me I am a messenger sent from God, be faithful and keep his commandments in all things,
he told me of a sacred record which was written on plates of gold, I saw in the
vision the place where they were deposited, he said the indians, were the literal descendants of Abraham he explained many ~~things~~ of the prophesies to
[p. 24] me, one I will mention which is ~~this~~ in Malachi 4 behold the day of
the Lord cometh &c; also that the Urim and Thumim,[184] was hid up with the
record, and that God would give me power to translate it, with the assistance

---

181. In his circa summer 1832 history, JS stated, "I saw the Lord and he spake unto me saying Joseph
my son thy sins are forgiven thee. . . . I am the Lord of glory I was crucified for the world . . . I come
quickly . . . in the glory of my Father." In the circa summer 1832 history, JS noted seeing Jesus Christ only.
All of JS's subsequent accounts, including this conversation with Matthews, record that he saw two
personages. (JS History, ca. Summer 1832, 3; JS History, vol. A-1, 3; JS, "Church History," *Times and
Seasons*, 1 Mar. 1842, 3:706–707, in *JSP*, H1:12–13, 214 [Draft 2], 494; Neibaur, Journal, 24 May 1844.)

182. Compare JS History, ca. Summer 1832, 2–3, in *JSP*, H1:11–12.

183. In a February 1835 letter, Oliver Cowdery described the angel as wearing a "garment" that was
"perfectly white." JS later clarified that the angel had appeared wearing a "robe of most exquisite whiteness." (Oliver Cowdery, "Letter IV," *LDS Messenger and Advocate*, Feb. 1835, 1:79; JS History, vol. A-1, 5, in
JSP, H1:58, 220–221 [Draft 2].)

184. JS earlier used the term "spectacles" to describe this instrument in his circa summer 1832
history. A January 1833 article in *The Evening and the Morning Star* explained that JS translated the Book
of Mormon "through the aid of a pair of Interpreters, or spectacles . . . known, perhaps, in ancient days as
Teraphim, or Urim and Thummim." (JS History, ca. Summer 1832, 5, in *JSP*, H1:15; "Book of Mormon,"
The Evening and the Morning Star, Jan. 1833, 58.)

of this instrument he then gradually vanished out of my sight, or the vision closed, while meditating on what I had seen, the Angel appeard to me again and related the same things and much more, also the third time bearing the same tidings, and departed; during the time I was in this vision I did not realize any thing else around me except what was shown me in this communication: after the vision had all passed, I found that it was nearly day-light, the family soon arose, I got up also:— on that day while in the field at work with my Father he asked me if I was sick I replyed, I had but little strenght, he told me to go to the house, I started and went part way and was finally deprived deprived of my strength and fell, but how long I remained I do not know; the Angel came to me again and commanded me to go and tell my Father, what I had seen and heard, I did so, he wept and told me that it was a vision from God to attend to it[185] I went and found the place, where the plates were, according to the direction of the Angel, also saw them, and the angel as before; the powers of darkness strove hard against me, I called on God, the Angel told me that the reason why I could not obtain the plates at this time was because I was under transgression,[186] but to come again in one year from that time, I did so, but did not obtain them [p. 25] also the third and the fourth year, at which time I obtained them, and translated them into the english language; by the gift and power of God and have been preaching it ever since.

While I was relating this brief history of the establishment of the Church of Christ in these last days, Joshua seemed to be highly entertained after I had got through I observed that, the hour of worship & time to dine had now arived and invited him to tarry, which he concented to,

After dinner the conversation was resumed and Joshua proceded to make some remarks on the prophesies, as follows:

He observed that he was aware that I could bear stronger meat than many others, therefore he should open his mind the more freely;— Daniel has told us that he is to stand in his proper lot, in the latter days according to his vision he had a right to shut it up and also to open it again after many days, or in the

---

185. JS's mother, Lucy Mack Smith, later recounted that the angel asked JS why he had not told his father, to which JS replied that "he was affraid his father would not believe him." The angel responded that his father would "believe every word you say to him." (Lucy Mack Smith, History, 1844–1845, bk. 3, [11].)

186. In 1832, JS explained that he attempted to remove the ancient record but was prohibited because he "saught the Plates to obtain riches and kept not the commandme[n]t that I should have an eye single to the Glory of God." (JS History, ca. Summer 1832, 4–5, in *JSP*, H1:14; compare JS History, vol. A-1, 7, in *JSP*, H1:232–234 [Draft 2]; Lucy Mack Smith, History, 1844–1845, bk. 4, [2]; and Jessee, "Joseph Knight's Recollection," 31.)

latter times;[187] Daniels Image whose head was gold, and body, armes, legs and feet was composed of the different materials described in his vision represents different governments, the golden head was ⟨to represent⟩ Nebuchodnazer King of Babylon, the other parts other kings & forms of government,[188] which I shall not now mention in detail, but confine my remarks, more particularly to the feet of the Image; The policy of the wicked spirit, is to separate what God has joined togather and unite what He has separated, which he has succeded in doing to admiration, in the present state of society, which is like unto Iron and clay, there is confusion in all things, both [p. 26] both Political and religious, and notwithstanding all the efforts that are made to bring about a union, society is remains disunited, and all attempts to ⟨unite her⟩ are as fruitless, as to attemp to unite Iron & Clay.

The feet of the Image, is the government of these united States,[189] other Nations & kingdoms are looking up to her for an example, of union fredom and equal rights, and therefore worship her, like as Daniel saw in the vision, although they are begining to loose confidence in her, seeing the broils and discord that distract, her political & religious horizon this Image is characteristic of all governments and institutions or most of them; as they begin with a head of gold and terminate in the contemp[t]ible feet of Iron & clay: making a splendid appearance at first, proposing to do much more than the[y] can perform, and finally end in degradation and sink, in infamy; we should not only start to come out of Babylon but leav it entirely lest we are overthrown in her ruins, we should keep improving and reforming, twenty-fours hours for improvement now is worth as much as a year a hundred years ago; the spirit of the Fathers that was cut down, or those that were under the altar,[190] are now rising this is the first resurection the Elder that fall's first will rise last;[191] we should not form any opinion only for the present, and leave the result of futurity with God: I have risen up out of obscurity, but was look^d. up to when but a youth, in temporal things:[192] It is not necessary that God should give us all things at first or in his first commission to us, but in his second. John saw

---

187. See Daniel 12:4.

188. See Daniel 2.

189. Matthews taught his followers that "President Jackson and his government were the toes of this image," that "this was the last of the republican governments," and that the United States federal government was "at an end." (Stone, *Matthias and His Impostures*, 167.)

190. See Revelation 6:9.

191. See Matthew 20:16.

192. Matthews was orphaned in his childhood and later became a farm laborer. However, during his mid- to late twenties he enjoyed a profitable enterprise as a storekeeper. (Johnson and Wilentz, *Kingdom of Matthias*, 57–62.)

the angel deliver the gospel in the last days,[193] which would not be necessary if [p. 27] it was already in the world this expression would be inconsistent, the small lights that God has given, is sufficient to lead us out of babylon, when we get out we shall have the greater light. I told Jo[s]hua that I did not understand him concerning the resurection and wishd him to be more explanatory on the subject; he replied that he did not feell impressed by the spirit to unfold it further at present, but perhaps he might at some other time.

I then withdrew to do some buisness with another gentleman that called to see me.

He [Robert Matthews] informed my Scribe that he was born in Washington County Town of Cambridge New York. he says that all the railroads canals and other improvements are performed by spirits of the resurection.

The silence spoken of by John the Revelator which is to be in heaven for the space of half an hour,[194] is between 1830 & 1851, during which time the judgments of God will be poured out after that time there will be peace.[195]

Curiosity to see a man that was reputed to be a jew caused many to call during the day and more particularly at evening suspicions were entertained that said Joshua was the noted Mathias of New York, spoken so much of in the public prints on account of the trials he underwent in that place before a court of justice, for murder manslaughter comtempt of court whip[p]ing his Daughter &c for the two last crimes he was imprisoned, and came out about 4, months [p. 28] since, after some, equivocating he confessed that he was realy Mathias: after supper I proposed that he should deliver a lecture to us, he did so sitting in his chair; he commenced by saying God said let there be light and there was light,[196] which he dwelt upon through his discource, he made some verry exelent remarks but his mind was evidently filled with darkness, after he dismissed his meeting, and the congregation disperced, he conversed freely upon the circumstances that transpired in New York,

His name is Robert Mathias, he say[s] that Joshua, is his priestly name.[197]

during all this time I did not contradict his sentiments, wishing to draw out all that I could concerning his faith; the next morning Tuesday 10th I resumed the conversation and desired him to enlighten my mind more on his views

---

193. See Revelation 14:6.

194. See Revelation 8:1.

195. In 1830, Matthews marked the beginning of his "Kingdom," then only an idea, by issuing a "Declaration of Judgement." He intended to preach until 1836, after which would follow fifteen years of turmoil before the world burned. (Johnson and Wilentz, *Kingdom of Matthias*, 79–81, 92, 96.)

196. See Genesis 1:3.

197. Matthews declared himself "chief high Priest of the Jews." (Johnson and Wilentz, *Kingdom of Matthias*, 145.)

respecting the resurection, he says that he poss[ess]es the spirit of his fathers, that he is a litteral decendant of Mathias the Apostle that was chosen in the place of Judas that fell[198] and that his spirit is resurected in him, and that this is the way or scheme of eternal life, this transmigration of soul or spirit from Father to Son: I told him that his doctrine was of the Devil that he was in reality in possession of wicked and depraved spirit, although he professed to be the spirit of truth, it self,[199] also that he possesses the soul of Christ; he tarried until Wednesday 11.th, after breckfast I told him, that my God told me that his God is the Devil, and I could not keep him any longer, and he must depart, and so I for once cast out the Devil in bodily shape, & I believe a murderer [p. 29]

———— ❧ ————

Discourse, 12 November 1835

Source Note

JS, Discourse, [Kirtland Township, Geauga Co., OH], 12 Nov. 1835. Featured version copied [ca. 12 Nov. 1835] in JS, Journal, 1835–1836, pp. 30–35; handwriting of Warren Parrish; JS Collection, CHL. For more information on JS, Journal, 1835–1836, see Source Notes for Multiple-Entry Documents, p. 524 herein.

Historical Introduction

On 12 November 1835, JS met with nine of the Twelve Apostles and counseled them to prepare for the solemn assembly to be held in the House of the Lord, when complete, and for the endowment of divine power that had been promised in earlier revelations.[200] The discourse he delivered that day, featured here, presented a more detailed description of the purposes for the House of the Lord and of the long-anticipated events that were to take place there.[201]

Since the Twelve's return to Kirtland, Ohio, in late September 1835 from a mission to the eastern United States, JS had instructed them several times regarding the solemn assembly and the endowment of power they were to receive in the House of the Lord.[202] On 5 October, he told them that they should "attend this fall the solemn assembly of the first Elders for the organization of the school of the prophets, and attend to the ordinance of the washing of feet and to prepare their hearts in all humility for an endowment with power

---

198. See Acts 1:15–26.

199. Matthews claimed to have the same "spirit of Truth" that was once within the New Testament apostle Matthias, whom the eleven apostles chose to replace Judas after Judas's betrayal. (Johnson and Wilentz, *Kingdom of Matthias*, 94–95; Acts 1:23–26.)

200. See, for example, Revelation, 27–28 Dec. 1832, in *JSP*, D2:334–346 [D&C 88:1–126]; Revelation, 3 Jan. 1833, in *JSP*, D2:346–348 [D&C 88:127–137]; and Revelation, 22 June 1834, in *JSP*, D4:69 [D&C 105:9–11].

201. Esplin, "Emergence of Brigham Young," 173–176.

202. JS, Journal, 26 Sept. 1835, in *JSP*, J1:64; Esplin and Nielsen, "Record of the Twelve, 1835," 48–51.

from on high." The apostles "all agreed with one accord" to follow this instruction.[203] About a month later, JS dictated a revelation that chastised the Twelve for being insufficiently humble and reminded them "they must all humble themselves before Me, before they will be accounted worthy to receive an endowment to go forth in my name unto all nations." The revelation encouraged the apostles to "repent speedily and prepare their hearts for the solem assembly and for the great day which is to come."[204] In the discourse featured here, JS continued to urge the Twelve to repent and prepare for the endowment of power, with the promise that "all who are prepared and are sufficiently pure to abide the presence of the Saviour will see him in the solem assembly."

In this 12 November discourse, JS gave, perhaps for the first time, specific details and instruction on what was to occur at the solemn assembly. He called particular attention to the purification ritual of foot washing. While other contemporary religious denominations viewed foot washing as an act of humility or as preparatory to receiving communion, JS and the Latter-day Saints focused on purification, understanding the washing of feet as a ritual to liberate recipients from the sins of the world.[205] In January 1833, at the formation of the School of the Prophets, JS formally received elders into the school by washing their feet.[206] According to Zebedee Coltrin, JS performed the ritual, or the "washing of the deciples feet," on each attendee of the inaugural class, following the precedent set by Jesus at the Last Supper.[207] Performance of foot washing ceased, however, after the initial term of the school. As demonstrated in the discourse featured here, JS was preparing to reintroduce the practice in the House of the Lord. Three days after the dedication of the House of the Lord on 27 March 1836, the long-awaited solemn assembly was held, and it included the washing of the feet of priesthood officers.[208]

JS's meeting with the apostles began at six o'clock in the evening and opened with singing and prayer before JS's discourse. Nine of the apostles attended, though which nine goes unspecified. Following JS's remarks, "the brethren expressed their gratifycation for the instruction [he] had given them."[209]

Document Transcript

This evening viz the 12th at 6 oclock meet with the council of 12. by their request, 9 of them were present [p. 30] council opened by singing & prayer, and I made some remarks as follows;— I am happy in the enjoyment of this opportunity of meeting with this council on this occasion, I am satisfyed that the spirit

203. JS, Journal, 5 Oct. 1835, in *JSP*, J1:68. A June 1834 revelation stated that an endowment of power for church leaders must be received in the House of the Lord before Zion could be redeemed. (Revelation, 22 June 1834, in *JSP*, D4:74 [D&C 105:9–11].)

204. Revelation, 3 Nov. 1835, pp. 35–36 herein.

205. Grow, "Clean from the Blood of This Generation," 131–134; see also Doctrine and Covenants 7:45–46, 1835 ed. [D&C 88:138–141].

206. Minutes, 22–23 Jan. 1833, in *JSP*, D2:381–382.

207. Coltrin, Diary and Notebook, 24 Jan. 1833; John 13:4–17.

208. Minutes, 30 Mar. 1836, pp. 216–221 herein; JS, Journal, 29 and 30 Mar. 1836, in *JSP*, J1:211–216.

209. JS, Journal, 12 Nov. 1835, in *JSP*, J1:96–99.

of the Lord is here, and I am satisfied with all the breth[r]en present, and I need not say that you have my utmost confidence, and that I intend to uphold, you to the uttermost, for I am well aware that you ~~do and delight in so doing~~ have to sustain my character ~~my charcter~~ against the vile calumnies and reproaches of this ungodly generation and that you delight in so doing:——²¹⁰ darkness prevails, at this time as it was, at the time Jesus Christ was about to be crucified, the powers of darkness strove to obscure the glorious sun of righteousness that began to dawn upon the world,²¹¹ and was soon to burst in great blessings upon the heads of the faithful, and let me tell you brethren that great blessings awate us at this time and will soon be poured out upon us if we are faithful in all things, for we are even entitled to greater blessings than they were, because the[y] had the person of Christ with them, to instruct them in the great plan of salvation, his personal presence we have not, therefore we need great faith on account of our peculiar circumstances and I am determined to do all that I can to uphold you, although I may do many things ⟨invertaintly [inadvertently]⟩ that are not right in the sight of God; you want to know many things that are before you, that you may know how ~~how~~ to prepare your selves for the [p. 31] great things that God is about to bring to pass; but there is on[e] great deficiency or obstruction, in the way that deprives us of the greater blessings, and in order to make the foundation of this church complete and permanent, we must remove this obstruction, which is to attend to certain duties that we have not as yet attended to; I supposed I had established this church on a permanent foundation when I went to the Missourie and indeed I did so, for if I had been taken away it would have been enough,²¹² but I yet live, and therefore God requires more at my hands:— The item to which I wish the more particularly to call your attention to night is the ordinance of washing of feet,²¹³ this we have not done as yet but it is necessary now as much as it was in the days of the Saviour, and we must have a place prepared, that we may attend to this ordinance, aside from the world; we have not desired much from the hand of the Lord, with that faith and obediance

---

210. See "A Summary," *LDS Messenger and Advocate,* Dec. 1834, 1:43–46; "A Summary," *LDS Messenger and Advocate,* Feb. 1835, 1:75–76; and Preface to the Doctrine and Covenants, 17 Feb. 1835, in *JSP,* D4:234–237.

211. See Malachi 4:2; and Book of Mormon, 1830 ed., 505 [3 Nephi 25:2].

212. Before leaving on the Camp of Israel expedition to Missouri in 1834, JS established a high council for church governance in Kirtland. While in Missouri in July, he similarly organized a high council and appointed David Whitmer, William W. Phelps, and John Whitmer as a local presidency to preside over the high council. JS also designated David Whitmer as a potential successor to the office of general church president. JS remarked on that occasion that "if he should now be taken away that he had accomplished the great work which the Lord had laid before him." (Minutes, 3 July 1834, in *JSP,* D4:88; Minutes and Discourse, ca. 7 July 1834, in *JSP,* D4:90; see also Minute Book 2, 15 Mar. 1838.)

213. See John 13:4–5; and Doctrine and Covenants 7:45–46, 1835 ed. [D&C 88:138–141].

that we ought, yet we have enjoyed great blessings, and we are not so sensible of this as we should be; When or wher has God suffered one of the witnesses or first Elders of this church ⟨to⟩ fall? never nor nowhere amidst all the calamities and judgments that have befallen the inhabitants of the earth his almighty arm has sustained us, men and Devils have raged and spent the malice in vain. [p. 32] we must have all things prepared and call our solem assembly as the Lord has commanded us,[214] that we may be able to accomplish his great work: and it must be done in Gods own way, the house of the Lord must be prepared, and the solem assembly called and organized in it according to the order of the house of God[215] and in it we must attend to the ordinance of washing of feet;[216] it was never intended for any but official members, it is calculated to unite our hearts, that we may be one in feeling and sentiment and that our faith may be strong, so that satan cannot over throw us, nor have any power over us,— the endowment you are so anxious about you cannot comprehend now, nor could Gabriel explain it to the understanding of your dark minds,[217] but strive to be prepared in your hearts, be faithful in all things that when we meet in the solem assembly that is such as God shall name out of all the official members, will meet, and we must be clean evry whit,[218] let us be faithful and silent brethren, ⟨and⟩ if God gives you a manifestation, keep it to yourselves, be watchful and prayerful, and you shall have a prelude of those joys that God will pour out on that day, do not watch for iniquity in each other if you do you will not get an endowment for God will not bestow it on such; but if we are faithful and live by every word that procedes forth from the mouth of God[219] I will venture to prophesy that we shall get a [p. 33] blessing that will be worth remembering if we should live as long as John the Revelator,[220] our blessings will be such as we have not realized before, nor in this generation. The order of the house of God has and ever will be the same, even after Christ comes, and after the termination of the thousand years it will be the same, and we shall finally roll into the celestial kingdom of God and enjoy it forever;— you need an endowment brethren in order that you may be prepared and able to overcome all things,[221] and those that

---

214. See Revelation, 27–28 Dec. 1832, in *JSP*, D2:341, 345 [D&C 88:70, 117]; and Revelation, 1 June 1833, in *JSP*, D3:106 [D&C 95:7–8].

215. See Revelation, 3 Nov. 1831, in *JSP*, D2:117 [D&C 133:6]; Revelation, 27–28 Dec. 1832, in *JSP*, D2:341 [D&C 88:70]; and Revelation, 1 June 1833, in *JSP*, D3:106 [D&C 95:7].

216. See Revelation, 27–28 Dec. 1832, in *JSP*, D2:341 [D&C 88:74].

217. See Luke 1:19.

218. See John 13:10.

219. See Deuteronomy 8:3; and Matthew 4:4.

220. See John 21:20–23; and Account of John, April 1829–C, in *JSP*, D1:47–48 [D&C 7].

221. See Revelation, 22 June 1834, in *JSP*, D4:74, 75, 77 [D&C 105:12, 18, 33].

reject your testimony will be damned the sick will be healed the lame made to walk the deaf to hear and the blind to see through your instrumentality;

But let me tell you that you will not have power after the endowment to heal those who have not faith, nor to benifit them, for you might as well expect to benefit a devil in hell as such a⟨n⟩ one, who is possessed of his spirit and are willing to keep it for they are habitations for devils and only fit for his society but when you are endowed and prepared to preach the gospel to all nations kindred and toungs in there own languages[222] you must faithfully warn all and bind up the testimony and seal up the law and the destroying angel will follow close at your heels and execute his tremendeous mission upon the children of disobediance, and destroy [p. 34] the workers of iniquity, while the saints will be gathered out from among them and stand in holy places[223] ready to meet the bride groom when he comes.—[224]

I feel disposed to speak a few words more to you my brethren concerning the endowment, all who are prepared and are sufficiently pure to abide the presence of the Saviour will see him in the solem assembly.[225]

———— ☙ ————

Revelation, 14 November 1835

Source Note

Revelation, [Kirtland Township, Geauga Co., OH], 14 Nov. 1835. Featured version copied [ca. 14 Nov. 1835] in JS, Journal, 1835–1836, pp. 35–36; handwriting of Warren Parrish; JS Collection, CHL. For more information on JS, Journal, 1835–1836, see Source Notes for Multiple-Entry Documents, p. 524 herein.

Historical Introduction

Dictated by JS on 14 November 1835, this revelation was directed to the man who recorded it, Warren Parrish. Since joining the church in 1833, Parrish had become a trusted

---

222. See Revelation, 3 Nov. 1831, in *JSP*, D2:118 [D&C 133:37].

223. See Matthew 24:15; and Psalm 24:3.

224. See Matthew 25:1–13; and Revelation, Oct. 1830–B, in *JSP*, D1:207–208 [D&C 33:17].

225. See Revelation, 2 Nov. 1831, in *JSP*, D2:109–110 [D&C 67:10]. JS's journal states that at the solemn assembly on 30 March 1836, JS left the "meeting in charge of the 12 and retired at about 9 o clock in the evening; the brethren continued exhorting, prophesying and speaking in tongues until 5 o clock in the morning—the Saviour made his appearance to some, while angels ministered unto others, and it was a penticost and enduement indeed, long to be remembered for the sound shall go forth from this place into all the world, and the occurrences of this day shall be handed down upon the pages of sacred history to all generations, as the day of Penecost." (JS, Journal, 30 Mar. 1836, in *JSP*, J1:215–216; see also Harper, "Pentecost and Endowment Indeed," 327–371.)

associate of JS and had already served informally as a clerk.[226] Less than a year after his
conversion, Parrish and his wife, Elizabeth Patten Parrish, marched with JS and approximately 225 other men, women, and children to Clay County, Missouri, on the Camp of
Israel expedition.[227] Sometime in late June or early July, Elizabeth Parrish died from
cholera, as did approximately twelve other members of the expedition.[228] Warren Parrish
likely remained in Missouri until 12 September, when he and his brother-in-law, David W.
Patten, left on a proselytizing mission that took them through Missouri, Kentucky, and
Tennessee.[229] Patten and Parrish, later joined by Wilford Woodruff, established several
small branches in those states between October 1834 and July 1835, when Parrish returned
to Kirtland.[230] Shortly after his return, Parrish was named to the First Quorum of the
Seventy.[231]

Upon his return, Parrish fulfilled a number of clerical responsibilities during fall 1835
and winter 1836. In addition to periodically taking minutes for the Kirtland high council,
acting as a scribe to the First Presidency, keeping a personal journal for JS, and copying
material from the journal and other records into JS's 1834–1836 history, Parrish acted as a
scribe as JS translated portions of the Egyptian papyri that had arrived in Kirtland sometime in late June.[232] It is to these "ancient records" that the following revelation most
likely refers.

Document Transcript

Thus came the word of the Lord unto me saying:

verily thus saith the ~~the~~ Lord unto my servant Joseph concerning my servant Warren [Parrish], behold [p. 35] his sins are forgiven him because of his
desires to do the works of righteousness therefore in as much as he will continue to hearken unto my voice he shall be blessed with wisdom and with a
sound mind even above his fellows, behold it shall come to pass in his day that
he shall ⟨see⟩ great things shew forth themselves unto my people, he shall see
much of my ancient records, and shall know of hid[d]en things, and shall be

226. Parrish was officially hired as JS's personal scribe sixteen days earlier. (JS, Journal, 29 Oct. 1835,
in *JSP*, J1:76.)

227. See "Joseph Smith Documents from April 1834 through September 1835," in *JSP*, D4:xix–xxii.

228. "Joseph Smith Documents from April 1834 through September 1835," in *JSP*, D4:xxii; Parkin,
"Zion's Camp Cholera Victims Monument Dedication," 4–5; Amasa Lyman, Journal, June 1834; Smith,
"History of George Albert Smith," 29–31; Bradley, *Zion's Camp 1834,* 261; Burgess, Autobiography, 3.

229. Patten, Journal, 12 Sept. 1834.

230. David W. Patten and Warren Parrish, Paris, TN, to Oliver Cowdery, 11 Oct. 1834, in *LDS
Messenger and Advocate,* Nov. 1834, 1:24; "A Summary," *LDS Messenger and Advocate,* Dec. 1834, 1:44; "A
Summary," *LDS Messenger and Advocate,* Feb. 1835, 1:76; "A Summary," *LDS Messenger and Advocate,* Apr.
1835, 1:104. According to Wilford Woodruff, he and Parrish parted company on 23 July 1835. (Woodruff,
Journal, 23 July 1835.)

231. Minutes, 17 Aug. 1835, in *JSP*, D4:390.

232. Minute Book 1, 17–19 Aug. and 28–29 Sept. 1835; 2 Jan. and 12 Feb. 1836; Partridge, Journal,
21 Jan. 1836; JS, Journal, 29 Oct. 1835, in *JSP*, J1:76; Jessee, "Writing of Joseph Smith's History," 446–449;
Hauglid, *Textual History of the Book of Abraham,* 110.

endowed with a knowledge of hiden languages,[233] and if he desires and shall seek it at my hand, he shall be privileged with writing much of my word, as a scribe unto me for the benefit of my people, therefore this shall be his calling until I shall order it otherwise[234] in my wisdom and it shall be said of him in a time to come, behold Warren the Lords Scribe, for the Lords Seer whom he hath appointed in Israel; Therefore ⟨if he will⟩ keep my commandments he shall be lifted up at the last day, even so Amen

———— ৩ ————

Letter to the Elders of the Church, 16 November 1835

Source Note

JS, Letter, Kirtland Township, Geauga Co., OH, to "the elders of the church of the Latter Day Saints," 16 Nov. 1835. Featured version published in "To the Elders of the Church of the Latter Day Saints," Latter Day Saints' Messenger and Advocate, Nov. 1835, 2:209–212. For more information on Latter Day Saints' Messenger and Advocate, see Source Notes for Multiple-Entry Documents, p. 527 herein.

Historical Introduction

This letter to the elders of the church is the second in a three-part series of open letters published in the September, November, and December 1835 issues of the church's newspaper, the *Latter Day Saints' Messenger and Advocate.* According to his journal, JS dictated a "letter for the Advocate" at his home on 16 November 1835, almost certainly referring to the installment featured here.[235]

In this letter, JS again discussed the concept of gathering, as he had in the letter published in the September issue.[236] Building on the doctrinal foundation of repentance and baptism outlined in the earlier letter and drawing heavily on biblical scripture, he asserted that the Latter-day Saints had begun fulfilling the commission to gather Israel to Zion, a New Jerusalem, in preparation for the second coming of Jesus Christ. By this time, the Saints had been driven out of Jackson County, Missouri, the revealed location for Zion,[237] but JS explained that it would still be established by and for the "elect" of God.

---

233. JS and other early church leaders demonstrated an abiding interest in ancient languages, including Egyptian, Hebrew, and even the "pure" or "Adamic" language believed to be spoken by Adam, Eve, and their children. (See Book of Abraham Manuscript, ca. Early July–ca. Nov. 1835–A [Abraham 1:4–2:6]; Letter to Henrietta Raphael Seixas, between 6 and 13 Feb. 1836, pp. 173–178 herein; and Sample of Pure Language, between ca. 4 and ca. 20 Mar. 1832, in *JSP,* D2:213–215.)

234. It appears Parrish kept JS's journal until Parrish left for a mission in May 1836. Upon his return in November 1836, he began to act as clerk for the Kirtland Safety Society. (Warren Parrish, "Mission in the South," *LDS Messenger and Advocate,* Nov. 1836, 3:404; Kirtland Safety Society, Stock Ledger, 1836–1837, Collection of Manuscripts about Mormons, Chicago History Museum, copy at CHL.)

235. JS, Journal, 16 Nov. 1835, in *JSP,* J1:101.

236. See Letter to the Elders of the Church, 2 Oct. 1835, pp. 6–15 herein.

237. Revelation, 20 July 1831, in *JSP,* D2:7–8 [D&C 57:1–3].

This second letter also instructed the traveling elders to obtain permission from the head of household before preaching to children or wives so as not to engender conflict between husband and wife or parents and children. The letter advised the same caution in preaching to slaves and servants. JS also provided practical instruction to the elders based on his understanding of the Bible and on past problems encountered by Latter-day Saint missionaries. Finally, JS's message encouraged the elders to provide a "warning voice" to all but to do so tactfully.

JS dictated this letter, probably to his scribe, Warren Parrish. The original is no longer extant. After JS dictated this letter, John Whitmer printed it in the November issue of the *Messenger and Advocate*. In the last installment of his three-part instruction, written on 30 November and 1 December, JS continued to highlight the importance of gathering and further advised the traveling elders on contending against religious misrepresentation.[238]

Document Transcript

To the elders of the church of the Latter Day Saints.

At the close of my letter in the September No. of the "Messenger and Advocate,"[239] I promised to continue the subject there commenced: I do so with a hope that it may be a benefit and a means of assistance to the elders in their labors, while they are combatting the prejudices of a crooked and perverse generation, by having in their possession, the facts of my religious principles, which are misrepresented by almost all those whose crafts are in danger by the same; and also to aid those who are anxiously inquiring, and have been excited to do so from rumor, in accertaining correctly, what my principles are.

I have been drawn into this course of proceeding, by persecution, that is brought upon us from false rumor, and misrepresentations concerning my sentiments.[240]

But to proceed, in the letter alluded to. The principles of repentance and baptism for the remission of sins, are not only set forth, but many passages of

238. JS, Journal, 30 Nov. and 1 Dec. 1835, in *JSP*, J1:113.

239. Letter to the Elders of the Church, 2 Oct. 1835, pp. 6–15 herein.

240. In his 2 October 1835 letter to the church, JS wrote, "We shall here show our faith, and thereby, as we humbly trust, put an end to these faults, and wicked misrepresentations." Church leaders published the Doctrine and Covenants earlier in 1835 in part to help clarify the beliefs of church members and thereby combat misrepresentations about the church. Over the previous year, the *Messenger and Advocate* published several letters from missionaries, some of which depicted the prejudices they encountered from the "enemies to the cause of truth." (Letter to the Elders of the Church, 2 Oct. 1835, p. 10 herein; Preface to Doctrine and Covenants, 17 Feb. 1835, in *JSP*, D4:234; "A Summary," *LDS Messenger and Advocate,* Dec. 1834, 43; see also Oliver Cowdery, "The Closing Year," *LDS Messenger and Advocate,* Dec. 1834, 47; "A Summary," *LDS Messenger and Advocate,* Feb. 1835, 75; and Lectures, *LDS Messenger and Advocate,* May 1835, 122.)

scripture, were quoted, clearly illucidating the subject; let me add, that I do positively rely upon the truth and veracity of those principles inculcated in the new testament;[241] and then pass from the above named items, on to the item or subject of the gathering, and show my views upon this point: which is an item which I esteem to be of the greatest importance to those who are looking for salvation in this generation, or in these what may be called "the latter times," as all the prophets that have written, from the days of righteous Abel down to the last man, that has left any testimony on record, for our consideration, in speaking of the salvation of Israel in the last days, goes directly to show, that it consists in the work of the gathering.

Firstly, I shall begin by quoting from the prophecy of Enoch, speaking of the last days: "Righteousness will I send down out of heaven, and truth will I send forth out of the earth, to bear testimony of mine Only Begotten, his resurrection from the dead, [this resurrection I understand to be the corporeal body][242] yea, and also the resurrection of all men, righteousness and truth will I cause to sweep the earth as with a flood, to gather out mine own elect from the four quarters of the earth, unto a place which I shall prepare; a holy city, that my people may gird up their loins, and be looking forth for the time of my coming: for there shall be my tabernacle; and it shall be called Zion, a New Jerusalem."[243]

Now I understand by this quotation, that God clearly manifested to Enoch, the redemption which he prepared, by offering the Messiah as a Lamb slain from before the foundation of the world: by virtue of the same, the glorious resurrection of the Savior, and the resurrection of all the human family,—even a resurrection of their corporeal bodies: and also righteousness and truth to sweep the earth as with a flood. Now I ask how righteousness and truth are agoing to sweep the earth as with a flood? I will answer:—Men and angels are to be co-workers in bringing to pass this great work: and a Zion is to be prepared; even a New Jerusalem, for the elect that are to be gathered from the four quarters of the earth,[244] and to be established an holy city: for the tabernacle of the Lord shall be with them.

---

241. See, for example, Luke 24:45–47; Acts 2:38–39; Revelation 22:17; Matthew 11:28–30; and Hebrews 5:12–14, 6:1–6.

242. This editorial insertion in the *Messenger and Advocate* is not found in other contemporary copies of JS's inspired revision of the Bible, from which the quotation is taken. (See Old Testament Revision 1, p. 19 [Moses 7:62]; "Extract from the Prophecy of Enoch," *The Evening and the Morning Star,* Aug. 1832, 18; and "Extract from the Prophecy of Enoch," *Evening and Morning Star,* Aug. 1832 [Mar. 1835], 47.)

243. See Old Testament Revision 1, p. 19 [Moses 7:62].

244. See Matthew 24:31; and Mark 13:27.

Now Enoch was in good company in his views upon this subject. See Revelations, 23:3.—"And I heard a great voice out of heaven saying, Behold the tabernacle of God is with men, and he will dwell with them, and they shall be his people, and God himself shall be with them, and be their God." I discover by this quotation, that John upon the isle of Patmos, saw the same things concerning the last days, which Enoch saw. But before the tabernacle can be with men, the elect must be gathered from the four quarters of the earth.

And to show further upon this subject of the gathering: Moses, after having pronounced the blessing and the cursing upon the children of Israel, for their obedience or disobedience, says thus:—"And it shall come to pass, when all these things are come upon thee, the blessing and the curse which I have set before thee; and thou shalt [p. [209]] call them to mind, among all the nations whither the Lord thy God hath driven thee, and shalt return unto the Lord thy God, and shalt obey his voice, according to all that I command thee, this day, thou and thy children, with all thine heart, and with all thy soul, that then the Lord thy God, will turn thy captivity, and have compassion upon thee, and will return and gather thee from all the nations whither the Lord thy God hath scattered thee; and if any of thine be driven out unto the utmost parts of heaven; from thence will the Lord thy God gather thee; and from thence will he fetch thee."[245]

It has been said by many of the learned, and wise men, or historians, that the Indians, or aboriginees of this continent, are of the scattered tribes of Israel. It has been conjectured by many others, that the aboriginees of this continent, are not of the tribes of Israel; but the ten tribes have been led away into some unknown regions of the north. Let this be as it may, the prophesy I have just quoted, "will fetch them" in the last days, and place them, in the land which their fathers possessed: and you will find in the 7th verse of the 30th chapt. quoted:—"And the Lord thy God will put all these curses upon thine enemies and on them that hate thee, which persecuted thee."[246]

Many may say that this scripture is fulfilled, but let them mark carefully what the prophet says: "If any are driven out unto the utmost parts of heaven;" (which must mean the breadths of the earth.) Now this promise is good to any, if there should be such, that are driven out, even in the last days: therefore, the children of the fathers have claim unto this day: and if these curses are to be laid over on the heads of their enemies, wo be unto the Gentiles: See book of Mormon, page 487,[247] Wo unto the unbelieving of the Gentiles, saith the Father. Again see book of Mormon, page 497, which says: "Behold this people

---

245. Deuteronomy 30:1–4.
246. Deuteronomy 30:7.
247. Book of Mormon, 1830 ed., 487 [3 Nephi 16, especially verses 4–12].

will I establish in this land, unto the fulfilling of the covenant which I made with your father Jacob: and it shall be a New Jerusalem."[248] Now we learn from the book of Mormon, the very identical continent and spot of land upon which the New Jerusalem is to stand,[249] and it must be caught up according to the vision of John upon the isle of Patmos. Now many will be disposed to say, that this New Jerusalem spoken of, is the Jerusalem that was built by the Jews on the eastern continent: but you will see from Revelations, 21:2, there was a New Jerusalem coming down from God out of heaven, adorned as a bride for her husband. That after this the Revelator was caught away in the Spirit to a great and high mountain, and saw the great and holy city descending out of heaven from God. Now there are two cities spoken of here, and as every thing cannot be had in so narrow a compass as a letter, I shall say with brevity, that there is a New Jerusalem to be established on this continent.— And also the Jerusalem shall be rebuilt on the eastern continent. See book of Mormon, page 566. Behold, Ether saw the days of Christ, and he spake also concerning the house of Israel, and the Jerusalem from whence Lehi should come: after it should be destroyed it should be built up again, a holy city unto the Lord: wherefore, it could not be a New Jerusalem, for it had been in a time of old.[250] This may suffice upon the subject of gathering until my next.

I now proceed, at the close of my letter, to make a few remarks on the duty of elders with regard to their teaching parents and children, husbands and wives, masters and slaves, or servants, &c. as I said I would in my former letter.[251] And firstly, it becomes an elder when he is travelling through the world, warning the inhabitants of the earth to gather together, that they may be built up an holy city unto the Lord,[252] instead of commencing with children, or those who look up to parents or guardians, to influence their minds, thereby drawing them from their duties, which they rightfully owe to such, they should commence their labors with parents, or guardians, and their teachings should be such as are calculated to turn the hearts of the fathers to the children, and the hearts of the children to the fathers.[253] And no influence should be used, with children contrary to the consent of their parents or

---

248. Book of Mormon, 1830 ed., 497 [3 Nephi 20:22].

249. The Book of Mormon identifies the American continent as the place where the New Jerusalem would stand, but the "spot of land" was revealed to be in Jackson County, Missouri, in a July 1831 JS revelation. (Revelation, 20 July 1831, in *JSP*, D2:7–8 [D&C 57:1–2]; Book of Mormon, 1830 ed., 566 [Ether 13:4–6]; see also Letter to the Elders of the Church, 30 Nov.–1 Dec. 1835, pp. 89–100 herein.)

250. Book of Mormon, 1830 ed., 566 [Ether 13:4–6]; see also Letter to the Elders of the Church, 30 Nov.–1 Dec. 1835, pp. 89–100 herein.

251. See Letter to the Elders of the Church, 2 Oct. 1835, pp. 6–15 herein.

252. See Isaiah 45:13.

253. See Malachi 4:6.

guardians.— But all such as can be persuaded in a lawful and righteous manner, and with common consent, we should feel it our duty to influence them to gather with the people of God. But otherwise let the responsibility rest upon the heads of parents or guardians, and all condemnation or consequences, be upon [p. 210] their heads, according to the dispensation which he hath committed unto us: for God has so ordained, that his work shall be cut short in righteousness, in the last days: therefore, first teach the parents, and then, with their consent, let him persuade the children to embrace the gospel also. And if children embrace the gospel, and their parents or guardians are unbelievers, teach them to stay at home and be obedient to their parents or guardians, if they require it; but if they consent to let them gather with the people of God let them do so and there shall be no wrong and let all things be done carefully, and righteously, and God will extend his guardian care to all such.

And secondly, it should be the duty of elders, when they enter into any house, to let their labors and warning voice, be unto the master of that house: and if he receive the gospel, then he may extend his influence to his wife also, with consent, that peradventure she may receive the gospel; but if a man receive not the gospel, but gives his consent that his wife may receive it, and she believes, then let her receive it. But if the man forbid his wife, or his children before they are of age, to receive the gospel, then it should be the duty of the elder to go his way and use no influence against him: and let the responsibility be upon his head—shake off the dust of thy feet as a testimony against him,[254] and thy skirts shall then be clear of their souls. Their sins are not to be answered upon such as God hath sent to warn them to flee the wrath to come, and save themselves from this untoward generation. The servants of God will not have gone over the nations of the Gentiles, with a warning voice, until the destroying angel will commence to waste the inhabitants of the earth; and as the prophet hath said, "It shall be a vexation to hear the report."[255] I speak because I feel for my fellow-men: I do it in the name of the Lord, being moved upon by the Holy Spirit. O that I could snatch them from the vortex of misery, into which I behold them plunging themselves, by their sins, that I may be enabled, by the warning voice, to be an instrument of bringing them to unfeigned repentance, that they may have faith to stand in the evil day.

Thirdly, it should be the duty of an elder, when he enters into a house to salute the master of that house, and if he gain his consent, then he may preach

---

254. See Matthew 10:14; Mark 6:11; Luke 9:5; Revelation, July 1830–A, in *JSP*, D1:159 [D&C 24:15]; and Revelation, 25 Jan. 1832–A, in *JSP*, D2:160 [D&C 75:20].

255. Isaiah 28:19.

to all that are in that house, but if he gain not his consent, let him go not unto his slaves or servants, but let the responsibility be upon the head of the master of that house, and the consequences thereof; and the guilt of that house is no longer upon thy skirts: Thou art free; therefore, shake off the dust of thy feet, and go thy way. But if the master of that house give consent, that thou mayest preach to his family, his wife, his children, and his servants, his man-servants, or his maid-servants, or his slaves, then it should be the duty of the elder to stand up boldly for the cause of Christ, and warn that people with one accord, to repent and be baptized for the remission of sins, and for the Holy Ghost, always commanding them in the name of the Lord, in the spirit of meekness to be kindly affected one towards another; that the fathers should be kind to their children, husbands to their wives; masters to their slaves or servants; children obedient to their parents, wives to their husbands, and slaves or servants to their masters:[256]

"Wives submit youselves unto your own husbands, as unto the Lord. For the husband is the head of the wife, even as Christ is the head of the church: and he is the Savior of the body. Therefore as the church is subject unto Christ, so let the wives be to their own husbands in every thing. Husbands, love your wives even as Christ also loved the church and gave himself for it; that he might sanctify and cleanse it with the washing of water by the word, that he might present it to himself a glorious church, not having spot, or wrinkle, or any such thing; but that it should be holy and without blemish. So ought men to love their wives as their own bodies. He that loveth his wife loveth himself. For no man ever yet hated his own flesh; but nourisheth and cherisheth it, even as the Lord the church: for we are members of his body, of his flesh, and of his bones.— For this cause shall a man leave his father and mother, and shall be joined unto his wife, and they two shall be one flesh."—Ephesians, Chapt. V. from the 22d to the end of the 21st [31st] verse.

"Wives submit yourselves unto your own husbands, as it is fit in the Lord. Husbands, love your wives, and be not bitter against them. Children, obey your parents in all things: for this is well pleasing unto the Lord. Fathers, provoke not your children to anger, lest they be discouraged. Servants, obey in all things your masters according to the flesh: not with eye service as menpleasers; but in singleness of heart,

---

256. For earlier statements on proselytizing to families, see Statement on Marriage, ca. Aug. 1835, in *JSP*, D4:475–478.

fearing God."—Colocians, Chapt. III. from the 18th to the end of the 22d verse. [p. 211]

But I must close this letter and resume the subject in another number.[257] In the bonds of the new and everlasting covenant

JOSEPH SMITH, jr.

To J[ohn] WHITMER, ESQ.

———— *୧୬* ————

Letter and Revelation to Harvey Whitlock, 16 November 1835

Source Note

JS, Letter and Revelation, Kirtland Township, Geauga Co., OH, to Harvey Whitlock, 16 Nov. 1835. Featured version copied [ca. 16 Nov. 1835] in JS, Journal, 1835–1836, pp. 42–44; handwriting of Warren Parrish; JS Collection, CHL. For more information on JS, Journal, 1835–1836, see Source Notes for Multiple-Entry Documents, p. 524 herein.

Historical Introduction

During fall 1835, JS received a contrite letter from Harvey Whitlock, who had become estranged from the church sometime during the previous two years. Though little is known about the circumstances surrounding his separation, he evidently had a change of heart during the latter part of 1835, which prompted him to write to JS. In a 28 September letter, he appealed to JS to let him know if he was still "within the reach of mercy" and requested that JS "enquire at the hand of the Lord in my behalf." Penitently, he told JS, "I am willing to receive any chastisement that the Lord sees I deserve."[258] On 16 November, JS responded to Whitlock's entreaty and informed him that he had inquired of God and received a revelation that Whitlock should "speedily" return from Missouri to Kirtland, Ohio. If he continued to heed JS's counsel, Whitlock was told, he would be "restored unto his former state."[259]

Prior to his estrangement, Whitlock had been a successful missionary, talented preacher, and prominent member of the Missouri branch of the church.[260] He settled in Jackson County, Missouri, following a summer 1831 mission to "regions west." Whitlock regularly participated in council meetings, but after his name is mentioned in minutes of

---

257. See Letter to the Elders of the Church, 30 Nov.–1 Dec. 1835, pp. 89–100 herein.

258. Letter from Harvey Whitlock, 28 Sept. 1835, in *JSP*, D4:445, 446.

259. The original letter is no longer extant, but a copy of the text was inserted into JS's 16 November journal entry by his scribe, Warren Parrish. (JS, Journal, 16 Nov. 1835, in *JSP*, J1:103–105.)

260. In early June 1831, Whitlock was ordained to the office of high priest and soon began proselytizing. As he preached throughout Ohio and Illinois, his sermons made a distinct impression on several early converts, including William E. McLellin and Joel Johnson. (Revelation, 6 June 1831, in *JSP*, D1:327–332 [D&C 52]; McLellin, Journal, 6–7; Johnson, Autobiographical Sketch, 8; *JSP*, D4:444n491.)

an 11 September 1833 meeting, he essentially disappears from the historical record for the next two years.[261] Whitlock's 28 September 1835 letter to JS offers only cryptic clues as to what might have caused him to distance himself from the church. In the letter, Whitlock obliquely mentions his "original difficulties with the church" and indicates that he was "charged with things" he was "not guilty of."[262]

JS's response to Whitlock's appeal offers insight into JS's personality and leadership style. Though JS condemned members of the church community who openly challenged the laws of God or questioned his authority, he quickly welcomed back those who admitted their faults and made restitution. After receiving JS's letter, Whitlock promptly obeyed the admonition to return to Kirtland. During a 30 January 1836 conference of the presidency of the church, Whitlock was officially restored to full fellowship.[263]

Document Transcript

Kirtland Nov. 16th 1835

Bro Harvey Whitlock

I have received your letter of the 28th Sept. 1835, and I have read it twice, and it gave me sensations that are better imagined than discribed; let it suffice, that I say the verry flood-gates of my heart were broken up: I could not refrain from weeping, I thank God, that it has entered into your heart, to try to return to the Lord, and to his people; if it so be, that he will have mercy upon you.

I have inquired of the Lord concerning your case, these words came to me

Verily thus saith the Lord unto you; let him who was my servant Harvey, return unto me;— and unto the bosom of my Church, and forsake all the sins wherewith he has offended against me and persue from hence forth a virtuous and upright life, and remain under the direction of those whom I have appointed to be pillars, and heads of my Church, and behold, saith the Lord, your God; his sins shall be blotted out from under heaven, and shall be forgotten from among men, and shall not come up in mine ears, nor be recorded as ⟨a⟩ memorial against him, but I will lift [p. 42] him up as out of deep mire, and he shall be exalted upon the high places, and shall be counted worthy to stand ammong princes, and shall yet be made a polished shaft in my quiver, of bringing down the strong holds of wickedness, among those who set themselves up on high, that they

---

261. Hancock, Autobiography, 92; Minute Book 2, 2 Aug. 1831 and 11 Sept. 1833; Letter from Oliver Cowdery, 28 Jan. 1832, in *JSP*, D2:165.

262. Letter from Harvey Whitlock, 28 Sept. 1835, in *JSP*, D4:445.

263. Minutes, 30 Jan. 1836, p. 165 herein.

may take council against me, and against annointed ones in the last days.

Therefore let him prepare himself speedily and come unto you; even to Kirtland and inasmuch as he shall harken unto all your council from henceforth he shall be restored unto his former state, and shall be saved unto the uttermost, even as the Lord your God liveth Amen.

Thus you see my dear Brother the willingness of our heavenly Father to forgive sins and restore to favour all those who are willing to humble themselves before him, and confess their sins and forsake them, and return to him with full purpose of heart (acting no hypocrisy) to serve him to the end.[264]

Marvle not that the Lord has condescended to speak from the heavens and give you instructions whereby you may learn your duty, he has heard your prayers, and witnessed your humility; and holds forth the hand of paternal affection, for your return; the angels rejoice over you, while the saints are willing to recieve you again into fellowship.

I hope on the rec[e]ipt of this, you will ~~not~~ loose ~~any~~ no time in coming to [p. 43] Kirtland: for if you get here in season, you will have the privelege of attending the School of the prophets, which has already commenced[265] and, also received instruction in doctrine, and principle, from those whom God has appointed whereby you may be qualified to go forth, and declare the true doctrines of the kingdom according to the ~~true doctrines of the~~ mind and, will of God. and when you come to Kirtland, it will be explained to you why God has condescended to give you a revelation according to your request.

please give my respects to you[r] family,[266] and bee assured I am yours in the bonds of the new and everlasting covenant

Joseph Smith Jun

—————— ⁓ ——————

264. See Book of Mormon, 1830 ed., 119 [2 Nephi 31:13].

265. JS had organized and called to order a session of the school, sometimes also referred to as the "Elders School," on 3 November 1835. (JS, Journal, 3 Nov. 1835, in *JSP*, J1:84.)

266. Harvey Whitlock married Minerva Abbott on 21 November 1830 in Cuyahoga County, Ohio. The 1850 census indicates that the couple had two or possibly three children by the time of this revelation: Almon, Sally Ann, and Sciota. (Cuyahoga Co., OH, Probate Court, Marriage Records, 1810–1941, vol. 2, p. 237, microfilm 877,912, U.S. and Canada Record Collection, FHL; 1850 U.S. Census, Great Salt Lake, Utah Territory, 56[A].)

Revelation, 16 November 1835

Source Note

Revelation, Kirtland Township, Geauga Co., OH, 16 Nov. 1835. Featured version copied [ca. 16 Nov. 1835] in JS, Journal, 1835–1836, pp. 44–45; handwriting of Warren Parrish; JS Collection, CHL. For more information on JS, Journal, 1835–1836, see Source Notes for Multiple-Entry Documents, p. 524 herein.

Historical Introduction

On the afternoon of 14 November 1835, JS was visited by Erastus Holmes of Miami Township, Clermont County, Ohio, some 230 miles southwest of Kirtland.[267] According to JS's journal, Holmes had called to "make enquiry about the establishment of the Church of the latter-day Saints and to be instructed more perfectly in our doctrine."[268] Holmes spent the next several days in Kirtland and, after learning more about the church, requested that JS ask God when and where he should be baptized.[269] On 16 November 1835, JS dictated the revelation presented here, which gave Holmes the personal instruction he sought.

Aside from the account of this visit recorded in JS's journal, little is known about Holmes. An 1880 county history indicates that he was a merchant in Clermont County, which is approximately sixteen miles northeast of Cincinnati; he also worked as a postmaster from 1837 to 1846.[270] According to JS's journal, Holmes had been a Methodist until he "was excommunicated for receiving, the Elders of the church of the latter-day Saints into his house."[271]

While it was not unusual for visitors who were curious about the Latter-day Saints to arrive in Kirtland unsolicited—between June 1835 and January 1836, JS entertained at least ten men of varying religious faiths who were interested in learning about him and the church[272]—JS seemed particularly interested in Holmes, perhaps because of his desire to "unite with the Church."[273] During Holmes's stay in Kirtland he dined with JS, attended a church meeting, and viewed the Egyptian mummies JS and others had recently purchased.[274] In a notable conversation between JS and Holmes, a brief summary of which was dictated to Warren Parrish and recorded in JS's journal, JS described his first vision of

---

267. Erastus Holmes to George Holmes, Indenture, Clermont Co., OH, 13 Jan. 1823, Clermont Co. Recorder, Deed Book, 1800–1877, vol. 21, pp. 259–260, microfilm 333,146, U.S. and Canada Record Collection, FHL; 1830 U.S. Census, Milford, Clermont Co., 267[A].

268. JS, Journal, 14 Nov. 1835, in *JSP*, J1:100.

269. JS, Journal, 16 Nov. 1835, in *JSP*, J1:105.

270. *History of Clermont County, Ohio*, 465, 466, 469; *Table of the Post Offices in the United States*, 113.

271. JS, Journal, 15 Nov. 1835, in *JSP*, J1:101.

272. From 24 October 1835 to 21 January 1836, JS's journal notes visits he received from at least nine people who were not members of the church (and several more whose religious identification is unclear); another visit is recorded in a 15 June 1835 letter. Some of the visitors came from cities in Ohio, while others trekked from neighboring states. (See JS, Journal, 30 Oct. and 9–11 Nov. 1835, in *JSP*, J1:79–80, 87–95; and Letter from Oliver Cowdery, 15 June 1835, in *JSP*, D4:342–344.)

273. JS, Journal, 14 Nov. 1835, in *JSP*, J1:100.

274. JS, Journal, 14–17 Nov. 1835, in *JSP*, J1:100–105.

Deity, the second time he recounted that event in less than a week: "I commenced and gave him a brief relation of my experience while in my juvenile years, say from 6, years old up to the time I received the first visitation of Angels which was when I was about 14, years old and also the visitations that I received afterward, concerning the book of Mormon, and a short account of the rise and progress of the church, up to this, date."[275]

On the evening of 16 November, JS dictated a revelation that advised Holmes that he "had better not be baptised here." The revelation was presumably delivered to Holmes that night or the next day. Warren Parrish copied the text into JS's journal, which represents the only extant copy. According to JS's journal, Holmes left Kirtland the next day, "being strong in the faith of the gospel of Christ and determined to obey the requirements of the same," but there is no evidence that he ever joined the church.[276]

Document Transcript

The same night ~~that~~ I received the word of the Lord on Mr. Hlmes [Erastus Holmes's] case, he had, desired that I would inquire at the hand of the Lord whether it was [p. 44] his duty to be baptised here, or wait until he returned home;— The word of the Lord came ~~to~~ unto me saying, that Mr. Holmes had better not be baptised here, and that he had better not return by water,[277] also that there were three men that were seeking his destruction, to be ware of his eneys [enemies]

———— ❧ ————

Marriage License for John F. Boynton and Susan Lowell, 17 November 1835

Source Note

Marriage License, for John F. Boynton and Susannah (Susan) Lowell, Geauga Co., OH, 17 Nov. 1835; printed form with manuscript additions in the handwriting of David D. Aiken; one page; Geauga Co., OH, Common Pleas Court Marriage Licenses, 1835–1836, CHL. Includes endorsement.

Single leaf, measuring 6⅛ × 7¾ inches (16 × 20 cm). The bottom and left sides of the recto have the square cut of manufactured paper. A line of ornamental type appears above and below the text block. Inspection of this form and other extant 1835 marriage licenses suggests two to three licenses were printed per page, with a black line between each form. To the left of the license text is an embossed seal. The document was trifolded in letter style.

---

275. JS, Journal, 14 Nov. 1835, in *JSP,* J1:100. He recounted these visions to another visitor, Robert Matthews, earlier that week. (Conversations with Robert Matthews, 9–11 Nov. 1835, pp. 42–44 herein.)

276. JS, Journal, 17 Nov. 1835, in *JSP,* J1:105.

277. Because Holmes lived in Miami Township, he may have traveled home by land or via the Ohio and Erie Canal (from Cleveland to Portsmouth) and the Ohio River. The admonition not to return by water may be related to an August 1831 revelation in which the Saints were warned of the "many dangers upon the waters"; the revelation also prophesied that "the days will come that no flesh shall be safe upon the waters." (Revelation, 12 Aug. 1831, in *JSP,* D2:37 [D&C 61].)

This license has been in institutional custody likely since the Kirtland period. Information from an old catalog folder suggests this and several other 1835 marriage licenses were banded together with a memorandum of agreement between Truman Angell and Zebedee Coltrin, 1836–1837, in the possession of the Church History Library.[278]

Historical Introduction

JS performed marriage ceremonies for eleven couples in late 1835 and early 1836. The license featured here, obtained on 17 November 1835 for John F. Boynton and Susan Lowell, is representative of marriage licenses from this period and was presented to and preserved by JS, who officiated at the couple's wedding. It does not, however, represent the first marriage solemnized by JS, which occurred on 24 November 1835, when he performed the marriage of Newel Knight and Lydia Goldthwaite Bailey. Boynton and Lowell were wed on 20 January 1836.[279]

A man and woman intending to wed were required to apply for a marriage license from the county court clerk. Once an application was approved, the clerk—in this instance, Geauga County Court clerk David D. Aiken—issued a license to the couple, which they then presented to a marriage officiator. The clerk also recorded the license into the county's marriage license ledger. Boynton and Lowell did not apply for their marriage license in person; on 17 November 1835, it was requested on their behalf by Edwin Webb, a church member who had gone to Chardon, Ohio, for his own marriage license.[280]

According to the wording on the license and Ohio's 1824 Act Regulating Marriages upon which the license was based, any minister with a license from an Ohio court of common pleas or any justice of the peace could perform marriages. The same Ohio statute had another provision that authorized "the several religious societies agreeably to the rules and regulations of their respective churches, to join together as husband and wife, all persons not prohibited by this act."[281] In other words, Ohio law allowed a minister to marry couples, even if he had not obtained a license by the local court of common pleas, as long as the ceremony was done according to his church's rules regarding marriage. JS qualified to perform marriages under this provision. In August 1835, the Church of the Latter Day Saints accepted a set of "rules and regulations" on marriage and included those articles in the 1835 edition of the Doctrine and Covenants.[282] JS's journal notes that he performed the

278. See full bibliographic entry for Geauga Co., OH, Common Pleas Court Marriage Licenses, 1835–1836, in the CHL catalog.

279. JS, Journal, 24 Nov. 1835 and 20 Jan. 1836, in *JSP*, J1:109–110, 165; Knight, Autobiography, 810–811. Notices of Boynton and Lowell's marriage were printed in Portland, Maine, newspapers, likely because Lowell hailed from nearby Saco, Maine. ("Married," *Eastern Argus* [Portland, ME], 9 Feb. 1836, [3]; "Married," *Portland [ME] Advertiser,* 16 Feb. 1836, [1].)

280. Geauga Co., OH, Probate Court, Marriage Records, 1833–1841, 17 Nov. 1835, microfilm 873,464, U.S. and Canada Record Collection, FHL.

281. An Act, Regulating Marriages [6 Jan. 1824], *Statutes of Ohio,* vol. 2, p. 1407, sec. 2; see also Bradshaw, "Joseph Smith's Performance of Marriages in Ohio," 28, 34–37, 57.

282. Statement on Marriage, ca. Aug. 1835, in *JSP,* D4:475–478.

Lowell-Boynton marriage "according to the rules and regulations of the church of the Latter-day-Saints."[283]

On 22 February 1836, JS made "returns to the county clerk on 11. marriages which I have solemnized within 3. months past 8, by license from the clerk of the court of common pleas in Geauga county Ohio, and 3, by publishment," and sent them to Chardon with Elijah Fuller.[284] Ohio state law required that a marriage certificate signed by the officiator be submitted to the county court clerk within three months of issuance of the marriage license; JS filled this requirement by signing a marriage certificate for each couple and having it delivered to the county office for recording.[285] JS's scribe, Warren Parrish, helped him write out the certificates and noted the returns made on each of the original licenses, as is demonstrated in the featured document. It is not clear when Aiken received the signed certificates from JS, but Aiken used the 22 February date when he recorded the certificates in the county marriage ledger. Once recorded, the marriages were legally valid.[286]

---

283. JS, Journal, 20 Jan. 1836, in *JSP*, J1:165. Despite the Ohio law's allowance for unlicensed ministers to perform marriages, reminiscent accounts cast doubt on JS's ability to legally solemnize marriages. John C. Dowen, a justice of the peace in Kirtland from 1833 to 1839, stated in 1885: "Mormons were not permitted to marry couples. They often had me perform the legal marriage ceremony, and afterward Joe Smith would, as he claimed, marry them according to the gospel." According to Lydia Knight, Ohio law "did not recognize the 'Mormon' Elders as ministers." Knight recalled that some unnamed Mormon elders were arrested and fined for performing marriages. Nevertheless, as M. Scott Bradshaw has argued, "Joseph was indeed within his statutory rights in assuming the authority to solemnize marriages. Moreover, he was correct when he stated that performing marriages was his 'religious privilege.'" (John C. Dowen, Statement, 5, microfilm, Chicago Historical Society, Collection of Mormon Materials, 1836–1886, CHL; Gates, *Lydia Knight's History*, 30; Bradshaw, "Joseph Smith's Performance of Marriages in Ohio," 31; see also Knight, Autobiography and Journal, [45]–[46].)

284. JS, Journal, 22 Feb. 1836, in *JSP*, J1:188. Regarding marriages for which the couples had obtained licenses, see JS, Journal, 24 Nov. 1835; 3 and 13 Dec. 1835; 14 and 20 Jan. 1836, in *JSP*, J1:109–110, 114–115, 121–122, 153, 165–166; and Cowdery, Diary, 3 Feb. 1836. Regarding marriages legitimized by publishment—that is, giving sufficient public notice of a couple's intent to marry without a license—see *JSP*, J1:161n297; and An Act, Regulating Marriages [6 Jan. 1824], *Statutes of Ohio*, vol. 2, p. 1407, sec. 8.

285. To meet the three-month deadline, JS had only two days left to file the certificate for Newel and Lydia Goldthwaite Bailey Knight, the first of the eleven marriages he solemnized. Though the marriage certificate for John F. Boynton and Susan Lowell is no longer extant, county clerk David D. Aiken recorded the certificate after 22 February 1836 in the ledger of solemnized marriages. The other ten marriages officiated by JS and recorded by Aiken in the official county record include Newel Knight and Lydia Goldthwaite Bailey (married 24 Nov. 1835); Warren Parrish and Martha H. Raymond (3 Dec. 1835); Ebenezer Robinson and Angeline Eliza Works (13 Dec. 1835); Edwin Webb and Eliza Ann McWithy (13 Dec. 1835); Thomas Carrico and Elizabeth (Betsey) Baker (14 Jan. 1836); John Webb and Catharine Wilcox (14 Jan. 1836); Joseph C. Kingsbury and Caroline Whitney (3 Feb. 1836); William Cahoon and Nancy Gibbs (17 Jan. 1836); Harvey Stanley and Lerona Cahoon (17 Jan. 1836); and Tunis Rappleye and Louisa Cutler (17 Jan. 1836). (Geauga Co., OH, Probate Court, Marriage Records, 1806–1920, vol. C, pp. 141–144, microfilm 873,461, U.S. and Canada Record Collection, FHL; see also JS, Journal, 17 and 19 Jan. 1836, in *JSP*, J1:161, 164.)

286. An Act, Regulating Marriages [6 Jan. 1824], *Statutes of Ohio*, vol. 2, p. 1407.

Document Transcript

THE STATE OF OHIO, ⎫
GEAUGA COUNTY, *SS.*[287] ⎭

PERMISSION IS HEREBY GIVEN TO John H. [F.] Boynton[288] & Susan Lowell Of the County of Geauga aforesaid, to be joined together in the bands of MATRIMONY; and any Minister of the Gospel, resident in the State of Ohio aforesaid, who has a license from any of the Courts of Common Pleas within said State, in conformity to the provisions of an act, entitled "An act to regulate Marriages";[289] or any Justice of the Peace in said County, who has been duly commissioned and sworn, is hereby authorised to solemnize the marriage contract between the parties aforesaid.[290]

GIVEN from under my hand, and the seal of my office, at the town of Chardon, in said county, the 17th day of November Anno Domini, one thousand eight hundred and thirty -five

D[avid] D. Aiken *Clerk.* [p. [1]]

⟨Made returns on the within Feb 22ᵈ 1836⟩
⟨J. Smith Jr⟩
⟨By W[arren] Parrish⟩[291]

———— ☙ ————

Minutes, 22 November 1835

Source Note

Minutes, Kirtland Township, Geauga Co., OH, 22 Nov. 1835. Featured version copied [between ca. 4 Apr. and ca. 16 May 1836] in Minute Book 1, pp. 130–131; handwriting of Warren A. Cowdery; CHL. For more information on Minute Book 1, see Source Notes for Multiple-Entry Documents, p. 527 herein.

Historical Introduction

On the evening of 22 November 1835, JS attended a meeting that examined the standing of Andrew Squires, a former elder "who had withdrawn from the church" but who had

---

287. An abbreviation for the Latin *scilicet,* meaning "namely" or "to wit."

288. "John H. Boynton" appears to be an error made by David D. Aiken. In the county record for marriages, Aiken wrote the names properly as John F. Boynton and Susan Lowell. (Geauga Co., OH, Probate Court, Marriage Records, 1806–1920, vol. C, p. 142, microfilm 873,461, U.S. and Canada Record Collection, FHL.)

289. An Act, Regulating Marriages [6 Jan. 1824], *Statutes of Ohio,* vol. 2, p. 1407.

290. TEXT: To the left of this paragraph is an embossed seal with the following text proceeding around the outside in a clockwise direction: "COMMON PLEAS OF THE COUNTY OF GEAUGA". The center of the seal is a sun peering over mountains or clouds with sheaves of bundled grain or grass below.

291. TEXT: Insertions in the handwriting of Warren Parrish.

recently appealed to return and be restored to his previous office.[292] Squires had been an energetic missionary for the Church of the Latter Day Saints. The minutes of the proceedings of a 24–25 January 1835 conference held in Freedom, New York, stated that Squires had recently established a branch of the church with nineteen members in good standing in Portage, Allegany County, New York.[293] A little more than two months later, minutes of another conference in Freedom recorded the creation of a church branch in Burns, Allegany County, and noted that it had been "raised and established almost wholly by the instrumentality of Elder A. J. Squires." The same minutes also indicated that Squires had "been the instrument in the hands of the Lord" in organizing the Rushford branch, also in Allegany County, on 23 March 1835 and that it had twenty-six members.[294]

Despite his proselytizing success, sometime between that April 1835 conference and this 22 November meeting, Squires mailed his priesthood license back to JS and joined the Methodists. At the time, Methodism constituted the largest Protestant denomination in the United States, and it was particularly prevalent in the New York areas where Squires preached.[295] Whatever attracted Squires to Methodism was apparently short lived—within months he journeyed to Kirtland, Ohio, to apologize to church leaders and to seek the restoration of his elder's license in order to recommence his missionary labors. After JS and Sidney Rigdon gave Squires "a severe chastisment" and a "keen rebuke" at the meeting featured here, the church and council voted to restore Squires to his office.[296] In the months following this 22 November 1835 meeting, Squires resumed proselytizing for the Latter-day Saints.[297]

Document Transcript

Council of High Priests and Elders, held in the presence of the members of the Church of the Latter-Day Saints Kirtland Nov 22ᵈ 1835.

President Joseph Smith Junᵣ. & Sidney Rigdon Presiding

Sylvester Smith appointed Clerk.

The case of A[ndrew] J. Squires presented by J. Smith Mr. Squires had been an ordained Elder in the Church and for a time preached the gospel successfully. but after a while sent his license in a letter ~~in a~~ to President Smith requesting to

292. JS, Journal, 22 Nov. 1835, in *JSP,* J1:109.

293. "A Summary," *LDS Messenger and Advocate,* Feb. 1835, 1:75.

294. Minutes, *LDS Messenger and Advocate,* Apr. 1835, 1:101.

295. Many early converts to the Church of the Latter Day Saints, including Brigham Young's family and Emma Smith, came from Methodist backgrounds. Several studies have examined the connections between and the parallel histories of Mormons and Methodists in the 1830s. (See Jones, "We Latter-day Saints Are Methodists," 3–20; Yorgason, "Some Demographic Aspects of One Hundred Early Mormon Converts," 42–43; Grandstaff and Backman, "Social Origins of the Kirtland Mormons," 56; Underwood, *Millenarian World of Early Mormonism,* 129–131; Underwood, "Millenarianism and Popular Methodism," 81–91; Jones, "Mormonism in the Methodist Marketplace," 83–90; and Hatch, "Mormon and Methodist," 24–44.)

296. JS, Journal, 22 Nov. 1835, in *JSP,* J1:109.

297. Andrew Squires, Euclid, NY, to John Whitmer, Kirtland, OH, Feb. 1836, in *LDS Messenger and Advocate,* Mar. 1836, 2:288; "Conference," *LDS Messenger and Advocate,* July 1836, 2:350.

be excused from laboring longer in the vineyard.[298] This evening he came forward before the church and confessed that he had been in temptation and fallen into Error, so much [p. 130] so as to go and join the Methodists, yet says he was not in faith with their doctrine. He now says he desires to return to the fellowship of the church and asks forgiveness of the brethren and a restoration of his license. President Smith arose & spoke at considerable length on the impropriety of turning away from the truth and going after a people so destitute, of the spirit of righteousness as the Methodists.[299] President Rigdon also labored quite lengthy to show the folly of fellowshiping any doctrine or spirit aside from that of Christ. After which Mr. Squires arose & said he felt firm in determination of doing the will of God in all things, or as far as in him lies, is sorry for his faults and by the grace of God will forsake them in future. President Rigdon then called for the vote of the Church & received it in favor of restoring him to fellowship, and the office of Elder also, and that the clerk give him a License.[300]

Sylvester Smith Clerk.

This certifies that the above named A. J. Squires received his License agreeably to the decision of the conference on the 22ᵈ of Nov. 1835

Sylvester Smith, Clerk

———— ☙ ————

Book of Abraham Manuscript, circa Early July–circa November 1835–A [Abraham 1:4–2:6]

Source Note

Book of Abraham, manuscript, [Kirtland Township, Geauga Co., OH], [ca. early July–ca. Nov. 1835]; handwriting of Frederick G. Williams; four pages; Book of Abraham Manuscripts, CHL. Includes archival marking.

Two leaves of different types of paper, the first measuring 12½ × 7⅝ inches (32 × 19 cm) and the second 12½ × 7¾ inches (32 × 20 cm). The first leaf is unlined; the second is ruled, bearing thirty-seven blue lines, now faded. The first three pages bear a hand-drawn margin line, separating hieratic characters

---

298. This letter, not located, was sent between early April 1835—when Squires was present and active in the Freedom, New York, conference—and this 22 November 1835 council meeting.

299. JS's thoughts on Methodism fluctuated. As a youth, his history stated, he was "somewhat partial to the Methodist sect." However, by the mid-1830s, his attitude toward Methodism became more negative. According to William E. McLellin, JS gave a sermon in 1834 in which he "exposed the Methodist Dicipline in its black deformity." (JS History, 1834–1836, 59; JS History, vol. A-1, 2, in *JSP,* H1:53, 210 [Draft 2]; McLellin, Journal, 5 Dec. 1834; see also JS, Journal, 30 Oct. and 15 Nov. 1835, in *JSP,* J1:79, 100–101.)

300. An addition to the church's governing Articles and Covenants, as published in the 1835 edition of the Doctrine and Covenants, instructed that "the elders are to receive their licences from other elders by vote of the church to which they belong, or from the conferences." The action taken at this meeting, calling for the church to vote on restoring Squires's elder's license, appears to be in adherence to that administrative policy. (Articles and Covenants, ca. Apr. 1830, in Doctrine and Covenants 2:14, 1835 ed. [D&C 20:63].)

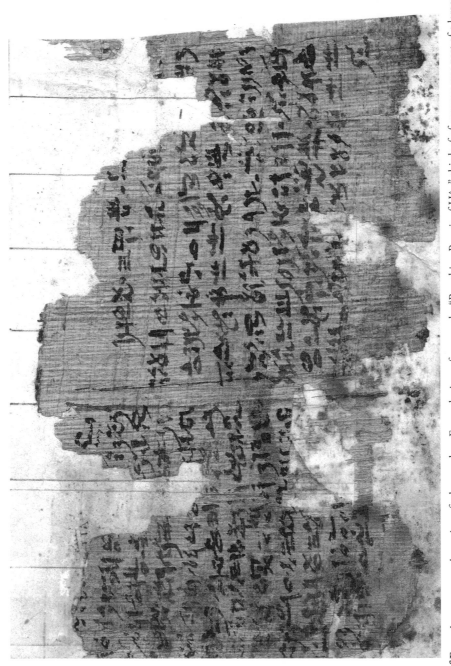

Fragment of Egyptian papyrus. A portion of what modern Egyptologists refer to as the "Breathing Permit of Hôr," this leaf of papyrus was part of a larger Egyptian collection that Joseph Smith and other investors purchased from traveling exhibitor Michael Chandler in summer 1835. This fragment is one of only a dozen that remain from the 1835 purchase. Second Fragment of the Breathing Permit of Hôr Papyrus, ca. 200–150 BC, Egyptian Papyri, Church History Library, Salt Lake City.

from the English text of the Book of Abraham. The leaves were folded in half once, the fold line running horizontally. The first leaf bears staining that appears to have been caused by water, mold, or possibly ink from another document. The second leaf bears staining that appears to be caused by oil-based material. The top of each recto is labeled with a letter in blue ink; the first is labeled "J", and the second, "L". These letters, which resemble markings on other Book of Abraham and Egyptian-language documents, served as a way to organize the documents. The markings were apparently written by assistant church historian Andrew Jenson and therefore show early custody of this document by the Historian's Office. This record was likely grouped with the records listed in early Historian's Office inventories as "Egyptian Grammar", which would also indicate continuous institutional custody.[301]

Historical Introduction

In summer 1835, traveling exhibitor Michael Chandler arrived in Kirtland, Ohio, with a collection of Egyptian antiquities, including four mummies and an assortment of papyri inscribed with hieroglyphic and hieratic characters.[302] After meeting Chandler and examining the papyri, JS identified some of the writings as accounts of the biblical patriarchs Abraham and Joseph, and JS and other investors purchased most or all of Chandler's antiquities.[303] Sometime between early July and late November 1835, JS produced a manuscript that became part of the Book of Abraham, a text considered by Latter-day Saints to be an inspired translation of portions of the papyri.[304] The featured text, in the handwriting of Frederick G. Williams, represents perhaps the earliest extant copy of the Book of Abraham.

Chandler arrived in Kirtland at a time when ancient Egyptian artifacts were generating tremendous excitement in Europe and America.[305] The mummies and papyri exhibited by

---

301. "Schedule of Church Records. Nauvoo 1846," [1]; "Inventory. Historian's Office. 4th April 1855," [1], Historian's Office, Catalogs and Inventories, 1846–1904, CHL.

302. Most contemporary accounts agree that four mummies were brought to Kirtland. However, observers described the form or number of Egyptian records variously as "some two or more rolls of papyrus," "two rolls of papyrus . . . [and] two or three other small pieces of papyrus," and "two papyrus rolls, besides some other ancient Egyptian writing."[a] It is not clear whether some of the records were sold before Chandler arrived in Kirtland. Newspaper accounts of the exhibit described some of the records variously as a "roll or book, having a little resemblance to birch bark," a "roll . . . filled with hieroglyphics," and a "*book* of ancient form and construction. . . . Its leaves were of bark."[b] (a. JS History, vol. B-1, 595–596; Oliver Cowdery, Kirtland, OH, to William Frye, Calhoun Co., IL, 22 Dec. 1835, in Cowdery, Letterbook, 70; William W. Phelps to Sally Waterman Phelps, 20 July 1835, in Historical Department, Journal History of the Church, 20 July 1835. b. "Mummies," *Painesville [OH] Telegraph,* 27 Mar. 1835, [3]; "A Rare Exhibition," *Cleveland Whig,* 25 Mar. 1835, 1, italics in original.)

303. Oliver Cowdery, Kirtland, OH, to William Frye, Lebanon, IL, 22 Dec. 1835, in Cowdery, Letterbook, 69–74; William W. Phelps to Sally Waterman Phelps, 20 July 1835, in Historical Department, Journal History of the Church, 20 July 1835; Corrill, *Brief History,* 45, in *JSP,* H2:192; JS History, vol. B-1, 595–596.

304. JS did not translate in the conventional sense of the word. For more on JS's use of the word *translation* as it applied to various projects, see "Joseph Smith Documents Dating through June 1831," in *JSP,* D1:xxix–xxxii; and "Joseph Smith as Revelator and Translator," in *JSP,* R1:xix–xxvi.

305. During the early nineteenth century, Europeans and Americans demonstrated a revived enthusiasm for Egyptian antiquities, an interest British architect and museum proprietor John Soane once referred to as "Egyptian mania." Several events contributed to this enthusiasm, including Napoleon Bonaparte's 1798 invasion of Egypt; a massive multivolume study of Egypt's ancient history and culture, known as

Chandler survived millennia and crossed oceans before arriving in the United States in the early 1830s. Exhumed by antiquities dealer Antonio Lebolo in the late 1810s or early 1820s, likely from tombs near the ancient Egyptian city of Thebes, the mummies and papyrus records became part of Lebolo's estate after his death in Italy in 1830.[306] Sometime before April 1833, Lebolo's Egyptian collection was sent to the shipping firms of Maitland & Kennedy and McLeod & Gillespie in New York City.[307]

Following their arrival in New York, the mummies and papyri once owned by Lebolo were exhibited in nearly a dozen cities across the United States. The collection was initially displayed at the Masonic Hall in Philadelphia, Pennsylvania, in early April and moved to the Baltimore Museum in Baltimore, Maryland, before 20 July 1833. From mid-August 1833 to February 1834, the artifacts were exhibited in museums and exhibition halls in Lancaster, Harrisburg, and Pittsburgh, Pennsylvania; Cincinnati, Ohio; Louisville, Kentucky; and New Orleans, Louisiana.[308] During the first year of the tour, as many as seven of the mummies were sold to museums or private collectors.[309]

The traveling exhibition reached the small township of Hudson, Ohio, by mid-February 1835, and in late March, four mummies were on display in Cleveland, where they

---

Description de l'Egypte, published by French scholars from 1809 to 1829; news that Thomas Young and Jean-Francois Champollion had independently deciphered some Egyptian hieroglyphs; and Egyptian antiquities that were exported to and exhibited in Europe and America from the 1800s through the 1830s and beyond. (Watkin, *Sir John Soane,* 36–37; Nina Burleigh, *Mirage: Napoleon's Scientists and the Unveiling of Egypt* [New York: Harper, 2007]; *Description de l'Égypte* [Paris: Imprimerie Impériale, 1809–1829]; Robinson, *Cracking the Egyptian Code,* 80–91, 127–150; Hume, *Belzoni,* 204–220; Wolfe, *Mummies in Nineteenth Century America,* 7–54.)

306. Born in the Piedmont region of Italy in 1781, Lebolo made his way to Egypt in his mid-thirties to work for Bernardino Drovetti, a French consul to Egypt and trusted adviser to the Egyptian viceroy Muhammad Ali. Employed by Drovetti through the mid-1820s, Lebolo was allowed to excavate and sell some objects on his own, which, according to one contemporary observer, brought him "a moderate fortune." Though the location of the tombs from which the mummies and records were exhumed is unclear, Lebolo spent time excavating artifacts on the west bank of the modern Egyptian city of Luxor. (Tyldesley, *Egypt,* 72–74; Count Carlo Vidua to Count Pio Vidua, 20 June 1820, in Pomba, *Letters of Count Caro Vidua,* 177; Peterson, *Story of the Book of Abraham,* 45–67.)

307. In November 1829, Lebolo prepared a will that included a lengthy inventory of his possessions. Attached to the will was a legal document, drawn up after Lebolo's death, listing additional assets held in Trieste, Italy; among these assets were eleven mummies entrusted to Albano Oblasser, who was authorized to sell them on behalf of Lebolo's four sons. Another legal document, written in 1833 on behalf of Lebolo's oldest son, Pietro, notes that the collection was sent to Maitland & Kennedy and McLeod & Gillespie. ("My Last Will, Antonio Lebolo" and "Special Power of Attorney from Pietro Lebolo to Bertola Francesco," photocopies, in Peterson, Research Collection on the Book of Abraham Papyri, BYU; Peterson, *Story of the Book of Abraham,* 76–80.)

308. *Daily Chronicle* (Philadelphia), 3–22 Apr. 1833; "Egyptian Mummies," *Daily Intelligencer* (Philadelphia), 9 Apr. 1833, [2]; *Baltimore (MD) Gazette,* 20 July–16 Aug. 1833; "Six Egyptian Mummies," *Lancaster (PA) Journal,* 30 Aug. 1833, [2]; "Six Egyptian Mummies," *Harrisburg (PA) Chronicle,* 9 Sept. 1833, [3]; *Daily Pittsburgh (PA) Gazette,* 21 Oct.–18 Nov. 1833; "Six Egyptian Mummies!," *Cincinnati Advertiser, and Ohio Phoenix,* 25 Dec. 1833, [2]; "Egyptian Mummies," *Daily Louisville (KY) Public Advertiser,* 10 Jan. 1834; Webb, "Mystery of the Mummies," 1–5.

309. Webb, "Mystery of the Mummies," 1–5; Wolfe, *Mummies in Nineteenth Century America,* 101–105.

received significant coverage in local newspapers.[310] In addition to reporting on the mummies, observers noted with curiosity the rolls or books of papyrus displayed along with the bodies. The *Cleveland Whig,* for example, observed, "There was found deposited in the arms of the old man . . . a *book* of ancient form and construction, which, to us, was by far the most interesting part of the exhibition."[311] On 26 March, the *Cleveland Advertiser* informed readers that "the collection is offered for sale by the proprietor."[312]

Though Michael Chandler was referred to as "proprietor" of the mummies, his relationship to the Egyptian collection is not fully understood. Born in Ireland around 1797, Chandler migrated with his family to the United States, likely in the late 1820s.[313] Chandler's profession and activities before 1835 are unknown. When he arrived in Kirtland in late June or early July, he informed Oliver Cowdery that he was Lebolo's nephew and had acquired the antiquities in New York City in 1833; however, there is no documentary evidence to support these claims.[314] According to a letter written by disaffected church member Joseph Coe in 1844, Chandler was acting as an agent for the collection's proprietors when he exhibited the mummies and papyri in Ohio in 1835.[315]

Whether owner of the collection or an agent for the owners, Chandler had apparently been referred to JS, who he was told could translate the hieroglyphic characters written on the papyri.[316] Shortly after JS's first meeting with Chandler in late June or early July 1835, JS, Joseph Coe, and an "S. Andrews" purchased Chandler's four mummies and some, if not all, of his Egyptian papyri for the substantial sum of $2,400.[317]

According to an entry in a later JS history, JS began "the translation of some of the characters or hieroglyphics" written on the ancient papyri in early July 1835.[318] In the months that followed, JS and four associates—William W. Phelps, Oliver Cowdery, Frederick G. Williams, and Warren Parrish—spent significant time engaged in two related endeavors: the translation and preparation of what would later be referred to as the Book of Abraham and a language-study effort that produced a number of Egyptian alphabet and grammar

---

310. Hudson, Journal, 19 Feb. 1835, David Hudson, Papers, Hudson Library and Historical Society, Hudson, Ohio; "A Rare Exhibition," *Cleveland Whig,* 25 Mar. 1835, [1]; "Egyptian Mummies," *Cleveland Daily Advertiser,* 26 Mar. 1835; "Mummies," *Painesville (OH) Telegraph,* 27 Mar. 1835, [3].

311. "A Rare Exhibition," *Cleveland Whig,* 25 Mar. 1835, [1], italics in original. A detailed description of the mummies published in the *Painesville Telegraph* noted that three of Chandler's mummies had with them a "roll . . . filled with hieroglyphics." ("Mummies," *Painesville [OH] Telegraph,* 27 Mar. 1835, [3].)

312. "Egyptian Mummies," *Cleveland Daily Advertiser,* 26 Mar. 1835. This is the earliest source to directly associate Chandler with the traveling exhibit.

313. Tinney, *Michael H. Chandler and the Pearl of Great Price,* 1–2.

314. Oliver Cowdery, Kirtland, OH, to William Frye, Lebanon, IL, 22 Dec. 1835, in Cowdery, Letterbook, 70.

315. Joseph Coe, Kirtland, OH, to JS, Nauvoo, IL, 1 Jan. 1844, JS Collection, CHL.

316. According to a certificate issued to JS and copied into Cowdery's letter to William Frye, Chandler had shown the hieroglyphics to scholars in other cities he had visited. (Oliver Cowdery, Kirtland, OH, to William Frye, Lebanon, IL, 22 Dec. 1835, in Cowdery, Letterbook, 71.)

317. Letter from Joseph Coe to JS, 1 Jan. 1844, JS Collection, CHL. According to a sermon delivered by Orson Pratt in 1878, Chandler told JS that "he would not sell the writings unless he could sell the mummies." (Orson Pratt, in *Journal of Discourses,* 25 Aug. 1878, 20:65.)

318. JS History, vol. B-1, 596. This entry in the history was penned by Willard Richards on 15 September 1843. (Richards, Journal, 15 Sept. 1843.)

manuscripts. While the unexpected acquisition of the papyri generated some excitement and curiosity in the community at large, it was not the sole catalyst for the interest that JS and other church members showed in language study and ancient texts; rather, the analysis and translation of those characters represented one part of a larger ongoing project to understand various ancient languages and texts during the early to mid-1830s.[319]

Seven brief entries in JS's journal offer the only contemporary firsthand account of his language-study and translation endeavors in 1835.[320] JS's 1835–1836 journal was begun on 22 September, more than two months after he apparently began his work with the papyri, but the first mention of ancient languages comes on 1 October, when the journal indicates that JS "labored on the Egyptian alphabet, in company with brsr O. Cowdery and W.W. Phelps." Entries from 7 October through 26 November are similarly concise, using language such as "spent the day in translating, and made rapid progress"; "translated some of the Egyptian records"; and "spent the day in transcribing Egyptian characters from the papyrus."[321] No contemporary document describes the method by which JS translated the Book of Abraham, and there is likewise no documentation of how he and associates produced the alphabet. Several months after Parrish was excommunicated from the church in December 1837, he informed the editor of the *Painesville Republican* that he had "penned down the translation of the Egyptian Hieroglyphicks as he [JS] claimed to receive it by direct inspiration from Heaven."[322]

Among the various Book of Abraham and Egyptian-related texts produced between circa early July and circa 26 November 1835 (the last date JS's journal mentions his work with the papyri) are three versions of portions of the Book of Abraham. In the Joseph Smith Papers, these are labeled as Book of Abraham Manuscript–A (the version featured here), –B, and –C, to differentiate between them. Textual evidence suggests that these Book of Abraham texts were based on an earlier manuscript that is no longer extant.[323] The copy

---

319. See Introduction to Part 1: 2 Oct.–1 Dec. 1835, pp. 3–6 herein.

320. Additionally, Willard Richards entered three July 1835 entries into JS's history in about September 1843. (JS History, vol. B-1, 595–596.)

321. JS, Journal, 1 and 7 Oct. 1835; 19, 20, and 24–26 Nov. 1835, in *JSP*, J1:67, 71, 109–111. After 26 November, there are no references to the translation of the Egyptian papyri in JS's journal until early 1842, when JS began preparing to publish the Book of Abraham. (JS, Journal, 23 Feb. and 8 Mar. 1842, in *JSP*, J2:36, 42.)

322. Warren Parrish, Letter to the Editor, 5 Feb. 1838, in *Painesville (OH) Republican*, 15 Feb. 1838, [3]. Two other reminiscent accounts noted various features of the translation process, but it is not always clear to which period they refer. As he helped set the type for the publication of the Book of Abraham in February 1842, Wilford Woodruff recorded in his journal, "The Lord is Blessing Joseph with Power to reveal the mysteries of the kingdom of God; to translate through the urim & Thummim Ancient records & Hyeroglyphics as old as Abraham or Adam." In a secondhand account recorded in the October 1846 issue of the *Friends' Weekly Intelligencer,* Lucy Mack Smith was quoted as saying that "when Joseph was reading the papyrus, he closed his eyes, and held a hat over his face, and that the revelation came to him; and where the papyrus was torn, he could read the parts that were destroyed equally as well as those that were there; and that scribes sat by him writing, as he expounded." (Woodruff, Journal, 19 Feb. 1842; "Correspondence of Friends' Weekly Intelligencer," *Friends' Weekly Intelligencer,* 3 Oct. 1846, 211.)

323. Documents directly dictated by JS typically had few paragraph breaks, punctuation marks, or contemporaneous alterations to the text. All the extant copies, including the featured text, have regular

presented here was inscribed by Frederick G. Williams and comprises what is today Abraham 1:4–2:6 in the Latter-day Saint scripture known as the Pearl of Great Price.[324] Written from Abraham's point of view, this passage depicts the biblical patriarch's calling to the priesthood, his escape from idolatrous priests in "the land of the Chaldeans," and his journey toward Egypt with his wife, Sarah.[325] Portions of the text parallel the account recorded in Genesis 11 and 12. Though not the most complete of the three extant versions, the featured text may be the earliest.[326]

Like the other two copies of the Book of Abraham manuscript, the featured document contains characters—many of which are hieratic characters, a cursive form of Egyptian hieroglyphs—in the left margin.[327] Many of the characters were copied from a portion of the papyri referred to by modern Egyptologists as the "Breathing Permit of Hôr."[328] Though the juxtaposition of the characters and Book of Abraham text implies a relationship between the two, the exact nature of that relationship is not stated. Modern Egyptologists agree that the Book of Abraham text is not a translation of the characters.[329]

News that JS was translating portions of the Egyptian papyri spread quickly through the church and the local community, but there is no evidence that anyone beyond those

---

paragraphing and punctuation included at the time of transcription, as well as several cancellations and insertions. (See examples throughout *JSP*, MRB; and *JSP*, R3; see also Hauglid, *Textual History of the Book of Abraham*, 58–59, 64–65, 84–85, 110–111.)

324. Williams served as a scribe for JS from early 1832 until the Hebrew School began in early January 1836. During fall 1835, Williams penned entries in JS's journal for 3–7 October, 16 November, and 23–26 December 1835. (Frederick G. Williams, Statement, no date, Frederick G. Williams, Papers, CHL; JS, Journal, 3–7 Oct., 16 Nov., and 23–26 Dec. 1835, in *JSP*, J1:67–71, 101–102, 135–138; see also Historical Introduction to Revelation, 15 Mar. 1832, in *JSP*, D2:207.)

325. "The Book of Abraham," *Times and Seasons*, 1 Mar. 1842, 3:704 [Abraham 1:1].

326. Williams's copy of the Book of Abraham exhibits a less refined orthography and more textual mistakes than the other two copies. Besides Williams's version, two other copies of the Book of Abraham manuscript were produced in 1835. One is in the handwriting of Warren Parrish and contains the text of what is today referred to as Abraham 1:4–2:2; the other, in the handwriting of both William W. Phelps and Warren Parrish, includes Abraham 1:1–2:18. (Hauglid, *Textual History of the Book of Abraham*, 6–9, 64–65; Book of Abraham Manuscript–B; Book of Abraham Manuscript–C, Book of Abraham Manuscripts, CHL.)

327. Two additional Book of Abraham manuscripts, produced in late 1841 or early 1842 by Willard Richards, do not contain hieratic characters. (Book of Abraham Manuscripts, CHL; see also Historical Introduction to Egyptian Alphabet, ca. Early July–ca. Nov. 1835–A, pp. 81–83 herein.)

328. Among the papyri purchased from Michael Chandler was a funerary text, derived from the Book of the Dead, for an Egyptian priest named Hôr. Fragments of this scroll were reacquired by The Church of Jesus Christ of Latter-day Saints from the New York Metropolitan Museum of Art in 1967 and are today housed in the Church History Library. Portions of the extant papyri are missing, likely due to deterioration. (Todd, "Egyptian Papyri Rediscovered," 12–16; Kirtland Egyptian Papers, CHL. For a brief history of the Egyptian Book of the Dead and the Breathing Permit of Hôr, see Ritner, *Joseph Smith Egyptian Papyri*, 86–89; for images of the papyri fragments, see the Joseph Smith Papers website, josephsmithpapers.org.)

329. For modern translations of the Breathing Permit of Hôr, see Ritner, *Joseph Smith Egyptian Papyri*, 81–149; Nibley, *Message of the Joseph Smith Papyri*, xix–xxiii, 33–50; and Rhodes, *Hor Book of Breathings*, 27–32.)

Book of Abraham manuscript inscribed by Frederick G. Williams. After Joseph Smith and others purchased a collection of Egyptian mummies and papyrus records from traveling exhibitor Michael Chandler in summer 1835, Joseph Smith and several close associates produced three extant manuscripts that became part of what is referred to as the Book of Abraham. The fourth page of the manuscript in Frederick G. Williams's copy, pictured here, includes hieratic characters copied from the papyrus scroll that is referred to by modern Egyptologists as the "Breathing Permit of Hôr." Book of Abraham Manuscript, ca. Early July–ca. Nov. 1835–A, p. 4, Book of Abraham Manuscripts, Church History Library, Salt Lake City.

working on the manuscripts in 1835 knew the details of the Abraham text.[330] In late 1837, it appears that church leaders planned to publish some of the Egyptian-related materials, likely the Book of Abraham. In a 5 November meeting, the church voted to "sanction the appointment of the Presidents in authorizing Brother [Willard] Richards & Brother Hadlock [Reuben Hedlock], to transact the business of the Church in procuring the means to translate & print those records taken from the chatacombs of Egypt, now in the temple."[331] It was not until March 1842, however, that the Book of Abraham was published in the church's publication the *Times and Seasons*.[332]

Document Transcript

✛ [333] sign of the fifth degree of the ~~first~~ ⟨Second⟩ part

✛ I sought for ⟨mine⟩ ~~the~~ appointment ~~whereunto~~ unto the priesthood according to the appointment of God unto the fathers concerning the seed

✛ my fathers having turned from their righteousness and from the holy commandments which the Lord their God had given unto them unto the worshiping of the Gods of the hethens

✛ utterly refused to harken to my voice for their hearts were set to do evil and were wholly turned to the God of Elk=Kener[334] and the God of Zibnah[335] and the God of Mah-mackrah and the God of Pharoah King of Egypt therefore they turned their hearts to the sacrafice of the heathens in offering up their children unto these[336] dumb Idols and harkened not unto my voice but indeovered to take away my life by the hand of the priest of Elk=Kener

✛ The priest of Elk=Keenah was also the priest of Pharoah, now at this time it was the custom of the priest of Pharaoh the King of Egypt to offer up upon the Alter which was built in the land of Chaldea for the offering unto these strange gods both men, women, and children— and it came to pass that the

---

330. William W. Phelps to Sally Waterman Phelps, 20 July 1835, in Historical Department, Journal History of the Church, 20 July 1835; Amasa Lyman, Journal, 11 July 1835; "Another Humbug," *Cleveland Whig,* 5 Aug. 1835, [1].

331. Minute Book 1, 5 Nov. 1837.

332. "The Book of Abraham," *Times and Seasons,* 1 Mar. 1842, 3:704–706 [Abraham 1–2:18]; "The Book of Abraham," *Times and Seasons,* 15 Mar. 1842, 3:718–722 [Abraham 2:18–5:21]. Though a notice printed in the 1 February 1843 issue of the *Times and Seasons* suggested that JS would publish "further extracts" from the Book of Abraham, there is no documentary evidence that other extracts were produced. All extant manuscripts generated by JS and his associates during their study of the Egyptian papyri, dated circa 1835 to circa 1842, are available on the Joseph Smith Papers website, josephsmithpapers.org. ("Notice," *Times and Seasons,* 1 Feb. 1843, 4:95.)

333. TEXT: This glyph stands in for the various hieratic and other characters found in the original document.

334. TEXT: Possibly "Elk=Kiner" or "Elk=Nene".

335. TEXT: Possibly "Zibrah".

336. TEXT: Possibly "their".

priest made an offering unto the god of Pharaoh and also unto the god of Shag=reel even after the manner of the Egyptians now the god of Shag-reel was the Sun—even a thank offering of a child did the priest of Pharaoh offer upon the Alter which stood by the hill called Potipher⟨s⟩ hill at the head of the plains of Olishem

✠ Now this priest had offered upon this alter three virgins at one time who were the daughters of ~~Onitus~~ Onitah— one of the ~~regular~~ royal discent directly from the loins of Ham these virgins were offered up because of their virtue they would not bow down to worship Gods of wood, or of stone therefore they were Killed upon this alter

✠ And it was done after the manner of the Egyptians and it came to pass ~~the~~ that the priests laid violence upon me that they might slay me also, as they did those virgins upon this alter, and that you might have a knowledge of this alter ⟨I will refer you to the representation that is at the commencement of this record⟩

✠ It was made after, the form of a bedsted such as was had among the Chaldeans and it stood before the Gods of Elk-keenah Zibnah Mah-Mach-rah—and als[o] a God like unto that of pharaoh King of Egypt [p. 1]

✠ ⟨That you may have an understanding of their gods I have given you the fashion of them in the figures at the begining which manner of figures is called by the Chaldians, Kah-lee-nos.[337] ——⟩

✠ And as they lifted up their hands upon me that they might offer me up ~~and~~[338] ⟨and⟩ take away my life behold I lifted up my voice unto the Lord my God; and the lord harkened, and heard and he filled me with a vision of the almighty and the angel of his presence stood by my feet and immediately loosed my bands

✠ And his voice was unto me. Abram Abram Behold my name is Jehovah. and I have heard thee and have come down to deliver thee. and to take thee away from thy fathers house, and from all thy Kinsfolks, in to a strange land which thou knowest not of, and this because ~~their hearts are turned~~ they have turned their hearts away from me to worship the god of Elk Kee-nah and the god of Zibnah— and of Mah-Mach-rah— and the god of pharaoh King of Egypt. Therefore I have come down to visit them. and to distroy him, who hath lifted up his hand against thee ~~Abraham~~ ⟨Abram⟩ my son to ~~distroy thy~~ take away thy life, Behold I will lead thee by my hand and I will take thee, to put upon thee my name even the priesthood of thy father, and my power shall be over thee; as it was with

---

337. TEXT: Possibly "Kah-be-nos."
338. TEXT: "and" written over "to" and then canceled.

Noah so shall it be with thee, that through thy ministry, my name shall be known, in the earth forever, for I am thy God

+ Behold Potiphers hill was in the land of Ur of Chaldea and the Lord broke down the alter of Elk-Keenah and of the gods[339] of the land, and utterly distroyed them ~~gods of the land~~ and smote the priests that he died and there was great morning in Chaldeea and also in the court of Pharaoh which Pharaoh signifies King by royal blood. Now this King of Egypt was a discendent from the loins of Ham and was a partaker of the blood of the Cananitess by birth: From this decent sprang all the Egyptians and thus the blood of the cannites was preserved in the land

+ [p. 2]

+ The land of Egypt being first discovered by a woman, who was the daughter

+ of Ham; and the daughter of Zep-tah. which in the Chaldea signifies Egypt, which sign[i]fies that which is forbidden. Whin this woman discovered the land it was under water, who after settled her sons in it: And thus from Ham sprang ~~the~~ that race which preserved the curse in the land.

+ Now the ⟨first⟩ government of Egypt, was established by Pharaoh the eldest son of Egyptes the daughter of Ham; and it was after the manner of the government of Ham, which was Patriarchal. Pharaoh being a righteous man established his kingdom, and Judged his people wisely and Justly all his days, seeking earnestly to imitate that order established by the fathers in the first generation in the days of the first Patriarchal reign, even in the reign of Adam. And also Noah his father. ~~For in his days~~ who blessed him with the blessings[340] of the earth, and ~~of~~ with the blessings of wisdom, but cursed him as pertaining to the priesthood.

+ Now Pharaoh being of that leniage by which he could not have the right of priesthood; notwithstanding the Pharaohs would fain claim it from Noah through Ham: Therefore, my father was led away by their— idolatry; but I shall indeaver hereafter to dilliniate the chronology running back from myself to the begining of ⟨the⟩ creation, for the reccords, have come into my hands which I hold unto this present time

+ Now after the priest of Elkkeenah was smitten that he died, there came a fulfilment of those things which were spoken unto me concerning the land of Chaldea, that there should be a famine in the land; and accordingly a famine prevailed throughout all the land of Chaldea: And my father was sorely tormented because of the famine, and he repented of the evil which he had determined against me, to take away my life: But the reccords of

339. TEXT: Possibly "god⟨s⟩".
340. TEXT: Possibly "blessing⟨s⟩".

the fathers even the patriarchs concerning the right of priesthood, the lord my god preserved in mine own hand⟨s⟩: [p. [3]] Therefore a knowledge of the begining of creation and also of the planets, and of the stars, as it was made known unto the fathers, have I kept even unto this day.

✦ And I shall endeaver to write some of these things, upon this reccord, for the benefit of my posterity, that shall come after me

✦ Now the Lord God caused the famine to wax soar in the land of Ur insomuch that Haran my brother died: but Terah my father yet lived in the land of Ur of the chaldees. And it came to pass; that I Abram took Sarai to wife, and Nahor my brother took Milcah to wife

✦ Who was the daughter of Haron

✦ Now the Lord had said unto me Abram get the[e] out of thy country, and from thy Kindred and from thy fathers home,[341] unto a land that I will shew thee: Therefore I left the land of Ur of the chaldees to go into the land of canaan; and I took Lot my brothers son, and his wife, and Sarai my wife; and also my father followed after me unto the land which we denominated Haran. And the famine abated, and my father tarried in Haran and dwelt there, as there were many flocks in Haran; And my father turned again unto his idolitry: Therefore he continued in Haran

Now the Lord had said unto Abram ⟨me⟩ get thee out of thy country, and from thy kindred and from thy fathers home[342] unto a land that I will shew thee. Therefore I left the land of Ur of the chaldees to go into the land of canaan, and I took Lot my bro son and his wife and sarah my wife and also my father follod me unto the land which we denominated Haran and the famine abated, and my father tarried in Haran and dwelt there as ~~they~~ ⟨there⟩ were ⟨many⟩ flock in Haran. and my father turned again unto his idolitry Therefore he continued in Haran but ⟨I⟩ Abram and and Lot my brothers son prayed unto the Lord, and the Lord appeared [p. 4]

———— ☙ ————

Egyptian Alphabet, circa Early July–circa November 1835–A

Source Note

Egyptian Alphabet, [Kirtland Township, Geauga Co., OH], [ca. early July–ca. Nov. 1835]; English in handwriting of JS, Oliver Cowdery, and Warren Parrish; copied characters in unidentified handwriting (likely JS and Oliver Cowdery); five pages; Kirtland Egyptian Papers, CHL. Includes archival marking.

---

341. TEXT: Or "house,".
342. TEXT: Or "house".

Four leaves of differing sizes and formats. The first leaf measures 12⅜ × 7¾ inches (31 × 20 cm) and has a blank verso. The second and third leaves both measure 12½ × 15⅝ inches (32 × 40 cm). Each of these two leaves has a blank verso. The leaves were folded in half with the crease running vertically. The fourth and final leaf measures 12½ × 15⅜ inches (32 × 39 cm) and has inscriptions on both sides. The first leaf appears to be ruled horizontally, though the lines are faded. The second and third leaves are ruled horizontally with forty blue lines, now faded. Some ruling is slightly visible on the fourth leaf, but the lines are almost all faded. The first leaf bears vertical ruling that organizes the characters, trans- literations, and meanings. The text has multiple ink flows, indicating it was likely inscribed in multiple writing sessions over a period of time. The leaves are stained throughout by an unidentified oil-based material; the leaves have also sustained water damage. There is additional damage to the outside edges of the leaves. Pinholes along the right side of each leaf align with pinholes on the other three leaves. Multiple sets of holes in the leaves indicate that the pages were fastened and unfastened several times. Green staining from an iron pin is visible on the first leaf, indicating these four leaves were fastened and stored together for significant time. Damage to the upper-right corner of the first two leaves resulted from the pinholes. When fastened, the pages of the three final leaves were folded in half and around the shorter first leaf, placing the first leaf in the middle of the packet of paper. No additional folding is evident. The top of each recto is labeled with a letter in blue ink, presumably to keep the pages in order; the first through fourth rectos are labeled "B", "T", "U", and "V", respectively. These letters, when compared with other similar markings on other Book of Abraham and Egyptian-language documents, served as a way to organize the documents. The markings were apparently written by assistant church historian Andrew Jenson, indicating this document was in the custody of the Historian's Office from an early time. This document was likely grouped with the records listed in early Historian's Office inventories as "Egyptian Grammar", further suggesting continuous institu- tional custody.[343]

Historical Introduction

After he purchased ancient Egyptian mummies and records from traveling exhibitor Michael Chandler in early July 1835,[344] JS and fellow church leaders Oliver Cowdery, William W. Phelps, Frederick G. Williams, and Warren Parrish embarked on two related endeavors: the translation of what would later be referred to as the Book of Abraham and an effort to study ancient languages. The latter initiative resulted in a number of documents that the men who created them considered to be Egyptian alphabet and grammar manuscripts.[345] The effort to understand the Egyptian language was part of a longer, ongoing endeavor to comprehend ancient languages and texts.[346]

As they studied the Egyptian papyri, JS and his associates generated a corpus of manuscripts, including portions of the Book of Abraham, an Egyptian grammar, and hieratic characters. Among these manuscripts were three copies of an "Egyptian alphabet" created by JS, Cowdery, and Phelps. In the Joseph Smith Papers, these are labeled as

---

343. "Schedule of Church Records. Nauvoo 1846," [1]; "Inventory. Historian's Office. 4th April 1855," [1], Historian's Office, Catalogs and Inventories, 1846–1904, CHL.

344. For more on the provenance of the mummies and records, see Historical Introduction to Book of Abraham Manuscript, ca. Early July–ca. Nov. 1835–A [Abraham 1:4–2:6], pp. 71–77 herein.

345. The translation of the Book of Abraham and the endeavor to study and understand ancient languages were partially influenced by JS's declaration that the papyri contained the writings and teach- ings of the ancient patriarchs Abraham and Joseph. (William W. Phelps to Sally Waterman Phelps, 20 July 1835, in Historical Department, Journal History of the Church, 20 July 1835.)

346. See Introduction to Part 1: 2 Oct.–1 Dec. 1835, pp. 3–6 herein.

Egyptian Alphabet–A (the version featured here), –B, and –C to differentiate between them.[347] An entry in JS's multivolume manuscript history notes that for nearly two weeks at the end of July 1835, JS was "continually engaged in translating an alphabet to the Book of Abraham, and arrangeing a grammar of the Egyptian language as practiced by the ancients."[348]

The Egyptian alphabet manuscript featured here is the only extant document among the larger collection of Egyptian-related materials that contains JS's handwriting; portions of the text are also in the handwriting of Cowdery and Parrish. Five pages in length, the manuscript contains various characters, some of which are followed by their pronunciation and interpretation.[349] The characters are divided into five groupings of varying lengths, each with its own heading. Most of the characters from the middle of page 2 through page 5 appear to be Egyptian hieratic characters copied from what modern Egyptologists refer to as the "Breathing Permit of Hôr."[350] Though the source texts for the characters from the beginning of page 1 through the middle of page 2 are largely unknown, six of the characters on page 1 appear in a 26 May 1835 letter from Phelps to his wife, Sally Waterman Phelps. The letter was written a month before JS acquired the Egyptian papyri, and in it, William Phelps described the characters he copied as "a specimen of some of the 'pure language.'"[351] That the characters in the Egyptian alphabet presented here were copied from more than one source suggests that what is termed an "Egyptian alphabet" may have been part of a comprehensive project that synthesized characters from various source texts.

The pronunciations and interpretations written to the right of the characters identified as Egyptian do not match translations rendered by modern Egyptologists, and the method by which JS and his associates produced this document is unclear, as there are no contemporary

---

347. The other two copies are in the hand of William W. Phelps and Oliver Cowdery, respectively, and are similar to the copy transcribed here. All of the extant manuscripts generated by JS and others' study of the Egyptian papyri, dated circa 1835–circa 1842, are available on the Joseph Smith Papers website, josephsmithpapers.org. (Egyptian Alphabet–B; Egyptian Alphabet–C, Kirtland Egyptian Papers, CHL.)

348. JS History, vol. B-1, July 1835, 597.

349. The Egyptian alphabet inscribed by William W. Phelps contains column headings such as "Character," "Sound," and "Explanation." (Egyptian Alphabet–B, Kirtland Egyptian Papers, CHL.)

350. Among the papyri purchased from Michael Chandler was a funerary text, derived from the Book of the Dead, for an Egyptian priest named Hôr. Fragments of this scroll were reacquired by The Church of Jesus Christ of Latter-day Saints from the New York Metropolitan Museum of Art in 1967 and are today housed in the Church History Library. Portions of the extant papyri are missing, likely due to deterioration. (Todd, "Egyptian Papyri Rediscovered," 12–16; Kirtland Egyptian Papers, CHL. For a brief history of the Egyptian Book of the Dead and the Breathing Permit of Hôr, see Ritner, *Joseph Smith Egyptian Papyri*, 86–89; for images of the papyri fragments, see the Joseph Smith Papers website, josephsmithpapers.org.)

351. William W. Phelps, Kirtland, OH, to Sally Waterman Phelps, Liberty, MO, 26 May 1835, William W. Phelps, Papers, BYU. The source text for William W. Phelps's characters is unknown, though some may have come from an 1832 document dictated by JS that revealed and defined some words from what he termed "the pure language of God." Some of the transliterated words in this document are also found in Phelps's letter. (Sample of Pure Language, between ca. 4 and ca. 20 Mar. 1832, in *JSP*, D2:213–215; see also 53n233 herein.)

firsthand descriptions of the process.[352] Though Egyptologists today understand hieroglyphs as essentially phonetic in nature, most scholars in the early nineteenth century believed that hieroglyphic characters were ideograms, which symbolized whole ideas or concepts rather than distinct sounds.[353] In this context, the Egyptian alphabet may have been an effort by JS and his associates to decode characters that they assumed stood for larger concepts. Though French scholar Jean-Francois Champollion came to recognize the phonetic nature of Egyptian hieroglyphics during the 1820s and early 1830s, his ideas were not fully embraced or widely published until decades after his death in 1832.[354]

Document Transcript

/[355]Egyptian[356] alphabet first degree[357]

+[358]   **ah the first being who exercises Supreme power [*page torn*][359]**

+   **pha-e the first man or one who has Kingly power or K[ing][360]**

+   **pha a more universal reighn having g[r]eater dom[in]ion or power**

+ + +   **⟨phatoeup⟩ rolyal [royal] family royal blood or pharaoah or supreme power ⟨or⟩ King**

---

352. For modern translations of the Breathing Permit of Hôr, see Ritner, *Joseph Smith Egyptian Papyri,* 81–149; Nibley, *Message of the Joseph Smith Papyri,* xix–xxiii, 33–50; and Rhodes, *Hor Book of Breathings,* 27–32.

353. Robinson, *Cracking the Egyptian Code,* 17–27; Singh, *Code Book,* 203–206.

354. Though news of Champollion's work had reached the United States by the 1830s, few Americans had access to or understood the significance of his work on Egyptian hieroglyphs, and there were no published dictionaries to aid in translating such characters. In 1830, Isaac Stuart translated an essay, written by French author J. G. H. Greppo, that described some of Champollion's early discoveries and the implications such discoveries might have for understanding ancient scripture. According to an 1831 article in the *North American Review,* Champollion's publications were "not translated into English, nor of common occurrence in this country." As late as the 1850s, scholars like Gustavus Seyffarth, a professor of archeology at Concordia College in St. Louis, Missouri, continued to oppose many of Champollion's theories about hieroglyphics. The first American translation of the Rosetta Stone, published by the Philomathean Society at the University of Pennsylvania, did not appear until 1858. (Robinson, *Cracking the Egyptian Code,* 237–242; Greppo, *Essay on the Hieroglyphic System of M. Champollion;* "Hieroglyphics," 96; Parkinson, *Cracking Codes,* 41.)

355. TEXT: JS handwriting begins.

356. TEXT: Upper portion of word missing because of damage to top edge of page.

357. TEXT: This page has three vertical lines running down the paper, dividing it into three columns and a wide left margin. The left column contains the characters. The middle column contains a phonetic spelling of each character and a description of its meaning, which runs across into the right column.

358. TEXT: This glyph stands in for the various hieratic and other characters found in the original document. The scribe or scribes for the characters in the left column cannot be identified. It may be that the respective characters were written by the same scribe who wrote the text that follows each.

359. Missing section may have contained additional writing; however, the copy of this alphabet in William W. Phelps's handwriting does not have other words for this phrase. (Egyptian Alphabet–B, Kirtland Egyptian Papers, CHL.)

360. TEXT: "K[*page torn*]". Text supplied based on Phelps copy. (Egyptian Alphabet–B, Kirtland Egyptian Papers, CHL.)

✢ ✢   ⟨ho up hah⟩ crown of a princess or queen or Stands for queen

✢   ⟨Zi⟩ Virgen unmaried or the pri[n]ciple of vi[r]tue

✢ ✢ ✢ ✢[361] Kah tou man the name of a royal family in female line

✢   Zie oop hah An unmaried woman and a vi[r]gin pri[n]cess

✢   ho-ee-oop young unmarried man a pri[n]cess

✢   Zip Zi woman married or unmarried ⟨or daughter⟩

✢   ho-ee oop hah Crown of a prince or King

✢   one-ahe or ohe the Earth

✢   tone tahe or ~~th~~ tohe ton-es beneath or under water

✢   Iota the eye or to see or sight sometimes me myself

✢   Iota tou-es[362] Zip-Zi~~p~~ the land of Egypt first seen under water

✢   Sue Eh ni what other person is that or who

✢   ho-ee oop-~~phare~~ hak[363] pha-e[364] goverment power or Kingdom

✢   Zub Zool oun the begining first before pointing to

✢   Zub Zool Eh in the begining of the E[a]rth ⟨or⟩ Creation

✢   Zool Eh Signifys to be in any as light in th[e earth][365]

✢   Zub the first Creation of any thing first insti[tu]tion[366]

✢   zub zool from the first to any Stated peried [period] after

✢   Zool from any or some fix⟨ed⟩ peried of time ⟨back⟩ to the begining ⟨of the creation⟩[367]

The second part first degree

✢   Ahnaios[368] God without begining or end

✢   Aleph in the begining with God the Son or ⟨first born⟩

✢   Albeth Angels or disimbodied spirits ⟨or⟩ Sainnts

✢[369]   ~~Alcatheth~~ Alcabeth Angels in an unattenable immortal ⟨state⟩

✢   ~~Achibeth~~ Achebeth minersters [ministers] of God high preasts ⟨Kings⟩

---

361. TEXT: The Phelps copy and the copy of the Egyptian alphabet in the handwriting of Oliver Cowdery both include only one symbol for "Kah tou man"; it is unclear why this document contains multiple characters. Perhaps it was an attempt to clarify or correct a malformed character. (Egyptian Alphabet–B; Egyptian Alphabet–C, Kirtland Egyptian Papers, CHL.)

362. TEXT: Possibly "ton-es".

363. TEXT: Possibly "hah".

364. TEXT: Possibly "~~phare~~ pha-".

365. TEXT: "th[*page torn*]". Text supplied based on Phelps copy. (Egyptian Alphabet–B, Kirtland Egyptian Papers, CHL.)

366. TEXT: "insti[*page torn*]tion".

367. TEXT: Possibly "peried of ⟨time ⟨back⟩ to the begining ⟨of the creation⟩⟩".

368. TEXT: Or "~~Ahnuos~~ Ahmios".

369. This character and the next five below it all appear in a 26 May 1835 letter from William W. Phelps to his wife and are described as a "specimen of some of the 'pure language.'" (William W. Phelps, Kirtland, OH, to Sally Waterman Phelps, Liberty, MO, 26 May 1835, William W. Phelps, Papers, BYU.)

+   ~~Alchobeth~~ Alchibeth ministers of God under or the less
+   ~~Alchubeth~~ Alchobeth ministers not ordained of God Sinful
+   ~~Alchybeth~~ Alchubeth ministers who are less sinful for want of ⟨power⟩
+   Baeth the name of all mankind man or men
+ +   Baeth Ka Adam or the first man or first King
+   Baeth Ke the next from Adam one ordained under ⟨him⟩[370]
+   Baeth Ki the third patrearck [patriarch][371]
+   Baeth Ko the fourth from Adam[372]
        ~~Baeth Ku~~ [p. [1]]

Egyptian alphabet first degree Second part
+   Baethchu the fifth high preast from Adam
+   Beth mans first residence fruiful garden A great val[le]y a place of
        hapiness 1 times
+   Bethcha an other place of residence or ~~an~~ ⟨a⟩ more fruitful Garden
        or larger place of hapiness greater hapiness 5 times
+   Bethche the third place 5 times Bethcha
+   Bethchi the fourth place 5 times Bethche
+ + + Bethcho the fifth place 5 times Bethchi
+   Bethchu the six place 5 Bethcho
+   Bethchu ain trieth the whole Earth or the largest ⟨place⟩ the greatest
        injoyment on Earth Ga[r]den of the Earth.
+   Ebethchuaintrieth Eternity
+   Ebethcha the greatest place of hapiness where God resides the
        Celesstial Kingdom
+   /[373]Kah-tu-ain-trieth-[374]
+   Kah-tu ain-
+   Dah-tu-hah-dees
+   Hah-dees
+   ~~De-en~~ De-eh
+   Zip-zi-iota-veh[375]

---

370. That is, Seth. (Instruction on Priesthood, between ca. 1 Mar. and ca. 4 May 1835, in *JSP*, D4:316 [D&C 107:42]; see also Genesis 5:3.)

371. That is, Enos. (Instruction on Priesthood, between ca. 1 Mar. and ca. 4 May 1835, in *JSP*, D4:316 [D&C 107:44]; see also Genesis 5:6.)

372. That is, Cainan. (Instruction on Priesthood, between 1 Mar. and ca. 4 May 1835, in *JSP*, D4:316 [D&C 107:21]; see also Genesis 5:9.)

373. TEXT: JS handwriting ends; Oliver Cowdery begins.

374. TEXT: Possibly "~~treeth~~ trieth".

375. TEXT: Or "aeh".

✛ Lish-zi-ho-e-oop-iota.[376]

✛ Gah-nel.

✛ Ho-hah-oop

✛ Io-ho-hah-oop

✛ Io-ho-hah-oop-zip-zi

✛ Jah-ho-e-oop

✛ ~~Jah-ho-hah~~ Jah-Ni-hah

✛ Jah-oh-eh

✛ Flo-ees

✛ Flos-isis.

✛ Kli-flos-isis

✛ ~~◊~~[377]

✛ Veh-kli-flos-isis

✛ ✛

✛ /[378]Kolob

✛ ✛

✛ ✛

✛

✛

✛

✛

✛ [p. 2]

/[379]Egyptian alphabet first degree

✛ ✛ ✛ ✛

✛ ✛ ✛

✛

✛

✛ ✛

✛

✛

✛

✛

✛ ✛ ✛ ✛

The third part of the first degree

✛

---

376. TEXT: Possibly a stray mark rather than a period.

377. TEXT: Possibly "K", "F", or "V".

378. TEXT: Oliver Cowdery handwriting ends; Warren Parrish begins.

379. TEXT: Warren Parrish handwriting ends; JS begins.

✦
✦
✦ ✦
✦ ✦
✦ ✦ ✦
✦ ✦
✦
✦
✦

✦ ✦   **Ah broam-ah brahoam Ki Ahbraoam**[380] /[381]Ki-ah-bram, Ki-ah-bra-
oam- Zub-sool-oan.

✦
✦
✦
✦

✦   /[382]**Iota nilah veh ah que**[383]

✦
✦ ✦

✦ ✦   **fourth part of the first degree**

✦ ✦
✦ ✦
✦

✦ ✦ ✦ ✦
✦ ✦ ✦
✦ ✦
✦ ✦ ✦ ✦ ✦ ✦ [p. 3]

Egyptian alphabet fourth part first degree

✦
✦ ✦
✦
✦
✦
✦
✦
✦ ✦

✦   **fifth part of the first degree**

---

380. TEXT: Possibly "Ahbraham" revised to "Ahbraoam" and then canceled.
381. TEXT: JS handwriting ends; Oliver Cowdery begins.
382. TEXT: Oliver Cowdery handwriting ends; JS begins.
383. TEXT: Phrase possibly in the handwriting of William W. Phelps.

+
+
+
+ + +
+
+
+ +
+ +
+
+ +
+ +
+ +
+
+
+ +
+ + + + +384
+
+
+
+
+ +
+ +
+ +

+ /385Ah braom—

+ Ah-bra-oam. Signifies father of the faithful— The first right— The elder [p. 4]

+ In the first degree Ah-broam— signifies The father of the faithful, the first right, the elders second degree— same sound— A follower of sig rightiousness— Third degree— same sound— One who possesses great Knowledge— Fourth degree— same sound— A follower of righteousness, a possessor of greater of knowledge. Fifth degree— Ah-bra-oam. The father of many nations, a prince of peace, one who keeps the commandments of God, a patriarch, a rightful heir, a high priest. [p. 5]

——— ❧ ———

---

384. TEXT: Canceled characters appear to be misformed versions of the final character.
385. TEXT: JS handwriting ends; Oliver Cowdery begins.

Letter to the Elders of the Church,
30 November–1 December 1835

Source Note

JS, Letter, Kirtland Township, Geauga Co., OH, to "the Elders of the Church of the Latter Day Saints," [30 Nov.–1 Dec. 1835]. Featured version published in "To the Elders of the Church of the Latter Day Saints," Latter Day Saints' Messenger and Advocate, *Dec. 1835, 2:225–230. For more information on* Latter Day Saints' Messenger and Advocate, *see Source Notes for Multiple-Entry Documents, p. 527 herein.*

Historical Introduction

This letter to the elders of the church was the last in a three-part series of open letters published in the September, November, and December 1835 issues of the church's newspaper, the *Latter Day Saints' Messenger and Advocate.*[386] In this installment, written on 30 November and 1 December 1835,[387] JS focused on biblical parables found in Matthew 13, on baptism and the Holy Ghost, and on the establishment of the kingdom of heaven. He also wrote on the gathering of Israel, a subject he discussed in the two previous letters in the series.

JS's remarks included a strident response to the recent and ongoing opposition from Alexander Campbell, Eber D. Howe, Doctor Philastus Hurlbut, and others. Campbell, Howe, and Hurlbut had repeatedly employed the power of print media to assail JS and the Church of the Latter Day Saints. Campbell led a sizable religious following known formally as the Disciples of Christ and informally as Campbellites. Soon after Sidney Rigdon and many other former Campbellites in northeastern Ohio converted to the Mormon faith in late 1830, Campbell used his newspaper, the *Millennial Harbinger,* and a printed pamphlet titled *Delusions: An Analysis of the Book of Mormon* to disparage JS.[388] In his writings, Campbell attacked the authenticity of the Book of Mormon and labeled JS an impostor.[389] In September 1834, after "perusing Mr. A. Campbell's 'Millennial Harbinger,'" JS wrote a letter to Oliver Cowdery that emphasized the difference in approach between himself and the combative Disciple of Christ leader; he further stated his expectation to see "truth triumph over error" when such men cry "delusion, deception, and false prophets."[390]

JS's letter featured here also dismissed the claims of Eber D. Howe and Doctor Philastus Hurlbut. The *Painesville Telegraph,* previously edited and published by Howe, had earlier reprinted some of Campbell's anti-Mormon polemics and included other articles and

---

386. See Letter to the Elders of the Church, 2 Oct. 1835, pp. 6–15 herein; and Letter to the Elders of the Church, 16 Nov. 1835, pp. 53–60 herein.

387. JS, Journal, 30 Nov. and 1 Dec. 1835, in *JSP,* J1:113.

388. "Delusions," *Millennial Harbinger,* 7 Feb. 1831, 85–95; Alexander Campbell, *Delusions* (Boston: Benjamin H. Greene, 1832). The *Millennial Harbinger,* a publication of the Disciples of Christ, was printed from 1830 to 1870 in Bethany, Virginia. Campbell first attacked JS personally by calling him ignorant, stupid, illiterate, and a false messiah. Campbell also analyzed the Book of Mormon, emphasizing that he considered it internally inconsistent. For more on Campbell, see Hughes, "From Primitive Church to Civil Religion," 87–103.

389. See "Christendom in Its Dotage," *Millennial Harbinger,* Aug. 1834, 374.

390. Letter to Oliver Cowdery, 24 Sept. 1834, in *JSP,* D4:169.

editorials belittling the church.[391] But Howe's book—*Mormonism Unvailed,* published in late 1834—attacked the reputation of JS and his role in founding the church more personally, partly through negative affidavits about JS and his family gathered by Hurlbut in New York. In 1833, Orris Clapp and other citizens of Geauga County, Ohio, employed Hurlbut to collect information about the Smith family and the origin of the Book of Mormon. While doing so, Hurlbut developed a new theory about the Book of Mormon: Sidney Rigdon, not JS, had produced it, and he had done so by plagiarizing an earlier manuscript written by Solomon Spalding.[392] Hearing rumors of a lost "romance," or novel, Hurlbut collected statements from Spalding's acquaintances that described the contents of the manuscript. He also claimed that he found the manuscript in Otsego County, New York, and that it contained a story that paralleled the Book of Mormon narrative.[393] Hurlbut supposedly delivered the manuscript to Howe, who chose not to publish the manuscript but instead used *Mormonism Unvailed* to introduce the Spalding theory and publish many of the affidavits Hurlbut collected about the Smith family and the Book of Mormon.[394]

JS may also have been reacting to attacks published even more recently. In a review of *Mormonism Unvailed* printed in the January 1835 issue of the *Millennial Harbinger,* Campbell wrote, "No man, *not already duped,* who has the half of five grains of common sense, can read this narrative of Mormonism without being converted to the belief that *Joseph Smith* and his colleagues in the plot are a band of the most unprincipled deceivers that ever disgraced any age or nation, and that his followers are a set of superlative fanatics."[395]

JS's letter was printed in the December issue of the *Messenger and Advocate,* which is the only known surviving version. With no original version extant, it is not clear whether JS or his scribe Warren Parrish penned this letter. JS's journal notes that he "spent the day in writing" for the *Messenger and Advocate* on both 30 November and 1 December.[396] If JS followed the procedure that produced his extensive diary entries during this period,

---

391. For instance, Campbell's *Delusions* was reprinted in the 8 and 15 March 1831 issues of the *Telegraph.* Oliver Cowdery responded to Campbell in his own article printed in the *Messenger and Advocate.* ("Delusions," *Painesville [OH] Telegraph,* 8 Mar. 1831, [1]–[2]; "Internal Evidences," *Painesville Telegraph,* 15 Mar. 1831, [1]–[2]; see also Letter to Oliver Cowdery, 24 Sept. 1834, in *JSP,* D4:168–171; Oliver Cowdery, "Delusion," *LDS Messenger and Advocate,* Mar. 1835, 1:90–93.)

392. Eber D. Howe, *Mormonism Unvailed* (Painesville, OH: By the author, 1834); see also "Mormonism Unvailed," *Painesville (OH) Telegraph,* 28 Nov. 1834, [3]. Hurlbut's theory would have required collusion between JS and Sidney Rigdon in the 1820s, but the two did not meet until Rigdon traveled to New York to meet JS in December 1830. Rigdon encountered the Book of Mormon and was baptized just prior to meeting JS. (See Letter from Oliver Cowdery, 12 Nov. 1830, in *JSP,* D1:211–213; Revelation, 7 Dec. 1830, in *JSP,* D1:219–223 [D&C 35]; and Pratt, *Autobiography,* 31–32, 49–50.)

393. When the Spalding manuscript was later rediscovered and published, it bore little resemblance to the Book of Mormon. (See Jackson, *Manuscript Found,* vii–xxviii.)

394. Howe, *Mormonism Unvailed,* 278–290; Winchester, *Plain Facts,* 8–9; Eber D. Howe, Statement, 8 Apr. 1885, Collection of Manuscripts about Mormons, 1832–1954, Chicago History Museum; for more information on Hurlbut, see "Joseph Smith Documents from February 1833 through March 1834," in *JSP,* D3:xxiv–xxvii.

395. "Mormonism Unveiled," *Millennial Harbinger,* Jan. 1835, 44–45, italics in original.

396. JS, Journal, 30 Nov. and 1 Dec. 1835, in *JSP,* J1:113.

he would have dictated to or otherwise worked with Parrish to compose the letter before submitting it to the editor, John Whitmer, for publication.

Document Transcript

To the Elders of the Church of the Latter Day Saints.

I have shown unto you, in my last,[397] that there are two Jerusalems spoken of in holy writ,[398] in a manner I think satisfactorily to your minds: At any rate I have given my views upon the subject. I shall now proceed to make some remarks from the sayings of the Savior, recorded in the 13th chapter of his gospel according to St Matthew, which in my mind affords us as clear an understanding, upon the important subject of the gathering, as any thing recorded in the bible. At the time the Savior spoke these beautiful sayings and parables, contained in the chapter above quoted, we find him seated in a ship, on the account of the multitude that pressed upon him to hear his words, and he commenced teaching them by saying: "Behold a sower went forth to sow, and when he sowed, some seeds fell by the way side, and the fowls came and devoured them up; some fell upon stony places, where they had not much earth, and forthwith they sprang up because they had no deepness of earth, and when the sun was up, they were scorched, and because they had not root they withered away; and some fell among thorns and the thorns sprang up and choked them; but other, fell into good ground and brought forth fruit, some an hundred fold, some sixty fold, some thirty fold: who hath ears to hear let him hear. And the disciples came and said unto him, why speakest thou unto them in parables, (I would remark here, that the "*them*," made use of, in this interrogation, is a personal pronoun and refers to the multitude,) he answered and said unto them, (that is the disciples,) it is given unto *you* to know the mysteries of the kingdom of heaven, but unto *them* (that is unbelievers) it is not given, for whosoever hath, to him shall be given, and he shall have more abundance; but whosoever hath not, shall be taken away, even that he hath."[399]

We understand from this saying, that those who had previously been looking for a Messiah to come, according to the testimony of the Prophets, and were then, at that time, looking for a Messiah, but had not sufficient light on the account of their unbelief, to discern him to be their Savior; and he being the true Messiah, consequently they must be disappointed and lose even all the knowledge, or have taken away from them, all the light, understanding and

---

397. See Letter to the Elders of the Church, 16 Nov. 1835, pp. 53–60 herein.

398. See Book of Mormon, 1830 ed., 501 [3 Nephi 21:23–24].

399. Matthew 13:3–12. In the weeks before he wrote this epistle, JS studied and taught basic English grammar. (See JS, Journal, 4 and 11 Nov. 1835, in *JSP*, J1:84, 96.)

faith, which they had upon this subject: therefore he that will not receive the greater light, must have taken away from him, all the light which he hath.[400] And if the light which is in you, become darkness, behold how great is that darkness?[401] Therefore says the Savior, speak I unto them in parables, because they, seeing, see not; and hearing, they hear not; neither do they understand: and in them is fulfilled the prophecy of Esaias, which saith: by hearing ye shall hear and shall not understand; and seeing ye shall see and not perceive.[402]

Now we discover, that the very reasons assigned by this prophet, why they would not receive the Messiah, was, because they did or would not understand; and seeing they did not perceive: for this people's heart is waxed gross; their ears are dull of hearing; their eyes they have closed, lest at any time, they should see with their eyes, and hear with their ears, and understand with their hearts, and should be converted and I should heal them.[403]

But what saith he to his disciples: Blessed are your eyes, for they see, and your ears, for they hear; for verily I say unto you, that many prophets and righteous men have desired to see those things which ye see, and have not seen them; and to hear those things which ye hear, and have not heard them.[404]

We again make a remark here, for we find that the very principles upon which the disciples were accounted blessed, was because they were permitted to see with their eyes, and hear with their ears, and the condemnation which rested upon the multitude, which received not his saying, was because they were not willing to see with their eyes and hear with their ears; not because they could not and were not privileged to see, and hear, but because their hearts were full of iniquity and abomi[p. [225]]nation: as your fathers did so do ye.— The prophet foreseeing that they would thus harden their hearts plainly declared it;[405] and herein is the condemnation of the world, that light hath come into the world, and men choose darkness rather than light because their deeds are evil: This is so plainly taught by the Savior, that a wayfaring man need not mistake it.[406]

And again hear ye the parable of the sower: Men are in the habit, when the truth is exhibited by the servants of God, of saying, all is mystery, they are spoken in parables, and, therefore, are not to be understood, it is true they have eyes to see, and see not; but none are so blind as those who will not see: And although the Savior spoke this parable to such characters, yet unto his disciples

---

400. See Matthew 13:12.
401. See Matthew 6:23.
402. See Matthew 13:14; see also Isaiah 6:9; and Jeremiah 5:21.
403. See Matthew 13:13–15.
404. See Matthew 13:16–17.
405. See Isaiah 6:9–10.
406. See John 3:19.

he expounded it plainly; and we have reason to be truly humble before the God of our fathers, that he hath left these things on record for us, so plain, that, notwithstanding the exertions and combined influence of the priests of Baal, they have not power to blind our eyes and darken our understanding, if we will but open our eyes and read with candor, for a moment. But listen to the explanation of the parable: when any one heareth the word of the kingdom, and understandeth it not, then cometh the wicked one and catcheth away that which was sown in his heart.[407] Now mark the expression; that which was before sown in his heart; this is he which received seed by the way side; men who have no principle of righteousness in themselves, and whose hearts are full of iniquity, and who have no desire for the principles of truth, do not understand the word of truth, when they hear it.— The devil taketh away the word of truth out of their hearts, because there is no desire for righteousness in them. But he that received the seed into stony places the same is he that heareth the word and, anon, with joy receiveth it, yet hath he not root in himself, but dureth for awhile; for when tribulation or persecution ariseth because of the word, by and by he is offended. He also that received seed among the thorns is he that receiveth the word, and the cares of this world, and the deceitfulness of riches choke the word, and he becometh unfruitful: but he that received seed into the good ground, is he that heareth the word and understandeth it which also beareth fruit and bringeth forth some an hundred fold, some sixty, some thirty.[408] Thus the Savior himself explains unto his disciples the parable, which he put forth and left no mystery or darkness upon the minds of those who firmly believe on his words.

We draw the conclusion then, that the very reason why the multitude, or the world, as they were designated by the Savior, did not receive an explanation upon his parables, was, because of unbelief. To you, he says, (speaking to his disciples) it is given to know the mysteries of the kingdom of God:[409] and why? because of the faith and confidence which they had in him. This parable was spoken to demonstrate the effects that are produced by the preaching of the word; and we believe that it has an allusion directly, to the commencement, or the setting up of the kingdom in that age: therefore, we shall continue to trace his sayings concerning this kingdom from that time forth, even unto the end of the world.

Another parable put he forth unto them, saying, (which parable has an allusion to the setting up of the kingdom, in that age of the world also) the

407. See Matthew 13:19.
408. See Matthew 13:20–23.
409. See Matthew 13:11.

kingdom of Heaven is likened unto a man which sowed good seed in his field, but while men slept an enemy came and sowed tares among the wheat and went his way; but when the blade was sprung up, and brought forth fruit, then appeared the tares also; so the servants of the householder came and said unto him, sir, didst not thou sow good seed in thy field? from whence then hath it tares? He said unto them, an enemy hath done this. The servants said unto him wilt thou then that we go and gather them up; but he said nay, lest while ye gather up the tares, ye root up also the wheat with them.— Let both grow together until the harvest, and in the time of the harvest, I will say to the reapers, gather ye together first the tares, and bind them in bundles, to burn them; but gather the wheat into my barn.[410]

Now we learn by this parable, not only the setting up of the kingdom in the days of the Savior, which is represented by the good seed, which produced fruit, but also the corruptions of the church, which is represented by the tares, which were sown by the enemy, which his disciples would fain [p. 226] have plucked up, or cleansed the church of, if their views had been favored by the Savior; but he, knowing all things, says not so; as much as to say, your views are not correct, the church is in its infancy, and if you take this rash step, you will destroy the wheat or the church with the tares: therefore it is better to let them grow together until the harvest, or the end of the world, which means the destruction of the wicked; which is not yet fulfilled; as we shall show hereafter, in the Savior's explanation of the parable, which is so plain, that there is no room left for dubiety upon the mind, notwithstanding the cry of the priests, parables, parables! figures, figures! mystery, mystery! all is mystery! but we find no room for doubt here, as the parables were all plainly elucidated.

And again, another parable put he forth unto them, having an allusion to the kingdom which should be set up, just previous or at the time of harvest, which reads as follows:—The kingdom of heaven is like to a grain of mustard seed, which a man took and sowed in his field, which indeed is the least of all seeds, but when it is grown it is the greatest among herbs, and becometh a tree, so that the birds of the air come and lodge in the branches thereof.[411] Now we can discover plainly, that this figure is given to represent the church as it shall come forth in the last days. Behold the kingdom of heaven is likened unto it. Now what is like unto it?

Let us take the book of Mormon, which a man took and hid in his field; securing it by his faith, to spring up in the last days, or in due time: let us behold it coming forth out of the ground, which is indeed accounted the least

---

410. See Matthew 13:24–30; see also Revelation, 6 Dec. 1832, in *JSP*, D2:326 [D&C 86:1–7].
411. See Matthew 13:31–32.

of all seeds, but behold it branching forth; yea, even towering, with lofty branches, and God-like majesty, until it becomes the greatest of all herbs: and it is truth, and it has sprouted and come forth out of the earth; and righteousness begins to look down from heaven; and God is sending down his powers, gifts and angels, to lodge in the branches thereof: The kingdom of heaven is like unto a mustard seed. Behold, then, is not this the kingdom of heaven that is raising its head in the last days, in the majesty of its God; even the church of the Latter day saints,—like an impenetrable, immovable rock in the midst of the mighty deep, exposed to storms and tempests of satan, but has, thus far, remained steadfast and is still braving the mountain waves of opposition, which are driven by the tempestuous winds of sinking crafts, have and are still dashing with tremendous foam, across its triumphing brow, urged onward with redoubled fury by the enemy of righteousness, with his pitchfork of lies, as you will see fairly represented in a cut, contained in Mr. [Eber D.] Howe's "Mormonism Unveiled?"[412]

And we hope that this adversary of truth will continue to stir up the sink of iniquity, that people may the more readily discern between the righteous and wicked. We also would notice one of the modern sons of Sceva,[413] who would fain have made people believe that he could cast out devils, by a certain pamphlet (viz. the "Millenial Harbinger,") that went the rounds through our country, who felt so fully authorized to brand Jo Smith, with the appellation of Elymus the sorcerer,[414] and to say with Paul, O full of all subtilty and all mischief, thou child of the devil, thou enemy of all righteousness, wilt thou not cease to pervert the right ways of the Lord![415] We would reply to this gentleman—Paul we know, and Christ we know, but who are ye?[416] And with the best of feelings, we would say to him, in the language of Paul to those who said they were John's disciples, but had not so much as heard there was a Holy Ghost, to repent and be baptised for the remission of sins by those who have legal authority, and under their hands you shall receive the Holy Ghost, according to the scriptures.[417]

---

412. On 28 November 1834, Eber D. Howe issued *Mormonism Unvailed* from his press in Painesville, Ohio. The book's frontispiece included a woodcut image of Satan holding a pitchfork and kicking JS on the backside through the air after JS had obtained the "gold bible." JS's comments here appear to reference that image and Howe's book generally as a "pitchfork of lies." (See "To the Public," *Painesville [OH] Telegraph*, 31 Jan. 1834, [3]; and Howe, *Mormonism Unvailed*, 275–276.)

413. See Acts 19:11–20.

414. See Acts 13:4–12.

415. See Acts 13:10; see also "Practical Thoughts and Reflections," *Millennial Harbinger*, May 1848, 288.

416. See Acts 19:15. In the book of Acts, chapter 19, seven sons of a Jewish priest try unsuccessfully to cast out an evil spirit by invoking Jesus's name.

417. See Acts 2:38. In the February 1831 issue of the *Millennial Harbinger*, Campbell's article "Delusions" includes this line: "I have never felt myself so fully authorized to address mortal man in the

Then laid they *their* hands on them, and they received the Holy Ghost.—Acts: ch. 8, v. 17.

And, when Paul had laid *his* hands upon them, the Holy Ghost came on them; and they spake with tongues, and prophesied.—Acts: ch. 19, v. 6.

Of the doctrine of baptisms, and of laying on of hands, and of resurrection of the dead, and of eternal judgment.—Heb. ch. 6, v.2.

How then shall they call on him in whom they have not believed? and how shall they believe in him of whom they have not heard? and how shall they hear without a preacher? And how shall they preach except they be sent? as it is written, How beautiful are the feet of them that preach the gospel of peace, and bring glad tidings of good things!—Rom. ch. 10, v. 14–15.

But if this man will not take our admonition, but will persist in his wicked course, we hope that he will continue trying to cast out devils, that we may [p. 227] have the clearer proof that the kingdom of satan is divided against itself, and consequently cannot stand: for a kingdom divided against itself, speedily hath an end.[418] If we were disposed to take this gentleman upon his own ground and justly heap upon him that which he so readily and unjustly heaps upon others, we might go farther; we might say that he has wickedly and maliciously lied about, vilified and traduced the characters of innocent men. We might invite the gentleman to a public investigation of these matters; yea, and we do challenge him to an investigation upon any or all principles wherein he feels opposed to us, in public or in private.

We might farther say that, we could introduce him to "Mormonism Unveiled." Also to the right honorable Doct. P. Hurlburt [Doctor Philastus Hurlbut], who is the legitimate author of the same, who is not so much a doctor of physic, as of falsehood, or by name[419] We could also give him an introduction to the reverend Mr. Howe, the illegitimate author of "Mormonism Unveiled," in order to give currency to the publication, as Mr. Hurlburt, about

---

style in which Paul addressed Elymas the sorcerer as I feel towards this Atheist [Joseph] Smith." Campbell referred to Acts 13:6–12. JS responded with his own references to the book of Acts, including Acts 19:2–15. Campbell and JS shared the belief in the doctrine of baptism by immersion for the remission of sins, but a December 1830 revelation to JS further instructed that following baptism came the conferral of the gift of the Holy Ghost through authority, "by the laying on of hands even as the Apostles of old." ("Delusions," *Millennial Harbinger*, 7 Feb. 1831, 96; Revelation, 7 Dec. 1830, in *JSP*, D1:220 [D&C 35:3–6].)

418. See Matthew 12:25–28.

419. "Doctor" was Hurlbut's given first name. He did not practice medicine.

this time, was bound over to court, for threatening life.[420] He is also an associate of the celebrated Mr. [Orris] Clapp, who has of late immortalised his name by swearing that he would not believe a Mormon under oath; and by his polite introduction to said Hurlburt's wife, which cost him (as we have been informed) a round sum.[421] Also his son Mathew [Matthew Clapp] testified that, the book of Mormon had been proved false an hundred times, by How's book: and also, that he would not believe a Mormon under oath.[422] And also we could mention the reverend Mr. [Adamson] Bentley, who, we believe, has been actively engaged in injuring the character of his brother-in-law, viz: Elder S[idney] Rigdon.[423]

Now, the above statements are according to our best information: and we believe them to be true; and this is as fair a sample of the doctrine of Campbellism, as we ask, taking the statements of these gentlemen, and judging them by their fruits. And we might add many more to the black catalogue; even the ringleaders, not of the Nazarenes, for how can any good thing come

---

420. JS here suggested that Hurlbut should have been credited as the author of *Mormonism Unvailed* because he provided the bulk of the research, developed the Spalding theory, and obtained the affidavits published in that book but that Howe was named as author because of court proceedings against Hurlbut in 1834 that might have discredited the book. Hurlbut faced charges and was fined and ordered to "keep the peace" on 9 April 1834, after he threatened to "beat wound or kill" JS. (Geauga Co., OH, Court of Common Pleas Record, vol. P, pp. 431–432, 31 Mar. 1834, microfilm 20,278, U.S. and Canada Record Collection, FHL; see also "Joseph Smith Documents from February 1833 through March 1834," in *JSP*, D3:xxv–xxvii; Note to Newel K. Whitney, ca. Oct. 1833–Early 1834, in *JSP*, D3:315–320; JS, Journal, 28 Jan. and 7–9 Apr. 1834, in *JSP*, J1:27, 38; and "Mormon Trial," *Chardon [OH] Spectator and Geauga Gazette,* 12 Apr. 1834, [3].)

421. Orris Clapp of Mentor, Ohio, was patriarch of a prominent family, a follower of Alexander Campbell, and formerly a neighbor of Sidney Rigdon. JS here appears to insinuate that Clapp had an affair with Maria Woodbury, Hurlbut's wife. Several later articles in the *Messenger and Advocate* referred to Clapp's immorality and used it to discredit Campbellism. (Sidney Rigdon to Oliver Cowdery, in *LDS Messenger and Advocate,* Apr. 1836, 2:298–299; "Persecution," *LDS Messenger and Advocate,* Jan. 1837, 3:436–439.)

422. Sidney Rigdon later reiterated this claim. He stated: "Old Clapp, with his two pious sons . . . did actually go and swear, before a justice of the peace, that they would not believe any of the saints under oath; when there was not one out of fifty of them, whose names they had ever heard, nor of whom they had the most distant knowledge; and knew nothing about them, still they were ready to swear, without the most distant knowledge of them, that they would not believe them under oath. If this does not amount to false swearing, in the sight of the great Jehovah, I must confess I do not know what does." ("Persecution," *LDS Messenger and Advocate,* Jan. 1837, 3:438.)

423. Adamson Bentley settled in Warren, Ohio, in 1810 and became the first minister of Concord Baptist Church. Rigdon lived with Bentley when he first moved to Ohio in 1819 or 1820. The two ministered together in the 1820s for northeastern Ohio's Reformed Baptist movement, which became affiliated with Campbell's Disciples of Christ in 1832. Both Bentley and Rigdon married daughters of Dorcas and Jeremiah Brooks, making them brothers-in-law after Rigdon's marriage in 1820. Their relationship became estranged when Rigdon converted to the Latter-day Saint faith in 1830. (See Hayden, *Early History of the Disciples in the Western Reserve,* 13–14, 102–109; and Rollmann, "Early Baptist Career of Sidney Rigdon," 39, 47–49.)

out of Nazareth,[424] but of the far-famed Mentor mob: all sons and legitimate heirs to the same spirit of Alexander Campbell, and "Mormonism Unveiled," according to the representation in the cut spoken of above.[425]

The above cloud of darkness has long been beating with mountain waves upon the immovable rock of the church of the Latter Day Saints, and notwithstanding all this, the mustard seed is still towering its lofty branches, higher and higher, and extending itself wider and wider, and the charriot wheels of the kingdom are still rolling on, impelled by the mighty arm of Jehovah; and in spite of all opposition will still roll on until his words are all fulfilled.

Our readers will excuse us for deviating from the subject, when they take into consideration the abuses, that have been heaped upon us heretofore, which we have tamely submitted to, until forbearance is no longer required at our hands, having frequently turned both the right and left cheek, we believe it our duty now to stand up in our own defence. With these remarks we shall proceed with the subject of the gathering.

And another parable spake he unto them: The kingdom of heaven is like unto leaven which a woman took and hid in three measures of meal, until the whole was leavened.[426] It may be understood that the church of the Latter Day Saints, has taken its rise from a little leaven that was put into three witnesses.[427] Behold, how much this is like the parable: it is fast leavening the lump, and will soon leaven the whole. But let us pass on.

All these things spake Jesus unto the multitudes, in parables, and without a parable spake he not unto them, that it might be fulfilled which was spoken by the prophet, saying: I will open my mouth in parables: I will utter things which have been kept secret from the foundation of the world: Then Jesus sent the multitude away and went into the house, and his disciples came unto him, saying, declare unto us the parable of the tares of the field. He answered and said unto them, he that soweth the good seed is the son of man; the field is the world; the good seed are the children of the kingdom, but the tares are the children of the wicked one.[428] Now let our readers mark the expression, the field is the world; the tares are the children of the wicked one: the enemy that sowed them is the devil; the harvest is the end of the world. Let them carefully

---

424. See John 1:46.

425. Mentor, Ohio, north of Kirtland, was home to a large congregation of Disciples of Christ, or Campbellites, and a stronghold for anti-Mormon activity. (See Pratt, *Short Account of a Shameful Outrage*, 3–11; and JS, Journal, 2 Dec. 1835, in *JSP*, J1:113–114.)

426. See Matthew 13:33.

427. See Testimony of Three Witnesses, Late June 1829, in *JSP*, D1:377–384. Eber D. Howe also published "The Testimony of Three Witnesses" in *Mormonism Unvailed*, 94–95.

428. See Matthew 13:34–38.

mark this [p. 228] expression also, *the end of the world*, and the reapers are the angels.[429] Now men cannot have any possible grounds to say that this is figurative, or that it does not mean what it says; for he is now explaining what he had previously spoken in parables; and according to this language, the end of the world is the destruction of the wicked; the harvest and the end of the world have an allusion directly to the human family in the last days, instead of the earth, as many have imagined, and that which shall precede the coming of the Son of man, and the restitution of all things spoken of by the mouth of all the holy prophets since the world began; and the angels are to have something to do in this great work, for they are the reapers: as therefore the tares are gathered and burned in the fire, so shall it be in the end of this world; that is, as the servants of God go forth warning the nations, both priests and people, and as they harden their hearts and reject the light of the truth, these first being delivered over unto the buffetings of satan, and the law and the testimony being closed up, as it was with the Jews, they are left in darkness, and delivered over unto the day of burning: thus being bound up by their creeds and their bands made strong by their *priests*, are prepared for the fulfilment of the saying of the Savior: the Son of man shall send forth his angels, and gather out of his kingdom all things that offend, and them which do iniquity, and shall cast them into a furnace of fire and there shall be wailing and gnashing of teeth.[430]

We understand, that the work of the gathering together of the wheat into barns, or garners, is to take place while the tares are being bound over, and preparing for the day of burning: that after the day of burnings, the righteous shall shine forth like the sun, in the kingdom of their Father: who hath ears to hear let him hear.

But to illustrate more clearly upon this gathering, we have another parable. Again the kingdom of heaven is like a treasure hid in a field, the which when a man hath found, he hideth and for joy thereof, goeth and selleth all that he hath and buyeth that field:[431] for the work after this pattern, see the church of the Latter Day Saints, selling all that they have and gathering themselves together unto a place that they may purchase for an inheritance, that they may be together and bear each other's afflictions in the day of calamity.

Again the kingdom of heaven is like unto a merchant man seeking goodly pearls, who when he had found one pearl of great price, went and sold all that he had, and bought it.[432] For the work of this example, see men travelling to

---

429. See Matthew 13:38–39.
430. See Matthew 13:41–42.
431. See Matthew 13:44.
432. See Matthew 13:45–46.

find places for Zion, and her stakes or remnants, who when they find the place for Zion, or the pearl of great price; straitway sell all that they have and buy it.

Again the kingdom of heaven is like unto a net that was cast into the sea, and gathered of every kind, which when it was full they drew to shore, and sat down and gathered the good into vessels, and cast the bad away.—[433] For the work of this pattern, behold the seed of Joseph, spreading forth the gospel net,[434] upon the face of the earth, gathering of every kind, that the good may be saved in vessels prepared for that purpose, and the angels will take care of the bad: so shall it be at the end of the world, the angels shall come forth, and sever the wicked from among the just, and cast them into the furnace of fire, and there shall be wailing and gnashing of teeth.

Jesus saith unto them, have you understood all these things? they say unto him yea Lord:[435] and we say yea Lord, and well might they say yea Lord, for these things are so plain and so glorious, that every Saint in the last days must respond with a hearty *amen* to them.

Then said he unto them, therefore every scribe which is instructed into the kingdom of heaven, is like unto a man that is an house holder; which bringeth forth out of his treasure things that are new and old.[436]

For the work of this example, see the book of Mormon, coming forth out of the treasure of the heart;[437] also the covenants given to the Latter Day Saints: also the translation of the bible: thus bringing forth out of the heart, things new and old: thus answering to three measures of meal, undergoing the purifying touch by a revelation of Jesus Christ, and the ministering of angels, who have already commenced this work in the last days, which will answer to the leaven which leavened the whole lump. Amen. [p. 229]

So I close but shall continue the subject in another number.[438]

In the bonds of the new and everlasting covenant.

JOSEPH SMITH, jr.

To J[ohn] WHITMER Esq.

---

433. See Matthew 13:47–48.

434. See Genesis 49:22.

435. See Matthew 13:51.

436. See Matthew 13:52.

437. See Matthew 12:35; and Luke 6:45.

438. No additional letter in this series appeared in the *Messenger and Advocate*.

PART 2: 5 DECEMBER 1835– 7 FEBRUARY 1836

As JS continued to prepare church leaders in Kirtland, Ohio, to receive an endowment of divine power in the nearly completed House of the Lord, jealousy and accusations of inequality persisted among some members of the Quorum of the Twelve. In a 15 December 1835 letter to JS, Orson Hyde accused Reynolds Cahoon of unfairly restricting Hyde's credit at the temple committee store while allowing JS's younger brother, William Smith, to accrue substantial debt.[1] A number of documents in this part also relate to a mid-December confrontation between JS and William. On 17 December, tension between the brothers erupted into violence during a session of the Kirtland debating school.[2] The fight, which left JS unable to "sit down, or rise up, without help," and subsequent events culminated in ecclesiastical charges against William Smith and a disciplinary hearing before the church presidency and other leaders.[3]

JS lamented the divisions that existed among the Twelve and within his own family, and his 1 January 1836 journal entry expressed hope that the Saints would "come forth like gold seven times tried in the fire, being made perfect throug[h] sufferings, and temptations, and the blessings of heaven and earth multiplyed upon our heads."[4] The new year did in fact usher in a period of relative calm for JS. In the weeks after reconciling with William, JS juggled various ecclesiastical responsibilities, including solemnizing several marriages and giving blessings to two men who had participated in the Camp of Israel expedition.[5] During the second week of January, JS also participated in a three-day feast for the poor, hosted by Bishop Newel K. Whitney and his wife, Elizabeth Ann Smith Whitney.[6] In addition to attending to church duties, JS devoted significant time to studying the Hebrew language. On 4 January, he organized a Hebrew School, which his peers asked him to lead

---

1. Letter from Orson Hyde, 15 Dec. 1835, pp. 107–108 herein.

2. Tension had been building between the two brothers for nearly six weeks. (See JS, Journal, 29 Oct. 1835, in *JSP*, J1:77–79; Minutes, 29 Oct. 1835, pp. 26–29 herein; and Letter from William Smith, 18 Dec. 1835, pp. 109–115 herein.)

3. Letter to William Smith, ca. 18 Dec. 1835, p. 119 herein; Charges against William Smith Preferred to the Church Presidency, 29 Dec. 1835, pp. 127–128 herein; Minutes, 2 Jan. 1836, pp. 128–131 herein.

4. JS, Journal, 1 Jan. 1836, in *JSP*, J1:141.

5. Historical Introduction to Marriage Certificate for William Cahoon and Nancy Gibbs, 18 Jan. 1836, pp. 154–155 herein; Blessing to Lorenzo Barnes, 3 Jan. 1836, pp. 131–135 herein; Blessing to Alvin Winegar, 7 Feb. 1836, pp. 165–168 herein.

6. Historical Introduction to Note from Newel K. Whitney, 9 Jan. 1836, pp. 135–137 herein.

until the school committee was able to identify and hire a trained teacher. On 26 January, a Hebrew scholar named Joshua Seixas arrived in Kirtland and began teaching the school, which included JS as a pupil.[7]

In mid-January, JS met with the presidency and other leaders of the church to "take into concideration the subject of the Solemn Assembly."[8] This "grand council"—consisting of the church presidency, the Missouri presidency, the Quorum of the Twelve, and the high councils and bishoprics of Kirtland and Missouri—voted on various administrative changes, including filling vacant leadership positions, and appointed JS, Sidney Rigdon, Hyrum Smith, William W. Phelps, and David Whitmer as a committee to draft rules of conduct for the House of the Lord. On 15 January, the committee presented their proposals—which stressed order and reverence while in the House of the Lord—to the grand council, which approved the rules.[9] The next day, JS and other members of the presidency met with the Twelve, who had requested an opportunity to air unresolved grievances. After listening to each of the men speak, JS acknowledged their concerns and asked forgiveness for sometimes speaking too harshly and injuring their feelings. It appears that the meeting largely resolved their differences; as JS's journal records, the men "took each others by the hand in confirmation of our covenant and their was a perfect unison of feeling on this occasion, and our hearts overflowed with blessings, which we pronounced upon eachothers heads."[10]

The spirit of unity continued into the following week. On 21 January, JS introduced to the presidency and other select men a new ritual in which they washed and perfumed their bodies and then anointed each other with pure oil, all in preparation for the solemn assembly and endowment of power.[11] After JS received blessings and prophecies from Joseph Smith Sr. and the presidency, he and several others reported that they saw a vision of God and the heavens and that angelic hosts ministered to them.[12] In the week following this heavenly manifestation, JS and the presidency continued to organize the church's priesthood officers and prepare them to receive the "holy anointing."[13]

———— ⁊ ————

7. JS, Journal, 4 and 26 Jan. 1836, in *JSP*, J1:143, 173.

8. JS, Journal, 12 Jan. 1836, in *JSP*, J1:147.

9. Minutes, 13 Jan. 1836, pp. 138–143 herein; Rules and Regulations, 14 Jan. 1836, pp. 143–145 herein; Minutes, 15 Jan. 1836, p. 147 herein.

10. Minutes, 16 Jan. 1836, p. 153 herein.

11. Historical Introduction to Visions, 21 Jan. 1836 [D&C 137], p. 157 herein. The House of the Lord in Kirtland was dedicated on 27 March 1836; three days later, JS and a group of approximately three hundred men met in a solemn assembly, where they participated in ordinances and experienced spiritual manifestations that they regarded as the long-promised endowment of power. (Minutes and Prayer of Dedication, 27 Mar. 1836, pp. 188–208 herein [D&C 109]; Minutes, 30 Mar. 1836, pp. 216–221 herein.)

12. Historical Introduction to Visions, 21 Jan. 1836 [D&C 137], pp. 157–158 herein.

13. Kirtland Elders Quorum, "Record," 25 Jan. 1836.

Letter to Editor, 5 December 1835

Source Note

JS, Letter, Kirtland Township, Geauga Co., OH, to the editor of Latter Day Saints' Messenger and Advocate *[John Whitmer], Kirtland Township, Geauga Co., OH, 5 Dec. 1835. Featured version published in "To the Editor of the Messenger and Advocate,"* Latter Day Saints' Messenger and Advocate, *Dec. 1835, 2:240. For more information on* Latter Day Saints' Messenger and Advocate, *see Source Notes for Multiple-Entry Documents, p. 527 herein.*

Historical Introduction

JS wrote this letter to John Whitmer, editor of the *Latter Day Saints' Messenger and Advocate,* to address the problem of his continually receiving letters with unpaid postage. Before an 1847 federal statute required postage stamps as proof of payment to send letters, the addressee rather than the sender of a letter could be liable for paying the postage.[14] Depending on the number of pages and the distance traveled, postage on a letter could cost anywhere from six cents to more than one dollar,[15] and pieces of mail often went unclaimed because the recipient could not or simply did not pay the postage. Single-page letters sent from church members in Missouri to Kirtland, Ohio, would have cost twenty-five cents; larger packages sent between the two church centers cost in excess of a dollar, which was more than the average daily wage of an agricultural laborer in the 1830s.[16]

This problem of unpaid postage on letters addressed to JS was not new. In an 1833 letter, he similarly urged those sending him letters through the post office to "pay the postage as we are receiving letters from all parts and have to pay a great sum of money otherwise we shall be under the necessity of letting them remain in the office as we are not able to pay so much."[17] Any party receiving a large number of postage-unpaid letters would have had a similar problem. In the July 1835 issue of the *Messenger and Advocate,* the editor printed the following notice: "Letters to the Editor, or publishers, of the Messenger and Advocate, must be *post paid*, or they will not be taken out of the office. Every honest man must see the propriety of our requiring the postage on letters, paid. If

---

14. An Act to Establish Certain Post Routes and for Other Purposes [3 Mar. 1847], *Statutes at Large and Treaties of the United States of America,* chap. 63, p. 201, sec. 11; see also Summerfield and Hurd, *U.S. Mail,* 45–46.

15. In the 1830s, a single-page letter sent less than thirty-six miles cost six cents. A single-page letter sent between 150 and 400 miles cost 18¾ cents, while the same letter sent more than 400 miles cost 25 cents. A two-page letter cost double, a three-page letter triple, and any letter four pages or more cost quadruple the rate of the single-page letter. Packages weighing more than an ounce started at one dollar. (Force, *National Calendar,* 227; An Act to Reduce into One the Several Acts Establishing and Regulating the Post-Office Department [3 Mar. 1825], *Public Statutes at Large,* 18th Cong., 2nd Sess., chap. 64, pp. 102–114; John, *Spreading the News,* 121–124, 159.)

16. See Letter to Church Leaders in Jackson County, MO, 25 June 1833, in *JSP,* D3:147–158; see also Margo, *Wages and Labor Markets in the United States,* 67, table 3A.5.

17. Letter to John S. Carter, 13 Apr. 1833, in *JSP,* D3:63–64.

we were to pay the postage on a hundred letters, each letter containing a subscriber, the sum might be *twenty five or fifty dollars*, and where is the profits?"[18]

The same day JS dictated this short letter to the editor, which he intended for public notice, he observed that receiving letters with the postage unpaid was a "common occurence." According to his journal entry for that day, JS was "subjected to a great deal of expence in this way, by those who I know nothing about, only that they are destitute of good manners, for if people wish to be benefited with information from me, common respect and good breeding would dictate, them to pay the postage on their letters."[19]

Despite these public notices in 1835, the problem continued. The *Messenger and Advocate* published a reminder in October 1836 that "all communications addressed to us, to ensure attention, must come free of postage."[20] By late January 1837, JS wrote yet another notice stating that he would not accept letters unless the sender paid the postage.[21]

Document Transcript

To the Editor of the Messenger and Advocate:

Dear Brother—I wish to inform my friends and all others, abroad, that whenever they wish to address me thro' the Post Office, they will be kind enough to pay the postage on the same.

My friends will excuse me in this matter, as I am willing to pay postage on letters to hear from *them;* but am unwilling to pay for insults and menaces,—consequently, must refuse *all*, unpaid.

Yours in the gospel,

JOSEPH SMITH, jr.

Kirtland, Dec. 5, 1835.

———— ℰↃ ————

Letter from Orson Hyde, 15 December 1835

Source Note

Orson Hyde, Letter, Kirtland Township, Geauga Co., OH, to JS, Kirtland Township, Geauga Co., OH, 15 Dec. 1835. Featured version copied [ca. 17 Dec. 1835] in JS, Journal, 1835–1836, pp. 70–74; handwriting of Warren Parrish; JS Collection, CHL. For more information on JS, Journal, 1835–1836, see Source Notes for Multiple-Entry Documents, p. 524 herein.

---

18. Notice, *LDS Messenger and Advocate,* July 1835, 1:160, italics in original.

19. JS, Journal, 5 Dec. 1835, in *JSP,* J1:116.

20. "Prospectus," *LDS Messenger and Advocate,* Oct. 1836, 3:386.

21. Notice, 24 Jan. 1837, p. 344 herein.

Historical Introduction

In the latter half of 1835, Orson Hyde was caught up in several disagreements involving the church's top leadership. As one of the Twelve Apostles, Hyde had been active in the quorum's mission to the eastern United States earlier in the year, during which he and William E. McLellin were reprimanded for criticizing Sidney Rigdon of the First Presidency. Church leaders suspended the two from their apostolic duties pending reconciliation.[22] The matter was resolved at a council meeting held in Kirtland, Ohio, on 26 September 1835, when Hyde and McLellin "frankly confessed" that they were at fault and the council forgave and reinstated them.[23] Another conflict arose several weeks later, however, after a 3 November revelation chastised the Twelve for inequality "in the division of the moneys which came into their hands." Hyde, McLellin, and David W. Patten were singled out for an unspecified sin, and all of the Twelve were encouraged to "humble themselves."[24] Two days later, on 5 November 1835, Hyde and McLellin visited JS and "expressed some little dissatisfaction" with the revelation. JS's journal notes that after the two apostles examined "their own hearts," they acknowledged the revelation "to be the word of the Lord and said they were satisfied."[25]

Nevertheless, on 15 December 1835, Hyde wrote to JS with a litany of complaints. Specifically, Hyde accused Reynolds Cahoon, a member of the committee to build the House of the Lord in Kirtland, of unfairly restricting credit to him at the committee store while allowing William Smith to accumulate a large debt.[26] Both Hyde and Smith were presumably expected to pay for anything they obtained from the committee store. However, Ira Ames, the store's clerk, later listed William Smith among the building committee members. If Smith was a part of the building committee in some fashion, it is possible that the store handled his debts differently than it did others.[27] In any case, Hyde was likely unaware of Smith's position or any special financial arrangement he had with the store.

---

22. Letter to Quorum of the Twelve, 4 Aug. 1835, in *JSP,* D4:375–376; Letter to the Editor, *LDS Messenger and Advocate,* Oct. 1835, 2:204–207.

23. Minutes, 26 Sept. 1835, in *JSP,* D4:441; JS, Journal, 26 Sept. 1835, in *JSP,* J1:64–66; see also Orson Hyde and William E. McLellin, Kirtland, OH, Letter to the Editor, Oct. 1835, in *LDS Messenger and Advocate,* Oct. 1835, 2:204–207.

24. Revelation, 3 Nov. 1835, pp. 32–36 herein. In a discourse given to the Quorum of the Twelve Apostles on 12 November 1835, JS continued to admonish them to repent, humble themselves, and prepare for the endowment of power in the House of the Lord. (Discourse, 12 Nov. 1835, pp. 49–51 herein.)

25. JS, Journal, 5 Nov. 1835, in *JSP,* J1:84.

26. The committee store in Kirtland, Ohio, was run by the committee to build the House of the Lord, which consisted of Hyrum Smith, Reynolds Cahoon, and Jared Carter. Cahoon appears to have been the store manager. By June 1835, the three joined together as a mercantile firm under the name Cahoon, Carter & Co. The store appears to have been in operation by October 1835, and it likely served two functions: it supported the construction of the House of the Lord by purchasing goods on credit or from donations obtained by the Twelve and others and then making those goods available in exchange for labor or payment, and it offered its stock for sale to anyone else in the area to turn a profit. (Advertisement, *Northern Times,* 9 Oct. 1835, [4]; "Anniversary of the Church of Latter Day Saints," *LDS Messenger and Advocate,* Apr. 1837, 3:488; JS, Journal, 7 Oct. 1835, in *JSP,* J1:69.)

27. Ames, Autobiography, [12]. Though William Smith's relationship with the building committee and its store is not known for certain, an 1838 legal document specifies that he was not a partner of the

In his letter to JS, Hyde invoked the 3 November revelation to demonstrate that the inequality it condemned still continued among the Twelve. Drawing on the parable of the twelve sons that is found in the 3 November revelation, Hyde suggested that each of the Twelve had a right to be treated equally by the committee store, particularly since they had all helped raise funds for the store—and for the completion of the House of the Lord—during their mission to the eastern United States.[28] Hyde further noted that while on their mission, the Twelve had been dependent upon donations to support themselves and their families but that he had given the committee "$275 in cash," thereby reducing himself to "nothing in a pecuniary point." He encouraged JS to uphold the principles of impartiality and equality.

The same day he wrote the letter, Hyde handed it to JS, whose journal notes that the letter "laserated" JS's feelings but did not weaken his conviction that he "had dealt in righteousness" with Hyde "in all things and endeavoured to promote his happiness and well being." JS felt that Hyde's reflections were "ungrateful and founded in jealousy and that the adversary is striving with all his subtle devises and influence to destroy him by causing a division amon[g] the twelve that God has chosen to open the gospel Kingdom in all the nations." JS's journal contains a prayer that Hyde would be "delivered from the power of the destroyer" so that he and all the apostles would be ready for the upcoming solemn assembly in the House of the Lord.[29]

The next day, 16 December, JS went to a meeting at the Kirtland schoolhouse to discuss Hyde's letter with the church's presidency. Upon his arrival at the meeting, JS realized that he had lost Hyde's letter, but he recounted what he could of it to those present. The council agreed to table the matter until 20 December as "they had not time to attend to it on the account of other buisness."[30] Before that occurred, Hyde visited JS on 17 December 1835 and presented him with a second copy of the letter. The two men conversed about Hyde's objections until Hyde was appeased and agreed to attend the Hebrew School in Kirtland. JS forgave Hyde "with every expression of friendship that a gentleman, and a Christian could manifest" and attributed Hyde's "ingratitude" to a lack of "correct information," possibly referring to Hyde being uninformed of William Smith's association with the building committee. JS also acknowledged that Reynolds Cahoon had mistreated Hyde. With the matter "settled amicably," JS and Hyde parted with mutual goodwill.[31] JS later spoke with Cahoon about extending credit to the Twelve Apostles on equal terms.[32]

---

mercantile firm Cahoon, Carter & Co., the entity responsible for running the committee store. (William W. Spencer v. Reynolds Cahoon et al., 25 Jan. 1838, in Cowdery, Docket Book, 349.)

28. Revelation, 3 Nov. 1835, pp. 35–36 herein; see also Revelation, 2 Jan. 1831, in *JSP*, D1:232 [D&C 38:26]. During their recent five-month mission, Hyde and his colleagues in the Quorum of the Twelve Apostles solicited funds for the House of the Lord, for purchasing lands in Zion, and for church publications. JS considered the committee store an integral part of financing construction on the House of the Lord. (Letter to Quorum of the Twelve, 4 Aug. 1835, in *JSP*, D4:371–378.)

29. JS, Journal, 15 Dec. 1835, in *JSP*, J1:123.

30. JS, Journal, 16 Dec. 1835, in *JSP*, J1:123.

31. JS, Journal, 17 Dec. 1835, in *JSP*, J1:128.

32. JS History, vol. B-1, addenda, 2.

The version of the letter presented here is the second copy of Hyde's letter, as copied into JS's journal by Warren Parrish, likely upon receipt on 17 December.

Document Transcript

Dec 15th 1835
President Smith

Sir you may esteem it a novel circumstance to receive a written communication from me at this time.

My reasons for writing are the following. I have some things which I wish to communicate to you, and feeling a greater liberty to do it by writing alone by myself, I take this method; and it is generally the case that you are thronged with buisness and not convenient to spend much time in conversing upon subjects of the following nature. Therefore let these excuses paliate the novelty of the circumstance and patiently hear my recital.

After the committee had received their stock of fall and winter goods, I went to Elder [Reynolds] Cahoon and told him that I was destitute of a cloak and wanted him to trust me until Spring for materials to make one. He told me that [p. 70] he would trust me until January, but must then have his pay as the payments for the goods become due at that time. I told him that I know not from whence the money would come and I could not promise it so soon.

But in a few weeks after I unexpectedly obtained the money to buy a cloak and applyed immediately to Elder C for one and told him that I had the cash to pay for it, but he said that the materials for cloaks were all sold and that he could not accommodately me, and I will here venture a guess that he has not realized the cash for one cloak pattern.

A few weeks after this I called on Elder Cahoon again and told him that I wanted cloth for some shirts to the amount of 4 or 5 Dollars I told him that I would pay him in the spring and sooner if I could.

He told me let me have it not long after, my school was established and some of the hands who laboured on the house attended and wished to pay me at the Committee Store for their tuition.— I called at the Store to see if any nego[ti]ation could be made and they take me off where I owed them, but no such negotiation could be made.[33] These with some other circumstances of like character called forth the following. reflections.

---

33. It appears that construction workers on the House of the Lord received credit from the committee store for the time they labored on the building. Hyde's students, some of whom also served as construction workers on the House of the Lord, apparently proposed an arrangement wherein they would pay Hyde for the education through their accounts at the committee store.

In the first place I gave the committee $275 in cash besides some more and during the last season have traveled thro the Middle and Eastern states to suport and uphold the store and in so doing have reduced myself to nothing in a pecuniary point.[34] Under [p. 71] these circumstances this establishment refused to render me that accomodation which a worldlings establishment would have gladly done, and one too, which never ⟨received⟩ a donation from ~~my~~ me nor in whose favour I never raised my voice or ~~extended~~ ⟨exerted⟩ my influence.

But after all this, thought I, it may be right and I will be still— Un[t]il not long since I asertained that Elder Wᵐ Smith could go to the store and get whatever he pleased, and no one to say why do ye so, until his account has amounted to seven Hundred Dollars or there abouts and that he was a silent partner in the conce[r]n yet not acknowledged ⟨as⟩ such fearing that his creditors would make a hawl upon the Store.

While we were abroad this last season we straind every nerve to obtain a little something for our familys and regularly divided the monies equally for ought that I know, not knowing that William had such a fountain at hom[e] from whence he drew his support. I then called to mind the revelation in which myself, McLellen [William E. McLellin] and [David W.] Patten were chastened and also the quotation in that revelation of the parable of the twelve sons; as if the original meaning referd directly to the twelve apostles of the church of the Latter day Saints,[35] I would now ask if each one of the twelve has not an equal right to the same accomodations from that Store provided they are alike faithful. If not, with such a combination [p. 72] mine honor be not thou united.

If each one has the same right, take the baskets off from our noses or put one to Williams nose or if this cannot be done, reconcile the parable of the twelve sons with the superior privileges that William has.

Pardon me if I speak in parables or parody.

A certain shepherd had twelve sons and he sent them out one day to go and gather his flock which were scattered upon the mountains and in the vallies afar off they were all obedient to their fathers mandate, and at Evening they returned with the flock, and one son received wool enough to make him warm and comfortable and also recᵈ of the flesh and milk of the flock, the other eleven received not so much as one kid to make merry with their freinds[36]

---

34. On fund-raising efforts by Hyde and the Twelve in summer 1835, see Letter to Quorum of the Twelve, 4 Aug. 1835, in *JSP*, D4:371–378; and Revelation, 3 Nov. 1835, pp. 32–36 herein.

35. Revelation, 3 Nov. 1835, pp. 32–36 herein.

36. See Luke 15:29.

These facts with some others have disqualified my mind for studying the Hebrew Language at present, and believing, as I do, that I must sink or swim, or in other words take care of myself, I have thought that I should take the most efficient means in my power to get out of debt, and to this end I proposed taking the school, but if I am not thought competent to take the charge of ~~the~~ it, or worthy to be placed in that station, I must devise some other means to help myself; altho having been ordained to that office under your own hand with a promise that it should not be taken from me.—[37] [p. 73]

Conclusion of the whole matter is sutch I am willing to continue and do all I can provided we can share equal benefits one with the other, and upon no other principle whatever. If one has his suport from the "publick crib" let them all have it. But if one is pinched I am willing to be, provided we are all alike.

If the principle of impartiality and equality can be observed by all I think that I will not peep again—

If I am damned it will be for doing what I think is right.— There have been two applications made to me to go into business since I talked of taking the school, but it is in the world and I had rather remain in Kirtland if I can consistently

All I ask is Right

I Am Sir with Respect Your ob^{t.} serv^{t.}

Orson Hyde

To President J. Smith jn

Kirtland Geauga C^{o.} Ohio [p. 74]

——— ☙ ———

Letter from William Smith, 18 December 1835

Source Note

William Smith, Letter, [Kirtland Township, Geauga Co., OH], to JS, [Kirtland Township, Geauga Co., OH], 18 Dec. 1835. Featured version copied [ca. 18 Dec. 1835] in JS, Journal, 1835–1836, pp. 77–79; handwriting of Warren Parrish; JS Collection, CHL. For more information on JS, Journal, 1835–1836, see Source Notes for Multiple-Entry Documents, p. 524 herein.

---

37. Hyde instructed the first term of the School of the Prophets in early 1833, along with JS and Sidney Rigdon. Apparently he anticipated a similar role in the winter 1835–1836 term of the Elders School. In fall 1835, after Oliver Cowdery returned from New York with Hebrew books to study, JS, Orson Hyde, and others began searching for a scholar who could teach them Hebrew. By January 1836, JS had organized a new school for the study of the Hebrew language. Hyde eventually enrolled in and attended the Hebrew School. (School of the Prophets Salt Lake City Minutes, 3 Oct. 1883; JS, Journal, 20–21 Nov. 1835; 4 Jan. and 19 Feb. 1836, in *JSP*, J1:107.)

Historical Introduction

In fall 1835, JS and his younger brother William had a series of altercations, culminat-ing on 16 December when William assaulted JS.[38] Two days later, William penned an apologetic letter begging his brother for forgiveness. While it was not uncommon for men of the age—or brothers, for that matter—to settle their differences by fighting, the dispute between the Smith brothers was complicated by the fact that JS was revered as a prophet and William was a member of the Quorum of the Twelve Apostles.[39]

Little is known about the relationship between the two brothers during their formative years in New York, but there is no record of unusual friction between them prior to 1835. In his memoir, published nearly fifty years later, William recalled that in his youth he was "quite wild and inconsiderate, paying no attention to religion of any kind, for which I received fre-quent lectures from my mother and my brother Joseph."[40] In the years prior to the conflict, JS seemed particularly concerned with his younger brother's spiritual welfare. In February 1835, JS charged the Three Witnesses of the Book of Mormon—Oliver Cowdery, David Whitmer, and Martin Harris—with selecting the members of the Quorum of the Twelve Apostles. According to reminiscent accounts written by Cowdery and Whitmer, the men chose Phineas Young to be one of the apostles, but JS requested that they instead select William Smith. Whitmer recalled JS saying that "it was only the way which he [William] could be saved."[41]

Contemporary accounts also indicate that JS and his father, Joseph Smith Sr., had long been concerned about William's defiant and prideful nature. An 1833 entry in JS's journal described William as a "fierce lion" who "in the pride of his heart . . . will neglect the more weighty matters until his soul is bowed down in sorrow." Despite this apprehension, JS believed that William would eventually repent, "find forgiveness . . . [and] wax valiant."[42] In a blessing pronounced on William in December 1834, Joseph Smith Sr. reminded his son, "Thou hast greatly desired to see thy father's family redeemed from trouble. . . . But thou hast not altogether desired this thing in meek[n]ess, because thou hast not always known the Lord."[43] In a 4 August 1835 letter to the Quorum of the Twelve, many of whom were then serving missions in the eastern United States, JS and the church's presidency reminded William specifically "to be very humble and prayerful, and to remember further, that he that humbleth himself shall be exalted."[44]

---

38. JS, Journal, 29 Oct. and 16 Dec. 1835, in *JSP*, J1:77–79, 124.

39. In nineteenth-century America, men often defended their reputation, honor, or masculinity when questioned or challenged by others, sometimes violently. Historian Richard Bushman stated that "any personal hurt, any damage to reputation called for an immediate response. Vengeance was to be sought for a hurt, and no insult was to go unchallenged." Men might defend their honor or sort out their differ-ences through various physical confrontations, including verbal debate, fistfights, or even armed duels. (Bushman, "Character of Joseph Smith," 27; see also Wyatt-Brown, *Honor and Violence in the Old South;* and Gorn, "Social Significance of Fighting in the Southern Backcountry," 18–43.)

40. Smith, *William Smith on Mormonism,* 10.

41. Minutes, Discourse, and Blessings, 14–15 Feb. 1835, in *JSP*, D4:219–234; Oliver Cowdery, Elk Horn, Wisconsin Territory, to Brigham Young, 27 Feb. 1848, Brigham Young Office Files, CHL; Gurley, "Questions Asked of David Whitmer," [7].

42. JS, Journal, 18 Dec. 1833, in *JSP*, J1:23–24.

43. Joseph Smith Sr. to William Smith, Blessing, 9 Dec. 1834, in Patriarchal Blessings, 1:6.

44. Letter to Quorum of the Twelve, 4 Aug. 1835, in *JSP*, D4:378.

For his part, JS at times reacted to insult with physical confrontation. In June 1835, for example, he had a violent clash with his brother-in-law Calvin Stoddard.[45] Over sixty years later, Benjamin Johnson, a friend and admirer of JS, recalled that JS "would allow no arrogance or undue liberties, and criticisms, even by his associates, was rarely acceptable; and contradictions would rouse in him the lion at once."[46]

Conflict between JS and William Smith had flared up earlier in 1835. During a disciplinary hearing for David and Mary Cahoon Elliott on 29 October, the two brothers engaged in a heated argument over a deposition offered by their mother, Lucy Mack Smith.[47] The day after this confrontation, William notified JS by letter (no longer extant) that the Kirtland high council had proposed to censure William. He called on JS on 31 October, and, in the presence of Hyrum Smith and Warren Parrish, the two men revisited their dispute. According to JS's journal, William insisted that "he had not done wrong" and that JS "was always determined to carry [his] points whether right or wrong." When Hyrum interceded, William became agitated. "His passion increased," the entry recorded, and he "arose abruptly and declared that he wanted no more to do with us or the church and said we might take his license for he would have nothing to do with us." William sent his ecclesiastical license to JS—an action that likely signaled his intention to resign from the Quorum of the Twelve or separate himself entirely from the church. He then began to speak publicly against JS, turning even their brother Samuel against the church president.[48] Despite his frustration with William, JS seems to have been more grieved than angry with his brother's actions. A 31 October entry in JS's journal implored the Lord to forgive William and Samuel "and give them humility and repentance . . . I can only pray my heavenly Father to open their eyes . . . that they may extricate themselves from the snare they have fallen into."[49]

JS's apprehension about his brother was compounded by the fact that William was also an apostle. Tensions within the Quorum of the Twelve Apostles, dating back to August, remained, and William's actions only added to the difficulties.[50] On 3 November, JS dictated

---

45. JS, Kirtland, OH, Letter to the Editor, 22 June 1835, in *Painesville (OH) Telegraph,* 26 June 1835, [3].

46. Benjamin F. Johnson, Mesa, AZ, to George S. Gibbs, Salt Lake City, UT, 1903, CHL.

47. See Minutes, 29 Oct. 1835, pp. 26–29 herein; and JS, Journal, 29 Oct. 1835, in *JSP,* J1:77–79.

48. JS, Journal, 31 Oct. 1835, in *JSP,* J1:80–81. A license demonstrated that the bearer had been granted the authority for a particular calling or office. Though William sent his license to JS, there is no extant evidence to suggest that JS accepted William's resignation from the Quorum of the Twelve. In the letter featured here, William proposed "withdrawing from the office of the apostleship . . . and remaining a member in the church." JS later responded that this idea was a "stratigem of the evil one" and counseled William that by "maintaining your apostleship in rising up, and making one tremendous effort, you may overcome your passions, and please God." (Historical Introduction to License for Frederick G. Williams, 20 Mar. 1833, in *JSP,* D3:43–44; Letter to William Smith, ca. 18 Dec. 1835, p. 120 herein.)

49. JS's journal records that as he prayed that night, JS received a witness that his brother "would return to the church and repair the wrong he had done." (JS, Journal, 31 Oct. 1835, in *JSP,* J1:80–81.)

50. On the recent issues with the Twelve Apostles, see Historical Introduction to Revelation, 3 Nov. 1835, pp. 32–35 herein; Letter from Orson Hyde, 15 Dec. 1835, pp. 104–109 herein; JS, Journal, 3 Nov. and 15 Dec. 1835, in *JSP,* J1:83–84, 100–101; and Esplin, "Emergence of Brigham Young," 150–223.

a revelation that condemned the quorum for failing to be "sufficiently humble" before God. The revelation also stated that if the other eleven members would pray in faith and humility, seeking unity as a body, William would return.[51]

On 18 November, JS attended a debate in the home that William and his wife, Caroline Grant Smith, shared with his parents, Joseph Sr. and Lucy Mack Smith. JS's journal indicates that he arrived to find William and several other "young Elders" discussing whether it was "the design of Christ to establish his gospel by miracles." Though he later said that he had attended the debating school with a genuine interest in learning from the exchange, JS apparently found this particular three-hour debate too argumentative and its participants self-serving. JS instructed the elders to give "due deference to the opinions of others" and be careful to "handle sacred things verry sacredly."[52] As he had done during the Elliott trial, JS freely corrected William, both as his older brother and as his ecclesiastical leader.[53]

After months of tension, the brothers came to blows on 16 December, following another session of the debating school. After the evening's formal discussion had concluded, an argument commenced, in the words of JS's journal, "upon the impropiety of continueing the school."[54] The journal records that Hyrum raised the issue, but when William insisted that he would not allow any man to speak ill of the school in his house, JS apparently took exception. Despite Joseph Smith Sr.'s attempt to intervene, a war of words quickly devolved into physical confrontation. As JS was removing his jacket, William attacked him. Though the exact nature of the fight is unclear, it appears several men were involved, including Jared Carter, a member of the Kirtland high council. In the end, JS left the house "bruised and wounded" and unable to "sit down or rise up without help." JS's history described him being "grieved beyond expr[e]ssion, at the wickedness of his brother, who Cain like had sought to kill him."[55]

News of JS and William's physical and verbal fights reverberated throughout the Kirtland community.[56] For church members, William's attack on a man considered a prophet

---

51. Revelation, 3 Nov. 1835, pp. 32–36 herein.

52. JS, Journal, 18 Nov. and 18 Dec. 1835, in *JSP*, J1:106, 131; Letter to William Smith, ca. 18 Dec. 1835, pp. 117–118 herein. Some church members participated in several sessions of a debating school in fall 1835. A nationwide "lyceum movement" in this period emphasized adult schooling and debates, influencing communities like Kirtland. (See JS, Journal, 18 Nov. 1835; 12 and 16 Dec. 1835, in *JSP*, J1:106, 120–121, 124; see also Stevens, "Science, Culture, and Morality," 69–83; and Bode, *American Lyceum*.)

53. See Smith, *William Smith on Mormonism*, 15.

54. JS, Journal, 16 Dec. 1835, in *JSP*, J1:123–124.

55. JS, Journal, 16 and 18 Dec. 1835, in *JSP*, J1:123–124, 131–134; JS History, 1834–1836, 149–150, in *JSP*, H1:148.

56. Nearly fifty years later, former Kirtland justice of the peace John Dowen remembered that "Jo, his brother Bil, and others had a fight. . . . They were raising the devil all the time." Church member Daniel Tyler was likely referring to this period of animosity when he later recalled a time when "William Smith and others rebelled against the Prophet." At a meeting held in the Kirtland schoolhouse, Tyler remembered, a solemn JS offered a sincere and humble prayer "in behalf of those who accused him of having gone astray and fallen into sin." JS then told those in attendance that these men would receive a testimony "*this night* that I am clear and stand approved before the Lord." Tyler added, "The next Sabbath his brother William and several others made humble confessions before the public." (John C. Dowen,

was a serious matter.[57] The Twelve quickly summoned their colleague William to a council meeting to account for his behavior. The following day, William penned a letter to JS in which he pleaded for his brother's forgiveness.

Though the original letter is no longer extant, JS's scribes recorded versions of the letter in three different church records. In mid-December 1835, Warren Parrish copied it into JS's 1835–1836 journal, and that copy is featured here. Wafer residue in JS's 1835–1836 journal suggests that Parrish may have attached the original letter to the journal while copying it. Parrish also copied the letter into JS's 1834–1836 history.[58] Then, in October 1843, Willard Richards copied the text of the letter, most likely from JS's journal, into the history begun in 1838.[59] Significant differences between the featured text and the copy in the 1834–1836 history are noted; the copy in JS's later history has no significant differences.

Document Transcript

18th Ins^{t.}

Copy of a letter from Br. William Smith

Br. Joseph— Though I do not know but I have forfeited all right and title to the word brother, in concequence of what I have done, for I concider myself; that I am unworthy to be called one, after coming to myself and concidering upon what I have done I feel as though it was a duty, to make a humble confession to you for what I have done or what took place the other evening,—[60] but leave this part of the subject at present,— I was called to an account by the 12, yesterday for my conduct;[61] or they desired to know my mind or determination and what I was going to do I told them that on reflection upon the many difficulties that I had had with the church and the much disgrace I had brought upon myself in concequence of these things[62] and also that my health would not permit me to go to school to ⟨make⟩ any preperations for the endument and that my health was such that I was not able to travel,[63] I told them that it would be better for them to appoint one in the office that would be better able

Statement, 2 Jan. 1885, Collection of Manuscripts about Mormons, 1832–1954, Chicago History Museum; Tyler, "Recollections of the Prophet," 127–128, italics in original.)

57. See Minutes, 28 Dec. 1835, pp. 124–127 herein; and Minutes, 2 Jan. 1836, pp. 128–131 herein.

58. JS History, 1834–1836, 155–156, in *JSP*, H1:152–153.

59. JS History, vol. B-1, 667–668.

60. The version copied into JS's 1834–1836 history reads, "what took place at my house the other evening." (JS History, 1834–1836, 155, in *JSP*, H1:152.)

61. There is no extant record of this meeting.

62. JS's 1834–1836 history reads, "in consequence of my bad conduct." (JS History, 1834–1836, 155, in *JSP*, H1:152.)

63. Though William references his poor health several times, no extant records shed light on what kind of condition he might have had.

to fill it, and by doing this they would throw me into the hands of the church, and leave me where I was before I was chosen—[64]

Then I would not be in a situation [p. 77] to bring so much disgrace upon the cause, when I fell into temptation, and perhaps by this I might obtain Salvation you know my passions and the danger of falling from so high a station, and thus by withdrawing from the office of the apostleship[65] while their is salvation for me, and remaining a member in the church;[66]

I feel a fraid if I do'nt do this it will be worse for me, some other day

And again my health is poor and I am not able to travel and it is necessary that the office, should not be idle—[67] And again I say you know my passions and I am a fraid it will be worse for me, by and by

do so if the Lord will have mercy on me and let me remain as a member in the church, and then I can travel and preach, when I am able— do not think that I am your enemy for what I have done, perhaps you may say or ask why I have not remembered the good that you have done to me—[68] When I reflect upon the ingury I have done you I must confess that I do not know what I have been ~~doing~~ about— I feel sorry for what I have done and humbly ask your forgiveness— I have not confidence as yet to come and see you for I feel ashamed of what I have done, and as I feel now I feel as thou[p. 78]gh all the confessions that I could make verbally or by writing would not be sufficient to atone for the transgression— be this as it may I am willing to make all the restitution you shall require, If I can stay in the church as a member— I will try to make all the satisfaction possible—

yours with respect
William Smith

do not cast me off for what I have done but strive to save me in the church as a member I do ~~repeat~~ repent of what I have done to you and ask your

---

64. JS's 1834–1836 history adds that William was chosen "among the twelve." (JS History, 1834–1836, 156, in *JSP*, H1:152.)

65. Instead of "and thus by withdrawing from the office of the apostleship," JS's 1834–1836 history has, "And therefore I chose to withdraw from the office of the Apostleship." (JS History, 1834–1836, 156, in *JSP*, H1:152.)

66. See Revelation, 26 Apr. 1832, in *JSP*, D2:235 [D&C 82:3].

67. On 27 February 1835, JS and the newly ordained apostles met to further discuss the role of the new priesthood body. During the meeting, JS declared that the Twelve were "called to a travelling high council to preside over all the churches of the saints among the gentiles where there is no presidency established. They are to travel and preach among the Gentiles." (Record of the Twelve, 27 Feb. 1835; see also Minutes and Discourses, 27 Feb. 1835, in *JSP*, D4:247–254.)

68. The version of the letter recorded in JS's 1834–1836 history reads, "Do not think that I am your enemy, for what I have done. perhaps the inquiry may arise in your mind, why I do not rem[em]ber the many good deeds you have done for me; or if I do remember them, why it is that I should treat you so basely." (JS History, 1834–1836, 156, in *JSP*, H1:153.)

forgiveness— I concider the transgression the other evening of no small magnitude,— but it is done and I cannot help it now— I know brother Joseph you are always willing to forgive.

But I sometimes think when I reflect upon the many inguries I have done you I feel as though a confession was not hardly sufficient— but have mercy on me this once and I will try to do so no more—

The 12, called a council yesterday and sent over after me and I went over

This council rem[em]ber was called together by themselves and not by me[69]

W[m.] S [p. 79]

———— ❧ ————

Letter to William Smith, circa 18 December 1835

Source Note

JS, Letter, Kirtland Township, Geauga Co., OH, to William Smith, [Kirtland Township, Geauga Co., OH], [ca. 18 Dec. 1835]. Featured version copied [ca. 19 Dec. 1835] in JS, Journal, 1835–1836, pp. 80–87; handwriting of Warren Parrish; JS Collection, CHL. For more information on JS, Journal, 1835–1836, see Source Notes for Multiple-Entry Documents, p. 524 herein.

Historical Introduction

Shortly after his dramatic confrontation with his younger brother William Smith on 16 December, JS responded to a contrite letter he had received from William.[70] According to his journal, JS had spent the day after the fight at home feeling "quite unwell."[71] On the following morning, 18 December, Hyrum visited JS's Kirtland, Ohio, home. Hyrum had also received an apologetic letter from William, which he read aloud to JS.[72] Hyrum and JS apparently spent the remainder of the morning discussing their younger brother's troubling behavior and his future welfare.[73]

The fight deeply wounded the Smith family. When Joseph Smith Sr. and Lucy Mack Smith called on JS the evening of 17 December, they were "sorely afflicted in mind on the account of that occurrence."[74] Hyrum felt that JS was justified in rebuking their younger brother, and he felt "wounded to the verry soul, with the conduct of William."[75] Despite the physical injuries that William had inflicted on him, JS expressed concern for his

---

69. JS's 1834–1836 history reads, "This council was called together without my knowledge, or concent." (JS History, 1834–1836, 157, in *JSP*, H1:153.)

70. Letter from William Smith, 18 Dec. 1835, pp. 109–115 herein.

71. JS, Journal, 17 Dec. 1835, in *JSP*, J1:124. The adaptation of JS's journal for his history confirms that his poor health was a result of the injuries he had sustained at William's hands. The exact nature of the injuries is not recorded. (JS History, 1834–1836, 150, 159, in *JSP*, H1:148, 156.)

72. JS, Journal, 18 Dec. 1835, in *JSP*, J1:129; this letter from William to Hyrum Smith is not extant.

73. JS, Journal, 18 Dec. 1835, in *JSP*, J1:129.

74. JS, Journal, 17 Dec. 1835, in *JSP*, J1:128–129.

75. JS, Journal, 18 Dec. 1835, in *JSP*, J1:129.

brother's spiritual welfare and optimism about his capacity to change. After writing to his brother, JS recorded in his journal: "I have had many solemn feelings this day Concerning my Brothe[r] William and have prayed in my heart to fervently that the Lord will not cast him off but he may return to the God of Jacob and magnify his apostleship and calling."[76]

The following letter to William offers the most detailed account of the 16 December fight and provides a glimpse of JS's feelings, personality, and demeanor. The letter also articulates some of JS's nascent ideas about the duty of priesthood leaders to reprove and counsel those under their stewardship, a teaching he would develop more fully in succeeding years.[77]

The dating of JS's letter to William is unclear. The letter, as it was copied in JS's journal by Warren Parrish, was originally inscribed with an incorrect date of 17 December; Parrish later changed the "7" to an "8" so the date read "Friday Dec. 18th 1835." The first line of the 19 December journal entry, in Parrish's handwriting, indicates that JS spent that day at home, where he "wrote the above letter to Br. Wm. Smith." The corresponding 19 December entry in JS's history, also penned by Parrish, is slightly different. It reads, "He was at home and wrote the above letter, or rather indited it, to his brother William."[78] In another, later JS history, Willard Richards copied William's 18 December letter and JS's response. Before recording the latter, Richards wrote that JS "gave the following answer the same day" he received William's letter of 18 December.[79] Given the aforementioned cancellation, insertion, and subsequent recording in JS's journal and histories, the letter is dated here as circa 18 December to reflect both the ambiguity of the dating and the date given by Parrish when he inscribed the letter into the journal.

JS's letter to William is no longer extant, but JS's scribes recorded three versions of the letter in various church records.[80] Significant differences between the featured text and the copy in JS's 1834–1836 history are noted; the copy in JS's later history has no significant differences.

Document Transcript

Kirtland Friday Dec ~~17th~~ ⟨18th⟩ 1835
Answer to the foregoing Letter from Br. William Smith a Copy
Br. William.

---

76. JS, Journal, 19 Dec. 1835, in *JSP*, J1:135.

77. Fifteen months after writing this letter, JS explained these responsibilities to a group of church members gathered in the Kirtland temple. He told them, "It is also the privilege of the Melchisedec priesthood, to reprove, rebuke and admonish, as well as to receive revelations." He himself "rebuked and admonished his brethren frequently, and that because he loved them." "These rebukes and admonitions," he continued, were "for their temporal as well as spiritual welfare. They actually constituted a part of the duties of his station and calling." (Discourse, 6 Apr. 1837, pp. 355–356 herein.)

78. JS, Journal, 19 Dec. 1835, in *JSP*, J1:135; JS History, 1834–1836, 162, in *JSP*, H1:158.

79. JS History, vol. B-1, 668–672.

80. JS, Journal, 19 Dec. 1835, in *JSP*, J1:135; JS History, 1834–1836, 157–162, in *JSP*, H1:153–158; JS History, vol. B-1, 668–672.

having received your letter I now procede to answer it, and shall first procede, to give a brief naration of my feelings and motives, since the night I first
came to the knowledge, of your having a debating school, which was at the
time I happened, in with, Bishop [Newel K.] Whitney his Father and Mother
&c⁸¹—which was the first that I knew any thing about it, and from that time I
took an interest in them, and was delighted with it, and formed a determination, to attend the school for the purpose of obtaining information, and with
the idea of imparting the same, through the assistance of the spirit of the Lord,
if by any means I should have faith to do so; and with this intent, I went to the
school on ⟨last⟩ Wedensday night, not with the idea of braking up the school,
neither did it enter into my heart,⁸² that there was any wrangling or jealousy's
in your heart, against me;

Notwithstanding previous to my leaving home there were feelings of
solemnity, rolling across my breast, which were unaccountable to me, and also
these feelings continued by spells to depress my ~~feelings~~ ⟨spirit⟩ and seemed to
manifest that all was not right, even after the ~~debate~~ school commenced, and
during the debate, yet I strove to believe that all would work together for good;
I was pleased with the power of the arguments, that were aduced,⁸³ and did
[p. 80] not feel to cast any reflections, upon any one that had spoken; but I felt
that it was ~~my~~ ⟨the⟩ duty of old men that set as presidents to be as grave, at least
as young men, and that it was our duty to smile at solid arguments, and sound
reasoning, and be impreesed, with solemnity, which should be manifest in our
countanance, when folly and that which militates against truth and righteousness, rears its head

Therefore in the spirit of my calling and in view of the authority of the
priesthood that has been confered upon me, it would be my duty to reprove
whatever I esteemed to be wrong fondly hoping in my heart that all parties,

---

81. On 18 November, JS, Newel K. and Elizabeth Ann Smith Whitney, and Newel's parents,
Samuel and Susanna Kimball Whitney, visited William Smith's home, where they were first introduced
to the debating school. (JS, Journal, 18 Nov. 1835, in *JSP*, J1:106.)

82. Despite JS's participation in the debating school, he had previously expressed reservations about it.
After attending the 18 November session, he noted in his journal, "I discovered in this debate, much
warmth displayed, to[o] much zeal for mastery, to[o] much of that enthusiasm that characterises a lawyer
at the bar, who is determined to defend his cause right or wrong." On that occasion, JS felt compelled to
"drop a few words upon this subject by way of advise." He told the participating elders that they should
"improve their minds and cultivate their powers of intellect in a proper manner" and "handle sacred
things verry sacredly, and with a due deference to the opinions of others and with an eye single to the
glory of God." (JS, Journal, 18 Nov. 1835, in *JSP*, J1:106.)

83. The 16 December debate focused on whether "it was necessary for God to reveal himself to man, in
order for their happiness." The journal noted that JS argued in favor of the question. (JS, Journal, 12 and
16 Dec. 1835, in *JSP*, J1:120–121, 124.)

would concider it right, and therefore humble themselves, that satan might not take the advantage of us, and hinder the progress of our School.

Now Br. William I want you should bear with me, notwithstanding my plainness—

I would say to you that my feelings, were grieved at the interuption you made upon Elder McLellen [William E. McLellin],[84] I thought, you should have concidered your relation, with him, in your Apostle ship, and not manifest any division of sentiment, between you, and him, for a surrounding multitude to take the advantage of you:—[85] Therefore by way of entreaty, on the account of the anxiety I had for your influence and wellfare,[86] I said, unto you, do not have any feelings, or something to that amount, why I am thus particular, is that if You, have misconstrued, my feelings, toward you,[87] you may be corrected.— [p. 81]

But to procede— after the school was closed Br. Hyrum [Smith], requested, the privilege, of speaking, you objected, however you said if he would not abuse the school, he might speak, and that you would not allow any man to abuse the school in your house,—

Now you had no reason to suspect that Hyrum, would abuse the school, therefore my feelings were mortifyed, at those unnecessa[r]y observations, I undertook to reason, with you but you manifisted, an inconciderate and stubourn spirit, I then dispared, of benefiting you, on the account of the spirit you manifested, which drew from, me the expression that you was as ugly as the Devil.

Father then commanded silence and I formed a determination, to obey his mandate, and was about to leave the house, with the impression, that You was under the influence of a wicked spirit, you replyed that you, would say what you pleased in your own house, Father replyed, say what you please, but let the rest hold their, toungs, then a reflection, rushed through my mind, of the, anxiety, and care I ~~had~~ ⟨hav⟩ had for you and your family, in doing what I did, in finishing your house[88] and providin flour for your family &c and also father

---

84. The version copied into JS's 1834–1836 history has "when you interrupted Eldr Mc Lellen in his speech." (JS History, 1834–1836, 158, in *JSP*, H1:154.)

85. For the past several months, JS had been troubled by what he perceived as jealousies between and disunity exhibited by the newly called members of the Quorum of the Twelve Apostles. (JS, Journal, 3 Nov. and 15 Dec. 1835, in *JSP*, J1:83–84, 122–123; see also Esplin, "Emergence of Brigham Young," 166–175.)

86. JS's 1834–1836 history records the statement as "the anxiety I had for you, & your influence & welfare in society." (JS History, 1834–1836, 158, in *JSP*, H1:155.)

87. The version in JS's 1834–1836 history states, "Why I am thus particular, is that if you have misunderstood my feelings or motives toward you." (JS History, 1834–1836, 158, in *JSP*, H1:155.)

88. In a 4 August 1835 letter written to certain members of the Quorum of the Twelve Apostles serving missions in the East, William was advised, "Your house is nearly finished, except plastering, a few days

had possession in the house, as well, as your self; and when at any time have I transgressed, the commandments of my father? or sold my birthright, that I should not have the privilege of speaking in my fathers house, or in other words in my fathers family, or in your house, [p. 82] (for so we will call it, and so it shall be,) that I should not have the privilege, of reproving a younger brother, therefore I said I will speak, for I built the house, and it is as much mine as yours, or something, to that effect, (I should have said that. I helped finish the house,) I said it merely to show that it could not be, the right spirit, that would rise up for trifling matters, and undertake to put me to silence, I saw that your indignation was kindled against me, and you made towards me, I was not then to be moved, and I thought, to pull off my loose coat, least it should tangle me, and you be left to hurt me, but not with the intention, of hurting You, but you was to[o] soon for me, and having once fallen into the hands of a mob, and ~~now~~ been wounded in my side,[89] and now into the hands of a brother, my side gave way, and after having been rescued, from your grasp,[90] I left your house, with, feelings that were indiscribale [indescribable], the scenery had changed, and all those expectations, that I had cherished, when going to your house, of brotherly kindness, charity forbearance and natural, affection, that in duty binds us not to make eachothers offenders for a word.[91] ~~but~~

But alass! abuse, anger, malice, hatred, and rage ⟨with a lame side⟩ with marks, of violence ⟨heaped⟩ upon ~~my body~~ me by a brother, were the reflections of my disapointment,[92] and with these I returned home, not able to sit down, or rise up, without help, but through the blessings of God I am now better.— [p. 83]

I have received your letter and purused it with care, I have not entertained a feeling of malice, against you, I am, older than your and have endured, more

---

will complete it except this: Whether it will [be] entirely finished by his return, or not, we cannot say. . . . Wm's, Father is soon to move in with Wm's wife." (Letter to Quorum of the Twelve, 4 Aug. 1835, in *JSP*, D4:378.)

89. JS was dragged from his bed, beaten by a mob, and tarred and feathered in Hiram, Ohio, on 24–25 March 1832, leaving him with a long-term side injury. In a June 1834 letter to Emma, he mentioned his "side complaint." (JS History, vol. A-1, 205–207; Letter to Emma Smith, 4 June 1834, in *JSP*, D4:54.)

90. The 16 December 1835 entry in JS's 1834–1836 history indicates that William had "Cain like . . . sought to kill him, and had conciderably wounded him, nothwithstanding the exertions of his brothren to prevent it." (JS History, 1834–1836, 150, in *JSP*, H1:148.)

91. See Isaiah 29:20–21.

92. In the version of the letter copied into JS's 1834–1836 history, the sentence reads, "But alas! abuse, anger, malice, hatred, and rage, are heaped upon me, by a brother; and with marks of violence upon my body, with a lame side, I left your habitation bruised and wounded; and not only oppressed with these, but more severely so in mind being born down under the reflection of my disappointment." (JS History, 1834–1836, 159, in *JSP*, H1:156.)

suffering, having been mar[r]ed by mobs, the labours of my calling, a series of persecution, and inguries, continually heaped upon me, all serve to debilitate, my body, and it may ⟨be⟩ that I cannot boast of being stronger, than you, if I could, or could not, would this be an honor, or dishonor to me,— if I could boast like David of slaying a Goliath, who defied the armies of the living God, or like Paul, of contending with Peter face to face, with sound arguments, it might be an honor, But to mangle the flesh or seek revenge upon one who never done you any wrong, can not be a source of sweet reflection, to you, nor to me, neither to an honorable father & mother, brothers, and sisters, and when we reflect, with what care ~~our parents~~ and with what unremiting diligence our parents, have strove to watch over us, and how many hours, of sorrow, and anxiety, they have spent over our cradles and bedsides, in times of sickness, how careful we ought to be of their feelings in their old age, it cannot be a source of sweet reflection to us to say or do any thing that will bring their grey hairs down with sorrow to the grave,

In your letter you asked my forgivness, which I readily grant, but it seems to me, that you still retain an idea, that I have given you reasons to be angry or disaffected with me,

Grant me the privilege of saying then, [p. 84] that however hasty, or harsh, I may have spoken, at any time to you, it has been done for the express purpose of endeavouring, to warn exhort, admonish, and rescue you, from falling into difficulties, and sorrows which I foresaw you plunging into, by giving way to that wicked spirit, which you call your passions, which you should curbe and break down, and put under your feet, which if you do not you, never can be saved, in my view, in the kingdom of God.

God requires the will of his creatures, to be swallowed up in his will.

You desire to remain in the church, but forsake your apostleship, this is a stratigem of the evil one, when he has gained one advantage, ~~your~~ he lays a plan for another, ~~by~~ ⟨but⟩ by maintaining your apostleship in rising up, and making one tremendeous effort, you may overcome your passions, and please God and by forsaking your apostleship, is not to be willing, to make that sacrafice that God requires at your hands[93] and is to incur his displeasure, and without pleasing God do not think, that it will be any better for you, when a man falls one step he must regain that step again, or fall another, he has still more to gain, or eventually all is lost.

---

93. Instead of "and by forsaking your apostleship, is not to be willing, to make that sacrafice that God requires at your hands," JS's 1834–1836 history is worded thus: "And by forsakeing your apostleship, you say that you are not willing to make that sacrifice that God requires at your hand." (JS History, 1834–1836, 161, in *JSP*, H1:157.)

I desire brother William that you will humble yourself, I freely forgive you[94] and you know, my unshaken and ~~unshaken~~ unchangable disposition I ~~think~~ know in whom I trust, I stand upon [p. 85] the rock, the floods cannot, no they shall not overthrow me, you know the doctrine I teach is true, and you know that God has blessed me, I brought salvation to my fathers house, as an instrument in the hand of God, when they were in a miserable situation, You know that it is my duty to admonish you when you do wrong this liberty I shall always take, and you shall have the same privelege, I take the privelege, to admonish you because of my birthright, and I grant you the privilege because it is my duty, to be humble and to receive rebuke, and instruction, from a brother or a friend.

As it regards, what course you shall persue hereafter, I do not pretend to say, I leave you in the hands of God and his church. Make your own desision, I will do you good altho you mar me, or slay me, by so doing my garments, shall be clear of your sins, and if at any time you should concider me to be an imposter, for heavens sake leave me in the hands of God, and not think to take vengance on me your self.

Tyrany ursurpation, and to take mens rights ever has and ever shall be banished from my heart.

David sought not to kill Saul, although he was guilty of crimes that never entered my heart.[95]

And now may God have mercy upon my fathers house, may God take [p. 86] away enmity, from betwe[e]n me and thee, and may all blessings be restored, and the past be forgotten forever, may humble repentance bring us both to thee ⟨O God⟩ and to thy power and protection, and a crown, to enjoy the society of father mother Alvin Hyrum Sophron[i]a Samuel Catharine [Katharine] Carloss [Don Carlos] Lucy[96] the Saints and all the sanctif[ie]d in peace forever⟨, is the prayer of⟩

~~This from~~ Your brother
Joseph Smith Jun

To William Smith

——— ⌘ ———

94. JS's 1834–1836 history renders this passage as "I feel for you, and freely forgive you all." (JS History, 1834–1836, 161, in *JSP*, H1:157.)

95. See 1 Samuel 24. Willard Richards copied this sentence into volume B-1 of JS's multivolume history, but Warren Parrish did not copy it into JS's 1834–1836 history. (JS History, vol. B-1, 671; JS History, 1834–1836, 161, in *JSP*, H1:157.)

96. The siblings of JS and William Smith, in order of age.

Revelation, 26 December 1835 [D&C 108]

Source Note

Revelation, [Kirtland Township, Geauga Co., OH], 26 Dec. 1835. Featured version copied [ca. 26 Dec. 1835] in JS, Journal, 1835–1836, p. 90; handwriting of Frederick G. Williams; JS Collection, CHL. For more information on JS, Journal, 1835–1836, see Source Notes for Multiple-Entry Documents, p. 524 herein.

Historical Introduction

On the morning after Christmas Day in 1835, Lyman Sherman, one of the presidents of the Seventy, asked JS to petition God for a revelation that "should make known [his] duty."[97] In response, JS dictated this revelation.

Sherman, then thirty-one years old, had distinguished himself as a faithful Latter-day Saint prior to his request. He joined the church in western New York in January 1832 and relocated his family 120 miles west to Kirtland, Ohio, sometime around June 1833.[98] Sherman marched to Missouri in May 1834 with about two hundred others as part of the Camp of Israel expedition.[99] In February 1835, he was called as one of seven presidents over the Seventy, a newly established priesthood office. In his ordination blessing, Sherman was told, "Your ministry shall be great and you shall proclaim to various nations. Your faith shall be unshaken and you shall be delivered from great afflictions."[100] At a May 1835 conference, church leaders voted that Sherman, along with the other presidents of the Seventy, should "hold himself in readiness to go at the call of the Twelve, when the Lord opens the way."[101] Sherman likely left Kirtland during summer 1835 to preach in local communities, though he may have remained in Kirtland and prepared himself to preach as he had been instructed.[102]

On 26 December, Sherman called on JS as he was studying Hebrew with Frederick G. Williams and Warren Parrish. According to JS's journal, Sherman entered the room in which they were studying and asked "to have the word of the lord" through JS. "I have been wrought upon to make known to you my feelings and desires," he told JS, adding that he had been promised by the Lord that "I should have a revelation which should make known my duty."[103] Sometime before the end of the day, JS dictated a revelation—presumably to Williams, who was acting temporarily as JS's scribe—that addressed

---

97. JS, Journal, 26 Dec. 1835, in *JSP,* J1:137.

98. Johnson, Reminiscences and Journals, 16–17. Lyman Sherman married Delcena Johnson in 1829 and was presumably living with or nearby his in-laws when missionaries converted several members of the family. Sherman likely arrived in Ohio at the same time that the rest of the Johnson family moved to Kirtland. (Johnson, "A Life Review," 9.)

99. Minutes, Discourse, and Blessings, 14–15 Feb. 1835, in *JSP,* D4:226.

100. Minutes and Blessings, 28 Feb.–1 Mar. 1835, in *JSP,* D4:258–259, 260–261.

101. Minutes and Discourse, 2 May 1835, in *JSP,* D4:302–303.

102. Though Sherman probably left with other elders to preach during the summer of 1835, minutes of the Kirtland high council indicate that he was in Kirtland during early May and late October. (Minutes and Discourse, 2 May 1835, in *JSP,* D4:303, 306; Minutes, 29 Oct. 1835, p. 27 herein.)

103. JS, Journal, 26 Dec. 1835, in *JSP,* J1:137.

Sherman's concerns.[104] Williams later copied the revelation into JS's journal. That copy, which is the earliest extant version, is featured here.

Document Transcript

The following is a revelation given to Lyman Sherman this day 26 Dec 1835

Verily thus saith the Lord unto you my servant Lyman your sins are forgiven you because you have obeyed my voice in coming up hither this morning to receive councel of him whom I have appointed

Therefore let your soul be at rest concerning your spiritual standing, and resist no more my voice, and arise up, and be more careful henceforth in observing your vows which you have made and do make, and you shall be blessed with exceding great blessings. Wait patiently untill the time when the solemn assembly[105] shall be called of my servants then you shall be numbered with the first of mine elders and receive right by ordination with the rest of mine elders whom I have chosen

Behold this is the promise of the father unto you if you continue faithful—

and it shall be fulfilled upon you in that day that you shall have right to preach my gospel wheresoever I shall send you from henceforth from that time,[106] Therefore strengthen your brethren in all your conversation in all your prayers, and in all your exhortations, and in all your doings, and behold and lo I am with you to bless you and deliver you forever Amen

———— ❧ ————

Charges against Almon Babbitt Preferred to Presidents of the High Council, circa 27–28 December 1835

Editorial Note

For the full text of this letter, see Minutes, 28 December 1835, p. 125 herein.

———— ❧ ————

---

104. JS, Journal, 19–26 Dec. 1835, in *JSP*, J1:135–138.

105. In the Old Testament, a solemn assembly was a "holy convocation" of individuals. For Latter-day Saints in 1835, the term had become closely associated with the House of the Lord at Kirtland. The House of the Lord was dedicated on 27 March 1836, and on 30 March a group of three hundred men met there to participate in a solemn assembly. (Leviticus 23:36; Joel 1:14; Revelation, 27–28 Dec. 1832, in *JSP*, D2:334–346 [D&C 88:70, 117–120]; JS, Journal, 27 and 30 Mar. 1836, in *JSP*, J1:97–98, 200–211, 213–216.)

106. During the 30 March 1836 solemn assembly, Sherman and the other members of the Seventy were instructed to "go to Zion if they please or go wheresoever they will and preach the gospel and let the redemtion of Zion be our object." (Minutes, 30 Mar. 1836, p. 220 herein.)

Minutes, 28 December 1835

Source Note

Kirtland high council, Minutes, Kirtland Township, Geauga Co., OH, 28 Dec. 1835. Featured version copied [between ca. 4 Apr. and ca. 16 May 1836] in Minute Book 1, pp. 131–134; handwriting of Warren A. Cowdery; CHL. For more information on Minute Book 1, see Source Notes for Multiple-Entry Documents, p. 527 herein.

Historical Introduction

Following the physical confrontation between JS and William Smith on 16 December,[107] Almon Babbitt, who was a member of the Quorum of the Seventy and an active participant in the debating school in Kirtland, Ohio, became outspoken in his view that JS had gotten angry simply because he had been "overpowered in argument." Upon hearing that Babbitt was publicly slandering him, JS referred the twenty-three-year-old to the Kirtland high council for a disciplinary hearing.

Despite having been reproved by church leaders several months earlier, Babbitt was presumably in good standing with his quorum and the church in December 1835.[108] During the previous months, Babbitt had witnessed two major confrontations between JS and William Smith. He was present during the 29 October trial of David and Mary Cahoon Elliott at which JS and William engaged in a heated verbal altercation. He also appears to have participated in the 16 December debate that provoked the brothers' fistfight, and his ongoing comments about JS's actions that evening prompted the 28 December council meeting featured here.[109]

After the council deliberated the charges, it ruled that Babbitt had "spoken things falsely to the injury" of JS and that he needed to acknowledge his error publicly. Though the minutes indicate that Babbitt confessed to the satisfaction of most of the council members in attendance, the charges were not fully resolved during the 28 December meeting. According to JS's journal, the council elected to adjourn the meeting without a full confession from Babbitt after "parleying with him a long time, and granting him every indulgence."[110] During the next council meeting, held on 2 January 1836, Babbitt fully confessed to the charges and was subsequently "restored to fellowship in the Church."[111]

---

107. JS, Journal, 16 Dec. 1835, in *JSP,* J1:124; see also Historical Introduction to Letter from William Smith, 18 Dec. 1835, pp. 110–113 herein.

108. In mid-August, Charles C. Rich preferred charges against Babbitt for failing to observe the church's health code (the Word of Wisdom) and for making statements that de-emphasized the doctrines contained in the Book of Mormon. Babbitt confessed to and apologized for breaking the Word of Wisdom but told the council that he had "taught the Book of Mormon & commandments as he had thought to be wisdom." The council reproved him and offered "good instruction." (Minute Book 1, 19 Aug. 1835.)

109. Minutes, 29 Oct. 1835, p. 28 herein; JS, Journal, 16 Dec. 1835, in *JSP,* J1:124; Historical Introduction to Letter from William Smith, 18 Dec. 1835, pp. 110–113 herein.

110. JS, Journal, 28 Dec. 1835, in *JSP,* J1:138.

111. Minutes, 2 Jan. 1836, p. 131 herein. In his journal, JS confirmed that Babbitt "confessed the charges which I prefered against him in a previous council, and was received into fellowship." (JS, Journal, 2 Jan. 1836, in *JSP,* J1:142.)

Document Transcript

At a meeting of the High Council of the church of the Latter Day Saints held in Kirtland December 28ᵗʰ 1835

President Sidney Rigdon presiding

Counsellors[112]

W. E. McLelin [William E. McLellin]	Orson Hyde
D[avid] W. Patten	Lyman Johnson
John Smith	Samuel H. Smith
Orson Johnson	Martin Harris
Jared Carter	Brigham Young
Luke Johnson	Parley P. Pratts [Pratt]

Prayer by President Rigdon. [p. 131]

The following complaint was presented by J. Smith Junʳ.

To the Presidents of the High Council,

Brethren, Almon Babbit[t] has been misrepresenting me to certain of the brethren. I therefore prefer a complaint to the council that the subject may be investigated, that my character and influence may be preserved as far as it can in righteousness.

Yours in the bonds of the New & everlasting covenant—

Joseph Smith Junʳ.

It was decided that three should speak on each side. Elder L[yman] Wight was called and stated what led to the affair was a difference in opinion respecting keeping their meeting.[113] Elder Babbit said J. Smith Junʳ. got mad because he got overpowered in argumint as Babbit had remarked before[.] L. Wight, said men would get over the mark, in advocating error. Babbit said a man must be a very weak man if he could not argue aginst the truth without being swerved Babbit said he (Smith) got mad because he was overpowered in argument. There would have been no disturbance if he had not got mad. Elder [Roger] Orton agreed with what L. Wight had stated. Dont know whether the conversation was heard by any one else. Babbit said he could read Tho. Paine or any other work without being swerved.[114] B. Said this by the door of the House,

---

112. Of the twelve counselors present at this meeting, six were members of the Quorum of the Twelve Apostles and six were members of the Kirtland high council.

113. In other words, JS and William Smith disagreed about the propriety of continuing the debates that were hosted in William's home.

114. Thomas Paine authored several works, including the influential *Age of Reason* (1795), in which he was critical of revealed religion, the Bible, and churches generally.

and appeared dissatisfied with J. Smith's bad spirit. Elder L. Wight thought Babbit showed a bad spirit against J. Smith.

Elder L[yman] Sherman called. Has not heard Babbit say any thing against J. Smith Junr Council asked Sherman if he had seen Babbit exhibit a restless or dissatisfied spirit Says, that on the Flats[115] one or two days after the transaction at the debate, Babbit said of his party. If it was not able one way, it was another, by knocking down. Sherman understood, that if they could not [p. 132] overpower by arguement, they would by knocking down, but said in a jesting way. Babbit said we would not have had any difficulty, if J. Smith had not have got mad. Babbit has a singular Spirit. Babbit gave him an idea that he had a difficulty with J. Smith. Benj[amin] Johnson called said ⟨he⟩ thought J. Smith was riled and Wm. Smith was mad. Brigham Young called. said that Eld. B. agreed with Bishop,[116] respecting being swerved when debating questions, must be weak minded. Babbit said [Joseph] Smith would not have wanted the school broke up, if they had not got defeated Young did not hear any thing from Smith at school that was calculated to hurt feelings and character, he also thinks he Babbit cast reflections on the whole Presidency, as well as J. Smith Junr. and that what Babbit said was calculated to hurt J. Smith. Babbit said that Smith was against the school.

Elder O. Hyde knows Babbit wants the school to continue and said Smith had tended school till the disturbance & had it not been for this circumstance he (Smith) would have been willing for it to continue heard this statement from Eld. Bishop and not from Babbit respecting reading Tho. Paine without having his faith shaken.

Eld. Sherman thinks if Babbit means all he says he is a singular man & Babbit said if it had not been for J. Smith's getting mad there would have been no difficulty Eld. Rich called stated that from what he heard from Babbit, he thought he had nothing against J. Smith Junr. Elder Orton stated that Babbit said the school would have continued if J. Smith Junr. had not got <u>mad</u>. He also thought that Babbit and Bishop had the spirit of the debating school.

Counsellors spoke to the case

President H[yrum] Smith addressed the council [p. 133]

President [Frederick G.] Williams then addressed the council

---

115. The "Flats" refers to the lowland area on the northern side of Kirtland through which the east branch of the Chagrin River flowed.

116. Likely Francis Gladden Bishop.

President S. Rigdon then rose and delivered the decision. That Eld. Babbit shall confess that for the want of conformity to the spirit of God he has let the adversary get the possession of his heart, in consequence of which, he has spoken things falsely to the injury of J. Smith Junr, and by injuring him he has insulted the feelings of the church of Christ and that he shall confess publicly to the satisfaction of his brethren.

This decision was confirmed by the whole council. Elder Babbit rose and confessed that he was to blame, for speaking about Brother Smith as he did, & that he said ~~him~~ them in anger, And that he never meant to rise up in rebelliong against the ~~church~~ government of the church. And that in a bad spirit he said what was proved and sees it. was wrong to talk as he did about brother J. Smith, and that he thought he would give B. J. Smith as good as he sent, as he did.

Elder Babbit confesses that he has injured J. S. character and is sorry for it, but is not willing to confess that he lied, and cannot confess all that President Rigdon has said in his speech Says he knows this council says he has done wrong and is willing to confess it. The decision is correct, Brother Babbit confessed to all present, the charges above stated to the satisfaction of most of the brethren present, [p. 134]

———— ✧ ————

Charges against William Smith Preferred to the Church Presidency, 29 December 1835

Source Note

Orson Johnson, Charges against William Smith Preferred to the Church Presidency, Kirtland Township, Geauga Co., OH, 29 Dec. 1835. Featured version copied [between ca. 4 Apr. and ca. 16 May 1836] in Minute Book 1, p. 135; handwriting of Warren A. Cowdery; CHL. For more information on Minute Book 1, see Source Notes for Multiple-Entry Documents, p. 527 herein.

Historical Introduction

On 29 December 1835, Orson Johnson, a member of the high council in Kirtland, Ohio, charged William Smith with "speaking disrespectfully" of and "attempting to inflict personal violence" upon JS and referred the matter to the presidency of the church. Nearly two weeks earlier, during a session of the debating school, the two brothers engaged in a verbal altercation that turned violent.[117] Though the 16 December fight was certainly one catalyst for Johnson's complaint, the charge that William had disparaged JS and "the revelations and commandments given through him" indicates that William had also

---

117. Historical Introduction to Letter to William Smith, ca. 18 Dec. 1835, pp. 115–116 herein.

challenged his brother's prophetic authority.[118] In response to Johnson's accusation, a disciplinary council assembled on 2 January 1836 to consider the charges.[119]

The original version of Johnson's charges is no longer extant, but at some point Warren A. Cowdery copied the charges into Minute Book 1.

Document Transcript

Kirtland Dec.[r.] 29th 1835

To the Honorable Presidency[120] of the Church of Christ of the Latter Day-Saints,

I prefer the following charges against Elder Wm. Smith

1[st.] Unchristian like conduct in speaking disrespectfully of President Joseph Smith [Junr.] and the revelations & commandments given through him.

2[d.] For attempting to inflict personal violence on President J. Smith [Junr.]

Orson Johnson

———— ⁊ ————

Minutes, 2 January 1836

Source Note

Kirtland high council, Minutes, Kirtland Township, Geauga Co., OH, 2 Jan. 1836. Featured version copied [between ca. 4 Apr. and ca. 16 May 1836] in Minute Book 1, pp. 135–136; handwriting of Warren A. Cowdery; CHL. For more information on Minute Book 1, see Source Notes for Multiple-Entry Documents, p. 527 herein.

Historical Introduction

On 2 January 1836, a disciplinary council—consisting of two members of the church presidency, the president of the Missouri high council, six of the seven senior members of the Quorum of the Twelve, and several members of the high councils of Kirtland, Ohio, and Clay County, Missouri—met to discuss charges filed by Orson Johnson against William Smith on 29 December.[121]

---

118. According to JS's journal, William had opposed JS publicly after a disagreement in October 1835. At the conclusion of a 29 October disciplinary council involving David and Mary Elliott, JS and William engaged in a fierce verbal dispute. The brothers attempted to settle their differences in a face-to-face meeting several days later, but, according to JS's journal, William left JS's house in a rage and was later "in the streets exclaiming against me." (See 29n113 herein; and JS, Journal, 29 and 31 Oct. 1835, in *JSP*, J1:76–79, 80–81.)

119. Minutes, 2 Jan. 1836, pp. 128–131 herein.

120. Though the complaint was directed to the "Presidency," the disciplinary council that met to discuss the charges consisted of two members of the presidency, six of the seven senior members of the Quorum of the Twelve Apostles, and members of the high councils of Kirtland and Clay County, Missouri. (JS, Journal, 2 Jan. 1836, in *JSP*, J1:142; Minutes, 2 Jan. 1836, p. 130 herein.)

121. Charges against William Smith Preferred to the Church Presidency, 29 Dec. 1835, p. 127 herein.

During the previous two months, JS and his brother William had engaged in a series of heated disputes, including one that ended in William attacking and injuring JS.[122] Though the brothers exchanged conciliatory letters in mid-December, JS's journal entry for the morning of New Year's Day indicates that conflict between the two of them continued to fester and had caused division within the Smith family.[123] "My heart is pained within me because of the difficulty that exists in my fathers family," JS dictated to his scribe. He added that "the Devil has made a violent attack" on William and Calvin Stoddard, their brother-in-law, and concluded, "The powers of Earth & hell seem combined to overthrow us and the Church by causing a division in the family."[124]

Later in the day on 1 January, the two brothers finally met in person at JS's Kirtland home; according to an account of the meeting recorded in JS's journal, Joseph Smith Sr., Hyrum Smith, John Smith, and Martin Harris were also present.[125] Joseph Smith Sr. opened the meeting with a prayer, after which he "expressed his feelings on the occasion in a verry feeling and pathetic manner even with all the sympathy of a father whose feeling were wounded deeply on the account of the difficulty that was existing in the family." The journal notes that as Joseph Smith Sr. spoke, "the spirit of God rested down upon us in mighty power, and our hearts were melted."[126] William Smith then "made an humble confession" and asked JS's forgiveness for "the abuse he had offered." For his part, JS asked William to forgive him "wherein [he] had been out of the way." The two men agreed to "build each other up in righteousness, in all things and not listen to evil reports concerning eachother, but like brethren, indeed to go to eachother, with our grievances in the spirit of meekness, and be reconciled and thereby promote our own happiness and the happiness of the family." Emma Smith, Lucy Mack Smith, and Warren Parrish, who had apparently been waiting in another room, were then called in to witness the brothers repeat the covenant. The journal documents the relief that JS and others felt, noting that "tears flowed from our eys . . . , and it was truly a jubilee and time of rejoiceing."[127]

Although the brothers had reconciled, the disciplinary council still met to discuss Johnson's charges. JS apparently recused himself from the trial but did attend the meeting.[128] Interspersed with more routine church business, the minutes featured here highlight William Smith's trial and confession before church leaders. The document also chronicles the confession of Almon Babbitt, who had appeared before the disciplinary council five days prior.[129]

---

122. JS, Journal, 29 and 31 Oct. 1835, in *JSP*, J1:77, 80–81; Letter from William Smith, 18 Dec. 1835, pp. 109–115 herein.

123. Letter from William Smith, 18 Dec. 1835, pp. 109–115 herein; Letter to William Smith, ca. 18 Dec. 1835, pp. 115–121 herein.

124. JS, Journal, 1 Jan. 1836, in *JSP*, J1:140–141; see also JS, Journal, 17–18 and 29 Dec. 1835; 1 Jan. 1836, in *JSP*, J1:128–129, 139–141; and Letter to Editor, 22 June 1835, in *JSP*, D4:347.

125. There is nothing in contemporary accounts to indicate who or what prompted the face-to-face meeting. Given that the disciplinary council was scheduled for the following morning, William may have felt compelled to privately reconcile with JS before appearing at the public council.

126. JS, Journal, 1 Jan. 1836, in *JSP*, J1:141. The account recorded in JS's history adds that "their hearts melted down in contrition and humility before the Lord." (JS History, 1834–1836, 168, in *JSP*, H1:165.)

127. JS, Journal, 1 Jan. 1836, in *JSP*, J1:141.

128. JS, Journal, 2 Jan. 1836, in *JSP*, J1:142.

129. Minutes, 28 Dec. 1835, pp. 125–127 herein.

Document Transcript

Kirtland January 2^d 1836

Kirtland January 2ᵈ 1836

High council met in the school Room agreeably to previous arrangement. Present.

F[rederick] G. Williams ⎫
Oliver Cowdery   ⎬ Presidents
David Whitmer   ⎭

Names of Counsellors

Brigham Young	Parley P. Pratt
Thomas B. Marsh	Heber C. Kimball
Wm. E. McLel[l]in	David W. Patten
Martin Harris	Simeon Carter
Solomon Hancock	Newel Knight
Levi Jackman	Calvin Bebee [Beebe]

President Williams arose and read the charge preferred against Wm. Smith by O[rson] Johnson bearing date Dec<u>r</u> 29th 1835, and proceeded to make some very appropriate remarks touching the case now before them, after which the council was opened by prayer.

Elder Wm. Smith then arose and asked permission to speak. He then in the spirit of meekness and humility confessed the charges [p. 135] pre-ferred against him ⟨by⟩ Elder Orson Johnson and asked the forgiveness of the Presidency & council and the whole congregation present,¹³⁰ He also covenant to make confession before the church the same as before this council.¹³¹

The council on the side of justice arose and expressed their entire satisfaction with his confession and resigned him into the hands of Mercy. A vote was then called of the council and congregation to raise hands if ~~their~~ they were

---

130. JS's journal notes that "before entering on the trial, Br. William arose and humbly confessed." Perhaps owing to this proactive confession, the high council may not have gone through with a formal trial—which according to established protocol should have included comments from members of the council assigned to "prevent insult or injustice" to the accused and from other high council members assigned to see that justice was done on behalf of the church. (JS, Journal, 2 Jan. 1836, in *JSP*, J1:142; Revised Minutes, 18–19 Feb. 1834, in *JSP*, D3:442 [D&C 102:15].)

131. According to JS's journal entry for 3 January 1836, William confessed to a larger body of Saints at a worship service the following day and was subsequently "received into fellowship again." William's confession, as well as his return to full fellowship with the Saints, lifted an onerous burden from the shoulders of JS. At the conclusion to his journal entry, he added, "This day has been a day of rejoicing to me, the cloud that has been hanging over us has burst with blessings on our heads . . . , and I thank my heavenly father for, the union and harmony which now prevails in the Church." (JS, Journal, 3 Jan. 1836, in *JSP*, J1:142–143.)

satisfied with his confession, which they did with apparent cheerfulness & with united consent.

President J. Smith Jun.ʳ then proposed that Vincent [Vinson] Knight & Thomas Grover be ordained to the office of Elders in the church of the Latter-Day-Saints on Sunday the 3ᵈ Inst. in the public congregation. A Vote was called & carried to that effect.

Elder Babbit [Almon Babbitt] arose & confessed the charges that were preferred against him by President J Smith ᴶᵘⁿ.ʳ in a former council.[132] A vote was called and carried in his favor and be restored to fellowship in the Church. Voted that Hiram Dayton be ordained to the office of an Elder

Council adjourned by Prayer

W[arren] Parrish, Clerk [p. 136]

———— ❧ ————

Blessing to Lorenzo Barnes, 3 January 1836

Source Note

JS, Sidney Rigdon, and Hyrum Smith, Blessing, to Lorenzo Barnes, Kirtland Township, Geauga Co., OH, 3 Jan. 1836. Featured version copied 24 Apr. 1836 in Lorenzo Barnes, Reminiscences and Diaries, [ca. 1 June 1835]–9 Jan. 1839, 9 May 1841; handwriting of Lorenzo Barnes; 188 pages; CHL.

Pocket-size, handmade blank book, 5⅝ × 3½ × ¾ inches (14 × 9 × 2 cm). The text block consists of ninety-four leaves measuring 5⅜ × 3⅜ inches (14 × 9 cm). The book has a tight-back rounded spine with a black, full-leather (likely calfskin) cover. Some pages appear hand cut with uneven edges.

The journal was inscribed in the book on pages 1–120; the pagination was inscribed in graphite at a later time. The next twenty-eight leaves (fifty-six pages) are blank. The remaining four leaves include four nonconsecutive blank pages, a list of subscribers to the *Latter Day Saints' Messenger and Advocate,* miscellaneous notations, and a 6 May 1841 journal entry.

The pastedown on the inside of the book's front cover contains inscriptions in the handwriting of Lorenzo Barnes: "Lorenzo Barnes | Norton Medina. Co | Ohio" and "His journal who was The | The Son of Phineas Barnes | whos father name was Phineas | also | and whos mothers name was | Abigal daughter of Ebenezer | Smith". The book suffered some moisture damage and staining on the front and back pastedowns.

This journal was in the possession of the Historian's Office by July 1858, and probably sooner.[133] The document may be one of the many journals categorized in earlier 1850s inventories as belonging to "private individuals."[134]

---

132. See Minutes, 28 Dec. 1835, p. 127 herein.

133. Contents of the Historian and Recorder's Office, July 1858, Historian's Office, Catalogs and Inventories, 1846–1904, CHL. The spine has labeling by Historian's Office clerk Leo Hawkins, dating from the 1850s.

134. "Inventory. Historian's Office. G. S. L. City April 1. 1857," [1]; "Historian's Office Inventory G. S. L. March 19. 1858," [1], Historian's Office, Catalogs and Inventories, 1846–1904, CHL.

Historical Introduction

On 3 January 1836, Lorenzo Barnes received a blessing from JS, Sidney Rigdon, and Hyrum Smith. When he copied the text of the blessing into his journal, Barnes described it as a "Zion Blessing"—a blessing given to some of the men who had participated in the Camp of Israel expedition in 1834.[135]

Like many converts, Barnes spent many of his early days in the church proselytizing in neighboring states. Baptized in Ohio on 16 June 1833, twenty-one-year-old Barnes left his parents' home in Norton, Ohio, on a mission to western New York less than six weeks later.[136] After returning to Ohio in early October, he spent three or four weeks working on construction of the House of the Lord in Kirtland, Ohio; during the winter, Barnes taught school and performed some manual labor.[137] In May 1834, he marched to Jackson County, Missouri, as a member of the Camp of Israel expedition.[138] In a 22 June revelation that effectively disbanded the expedition, participants were promised that the Lord had "prepared a blessing and an endowment" for those who remained faithful.[139]

Instead of returning immediately to Ohio in 1834 as many did, Barnes remained in Clay County, Missouri, until October before once again setting out on a "mission to the East."[140] Over the next six and a half months, Barnes and various companions trekked across Missouri, Illinois, Indiana, and Ohio, preaching and baptizing.[141] By the time Barnes returned to his home in Norton on 30 April, he had been away for nearly a year. During that period, he estimated that he had traveled about 2,000 miles, held 105 meetings, and "in company with brother O[rson] Pratt baptized 14 persons."[142]

As Barnes preached near Cincinnati in February 1835, the Quorum of the Twelve Apostles and Quorum of the Seventy were being called and ordained in Kirtland. On 14 February, "a meeting was called of those who journeyed to Zion for the purpose of laying the foundation of its redemption." Explaining that God had not forgotten the sacrifice of those who had participated in the expedition, JS reportedly told those in attendance that "it was the Will of God, that they should be ordained to the ministry."[143] As a result, many of the men who participated in the Camp of Israel expedition were given blessings in this meeting and in others held in subsequent weeks. Some of these blessings were given in conjunction with ordination as an apostle or seventy and were referred to as "ordination

135. See Historical Introduction to Minutes, 8 Aug. 1835, in *JSP*, D4:379; and Park, "Thou Wast Willing to Lay Down Thy Life for Thy Brethren," 27–37.

136. Barnes, Reminiscences and Diaries, vol. 1, p. 1.

137. Barnes, Reminiscences and Diaries, vol. 1, p. 2.

138. Barnes, Reminiscences and Diaries, vol. 1, p. 2.

139. Revelation, 22 June 1834, in *JSP*, D4:75 [D&C 105:12].

140. Barnes, Reminiscences and Diaries, vol. 1, pp. 2–3. Barnes received a license to preach from the Missouri high council on 7 August. (Minute Book 2, 6–7 Aug. 1834.)

141. Barnes, Reminiscences and Diaries, vol. 1, pp. 2–10. Barnes began his journey with Lewis Robbins; in Sugar Creek, Illinois, he and Robbins parted ways, and Barnes continued on with Orson Pratt.

142. Barnes, Reminiscences and Diaries, vol. 1, p. 10.

143. Minutes, Discourse, and Blessings, 14–15 Feb. 1835, in *JSP*, D4:224, 225.

blessings."[144] Many members of the Camp of Israel who were not ordained to leadership positions during spring 1835 also received blessings during the subsequent year, and these were often referred to as "Zion blessings."[145]

Barnes returned to Kirtland just in time to attend an important "grand council" on 2 May 1835, during which he was ordained to the Seventy.[146] After a short stay in Kirtland, he departed on another lengthy mission that took him through Ohio, western Pennsylvania, and New York.[147] He enrolled in several educational institutions after returning to Kirtland in mid-November 1835, and it was during this time that he received his Zion blessing on 3 January 1836.[148] He copied the blessing into his journal on 24 April 1836.[149]

Document Transcript

L[orenzo] Barnes, Zion Blessing received under the[150] hands of Joseph Smith J[r.] Sidney Rigdon & Hyram [Hyrum] Smith Presidents of the church of Latter Day Saints Kirtland Ohio J[an.] 3[d] 1836

Brother Barnes

we lay our hands ⟨up⟩on thy head in the name of the Lord & in his name we say unto thee thou art excepted [accepted] before him [p. [47]] The Eyes of the Lord thy God hav been upon thee & thou hast done that which was most pleasing in his sight for thou hast in thy youth set out in his serves [service] & Thy Prayers & suplications hav been herd & thy Name is writen in Heaven for Angels to gaze upon and thou shalt be a swift messinger to the Nations.[151]

---

144. Warren A. Cowdery copied many of the blessings associated with an ordination to the Quorum of the Twelve or Quorum of the Seventy into Minute Book 1. (Minute Book 1, pp. 147–158, 165–186.)

145. Many of these blessings were recorded in the Patriarchal Blessing Book; other blessings, including Barnes's, were recorded in private journals. (Patriarchal Blessings, vol. 1; Barnes, Reminiscences and Diaries, vol. 2, pp. 43, 47.)

146. Barnes, Reminiscences and Diaries, vol. 1, p. 10; Minutes, 2 May 1835–B, in *JSP*, D4:304; Minute Book 1, 2 May 1835. It is not clear whether Barnes was selected by JS and the church presidency before he returned home from his second mission or whether he was chosen that day.

147. Barnes, Reminiscences and Diaries, vol. 2, pp. 1–40.

148. Barnes began studying grammar under Sidney Rigdon on 9 December and continued under Vinson Knight; in February 1836 he studied Hebrew under the tutelage of Joshua Seixas. (Barnes, Reminiscences and Diaries, vol. 2, pp. 41–43.)

149. The blessing was copied into Barnes's journal following a copy of his patriarchal blessing, which had been given by Joseph Smith Sr. eight months earlier. Barnes copied the Zion blessing while preaching near Canfield, Ohio. (Barnes, Reminiscences and Diaries, vol. 2, pp. 43–52, 57–58.)

150. TEXT: When found at the start of a word, Lorenzo Barnes's capital and lowercase *t*'s are indistinguishable. They have been rendered according to conventional usage throughout this document.

151. See Isaiah 18:2. The term "swift messenger" also appears in two other contemporary blessings. In a May 1835 patriarchal blessing, Barnes was told that he would "go forward and proclaim the gospel and win thousands of souls" and was promised, "Thy Name is written in Heaven." (Minute Book 1, 1 Mar. 1835, 174; Blessing to Alvin Winegar, 7 Feb. 1836, p. 167 herein; Barnes, Reminiscences and Diaries, vol. 2, pp. 44–47.)

Thou art a desendant of Joseph & of the Tribe of Ep[h]raim[152] & the blessings of Jacob & Joseph are thine even the choise Blessings of Heaven above & the Earth beneath & the fullness there of Because thou hast been faithful and hast not withheld thy Life from layinging it down for thy breathren[153] Thou art a chosen vessel unto the Lord[154] to bare the fullness of [p. [48]] the Gosple unto people & Nations a far off Be faithful & thou shalt be endowed with power from on high[155] for the spirit of the highest shall rest upon thee & thou shalt go forth from Land to Land from Nation to Nation & from Kingdom to Kingdom Thou shalt Stand before Kings & ~~rulers~~ ⟨Princes⟩ the rich & the great & they shall be estonished at thy wisdom & tremble ~~at~~ at thy words for the Lord thy God will unloos thy tongue hitherto thou hast been week but thou shalt be made strong Thou shalt be mighty in speaking Thy voice shall bee like the voice of an Angel of God Thy faith shall be mighty in the Earth Thou shalt lift up thy voice & the hills shall tremble before the[e] & the Earth shall quake [p. [49]] under thy feet Prison walls shall not hold thee watters shall not stay thee The sea & the wind shall obey thy command Thou shalt lay thine hands on the sick & they shall recover Thou shalt hav power to open the eyes of the blind & unstop the ears of the deaf Thou shalt cause the lame to leap as an heart [hart] & the tongue of the dumb to sing yea thou shalt bring thy thousands & thy & thy tens of thousands from the Nations to Zion with rejoicing & sit down with them ~~in~~ ⟨&⟩ with Abraham Isaac & Jacob in the Kingdom of God

Therefore be faithful & thy God shall lift the[e] up & thou shalt be exalted & he shall say of ⟨thee⟩ This is my servant ⟨in my sight⟩ he is highley exalted ~~in my sight~~ Therefore we say unto thee our brother [p. [50]] let thy mind expand for it is thy privaleg to behold the Heavens opened over thy head to see & converce with the Angel of God for they shall appear unto thee in thy ministry y[e]a thou shalt behold the fase of thy Redeemer in the flesh Thou

---

152. For some reason, Barnes was not previously assigned a tribe in his patriarchal blessing, as was the custom at the time. (Barnes, Reminiscences and Diaries, vol. 2, pp. 44–47.)

153. Similar language was used in sermons about and blessings given to members of the Camp of Israel expedition. While addressing former members of the expedition on 14 February 1835, JS remarked, "Those who went to Zion, with a determination to lay down their lives, if necessary, it was the Will of God, that they should be ordained to the ministry." A line from Barnes's patriarchal blessing expresses a similar sentiment: "Thou has taken thy life in thine hand & hast not withheld it even from laying it down for thy brethren." Other Zion blessings included similar language. (Minutes and Blessings, 14–15 Feb. 1835, in *JSP*, D4:225; Barnes, Reminiscences and Diaries, vol. 2, p. 44; see also Minute Book 1, 17 Aug. 1835, 101; 1 Mar. 1835, 175, 177, 186; and Blessing to Alvin Winegar, 7 Feb. 1836, pp. 166–168 herein.)

154. See Acts 9:15. Joseph Smith Sr. had also referred to Barnes as a "chosen vessel" in his patriarchal blessing. (Barnes, Reminiscences and Diaries, vol. 2, p. 46.)

155. See Revelation, 22 June 1834, in *JSP*, D4:74 [D&C 105:11–12].

shalt hav communion with the general assembly & Church of the first born in Heaven[156] y[e]a thou shalt behold with thine eyes the glory of ~~thy~~ the Lord untill thou shhalt be satisfied & thou shalt say it is ~~a~~ enough O Lord it is enough Thou shalt hav all the desires of thy heart Thou shalt hav length of days & thy years shall be many

When thy hears [hairs] shall be gray thou shalt be as in the vigur of youth & thy mind unimpared Thou shalt remane untill the coming of the Son of man in [p. [51]] the clowds of heaven y[e]a thou shalt see ⟨view⟩ the winding up seen of all things & stand with the hundred forty & four thousand on Mount Zion[157] These blessings & many others which tongue cannot express & all the powers of the priesthood we seal upon thy head & upon thy sead forever in the name of Jesus Christ & by the ~~power~~ arthority of the High Priesthood even so amen

A$^{pr.}$ 24th 1836 [*1/3 page blank*] [p. [52]]

———— ☙ ————

Note from Newel K. Whitney, 9 January 1836

Source Note

Newel K. Whitney, Note, [Kirtland Township, Geauga Co., OH], to JS, [Kirtland Township, Geauga Co., OH], 9 Jan. 1836. Featured version copied [ca. 9 Jan. 1836] in JS, Journal, 1835–1836, p. 102; handwriting of Warren Parrish; JS Collection, CHL. For more information on JS, Journal, 1835–1836, see Source Notes for Multiple-Entry Documents, p. 524 herein.

Historical Introduction

At "about 11, oclock" in the morning on 9 January 1836, JS was attending the Hebrew School when he received a note from Newel K. Whitney, asking him to attend a feast for the "poor & lame" at Whitney's home. JS then "dismissed the School in order to attend to this polite invitation with [his] wife father & mother."[158]

As the church's bishop in Kirtland, Ohio, Whitney had the responsibility to care for the poor and support those in need. When he was appointed bishop on 4 December 1831, Whitney was directed to "receive the funds of the church" and then to reallocate money

---

156. See Vision, 16 Feb. 1832, in *JSP*, D2:179–192 [D&C 76].

157. See Revelation 7:4; 14:1; and Answers to Questions, between ca. 4 and ca. 20 Mar. 1832, in *JSP*, D2:208–213 [D&C 77]. In the same 2 May 1835 meeting at which Barnes was ordained to the Seventy, JS taught that there may be set apart "seven times Seventy, even until there shall be one hundred & forty and four thousand." Barnes's patriarchal blessing also mentions the hundred and forty-four thousand: "Thou shalt stand when wickedness is swept of[f] from the Earth even with thy breathren the hundred forty & four thousand sealed out of . . . the twelve tribes of Israel." (Minutes, 2 May 1835, in *JSP*, D4:302; Barnes, Reminiscences and Diaries, vol. 2, pp. 46–47.)

158. JS, Journal, 9 Jan. 1836, in *JSP*, J1:146–147.

Elizabeth Ann Smith Whitney. 1867. Along with her husband, Kirtland bishop Newel K. Whitney, Elizabeth hosted a three-day gathering for the church community's poor in Kirtland. Elizabeth and Newel often spent their "means and time" to benefit "the lame, the halt, the deaf, the blind, the aged and infirm" ([Elizabeth Ann Smith Whitney], "A Leaf from an Autobiography," *Woman's Exponent,* 1 Oct. and 1 Nov. 1878, 7:71). (Church History Library, Salt Lake City. Photograph from studio of Edward Martin.)

and goods to the "poor and needy and he who hath not wherewith to pay."[159] As early as September 1832, a revelation commanded Whitney, as bishop, to "travel round about and among all the churches searching after the poor to administer to ther wants by humbling the rich and the proud."[160] On 7 October 1835, JS gave a blessing to Whitney that focused on his role as bishop and reminded him of his responsibility to the poor in Kirtland. That blessing also contained spiritual promises for Whitney if he would "deal with a liberal hand to the poor" and "exalt the poor and humble the rich."[161] The December 1835 issue of the *Messenger and Advocate* likewise featured an article that alluded to teachings about charity found in the Old Testament and JS's revelations. It admonished church members generally to "remember the poor, and consecrate of thy properties for their support."[162]

In early January 1836, Bishop Whitney and his wife, Elizabeth Ann Smith Whitney, hosted a three-day gathering of the church community's poor in Kirtland. After attending the first day of the event on 7 January, JS wrote in his journal that he "attended a sumptuous feast at Bishop N. K. Whitneys this feast was after the order of the Son of God the lame the halt and blind wer invited according to the instruction of the Saviour." The "bountiful refreshment, furnished by the liberality of the Bishop" was accompanied with joyful prayer and song, and Joseph Smith Sr. gave patriarchal blessings to Newel K. Whitney's parents and others in attendance.[163] Though Elizabeth Ann Whitney later remembered that JS and his two counselors were "present each day, talking, blessing, and comforting the poor," JS's journal indicates that he instead studied at the Hebrew School on the second day of the feast, 8 January 1836.[164] Perhaps Newel K. Whitney sent the 9 January note featured here because of JS's absence the previous day. In any case, Whitney explained that "the voice of the spirit" told him that the poor would be blessed if JS came to the final day of the gathering. According to JS's journal, he "attended the feast" on 9 January at which "a large congregation assembled a number was blessed under the hands of father Smith, and we had a good time."[165]

The original note is no longer extant, and JS's journal preserves the only known copy. The residue of an adhesive wafer in the journal suggests that the original, likely written by Whitney on the morning of 9 January 1836, was temporarily attached to a journal page while JS's scribe Warren Parrish copied the note into the journal.[166]

---

159. Revelation, 4 Dec. 1831–A; and Revelation, 4 Dec. 1831–B, in *JSP,* D2:146–153 [D&C 72:1–23].

160. Revelation, 22–23 Sept. 1832, in *JSP,* D2:303 [D&C 84:112].

161. Blessing to Newel K. Whitney, 7 Oct. 1835, pp. 20–21 herein.

162. "Good Understanding Giveth Favor," *LDS Messenger and Advocate,* Dec. 1835, 2:239. The wording found in the *Messenger and Advocate* article is similar to that found in a 9 February 1831 revelation, especially to the later version of that revelation found in the 1835 edition of the Doctrine and Covenants, which stated, "Thou wilt remember the poor, and consecrate of thy properties, for their support." (Revelation, 9 Feb. 1831, in *JSP,* D1:252 [D&C 42:30–31]; Doctrine and Covenants 13:8, 1835 ed. [D&C 42:30].)

163. JS, Journal, 7 Jan. 1836, in *JSP,* J1:146.

164. [Elizabeth Ann Smith Whitney], "A Leaf from an Autobiography," *Woman's Exponent,* 1 Nov. 1878, 7:83; JS, Journal, 8 Jan. 1836, in *JSP,* J1:146.

165. JS, Journal, 9 Jan. 1836, in *JSP,* J1:146–147.

166. See *JSP,* J1:146n254.

Document Transcript

Thus saith the voice of the spirit to me, if thy Brother Joseph Smith jr will attend the feast at thy house[167] this day (at 12 ocl) the poor & lame will rejoice at his presence & also think themselves honored—

Yours in friendship & Love

9th Jan[y] 1836

N.K. W [Newel K. Whitney]

——— ☙ ———

Minutes, 13 January 1836

Source Note

Minutes, Kirtland Township, Geauga Co., OH, 13 Jan. 1836. Featured version copied [between ca. 4 Apr. and ca. 16 May 1836] in Minute Book 1, pp. 200–203; handwriting of Warren A. Cowdery; CHL. For more information on Minute Book 1, see Source Notes for Multiple-Entry Documents, p. 527 herein.

Historical Introduction

On Tuesday, 12 January 1836, JS invited the church presidency and other leaders to meet at ten o'clock the next morning "to take into concideration the subject of the Solemn Assembly."[168] Several changes had been made to the church's administrative structure in the previous thirteen months because of deaths, disciplinary removal, and the creation of two new governing bodies: the Quorum of the Twelve Apostles and the First Quorum of the Seventy.[169] Formally filling all vacancies in church councils and quorums was a key part of the church's preparation for the anticipated solemn assembly in the House of the Lord in Kirtland, Ohio.

Several men were serving simultaneously in two or more church governing offices prior to the 13 January 1836 meeting. For instance, Orson Hyde and Luke Johnson had held positions in both the Kirtland high council and the Quorum of the Twelve Apostles since February 1835. Likewise, Hyrum Smith, Oliver Cowdery, and Joseph Smith Sr. had been serving since early December 1834 as assistant presidents in the church's presidency in addition to their positions on the Kirtland high council and Joseph Smith Sr.'s role as church patriarch.[170] It appears that after this 13 January grand council, men ordained to the priesthood no longer held multiple offices.

---

167. The modest house of Newel K. and Elizabeth Ann Whitney, located across the road from their store, measured 28½ feet by 25½ feet, with a 20-by-12-foot summer kitchen attached in the rear. (Staker, "Thou Art the Man," 88.)

168. JS, Journal, 12 Jan. 1836, in *JSP*, J1:147.

169. Minutes, 17 Feb. 1834, in *JSP*, D3:435; Minutes, 28–29 Aug. 1834, in *JSP*, D4:120; Minutes, 24 Sept. 1834, in *JSP*, D4:171–176; Minutes, Discourse, and Blessings, 14–15 Feb. 1835, in *JSP*, D4:219–234; Minutes and Blessings, 28 Feb.–1 Mar. 1835, in *JSP*, D4:255–264.

170. JS, Journal, 5 Dec. 1834, in *JSP*, J1:47; Account of Meetings, Revelation, and Blessing, 5–6 Dec. 1834, in *JSP*, D4:191–200; Minutes, Discourse, and Blessings, 14–15 Feb. 1835, in *JSP*, D4:219–234.

The 13 January grand council meeting became the first in a series of meetings preparatory to the solemn assembly and the promised endowment of power in the House of the Lord. The grand council consisted of the presidencies of Kirtland and Missouri, the Quorum of the Twelve, and the high councils and bishoprics of Kirtland and Missouri. JS's journal notes that "the presidency of the Seventy were also present, and many more of the Elders of the church of the latterday Saints."[171] At this meeting, the grand council further organized the church's leadership structure, continued setting the quorums of the priesthood in order, ordained several men to priesthood offices, and established a committee to draft rules of conduct for use in the nearly finished House of the Lord. Supplementing the official minutes presented here, JS's journal records that the meeting also featured blessings and prayers for the sick.[172] JS's journal also notes his optimism and joy following the meeting: "This has been one of the best days that I ever spent, there has been an entire unison of feeling expressed in all our proceedings this day, and the Spirit of the God of Israel has rested upon us in mighty power, and it has been good for us to be here, in this heavenly place in Christ Jesus, and altho much fatiegued with the labours of the day, yet my spiritual reward has been verry great indeed."[173]

There are two extant accounts of the 13 January meeting, both based on the official minutes that Orson Hyde recorded at the meeting, probably on loose paper. Warren A. Cowdery copied the minutes into Minute Book 1 sometime in the spring of 1836, and Warren Parrish penned an alternate account in JS's journal sometime shortly after the meeting took place.[174] Because Minute Book 1 represents the official record of meetings on church governance in Kirtland, the minutes as written into that record are featured here. Significant differences between the featured text and JS's journal are noted.

Document Transcript

Kirtland Jany. 13th 1836

The grand council met this day in the attic story of the printing office, consisting of the following Authoroties, (viz.) Presidents. Joseph Smith Senior, Sidney Rigdon, Hyrum Smith, David Whitmer, John Whitmer, Joseph Smith Junr and W[illiam] W. Phelps. Also the twelve Apostles, The High council of Zion and a part of the high council of Kirtland[175]

---

171. JS, Journal, 13 Jan. 1836, in *JSP*, J1:148; for more on the various quorums and presidencies of the church, see the charts on pages 601–614 herein.

172. JS, Journal, 13 Jan. 1836, in *JSP*, J1:151.

173. JS, Journal, 13 Jan. 1836, in *JSP*, J1:151.

174. See JS, Journal, 13 Jan. 1836, in *JSP*, J1:148–151.

175. The Whitmers and William W. Phelps constituted the presidency of Missouri, or Zion. Some of the men in these various offices were unable to attend the meeting. Oliver Cowdery was one of those absent leaders; he did not return from Newark, Licking County, Ohio, until the following day. (JS, Journal, 13 Jan. 1836, in *JSP*, J1:148; Cowdery, Diary, 11–14 Jan. 1836.)

The Bishop of Zion and his counsellors,[176] also the Bishop of Kirtland and one Counsellor[177] and one to be appointed instead of Hyrum Smith now belonging to the Presidency.[178]

Council opened by prayer of J. Smith Senior. J. Smith Jun[r.] presiding. Elder Vinson Knight was nominated by the Bishop of Kirtland as a counsellor to fill the vacancy in his court occasioned by the elevation of Hyrum Smith to the presidency. The move was seconded and carried by a unanimous vote of all[179] [p. 200]

Bishop Whitney then proceeded to ordain Elder Night to the high Priesthood and also to be a counsellor, after which all the congregation said amen with a loud voice. After singing a Hymn they adjourned for one hour.[180]

At the expiration of the time met again pursuant to adjournment, and proceeded to fill the vacancies in the high council. The standing high counsellors were John Smith, John Johnson, Orson Johnson, Martin Harris, Samuel H. Smith Jared Carter and Joseph Coe[181]

The names of those who had been called to fill other offices were Joseph Smith Sen[r.] Hyrum Smith Orson Hyde Luke Johnson and Oliver Cowdery It was then moved, seconded & voted unanimously that Elder J. P. Green [John P. Greene] be appointed a high counseller in the place of Oliver Cowdery.[182] Elder Thomas Grover was nominated in the room of Elder Luke Johnson.[183] This motion was carried unanimously by all the quorums present. It was then moved, seconded, and voted unanimously that Noah Packard be a counsellor in

176. Edward Partridge, John Corrill, and Isaac Morley.

177. Newel K. Whitney and Reynolds Cahoon.

178. Hyrum Smith was called as "assistant for the Bishop" in Kirtland on 10 February 1832. He was appointed an assistant president in the presidency of the high priesthood—and therefore in the presidency of the church—on 6 December 1834. (Hyrum Smith, Diary and Account Book, 10 Feb. 1832; Cahoon, Diary, 10 Feb. 1832; Account of Meetings, Revelation, and Blessing, 5–6 Dec. 1834, in *JSP*, D4:200; JS, Journal, 16 Jan. 1836, in *JSP*, J1:156–160.)

179. Knight was ordained to the office of elder on 2 January 1836. (Minutes, 2 Jan. 1836, p. 131 herein.)

180. According to JS's journal, the council sang "Come let us rejoice in the day of salvation." William W. Phelps, a member of the Missouri presidency in attendance at this council, authored the text of this hymn. (JS, Journal, 13 Jan. 1836, in *JSP*, J1:149; Hymn 18, *Collection of Sacred Hymns*, 24–25.)

181. All these men except Orson Johnson were original members of the Kirtland high council. Johnson replaced John S. Carter in August 1834 after Carter died during the Camp of Israel expedition. (Minutes, 17 Feb. 1834, in *JSP*, D3:436; Minutes, 28–29 Aug. 1834, in *JSP*, D4:123.)

182. Cowdery had served on the Kirtland high council since its creation. JS ordained him "assistant President of the High and Holy Priesthood . . . to assist in presiding over the whole chu[r]ch" in December 1834. (Minutes, 17 Feb. 1834, in *JSP*, D3:436; Account of Meetings, Revelation, and Blessing, 5–6 Dec. 1834, in *JSP*, D4:194–196.)

183. Luke Johnson had served on the Kirtland high council since its creation. He was later ordained as one of the original members of the Quorum of the Twelve Apostles, eleven months before this grand council. (Minutes, 17 Feb. 1834, in *JSP*, D3:436; Minutes, Discourse, and Blessings, 14–15 Feb. 1835, in *JSP*, D4:228.)

the room of Hyrum Smith.[184] Moved, seconded and voted that Elder Joseph Kingsbury be appointed a high counsellor in the room of Orson Hyde.[185] Moved, seconded and carried that Samuel James be appointed a high counsellor in the room of Joseph Smith Senior.[186] Motioned seconded and voted that Joseph Smith Senr S. Rigdon and Hyrum Smith proceed to ordain the foregoing persons to the respective offices to which they been appointed.[187]

1st Proceeded to ordain Elder John P. Green.

We lay our hands on the thy head and ordain thee to this high and conspicuous office and pray that our heavenly Father will give thee great wisdom in counsel and make thee of deep penetration, and fill thy heart with compassion and love that all thy decisions may be just and true [p. 201]

Brother Grover, we ordain thee to be an high priest in the church of Christ and pray that thou mayest have all the power of thy ministry, we also ordain thee a high counsellor in the High council at Kirtland, and we pray that thou mayest have great wisdom and be very useful in the church and through faithfulness thou shalt have all the blessings of heaven and of earth and no man shall take them from thee.

Noah Packard we also ordain thee to be a high priest and pray that thou mayest be a minister in Righteousness and go forth and proclaim the gospel with great power. We also ordain thee to be a high counsellor in the high counsil of Kirtland and we say, if thou art faithful great blessings shall be given to you.

Joseph Kingsbury, We ordain thee to be an high priest and pray that thy crown be made to shine as the stars that thou mayest always bear off the gospel triumphly in in the face of all opposition, We also ordain thee to be a high counsellor at that stake at Kirtland, praying that you may have the spirit of these offices to which you are now ordained, and this shall be the case through your faithfulness.

---

184. Hyrum Smith was called to the Kirtland high council on 24 September 1834 to replace Sylvester Smith, who had been removed from the council for making unfounded accusations against JS. (Minutes, 24 Sept. 1834, in *JSP,* D4:174.)

185. Hyde had served on the Kirtland high council since its creation. He was later ordained as one of the original members of the Quorum of the Twelve Apostles, eleven months before this grand council. (Minutes, 17 Feb. 1834, in *JSP,* D3:436; Minutes, Discourse, and Blessings, 14–15 Feb. 1835, in *JSP,* D4:228.)

186. Joseph Smith Sr. had served on the Kirtland high council since its creation. He was then appointed to the church's presidency, thirteen months before this grand council. (Minutes, 17 Feb. 1834, in *JSP,* D3:436; Account of Meetings, Revelation, and Blessing, 5–6 Dec. 1834, in *JSP,* D4:200.)

187. JS's journal adds that "many great and glorious blessings were pronounced upon the heads of thes[e] councilors by president S. Rigdon who was spokesman on the occasion." (JS, Journal, 13 Jan. 1836, in *JSP,* J1:150.)

Samuel James, We ordain thee to be an high priest in the Church of the Latter day Saints, and pray that all the powers of thy mind may be enlisted in building up the kingdom of God, that thou mayest be consecrated to God from this very hour: We also ordain thee to be a high counsellor at the stake of Kirtland and we say to thee, if thou wilt be faithful, thou shalt have all the blessings pertaining to the offices to which you have been ordained and no power shall take them from thee. amen.

Alvah Beeman [Beman][188] and Isaac McWithy[189] were appointed counsellors pro tem in the place of Elders [p. 202] John Murdock and Solomon Hancock who were absent in the council of Zion.[190]

Thomas Carrico [Jr.][191] was appointed Door Keeper in the house of the Lord by unanimous vote of the assembly

Motioned, seconded and voted unanimously that J. Smith Jun.' S. Rigdon, Hyrum Smith, W. W. Phelps and David Whitmer, be a committee to draft a code of rules or laws for the regulation of the house of the Lord in times of worship.[192]

Nominated, Seconded and carried unanimously that no whispering shall be allowed in the council nor any loud talking by any one except when called upon, or when he asks the privelege of so doing;[193]

---

188. Beman arrived in Kirtland two days earlier from Genesee County, New York, to prepare to attend the upcoming solemn assembly. (JS, Journal, 11 Jan. 1836, in *JSP*, J1:147.)

189. McWithy was ordained an elder on 15 February 1833 and had lived in Kirtland since 1835. JS performed a marriage at McWithy's house in December 1835. (Minutes, 15 Feb. 1833, in *JSP*, D3:10; Geauga Co., OH, Deed Records, 1795–1921, vol. 20, pp. 299–300, 15 July 1835, microfilm 20,238, U.S. and Canada Record Collection, FHL; JS, Journal, 13 Dec. 1835, in *JSP*, J1:121.)

190. A week earlier, a council at Kirtland permanently replaced five other members of the Missouri high council, four of whom had been called to the Quorum of the Twelve. (Minute Book 2, 6 Jan. 1836; JS, Journal, 13 Jan. 1836, in *JSP*, J1:150.)

191. Carrico moved to Kirtland in August 1835. The day after this meeting, he married Elizabeth Baker in a ceremony performed by JS. (Nauvoo Ninth Ward High Priests Quorum, Minutes, [14]; JS, Journal, 14 Jan. 1836, in *JSP*, J1:153.)

192. See Rules and Regulations, 14 Jan. 1836, pp. 143–145 herein.

193. JS's journal expands upon this point: "The question was agitate[d] whether whispering, should be allowed in our councils and assemblys a vote was called from the whole assembly and carried in the negative, that no whispering shall be allowed nor any one allowed, (except he is called upon or asks permission,) to speak loud in our councils or assemblies, upon any concideration whatever, and no man shall be interupted while speaking unless he is speaking out of place, and every man, shall be allowed to speak in his turn." The vote and decision made here were in harmony with a December 1832 revelation that gave instructions for the School of the Prophets and for the "house of God." The revelation stated: "Lit [let] not all be spokesmen at once, but let one speak at a time, and lit [let] all listen, unto his sayings, that when all have spoken, that all may be edified, of all, and that evry man, may have an equal privelege." (JS, Journal, 13 Jan. 1836, in *JSP*, J1:150; Revelation, 27–28 Dec. 1832, in *JSP*, D2:345 [D&C 88:122]; for more on conduct in church councils, see Minutes, 12 Feb. 1834, in *JSP*, D3:427.)

President Rigdon rose up and made some general remarks in relation to the building up of the Kingdom of God, which were very appropriate and timely.[194] He then closed by prayer——

adjourned till Friday the 15th inst at 9 °-clock A.M. to meet in the stone house[195]

Orson Hyde, Clerk

————— ❧ —————

Rules and Regulations, 14 January 1836

Source Note

Rules and Regulations, Kirtland Township, Geauga Co., OH, 14 Jan. 1836. Featured version copied [ca. 15 Jan. 1836] in JS, Journal, 1835–1836, pp. 111–113; handwriting of Warren Parrish; JS Collection, CHL. For more information on JS, Journal, 1835–1836, see Source Notes for Multiple-Entry Documents, p. 524 herein.

Historical Introduction

Church leaders from Ohio and Missouri gathered in Kirtland, Ohio, on 13 January 1836 to form a grand council. That council appointed JS, Sidney Rigdon, Hyrum Smith, William W. Phelps, and David Whitmer to write a set of rules "for the regulation of the house of the Lord in times of worship."[196]

On 27 December 1832, JS had dictated a revelation that commanded church members to build a religious structure for educational purposes as well as for worship.[197] By mid-January 1836, the House of the Lord was nearly finished. As interior rooms were completed, church leaders and members began to use them for administrative, religious, and educational activities, even before the formal dedication of the building.[198]

With the House of the Lord already being used, the grand council discussed the need to establish rules for use of and conduct in the building, particularly during times of worship.[199] On 14 January 1836, the committee appointed by the grand council met in the

---

194. According to JS's journal, Rigdon "made some verry appropriate remarks touching the enduement." (JS, Journal, 13 Jan. 1836, in *JSP*, J1:151.)

195. The building referred to here is the House of the Lord in Kirtland, also sometimes called the "stone meeting house," "chapel," or "chapel house." (See Minutes, 15 Jan. 1836, pp. 146–148 herein; Geauga Co., OH, Deed Records, 1795–1921, vol. 24, p. 353, 10 Apr. 1837, microfilm 20,240, U.S. and Canada Record Collection, FHL.)

196. Minutes, 13 Jan. 1836, p. 142 herein.

197. Revelation, 27–28 Dec. 1832, in *JSP*, D2:345 [D&C 88:119]; see also Letter to William W. Phelps, 11 Jan. 1833, in *JSP*, D2:367.

198. JS, Journal, 18 Oct. 1835; 12 and 19 Nov. 1835; 10 Dec. 1835; 4 and 15 Jan. 1836, in *JSP*, J1:72, 96, 107, 119–120, 143, 153; Angell, Autobiography, 2–5.

199. Minutes, 13 Jan. 1836, p. 142 herein.

printing office to draft these rules of conduct.[200] The committee presented these rules and regulations to the grand council in a meeting in the attic of the House of the Lord on 15 January 1836. After reading the rules, the grand council vigorously debated them before ultimately approving them.[201]

There are two extant versions of these rules and regulations: one in Minute Book 1 and one in JS's journal. While Minute Book 1 is the official record, the minutes that contain the rules are misdated to 12 January 1836 and are combined with a shortened version of the minutes dated 13 January 1836. Those minutes were entered into Minute Book 1 in May 1837 and appear to be copied from the version in JS's journal, which Warren Parrish recorded soon after the grand council approved the rules and regulations.[202] Therefore, the version from JS's journal appears to be closer to the original document and is featured here. The Minute Book 1 version contains a few variations in text and punctuation; significant differences are noted.

Document Transcript

1st— It is according to the rules and regulations of all regular and legal organized bodies to have a president to keep order.—

2ond— The body thus organized are under obligation to be in subjection to that authority—

3d— When a congregation assembles in this house they shall submit to the following rules, that due respect may be paid to the order of the worship—viz.

1st— no man shall be interupted who is appointed to speak by the presidency of the Church,[203] by any disorderly person or persons in the congregation, by whispering by laughing by talking[204] by menacing Jestures by getting up and running out in a disorderly manner or by offering indignity to the manner of worship or the religion or to any officer of said church while officiating in his office in any wise whatever by any display of ill manners or ill breeding from old or young rich or poor male or female bond or free black or white believer or unbeliever and if any of the above insults are offered such measures will be taken as are lawful to punish the aggressor or aggressors and eject them out of the house

---

200. JS, Journal, 14 Jan. 1836, in *JSP*, J1:151–153.

201. JS, Journal, 15 Jan. 1836, in *JSP*, J1:153–154; see also Minutes, 13 Jan. 1836, pp. 138–143 herein; and Minutes, 15 Jan. 1836, pp. 146–148 herein.

202. Minute Book 1, 12 Jan. 1836; Minutes, 15 Jan. 1836, p. 148 herein; JS, Journal, 14 Jan. 1836, in *JSP*, J1:152–153.

203. The copy of the rules found in Minute Book 1 reads, "by the permission of the church." (Minute Book 1, 12 Jan. 1836.)

204. At the previous day's meeting of the grand council, a measure was unanimously approved that no whispering would be allowed and that only after requesting and obtaining permission would anyone be permitted to speak aloud in church councils or assemblies. (Minutes, 13 Jan. 1836, p. 142 herein.)

2^{ond}— An insult offered to the ~~presidency~~ ⟨presiding⟩ Elder of said Church, shall be concidered an insult to the whole [p. 111] body, also an insult offered to any of the officers of said Church while officiating shall be considered an insult to the whole body—

3^{d}— All persons are prohibited from going up the stairs in times of worship[205]

4th— all persons are prohibited from exploring the house except waited upon by a person appointed for that purpose—

5th— all persons are prohibited from going ⟨in⟩to the several pulpits[206] except the officers who are appointed to officiate in the same[207]

6th— All persons are prohibited from cutting marking or marring the inside or outside of the house with a knife pencil or any other instrument whatever, under pain of such penalty as the law shall inflict—

7th— All children are prohibited from assembling in the house above or below or any part of it to play or for recreation at any time, and all parents guardians or masters shall be ameneable for all damage that shall accrue in consequence of their children—[208]

8th— All persons whether believers or unbelievers shall be treated with due respect by the ~~authority~~ ⟨authorities⟩ of the Church— [p. 112]

9th— no imposition shall be practiced upon any member of the church by depriving them of their ⟨rights⟩ in the house— council adjourned sini di [sine die][209]

———— ❧ ————

205. Besides general worship meetings on the first and second floors of the temple, the third or attic floor with its dormer windows and five offices, or classrooms, provided meeting places for smaller gatherings, such as priesthood quorums, high council meetings, and the Hebrew School.

206. The two general assembly floors were designed with sets of three-tiered pulpits at each end of the large assembly rooms. (See Plan of the House of the Lord, between 1 and 25 June 1833, in *JSP,* D3:131.)

207. Various church officers were to occupy the two tiers of pulpits in the House of the Lord. (See Plan of the House of the Lord, between 1 and 25 June 1833, in *JSP,* D3:141–142.)

208. Perhaps the committee foresaw the use of the building by scores of young students. Though this seems to be a general rule to regulate the behavior of children and their parents in worship in the House of the Lord, it was particularly pertinent later in 1836: by November, the attic floor was being used by the church's Kirtland High School with "135 or 40 students" as well as a "Juvenile" school. ("Our Village," *LDS Messenger and Advocate,* Jan. 1837, 3:444.)

209. The grand council adjourned 15 January after it approved these rules, but JS's scribe copied the approved rules into JS's journal using the date that he and his committee drafted them—14 January 1836—suggesting that Parrish copied these rules into JS's journal no earlier than 15 January.

Minutes, 15 January 1836

Source Note

Minutes, Kirtland Township, Geauga Co., OH, 15 Jan. 1836. Featured version copied [between ca. 4 Apr. and ca. 16 May 1836] in Minute Book 1, pp. 203–205; handwriting of Warren A. Cowdery; CHL. For more information on Minute Book 1, see Source Notes for Multiple-Entry Documents, p. 527 herein.

Historical Introduction

The grand council of church leaders that met in the attic of the printing office on 13 January 1836 reconvened two days later in a council room on the third floor of the House of the Lord. The council discussed and voted on the rules and regulations that a committee led by JS had drafted the previous day.[210] The church leaders at the meeting further organized the priesthood quorums preparatory to the solemn assembly and the promised endowment of power. Presidents were then appointed and ordained to lead the various quorums of the priesthood. This structure—each quorum overseen by a presiding official—had been described in a November 1831 revelation that was later incorporated into the instruction on priesthood published in the 1835 edition of the Doctrine and Covenants.[211] The council also oversaw the bestowal of blessings on certain individuals and conducted other business concerning the House of the Lord.

There are two extant accounts of the 15 January meeting. Orson Hyde took the official minutes, probably on loose paper, but that original version has not survived. Warren A. Cowdery copied the minutes into Minute Book 1 sometime in the spring of 1836. Warren Parrish penned an alternate account in JS's journal sometime shortly after the meeting took place.[212] Because Minute Book 1 represents the official record of meetings of church governance in Kirtland and both extant versions are contemporaneous, the Minute Book 1 version is presented here. Significant differences between the two versions are noted.

Document Transcript

Friday Morning January 15, 1836, council met pursuant to adjournment[213] and after President J. Smith Junʳ had organized the council, he proceeded to give many good instructions in relation to the order & manner of conducting the council and also delivered a solemn charge to the counsel[214] after which he opened by prayer and presided as before.

---

210. Minutes, 13 Jan. 1836, p. 139 herein; Rules and Regulations, 14 Jan. 1836, pp. 144–145 herein.

211. Revelation, 11 Nov. 1831–B, in *JSP,* D2:133–134 [D&C 107:60–66]; Instruction on Priesthood, between ca. 1 Mar. and ca. 4 May 1835, in *JSP,* D4:317–318 [D&C 107:60–66].

212. JS, Journal, 15 Jan. 1836, in *JSP,* J1:153–156.

213. See Minutes, 13 Jan. 1836, pp. 138–143 herein. According to JS's journal, the meeting commenced at nine in the morning. (JS, Journal, 15 Jan. 1836, in *JSP,* J1:153.)

214. According to JS's journal, JS "made some observation respecting the order of the day, and the great responsibility we are under to transact all our business, in righteousness before God, inasmuch as

President J. Smith Jun[r] one of the committee to draft rules for the regulation of the House of the Lord, made the report of said committee by reading the laws or rules they had drafted three times.[215] Th[e]y were approved and unanimously adopted.[216] and the counsil adjourned one hour.[217]

Met at the expiration of the time aforesaid and proceeded to business without ceremony. [p. 203]

Don Carlos Smith was nominated to be president of the high priest hood in Kirtland, Seconded and carried with out opposition.[218]

Alvah Beeman [Beman], was nominated for president of the quorum of Elders in Kirtland, seconded and voted unanimously that he serve in that capacity.

The Bishop of Kirtland[219] nominated William Cowdery [Jr.] to be president of the priests in Kirtland. This nomination was seconded and carried unanimously.

Thomas Gates was nominated for president of the teachers, vote not carried[220]

Oliver Olney was nominated for president of the Teachers, seconded and vote carried unanimously

Ira Bond was nominated to be president of the Deacons in this place, motion seconded and carried by a unanimous vote.

President Joseph Smith Sen[r.] Sidney Rigdon proceeded to ordain Don Carlos Smith and Alvah Beeman to the respective offices to which they had been chosen, and pronounced great blessings upon them.[221]

Bishop [Newel K.] Whitney of Kirtland then proceeded to ordain William Cowdery, Oliver Olney & Ira Bond and pronounced many blessings upon them, according to their offices & standing.[222]

----

our desisions will have a bearing upon all mankind and upon all generations to come." (JS, Journal, 15 Jan. 1836, in *JSP*, J1:153.)

215. See Rules and Regulations, 14 Jan. 1836, pp. 144–145 herein.

216. The account in JS's journal indicates that there was some disagreement and discussion about the rules and regulations before they were finally adopted by a unanimous vote. (JS, Journal, 15 Jan. 1836, in *JSP*, J1:154.)

217. According to JS's journal, the council adjourned at noon and resumed its meeting at one in the afternoon. (JS, Journal, 15 Jan. 1836, in *JSP*, J1:154.)

218. Don Carlos Smith was first nominated to be ordained a high priest before being nominated and accepted to serve as the president of the high priests quorum. (JS, Journal, 15 Jan. 1836, in *JSP*, J1:155.)

219. Newel K. Whitney.

220. Meaning, the vote was not unanimous, as required by previous revelation. (See Revelation, July 1830–B, in *JSP*, D1:161 [D&C 26:2]; and Revelation, Sept. 1830–B, in *JSP*, D1:186 [D&C 28:13].)

221. JS's journal notes that Hyrum Smith also participated in the ordinations of and blessings given to Don Carlos Smith and Beman. (JS, Journal, 15 Jan. 1836, in *JSP*, J1:155.)

222. JS's journal notes that Whitney's counselors in the bishopric, Reynolds Cahoon and Vinson

Moved seconded & voted that all the quorums take their turn in performing the office of door keeper in the house of the Lord.

Moved seconded and voted ~~that~~ by each quorum that Amos Orton, Samuel Rolfe Thomas Carico [Carrico Jr.] & Nathaniel Milliken[223] be appointed assistant door keepers

Motioned, seconded & voted that the Presidencey of the high council[224] hold the keys of the house of the Lord except the keys of one vestry which shall be held by the Bishop of Kirtland [p. 204]

Motioned and seconded that the Laws regulating the house of the Lord go into effect from this time, and that Elder John Corril[l] take it upon him to see that they are enforced, giving him the privilege of calling as many as he choose to assist him.[225]——

Moved, seconded and voted that this council adjourn sine die— Charge & Prayer By President S. Rigdon.

O[rson] Hyde, Clerk.

———— ❧ ————

Minutes, 16 January 1836

Source Note

Minutes, Kirtland Township, Geauga Co., OH, 16 Jan. 1836. Featured version copied [ca. 16 Jan. 1836] in JS, Journal, 1835–1836, pp. 119–126; handwriting of unidentified scribe and Warren Parrish; JS Collection, CHL. For more information on JS, Journal, 1835–1836, see Source Notes for Multiple-Entry Documents, p. 524 herein.

Historical Introduction

On Saturday, 16 January 1836, JS, Frederick G. Williams, and Sidney Rigdon met in Kirtland, Ohio, with the Quorum of the Twelve Apostles, who had requested a conference to air their grievances to the church's presidency.[226] Warren Parrish, the clerk at the

---

Knight, also participated in the ordination and blessing of Cowdery, Olney, and Bond. (JS, Journal, 15 Jan. 1836, in *JSP*, J1:155.)

223. On 13 January 1836, the grand council appointed Milliken and Carico as doorkeepers. Milliken declined the appointment for health reasons, and he was released from the position. Milliken may have reconsidered declining the office and accepted the appointment given this day. (JS, Journal, 13 Jan. 1836, in *JSP*, J1:150–151.)

224. JS, Sidney Rigdon, and Frederick G. Williams presided over the Kirtland high council. (Minutes, 17 Feb. 1834, in *JSP*, D3:435–439; see also "Church Officers in the Kirtland Stake," p. 609 herein.)

225. Corrill, a member of the Missouri bishopric, had been appointed to oversee "the finishing of the Lord's house." (Corrill, *Brief History*, 22, in *JSP*, H2:153.)

226. Oliver Cowdery was not present for the meeting, though he was in Kirtland on this date. He was evidently informed of the meeting's discussion and outcome that evening when he met in the House of the Lord with JS and others. Cowdery's diary notes that he "wrote a letter to my brother Warren on the

gathering, wrote that Thomas B. Marsh, the president of the Twelve, "arose and requested the privilege in behalf of his colleagues of speaking, each in his turn without being interrupted." Marsh presented three issues that were particularly troubling the Twelve. First, notwithstanding earlier attempts to resolve the matter, they remained disturbed by a letter of reprimand that had been sent to them by church leaders while they were in Maine proselytizing in August 1835.[227] Second, despite normally being placed next to the presidency in voting at council meetings, they had voted after the high councils of both Missouri and Kirtland at the grand council held the previous day.[228] Finally, Marsh was doubly upset about the Kirtland high council's recent trial of Francis Gladden Bishop, who had been accused of "advancing heretical doctrines." Marsh felt that Hyrum Smith had wronged the Twelve at the trial by speaking against them, and the fact that the trial had occurred at all, after Bishop had already been tried and disciplined by the Twelve, further incensed Marsh.[229]

Despite confessions and expressions of forgiveness at a September 1835 meeting between the Twelve and the presidency, problems continued to surface, and JS had disagreements with individual members of the Twelve, including his brother William.[230] At the 16 January meeting, the church presidency granted each of the Twelve, starting with Thomas B. Marsh, the opportunity to be heard. JS's journal notes that Marsh preferred charges against Warren A. Cowdery for making false accusations against the Twelve and for unchristian conduct.[231] Marsh also singled out Oliver Cowdery for using language "to one of the twelve that was unchristian and unbecoming [of] any man, and that they would not submit to such treatment." After Marsh finished his remarks, each of the other apostles spoke.

After each member of the Twelve spoke, JS responded and gave the instruction found in the first-person voice in the minutes featured here. JS explained that the authority of the Twelve "is next to the present presidency," and he renounced Oliver Cowdery's "harsh language" and moved toward a reconciliation between the presidency and the Twelve. He sought forgiveness from the Twelve and informed them that he had "unlimited confidence" in them and their word. The Twelve accepted JS's words and those of Sidney Rigdon and Frederick G. Williams; all "the difficulties that were on their minds" were satisfactorily settled. Reflecting on this meeting, JS's 17 January journal entry recounts that "some of our hearts were too big for utterance . . . and my soul was filled with the glory of God."[232] Six

subject of a difficulty which exists between him and the Twelve," a subject that was addressed at the meeting. (Cowdery, Diary, 16 Jan. 1836.)

227. Letter to Quorum of the Twelve, 4 Aug. 1835, in *JSP*, D4:371; see also Record of the Twelve, 4 May 1835–28 Aug. 1835.

228. Minutes, 13 Jan. 1836, p. 139 herein.

229. Minutes, 28–29 Sept. 1835, in *JSP*, D4:449–451; Orson Hyde and William E. McLellin to Oliver Cowdery, 27 Apr. 1835, in *LDS Messenger and Advocate*, Apr. 1835, 1:103; Record of the Twelve, 7 Aug. 1835.

230. Minutes, 26 Sept. 1835, in *JSP*, D4:441–442; Revelation, 3 Nov. 1835, pp. 32–36 herein; JS, Journal, 3 Nov. 1835, in *JSP*, J1:83; Discourse, 12 Nov. 1835, pp. 48–49 herein; Letter from William Smith, ca. 18 Dec. 1835, pp. 109–115 herein.

231. Cowdery, Diary, 16 Jan. 1836; "Notice," *LDS Messenger and Advocate*, Feb. 1836, 2:263.

232. JS, Journal, 16 and 17 Jan. 1836, in *JSP*, J1:156–160; Cowdery, Diary, 17 Jan. 1836; William W. Phelps, [Kirtland, OH], to Sally Waterman Phelps, [Liberty, MO], [18 Jan. 1836], William W. Phelps, Papers, BYU.

days later, the Twelve received their anointing, preparatory to the solemn assembly and the anticipated endowment of power in the House of the Lord in Kirtland.[233]

Document Transcript

/[234]Saturday morning the 16th by request I meet with the council of the 12 in company with my colleagues F[rederick] G Williams and S[idney] Rigdon

Council organized and opened by singing and prayer offered up by Thomas B. Marsh president of the 12

He arose and requested the privilege in behalf of his colleagues of speaking, each in his turn without being interupted; which was granted them— Elder Marsh proceeded [p. 119] to unbosom his feelings touching the mission of the 12, and more particularly respecting a certain letter which they recieved from the presidency of the high council in Kirtland, while attending a conference in the ~~East~~ State of Maine—[235] also spoke of being plased in our council, on Friday last below the council's of Kirtland and Zion having been previously placed next [to] the presidency, in our assemblies—[236] also observed that they were hurt on account of some remarks made by President H[yrum] Smith on the trial of [Francis] Gladden Bishop who had been previously tried before the council of the 12, while on their mission in the east, who had by their request thrown his case before the high council in Kirtland for investigation, and the 12 concidered that their proceedings with him were in some degree, discountenanced—[237]

~~The rest~~ ⟨remaining⟩ Elder Marsh then gave way to his brethren and they arose and spoke in turn untill they had all spoken acquiessing in the observations of Elder Marsh and mad[e] some additions to his remarks which are as follows— That the letter in question which they received from the presidency, in which two of their numbers were suspended,[238] and the rest severely chastened,

233. JS, Journal, 22 Jan. 1836, in *JSP*, J1:171–172.

234. TEXT: Warren Parrish handwriting begins.

235. The Quorum of the Twelve Apostles held conferences in Maine on 21 and 28 August 1835 after having held conferences in the state of New York the previous month. On 4 August 1835, a high council consisting of the First Presidency and the presidency of the Missouri high council composed a letter to the Twelve reprimanding the quorum for neglecting their duties. (Record of the Twelve, 21 and 28 Aug. 1835; Letter to Quorum of the Twelve, 4 Aug. 1835, in *JSP*, D4:371–378.)

236. See Minutes, 15 Jan. 1836, pp. 146–148 herein.

237. While on their mission to the eastern states, the Twelve disciplined Bishop, whose case was reheard in Kirtland by the high council on 28 September 1835 with some apostles as witnesses. (Minutes, 28–29 Sept. 1835, in *JSP*, D4:449–451; JS, Journal, 28 Sept. 1835, in *JSP*, J1:66.)

238. The two were William E. McLellin and Orson Hyde. (Letter to Quorum of the Twelve, 4 Aug. 1835, in *JSP*, D4:375–376; Revelation, 3 Nov. 1835, pp. 35–36 herein; see also Letter from Orson Hyde, 15 Dec. 1835, pp. 104–109 herein.)

and that too upon testimony which was unwarantable, and particularly stress was laid upon a certain letter which the presidency had received from Dr. [p. 120] W[arren] A. Cowdery of Freedom New York in which he prefered charges against them[239] which were false, and upon which ~~they~~ ⟨we⟩ (the presiders[240]) had acted in chastning them and therefore, the 12, had concluded that the presidency had lost confidence in them, and that whereas the church in this place, had carressed them, at the time of their appointment, to the appostleship they now treated them coolly and appear to have lost confidence in them also—

They spoke of their having been in this work from the beginning almost and had born the burden in the heat of the day and passed through many trials and that the presidency ought not to ~~have~~ suspect their fidelity nor loose confidence in them, neither have chastised them upon such testimony as was lying ~~before~~ before them— also urged the necessity of an explinition upon the letter which they received from the presidency, and the propriety of their having information as it respects their duties, authority &c— that they might come to ⟨an⟩ understanding in all things, that they migh[t] act in perfect unison and harmony before the Lord and be prepared for the endument— also that they had prefered a charge against Dr [Warren A.] Cowdery for his unchristian conduct which the presidency had disregarded— also that President O[liver] Cowdery on a certain occasion had made use of language to one of the [p. 121] twelve that was unchristian and unbecoming any man, and that they would not submit to such treatment

The remarks of all the 12 were made in a verry forcible and explicit manner yet cool and deliberate; /[241]~~I arose~~

I observed that we had heard them patiently and in turn should expect to be heard patiently also; and first I remarked that it was necessary that the 12 should state whether they were determined to persevere in the work of the Lord, whether the presidency are able to satisfy them or not; vote called and carried in the affirmative unaminously; I then said to them that I had not lost confidence in them, and that they had no reason to suspect my confidence, and that I would be willing to be weighed in the scale of truth today in this matter, and risk it in the day of judgment; and as it respects the chastning contained in the letter in question which I acknowledge might have been expressed in too harsh

---

239. After the Twelve departed Freedom, Warren A. Cowdery wrote a letter to his brother Oliver in late July 1835 complaining that the Twelve had neglected to instruct the branch's members on the necessity of gathering donations for the construction on the House of the Lord in Kirtland. According to Warren, this dereliction of duty by the Twelve prevented the church members in Freedom from making more substantial donations. (Letter to Quorum of the Twelve, 4 Aug. 1835, in *JSP*, D4:374–375.)

240. TEXT: Possibly "presiden".

241. TEXT: Warren Parrish handwriting ends; unidentified begins.

language; which was not intentional and I ask your forgiveness in as much as I have hurt your feelings; but nevertheless, the letter ~~that~~ that Elder Mc.lellen [William E. McLellin] wrote back[242] to Kirtland while the twelve were at the east was harsh also and I was willing to set the one against the other; I next proceeded to explain the subject of the duty of the twelve;[243] and their authority which is next to the present presidency, and that the arangement of the assembly[244] in this place on the 15[inst] /[245] in placing the high councils of Kirtland ~~and~~ next [to] the presidency[246] was because the buisness to be transacted was buisness that related to that body in particular which was to [p. 122] fill the several quorum's in Kirtland; not beca[u]se they were first in office, and that the arangement was most Judicious that could be made on the occassion also the 12, are not subject to any other than the first presidency; viz. myself S. Rigdon and F. G. Williams— I also stated to the 12, that I do not ~~continue~~ countinance the harsh language of President [Oliver] Cowdery to them neither in myself nor any other man, although I have sometimes spoken to[o] harsh from the impulse of the moment and inasmuch as I have wounded your feelings brethren I ask your forgivness, for I love you and will hold you up with all my heart in all righteousness before the Lord, and before all men, for be assured brethren I am willing to stem the torrent of all opposition; in storms in tempests in thunders and lightning by sea and by land in the wilderness or among fals brethren, or mobs or wherever God in his providence may call us and I am determined that neither hights nor depths principalities nor powers things present or to come nor any other creature shall separate me from you;[247] and I will now covenant with you before God that I will not listen too nor credit, any derogatory report against any of you nor condemn you upon any testimony beneath the heavens,

---

242. In a letter (no longer extant) to his wife, McLellin expressed his displeasure at the manner in which a school at Kirtland was being conducted. McLellin had formed his critical view of the school from a report by Orson Hyde, who had returned east from a recent visit to Kirtland. The charges against the Twelve were heard 26 September 1835, the day the Twelve returned to Kirtland, when Hyde and McLellin "frankly confessed" the impropriety of what they had said about "President Rigdon's school" and "were forgiven." (Minutes, 26 Sept. 1835, in *JSP,* D4:442.)

243. For documents related to the responsibilities and administrative jurisdiction of the Twelve, see Minutes, 27 Feb. 1835, in *JSP,* D4:247–254; Instruction on Priesthood, between ca. 1 Mar. and ca. 4 May 1835, in *JSP,* D4:308–321 [D&C 107]; Letter to Quorum of the Twelve, 4 Aug. 1835, in *JSP,* D4:371–378; and Record of the Twelve, 27 Feb. and 2 May 1835.

244. See Minutes, 15 Jan. 1836, pp. 146–148 herein.

245. TEXT: Unidentified handwriting ends; Warren Parrish begins.

246. During the discussion the previous day on the regulations governing the House of the Lord, JS presented the rules for a vote by the Twelve only after presenting them to the high councils of Kirtland and Missouri. (Minutes, 15 Jan. 1836, pp. 146–148 herein; see also Esplin, "Emergence of Brigham Young," 184–185, 216–217nn84–86.)

247. See Romans 8:38–39.

short of that testimony which is infalible, untill I can see you face to face and know of a surity [p. 123] and I do place unlimited confidence in your word for I believe you to be men of truth, and I ask the same of you, when I tell you any thing that you place equal confidence in my word for I will not tell you I know anything which I do not know— but I have already consumed more time than I intended to when I commenced and I will now give way to my colleagues

President Rigdon arose next and acquiessed in what I had said and acknowledged to the 12, that he had not done as he ought, in not citing Dr. Cowdery to trial on the charges that were put into his hands by the 12, that he had neglected his duty in this thing, for which he asked their forgiveness, and would now attend to it if they desired him to do so,[248] and ~~Elder~~ ⟨Presdt⟩ Rigdon also observed to the 12 ~~that~~ ⟨if he⟩ ~~he might have~~ ⟨had⟩ spoken, or reproved too ~~harshe,~~ ⟨harshly,⟩ at any time and had injured their feelings by so doing he asked their forgivness.—

President Williams arose and acquiessed in the above sentiment's expressed by myself and President Rigdon, in full and said many good things

The President of the 12, then called a vote of that body to know whether they were perfectly satisfied with the [p. 124] explenation which we had given them and whether they would enter into the covenant we had proposed to them, which was most readily manifested in the affirmative by raising their hands to heaven, in testimony of their willingness and desire to enter into this covenant and their entire satisfaction with our explanation, upon all the difficulties that were on their minds, we then took each others by the hand in confirmation of our covenant and their was a perfect unison of feeling on this occasion, and our hearts overflowed with blessings, which we pronounced upon eachothers heads as the Spirit gave us utterance my scribe[249] is included in this covenant ~~with~~ and blessings with us, for I love him, for ⟨the⟩ truth and integrity that dwelleth in him and may God enable us all, to perform our vows and covenants with each other in all fidelity and rightiousness before Him, that our influence may be felt among the nations of the earth in mighty power, even to rend the kingdom of darkness in sunder, and triumph over priestcraft and

---

248. This occurred on 5 March 1836, when JS met with Oliver Cowdery, Sidney Rigdon, the Quorum of the Twelve, and Warren A. Cowdery. According to Oliver Cowdery, "The Twelve had prefered a charge against my brother [Warren A. Cowdery] for a letter he wrote last summer upon the subject of their teaching while at the Freedom conference. My brother confessed his mistake, upon the testimony of the Twelve, and said he was willing to publish that they were not in the fault, but that he was satisfied they delivered those instructions which he had supposed they had not." Warren A. Cowdery wrote a statement of apology, which the *Messenger and Advocate* printed in its February 1836 issue. (Cowdery, Diary, 5 Mar. 1836; "Notice," *LDS Messenger and Advocate,* Feb. 1836, 2:263.)

249. Warren Parrish.

spiritual wickedness in high places,²⁵⁰ and brake in pieces all ~~other~~ kingdoms that are opposed to the Kingdom of Christ, and spread the light and truth of the everlasting gospel from the rivers to the ends of the earth²⁵¹

Elder Beemon [Alvah Beman] call[ed] for council upon the subject of his returning home he wished to know whether it was best for him to return before the Solemn Assembly [p. 125] or not, after taking it into concideration the council advised him to tarry²⁵² we dismissed by singing and prayer and retired²⁵³

W[arren] Parrish <u>scribe</u>

———— ⁊ ————

Marriage Certificate for William Cahoon and Nancy Gibbs, 18 January 1836

Source Note

JS, Marriage Certificate, for William Cahoon and Nancy Gibbs, Kirtland Township, Geauga Co., OH, 18 Jan. 1836. Featured version copied [ca. 19 Jan. 1836] in JS, Journal, 1835–1836, p. 131; handwriting of Warren Parrish; JS Collection, CHL. For more information on JS, Journal, 1835–1836, see Source Notes for Multiple-Entry Documents, p. 524 herein.

Historical Introduction

JS performed marriages in late 1835 and early 1836 for members of the Church of the Latter Day Saints according to the church's rules and regulations.²⁵⁴ On the afternoon of 17 January 1836, JS solemnized three marriages, including that of William F. Cahoon and Nancy Gibbs.²⁵⁵ Cahoon, the son of Reynolds and Thirza Stiles Cahoon, was twenty-two years old at the time of his marriage to Gibbs. He had traveled and proselytized in New York with David W. Patten and Amasa Lyman in 1832 and 1833 and had participated in the 1834 Camp of Israel expedition before returning to Kirtland to labor as a carpenter on the House of the Lord.²⁵⁶ He was ordained a member of the Seventy on 28 February 1835.²⁵⁷ Little is known about Gibbs at this time. She was eighteen years old

---

250. See Ephesians 6:12.

251. See Daniel 2:45; and Zechariah 9:10.

252. It appears that Beman remained in Kirtland and attended to the business of organizing the Kirtland elders quorum. (See Letter from the Presidency of Elders, 29 Jan. 1836, pp. 162–163 herein.)

253. Following this day of reconciliation, JS retired to his home, where he was joined by Oliver Cowdery, John Corrill, and later Martin Harris. They performed ritual washings that they "might be clean before the Lord for the Sabbath, confessing our sins and covenanting to be faithful to God." (Cowdery, Diary, 16 Jan. 1836.)

254. See Marriage License for John F. Boynton and Susan Lowell, 17 Nov. 1835, pp. 64–67 herein.

255. JS, Journal, 17 Jan. 1836, in *JSP,* J1:161.

256. Cahoon, Autobiography and Family Records, 22–25; see also Minutes, Discourse, and Blessings, 14–15 Feb. 1835, in *JSP,* D4:227.

257. Minutes and Blessings, 28 Feb.–1 Mar. 1835, in *JSP,* D4:259.

on her wedding day and had lived in Kirtland since the fall of 1833, having previously resided in Benson, Vermont.[258]

Although a couple intending to marry could obtain a license from the county clerk for permission to wed, they could also gain authorization to enter into marriage through publishment, or giving sufficient public notice of their intent to marry. According to Ohio state law, this required giving notice "in the presence of the congregation" on "two different days of public worship" with the first notice occurring "at least ten days previous to such marriage."[259] In his autobiography, William Cahoon noted that he and Gibbs did not obtain a license but that notice of their marriage was "published several times previously in the church which custom was allowed by the laws of the state."[260] After JS performed the ceremonies and dismissed the "publick congregation" of about three thousand that had assembled for the day's weddings, he and many others attended a feast at the home of Reynolds and Thirza Cahoon.[261] JS's journal notes that he enjoyed the "rich repast" and good company at the gathering.[262]

On 18 January 1836, the day after the wedding, JS signed a marriage certificate for Cahoon and Gibbs, and the day after that, 19 January, Warren Parrish made a copy of it in JS's journal. JS was required by law to file a marriage certificate with the county clerk within three months of a wedding.[263] On 22 February 1836, JS sent Elijah Fuller to Chardon with a copy of Cahoon and Gibbs's marriage certificate along with certificates for ten other couples.[264] Fuller delivered the certificates to Geauga County clerk David D. Aiken, who subsequently recorded the marriages in the county's marriage record ledger.[265]

Document Transcript

I hereby certify that agreeably to the rules and regulations of the church of christ of Latter-Day Saints,[266] on matrimony,[267] were joined in marriage Mr. William F. Cahoon and Miss Nancy M. Gibbs, both of this place, on Sabbath the 17th instant.

Joseph Smith Jun
Presiding Elder of said church

Kirtland Ohio Jan. 18th 1836 [p. 131]

———— ⁊ ————

258. Obituary for Nancy Miranda Cahoon, *Deseret News*, 25 Dec. 1867, 368.

259. An Act, Regulating Marriages [6 Jan. 1824], *Statutes of Ohio*, vol. 2, chap. 623, p. 1407, sec. 6.

260. Cahoon, Autobiography, 44–45.

261. Cahoon, Autobiography, 45.

262. JS, Journal, 17 Jan. 1836, in *JSP*, J1:161.

263. An Act, Regulating Marriages [6 Jan. 1824], *Statutes of Ohio*, vol. 2, chap. 623, p. 1407, sec. 8.

264. JS, Journal, 22 Feb. 1836, in *JSP*, J1:188.

265. Geauga Co., OH, Probate Court, Marriage Records, 1806–1920, vol. C, p. 144, 17 Jan. 1835, microfilm 873,461, U.S. and Canada Record Collection, FHL.

266. For more on changes to the name of the church, see Historical Introduction to Minutes, 3 May 1834, in *JSP*, D4:42–44.

267. For the published rules and regulations of the church, see Statement on Marriage, ca. Aug. 1835, in *JSP*, D4:475–478.

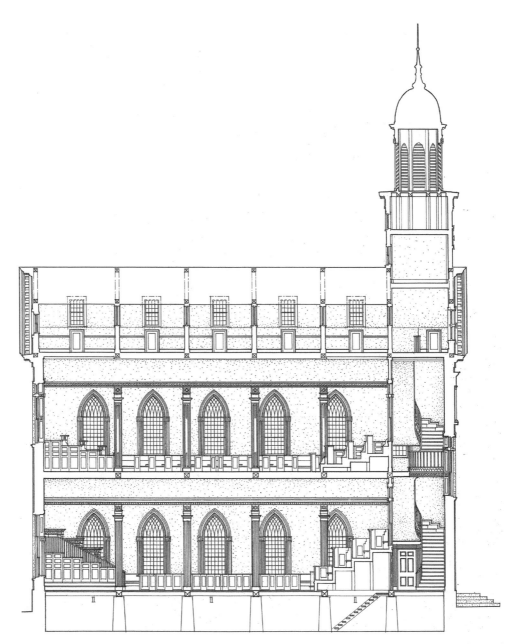

Interior of the House of the Lord, Kirtland, Ohio. This longitudinal section shows the first and second floors of the building, each of which had an assembly room or court with terraced pulpits on each end, and the five rooms of the third story. Joseph Smith used the top left room on the third floor for an office; schools and priesthood officers met in other third-floor rooms. (Courtesy Library of Congress, Washington DC. Drawing by Verdon W. Upham, Historic American Building Survey, 1934.)

Visions, 21 January 1836 [D&C 137]

Source Note

Visions, [Kirtland Township, Geauga Co., OH], 21 Jan. 1836. Featured version copied [ca. 21 Jan. 1836] in JS, Journal, 1835–1836, pp. 136–138; handwriting of Warren Parrish; JS Collection, CHL. For more information on JS, Journal, 1835–1836, see Source Notes for Multiple-Entry Documents, p. 524 herein.

Historical Introduction

The winter of 1835–1836 was a time of meetings and instruction in Kirtland, Ohio, as the Latter-day Saints prepared for the forthcoming solemn assembly in the House of the Lord and for the divine endowment of power long promised to be received there. On the afternoon of 21 January 1836, JS and the church presidency met in the council room above the printing office to take another step in preparation for the endowment.[268] Following biblical precedent, these church leaders washed their bodies with water and perfumed themselves with a sweet-smelling wash "preparatory to the annointing with the holy oil."[269] At sunset the church presidency and several others, including JS's scribe Warren Parrish and the bishoprics of Missouri and Kirtland, met on the third floor of the Kirtland House of the Lord in the "president's room," also called the "west school room," to administer the anointing ordinance. The Kirtland and Missouri high councils also came to the House of the Lord, but they "waited in prayer" separately until after the first anointings.[270] According to Oliver Cowdery, the members of the church presidency were "annointed with the same kind of oil and in the man[ner] that were Moses and Aaron, and those who stood before the Lord in ancient days."[271] The presidency first anointed church patriarch Joseph Smith Sr.'s head with consecrated oil and gave him a blessing. The patriarch then anointed the church's presidents in the order of their ages. When Joseph Smith Sr. anointed the head of JS, he "sealed upon [him], the blessings, of Moses, to lead Israel in the latter days."[272]

After the patriarch blessed his son, JS received blessings and prophecies under the hands of "all of the presidency," after which the "heavens were opened" and JS and others beheld "visions and revelations."[273] Warren Parrish recorded JS's narrative of those heavenly manifestations, including a description of the celestial kingdom and the individuals who would dwell therein, in JS's journal; that text is featured here. This vision of the celestial

---

268. For earlier meetings, see Minutes, 13 Jan. 1836, pp. 138–143 herein; Minutes, 15 Jan. 1836, pp. 146–148 herein; and Minutes, 16 Jan. 1836, pp. 148–154 herein.

269. Cowdery, Diary, 21 Jan. 1836.

270. JS, Journal, 21 Jan. 1836, in *JSP,* J1:167. As Oliver Cowdery explained, the high councils of Kirtland and Missouri were anointed in separate rooms. (Cowdery, Diary, 21 Jan. 1836.)

271. Cowdery, Diary, 21 Jan. 1836; see also Whitmer, History, 83, in *JSP,* H2:91–92. For the instructions to Moses to wash and anoint Aaron before allowing him to enter the holy tabernacle, see Exodus 40:9–15.

272. JS, Journal, 21 Jan. 1836, in *JSP,* J1:167.

273. JS, Journal, 21 Jan. 1836, in *JSP,* J1:167; Cowdery, Diary, 21 Jan. 1836.

kingdom added details to JS's 1832 vision that depicted the separation of the afterlife into three kingdoms of heavenly glory: celestial, terrestrial, and telestial.[274]

Bishop Edward Partridge recorded that a number of others present at the evening meeting also saw visions.[275] JS's journal notes that "some of them saw the face of the Saviour, and others were ministered unto by holy angels," and also that "the power of the highest rested upon, us the house was filled with the glory of God, and we shouted Hosanah to God and the Lamb."[276] The next morning, instead of studying as usual, JS and others "spent the time in rehearsing to each other the glorious scenes that transpired" the evening before.[277]

Cowdery demurred to record the details of the evening's events in his journal. "The glorious scene is too great to be described in this book," he wrote, "therefore, I only say, that the heavens were opened to many, and great and marvelous things were shown."[278] JS's journal reports additional visionary experiences that were had during the week following 21 January 1836.[279] Between 21 January and 6 February, JS and other senior church leaders gave instruction and performed washings, anointings, and other blessings as the solemn assembly neared.[280]

Document Transcript

The heavens were opened upon us and I beheld the celestial kingdom of God,[281] and the glory thereof, whether in the body or out I cannot tell,—[282] I saw the transcendant beauty of the gate ~~that enters~~, through which the heirs of that kingdom will enter, which was like unto circling flames of fire, also the blasing throne of God, whereon was seated the Father and the Son,— I saw the beautiful streets of that kingdom, which had the appearance of being paved with gold— I saw father Adam, and Abraham and Michael[283] and my father

---

274. Vision, 16 Feb. 1832, in *JSP*, D2:179–192 [D&C 76].

275. Partridge, Journal, 21 Jan. 1836.

276. JS, Journal, 21 Jan. 1836, in *JSP*, J1:170.

277. JS, Journal, 22 Jan. 1836, in *JSP*, J1:171.

278. Cowdery, Diary, 21 Jan. 1836.

279. See JS, Journal, 22–23 and 28–29 Jan. 1836, in *JSP*, J1:172, 174–175.

280. JS, Journal, 22–23 and 28–29 Jan. 1836; 6 Feb. 1836, in *JSP*, J1:172, 174–175, 181–182.

281. In 1832, JS and Sidney Rigdon recorded a vision describing the celestial realm in terms of "the glory of the sun" and outlining requirements to attain that kingdom. (Vision, 16 Feb. 1832, in *JSP*, D2:179–192 [D&C 76:50–70, 92–96].)

282. See 2 Corinthians 12:1–4.

283. Although Adam and Michael, the archangel, are designated here as separate persons, the previous year JS approved publication of the Doctrine and Covenants, which described them as the same person: "Michael, or Adam, the father of all, the prince of all, the ancient of days." Likewise, in a 1 January 1834 letter to John Whitmer, Oliver Cowdery wrote that he had "been informed from a proper source that the Angel Michael is no less than our father Adam." (Doctrine and Covenants 50:2, 1835 ed. [D&C 27:11]; Oliver Cowdery, Kirtland, OH, to John Whitmer, Missouri, 1 Jan. 1834, in Cowdery, Letterbook, 15; see also Richards, "Pocket Companion," 74–75; and Robert B. Thompson, Sermon Notes, 5 Oct. 1840, JS Collection, CHL.)

and mother, my brother Alvin that has long since slept,[284] and marvled how it was that he had obtained ~~this~~ an inheritance ⟨in⟩ ~~this~~ ⟨that⟩ kingdom, seeing that he had departed this life, before the Lord ⟨had⟩ set his hand to gather Israel[285] ⟨the second time⟩ and had not been baptized for the remission of sins—[286] Thus ~~said~~ came the voice ⟨of the Lord un⟩to me saying all who have [p. 136] died with[out] a knowledge of this gospel, who would have received it, if they had been permited to tarry, shall be heirs of the celestial kingdom of God— also all that shall die henseforth, with⟨out⟩ a knowledge of it, who would have received it, with all their hearts, shall be heirs of that kingdom, for I the Lord ⟨will⟩ judge all men according to their works[287] according to the desires of their hearts— and ~~again I also beheld the Terrestial kingdom~~ I also beheld that all children who die before they arive to the years of accountability, are saved in the celestial kingdom of heaven—[288] I saw the 12, apostles of the Lamb, who are now upon the earth[289] who hold the keys of this last ministry,[290] in foreign lands, standing together in a circle much fatiegued, with their clothes tattered and feet swolen, with their eyes cast downward, and Jesus ⟨standing⟩ in their midst, and they did not behold him, ~~he~~ the Saviour looked upon them and wept— I also beheld Elder McLellen [William E. McLellin] in the south,[291] standing upon a hill surrounded with a vast multitude, preaching

---

284. Born 11 February 1798, JS's oldest brother, Alvin, died near Palmyra, New York, on 19 November 1823, probably from a deadly dose of calomel administered by a physician, possibly for a ruptured appendix. In August 1842, JS stated concerning Alvin: "He was the oldest, and the noblest of my fathers family. He was one of the noblest of the sons of men. . . . In him there was no guile. He lived without spot from the time he was a child." Lucy Mack Smith wrote that Alvin "was a youth of singular goodness of disposition Kind and amiable" so that when he died, "lamentation and Mourning filled the whole neighborhood where we lived." (JS Family Bible; Tunbridge, VT, Town and Vital Records, 1785–1878, vol. A, p. 130, microfilm 28,990, U.S. and Canada Record Collection, FHL; JS History, 1834–1836, 10, in *JSP*, H1:30; Lucy Mack Smith, *Biographical Sketches*, 87–89; JS, Journal, 23 Aug. 1842, in *JSP*, J2:116–117; Lucy Mack Smith, History, 1844–1845, bk. 4, [5].)

285. See Visions, 3 Apr. 1836, p. 228 herein [D&C 110:11].

286. See John 3:3–5; and Book of Mormon, 1830 ed., 508 [3 Nephi 27:19–21].

287. See Romans 1:28–32; 2:10–13.

288. See Revelation, ca. June 1835, in *JSP*, D4:358–359 [D&C 68:25–28]; and Book of Mormon, 1830 ed., 581–582 [Moroni 8:10–14, 22].

289. JS called the Twelve Apostles nearly one year earlier. (Minutes, Discourse, and Blessings, 14–15 Feb. 1835, in *JSP*, D4:228, 233–234.)

290. Following biblical precedent, JS designated the Twelve as a "traveling high council," responsible for "presid[ing] over all the churches of the Saints among the Gentiles, where there is no presidency established." The Twelve were also to hold "the keys of this ministry—to unlock the door of the kingdom of heaven unto all nations and preach the Gospel unto every creation." (Minutes, 27 Feb. 1835, in *JSP*, D4:252, 254; see also Mark 16:15; and Luke 9:1–2, 6.)

291. In April 1836 McLellin journeyed south and eventually reached Kentucky on a proselytizing mission. (McLellin, Journal, 9 Apr. 1836–7 June 1836; Shipps and Welch, *Journals of William E. McLellin*, 320–321.)

to them, and a lame man standing before him, supported by his crutches, he threw them down at his word, and leaped as an heart [hart] by the mighty power of God

Also Eldr Brigham Young standing in a strange land, in the far southwest, in a desert place, upon a rock in the midst of about a dozen men of colour, who, appeared hostile [p. 137] He was preaching to them in their own toung, and the angel of God standing above his head with a drawn sword in his hand protecting him, but he did not see it,— and I finally saw the 12 in the celestial kingdom of God,— I also beheld the redemption of Zion, and many things which the toung of man, cannot discribe in full,

—————— ☙ ——————

Letter from Warren Parrish, 25 January 1836

Source Note

Warren Parrish, Letter, [Kirtland Township, Geauga Co., OH], to JS, [Kirtland Township, Geauga Co., OH], 25 Jan. 1836. Featured version copied [ca. 25 Jan. 1836] in JS, Journal, 1835–1836, p. 142; handwriting of Sylvester Smith; JS Collection, CHL. For more information on JS, Journal, 1835–1836, see Source Notes for Multiple-Entry Documents, p. 524 herein.

Historical Introduction

JS hired Warren Parrish as a scribe on 29 October 1835 for fifteen dollars a month plus a four-dollar monthly allowance for meals.[292] On 14 November 1835, JS dictated a revelation that proclaimed Parrish as "the Lords Scribe, for the Lords Seer."[293] In his scribal responsibilities, Parrish primarily maintained JS's journal, though he also wrote in other church records including Minute Book 1 and JS's 1834–1836 history.[294]

In December 1835, Parrish's ill health sometimes interfered with his work.[295] Parrish's health returned by 30 December and remained strong enough for him to continue his writing duties for most of January; he even participated in the anointing ordinance that took place in the House of the Lord on 21 January 1836.[296] However, on 25 January 1836, his health worsened, and he wrote JS to request a temporary leave of absence from his scribal duties.

---

292. JS, Journal, 29 Oct. 1835, in *JSP*, J1:76; see also Historical Introduction to Revelation, 14 Nov. 1835, pp. 51–52 herein.

293. JS, Journal, 14 Nov. 1835, in *JSP*, J1:99–100.

294. Historical Introduction to JS, Journal, 1835–1836, in *JSP*, J1:55–56; Minute Book 1, 2 Jan. and 12 Feb. 1836; Source Note for JS History, 1834–1836, in *JSP*, H1:23.

295. JS, Journal, 22 Dec. 1836, in *JSP*, J1:135.

296. JS, Journal, 30 Dec. 1835, in *JSP*, J1:140; see also Historical Introduction to Visions, 21 Jan. 1836 [D&C 137], pp. 157–158 herein.

Sylvester Smith copied Parrish's letter into JS's journal shortly after JS received it. Smith acted as interim scribe for JS from 25 January until 8 February 1836, when Parrish resumed his labors.[297]

Document Transcript

Brother Joseph,

My great desire to be in your company[298] & in the Assembly of the Saints where God opnes [opens] the heavens & exhibits the treasures of eternity is the only thing that has stimulated me for a number of days past to leave my house;[299] for be assured, dear brother, my bodily affliction is severe; I have a violent ⟨cough⟩ more especially nights, which deprives me of my appetite, & my strength fails, & writing has a particular tendency to injure my lungs while I am under the influence of such a cough I therefore, with reluctance send your journal[300] to you untill my health improves[301]

Yours in heart
Warren Parrish

P.S.
Brother Joseph,
pray for me, & ask the prayers of the class on my account also.[302]

———— ❧ ————

297. JS, Journal, 25 Jan. and 8 Feb. 1836, in *JSP,* J1:173, 183.

298. JS and Parrish had developed a close relationship. Parrish was included in a covenant JS made with the Twelve on 16 January 1836 and on that day received a blessing that commended him for the "truth and integrity that dwelleth in him." (Minutes, 16 Jan. 1836, p. 153 herein; JS, Journal, 16 Jan. 1836, in *JSP,* J1:160.)

299. This likely referred to the group of priesthood holders and church leaders present at the anointing that took place a few days earlier, on 21 and 22 January 1836, which Parrish attended despite his illness. JS's journal records that when Parrish received the ordinance of anointing with holy oil in the House of the Lord on 21 January 1836, he "saw in a vision the armies of heaven protecting the Saints in their return to Zion." (JS, Journal, 21–22 and 24 Jan. 1836, in *JSP,* J1:166–172; see also Historical Introduction to Visions, 21 Jan. 1836 [D&C 137], pp. 157–158 herein.)

300. This likely refers to the bound volume containing JS's Ohio journal, covering September 1835– April 1836, much of which was dictated daily by JS to Parrish. Though less likely, this may instead reference JS's 1834–1836 history, on which Parrish also served contemporaneously as a scribe and which was referred to as JS's "large journal." (See Historical Introduction to JS, Journal, 1835–1836, in *JSP,* J1:55–61; and JS History, 1834–1836, in *JSP,* H1:24, 105.)

301. On 8 February 1836, JS's journal records, "Elder Parrish my scribe, received my journal again, his health is so much improved that he thinks he will be able, with the blessing of God to perform this duty." (JS, Journal, 8 Feb. 1836, in *JSP,* J1:183.)

302. Parrish here referred to the Hebrew School, which met for the next several days. (JS, Journal, 26 Jan.–1 Feb. 1836, in *JSP,* J1:173–179.)

Letter from the Presidency of Elders, 29 January 1836

Source Note

Alvah Beman, Reuben Hedlock, John Morton, and Evan M. Greene, Letter, Kirtland Township, Geauga Co., OH, to JS, [Kirtland Township, Geauga Co., OH], 29 Jan. 1836. Featured version copied [ca. 29 Jan. 1836] in JS, Journal, 1835–1836, p. 145; handwriting of Sylvester Smith; JS Collection, CHL. For more information on JS, Journal, 1835–1836, see Source Notes for Multiple-Entry Documents, p. 524 herein.

Historical Introduction

At a grand council on 15 January 1836, as they filled vacancies in the several priesthood quorums, JS and other church leaders appointed a presidency for the elders.[303] Alvah Beman, who had arrived in Kirtland, Ohio, from Avon, Livingston County, New York, on 11 January 1836, received a unanimous vote to officiate as president of the Kirtland quorum of elders. JS, Sidney Rigdon, and Hyrum Smith then ordained him to that position.[304]

Following his appointment, Beman worked to organize the Kirtland elders and prepare them to receive the promised endowment of power.[305] At a meeting of the Kirtland elders on 25 January 1836, Sidney Rigdon, Frederick G. Williams, and Hyrum Smith gave instructions respecting the elders' preparation to receive the "holy anointing."[306] At that meeting, Beman chose Reuben Hedlock and John Morton as his counselors; he then "organized the quorum according to age" and recorded their names.[307] On 28 January, JS "assisted in anointing the counsellors of the President of the Elders & gave them the instruction necessary for the occasion" so that they could anoint others in the quorum.[308] The next day, Beman, Hedlock, and Morton, with Evan M. Greene as their clerk, wrote to the church's First Presidency seeking further clarity about putting the elders quorum in order as JS had directed. They wrote specifically requesting instruction on receiving and ordaining new candidates to the office of elder.[309] Though no written response from the First Presidency has been found, JS and other leaders may have had this letter in mind

---

303. Minutes, 13 Jan. 1836, pp. 138–143 herein; JS, Journal, 15 Jan. 1836, in *JSP*, J1:153–156; Kirtland Elders Quorum, "Record," 30 Jan. 1836.

304. JS's journal incorrectly states that Beman lived in Genesee County, New York, at this time. Mary A. Noble, Beman's daughter, and county deed records indicate that Beman resided in Avon, Livingston County, approximately twenty-five miles from Batavia, the seat of Genesee County. (JS, Journal, 11 and 15 Jan. 1836, in *JSP*, J1:147, 155; Noble, Reminiscences, [2]; Livingston Co., NY, Deed Records, 1820–1901, vol. 8, p. 593, 22 Jan. 1831, microfilm 510,038, U.S. and Canada Record Collection, FHL; Minutes, 13 Jan. 1836, p. 142 herein; Minutes, 15 Jan. 1836, p. 147 herein.)

305. JS, Journal, 21–23 Jan. 1836, in *JSP*, J1:166–172; Kirtland Elders Quorum, "Record," 30 Jan.–6 Feb. 1836; Revelation, 2 Jan. 1831, in *JSP*, D1:232–233 [D&C 38:32, 38].

306. Kirtland Elders Quorum, "Record," 25 Jan. 1836. The "ordinance of annointing our heads with holy oil" was a ritual to prepare men who had been ordained to priesthood office to receive the promised endowment of power at the solemn assembly. (JS, Journal, 21 Jan. 1836, in *JSP*, J1:166–171; Whitmer, History, 83, in *JSP*, H2:92; Revelation, 27–28 Dec. 1832, in *JSP*, D2:341 [D&C 88:70].)

307. Kirtland Elders Quorum, "Record," 25 Jan. 1836.

308. JS, Journal, 28 Jan. 1836, in *JSP*, J1:174–175; Kirtland Elders Quorum, "Record," 28 Jan. 1836.

309. JS, Journal, 21–22, 25, 28, and 30 Jan. 1836, in *JSP*, J1:166–175, 178.

at a conference of the church presidency the next day, when they passed a resolution "that no one be ordained to an office in the Church in Kirtland without the voice of the several quorums when assembled for church business."[310]

Sylvester Smith copied the letter from the presidency of elders into JS's journal sometime before 8 February 1836, when Warren Parrish resumed his scribal duties.[311]

Document Transcript

Kirtland Jany. 29. AD. 1836

To the Presidents of the church of Latter day Saints. Beloved Bret[hren] feeling ourselves amenable to you for our proceedings as the presidency of the first quorem of Elders[312] in Kirtland, & believing that we are to be govorned by you;[313] we desire to know if we are to receive all those who are recommended to us by Elders for ordination, or shall we receive none only those who have written recommendations from you.[314] please answer our request

Alvah Beman   Pres.

Reuben Hadlock [Hedlock]
John Morton   Counsel

E. M. Green [Evan Greene]   Ck

———— ∾ ————

Minutes, 30 January 1836

Source Note

Church presidency (including JS), Minutes, Kirtland Township, Geauga Co., OH, 30 Jan. 1836. Featured version copied [between ca. 4 Apr. and ca. 16 May 1836] in Minute Book 1, p. 137; handwriting of Warren A. Cowdery; CHL. For more information on Minute Book 1, see Source Notes for Multiple-Entry Documents, p. 527 herein.

---

310. Minutes, 30 Jan. 1836, p. 164 herein.

311. JS, Journal, 8 Feb. 1836, in *JSP*, J1:183; see also Letter from Warren Parrish, 25 Jan. 1836, pp. 160–161 herein.

312. There was only one quorum of elders at this time. A record of its proceedings was kept between 15 January 1836 and 5 October 1841. Beman served as president of the quorum until his death in November 1837. (Kirtland Elders Quorum, "Record," 1.)

313. Earlier instruction from JS designated the presidency of the high priesthood, or the church presidency, as the highest body to preside over the priesthood office and officers. (Instruction on Priesthood, between ca. 1 Mar. and ca. 4 May 1835, in *JSP*, D4:312, 317–318 [D&C 107:7, 60–66].)

314. The 1835 edition of the Doctrine and Covenants did not definitively answer the question of whether explicit approval from the church presidency was necessary to ordain any man to the office of elder. One relevant, though potentially ambiguous, passage in the Doctrine and Covenants stated, "No person is to be ordained to any office in this church, where there is a regularly organized branch of the same, without the vote of that church; but the presiding elders, traveling bishops, high counsellors, high priests, and elders, may have the privilege of ordaining, where there is no branch of the church, that a vote may be called." (Doctrine and Covenants 2:16, 1835 ed. [D&C 20:65–66].)

Historical Introduction

In continuing the effort to organize the church's priesthood officers and instruct the church membership to prepare for the forthcoming solemn assembly, the church's presidency, including JS, met on the evening of 30 January 1836 in the upper floor of the House of the Lord in Kirtland, Ohio. They passed three resolutions at the meeting.[315] The first, instituting a new policy on ordination to priesthood offices, may have been prompted in part by a letter the presidency of the Kirtland elders quorum wrote to the "Presidents of the church" the day before.[316] This resolution put in place a new requirement: only at a business meeting of the several priesthood quorums could a recommendation for priesthood ordination be approved.[317] The second resolution assigned the elders quorum president, Alvah Beman, to compile a list of elders. The final resolution concerned Harvey Whitlock, with whom JS exchanged letters several weeks earlier regarding Whitlock's separation from the church. JS had written the contrite Whitlock on 16 November 1835 and informed him that he should return to Kirtland and humble himself according to JS's counsel in order to be "restored unto his former state" as a church member and high priest.[318] Whitlock apparently did come to Kirtland from Missouri, and at this 30 January 1836 meeting, the church's presidency passed a resolution indicating the next steps he should take to "be restored to the church."

Document Transcript

Kirtland Ohio January 30th 1836

At a conference of the Presidency of the church of the Latter Day-Saints, it resolved, that no one be ordained to an office in the Church in Kirtland without the voice of the several quorums when assembled for church business.[319]

Carried unanimously.

2^d Resolved, that Alvah Beaman, the Presidents of the Elders, be directed to give to the Presidents of the church, a list of the names of the several Elders comprising his quorum and all other Elders in Kirtland not belonging to any quorum now established.[320] Carried unanimously.

---

315. JS, Journal, 30 Jan. 1836, in *JSP*, J1:178; Cowdery, Diary, 30 Jan. 1836; Post, Journal, 30 Jan. 1836.

316. See Letter from the Presidency of Elders, 29 Jan. 1836, pp. 162–163 herein.

317. This matter of procedures for approval of ordinations remained an issue for more than two weeks hereafter. (See Minutes, 12 Feb. 1836, pp. 170–173 herein.)

318. Letter and Revelation to Harvey Whitlock, 16 Nov. 1835, p. 62 herein.

319. This instruction appears to refine the practice of ordination adopted in the 1835 version of the church's founding "Articles and Covenants," which stated, "No person is to be ordained to any office in this church, where there is a regularly organized branch of the same, without the vote of that church." In addition to the local vote, the resolution here required the priesthood quorums in Kirtland to vote to sanction the ordination of any new official member. The procedure for approving ordinations was further clarified on 12 February 1836. (Articles and Covenants, ca. Apr. 1830, in Doctrine and Covenants 2:16, 1835 ed. [D&C 20:65–66]; Minutes, 12 Feb. 1836, pp. 170–173 herein.)

320. It appears that the church's presidency had not realized until a few days earlier how many elders in Kirtland did not belong to a quorum. According to Oliver Cowdery, on the evening of 25 January 1836,

3[d] Resolved, that Harvey Whitlock be restored to the church in full fellowship on his being rebaptized, and after be ordained to the High Priest-hood.[321] carried unanimously

Oliver Cowdery
Clerk of conference

———— ℰ ————

Blessing to Alvin Winegar, 7 February 1836

Source Note

JS, Sidney Rigdon, and Hyrum Smith, Blessing, to Alvin Winegar, Kirtland Township, Geauga Co., OH, 7 Feb. 1836. Featured version copied in Alvin Winegar, Emigration Record Book, [ca. 1850s]; handwriting probably of John Winegar; private possession; photocopy in Alvin Winegar, Papers, CHL.

Handmade book measuring 9¼ × 7¾ inches (24 × 20 cm). The book is not paginated, and the number of pages is unknown. The covers are constructed of heavy brown paper. Winegar primarily used the book as an emigration record book while migrating to Utah Territory in 1852; the book also contains a company roster, Winegar family genealogy, and the blessing Winegar received from the First Presidency in Kirtland, Ohio, in 1836.

Joseph Smith Papers staff accessed the original in 2005 from a Winegar descendant; subsequent attempts to access the original and obtain additional physical information were unsuccessful.

Historical Introduction

Alvin Winegar likely joined the church along with his parents, Rhoda and Samuel Winegar, in the town of Springfield, Erie County, Pennsylvania, sometime in early 1833.[322] In March 1834, JS and Parley P. Pratt passed through Springfield and nearby Elk Creek, recruiting volunteers and raising money for the Camp of Israel expedition to Missouri.[323] Eighteen-year-old Alvin and his father soon volunteered to join the expedition

---

"the high priests and elders, all who did not belong to the quorums, met in the Lord's house" and a "large number of elders convened; more than I had supposed resided in Kirtland." On 25 January, Alvah Beman "organized the quorum according to age" and took their names. From the list of elders, the church presidency selected men for a second Quorum of the Seventy in early February 1836. On 3 February, Beman "handed in the names of seventy of his quorem—designed for another seventy if God will." The following day, 4 February, the names of seventy elders were presented to the presidents of the Seventy and accepted. The church presidency met to approve the ordinations of the elders to the Seventy on Sunday, 7 February. (Cowdery, Diary, 25 and 26 Jan. 1836; Kirtland Elders Quorum, "Record," 25 Jan. 1836; Post, Journal, 1 and 4 Feb. 1836; JS, Journal, 3 and 7 Feb. 1836, in *JSP*, J1:180–182; Cowdery, Diary, 7 Feb. 1836; Record of Seventies, bk. A, 6–9.)

321. Whitlock had previously been ordained to the office of high priest in June 1831. (Minutes, ca. 3–4 June 1831, in *JSP*, D1:324–326; Whitmer, History, 28, in *JSP*, H2:40.)

322. Winegar was born in the town of German, New York, on 13 May 1816. According to the journal of Evan Greene, Rhoda and Samuel Winegar were baptized by either Greene or John F. Boynton on 20 June 1833. In a list near the end of his journal, Greene also noted that Alvin's siblings Almira and John were baptized on the same day. ("Names of Those Baptised," in Greene, Diary, vol. 1, 1833–1835.)

323. JS, Journal, 26 and 27 Mar. 1834, in *JSP*, J1:36.

and subsequently marched to Missouri.[324] Along with many of the other participants in the expedition, Alvin likely returned home by early 1835. He was in Kirtland, Ohio, by early February 1836.[325]

On 7 February, Winegar received his Zion blessing from a member of the First Presidency, likely JS.[326] JS's journal entry for 7 February indicates that he spent the majority of that day engaged in church meetings. Following an "evening meet[ing] with the presidency in the loft of the Printing-office, in company with the presidency of the 70," JS "blessed one of the Zion brethren"—presumably Winegar.[327] Sylvester Smith, who temporarily served as JS's scribe from 25 January to 8 February 1836, recorded the blessing. Although that original is no longer extant and was not copied into any of the church's official blessing books, a copy of the blessing—likely written in the handwriting of Winegar's son John—was preserved and retained in private possession.

Document Transcript

A blessing— Pronounced by the first Presidency[328] upon the head of Alvin Winegar— F͟e͟b͟y͟ 7͟t͟h͟ 1836.

We lay our hands upon thy head in the name of Jesus and ask our Heavenly Father to bestow many blessings upon thee, both in this life— and in that which is to come— we seal many blessings in time upon thee, and in Eternity an exceeding rich reward. Thou wast willing to lay down thy life for thy brethren[329] and the Lord shall cho[o]se thee for his own— Even as a vessel in the

---

324. "Festival of the Camp of Zion," *Deseret News,* 12 Oct. 1864, 13; Bradley, *Zion's Camp 1834,* 275–280; "A Synopsis of Remarks Made by Prests. Brigham Young and Geo. A. Smith," 14 June 1874, pp. 1–3, in Historian's Office, Reports of Speeches, 1845–1885, CHL. For more on the Camp of Israel expedition—later referred to as "Zion's Camp"—see Revelation, 16–17 Dec. 1833, in *JSP,* D3:386–397 [D&C 101]; Revelation, 24 Feb. 1834, in *JSP,* D3:457–463 [D&C 103]; and Minutes, 24 Feb. 1834, in *JSP,* D3:453–457.

325. Winegar's whereabouts following the 1834 expedition are largely unknown. He was in Kirtland at the time of this blessing and married Mary Judd in Henry County, Indiana, on 31 August 1837; their first child, John, was born in Clay County, Missouri, on 28 September 1838. (Henry Co., IN, Clerk of the Circuit Court, Marriage Records, 1823–1951, vol. C, p. 298, microfilm 1,870,202, U.S. and Canada Record Collection, FHL; Esshom, *Pioneers and Prominent Men of Utah,* 1255.)

326. Many members of the Camp of Israel expedition who were not ordained to a leadership calling during spring 1835 received blessings, often referred to as Zion blessings, during the subsequent years. Many of these blessings were recorded in Patriarchal Blessing Book 1; others, such as Lorenzo Barnes's blessing, were recorded in private journals. (Patriarchal Blessings, vol. 1; Blessing to Lorenzo Barnes, 3 Jan. 1836, pp. 131–135 herein.)

327. JS, Journal, 7 Feb. 1836, in *JSP,* J1:182.

328. In January 1836, the presidency consisted of JS, Oliver Cowdery, Sidney Rigdon, Frederick G. Williams, Hyrum Smith, and Joseph Smith Sr. (Account of Meetings, Revelation, and Blessing, 5–6 Dec. 1834, in *JSP,* D4:194, 200.)

329. Similar language was used in sermons about the Camp of Israel expedition and in other blessings given to its participants. While addressing former members of the expedition on 14 February 1835, JS remarked, "Those who went to Zion, with a determination to lay down their lives, if necessary, it was the Will of God, that they should be ordained to the ministry." Other Zion blessings expressed similar language, including blessings for Sherman Gilbert, Charles Kelly, Salmon Warner,

House of God—[330] The Lord shall seal blesings for thee in Heaven— and look upon them and none shall fail— thy mind shall be strengthened— faith encreased— receive much wisdom— power and understanding— must offer all that thou hast a sacrifice to thy God, even all thy mind and strengt[h]— and give thy self up to him without reserve. body and spirit— go at his command and he will loose thy tongue and make thee a swift Messenger—[331] an instrument of much good on the Earth— see great disolations come upon the wicked and glory to the righteous— and his power manifested in blessings and in cureings— Shall be lifted up and shout hosannah among the heavenly hosts— see the Heavens opened. The charriots of Israel and the Horsemen thereof—[332] and great shall be thy rejoicings— Shall receive the holy Priesthood in due time, which shall never be taken from thee in time or in Eternity— Stand upon the Earth till the son of man comes— see the end of this generation— do much good in proclaiming the gospel carried to Nations afar off— preach in all languages and tongues— power to resist the power of floods and flames— overcome the destroyer— and the pestilence shall not harm thee— power to heal the sick— open the blind eyes— unstop the deaf ears— Cause the ~~dumb~~ Tongue of the dumb to sing for joy— many shall seek to touch thy garments—[333] and others shall send handkerchiefs, and Aprons to thee and be healed by this means.[334] Thou shalt have all the power that thou needest to fill thy Ministry[.] Angels shall minister unto thee— and thy saviour shall stand before thee, and thou shalt be able to Certify to the Nations of things which thou hast seen, and doest most assuredly know. The Heavenly Hosts shall be round about thee, to deliver thee out of all thy afflictions— and thy soul shall Shout Hosannah to God and the Lamb[335] and nothing shall

---

and Hyrum Smith. (Minute Book 1, 14–15 Feb. 1835; 1 Mar. 1835; 17 Aug. 1835; see also Park, "Thou Wast Willing to Lay Down Thy Life for Thy Brethren," 27–37.)

330. See 2 Timothy 2:20–21.

331. See Isaiah 18:2. The term "swift messenger" also appears in two other contemporary Zion blessings, for Hazen Aldrich and Lorenzo Barnes. (Minutes, Discourse, and Blessings, 1 Mar. 1835, in *JSP*, D4:267; Blessing to Lorenzo Barnes, 3 Jan. 1836, p. 133 herein.)

332. See 2 Kings 2:12, 13:14; and JS, Journal, 22 Jan. 1836, in *JSP*, J1:171.

333. See Matthew 9:20–22; and Luke 8:43–48.

334. See Acts 19:11–12.

335. JS and others used the phrase "shout Hosanna to God and the Lamb" elsewhere during this period. In a 21 January 1836 journal entry, JS recorded a vision in which "the power of the highest rested upon, us the house was filled with the glory of God, and we shouted Hosanah to God and the Lamb." The phrase also appeared in a hymn penned by William W. Phelps sometime in 1835 and was included in the church's first hymnal. The hymn—referred to as "Hosanah to God and the Lamb" in JS's journal— was sung following the dedication of the House of the Lord in Kirtland on 27 March. (JS, Journal, 26 and 27 Mar. 1836, in *JSP*, J1:170, 210; see also Visions, 21 Jan. 1836 [D&C 137], pp. 157–160 herein; and Hymn 90, *Collection of Sacred Hymns*, 120.)

prevail against thee to harm thee— These blessings dear brother if thou art faithful Shall rest upon thy head and be ⟨all⟩ fulfilled— for we seal them upon the[e] in the name of Jesus by the authority of the Holy Priesthood even so Amen.—— Kertland Ohio—— Sylvester Smith / scribe. JW^sr last scribe.[336]

---

336. This is likely Alvin Winegar's son John Alvin Winegar. (Esshom, *Pioneers and Prominent Men of Utah*, 1255.)

PART 3: 12 FEBRUARY– 28 MARCH 1836

During this period of about six weeks, JS spent much of his time studying the Hebrew language under the instruction of Joshua Seixas.[1] He also saw to his familial and domestic concerns and at the same time entertained visitors in Kirtland, Ohio, who were interested in the Egyptian artifacts, the House of the Lord, or "the work of the Lord" generally.[2]

The majority of the documents in this part highlight JS attending to the "duties of the church" as the House of the Lord neared completion and the anticipated solemn assembly approached. During this time of preparation, JS continued to instruct and organize the church, and he oversaw the passage of resolutions that standardized the ordination of men to priesthood offices and centralized priesthood licensing to a more formal system of tracking the growing body of ordained men.[3]

A historic event came at the end of these six weeks: after more than three years of fund raising, construction work, and high expectations, the House of the Lord was completed, and JS led the dedicatory services on 27 March 1836. Participants recorded that a spiritual outpouring transpired that day. Frederick G. Williams stated "that a Holy Angel of God" entered the building and sat next to him and Joseph Smith Sr. during the dedicatory prayer offered by JS.[4] Benjamin Brown recorded that at a meeting of the priesthood on the evening of the dedication, several in attendance had "Miracilous Experiences" and saw "Many Visions" during a Pentecostal event in the House of the Lord.[5]

───────── ❧ ─────────

1. See Letter to Henrietta Raphael Seixas, between 6 and 13 Feb. 1836, pp. 173–178 herein; and JS, Journal, 24 and 25 Feb. 1836; 2 and 3 Mar. 1836, in *JSP*, J1:189, 191.

2. See JS, Journal, 12, 15, 16, 28, and 29 Feb. 1836, in *JSP*, J1:184, 186, 190–191.

3. See, for example, Minutes, 12 Feb. 1836, pp. 170–173 herein; Minutes, 22 Feb. 1836, pp. 179–180 herein; and License, 21 Mar. 1836, pp. 186–188 herein.

4. Minutes and Prayer of Dedication, 27 Mar. 1836 [D&C 109], p. 209 herein.

5. Benjamin Brown to Sarah Mumford Brown, ca. Apr. 1836, Benjamin Brown Family Collection, CHL.

Minutes, 12 February 1836

Source Note

Minutes, [Kirtland Township, Geauga Co., OH], 12 Feb. 1836. Featured version copied [between ca. 4 Apr. and ca. 16 May 1836] in Minute Book 1, pp. 137–138; handwriting of Warren A. Cowdery; CHL. For more information on Minute Book 1, see Source Notes for Multiple-Entry Documents, p. 527 herein.

Historical Introduction

Since fall 1835, JS had talked of a solemn assembly to be held in the House of the Lord in which men ordained to the priesthood in the Church of the Latter Day Saints would be endowed with divine power for their ministry. In anticipation of such a meeting—planned to be held in spring 1836, after the dedication of the House of the Lord—JS began in early 1836 to organize and prepare the priesthood quorums. On 30 January 1836, the church's presidency unanimously passed a resolution that "no one be ordained to an office in the Church in Kirtland without the voice of the several quorums when assembled for church business."[6] In early February, JS continued to attend to the business of "organizing of the quorems of High priests— Elders— Seventy & Bishops," beginning with meetings prior to the one featured here.[7] At a meeting on 6 February that included the bishoprics of Kirtland and Zion (Missouri), elders, high priests, seventies, the high councils of Kirtland and Zion, the Quorum of the Twelve Apostles, and the church's presidency, JS "laboured with each of these quorems for some time to bring [them] to the order which God had shown to me."[8] At the same meeting, JS reprimanded the elders for "evil deeds" and for having failed to observe "the order which [he] had given them," and he instructed them concerning the proselytizing work they would commence after they received the endowment of power. JS stated, "This night the key is turned to the nations; and the angel John is about commencing his mission to prophesy before kings, and rulers, nations tongues and people."[9] On 11 February, the instruction continued in a meeting of the elders quorum. According to the elders quorum record, "president [Alvah] Beman gave some instructions respecting the duty of the officers, and made some confession and was followed by president Joseph Smith jr. in giving instruction to the quorum."[10]

---

6. Minutes, 30 Jan. 1836, p. 164 herein.

7. JS, Journal, 1 Feb. 1836, in *JSP*, J1:179.

8. JS, Journal, 6 Feb. 1836, in *JSP*, J1:181.

9. JS, Journal, 6 Feb. 1836, in *JSP*, J1:181; Kirtland Elders Quorum, "Record," 6 Feb. 1836; see also Revelation 10:11; and Answers to Questions, between ca. 4 and ca. 20 Mar. 1832, in *JSP*, D2:213 [D&C 77:14]. According to the Kirtland elders quorum record, at least ninety-seven elders had been anointed with oil from 28 January to 4 February 1836. The elders quorum minutes for 6 February record that JS and his counselors in the presidency "came and sealed our anointing by prayer and shout of Hosanna" and then "gave us some instructions and left us." Alvah Beman then addressed those present, and "several spoke and there seemed to be a cloud of darkness in the room." After Oliver Cowdery and Hyrum Smith came into the room to resolve the problem, "the cloud was broken and some shouted, Hosanna and others spake with tongues." (Kirtland Elders Quorum, "Record," 28 Jan.–6 Feb. 1836; see also JS, Journal, 3 Apr. 1836, in *JSP*, J1:219–222.)

10. Kirtland Elders Quorum, "Record," 11 Feb. 1836.

In the House of the Lord on 12 February 1836, JS met again with the council comprising the several quorums of the priesthood, to whom he presented some specific problems and possible solutions on the subject of ordinations. The church leaders discussed regulating the "manner and power to ordain" men to various priesthood offices and quorums.[11] After those in attendance rejected a preliminary set of resolutions, the council asked JS alone to compose new governing measures, which he did.[12] As a part of this discussion, JS then offered two resolutions that further clarified the 30 January 1836 resolution on ordinations.[13]

There are two extant versions of the minutes: one was recorded in JS's 1835–1836 journal and the other in Minute Book 1. The version in Minute Book 1 is featured here as the official minutes; footnotes detail differences between the two versions. Warren Parrish was both the clerk for the council meeting who wrote the original minutes (no longer extant) and the scribe for the copy found in JS's journal. Parrish also recorded JS's instructions and the resolutions presented on 12 February 1836 into the 14 February 1836 entry of JS's journal.[14] Warren A. Cowdery recorded the minutes in Minute Book 1 in the spring of 1836. Both the Minute Book 1 version and the version in JS's journal may have been copied from the original minutes, or Cowdery may have relied solely on JS's journal when he penned his version a couple of months later.[15]

Document Transcript

Friday evening, February 12$^{\underline{th}}$ 1836

Council convened in the House of the Lord[16] for the purpose of taking into consideration the subject of ordaining men to the office of Elder and other offices in the Church of Christ of Latter Day Saints.

Opened by singing and prayer[17]

---

11. Cowdery, Diary, 12 Feb. 1836.

12. Minutes, 12 Feb. 1836, in *JSP*, J1:184–185.

13. See JS, Journal, 12 and 14 Feb. 1836, in *JSP*, J1:184–185.

14. JS, Journal, 12 and 14 Feb. 1836, in *JSP*, J1:184–185.

15. See *JSP*, J1:185n376.

16. The copy of the minutes in JS's journal specifies that JS "met in the School room in the chapel in company with the several quorums." The "several quorums" likely included those entities listed in the first resolution in the featured text. These several quorums also constituted the church's "grand council," which met regularly during the months when Missouri church leaders were in Kirtland to prepare for the March dedication of the House of the Lord. (Minutes, 13 Jan. and 12 Feb. 1836, in *JSP*, J1:148, 184; Minutes, 13 Jan. 1836, p. 139 herein.)

17. The minutes in JS's journal state the following: "I then arose and made some remarks upon the object of our meeting, which were as follows— first that many are desiring to be ordained to the ministry, who are not called and consequntly the Lord is displeased."[a] This may have been connected to the ongoing difficulties and questions raised about ordinations to the elders quorum.[b] It is also possible that JS suggested here that the Lord was displeased that so many who desired ordination had not adequately prepared for the ministry and were, therefore, not properly called and ordained to the work. As a February 1829 revelation stated, "If ye have desires to serve God ye are called to the work."[c] The journal continues: "Secondly, many already have been ordained who ought [not] to hold official stations in the church because they dishonour themselves and the church and bring persecution swiftly upon us, in consequence of their zeal without k[n]owledge— I requested the quorum's to take some measures to regulate the same."[d] The

The following resolutions were offered by the Presidency for discussion.[18]

1<u>st</u> Resolved that no one be ordained to any office in the Church in this stake of Zion at Kirtland without the unanimous voice of the several bodies that constitute this quorum, who are appointed to do church business in the name of ~~the~~ ⟨said⟩ church. (Viz) The Presidency of the Church and Council. The twelve Apostles of the Lamb. The twelve High Counsellors of Kirtland. The twelve High Counsellors— [p. 137] of Zion, The Bishop of Kirtland, and his counsellors The Bishop of Zion and his counsellors, and the seven Presidents of Seventies, until otherwise ordered by said quorum.[19]

2<u>dly.</u> Resolved that none be ordained in the branches of said church abroad, unless they are recommended by the voice of the respective branches of the church to which they belong to the general conference appointed by the heads of the Church,[20] and from that conference receive their ordination.[21]

"official stations" likely referred to various priesthood offices. Church leaders had cautioned local leaders two years earlier to be "exceedingly careful" when they ordained an elder to the ministry. "Let it be a *faithful man*," they counseled, and they admonished the local authorities to instruct those ordained to "avoid contentions and vain disputes."*e* In a 2 October 1835 letter instructing the "elders, traveling through the world," JS cautioned against those who had a "zeal not according to knowledge" and who "in the heat of enthusiasm, taught and said many things which are derogatory to the genuine character and principles of the church."*f* (*a*. Minutes, 12 Feb. 1836, in *JSP*, J1:184–185. *b*. See Letter from the Presidency of Elders, 29 Jan. 1836, pp. 162–163 herein. *c*. Revelation, Feb. 1829, in *JSP*, D1:13 [D&C 4:3]. *d*. Minutes, 12 Feb. 1836, in *JSP*, J1:185. *e*. Letter to the Church, not after 18 Dec. 1833, in *JSP*, D3:397–401, italics in original; see also Romans 10:2. *f*. Letter to the Elders of the Church, 2 Oct. 1835, pp. 7, 10 herein.)

18. According to the minutes in JS's journal, JS "proposed some resolutions and remarked to the brethren that the subject was now before them and open for discussion[.] The subject was taken up and discussed by President's S[idney] Rigdon O[liver] Cowdery Eldr. M[artin] Harris and some others, and resolutions drafted, by my scribe [Warren Parrish] who served as clerk on the occasion— read and rejected— it was then proposed that I should indite resolutions which I did as follows." (Minutes, 12 Feb. 1836, in *JSP*, J1:185.)

19. This restated and clarified a resolution passed by a conference of the church presidency on 30 January 1836. (Minutes, 30 Jan. 1836, p. 164 herein.)

20. The following day, 13 February, the Quorum of the Twelve Apostles proposed an amendment to this part of the second resolution that named themselves, instead of local leaders presiding at outlying church conferences, as "having authority to ordain and set in order all the Officers of the church abroad," in accordance with the Doctrine and Covenants published the previous year. The Twelve's amendment was discussed at a meeting ten days later. (Minute Book 1, 13 Feb. 1836; Doctrine and Covenants 3:12, 17, 30, 1835 ed. [D&C 107:33, 39, 58]; Minutes, 22 Feb. 1836, pp. 179–180 herein; see also Minutes and Discourse, 2 May 1835, in *JSP*, D4:307; and Record of the Twelve, 2 May 1835.)

21. This resolution modified the 1835 edition of the Doctrine and Covenants regarding ordinations for the church by adding the clause that ordinations were to be approved at a general conference of the church "and from that conference receive their ordination." The 1835 Doctrine and Covenants stated, "No person is to be ordained to any office in this church, where there is a regularly organized branch of the same, without the vote of that church; but the presiding elders, travelling bishops, high counsellors, high priests, and elders, may have the privilege of ordaining, where there is no branch of the church, that a vote may be called." (Articles and Covenants, ca. Apr. 1830, in Doctrine and Covenants 2:16, 1835 ed. [D&C 20:65–66].)

The foregoing were concurred in by the Presidents of the Seventies.

W[arren] Parrish Clerk.

——————— ✑ ———————

Letter to Henrietta Raphael Seixas, between 6 and 13 February 1836

Source Note

JS, Sidney Rigdon, Frederick G. Williams, and Oliver Cowdery, Letter, Kirtland Township, Geauga Co., OH, to Henrietta Raphael Seixas, Hudson, Summit Co., OH, [between 6 and 13 Feb. 1836]. Featured version copied [ca. 13 Feb. 1836] in Oliver Cowdery, Letterbook, pp. [77]–[78]; handwriting of Warren F. Cowdery; Henry E. Huntington Library, San Marino, CA. For more information on Oliver Cowdery, Letterbook, see Source Notes for Multiple-Entry Documents, p. 531 herein.

Historical Introduction

On 4 January 1836, JS and several other elders met in the attic of the House of the Lord to formally organize a Hebrew school, one of various educational institutions established in Kirtland, Ohio, during fall and winter 1835–1836.[22] Toward the end of January, noted Hebrew scholar Joshua Seixas began teaching the school.[23] By February, the number of students in the Hebrew School had grown substantially, leading the "school committee"— composed of JS, Sidney Rigdon, Frederick G. Williams, and Oliver Cowdery—to seek out additional study materials.[24] Sometime between 6 and 13 February, apparently at the request of Professor Seixas, the committee wrote a letter to his wife, Henrietta Raphael Seixas, requesting to acquire her "valuable lexicon," which her husband had brought to Kirtland.

Though not the first person recruited for the position, Joshua Seixas taught Hebrew classes at the school from 26 January to 29 March 1836.[25] He was born in New York City in

---

22. JS, Journal, 4 Jan. 1836, in *JSP*, J1:143. Though the school was officially organized on that day, JS's journal indicates that he began studying Hebrew informally as early as late November 1835—sometimes alone and sometimes in the company of others—and more "regularly, & systematically" after 26 December 1835. In addition to studying Hebrew, Kirtland residents were taking classes in subjects such as theology, English grammar, geography, writing, and history by January 1836. (JS, Journal, 21 Nov. and 26 Dec. 1835, in *JSP*, J1:107–109, 137; JS History, 1834–1836, 163, in *JSP*, H1:160; Satterfield, "History of Adult Education in Kirtland," 97–130.)

23. JS, Journal, 26 Jan. 1836, in *JSP*, J1:173.

24. Cowdery, Diary, 1, 6, and 7 Feb. 1836; JS, Journal, 4 Feb. 1836, in *JSP*, J1:180.

25. JS, Journal, 26 Jan. and 29 Mar. 1836, in *JSP*, J1:173, 211. In October 1835, Oliver Cowdery exchanged letters with Lucius Parker of Southborough, Massachusetts, about teaching the class, but the school committee rejected his candidacy after learning that he could teach only the "rudiments of Hebrew." In early November, the committee arranged for Daniel Peixotto, a Jew and professor of medicine and obstetrics at the nearby Willoughby Medical College, to teach the class. Peixotto ultimately failed to fulfill his agreement. (Oliver Cowdery, Kirtland, OH, to Lucius Parker, Southborough, MA, 28 Oct. 1835, in Cowdery, Letterbook, 57; Historical Introduction to Revelation, 2 Nov. 1835, pp. 30–32 herein; Daniel Peixotto, Willoughby, OH, to Warren Parrish, Kirtland, OH, 5 Jan. 1836; Warren Parrish, Kirtland, OH, to Daniel Peixotto, Willoughby, OH, 11 Jan. 1836, in JS, Journal, 18 Jan. 1836, in *JSP*, J1:161–164.)

1802 into a family of Sephardic Jews who immigrated to the United States from Portugal in the 1730s. The son of Gershom Mendes Seixas, communal and religious leader of Congregation Shearith Israel in New York City, Seixas became an accomplished Hebraist.[26] During the late 1820s and early 1830s, he taught Hebrew at institutions from New York City to Washington DC; in 1833, he published his own textbook, *Manual Hebrew Grammar.*[27] In the preface to the grammar book's second edition, released in 1834, Seixas promoted his teaching methodology. "With proper attention to the following rules, and with the aids of oral instruction as given to my classes," he asserted, "any one desirous to become acquainted with this language may be enabled in a short time and with little trouble, to read with much pleasure and satisfaction."[28]

In the fall of 1835, Seixas moved his family of nine to Ohio, where he taught Hebrew at several newly established institutions of higher learning, including the Oberlin Collegiate Institute and the Western Reserve College.[29] John Bus, a pupil who left a detailed journal account of his studies under Seixas at Western Reserve College, said of the professor in December 1835, "I never saw any man talk and have so much to say as Mr. Seixas in recitation in my life before." When the class adjourned in January, Bus commented, "I am very well satisfied that he is a man of great learning."[30] While Seixas was teaching at Western Reserve College—which JS referred to as Hudson Seminary—he was recruited by William E. McLellin, a member of the Quorum of the Twelve Apostles, to teach a seven-week course in Kirtland.[31]

---

26. Phillips, "Levy and Seixas Families of Newport and New York," 208; Stern, *First American Jewish Families,* 264; "Seixas," in *Encyclopedia Judaica,* 255–256.

27. "Testimonials," verso of Joshua Seixas, Utica, NY, to John Shipherd, Oberlin, OH, 29 May 1835, Office of the Treasurer, Record Group 7, Series 7/1/5, Letters Received by Oberlin College, 1822–1907, Subseries 1, Oberlin College Archives, Oberlin, OH; Longworth, *Longworth's American Almanac* [1829], 502; Moses Stuart, Andover, MA, to Joshua Seixas, Charlestown, MA, 6 Sept. 1832, Nathan/Kraus Family Collection, 1738–1929, Jacob Rader Marcus Center of the Jewish American Archives, Cincinnati, OH; Joshua Seixas, *Manual Hebrew Grammar for the Use of Beginners* (Andover, MA: Gould and Newman, 1834).

28. Seixas, *Manual Hebrew Grammar,* iii. Former students endorsed the professor's teaching methods as effective, and before moving to Ohio to teach at Oberlin, Seixas forwarded to the college's president a list of enthusiastic testimonials gleaned from past students. ("Testimonials," verso of Joshua Seixas, Utica, NY, to John Shipherd, Oberlin, OH, 29 May 1835, Office of the Treasurer, Record Group 7, Series 7/1/5, Letters Received by Oberlin College, 1822–1907, Subseries 1, Oberlin College Archives, Oberlin, OH.)

29. Seixas arrived in Oberlin, Ohio, during the summer of 1835 and, though not an official faculty member, taught classes at the Oberlin Collegiate Institute during the fall. From 8 December 1835 to 23 January 1836, he taught Hebrew to students at the Western Reserve College in Hudson, Ohio. (Joshua Seixas, Utica, NY, to John Shipherd, Oberlin, OH, 29 May 1835, Record Group 7, Series 7/1/5, Letters Received by Oberlin College, 1822–1907, Subseries 1, Oberlin College Archives, Oberlin, OH; Faculty Minutes, 14 July 1835, Board of Trustees Records, 1833–1982, Record Group 1, Series 2, Oberlin College Archives, Oberlin, OH; Fletcher, *History of Oberlin College,* 368–370; "Hebrew Lectures," *Ohio Observer* [Hudson], 7 Jan. 1836, [2]; "Extracts from the Daily Journal of John Bus," Enclosure, in F. C. Waite, Cleveland, OH, to Joseph L. Rubin, Washington DC, 8 Nov. 1933, Western Reserve Historical Society, Cleveland, OH.)

30. "Extracts from the Daily Journal of John Bus," Enclosure, in F. C. Waite, Cleveland, OH, to Joseph L. Rubin, Washington DC, 8 Nov. 1933, Western Reserve Historical Society, Cleveland, OH.

31. JS, Journal, 4–6 Jan. 1836, in *JSP,* J1:143–145. In January 1836, McLellin and Orson Hyde had been sent by the school committee to hire an instructor. McLellin described Seixas as a "highly

Seixas began his instruction in Kirtland on 26 January 1836. JS's journal entry for the day commented, "His introduction pleased me much. I think he will be a help to the class in learning the Hebrew."[32] Though the school committee initially organized a class of approximately forty students (which they may have divided into two sections), another class of thirty was instituted just six days later; according to Oliver Cowdery, the second class commenced on 2 February.[33] The committee apparently selected another class of fifteen students on 4 February, combined it with the class organized two days earlier, and divided the students into two classes, one of twenty-two and one of twenty-three.[34] With as many as four classes running concurrently, study materials—including grammar books and Hebrew Bibles—became scarce.[35] JS's 4 February journal entry reports, "We have a great want of books but are determined to do the best we can." On the following day, the journal notes, JS "assisted the committe to make arangements for supplying the third & Fourth classes with books— concluded to divide a bible into several parts for the benefit of said classes."[36] Perhaps to compensate for a lack of grammar books, a supplement to Seixas's *Manual Hebrew Grammar* was printed in 1836 expressly for the Kirtland school.[37]

On 6 February, Cowdery, acting on behalf of the school committee, wrote a letter to Henrietta Seixas asking if she would be willing to lend or sell her Hebrew dictionary.[38] Henrietta Raphael, formerly of Richmond, Virginia, married Joshua Seixas sometime before 1822.[39] By 1835, the couple had seven children; their eighth child, James, was likely born during their time in Ohio.[40] According to JS's journal, Henrietta and the children were living in Hudson, Ohio, when Seixas began teaching in Kirtland.[41]

---

celebrated . . . hebrew schollar" who "proposes to give us sufficient knowledge to read and translate the language" in seven weeks. (JS, Journal, 4, 6, and 26 Jan. 1836, in *JSP*, J1:143, 145, 173.)

32. JS, Journal, 26 Jan. 1836, in *JSP*, J1:173.

33. JS, Journal, 26 Jan. and 1 Feb. 1836, in *JSP*, J1:173, 179; Cowdery, Diary, 1–2 Feb. 1836.

34. JS, Journal, 4 Feb. 1836, in *JSP*, J1:180; Cowdery, Diary, 4 Feb. 1836.

35. JS and the committee did have a limited number of books in their possession. In November 1835, Oliver Cowdery had traveled to New York, in part to purchase Hebrew study materials, and JS's journal notes that he returned with a "Hebrew bible, lexicon & Grammar, also a Greek Lexicon and Websters English Lexicon." (JS, Journal, 20 Nov. 1835, in *JSP*, J1:107.)

36. JS, Journal, 4 and 5 Feb. 1836, in *JSP*, J1:180. Apparently Hebrew Bibles were scarce in 1835; in a letter to a trustee at Oberlin, written in May 1835, Seixas remarked that the Bibles "cost rather more than I had anticipated on account of their scarcity. Perhaps there are not ten copies for sale in the U. States." (Joshua Seixas, Utica, NY, to John Shipherd, Oberlin, OH, 29 May 1835, Office of the Treasurer, Record Group 7, Series 7/1/5, Letters Received by Oberlin College, 1822–1907, Subseries 1, Oberlin College Archives, Oberlin, OH.)

37. Joshua Seixas, *Supplement to J. Seixas' Manual Hebrew Grammar* (New York: West and Trow, 1836).

38. Cowdery, Diary, 6 Feb. 1836.

39. Stern, *First American Jewish Families*, 264, 326; Phillips, "Levy and Seixas Families of Newport and New York," 208.

40. Stern, *First American Jewish Families*, 264; Fletcher, *History of Oberlin College*, 369.

41. JS, Journal, 13 Feb. 1836, in *JSP*, J1:184; Cowdery, Diary, 13 Feb. 1836. According to JS's journal, JS and the school committee "made arrangements with Mr. Seixas about continuing longer with us & bringing his family to this place" on 11 March. The family arrived three days later, though it is not clear how long they remained. (JS, Journal, 11–14 Mar. 1836, in *JSP*, J1:196–197.)

Henrietta Raphael Seixas. Between 1851 and 1867. Joseph Smith and others wrote a letter to Henrietta Seixas asking that she allow her husband, Joshua Seixas, who was teaching Hebrew to the Saints in Kirtland, Ohio, to sell to them her "valuable Lexicon" to aid in their continuing language study. (Courtesy American Jewish Historical Society, New York City. Photograph by Rufus P. Anson.)

The text featured below is a copy of Cowdery's letter that was inscribed into his letter-book by his nephew Warren F. Cowdery.[42] Though the letterbook version is dated 13 February, entries in Oliver Cowdery's journal indicate that the original was drafted earlier. Cowdery's 6 February journal entry states, "In the afternoon wrote a letter in the name of the committee containing a request to Professor Seixa's wife, for a valuable Lexicon."[43] Cowdery's entry for the following day confirms that he "copied the committee's letter to Mrs. Seixas, as her husband was urging for it."[44] The letter was probably delivered to Henrietta Seixas by her husband, who apparently left Kirtland around midday on 13 February to visit his family in Hudson for the weekend.[45] Extant records do not include a response, nor is it clear whether the school committee was ultimately able to obtain the lexicon.

Document Transcript

Kirtland Ohio Feb. 13th. 1836.

Dear Madam

We have the privilege of addressing you a few lines through the kindness of Professor Sexias [Joshua Seixas] who we believe has been sent to this institution[46] through the immediate directions of God to promote the cause of truth and benefit a fallen world. We are in this led to be ~~believe~~ thankful to our Redeemer in whose Glorious cause we are engaged as we are anxiously desiring to become acquainted with an individual of virtue & piety who understood perfectly those languages in which the Scriptures of the Old and New Testaments were originally written[47] as our only object is to do good to

---

42. Warren F. Cowdery was the son of Warren A. Cowdery, Oliver Cowdery's older brother.

43. Cowdery, Diary, 6 Feb. 1836.

44. Cowdery, Diary, 7 Feb. 1836.

45. JS, Journal, 13 Feb. 1836, in *JSP,* J1:184.

46. The Hebrew School. In the preface to Joshua Seixas's *Supplement to J. Seixas' Manual Hebrew Grammar,* Oliver Cowdery used the term "Kirtland Theological Institution." This may have referred to the Hebrew School specifically or to the Elders School generally. (Seixas, *Supplement to J. Seixas' Manual Hebrew Grammar,* 7.)

47. The Old Testament was written in Hebrew; the New Testament was written in Greek. Like his contemporaries, JS saw learning Hebrew as a means to read and understand the scriptures "in the language in which they were givn." Following the sixteenth-century Protestant Reformation, a movement to study Hebrew began on the European continent and spread to universities in England, such as Cambridge and Oxford. In America, Harvard, Yale, and other prominent Protestant universities trained religious students in Hebrew during the colonial era. Though the study of Hebrew at American universities had diminished by the 1780s, a resurgence of biblical study—sparked by the Second Great Awakening, the professionalization of college teaching, and the revival of seminary education in the first decades of the nineteenth century—created a renewed interest in Hebrew among Christian intellectuals. Amid this revival, newly established religious institutions in Ohio, such as Oberlin and Western Reserve College, offered courses in Hebrew to their students. JS had studied Greek prior to this time, though it is unclear if and to what extent his study was done in order to understand the New Testament in its original language. (JS, Journal, 23 Dec. 1835 and 4 Feb. 1836, in *JSP,* J1:135, 180; Jones, *Discovery of Hebrew in Tudor England,* 180–220; Goldman, *God's Sacred Tongue,* 116–118, 129, 147–150; Fletcher, *History of Oberlin*

lay aside error when we discover it forsake evil and follow righteousness and truly be the better prepared and qualified to render assistance to our fellow men and glorify the name of the Lord: in this our expectations are fully realized and we trust through the goodness of ~~Good~~ God to make a proper improvement of the blessing thus given. And we sincerely pray that on the part of your husband our acquaintance may be of that kind that we shall ever have cause to bless and adore God for thus guiding him to this place by his unseen hand.

We have seen the possession of Mr. Seixas a very valuable Lexicon which he informs us is your individual property. We have no hesitation in saying that is highly valuable by yourself for the convenience and use of a private family; but we do believe that the wisdom and philanthropy which error inspires the heart of the pure and good will forego for a few months these <u>special</u> benefits which may be derived from it for a few for the pleasure of beneftting the many. As the Trustees of this institution[48] we have by the request of others as well as expressing [p. [77]] our own individual desires to have it the same taken the liberty to thus tresspass upon your time and patience and request the privilege of purchaseing of you through Professor Seixas this Lexicon. It is unnecessary to wholly unnecessary for us to communicate or attempt to the great worth this Lexicon would be to this Institution in our present and future studies as yourself of the fact and we only say that we hope that God may direct you by his Holy Spirit to do right, and we trust the issue in his hands believing you will call to mind the flood of reproach heaped upon us as a people the few advantages we profess in comparison with others institution in consequence of the same and that all favors thus bestowed will be only appreciated and thankfully remembered.

We are most respectfully.

Your Obt. Servants.

Joseph Smith Junr.

Sidney Rigdon

F[rederick] G. Williams

Oliver Cowdery

Kirtland Ohio, Feb. 1836

A true copy from the original.

W[arren] F. Cowdery <u>Rec.</u> [p. [78]]

———— ℰↄ ————

College, 367; Cutler, *History of Western Reserve College,* 21; see also Grey, "Word of the Lord in the Original," 249–275; and Welch, "Joseph Smith's Awareness of Greek and Latin," 310–316.)

48. As members of the school committee, JS, Sidney Rigdon, Frederick G. Williams, and Oliver Cowdery acted as trustees of the Hebrew School.

Minutes, 22 February 1836

Source Note

Church presidency (including JS), Minutes, Kirtland Township, Geauga Co., OH, 22 Feb. 1836. Featured version copied [between ca. 4 Apr. and ca. 16 May 1836] in Minute Book 1, p. 139; handwriting of Warren A. Cowdery; CHL. For more information on Minute Book 1, see Source Notes for Multiple-Entry Documents, p. 527 herein.

Historical Introduction

At a council meeting on 12 February 1836, JS proposed two resolutions to standardize the ordaining of men to priesthood offices. The afternoon following JS's proposal, the Quorum of the Twelve Apostles considered the resolutions; they agreed with the first resolution but objected to the second, which altered the method for ordinations in "branches of said church abroad."[49] The Twelve had jurisdiction over ordinations of church officers in all nations, but the proposed 12 February resolution required that "the heads of the church" in a given branch call a conference to ratify the recommendation of the branch to ordain a church member to a priesthood office. The Twelve offered an amendment to the resolution that would maintain their authority. The Twelve's proposed change contained the following language: "That none be ordained to any office in the branches to which they belong to a general conference, appointed by those, or under the direction of those who are designated in the Book of Covenants as having authority to ordain and set in order all the Officers of the church abroad"—that is, by the authority of the Twelve.[50]

On 17 February, the Kirtland high council discussed JS's 12 February resolutions and the Twelve's proposed amendment. That entity unanimously endorsed the earlier resolution and agreed that the amendment "should be rejected."[51] The next day, the high council of Zion also discussed the resolutions and voted unanimously that the 12 February resolutions should remain "without any alteration or amendment."[52] On 22 February 1836, as described in the minutes presented here, JS and the other members of the church's presidency met again to confer on the subject of ordinations and affirmed the original resolutions. Two days later, the several quorums met in the House of the Lord and implemented the new guidelines for approving ordinations.[53] Notwithstanding the decision in the 22 February presidency meeting, members of the Twelve continued to

---

49. JS, Journal, 12 Feb. 1836, in *JSP*, J1:185.

50. JS, Journal, 12 Feb. 1836, in *JSP*, J1:185; Minute Book 1, 13 Feb. 1836; see also Instruction on Priesthood, between ca. 1 Mar. and ca. 4 May 1835, in *JSP*, D4:315, 317 [D&C 107:33, 58]; Minutes and Discourse, 2 May 1835, in *JSP*, D4:307; and Quorum of the Twelve, Record of the Twelve, 2 May 1835.

51. Minute Book 1, 17 Feb. 1836.

52. Minute Book 1, 18 Feb. 1836. The presidents of the Seventy explicitly concurred with the presidency at the 12 February meeting at which the two resolutions were presented and thus, unlike the high councils, may not have held any separate meeting to discuss the amendment proposed by the Twelve. (Minutes, 12 Feb. 1836, p. 173 herein.)

53. This meeting considered the "propriety or impropriety of ordaining a large number of individuals who wish to be ordained to official stations in the church— each individual's nam[e] was presented and

support their proposed modification. However, nine of the Twelve Apostles joined with other ecclesiastical bodies in approving the resolutions on 3 March 1836, and the remaining three eventually withdrew their objections in a meeting with the presidency on 19 March 1836.[54]

Oliver Cowdery wrote the original minutes (no longer extant), likely on a loose sheet of paper. The minutes were later recorded into Minute Book 1 by Warren A. Cowdery.

Document Transcript

Kirtland Ohio Feb. 22[d] 1836

The Presidency of the Church met and took into consideration the foregoing resolutions previously presented to the Twelve Apostles, (Dated Feb. 12th 1836) the Presidents of the seventies, The High council of the church for Zion & for Kirtland and after due deliberation it was unanimously agreed that the original resolutions be adopted without amendments.[55]

Oliver Cowdery Clerk of council [p. 139]

———— ☙ ————

Minutes, 3 March 1836

Source Note

Minutes, Kirtland Township, Geauga Co., OH, 3 Mar. 1836. Featured version copied [between ca. 4 Apr. and ca. 16 May 1836] in Minute Book 1, pp. 140–143; handwriting of Warren A. Cowdery; CHL. For more information on Minute Book 1, see Source Notes for Multiple-Entry Documents, p. 527 herein.

Historical Introduction

On 24 February 1836, all of the quorums and councils of the church met in the House of the Lord in Kirtland, Ohio, "to conclude the business concerning the ordination" of men to priesthood offices.[56] Recognizing the imperfect state of record keeping in the church's conferences and branches, church authorities believed that new rules and regulations on the issuance and recording of licenses were needed to standardize, organize, and better supervise the ordaining of priesthood holders to various offices. This task was made more urgent because of the extensive ministry that

---

the voice of the assembly called." Participants at the meeting approved seven men for ordination and rejected nineteen others. (JS, Journal, 24 Feb. 1836, in *JSP*, J1:189; Minute Book 1, 24 Feb. 1836.)

54. The three were Orson Pratt, John F. Boynton, and Lyman E. Johnson. (Minutes, 3 Mar. 1836, p. 184 herein; JS, Journal, 3 Mar. 1836, in *JSP*, J1:193–194; Minutes, 19 Mar. 1836, p. 185 herein.)

55. The original resolutions were recorded in Minutes, 12 Feb. 1836, pp. 171–173 herein.

56. Minute Book 1, 24 Feb. 1836. Deliberations concerning ordinations had been ongoing since 30 January 1836. (Minutes, 30 Jan. 1836, pp. 163–165 herein; Minutes, 12 Feb. 1836, pp. 170–173 herein; Minutes, 22 Feb. 1836, pp. 179–180 herein.)

traveling elders were expected to assume after the solemn assembly and endowment of power from on high. At the 24 February meeting, the church's governing bodies appointed Oliver Cowdery, Orson Hyde, and Sylvester Smith as a committee to draft "regulations concerning licenses" and selected Thomas Burdick to officiate as the clerk responsible for recording licenses in Kirtland.[57] The committee drafted resolutions on 27 February 1836 and presented them at the meeting featured here, held on the evening of 3 March 1836.[58]

After the meeting commenced, Cowdery, who served as the chair of the committee, presented the draft of the resolutions for centralizing priesthood licensing.[59] The resolutions called for all licenses to be signed by proper authority, issued by the chairman and clerk of each conference, and recorded, thereby establishing an organized system of licensing in the growing church.[60]

Two contemporary versions of the 3 March 1836 minutes are extant. One version is found in the February 1836 issue of the church newspaper, the *Latter Day Saints' Messenger and Advocate,* which was not published until early March. The other is found in Minute Book 1, the official record for meeting minutes. Both of these copies may have derived from the original text, no longer extant, which was written by Oliver Cowdery, who served as the meeting's clerk. The copy in Minute Book 1 was made by Warren A. Cowdery sometime after he began his scribal duties in April 1836. There are slight differences in capitalization, punctuation, and words used between the two extant versions, suggesting that Warren A. Cowdery did not copy the minutes from the *Messenger and Advocate* version. Because Minute Book 1 was the official record for meetings held in Kirtland, it is the version featured here. Significant differences between the two copies are noted below.

Document Transcript

Kirtland Ohio March 3ᵈ 1836

The following Authorities of the Church of Latter-Day-Saints assembled in the House of the Lord according to adjournment for the purpose of tra[n]sacting business for the Church (Viz.) The Presidency of the church, The Twelve Apostles of the Lamb, the twelve high counsellors of the Church in Kirtland, The twelve High Counsellors of the church in Zion, The Bishop and his counsellors of Kirtland. The Bishop and counsellors of Zion. The seven Presidents of the Seventies. The President and Counsellors of the High Priests The President and counsellors of the Elders, The President and counsellors of

---

57. Minute Book 1, 24 Feb. 1836; JS, Journal, 24 Feb. 1836, in *JSP,* J1:189; Minutes, *LDS Messenger and Advocate,* Feb. 1836, 2:266. The *Messenger and Advocate* version of the minutes erroneously indicates that the 24 February meeting occurred on 26 February.

58. Cowdery, Diary, 27 Feb. 1836.

59. JS, Journal, 3 Mar. 1836, in *JSP,* J1:193.

60. Cannon, "Licensing in the Early Church," 105.

the Priests: The President and counsellors of the Teachers. and the President and counsellors of the Deacons.[61] Opened by singing & Prayer.

The Committee appointed on the 24th of February to draft resolutions for the better regulation of Licensing the official Members of said church, made their report, which was read three times by the chairman of said Committee, After which an addition was made to the 6th article, extending the power of the chairman & Clerk pro-tempore, to act in the absence of the standing chairman & Clerk. The following is a copy of the Report of a Committee appointed by the authorities of the church Latter-Day-Saints, assembled in the House of the Lord in Kirtland. Feb. 24th 1836, for the purpose of drafting [p. 140] resolutions to regulate the manner of licences to the official members of said church which were to be presented to said authorities for their consideration.[62]

Whereas the records of the several conferences, held by the Elders of the church, and the ordination of many of the official members of the same, in many cases have been imperfectly kept since its organization,[63] to avoid ever after, any inconvenience, difficulty or injury in consequence of such neglect your committee recommend.

1st That all licences hereafter granted by these authoroties assembled as a quorum or by general conference held for the purpose of transacting the business of the church, be recorded at full length ⟨by a clerk⟩ appointed for that purpose in a in a book to be kept in this branch of the church until it shall be thought advisable by the heads of the church, to order other books and appoint other clerks to record record licences as above. And that said recording clerk be required to endorse a certificate under his own hand and signature on the back of said licences, specifying the time when & place where such license was

---

61. Prior to the singing and prayer, JS "arose and made some remarks on the object of our meeting," which he identified as "1st To receive or reject certain resolutions that were drafted by a commitee chosen for that purpose at a preceeding meeting respecting licenses for elders and other official members. 2nd To sanction by the united voice of the quorum certain resolutions respecting ordaining members; that had passed through each quorum seperately without any alteration or amendment excepting in the quorum of the twelve." (JS, Journal, 3 Mar. 1836, in *JSP*, J1:193.)

62. See Minute Book 1, 24 Feb. 1836; and JS, Journal, 24 Feb. 1836, in *JSP*, J1:189.

63. A resolution offered on 30 January 1836 provides another example of church leaders' concern about imperfect record keeping. At a meeting held that day, JS and the church's presidency charged Alvah Beman with creating a "list of the names of the several Elders comprising his quorum and all other Elders in Kirtland"—a directive indicating that neither Beman nor the church presidency had a complete list of who had been ordained to that office. (Minutes, 30 Jan. 1836, p. 164 herein.)

recorded, and also a reference to the letter and page of the Book containing the same;

2ᵈ That this quorum appoint two persons to sign Licences given as aforesaid. one as chairman, and the other as clerk of conference, and that it shall be the duty of said person appointed to sign licences as clerk of Conference, immediately thereafter, to deliver the same into the hands of the recording Clerk,

3ᵈ That all general conferences abroad give each individual, whom they ordain a certificate signed by the chairman & clerk of said conference, stating the time and place of such conference, and the office to which the individual has been ordained; and that when such certificate has been forwarded to [p. 141] to the person hereafter authorized to sign licences as clerk of conference, such person shall, together with the chairman of conference, immediately sign a license, and said clerk of conference shall, after the same has been recorded, forward it to the proper person.

4ᵗʰ That all official members in good standing & fellowship in the various branches of this church, be requested to forward their present licences accompanied accompanied by their ⟨a certificate of their virtuous &⟩ faithful⁶⁴ walk before the Lord, signed by the chairman and clerk, of a general conference, or by the clerk of the branch of the church in which such official member resides, by the advic[e] & direction of such Church, to the clerk of conference, whose duty it shall be to fill a new licence as directed in the 3ᵈ· article: And that all licences signed recorded and endorsed, as specified in the first article shall be considered good and valid to all intents & purposes in the business, in and spiritual affairs of this church as a religious society, or before any court of record of this or any court of record of this or any court of other country wherein preachers of the Gospel are entitled to special privileges, answering in all respects as an original record without the necessity of refering to any other document.

5 That the recording clerk be required to publish quarterly in a paper published by some member or members of this church, a list of the names of the several persons for whom he has recorded licences within the last quarter.⁶⁵

---

64. The words "& faithful" are not present in the *Messenger and Advocate* version. (Minutes, *LDS Messenger and Advocate,* Feb. 1836, 2:267.)

65. On 3 June 1836, Thomas Burdick wrote a list "containing the names of Ministers of the Gospel, belonging to the church of the Latter Day Saints, whose Licenses were recorded, the preceeding Quarter, in the License Records, in Kirtland, Ohio." The *Messenger and Advocate* published that list in its

6 That this quorum appoint two persons to sign as chairman and clerk of conference, Pro. Tempore licencens for the standing chairman and clerk, who shall be appointed as named in the 2ᵈ article and also to act in their absence in signing other licences. [p. 142] as specified in the foregoing article

Kirtland Feb. 27 1836

Oliver Cowdery ⎫
Orson Hyde ⎬ Committee
Sylvester Smith ⎭

The several bodies were then called upon for their decision upon the foregoing report. The Deacons being first called upon gave a unanimous vote in favor of the same. The teachers were then called upon, and voted unanimously in favor of the report. The quorum of Priests received it by a ~~unanimously~~ vote. The Bishop & council of Kirtland received it unanimously. The Bishop and council of Zion received it without a dissenting voice. The Elders passed it unanimously. The High Priests also. The President of the seventies, The High counsellors of Zion, The High counsellors of Kirtland. The Twelve Apostles and the Presidency, all concurred in the reception of said report.

Joseph Smith Junʳ· was nominated as standing chairman & Frederick G. Williams as clerk.

Sidney Rigdon as chairman and Oliver Cowdery as Clerk pro tempore—

The several bodies were then called to vote upon the above nominations which passed by unanimous vote.

The resolutions offered to the quorums on the 12ᵗʰ of February regulating ordinations[66] were then read, when a discussion was had after which, the Twelve recalled their previous amendments[67] except three, (Viz.) John F. Boynton, Orson Pratt & Lyman Johnson,[68]

June issue. Burdick submitted another list to the *Messenger and Advocate* on 3 September 1836. (List, *LDS Messenger and Advocate,* June 1836, 2:335–336; see also Minute Book 1, 24 Feb. 1836; and List, *LDS Messenger and Advocate,* Sept. 1836, 2:383.)

66. Minutes, 12 Feb. 1836, pp. 171–173 herein.

67. According to his journal, JS "made some remarks on the amendment of the 12," after which Thomas B. Marsh "made some observations." JS then called for the vote of the Twelve "to asertain whether they would repeal their amendment or not." (JS, Journal, 3 Mar. 1836, in *JSP,* J1:194; see also Historical Introduction to Minutes, 22 Feb. 1836, pp. 179–180 herein; and Minute Book 1, 17 Feb. 1836.)

68. From "when a discussion was had" to this point, the *Messenger and Advocate* instead has "a decision was had after which they passed unanimously." Boynton, Pratt, and Johnson met with JS and the church

Council closed by prayer of Bishop [Edward] Partridge

Oliver Cowdery }

Clerk }   [p. 143]

———— ∞ ————

Minutes, 19 March 1836

Source Note

Minutes, Kirtland Township, Geauga Co., OH, 19 Mar. 1836. Featured version copied [between ca. 4 Apr. and ca. 16 May 1836] in Minute Book 1, p. 144; handwriting of Warren A. Cowdery; CHL. For more information on Minute Book 1, see Source Notes for Multiple-Entry Documents, p. 527 herein.

Historical Introduction

JS and the church presidency met with Orson Pratt, John F. Boynton, and Lyman Johnson, three members of the Quorum of the Twelve Apostles, on 19 March 1836 to discuss their continued opposition to a resolution on priesthood ordinations, which was passed on 12 February.[69]

Document Transcript

Kirtland Ohio March 19th 1836

Elders, Orson Pratt, John F. Boynton, and Lyman Johnson met the Presidency of the church and verbally withdrew all objections to the first resolution[70] presented to the quorums. by the Presidency on the 12th of February for the regulation of ordinations[71]

Oliver Cowdery
Clerk of conference

———— ∞ ————

---

presidency to resolve this matter about two weeks after the 3 March meeting. (Minutes, *LDS Messenger and Advocate,* Feb. 1836, 2:268; Minutes, 19 Mar. 1836, p. 185 herein.)

69. See Historical Introduction to Minutes, 12 Feb. 1836, pp. 170–171 herein; Historical Introduction to Minutes, 22 Feb. 1836, pp. 179–180 herein; and Historical Introduction to Minutes, 3 Mar. 1836, pp. 180–181 herein.

70. This appears to be a scribal error; the Twelve had objected to "the 2d resolution." (Minute Book 1, 13 Feb. 1836.)

71. Minutes, 12 Feb. 1836, pp. 171–173 herein.

License, 21 March 1836

Source Note

Sidney Rigdon and Oliver Cowdery, License, for JS, Kirtland Township, Geauga Co., OH, 21 Mar. 1836; printed form with manuscript additions in the handwriting of Oliver Cowdery; signatures of Oliver Cowdery, Sidney Rigdon, and Thomas Burdick; endorsed by Thomas Burdick; two pages; JS Collection, CHL.

One leaf, measuring 5 × 8 inches (13 × 20 cm). The document has three vertical folds. It was printed on the press of the *Latter Day Saints' Messenger and Advocate*. The document was signed by Oliver Cowdery, Sidney Rigdon, and Thomas Burdick on 21 March 1836. The provenance of this document is unknown; it is assumed that the document has remained in continuous institutional custody since its creation.

Historical Introduction

The church's founding "Articles and Covenants" allowed for licenses to be issued to deacons, teachers, priests, and elders, declaring their priesthood office.[72] A license demonstrated to those both inside and outside the church that an individual had been granted authority for a particular assignment or office. A JS revelation from February 1831 required that no one "go forth to preach my gospel or to build up my church except they be ordained by some one that hath authority & it is known to the church that he hath authority & have been regularly ordained by the leaders of the church."[73] As early as March 1833, licenses issued by the church began attesting to moral character and spiritual worthiness.[74] Whereas earlier licenses were handwritten documents, in February 1834 individuals began receiving printed licenses with blank lines on which the issuer wrote in his name, the date, and the name of the person receiving the license.[75]

At a 3 March 1836 council of church leaders, a committee consisting of Oliver Cowdery, Orson Hyde, and Sylvester Smith presented its draft of regulations for licensing priesthood holders.[76] After the council unanimously accepted the licensing resolutions, all "official members"—that is, men ordained to a priesthood office—were evaluated for worthiness and obtained a new license. In this system, men ordained to offices of the Melchizedek, or higher, priesthood were issued an elder's license, even if they had already been ordained as a high priest or to another office. The term *elder* was used in two ways: sometimes it referred generically to all men ordained to the Melchizedek priesthood, and in other cases it pertained specifically to the particular priesthood office of elder. Once an official member received the signed license from the chairman and clerk, it was his responsibility to have it copied into a record book maintained by Thomas Burdick as part of the church's larger effort to standardize licensing and track the growing body of men ordained to offices in the higher priesthood. The recipient would retain possession of the original license, such as the one featured here, as proof of his authority.

---

72. Articles and Covenants, ca. Apr. 1830, in *JSP*, D1:124 [D&C 20:64].
73. Revelation, 9 Feb. 1831, in *JSP*, D1:250–251 [D&C 42:11].
74. License for Frederick G. Williams, 20 Mar. 1833, in *JSP*, D3:43–46.
75. License for Frederick G. Williams, 25 Feb. 1834, in *JSP*, D3:463–465.
76. Minutes, 3 Mar. 1836, pp. 182–184 herein.

The license featured here is representative of hundreds of similar licenses that bear JS's signature; as chairman appointed on 3 March 1836 to sign licenses, JS signed nearly 250 of these new licenses before the end of May 1836.[77] Unlike those licenses, however, JS was the recipient of this license, rather than the signatory.

Document Transcript

TO WHOM IT MAY CONCERN:

THIS Certifies that [78] Joseph Smith, Jr. *has been received into the church of the Latter Day Saints, organized on the sixth of April, in the year of our Lord, one thousand, eight hundred, and thirty,*[79] *and has been ordained an elder according to the rules and regulations of said church,*[80] *and is duly authorized to preach the gospel, agreeably to the authority of that office.*[81]

From the satisfactory evidence which we have of his good moral character, and his zeal for the cause of righteousness, and diligent desire to persuade men to forsake evil and embrace truth, we confidently recommend him to all candid and upright people, as a worthy member of society.

We, therefore, in the name, and by the authority of this church, grant unto this, our worthy brother in the Lord, this letter of commendation as a proof of our fellowship and esteem: praying for his success and prosperity in our Redeemer's cause.

Given by the direction of a conference of elders of said church, assembled in Kirtland, Geauga county, Ohio, ~~this~~ ⟨the⟩ 3rd day of March in the year of our Lord, one thousand, eight hundred, and thirty- six.

---

77. Of the licenses recorded in the Kirtland Elders' Certificate record book, only thirteen originals from the period covered in this volume are known to be extant. (See Kirtland Elders' Certificates; and Calendar of Documents, at josephsmithpapers.org.)

78. TEXT: Underlined text with leading and trailing spaces indicates handwritten portions of the pre-printed form. Handwriting of Oliver Cowdery.

79. The church was organized on this date as the "Church of Christ." The church officially changed its name in May 1834 to the "Church of the Latter Day Saints." (Articles and Covenants, ca. Apr. 1830, in *JSP,* D1:120 [D&C 20:1]; Minutes, 3 May 1834, in *JSP,* D4:44.)

80. The "articles and covenants of the Church of Christ," containing the founding principles for governing the priesthood, were presented to members at the first conference of the church, held 9 June 1830 at Fayette, New York. (Articles and Covenants, ca. Apr. 1830, in *JSP,* D1:116–126.)

81. These new licenses, with the wording presented in this first paragraph, could be used to demonstrate that their holders were ordained ministers of the Church of the Latter Day Saints and, therefore, eligible for licenses to perform marriages in accordance with Ohio state law. On 21 March 1836, JS's journal states that JS "went to the printing office and prepared, a number of Elders licinses, to send by Elder [Ambrose] Palmer to the court [in] Medina County in order to obtain licenses to marry." (JS, Journal, 21 Mar. 1836, in *JSP,* J1:198–199; An Act, Regulating Marriages [6 Jan. 1824], *Statutes of Ohio,* vol. 2, chap. 623, pp. 1407–1408; see also Historical Introduction to Marriage License for John F. Boynton and Susan Lowell, 17 Nov. 1835, pp. 65–66 herein.)

⁸²‾Sidney Rigdon‾ Chairman.
⟨Pro. Tem.⟩

‾Oliver Cowdery,‾ Clerk.
⟨Pro Tempore.⟩⁸³
⟨Kirtland, Ohio. March 21, 1836.⟩ [p. [1]]
⁸⁴⟨This certifies that the within Licence was recorded on the 21ˢᵗ· day of
March, 1836, in Kirtland, Ohio, in the Licence Records' Book A. page 1.——⟩⁸⁵
⟨Thomas Burdick⟩⁸⁶
⟨Recording Clerk.⟩

———— ❧ ————

Minutes and Prayer of Dedication, 27 March 1836 [D&C 109]

Source Note

Minutes and Prayer of Dedication, Kirtland Township, Geauga Co., OH, 27 Mar. 1836. Featured version published in "Kirtland, Ohio, March 27th 1836," Latter Day Saints' Messenger and Advocate, *Mar. 1836, 2:274–281. For more information on* Latter Day Saints' Messenger and Advocate, *see Source Notes for Multiple-Entry Documents, p. 527 herein.*

Historical Introduction

The dedication of the House of the Lord in Kirtland, Ohio, on 27 March 1836 was the result of years of devoted effort. In summer and fall 1835, men and women worked side by side to complete the temple. Men generally did masonry work, drove cattle, and hauled rock, while women generally spun, knit, and wove clothes for workers, "us[ing] every exertion in their power to forward the work."⁸⁷ Women also worked on the veils, or curtains, that hung in the House of the Lord, and JS "pronounced a blessing upon the Sisters for the liberality in

---

82. TEXT: Signatures of Sidney Rigdon and Oliver Cowdery.

83. The resolutions to regulate licenses specified that both a chairman "Pro. Tempore" and temporary clerk could sign the licenses for the standing chairman and clerk. At the meeting on 3 March 1836 when the regulations on licensing were approved, JS was appointed as the "standing chairman" and Sidney Rigdon as "chairman protem." Frederick G. Williams served as the standing clerk to sign licenses, and the authorities of the church appointed Oliver Cowdery as clerk pro tempore. (See Minutes, 3 Mar. 1836, pp. 182–184 herein; JS, Journal, 3 Mar. 1836, in *JSP,* J1:194.)

84. TEXT: Certification and accompanying signature in the handwriting of Thomas Burdick.

85. This notation on the license's verso was made in accordance with the first article of the regulations on licensing approved on 3 March 1836. That article required the recording clerk "to endorse a certificate under his own hand and signature on the back of said licences, specifying the time when & place where such license was recorded." (Minutes, 3 Mar. 1836, pp. 182–183 herein.)

86. On 24 February 1836, the day they appointed the committee to write the resolutions on licensing, the priesthood quorums appointed Thomas Burdick "to officiate as clerk to record licenses, and to receive pay for his services accordingly." (JS, Journal, 24 Feb. 1836, in *JSP,* J1:189.)

87. Kimball, "History," 26; Helen Mar Whitney, "Life Incidents," *Woman's Exponent,* 15 Aug. 1880, 9:42.

giving their servises so cheerfully."[88] Men likewise found great satisfaction in their work building the religious edifice. Newel Knight, for instance, rejoiced in his labors because it had been "a long time since the Lord had a house on the Earth" and he believed that in the House of the Lord, the Saints would receive the promised endowment of divine power.[89]

By late March 1836, the building and the church members were prepared for a dedicatory meeting. On 26 March, the day before the dedication, JS, Oliver Cowdery, Sidney Rigdon, and JS's two scribes, Warren A. Cowdery and Warren Parrish, met in the president's room on the attic floor of the temple to prepare for the dedication. Oliver Cowdery noted in his diary that at this meeting he "assisted in writing a prayer for the dedication of the house." The text of the prayer, likely set in type on the printing press of the *Messenger and Advocate* that night, was printed as a broadside for JS to read at the dedication the following day.[90]

On Sunday morning, 27 March, a crowd of approximately one thousand people filled the building to capacity. Some of those unable to enter held a meeting in the adjacent schoolhouse while others returned home to await a second dedicatory event.[91] At nine o'clock, Rigdon commenced the meeting with an opening prayer and preliminary remarks. Following a hymn, Rigdon addressed the congregation for two and a half hours on a variety of topics. Rigdon then presented JS's name to the congregation as "Prophet and Seer," followed by a systematic vote by each quorum of the church and others in attendance. All voted unanimously in the affirmative. In the afternoon session, JS addressed the congregation first. He presented the names of the church's First Presidency "as Prophets and Seers" and the Twelve Apostles "as Prophets and Seers and special witnesses to all the nations of the earth," and he invited the congregation to signify their support for these officers by rising. He then similarly presented the other quorums and officers. Each group was upheld separately by a systematic vote similar to the vote Rigdon presented in the morning session.[92] After another hymn, JS stood at the pulpit and read the prayer of dedication—the first dedication of a temple in Latter-day Saint history.

The dedicatory prayer alluded to earlier revelations and events and petitioned both God and Jesus Christ for blessings, mercy, and deliverance for the Saints. In particular, the prayer referenced JS's late December 1832 revelation commanding the Saints to build the "house of God," and it also recounted the 1833 violence against the Latter-day Saints in Jackson County, Missouri.[93] In the prayer, JS asked that the House of the Lord be accepted and that it be a place where the glory of God could rest down upon his children. JS also requested that God remember the oppression the Saints had faced in their efforts to follow his commandments. He pleaded for priesthood holders to be protected and empowered with spiritual gifts and power so that they might be better equipped to go out preaching. The prayer

---

88. JS, Journal, 23 Feb. 1836, in *JSP*, J1:188–189; see also Plan of the House of the Lord, between 1 and 25 June 1833, in *JSP*, D3:141.

89. Knight, Autobiographical Sketch, [4].

90. Cowdery, Diary, 26 Mar. 1836; JS, Journal, 26 Mar. 1836, in *JSP*, J1:199; George A. Smith, in *Journal of Discourses*, 15 Nov. 1864, 11:9; Prayer, 27 Mar. 1836, in *Prayer, at the Dedication of the Lord's House in Kirtland, Ohio, March 27, 1836* (Kirtland, OH: 1836), copy at CHL [D&C 109].

91. JS, Journal, 27 Mar. 1836, in *JSP*, J1:200; Post, Journal, 27 Mar. 1836.

92. JS, Journal, 27 Mar. 1836, in *JSP*, J1:203–204; Post, Journal, 27 Mar. 1836.

93. Revelation, 27–28 Dec. 1832, in *JSP*, D2:334–346 [D&C 88:1–126].

also expressed desire that the Saints might be blessed to grow up in the ways of God. All those in attendance unanimously accepted the prayer by vote.

Both the minutes of this meeting and accounts by Latter-day Saints who attended the dedication report miracles, heavenly visitations, and a spiritual outpouring. Frederick G. Williams reported that a "Holy Angel of God" entered the temple during the prayer of dedication. Following the prayer, Brigham Young "gave a short address in tongues." At the conclusion of the day's events, JS "blessed the congregation in the name of the Lord" and ended the meeting "a little past four P. M."[94]

The importance the Saints placed on attending the dedication of the House of the Lord is manifest in participant accounts. For example, according to Benjamin Brown and Eliza R. Snow, one woman could not find anyone with whom to leave her two-month-old child so that she could attend the dedication. She implored Joseph Smith Sr. to allow her to enter the House of the Lord with her child even though young children were not allowed at the meeting. Upon this request, Joseph Smith Sr. reportedly said to the doorkeepers on duty, "Brethren we do not Exercise faith[;] my faith is this child will not cry a word in the House to day." Brown observed, "On this the woman & child entered and the child did not cry a word from 8 till 4 in the after noon. But when the saints all shouted Hosana the child was nursing But let go & shouted also when the saints paused it paused when they shouted it shouted for three times when they shouted amen it shouted also for three times then it resumed its nursing without any alarm."[95]

According to participants, the events following the dedicatory meeting included an outpouring of spiritual gifts similar to that experienced by the apostles in the New Testament on the day of Pentecost.[96] JS requested that "all official members," meaning men who had been ordained to the priesthood, meet again in the House of the Lord that evening for instruction "respecting the ordinance of washing of feet."[97] That evening meeting "was designed as a continuation of our pentecost," wrote participant Stephen Post, and according to his journal, "Angels of God came into the room, cloven tongues rested upon some of the servants of the Lord like unto fire, & they spake with tongues and prophesied."[98] In another description of the evening meeting, Oliver Cowdery wrote, "The spirit was poured out—I saw the glory of God, like a great cloud, come down and rest upon the house, and fill the same like a mighty rushing wind. I also saw cloven tongues, like as of fire rest upon many, (for there were 316 present,) while they spake with other tongues and prophesied."[99] Levi Jackman similarly declared, "I believe that as great things were heard and felt and seen as there was on the day of Pentecost with the apostles."[100] Writing to his wife, Sarah Brown, Benjamin Brown recorded that on the evening of the dedication, "one saw a pillar or cloud

94. JS, Journal, 27 Mar. 1836, in *JSP*, J1:210–211.

95. Benjamin Brown to Sarah Mumford Brown, [ca. Apr. 1836], Benjamin Brown Family Collection, CHL; Tullidge, *Women of Mormondom*, 94–95.

96. See Acts 2:1–18.

97. JS, Journal, 27 Mar. 1836, in *JSP*, J1:211.

98. Post, Journal, 27 Mar. 1836.

99. Cowdery, Diary, 27 Mar. 1836.

100. Jackman, Diary, 17.

rest down upon the house bright as when the sun shines on a cloud like as gold, two others saw three personages hovering in the room with bright keys in their hands."[101]

On Thursday, 31 March, JS and the First Presidency again performed the dedicatory ceremonies "for the benefit of those who could not get into the house on the preceeding Sabbath." According to JS's journal, the services that day were "prosecuted and terminated in the same manner as at the former dedication and the spirit of God rested upon the congregation and great solemnity prevailed."[102]

There are two extant versions of the minutes of the 27 March dedication, one in manuscript and the other in print. JS's scribe Warren Parrish made a record of the meeting that he copied into JS's journal.[103] Though not credited, Oliver Cowdery created the official minutes, featured here, which were then published in the *Messenger and Advocate*.[104] The original minutes are no longer extant, and, unlike other minutes Oliver Cowdery kept in this period, these minutes were never copied into Minute Book 1. The lack of an original copy and minute book entry may be accounted for by the timely publication of the minutes. Substantive differences between the two extant versions are noted below.

Document Transcript

Kirtland, Ohio, March 27th, 1836.

Previous notice having been given, the Church of the Latter Day Saints met this day in the House of the Lord to dedicate it to him. The congregation began to assemble before 8 o'clock A. M.[105] and thronged the doors until 9, when the Presidents of the church who assisted in seating the congregation, were reluctantly compelled to order the door-keepers to close the doors; every seat and aisle were crowded.— One thousand persons were now silently and solemnly waiting to hear the word of the Lord from the mouth of his servants in the sacred desk. President S[idney] Rigdon began the services of the day, by reading the 96th and 24th Psalms.[106] An excellent choir of singers, led by M[arvel] C. Davis sung the following Hymn:[107]

---

101. Benjamin Brown to Sarah Mumford Brown, [ca. Apr. 1836], Benjamin Brown Family Collection, CHL; see also Harper, "Pentecost Continued," 4–22.

102. JS, Journal, 31 Mar. 1836, in *JSP*, J1:216.

103. JS, Journal, 27 Mar. 1836, in *JSP*, J1:200–211.

104. Cowdery, Diary, 27 Mar. 1836.

105. According to JS's journal, the congregation began to assemble "at about 7 oclock," one hour before "the doors were to be opened." (JS, Journal, 27 Mar. 1836, in *JSP*, J1:200.)

106. Psalm 96 admonishes its hearers to praise the Lord, for "strength and beauty are in his sanctuary," and to "come into his courts." Latter-day Saints called the main floors of the House of the Lord "courts," as with the courts of Solomon's temple. Psalm 24 states that only those with "clean hands, and a pure heart" should enter the Lord's "holy place," where "the King of glory shall come in." (Psalms 24:3–7, 96:4–8; Revelation, 1 June 1833, in *JSP*, D3:107–108 [D&C 95:15–17]; see also 2 Chronicles 4:9.)

107. This hymn, Hymn 19 in the recently published Latter-day Saint hymnal, was written by apostle Parley P. Pratt. According to JS's journal, the choir sang the "hymn on the 29th page of Latter day Saints collection of hymn's." Page 29 contains the beginning of Hymn 23, "Adam-ondi-Ahman," which actually

TUNE—*Sterling.*

Ere long the vail will rend in twain,
The King descend with all his train;
The earth shall shake with awful fright,
And all creation feel his might.

The trump of God, it long shall sound,
And raise the nations under ground;
Throughout the vast domain of heav'n
The voice echoes, the sound is given.

Lift up your heads ye saints in peace,
The Savior comes for your release;
The day of the redeem'd has come,
The saints shall all be welcom'd home.

behold the church, it soars on high,
To meet the saints amid the sky;
To hail the King in clouds of fire,
And strike and tune th' immortal lyre.

Hosanna now the trump shall sound,
Proclaim the joys of heav'n around,
When all the saints together join,
In songs of love, and all divine.

With Enoch here we all shall meet,
And worship at Messiah's feet,
Unite our hands and hearts in love,
And reign on thrones with Christ above.

The city that was seen of old
Whose walls were jasper, and streets gold
We'll now inherit thron'd in might:
The Father and the Son's delight.

Celestial crowns we shall receive,
And glories great our God shall give,

opened the second session of the services. (JS, Journal, 27 Mar. 1836, in *JSP*, J1:203; Hymns 19 and 23, *Collection of Sacred Hymns*, 25–27, 29.)

While loud hosannas we'll proclaim,
And sound aloud the Saviors name. [p. 274]

Our hearts and tongues all joined in one,
A loud hosanna to proclaim,
While all the heav'ns shall shout again,
And all creation say, Amen.

President Rigdon then in an able, devout and appropriate manner, addressed the throne of Grace. The following Hymn was then sung:[108]

TUNE—*Weymouth.*

O happy souls who pray
    Where God appoints to hear!
O happy saints who pay
    Their constant service there!

        We praise him still;
        And happy we;
        We love the way
        To Zion's hill.

No burning heats by day,
    Nor blasts of evening air,
Shall take our health away,
    If God be with us there:

        He is our sun,
        And he our shade,
        To guard the head
        By night or noon.

God is the only Lord,
    Our shield and our defence;
With gifts his hand is stor'd:
    We draw our blessings thence.

        He will bestow
        On Jacobs race,

---

108. Hymn 8, written by William W. Phelps. (*Collection of Sacred Hymns,* 14–15.)

Pecu[l]iar grace,
And glory, too—

The speaker (S. Rigdon,) selected the 8th chapter of Matthew, the 18, 19 and 20th verses from which, he proposed to address the congregation, confining himself more closely to the 20th verse— He spoke two hours and a half in his usual, forcible and logical manner.[109] At one time in the course of his remarks he was rather pathetic, than otherwise, which drew tears from many eyes. He was then taking a retrospective view of the toils, privations and anxieties of those who had labored upon the walls of the house to erect them. And added, there were those who had wet them with their tears, in the silent shades of night, while they were praying to the God of Heaven, to protect them, and stay the unhallowed hands of ruthless spoilers, who had uttered a prophecy when the foundation was laid, that the walls would never be reared. This was only a short digression from the main thread of his discourse, which he soon resumed.

Here it may not be improper to give a synopsis of the discourse for the satisfaction of our readers who were not privileged as we were with hearing it. The speaker assumed as a postulate, what we presume no one was disposed to deny, (viz:) that in the days of the Savior there were Synagogues, where the Jews worshipped God, and in addition to them, the splendid Temple at Jerusalem. Yet, when on a certain occasion, one proposed to follow him withersoever he went, He though heir of all things cried out like one in the bitterness of his soul in abject poverty, The Foxes have holes, &c.—[110] This, said the speaker, was evidence to his mind, that the Most High did not put his name there, and that he did not accept the worship of those who payed their vows and adorations there. This was evident from the fact that they would not receive him, but thrust him from them, saying, away with him, crucify him! crucify him! It was therefore abundantly evident that his spirit did not dwell in them. They were the degenerate sons of noble sires: but they had long since slain the Prophets and Seers through whom the Lord revealed himself to the children of men. They were not led by revelation, *This*, said the speaker, was the grand difficulty among them. Their unbelief in present revelation. He further remarked, that, their unbelief in present revelation was the means of dividing that generation into the various sects and parties that existed. They were sincere worshipers, but their worship was not required of them, nor was it acceptable to God.— The Redeemer himself who knew the hearts of all men,

109. JS's journal notes that Rigdon's sermon was "sublime, and well adapted to the occasion." (JS, Journal, 27 Mar. 1836, in *JSP*, J1:203.)

110. See Matthew 8:20; and Luke 9:58.

called them a generation of vipers.[111] It was proof positive to his mind, that there being Pharisees, Sadducees, Herodians and Essen[e]s, and all differing from each other, that they were led by the precepts and commandments of men. Each had something peculiar to himself, but all agreed in one point, (viz:) to oppose the Redeemer. So that we discover he could with the utmost propriety, exclaim, notwithstanding their synagogue and Temple worship, The foxes have holes, the birds of the air have nests, but the Son of man hath not where to lay his head. He took occasion here to remark that such diversity of sentiment ever had, and ever would obtain when people were not led by present revelation. This brought him to the inevitable conclusion that the various sects of the pres[p. 275]ent day, from their manifesting the same spirit, rested under the same condemnation with those who were coeval with the Savior. He admitted there were many houses: many sufficiently great, built for the worship of God, but not one except this, on the face of the whole earth, that was built by divine revelation, and were it not for this, the dear Redeemer might in this day of science, this day of intelligence, this day of religion, say to those who would follow him, The foxes have holes, the birds of the air have nests, but the Son of man hath not where to lay his head.

Here his whole soul appeared to be fired with his subject. Arguments, strong and conclusive seemed almost to vie with each other for utterance. Indeed, there was no sophistry in his reasoning, no plausible hypothesis on which the whole rested, but on the contrary plain scripture facts. Therefore his deductions and inferences were logical and conclusive.

The comparison drawn between the different religious sects of ancient and modern times, was perfectly natural, and simple yet it was done in that confident, masterly manner, accompanied with those incontrovertable proofs of his position, that was directly calculated to cheer and gladden the hearts of the Saints, but to draw down the indignation of the sectarian world upon him, and we have no doubt, had our speaker uttered the same sentiments, with the same proof of their correctness, had there been those present that we might name, his voice would doubtless have been drowned as was that of the ancient apostle in the Athenian Temple, when his auditors cried incessantly for about two hours "Great is Diana of the Ephesians."[112]

But to conclude, we can truly say no one unacquainted with the manner of delivery and style of our speaker can, from reading form any adequate idea of the powerful effect he is capable of producing in the minds of his hearers: And to say on this occasion he showed himself master of his subject and

---

111. See Matthew 12:34; 23:33; and Luke 3:7.
112. See Acts 19:28.

did well, would be doing him injustice; to say he acquitted himself with honor
or did very well, would be detracting from his real merit; and to say that he did
exceeding well; would be only halting praise.

After closing his discourse he presented Joseph Smith jr. to the church
as a Prophet and Seer. The Presidents of the church then all in their seats, acknowledged him as such by rising. The vote was unanimous in the affirmative.

The question was then put, and carried without a manifest dissenting sentiment to each of the different grades or quorums of church officers respectively
and then to the congregation.— The following hymn was then sung:[113]

TUNE—*Hosanna.*

Now let us rejoice in the day of salvation,
No longer as strangers on earth need we roam;
Good tidings are sounding to us and each nation,
And shortly the hour of redemption will come:

When all that was promis'd the saints will be given,
And none will molest them from morn until even,
And earth will appear as the garden of Eden,
And Jesus will say to all Israel: Come home!

We'll love one another and never dissemble,
But cease to do evil and ever be one;
And while the ungodly are fearing and tremble.
We'll watch for the day when the Savior shall come:

When all that was promis'd the saints will be given,
And none will molest them from morn until even,
And earth will appear as the garden of Eden,
And Jesus will say to all Israel: Come home!

In faith we'll rely on the arm of Jehovah,
To guide through these last days of trouble and gloom;
And after the scourges and harvest are over,
We'll rise with the just, when the Savior doth come:

Then all that was promis'd the saints will be given,
And they will be crown'd as the angel of heaven:

---

113. Hymn 18, by William W. Phelps. (*Collection of Sacred Hymns*, 24–25.)

And earth will appear as the garden of Eden,
And Christ and his people will ever be one.

Services closed for the forenoon.

Intermission was about 15 minutes[114] during which none left their seats except a few females, who from having left their infants with their friends, were compelled to do so to take care of them. The P. M. services commenced by singing the following hymn:[115]

TUNE—*Adam-ondi-Ahman.*

This earth was once a garden place,
    Wi[t]h all her glories common;
And men did live a holy race,
And worship Jesus face to face,
    In Adam-ondi-Ahman. [p. 276]

We read that Enoch walk'd with God,
    Above the power of Mammon:
While Zion spread herself abroad,
And saints and angels sung aloud,
    In Adam-ondi-Ahman.

Her land was good and greatly blest,
    Beyond old Israel's Canaan:
Her fame was known from east to west;
Her peace was great, and pure the rest
    Of Adam-ondi-Ahman.

Hosanna to such days to come—
    The Savior's second comin'—
When all the earth in glorious bloom,
Affords the saints a holy home
    Like Adam-ondi-Ahman.

President J. Smith jr. then rose, and after a few preliminary remarks, presented the several Presidents of the church, then present, to the several quorums

---

114. According to JS's journal, the intermission lasted twenty minutes. (JS, Journal, 27 Mar. 1836, in *JSP,* J1:203; for other accounts of the intermission, see Post, Journal, 27 Mar. 1836; and Benjamin Brown to Sarah Mumford Brown, Mar. 1836, Benjamin Brown Family Collection, CHL.)
115. Hymn 23, by William W. Phelps. (*Collection of Sacred Hymns,* 29–30.)

respectively, and then to the church as being equal with himself, acknowledging them to be Prophets and Seers.[116] The vote was unanimous in the affirmative in every instance.— Each of the different quorums was presented
in its turn to all the rest, and then to the church, and received and acknowledged by all the rest, in their several stations without a manifest dissenting
sentiment.

President J. Smith jr. then addressed the congregation in a manner calculated to instruct the understanding, rather than please the ear, and at or about
the close of his remarks, he prophesied to all, that inasmuch as they would
uphold these men in their several stations, alluding to the different quo[r]ums
in the church, the Lord would bless them; yea, in the name of Christ, the
blessings of Heaven shall be yours. And when the Lord's annointed go forth to
proclaim the word, bearing testimony to this generation, if they receive it, they
shall be blessed, but if not, the judgments of God will follow close upon them,
until *that* city or *that* house, that rejects them, shall be left desolate. The following hymn was then sung:[117]

TUNE—*Dalston.*

How pleasd and blest was I,
To hear the people cry,
"Come, let us seek our God to-day!"
Yes, with a cheerful zeal,
We'll haste to Zion's hill,
And there our vows and honors pay.

Zion thrice happy place,
Adorn'd with wondrous grace,
And walls of strength embrace thee round!
In thee our tribes appear,
To pray, and praise, and hear
The sacred gospel's joyful sound.

There David's greater Son
Has fix'd his royal throne;
He sits for grace and judgment there:
He bids the saint be glad,

---

116. On the authority and composition of the various priesthood quorums, see Instruction on
Priesthood, between ca. 1 Mar. and ca. 4 May 1835, in *JSP*, D4:314 [D&C 107:21–27].

117. Hymn 84, by Isaac Watts. (*Collection of Sacred Hymns,* 114–115.)

He makes the sinner sad,
And humble souls rejoice with fear.

May peace attend thy gate,
And joy within thee wait,
To bless the soul of every guest:
The man that seeks thy peace,
And wishes thine increase,
A thousand blessings on him rest!

My tongue repeats her vows,
"Peace to this sacred house!
For here my friends and kindred dwell."
And since my glorious God
Makes thee his blest abode,
My soul shall ever love thee well.

He then offered the dedication prayer, which was as follows:[118]

THANKS be to thy name, O Lord God of Israel, who keepest covenant and shewest mercy unto thy servants, who walk uprightly before thee with all their hearts: thou who hast commanded thy servants to build an house to thy name in this place. (Kirtland.) And now thou beholdest, O Lord, that so thy servants have done, according to thy commandment.[119] And now we ask thee, holy Father, in the name of Jesus Christ, the Son of thy bosom, in whose name alone salvation can be administered to the children of men: we ask thee, O Lord, to accept of this house, the workmanship of the hands of us, thy servants, which thou didst command us to build; for thou knowest that we have done this work through great tribulation: and out of our poverty we have given of our substance to build a house to thy name,[120] that the Son of Man might have a place to manifest himself to his people.

---

118. Besides the featured text, there are two contemporaneous versions of the prayer of dedication: the one found in JS's journal and the published broadside JS read from at the dedicatory meeting. There are only a few minor spelling and punctuation differences between the featured text and the JS journal version; those differences are not noted. The version printed on the broadside is nearly identical to the version featured here. Both the broadside and featured text were printed on the church's printing press, probably from the same typesetting. (JS, Journal, 27 Mar. 1836, in *JSP*, J1:204–210; Prayer, 27 Mar. 1836, in *Prayer, at the Dedication of the Lord's House in Kirtland, Ohio, March 27, 1836* [Kirtland, OH: 1836], copy at CHL [D&C 109].)

119. See Revelation, 27–28 Dec. 1832, in *JSP*, D2:345 [D&C 88:117–119]; and Revelation, 1 June 1833, in *JSP*, D3:106 [D&C 95:3, 7–8].

120. In a description of the House of the Lord in July 1835, Oliver Cowdery noted, "The sum expended, thus far, towards its erection, may be computed at about *ten thousand dollars,* and the whole cost,

And as thou hast said, in a revelation given unto us, calling us thy friends, saying—"Call your solemn assembly, as I have commanded you; and as all have not faith, seek ye diligently and teach one another words of wisdom; yea, seek ye out of the best books words of wisdom: Seek learning, even by study, and also by faith.

"Organize yourselves; prepare every needful thing, and establish a house, even a house of prayer, a house of fasting, a house of faith, a house of learning, a house of glory, a house of order, a house of God: that your incomings may be in the name of the [p. 277] Lord; that your out goings may be in the name of the Lord: that all your salutations may be in the name of the Lord, with uplifted hands to the Most High."[121]

And now, holy Father, we ask thee to assist us, thy people with thy grace in calling our solemn assembly, that it may be done to thy honor, and to thy divine acceptance, and in a manner that we may be found worthy, in thy sight, to secure a fulfilment of the promises which thou hast made unto us thy people, in the revelations given unto us: that thy glory may rest down upon thy people, and upon this thy house, which we now dedicate to thee, that it may be sanctified and consecrated to be holy, and that thy holy presence may be continually in this house; and that all people who shall enter upon the threshhold of the Lord's house may feel thy power and be constrained to acknowledge that thou hast sanctified it, and that it is thy house, a place of thy holiness.

And do thou grant, holy Father, that all those who shall worship in this house, may be taught words of wisdom out of the best books, and that they may seek learning, even by study, and also by faith; as thou hast said; and that they may grow up in thee and receive a fulness of the Holy Ghost, and be organized according to thy laws, and be prepared to obtain every needful thing: and that this house may be a house of prayer, a house of fasting, a house of faith, a house of glory, and of God, even thy house: that all the incomings of thy people, into this house, may be in the name of the Lord; that all their outgoings, from this house, may be in the name of the Lord; that all their salutations may

---

when finished, will probably be from twenty to thirty thousand." John Corrill later wrote that the building cost "nearly $40,000" and that the building committee "found themselves 13 or $14,000 in debt." JS's journal notes that church leaders received voluntary contributions amounting to $960.00 from those attending the dedication that day. Debts associated with land transactions, expulsion from Jackson County and the subsequent Camp of Israel expedition, publication of the Doctrine and Covenants, and construction of the House of the Lord contributed to the impoverished circumstances of many of the Saints. (Oliver Cowdery, "The House of God," *LDS Messenger and Advocate,* July 1835, 147, italics in original; Corrill, *Brief History,* 21, in *JSP,* H2:151; JS, Journal, 27 Mar. 1836, in *JSP,* J1:201; see also, for example, Letters to John Burk, Sally Waterman Phelps, and Almira Mack Scobey, 1–2 June 1835, in *JSP,* D4:334; Letter to Quorum of the Twelve, 4 Aug. 1835, in *JSP,* D4:374–375; and Minutes, 2 Apr. 1836, pp. 222–224 herein.)

121. Revelation, 27–28 Dec. 1832, in *JSP,* D2:345 [D&C 88:118–120].

PRAYER.

At the Dedication of the Lord's House in Kirtland, Ohio, March 27, 1836,—By JOSEPH SMITH, jr.
President of the Church of the Latter Day Saints.

Thanks be to thy name, O Lord God of Israel, who keepest covenant and showest mercy unto thy servants, who walk uprightly before thee with all their hearts: thou who hast commanded thy servants to build an house to thy name in this place. (Kirtland.) And now thou beholdest, O Lord, that so thy servants have done, according to thy commandment. And now we ask thee, holy Father, in the name of Jesus Christ, the Son of thy bosom, in whose name alone salvation can be administered to the children of men: we ask thee, O Lord, to accept of this house, the workmanship of the hands of us, thy servants, which thou didst command us to build; for thou knowest that we have done this work through great tribulation: and out of our poverty we have given of our substance to build a house to thy name, that the Son of Man might have a place to manifest himself to his people.

And as thou hast said, in a revelation given unto us, calling us thy friends, saying—"Call your solemn assembly, as I have commanded you; and as all have not faith, seek ye diligently and teach one another words of wisdom; yea, seek ye out of the best books words of wisdom: Seek learning, even by study, and also by faith.

"Organize yourselves; prepare every needful thing, and establish a house, even a house of prayer, a house of fasting, a house of faith, a house of learning, a house of glory, a house of order, a house of God: that your incomings may be in the name of the Lord; that your out goings may be in the name of the Lord: that all your salutations may be in the name of the Lord, with uplifted hands to the Most High."

And now, holy Father, we ask thee to assist us, thy people with thy grace in calling our solemn assembly, that it may be done to thy honor, and to thy divine acceptance, and in a manner that we may be found worthy, in thy sight, to secure a fulfilment of the promises which thou hast made unto us thy people, in the revelations given unto us: that thy glory may rest down upon thy people, and upon this thy house, which we now dedicate to thee, that it may be sanctified and consecrated to be holy, and that thy holy presence may be continually in this house; and that all people who shall enter upon the threshhold of the Lord's house may feel thy power and be constrained to acknowledge that thou hast sanctified it, and that it is thy house, a place of thy holiness.

And do thou grant, holy Father, that all those who shall worship in this house, may be taught words of wisdom out of the best books, and that they may seek learning, even by study, and also by faith; as thou hast said; and that they may grow up in thee and receive a fulness of the Holy Ghost, and be organized according to thy laws, and be prepared to obtain every needful thing: and that this house may be a house of prayer, a house of fasting, a house of faith, a house of glory, and of God, even thy house: that all the incomings of thy people, into this house, may be in the name of the Lord; that all their outgoings, from this house, may be in the name of the Lord; that all their salutations may be in the name of the Lord, with holy hands, uplifted to the Most High; and that no unclean thing shall be permitted to come into thy house to pollute it.

And when thy people transgress, any of them, they may speedily repent and return unto thee, and find favor in thy sight, and be restored to the blessings which thou hast ordained, to be poured out upon those who shall reverence thee in this thy house.

And we ask thee, holy Father, that thy servants may go forth from this house, armed with thy power, and that thy name may be upon them and thy glory be round about them, and thine angels have charge over them; and from this place they may bear exceeding great and glorious tidings, in truth, unto the ends of the earth, that they may know that this is thy work, and that thou hast put forth thy hand, to fulfil that which thou has spoken by the mouths of thy prophets concerning the last days.

We ask thee, holy Father, to establish the people that shall worship and honorably hold a name and standing in this thy house, to all generations, and for eternity, that no weapon formed against them shall prosper; that he who diggeth a pit for them shall fall into the same himself; that no combination of wickedness shall have power to rise up and prevail over thy people, upon whom thy name shall be put in this house: and if any people shall rise against this people, that thine anger be kindled against them: and if they shall smite this people, thou wilt smite them—thou wilt fight for thy people as thou didst in the day of battle, that they may be delivered from the hands of all their enemies.

We ask thee, holy Father, to confound, and astonish, and bring to shame, and confusion, all those who have spread lying reports abroad over the world against thy servant, or servants, if they will not repent when the everlasting gospel shall be proclaimed in their ears, and that all their works may be brought to nought, and be swept away by the hail, and by the judgments, which thou wilt send upon them in thine anger, that there may be an end to lyings and slanders against thy people: for thou knowest, O Lord, that thy servants have been innocent before thee in bearing record of thy name for which they have suffered these things; therefore we plead before thee for a full and complete deliverance from under this yoke. Break it off O Lord: break it off from the necks of thy servants, by thy power, that we may rise up in the midst of this generation and do thy work!

O Jehovah, have mercy upon this people, and as all men sin, forgive the transgressions of thy people, and let them be blotted out forever. Let the annointing of thy ministers be sealed upon them with power from on high: let it be fulfilled upon them as upon those on the day of Pentacost: let the gift of tongues be poured out upon thy people, even cloven tongues as of fire, and the interpretation thereof. And let thy house be filled, as with a rushing mighty wind, with thy glory.

Put upon thy servants the testimony of the covenant, that when they go out and proclaim thy word, they may seal up the law, and prepare the hearts of thy saints for all those judgements thou art about to send, in thy wrath, upon the inhabitants of the earth, because of their transgressions, that thy people may not faint in the day of trouble.

And whatever city thy servants shall enter, and the people of that city receive their testimony, let thy peace and thy salvation be upon that city, that they may gather out of that city the righteous, that they may come forth to Zion, or to her stakes, the places of thine appointment, with songs of everlasting joy,—and until this be accomplished let not thy judgments fall upon that city.

Prayer of dedication. Joseph Smith delivered the dedicatory prayer for the Kirtland, Ohio, House of the Lord on 27 March 1836. This loose-leaf broadside containing the text of the dedicatory prayer was prepared and printed the night before on the printing press of the *Latter Day Saints' Messenger and Advocate*. *Prayer, at the Dedication of the Lord's House in Kirtland, Ohio, March 27, 1836* (Kirtland, OH: 1836), Church History Library, Salt Lake City.

be in the name of the Lord, with holy hands, uplifted to the Most High; and that no unclean thing shall be permitted to come into thy house to pollute it.[122]

And when thy people transgress, any of them, they may speedily repent and return unto thee, and find favor in thy sight, and be restored to the blessings which thou hast ordained, to be poured out upon those who shall reverence thee in this thy house.

And we ask thee, holy Father, that thy servants may go forth from this house, armed with thy power, and that thy name may be upon them and thy glory be round about them, and thin[e] angels have charge over them; and from this place they may bear exceeding great and glorious tidings, in truth, unto the ends of the earth,[123] that they may know that this is thy work, and that thou hast put forth thy hand, to fulfil that which thou has spoken by the mouths of thy prophets concerning the last days.

We ask thee, holy Father, to establish the people that shall worship and honorably hold a name and standing in this thy house, to all generations, and for eternity, that no weapon formed against them shall prosper; that he who diggeth a pit for them shall fall into the same himself; that no combination of wickedness shall have power to rise up and prevail over thy people, upon whom thy name shall be put in this house: and if any people shall rise against this people, that thine anger be kindled against them: and if they shall smite this people, thou wilt smite them—thou wilt fight for thy people as thou didst in the day of battle, that they may be delivered from the hands of all their enemies.

We ask thee, holy Father, to confound, and astonish, and bring to shame, and confusion, all those who have spread lying reports abroad over the world against thy servant, or servants, if they will not repent when the everlasting gospel shall be proclaimed in their ears, and that all their works may be brought to nought, and be swept away by the hail, and by the judgments,[124] which thou wilt send upon them in thine anger, that there may be an end to lyings and slanders against thy people:[125] for thou knowest, O Lord, that thy servants have been innocent before thee in bearing record of thy name for which they have suffered these things; therefore we plead before thee for a full

---

122. See 2 Chronicles 23:19; Psalm 24:3–4; and Revelation, 2 Aug. 1833–A, in *JSP*, D3:202 [D&C 97:15–17].

123. See Revelation, 2 Jan. 1831, in *JSP*, D1:232 [D&C 38:32–33].

124. For JS revelations warning of disasters at the end of time, see, for example, Revelation, Sept. 1830–A, in *JSP*, D1:179–181 [D&C 29:14–28]; Revelation, 2 Jan. 1831, in *JSP*, D1:231 [D&C 38:5]; Revelation, February 1831–A, in *JSP*, D1:259 [D&C 43:25–30]; and Revelation, 1 Nov. 1831–B, in *JSP*, D2:103–107 [D&C 1].

125. JS had recently written a letter published in the *Messenger and Advocate* addressing the ongoing opposition of individuals to the Latter-day Saints and affirming the authenticity of the Book of Mormon. (See Letter to the Elders of the Church, 30 Nov.–1 Dec. 1835, pp. 89–100 herein.)

and complete deliverance from under this yoke. Break it off O Lord: break it off from the necks of thy servants, by thy power, that we may rise up in the midst of this generation and do thy work!

O Jehovah, have mercy upon this people, and as all men sin, forgive the transgressions of thy people, and let them be blotted out forever. Let the annointing of thy ministers be sealed upon them with power from on high: let it be fulfilled upon them as upon those on the day of Pentecost: let the gift of tongues be poured out upon thy [p. 278] people, even cloven tongues as of fire, and the interpretation thereof. And let thy house be filled, as with a rushing mighty wind, with thy glory.[126]

Put upon thy servants the testimony of the covenant, that when they go out and proclaim thy word, they may seal up the law, and prepare the hearts of thy saints for all those judgements thou art about to send, in thy wrath, upon the inhabitants of the earth, because of their transgressions, that thy people may not faint in the day of trouble.

And whatever city thy servants shall enter, and the people of that city receive their testimony, let thy peace and thy salvation be upon that city, that they may gather out of that city the righteous, that they may come forth to Zion, or to her stakes,[127] the places of thine appointment, with songs of everlasting joy,—and until this be accomplished let not thy judgments fall upon that city.

And whatever city thy servants shall enter, and the people of that city receive not the testimony of thy servants, and thy servants warn them to save themselves from this untoward generation, let it be upon that city according to that which thou hast spoken, by the mouths of thy prophets; but deliver thou, O Jehovah, we beseech thee, thy servants from their hands, and cleanse them from their blood. O Lord, we delight not in the destruction of our fellow men: their souls are precious before thee;[128] but thy word must be fulfilled:—help thy servants to say, with thy grace assisting them, thy will be done, O Lord, and not ours.

We know that thou hast spoken by the mouth of thy prophets, terrible things concerning the wicked, in the last days, that thou wilt pour out thy judgments, without measure: therefore, O Lord, deliver thy people from the calamity of the wicked; enable thy servants to seal up the law and bind up the testimony, that they may be prepared against the day of burning.

We ask thee, holy Father, to remember those who have been driven by the inhabitants of Jackson county, Missouri, from the lands of their inheritance, and

---

126. The day of Pentecost is depicted in Acts 2:1–18.

127. For more on Zion and its stakes, see, for example, Revelation, ca. 7 Mar. 1831, in *JSP*, D1:280 [D&C 45:65–67]; Revelation, 20 July 1831, in *JSP*, D2:7–8, 12 [D&C 57:1–3, 14]; Revelation, 1 Nov. 1831–A, in *JSP*, D2:104 [D&C 68:26]; and Revelation, 2 Aug. 1833–B, in *JSP*, D3:205 [D&C 94:1].

128. See Revelation, June 1829–B, in *JSP*, D1:71 [D&C 18:10].

break off, O Lord, this yoke of affliction, that has been put upon them. Thou knowest, O Lord, that they have been greatly oppressed, and afflicted, by wicked men, and our hearts flow out in sorrow because of their grievous burdens. O Lord, how long wilt thou suffer this people to bear this affliction, and the cries of their innocent ones to ascend up in thine ears, and their blood to come up in testimony before thee, and not make a display of thy power in their behalf?[129]

Have mercy, O Lord, upon that wicked mob, who have driven thy people, that they may cease to spoil, that they may repent of their sins, if repentance is to be found; but if they will not, make bear thine arm O Lord, and redeem that which thou didst appoint a Zion unto thy people!

And if it can not be otherwise, that the cause of thy people may not fail before thee, may thine anger be kindled and thine indignation fall upon them, that they may be wasted away, both root and branch from under heaven; but in as much as they will repent, thou art gracious and merciful, and will turn away thy wrath, when thou lookest upon the face of thine annointed.[130]

Have mercy, O Lord, upon all the nations of the earth: have mercy upon the rulers of our land: may those principles which were so honorably and nobly defended: viz, the constitution of our land, by our fathers, be established forever.[131] Remember the kings, the princes, the nobles, and the great ones of the earth, and all people; and the churches: all the poor, the needy and the afflicted ones of the earth, that their hearts may be softened when thy servants shall go out from thy house, O Jehovah, to bear testimony of thy name, that their prejudices may give way before the truth, and thy people may obtain favor in the sight of all, that all the ends of the earth may know that we thy servants have heard thy voice, and that thou hast sent us, that from among all these thy servants, the sons of Jacob, may gather out the righteous to build a holy city to thy name, as thou hast commanded them.

We ask thee to appoint unto Zion other stakes besides this one, which thou hast appointed,[132] that the gathering of thy people may roll on in great power and majesty, that thy work may be cut short in righteousness.

---

129. Several earlier revelations chastised the Saints for their disobedience but promised a future redemption of Zion. (See, for example, Revelation, 24 Feb. 1834, in *JSP*, D3:459–460 [D&C 103:4–9]; and Revelation, 22 June 1834, in *JSP*, D4:73–74 [D&C 105:2–9]; on violence against the Saints in Missouri and their expulsion from Jackson County in November 1833, see "Joseph Smith Documents from February 1833 through March 1834," in *JSP*, D3:xvii–xxxii; see also "A History, of the Persecution," *Times and Seasons*, Dec. 1839–Feb. 1840, 1:17–20, 33–36, 49–50, in *JSP*, H2:203–227.)

130. See 2 Chronicles 6:42; and Psalms 84:9; 132:10.

131. For an earlier revelation concerning the U.S. Constitution, see Revelation, 16–17 Dec. 1833, in *JSP*, D3:395 [D&C 101:77–80].

132. At the time of this prayer, Kirtland was the only appointed stake of Zion. (See Revelation, 2 Aug. 1833–B, in *JSP*, D3:205 [D&C 94:1]; and Revelation, 11 Sept. 1831, in *JSP*, D2:65 [D&C 64:21–22].)

Now these words, O Lord, we have spoken before thee, concerning the [r]evelations and commandments which [p. 279] thou hast given unto us, who are identified with the Gentiles;—But thou knowest that we have a great love for the children of Jacob who have been scattered upon the mountains; for a long time in a cloudy and dark day.[133]

We therefore ask thee to have mercy upon the children of Jacob, that Jerusalem, from this hour, may begin to be redeemed; and the yoke of bondage may begin to be broken off from the house of David, and the children of Judah may begin to return to the lands which thou didst give to Abraham,[134] their father, and cause that the remnants of Jacob, who have been cursed and smitten, because of their transgression, to be converted from their wild and savage condition, to the fulness of the everlasting gospel, that they may lay down their weapons of bloodshed and cease their rebellions. And may all the scattered remnants of Israel, who have been driven to the ends of the earth,[135] come to a knowledge of the truth, believe in the Messiah, and be redeemed from oppression, and rejoice before thee.

O Lord, remember thy servant Joseph Smith, jr. and all his afflictions and persecutions, how he has covenanted with Jehovah and vowed to thee, O mighty God of Jacob, and the commandments which thou hast given unto him, and that he hath sincerely strove to do thy will.—Have mercy, O Lord, upon his wife and children, that they may be exalted in thy presence, and preserved by thy fostering hand. Have mercy upon all their immediate connexions, that their prejudices may be broken up, and swept away as with a flood, that they may be converted and redeemed with Israel and know that thou art God. Remember, O Lord, the presidents, even all the presidents of thy church, that thy right hand may exalt them with all their families, and their immediate connexions, that their names may be perpetuated and had in everlasting remembrance from generation to generation.

Remember all thy church, O Lord, with all their families, and all their immediate connexions, with all their sick and afflicted ones, with all the poor and meek of the earth, that the kingdom which thou hast set up without hands, may become a great mountain and fill the whole earth,[136] that thy church may come forth out of the wilderness of darkness, and shine forth fair as the moon, clear as the sun, and terrible as an army with banners, and be addorned as a bride for that day when thou shalt unveil the heavens, and cause the mountains

---

133. See 2 Chronicles 18:16; Ezekiel 34:12; and Nahum 3:18.

134. See Genesis 12:7.

135. For references to scattered Israel, see, for example, 2 Kings 17:1–6, 18; 18:11; Hosea 9:17; Amos 9:9; and Book of Mormon, 1830 ed., 56, 85 [1 Nephi 22:3–5; 2 Nephi 10:20–22].

136. See Daniel 2:34–35, 44–45; and Revelation, 30 Oct. 1831, in *JSP*, D2:93–94 [D&C 65:2–6].

to flow down at thy presence,[137] and the valleys to be exalted, the rough places made smooth, that thy glory may fill the earth.

That when the trump shall sound for the dead, we shall be caught up in the cloud to meet thee,[138] that we may ever be with the Lord, that our garments may be pure, that we may be clothed upon with robes of righteousness,[139] with palms in our hands, and crowns of glory upon our heads, and reap eternal joy for all our sufferngs. O Lord, God Almighty, hear us in these our petitions, and answer us from heaven, thy holy habitation, where thou sittest enthroned, with glory, honor, power, majesty, might, dominion, truth, justice, judgement, mercy and an infinity of fulness, from everlasting to everlasting.

O hear, O hear, O hear us, O Lord, and answer these petitions, and accept the dedication of this house, unto thee, the work of our hands, which we have built unto thy name; and also this church to put upon it thy name. And help us by the power of thy Spirit, that we may mingle our voices with those bright shining seraphs, around thy throne with acclamations of praise, singing hosanna to God and the Lamb: and let these thine annointed ones be clothed with salvation, and thy saints shout aloud for joy. AMEN AND AMEN.

The choir then sung a hymn.[140]

TUNE—*Hosanna.*

The Spirit of God like a fire is burning;
    The latter day glory begins to come forth;
The visions and blessings of old are retuning;
    The angels are coming to visit the earth.
We'll sing & we'll shout with the armies of heaven;
    Hosanna, hosanna to God and the Lamb!
Let glory to them in the highest be given,
    Henceforth and forever: amen and amen!

The Lord is extending the saints' understanding—
    Restoring their judges and all as at first;
The knowledge and power of God are expanding:
    The vail o'er the earth is beginning to burst.
We'll sing and we'll shout &c.

---

137. See Isaiah 64:1; and Revelation, 3 Nov. 1833, in *JSP,* D2:119 [D&C 133:44].

138. See 1 Corinthians 15:52; Revelation, Sept. 1830–A, in *JSP,* D1:179–180 [D&C 29:13, 26]; 1 Thessalonians 4:16–17; and Revelation, 27–28 Dec. 1832, in *JSP,* D2:344 [D&C 88:94–97].

139. See Book of Mormon, 1830 ed., 80 [2 Nephi 9:14].

140. Hymn 90, by William W. Phelps. (*Collection of Sacred Hymns,* 120–121.)

Kirtland House of the Lord. Circa 1875. Joseph Smith dedicated this sacred edifice on 27 March 1836 after nearly three years of construction. The Latter-day Saints sacrificed much to build this House of the Lord and rejoiced at its dedication and the spiritual promise it represented. (Courtesy Community of Christ Library-Archives, Independence, MO. Stereograph by W. A. Faze.)

We call in our solemn assemblies, in spirit,
    To spread forth the kingdom of heaven abroad,
That we through our faith may begin to inherit
    The visions, and blessings, and glories of God.
We'll sing and we'll shout &c.

We'll wash, and be wash'd and with oil be anointed
    Withal not omitting the washing of feet:
For he that receiveth his PENNY appointed,
    Must surely be clean at the harvest of wheat
We'll sing and we'll shout &c. [p. 280]

Old Israel that fled from the world for his freedom,
    Must come with the cloud and the pillar, amain:
A Moses, and Aaron, and Joshua lead him,
    And feed him on manna from heaven again.
We'll sing and we'll shout &c.

How blessed the day when the lamb and the lion
    Shall lie down together without any ir[e];
And Ephraim be crown'd with his blessing in Zion,
    As Jesus descends with his chariots of fire!
We'll sing & we'll shout with *His* armies of heaven:
    Hosanna, hosanna to God and the Lamb!
Let glory to them in the highest be given,
    Henceforth and forever: amen and amen.

President Smith then asked the several quorums separately and then the congregation, if they accepted the prayer. The vote was, in every instance, unanimous in the affirmative.

The Eucharist[141] was administered.— D. C. [Don Carlos] Smith blessed the bread and wine and they were distributed by several Elders present, to the church.[142]

President J. Smith jr. then arose and bore record of his mission. D. C. Smith bore record of the truth of the work of the Lord in which we are engaged.

---

141. The account in JS's journal calls this the "Lords supper," a much more common term in Latter-day Saint texts. (JS, Journal, 27 Mar. 1836, in *JSP,* J1:210.)

142. The church's "Articles and Covenants" as well as the Book of Mormon assigned the task of administering the sacrament to elders and priests. (Articles and Covenants, ca. Apr. 1830, in *JSP,* D1:122–125 [D&C 20:40, 46]; Book of Mormon, 1830 ed., 575–576 [Moroni 4–5].)

President O[liver] Cowdery spoke and testified of the truth of the book of Mormon, and of the work of the Lord in these last days.

President F[rederick] G. Williams bore record that a Holy Angel of God, came and set between him and J[oseph] Smith sen. while the house was being dedicated.[143]

President Hyrum Smith, (one of the building committee)[144] made some appropriate remarks concerning the house, congratulating those who had endured so many toils and privations to erect it. That it was the Lord's house built by his commandment and he would bless them.

President S. Rigdon then made a few appropriate closing remarks; and a short prayer which was ended with loud acclamations of Hosanna! Hosanna! Hosanna to God and the Lamb, Amen, Amen and Amen![145] Three times. Elder B[righam] Young, one of the Twelve, gave a short address in tongues; Elder D[avid] W. Patten interpreted and gave a short exhortation in tongues himself; after which, President J. Smith jr. blessed the congregation in the name of the Lord, and at a little past four P. M. the whole exercise closed and the congregation dispersed.

We further add that we should do violence to our own feelings and injustice to the real merit of our brethren and friends who attended the meeting, were we here to withhold a meed of praise, which we think is their just due; not only for their quiet demeanor during the whole exercise, which lasted more than eight hours, but for their great liberality in contributing of their earthly substance for the relief of the building committee, who were yet somewhat involved. As this was to be a day of sacrifice, as well as of fasting,— There was a man placed at each door in the morning to receive the voluntary donations of those who entered. On counting the collection it amounted to nine hundred and sixty three dollars.[146]

---

143. Stephen Post recorded Williams stating that the angel came through the window behind the pulpit. Edward Partridge recorded that "Williams saw an angel" but interlinearly inserted "or rather the Savior"—possibly conflating Williams's vision of an angel with the vision of Jesus Christ shared by JS and Oliver Cowdery a week later. Years later, Truman Angell recalled that JS identified this angel as the apostle Peter. After mentioning Williams's vision, JS's journal notes that "Presdt David Whitmer also saw angels in the house." (Post, Journal, 27 Mar. 1836; Minutes, *LDS Messenger and Advocate,* Mar. 1836, 2:281; Partridge, Journal, 27 Mar. 1836; Angell, Autobiography, 16; JS, Journal, 27 Mar. 1836, in *JSP,* J1:211.)

144. Along with Jared Carter and Reynolds Cahoon, Hyrum Smith was assigned in 1833 to raise funds for construction of the House of the Lord. (Minutes, 4 May 1833, in *JSP,* D3:81–82; Minutes, 6 June 1833, in *JSP,* D3:112–115.)

145. JS's journal records, "We then sealed the proceedings of the day by a shouting hosanah to God and the Lamb 3 times sealing it each time with Amen, Amen, and Amen." (JS, Journal, 27 Mar. 1836, in *JSP,* J1:211.)

146. JS's journal puts the amount collected at $960. (JS, Journal, 27 Mar. 1836, in *JSP,* J1:201.)

Letter from the Quorum of the Twelve Apostles, 28 March 1836

Source Note

Quorum of the Twelve Apostles, Letter, Kirtland Township, Geauga Co., OH, to JS, Kirtland Township, Geauga Co., OH, 28 Mar. 1836. Featured version copied [between ca. 4 Apr. and ca. 16 May 1836] in Minute Book 1, p. 198; handwriting of Warren A. Cowdery; CHL. For more information on Minute Book 1, see Source Notes for Multiple-Entry Documents, p. 527 herein.

Historical Introduction

One day after the dedication of the House of the Lord, the Quorum of the Twelve Apostles met together for a "time of general confession" and drafted a letter to JS. In the letter, penned by Orson Hyde and William E. McLellin, the quorum acknowledged their shortcomings, sought the forgiveness of the church presidency, and asked JS for a written revelation to carry with them as they departed Kirtland, Ohio, to preach during spring 1836.

The circumstances that prompted the apostles' confession and letter to JS are unclear. Quorum members likely felt compelled to acknowledge their faults and express their humility in preparation for receiving the long-promised endowment of power associated with the completion of the House of the Lord. Since 1831, JS had urged church leaders to sanctify themselves in preparation for the endowment, and his efforts to prepare them continued through fall and winter 1835–1836.[147] The spiritual outpouring many experienced during and after the dedication of the House of the Lord on 27 March may have also contributed to the apostles' show of humility.[148] Another factor may have been the opposition of some of the Twelve to a resolution regarding priesthood ordinations that JS drafted in February 1836; a few members of the quorum did not formally withdraw their objections until 19 March.[149]

The original letter is no longer extant. The version featured here was copied into Minute Book 1 by Warren A. Cowdery around the time it was created. Though the letter is dated 28 March 1836, scribes later inserted a copy of the text into JS's history under the date 28 March 1835 and directly connected it to JS's spring 1835 instruction on priesthood.[150] However, JS and five members of the Twelve—including William E. McLellin, who was

---

147. Revelation, 2 Jan. 1831, in *JSP*, D1:232 [D&C 38:32]; Revelation, 27–28 Dec. 1832; Revelation, 3 Jan. 1833, in *JSP*, D2:334–348 [D&C 88:1–137]. A 3 November 1835 revelation, for example, admonished the Twelve to humble themselves before God before they would "be accounted worthy to receive an endowment to go forth in my name unto all nations"; on 12 November JS promised the quorum, "All who are prepared and are sufficiently pure to abide the presence of the Saviour will see him in the solem assembly." (Revelation, 3 Nov. 1835, p. 35 herein; Discourse, 12 Nov. 1835, p. 51 herein.)

148. Minutes and Prayer of Dedication, 27 Mar. 1836 [D&C 109], pp. 188–210 herein; Minutes, *LDS Messenger and Advocate*, Mar. 1836, 2:281.

149. Minutes, 12 Feb. 1836, pp. 170–173 herein; Minutes, 22 Feb. 1836, p. 180 herein; Minutes, 19 Mar. 1836, p. 185 herein. This was not the first instance of tension between the presidency and the Twelve. During the fall and winter of 1835–1836, for example, a series of misunderstandings strained their relationship. Most of these issues were apparently resolved during a face-to-face discussion on 16 January 1836. (Minutes, 16 Jan. 1836, pp. 148–154 herein.)

150. Willard Richards copied the letter into JS's manuscript history sometime between 1 October

identified as one of the meeting's clerks—were preaching and baptizing in Huntsburgh, Ohio, on 28 March 1835 and did not return to Kirtland until 30 March.[151] This evidence supports the 1836 date found in the minute book.

Document Transcript

Kirtland March 28th 1836

This afternoon the Twelve met in council and had a time of general confession.

On reviewing our past course we are satisfied and feel to confess also that we have not realized the importance of our calling to that degree that we ought; we have been light minded and vain and in many things done <u>wrong</u>, <u>wrong</u>. For all these things we have asked the forgiveness of our Heavenly Father, and wherein we have grieved or wounded the feelings of the Presidency we ask their forgiveness.

The time has come when we are about to seperate, and when we shall meet again, God only knows,[152] We therefore feel to ask of him whom we have acknowledged to be our Prophet and Seer that he enquire of God for us and obtain a written revelation,[153] (if consistent) that we may look upon it when we are seperated. that our hearts may be comforted. Our worthiness has not inspired us to make this request but our unworthiness.

We have unitedly asked God, our Heavenly Father to grant unto us through his Seer, a revelation of his mind and will concerning our duty the coming season even a great revelation that will enlarge our hearts, comfort us in adversity and brighten our hopes amidst the powers of Darkness.

To President J. Smith Jun[r.]   Orson Hyde
            Kirtland Ohio   Wm E. M[c]Lel[l]in } Clerks[154] [p. 198]

1843 and 24 February 1845. (JS History, vol. B-1, 581–582; see also Instruction on Priesthood, between ca. 1 Mar. and ca. 4 May 1835, in *JSP*, D4:308–321 [D&C 107].)

151. McLellin, Journal, 30 Mar. 1835; Historical Introduction to Instruction on Priesthood, between ca. 1 Mar. and ca. 4 May 1835 [D&C 107], in *JSP*, D4:310.

152. During the solemn assembly, convened in the House of the Lord two days later, JS told those assembled, "The time that we were required to tarry in Kirtland to be endued would be fulfilled in a few days, and then the Elders would go forth and each must stand for himself, that it was not necessary for them to be sent out two by two as in former times. . . . The 12 are at liberty to go wheresoever they will." The Twelve began to separate several weeks later. Thomas B. Marsh and David W. Patten returned to Missouri, while other members of the quorum, including Brigham Young, Heber C. Kimball, Orson Hyde, William E. McLellin, and Parley P. Pratt, left Kirtland to preach. (Minutes, 30 Mar. 1836, pp. 219–220 herein; Esplin, "Emergence of Brigham Young," 203–204.)

153. It is unclear whether a written revelation resulted from this request.

154. The members of the Twelve had been selected in a church conference held in Kirtland on 14 February 1835. Two weeks later, William E. McLellin and Orson Hyde were nominated and appointed to act as clerks for the Twelve. (Record of the Twelve, 14 and 27 Feb. 1835.)

PART 4: 30 MARCH–
19 AUGUST 1836

The spiritual outpouring that occurred in Kirtland, Ohio, when the House of the Lord was dedicated on 27 March 1836 continued in the days following that special event. Three days after the dedication, participants reported, the promised endowment of power occurred at a solemn assembly. This event marked the culmination of a series of instruction from JS and other church leaders, the organizing of the church's priesthood structure, and the administration of rituals.[1] JS's journal records that another significant event took place on the afternoon of 3 April: JS and Oliver Cowdery experienced a vision of Jesus Christ and visitations from Moses, Elias, and Elijah.[2] This entry is the last entry in JS's 1835–1836 Kirtland journal, the most detailed of his journals. Finally, 6 April 1836, the sixth anniversary of the church's organization, was "set apart as a day of prayer to end the feast of the Passover and in honor of the jubilee of the church."[3] That day men ordained to the priesthood met to observe and participate in sacred ordinances. According to Heber C. Kimball, as the meeting continued, "the spirit of prophecy was poured out upon the Assembly," and this "marvellous spirit" continued for several days.[4]

At about the same time that church members in Kirtland witnessed and were celebrating this spiritual feast, church members in Clay County, Missouri, saw a rise in tension with their non-Mormon neighbors, similar to the events that led to violence in Jackson County three years earlier. Clay County residents charged, as had their Jackson County counterparts, that the Mormon population opposed slavery and had unauthorized communications with American Indians.[5] In late June 1836 at the Liberty courthouse, Clay County citizens organized a "Committee of nine," composed of community leaders, to persuade church members to leave the county peaceably. Led by William W. Phelps, church leaders in Clay County ultimately acquiesced. In a letter written 25 July 1836, JS and his associates in Kirtland approved that decision.[6]

---

1. Minutes, 30 Mar. 1836, pp. 216–221 herein.

2. Visions, 3 Apr. 1836, pp. 224–229 herein [D&C 110].

3. William W. Phelps, Kirtland, OH, to Sally Waterman Phelps, Liberty, MO, Apr. 1836, William W. Phelps, Papers, BYU.

4. Kimball, "History," 42–43.

5. Letter to John Thornton and Others, 25 July 1836, pp. 262–265 herein; see also 264n201 herein; and Historical Introduction to Letter to Oliver Cowdery, ca. 9 Apr. 1836, pp. 234–235 herein.

6. "Public Meeting," *LDS Messenger and Advocate,* Aug. 1836, 2:353–355; Letter to William W. Phelps and Others, 25 July 1836, pp. 268–271 herein.

The same day that JS wrote to church leaders in Missouri, he, along with Hyrum Smith, Oliver Cowdery, and Sidney Rigdon, departed Kirtland for the eastern United States. The indebtedness of the church and the pressing need to aid church members in Missouri were at the forefront of JS's thoughts as he traveled east, and these concerns were major factors motivating this journey. The men visited New York City, and saw its famous financial district that had recently burned down, before traveling to Boston and ultimately reaching Salem, Massachusetts, on 5 August. While there, JS produced three documents, including a revelation indicating that "treasures" would be available to the Latter-day Saints in that city. The four church leaders spent time preaching as well as visiting museums and touring historic sites. They sojourned in the Salem area for most of August before returning to Kirtland, arriving by mid-September.[7]

——— ℰℐ ———

Certificate from Joshua Seixas, 30 March 1836

Source Note

Joshua Seixas, Certificate, to JS, Kirtland Township, Geauga Co., OH, 30 Mar. 1836; handwriting of Joshua Seixas; one page; JS Collection, CHL. Includes dockets.

One leaf, measuring 9¾ × 7⅞ inches (25 × 20 cm). The top, bottom, and right edges of the recto have the square cut of manufactured paper; the left edge is torn. The leaf contains a watermark: "DEWDNEY & TREMLETT | 1831". Dewdney & Tremlett was a papermaker in Bradninch, Devon, England.[8] The embossed left corner of the recto is now illegible. The verso of the certificate was docketed by Joshua Seixas prior to folding. The certificate was folded in a parallel fold twice, then folded again to 3⅞ × 2½ inches (10 × 6 cm). The placement of Warren Parrish's docket suggests the certificate was folded when it was docketed. It also suggests the certificate was in institutional custody as early as the Kirtland, Ohio, period.

Historical Introduction

On 29 March 1835, JS and other members of the Hebrew School in Kirtland, Ohio, finished their seven-week course of study under Joshua Seixas, the Hebraist who began teaching the class on 26 January.[9] JS and the other students of the school—which had grown from a single class to four classes by early February—gathered each Monday through Saturday to receive oral instruction in Hebrew grammar; pupils also read aloud from and translated parts of the Hebrew Bible.[10] On 30 March, Seixas issued a certificate to JS verifying that he had completed the Hebrew course to Seixas's satisfaction and had been "indefatigable in acquiring the principles of the sacred language."

---

7. See Revelation, 6 Aug. 1836, pp. 271–278 herein [D&C 111]; Promissory Note to Jonathan Burgess, 17 Aug. 1836, pp. 278–280 herein; and Letter to Emma Smith, 19 Aug. 1836, pp. 280–283 herein.

8. "Dewdney & Tremlett," Yoward/Logan database no. 4206, Mills Archive.

9. See Letter to Henrietta Raphael Seixas, between 6 and 13 Feb. 1836, pp. 173–178 herein.

10. JS, Journal, 1 and 4–5 Feb. 1836; 7–8 Mar. 1836, in *JSP*, J1:179–180, 195; Cowdery, Diary, 1–2 and 4 Feb. 1836, 10–11; Seixas, *Manual Hebrew Grammar*, iii–iv; Joshua Seixas, *Supplement to J. Seixas' Manual Hebrew Grammar* (New York: West and Trow, 1836).

Mr Joseph Smith Junr has attended a full course of Hebrew Lessons under my tuition; & has been indefatigable in acquiring the principles of the sacred language of the Old Testament scriptures in their original tongue. He has so far accomplished a knowledge of it, that he is able to translate to my entire satisfaction; & by prosecuting the study he will be able to become a proficient in Hebrew. I take this opportunity of thanking him for his industry, & his marked kindness towards me

J Seixas

Kirtland Ohio March 30th
1836

Joseph Smith's certificate of completion of Hebrew study. Joshua Seixas wrote this certificate for Joseph Smith on 30 March 1836. Seixas noted that Smith was "indefatigable in acquiring the principles of the sacred language of the Old Testament Scriptures in their original tongue." Certificate from Joshua Seixas, 30 Mar. 1836, JS Collection, Church History Library, Salt Lake City.

By all accounts, JS was a diligent student of Hebrew. After Oliver Cowdery returned to Kirtland with "a quantity of Hebrew books" on 20 November 1835, JS commenced an earnest study of the language. Though he participated in the formal classes taught by Seixas, he also devoted considerable time to studying the language on his own. Between 23 November 1835 and 29 March 1836, JS's journal mentions his studying of Hebrew—whether in class, with colleagues, or by himself—no fewer than seventy times.[11] JS was apparently among a small group of students selected by Seixas for private instruction beyond regular class time; he may have also received individual instruction from the Hebrew teacher on occasion.[12] According to JS's journal, Seixas remarked that JS and the other students in the class were "the most forward of any class he ever taught, the same length of time."[13] The document featured here affirms JS's progress in learning the Hebrew language. Besides JS, at least one other student, Orson Pratt, was issued a similar certificate by Seixas attesting to his linguistic proficiency.[14]

Document Transcript

Mr Joseph Smith Jun[r] has attended a full course of Hebrew lessons under my tuition; & has been indefatigable in acquiring the principles of the sacred language of the Old Testament Scriptures in their original tongue.[15] He has so far accomplished a knowledge of it, that he is able to translate to my entire satisfaction; & by prosecuting the study he will be able to become a proficient in Hebrew. I take this opportunity of thanking him for his industry, & his marked kindness towards me

J[oshua] Seixas

Kirtland Ohio March 30th 1836 [*1/3 page blank*] [p. [1]]
⟨J. Seixas Recommendation⟩[16]
⟨Joseph Smith Junr.⟩[17]

——————— ℰↄ ———————

Minutes, 30 March 1836

Source Note

Solemn Assembly, Minutes, Kirtland Township, Geauga Co., OH, 30 Mar. 1836. Featured version copied [ca. 30 Mar. 1836] in JS, Journal, 1835–1836, pp. 187–190; unidentified handwriting; JS Collection,

———————————

11. See various JS journal entries, 20 Nov. 1835–29 Mar. 1836, in *JSP,* J1:107–211.

12. JS, Journal, 19 Feb. 1836; 10 and 11 Mar. 1836, in *JSP,* J1:187, 195–196.

13. JS, Journal, 15 Feb. 1836, in *JSP,* J1:186.

14. "History of Orson Pratt," *LDS Millennial Star,* 11 Feb. 1865, 27:87.

15. Concerning his study of Hebrew, JS's 17 February 1836 journal entry notes, "Read and translated with my class as usual, and my soul delights in reading the word of the Lord in the original, and I am determined to persue the study of languages untill I shall become master of them." (JS, Journal, 17 Feb. 1836, in *JSP,* J1:186.)

16. TEXT: Docketing in handwriting of Warren Parrish.

17. TEXT: Docketing in handwriting of Joshua Seixas.

CHL. *For more information on JS, Journal, 1835–1836, see Source Notes for Multiple-Entry Documents, p. 524 herein.*

Historical Introduction

On 30 March 1836, ordained men in the Church of the Latter Day Saints attended the long-anticipated solemn assembly in the House of the Lord in Kirtland, Ohio. At the dedication of the House of the Lord three days earlier, church members had experienced spiritual outpourings, which continued in the hours and days leading up to the solemn assembly.[18] For the men in attendance, the 30 March meeting was the pinnacle of a progression of washings, anointings, and blessings in preparation for the promised endowment of "power from on high." At the solemn assembly, JS and the church's elders participated in a ritual foot washing, prophesied, and received blessings that empowered them to go forth and preach the gospel.[19]

In the unfinished House of the Lord on 12 November 1835, JS informed the Quorum of the Twelve Apostles that he wanted to make "the foundation of this church complete and permanent," a process that included administering the ordinance of "washing of feet." JS desired that "all the official members" of the church, or men who held priesthood office, participate in this ordinance. Furthermore, he told the Twelve on that November day that the washing of feet was "necessary now as much as it was in the days of the Saviour." JS instructed them, however, that "the house of the Lord must be prepared, and the solem assembly called" so that the ordinance could be administered there, "aside from the world." He admonished that the ordained men needed a heavenly enrichment, an instruction or endowment of power at the solemn assembly to help them preach the gospel and "overcome all things" while on their future missions.[20]

On Tuesday, 29 March 1836, two days after the dedication of the Kirtland temple, JS and a select group of church leaders met in the House of the Lord to finalize preparations for the solemn assembly. Participants included the church presidency—JS, Oliver Cowdery, Sidney Rigdon, Frederick G. Williams, Joseph Smith Sr., and Hyrum Smith— the presidency of Zion (Missouri), and the two bishoprics of the church. At this, the first of two days and nights of meetings, the church leaders received instruction about their going to Zion, and they also ceremoniously washed one another's feet in what William W. Phelps described as "a solemn scene."[21] They then partook of the Lord's Supper of bread and wine and spent the night in the House of the Lord "prophesying and giving glory to God."[22]

---

18. Historical Introduction to Minutes and Prayer of Dedication, 27 Mar. 1836 [D&C 109], pp. 189–190 herein.

19. Revelation, 2 Jan. 1831, in *JSP*, D1:232–233 [D&C 38:32]; Revelation, Feb. 1831–A, in *JSP*, D1:258–259 [D&C 43:16]; Luke 24:49; Revelation, 1 June 1833, in *JSP*, D3:106–107 [D&C 95:8–9]; see also Revelation, 2 Aug. 1833–A, in *JSP*, D3:201–202 [D&C 97:12–16]; Minutes, 3 Mar. 1836, pp. 180–185 herein; Minutes and Prayer of Dedication, 27 Mar. 1836, pp. 188–208 herein [D&C 109]; and Corrill, *Brief History*, 23, in *JSP*, H2:155.

20. JS, Journal, 12 Nov. 1835, in *JSP*, J1:96–99; Discourse, 12 Nov. 1835, p. 50 herein.

21. JS, Journal, 29 Mar. 1836, in *JSP*, J1:212; Partridge, Journal, 29 Mar. 1836; William W. Phelps, Kirtland, OH, to Sally Waterman Phelps, Liberty, MO, Apr. 1836, William W. Phelps, Papers, BYU.

22. JS, Journal, 29 Mar. 1836, in *JSP*, J1:212–213; Post, Journal, 29 Mar. 1836.

Early the following morning, the Twelve, the Seventy, and other priesthood quorums gathered for the solemn assembly. They joined JS and the other church leaders in the House of the Lord and participated in the washing of feet, which one participant referred to as "the last ordinance of the endowment." In the afternoon, the church leaders "commenced prophesying" and "the Spirit of prophecy was poured out upon the congregation," including "shouts of hosanna, to God and the Lamb with amen and amen."[23]

During the meeting, JS stated that he "had now completed the organization of the church" and that the church leaders and official members "had passed through all the necessary ceremonies." Soon after this 30 March session, JS declared that those ordained men, armed with new knowledge and divinely empowered, "now were at liberty . . . to go forth and build up the kingdom of God."[24] In the weeks following the meeting featured here, most of the ordained men left Kirtland to proselytize and to "raise Money to purchase land" for the church in Missouri.[25]

The proceedings of the solemn assembly as featured here were recorded in JS's journal. The scribe is not known, and no other version of the minutes is known to exist.

Document Transcript

Wedensday morning 8 o clock March 30th 1836 According to appointment the presidency, the 12, the seventies, the high ~~councils~~ councils, the Bishops and their entire quorums, the Elders, and all the official members in this stake of Zion amounting to about 300 met in the temple of the Lord to attend to the ordinance of washing of feet, I ascended the pulpit and remarked to the congregation that we had passed through many trials and afflictions since the organization of this church and that this is a year of Jubilee to us and a time of rejoicing,[26] and that it was expedient for us to prepare bread and wine sufficient to make our hearts glad, as we should not probably leave this house until morning; to this end we should call on the brethren to make a contribution, the stewards passed round and took up a liberal contribution and messengers were dispatched for bread and wine; tubs water and towels were prepared ⟨and⟩ I called the house to order, and the presidency

---

23. Post, Journal, 30 Mar. 1836; Partridge, Journal, 30 Mar. 1836.

24. This declaration on 30 March fulfilled the instruction JS gave on 12 November 1835 that after ordained men were endowed with power they would be prepared to go forth to "preach the gospel to all nations kindred and toungs in there own languages." (Discourse, 12 Nov. 1835, p. 51 herein.)

25. W. Phelps to S. Phelps, Apr. 1836.

26. An allusion to the Israelite year of Jubilee, a sabbatical year of liberty and hope occurring every fifty years. The sabbatical year followed the seventh cycle of seven years. The Mormon jubilee paralleled in some respects the Israelite Jubilee, which was begun at the temple on the Day of Atonement—a day of fasting on which the high priest of Israel performed ritual purifications in the temple for the redemption of Israel and its priests. The church celebrated the jubilee for the seven days preceding the beginning of the church's seventh year since organization. (Leviticus 16; 25:4–5, 8–17; W. Phelps to S. Phelps, Apr. 1836.)

proceeded to wash the feet of the 12[27] pronouncing many prophecy's and blessings upon them in the name of the Lord Jesus, the brethren began to prophesy
[p. 187] upon each others heads, and cursings upon the enimies of Christ who
inhabit Jackson county Missouri[.] continued prophesying and blessing and
sealing them with Hosanna and Amen until nearly 7 o clock P.M.[28] the bread
⟨& wine⟩ was then brought in, and I observed that we had fasted all the day;
and lest we faint; as the Saviour did so shall we do on this occasion, we shall
bless the bread and give it to the 12 and they to the multitude, after which we
shall bless the wine and do likewise;[29] while waiting ~~for the wine~~ I made the following remarks, that the time that we were required to tarry in Kirtland to be
endued would be fulfilled in a few days,[30] and then the Elders would go forth
and each must stand for himself, that it was not necessary for them to be sent
out two by two as in former times;[31] but to go in all meekness in sobriety and
preach Jesus Christ & him crucified[32] not to contend with others on the account
of their faith or systems of religion[33] but pursue a steady course, this I delivered

---

27. Stephen Post, a participant at this solemn assembly, reported, "The washing was commenced by the
presidents who first washed the 12 & 7 presidents of the seventies the 12 & 7 then commenced washing
until the whole were washed." (Post, Journal, 30 Mar. 1836; see also W. Phelps to S. Phelps, Apr. 1836.)

28. Edward Partridge recorded that "the priests teachers & deacons [were] in one corner the vails having
been let down, and the other officers occupied the rest of the lower room." According to Partridge, "The
washing of feet was performed by noon, then they began to prophecy and speak in tongues adding shouts
of hosanna, to God and the Lamb with amen and amen this continued till dark." Similarly, Stephen Post
recorded that the men "prophesied, spake and sang in tongues" in the four parts of the curtained lower
court. (Partridge, Journal, 30 Mar. 1836; Post, Journal, 30 Mar. 1836.)

29. An allusion not only to Matthew 15:32–38—when Jesus fed the multitude bread and fish "lest they
faint"—but also to the Book of Mormon, 1830 ed., 490–491, 496 [3 Nephi 18:1–11; 20:1–9]—when Jesus
administered bread and wine as the sacrament of the Lord's Supper. A February 1833 revelation stated that
homemade wine could be used for the sacrament of the Lord's Supper.[a] William W. Phelps wrote that "the
sacrament was administered, as the feast of the Passover for the first time in more than 1800 years."[b] Stephen
Post recorded that the men "partook of bread & wine in commemoration of the marriage supper of the
Lamb," a phrase mentioned in Revelation 19:9 as a symbolic representation of the second coming of Jesus
Christ.[c] In November 1835, JS taught that after the completion of the temple, Latter-day Saints would "stand
in holy places ready to meet the bride groom when he comes."[d] (a. Revelation, 27 Feb. 1833, in *JSP*, D3:20–21
[D&C 89:5–6]. b. W. Phelps to S. Phelps, Apr. 1836; compare Snow, Journal, 1835–1837, [24]. c. Post,
Journal, 30 Mar. 1836. d. JS, Journal, 12 Nov. 1835, in *JSP*, J1:99.)

30. William W. Phelps wrote that the jubilee and Passover that began at the solemn assembly ended a
week later on 6 April, which date was the sixth anniversary of the church's organization and was "set apart
as a day of prayer, to end The feast of the passover. and in honor of the Jubilee of the church." However,
Phelps also wrote that elders began leaving Kirtland on 1 April. (W. Phelps to S. Phelps, Apr. 1836; see also
Partridge, Journal, 6 Apr. 1836.)

31. See Revelation, 9 Feb. 1831, in *JSP*, D1:250 [D&C 42:6]; and Revelation, 12 Aug. 1831, in *JSP*, D2:42
[D&C 61:35].

32. See 1 Corinthians 2:1–8.

33. John Corrill explained that JS told the elders, who were now "endowed with power to go forth
[from Kirtland] and build up the Kingdom," to act cautiously "and avoid contention, and not to meddle

by way of commandment,[34] and all that observe them not will pull down persecution upon ~~your~~ ⟨thier⟩ heads, while those who do shall always be filled with the Holy Ghost, this I pronounced as a prophesy, sealed with a Hosanna & amen. Also that the seventies are not called to serve tables[35] or preside over churches to settle difficulties, but to preach the gospel and build them up, and set others who do not belong to these quorums to preside over them who are high priests— the twelve also are not to serve tables, but to bear the keys of the kingdom to all nations, and unlock them and call upon the seventies to follow after them and assist them.[36] The 12 are at liberty to go wheresoever they will [p. 188] and if one shall say, I wish to go to such a place let all the rest say Amen.

The seventies are at liberty to go to Zion if they please or go wheresoever they will and preach the gospel and let the redemtion of Zion be our object, and strive to affect it by sending up all the strength of the Lords house wherever we find them,[37] and I want to enter into the following covenant, that if any more of our brethren are slain or driven from their lands in Missouri by the mob that we will give ourselves no rest until we are avenged of our enimies to the uttermost, this covenant was sealed unaminously by a hosanna and Amen.— I then observed to the ~~quorums~~— quorum⟨s⟩ that I had now completed ~~their~~ organization of the church[38] and we had passed through all

---

with other orders of Christians, nor proclaim against their doctrines, but to preach the gospel in its simplicity, and let others alone." (Corrill, *Brief History*, 26, in *JSP*, H2:158.)

34. In response, many who attended the solemn assembly departed immediately to preach the gospel. William W. Phelps wrote, "On Friday, April 1, the elders began to go forth to bind up the [law] and seal up their testimony: and though the going was very hard, not a word was heard, every [one] was anxious to be in the field." Erastus Snow, who left Kirtland on 16 April, reported that while "laboring entirely alone" he baptized fifty people and organized three branches of the church in Indiana, returning to Kirtland in December. Ebenezer Robinson departed on his mission 2 June 1836 and said that he "took leave of wife and home, and with valise in hand, started out on foot, without purse or script. (leaving the last penny at home.) being only twenty years and eight days old. trusting solely on the Lord." (W. Phelps to S. Phelps, Apr. 1836; Erastus Snow, Kirtland, OH, 30 Dec. 1836, Letter to the Editor, *LDS Messenger and Advocate*, Jan. 1837, 3:440; Ebenezer Robinson, "Items of Personal History of the Editor," *Return,* June 1889, 90–91.)

35. That is, to involve themselves in local ministry—see Acts 6:1–4. Jesus charged the seventy to preach the gospel in Luke 10:1–16.

36. The spring 1835 "Instruction on Priesthood" stated that the Seventy formed "a quorum equal in authority to that of the twelve" and under the direction of the Twelve were to be "especial witnesses unto the Gentiles and in all the world." (Instruction on Priesthood, between ca. 1 Mar. and ca. 4 May 1835, in *JSP*, D4:314 [D&C 107:25–26]; see also Minutes and Blessings, 28 Feb.–1 Mar. 1835, in *JSP*, D4:255.)

37. This reflects the language in several JS revelations. (See Revelation, 16–17 Dec. 1833, in *JSP*, D3:393–394 [D&C 101:55–58]; Revelation, 24 Feb. 1834, in *JSP*, D3:461 [D&C 103:22]; and Revelation, 22 June 1834, in *JSP*, D4:75 [D&C 105:16].)

38. In the three years preceding this discourse, the church saw a proliferation of offices in its organizations, including the creation of a high council in Kirtland, a presidency and high council in Missouri, the Quorum of the Twelve Apostles, the Seventy, and presidencies for the various priesthood quorums. All

the necessary ceremonies, that I had given them all the instruction they needed and that they now were at liberty after obtaining their lisences[39] to go forth and build up the kingdom of God, and that it was expedient for me and the presidency to retire, having spent the night previous in waiting upon the Lord in his temple, and having to attend another dedication on the morrow,[40] or conclude the one commenced on the last sabbath for the benifit of those of my brethren and sisters who could not get into the house on the former occasion but that it was expedient for the brethren to tarry all night and worship before the Lord in his house I left the meeting in the charge of the 12[41] and retired at about 9 o clock in the evening; the brethren continued exhorting, prophesying and speaking in tongues until 5 o clock in the morning— the Saviour made his appearance to some,[42] while angels minestered unto others, and it was a penticost and enduement indeed, long to be remembered for the sound shall go forth from this place into all the [p. 189] world, and the occurrences of this day shall be handed down upon the pages of sacred history to all generations, as the day of Pentecost,[43] so shall this day be numbered and celebrated as a year of Jubilee and time of rejoicing to the saints of the most high God.

———— ⌁ ————

these quorums were set in order in preparation for the solemn assembly. (Minutes, 17 Feb. 1834, in *JSP*, D3:435–439; Minutes, 3 July 1834, in *JSP*, D4:88–90; Minutes, Discourse, and Blessings, 14–15 Feb. 1835, in *JSP*, D4:219–234; JS, Journal, 15 Jan. 1836, in *JSP*, J1:153–156; Kirtland Elders Quorum, "Record," 28 Jan. 1836.)

39. For more information on licensing, see License, 21 Mar. 1836, pp. 186–188 herein.

40. The 31 March entry in JS's journal records, "This day being set apart to perform again the ceremonies of the dedication for the benifit of those who could not get into the house on the preceeding sabbath I repaired to the temple at 8 o clock A.M. in company with the presidency." William W. Phelps wrote that the second dedicatory service "was a sublime scene, surpassing the first in sublimity and solemnity as well as in order. The singing was grand. The Addresses were the best that could be and majesty exceeded any thing I have witnessed in the last days." (JS, Journal, 31 Mar. 1836, in *JSP*, J1:216; W. Phelps to S. Phelps, Apr. 1836; see also Partridge, Journal, 31 Mar. 1836; and Post, Journal, 31 Mar. 1836.)

41. Benjamin Brown confirmed that after JS departed, "two [quorums] continued all night in the House the twelve guarded it." (Benjamin Brown to Sarah Mumford Brown, Mar. 1836, Benjamin Brown Family Collection, CHL.)

42. Four months earlier, JS taught the Quorum of the Twelve that "all who are prepared and are sufficiently pure to abide the presence of the Saviour will see him in the solem assembly." (JS, Journal, 12 Nov. 1835, in *JSP*, J1:99.)

43. See Acts 2:1–18; and Minutes and Prayer of Dedication, 27 Mar. 1836, pp. 188–210 herein [D&C 109].

Minutes, 2 April 1836

Source Note

F. G. Williams & Co., Minutes, Kirtland Township, Geauga Co., OH, 2 Apr. 1836. Featured version copied [between ca. 4 Apr. and ca. 16 May 1836] in Minute Book 1, p. 199; handwriting of Warren A. Cowdery; CHL. For more information on Minute Book 1, see Source Notes for Multiple-Entry Documents, p. 527 herein.

Historical Introduction

On 2 April 1836, JS met with other members of F. G. Williams & Co., the church's printing firm. The company's principals, Frederick G. Williams and Oliver Cowdery, had been in charge of the church's printing operations in Kirtland, Ohio, beginning with its organization on 11 September 1833.[44] Since its inception, F. G. Williams & Co. had taken on several publishing endeavors, including the publication of church newspapers, the Doctrine and Covenants, and the church's first hymnal.[45] By fall 1835, monthly expenditures exceeded the company's receipts, and F. G. Williams & Co. had to rely on donations and loans from church members to remain solvent.[46]

In spring 1836, after the dedication of the House of the Lord in Kirtland, church leaders turned their attention to temporal needs, including the church's printing efforts and fund raising for the redemption of Zion. On 29 March 1836, JS, Williams, Cowdery, Sidney Rigdon, and Hyrum Smith met in the House of the Lord and "sought for a revelation from Him, to teach us concerning our going to Zion."[47] The next day, they resolved to "let the redemtion of Zion be our object, and strive to affect it by sending up all the strength of the Lords house whereever we find them."[48] Then, three days later, JS met with "many brethren" on temporal and spiritual business, and the next day, 2 April 1836, he and the other members of F. G. Williams & Co. met to transact temporal business that would "have a bearing upon the redemption of Zion."[49] At the 2 April meeting, the members of the firm designated JS and Cowdery to raise money to purchase land in Zion and contribute "all in [their] power" for its redemption. Although Warren A. Cowdery noted that JS and Oliver Cowdery had great success initially, which gave them "pleasing anticipations," they appear to have encountered difficulties in finding members willing to give their money or land for the cause of Zion.[50]

---

44. Minutes, 11 Sept. 1833, in *JSP,* D3:297–301; Note, 16 Sept. 1835, in *JSP,* D4:420–422.

45. Church newspapers included *The Evening and the Morning Star,* which was replaced by the *Latter Day Saints' Messenger and Advocate* in 1834, and the *Northern Times,* a periodical dedicated to political issues.

46. See Covenant, 29 Nov. 1834, in *JSP,* D4:188–191; F. G. Williams & Co., Account Book, 3 (second numbering); and JS, Journal, 6 Oct. 1835, in *JSP,* J1:68–69.

47. JS, Journal, 29 Mar. 1836, in *JSP,* J1:212.

48. JS, Journal, 30 Mar. 1836, in *JSP,* J1:215.

49. JS, Journal, 1 and 2 Apr. 1836, in *JSP,* J1:216–219.

50. JS, Journal, 2 Apr. 1836, in *JSP,* J1:217–219. Several unwilling individuals were brought before the Kirtland high council in summer 1836. (See Minutes, 16 June 1836, pp. 247–253 herein.)

In the 2 April meeting, William W. Phelps and John Whitmer, members of the Missouri presidency who would soon leave Kirtland to return to Missouri, were released from future responsibilities and debts of the firm. Frederick G. Williams and Sidney Rigdon were charged with collecting on the firm's "outstanding claims" as a way to "discharge the company debts." Collecting funds from those who were in arrears for their newspaper subscriptions would have likely helped keep the printing establishment afloat and alleviated the church's poor financial circumstances as church leaders focused on diverting resources to the redemption of Zion.[51]

F. G. Williams & Co. eventually dissolved on 7 June 1836, when Oliver Cowdery "purchased the entire establishment."[52]

Document Transcript

Kirtland April 2ᵈ 1836

The following individuals comprising the firm of F. G. Williams & co. (viz.) Joseph Smith ᴶᵘⁿʳ· Sidney Rigdon Oliver Cowdery, W[illiam] W. Phelps, John Whitmer, and F[rederick] G. Williams,[53] met in the upper room in the printing office to take into consideration, the situation of the firm in a pecuniary point of view, to devise ways & means to discharge the debts,[54] to make a partial division of stock, and to release from the responsibility of the company Messrs. Wm. W. Phelps & John Whitmer.

First. We deem it wisdom, considering the importance of our contributing all in our power for the redemption of Zion, that J. Smith Junʳ and Oliver Cowdery, be a board or committee whose duty it shall be to raise all the money they can in Righteousness, for a season, to send by, or to certain wise men, appointed to purchase land in Zion, in obedience to a revelation[55] or

---

51. In the March 1836 issue of the *Messenger and Advocate,* which was likely published sometime after the meeting featured here, the editors published the following notice in an effort to collect on debts: "Those who are in arrears for the Messenger and Advocate, will please forward the amount to Oliver Cowdery; with the exception of those who reside in Missouri, they will please settle their arrears with John Whitmer. We hope that our friends will bear in mind, that paper, ink, and labor, cannot be obtained without the money; therefore, we are under the necessity to call on those who are indebted to us for assistance, which will be thankfully received." (Notice, *LDS Messenger and Advocate,* Mar. 1836, 2:288.)

52. "Notice," *LDS Messenger and Advocate,* June 1836, 2:329. After the purchase, Cowdery named the firm O. Cowdery & Co., which appears to have included JS and Rigdon by February 1837. The printing office changed hands twice more in the next year. ("Notice," *LDS Messenger and Advocate,* Feb. 1837, 3:458; "Notice," *LDS Messenger and Advocate,* Apr. 1837, 3:496.)

53. All of these men, except Frederick G. Williams, had been designated as original members of the Literary Firm, along with Martin Harris. (See Revelation, 26 Apr. 1832, in *JSP,* D2:234–236.)

54. Entries in the F. G. Williams & Co. cash book end in November 1835, so the extent of the firm's debt at the time of this meeting is not known. (F. G. Williams & Co., Account Book, in Patience Cowdery, Diary, CHL.)

55. Previous revelations outlined the need for the church to send "wise men" to purchase land in Zion.ᵃ According to John Whitmer's history, on 11 March 1836, JS appointed Edward Partridge, Isaac Morley,

command of the Lord for the mutual benefit of the said company or firm aforesaid.

Second. It is mutually agreed that Sidney Rigdon & F. G. Williams exert themselves in devising ways & means with the stock on hand, the available outstanding claims of the firm and such other means as they may deem most proper to discharge the company debts.

Third. It is also mutually understood & agreed, that W. W. Phelps, J. Whitmer & David Whitmer,[56] have five hundred Books of Doctrine & Covenants, when bound and five hundred hymn books[57] together with the subscription list for the Messenger & Advocate and Northern Times now due the firm in Clay Co. Missouri, and that Messrs. W. W. Phelps & John Whitmer be released from all ⟨the⟩ responsibility of all claims on them or either of them, as joint partners in the firm aforsaid.[58]

W[arren] A. Cowdery Clerk [p. 199]

———— ☙ ————

Visions, 3 April 1836 [D&C 110]

Source Note

Visions, [Kirtland Township, Geauga Co., OH], 3 Apr. 1836. Featured version copied [ca. 3 Apr. 1836] in JS, Journal, 1835–1836, pp. 192–193; handwriting of Warren A. Cowdery; JS Collection, CHL. For more information on JS, Journal, 1835–1836, see Source Notes for Multiple-Entry Documents, p. 524 herein.

John Corrill, and William W. Phelps as "wise men" sent to Missouri "with some money [to] purchase land for the saints—to seek a place for them &c."[b] In a letter sent the following day to his wife, Sally Waterman Phelps, William W. Phelps wrote that he "could not get ready to start for Missouri, on Monday—had to wait to raise Money to purchase land."[c] (a. See, for example, Revelation, 16–17 Dec. 1833, in *JSP,* D3:395 [D&C 101:73]; Revelation, 23 Feb. 1834, in *JSP,* D3:461 [D&C 103:23]; and Revelation, 22 June 1834, in *JSP,* D4:76 [D&C 105:28]. b. Whitmer, History, 83, in *JSP,* H2:92. c. William W. Phelps, Kirtland, OH, to Sally Waterman Phelps, Liberty, MO, Apr. 1836, William W. Phelps, Papers, BYU.)

56. These men constituted the presidency of the Missouri high council. With the exception of David Whitmer, they were planning to depart Kirtland to return to Clay County, Missouri, immediately.

57. The 1835 edition of the Doctrine and Covenants was published by F. G. Williams & Co. during the summer of 1835, and contemporary accounts suggest that at least one thousand copies were bound in Cleveland; it appears that at least five hundred, however, were left unbound by the time of the 2 April 1836 meeting featured here. *A Collection of Sacred Hymns* was published by F. G. Williams & Co. in 1835 and became available sometime in early 1836. ([William W. Phelps], "Doctrine and Covenants," *LDS Messenger and Advocate,* Aug. 1835, 1:170; William W. Phelps, Kirtland Mills, OH, to Sally Waterman Phelps, Liberty, MO, 16–18 Sept. 1835, private possession, copy at CHL.)

58. John Whitmer served as the editor of the *Messenger and Advocate* through the March 1836 issue, after which time the duties of editor transferred to Oliver Cowdery, though the paper was still published under the F. G. Williams & Co. name. (Masthead, *LDS Messenger and Advocate,* Mar. 1836, 2:288; Masthead, *LDS Messenger and Advocate,* Apr. 1836, 2:304.)

Historical Introduction

A few days following the temple dedication in Kirtland, Ohio, and the solemn assembly that empowered church elders for the ministry, JS's journal records that JS and Oliver Cowdery had a vision of heavenly messengers in the House of the Lord.[59] On the afternoon of Easter Sunday, 3 April 1836, JS helped other members of the church presidency distribute the sacrament of the Lord's Supper to the congregation that had assembled in the lower court of the House of the Lord. After the sacrament, the curtains were dropped, dividing the court into four quarters. According to Stephen Post, who participated in the day's meetings, the presidency then went to the pulpits for "the confirmation & blessing of the children."[60] At some point during the meeting, more veils were lowered, enclosing the west pulpits and dividing them into their four levels. JS and Cowdery "retired to the pulpit"—apparently the top tier, which was reserved for the presidency—where they bowed "in solemn, but silent prayer to the Most High."[61]

According to the journal, after JS and Cowdery prayed, secluded in the curtains and pulpits of the temple, they had a miraculous vision of Jesus Christ, who accepted the House of the Lord as JS had prayed for at the dedication.[62] The appearance was a fulfillment of a promise made in earlier JS revelations, that the Lord would show himself in the temple.[63] Following the appearance of Christ, the journal records, JS and Cowdery also received visitations from the biblical prophets Moses, Elias, and Elijah, who bestowed upon the two church leaders "the Keys of this dispensation." These keys authorized JS and Cowdery to exercise in new ways the priesthood they had received from the apostles Peter, James, and John in 1829.[64] The bestowal of "the Keys of this dispensation," particularly those concerning the gathering of Israel and turning "the hearts of the Fathers to the children," marked a vital moment for Latter-day Saint missionary work and temple ordinances. Just over a year after receiving these keys, JS sent preachers to England to begin the gathering of Israel from abroad.[65] Later, in Nauvoo, Illinois, he would teach and administer new temple ordinances that offered salvation to the deceased and bound them to the living, including

---

59. JS, Journal, 3 Apr. 1836, in *JSP*, J1:219–222.

60. Post, Journal, 3 Apr. 1836; see also William W. Phelps, Kirtland, OH, to Sally Waterman Phelps, Liberty, MO, Apr. 1836, William W. Phelps, Papers, BYU.

61. JS, Journal, 3 Apr. 1836, in *JSP*, J1:219; Robison, *First Mormon Temple*, 19, 85. The pulpits at the west end of the House of the Lord were dedicated for the Melchizedek priesthood. In November 1836, Wilford Woodruff, who had not previously seen the finished temple, wrote, "I must confess the scenery is indisscribable . . . After walking into the Pulpets, erected for the Priesthoods & viewing the curtains all bespeaking that grandure, solemnity & order that nothing Short of wisdom from God could invent." (Plan of the House of the Lord, between 1 and 25 June 1833, in *JSP*, D3:141–142; Woodruff, Journal, 25 Nov. 1836.)

62. Minutes and Prayer of Dedication, 27 Mar. 1836, p. 199 herein [D&C 109].

63. See Revelation, ca. 2 Nov. 1831, in *JSP*, D2:109–110 [D&C 67:10]; Revelation, 27–28 Dec. 1832, in *JSP*, D2:341 [D&C 88:68]. In a letter written to William W. Phelps on 11 January 1833, JS stated that inasmuch as church members remained obedient the Lord had promised "great things, yea even a visit from the heavens to honor us with his own presence." (Letter to William W. Phelps, 11 Jan. 1833, in *JSP*, D2:367.)

64. See "Joseph Smith Documents Dating through June 1831," in *JSP*, D1:xxxviii.

65. See Recommendation for Heber C. Kimball, between 2 and 13 June 1837, p. 400 herein.

baptisms for the dead, endowments, and sealings. The Latter-day Saints had shown their willingness to build the Lord a house, and these visitations on 3 April 1836 were not only a continuation of great spiritual outpouring; they were also a beginning for Latter-day Saint understanding of the purpose and power of temples.

JS and Cowdery recounted their visions to some associates shortly after they occurred. In a letter to his wife, Sally Waterman Phelps, written on the same day, William W. Phelps stated that JS and Cowdery experienced "a manifestation of the Lord" in which they learned that "the great & terrible day of the Lord as mentioned by Malichi, was near, even at the doors."[66]

Sometime shortly after, Warren A. Cowdery, JS's scribe and Oliver's brother, recorded the experience in JS's journal, which is the source for the text below. Warren wrote the entry referring to JS in the third person, in contrast to the first-person language found throughout the journal.[67] He may have relied on another original text, no longer extant, or on oral reports from either or both of the participants. If he was working from a prior text, it would directly parallel the method that produced the third-person 1834–1836 history, which he was composing in early April using JS's journal.[68] By 7 November 1843, Willard Richards, church historian and personal secretary to JS, changed the account into first person for JS's multivolume history.[69] JS and Oliver Cowdery's vision was added to the Doctrine and Covenants in 1876. That version, and published versions to follow, contained first-person language.

This account of visitations closes JS's 1835–1836 journal. After more than six months of almost daily recording of developments in Kirtland, entries ceased, and for nearly two years there were no entries written in this or in any other extant JS journal.

Document Transcript

The vail was taken from their minds and the eyes of their understandings were opened. They saw the Lord standing upon the breast work of the pulpit before them.[70] and under his feet was a paved work of pure gold,[71] in color like amber: his eyes were as a flame of fire; the hair of his head was like the pure snow,[72] his countenance shone above the brightness of the sun,[73] and his voice

---

66. W. Phelps to S. Phelps, Apr. 1836.

67. Warren A. Cowdery also penned the 2 April 1836 journal entry in third person. (See Editorial Note in JS, Journal, 1835–1836, in *JSP*, J1:217.)

68. See Editorial Note in JS, Journal, 1835–1836, in *JSP*, J1:217. For more information on JS's 1834–1836 history, see Historical Introduction to JS History, 1834–1836, in *JSP*, H1:25–28; and Editorial Note in JS History, 1834–1836, in *JSP*, H1:91.

69. Richards, Journal, 7 Nov. 1843; JS History, vol. B-1, 727–728.

70. A week earlier, JS prayed that the House of the Lord would be a place that the Son of Man would manifest himself to his people. (Minutes and Prayer of Dedication, 27 Mar. 1836, p. 199 herein [D&C 109:5].)

71. Earlier in 1836, JS saw in vision "the beautiful streets of that kingdom, which had the appearance of being paved with gold." (Visions, 21 Jan. 1836, p. 158 herein [D&C 137:4].)

72. See Revelation 1:14; 2:18; 19:12; and Historical Introduction to Minutes, 18 Mar. 1833, in JSP, D3:39–40, 43n259.

73. See Acts 26:13.

West pulpits, lower court, Kirtland House of the Lord. 1934. Joseph Smith and Oliver Cowdery reported that while secluded in these pulpits on Sunday, 3 April 1836, they received a vision of Jesus Christ and visitations from ancient biblical prophets. Warren A. Cowdery recorded their experience in Joseph Smith's 1835–1836 journal. (Courtesy Library of Congress, Washington DC. Photograph by Carl F. Waite.)

was as the sound of the rushing of great waters, even the Voice of Jehovah, saying, I am the first and the last. I am he who liveth. I am he who was slain.[74] I
am your Advocate with the Father.[75] Behold your sins are forgiven you. You are
clean before me, therefore, lift up your heads and rejoice, let the hearts of your
brethren rejoice and let the hearts of all my ~~brethren~~ ⟨people⟩ rejoice, who have
with their might, built this house to my name. For behold I have accepted this
house and my name shall be here; and I will manifest myself to my people, in
mercy, in this House, Yea I will appear unto my servants and speak unto them
with mine own voice, if my people will keep my commandments and do not
pollute this Holy House. Yea the hearts of thousands and tens of thousands
shall greatly rejoice in consequence of the blessings which shall be poured out,
and the endowment with which my servants have already been endowed and
shall hereafter be endowed in this House. and the fame of this House shall
spread to foreign lands, and this is the beginning of the blessing, which
shall [p. 192] be poured out upon the heads of my people. even so amen. After this vision closed, the Heavens were again opened unto them and Moses
appeared before them and committed unto them the Keys of the gathering of
Israel from the four parts of the Eearth and the leading of the ten tribes from
the Land of the North.[76] After this Elias appeared and committed the dispensation of the gospel of Abraham, saying, that in them and their seed all generations after them should be blessed.[77] After this vision had closed, another great
and glorious vision burts [burst] upon them, for Elijah, the Prophet, who was
taken to Heaven without tasting death,[78] also stood before them, and said,
behold the time has fully come which was spoken of by the mouth of Malachi,
testifying, that he should be sent before the great and dreadful day of the
Lord come, to turn the hearts of the Fathers to the children, and the children

---

74. See John 19:19–23; and Revelation 13:8.

75. See Revelation, Sept. 1830–A, in *JSP,* D1:179 [D&C 29:5]; and Revelation, ca. 7 Mar. 1831, in *JSP,*
D1:275 [D&C 45:3–5].

76. See Ezekiel 37:21–22; Jeremiah 3:18–19; and Amos 9:9, 14–15. JS's translation of the Book of
Mormon, as well as subsequent prophecies, stated that in the last days the lost ten tribes would return
from the "north countries." (Book of Mormon, 1830 ed., 488, 567 [3 Nephi 17:4; Ether 13:11]; Revelation,
3 Nov. 1831, in Doctrine and Covenants 100:3, 1835 ed. [D&C 133:26]; Revelation, 3 Nov. 1831, in *JSP,*
D2:118–119 [D&C 133:26–32]; JS, Kirtland, OH, to Noah C. Saxton, Rochester, NY, 4 Jan. 1833, in JS
Letterbook 1, pp. 14–18.)

77. JS's revelations used the generic name "Elias" to refer to various messengers who appeared as "forerunners" to the first or second comings of Jesus Christ. (See, for example, New Testament Revision 2,
part 2, p. 106 [Joseph Smith Translation, John 1:26]; New Testament Revision 1, p. 42 [Joseph Smith
Translation, Matthew 17:13]; Revelation, ca. Aug. 1830, in Doctrine and Covenants 50:2, 1835 ed. [D&C
27:6–7]; see also Genesis 13–15; 17; 22:17–18, 28; Galatians 3:6–18; and Matthew 17:10–13.)

78. See 2 Kings 2:8–15.

to the fathers, lest the whole earth be smitten with a curse.[79] Therefore, the Keys of this dispensation are committed into your hands, and by this ye may know that the great and the dreadful day[80] of the Lord is near, even at the doors[81] [p. 193]

———— ℰℛ ————

Recommendation for Lyman Wight, 4 April 1836

Source Note

JS, Oliver Cowdery, Hyrum Smith, Reynolds Cahoon, and Jared Carter, Recommendation, for Lyman Wight, Kirtland Township, Geauga Co., OH, 4 Apr. 1836. Featured version copied [between ca. 4 Apr. and ca. 16 May 1836] in Minute Book 1, p. 200; handwriting of Warren A. Cowdery; CHL. For more information on Minute Book 1, see Source Notes for Multiple-Entry Documents, p. 527 herein.

Historical Introduction

Six days after he participated in the solemn assembly in the House of the Lord, Lyman Wight left Kirtland, Ohio, for his home in Clay County, Missouri. In his possession was a short document, signed by church leaders the previous day, that recommended him—and his advice concerning "temporal matters"—to members of the church.

The recommendation includes references to Zion and the "upbuilding of the cause," suggesting that church leaders had entrusted Wight with duties related to the redemption or building up of Zion. The list of signatures on the document supports this possibility. Three of the signers, Hyrum Smith, Reynolds Cahoon, and Jared Carter, made up the committee to build the House of the Lord, which was responsible for financing the building's construction. This recommendation may be related to a 2 April 1836 meeting at which the partners of F. G. Williams & Co. considered "the situation of the firm in a pecuniary point of view." During that meeting, in an effort to contribute "all in our power for the redemption of Zion," the partners appointed JS and Oliver Cowdery to "raise all the money they can in Righteousness, for a season, to send by, or to certain wise men, appointed to purchase land in Zion." Given that JS and Cowdery were the first two signatories to Wight's recommendation, it is possible that they selected Wight as one of these "wise men."[82] In addition to raising funds in New York for the redemption of Zion during the

---

79. See Malachi 4:5–6; and Revelation, ca. Aug. 1830, in Doctrine and Covenants 50:2, 1835 ed. [D&C 27:9]. JS later recounted that the visit of Elijah was foretold by the angel Moroni in 1823. He also taught that Elijah restored the keys "of the fulness of the Melchezedek Priesthood," including the authority to perform ceremonies that would "seal" for eternal duration marriages and parent-child relationships for both the living and the dead. (JS History, vol. A-1, 5–6, in *JSP*, H1:224 [Draft 2]; Robert B. Thompson, Sermon Notes, 5 Oct. 1840, JS Collection, CHL; Coray, Notebook, 13 Aug. 1843; JS, Journal, 27 Aug. 1843, in *JSP*, J3:86–87; Woodruff, Journal, 10 Mar. 1844.)

80. See Revelation, 3 Nov. 1831, in *JSP*, D2:120 [D&C 133:48–52, 56]; and Isaiah 64:1–7.

81. See Malachi 4:5; Matthew 24:33; and Mark 13:29.

82. Minutes, 2 Apr. 1836, p. 223 herein.

summer of 1834, Wight had been entrusted with collecting money for JS (or perhaps the church) during early 1836.[83] Wight later recalled that after arriving back in Missouri on 6 May 1836, he did "much to help the Br[ethren] enter land in Caldwell Co," where the Missouri Saints began settling.[84]

Lyman Wight had deep connections to the cause of redeeming Zion. After Wight and most other members of the church in Jackson County, Missouri, were driven from their homes in November 1833, he and Parley P. Pratt traveled to Kirtland in January 1834 to counsel with church leaders.[85] Wight was then among eight men chosen to recruit volunteers and raise money to redeem Zion after a 24 February 1834 JS revelation led to the organization of the Camp of Israel expedition.[86] He participated in that expedition and was chosen as the group's general.[87] After a 22 June 1834 revelation stated that the redemption of Zion could not occur until after church leaders were "endowed with power from on high," Wight was among the men chosen to travel from Missouri to Kirtland to receive this endowment in the House of the Lord.[88] Shortly after taking part in the 30 March 1836 solemn assembly, Wight received this letter of recommendation; the following day, he began his journey back to Missouri.[89]

Though the original recommendation is no longer extant, Warren A. Cowdery copied it into Minute Book 1, the version featured here.

Document Transcript

We the undersigned from a long and intimate acquaintance with the Bearer, brother Lyman Wight, from the instructions he has received, the accurate knowledge he has of Zion and her present situation, we cheerfully recommend him to the fullest confidence, of the brethren of the Church of the Latter-Day-Saints, and any advice he may give relative to temporal matters, the upbuilding of the cause or the furtherance of the Gospel may be safely followed,

---

83. In a letter written to Wilford Woodruff in 1857, Wight recalled that he departed Kirtland "the 13th of Jan and went south 120 miles to collect some money for Br Joseph, got $500 returned on the 27th of Feb." Neither Wight's letter to Woodruff nor any other extant document offers an explanation as to what the money might have been for. (Lyman Wight, Mountain Valley, TX, to Wilford Woodruff, 24 Aug. 1857, p. 9, Historian's Office, Histories of the Twelve, 1856–1858, 1861, CHL.)

84. Lyman Wight, Mountain Valley, TX, to Wilford Woodruff, 24 Aug. 1857, p. 9, Historian's Office, Histories of the Twelve, 1856–1858, 1861, CHL.

85. Parley P. Pratt et al., "'The Mormons' So Called," *The Evening and the Morning Star,* Extra, Feb. 1834, [1]–[2]; Lyman Wight, Journal, in *History of the Reorganized Church,* 1:401–402.

86. Revelation, 24 Feb. 1834, in *JSP,* D3:457–463 [D&C 103]; JS, Journal, 15–17 Mar. 1834, in *JSP,* J1:34–35.

87. Kimball, "Journal and Record," 11–12. JS served as commander-in-chief of the Camp of Israel expedition.

88. Revelation, 22 June 1834, in *JSP,* D4:74 [D&C 105:11]; Minutes, 23 June 1834, in *JSP,* D4:84; Letter to Lyman Wight and Others, 16 Aug. 1834, in *JSP,* D4:104–105.

89. Wight left Kirtland on 5 April 1836. (Lyman Wight, Mountain Valley, TX, to Wilford Woodruff, 24 Aug. 1857, p. 9, Historian's Office, Histories of the Twelve, 1856–1858, 1861, CHL.)

J. Smith ^{Junr.}

Oliver Cowdery

~~Hiram~~ Hyrum Smith

Reynolds Cahoon

Jared Carter

Kirtland April 4th. 1836

———— ∾ ————

Letter to Oliver Cowdery, circa 9 April 1836

Source Note

JS, Letter, [Kirtland Township, Geauga Co., OH], to Oliver Cowdery, [Kirtland Township, Geauga Co., OH], ca. 9 Apr. 1836. Featured version published in "For the Messenger and Advocate," Latter Day Saints' Messenger and Advocate, Apr. 1836, 2:289–291. For more information on Latter Day Saints' Messenger and Advocate, see Source Notes for Multiple-Entry Documents, p. 527 herein.

Historical Introduction

A series of three articles addressing slavery and abolitionism appeared in the April 1836 issue of the church newspaper, the *Latter Day Saints' Messenger and Advocate.* Among these pieces was a letter JS wrote to the paper's editor, Oliver Cowdery, in which he stated his view on the right of citizens of the United States to own slaves and addressed the spread of radical abolitionism in Ohio and other western states.[90]

Though Americans had been debating the morality of slavery since before the country's founding, the rhetoric of William Lloyd Garrison and other antislavery activists in the early 1830s prompted many Northerners to take a more pronounced stand on slavery and emancipation. Distancing themselves from the faction of the antislavery movement that advocated gradual emancipation and sending the slaves to colonies in Africa, abolitionists like Garrison condemned slavery on moral grounds and demanded the immediate emancipation and enfranchisement of black slaves.[91] Using passionate public speeches and his abolitionist newspaper, the *Liberator,* Garrison sought to "lift up the standard of emancipation in the eyes of the nation."[92] In December 1833, Garrison joined other prominent abolitionists, such as Theodore Weld and Arthur Tappan, to found the American Anti-Slavery Society (AASS), an organization that advocated for the "immediate abandonment" of slavery "without expatriation." The number of local antislavery societies grew rapidly. By 1836,

---

90. The other two articles are Warren Parrish, "For the Messenger and Advocate"; and "The Abolitionists," *LDS Messenger and Advocate,* Apr. 1836, 2:295–296, 299–301.

91. Motivated by the presumption that black slaves could not assimilate into white American society, the American Colonization Society, founded in 1816, promoted freeing slaves and then recolonizing them in Africa. Though Garrison and other abolitionists originally supported colonization, they later condemned the society's efforts as a "conspiracy against human rights." (Sewall, *Selling of Joseph,* 1–3; *Twelfth Annual Report,* 57–58; "Christian Secretary—Colonization Society," *Liberator* [Boston], 23 Apr. 1831, [1].)

92. William Lloyd Garrison, "To the Public," *Liberator,* 1 Jan. 1831, 1.

the AASS itself had organized well over 500 branches in communities across the United States, including 133 in Ohio—the most in any state.[93]

As abolitionists began to grow in number, the movement's leaders launched an ambitious campaign to persuade more Americans to embrace their cause. This campaign generated the desired publicity, but it also resulted in significant social and political backlash. In 1834 and 1835, the AASS began mailing abolitionist literature en masse to members of Congress and to prominent citizens in the South. Letters to legislators urged national leaders to end slavery in the District of Columbia, while mass-produced tracts, directed to thousands of individuals, vividly depicted the cruelties of American slavery.[94] The postal campaign generated intense controversy in the South; in July 1835, a mob ransacked the post office in Charleston, South Carolina, burned abolitionist literature, and hanged Garrison and Tappan in effigy.[95] In 1836, the House of Representatives passed a resolution—later referred to as the "gag rule"—mandating that all petitions relating to slavery or abolition be tabled immediately and not receive further action.[96] The resolution was renewed yearly until Congress rescinded it in 1844.[97] Though Northerners largely condemned southern slavery, most remained indifferent, if not opposed, to the "radical" cries of the abolitionists. From 1834 to 1835, anti-abolitionist riots broke out in New York, Philadelphia, Boston, and other cities across the North; in July 1836, a mob destroyed an abolitionist press in Cincinnati and then turned on local black residents.[98] The pervasiveness of anti-abolitionist violence meant Mormon leaders were keenly aware that if they so much as hinted at support for abolitionism, there could be violent repercussions—even in the northern states.

Despite social and political resistance to abolitionist ideas, support for the movement grew steadily throughout the western frontier. Ohio in particular became a stronghold of abolitionism during the 1830s, attracting a vocal group of students and professors from local religiously affiliated institutions. In 1831, several prominent faculty members at Western Reserve College in Hudson (thirty-five miles south of Kirtland) embraced and promoted Garrison's brand of abolitionism, leading many students to join local abolitionist societies. In the winter of 1833, some of these students even traveled through nearby towns delivering abolitionist speeches.[99] Following a series of debates between abolitionists and colonizationists at

---

93. *Constitution of the American Anti-Slavery Society*, 4; *Second Annual Report of the American Anti-Slavery Society*, 83–87; *Third Annual Report of the American Anti-Slavery Society*, 5, 89–99. Between the 1835 and 1836 annual meetings, the number of chapters grew from 225 to 527.

94. Feldman, *Free Expression and Democracy in America*, 129–136; Wyatt-Brown, "Abolitionists' Postal Campaign of 1835," 227–238.

95. "From the Courier of Friday," *Liberator*, 15 Aug. 1835, [1].

96. *Journal of the House of Representatives of the United States* [1835], 25 May 1836, 876.

97. *Journal of the House of Representatives of the United States* [1844–1845], 3 Dec. 1844, 9–12.

98. The North's lack of support for abolitionism was partly due to racism and a deep-seated fear of miscegenation. Rumors that abolitionists were promoting interracial marriage, for example, helped spark the anti-abolitionist riot in New York. For contemporary accounts of the riots, see "Disgraceful Proceedings," *New York Journal of Commerce*, 11 July 1834, [2]; "Charlestown Riots Renewed," *Philadelphia Gazette and Universal Daily Advertiser*, 15 Aug. 1834, [2]; "Abolition," *Hampshire Gazette* (Northampton, MA), 28 Oct. 1835, [2]; and Ohio Anti-Slavery Society, *Narrative of the Late Riotous Proceedings*, 15, 39–40.

99. Waite, *Western Reserve University*, 95–102.

LATTER DAY SAINTS'
MESSENGER AND ADVOCATE.

VOL. II. No. 7.]   KIRTLAND, OHIO, APRIL, 1836.   [Whole No. 19.

For the Messenger and Advocate.

BROTHER O. COWDERY:

    Dear Sir—This place having recently been visited by a gentleman who advocated the principles or doctrines of those who are called abolitionists; if you deem the following reflections of any service, or think they will have a tendency to correct the opinions of the southern public, relative to the views and sentiments I believe, as an individual, and am able to say, from personal knowledge, are the feelings of others, you are at liberty to give them publicity in the columns of the Advocate. I am prompted to this course in consequence, in one respect, of many elders having gone into the Southern States, besides, there now being many in that country who have already embraced the fulness of the gospel, as revealed through the book of Mormon,—having learned, by experience, that the enemy of truth does not slumber, nor cease his exertions to bias the minds of communities against the servants of the Lord, by stirring up the indignation of men upon all matters of importance or interest.

    Thinking, perhaps, that the sound might go out, that "an abolitionist" had held forth several times to this community, and that the public feeling was not aroused to create mobs or disturbances, leaving the impression that all he said was concurred in, and received as gospel and the word of salvation. I am happy to say, that no violence or breach of the public peace was attempted, so far from this, that all except a very few, attended to their own avocations and left the gentleman to hold forth his own arguments to nearly naked walls.

    I am aware, that many who profess to preach the gospel, complain against their brethren of the same faith, who reside in the south, and are ready to withdraw the hand of fellowship because they will not renounce the principle of slavery and raise their voice against every thing of the kind. This must be a tender point, and one which should call forth the candid reflection of all men, and especially before they advance in an opposition calculated to lay waste the fair States of the South, and set loose, upon the world a community of people who might peradventure, overrun our country and violate the most sacred principles of human society,—chastity and virtue.

    No one will pretend to say, that the people of the free states are as capable of knowing the evils of slavery as those who hold them. If slavery is an evil, who, could we expect, would first learn it? Would the people of the free states, or would the slave states? All must readily admit, that the latter would first learn this fact. If the fact was learned first by those immediately concerned, who would be more capable than they of prescribing a remedy?

    And besides, are not those who hold slaves, persons of ability, discernment and candor? Do they not expect to give an account at the bar of God for their conduct in this life? It may, no doubt, with propriety be said, that many who hold slaves live without the fear of God before their eyes, and, the same may be said of many in the free states. Then who is to be the judge in this matter?

    So long, then, as those of the free states are not interested in the freedom of the slaves, any other than upon the mere principles of equal rights and of the gospel, and are ready to admit that there are men of piety who reside in the South, who are immediately concerned, and until *they* complain, and call for assistance, why not cease their clamor, and no further urge the slave to acts of murder, and the master to vigorous discipline, rendering both miserable, and unprepared to pursue that course which might otherwise lead them both to better their condition? I do not believe that the people of the North have any more right to say that the South *shall not* hold slaves, than the South have to say the North *shall.*

    And further, what benefit will it ever be to the slave for persons to run over the free states, and excite indignation against their masters in the minds of thousands and tens of thousands who understand nothing relative

Letter on slavery and abolition. The April 1836 issue of the *Latter Day Saints' Messenger and Advocate* included the printed text of a letter Joseph Smith wrote to Oliver Cowdery, the newspaper's editor. This letter, which discussed slavery, emancipation, and abolition, was one of a few writings that addressed these contentious topics in the church's newspaper. Letter to Oliver Cowdery, ca. 9 Apr. 1836, *LDS Messenger and Advocate,* Apr. 1836, 2:289. (Church History Library, Salt Lake City.)

Cincinnati's Lane Seminary in February 1834, sympathetic students began to actively work and lecture for abolition in surrounding communities. This angered local residents, who put pressure on the institution's trustees to fire professors and ban abolitionist activities. During fall 1834, more than fifty students, later referred to as "Lane rebels," left the institution in protest. The Oberlin Institute welcomed the Lane abolitionists, more than two dozen of whom enrolled at the school by summer 1835. By the spring of 1836, Oberlin—located fifty miles from Kirtland—had become a local center of abolitionism.[100]

Students affiliated with these three institutions played a significant role in spreading abolitionism from college campuses to communities throughout Ohio. One student at Oberlin, John W. Alvord, embarked on a lecture circuit in December 1835 that took him through various communities in northeastern Ohio, including Willoughby and Kirtland. Alvord, who was employed by the AASS, is likely the "gentleman" referred to by JS in the featured text. Though he had been pelted with stones and threatened with tarring and feathering in Willoughby several months before, Alvord returned in April to give several speeches there; he also helped establish a local antislavery society. According to the abolitionist newspaper *Philanthropist,* Alvord also lectured in Kirtland in April 1836 and organized a society there.[101]

The experiences of Latter-day Saints in Jackson County, Missouri, in 1833, as well as missionary efforts in the South from 1834 to 1836, also shaped the way in which JS and other church leaders responded to the spread of abolitionism in Ohio. In July 1833, William W. Phelps wrote an editorial in the church's newspaper *The Evening and the Morning Star* that was interpreted by the citizens in Jackson County as being an invitation for free blacks to migrate to the state.[102] Asserting that his article had been misunderstood, Phelps issued an extra edition of the *Star* several days later in which he claimed that "our intention was not only to stop free people of color from emigrating to this state, but to prevent them from being admitted as members of the church."[103] Phelps's extra did little to allay the outrage of local citizens. On 18 July, local residents circulated a document that decried church members as "deluded fanatics" and accused them of "tampering with our slaves and endeavoring to sow dissensions & raise seditions among them."[104] Two days later, a mob destroyed the church's print shop and tarred and feathered two local members, Edward Partridge and Charles Allen. The perception that the church supported the migration of free blacks into Missouri ultimately contributed to the mass expulsion of church members from Jackson County. Violent opposition and a traumatic uprooting—felt collectively by church members from Missouri to Ohio—undoubtedly discouraged church leaders from actively engaging in

---

100. Fletcher, *History of Oberlin College,* 151–166, 183, 236–239; *Statement of the Reasons,* 3–5, 28; Morris, *Oberlin,* 23–37.

101. Myers, "Antislavery Activities of Five Lane Seminary Boys in 1835–36," 98–102; "Anti-Slavery Intelligence," *Philanthropist* (Cincinnati), 22 Apr. 1836, [2].

102. "Free People of Color," *The Evening and the Morning Star,* July 1833, 109; "We the Undersigned Citizens of Jackson County," [July 1833], Edward Partridge, Papers, CHL; "To His Excellency, Daniel Dunklin," *The Evening and the Morning Star,* Dec. 1833, 114.

103. *The Evening and the Morning Star,* Extra, 16 July 1833, [1].

104. The document, later referred to by members of the church as the "manifesto," is reproduced in Letter from John Whitmer, 29 July 1833, in *JSP,* D3:186–198.

issues of slavery and race from 1833 onward. In addition to their experiences in Missouri, successful missionary efforts in Tennessee and Kentucky from 1834 to 1836 likely made JS and other leaders wary of openly supporting any antislavery movement that could potentially hinder proselytizing or ignite tensions between new converts and their Southern neighbors.[105]

These experiences, along with the spread of abolitionism in Ohio during the mid-1830s, compelled church leaders to periodically reiterate their views on slavery and emancipation. In distancing themselves from abolitionism, Mormon leaders were not alone in eschewing what was then considered a radical movement, even among those who regarded themselves as antislavery. The "Declaration on Government and Law," issued in August 1835 and published in the Doctrine and Covenants, codified the policy that slaves should not be preached to or baptized "contrary to the will and wish of their masters."[106] A 9 October 1835 editorial in the *Northern Times* (likely authored by Oliver Cowdery or Frederick G. Williams) informed readers that "several communications have been sent . . . in favor of antislavery—or the abolition of slavery." The editor asserted that the church would have nothing to do with the matter. "We are opposed to abolition, and whatever is calculated to disturb the peace and harmony of our Constitution and country," the editorial continued. "Abolition does hardly belong to law or religion, politics or gospel."[107] The subject continued to generate discussion within church circles. On 2 February 1836, Oliver Cowdery recorded in his journal that he wrote an "article on the present agitating question of slavery and antislavery." Regarding the slavery issue, Cowdery further noted, "There is a hostill spirit exhibited between the North and South, and ere long must make disturbances of a serious nature."[108]

John Alvord's spring 1836 lecture in Kirtland likely prompted JS to write the featured letter to Oliver Cowdery. The original letter is not extant, and the text presented here is the version that was printed in the April issue of the *Messenger and Advocate*. In his letter, JS carefully outlined his position on slavery and emancipation. JS's views recorded here were expressed in response to a specific geographical, political, and cultural milieu. His ideas about black Americans and slavery were not static. During the 1830s and 1840s, a small number of former slaves or free blacks were baptized into the Latter-day Saint church.[109] During JS's tenure as church president, at least two black converts were ordained to the priesthood in Kirtland, and one man, Elijah Abel, was selected as a member of the Quorum

---

105. Between 1834 and 1836, missionaries such as David W. Patten, Warren Parrish, and Wilford Woodruff established eight branches, consisting of approximately 130 members, in three counties in Tennessee and two counties in Kentucky. (Berrett, "History of the Southern States Mission," 68–123.)

106. Declaration on Government and Law, ca. Aug. 1835, in *JSP*, D4:484 [D&C 134:12].

107. "Abolition," *Northern Times,* 9 Oct. 1835, [2].

108. Two days later Cowdery wrote another article "upon the subject of slavery." It is unknown if Cowdery published either of these articles. (Cowdery, Diary, 2 and 4 Feb. 1836.)

109. This included individuals such as "Black Pete," Elijah Abel, Q. Walker Lewis, Jane Manning James, and William McCary. ("Fanaticism," *Albany [NY] Evening Journal,* 16 Feb. 1831, [2]; "Elders License Elijah Abel Certificate," James D. Wardle, Papers, 1812–2001, Special Collections, J. Willard Marriott Library, University of Utah, Salt Lake City; James, Autobiography, 1893, 15; William Appleby, Batavia, NY, to Brigham Young, 2 June 1847, Brigham Young Office Files, CHL; see also Reeve, *Religion of a Different Color,* 106–114, 128–129.)

of the Seventy in 1836.[110] In the years after church members were expelled from Missouri and settled in Nauvoo, Illinois, JS expressed a progressive view of the intellectual capacities of black slaves, advocated granting them certain civil rights, and, as a presidential candidate in 1844, campaigned for their emancipation.[111]

The original letter, written circa 9 April 1836 and addressed to Cowdery, is not extant, but a copy was subsequently published in the April issue of the *Messenger and Advocate*.[112]

Document Transcript

For the Messenger and Advocate.

BROTHER O[liver] COWDERY:[113]

Dear Sir—This place having recently been visited by a gentleman[114] who advocated the principles or doctrines of those who are called abolitionists; if you deem the following reflections of any service, or think they will have a tendency to correct the opinions of the southern public, relative to the views and sentiments I believe, as an individual, and am able to say, from personal knowledge, are the feelings of others, you are at liberty to give them publicity in the

---

110. Elders License for Elijah Abel, 31 Mar. 1836, in Kirtland Elders' Certificates, 61; Record of Seventies, bk. A, 11; William Appleby, Batavia, NY, to Brigham Young, 2 June 1847, Brigham Young Office Files, CHL.

111. JS's position on racial characteristics can be contrasted to theories of the time that immutable racial biology (cranial size) ultimately determined intellectual capacity; such scientific racism put the "Negro race" at the bottom of a racial hierarchy. In a 30 December 1843 conversation with apostle Orson Hyde recorded in his journal, JS asserted that slaveholders should "bring their slaves into a free country— & set them free— Educate them & give them equal Rights." While JS favored granting black slaves certain rights, the same entry suggests that he, like many of his contemporaries, remained apprehensive about miscegenation. In his presidential platform, JS proposed to "break off the shackles from the poor black man, and hire him to labor like other human beings." Walking an ideological line between radical abolitionists and proponents of slavery, he suggested using the revenue from public land sales to reimburse southern slaveholders for their property, thus enabling them to "rid so *free* a country of every vestige of slavery." (JS, Journal, 30 Dec. 1842 and 2 Jan. 1843, in *JSP*, J2:197, 212; JS, *General Smith's Views of the Powers and Policy of the Government of the United States,* 9, 10, italics in original; see also Samuel George Morton, *Crania Americana* [Philadelphia, PA: J. Dobson; London: Simpkin, Marshall and Company, 1839]; Samuel George Morton, *Crania Aegyptiaca* [Philadelphia, PA: John Penington; London: Madden and Company, 1844]; and Samuel George Morton, *Catalogue of Skulls of Man and the Inferior Animals* [Philadelphia, PA: Merrihew and Thomson, 1849].)

112. John Alvord certainly lectured in Kirtland before 22 April, the date an account of that visit was published in the abolitionist periodical *Philanthropist*. An entry in a later JS history, inscribed by Willard Richards in early November 1843, indicates that JS composed the letter "soon after" 9 April 1836. ("Anti-Slavery Intelligence," *Philanthropist*, Apr. 22, 1836, 2; Myers, "Antislavery Activities of Five Lane Seminary Boys in 1835–36," 100–102; JS History, vol. B-1, 728.)

113. Oliver Cowdery was the editor of the *Messenger and Advocate* in April 1836, having taken over for John Whitmer (and William W. Phelps, who aided Whitmer to a great extent) sometime that month. Cowdery's brother, Warren, was largely responsible for editing the next nine issues of the paper. (Masthead, *LDS Messenger and Advocate,* Apr. 1836, 2:304.)

114. Likely John W. Alvord.

columns of the Advocate. I am prompted to this course in consequence, in one respect, of many elders having gone into the Southern States, besides, there now being many in that country who have already embraced the fulness of the gospel, as revealed through the book of Mormon,—having learned, by experience, that the enemy of truth does not slumber, nor cease his exertions to bias the minds of communities against the servants of the Lord, by stiring up the indignation of men upon all matters of importance or interest.[115]

Thinking, perhaps, that the sound might go out, that "an abolitionist" had held forth several times to this community, and that the public feeling was not aroused to create mobs or disturbances, leaving the impression that all he said was concurred in, and received as gospel and the word of salvation. I am happy to say, that no violence or breach of the public peace was attempted, so far from this, that all except a very few, attended to their own avocations and left the gentleman to hold forth his own arguments to nearly naked walls.[116]

I am aware, that many who profess to preach the gospel, complain against their brethren of the same faith, who reside in the south, and are ready to withdraw the hand of fellowship because they will not renounce the principle of slavery and raise their voice against every thing of the kind.[117] This must be a tender point, and one which should call forth the candid reflection of all men, and especially before they advance in an opposition calculated to lay waste the

---

115. An unattributed letter, published in the May 1836 issue of the *Messenger and Advocate,* confirms the anxiety of church leaders regarding abolitionism. Apparently written to an individual who was not a member of the church, the letter notes, "Being aware that our brethren are numerous in the South . . . it was thought advisable to come out decidedly in relation to this matter, that our brethren might not be subjected to persecution on this account—and the lives of our traveling elders put in jeopardy." (Letter, *LDS Messenger and Advocate,* May 1836, 2:313.)

116. An article printed in the April edition of the abolitionist publication *Philanthropist* offered a more positive assessment of John Alvord's time in Kirtland. The article noted that Alvord was "well received" and that he was able to form an antislavery society with as many as eighty-six members. It is unclear whether any Mormons were among those who listened to the lecture or later joined the abolitionist society Alvord established. ("Anti-Slavery Intelligence," *Philanthropist* [Cincinnati], 22 Apr. 1836, [2].)

117. For decades before and after the 1830s, ministers and religious scholars in both the northern and southern United States used portions of the Old and New Testaments to either condemn or legitimate the practice of slavery. Even within the largely antislavery North, however, interpretations of biblical passages regarding slavery varied. The ideology of radical abolitionists—largely inspired by Christ's teachings generally and the enlightenment doctrine of natural rights—alienated some antislavery moderates in the North who espoused more literal interpretations of the Bible. Slavery exacerbated existing schisms within American religions, eventually leading some churches, including the Presbyterian, Methodist, Episcopal, and Baptist denominations, to divide along sectional lines during the late 1830s and early 1840s. (Genovese, "Religion in the Collapse of the American Union," 78–79; see also Noll, *Civil War as a Theological Crisis,* 1–6, 33–46.)

fair States of the South,[118] and set loose, upon the world a community of people who might peradventure, overrun our country and violate the most sacred principles of human society,—chastity and virtue.[119]

No one will pretend to say, that the people of the free states are as capable of knowing the evils of slavery as those who hold them. If slavery is an evil, who, could we expect, would first learn it? Would the people of the free states, or would the slave states? All must readily admit, that th[e] latter would first learn this fact. If the fact was learned first by those immediately concerned, who would be more capable than they of prescribing a remedy?

And besides, are not those who hold slaves, persons of ability, discernment and candor? Do they not expect to give an account at the bar of God for their conduct in this life? It may, no doubt, with propriety be said, that many who hold slaves live without the fear of God before their eyes, and, the same may be said of many in the free states. Then who is to be the judge in this matter?

So long, then, as those of the free states are not interested in the freedom of the slaves, any other than upon the mere principles of equal rights and of the gospel, and are ready to admit that there are men of piety who reside in the South, who are immediately concerned, and until *they* complain, and call for assistance, why not cease their clamor, and no further urge the slave to acts of murder,[120] and the master to vigorous discipline, rendering both miserable, and unprepared to pursue that course which might otherwise lead them both to better their condition? I do not believe that the people of the North have any more right to say that the South *shall not* hold slaves, than the South have to say the North *shall*.

---

118. In December 1832, JS dictated a revelation warning of a war in which "the southern states shall be divided against the Northern states." The prophecy continued, "Slaves shall rise up against there Masters who shall be Martialed and disaplined for war." (Revelation, 25 Dec. 1832, in *JSP*, D2:328–331 [D&C 87].)

119. Apprehensions about interracial mixing were common among white Americans in the 1830s. Historian Elise Lemire argues that the growth of abolitionist societies in the 1830s precipitated an "explosion of anxiety about black political rights" and miscegenation. Detractors of abolitionism, she contends, "repeatedly and vociferously called them 'amalgamationists.'" An editorial in the April 1836 *Messenger and Advocate* also expressed fear that "amalgamation" could potentially endanger "the chastity of every female." (Lemire, *Miscegenation*, 1–2, 54–55; "The Abolitionists," *LDS Messenger and Advocate*, Apr. 1836, 2:300.)

120. Virginian slave Nat Turner led a bloody slave rebellion five years earlier. For two days in August 1831, Turner and a "posse" of nearly sixty armed men (comprising both slaves and free blacks) marched through the countryside killing white inhabitants indiscriminately. By the time he was captured on 30 October, some fifty-seven white people, nearly four dozen of whom were women and children, had lost their lives. Though Turner and his followers were tried and summarily executed for their crimes, the specter of slave rebellion haunted Americans in the North and South during the 1830s and beyond. (Howe, *What Hath God Wrought*, 323–325.)

And further, what benefit will it ever be to the slave for persons to run over the free states, and excite indignation against their masters in the minds of thousands and tens of thousands who understand nothing relative [p. [289]] to their circumstances or conditions? I mean particularly those who have never travelled in the South, and scarcely seen a negro in all their life. How any community can ever be excited with the chatter of such persons—boys and others who are too indolent to obtain their living by honest industry, and are incapable of pursuing any occupation of a professional nature, is unaccountable to me. And when I see persons in the free states signing documents against slavery,[121] it is no less, in my mind, than an array of influence, and a declaration of hostilities against the people of the South! What can divide our Union sooner, God only knows!

After having expressed myself so freely upon this subject, I do not doubt but those who have been forward in raising their voice against the South, will cry out against me as being uncharitable, unfeeling and unkind—wholly unacquainted with the gospel of Christ. It is my privilege then, to name certain passages from the bible, and examine the teachings of the ancients upon this matter, as the fact is uncontrovertable, that the first mention we have of slavery is found in the holy bible, pronounced by a man who was perfect in his generation and walked with God. And so far from that prediction's being averse from the mind of God it remains as a lasting monument of the decree of Jehovah, to the shame and confusion of all who have cried out against the South, in consequence of their holding the sons of Ham in servitude![122]

"And he said cursed *be* Canaan;[123] a servant of servants shall he be unto his brethren. And he said, Blessed *be* the Lord God of Shem; and

---

121. This may be a general reference to various abolitionist societies' adoption of a constitution or "declaration of sentiment," which defined a society's abolitionist creed and was often signed by its members. The 1833 constitution of the American Anti-Slavery Society, for example, denounced slaveholding as a "heinous crime in the sight of God" and declared the society's intention to "put an end to the domestic slave-trade, and to abolish Slavery in all those portions of our common country which come under its control, especially in the District of Columbia,—and likewise to prevent the extension of it to any State that may be hereafter admitted to the Union." The Ohio Anti-Slavery Society's 1835 Declaration of Sentiment implored churches to "purge [themselves] from the sin of slavery, disowning all fellowship with 'the unfruitful works of darkness' and 'hating the garment spotted with the flesh.'" (*Constitution of the American Anti-Slavery Society*, 2–5; *Proceedings of the Ohio Anti-Slavery Convention*, 9.)

122. The notion that black slaves descended from the sons of Ham, who were cursed by Ham's father, Noah, had been a part of some Christian, Jewish, and Muslim traditions for centuries, and nineteenth-century slaveholders often cited the biblical story as a justification for the practice of slavery in the United States. (Haynes, *Noah's Curse*, 7–8; Goldenberg, *Curse of Ham*, 168–177.)

123. Canaan was the fourth son of Ham. (Genesis 10:6.)

Canaan shall be his servant.— God shall enlarge Japheth, and he shall dwell in the tents of Shem; and Canaan shall be his servant."—Gen, 8:25, 26, 27.[124]

Trace the history of the world from this notable event down to this day, and you will find the fulfilment of this singular prophecy. What could have been the design of the Almighty in this wonderful occurrence is not for me to say; but I can say, that the curse is not yet taken off the sons of Canaan, neither will be until it is affected by as great power as caused it to come;[125] and the people who interfere the least with the decrees and purposes of God in this matter, will come under the least condemnation before him; and those who are determined to pursue a course which shows an opposition and a feverish rest-lessness against the designs of the Lord, will learn, when perhaps it is too late for their own good, that God can do his own work without the aid of those who are not dictated by his counsel.

I must not pass over a notice of the history of Abraham, of whom so much is spoken in the scriptures. If we can credit the account, God conversed with him from time to time, and directed him in the way he should walk, saying, "I am the Almighty God: walk before me and be thou perfect."[126] Paul says that the gospel was preached to this man. And it is further said, that he had sheep and oxen, men-servants and maid-servants, &c.[127] From this I conclude, that if the principle had been an evil one, in the midst of the communications made to this holy man, he would have been instructed differently. And if he was instructed against holding men-servants and maid-servants, he never ceased to do it; consequently must have incurred the displeasure of the Lord and thereby lost his blessings—which was not the fact.

Some may urge, that the names, man-servant and maid-servant, only mean hired persons who were at liberty to leave their masters or employers at any time. But we can easily settle this point by turning to the history of Abraham's descendants, when governed by a law given from the mouth of the Lord him-self. I know that when an Israelite had been brought into servitude in conse-quence of debt, or otherwise, at the seventh year he went from the task of his former master or employer; but to no other people or nation was this granted in the law to Israel. And if, after a man had served six years, he did not wish to be

---

124. The quoted passage is found in Genesis 9:25–27.

125. The two other authors of anti-abolitionist articles in the April 1836 *Messenger and Advocate* expressed similar sentiments. (See Warren Parrish, "For the Messenger and Advocate"; and "The Abolitionists," *LDS Messenger and Advocate,* Apr. 1836, 2:295–296, 301.)

126. Genesis 17:1.

127. See Genesis 12:16; Romans 4; and Galatians 3.

free, then the master was to bring him unto the judges, boar his ear with an awl, and that man was "to serve him forever."[128] The conclusion I draw from this, is that this people were led and governed by revelation and if such a law was wrong God only is to be blamed, and abolitionists are not responsible.

Now, before proceeding any farther, I wish to ask one or two questions:—Were the apostles men of God, and did they preach the gospel? I have no [p. 290] doubt but those who believe the bible will admit these facts, and that they also knew the mind and will of God concerning what they wrote to the churches which they were instrumental in building up.

This being admitted, the matter can be put to rest without much argument, if we look at a few items in the New Testament. Paul says:

> "Servants, be obedient to them that are *your* masters according to the flesh, with fear and trembling, in singleness of your heart, as unto Christ: Not with eye service, as men-pleasers: but as the servants of Christ, doing the will of God from the heart: With good will doing service, as to the Lord, and not to men. Knowing that whatsoever good thing any man doeth, the same shall he receive of the Lord, whether *he be* bond or free. And, ye masters, do the same things unto them, forbearing threatening: knowing that your Master also is in heaven; neither is there respect of persons with him." Eph. 6:5, 6, 7, 8, 9.

Here is a lesson which might be profitable for all to learn, and the principle upon which the church was anciently governed, is so plainly set forth, that an eye of truth might see and understand. Here, certainly are represented the master and servant; and so far from instructions to the servant to leave his master, he is commanded to be in obedience,[129] as unto the Lord: the master in turn is required to treat them with kindness before God, understanding at the same time that he is to give an account.— The hand of fellowship is not withdrawn from him in consequence of having servants.

The same wri[t]er, in his first epistle to Timothy, the sixth chapter, and the five first verses, says:

> "Let as many servants as are under the yoke count their own masters worthy of all honor, that the name of God and *his* doctrine be not blasphemed. And they that have believing masters, let them not

---

128. Exodus 21:5–6.
129. See Colossians 3:22. In November 1835, JS advised missionaries to avoid preaching to slaves or servants without obtaining permission from their master. (Letter to the Elders of the Church, 16 Nov. 1835, pp. 58–59 herein.)

despise *them*, because they are brethren: but rather do *them* service, because they are faithful and beloved, partakers of the benefit These things teach and exhort. If any man teach otherwise, and consent not to wholesome words, *even* the words of our Lord Jesus Christ, and to the doctrine which is according to godliness: he is proud, knowing nothing but doting about questions and strifes of words, whereof cometh envy, strife, railings, evil surmisings, Perverse disputings of men of corrupt minds, and destitute of the truth, supposing that gain is godliness: from such withdraw thyself."

This is so perfectly plain, that I see no need of comment. The scripture stands for itself, and I believe that these men were better qualified to teach the will of God, than all the abolitionists in the world.

Before closing this communication, I beg leave to drop a word to the travelling elders: You know, brethren, that great responsibility rests upon you, and that you are accountable to God for all you teach the world. In my opinion, you will do well to search the book of Covenants,[130] in which you will see the belief of the church concerning masters and servants.[131] All men are to be taught to repent; but we have no right to interfere with slaves contrary to the mind and will of their masters. In fact, it would be much better and more prudent, not to preach at all to slaves, until after their masters are converted: and then, teach the master to use them with kindness, remembering that they are accountable to God, and that servants are bound to serve their masters, with singleness of heart, without murmuring. I do, most sincerely hope, that no one who is authorized from this church to preach the gospel, will so far depart from the scripture as to be found stirring up strife and sedition against our brethren of the South.[132]

---

130. That is, the Doctrine and Covenants.

131. An August 1835 declaration, which was included in the 1835 edition of the Doctrine and Covenants, outlined the church's belief regarding the proper role of government in society. Among twelve declarations was a clause asserting, "We do not believe it right to interfere with bond-servants, neither preach the gospel to, nor baptize them, contrary to the will and wish of their masters, nor to meddle with, or influence them in the least to cause them to be dissatisfied with their situations in this life, thereby jeopardizing the lives of men." In his article published in the same issue of the *Messenger and Advocate,* Warren Parrish observed, "God . . . teaches us to pay due defference and respect to magistrates, and rulers, and to be in subjection to the powers that be." (Declaration on Government and Law, ca. Aug. 1835, in *JSP,* D4:484 [D&C 134:12]; Warren Parrish, "For the Messenger and Advocate," *LDS Messenger and Advocate,* Apr. 1836, 2:295.)

132. A Lutheran synod in South Carolina in 1836 similarly protested against the "injustice of the interference or intermeddling of any religious or deliberative body with the subject of slavery or slaveholding." A clause in the August 1835 "Declaration on Government and Law" stated that "sedition and rebellion are unbecoming every citizen" and that the church did not "justify sedition nor conspiracy." (Gaustad, *Religious History of America,* 169; Declaration on Government and Law, ca. Aug. 1835, in *JSP,* D4:483 [D&C 134:5].)

Having spoken frankly and freely, I leave all in the hands of God, who will direct all things for his glory and the accomplishment of his work.

Praying that God may spare you to do much good in this life, I subscribe myself your brother in the Lord.

JOSEPH SMITH, jr.

———— ∾ ————

Charges against Wilkins Jenkins Salisbury and Charles Kelly Preferred to the Presidency of the High Council, 14 May 1836

Editorial Note

For the full text of this letter, see Minutes, 16 May 1836, p. 245 herein.

———— ∾ ————

Charges against Hannah Brown and Lucena Elliott Preferred to the Church Presidency, 16 May 1836

Editorial Note

For the full text of this letter, see Minutes, 16 May 1836, p. 247 herein.

———— ∾ ————

Minutes, 16 May 1836

Source Note

Kirtland high council, Minutes, Kirtland Township, Geauga Co., OH, 16 May 1836. Featured version copied [ca. 16 May 1836] in Minute Book 1, pp. 205–207; handwriting of Warren A. Cowdery; CHL. For more information on Minute Book 1, see Source Notes for Multiple-Entry Documents, p. 527 herein.

Historical Introduction

On 14 May 1836, Oliver Cowdery, a member of the church presidency, preferred charges against Wilkins Jenkins Salisbury and Charles Kelly of the Quorum of the Seventy for "unchristian like conduct." Two days later, a high council consisting of church leaders from Ohio and Missouri met in the House of the Lord in Kirtland, Ohio, to address Cowdery's allegations, during which JS testified against Salisbury, who was his brother-in-law. In addition to considering testimony for and against Salisbury, the council deliberated over a complaint against two women, Hannah Brown and Lucena Elliott.

Jenkins Salisbury, as he was generally known, joined the church in New York and migrated to Ohio with a group of converts from Fayette, New York, during the spring of 1831.[133] On 8 June 1831, he married JS's sister Katharine in Kirtland.[134] In 1834, Salisbury marched with JS and others to Missouri as part of the Camp of Israel expedition.[135] Salisbury apparently had a propensity for hard liquor, and according to Oliver Cowdery, he was excommunicated from the church sometime before December 1834.[136] He had regained his membership by early spring 1835, and on 1 March he was ordained to the office of seventy.[137] In the spring of 1836, Salisbury again faced church discipline. In the minutes of the high council meeting presented here, both JS and Hyrum Smith testified against their brother-in-law, accusing him of leaving his family without adequate food and firewood during harsh, wintry weather and suggesting that he had been unfaithful to his wife.[138]

In his complaint of 14 May, Cowdery also accused "Charels Kellogg" of "unchristian" behavior. There is no record of a Charles Kellogg belonging to the church in 1836. A later revision in JS's history indicates that the individual referred to in the minutes was actually Charles Kelly.[139] Kelly, like Salisbury, participated in the Camp of Israel expedition in 1834 and was ordained a seventy in March 1835.[140] Although there is no evidence the high council conducted a trial for Kelly during the 16 May meeting, the minutes close with a statement that the council unanimously "withdrew their fellowship" from him. The two other trials may have taken longer than expected, delaying Kelly's hearing; it is also possible that he failed to appear before the council and was therefore temporarily disfellowshipped.[141] On 23 May 1836, the high council did in fact hold a formal trial for Charles Kelly, in which he, like Salisbury the previous week, was excommunicated for leaving his family "in a destitute situation about the time of the solemn assembly."[142]

Little is known about the female subjects of Cowdery's 16 May complaint, Hannah Brown and Lucena Elliott, who were both tried in the afternoon session. Lucena was the teenage daughter of David and Mary Cahoon Elliott of Chagrin, Ohio. In late October,

---

133. Smith, *William Smith on Mormonism*, 19; Walker, "Katharine Smith Salisbury," 9–10.

134. Geauga County, OH, Probate Court, Marriage Records, 1806–1920, Marriage License, 1829–1833, 8 June 1831, microfilm 873,464, U.S. and Canada Record Collection, FHL.

135. Minutes, Discourse, and Blessings, 14–15 Feb. 1835, in *JSP*, D4:226.

136. In December 1834, Joseph Smith Sr. gave patriarchal blessings to his children and their spouses. While copying Salisbury's blessing into Patriarchal Blessing Book 1, Cowdery inscribed a short preface which read, "This man, at the time of receiving his blessing, was not a member of the church, having been cast out because of intemperance." (Joseph Smith Sr. to Wilkins Jenkins Salisbury, Blessing, 9 Dec. 1835 [1834], in Patriarchal Blessings, 1:7.)

137. Minutes and Blessings, 28 Feb.–1 Mar. 1835, in *JSP*, D4:259; Minutes, Discourse, and Blessing, 1 Mar. 1835, in *JSP*, D4:269.

138. Though it is not clear exactly when Salisbury left his family, the minutes indicate it was just before the solemn assembly on 30 March. According to JS's journal, Kirtland experienced an "uncommon storm for this season" on 22 March, which left Kirtland covered with a foot of snow; later entries suggest that temperatures remained cold enough for the snow to persist. (JS, Journal, 22–26 Mar. 1836, in *JSP*, J1:199.)

139. JS History, vol. B-1, 733.

140. Minutes, Discourse, and Blessings, 14–15 Feb. 1835, in *JSP*, D4:227; Minutes, Discourse, and Blessings, 1 Mar. 1835, in *JSP*, D4:268.

141. Minutes, 16 May 1836, pp. 245–247 herein.

142. Minute Book 1, 23 May 1836, p. 208.

the Elliott family became the subject of some controversy when William Smith accused the Elliott parents of beating and whipping their teenage daughter, presumably Lucena.[143] Nothing is known about the other defendant, Hannah Brown. The two women were also accused of "unchristianlike conduct"; the minutes indicate that they confessed to "telling . . . falsehoods."

The original copy of Oliver Cowdery's 14 May charges against Salisbury and Kelly, as well as his 16 May charges against Brown and Elliott, are no longer extant. Warren A. Cowdery later copied Oliver Cowdery's charges and the minutes of the disciplinary council's 16 May meeting into Minute Book 1.

Document Transcript

Kirtland May 16th. 1836, high council met in the house of the Lord. President S[idney] Rigdon Presiding

Counsellors

Jared Carter	Noah Packard
John Murdock	Joseph Kingsbury
Samuel H. Smith	Joseph Coe
⟨Prest.⟩ David Whitmer	John Gould
Josiah Butterfield	Isaac H. Bishop
James Foster	Truman Angel[l]

The following charge was read by President S. Rigdon

Kirtland May 14th 1836

To the presidency of the high council of the church of Latter Day Saints: I prefer a charge of unchristian like conduct against ⟨Elders⟩ [Wilkins] Jenkins Salisbury and Charels Kellogg [Charles Kelly].[144]

Your Obt. Servant
Oliver Cowdery

It was voted that one counsellor speak on each side of the case before the counsel. Prayer and some appropriate remarks were made by S. Rigdon, relative to the importance of the cases now defending.

Complainant now stated in short what he expected to prove and then called on J. Smith Junr. to testify. He stated that said Salisbury has not walked orderly, but has pursued such a course as to bring unnecessary persecution on him that he neglected his family [p. 205] left them in a starving ~~them~~ condition and without Wood just before the solemn assembly, when he ought to have been home. Question by complainant relative to the use of tobacco

---

143. Minutes, 29 Oct. 1835, pp. 28–29 herein.
144. See JS History, vol. B-1, 733.

⟨liquor.⟩ ~~&c.~~ ~~&c.~~ John Johnson called on to testify relative to the use of strong liquor says that defendant had taken some once or twice in a few mont[h]s past.[145] Hyrum Smith testifies that he left his family without sufficient wood to last more than two days, and no provision of any consequence in the house. He gave his <u>family</u> no intimation where he was going or when he should return, he also states that it is his full belief that when he went away he never intended to return.

J. Smith Jun[r.] Stated that Elder Wm. E. M[c]Lel[l]in had learned from defendant that he had been intimate with every woman he could since he belonged to the church David Elliot[t] States that he had not heard any complaaint of J. Salsibury since he belonged to the Seventy.

Testimony closed—

Elder J Carter spoke at some length touching the evidence setting it in a clear light, and pointing out the criminality before the court. Elder Coe Spoke on the other part and touched the case but lightly.

O. Cowdery Complainant spoke on part of the prosecution ⟨in⟩ setting the whole case in a clear light before the court according to the evidence addressed.

J. Salsibury then Spoke in his own defence confesses his strong propensity to talebearing[146] and drinking strong liquor, but denies the charge or unchastity to his wife, ~~stated~~ suggested by J. Smith Jun[r.] as stated by Wm. E. M[c]Lelin

President S. Rigdon then rose to give decision in the case before the council. He expressed his deep regret to have to act in this case. Guilt he said was fixed on the head of the defendant and not rebutted. [p. 206]

He therefore decided that Jenkins Salsibury can be ⟨no⟩ longer an Elder or a member in this church until there be a thorough reformation.— Council all concurred

adjourned for one hour—

W[arren] A. Cowdery ⎫
Clerk of Counsel ⎭

Met in the afternoon pursuant to adjournment when the following charge was read by President Sidney Rigdon.

---

145. John Johnson Sr. (and later his son, John Johnson Jr.) operated the Johnson Inn, located on the Kirtland Flats. Johnson Sr. was granted a license to keep a tavern on 5 April 1834. The account book of Gilbert Belnap, manager of and accountant for the inn, documents the inn's sale of alcohol, which continued through at least fall 1837. (Geauga Co., OH, Court of Common Pleas, Court Records, 1807–1904, vol. M, p. 184, 5 Apr. 1834, microfilm 20,277, U.S. and Canada Record Collection, FHL; Belnap, Account Book, CHL; Minute Book 1, 23 Oct. 1837.)

146. Webster's 1828 dictionary defines *talebearing* as "the act of informing officiously; communication of secrets maliciously." ("Talebearing," in *American Dictionary*.)

Kirtland Ohio May 16th 1836

To the Presidency of the High priesthood of the church of Latter Day-Saints, I prefer a charge of unchristianlike conduct against Sisters, Hannah Brown & Lucenia Elliot [Lucena Elliott], both members of this church

Oliver Cowdery

The counsellors who set on this case were as follows

Jared Carter—	Noah Packard
John Murdock	Joseph Kingsbury
S[amuel] H. Smith	Joseph Coe
John Johnson	George Morey
Josiah Butterfield	Isaac H. Bishop
Giles Cook	Truman Angel[l]

Defendants confessed having been guilty of telling a number of falsehoods, Counsel called on to give their assent to the confission [confession] and the sisters retain their standing in the church

They were reproved and permitted to retain their standing in the church.

Counsel then withdrew their fellowship from from Charles Kellogg an Elder in this Church by a unanimous vote—

dismissed by Prayer of Brother Coe. [p. 207]

———— ℰℐ ————

Minutes, 16 June 1836

Source Note

Kirtland high council, Minutes, Kirtland Township, Geauga Co., OH, 16 June 1836. Featured version copied [ca. 16 June 1836] in Minute Book 1, pp. 212–218; handwriting of Warren A. Cowdery; CHL. For more information on Minute Book 1, see Source Notes for Multiple-Entry Documents, p. 527 herein.

Historical Introduction

On 16 June 1836, JS met with members of the high council of Kirtland, Ohio, to consider accusations he had made against two church members, Preserved Harris and Isaac McWithy, for "a want of benevolence to the poor and charity to the church." Since he himself had brought the charges, JS may have recused himself from presiding at this meeting, though he actively participated. The council first considered Harris's case and then, after adjourning for an hour, returned and considered McWithy's case.

The cases heard on 16 June highlight two concerns church leaders had at the time: providing for the destitute Saints in Kirtland and supporting the church in Zion—that is, Missouri. Bishop Newel K. Whitney testified in both cases that the men had contributed very little to the poor, and he concluded that neither had borne an appropriate portion of the financial burden of caring for impoverished Kirtland church members.[147] Harris and McWithy were also tried for their reluctance to financially support church endeavors, including construction of the House of the Lord in Kirtland and purchasing land in Zion.[148] In the trials, JS specifically mentioned Harris's and McWithy's refusals to send money or move to Zion; Frederick G. Williams stated that such unwillingness had forced church leaders into debt. Sidney Rigdon reminded those present of the need to consecrate all they had to building Zion, adding that if they refused, they were "unworthy of the fellowship of the Saints."

During the meeting, the charges against Preserved Harris were deemed fully sustained and he was disfellowshipped. Isaac McWithy defended himself against the accusations, claiming he had acted charitably, and asked the council for forgiveness. No verdict was recorded in the minutes for McWithy's case.[149] Harris appears to have been unwilling to change his conduct; he accepted the council's decision and left the church. Although the extant minutes do not officially disfellowship McWithy, he also seems to have distanced himself from the church after this trial.

Throughout summer and fall 1836, JS and his fellow church leaders grappled with the competing priorities of providing for the poor Saints in Kirtland while raising money and support for Zion. Both concerns would again be addressed in December 1836, when a conference was held for the church leadership in Kirtland to consider the difficulties of additional impoverished church members moving there.[150]

Document Transcript

High Council Met in the Lord's house in Kirtland June ⟨16ᵗʰ⟩ 1836. S[idney] Rigdon and F[rederick] G. Williams Presiding.

Counsellors. J[oseph] Coe C[yrus] Smalling, Wm. Smith N[oah] Packard L. Shearman [Lyman Sherman], J[oseph] Kingsbury T[homas] Burdick J[ohn] Johnson, J[ohn] Smith J[ared] Carter H[enry] G. Sherwood J[osiah] Butterfield— Appointed Sylvester Smith Clerk

Council opened by prayer by S. Rigdon and the counsellors charged according to the law of God.

---

147. Whitney, as the bishop in Kirtland, had firsthand knowledge of both the needs of the Saints and the charity that had been provided. (Revelation, 4 Dec. 1831–A, in *JSP*, D2:146 [D&C 72:1–8]; see also Revelation, 22–23 Sept. 1832, in *JSP*, D2:289 [D&C 84].)

148. At an April 1836 meeting of F. G. Williams & Co., JS and Cowdery resolved to raise money to purchase land in Missouri. (Minutes, 2 Apr. 1836, p. 223 herein.)

149. Unfortunately, the minutes featured here are the last entries in the Kirtland high council records until May 1837. The handwriting of Warren A. Cowdery, who had acted as the scribe recording Minute Book 1 in 1836, ends with this entry, and Marcellus Cowdery's handwriting begins with the next entry, dated 11 May 1837. The entry for the 16 June 1836 meeting featured here is followed by a blank half page, possibly indicating room was left to record additional information on the case. (Minute Book 1, 16 June 1836–29 May 1837.)

150. Minutes, 22 Dec. 1836, pp. 322–323 herein.

The case of brother Preserved Harris was first considered.

He was charged by J. Smith <u>Junr</u> with a want of benevolence to the poor and charity to the church.

Bishop N[ewel] K. Whitney testifies that he does not know that Brother Harris has assisted him in relieving the poor or in assisting the church. He once gave 50. to send to Zion but thinks he has not been as liberal as others in these matters. Counsellors appointed three of the counsellors to speak on each side.

Elder J. Carter says he has been in a situation to know of the liberality of the Saints, being one of a committee to build the Lords house.[151] P. Harris donated some but too little for one who knows & intends to do his duty in this respect: seeing so many loud calls have been given for the rich to assist the poor,[152] he knows not that he has assisted.

There is a general complaint against him in the church, from Spiritual men, men of God, knows that some individuals have suffered for want of assistance, and he has not heard them thank God for Brother Harris' liberality as they did for the liberality of others.

Elder L◊◊◊ [Leonard] Rich says he lives near Brother Fisher[153] who has lived for the most part on the charity of the ~~church~~ saints. Many have assisted him [p. 212] in getting wood. Brother Harris was never present, although a public call had been given out frequently; he thinks the poor have generally been the most forward to assist the needy, he once gave a half a dollar to assist Eld. [Thomas B.] Marsh. Many of the poor gave much more. J. Coe says he is knowing to the accused giving about 35. some time since— in may, yet did not feel that he has been sufficiently liberal according to his circumstances and the wants of the brethren. J[onathan] Hampton says he is acquainted with brother Fisher's poverty. he took it upon himself to call for a donation to get him a cow, did not call on brother Harris nor receive any thing from him.

---

151. Jared Carter was appointed to receive contributions to help build the House of the Lord in April 1834. He and Hyrum Smith traveled to the eastern United States soliciting donations in August 1835. After returning from the trip, Carter gave a sermon rebuking church members for their unwillingness to donate and was brought before the Kirtland high council for correction. (Notice, *The Evening and the Morning Star*, Apr. 1834, 151; Minutes, 19 Sept. 1835, in *JSP*, D4:422–427.)

152. No contemporary calls for assistance of the poor are extant, but Newel K. Whitney was reminded of the need to care for the destitute in Kirtland in a blessing on 7 October 1835. Whitney with the help of other church members held a feast for the poor in January 1836. (Blessing to Newel K. Whitney, 7 Oct. 1835, pp. 20–21 herein; Note from Newel K. Whitney, 9 Jan. 1836, p. 138 herein; JS, Journal, 7–9 Jan. 1836, in *JSP*, J1:146.)

153. The identity and residence of "Brother Fisher" are not known. Four men with the surname Fisher were members of the church in Kirtland: Cyrus B. Fisher, Edmund Fisher, Jonathan Fisher, and Thomas G. Fisher. (Backman, *Profile*, 24–25.)

The counsellors proceeded to speak according to their impressions made by the testimony, 1 J. Smith 2ᵈ, J. Coe said the charge of a want of charity to the church was not sustained. The accusor called Brother Whitney to say whether the church was not poor, he answered yes, then says the accusor I have sustained the charge. 3ᵈ J. Carter, 4ᵗʰ C. Smalling 5.ᵗʰ H. G. Sherwood & 6ᵗʰ Wm. Smith. When the counsellors appointed to speak were through, the accusor rose & spoke concerning the sin of a want of charity to the the poor and quoted several instances to prove the fact, &c. such as feed the hungry, clothe the naked administer to the wants of the widow and fatherless, &c. He also testified that himself in Co. with Pres. O[liver] Cowdery did once call on Brother Harris for a donation to assist the poor & gave him a plan which (to me said he) was the most noble, Which was to send up money to help build up Zion, purchase land &c.¹⁵⁴ He referred us to his wife,¹⁵⁵ we could not reconcile her to the plan, which we laid before her. H said that he had promised her that [p. 213] if she would come to this place, he would settle down and not remove again, & therefore he could not help us as we wished in building up Zion. Whe[n] he P. Smith had closed his remarks. The accused arose and spoke for himself. says he has a considerable property in his hand has helped the poor some, got his property by hard work, Some that are liberal with others property, do not labor to get much to give to the poor themselves: he may have failed in some things, but has done as he felt before God.

The case was then submitted.

P. F. G. Williams arose and said the case before us is an important one. The church poor, Zion to be built and we have not means to do it unless the rich assist. & because the rich have not assisted, the heads of the church have to suffer and are now suffering under severe embarrassments and are much in debt.¹⁵⁶ In regard to the charge preferred against brother P. Harris by P. J. S. ᴶᵘⁿʳ· it is my opinion they are fully sustained to the satisfaction of the council.

President S. Rigdon arose and said many things concerning the law of God upon the subject of property,¹⁵⁷ showing clearly that it is the duty of the saints to offer their all to the will of God for the building up of the Kingdom & for

---

154. Financial needs related to Missouri included money to purchase land, help poor Saints, and fund church members migrating from Kirtland. (See Prayer, 23 Oct. 1835, pp. 23–25 herein; Minutes, 2 Apr. 1836, pp. 222–224 herein; and Minutes, 22 Dec. 1836, pp. 321–323 herein.)

155. Nancy Warren Harris.

156. The church was in debt from building the House of the Lord, purchasing goods in New York, and printing the Doctrine and Covenants and Book of Mormon. (See Revelation, 23 Apr. 1834, in JSP, D4:19–31 [D&C 104]; Prayer, 23 Oct. 1835, pp. 23–25 herein; Minutes and Prayer of Dedication, 27 Mar. 1836, pp. 188–210 herein [D&C 109].)

157. Revelations commanding the Saints to consecrate their property to the church and receive inheritances in land were dictated in February and August 1831 and in November 1832. (Revelation, 9 Feb. 1831,

the sustenance of the poor, of property, life & all that he possesses, & he that is not willing to make this sacrifice cannot be considered a saint of the most High God & unworthy of the fellowship of the Saints, Christ suffered the loss of all things, that he might save all, We must follow him and be made perfect through sufferings also, or lose all.[158] As to the charges preferred against brother Harris it is the decision of this council that they are fully sustained and that the hand of fellowship is with[p. 214]drawn from him until he shall see that the course he is pursuing is contrary to the gospel of Jesus.

The decision of the presidency was concurred in by the 12 councellors unanimously and the council adjourned for one hour.

P.M. met according to adjournment in the council room and proceeded to examine a complaint preferred by Prest. J. Smith Junr against Eld. Isaac McWithy for a want of benevolence to the poor and charity to the church. Voted that the six counsellors who did not speak in the former case take the lead in the investigation of this case. Bishop N. K. Whitney says that Elder McWithy has never given any thing for the poor to his knowledge though there may be many in the church who stand in need of the charity of the Saints, and he thinks Eld. McWithy has not born his proportion of the burden of the poor and this complaint is pretty general in the church. Elder J. Hampton says, that he wished to obtain money to buy a cow for brother Fisher, who had fallen from a house and sustained a great injury personally and stood in need, he called on the accused for help for this poor brother, but he only received excuses &c. but no help from him. & it was returned for he did not with all his exertions get enough to buy a cow, and further said that he could more easily get two dollars from a poor man than one from the rich. He considerd Eld. McWithy to be rich. Eld. Josiah Butterfield says that he heard the accused say that he brought two thousand dollars from the East.[159] Prest. J[oseph] Smith Senr says that he blessed the accused with a patriarchal blessing but thinks that he received nothing from [p. 215] him for the poor as it was usual for him on such occasions.[160] Eld. Edmund Bosley says he thinks from what he told him, he was worth at least two thousand dollars. Eld. Rich says he has been

---

in *JSP,* D1:251–252 [D&C 42:30–36]; Revelation, 1 Aug. 1831, in *JSP,* D2:17 [D&C 58:35–36]; Letter to William W. Phelps, 27 Nov. 1832, in *JSP,* D2:319–320.)

158. See Mark 8:34–36.

159. Isaac McWithy was born in New York and lived in towns in Genesee County before moving to Kirtland. (1820 U.S. Census, Covington, Genesee Co., NY, 83; 1830 U.S. Census, Bennington, Genesee Co., NY, 136[A]; Genesee Co., NY, Deed Records, 1792–1901, vol. 29, p. 337, 7 Apr. 1832, microfilm 987,179, U.S. and Canada Record Collection, FHL.)

160. Patriarch Joseph Smith Sr. was to be paid ten dollars a week by the church for the time he spent giving patriarchal blessings. Recipients of patriarchal blessings paid a fee to have them written in Patriarchal Blessing Book 1, and they may have also been charged for personal copies of the blessing. Here

acquainted with the accused for several years before and after he came into the church and thinks he has always been two covetous he has been compelled to doubt at times whether he was a full believer in the Latter Day work in consequence, yet he had sometimes known him to give a little, but it always came hard. He had a considerable property or had given it to his unbelieving son! thinks that he does not deal with that liberally as a man of God should do. He once took a dollar from brother Hadlock for the use of a few dollars a little time but afterwards restored four dollars fearing the fulfilment of a prophecy delivered against him at the dedication.[161] that requested security of him and Eld. Lyon[162] for about $,.20. whe [which?] he obtained of him for the expenses which they bore in taking care of Eld. Coltrin who had the small pox at Eld. Lyon's The Elders frequently complaned of his want of liberality. Brother Joel Haskins says, that his circumstances are pretty low, has one cow & works for bread. A brother lent a horse & waggon to him to go to Zion. The accused has never given him any bread or other things necessary. he lives in a small cabin on his farm and occupy a little yard for vines, he knows not whether he will charge him for it or not. It is less than a quarter of an acre. He expects to pay him for pasturing a cow. Accused said he wished to be a a steward over his own and rather felt ~~indignant~~ ⟨repugnant⟩ at the idea of giving all for the good of the church [p. 216] Never saw him give any thing for the help of the poor. thinks he is in good temporal circumstances.

Wm. Smith says he heard the accused say that he did not believe that a Saint ever accused his enemies. Witness[163] labored to show him his error, he said he did not ~~believing~~ believe in this kind of interpreting scripture. Eld A Brown says he called on the accused for help for a poor brother and could get none but observed that the accused manifested a kind of angry spirit rather than a spirit of love; he frequently heard complaints against him for not assisting the poor, he is considerable rich, he once gave Eld Green about six dollars considered him to be a covetous man. The testimony here closed and the counsellors were here called upon to speak. 1.ˢᵗ Joseph Kingsbury considered the case clearly proven according to the nature of the charges. 2ᵈ Noah Packard considered that he was liberal in some things but still the case was clear and the charges

---

Joseph Smith Sr. suggests that he often received donations for the poor from church members when he gave patriarchal blessings; no other extant records mention this. (Minutes, 14 Sept. 1835, in *JSP*, D4:414.)

161. Likely a reference to the dedication of the House of the Lord in Kirtland on 27 March 1836. (See Minutes and Prayer of Dedication, 27 Mar. 1836, pp. 188–210 herein [D&C 109].)

162. Probably Aaron C. Lyon, who received an elder's license on 3 June 1836. Aaron Lyon and Leonard Rich preached and proselytized together in Warsaw, Genesee County, New York, in the winter of 1832–1833. ("Conference," *LDS Messenger and Advocate*, June 1836, 2:336; *JSP*, D3:431n103.)

163. William Smith.

fully sustained. J. Smith Senr thought the case a clear one. Leonard Rich thought the case clear. Josiah Butterfield, clear, Thomas Burdick also concurred in opinion with his brother counsellors. The accusor arose and spoke as he felt stating that he in company with Prest. O. Cowdery called upon the accused for money to send up to Zion but, could get none, afterwards saw him and asked him if he would sell his farm. He at first seemed willing, he wished to build up Zion He plead excuse in consequence of his liberality to the poor. We offered him $.3000. for his farm. would give him $.400. or 500. to take him to Zion and settle him there and obligation for the remainder with good security, and interest. He went & [p. 217] told father Lyon that we demanded all his property a[nd] so we lost 4 or 500. dollars because the accused told him such a story he calculated to keep it himself The accused then arose and said it was the first time he had been called upon to clear himself before a High Council. He complained of being called contrary to the rules of the Gospel before the council The President decided that as the case was now before the council it could not now be urged but should have been made in the beginning. He plead that he had relieved the wants of the poor. and did so many good things that he was astonished that he should hear such things as he had heard today, because he did not give all he had got to one man. If he had done wrong he asked forgiveness of God and the church. [p. 218]

———— ∾ ————

Application for Land Patent, 22 June 1836

Historical Introduction

In early summer 1836, agents acting on behalf of JS purchased land in what became Caldwell County, Missouri. Many Latter-day Saints in Missouri had been exiled from their homes twice in the last three years. In 1833, Saints living in Jackson County fled to neighboring Clay County seeking refuge, and from 1834 to 1836 additional church members immigrated there at the encouragement of church leaders, who were hoping for an eventual return to Jackson County.[164] In 1834, Saints began acquiring land for church settlements in the southern and eastern areas of Clay County.[165] By the summer of 1836, church members

---

164. See Letter from William W. Phelps, 6–7 Nov. 1833, in *JSP*, D3:336–341; Letter from William W. Phelps, 14 Nov. 1833, in *JSP*, D3:343; Letter from Edward Partridge, between 14 and 19 Nov. 1833, in *JSP*, D3:344–351; Revelation, 22 June 1834, in *JSP*, D4:76 [D&C 105:28–29]; and Letter to Lyman Wight and Others, 16 Aug. 1834, in *JSP*, D4:102–108.

165. Some church members rented land from original settlers in Clay County. Other church members purchased land from settlers or from the government through land patents or preemption claims that allowed them to live on the land before paying for it. (See Parkin, "History of the Latter-day Saints in Clay County," 200–208.)

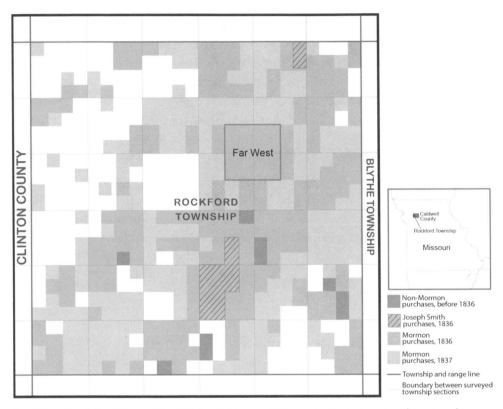

Far West, Rockford Township, Caldwell County, Missouri, 1836–1837. Amid tensions between church members and their neighbors in Clay County, Missouri, church leaders began to scout new locations for a permanent settlement for the Latter-day Saints. By June 1836 church leaders made initial land purchases in northwest Missouri in what would become Rockford (and later Mirabile) Township, Caldwell County. On 8 August 1836 John Whitmer and William W. Phelps made a substantial purchase in the township for a city that would become the church's new gathering place in Missouri, called Far West. In June and September 1836, agents acting on behalf of Joseph Smith applied for three land patents, totaling approximately 560 acres in the area. From 1836 to 1837, church members living in Missouri and Ohio purchased large swaths of land in and around Far West, though it was not an exclusively Mormon settlement.

owned nearly one thousand acres in the county.[166] Facing their neighbors' growing unrest over the continuing influx of Mormons and fears that the church was making Clay County a more permanent gathering place, in May 1836 church leaders began scouting new locations north and east of Clay County where the Saints could settle.[167]

After returning to Missouri from Kirtland, Ohio, in early May 1836, Missouri bishop Edward Partridge and William W. Phelps led the effort to locate new settlements.[168] Phelps wrote to Oliver Cowdery on 2 June that he had been "constantly engaged in viewing the country" since his return; Phelps had completed two tours of northern Missouri with Partridge by the time he wrote to Cowdery. The two men first traveled through northern Clay County into Clinton County and northern Ray County, eventually locating a desirable "mill seat on Shoal creek" approximately thirty-five miles northeast of Liberty, Missouri.[169] On their second tour, Partridge and Phelps—accompanied by Isaac Morley and John Corrill—scouted available land north of Ray County. Corrill then purchased seven eighty-acre lots in what became Caldwell County and an additional thirteen lots in the same area shortly thereafter. The Missouri church "made preperations to begin a settlement upon the new purchase" and hoped to move to these new areas before July 1836, but they were delayed by increasing tension in Clay County and by impending lawsuits.[170]

Although JS did not travel to Missouri in 1836 or make land purchases there himself, he appears to have appointed agents, including John Corrill, to purchase land in his name. On 22 June 1836, Corrill purchased land for himself and appears to have submitted applications for Cowdery and JS.[171] Two applications were made in JS's name for around 478 acres of

---

166. Parkin, "History of the Latter-day Saints in Clay County," 207.

167. For more on the tensions in Clay County, see Historical Introduction to Letter to John Thornton and Others, 25 July 1836, pp. 258–260 herein; and William W. Phelps et al., Liberty, MO, to Daniel Dunklin, 7 July 1836, copy, William W. Phelps, Collection of Missouri Documents, CHL.

168. Partridge, Phelps, and other Missouri church leaders had traveled to Kirtland in early 1835 and remained there until the dedication of the House of the Lord and the solemn assembly held in spring 1836. (Partridge, Journal, 27 Mar.–6 May 1836; William W. Phelps, Liberty, MO, to Oliver Cowdery, 2 June 1836, in *LDS Messenger and Advocate,* July 1836, 2:341.)

169. Partridge, Journal, 6 May–29 June 1836; William W. Phelps, Liberty, MO, to Oliver Cowdery, 2 June 1836, in *LDS Messenger and Advocate,* July 1836, 2:340–341.

170. Partridge, Journal, 6 May–29 June 1836. Partridge wrote that a "mob began to appear, and our suits were coming on, at Richmond on the 6th July, which both together made us delay moving to the North." On 26 May 1835, Judge John F. Ryland granted a change of venue from Jackson County, Missouri, to Ray County, Missouri, for two lawsuits growing out of the violent expulsion of Mormons from Jackson County in 1833; Phelps and Partridge were involved in both lawsuits. (Partridge, Journal, 6 May–29 June 1836; *JSP,* H2:227n101; for more on the Saints' move from Clay County, see Historical Introduction to Letter to John Thornton and Others, 25 July 1836, pp. 258–260 herein; and Historical Introduction to Letter to William W. Phelps and Others, 25 July 1836, pp. 268–269 herein.)

171. It is likely that JS appointed Corrill and provided him with a power of attorney, though no documents giving power of attorney to Corrill or another agent are extant for the Missouri land transactions. A power of attorney was necessary for an agent to purchase land and conduct business for another individual. In his 1839 redress petition, Corrill stated, "Your petitioner further testifies that he acted as Agent, and entered some 2000 acres of land lying in Caldwell county for, and took Duplicates in the names of Joseph Smith Jun, Hirum [Hyrum] Smith & Oliver Cowdery." Corrill may have acted as the agent who

land in what would become Caldwell County.[172] In order to purchase the land, which was owned by the federal government, Corrill traveled to the land office in Lexington, Missouri, to apply for the patents. Individuals interested in obtaining land could satisfy the legal requirements in one of three ways: making a cash payment, presenting a bounty warrant given for military service, or claiming preemption rights through proof of residency and improvements on the land the individual wanted to purchase.[173] The applications submitted by Corrill were completed by cash payment.

Records exist for both land applications Corrill made for JS on 22 June 1836, but only the records for the second of the two land purchases (the purchase represented here) contain the federally approved patent, granting title to the land, that was sent with the application. The certificate and receipt featured here represent JS's application for the second purchase. The first receipt indicates that the land claim was recorded by the register's office, and the second verifies that payment for the land was received by the receiver's office. The application forms completed by the register and receiver were each assigned a number, and together they formed a land entry case file, which was sent by the Lexington, Missouri, land office to the General Land Office in Washington DC. Applications were then reviewed in Washington; if a case was found valid, with no conflicting claims to the land, the patent was approved and returned to the local land office to be given to the applicant as a deed of title.[174] JS's patent for this land was processed by the federal land office in September 1838.[175]

I. Register's Office, Certificate
Source Note

Register's Office, Certificate, to JS, Lexington, Lafayette Co., MO, 22 June 1836; printed form with manuscript additions in unidentified handwriting; signature of Finis Ewing; Land Entry Case File 7874, Record Group 49, Records of the Bureau of Land Management, National Archives and Records Administration, Washington DC. Includes docket.

One leaf, measuring 6½ × 8 inches (17 × 20 cm). The document appears to have been cut out of an unknown ledger, with the left and bottom sides of the recto unevenly cut. The document is folded in half. Two diagonal cuts in the shape of an "X" were made through the signature of Finis Ewing.

---

purchased land for Hyrum Smith in May and early June 1836. These land purchases were the earliest made by a church member in what would become Caldwell and Daviess counties. (John Corrill, Affidavit, Quincy, IL, 9 Jan. 1840, photocopy, Material Relating to Mormon Expulsion from Missouri, CHL; Johnson and Romig, *Index to Early Caldwell County,* 202; Land Patents for Hyrum Smith, Caldwell Co., MO, nos. 7548, 7549, 7550, 7551, 7552, General Land Office Records, Bureau of Land Management, U.S. Department of the Interior; for more on the appointment of an agent through a power of attorney, see Power of Attorney to Hyrum Smith, 5 Sept. 1837, pp. 433–437 herein.)

172. The first application for JS, assigned the land entry case file number 7873, involved a patent for four hundred acres of land in Rockford Township, in what would become Caldwell County. (Land Entry Case File no. 7873, in Record Group 49, Records of the Bureau of Land Management, National Archives and Records Administration, Washington DC.)

173. Hawkins, *Research in the Land Entry Files of the General Land Office,* 2.

174. Hawkins, *Research in the Land Entry Files of the General Land Office,* 2–3.

175. Land Patents for JS, Caldwell Co., MO, nos. 7873 and 7874, General Land Office Records, Bureau of Land Management, U.S. Department of the Interior. For more on the process and potential delays in obtaining land patents, see Rohrbough, *Land Office Business,* 221–249.

The docket on the verso is in the handwriting of E. M. Ryland and reads, "7874 | Lexington | Pat[ent] dat[e] 7th Nov. 1837 | 7th Sept 1838 | Rec[orde]d Vol. 18 | Page 448".

This document and a receiver's office receipt were sent together to the General Land Office in Washington DC for approval, then returned to the Land Office in Lexington, Missouri, and filed there. Records from the Lexington Land Office were relocated to the Bureau of Land Management when the Lexington Land Office closed in 1922. By 1953 the land records held by the Bureau of Land Management had been transferred to the National Archives and Records Administration in Washington DC.

Document Transcript

[176] No 7874

LAND OFFICE, *At Lexington Missouri.*
REGISTER'S OFFICE, June 22nd 183 6 .
IT IS HEREBY CERTIFIED, that in pursuance of law, Joseph Smith Jr
of Ohio county
has this day purchased of the Register of this office, the West half of Southeast Quarter *of section No.* 22 *of township No.* Fifty six *north of the base line,* ([blank] *of the* [blank] *river) of range No.* Twenty nine *west of the fifth principal meridian, containing* Seventy eight *acres and* 56 *hundredths,*[177] *at the rate of $* 1.25 [178] *per acre, amounting in the whole to $* 98.20 *for which the said* Joseph Smith Jr *has made payment in full agreeably to law.*

NOW THEREFORE, BE IT KNOWN, *that on presentation of this certificate to the Commissioner of the General Land Office, the said* Joseph Smith Jr *shall be entitled to receive a patent for the land above described.*

[179] Finis Ewing *Register.*

II. Receiver's Office, Receipt
Source Note

Receiver's Office, Receipt, to JS, Lexington, Lafayette Co., MO, 22 June 1836; printed form with manuscript additions in the handwriting of E. M. Ryland; signature and endorsement in handwriting of E. M. Ryland; Land Entry Case File 7874; Record Group 49, Records of the Bureau of Land Management, National Archives and Records Administration, Washington DC.

One leaf, measuring 4½ × 7¾ inches (11 × 20 cm). The document appears to have been cut out of an unknown ledger, with the left and bottom sides of the recto unevenly cut. The document was folded once at the bottom third of the leaf. Two diagonal cuts in the shape of an "X" were made through the signature of E. M. Ryland.

---

176. TEXT: Manuscript additions in unidentified handwriting.

177. Although each quarter should have been eighty acres, it appears that the lot Corrill purchased for JS was slightly smaller than the intended acreage.

178. The Land Act of 1820 set a standard price for government-owned land at $1.25 per acre. (See An Act Making Further Provision for the Sale of Public Lands [24 Apr. 1820], *Public Statutes at Large,* 16th Cong., 1st Sess., chap. 51, p. 566, sec. 3.)

179. TEXT: Signature of Finis Ewing.

This document and a register's office certificate were sent together to the General Land Office in Washington DC for approval, then returned to the Land Office in Lexington, Missouri, and filed there. Records from the Lexington Land Office were relocated to the Bureau of Land Management when the Lexington Land Office closed in 1922. By 1953 the land records held by the Bureau of Land Management had been transferred to the National Archives and Records Administration in Washington DC.

Document Transcript

No. [180] _7874_

LAND OFFICE, *Lexington, Missouri.*

RECEIVER'S OFFICE, _June 22nd_ 183_6_ .

RECEIVED from _Joseph Smith Jr._ *of* _[blank]_ *county* _Ohio_ *the sum of* _Ninety eight & 20/100_ *dollars, being in full for* _W[est] 1/2 of the s.E. [southeast] 1/4 of section no Twenty two_ *township No.* _Fifty six_ (_[blank]_) *north of the base line and west of the fifth principal meridian, range No.* _Twenty nine_ *containing* _seventy eight & 56/100_ *acres, at the rate of $* _1²⁵_ *per acre.*

$ _98.20_

E M Ryland *Receiver.*

⟨Silver $98.20⟩[181]

———— ⌘ ————

Letter to John Thornton and Others, 25 July 1836

Source Note

Sidney Rigdon, JS, Oliver Cowdery, Frederick G. Williams, and Hyrum Smith, Letter, Kirtland Township, Geauga Co., OH, to John Thornton, Peter Rogers, Andrew Robertson, James Thompson, William Wood, Woodson Moss, James Hughs, David R. Atchison, and Alexander Doniphan, Clay Co., MO, 25 July 1836. Featured version published in "Kirtland, Geauga County, Ohio," Latter Day Saints' Messenger and Advocate, *Aug. 1836, 2:355–359. For more information on* Latter Day Saints' Messenger and Advocate, *see Source Notes for Multiple-Entry Documents, p. 527 herein.*

Historical Introduction

After disbanding the Camp of Israel in Clay County, Missouri, in 1834, JS encouraged Latter-day Saints to emigrate there.[182] The revelation calling for the discontinuance of the camp directed the Saints "to gather up the strength of my house" into the county, and a letter JS wrote the following August instructed church leaders in Missouri to "prevail on

---

180. TEXT: Manuscript additions in handwriting of E. M. Ryland.

181. This endorsement, recorded on the verso of the certificate, indicates that payment for the land was made in silver coins.

182. See "Joseph Smith Documents from April 1834 through September 1835," in *JSP,* D4:xix–xxii.

the churches to gather to those regions and situate themselves to be in readiness" to return to Jackson County by the fall of 1836.[183]

By summer 1836, more than 100 Latter-day Saint families joined the 250 families already residing in Clay County, many of whom had been forced out of Jackson County in 1833.[184] With this immigration, unrest grew among the non-Mormon citizens of the county. The factors that gave rise to the tension in Clay County had marked similarities to the causes of earlier violence in Jackson County. In late 1833 and early 1834, Clay County residents who were sympathetic to the Mormon exiles had agreed to give them temporary asylum after their troubles in Jackson County. By mid-1836, however, because of the rapid and increasing immigration of church members to the county and their extensive land purchases, non-Mormon Clay County residents feared that their county was becoming the new Zion, or permanent church center.[185] They also accused Mormons of opposing slavery and causing problems for slaveholders, as well as having unauthorized communications with American Indians in the area to turn them against non-Mormon whites.[186]

By late June 1836, violence broke out between the communities. Anderson Wilson, a Clay County citizen who organized forces against the Saints, wrote, "There were Several outrages Committed on the night of the 28 [June 1836]. Six of our party went to a mormon town. Several mormons Cocked their guns & Swore they would Shoot them. After Some Scrimiging two white men took a mormon out of Company & give him 100 lashes & it is thought he will Die of this Beating."[187] Missouri Latter-day Saint Joseph Holbrook remembered that in late spring 1836, "it appeared that war was even at our doors."[188] Believing that the Mormons' increased immigration, efforts to redeem Zion, and apparent sympathy for slaves and Indians would lead to bloodshed and "civil war" in Clay County, local citizens and community leaders met in Liberty to devise a resolution to the impending conflict.

At the meeting, held 29 June 1836 at the Liberty courthouse, Clay County citizens organized a "Committee of nine." This body was composed of community leaders and included John Thornton, a Democrat and former judge in Ray County who served as the committee chair, and three attorneys previously employed by the Saints during their efforts to obtain redress and justice for their expulsion from Jackson County—David R.

---

183. JS, Journal, 30 Mar. 1836, in *JSP*, J1:215; Revelation, 22 June 1834, in *JSP*, D4:75–77 [D&C 105:24, 27–31]; Letter to Lyman Wight and Others, 16 Aug. 1834, in *JSP*, D4:106; Minutes, 2 Apr. 1836, pp. 222–224 herein.

184. Murdock, Journal, 27 July 1836; Parkin, "History of the Latter-day Saints in Clay County," 269, 318–319.

185. Lewis, "Mormon Land Ownership," 25–28; Parkin, "History of the Latter-day Saints in Clay County," 318–319; Berrett, *Sacred Places*, 4:162–190.

186. "Public Meeting," *LDS Messenger and Advocate*, Aug. 1836, 2:359–360; "Another Mormon Invasion," *Daily Missouri Republican*, 17 May 1836, [2]; see also "Joseph Smith Documents from February 1833 through March 1834," in *JSP*, D3:xvii–xxxii.

187. Anderson Wilson and Emelia Wilson, Clay Co., MO, to Samuel Turrentine, Orange Co., NC, 4 July 1836, Wilson Family Papers, Southern Historical Collection, Louis Round Wilson Special Collections Library, University of North Carolina, Chapel Hill; see also Parkin, "History of the Latter-day Saints in Clay County," 242–279.

188. Holbrook, Reminiscences, 41.

Atchison, William T. Wood, and Alexander Doniphan.[189] The committee wrote a preamble and resolutions to present to the Saints. The preamble expressed residents' belief that a crisis had arrived and that if it was not resolved, harmony, good order, and peace would no longer exist in the county. The committee listed what they believed were the county residents' collective complaints against the Saints and requested as a solution that church members stop immigrating to the county and completely withdraw from it.[190] The resolutions detailed how they would negotiate the departure of the Latter-day Saints from the county.[191]

While the Clay County committee did not intend to include JS as part of these negotiations, William W. Phelps, assistant church president in Missouri, forwarded to him the committee's preamble and resolutions, which had been published in a local newspaper. The letter featured here is the response JS and other members of the church presidency in Kirtland wrote directly to the committee led by John Thornton. The letter from the Kirtland leaders countered rumors about the Missouri Saints and explained their defensive actions, addressing issues that had spurred tensions leading to the request for them to vacate the county. This letter was sent along with another letter JS and the other church leaders wrote to Phelps and the Missouri church leaders on the same date.[192] Wording in the Phelps letter indicates that it was written after the letter featured here. Both letters were apparently sent to Phelps, with the intent that he pass on the letter addressed to Thornton and the rest of the committee. Both letters were printed in the August issue of the *Latter Day Saints' Messenger and Advocate;* the printed copies are the only known extant versions.

Document Transcript

Kirtland, Geauga County, Ohio,
JULY 25, 1836.

To John Thornton, Esq., Peter Rogers, Esq., Andrew Robertson, Esq., James T. V. Thompson, Esq., Col. William T. Wood, Doct Woodson J. Moss, James M. Hughs, Esq., David R. Atchison, Esq. and A[lexander] W. Doniphan, Esq.

GENTLEMEN,—

We have just perused, with feelings of deep interest, an article in the "Far West," printed at Liberty, Clay County, Mo. containing the proceedings of a public meeting of the citizens of said county,[193] upon the subject of an excitement now prevailing among you occasioned, either from false reports against

---

189. "Public Meeting," *LDS Messenger and Advocate,* Aug. 1836, 353–355; "Public Meeting," *Far West* (Liberty, MO), 30 June 1836; see also Historical Introduction to Letter to John Thornton and Others, 25 June 1834, in *JSP,* D4:85–86.

190. "Public Meeting," *LDS Messenger and Advocate,* Aug. 1836, 2:353–355.

191. For the response of the Saints in Clay County, see Historical Introduction to Letter to William W. Phelps and Others, 25 July 1836, pp. 268–269 herein.

192. Letter to William W. Phelps and Others, 25 July 1836, pp. 268–271 herein.

193. Church leaders at Kirtland read the report of the proceedings of the 29 June 1836 meeting in Liberty as printed in the newspaper *Far West,* which they received from Phelps. The proceedings were reprinted alongside the letters to Phelps and Thornton in *LDS Messenger and Advocate,* Aug. 1836, 2:353–361.

the church of Latter Day Saints, or from the fact, that said church is [p. 355] dangerous to the welfare of your country, and will, if suffered among you, cause the ties of peace and friendship, so desirable among all men, to be burst asunder, and bring war and desolation upon your now pleasant homes.

Under existing circumstances, while rumor is afloat with her accustomed cunning, and while public opinion is fast setting, like a flood-tide against the members of said church, we cannot but admire the candor with which your preamble and resolutions were clothed, as presented to the meeting of the citizens of Clay county, on the 29th of June last.[194] Though, as you expressed in your report to said meeting—"We do not contend that we have the least right, under the constitution and laws of the country, to expel them by force,"—yet communities may be, at times, unexpectedly thrown into a situation, when wisdom, prudence, and that first item in nature's law, SELF-DEFENCE, would dictate that the responsible and influential part should step forward and guide the public mind in a course to save difficulty, preserve rights, and spare the innocent blood from staining that soil so dearly purchased with the fortunes and lives of our fathers. And as you have come forward as "mediators," to prevent the effusion of blood, and save disasters consequent upon civil war,[195] we take this opportunity to present to you, though strangers, and through you, if you wish, to the people of Clay county, our heart-felt gratitude for every kindness rendered our friends in affliction, when driven from their peaceful homes, and to yourselves, also, for the prudent course in the present excited state of your community.[196] But, in doing this, justice to ourselves, as communicants of that church to which our friends belong, and duty towards them as acquaintances and former fellow citizens, require us to say something to exonerate them from the foul charges brought against them, to

194. See "Public Meeting," *LDS Messenger and Advocate*, Aug. 1836, 2:353–354; and "Public Meeting," *Far West* (Liberty, MO), 30 June 1836.

195. The resolutions of the committee expressed the fear that "the horrors and desolations of a civil war" would befall Clay County if Mormons did not stop migrating to the county. ("Public Meeting," *LDS Messenger and Advocate*, Aug. 1836, 2:354.)

196. Speaking of the "excited state" of the Clay County community, Latter-day Saint Drusilla Hendricks, who relocated from Simpson County, Kentucky, in spring 1836, recalled, "Our wagons, some five or six in number, had stirred up the mob spirit for fear the Mormons would come and take away their place and nation." On 4 July 1836, Clay County citizen Anderson Wilson described the unrest in a letter, stating that the Saints "have been flocking in here faster than ever and making great talk what they would do. . . . We are to Submit to a mormon government or trample under foot the laws of our Co[u]ntry. To go away was to Just give up all for if emigration once Begun none would buy our land but mormons and they would have it at their own price So we were resolved . . . [to] fight by each others Side & die like Ishmael." (Hendricks, Reminiscences, 17; Anderson Wilson and Emelia Wilson, Clay Co., MO, to Samuel Turrentine, Orange Co., NC, 4 July 1836, Wilson Family Papers, Southern Historical Collection, Louis Round Wilson Special Collections Library, University of North Carolina, Chapel Hill.)

deprive them of their constitutional privileges, and drive them from the face of society:

They have been charged, in consequence of the whims and vain notions of some few uninformed, with claiming that upper country, and that ere long they were to possess it, at all hazards, and in defiance of all consequences.—[197] This is unjust and far from a foundation, in truth. A thing not expected, not looked for, not desired by this society, as a people, and where the idea could have originated is unknown to us—We do not, neither did we ever insinuate a thing of this kind, or hear it from the leading men of the society, now in your country. There is nothing in all our religious faith to warrant it, but on the contrary, the most strict injunctions to live in obedience to the laws, and follow peace with all men.[198] And we doubt not, but a recurrence to the Jackson county difficulties, with our friends, will fully satisfy you, that at least, heretofore, such has been the course followed by them. That instead of fighting for their own rights, they have sacrificed them for a season, to wait the redress guaranteed in the law, and so anxiously looked for at a time distant from this. We have been, & are still, clearly under the conviction, that had our friends been disposed, they might have maintained their possessions in Jackson county. They might have resorted to the same barbarous means with their neighbors, throwing down dwellings, threatening lives, driving innocent women and children from their homes, and thereby have annoyed their ene-

---

197. Joseph Thorp, a Clay County resident who was sometimes a friendly employer of the Saints, said, "The poor, deluded mortals, with all their experience in Jackson, began to tell the citizens of Clay the same old tale; that this country was theirs by gift of the Lord, and it was folly for them to improve their lands, they would not enjoy the fruits of their labor; that it would finally fall into the hands of the saints. . . . This kind of talk, with their insolence and impudent behavior, so enraged the citizens that they began to consult about the best course to take to rid themselves of a set of religious fanatics, for they found that their faith was so strong that not only the land was theirs, but the goods and chattels of the ungodly Gentiles was theirs." This was similar to explanations given for some of the animosity against the Saints in Jackson County. David Whitmer remembered that "there were among us a few ignorant and simple-minded persons who were continually making boasts to the Jackson county people that they intended to possess the entire county." Similarly, Isaac McCoy, who rode with the mobs in Jackson County, remembered of the earlier conflict, "[The Mormons] grew bolder as they grew stronger, and daily proclaimed to the older settlers that the Lord had given them the whole land of Missouri." They "had not so much violated law," said McCoy, as become "arrogant and unbearable." A JS revelation in 1834 had counseled the Saints to be prudent in the words they used with their Clay County neighbors. (Thorp, *Early Days in the West*, 79–80; "Mormonism," *Kansas City Daily Journal*, 5 June 1881, 1; *History of Jackson County, Missouri*, 253, 257; Revelation, 22 June 1834, in *JSP*, D4:75–76 [D&C 105:23–25]; Letter to Lyman Wight and Others, 16 Aug. 1834, in *JSP*, D4:102; see also "The Other Side," *Kansas City Daily Journal*, 24 Apr. 1881, 9.)

198. For JS revelations to this effect, see, for example, Revelation, 6 Aug. 1833, in *JSP*, D3:224, 227 [D&C 98:4–5, 34–35]; Revelation, 16–17 Dec. 1833, in *JSP*, D3:395 [D&C 101:77–80]; and Revelation, 22 June 1834, in *JSP*, D4:77 [D&C 105:38–40].

mies equally, at least—But, this to their credit, and which must ever remain upon the pages of time, to their honor, they did not. They had possessions, they had homes, they had sacred rights, and more still, they had helpless harmless innocence, with an approving conscience that they had violated no law of their country or their God, to urge them forward—But, to show to all that they were willing to forego these for the peace of their country, they tamely submitted, and have since been wanderers among strangers, (though hospitable,) without homes. We think these sufficient reasons, to show to your patriotic minds, that our friends, instead of having a wish to expel a community by force of arms, would suffer their rights to be taken from them before shedding blood.[199]

Another charge brought against our friends is that of being dangerous in societies "where slavery is tolerated and practiced." Without occupying time here, we refer you to the April (1836) No. of the "Latter Day Saints' Messenger and Advocate,"[200] printed at this place, a copy of which we forward to each of you. From the length of [p. 356] time which has transpired since its publication, you can easily see, that it was put forth for no other reason than to correct the public mind generally, without a reference or expectation of an excitement of the nature of the one now in your country. Why we refer you to this publication, particularly, is because many of our friends who are now at the west, were in this place when this paper made its appearance, and from personal observation gave it their decided approbation, and expressed those sentiments to be their own, in the fullest particular.

Another charge of great magnitude is brought against our friends in the west—of "keeping up a constant communication with the Indian tribes on our frontier, with declaring, even from the pulpit, that the Indians are a part of God's chosen people, and are destined, by heaven, to inherit this land, in com-

---

199. The response of William W. Phelps and the other Missouri Saints to the citizens' committee similarly stated, "That we (the Mormons so called,) are grateful for the kindness which has been shown to us by the citizens of Clay, since we have resided with them, and being desirous for peace and wishing the good rather than the ill-will of mankind, will use all honorable means to allay the excitement, and so far as we can, remove any foundation for jealousies against us as a people." ("Public Meeting," *LDS Messenger and Advocate,* Aug. 1836, 2:359–360.)

200. The April 1836 *Messenger and Advocate* included several articles arguing against abolition, including Letter to Oliver Cowdery, ca. 9 Apr. 1836, pp. 231–243 herein. On 1 July, William W. Phelps stated, "We have taken no part for or against slavery, but are opposed to the abolitionists, and consider that men have a right to hold slaves or not according to law." In earlier statements, the church had declared itself as "opposed to abolition," stating that it disturbed "the peace and harmony of our Constitution and country." Jackson County residents also considered Mormon views on slavery to be a threat to society in Missouri. ("Public Notice," *LDS Messenger and Advocate,* Aug. 1836, 2:360; "Abolition," *Northern Times,* 9 Oct. 1835, 2; Letter from John Whitmer, 29 July 1833, in *JSP,* D3:186–198.)

mon with themselves."[201] We know of nothing, under the present aspect of our Indian relations, calculated to rouse the fears of the people of the Upper Missouri, more than a combination or influence of this nature; and we cannot look upon it other than one of the most subtle purposes of those whose feelings are embittered against our friends, to turn the eye of suspicion upon them from every man who is acquainted with the barbarous cruelty of rude savages. Since a rumor was afloat that the Western Indians were showing signs of war, we have received frequent private letters from our friends, who have not only expressed fears for their own safety, in case the Indians should break out, but a decided determination to be among the first to repel any invasion, and defend the frontier from all hostilities.[202] We mention the last fact, because it was wholly uncalled for on our part, and came previous to any excitement on the part of the people of Clay county, against our friends, and must definitively show, that this charge is also untrue.[203]

Another charge against our friends, and one that is urged as a reason why they must immediately leave the county of Clay, is, that they are making or are like to, the same "their permanent home, the center and general rendez- vous of their people."[204] We have never understood such to be the purpose, wish or design of this society; but on the contrary, have ever supposed, that

---

201. Similar charges of objectionable interaction between Latter-day Saints and American Indians had been made during the conflict in Jackson County. Shortly after the Mormons' expulsion from Jackson County in 1833, Isaac McCoy, a Baptist missionary who preached among the American Indians in Independence and present-day eastern Kansas in the early 1830s, accused the Mormons of seeking aid from the Indians west of the Missouri River during the Jackson County struggles, of violating federal Indian law, and of possibly tampering with Indians and attempting to ally with them against non-Mormon whites. McCoy explained that he and his white neighbors "strongly suspected" that the Mormons were "secretly tampering with the neighboring Indians, to induce them to aid in the event of open hostility; for myself, I could not resist the belief that they had sought aid from the Indians though I have not ascertained that legal evidence of the fact could be obtained." (Isaac McCoy, "The Disturbances in Jackson County," *Missouri Republican* [St. Louis], 20 Dec. 1833, [2]–[3]; Jennings, "Isaac McCoy and the Mormons," 62–82.)

202. These letters have not been located.

203. William W. Phelps and a committee of Saints also responded to this accusation: "We deny holding any communications with the Indians, & mean to hold ourselves as ready to defend our country against their barbarous ravages as any other people." ("Public Meeting," *LDS Messenger and Advocate,* Aug. 1836, 2:360.)

204. Preliminary studies identify more than 3,600 acres purchased by the Saints in Clay County, usually in 40- or 80-acre parcels. Of the approximately 250 Latter-day Saint families that resided in the county through 1836, about a third of them owned land. The rest rented, squatted on government land, or lived on the land of other Saints. Most of the land owned by the Saints was located within three miles of the main east-west road that passed through the southern part of the county. Examples are Newel Knight's forty acres, the holdings of the Colesville branch at the southwest corner of the county, Edward Partridge's rented land two miles south of Liberty, Lyman Wight's 130 acres near the Fishing River in the eastern part of the county, and John Cooper's eighty acres on the eastern edge of the county. (Lewis, "Mormon Land Ownership," 25–28; Parkin, "History of the Latter-day Saints in Clay County," 318–319;

those who resided in Clay county, only designed it as a temporary residence, until the law and authority of our country should put them in the quiet possession of their homes in Jackson county.[205] And such as had not possessions there, could purchase to the entire satisfaction and interest of the people of Jackson county.

Having partially mentioned the leading objections urged against our friends, we would here add, that it has not been done with a view on our part, to dissuade you from acting in strict conformity with your preamble and resolutions, offered to the people of Clay county, on the 29th ult. but from a sense of duty to a people embarrassed, persecuted and afflicted. For you are aware, gentlemen, that in times of excitement, virtues are transformed into vices, acts, which in other cases, and under other circumstances, would be considered upright and honorable, interpreted contrary from their real intent, and made objectional and criminal; and from whom could we look for forbearance and compassion with confidence and assurance, more than from those whose bosoms are warmed with those pure principles of patriotism with which you have been guided in the present instance, to secure the peace of your county, and save a persecuted people from further violence, and destruction?

It is said that our friends are poor; that they have but little or nothing to bind their feelings or wishes to Clay county, and that in consequence, have a less claim upon that county. We do not deny the fact, that our friends are poor; but their persecutions have helped to render them so. While other men were peacefully following their avocations, and extending their interest, they have been deprived of the right of citizenship, prevented from enjoying their own, charged with violating the sacred principles of our constitution and laws; made to feel the keenest aspersions of the tongue of slander, waded through all but death, and, are now suffering under calumnies calculated to excite the indignation and hatred of every people among whom they may dwell, thereby exposing them to destruction and inevitable ruin!

If a people, a community, or a society, can accumulate wealth, increase [p. 357] in worldly fortune, improve in science and arts, rise to eminence in the

---

Berrett, *Sacred Places*, 4:161–190; Clay County Land Deed Record, vol. D, pp. 197, 256; vol. E, pp. 170, 399; Eliza Partridge Lyman, Journal, 10; Young, "What I Remember," 13.)

205. Church leaders continued to encourage Saints to gather to Missouri until their numbers were sufficient to reclaim their lands in Jackson County. Though considered a temporary home, Clay County had become the main Missouri gathering place for the Saints. Following the endowment in the Kirtland House of the Lord, church leaders set in motion greater proselytizing and fund-raising efforts to purchase lands in Missouri as part of their greater focus on redeeming Zion. (Minutes, 30 Mar. 1836, pp. 218–221 herein; Minutes, 2 Apr. 1836, pp. 223–224 herein; JS, Journal, 2 Apr. 1836, in *JSP*, J1:217–219.)

eyes of the public, surmount these difficulties, so much as to bid defiance to poverty and wretchedness, it must be a new creation, a race of beings super-human. But in all their poverty and want, we have yet to learn, for the first time, that our friends are not industrious, and temperate,[206] and wherein they have not always been the *last* to retaliate or resent an injury, and the *first* to overlook and forgive.[207] We do not urge that there are not exceptions to be found: all communities, all societies and associations, are cumbered with dis-orderly and less virtuous members—members who violate in a greater or less degree the principles of the same. But this can be no just criterion by which to judge a whole society. And further still, where a people are laboring under con-stant fear of being dispossessed, very little inducement is held out to excite them to be industrious.

We think, gentlemen, that we have pursued this subject far enough, and we here express to you, as we have in a letter accompanying this, to our friends, our decided disapprobation to the idea of shedding blood, if any other course can be followed to avoid it; in which case, and which alone, we have urged upon our friends to desist, only in *extreme* cases of self-defence;[208] and in this case not to *give* the offence or provoke their fellow men to acts of violence,—which we have no doubt they will observe, as they ever have. For you may rest assured, gentlemen, that we would be the last to advise our friends to shed the blood of men, or commit one act to endanger the public peace.

We have no doubt but our friends will leave your county, sooner or later,—they have not only signified the same to us, but we have advised them so to do, as fast as they can without incurring too much loss.[209] It may be said that they have but *little* to lose if they lose the whole. But if they have but *little, that little is their all*, and the imperious demands of the helpless, urge them to make a prudent disposal of the same. And we are highly pleased with a propo-sition in your preamble, suffering them to remain peaceably till a disposition can be made of their land, &c. which if suffered, our fears are at once hushed, and we have every reason to believe, that during the remaining part of the residence of our friends in your county, the same feelings of friendship and

---

206. Of the Saints in Clay County, Joseph Thorp wrote, "The Mormons, in the main, were industri-ous, good workers, and gave general satisfaction to their employers, and could live on less than any people I ever knew. . . . They had the knack of economizing in the larder, which was a great help to the men, as they had mostly to earn their bread and butter by day's work." (Thorp, *Early Days in the West*, 76.)

207. An August 1833 revelation counseled the Saints to bear repeated offenses from their enemies. (Revelation, 6 Aug. 1833, in *JSP*, D3:227 [D&C 98:39–45].)

208. On instructions to the Saints regarding self-defense, see Letter to William W. Phelps and Others, 25 July 1836, p. 269 herein; and Revelation, 6 Aug. 1833, in *JSP*, D3:226–227 [D&C 98:23–31].

209. See Letter to William W. Phelps and Others, 25 July 1836, pp. 269–270 herein.

kindness will continue to exist, that have heretofore, and that when they leave you, you will have no reflection of sorrow to cast, that they have been sojourners among you.

To what distance or place they will remove, we are unable to say: in this they must be dictated with judgment and prudence. They may explore the Territory of Wisconsin[210]—they may remove there, or they may stop on the other side—of this we are unable to say; but be they where they will, we have this gratifying reflection, that they have never been the first, in an unjust manner, to violate the laws, injure their fellow men, or disturb the tranquility and peace under which any part of our country has heretofore reposed. And we cannot but believe, that ere long the public mind must undergo a change, when it will appear to the satisfaction of all that this people have been illy treated and abused without cause, and when, as justice would demand, those who have been the instigators of their sufferings will be regarded as their true characters demand.

Though our religious principles are before the world, ready for the investigation of all men, yet we are aware that the sole foundation of all the persecution against our friends, has arisen in consequence of the calumnies and misconstructions, without foundation in truth, or righteousness, in common with all other religious societies, at their first commencement; and should Providence order that we rise not as others before us, to respectability and esteem, but be trodden down by the ruthless hand of extermination, *posterity* will do us the justice, when our persecutors are equally low in the dust, with ourselves, to hand down to succeeding generations, the virtuous acts and forbearance of a people, who sacrificed their reputation for their religion, and their earthly fortunes and happiness, to preserve peace, and save this land from being further drenched in blood.

We have no doubt but your very seasonable mediation, in the time of so great an excitement, will accomplish your most sanguine desire, in preventing

---

210. The United States Congress passed an act establishing Wisconsin Territory on 20 April 1836, which took effect on 4 July 1836. The Clay County citizens' committee recommended that the Saints investigate and remove to Wisconsin, "which is peculiarly suited to their conditions and their wants." The Clay County committee further said of Wisconsin, "It is almost entirely unsettled; they [the Mormons] can there procure large bodies of land together, where there are no settlements, and none to interfere with them. . . . We therefore, in a spirit of frank and friendly kindness, do advise them to seek a home where they may obtain large and separate bodies of land, and have a community of their own." A short time later, a resident of Wisconsin Territory wrote, "Gentleman Mormons, we pray you to be assured, that your 'promised land' is not in Wisconsin." ("Public Notice," *LDS Messenger and Advocate,* Aug. 1836, 354; An Act Establishing the Territorial Government of Wisconsin [20 Apr. 1836], *Public Statutes at Large,* 24th Cong., 1st Sess., chap. 54, p. 10; "The Mormons—Unparalleled Impudence," *Far West* [Liberty, MO], 18 Aug. 1836, 1.)

further disorder; and we hope, [p. 358] gentlemen, that while you reflect upon the fact, that the citizens of Clay county are *urgent* for our friends to leave you, that you will also bear in mind, that by their complying with your request to leave, is surrendering some of the dearest rights and first, among those inherent principles, guaranteed in the constitution of our country; and that human nature can be driven to a certain extent, when it will yield no farther. Therefore, while our friends *suffer* so much, and forego so many sacred rights, we sincerely hope, and we have every reason to expect it, that a suitable forbearance may be shown by the people of Clay, which if done, the cloud that has been obscuring your horizon, will disperse, and you be left to enjoy peace, harmony and prosperity.

With sentiments of esteem and profound respect, we are, gentlemen, your obedient servants.

SIDNEY RIGDON,
JOSEPH SMITH, Jr.
O[liver] COWDERY,
F[rederick] G. WILLIAMS,
HYRUM SMITH.

———— ☙ ————

Letter to William W. Phelps and Others, 25 July 1836

Source Note

Sidney Rigdon, JS, Oliver Cowdery, Frederick G. Williams, and Hyrum Smith, Letter, Kirtland Township, Geauga Co., OH, to William W. Phelps and others [likely John Corrill, Edward Partridge, Isaac Morley, Lyman Wight, Thomas B. Marsh, Elias Higbee, Calvin Beebe, Jesse Hitchcock, Isaac Higbee, Samuel Bent, Titus Billings, James Emmett, and R. Evans], Liberty, Clay Co., MO, 25 July 1836. Featured version published in "Kirtland, Ohio, July 25, 1836," Latter Day Saints' Messenger and Advocate, *Aug. 1836, 2:359. For more information on* Latter Day Saints' Messenger and Advocate, *see Source Notes for Multiple-Entry Documents, p. 527 herein.*

Historical Introduction

On 1 July 1836, church leaders in Clay County, Missouri, under William W. Phelps as chairman, met and discussed the 29 June resolutions presented to them by the Clay County citizens' committee that had demanded the Mormons leave the county.[211] It was "for the sake of friendship," the church leaders said, "and to be in a covenant of peace with the citizens of Clay county" that they acquiesced to the committee's request.[212] On 2 July, the church leaders met with the citizens' committee, which accepted their commitment to leave

---

211. For more information on the situation in Clay County leading to these resolutions, see Letter to John Thornton and Others, 25 July 1836, pp. 258–268 herein.

212. "Public Meeting," *LDS Messenger and Advocate,* Aug. 1836, 2:359–361. Edward Partridge also reported that on 30 June 1836, before the official statement by the Saints was delivered to the citizens'

and further resolved to "assist the Mormons in selecting some abiding place where they will be in a measure the only occupants" and where "none will be anxious to molest them."[213] At the end of 1836, Alexander Doniphan and others from Clay County helped push forward a statute in the Missouri state legislature that created Caldwell County specifically for Mormon settlement.[214]

Phelps and other church leaders in Clay County wrote to JS and the church presidency in Kirtland, Ohio, on 1 July 1836 to inform them of these developments and the agreement to vacate the county.[215] In the church presidency's reply, presented here, JS and the presidency approved the decision made by Phelps and the Missouri Latter-day Saints to peaceably leave the county.

The original letter is no longer extant; the version featured here was printed in the August 1836 issue of the *Latter Day Saints' Messenger and Advocate*.

Document Transcript

Kirtland, Ohio, July 25, 1836.

DEAR BRETHREN:[216]—Yours of the 1st inst. accompanying the proceedings of a public meeting, held by the people of Clay, was duly received.[217] We are sorry that this disturbance has broken out—we do not consider it our fault. You are better acquainted with circumstances than we are, and of course have been directed in wisdom in your moves, relative to leaving the county. We forward you our letter to Mr. [John] Thornton and others,[218] that you may know all we have said. We advise that you be not the first aggressors—give no

committee, he, his counselors, and others met the committee and reported that they "wanted peace and were willing to make sacrifices, to keep it." (Partridge, Journal, 30 June 1836.)

213. "Public Meeting," *LDS Messenger and Advocate,* Aug. 1836, 2:361.

214. An Act to Organize the Counties of Caldwell and Daviess [29 Dec. 1836], *Laws of the State of Missouri* [1836], 46–47; Alexander Doniphan, Jefferson City, MO, to William W. Phelps, Shoal Creek, MO, 8 Jan. 1837, William W. Phelps, Collection of Missouri Documents, CHL.

215. No copy of the 1 July 1836 letter from Phelps to JS has been located.

216. In addition to William W. Phelps, who was named at the end of the letter, the intended recipients likely included Edward Partridge, Isaac Morley, Lyman Wight, Thomas B. Marsh, Elias Higbee, Calvin Beebe, Jesse Hitchcock, Isaac Higbee, Samuel Bent, Titus Billings, James Emmett, and R. Evans, all of whom made up the committee of twelve Latter-day Saints appointed to respond to the demands of the Clay County citizens' committee. John Corrill was likely also an intended recipient; he was secretary at the meeting where the committee was appointed. ("Public Meeting," *LDS Messenger and Advocate,* Aug. 1836, 2:359.)

217. William W. Phelps's report of the Clay County citizens' meeting, held 29 June, is found in the August issue of the *Messenger and Advocate.* The Clay County committee's resolutions were also printed in the newspaper *Far West*—a Liberty, Clay County, paper owned by Peter Rogers, a member of the citizens' committee—on 30 June 1836. ("Public Meeting," *LDS Messenger and Advocate,* Aug. 1836, 2:359–361; "Public Meeting," *Far West* [Liberty, MO], 30 June 1836; for more information on the meeting, see Letter to John Thornton and Others, 25 July 1836, pp. 258–268 herein.)

218. John Thornton was chairman of the "Committee of nine" that wrote the appeal requesting that the Latter-day Saints leave Clay County. The 25 July letter to Thornton and others is found on pp. 258–268 herein. ("Public Meeting," *LDS Messenger and Advocate,* Aug. 1836, 2:353.)

occasion, and if the people will let you dispose of your property, settle your affairs, and go in peace, go. You have thus far had an asylum,[219] and now seek another as God may direct.[220] Relative to your going to Wisconsin,[221] we cannot say, we should think if you could stop short, in peace you had better. You know our feelings relative to not giving the first offence, and also of protecting your wives and little ones in case a mob should seek their lives. We shall publish the proceedings of the public meeting, with your answer, as well as our letter. We mean that the world shall know all things as they transpire. If we are persecuted and driven men shall know it!

Be wise, let prudence dictate all your counsels, preserve peace with all men, if possible, stand by the constitution of your country, observe its principles,

---

219. In their proposition, the "Committee of nine" wrote that the Latter-day Saints "came to our county, thus friendless and pennyless, seeking (as they said) but a temporary asylum, from the storms of persecution." The Clay County citizens had been willing to offer a "temporary asylum," but the growing population of and extensive land purchases by Latter-day Saints in the county raised substantial concerns. By summer 1836 church members had acquired some 3,640 acres in Clay County, in accordance with instructions in a 22 June 1834 revelation that commanded church members to purchase lands in Jackson County "and in the adjoining Counties round about." ("Public Meeting," *LDS Messenger and Advocate,* Aug. 1836, 2:353; Plewe, *Mapping Mormonism,* 34–35; [Edward Partridge], "A History, of the Persecution," *Times and Seasons,* Dec. 1839, 1:50–51, in *JSP,* H2:228–229; Revelation, 22 June 1834, in *JSP,* D4:69–77 [D&C 105].)

220. Since at least 1834, church leaders had looked for lands where the church could relocate. On 24 August 1834, William W. Phelps wrote a letter to church leaders in Kirtland apprising them of developments that might affect land availability along Clay County's northwestern border, land generally known as the Platte country.[a] When Phelps and his compatriots returned to Missouri after a stay in Kirtland for the temple dedication and solemn assembly, he and Edward Partridge began looking for a new location in Missouri for the Saints. As a result of their scouting, John Corrill on 22 June 1836 applied for several land patents in the area north of Ray County for himself and on behalf of JS and Oliver Cowdery.[b] Between 13 and 21 July, non-Mormon guides Elisha Cameron and Cornelius Gilliam traveled with Partridge, Phelps, and John Whitmer to explore the land in northwest Missouri for the possible purchase of enough land in that region to relocate the Saints from Clay County.[c] On 25 July 1836, a general church assembly in Clay County resolved to send out a committee consisting of Phelps, Whitmer, Partridge, Isaac Morley, and Corrill "to search out land for the Church to settle upon &c."[d] Church leaders in Missouri eventually chose the area north of Ray County, which became Caldwell County in December 1836, as the place to which the Saints would relocate.[e] (a. Letter from William W. Phelps, 24 Aug. 1834, in *JSP,* D4:114–119; U.S. Senate, *Memorial of the General Assembly of Missouri,* 28 Feb. 1831, 21st Cong., S. Doc. No. 71, p. 3; McKee, "Platte Purchase," 134–135. b. Application for Land Patent, 22 June 1836, pp. 257–258 herein; "2d Series—Letter No. I," *LDS Messenger and Advocate,* July 1836, 2:341; Partridge, Journal, [46]–[50]; see also William W. Phelps et al., Liberty, MO, to Daniel Dunklin, 7 July 1836, copy, William W. Phelps, Collection of Missouri Documents, CHL. c. Edward Partridge, Miscellaneous Papers, CHL; Parkin, "History of the Latter-day Saints in Clay County," 268; [Edward Partridge], "A History, of the Persecution," *Times and Seasons,* Dec. 1839, 1:51, in *JSP,* H2:229. d. Minute Book 2, 25 July 1836. e. [Edward Partridge], "A History, of the Persecution," *Times and Seasons,* Dec. 1839, 1:51, in *JSP,* H2:229.)

221. The citizens' committee had recommended Wisconsin as a potential settlement location for the Mormons. (See 267n210 herein.)

and above all, show yourselves men of God, worthy citizens, and we doubt not, community ere long, will do you justice, and rise in indignation against those who are the instigators of your suffering and affliction.[222]

In the bonds of brotherly love we subscribe ourselves, as ever.

SIDNEY RIGDON,
JOSEPH SMITH, J.
OLIVER COWDERY,
F[rederick] G. WILLIAMS,
HYRUM SMITH.

To W[illiam] W. PHELPS and others.

———— ☙ ————

Revelation, 6 August 1836 [D&C 111]

Source Note

Revelation, Salem, Essex Co., MA, 6 Aug. 1836. Featured version copied [between ca. Sept. 1836 and ca. early 1840s] in William W. Phelps, Diary, 1835–1864, pp. 35–[37]; handwriting of William W. Phelps; CHL.

Handmade booklet measuring 5⅞ × 4⅜ × ¼ inches (15 × 11 × 1 cm). The text block consists of forty-six leaves measuring 5⅜ × 4⅛ inches (14 × 10 cm) or smaller. The cover is made of a cream-colored fabric now worn to a tan color. The book flap wraps around the fore edge of the text block, with a loop fastening to a button sewn on the front cover. An inscription in black ink on the front cover reads, "W.W. Phelps' Diary. & c. | 1835". On the front pastedown is the following inscription, also in black ink: "W.W Phelps' Diary | Liberty Mo. 1835".

The diary portion of the booklet contains sixty-one pages, with two pagination sequences. Pages 1–13 contain memorandum-like entries; pagination then begins again with copies of revelations. Additional scriptural passages, miscellaneous notations, and poetry were inscribed in the remaining pages of the booklet as late as 1864.

The Historian's Office received Phelps's diary before 1978, and it contains archival stickers and other archival markings.

Historical Introduction

On 25 July 1836, after writing two letters concerning church members in Missouri, JS, Hyrum Smith, Oliver Cowdery, and Sidney Rigdon left Kirtland, Ohio, to travel to the eastern United States, briefly visiting New York City and Boston and staying in Salem, Massachusetts, before returning to Kirtland in mid-September.[223] Salem, which was offi-cially incorporated as a city in May 1836, was described by Oliver Cowdery as a "pleasantly

---

222. See Revelation, 16–17 Dec. 1833, in *JSP*, D3:395, 397 [D&C 101:77, 80, 95]; and Revelation, 6 Aug. 1833, in *JSP*, D3:224 [D&C 98:4–6].

223. Letter to William W. Phelps and Others, 25 July 1836, pp. 268–271 herein; Letter to John Thornton and Others, 25 July 1836, pp. 258–268 herein; Letter from the Editor, *LDS Messenger and Advocate,* Sept. 1836, 2:372–375; Letter from the Editor, *LDS Messenger and Advocate,* Oct. 1836, 3:386–393. Hyrum Smith departed for Kirtland shortly after 19 August; the other three men left Salem by 26 August. This was JS's second trip to Salem. He had first visited the city as a young boy with his uncle Jesse Smith

situated town with fifteen thousand inhabitants."[224] Located on Massachusetts Bay about fifteen miles north of the larger city of Boston, Salem's busy port held a prominent place in the domestic and international commercial shipping trade of the United States.[225] JS and his three companions arrived in Salem on 5 August and rented a house on Union Street for three weeks. The house may have been where JS dictated this revelation a day later.[226]

No known contemporary documents specify church leaders' reasons for visiting the eastern United States, and few records discuss the trip. The main contemporary sources of information are two letters written by Oliver Cowdery to his brother Warren A. Cowdery, which were published in the church's newspaper, and a letter JS wrote to his wife Emma while in Salem. Oliver Cowdery's letters indicate that their time in New England was spent preaching and occasionally visiting historic places.[227] The four church leaders were likely motivated by a concern about Zion and the financial situation of the church, particularly a need to reduce debts of church leaders. The financial burden placed on them by finishing the House of the Lord in Kirtland and purchasing land in Ohio and Missouri had added significantly to the church's existing debts. Following a 2 April 1836 meeting at which JS and Cowdery were assigned to raise money to purchase land in Missouri, the men appear to have encountered difficulties in finding members willing to give their money or land for the cause of Zion.[228] With the citizens of Clay County, Missouri, requesting that church members living there relocate, the need for temporal means to aid church members in Missouri grew even more pressing. JS and his colleagues may have raised money as they preached during their trip east in 1836, as it was not uncommon for missionaries to have the dual objectives of proselytizing and collecting funds for the church. This 6 August revelation addresses the church leaders' financial concerns. It informed the men that they would

---

while recovering from leg surgery to remove diseased bone. (Letter to Emma Smith, 19 Aug. 1836, p. 282 herein; Lucy Mack Smith, History, 1844–1845, bk. 3, [2].)

224. Letter from the Editor, *LDS Messenger and Advocate,* Oct. 1836, 3:388, 391; "Salem," *Christian Register and Boston Observer,* 8 Aug. 1836, [3]; Saltonstall, *Address to the City Council.*

225. Most of Salem's residents were involved in seafaring and commercial trade. In his May 1836 address at the city's incorporation, Mayor Leverett Saltonstall stated, "In maritime enterprize, Salem is still unsurpassed. . . . We now hold, as we have always held, a respectable rank among the principal commercial places in the country." The East India Marine Society Museum (now the Peabody Essex Museum) in Salem was founded by local mariners involved in international trade in Asia and the Pacific Rim. (Saltonstall, *Address to the City Council,* 22; Whitehill, *East India Marine Society and the Peabody Museum of Salem,* 3–15.)

226. Letter from the Editor, *LDS Messenger and Advocate,* Oct. 1836, 3:386–388; JS History, vol. B-1, 749. An *Essex Register* article reported that the four men rented a house on Union Street and may have planned to return the next year. In the nineteenth century some properties on Union Street in Salem were resident houses and others were rooming houses. (News Item, *Essex Register* [Salem, MA], 25 Aug 1836, [2]; Proper, "Joseph Smith and Salem," 97n27.)

227. Letter to Emma Smith, 19 Aug. 1836, pp. 280–283 herein; Letter from the Editor, *LDS Messenger and Advocate,* Sept. 1836, 2:372–375; Letter from the Editor, *LDS Messenger and Advocate,* Oct. 1836, 3:386–393. Cowdery's "letters from the editor" were used as a source for JS's history. (JS History, vol. B-1, 749.)

228. Minutes, 2 Apr. 1836, p. 223 herein. Some individuals unwilling to donate funds were brought before the Kirtland high council. (Minutes, 16 June 1836, pp. 247–253 herein.)

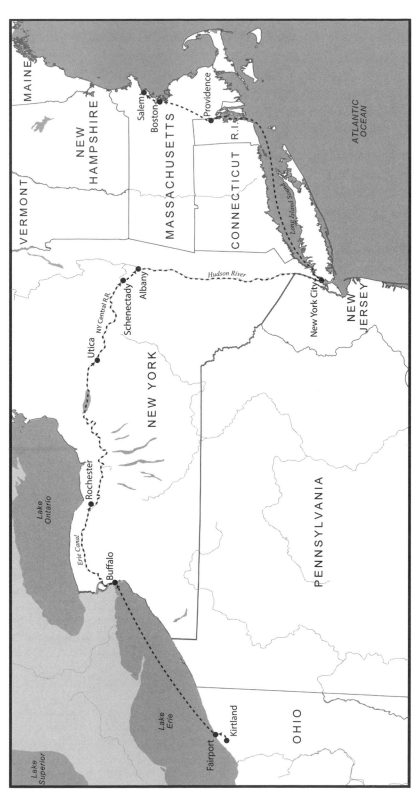

Trip to eastern United States, July–September 1836. Joseph Smith, Oliver Cowdery, Sidney Rigdon, and Hyrum Smith left Kirtland, Ohio, on 25 July 1836, traveling across Lake Erie and then through New York. The men stopped for a short time in New York City before heading northeast and ultimately arriving in Salem, Massachusetts, on 5 August. A revelation Joseph Smith dictated the next day instructed the men to remain in Salem for a time. After spending three or four weeks in Salem, the men stayed briefly in Boston before returning home to Kirtland in September.

have the power to pay their debts and instructed them to "concern not yourselves about Zion" for there were people and money in Salem "for the benefit of Zion."

Related to the revelation's statement that there was "much treasure" in Salem, two later accounts from individuals not directly involved in the journey state that JS traveled to the eastern United States to search for treasure or hidden money. In an 1843 pamphlet, sixteen-year-old dissident James C. Brewster briefly mentioned treasure hunting in relation to JS's 1836 trip.[229] Ebenezer Robinson wrote an account in 1889, fifty-three years after JS's trip, that also linked the 1836 trip and searching for treasure—in fact, he claimed that the single objective of the trip was to look for hidden money in Salem.[230] Robinson printed his account as the editor of the *Return,* a publication for David Whitmer's Church of Christ.[231] Robinson, who joined the Church of the Latter Day Saints in 1836 while working in the Kirtland printing office, stated in his reminiscences that Don Carlos Smith, who worked with him, told him that JS had learned about possible treasure from "a brother in the church, by the name of Burgess" who had come to Kirtland and "stated that a large amount of money had been secreted in the cellar of a certain house in Salem, Massachusetts, which had belonged to a widow, and he thought he was the only person now living, who had knowledge of it, or the location of the house." Robinson claimed he was also told that Burgess met JS in Salem but that Burgess was unable to identify the house after so many years and left. Continuing their search, according to Robinson, JS and the three other men found and rented a house they thought contained the hidden money, but they were unsuccessful in finding it.[232]

It is possible that JS had been told about hidden money in Salem and decided to pursue it to aid the church and relieve the financial and temporal pressure weighing down the branches in Kirtland and Missouri, and two contemporary documents may provide support for the statements of Brewster and Robinson. First, a promissory note was made out to a

---

229. As a young man in Kirtland in 1837, Brewster claimed to have visions of ancient scriptures, and he and his small group of followers were disfellowshipped. He published his extra-scriptural Book of Esdras in 1842, which was the subject of a notice written by editor John Taylor in the December 1842 issue of the *Times and Seasons.* Responding to Taylor's description of treasure hunting as a "ridiculous and pernicious" practice, Brewster wrote: "I would ask him who was the author of this practice among the Mormons? If he has a good memory, he will remember the house that was rented in the city of Boston, with the expectation of finding a large sum of money buried in or near the cellar." (Minute Book 1, 20 Nov. 1837; "Notice," *Times and Seasons,* 1 Dec. 1842, 4:32; Brewster, *Very Important! To the Mormon Money Diggers,* 4; see also Vogel, "James Colin Brewster," 120–139.)

230. Robinson wrote that he learned of JS's 6 August 1836 revelation many years after JS's trip to New England. It is not clear when Robinson first read the revelation, but he stated in 1889 that he had first heard of it only "recently," when he saw it printed in an 1853 issue of the *Millennial Star.* (Ebenezer Robinson, "Items of Personal History of the Editor," *Return,* July 1889, 104–108.)

231. Robinson remained a Latter-day Saint during JS's life, though he seems to have become disillusioned by JS's financial dealings as well as his teachings about plural marriage in the 1840s. After JS's death, Robinson first followed Sidney Rigdon, serving as his counselor for a time, and was then baptized into the Reorganized Church of Jesus Christ of Latter Day Saints in 1863. In 1888, he was affiliated with David Whitmer's Church of Christ and served as the editor of the *Return* until his death in 1891. (Ebenezer Robinson, "Items of Personal History of the Editor," *Return,* July 1889, 105–108; Nov. 1889, 173–174; *Biographical and Historical Record of Ringgold and Decatur Counties, Iowa,* 543–544.)

232. Ebenezer Robinson, "Items of Personal History of the Editor," *Return,* July 1889, 105–106.

Jonathan Burgess in Salem, a tentative connection to the Burgess of Robinson's account.[233] Second, JS mentioned looking for a specific house in Salem in his 19 August letter to Emma Smith. Robinson's account stated that JS rented the house and failed to find any treasure, but JS's letter to Emma reveals that he had not been able to rent or gain access to the house.[234] While JS seemed hopeful the situation would change, the men left Salem only a few days later and offered no indication that they had rented or even visited the sought-after house, nor is there any evidence that they later returned.

Aside from alluding to "more treasures than one," the revelation makes other references to the people of Salem and their significance to the growing church. In the three weeks following the revelation, JS and the others in the church presidency spent much of their time in Salem and in Boston preaching to the people.[235] By the early 1840s, church leaders in Nauvoo focused on the proselytizing aspects of the 6 August 1836 revelation. In 1841, Hyrum Smith and William Law of the First Presidency visited the eastern United States and left instructions at a church conference in Philadelphia for Erastus Snow and Benjamin Winchester to extend their missions and begin preaching in Salem. Snow recorded in his journal that Smith and Law "left with us a copy of a Revelation given about that people in 1836 which said the Lord had much people there whom he would gather into his kingdom in his Own due time and they thought the due time of the Lord had come." Snow and Winchester arrived in Salem on 3 September 1841.[236] After a week, Winchester returned to Philadelphia while Snow preached in Salem and the surrounding area.[237] Snow organized the Salem branch on 5 March 1842, and by the end of his mission more than one hundred people had joined the church.[238] When Snow and his family left in the fall of 1843, seventy-five members from "Boston and the eastern churches" traveled with them to Nauvoo.[239]

The original text of the revelation has not been found, but four copies are extant. The version presented here comes from a diary kept by William W. Phelps. Phelps's diary also contains earlier JS revelations, Phelps's September 1835 patriarchal blessing, and later material from the Illinois and Utah eras of the church. Although Phelps was in Kirtland for the March 1836 dedication of the House of the Lord, he had returned to Missouri before the date of this revelation. He likely copied the revelation into his diary in the late 1830s or early 1840s. Based on textual comparison, Phelps's copy appears to be the earliest

233. Promissory Note to Jonathan Burgess, 17 Aug. 1836, p. 280 herein.

234. Ebenezer Robinson, "Items of Personal History of the Editor," *Return,* July 1889, 105–106; Letter to Emma Smith, 19 Aug. 1836, pp. 282–283 herein.

235. "Mormonism," *Essex Register* (Salem, MA), 22 Aug. 1836, [3]; "Mormonism," *Boston Daily Times,* 24 Aug. 1836, [2]; "Mormonism—Again," *Boston Daily Times,* 26 Aug. 1836, [2].

236. Snow, Journal, 1841–1847, 3–4, 11.

237. Snow, Journal, 1841–1847, 13–22. Snow spent most of his time in Salem, but he also traveled to other areas in Massachusetts, including Boston, Lynn, Marblehead, Northbridge, and Lowell, as well as Peterboro, New Hampshire, and Woonsocket, Rhode Island.

238. Snow, Journal, 1841–1847, 21, 27; "The Mormons in Salem," *Salem (MA) Register,* 2 June 1842, [2]. Snow recorded that there were fifty-three members at the organization of the Salem branch on 5 March 1842. By June 1842 the branch had grown to ninety members.

239. Snow, Journal, 1841–1847, 44. For more detail on Snow's mission in Salem, see Godfrey, "More Treasures Than One," 196–204.

Peabody Essex Museum register. August 1836. On 9 August 1836 Joseph Smith visited the East India Marine Society Museum (now known as the Peabody Essex Museum) in Salem, Massachusetts. This page includes Joseph Smith's signature in the museum's guest register. Oliver Cowdery and Sidney Rigdon visited the museum on 6 August 1836, the same day Joseph Smith dictated a revelation relative to their visit in Salem. (Courtesy Phillips Library, Peabody Essex Museum, Salem, MA.)

version, and it matches the text of later printed versions. Another version, made by Erastus Snow, was likely copied in 1841 from a copy that was left for him in Philadelphia by Hyrum Smith and William Law. Snow's copy matches the wording used in Phelps's inscription, with only minor exceptions. A third copy is in the Book of the Law of the Lord, inscribed by Robert B. Thompson in Nauvoo between 1840 and 1841.[240] A fourth inscription of the revelation is found in volume B-1 of JS's history and was written by Willard Richards between 1842 and 1844.[241] The version in JS's history is textually similar to both the Phelps and Book of the Law of the Lord inscriptions, with punctuation and spelling in the first six lines of the revelation that match the Book of the Law of the Lord inscription.

This revelation was not published in JS's lifetime. It first appeared in print in the 1850s with the printing of the "History of Joseph Smith" in the *Deseret News* and the *Millennial Star*.[242] It was first included in the Doctrine and Covenants in the 1876 edition, and the canonized version follows the text of the Phelps inscription featured here. Significant differences between Phelps's copy and other early copies of this revelation are described in footnotes below.

Document Transcript

A revelation

Salem (Mss.) [Massachusetts] August 6, 1836.

I the Lord your God am not displeased with your coming[243] this Journey, notwithstandi[n]g your follies. I have much treasure in this city for you, for the benefit of Zion; and many people in this city whom I will gather out in due time for the benefit of Zion, through your instrumentality: Therefore it is expedient that you should form acquaintance with men in this city, as you shall be lead, and as it shall be be given you.[244] And it shall come to pass, in

240. Snow, Journal, 1841–1847, 3–4. The copy found in the Book of the Law of the Lord omits two clauses in the last few lines of the revelation, as described in footnotes below. One of these omissions can be explained as a scribal error, due to the repetitive nature of the first words of two adjacent sentences, but the omissions could also reflect a different version of the revelation. However, unlike Erastus Snow's copy, the inscription in the Book of the Law of the Lord has the same first line as the Phelps copy, and it includes grammatical errors found in Phelps's copy but not in Snow's. (Book of the Law of the Lord, 22.)

241. JS History, vol. B-1, 750; Searle, "Authorship of the History of Joseph Smith," 110–112.

242. "History of Joseph Smith," *Deseret News,* 25 Dec. 1852, [1]; "History of Joseph Smith," *LDS Millennial Star,* 17 Dec. 1853, 15:51.

243. Erastus Snow's copy of the revelation reads "you concerning" in place of "your coming." ("Revelation given August 6, 1836 in Salem, Ma," in Snow, Journals, 1835–1851, 1856–1857, CHL.)

244. One way JS and his companions may have tried to accomplish this directive to make acquaintances in the Boston-Salem area was by holding meetings. Their most publicized meeting in Salem was held at the Lyceum Hall on 20 August, where Rigdon spoke on Christianity. The *Essex Register* described Rigdon favorably as "a man of very respectable appearance" and "very fluent in his language." Several Salem and Boston newspapers mentioned the meeting. The men also held several meetings in Boston after leaving Salem. According to local newspapers they held meetings at the house of a Fanny Brewer, and Rigdon spoke publicly on 22 and 24 August. ("Mormonism," *Essex Register*

due time, that I will give this city into your hands, that you shall have power over it, insomuch that they shall not discover your secret [p. 35] parts;²⁴⁵ and its wealth, pertaining to gold and silver, shall be yours. Concern not yourselves about your debts, for I will give you power to pay them.²⁴⁶ Concern not yourselves about Zion, for I will deal merciful with her. Tarry in this place and in the regions round about, and the place where it is my will that you should tarry, for the main, shall be signalized unto you by the peace and power of ~~the~~ my Spirit, that shall flow unto you. This place you may obtain by hire, &c . . .²⁴⁷ And inquire [p. [36]] diligently concerning the more ancient inhabitants and founders of this city,²⁴⁸ for there are more treasures than one for you, in this city:²⁴⁹ Therefore be ye as wise as serpents²⁵⁰ and yet without sin, and I will order all things for your good as fast as ye are able to receive them. Amen. [p. [37]]

———— ☙ ————

Promissory Note to Jonathan Burgess, 17 August 1836

Source Note

JS, Oliver Cowdery, Sidney Rigdon, and Hyrum Smith, Promissory Note, Salem, Essex Co., MA, to Jonathan Burgess, Salem, Essex Co., MA, 17 Aug. 1836; handwriting of Oliver Cowdery; signatures of Oliver Cowdery and Sidney Rigdon and partial signatures of Hyrum Smith and JS; endorsed by unidentified scribe; one page; JS Collection, CHL.

[Salem, MA], 22 Aug. 1836, [3]; News Item, *Salem [MA] Gazette,* 23 Aug. 1836, [2]; "Mormonism," *Boston Daily Times,* 24 Aug. 1836, [2]; "Mormonism," *Salem [MA] Observer,* 27 Aug. 1836, [3]; Joshua Himes, "Joe Smith-ism, Alias Mormonism," *Christian Palladium* [Union Mills, NY], 15 Dec. 1836, 5:243–244; "Mormonism—Again," *Boston Daily Times,* 26 Aug. 1836, [2]; News Item, *Boston Daily Times,* 25 Aug. 1836, [2].)

245. See Isaiah 3:17. A blessing given to Hyrum Smith by JS on 18 Dec. 1833 stated, "He shall be hid by the hand of the Lord that none of his secret parts shall be discovered unto his hu[r]t." (Blessing to Hyrum Smith, 18 Dec. 1833, in *JSP,* D4:491.)

246. The clause "Concern not yourselves about your debts, for I will give you power to pay them" is omitted in the copy found in the Book of the Law of the Lord. (Book of the Law of the Lord, 22.)

247. TEXT: Ellipses in original.

248. JS, Hyrum Smith, Oliver Cowdery, and Sidney Rigdon visited museums and historic sites in Salem and Boston. On the day that JS dictated the revelation, Rigdon and Cowdery toured the East India Marine Society Museum and signed the guest register; JS visited the same museum on 9 August. Cowdery and possibly the other men also visited places in Salem related to the seventeenth-century witchcraft trials. They also visited the Boston naval yard, Bunker Hill, and the ruins of the Charlestown Ursuline Convent, which had been destroyed by a mob in 1834. ("Album, for the Use of Visitors," series 5, vol. 4, 6 and 9 Aug. 1836, East India Marine Society Records, Phillips Library, Peabody Essex Museum, Salem, MA; Letter from the Editor, *LDS Messenger and Advocate,* Oct. 1836, 3:388–393.)

249. The clause "for there are more treasures than one for you in this city" does not appear in the copy of the revelation in the Book of the Law of the Lord. (Book of the Law of the Lord, 22.)

250. See Matthew 10:16.

This note is written on an irregular-shaped page measuring 1¾–3 × 7¾ inches (5–8 × 20 cm). The single leaf has one horizontal fold and three vertical folds. The signatures of Oliver Cowdery and Sidney Rigdon are fully visible. Because the bottom right corner is torn, all that remains of the other signatures (those of Hyrum Smith and JS) are parts of the "H" and the "J". This document is discolored in some areas and has undergone preservation work; it is mounted on Japanese paper to prevent further tearing. The provenance of this document is unknown; it is assumed that the document has remained in continuous institutional custody since its creation.

Historical Introduction

Nearly two weeks after their arrival in Salem, Massachusetts, JS, Sidney Rigdon, Oliver Cowdery, and Hyrum Smith signed a promissory note agreeing to pay Jonathan Burgess $100 plus interest for financial assistance that he had provided them. This Jonathan Burgess has not been identified, but he may be the same "Brother Burjece" JS referred to in a letter to his wife Emma two days later, a man who had been with them in Salem but had left the city by 19 August.[251] He may also possibly be the "Brother Burgess" who, according to Ebenezer Robinson's reminiscent account, written fifty-three years later, came to Kirtland, Ohio, and provided information setting JS's trip to New England in motion.[252] None of this is certain, and no evidence exists to confirm whether these were in fact the same individual. Burgess was a relatively common surname in New England in the nineteenth century, and more than one individual named Burgess lived in the vicinity of Salem at this time.[253] A family with the surname of Burgess also lived in Kirtland, Ohio, in 1836, but none of the men for whom there is biographical information were named Jonathan, and it is not known if any member of the Kirtland Burgess family had lived in Salem or had any relations there.[254] A Jonathan Burgess is listed as attending a church council in Kirtland in 1837 and being ordained a priest, but nothing else is known of this individual.[255]

---

251. Letter to Emma Smith, 19 Aug. 1836, p. 282 herein.

252. Ebenezer Robinson, "Items of Personal History of the Editor," *Return*, July 1889, 104–106; see also Historical Introduction to Revelation, 6 Aug. 1836 [D&C 111], pp. 271–276 herein. Robinson's account suggests that Burgess told JS about hidden money or treasure in Salem, motivating the trip to the eastern United States. Robinson implied that Burgess lived in Salem previously, but he did not include any information that might help identify the man, such as his age or when he might have lived there.

253. The federal census for 1820 lists about sixty men in Massachusetts with the surname of Burgess, and the census for 1830 includes about seventy men with the surname of Burgess. No city directories exist for Salem before 1837, but Salem's vital records name a William Burgess, baptized 22 November 1803, son of William. It also names a Jonathan Burges baptized at two years of age in September 1786. The marriage record also names the marriages of William Burgess and Mary Joseph, 6 November 1798, and a William Burges with intent to marry Mary Underwood, 15 September 1832, without giving the relationship of the two Williams. (1820 U.S. Census, MA; 1830 U.S. Census, MA; *Vital Records of Salem Massachusetts*, 1:140; 3:166–167.)

254. Historian Milton Backman identifies the family of William Burgess, including four men, all born in New York: William Burgess, Harrison Burgess, Horace Burgess, and William Burgess Jr. William, Harrison, and Horace Burgess are also mentioned in the Kirtland high council minutes. Harrison left an autobiographical sketch later in his life, and he did not refer to Salem, Massachusetts. (Backman, *Profile,* 11; Minute Book 1, 14–15 Feb. 1835; 28 Feb.–1 Mar. 1835; 7–8 Mar. 1835; 2 May 1835; 17 Aug. 1835; Burgess, Autobiography, ca. 1883, CHL.)

255. Minute Book 1, 2 Nov. 1837.

It appears that the promissory note was paid, since the signatures of Hyrum Smith and JS have been torn from the bottom of the note. When a promissory note was paid, the names or signatures of the endorsers were often torn from the note, canceling or invalidating the note so it was no longer negotiable.[256] The note would then act as a receipt for the individual who paid the debt.

Document Transcript

Salem, Mss. [Massachusetts] August 17, 1836.

$100=

For value received we promise to pay Jonathan Burgess, one hundred dollars, one year from date, with use.

[257]O[liver] COWDERY
Sidney Rigdon
H[yrum Smith]
J[oseph Smith]

⟨Interest of $22,00⟩[258]

———— ℰᴐ ————

Letter to Emma Smith, 19 August 1836

Source Note

JS, Letter, Salem, Essex Co., MA, to Emma Smith, [Kirtland Township], Geauga Co., OH, 19 Aug. 1836; handwriting of JS; one page; Charles Aldrich Autograph Collection, State Historical Society of Iowa, Des Moines. Includes address and dockets.

The leaf is ruled with twenty-nine blue horizontal lines (now faded) and measures 9¾ × 7¾ inches (25 × 20 cm). The top, bottom, and right sides of the recto have the square cut of manufactured paper; the left side is uneven. Notations on the back of the document correspond with two folding patterns. The first pattern was a trifold in letter style, addressed by JS and sealed with an adhesive wafer. At the edge of the address panel is a docket, "Salem Aug. 19./36 | Joseph Smith Jr", in the handwriting of Willard Richards. The placement of the docket suggests the letter was initially kept folded for storage. The second folding was a trifold with a docket in unknown handwriting: "Joseph Smith Jr | Letter". Two small holes are 1/4 inch (1 cm) from the top and bottom of the page.

The letter contains no postmark; presumably, the letter was carried by Hyrum Smith.[259] The docket by Willard Richards suggests the letter was kept for a time in JS's Nauvoo, Illinois, office. If so, the letter was eventually returned to Smith family possession. Joseph Smith III donated the letter to Iowa's collection of letters and autographs in 1891.[260] The state's collection, which included the exten-

---

256. "Cancellation," in Bouvier, *Law Dictionary* [1839], 1:151–152; Chitty, *Practical Treatise on Bills of Exchange,* 214.

257. TEXT: Original signatures of Oliver Cowdery, Sidney Rigdon, Hyrum Smith, and JS.

258. TEXT: Endorsement in unidentified handwriting.

259. "Letters of Joseph Smith, the Martyr," *Saints Herald,* 1 Dec. 1879, 356–357.

260. "The Mormon Prophet," *Des Moines (IA) Register,* 13 Mar. 1891, in Newspaper clippings 1831–1993, miscellaneous volumes 1891–1907, Oct. 1890–June 1892 volume, 44, CHL.

Salem Mass— August 19th 1836

My beloved Wife

Brother Hyram is about to Start for home before the rest of us, which Seems wisdom in God, as our buisness here cannot be determined assoon as we could wish it, I thought a line from me by him would not be acceptable to you, even if it did not contain but little, that you may know that you and the children are much on my mind, with regard to the great object of our mission you will be anxious to know, we have found the house Since Brother Burgess left us, very luck =ily and providentialy, as we had one Spell been most discouraged, but the house is ocupied and it will require much care and patience to rent or buy it, we think we shall be able to effect it if not now within the course of a few months, we think we shall be at home about the middle of September, I can think of many things concerning our busi =ness but can only pray that you may have wisdom to manage the concerns that involve on you and want you should believe me that I am your sincere friend and husband in hast yours &c—

Emma Smith   Joseph Smith Jr

Letter written to Emma Smith from Salem, Massachusetts. Joseph Smith wrote this letter while travel-ing with Hyrum Smith, Sidney Rigdon, and Oliver Cowdery in the eastern United States. While in Salem, he penned this heartfelt and informational letter to Emma, who remained in Kirtland with their children. The letter is one of the few sources of contemporary evidence about Joseph Smith's trip east in the summer of 1836. It is also one of only a handful of documents from the period covered by this volume that includes his handwriting. Letter to Emma Smith, 19 Aug. 1836, Charles Aldrich Autograph Collection, State Historical Society of Iowa, Des Moines.

sive compendium of autograph collector Charles Aldrich (1828–1908), was deposited with the newly organized Iowa State Historical Department (now the State Historical Society of Iowa) in 1892.[261] It is unknown when the letter was interfiled with the Aldrich collection.

Historical Introduction

JS, Hyrum Smith, Sidney Rigdon, and Oliver Cowdery traveled to the eastern United States in summer 1836 to proselytize and obtain financial support for the church. While in Salem, Massachusetts, JS wrote a letter to his wife Emma conveying his affection for her and their children and informing her about the progress of the trip.

JS wrote that they had found a particular house in Salem that they had been searching for, but the letter provides no details concerning the reason for locating the house.[262] In the letter, JS expressed uncertainty but also hope that they would gain access to the house at some point. However, they left Salem before doing so, and there is no record that they returned.

Hyrum Smith left to return to Kirtland, Ohio, shortly after the letter was written, likely taking the letter with him. JS, Oliver Cowdery, and Sidney Rigdon remained in Salem as late as 22 August and spent some time in Boston during their return trip.[263] They arrived in Kirtland by 13 September 1836.[264]

Document Transcript
Salem, Mss. [Massachusetts], August 19th, 1836.

My beloved wife

Brother Hyram [Hyrum Smith] is about ~~to start for home~~[265] **to start for home before the rest of us, which seems wisdom in God, as our buisness here cannot be determined as soon as we could wish to ⟨have it⟩, I thaught a line from me by him would ~~not~~ be acceptible to you, even if it did not contain but little, that you may know that you and the children are much on my mind, with regard to the graat [great] object of our mishion you will be anxtiou [anxious] to know, we have found the house since Brother Burjece[266] left us, very luckily and providentialy, as we had one spell been**

---

261. "Signed on the Dotted Line: The Charles Aldrich Autograph Collection," [6]–[7].

262. See Historical Introduction to Revelation, 6 Aug. 1836 [D&C 111], pp. 271–276 herein.

263. Letter from the Editor, *LDS Messenger and Advocate,* Oct. 1836, 3:386; "Mormonism," *Boston Daily Times,* 24 Aug. 1836, [2]; "Mormonism—Again," *Boston Daily Times,* 26 Aug. 1836, [2].

264. The exact date of their return is not known, but the three men purchased land in Kirtland from Hiram Dayton on 13 September 1836. JS also bought another tract of land in Kirtland from William Draper Jr. on 14 September 1836. (Geauga Co., Deed Records, 1795–1921, vol. 22, p. 305, 13 Sept. 1836; pp. 428–429, 14 Sept. 1836, microfilm 20,239, U.S. and Canada Record Collection, FHL.)

265. TEXT: After reaching the end of the line at "is about", JS mistakenly inscribed "to start for home" at the beginning of the same line, in the space created by the paragraph indention. He then canceled the four words and continued the inscription on the next line.

266. On the possible identity of "Brother Burjece," see Historical Introduction to Promissory Note to Jonathan Burgess, 17 Aug. 1836, p. 279 herein.

most discouraged, ~~but~~ the house is ocupied and it will require much care and patience to rent or b[u]y it, we think we shall be able to effect it if not now within the course of a few months, we think we shall be at home about the midle of septtember, I can think of many things concerning our business but can only pray that you may have wisdom to manage the concerns that involve on you[267] and want you should believe me that I am your sincere friend and husband in hast yours &c—

Joseph Smith Jr

Emma Smith [p. [1]]

✉

Mrs Emma Smith
Geauga Co—
Ohio

---

267. JS's reluctance to discuss the business concerns on his mind mirrors his decision in an earlier letter to Emma, in which he wrote that he felt it was "not prudent" to write on such matters. In that letter, he told her, "I omit all the important things which could I See you I could make you aquainted with." (Letter to Emma Smith, 6 June 1832, in *JSP*, D2:256.)

PART 5: 5 OCTOBER 1836– 10 APRIL 1837

From fall 1836 to early spring 1837, JS and other church leaders focused on developing the town of Kirtland, Ohio, and finding means to pay church debts. JS was involved in several large land transactions and, according to extant records, purchased about 440 acres in fall 1836.[1] A primary motivation for these acquisitions was expanding the amount of land the church had available for newly arriving members to purchase.[2] Some of these purchases may also have acted as financial security for JS's other major endeavor in this period, the Kirtland Safety Society Bank.[3] An ambitious endeavor, the Safety Society was never able to realize its founders' aspirations because of the insurmountable obstacles it faced, including underfunding, opposition, the lack of a bank charter, and the financial panic of 1837.[4]

JS and other church leaders in Kirtland began making plans for a bank in October 1836. By mid-October they had chosen the name of the institution, the Kirtland Safety Society Bank, and had begun taking subscriptions for stock.[5] On 2 November 1836 the stockholders met and ratified the Kirtland Safety Society's constitution. Thirty-two stockholders were then elected as bank directors, likely at this same meeting, and they elected two primary officers for the society, Sidney Rigdon as president and JS as cashier.[6]

Ohio, like many other states, required parties intending to establish a bank to petition the state legislature for an act of incorporation. If approved, the bank would receive

---

1. See Historical Introduction to Mortgage to Peter French, 5 Oct. 1836, pp. 294–295 herein.

2. See Historical Introduction to Minutes, 22 Dec. 1836, p. 321 herein; and Historical Introduction to Discourse, 6 Apr. 1837, p. 354 herein.

3. See Willard Richards, Kirtland, OH, to Hepzibah Richards, Hamilton, NY, 20 Jan. 1837, Levi Richards Family Correspondence, CHL; and Warren A. Cowdery, Editorial, *LDS Messenger and Advocate,* July 1837, 3:535.

4. See Historical Introduction to Constitution of the Kirtland Safety Society Bank, 2 Nov. 1836, pp. 300–304 herein. For more on the financial panic of 1837, see "Joseph Smith Documents from October 1835 through January 1838," pp. xxviii–xxxii herein.

5. Winthrop Eaton, Bill of Goods, 11 Oct. 1836, JS Office Papers, CHL; Kirtland Safety Society, Stock Ledger, 1–2; see also Historical Introduction to Constitution of the Kirtland Safety Society Bank, 2 Nov. 1836, pp. 301–304 herein.

6. Historical Introduction to Constitution of the Kirtland Safety Society Bank, 2 Nov. 1836, pp. 300–303 herein.

a charter granting it banking privileges.[7] After the 2 November organization of the Safety Society, apostle Orson Hyde was assigned to go to Columbus, Ohio, where the legislature met, to find a politician willing to present the society's petition for a charter. Although the Kirtland Safety Society directors may have hoped for a quick approval, Hyde was not able to find a legislative sponsor until February 1837.[8] In the meantime, JS, Rigdon, and the society's stockholders reorganized their institution on 2 January 1837. They restructured the society as an unincorporated bank, renamed it the Kirtland Safety Society Anti-Banking Company, and drafted new articles of agreement to replace the original constitution.[9] This change in structure led to new titles for the society's officers: Rigdon became the secretary and JS the treasurer. After this reorganization, the society conducted banking services in an unofficial capacity while Hyde continued pursuing a bank charter.

A record of loans from the institution bears the date of 7 January, but the institution may have opened for business as early as 4 January, the date found on the earliest extant Kirtland Safety Society notes.[10] When individuals took out a loan, they received the amount borrowed in the form of Kirtland Safety Society notes.[11] The clerks and officers of the society also exchanged the society's notes for the notes of other banks, thereby increasing the circulation of the society's notes and its financial reserves.[12] According to the extant records, most of the individuals involved in financial transactions with the Kirtland Safety Society were Kirtland residents, along with a few people from Willoughby and Cleveland. Nearly all stockholders and loan recipients were church members.[13]

---

7. An Act to Prohibit the Issuing and Circulating of Unauthorized Bank Paper [27 Jan. 1816], *Statutes of the State of Ohio* [1841], 136–139, 154; see also Bodenhorn, "Bank Chartering and Political Corruption in Antebellum New York," 231–257.

8. No extant documents record Hyde's efforts in Columbus. He may have begun as early as November, but there is no evidence that he traveled to Columbus before the beginning of the 1836–1837 legislative session on 5 December 1836.

9. Articles of Agreement for the Kirtland Safety Society Anti-Banking Company, 2 Jan. 1837, pp. 324–325 herein. Warren A. Cowdery described the society as a "bank, or monied institution," that was "considered a kind of joint stock association." (Warren A. Cowdery, Editorial, *LDS Messenger and Advocate,* July 1837, 3:535; see also Walker, "Kirtland Safety Society and the Fraud of Grandison Newell," 44–47.)

10. These loans are recorded in the discount book and loan papers. The earliest loans are undated and some are dated 7 January 1837. In the charges filed against JS and Sidney Rigdon for issuing banknotes, 4 January 1837 was listed as the first day JS and Rigdon acted as bank officers. (Kirtland Safety Society, Loan Transactions, JS Office Papers, CHL; Transcript of Proceedings, 24 Oct. 1837, Rounds Qui Tam v. JS [Geauga Co. C.P. 1837], Record Book U, pp. 359–364; Transcript of Proceedings, 24 Oct. 1837, Rounds Qui Tam v. Rigdon [Geauga Co. C.P. 1837], Record Book U, pp. 359–362, Geauga County Archives and Records Center, Chardon, OH; see also Kirtland Safety Society Notes, 4 Jan.–9. Mar. 1837, pp. 331–340 herein.)

11. See Kirtland Safety Society Notes, 4 Jan.–9 Mar. 1837, pp. 331–340 herein. Often banks followed a practice called discounting, in which the interest from the loan was subtracted from the loan total at the time the borrower was given the money for the loan. From the few extant records, it appears that the Safety Society was practicing discounting on at least the early loans it financed. (See Kirtland Safety Society, "List of Notes for Discounting Jany. 1837," JS Office Papers, CHL.)

12. Woodruff, Journal, 6 Jan. 1837; Agreement with David Cartter, 14 Jan. 1837, pp. 341–343 herein.

13. Kirtland Safety Society, Loan Transactions, JS Office Papers, CHL. A small number were apparently unknown to the recording clerks, who in place of a name wrote "stranger." Most of the transactions

After opening in early January, the Kirtland Safety Society quickly garnered both popular interest and hostility. Contemporary and reminiscent accounts indicate there was general acceptance and circulation of the society's notes in the first weeks of the institution's operation.[14] Early on, however, several newspapers concentrated on the solvency of the institution. Editors for the *Cleveland Gazette* expressed surprise at "the readiness with which these anti-banking *bank* bills are thrown into circulation without any *evidence* or *knowledge* of the solvency of the issues" and considered it "a most reprehensible fraud on the public," since "as far as we can learn there is no property bound for their redemption, no coin on hand to redeem them with, and no responsible individuals whose honor or whose honesty is pledged for their payment."[15] The *Ohio Star,* a Ravenna newspaper that frequently criticized JS and the church, printed an article warning readers of the "emission of Mormon money, purporting to be bank paper."[16] In contrast, a few newspapers defended the society. Although skeptical about the institution, the editors of the *Painesville Republican* wrote in mid-January that they had been informed that Safety Society officers "have a large amount in specie on hand and have the means of obtaining much more, if necessary," and, if this were the case, the circulation of the society's notes "would be beneficial to [the] community, and sensibly relieve the pressure in the money market."[17] The editors of the *Cleveland Weekly Advertiser* wrote an outright defense of the society, which they believed was "most shamefully and cruelly persecuted; whose motives and intentions were totally misconstrued and misrepresented" by other newspapers, particularly the *Cleveland Gazette.*[18]

Newspapers were not the only source of hostility; some individuals in Geauga County actively campaigned against the Kirtland Safety Society, with prominent county resident Grandison Newell apparently taking a lead role.[19] Amid heightened opposition in late January came rumors that the Safety Society had closed its doors. It is unclear whether or not the business did temporarily close, and if it did, what led to the closure. Wilford

---

where clerks used "stranger" involved an individual exchanging banknotes or redeeming Safety Society notes.

14. "Rags! Mere Rags!!," *Ohio Star* (Ravenna), 19 Jan. 1837, [3]; Kennedy, *Early Days of Mormonism,* 162.

15. "Mormon Currency," *Cleveland Daily Gazette,* 20 Jan. 1837, [2], italics in original; "A New Revelation—Morman Money," *Cleveland Daily Gazette,* 12 Jan. 1837, [2].

16. "Rags! Mere Rags!!," *Ohio Star* (Ravenna), 19 Jan. 1837, [3].

17. "Anti-Banking Company," *Painesville (OH) Republican,* 19 Jan. 1837, [2].

18. "Kirtland Safety Society," *Cleveland Weekly Advertiser,* 2 Feb. 1837, [3].

19. A former employee of Newell's, James Thompson, claimed Newell actively worked against the Safety Society: "I worked for Grandison Newell considerable. He used to drive about the country and buy up all the Mormon money possible, and the next morning go to the bank and obtain the specie." At the end of his life, Newell claimed that the actions he initiated against the Kirtland Safety Society were largely responsible for driving the church and its members out of Kirtland. Henry Holcomb, who was married to Newell's great-granddaughter, recorded, "He early became involved in serious controversies with the Mormons, located at Kirtland, and after a series of litigations succeeded, in consequence of their violation of the currency laws, in expelling them from the state." (James Thompson, Statement, *Naked Truths about Mormonism* [Oakland, CA], Apr. 1888, 3; Henry Holcomb, "Personal Experience's after the Civil War," in "Personal and Family History 1865–1903," p. 52, in Henry Holcomb Papers, Western Reserve Historical Society, Cleveland, OH.)

Woodruff recounted in his journal hearing that a mob from Painesville was coming to destroy the society's office.[20] Though it is not known whether the mob materialized in Kirtland, fear of violence may have led the directors to close the office temporarily. Writing about events at a distance, the *Cleveland Weekly Advertiser* described a "furious and insulting mob" gathering in Kirtland and threatening to destroy the society.[21] In a July 1837 editorial in the *Messenger and Advocate,* Warren A. Cowdery reported that "hundreds who were enemies, either came or sent their agents and demanded specie till the officers thought best to refuse payment."[22]

Rumors that the society had closed and was refusing to redeem notes for specie damaged its reputation and led some to assume the worst.[23] In response to the reported closing of the society's office, the *Cleveland Gazette* announced the failure of the institution, and other papers echoed this conclusion.[24] Such news may have been based on false stories devised by opponents to harm the institution and discredit JS as its officer. If the Safety Society did close in late January, it was a brief closure, probably around 23 or 24 January. Even though a few newspapers continued to insist that it had failed, the society made loans and accepted payments for stock after January 1837.[25]

The success of the Safety Society was also hampered by the terms of its incorporation. The articles of agreement set the original capital stock for the institution at $4 million, a considerably higher amount than that of other community banks in the period, which ranged from $100,000 to $300,000.[26] The capital stock was divided into 80,000 shares of

---

20. Woodruff wrote in his journal, "We had been threatened by a mob from Panesville to visit us that night & demolish our Bank & take our property but they did not appeare but the wrath of our enemies appears to be kindled against us." (Woodruff, Journal, 24 Jan. 1837.)

21. "Kirtland Safety Society," *Cleveland Weekly Advertiser,* 2 Feb. 1837, [3].

22. Warren A. Cowdery, Editorial, *LDS Messenger and Advocate,* July 1837, 3:536. The editors of the *Cleveland Weekly Advertiser* claimed that the accounts by other regional newspapers that the bank could not redeem its notes for specie were incorrect and that the office was closed for only a day. ("Kirtland Safety Society," *Cleveland Weekly Advertiser,* 2 Feb. 1837, [3].)

23. Warren A. Cowdery, Editorial, *LDS Messenger and Advocate,* July 1837, 3:536–537.

24. "A Piece of News for the Herald," *Cleveland Daily Gazette,* 24 Jan. 1837, [2]. For newspapers relaying this news, see the *Western Reserve Chronicle,* which reports to have gotten its information from the *Painesville Telegraph.* ("How Have the Mighty Fallen!!," *Western Reserve Chronicle* [Warren, OH], 7 Feb. 1837, [3].)

25. Kirtland Safety Society, Stock Ledger, 2, 14, 84.

26. As part of the process of granting a bank charter, the state legislature approved the proposed capital stock and determined the amount of capital a bank would be required to have before being allowed to operate. The required amount varied widely, ranging from five to twenty percent of the bank's capital stock. A banking reform bill by Ohio state senator Alfred Kelley—presented to the Ohio senate in January 1837 but not passed until 1845—stipulated a standard amount that subscribers would be required to pay to the bank: ten percent of each share when they subscribed for stock, thirty percent after directors were elected, and twenty percent every ninety days until the full amount they owed was paid. There was often not enough local capital on the frontier to provide the financial backing needed to establish most banks, and eastern investors were often needed to provide capital. ("A Bill for the Regulation of Banks within This State," sec. 10, *Ohio State Journal and Columbus Gazette,* 13 Jan. 1837, [2]; see also An Act to Incorporate the State Bank of Ohio and Other Banking Companies [24 Feb. 1845], *Acts of a General*

stock valued at $50 each.²⁷ Stockholders were required to pay a first installment of twenty-six cents per share of stock, and these subscription payments were intended to provide the reserves that would give the society financial stability, allowing the officers to exchange the society's paper notes for specie when customers presented them for redemption. By the beginning of January, the society had received almost $12,000 in specie or banknotes, as more than one hundred investors paid some portion of the first installment due on their stock subscriptions.²⁸ It is unclear how many Kirtland Safety Society notes were put in circulation,²⁹ but based on banking practices of the time, the society would have needed enough reserves to repay ten to thirty percent of the notes it issued, meaning its officers could feasibly have issued notes for between $40,000 and $120,000.³⁰

Nevertheless, the society was significantly underfunded, in large part because of the small amount that stockholders were required to pay for their stock. At fifty dollars per share, the price of stock for the Kirtland Safety Society was lower than average, but not unusually low when compared with similar financial institutions.³¹ What was substantially reduced for the society's stockholders was the amount they were required to pay when they first subscribed for stock.³² At twenty-six cents per share, this initial payment was

---

Nature [1845], p. 27, sec. 8. For an example of a failed bank revived by eastern investment, see Scheiber, "Commercial Bank of Lake Erie," 49–52.)

27. See Historical Introduction to Constitution of the Kirtland Safety Society Bank, 2 Nov. 1836, p. 302 herein.

28. Kirtland Safety Society, Stock Ledger, 1836–1837, in Chicago Historical Society, Collection of Mormon Materials, microfilm, CHL. In the stock ledger these payments are recorded as being made in "cash," which in nineteenth-century banking and accounting terminology could mean either specie, such as gold or silver coins, or banknotes. (Coffin, *Progressive Exercises in Book Keeping,* 10–39.)

29. The few contemporary records that discuss the number of the society's notes in circulation provide conflicting accounts of the society's financial stability and may not be reliable. (See "Kirtland Safety Society," *Cleveland Weekly Advertiser,* 2 Feb. 1837, [3]; and Warren Parrish, Kirtland, OH, 5 Feb. 1838, Letter to the Editor, *Painesville [OH] Republican,* 15 Feb. 1838, [3]; see also Hill et al., *Kirtland Economy Revisited,* 53–58.)

30. Fifty percent was considered a conservative amount for specie reserves, with most banks attempting to maintain reserves between ten to thirty percent. In Ohio, senator Alfred Kelley's banking reform bill required a fifty percent specie backing for the notes and bills issued by a banking institution. ("A Bill for the Regulation of Banks within This State," secs. 34, 41, *Ohio State Journal and Columbus Gazette,* 13 Jan. 1837, [2].)

31. In the 1836 Ohio legislature proceedings, the most common cost of stock shares for banks in Ohio towns was $100. Stock shares in larger, well-established areas varied from $100 to $500 per share, but most community banks on the western frontier could not demand such elevated prices. Shares in the stock of the Commercial Bank of Lake Erie were $100 and required five percent to be paid upon subscription. ("A Bill for the Regulation of Banks within This State," sec. 7, *Ohio State Journal and Columbus Gazette,* 13 Jan. 1837, [2]; Bodenhorn, *State Banking in Early America,* 19–20; Charter Acceptance, Letterbook, vol. 1, 1816–1839, [1], Commercial Bank of Lake Erie Records, Western Reserve Historical Society, Cleveland, OH.)

32. The Kirtland Safety Society charged $0.26¼ per share of stock. This amount was not a published figure but can be calculated based on stockholders' payments recorded in the society's stock ledger. Stockholders paid $2.63 for 10 shares of stock, $5.25 for 20 shares, $10.50 for 40 shares, $15.75 for 60 shares, $26.25 for 100 shares, $52.50 for 200 shares, and $105 for 400 shares. When the amount paid is divided by the number of shares, the price of an individual share comes to $0.26¼. While some individuals paid

significantly lower than what other banks or banking companies charged, which typically required between five and fifty dollars' initial payment per share.[33] The Kirtland Safety Society officers showed leniency to those who could not pay their full initial payment, and several stockholders made only partial payments, while a few never paid anything.[34] Individuals who subscribed for one thousand shares should have made an initial payment of $262.50, but many with subscriptions of a thousand or more shares of stock only ever paid a few dollars.[35] The combination of relatively low share prices, an unusually high capital stock, and a very low initial installment payment for stock, some of which was never paid, meant that the society was low on funds from the outset.

JS and other stockholders appear to have obtained additional funding by taking out loans from two nearby banking institutions. These loans would not have significantly improved the society's solvency but would likely have increased its available specie, which was needed for the redemption of notes. On 2 January, JS, Rigdon, and Newel K. Whitney received a loan for $3,000 from the Bank of Geauga in Painesville, due in forty-five days.[36] The second loan was taken out on 10 January from the Commercial Bank of Lake Erie in Cleveland for $1,200, due in four months.[37] This second loan was likely taken out by JS and Rigdon as officers of the Safety Society, but it is not certain, since the signatures on the promissory note were removed—a common practice when a loan was repaid.

---

more than the required amount, many others paid less than they owed for their initial payment on stock. (Kirtland Safety Society, Stock Ledger, 33–34, 43–44, 81–82, 183–184, 191–192, 195–196.)

33. No compilations of data for installment payments have been created for nineteenth-century banks, but the Bank of Geauga in Painesville, Ohio, notified stockholders that an installment of $6.50 was due on each share on 20 January 1837. The bank charter for the Commercial Bank of Lake Erie in Cleveland, Ohio, required an installment of five percent, or five dollars on each share. The Bank of Monroe in Michigan notified stockholders of monthly installments of five dollars per share after the bank's 10 February 1837 meeting. (Notice from Bank of Geauga, 16 Nov. 1836, in *Painesville [OH] Telegraph*, 30 Dec. 1836, [4]; Charter Acceptance, Letterbook, vol. 1, 1816–1839, [1], Commercial Bank of Lake Erie Records, Western Reserve Historical Society, Cleveland, OH; "Bank of Monroe," *Painesville [OH] Republican*, 29 Feb. 1837.)

34. Five individuals who subscribed for stock have no recorded payments in the extant stock ledger: Joseph Brayn, Frederick G. Williams, Samuel Willard, Luther P. Bates, and Samuel Wittemore. (Kirtland Safety Society, Stock Ledger, 159–160, 197–198, 199–200, 207–208, 213–214.)

35. See, for example, Kirtland Safety Society, Stock Ledger, 37–38, 57–58, 209–210, 237–238, 243–244. This was not the only time that subscriptions caused financial difficulties for the church in Kirtland. During the construction of the House of the Lord in Kirtland, missionaries gathered subscriptions from church members for the temple only to find later that many were not honored. (Bishop's Appeal, *LDS Messenger and Advocate*, Sept. 1837, 3:561; Hyrum Smith, Reynolds Cahoon, and Jared Carter, Kirtland, OH, to "the Churches of Christ," 1 June 1833, in JS Letterbook 1, pp. 36–38.)

36. The promissory note for this loan is not extant, but the record of the loan appears in the Bank of Geauga Discount Book. The Bank of Geauga was the closest banking institution to Kirtland. (Bank of Geauga, Discount Book, 2 Jan. 1837.)

37. JS and Others, Cleveland, OH, to Commercial Bank of Lake Erie, Promissory Note, 10 Jan. 1837, JS Collection, CHL. The Commercial Bank of Lake Erie was another bank located relatively close to Kirtland. The substantial investments of the Dwights, a New York banking family, ensured the financial reserves and stability of the bank. It held deposits from the Ohio government and the federal government and provided much of northern Ohio's paper currency from 1831 to 1843. (Scheiber, "Commercial Bank of Lake Erie," 47, 49–53.)

By mid-January, JS, Rigdon, and managers of the Kirtland Safety Society began making arrangements to expand its reach outside of Kirtland. On 14 January the managers signed a contract with David Cartter, a lawyer in Akron, Ohio, designating him an agent of the society,[38] and later that month, the officers made business arrangements with the Bank of Monroe in Monroe, Michigan. They appear to have bought stock in the bank and reached an agreement to partner with its officers, perhaps intending to become a branch of the Bank of Monroe and act under its charter.[39] In early February, JS, Rigdon, Hyrum Smith, and Oliver Cowdery traveled to Michigan for a stockholders' meeting of the bank. At this meeting, Cowdery was made vice president and a bank director of the Bank of Monroe.[40] While in Monroe in February, Hyrum Smith and Rigdon each borrowed notes from the Bank of Monroe, likely taking these notes back to Kirtland and using them in the society's office.[41] By the end of March the Bank of Monroe suspended specie payments, and it appears to have failed by the end of the year.[42]

Two events in February significantly affected the development of the Kirtland Safety Society and its ability to gain public support. First, Samuel D. Rounds brought charges against JS, Sidney Rigdon, Warren Parrish, Newel K. Whitney, Frederick G. Williams, and Horace Kingsbury under an 1816 Ohio statute that made it a finable offense for an unchartered bank to perform banking services, including the issuing of notes.[43] Public understanding of Ohio banking laws in 1837 was muddled, and there was disagreement

---

38. Agreement with David Cartter, 14 Jan. 1837, pp. 341–343 herein.

39. The earliest extant record of a transaction between the Kirtland Safety Society and the Bank of Monroe is a receipt dated 25 January 1837. This receipt was signed by Sidney Rigdon, identifying himself as the president of the Kirtland Safety Society, and Bailey J. Hathaway, a bank director for the Bank of Monroe, who replaced G. B. Harleston as the bank's cashier. (B. J. Hathaway, Receipt, 25 Jan. 1837, JS Office Papers, CHL; "Bank of Monroe," *Painesville [OH] Republican,* 29 Feb. 1837.)

40. "Bank of Monroe," *Painesville (OH) Telegraph,* 24 Feb. 1837, [3]. Bailey J. Hathaway, who was appointed cashier at the same gathering, announced the new positions to the public. S. A. Davis, the editor of the Universalist paper *Glad Tidings, and Ohio Christian Telescope,* visited Kirtland in February or March 1837 and wrote, "We had not the pleasure of seeing Joseph Smith Jr. Sidney Rigdon, or O. Cowdery, three leading men of this sect, as they had gone to Michigan on business for their Banking Institution." ("Bank of Monroe," *Painesville [OH] Republican,* 29 Feb. 1837; "Kirtland,—Mormonism, &c.," *LDS Messenger and Advocate,* Apr. 1837, 3:491.)

41. Bank of Monroe, Account Statement, [Monroe, MI], for Kirtland Safety Society, ca. Apr. 1837, CHL.

42. "Monroe Bank," *Daily Cleveland Herald,* 18 Mar. 1837, [2]; "Monroe Bank," *Ohio Star* (Ravenna), 30 Mar. 1837; "Bank of Monroe, Michigan," *Herald* (New York), 12 Apr. 1837, [2]; "Broken Banks and Fraudulent Institutions," *Daily Herald and Gazette* (Cleveland, OH), 4 Dec. 1837, [1].

43. See An Act to Prohibit the Issuing and Circulating of Unauthorized Bank Paper [27 Jan. 1816], *Statutes of the State of Ohio, of a General Nature* [1841], pp. 136, 137, secs. 1–4, 12. The charges were first brought 9 February, with an additional lawsuit adding Parrish as a defendant on 14 March. Rounds charged these individuals because, in their positions in the Kirtland Safety Society, they had signed notes issued for loans or exchanges. JS and Rigdon were elected officers, Parrish served as the main clerk, and Whitney, Williams, and Kingsbury acted as temporary officers in January. Rounds may have been encouraged in pursuing this litigation by Grandison Newell. After the trials for JS and Rigdon, Rounds transferred the judgments to Newell, suggesting he had an interest in the case. (Case Costs, 24 Oct. 1837, Rounds Qui Tam v. JS [Geauga Co. C.P. 1837], Execution Docket G, p. 105; Case Costs, 24 Oct. 1837, Rounds Qui Tam v. Rigdon [Geauga Co. C.P. 1837], Execution Docket G, p. 106, Geauga County Archives and Records Center, Chardon, OH.)

regarding the enforcement of the 1816 statute, in large part due to an 1824 statute that had prohibited lawsuits against the notes of unauthorized or unincorporated banks.[44] The legal disjuncture between the two statutes was not formally resolved until 1840.[45] Though the other four church members were not prosecuted,[46] JS and Rigdon were tried in absentia in October 1837. In the trials, "the Court charged the Jury that said Statute was in force," and JS and Rigdon were both found guilty according to the Act of 1816 and fined $1,000 each.[47]

The second significant event in February occurred when Samuel Medary presented the society's petition for a bank charter in the Ohio senate. The petition was presented as an amendment to a bill to create a state bank in Ohio, and some aspects of the proposal differed from the society's articles, possibly to make the legislature more amenable to granting a charter.[48] The most significant change was a decrease in the society's capital stock from $4 million to $300,000, which, although still higher than most, was within the range of other community banks. The Safety Society's petition failed to pass, on a vote of eleven in favor and twenty-four opposed.[49] In fact, the legislature did not approve the incorporation of a single bank in its 1836–1837 session. Some banks were approved for a charter by virtue of being added to the bill for a state bank, but that bill was not passed until 1845.[50] There were no other documented attempts to obtain a banking charter for the Kirtland Safety Society from the Ohio legislature.

Despite these setbacks, the society continued to expand its economic reach and acquire financial supporters inside and outside of Kirtland. In March two additional contracts were

---

44. See "Anti-Banking Company," *Painesville (OH) Republican,* 19 Jan. 1837, [2]–[3]; "A New Revelation—Morman Money," *Cleveland Daily Gazette,* 12 Jan. 1837, [2]; "Mormon Currency," *Cleveland Daily Gazette,* 20 Jan. 1837, [2]; and "For the Republican," *Painesville Republican,* 16 Feb. 1837, [2]–[3]; see also Walker, "Kirtland Safety Society and the Fraud of Grandison Newell," 60–105; and Hill et al., *Kirtland Economy Revisited,* 49–50.

45. An Act Further to Amend the Act Entitled, "An Act to Prohibit the Issuing and Circulating of Unauthorized Bank Paper," Passed January 27, 1816, and to Repeal Certain Acts and Parts of Acts Therein Named [23 Mar. 1840], *Statutes of the State of Ohio* [1841], p. 144, sec. 8.

46. Geauga Co., OH, Court of Common Pleas, Record Book U, pp. 353–359, Geauga County Archives and Records Center, Chardon, OH.

47. Transcript of Proceedings, 24 Oct. 1837, Rounds Qui Tam v. JS [Geauga Co. C.P. 1837], Record Book U, pp. 362–364; Transcript of Proceedings, 24 Oct. 1837, Rounds Qui Tam v. Rigdon [Geauga Co. C.P. 1837], Record Book U, pp. 359–362, Geauga County Archives and Records Center, Chardon, OH; Account Statement from Perkins & Osborn, 28 Oct. 1838, JS Collection, CHL. Perhaps because of the confusing and contradictory nature of Ohio banking laws, JS and Rigdon's lawyers, William L. Perkins and Salmon Osborn, submitted a bill of exceptions, the first step in appealing the judgment, but no formal appeal was ever made.

48. The charter also included the names of Benjamin Adams, Nehemiah Allen, and Benjamin Bissel, who were not members of the church and were not stockholders in the society. These individuals, all influential men from Painesville, may have been added in hopes of strengthening the petition or lessening religious prejudice. (*Journal of the Senate of the State of Ohio,* 365; Letter to the Editor, *Daily Herald and Gazette* [Cleveland, OH], 8 Sept. 1837, [2].)

49. *Journal of the Senate of the State of Ohio,* 366.

50. See An Act to Incorporate the State Bank of Ohio and Other Banking Companies [24 Feb. 1845], *Acts of a General Nature* [1845], p. 51, sec. 69.

signed, establishing individuals in Painesville, Ohio, and Beaver County, Pennsylvania, as agents of the Safety Society.[51] In discourses given on 6 April 1837, JS, Hyrum Smith, and Sidney Rigdon each focused on debt and the need for church members to support the Kirtland Safety Society financially.[52] In his address, Rigdon identified three distinct sources of the church's debt: building the Kirtland House of the Lord, losing property in Missouri, and purchasing land in Kirtland for the Saints.[53] A few days later, on 9 April, JS and Rigdon again spoke on the financial situation of the church and urged members to accept the notes of the Kirtland Safety Society and support the institution.[54] Possibly fearing the seizure of his property to pay outstanding debts, JS on 7 and 10 April sold or transferred several large properties he owned to William Marks, who appears to have acted as his agent.[55]

From November 1836 to April 1837 financial matters were one of JS's greatest concerns. Over these six months he struggled to repay the debts of the church while attempting to establish a new banking company. The documents concerning the Kirtland Safety Society demonstrate its tumultuous period of operation, from an ambitious beginning in November 1836, through reorganization in January 1837, and into a constant struggle for investors and support in spring 1837. Despite JS's efforts, the society faced frequent opposition and received only limited support.

------------------- ☙ -------------------

Mortgage to Peter French, 5 October 1836

Source Note

William Miller, William Smith, Don Carlos Smith, and JS, Mortgage for property in Kirtland Township, Geauga Co., OH, to Peter French, 5 Oct. 1836; signed by Phebe Scott Miller, William Miller, Caroline Grant Smith, William Smith, Agnes Coolbrith Smith, Don Carlos Smith, Emma Smith, and JS; witnessed by Joseph Pine and Arial Hanson; certified by Arial Hanson. Featured version copied in Geauga County Deed Record, vol. 22, pp. 383–384; handwriting of Ralph Cowles; Geauga County Archives and Records Center, Chardon, OH. Transcription from a digital color image made of original in 2011.

Volume measuring 18¼ × 13 × 3 inches (46 × 33 × 8 cm) and including 618 pages, plus 15 pages of an index of grantors and grantees. At an unknown time, the original cover and binding were replaced with a cream canvas cover with maroon leather corners. The volume contains 318 leaves measuring 17¾ × 11½ inches (45 × 29 cm). In the mid- to late nineteenth century, a page-for-page transcript of the volume was created; the transcript is also housed at the Geauga County Archives and Records Center.

This volume was in the possession of the Geauga County Recorder from its creation until 1996, when it was transferred to the newly organized Geauga County Archives and Records Center. Includes tipped-in documents, notations, redactions, and archival marking.

---

51. Agreement with Ovid Pinney and Stephen Phillips, 14 Mar. 1837, pp. 344–348 herein; J. W. Briggs, Bond, Kirtland, OH, 8 Mar. 1837, JS Office Papers, CHL.

52. See Historical Introduction to Discourse, 6 Apr. 1837, p. 354 herein.

53. "Anniversary of the Church of Latter Day Saints," *LDS Messenger and Advocate,* Apr. 1837, 3:488.

54. Woodruff, Journal, 9 Apr. 1837.

55. See Historical Introduction to Deed to William Marks, 10 Apr. 1837, pp. 358–359 herein.

Historical Introduction

On 5 October 1836, JS, William Miller,[56] William Smith, and Don Carlos Smith purchased just over 239 acres of land located at the intersection of Eagle Mills Road and Russell Road in southwestern Kirtland Township, Ohio, from Peter and Sarah French for $11,777.50.[57] The same day, the four men signed a mortgage agreement, presented here, with Peter French for that land.[58] The mortgage agreement was for $9,777.50; the $2,000 difference may reflect a down payment or may have been a discount to cover the interest JS and the others would pay, although neither is specified in extant records.

Traditionally mortgaged property provided the creditor a guarantee or security for repayment without denying the debtor use of the property. According to John Bouvier's 1839 legal dictionary, a mortgage was "a conveyance of lands by a debtor to his creditor as a pledge and security for the repayment of a sum of money borrowed, or performance of a covenant . . . with a proviso that such conveyance shall be void on payment of the money and interest on a certain day." In courts following English legal traditions, mortgaged land was held "merely as a pledge or security" and the person paying the mortgage "is held to be the real owner of the land, the debt being considered the principal, and the land the accessory."[59] In the case of the mortgage featured here, the agreement with Peter French gave JS and his fellow purchasers immediate access to the title and the legal right to the land but required them to pay for the property over an extended length of time. As part of the mortgage, the four men agreed to yearly payments of $1,000 to French for thirteen years beginning on 5 April 1838, with a final payment on 5 April 1851 of around $400.

---

56. William Miller was born in Avon, New York, in 1814. He married Phebe Scott in May 1834 and was baptized into the Latter-day Saint church on 28 October 1834. He first bought land in Kirtland in November 1834, and he and his wife moved there in fall 1835. Miller may have been involved because he was in a position to help finance the purchase. He may have also been intended to act as a caretaker or overseer since he owned land in an adjacent lot. (Jenson, *LDS Biographical Encyclopedia,* 1:481–482; Geauga Co., OH, Deed Records, 1795–1921, vol. 19, pp. 178–179, 1 Nov. 1834, microfilm 20,238, U.S. and Canada Record Collection, FHL.)

57. Peter and Sarah French to William Miller et al., Deed, Kirtland, OH, 5 Oct. 1836, Geauga County Deed Record, vol. 23, pp. 94–95, Geauga County Archives and Records Center, Chardon, OH. Peter French was one of the earliest settlers of Kirtland, moving there in 1811, and was a major property owner in Kirtland. The church had purchased 103 acres from him in 1833, including the land on which the House of the Lord had been built as well as part of the area JS and other church leaders platted for the use of the Saints. (Crary, *Pioneer and Personal Reminiscences,* 6; Geauga Co., OH, Deed Records, 1795–1921, vol. 17, pp. 38–39, 359–361, 10 Apr. and 17 June 1833, microfilm 20,237, U.S. and Canada Record Collection, FHL; Minutes, 23 Mar. 1833–A and 23 Mar. 1833–B, in *JSP,* D3:46–54; *JSP,* D4:176n286; Historical Introduction to Covenant, 29 Nov. 1834, in *JSP,* D4:188–189; Historical Introduction to Minutes, 18 Jan. 1835, in *JSP,* D4:216–217.)

58. This was the first of two extant mortgage agreements JS and others made for land bought in fall 1836. The second mortgage was for over 132 acres, purchased from Alpheus Russell by JS and Jacob Bump on 10 October 1836. (Geauga Co., OH, Deed Records, 1795–1921, vol. 23, pp. 539–540, 10 Oct. 1836, microfilm 20,240, U.S. and Canada Record Collection, FHL.)

59. "Mortgage," in Bouvier, *Law Dictionary* [1839], 2:150–151.

This transaction with Peter French was the largest documented land purchase JS made in Ohio. During a three-month period in the fall of 1836, JS (individually and in connection with other church members) purchased several documented tracts of land totaling approximately 440 acres in and around Kirtland.[60] The French land transaction is representative of these land purchases and illustrates JS's increased involvement in temporal and financial affairs and his personal investment in facilitating the development of Kirtland.[61] The land purchased in the fall of 1836 appears to have provided space for newly arrived members of the church as well as increased the church's assets. The French mortgage may have also provided financial security for the Kirtland Safety Society. JS sold land at this time, though primarily in small sections in the platted area of Kirtland near the House of the Lord and not from his recent purchases. Just over six months later, on 10 April 1837, JS transferred his interest in the French land to William Marks in the form of a quitclaim deed.[62] This was part of several land transactions made between JS and Marks in early April 1837.[63]

Document Transcript

W^m. Miller, W^m. Smith, Don C[arlos] Smith & Joseph Smith Jr. To Peter French

To all people to whom these presents shall come Greeting Know Ye that we William Miller William Smith & Don Carlos Smith, Joseph Smith Jun. of Kirtland in the ⟨County of Geauga &⟩ State of Ohio for the consideration

---

60. For the recorded land purchases by JS between September and November 1836, see Geauga Co., OH, Deed Records, 1795–1921, vol. 22, p. 305, 13 Sept. 1836; pp. 428–429, 14 Sept. 1836; pp. 430–431, 1 Oct. 1836; p. 430, 14 Oct. 1836; pp. 567–568, 2 Nov. 1836, microfilm 20,239, U.S. and Canada Record Collection, FHL; and Alpheus Russell to JS et al., Deed, Kirtland, OH, 10 Oct. 1836, Geauga County Deed Record, vol. 23, p. 539, Geauga County Archives and Record Center, Chardon, OH. Images of these records are available on the Joseph Smith Papers website, josephsmithpapers.org.

61. See JS History, vol. B-1, 733. The population of Ohio grew significantly in the 1830s, as did the number of Latter-day Saints in Kirtland. Milton Backman estimated the number of Saints in Kirtland in 1836 at 1,300, with an annual growth of 200 to 500 members and the period of 1835 to 1837 seeing the greatest amount of growth. By December 1836 there was a shortage of land for arriving church members, and guidelines were established for those intending to move to Kirtland. Sidney Rigdon later described the objective of purchasing land: "that there might be a place of rest, a place of safety, a place that the saints might lawfully call their own." He instructed the elders to discuss the gathering of the Saints and "urge the necessity and propriety of the measure from the fact that we have a place *for them,* and not only so, it is the will of God that they should come." (Backman, *Heavens Resound,* 139–140; Minutes, 22 Dec. 1836, p. 323 herein; "Anniversary of the Church of Latter Day Saints," *LDS Messenger and Advocate,* Apr. 1837, 3:488–489, italics in original.)

62. Geauga Co., OH, Deed Records, 1795–1921, vol. 23, p. 539, 10 Apr. 1837, microfilm 20,240, U.S. and Canada Record Collection, FHL. Bouvier's legal dictionary defines a quitclaim deed as a release of the possession of land by the owner. A quitclaim deed was used to release an individual's title, interest, or claims to property. It did not act as a warranty deed granting title but merely conveyed all of that individual's ties, if any, to another person. ("Quit claim," in Bouvier, *Law Dictionary* [1839], 2:321; Greenwood, *Researcher's Guide to American Genealogy,* 409.)

63. See Historical Introduction to Deed to William Marks, 10 Apr. 1837, p. 358 herein.

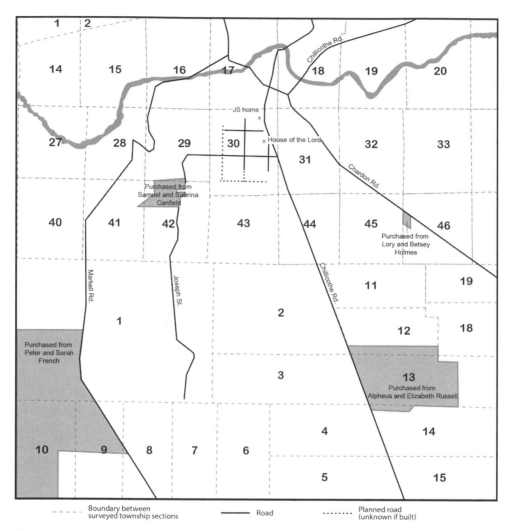

Selected land purchases, Kirtland, Ohio, September–November 1836. Beginning in mid-September, Joseph Smith, individually and jointly with other church members, purchased approximately 440 acres of land in the Kirtland area. Four of the more substantial purchases are highlighted here. Joseph Smith appears to have purchased this land for incoming Latter-day Saints and may also have used it to back the Kirtland Safety Society Bank.

of nine thousand, seven hundred, and Seventy seven dollars 50/100 received to our full satisfaction of Peter French, do give grant, bargain sell & confirm unto him the said Peter French the following described Tract or lot of land situate in the township of Kirtland being number nine in the ninth Range of Townships ~~in~~ of the Connecticut Western Reserve in the State of Ohio, and which is also in the County of Geauga and is known by being a part of Lots Nᵒ· one, nine and ten and is bounded as follows, beginning at the S.W. corner of Tract Nᵒ· two thence E on the line of said tract Eighty rods sixteen and a half links, thence northerly on the W. line of a lot of land now owned by Eli Bunnell to said Bunnells N.W. corner, thence E to the centre of the highway leading from Kirtland Mills to the Metcalf Settlement so called, thence northerly on said highway to the S. E. corner of a lot of land now owned by Joshua Roberts;[64] thence westerly on the S. line of said Roberts land one hundred and eighteen rods and six links to the W. line of said Tract Nᵒ· two thence S. on said line, two hundred and ninety two rods and twenty two links to the place of beginning. Also another piece beginning at the N W. corner of land now owned by Ezekiel Rider,[65] thence south on said Riders and John Huffmans[66] land, to the corner of the sixty acres formerly owned by Joel Roberts[67] thence W. parallel with the N. line of said lot to the centre of the Road thence N westerly on the centre of said Road to the centre of the E & W. (County) Road thence E on said Road far enough so that a line drawn N. parallel with the E line of said Lot shall contain thirty acres; thence north on said line to the N. line of the Gore or lot, thence East on said Lot line to the place of beginning, containing in all the two above Surveys two hundred thirty nine acres and ninety one rods, be the same more or less, but subject to all legal highways. To have and to hold the above granted and bargained premises with the appurtenances thereof unto him the said Peter French his heirs and assigns forever to his own proper use and behoof. And we the said Wᵐ Miller Wᵐ Smith, Don C. Smith & Joseph Smith Junʳ· do for ourselves our heirs executors and administrators, covenant with the said Peter French his heirs and assigns that at and until the ensealing of these presents we

---

64. Joshua Roberts purchased this land, totaling one hundred acres, from Arial Cornings on 15 September 1834. (Geauga Co., OH, Deed Records, 1795–1921, vol. 19, pp. 73–74, 15 Sept. 1834, microfilm 20,238, U.S. and Canada Record Collection, FHL.)

65. Ezekiel Rider may have owned or rented the land at the time of this transaction, but no deed in his name appears in Geauga County Deed Records for Kirtland.

66. John Huffman owned an adjoining lot. (Geauga Co., OH, Deed Records, 1795–1921, vol. 16, pp. 292–293, 17 Mar. 1832, microfilm 20,236, U.S. and Canada Record Collection, FHL.)

67. Joel Roberts sold sixty acres of land to Joseph Robinson and David Lafler on 15 March 1833, and on 13 April 1833 Robinson obtained a quitclaim deed on thirty acres from Lafler, presumably Lafler's half of the sixty acres they purchased jointly from Roberts. (Geauga Co., OH, Deed Records, 1795–1921, vol. 17, pp. 366–368, 15 Mar. and 13 Apr. 1833, microfilm 20,237, U.S. and Canada Record Collection, FHL.)

were well seized of the premises, as a good indefeasible estate in fee simple and have good right to bargain and sell the same in manner and form as above written, and that the same be free of all incumbrances, whatsoever. And furthermore we the said Wm Miller W^m. Smith, Don C Smith and Joseph Smith Junr. do by these presents bind ourselves and our heirs, forever to Warrant and defend the above granted and bargained premises to him the said Peter French his heirs and assigns, against all lawful claims and demands whatsoever. And we the said Phebe Miller,[68] Caroline [Grant] Smith,[69] Agnes M. [Coolbrith] Smith[70] & Emma Smith, do hereby remise, release, and forever quit-claim unto the said Peter French his heirs and assigns, all my right and title of dower [p. 383] in and to the above described premises.[71] The condition of this deed is such that whereas the said Wm Miller Wm Smith, Don C Smith & Joseph Smith Jr. have executed and delivered to the said Peter French, fourteen promissory notes payable to him or bearer as follows: (to wit,) one of One thousand dollars on the fifth of April in the year one thousand Eight hundred and thirty Eight, & one of one thousand dollars in on each successive fifth of April thereafter until the fifth of April in the year one thousand Eight hundred and fifty one when they are to pay one of three hundred and ninety Eight dollars and Eighty cents. Now if the said Wm. Miller William Smith, D. C. Smith & J. Smith Junr. their heirs assigns, executors, or administrators, shall well and truly pay the aforesaid Notes, according to the tenor thereof to the said Peter French his heirs or assigns, then the above deed shall be void, otherwise to remain in full force and virtue In witness whereof we have hereunto set our hands and seals,

---

68. Phebe Scott was born in 1816 in Avon, New York. She married William Miller in May 1834, was baptized into the church in June 1834, and moved to Kirtland with her husband in autumn 1835. (Jenson, *LDS Biographical Encyclopedia,* 1:481–482; Backman, *Profile,* 48.)

69. Caroline Amanda Grant was born in 1814. She and her sister Roxie Ann Grant were baptized in 1833 near Erie, Pennsylvania. Their father, Joshua Grant, was also baptized in 1833. She married William Smith, JS's brother, in February 1833, and the couple moved to Kirtland shortly thereafter. They had two daughters, Mary Jane and Caroline. ("Records of Early Church Families," *Utah Genealogical and Historical Magazine,* July 1935, 104–105; Smith, *William Smith on Mormonism,* 22.)

70. Agnes Moulton Coolbrith was born in Scarborough, Maine, in July 1811. She was baptized into the church in Boston on 30 July 1832 and moved to Kirtland by 1833. She married Don Carlos Smith at the end of July 1835. ("Smith, Agnes M. Cool[b]rith," Patriarchal Blessing Index, 1833–1963, microfilm 392,685, U.S. and Canada Record Collection, FHL; Temple Records Index Bureau, *Nauvoo Temple Endowment Register,* 2; Samuel Smith, Diary, 30 July 1832; Lucy Mack Smith, History, 1844–1845, bk. 13, [11]; bk. 14, [3]; Geauga Co., OH, Probate Court, Marriage Records, 1806–1920, vol. C, p. 108, 30 July 1835, microfilm 873,461, U.S. and Canada Record Collection, FHL.)

71. This section of the deed specifies that the wives of the sellers were relinquishing their dower rights, or rights to the property after their husband's death, to Peter French. To ensure the release of dower rights was a voluntary action, the justice of the peace would ask each wife individually to acknowledge that she understood the terms of the release and willingly agreed to it. A similar section was included in most deeds that involved a married man.

this fifth day of October in the year of Our Lord One thousand eight hundred and thirty six.

Phebe Miller Seal[72]	Wm. Miller Seal
Caroline Smith Seal	Wm Smith Seal
Agnes M. Smith Seal	Don C. Smith Seal
Emma Smith Seal	Joseph Smith Jr Seal

Signed sealed and delivered in presence of Joseph Pine
Arial Hanson

The State of Ohio
Geauga County ss.   Oct. 5. 1836

Personally appeared Wm. Miller Wm. Smith Don C. Smith & Joseph Smith Jr. who acknowledged that they did Sign and seal the foregoing instrument; and that the same is their free act and deed. I further certify that I did examine the said Phebe Miller, Caroline Smith Agnes M Smith & Emma Smith separate and apart from her said husband and did then and there make known to her the contents of the foregoing instrument; and upon that examination she declared that she did voluntarily sign seal and acknowledge the same and that she was still satisfied therewith

Before me Arial Hanson Justice of the peace

Rec^{d.} 24th. at 1/2 past 2 o'clock PM & Recorded 26 Octr. AD 1836 Ralph Cowles Recorder

———— ℰℐ ————

Constitution of the Kirtland Safety Society Bank, 2 November 1836

Source Note

Constitution of the Kirtland Safety Society Bank, Kirtland Township, Geauga Co., OH, 2 Nov. 1836. Featured version printed [ca. Dec. 1836] as an extra of Latter Day Saints' Messenger and Advocate, *Dec. 1836; endorsed by unidentified scribe; one page; CHL.*

Single leaf, measuring 12⅝ × 6¾ inches (32 × 17 cm); text area measures 9½ × 4¼ inches (24 × 11 cm). The copy used for transcription has undergone archival preservation work to fix a tear at the document's top. On the verso, two ink notations in unidentified handwriting read, "Nov 2 1836 | Minutes of meeting | of Kirtland Safety | Society" and "Kirtland | Bank". The provenance of this document is unknown; it is assumed that the document has remained in continuous institutional custody since its creation.

---

72. TEXT: Each instance of "Seal" is enclosed in a hand-drawn representation of a seal.

Historical Introduction

On 2 November 1836, JS, Sidney Rigdon, and other stockholders of the Kirtland Safety Society Bank voted on and approved a constitution to organize and govern the new financial institution.[73] Though established primarily for the church, the bank was not exclusively for church members' use; JS and others likely saw the creation of a bank as a way to improve the local economy and raise money for destitute Saints. At this time, church leaders were also seeking ways to pay off their considerable debt, which resulted from the construction of the House of the Lord in Kirtland, Ohio; efforts to redeem Zion in Missouri; purchases of land in Kirtland and Missouri; and the recent printing of the Doctrine and Covenants and other publications.[74]

The establishment of a bank was a natural development for a growing community like Kirtland. Community banks sought profits by charging interest on the loans they made, discounting the notes of other banks, and making investments. In addition, banks stimulated local economies in two important ways: they provided the credit and liquidity necessary to allow a larger portion of a community to be involved in economic endeavors, such as funding land improvements or new companies, and they facilitated opportunities to exchange goods and services.[75]

JS and others had decided to establish a bank by late September or early October. Around that time, purchasing agents—likely Oliver Cowdery and Hyrum Smith—left for New York City to buy goods and negotiate credit for at least two Kirtland-area mercantile firms.[76] On 11 October the agents purchased goods from New York City merchant Winthrop Eaton, and for payment they gave Eaton a promissory note that was payable in six months at the "Kirtland Safety Society Bank,"[77] confirming that church leaders had developed plans for such an institution before the agents left. While in New York, the agents purchased safes—which were probably intended to hold the Kirtland Safety Society's

---

73. JS's history later recorded that "on the 2ᵈ of November the Brethren at Kirtland drew up certain articles of Agreement, preparatory to the organization of a Banking Institution." The majority of stockholders in the Kirtland Safety Society were members of the church living in Kirtland, though a small number of Painesville, Ohio, residents also invested, as did a few individuals who were not church members. Most stockholders were men, though six women had subscribed for stock by November 1836. Most subscribers had modest means and paid only a small portion of the price for the shares they were purchasing; the constitution required stockholders to pay additional installments when called upon to do so. (JS History, vol. B-1, 750; Kirtland Safety Society, Stock Ledger, 1836–1837, in Collection of Manuscripts about Mormons, Chicago History Museum.)

74. See Historical Introduction to Revelation, 6 Aug. 1836 [D&C 111], pp. 272–274 herein; see also Angell, Autobiography, 13; Johnson, Reminiscences and Journals, 25; Joseph Young, Salt Lake City, to Lewis Harvey, 16–18 Nov. 1880, CHL; Kennedy, *Early Days of Mormonism*, 111–112; and Olney, *Absurdities of Mormonism Portrayed*, 4.

75. Bodenhorn, *History of Banking*, 17–20, 46–47.

76. Both Ira Ames and Cyrus Smalling suggest in reminiscent accounts that Cowdery and Hyrum Smith made a trip to New York City to purchase goods for the Kirtland mercantile firms of Rigdon, Smith & Cowdery and Cahoon, Carter & Co., though neither provided a specific date for the journey. (Ames, Autobiography and Journal, [12]; Cyrus Smalling, Letter, Kirtland, OH, 10 Mar. 1841, in "Banking and Financiering at Kirtland," 668–670.)

77. Winthrop Eaton, Bill of Goods, 11 Oct. 1836, JS Office Papers, CHL.

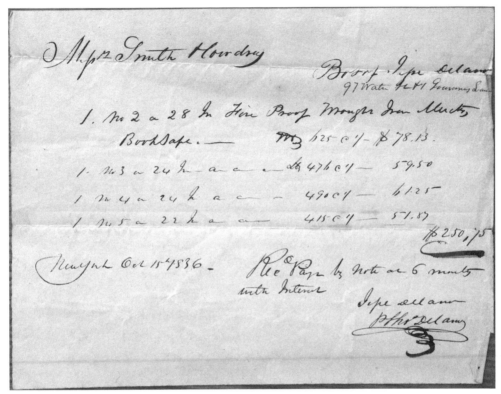

Invoice from Jesse Delano. 15 October 1836. New York City merchant Jesse Delano sold four "booksafes" to Hyrum Smith and Oliver Cowdery, at least one of which was probably intended for use by the Kirtland Safety Society. This and other invoices from Smith and Cowdery's trip to New York provide fragmentary evidence of the planning efforts for the Kirtland Safety Society in early fall 1836. Many of the goods purchased on credit by Smith and Cowdery were sold in the stores in and around Kirtland, Ohio, run by the firms Rigdon, Smith & Co.; Cahoon, Carter & Co.; and H. Smith & Co. Jesse Delano, Bill, 15 Oct. 1836, JS Office Papers, Church History Library, Salt Lake City. (Photograph by Welden C. Andersen.)

books and specie—from merchant Jesse Delano.[78] It may also have been during this trip that Cowdery arranged to have printing plates for Kirtland Safety Society banknotes made by the printing and engraving firm of Underwood, Spencer, Bald & Hufty.[79]

The Kirtland Safety Society began collecting subscriptions to purchase shares of the bank's stock in mid-October, and these stock subscriptions accounted for most of the society's operating capital.[80] The capital stock for the society was set at $4 million and divided into 80,000 shares valued at $50 each. The first subscription recorded in the society's stock ledger, dated 18 October 1836, was for 2,000 shares of stock for Sidney Rigdon, who paid $630 on his subscription by 22 October. He continued to pay the bank for his stock, and sometime later he subscribed for an additional 1,000 shares, thus reaching the maximum number of 3,000 shares a single stockholder could hold. JS also subscribed for 3,000 shares and made an initial payment of $1,342.69 on 22 October.[81] By 1 November, thirty-six subscribers had paid more than $5,000 on their 27,105 shares of stock.[82] An additional twenty-four individuals paid for stock on 2 November, possibly in connection with the stockholder meeting held that same day, increasing the bank's collections on stock to nearly $7,000. These payments were recorded in the society's stock ledger as being made in "cash," which in nineteenth-century banking terminology could mean either specie or banknotes.[83] The majority of stockholders in the bank subscribed for their shares of stock between October and December 1836.

The constitution of the Kirtland Safety Society Bank, featured here, is the only extant record of the 2 November 1836 stockholders' meeting. Presented to the gathering by Orson

---

78. Jesse Delano, Bill, 15 Oct. 1836, JS Office Papers, CHL.

79. Underwood, Spencer, Bald & Hufty had offices in New York City and Philadelphia. A 14 November letter to the editor of the newspaper *Aurora* noted that the Latter-day Saints had ordered plates in New York City. The plates were apparently picked up in Philadelphia. JS's history implies that Cowdery was given the task of acquiring banknotes after the society was formally organized on 2 November 1836. ("Mormonism in Ohio," *Aurora* [New Lisbon, OH], 19 Jan. 1837, [3]; "Bank at Kirtland," *Cleveland Weekly Advertiser*, 29 Dec. 1836, [1]; Kirtland Safety Society Notes, 4 Jan.–9 Mar. 1837, pp. 331–340 herein; JS History, vol. B-1, 750.)

80. A complete list of initial stockholders was never created, but a partial list, including later subscribers, was printed in the March 1837 issue of the *Messenger and Advocate*. The extant stock ledger for the Kirtland Safety Society serves as the main source for identifying those involved with the society. However, the ledger may be incomplete; some individuals named as subscribers at the 2 January meeting do not appear in the book and some stockholders' names appear to have been erased or written over. ("Minutes of a Meeting," *LDS Messenger and Advocate*, Mar. 1837, 3:476–477; Kirtland Safety Society, Stock Ledger, 1836–1837, in Collection of Manuscripts about Mormons, Chicago History Museum.)

81. Kirtland Safety Society, Stock Ledger, 1–2, 13–14; see also Young, Account Book, [2].

82. Kirtland Safety Society, Stock Ledger, 1836–1837, in Collection of Manuscripts about Mormons, Chicago History Museum.

83. James H. Coffin, *Progressive Exercises in Book Keeping* (Greenfield, MA: A. Phelps; Boston: Crocker and Brewster, 1836). Only one stock ledger is extant for the Kirtland Safety Society, containing the accounts for 205 stockholders from October 1836 to July 1837. It records the amount of stock purchased and payments made on the cost of that stock but no other financial transactions of the institution. Some individuals borrowed money against their stock subscriptions, a common practice in this period. (Kirtland Safety Society, Stock Ledger, 1836–1837, in Collection of Manuscripts about Mormons, Chicago History Museum.)

Hyde and unanimously approved by participants, the constitution established rules to govern the bank, its officers, and its stockholders preparatory to receiving a bank charter from the state legislature.[84] The authors of the constitution are unknown, but it was a group endeavor, likely headed by JS and Rigdon.[85] This constitution governed the Kirtland Safety Society until 2 January 1837, when the officers and stockholders reorganized the structure of their institution in the absence of a bank charter.[86]

In accordance with the guidelines established in the constitution, the stockholders held an election for officers and directors. This likely took place during the 2 November meeting or shortly thereafter. Thirty-two directors were elected from the stockholders present, and from this group a committee of six was appointed to act collectively for the entire group of directors.[87] The choice of directors for a local bank was in many ways as significant as the choice of officers, since the directors usually included prominent individuals able to inspire confidence in the bank and use their political connections on the bank's behalf.[88] The thirty-two directors then elected the bank officers. Rigdon was elected president and JS was elected cashier.[89]

The society's constitution was printed as an extra to the *Latter Day Saints' Messenger and Advocate* between the November and December issues of the newspaper. The extra was a single broadside dated December 1836 but possibly printed in November 1836. The

---

84. The language and terminology used in the constitution suggest that those involved in drafting it may have sought help from someone with legal or banking experience, though they may have also drawn on their own knowledge or consulted templates for legal forms that were available at the time. Handbooks such as *Every Man His Own Lawyer* and *The Business Man's Assistant* contained legal forms that clerks or others could copy for their own use. There was little standardization of banking practices in the United States in this period, and regulation of banking was managed at a state level. The regulations outlined in the constitution appear to have been consistent with other banking operations of the day. In January 1837, state senator Alfred Kelley introduced a banking reform bill that outlined articles to regulate and standardize banking practices in Ohio. The constitution for the Kirtland Safety Society uses the same terminology and many of the same practices and bylaws as those found in Kelley's bill, with a few exceptions in the number of directors appointed and the amount of the society's capital stock. Kelley's bill was not passed by the Ohio legislature until 1845. (Paraclete Potter, *Every Man His Own Lawyer* [Poughkeepsie, NY: By the author, 1836]; I. R. Butts, *Business Man's Assistant* [Boston: By the author, 1847]; "A Bill for the Regulation of Banks within This State," *Ohio State Journal and Columbus Gazette,* 13 Jan. 1837, [2]; An Act to Incorporate the State Bank of Ohio and Other Banking Companies [24 Feb. 1845], Swan, *Statutes of the State of Ohio,* 80–103.)

85. JS History, vol. B-1, 750.

86. See Historical Introduction to Articles of Agreement for the Kirtland Safety Society Anti-Banking Company, 2 Jan. 1837, p. 324 herein.

87. The members of the committee of directors were not named in the constitution, but an agreement signed by JS, Sidney Rigdon, Frederick G. Williams, David Whitmer, Oliver Cowdery, and Reynolds Cahoon in January 1837 identifies these men as managers of the society and may indicate that they were members of the committee of directors. (Agreement with David Cartter, 14 Jan. 1837, p. 343 herein.)

88. Scheiber, "Commercial Bank of Lake Erie," 51.

89. See Historical Introduction to Kirtland Safety Society Notes, 4 Jan.–9 Mar. 1837, p. 332 herein; Transcript of Proceedings, 24 Oct. 1837, Rounds v. JS [Geauga Co. C.P. 1837], Geauga Co., OH, Court of Common Pleas, Record Book U, pp. 362–364; and Transcript of Proceedings, 24 Oct. 1837, Rounds Qui Tam v. Rigdon [Geauga Co. C.P. 1837], Geauga Co., OH, Court of Common Pleas, Record Book U, pp. 359–362, Geauga County Archives and Records Center, Chardon, OH.

fact that the constitution was printed as an extra suggests that the society's officers and stockholders were unwilling to wait for it to be included in the normal issue of the paper and wanted to have copies available soon after the November meeting.

Document Transcript

Minutes of a meeting of the Stockholders of the Kirtland Safety Society Bank; held on the 2nd day of November, A. D. 1836. When the following preamble and articles were read three times by Orson Hyde, and unanimously adopted.

We the Stockholders of the Kirtland Safety Society Bank, for the more perfect government and regulation of the same, do ordain and establish the following constitution.

ARTICLE I.

The capital stock of said Bank shall not be less than four millions of dollars;[90] to be divided into shares of fifty dollars each; and may be increased to any amount, at the discretion of the directors.

ARTICLE II.

The management of said Bank shall be under the superintendence of thirty two directors, to be chosen annually by, and from among the Stockholders of the same; each Stockholder being entitled to one vote for each share, which he, she or they may hold in said Bank; and said votes may be given by proxy or in *propria persona.*

ARTICLE III.

It shall be the duty of said directors when chosen to elect from their number a President, Cashier, and chief Clerk.[91] It shall be the further duty of said directors to meet in the Director's Room, in said Banking house,[92] on the first Mondays of November and May of each year, at 9 o'clock A. M. to inspect the books of said Bank, and transact such other business as may be deemed necessary.

---

90. A capital stock of $4 million was significantly higher than that of other community banks in the period. The amount of the Kirtland Safety Society's capital stock was an ambitious and unlikely, if not impossible, objective. When the Kirtland Safety Society's charter was considered by the state senate in February 1837, the amount of its capital stock had been reduced to $300,000, which was still high but within the range of other community banks. (See Introduction to Part 5: 5 Oct. 1836–10 Apr. 1837, pp. 289–290 herein; "In Senate," *Ohio State Journal and Columbus Gazette,* 14 Feb. 1837, [2].)

91. In addition to electing Sidney Rigdon president and JS cashier, the directors made Warren Parrish the chief clerk, but it is not clear if he was elected in November or at a later point. Parrish's handwriting in the Safety Society's stock ledger begins by 21 November 1836, likely the same time he began acting as chief clerk. (Kirtland Safety Society, Stock Ledger, 13–14.)

92. The society's office was located close to the House of the Lord, likely in a lot to the south. (Woodruff, Journal, 25 Nov. 1836; see also Staker, *Hearken, O Ye People,* 413; and Plewe, *Mapping Mormonism,* 31.)

ARTICLE IV.

It shall be the duty of said directors to cho[o]se from among their number six men, who shall meet in the Banking house on Tuesday of each week, at 4 o'clock P. M. to examine all notes presented for discounting,[93] and enquire into, and assist in all matters pertaining to the Bank.

ARTICLE V.

Each director shall receive from the Bank one dollar per day for his services when called together at the semi-annual and annual meetings. The President, Cashier, chief Clerk and the six, the committee of the directors, shall receive a compensation for their services as shall be agreed by the directors at their semi-annual meetings.[94]

ARTICLE VI.

The first election of directors as set forth in the second article, shall take place at the meeting of the Stockholders to adopt this constitution, who shall hold their office until the first Monday of November, 1837 unless removed by death, or misdemeanor, and until others are duly elected. Every annual election of directors shall take place on the first Monday of November of each year.— It shall be the duty of the President, Cashier, and chief Clerk, of said Bank to receive the votes of the Stockholders by ballot, and declare the election.

ARTICLE VII.

The books of the Bank shall be always open for the inspection of the Stockholders.

ARTICLE VIII.

It shall be the duty of the officers of the Bank, to declare a dividend once in six months; which dividend shall be apportioned among the Stockholders, according to the installments by them paid in.

ARTICLE IX.

All persons subscribing stock in said Bank shall pay their first installment at the time of subscribing; and other installments from time to time, as shall be required by the directors.[95]

---

93. Discounting involved paying specie for less than the face value of notes from other banks and financial institutions. A discount was taken because the notes did not belong to the bank at which they were presented. If the credibility of the bank was in question, or if it was located far from the accepting bank, then a larger discount might be assessed. (Bodenhorn, *State Banking in Early America,* 48–49; Bodenhorn, *History of Banking,* 100, 149.)

94. Fredrick G. Williams recorded compensation from the Kirtland Safety Society Bank for three days "as director" and one day of labor, possibly referring to his work as treasurer pro tem in January 1837. (Williams, Account Book, 22; Kirtland Safety Society Notes, 4 Jan.–9 Mar. 1837, p. 332 herein.)

95. The first installment required for stock was twenty-six cents per share. This was an uncommonly low installment for initial subscriptions, yet many subscribers struggled to pay even this small amount. (Kirtland

ARTICLE X.

The directors shall give thirty days notice in some public paper, printed in this county, previous to an installment being paid in. All subscribers residing out of this State, shall be required to pay in half the amount of their subscriptions at the time of subscribing, and the remainder, or such part thereof as shall be required at any time by the directors after thirty days notice.

ARTICLE XI.

The President shall be empowered to call special meetings of the directors, whenever he shall deem it necessary; separate and aside from the annual and semi-annual meetings.

ARTICLE XII.

Two thirds of the directors shall form a quorum to act at the semi-annual meetings; and any number of the six, the committee of the directors, with the officers of the Bank, or any one of them may form a quorum to transact business at the weekly meetings; and in case none of the six are present at the weekly meetings the officers of the Bank must transact the business.

ARTICLE XIII.

The directors shall have power to enact such by-laws as they may deem necessary from time to time, providing they do not infringe upon this constitution.

ARTICLE XIV.

Any article in this constitution may be altered at any time, amended, added unto, or expunged by the vote of two thirds of the Stockholders.

SIDNEY RIGDON, *Ch'n,*

Attest OLIVER COWDERY, *Cl'k.*

———— ∽ ————

Petition to Arial Hanson, 7 November 1836

Source Note

JS and others, Petition, Kirtland Township, Geauga Co., OH, to Arial Hanson, [Kirtland Township, Geauga Co., OH], 7 Nov. 1836. Featured version copied [ca. 1837–1838]; handwriting likely of Elijah A. Ward; one page; Lake County Historical Society, Painesville, OH. Includes docket and redaction. Transcription from a digital color image made of original in 2001.

Three conjoined leaves; the first measures 12 × 7¾ inches (30 × 20 cm), the second 11¾ × 7¾ inches (29 × 20 cm), and the third 12 × 7¾ inches (30 × 20 cm). The three leaves were made into one cohesive document measuring 34⅜ × 7¾ inches (87 × 20 cm) by joining the bottom of the first leaf and the top of the second leaf with three adhesive wafers and by joining the bottom of the second leaf and the top of

Safety Society, Stock Ledger, 1836–1837, in Chicago Historical Society, Collection of Mormon Materials, microfilm, CHL; see also Introduction to Part 5: 5 Oct. 1836–10 Apr. 1837, p. 290 herein.)

the third leaf with three additional adhesive wafers. The first leaf contains thirty-seven brown lines; the second and third leaves have thirty-six brown lines each. The petition was likely folded into fourths and then trifolded to form three panels. It was docketed on the right side of the left panel. A bottom segment of the petition is torn entirely at a fold. This copy of the original letter was likely created by Elijah A. Ward, the brother-in-law of Arial Hanson, while serving as deputy sheriff in Cuyahoga County, Ohio. The location of the original letter is unknown.

A typed note accompanying the letter states it was donated by Philip Ward, a grandson of Elijah A. Ward, to the Lake County Historical Society.[96] The donation occurred between 1938, when the historical society was organized, and 1954, when Ward died.[97]

Historical Introduction

In early November 1836, JS and other residents of Kirtland, Ohio, drafted a petition to Arial Hanson, a justice of the peace in Kirtland, asking him to resign his office and leave the county.[98] The petition was signed by seventy-two Kirtland residents; all but a few are known to have been members of the Church of the Latter Day Saints.[99] In scathing language, they charged Hanson with incompetence as a justice of the peace and with acting contrary to his duties in that office, especially regarding his actions toward church members.

Justices of the peace were important figures in antebellum towns and were recognized as local government officials by their communities. Elected by the residents of their township, justices of the peace oversaw the local court, also called the "justice of the peace court" or "small claims court," which heard civil cases for debts of less than one hundred dollars. Justices had jurisdiction in criminal cases relating to assault and battery or fear of violence and in this role were appointed "conservators of the peace." The position also included record-keeping responsibilities. Justices were required to keep a docket recording the lawsuits and other actions that related to their court duties; they also administered oaths and acknowledged contracts, such as deeds and mortgages.

The petition featured here notes several ways in which the signers felt Hanson had acted contrary to his elected position as a peacekeeper, impartial judge, and arbiter of community conflicts.[100] According to the petition, Hanson encouraged mob violence, wrote slanderous statements, and aided enemies of church members in acting against them.

---

96. Upton, *History of the Western Reserve*, 758–760.

97. "Philip Emmerson Ward," Melbourne Cemetery, Melbourne, Brevard Co., FL, U.S. Find a Grave Index.

98. Arial Hanson, born in Massachusetts in 1800, moved to Kirtland in 1821. He married Sally Ward on 4 October 1829 in Cuyahoga County, Ohio. He served as overseer of the poor in Kirtland from 1834 to 1835 and justice of the peace in Kirtland from 1834 to 1837. (Upton, *History of the Western Reserve*, 759; List of Letters, *Painesville [OH] Telegraph*, 7 Apr. 1837, [3].)

99. Five of the signers cannot be confirmed as members of the church: John Davidson, Joseph Willard, L. J. Reave, John Gamble, and Jacob Harvey.

100. The Ohio legislature clarified the duties of justices of the peace in 1831. (An Act Defining the Powers and Duties of Justices of the Peace and Constables, in Criminal Cases [11 Mar. 1831]; An Act Defining the Powers and Duties of Justices of the Peace and Constables, in Civil Cases [14 Mar. 1831]; An Act to Regulate the Action for Forcible Entry and Detainer [25 Feb. 1831], *Acts of a General Nature* [1831], pp. 170–214.)

Though there is little extant evidence regarding the allegations found in the petition, some reminiscent accounts support the claims that Hanson was antagonistic toward church members.

In an autobiographical letter possibly written several decades after he left Kirtland, church member Daniel Wood related an instance when the justice of the peace seized his property in 1837. Wood had acted as the surety for another church member's promissory note and later had his wagon confiscated by Hanson. Wood felt this was done unfairly, since the church member who issued the note had also provided ample land as security. Wood's letter further described the arbitrary property seizures by some local constables and justices of the peace, likely including Hanson, that became so severe by 1837–1838 that "no Latter Day Saint could consider any property secure which he possessed."[101] Wood noted that constables would find any excuse to confiscate a Mormon's property. Should the owner object, arguing that he did not owe anyone money, then "the constable would curse and swear that they were Jo Smiths goods and they would take them to pay his debts or somebody else." Confiscating good[s] for outstanding debts would be legal if church members had been acting as sureties on promissory notes of JS or other members. But Wood implied that Mormons' goods were routinely confiscated even when not used to secure promissory notes, and he claimed that it was a common practice for some local officials to unfairly require additional security for promissory notes or other financial transactions involving church members. These abuses occurred, according to Wood, because of religious bias against the Church of the Latter Day Saints.[102]

No statements by Arial Hanson are extant, but there is evidence that his family members were opposed to JS and the church. A reminiscent statement by his wife, Sally Ward Hanson, was printed in Arthur Deming's *Naked Truths about Mormonism* in 1888. In it, she claimed that when church members' appeals to appoint a Mormon postmaster failed, they threatened her husband.[103] Arial Hanson's father-in-law, Reverend Elijah Ward, was a minister for the Methodist Episcopal Church in neighboring Willoughby and preached against the Church of the Latter Day Saints.[104]

---

101. Wood, "Letter to Daniel Wood's Brother Hosea Wood," 3–4. A constable was a town officer of the peace and had the authority to carry out civil and criminal judgments under the direction of justices of the peace.

102. Wood, "Letter to Daniel Wood's Brother Hosea Wood," 4.

103. "Mrs. S. W. Hanson's Statement," *Naked Truths about Mormonism,* Apr. 1888, 3.

104. Upton, *History of the Western Reserve,* 758. Isaac Russell, a church member living in Upper Canada, wrote to the editor of the *Christian Guardian* in Toronto, Canada, defending the Kirtland Safety Society—and by extension, the church—from earlier statements printed in the *Christian Guardian* from a "Methodist Minister who, it is stated, resided in the vicinity of Kirtland." This minister might have been Reverend Elijah Ward, who lived with his son Elijah A. Ward in Willoughby, Ohio. According to Harriet Upton, Hanson donated land to the Methodist Episcopal Church. An 1839 Geauga County deed shows that Hanson and his brother-in-law Elijah A. Ward jointly transferred land to the trustees of the Kirtland Methodist Episcopal Church. This appears to be the land on which the Methodist Episcopal chapel was located. (Isaac Russell to Editor of the *Christian Guardian,* Toronto, Upper Canada, 11 Mar. 1837, Isaac Russell Correspondence, CHL; Upton, *History of the Western Reserve,* 757, 759; Geauga Co., OH, Deed Records, 1795–1921, vol. 30, pp. 361–362, 21 June 1839, microfilm 20,242, U.S. and Canada Record Collection, FHL.)

Despite the demands made in the petition, Hanson did not resign as justice of the peace in Kirtland but remained in the position until his term ended in May 1837, when he was replaced by Oliver Cowdery. Hanson continued to live in Kirtland into the 1840s and remained in northeastern Ohio until his death in 1862.[105]

Document Transcript

Kirtland Nov 7th 1836,

Mr A[rial] Hanson Esqr[106]

 Sir

The undersigned Subscribers inhabitants of Kirtland being among the number of those or at least some of us who elevated you to the honourable office of Justis of the Peace[107] feeling themselves openly disgraced by your ignorance stupidity & in competency which has ben clearly manifested by the contempt that has been shown to your decisions in Law in the Court of the County in which you live concider it an indispensable duty they owe to <u>themselves</u> & there families to request you by way of petition to resign the office with which you have ben honaured— & deliver them & there posterity from this open disgrace,— You must be sensible Sir that you have openly desgraced your friends that elivated you to office by reason of your incompetency & inability to discharge the duties of the same & that your continuanc[e] in office will bee heaping disgrace upon disgrace— We pray you there fore if there is yet remaining one spark of compassion in your ~~sole~~ soul that you will have mercy upon us & our children & our childrens children to the latest generation and suffer not this disgrace to be entailed upon our heads & upon the heads of our Children forever lest you bring down our gray hairs with sorrow to the grave—

You must also be sensible Sir that your continuance in this Town ~~of~~ or County must be an open rebuke & perpetual chastisement to those who were so far blinded to your abilities & to there own reputation as as to confer upon you the office of Justice of the Peace We therefore in the most solemn & aganising manner pray you as an act of duty you owe to us to our children forever that you ~~that you~~ with all possible speed & the greatest posible ~~secrecy~~ ⟨secrecy⟩ not even letting your right hand Know what you[r] left hand doeth[108]

---

105. Upton, *History of the Western Reserve,* 758; "Death Notice," *Painesville (OH) Telegraph,* 4 Sept. 1862, [3]; 1840 U.S. Census, Kirtland, Lake Co., OH, 97; 1850 U.S. Census, Mentor, Lake Co., OH, 277[B]; 1860 U.S. Census, Willoughby, Lake Co., OH, 172.

106. "Esquire" in this case was a customary title given to Hanson because of his position as justice of the peace.

107. In the 1834 vote for justice of the peace, Hanson received fifty-six votes to Lyman Pitcher's four votes and Oliver Hamon's two. (Kirtland Township Trustees' Minutes and Poll Book, 127.)

108. See Matthew 6:3; and Book of Mormon, 1830 ed., 482 [3 Nephi 13:3].

depart out of Geauga County & seek your residence elsewhere— In doing this we wish to be distinctly understood that we intend no injury to your person property or Carracter in public or in private— but from a sense of duty we owe ⟨owe⟩ ourselves & families— For be assurid Sir we your humble petitioners concider you a pest & public nuisance to society Therefore we do again most sincearly adjure you to depart out of our coasts & deliver us from this evil that we have so Long groaned under in pain to be released— be assured Sir in the midst of all your slander misrepresentations & abuse we have paid you well for your nominal servises as a magistrate[109] & finally that society of people that you have so much persecuted have purchased your possessions & plased you in easy circumstances:[110] there fore we have claims ~~on~~ upon your Clemency & besech of you to not disregard our suplication but pity our deplorable condi-tion & grant us this our last request do not longer harden your hart & stifen your <u>neck</u> against <u>us</u> Comply with our prayers for <u>mercy</u> sake In adition to you[r] ignoranc[e] & in competancy have you not Sir forgotten the duties of a peace maker & the solemnities of an oath[111] that bound you to lift your voice against all violation of law & acts of violence against the peace & happiness of the citizens of the united States by making a league with a mob who have driven defensless women & children from their houses & hom[e]s & trampled upon the rights ~~against~~ granted to them by the Laws of God & man and have you not Sir used all your influence to increace there miseries by encourageing mobs & inflaming the indignation of a lawless banditti by conveying secret letters full of falsehood & misrepresentations to increase there suffering & to strengthen the hands of ~~murderers~~ mourauders to put at defiance the constitu-tion of the United States which you Sir was bound by the solemnities of an oath[112] to defend In thus saying we arraign you before the bar of your own

---

109. Justices of the peace were paid for each action they performed: issuing writs such as summons, subpoenas, or warrants; recording judgments on cases and other information in their docket; certifying deeds or other financial instruments; and fulfilling other duties such as performing marriages or swearing in witnesses. Each of these tasks was assigned a fee that generally ranged from ten cents to seventy-five cents; performing a marriage paid $1.50. (See Swan, *Treatise on the Law,* 101–102.)

110. Some church members bought land from Hanson, including John F. Boynton and Luke Johnson. Reminiscent accounts by Ira Ames and Sally Ward Hanson note that Hanson regained possession of much of the land he had sold to church members in Kirtland when they defaulted on their payments or left Kirtland to move to Missouri. (Geauga Co., OH, Deed Records, 1795–1921, vol. 22, pp. 71–72, 28 June 1836, microfilm 20,239, U.S. and Canada Record Collection, FHL; Lake Co., OH, Deed Records, 1840–1950, bk. A, 429–431, microfilm 974,393, U.S. and Canada Record Collection, FHL; Ames, Autobiography and Journal, [13]; "Mrs. S. W. Hanson's Statement," *Naked Truths about Mormonism,* Apr. 1888, 3.)

111. Ohio state law required that a justice of the peace take an oath of office. (An Act to Provide for the Election and Resignation of Justices of the Peace [31 Jan. 1831], *Acts of a General Nature* [1831], p. 169, sec. 11.)

112. TEXT: Or "oaths".

conscience & ask you in the presence of the searcher of all hearts are not thes[e] eternal realities do you not know Sir that when the great Orbiter of heaven & earth Judges your case that he will pronounce you guilty of these blackest of crimes & that you will be left with out excuse— Therefore be not surprised that we your petitioners should urge upon you in the most powerful manner in which language can express that you should depart forthwith out of Kirtland and we presume that your ~~presents~~ presence would be as little mesed [missed] as any other man that ever left this place except that injustice & cruelty might find them selvs deprived of one of there strongest advocates and righteousness might find it self an abode in a place where it never bifore was priviledged to show its <u>head</u>.— Should you be so kind as to comply with this our humble petition we will ever pray that you may never com[e] back again

Joseph Smith J^r	John Davidson
F. G. Willians [Frederick G. Williams]	Christopher W Stillwell
Sidney Rigdon	David Dart [Dort]
Edmund Bosley	Solomon Angell
D. H. Reedfide [David Harvey Redfield]	Jared Carter
Beihias [Bechias] Dustin	Edwin Webb
Lyman Sherman	Artemus Millet
Brigham Young	John Read [Reed]
Roger Orton	Georg[e] A. Smith
W^m· Smith	I[saac] H Bishop
Jacob Bump	Reynolds Cahoon
W A Cowdry [Warren A. Cowdery]	V[inson] Knight
Jacob Parker	John Smith
Martin D. Cowdry	Joseph Willard
Warrn F Cowdry [Warren F. Cowdery]	Hiram Clark
Benj^a[min] Sweat	Solomon Fre[e]man
L J Reave	Roswell Blood
John Gamble	W^m F Cahoon
Ebenezer Robinson	Harv[e]y Stanley
Willard Woodstock	Hyrum Struttan [Hiram Stratton]
P[arley] P. Pratt	Horace Burges[s]
R[oyal] Barney J^r·	Lorren [Loren] Babbit
Nathan Haskins	Normen Ruall[113]
Edson Barney	Ezra Strong

---

113. Possibly Norman Buell. (See "Death of Presendia Kimball," *Deseret Evening News*, 6 Feb. 1892, 4.)

Chancy [Chauncey] G Webb
Burton H. Phelps
Sterry Fisk
Peter Shirts
W^m. Felshaw
Jacob Harvey
Joseph Young
Z Coltrain [Zebedee Coltrin]
E[zekiel] Rider

Lysandar M Davis
Asahel Smith
Jonathan H. Holm[e]s
Williams [William] D Pratt
George W Gee
Samuel H Smith
Don C[arlos] Smith
John P Green[e]
Oliver Cowdrey [Cowdery]
Leonard Rich
Lorenzo L Lewis
M[arvel] C Davis
G W Meelks [Garland W. Meeks]
Ebenezer Borr [Barr]

James M Carrel[l] printer[114]
A tru[e] copy of the origional by E[lijah] A Ward[115] Dep Sheriff [p. [1]]
Joseph Smith j^r. F. G. Willim S. Rigdon & othr
To
Arial Hanson Esqr.
Complements

———— ⁊ ————

Indenture from Warren A. Cowdery, 23 November 1836

Source Note

Warren A. Cowdery, Indenture, Kirtland Township, Geauga Co., OH, to JS, Kirtland Township, Geauga Co., OH, 23 Nov. 1836; handwriting of Warren A. Cowdery; signatures of Warren A. Cowdery, Lyman Cowdery, and JS; witnessed by Warren Parrish; two pages; JS Collection, CHL. Includes docket and archival marking.

One leaf, measuring 10 × 7⅞ inches (25 × 20 cm). The document was trifolded for filing and was docketed by William Clayton as follows: "Wn A. Cowdery's | Indenture | To Joseph Smith". After being trifolded, the document was folded again to form a square measuring 4 × 3¼ inches (10 × 8 cm).

Clayton's docket on the verso suggests the indenture was in institutional custody as early as the Nauvoo, Illinois, period. Graphite notations by Andrew Jenson on the recto indicate institutional custody into the early 1940s.

---

114. TEXT: This line was written vertically between the two columns of names. James M. Carrell was a member of the church and a foreman in the Kirtland printing office in 1835–1836. It is not clear if Carrell's name appears here as a signature to the petition or if he is identified for printing an unlocated copy of the petition. (Historical Introduction to Doctrine and Covenants, 1835 ed., in *JSP*, R2:305; Ebenezer Robinson, "Items of Personal History of the Editor," *Return*, May 1889, 76; July 1889, 104.)

115. Elijah A. Ward was the brother of Arial Hanson's wife, Sally Ward Hanson.

Historical Introduction

Warren A. Cowdery, Oliver Cowdery's oldest brother, moved to Kirtland, Ohio, from Freedom, New York, on 25 February 1836, with his wife, Patience Simmonds Cowdery, and their ten children.[116] In Kirtland, Warren began working in the printing office and as a scribe for JS.[117] This was a departure from his previous employment in New York, where he had been a physician and the local postmaster.[118] On 23 November 1836, Warren and his fourth son, Lyman Hervy Cowdery, entered into an indenture with JS. It was Lyman's fifteenth birthday.[119]

An indenture for a child in nineteenth-century America was a legal contract made between a parent or government official and another adult for whom the child would provide labor or serve as an apprentice; this practice was sometimes called "binding out." Indentures and apprenticeships were arranged for children from colonial settlement to the mid-nineteenth century; the practice increased in the eighteenth century and declined over the course of the nineteenth century.[120] Indentures took many forms, such as immigrants indentured to pay for their travel to America, craft apprentices indentured to study and work under master craftsmen and learn a specific trade, and children bound to an adult to labor and possibly learn trade skills. The most common forms of indenture for children in the 1800s were apprenticeships and binding out. Binding out was particularly common for children who were orphaned, abandoned, or otherwise left without caretakers.[121]

An indenture specified the conditions and duration of the child's term of service, which generally involved some type of artisanal or vocational training. Under the terms of an indenture, the adult supervisor, often referred to as a master, was obligated to care for

---

116. Cowdery, Diary, 25 Feb. 1836; Mehling, *Cowdrey-Cowdery-Cowdray Genealogy,* 170–171.

117. In the printing office, Warren A. Cowdery helped his brother Oliver with the *Messenger and Advocate,* taking over his duties as editor during Oliver's trip with JS, Hyrum Smith, and Sidney Ridgon to the East Coast of the United States in summer 1836. In February 1837, when Oliver moved to Michigan to serve on the board of directors for the Bank of Monroe, Warren took over as the editor of the *Messenger and Advocate* and became the agent for JS and Sidney Rigdon in the printing office. It is not certain when Warren began serving as a scribe for JS, but he worked on JS's 1834–1836 history and inscribed some early April 1836 entries in JS's journal. (Oliver Cowdery, Long Island Sound, NY, to Warren A. Cowdery, Kirtland, OH, [4] Aug. 1836, in *LDS Messenger and Advocate,* Sept. 1836, 2:373–375; Notice, *LDS Messenger and Advocate,* Feb. 1837, 3:458–459; JS History, 1834–1836, 105, in *JSP,* H1:216; JS, Journal, 2–3 Apr. 1836, in *JSP,* J1:217–222.)

118. Warren A. Cowdery may have also had an apothecary business in New York. (Mehling, *Cowdrey-Cowdery-Cowdray Genealogy,* 170.)

119. Lyman Hervy Cowdery was born 23 November 1821 in Leroy, Genesee County, New York. He married Sarah H. Holmes in Kirtland, Ohio, on 30 August 1849. Together they had eight children. He worked for the Lake Shore Railroad and at one point was a station agent in Perry, Ohio. He died 24 March 1906 in Rochester, New York. (Mehling, *Cowdrey-Cowdery-Cowdray Genealogy,* 171, 253.)

120. Herndon, "'Proper' Magistrates and Masters," 40–42.

121. Herndon and Murray, *Children Bound to Labor,* 2. Government officials often placed children without caretakers into indentures. When government officials were not involved, indentures were generally voluntary, though often still motivated by financial difficulties. (Zipf, "Labor of Innocents"; Herndon and Murray, "Proper and Instructive Education," 4–5.)

the child, providing food, quarters, clothing, and other basic necessities in exchange for the child's labor.[122] The arrangement documented here appears to be the only time a youth was formally indentured to JS as a servant. While at other times JS may have agreed to informal indentures, with individuals working as servants in his household, such arrangements were probably not documented as indentures with a specified term of service.[123]

This indenture for Lyman Cowdery differs from more traditional apprentice or master-servant relationships. It does not stipulate that JS provide any form of artisanal or vocational training but does, perhaps as a substitute, require that he fund Cowdery's education. Though most nineteenth-century indentures required masters to provide a minimum education of reading, writing, and basic arithmetic for their indentured children, the agreement with JS specified that Cowdery should receive a classical—or collegiate-level—education.[124] Tuition and books were also included in the expenses to be covered by JS. Lyman's oldest brother, Marcellus, was a schoolteacher, as were some of his uncles, and this might have been a vocation Lyman's father considered for him.[125] The Cowderys might not have been able to afford tuition at that time, however, because of the family's apparent financial difficulties after their move to Ohio.[126] JS's reasons for agreeing to the indenture are not clear. He may have needed additional labor in his household, on his lands, or in one of the mercantile stores he was associated with. The agreement may have simply formalized an existing working relationship between Lyman Cowdery and the Smiths, binding Lyman to work for JS for five years, until he reached twenty years of age.

Shortly after the indenture was signed, JS began to fulfill his commitment to Lyman's education. Lyman attended the Kirtland High School, held in the attic of the House of the Lord, beginning in the winter of 1836–1837. JS paid the six-dollar tuition for Lyman, who enrolled as a student in the Classical department, taught by Professor H. M. Hawes. Students in the Classical department studied Latin and Greek, while those in the English department were less advanced and had a broader range of study that included reading, writing, English grammar, geography, and mathematics.[127]

---

122. The term *master* used here originates from medieval indentures that involved an apprentice being bound to a master craftsman in the guild of the trade he was being taught.

123. In his memoirs, Joseph Smith III mentions several individuals who worked for his parents in Nauvoo, Illinois, as servants. One young woman, Lucy Walker, served as a maid and worked for her board and education. This may have been something like an informal indenture, where Lucy's necessities and the cost of her education were provided in exchange for her work. (Mary Audentia Smith Anderson, "The Memoirs of President Joseph Smith," *Saints' Herald,* 18 Dec. 1934, 1614.)

124. Herndon and Murray, "Proper and Instructive Education," 4, 13.

125. Oliver Cowdery boarded with the family of Joseph Sr. and Lucy Mack Smith while he taught school in the Palmyra, New York, area in 1828 and 1829. Marcellus Cowdery became a widely recognized educator in Ohio, established some of the first teachers institutes there, and served as the superintendent of city schools in Sandusky, Ohio, for twenty-three years. (Mehling, *Cowdrey-Cowdery-Cowdray Genealogy,* 170.)

126. See "To the Subscribers of the Journal," *Elders' Journal,* Aug. 1838, 54–55.

127. "Our Village," *LDS Messenger and Advocate,* Jan. 1837, 3:441; Kirtland High School Register, ca. 1836–1837, CHL. According to George A. Smith, Marcellus Cowdery taught in the English department at the Kirtland High School in 1836 and 1837. (George A. Smith, "My Journal," *Instructor,* Nov. 1946, 528.)

Classical Department

George W. Robinson			$6.00
Samuel James			6
Perpoint & Amos Orton } Roger Orton 2			12
Milton Holmes			6
Abram C Smoot			6
Miron W. Rine			6
John Parkin			6
John M Davis			6
Harry Brown			6
George P Stiles			
Lovina Smith Hyrum Smith			6
Andrew Cahoon F. Cahoon			6
Horace Whitney N K Whiting			6
Reuben McBride do			6
Marcus J Bicknal Calvin Bicknal			6
Orlando }			
Coelim & }			
Ellen bartz } Jared Carter			18
Sarat			
Sidny &			
Eliza Rigdon Sidney Rigdon			18
George Barley C Barly			6
Lorenzo Snow Esq. Snow			6
Julian Moses do			6
Lyman H Cowdery , Joseph Smith Jr			6
Almira Knight , V Knight			6

Kirtland High School register. The indenture for Lyman Cowdery specified that Joseph Smith would fund fifteen-year-old Cowdery's education. This Kirtland High School register provides evidence that Joseph Smith fulfilled his end of the agreement by paying Cowdery's six-dollar tuition to study in the Classical department. Cowdery attended the school, which met in the attic of the House of the Lord, beginning in the winter of 1836–1837. Kirtland High School Register, ca. 1836–1837, p. [1], Church History Library, Salt Lake City.

Within months of entering into this indenture, Lyman appears to have been integrated into JS's household. He was referred to by his middle name, Hervy, in a letter from Emma Smith to JS in May 1837. Emma praised Lyman and suggested that JS offer him some encouragement since "he is very faithful not only in business, but in taking up his cross in the family."[128]

The arrangement did not last the full five years. Warren A. Cowdery became disaffected with church leaders by summer 1837 and distanced himself from the church in 1838. His family, including Lyman, remained in Kirtland after JS and the majority of church members moved to Missouri in early 1838. It is unknown what became of this indenture after JS's move. Apprentices were not required to follow their masters out of the state;[129] the Cowderys and JS may have mutually agreed to annul the indenture, or they may have simply allowed the agreement to lapse when JS departed to Missouri.

Document Transcript

This indenture made and entered into this twenty third day of November in the year one thousand eight hundred & thirty six between W[arren] A. Cowdery and Lyman H. Cowdery, his son, of the town of Kirtland, county of Geauga and State of Ohio of the first part & Joseph Smith Junr of the town county and State aforesaid of the second part Witnesseth, that said W. A. Cowdery of the first part agrees for the consideration herein after named to put, place and bind to said party of the second part his son, Lyman H. Cowdery, for the full term of five years from the twenty third day of November A.D. 1836 and until he the said Lyman H. Cowdery shall be twenty years of age—[130] And the said Lyman H. Cowdery also voluntarily places, himself under the care, protection superintendence and control of said party of the second part, for the term of five years from the twenty third day of November aforesaid, during which time he promises to be faithful, obedient and attentive to all the lawful command of said party of the second part reserving only and excepting the hours of devotion, school, refreshment and repose. Said party of the second part promises and agrees that he will, during the term of five years aforesaid board the said L. H. Cowdery, clothe him in a respectful manner, and defray all his necessary and contingent expenses, for books tuition and maintainence in sickness and in health, until the expiration of the five years, aforesaid, It is expressly understood by the contracting parties [p. [1]] that said party of the second part is to continue to ~~said~~ send said Lyman H. Cowdery to such a school as in it he

---

128. Letter from Emma Smith, 3 May 1837, p. 376 herein.

129. Butts, *Business Man's Assistant*, 15.

130. A more traditional age for a young man to be released from an indenture was 21, when he was considered to have reached adulthood, but there is record of some indentures releasing boys at older or younger ages. (Herndon and Murray, *Children Bound to Labor*, 1; Herndon and Murray, "Proper and Instructive Education," 16–17; Hindle and Herndon, "Recreating Proper Families," 34.)

may obtain, in the five years aforesaid, a full and competent knowledge of the circle of sciences embraced in a collegiate or classical education.[131]

In witness whereof we have hereunto set our hands and seals——

[132]W. A. Cowdery L.S.[133]

Lyman H. Cowdery LS.

Joseph Smith Jr L.S.

In presence of W[arren] Parrish [p. [2]]

——— ∾ ———

Deed to Caroline Grant Smith, 11 December 1836

Source Note

JS and Emma Smith, Deed for property in Kirtland Township, Geauga Co., OH, to Caroline Grant Smith, 11 Dec. 1836; signed by JS and Emma Smith; witnessed by William Tenney Jr. and Josiah Butterfield; certified by Frederick G. Williams. Featured version copied 18 Mar. 1837 in Geauga County Deed Record, vol. 24, p. 25; handwriting of Ralph Cowles; Geauga County Archives and Records Center, Chardon, OH. Transcription from a digital color image made of original in 2011. For more information on Geauga County Deed Record, Volume 24, see Source Notes for Multiple-Entry Documents, p. 521 herein.

Historical Introduction

On 11 December 1836, JS and Emma Smith sold land to Caroline Grant Smith, the wife of JS's brother William.[134] In this transaction Caroline Smith purchased nearly one acre of land, 142 of 160 rods, for fifty dollars. This land was located in a growing area of Kirtland, Ohio, near the recently completed House of the Lord, and was part of land that had been deeded to JS by Fredrick G. Williams in 1834.[135]

JS was closely involved in purchasing land and developing Kirtland in fall and winter 1836.[136] In order to aid growth in Kirtland and provide land for the Saints, church leaders divided the large tracts of land they had purchased or received by deed and then distributed

---

131. The majority of indentures made with children included freedom dues, or payment given to them when their term of service ended. Freedom dues might be a suit of clothing, land, tools necessary for their trade, or livestock in rural areas. Lyman's indenture does not include any freedom dues, likely because he was bound at an older age. Children who were older when bound usually served shorter indentures and their freedom dues were lower or omitted because they had deprived their master of profits from being bound for a longer period of time. (Herndon and Murray, "Proper and Instructive Education," 14–16; Whitman, "Orphans in the City and Countryside in Maryland," 59.)

132. TEXT: Signatures of Warren A. Cowdery, Lyman Cowdery, JS, and Warren Parrish.

133. TEXT: Instances of "L.S." (*locus sigilli,* in place of the seal) are enclosed in hand-drawn representations of seals. Handwriting of Warren A. Cowdery.

134. For biographical information on Caroline Grant Smith, see 298n69 herein.

135. Geauga Co., OH, Deed Records, 1795–1921, vol. 18, pp. 477–478, 5 May 1834, microfilm 20,237, U.S. and Canada Record Collection, FHL.

136. See Historical Introduction to Mortgage to Peter French, 5 Oct. 1836, pp. 294–295 herein.

or sold the smaller allotments to members of the church.[137] On the Kirtland plat created by church leaders in summer 1833, the area around the House of the Lord in Kirtland was primarily divided into half-acre lots.[138]

Caroline Smith alone is identified as holding the title to this land. While William Smith is mentioned in the deed as her husband, he was not a party in the transaction, nor was he named as a holder of the title. The reasons for her individually purchasing this land are not clear. In nineteenth-century America, when a woman married, her legal identity was subsumed into that of her husband, and she could not act on her own in legal matters. This legal principle, called coverture or unity of persons, also meant that a woman's property and earnings were transferred to her husband upon marriage and no longer belonged to her.[139] Given these restrictions, Caroline may have purchased this land as an agent for her husband. Wives often engaged in financial transactions for their husbands, especially if their husbands traveled or engaged in other business that involved frequent absences.[140] However, William Smith may have been in Kirtland in December 1836 and able to purchase the land himself. Thus, there remains a possibility that Caroline was buying the land for her own use. The western frontier of the United States provided opportunities for a relaxation of gendered norms, and some local government officials may have been willing to allow married women to be involved in legal or financial matters.[141] Over the next several years many states began to pass laws granting women the right to own property and have their own legal and financial identities independent of their husbands.[142]

Contemporary deed records in Geauga County, Ohio, demonstrate instances of other married women—at least eighteen—buying and selling land in their name alone, with no apparent involvement by their husbands.[143] One of these women was Martha H. Raymond

---

137. The division of larger tracts into smaller lots for the use of church members may have followed a pattern set forth by the 4 June 1833 revelation, which commanded Newel K. Whitney to divide lots for inheritances for church members. However, in 1836 lots were sold to church members rather than given to them as an inheritance. (Revelation, 4 June 1833, in *JSP*, D3:111 [D&C 96:2–3].)

138. Plat of Kirtland, OH, not before 2 Aug. 1833, in *JSP*, D3:208–221.

139. American coverture laws originated with English common law. (Bouvier, *Law Dictionary* [1843], 1:392; Salmon, *Women and the Law of Property*, 14–18; Kerber, "Constitutional Right to Be Treated like American Ladies," 20–22.)

140. Salmon, *Women and the Law of Property*, 53–55.

141. See, for example, Harris, "Homesteading in Northeastern Colorado," 165–178. One way for married women to be involved in financial or business matters was to file a petition with a county court to be recognized as a "feme sole trader." This status was often given to married women who faced long absences from or desertion by their husbands. In other instances a woman might become a "sole trader" with her husband's consent. (Salmon, *Women and the Law of Property*, 44–49.)

142. Laws granting married women property rights were enacted in the United States beginning in 1839. Married women could own property in Ohio starting in the mid-1840s. (Speth, "Married Women's Property Acts," 74.)

143. Examples of married women executing land transactions in the deed records for Geauga County for 1835–1837 include Mary Beebee, Marinda N. Hyde, Martha H. Parrish, Sophia Coe, Sarah A. Lowell, Sally Brown, Sophia Robinson, Caroline Kingsbury, Miranda Todd, Susannah Boynton, Hannah Pratt, and Hannah Ward.[a] One notable female land holder in the Kirtland area was Abigail Champion Deming, who was involved with land transactions from 1826 to 1839.[b] (a. Geauga Co., OH, Deed Records, 1795–1921,

Parrish, who purchased just over a half an acre of land near the House of the Lord from JS on 8 December 1836.[144] Parrish, like other women in Kirtland, had purchased land as a single woman, and her independent land transactions continued after her December 1835 marriage to Warren Parrish, despite coverture restrictions.[145] As with Caroline Smith, it is unclear if Martha Parrish completed this December 1836 land transaction as an agent for her husband, who was likely in Kirtland at the time, or in her own stead.[146]

William Smith later sold or transferred the title of the land Caroline Smith had purchased to William Marks on 15 February 1838.[147] It is not known if William Smith's ownership of the land was implied through laws of female coverture or if Caroline Smith had deeded the land to her husband or amended the original deed to include him.

Document Transcript

Joseph Smith Jun To Caroline [Grant] Smith.

To all People to whom these presents shall come Greeting Know Ye that I Joseph Smith Jun & Emma wife of said Joseph of the town of Kirtland Geauga County & State of Ohio for the consideration of Fifty dollars received to our full satisfaction of Caroline— Smith wife of William Smith of the town of Kirtland County of Geauga and State of Ohio do give grant bargain sell and confirm unto the said Caroline Smith her heirs & assigns the following described tract or lot of land Situate in Kirtland township No Nine in the Ninth range of townships in the Connecticut Western Reserve in the State of Ohio and which is also in the County of Geauga and is known as part of Lot No thirty tract 1 and is bounded as follows to wit. Beginning at the centre of the road leading from Kirtland Mills to Aurora Nineteen rods & Seven links Southerly from the North east corner of that part of Said lot No 30 which was deeded to me said Joseph Smith Jun by F[rederick] G Williams & running thence southerly along the Centre of said road ten rods & twenty one

---

vol. 23, pp. 72–73, 30 Apr. 1836; pp. 451–452, 16 Jan. 1837; vol. 24, p. 95, 8 Dec. 1836; pp. 113–114, 28 Feb. 1837; pp. 259–260, 29 May 1837; pp. 381–382, 24 Oct. 1836; pp. 521–522, 17 Oct. 1837, microfilm 20,240; vol. 25, pp. 143–144, 22 May 1837; p. 351, 8 Apr. 1837; pp. 379–380, 25 Sept. 1837; p. 420, 30 May 1837; p. 421, 9 Feb. 1837, microfilm 20,241, U.S. and Canada Record Collection, FHL. *b*. See Geauga Co., OH, Deed Records, 1795–1921, vol. 21, pp. 364–365, 4 Feb. 1836, microfilm 20,239; vol. 23, pp. 578–579, 21 Apr. 1837; vol. 24, p. 51, 4 Feb. 1836, microfilm 20,240, U.S. and Canada Record Collection, FHL.)

144. Geauga Co., OH, Deed Records, 1795–1921, vol. 24, p. 95, 8 Dec. 1836, microfilm 20,240, U.S. and Canada Record Collection, FHL.

145. Geauga Co., OH, Deed Records, 1795–1921, vol. 23, p. 492, 31 Aug. 1835, microfilm 20,240, U.S. and Canada Record Collection, FHL.

146. Warren Parrish was acting as a clerk for the Kirtland Safety Society at this time, and his handwriting is found in the society's stock ledger for entries dated December 1836. (Kirtland Safety Society, Stock Ledger, Dec. 1836.)

147. William Smith sold this land to Marks along with an adjacent half-acre lot. (Geauga Co., OH, Deed Records, 1795–1921, vol. 30, p. 383, 15 Feb. 1838, microfilm 20,242, U.S. and Canada Record Collection, FHL.)

links thence west Sixteen rods & ten links thence north ten rods thence East twelve rods & two links to the place of beginning. Containing about One hundred & forty two rods of Land Be the same more or less. To have and to hold the above granted and bargained premises with the appurtenances thereof unto the said Caroline Smith her heirs and assigns forever to their own proper use and behoof And also I the said Joseph Smith Jun do for myself and my heirs executors and administrators covenant with the said Caroline Smith her heirs and assigns that at and until the ensealing of these presents I was well seized of these premises and as a good indefeasible estate in fee simple and have good right to bargain and sell the same in manner and form as is above written And that the same is free from all incumbrances whatsoever. And furthermore I the said Joseph Smith Jun do by these presents bind myself & my heirs forever to warrant and defend the above granted and bargained premises to her the said Caroline Smith her heirs and assigns against all lawful claims and demands whatsoever And I the said Emma Smith do hereby remise release and forever quit claim unto the said Caroline Smith her heirs and assigns all my right and title of dower in and to the above described premises. In witness whereof we have hereunto set our hands and seals this Eleventh day of December AD One Thousand Eight hundred & Thirty Six.

Joseph Smith Junr seal[148]

Emma Smith seal

Signed Sealed Acknowledged and Delivered in presence of Wm. Tenney Jr. Josiah Butterfield. The State of Ohio Geauga County SS Personally appeared Joseph Smith Jun & Emma Smith to me personally known as the signers and sealers of the above instrument and acknowledged that they did voluntarily sign and seal the same and that the same is their free act and ~~deed~~ ⟨will⟩ and I having fully made known and explained to the said Emma Smith the contents of the above deed and having likewise examined her separate & apart from her said husband she declared that she did of her own free will and accord voluntarily sign seal acknowledge and as her free act and deed deliver the same without the force coercion or compulsion of her said husband & that she is still satisfied with the same Before me Kirtland 11 day of Decr. AD 1836 F G Williams Justice of the Peace seal

Rec^d 17th & Recorded 18th March AD 1837. Ralph Cowles. Recorder. [p. 25]

————— ☙ —————

---

148. TEXT: Each instance of "seal" (including at the end of the following paragraph) is enclosed in a hand-drawn representation of a seal.

Minutes, 22 December 1836

Source Note

Minutes, [Kirtland Township, Geauga Co., OH], 22 Dec. 1836. Featured version published in "Minutes of a Conference," Latter Day Saints' Messenger and Advocate, *Jan. 1837, 3:443–444. For more information on* Latter Day Saints' Messenger and Advocate, *see Source Notes for Multiple-Entry Documents, p. 527 herein.*

Historical Introduction

On 22 December 1836 a conference of church authorities was held in the Kirtland, Ohio, House of the Lord to address difficulties created by the growth of the church in the area, a problem made worse by the the influx of impoverished Saints moving to Kirtland.

Over the course of 1836, the number of Latter-day Saints living in Kirtland and the surrounding area expanded significantly.[149] Writing in the December issue of the *Latter Day Saints' Messenger and Advocate,* Oliver Cowdery noted, "It is impossible to give an accurate account of the increase of members to this church during the last year; but we feel authorized to say, that during no preceeding year since the same was organized have their numbers been so great."[150] Concurrent with this growth was an increase in the number of church members in Kirtland in need of financial assistance. Many had used all or most of their means to move to Ohio; others, such as missionaries and their wives, were trying to care for their families with little or no income. Church leaders, who themselves were in substantial debt, found it difficult to provide for the destitute already living in their community as well as the new members arriving with little money.

To improve the situation, church leaders relied on other members, particularly the affluent, to provide charity, but some members proved less than willing to contribute to the poor.[151] The church leaders in attendance at the 22 December meeting discussed the problem, established procedures for the care of the poor, and provided instructions for those who wished to move to Kirtland. Notably, the conference referred to principles from a December 1833 revelation originally intended for those moving to Zion and used these principles to direct members on how they should gather to Kirtland.[152] The objective of the conference was not to dissuade church members from moving to Kirtland but to create guidelines for those moving so that they might be adequately cared for and not become a financial burden to the church.

Church leaders informed members of the new policies by publishing the minutes of this conference in the January 1837 issue of the *Messenger and Advocate,* the version featured

---

149. JS's journal notes that in October 1835, the number of church members in the Kirtland area was "about five or six hundred who commune at our chapel and perhaps a thousand in this vicinity." Milton Backman estimated the number of Saints in Kirtland in 1836 at 1,300, with an annual growth of 200 to 500 members from 1833 to 1838 and the period of 1835–1837 experiencing the greatest amount of growth. (JS, Journal, 30 Oct. 1835, in *JSP,* J1:79; Backman, *Heavens Resound,* 139–140.)

150. "The Closing Year," *LDS Messenger and Advocate,* Dec. 1836, 3:426.

151. See Minutes, 16 June 1836, pp. 247–253 herein.

152. See Revelation, 16–17 Dec. 1833, in *JSP,* D3:394–395 [D&C 101:63–74].

here. In the newspaper, the minutes were immediately preceded by the 2 January 1837 "Articles of Agreement for the Kirtland Safety Society Anti-Banking Company" and by remarks from JS appended to the articles. In language similar to that of the conference minutes, JS's remarks addressed all those intending to help build Zion. He instructed that "wise men" should be appointed by their families or local congregations to come to Kirtland, where they could receive further counsel and likely purchase land.[153] With such encouragement from church leaders, Saints moved to Kirtland throughout 1837 and continued to increase the number of church members living there.[154]

Document Transcript

MINUTES OF A CONFERENCE, HELD IN THE HOUSE OF THE LORD, ON THE 22d DAY OF DECEMBER, 1836.

The authorities of the church being present; viz: the first Presidency, the High Council of Kirtland, the quorum of the Twelve, the Presidents of the Seventies, the President of the Elders and his counsellors,[155] and many other official members, such as Priests, Teachers, Deacons, &c.:—The house was called to order, and the following motions were made, seconded, and carried by the unanimous voice of the Assembly.

1st. That it has been the case, that a very improper and unchristian-like course of conduct, by the Elders of this church, and the churches abroad, in sending their poor from among them, and moving to this place, without the necessary means of subsistence:[156] whereas the church in this place being poor from the beginning, having had to pay an extortionary price for their lands, provisions, &c.;[157] and having a serious burthen imposed upon them by comers and goers from most parts of the world, and in assisting the travelling Elders and their families,[158] while they themselves have been laboring in the vineyard of the Lord, to preach the gospel; and also having suffered great loss

---

153. See Articles of Agreement for the Kirtland Safety Society Anti-Banking Company, 2 Jan. 1837, p. 329 herein.

154. See Backman, *Heavens Resound,* 139–140.

155. For a list of the men in these positions, see the charts on pages 601–614 herein. John Morton, the second counselor in the elders quorum presidency, was not in Kirtland for this meeting or others at the end of December 1836, and Edmund Bosley was made a temporary counselor in his absence. (Kirtland Elders Quorum, "Record," 21 Dec. 1836.)

156. Town officials called "overseers to the poor" could "warn out" indigent new arrivals in order to absolve the town from the responsibility of providing for them. In 1833 some members of the church in Kirtland, including JS, were "warned out." (Historical Introduction to Warrant, 21 Oct. 1833, in *JSP,* D3:325.)

157. Frederick G. Williams made a similar argument in a June 1836 meeting. (Minutes, 16 June 1836, p. 250 herein.)

158. Newel K. Whitney, as bishop in Kirtland, had been instructed to assist the traveling elders and their families. (Revelation, 9 Feb. 1831, in *JSP,* D1:255 [D&C 42:71]; Revelation, 4 Dec. 1831–B, in *JSP,* D2:151–153 [D&C 72:9–23].)

in endeavoring to benefit Zion: it has become a serious matter, which ought well to be considered by us—

Therefore, after deliberate discussion upon the subject, it was motioned, seconded and unanimously carried, that we have borne our part of this burthen, and that it becomes the duty, henceforth, of all the churches abroad, to provide for those who are objects of charity, that are not able to provide for themselves; and not send them from their midst, to burthen the church in this place, unless they come and prepare a place for them, and means for their support.

2nd. That there be a stop put to churches or families gathering or moving to this place, without their first coming or sending their wise men, to prepare a place for them, as our houses are all full, and our lands mostly occupied, except those houses and lands that do not belong to the church, which cannot be obtained without great sacrifice,[159] especially when brethren with their families, are crowding in upon us, and are compelled to purchase at any rate; and consequently are thrown into the hands of speculators, and extortioners,[160] with which the Lord is not well pleased. Also, that the churches abroad do according to the revelation contained in the Book of Commandments, page 238, commencing at section 10,[161] which is as follows:

"Now verily I say unto you, let all the churches gather together all their moneys; let these things be done in their time, be not in haste; and observe to have all these things prepared before [p. 443] you. And let honorable men be appointed, even wise men, and send them to purchase these lands; and every church in the eastern countries when they are built up, if they will hearken unto this counsel, they may buy lands and gather together upon them, and in this way they may establish Zion."

Pres't JOSFPH SMITH,
Chairman.

Warren Parrish, *Clerk.*

---

159. In the months preceding this conference, JS bought hundreds of acres of land in Kirtland at considerable expense to himself and other church members. (See Mortgage to Peter French, 5 Oct. 1836, pp. 293–299 herein.)

160. Warren A. Cowdery, in the May 1837 *Messenger and Advocate,* advised new arrivals to Kirtland not to assume they could trust everyone there and specifically cautioned them about speculators. He suggested they ask only trusted friends for advice about land purchases. Cowdery warned them to "beware of such as attack you as soon as you enter this place, and begin to interrogate you about the amount of money you have," since they would "take advantage of your honest simplicity, obtain your available means, and then desert you." (Editorial, *LDS Messenger and Advocate,* May 1837, 3:505.)

161. Revelation, 16–17 Dec. 1833, in *JSP,* D3:395 [D&C 101:72]. Here "Book of Commandments" refers to the 1835 edition of the Doctrine and Covenants.

Articles of Agreement for the Kirtland Safety Society Anti-Banking Company, 2 January 1837

Source Note

Articles of Agreement for the Kirtland Safety Society Anti-Banking Company, Kirtland Township, Geauga Co., OH, 2 Jan. 1837. Featured version published in "Articles of Agreement," Latter Day Saints' Messenger and Advocate, *Jan. 1837, 3:441–443. For more information on* Latter Day Saints' Messenger and Advocate, *see Source Notes for Multiple-Entry Documents, p. 527 herein.*

Historical Introduction

On 2 January 1837, Kirtland Safety Society officers Sidney Rigdon and JS, along with the society's directors, met with stockholders in Kirtland, Ohio, to replace their November 1836 constitution with new articles of agreement to govern the society.[162] Because only the Ohio legislature could grant banking privileges, those interested in establishing a bank were required to petition the legislature for an act of incorporation, also known as a charter. Orson Hyde had been assigned in November 1836 to find a politician to present the society's petition for a charter, but the only petition on record was not presented to the Ohio senate until 10 February 1837.[163] When the society met on 2 January, it was uncertain whether the Democratic majority (with its aversion to private banking and paper currency) in the state legislature would approve a charter for the Kirtland Safety Society. The articles of agreement featured here were created to allow the society to act as an unincorporated bank, which they called an "anti-banking company" but which may have functioned as a joint-stock company.[164] Despite this restructuring, the society continued to seek a banking charter after 2 January and continued to conduct banking services.

In drafting this new document, the authors reused many of the original articles from the 2 November 1836 constitution, though they also made changes, such as adding a new

---

162. Between the 2 November 1836 stockholders' meeting and the 2 January 1837 meeting, seventy-four more individuals subscribed for stock in the society, making a total of around 137 stockholders at the beginning of January. This number included seventeen women who subscribed for stock in their own name. Many of these women were married yet seem to have had an independent financial role in the Kirtland Safety Society. The demographics of the stockholders remained similar to the earlier composition of stockholders in November 1836, with most stockholders living in Kirtland and having ties to the Church of the Latter Day Saints. (Kirtland Safety Society, Stock Ledger, 1836–1837, in Collection of Manuscripts about Mormons, Chicago History Museum; Historical Introduction to Constitution of the Kirtland Safety Society Bank, 2 Nov. 1836, pp. 300–304 herein.)

163. "In Senate," *Ohio State Journal and Columbus Gazette,* 14 Feb. 1837, [2]; *Journal of the Senate of the State of Ohio,* 365–366. JS's history suggests that Hyde was given this task sometime after the 2 November meeting of the society's stockholders. (JS History, vol. B-1, 750; see also Introduction to Part 5: 5 Oct. 1836–10 Apr. 1837, p. 286 herein.)

164. Webster's 1828 dictionary defines *society* as "any number of persons associated for a particular purpose, whether incorporated by law, or only united by articles of agreement; a fraternity." The articles of agreement served to bind the stockholders together in place of legal incorporation. For more information on the Safety Society possibly functioning as a joint-stock company, see Walker, "Kirtland Safety Society and the Fraud of Grandison Newell," 44–48. ("Society," in *American Dictionary.*)

introduction and changing the terminology used in the text. Banking-specific terminology was replaced with generic business terms; for instance, references to the "bank" were changed to "company" and "stockholders" became "managers." New articles were also added, including one that addressed the wording to be used for promissory notes made to the society. The officers may have received legal counsel in the process of drafting new articles of agreement, as reported by one contemporary observer.[165] As had perhaps been the case with the original constitution, they may have also relied on their general knowledge of business and legal structures, supplemented by the language found in legal handbooks of the time.[166] Footnotes to the text presented here identify substantive differences between the articles of the November 1836 constitution and those of the January 1837 articles of agreement.

The articles of agreement were printed in the January 1837 issue of the *Messenger and Advocate,* with a postscript by JS that asked members of the church to invest in the Kirtland Safety Society. JS's quotations from the book of Isaiah suggest he envisioned a spiritual purpose for the Kirtland Safety Society in conjunction with its temporal benefits. The establishment of the Safety Society was tied to JS's goals of developing Kirtland into a large city and gathering the Saints there. JS and others may have had ambitious hopes that by developing Kirtland, and especially the Safety Society, funds could be raised for the church and for the redemption of Zion.[167]

The articles of agreement featured here were also reprinted in newspapers in Painesville and Cleveland, Ohio.[168] The March 1837 issue of the *Messenger and Advocate* published a slightly different version of these articles of agreement, along with the names of 187 individuals who identified themselves as stockholders. The version of the articles of agreement published in March 1837 reintroduced banking terminology that was altered in the text featured here. It also called the institution the "Kirtland Safety Society Banking Company," and other records vary in usage of "anti-banking company" and "banking company."[169]

Document Transcript

ARTICLES OF AGREEMENT.

Minutes of a meeting of the members of the "Kirtland Safety Society," *held on the 2d day of January,* 1837.

At a special meeting of the Kirtland Safety Society, two thirds of the members being present, S[idney] Rigdon was called to the Chair, and W[arren] Parrish chosen Secretary.

---

165. "About Matters in Kirtland," *Ohio Observer* (Hudson), 2 Mar. 1837, [2].

166. See 303n84 herein.

167. Woodruff, Journal, 9 Apr. 1837; "Anniversary of the Church," *LDS Messenger and Advocate,* Apr. 1837, 3:486–489.

168. "Kirtland Safety Society," *Cleveland Weekly Advertiser,* 19 Jan. 1837, 1; "Anti-Banking Company," *Painesville (OH) Republican,* 19 Jan. 1837, [2]–[3].

169. "Minutes of a Meeting," *LDS Messenger and Advocate,* Mar. 1837, 3:475–477. Terminology such as the titles of president, cashier, and directors were reintroduced, replacing the neutral language in the version of the articles of agreement featured here. This may have resulted from the decision of the society's officers by March 1837 to operate the society more explicitly in the style of a bank rather than a company.

The house was called to order, and the object of the meeting explained by the chairman; which was:

1st. To annul the old constitution, which was adopted by the society, on the 2d day of November, 1836:[170] which was, on motion, by the unanimous voice of the meeting, annulled.

2nd. To adopt Articles of Agreement, by which the Kirtland Safety Society are to be governed.

After much discussion and investigation, the following Preamble and Articles of Agreement were adopted, by the unanimous voice of the meeting.

We, the undersigned subscribers, for the promotion of our temporal interests, and for the better management of our different occupations, which consist in agriculture, mechanical arts, and merchandising; do hereby form ourselves into a firm or company for the before mentioned objects, by the name of the "Kirtland Safety Society Anti-Banking Company," and for the proper management of said firm, we individually and jointly enter into, and adopt, the following Articles of Agreement.

Art. 1st. The capital stock of said society or firm[171] shall not be less than four millions of dollars;[172] to be divided into shares of fifty dollars each; and may be increased to any amount, at the discretion of the managers.[173]

Art. 2d. The management of said company[174] shall be under the superintendence of thirty-two managers, to be chosen annually by, and from among the members[175] of the same; each member being entitled to one vote for each [p. 441] share, which he, she, or they may hold in said company; and said votes may be given by proxy, or in *propria persona*.

Art. 3d. It shall be the duty of said managers, when chosen, to elect from their number, a Treasurer and Secretary.[176] It shall be the further duty of said

---

170. Constitution of the Kirtland Safety Society Bank, 2 Nov. 1836, pp. 299–306 herein.

171. In this and subsequent instances, the November 1836 constitution has "Bank" instead of "society or firm."

172. When the Kirtland Safety Society charter was presented before the state senate on 10 February 1837, the capital stock was set at $300,000 instead of the $4 million stated here and in the earlier constitution. The revised figure was within the range of the capital stocks of other community banks in the West. (*Journal of the Senate of the State of Ohio*, 365–366; see also Historical Introduction to Constitution of the Kirtland Safety Society Bank, 2 Nov. 1836, p. 302 herein; and Introduction to Part 5: 5 Oct. 1836–10 Apr. 1837, pp. 288–291 herein.)

173. Except where noted, the November 1836 constitution has "directors" instead of "managers" throughout the text.

174. In this and subsequent instances, the November 1836 constitution has "Bank" instead of "company."

175. In this and subsequent instances, the November 1836 constitution uses "Stockholders" rather than "members."

176. Starting here, "Treasurer" and "Secretary" replace instances of "President" and "Cashier" found

managers to meet in the upper room of the office of said company,[177] on the first Mondays of November and May of each year, at nine o'clock, A. M. to inspect the books of said company and transact such other business as may be deemed necessary.

Art 4th. It shall be the duty of said managers to choose from among their number, seven men, who shall meet in the upper room of said office, on Tuesday of each week, at 4 o'clock, P.M. to inquire into and assist in all matters pertaining to said company.[178]

Art. 5th. Each manager shall receive from the company one dollar per day for his services when called together at the annual and semi-annual meetings. The Treasurer and Secretary, and the seven, the committee of the managers, shall receive a compensation for their services as shall be agreed by the managers at their semi-annual meetings.

Art. 6th. The first election of managers, as set forth in the second article, shall take place at the meeting of the members to adopt this agreement,[179] who shall hold their office until the first Monday of November, 1837, unless removed by death or misdemeanor, and until others are duly elected. Every annual election of managers shall take place on the first Monday of November, of each year. It shall be the duty of the Treasurer and Secretary of said company, to receive the votes of the members by ballot, and declare the election.

Art. 7th. The books of the company shall be always open for the inspection of the members.

Art. 8th. It shall be the duty of the managers[180] of the company, to declare a dividend once in six months; which dividend shall be apportioned among the members, according to the installments by them paid in.

Art. 9. All persons subscribing stock in said firm, shall pay their first installment at the time of subscribing; and other installments from time to time, as shall be required by the managers.

---

in the November 1836 constitution. The change to a banking company entailed new titles for the officers. Despite this change, it appears that Rigdon continued to act as the head of the company and JS continued to perform the duties of a cashier, with help from clerks.

177. This article in the November constitution required directors to meet "in the Director's Room in said Banking house." The change removes all mentions of the earlier bank, even though the managers were likely meeting in the same place designated by the November 1836 constitution.

178. The earlier November 1836 constitution called for six men. The duty originally assigned the group of six men to "examine all notes presented for discounting," was removed from these January articles of agreement. While this was likely a move to distance the company from banking ties, it may also have meant that the Kirtland Safety Society did not intend to accept and discount the notes of other banks. For a definition of discounting, see 305n93 herein.

179. The November 1836 constitution has "constitution" rather than "agreement."

180. Here the November 1836 constitution has "officers" rather than "managers."

Art. 10. The managers shall give thirty days notice in some public paper, printed in this county, previous to an installment being paid in. All subscribers residing out of the State, shall be required to pay in half the amount of their subscriptions at the time of subscribing, and the remainder, or such part thereof, as shall be required at any time by the managers, after thirty days notice.

Art. 11th. The Treasurer shall be empowered to call special meetings of the managers, whenever he shall deem it necessary; seperate and aside from the annual and semi-annual meetings.

Art. 12. Two thirds of the managers shall form a quorum to act at the semi-annual meetings, and any number of the seven, the committee of the managers, with the Treasurer and Secretary,[181] or either of them, may form a quorum to transact business at the weekly meetings; and in case none of the seven are present at the weekly meetings, the Treasurer and Secretary must transact the business.

Art. 13th. The managers shall have power to enact such by-laws as they may deem necessary, from time to time, providing they do not infringe upon these Articles of Agreement.[182]

Art. 14th. All notes given by said society, shall be signed by the Treasurer and Secretary thereof, and we the individual members of said firm, hereby hold ourselves bound for the redemption of all such notes.[183]

Art. 15. The notes given for the benefit of said society, shall be given to the Treasurer, in the following form:

"Ninety days after date, we jointly and severally promise to pay A. B.[184] or order [blank] dollars and [blank] cents, value received."

A record of which shall be made in the books at the time, of the amount, and by whom given, and when due—and deposited with the files and papers of said society.[185]

Art. 16. Any article in this agreement may be altered at any time, annulled, added unto or expunged, by the vote of two-thirds of the members of said society; except the fourteenth article, that shall remain unaltered during the

---

181. From this point on in the document, "Treasurer and Secretary" replaces "officers of the Bank" used in the November 1836 constitution.

182. The November 1836 constitution has "constitution" instead of "Articles of Agreement."

183. This is a new article written for the 2 January articles of agreement; it is not found in the November 1836 constitution.

184. In this template, "A. B." stands for the name of the bearer of the note.

185. This is a new article not found in the November 1836 constitution. The notes mentioned here are promissory notes made by those taking out loans from the Kirtland Safety Society. These articles of agreement set a ninety-day loan period and required that a record of the loan be made in the books of the society. Wording that is copied almost verbatim from this article appears on a sheet found among records of early January loans made by the Kirtland Safety Society. ("List of Notes for Discounting," Jan. 1837, JS Office Collection, CHL.)

existence of said company. For the true and faithful fulfillment of the above covenant and agreement, we in[p. 442]dividually bind ourselves to each other under the penal sum of one hundred thousand dollars. In witness whereof we have hereunto set our hands and seals the day and date first written above.

In connexion with the above Articles of Agreement of the Kirtland Safety Society, I beg leave to make a few remarks to all those who are preparing themselves, and appointing their wise men, for the purpose of building up Zion and her Stakes. It is wisdom and according to the mind of the Holy Spirit, that you should call at Kirtland,[186] and receive counsel and instruction upon those principles that are necessary to further the great work of the Lord, and to establish the children of the Kingdom, according to the oracles of God, as they are had among us. And further, we invite the brethren from abroad, to call on us, and take stock in our Safety Society. And we would remind them also of the sayings of the prophet Isaiah, contained in the 60th chapter, and more particularly the 9th and 17th verses, which are as follows: "Surely the isles shall wait for me, and the ships of Tarshish first, and to bring thy sons from far, their silver and their gold (not their bank notes)[187] with them, unto the name of the Lord thy God, and to the holy one of Israel, because he hath glorified thee.

["]For brass I will bring gold, and for iron I will bring silver, and wood brass and for stones iron: I will also make thy officers peace, and thine exactors righteousness." Also 62 ch. 1st vrs. "For Zion's sake will I not hold my peace,

---

186. This echoes the December 1833 and February 1834 revelatory injunctions to select wise men from the churches to purchase land in order to establish Zion. The phrasing JS uses here regarding the appointment of "wise men" is also similar to conference minutes from December 1836 that established guidelines for those Saints interested in moving to Kirtland. (Revelation, 16–17 Dec. 1833, in *JSP*, D3:395 [D&C 101:73]; Revelation, 24 Feb. 1834, in *JSP*, D3:461 [D&C 103:23]; Minutes, 22 Dec. 1836, p. 323 herein.)

187. Though JS may have added this parenthetical in jest, it demonstrates the Kirtland Safety Society's need for specie and not simply payment in banknotes. It is difficult to know how much coinage the Safety Society had at any given time, and reports of the amount held differ dramatically. The *Cleveland Weekly Advertiser* stated that the society had $16,000 in "specie and bankable funds" in January 1837. Warren Parrish, the clerk for the society who was elected to replace JS as cashier in summer 1837, later wrote, "I have been astonished to hear him [JS] declare that we had 60,000 Dollars in specie in our vaults and $600,000 at our command, when we had not to exceed $6,000 and could not command any more." Parrish's claims may have been colored by his objections to JS's leadership and his excommunication from the church. No other sources exist to substantiate any of these amounts. The society likely had the ten percent necessary to redeem a portion of their notes when they opened their office at the beginning of January 1837, but they did not have a substantial specie reserve. The public's widespread reluctance to use or accept the society's notes, and the efforts of opponents like Grandison Newell to demand the redemption of hundreds of dollars of notes at one time, worked to deplete what reserves they had gathered. ("Kirtland Safety Society," *Cleveland Weekly Advertiser*, 2 Feb. 1837, [3]; Warren Parrish, Kirtland, OH, 5 Feb. 1838, Letter to the Editor, *Painesville [OH] Republican*, 15 Feb. 1838, [3]; John Smith and Clarissa Lyman Smith, Kirtland, OH, to George A. Smith, Shinnston, VA, 1 Jan. 1838, George Albert Smith, Papers, CHL.)

Uncut sheet of Kirtland Safety Society notes. 1837. This document offers insight into the process of creating Kirtland Safety Society notes. Sheets such as the one shown here were printed from plates. Each printing plate contained the engravings for four individual notes. The letter A, B, or C was included in the image of each note, designating whether it was the first, second, or third note of that denomination on the printing plates. Most of the engraved notes contained the letter A, meaning that they were the first or only image of that denomination included on the printing plates. After printing, the notes were signed by the officers of the society before the sheets were detached into separate notes. Coin and Currency Collection, Church History Library, Salt Lake City.

and for Jerusalem's sake I will not rest, until the righteousness thereof go forth as brightness, and the salvation thereof as a lamp that burneth.["]

J. SMITH jr.

———— ⁊ ————

Kirtland Safety Society Notes, 4 January–9 March 1837

Historical Introduction

In early January 1837 the Kirtland Safety Society opened for business and began issuing notes through loans or in exchange for the notes of other banks. The notes then functioned as currency. Through its agents and other business arrangements, the society tried in the following months to introduce notes into circulation across northern Ohio and in parts of Pennsylvania, Michigan, and New York.[188]

Notes for the Kirtland Safety Society were engraved by the printing and engraving firm Underwood, Bald, Spencer & Hufty in late 1836. Oliver Cowdery likely commissioned the printing plates for the notes in October 1836 while on a trip to New York City to purchase goods for mercantile firms in Kirtland, including the firm of Rigdon, Smith & Cowdery.[189] Cowdery appears to have left Kirtland in December 1836 to collect the finished printing plates; he likely also had the Underwood engraving firm print a significant quantity of paper notes.[190] According to newspaper reports, Cowdery picked up the plates at the firm's Philadelphia office—rather than their New York office, where he presumably ordered them—and he returned to Kirtland by the end of December.[191]

The notes for the Kirtland Safety Society were engraved on three, or possibly four, printing plates.[192] Each plate contained the engraving for four notes. The letter A, B, or C was included on the upper right or left of each note, designating whether it was the first, second, or

---

188. See Introduction to Part 5: 5 Oct. 1836–10 Apr. 1837, pp. 286–287 herein.

189. The engraving firm took Cowdery, JS, and fifteen other Kirtland residents to court in June 1837 for defaulting on a promissory note for $1,450, likely the cost of the engraved plates and any printing done by the firm. (Transcript of Proceedings, 16 Apr. 1839, Underwood et al. v. Rigdon et al. [Geauga Co. C.P. 1839], Geauga Co., OH, Court of Common Pleas, Record Book X, pp. 34–36, Geauga County Archives and Records Center, Chardon, OH.)

190. Cowdery's trip to Philadelphia likely occurred between 7 and 22 December, since he withdrew money from his account with the Kirtland Safety Society on those dates. (Kirtland Safety Society, Stock Ledger, 231.)

191. A 14 November 1836 letter to the editor of an Ohio newspaper states that Kirtland residents had "procured plates from New York," but several contemporary accounts indicate the plates came from Philadelphia, including a late December 1836 article in the *Cleveland Weekly Advertiser* announcing that "the bank will go into operation immediately, the plates for bills being soon expected from Philadelphia." ("Mormonism in Ohio," *Aurora* [New Lisbon, OH], 19 Jan. 1837, [3]; "Bank at Kirtland," *Cleveland Weekly Advertiser,* 29 Dec. 1836, [1]; see also Editorial, *LDS Messenger and Advocate,* July 1837, 3:535; and JS History, vol. B-1, 750.)

192. Uncut sheets exist for two plates; the arrangement of the third plate is not certain, and partially uncut sheets containing ten- and twenty-dollar bills suggest there may have also been a fourth plate of

third note of that denomination on the printing plates. After printing, the notes were signed by the officers of the Kirtland Safety Society before the sheets were cut into individual notes.

Because the name and organization of the Safety Society changed on 2 January, the first notes it issued were modified. The characters "ANTI" and "ING CO." were hand stamped onto the original printed notes to reflect the institution's revised title, the Kirtland Safety Society Anti-Banking Company.[193] Stamps were also used to cancel the titles of president and cashier printed on the notes. The society hand stamped only the earliest bills it issued and abandoned the practice in early January, possibly by 5 January. The only extant notes that bear these hand-stamped alterations are one-dollar, two-dollar, and three-dollar denominations. Despite the brief time the society hand stamped alterations on its notes, some newspapers in northeastern Ohio reacted strongly to the practice. For instance, an article in the *Cleveland Weekly Gazette* discussed the perceived deception:

> We look upon the whole as a most reprehensible fraud on the public, and cannot conceal our surprise that they should circulate at all. For instance, the large letters engraved on the bills appear, on a casual examination, to read like a Bank bill, and the unsuspecting would in the hurry of business, take them as ordinary Bank bills. But on scrutiny it will be found that previous to the word "Bank" in capitals, the word "anti" in fine letters is inserted, and after the word "Bank," the syllable "ing" is affixed in small letters also, so as to read in fact, instead of Bank, "ANTIBANKING." We do not object to private or company banking, as a system, provided it is done *upon* a *system* and *made safe*, but we consider this whole affair a deception.[194]

Although JS and Sidney Rigdon appear to have signed most of the extant notes, others were also involved in writing additional information on, signing, and recording the distribution of the notes. Clerks for the society often wrote the date, serial number, or name of the bearer on the notes. Notes bearing the date of 4 January 1837 were signed by three interim officers for the society—Newel K. Whitney, Frederick G. Williams, and Horace Kingsbury—who assisted the elected officers by signing notes. In each case the men wrote their position as treasurer or secretary after their signature and added "PT," an abbreviation for *pro tempore,* demonstrating their temporary status as officers.

Notes were issued by the society from January to July 1837. The notes featured here, dated between 4 January and 9 March, are the earliest known examples of each denomination currently held by the Church History Library of The Church of Jesus Christ of Latter-day Saints. JS and Rigdon resigned as officers of the society sometime between 8 June and 7 July

---

notes. (Kirtland Safety Society Notes, Jan.–Mar. 1837, Coin and Currency Collection, CHL; Nyholm, *Mormon Currency,* 17–22.)

193. See Historical Introduction to Articles of Agreement for the Kirtland Safety Society Anti-Banking Company, 2 Jan. 1837, p. 324 herein.

194. "A New Revelation—Mormon Money," *Cleveland Weekly Gazette,* 18 Jan. 1837, [3], italics in original. This article was reprinted in several Ohio newspapers. (See, for example, "A New Revolution.—Mormon Money," *Huron Reflector* [Norwalk, OH], 24 Jan. 1837, [3]; and "A New Revolution.—Morman Money," *Painesville [OH] Telegraph,* 20 Jan. 1837, [3]; see also "Rags! Mere Rags!!," *Ohio Star* [Ravenna], 19 Jan. 1837, [3].)

1837, and the new officers, Frederick G. Williams and Warren A. Parrish, issued additional notes in July 1837. No extant notes bear dates after 20 July 1837, and the institution soon closed, likely by August 1837.[195]

I. One-Dollar Note
Source Note

One-dollar note, Kirtland Township, Geauga Co., OH, 4 Jan. 1837; printed note with additions in handwriting of Newel K. Whitney and an unidentified scribe; signatures of Sidney Rigdon and JS; one page; Coin and Currency Collection,CHL.

Single leaf measuring 3 × 6⅞ inches (8 × 17 cm). The lines on the form for names, dates, and serial numbers are filled in. The paper is discolored.

Document Transcript

1 No. _309_   A 1
THE KIRTLAND SAFETY SOCIETY ⟨ANTI-⟩BANK⟨ING CO.⟩[196]
      I   I

Will pay ONE DOLLAR on demand
to _W[arren] Parrish_ or bearer
KIRTLAND OHIO _4 Jan^y_ 18_37_

I   I

S[idney] Rigdon Sec ~~Cash^r~~ **J Smith Jr.** Treas [197] ~~Pres^t~~
Underwood Bald Spencer & Hufty N. York & Philad^a.

One-dollar note, Kirtland Safety Society. Coin and Currency Collection, Church History Library, Salt Lake City.

---

195. For more on the end of the Kirtland Safety Society, see Introduction to Part 6: 20 Apr.–14 Sept. 1837, pp. 365–366 herein; and Historical Introduction to Notice, ca. Late Aug. 1837, pp. 418–420 herein.
196. TEXT: Insertions in this line made interlinearly with a stamp.
197. TEXT: Signatures of Sidney Rigdon and JS. "Sec" and "Treas" in unidentified handwriting.

II. Two-Dollar Note

Source Note

Two-dollar note, Kirtland Township, Geauga Co., OH, 4 Jan. 1837; printed note with additions in handwriting of Newel K. Whitney and Warren Parrish; signatures of Sidney Rigdon and JS; one page; Coin and Currency Collection, CHL.

Single leaf measuring 3 × 6¾ inches (8 × 17 cm). The lines on the form for names and dates are filled in.

Document Transcript

2   Kirtland   _4 Jan_ 18_37_ [198]   2
OHIO   N° _1897_ [199] A
    2   2

THE KIRTLAND SAFETY SOCIETY ⟨ANTI-⟩BANK⟨ING CO.⟩ [200]
Will pay TWO DOLLARS on demand
to _O[rson] Hyde_ or bearer

2   2

  S[idney] Rigdon Sec [201] ~~Cash^f.~~   **J Smith Jr. Treas.** [202] ~~Pres^t.~~
Underwood Bald Spencer & Hufty N. York & Philad^a.

Two-dollar note, Kirtland Safety Society. Coin and Currency Collection, Church History Library, Salt Lake City.

---

198. TEXT: Additions in handwriting of Newel K. Whitney unless otherwise noted.
199. TEXT: Addition in handwriting of Warren Parrish.
200. TEXT: Insertions in this line made interlinearly with a stamp.
201. TEXT: Signature and "Sec" in handwriting of Sidney Rigdon.
202. TEXT: Signature and "Treas." in handwriting of JS.

III. Three-Dollar Note
Source Note

Three-dollar note, Kirtland Township, Geauga Co., OH, 4 Jan. 1837; printed note with additions in handwriting of Oliver Cowdery; signatures of Sidney Rigdon and JS; one page; Coin and Currency Collection, CHL.

Single leaf measuring 3 × 6⅞ inches (8 × 17 cm). The lines on the form for names and dates are filled in.

Document Transcript

A   No. _89_

THE KIRTLAND
SAFETY SOCIETY

3   3

⟨ANTI-⟩BANK⟨ING CO.⟩[203] Will pay on demand
to _W[arren] Parrish_ or bearer THREE DOLLARS
Kirtland Ohio _4. Jany_ 18_37_
S[idney] Rigdon Sec. ~~Cash[r.]~~ **J Smith Jr.** Tres. [204] ~~Pres[t.]~~
Underwood Bald Spencer & Hufty N. York & Philad[a.]

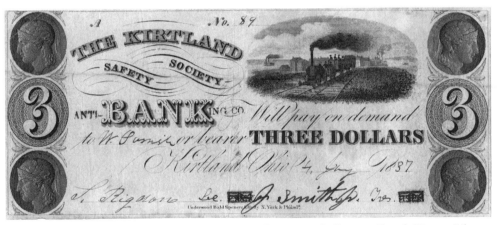

Three-dollar note, Kirtland Safety Society. Coin and Currency Collection, Church History Library, Salt Lake City.

---

203. TEXT: Insertions in this line made interlinearly with a stamp.
204. TEXT: Signatures of Sidney Rigdon and JS.

IV. Five-Dollar Note

Source Note

Five-dollar note, Kirtland Township, Geauga Co., OH, 10 Feb. 1837; printed note with additions in handwriting of Oliver Cowdery and Newel K. Whitney; signatures of A. B. Hull, JS, and Sidney Rigdon; one page; Coin and Currency Collection, CHL.

Single leaf measuring 3 × 6⅞ inches (8 × 17 cm). The lines on the form for names and dates are filled in.

Document Transcript

V   No. 1005 [205]   B   V

⟨AB Hull⟩[206]

    5   5

THE KIRTLAND SAFETY SOCIETY BANK
Will pay FIVE DOLLARS on demand
to O Gates [207] or bearer
KIRTLAND OHIO 10 Feb 18 37

5   5

J Smith Jr Cash[r.]   S[idney] Rigdon [208] Pres[t.]
Underwood Bald Spencer & Hufty N. York & Philad[a.]

Five-dollar note, Kirtland Safety Society. Coin and Currency Collection, Church History Library, Salt Lake City.

---

205. TEXT: Addition in handwriting of Oliver Cowdery.

206. TEXT: Signature of A. B. Hull written vertically on note. For more information on A. B. Hull, see Historical Introduction to Agreement with Ovid Pinney and Stephen Phillips, 14 Mar. 1837, pp. 345–346 herein.

207. TEXT: This and the following addition in handwriting of Newel K. Whitney.

208. TEXT: Signatures of JS and Sidney Rigdon.

V. Ten-Dollar Note

Source Note

Ten-dollar note, Kirtland Township, Geauga Co., OH, 1 Mar. 1837; printed note with additions in handwriting of Warren Parrish, Oliver Cowdery, and Newel K. Whitney; signatures of Ovid Pinney, JS, and Sidney Rigdon; one page; Coin and Currency Collection, CHL.

Single leaf measuring 3 × 6¾ inches (8 × 17 cm). The lines on the form for names and dates are filled in.

Document Transcript

X   Kirtland Ohio   <u>March 1,</u> 18<u>_37_</u>[209]   X
          Nº. <u>_913_</u>[210]   B
⟨Ovid Pinney 913⟩[211]
          TEN   TEN

THE KIRTLAND
SAFETY SOCIETY
Bank Will pay TEN dollars on demand
to <u> O Gates </u>[212] or bearer.

IO   IO

<u>**J Smith Jr**</u> Cashr. <u>S[idney] Rigdon</u>[213] Prest.
Underwood Bald Spencer & Hufty N. York & Philada.

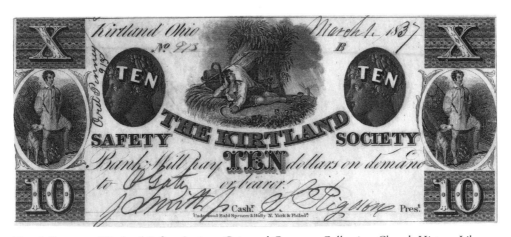

Ten-dollar note, Kirtland Safety Society. Coin and Currency Collection, Church History Library, Salt Lake City.

---

209. TEXT: Additions in handwriting of Warren Parrish.

210. TEXT: Addition in handwriting of Oliver Cowdery.

211. TEXT: Signature of Ovid Pinney written vertically on note. For more information on Ovid Pinney, see Historical Introduction to Agreement with Ovid Pinney and Stephen Phillips, 14 Mar. 1837, pp. 345–346 herein.

212. TEXT: Addition in handwriting of Newel K. Whitney.

213. TEXT: Signatures of JS and Sidney Rigdon.

VI. Twenty-Dollar Note

Source Note

Twenty-dollar note, Kirtland Township, Geauga Co., OH, 20 Feb. 1837; printed note with additions in handwriting of an unidentified scribe and Newel K. Whitney; signatures of JS and Sidney Rigdon; one page; Coin and Currency Collection, CHL.

Single leaf measuring 3 × 6⅞ inches (8 × 17 cm). The lines on the form for names and dates are filled in.

Document Transcript

20   20

No. __439__ [214]   A

20   20

THE KIRTLAND SAFETY SOCIETY BANK
Will pay TWENTY dollars on
demand to __O P Good__ [215] or bearer.
Kirtland Ohio __20 Feb__ 18__37__
__J Smith Jr__ Cashr.   __S[idney] Rigdon__ [216] Prest.

20   20

Underwood Bald Spencer & Hufty N. York & Philada.

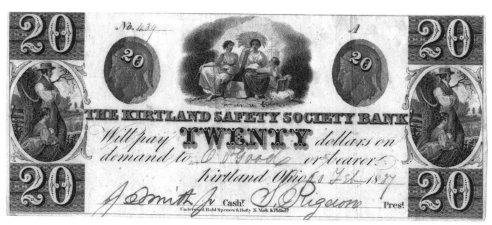

Twenty-dollar note, Kirtland Safety Society. Coin and Currency Collection, Church History Library, Salt Lake City.

---

214. TEXT: Addition in unidentified handwriting.
215. TEXT: This and following additions in handwriting of Newel K. Whitney.
216. TEXT: Signatures of JS and Sidney Rigdon.

VII. Fifty-Dollar Note

Source Note

Fifty-dollar note, Kirtland Township, Geauga Co., OH, 9 Mar. 1837; printed note with additions in handwriting of Warren Parrish and Newel K. Whitney; signatures of JS and Sidney Rigdon; one page; Coin and Currency Collection, CHL.

Single leaf measuring 2⅞ × 6⅞ inches (7 × 17 cm). The lines on the form for names and dates are filled in.

Document Transcript

50   50

    No. __35__ [217]   A

    50   50

THE KIRTLAND
SAFETY SOCIETY BANK
Will pay FIFTY dollars on demand
to __O[rson] Pratt__ [218] or bearer

                        Kirtland Ohio. __9 Mar__ 18_37_ [219]

    __J Smith Jr__ Cash[r.]   __S[idney] Rigdon__ [220] Pres[t.]

50   50

Underwood Bald Spencer & Hufty N. York & Philad[a.]

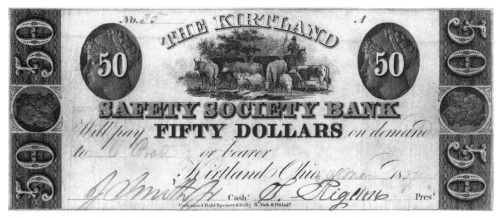

Fifty-dollar note, Kirtland Safety Society. Coin and Currency Collection, Church History Library, Salt Lake City.

---

217. TEXT: Addition in handwriting of Warren Parrish.
218. TEXT: Addition possibly in handwriting of Warren Parrish.
219. TEXT: Additions likely in handwriting of Newel K. Whitney.
220. TEXT: Signatures of JS and Sidney Rigdon.

VIII. One-Hundred-Dollar Note
Source Note

One-hundred-dollar note, Kirtland Township, Geauga Co., OH, 9 Mar. 1837; printed note with additions in handwriting of Warren Parrish and an unidentified scribe; signatures of JS and Sidney Rigdon; one page; Coin and Currency Collection, CHL.

Single leaf measuring 2⅞ × 6⅞ inches (7 × 17 cm). The lines on the form for names and dates are filled in.

Document Transcript

100   100

Kirtland   9 Mar   18_37_ [221]
OHIO   Nᵒ· _209_ [222] A

    100   100

C   THE KIRTLAND SAFETY SOCIETY BANK   C

Will pay ONE HUNDRED Dollars
on demand to _O[rson] Pratt_ or bearer

100   100

J Smith Jr   Cashʳ·   S[idney] Rigdon [223] Presᵗ·
Underwood Bald Spencer & Hufty N. York & Philadᵃ·

One-hundred-dollar note, Kirtland Safety Society. Coin and Currency Collection, Church History Library, Salt Lake City.

———— ☙ ————

221. TEXT: Addition in handwriting of Warren Parrish.
222. TEXT: This and following addition in unidentified handwriting.
223. TEXT: Signatures of JS and Sidney Rigdon.

Agreement with David Cartter, 14 January 1837

Source Note

Sidney Rigdon, JS, Frederick G. Williams, Reynolds Cahoon, David Whitmer, and Oliver Cowdery, Agreement, with David Cartter, [Kirtland Township, Geauga Co., OH], 14 Jan. 1837; handwriting of unidentified scribe and David Cartter; signatures of Sidney Rigdon, JS, Frederick G. Williams, Reynolds Cahoon, David Whitmer, Oliver Cowdery, and David Cartter; two pages; JS Collection, CHL. Includes docket.

Bifolium measuring 9⅞ × 7⅞ inches (25 × 20 cm) when folded. Pages are ruled with twenty-eight horizontal, watermarked lines and one watermarked margin line. A watermark placed at the bifolium fold reads "LOCo." and is circumscribed by a faint circle. The scribe did not write on the watermarked lines. The first two pages are inscribed, the third is blank, and the fourth contains a docket in the handwriting of David Cartter. The document was folded in three patterns. The first pattern is a trifold with the agreement facing outward. The second pattern is a five-panel roll fold with the endorsement facing inward. Marked staining, soot, fingerprints, and fly specks on the third page suggest that the agreement was folded at one time so the third page was an exterior page.

The provenance of this document is unknown; however, given the pattern of extant Kirtland-era documents in possession of the Church History Library, this document was probably bundled and stored with other loose Kirtland financial material and was likely in continuous institutional custody.

Historical Introduction

On 14 January 1837, shortly after the Kirtland Safety Society opened for business, society officers Sidney Rigdon and JS and managers Frederick G. Williams, Reynolds Cahoon, David Whitmer, and Oliver Cowdery entered into an agreement with David K. Cartter—a young lawyer who had recently moved to Akron, Ohio—to become an agent of the society.[224] Banks generally appointed agents to extend their influence to additional markets through loans and through a wider circulation of their notes. A broader distribution of notes and the contracting of local agents who were known in their own communities increased the likelihood that notes of distant or lesser-known financial institutions would be accepted outside of the issuing bank's immediate vicinity. A later agreement between the Kirtland Safety Society and another agent stipulated that the agent should "use his influence at all times & in all places at home & abroad both directly and indirectly to sustain the above named institution & promote its interest, by putting into the hands of the Cashier of the Same all the Spices [specie] & Bankable money that comes into his hands."[225]

Cartter's contract specified that he was to extend the influence of the Kirtland Safety Society to Akron, a burgeoning town approximately forty-five miles south of Kirtland. Cartter's role involved making loans and exchanging the notes of the Kirtland Safety Society for the notes of other banks. To enable him to make loans and exchanges, the

---

224. David Kellogg Cartter, born in New York in 1812, served as a representative from Ohio to the United States Congress, 1849–1853. Cartter moved to Cleveland in 1856 and continued to practice law. He served as U.S. minister to Bolivia from 1861 to 1862 and was appointed chief justice of the Supreme Court of the District of Columbia in 1863, serving in that capacity until his death in Washington DC in 1887. (*Biographical Directory of the United States Congress,* 751; 1870 U.S. Census, 552686, M593_1187, p. 57A; 1880 U.S. Census, Washington DC, 56B.)

225. J. W. Briggs, Bond, Kirtland, OH, 8 Mar. 1837, JS Office Papers, CHL.

Kirtland Safety Society agreed to provide Cartter with up to $30,000 in society notes, for which Cartter would be held liable. Cartter would earn a commission of one and a half percent on the loans and exchanges he made. On the same day this agreement was signed, Cartter drew up a bond between himself and two other Akron residents, Eliakim Crosby and James W. Philips, binding the three men to the repayment of the $30,000 entrusted to him by the Kirtland Safety Society.[226] In addition to making Cartter and his partners jointly liable for the repayment of the $30,000, the bond may have allowed Crosby and Philips to partner with Cartter and receive a portion of his commission.

Extant records give no further information about Cartter's role as an agent or how the notes of the Safety Society were received in Akron. This is the earliest extant agreement made between the Kirtland Safety Society and an agent. By March the society had made at least two additional agreements establishing agents for the society outside of Kirtland.[227]

Document Transcript

/[228]This agreement made & entered into this fourteenth day of January A.D. 1837.— witnesseth that We the Undersigned Managers of the Kirtland-safety-society-Bank[229] of the Township of Kirtland, County of Geauga and State of Ohio hereby authorize, constitute and appoint David K. Cartter of the Village of Akron, County of Portage & State aforesaid, our Banking Agent at Akron aforesaid to loan and Exchange the Notes of said Bank.— And we hereby covenant and agree to furnish said Cartter with the Notes aforesaid from time to time as said Cartter may require, to the amount of Thirty Thousand Dollars, It is further stipulated by the parties of to these presents that said Cartter in

---

226. David K. Cartter, Bond, 14 Jan. 1837, JS Office Papers, CHL. Eliakim Crosby was born in Connecticut in 1779, trained as a physician in New York, and moved with his family to Ohio in 1820. He helped found the town of Cascade, which became Akron, and was one of its most prominent residents. James W. Philips was a member of a committee that unsuccessfully petitioned the Ohio legislature for a bank in Akron in December 1835. In February 1837, a new firm called the Portage Canal and Manufacturing Company was incorporated by the legislature and was granted permission to issue bonds. Eliakim Crosby was the first president of this company, and James Philips served as a "special agent" for its business in New York. David Cartter is not listed as an officer of the new firm, but he may have been a stockholder. (Lane, *Fifty Years and Over of Akron and Summit County,* 41–45, 82–83.)

227. Agreement with Ovid Pinney and Stephen Phillips, 14 Mar. 1837, pp. 344–348 herein; J. W. Briggs, Bond, Kirtland, OH, 8 Mar. 1837, JS Office Papers, CHL.

228. TEXT: Unidentified handwriting begins.

229. As this agreement was created after the 2 January 1837 reorganization of the society into the Kirtland Safety Society Anti-Banking Company, the society in its official structure was no longer a bank. However, the wording of this agreement follows the banking-specific terminology used in the 2 November 1836 constitution of the Kirtland Safety Society, with the exception of the term "managers," which was introduced in the 2 January 1837 articles of agreement. This use of the earlier-employed banking terminology suggests that the Kirtland Safety Society officers considered the institution a bank, despite its not yet being granted a charter by the Ohio legislature. (Constitution of the Kirtland Safety Society Bank, 2 Nov. 1836, pp. 304–306 herein; Articles of Agreement for the Kirtland Safety Society Anti-Banking Company, 2 Jan. 1837, pp. 325–331 herein.)

loaning said money shall not receive notes or other obligations therefor made payable, at a longer period than ninety Days from the date thereof ⟨and renew the same from time to time at his discression Except otherwise directed by said Managers⟩²³⁰.— Also that said Cartter shall report and make a full exhibit of his business as such agent to the President of said Bank by letter or otherwise once in every two weeks.— Also that said Cartter shall be limited to and governed in the amount of his loans, by the amount of his Exchanges.—

Also that the amount of said Exchanges shall be subject to the order of said Managers.— [p. [1]]

Also that said Cartter shall receive & retain One and a half per cent upon all loans & Exchanges so as aforesaid made.— Also that this Agency shall continue from the date hereof until the first day of Nov.ᴵ 1837.²³¹

/²³²Witness our Hands and seals this fourteenth day of January A.D. 1837.

²³³Sidney Rigdon LS²³⁴

Joseph Smith Jr LS

F[rederick] G Williams LS

Reynolds Cahoon LS

David Whitmer LS

O[liver] Cowdery LS

LS.

D K Cartter LS. [1/2 page blank] [p. [2]]

[page [3] blank]

²³⁵D K Cartter

To

Managers &c [p. [4]]

———— ❧ ————

---

230. TEXT: Insertion in the handwriting of David Cartter.

231. This date for the end of Cartter's tenure as an agent for the Kirtland Safety Society was the same date the 2 January 1837 articles of agreement required new elections for the society's officers. This was possibly a measure to ensure that the newly elected officers would be aware of each of the society's agents and could renew agents or appoint new ones as needed. (Articles of Agreement for the Kirtland Safety Society Anti-Banking Company, 2 Jan. 1837, p. 327 herein.)

232. TEXT: Unidentified handwriting ends; David Cartter begins.

233. TEXT: Signatures of Sidney Rigdon, JS, Frederick G. Williams, Reynolds Cahoon, David Whitmer, Oliver Cowdery, and David Cartter.

234. TEXT: All instances of "LS" are enclosed in hand-drawn boxes. Handwriting of David Cartter. "LS" here is short for a Latin legal term, *locus sigilli*, denoting the area on a contract to affix a seal. The use of LS replaces the actual seal on the document.

235. TEXT: Docket in handwriting of David Cartter.

Notice, 24 January 1837

Source Note

JS, Notice, "To All Concerned," Kirtland Township, Geauga Co., OH, 24 Jan. 1837. Featured version published in "To All Concerned," Latter Day Saints' Messenger and Advocate, *Jan. 1837, 3:447. For more information on* Latter Day Saints' Messenger and Advocate, *see Source Notes for Multiple-Entry Documents, p. 527 herein.*

Historical Introduction

On 5 December 1835, JS sent a letter to the editor of the *Latter Day Saints' Messenger and Advocate* stating that he would refuse all unpaid mail addressed to him.[236] Yet he and other church leaders in Kirtland, Ohio, continued receiving mail with unpaid postage, an issue apparently compounded by an increasing quantity of incoming letters in late 1836 and early 1837.[237] In the notice featured here, JS again took space in the *Messenger and Advocate* to remind anyone sending mail to him to pay the postage on their letters. It appears that JS did in fact decline to pay the postage on unpaid letters in the months following the notice's publication. By July 1837, according to the *Painesville Telegraph,* the Kirtland Mills post office held eight letters addressed to JS, and another dozen addressed to him and his associates, for which the postage had not been paid.[238]

Document Transcript

TO ALL CONCERNED.

Owing to the multiplicity of Letters with which I am crowded, I am *again* under the necessity of saying, through the medium of the Messenger, that I will *not*, hereafter, take *any* letters from the Post-office, unless they are *post-paid*.

JOSEPH SMITH, Jr.

Kirtland, Jan. 24, 1837.

———— ☙ ————

Agreement with Ovid Pinney and Stephen Phillips,
14 March 1837

Source Note

Sampson Avard, agent, on behalf of JS and Sidney Rigdon, Agreement, with Ovid Pinney and Stephen Phillips, possibly Beaver Co., PA, 14 Mar. 1837; handwriting of A. B. Hull; signatures of Sampson Avard, Ovid Pinney, and Stephen Phillips; witnessed by A. B. Hull and James McConnel; two pages; JS Office Papers, CHL. Includes docket.

---

236. Letter to Editor, 5 Dec. 1835, pp. 103–104 herein.

237. See "Prospectus," *LDS Messenger and Advocate,* Oct. 1836, 3:386.

238. "List of Letters," *Painesville (OH) Telegraph,* 14 July 1837, [3].

Single bifolium, measuring 12¼ × 7½ inches (31 × 19 cm) when folded. The bifolium is ruled with thirty-eight horizontal, blue lines, nearly faded. After inscription, the agreement was ordered so the docket and second page were the exterior folio leaves. The document was then folded in a parallel fold twice and was docketed. Marked soiling is present on the page containing the docket.

The provenance of this document is unknown; however, given the pattern of extant Kirtland-era documents in possession of the Church History Library, this document was probably bundled and stored with other loose Kirtland financial material and was likely in continuous institutional custody.

Historical Introduction

On 14 March 1837, Sampson Avard, acting as an agent for Kirtland Safety Society officers JS and Sidney Rigdon, signed the agreement featured here with Pennsylvania businessmen Ovid Pinney and Stephen Phillips and their agents A. B. Hull and James McConnel. The agreement outlined Pinney and Phillips's commitment to circulate the notes of the society in Beaver County, Pennsylvania.[239]

This agreement was one of several contracts the officers and managers of the Kirtland Safety Society made with their appointed agents between January and March 1837 to expand the reach of the institution and find financial support outside of the Kirtland, Ohio, area.[240] On 8 March, a week earlier, J. W. Briggs, a merchant from Painesville, Ohio, signed an agreement to act as an agent for the society in Painesville.[241] Unlike the January agreement with David Cartter and the agreement featured here, both of which involved tens of thousands of dollars in Kirtland Safety Society notes, Briggs was given only one thousand dollars.[242]

Compared to the earlier agreements, the arrangement with Pinney, Phillips, and their agents gave them significant autonomy, more time to circulate the society's notes, and a larger amount of capital from which to base their loans. The Kirtland Safety Society committed to provide $40,000 in the society's notes to Pinney and Phillips over the next four years. The independence given to Pinney and Phillips suggests a different role than agents had previously played in the circulation of the society's notes. Additionally, they were required to mark the

---

239. Both Ovid Pinney and Stephen Phillips are described as capitalists in a history of Beaver County. After moving to Pennsylvania, Pinney had purchased land and tried to create a new town in Beaver County. He was also involved in efforts to establish the Conneaut Railroad, intended to connect Pennsylvania and Ohio, beginning in 1835. Phillips, a carpenter who was a partner in a steamboat-building firm, helped found the town of Freedom, Pennsylvania, in 1832. (Patterson, "Beaver County," 359–360.)

240. See Introduction to Part 5: 5 Oct. 1836–10 Apr. 1837, pp. 291–292 herein; Agreement with David Cartter, 14 Jan. 1837, pp. 341–343 herein; and J. W. Briggs, Bond, Kirtland, OH, 8 Mar. 1837, JS Office Papers, CHL.

241. J. W. Briggs, Bond, Kirtland, OH, 8 Mar. 1837, JS Office Papers, CHL. This bond was witnessed by Warren Parrish alone, and neither of the society's officers were recorded as being involved with the agent agreement.

242. Painesville was a large market town in Geauga County and could have generated some economic support, but significant opposition against JS and the church existed there. Additionally, the Bank of Geauga was located in Painesville, and the banks' officers likely had no desire to compete with another banking institution in Geauga County and may have worked against the Safety Society politically and economically. Grandison Newell, a determined opponent to JS and the church, was on the Bank of Geauga's board of directors. ("Bank of Geauga," *Geauga [OH] Gazette,* 28 Feb. 1832, [3]; Adams, "Grandison Newell's Obsession," 159–188; Agreement with David Cartter, 14 Jan. 1837, pp. 341–343 herein; Historical Introduction to Letter from Newel K. Whitney, 20 Apr. 1837, pp. 367–368 herein.)

Kirtland Safety Society notes given to them with their names and to deposit money with the society to redeem those notes.

The arrangement appears to have been at least partially successful: several extant notes bear the names of Pinney and his agent Hull, suggesting that the notes held by the Pennsylvania businessmen were put into circulation for a time, thereby extending the society's access to western Pennsylvania and eastern Ohio.[243] No further records of transactions between Pinney and Phillips and the Kirtland Safety Society exist. The closure of the society by August 1837 ended this arrangement long before the four-year period outlined in the contract was over.

Document Transcript

Article of an Agreement Made and entered into this Fourteenth day of March in the Year of our Lord one Thousand Eight Hundred and Thirty Seven between Joseph Smith Jr. Cashier of the Kirkland [Kirtland] Safety Society Bank or Kirkland Safety Society Anti Banking and Sidney Rigdon President of the same——— by their Agent Sampson Avard of the Town of Kirkland County of Geauga——— and State of ohio of the first party And Ovid Pinney & Stephen Phillips of the Township of New Seweekly [New Sewickley] County of Beaver and State of Pennsylvania of the Second part

—Witnesseth—

That the partys of the first part for and in consideration hereafter mentioned hath and doth agree that they will furnish of the Bills of the Kirkland Safety Soeciety Bank or Anti Banking the Sum of——— Forty Thousand Dollars to the Second party and let them have the same and put them in circulation for four Years from this date— Ten Thousand Dollars they are to have on Signing this agreement——— Ten Thousand Dollars as soon as they can get the first in circulation or within two months or at any time when Call^d. for, ⟨and Twenty Thousand Dollars also when called for⟩ The two last Sums are to be called for at the Banking House in Kirkland. And the party of the first part do further agree that they will alwais redeem the same money at their office in the Township of Kirkland County of— Geauga— and State of ohio Whenever offered and pay Current Money for the same and that ~~we~~ ⟨they⟩ will at all times take ~~our~~ ⟨their⟩ own notes as paymen[t] for any debts that Pinney & Phillips are bound to ~~us~~ ⟨them⟩ for the payment off. And we do further agree with the Second party that all money marked for them when redeemed at our office we will let them have it again for circulation.

---

243. Kirtland Safety Society Notes, 4 Jan.–9 Mar. 1837, pp. 336–337 herein; No. 735, No. 948, No. 1005, No. 913, No. 551, No. 1090, Kirtland Safety Society Notes, Jan. 1837–Mar. 1837, Coin and Currency Collection, CHL.

The second party doth agree with the first party that they will take their Bills and try to put them in circulation and at the expiration of the four Years we bind ourselves to pay to the Said party of the first [p. [1]] part the Sum of Forty Thousand Dollars if we receive the Same either in paper we receive or Their own Bills or Current Money of the State of Ohio or Pennsylvania, and we do further agree if the Bills are got in Circulation and the same or any of them are returned and redeemed by the first party on being notified by the Cashier of the Bank by Letter directed to Beaver Post Office Penn if we have not the Same amt. of their Bills in our possessi[o]n and not our Signature we will immediately Send to him a check on the Branch Bank of the United States at New Brighton to redeem the Same or one on the Branch Bank of Pittsburgh at Beaver

we do further agree that we will on receiving the Bills write one of our names across the face of the Bills or cause Some other person his— whose Signature we will acknowledge as one of ours by which our Bills may at all times be designated.[244]

We do further agree on receiving the next Ten Thousand Dollars if this Can be put into circulation we will make a deposite of Three Thousand Dollars in the Bank of the first party to redeem our Bills when they Come in—

The fir[s]t Ten Thousand Dollars is received and acknowledged on this agreement with the following Signatures one half is Signed by Stephen Phillips or James McConnel and the other half is Signd by Ovid Pinney or AB Hull whose names one of them is on each bill and each mans names & Signature is on this Article.

The interlining on the opposite Side was done before the Signing of this agreement

In Witness whereof we have hereunto Set our hands and Seals the day & year first above written

[245]<u>Sampson Avard</u> agent Seal[246]
Ovid Pinney Seal
S Phillips Seal

In Pressce of}
AB Hull
JM Cannel [James McConnel] [p. [2]]

---

244. Several extant Kirtland Safety Society notes bear the names of Ovid Pinney and A. B. Hull, demonstrating that they wrote their names on the notes that were given to them as they agreed to do. (See Kirtland Safety Society Notes, 4 Jan.–9 Mar. 1837, pp. 336–337 herein; No. 735, No. 948, No. 1005, No. 913, No. 551, No. 1090, Kirtland Safety Society Notes, Jan. 1837–Mar. 1837, Coin and Currency Collection, CHL.)

245. TEXT: Signatures of Sampson Avard and Ovid Pinney.

246. TEXT: Each instance of "Seal" is enclosed in a hand-drawn seal. Handwriting of A. B. Hull.

Article of Agreement between Joseph Smith J. & Ovid Pinney Stephen
Phillips

——————— ✑ ———————

Letter from A. Miles, 21 March 1837

Source Note

*A. Miles, Letter, Brunswick, Medina Co., OH, to JS, Kirtland Township, Geauga Co., OH, 21 Mar.
1837; manuscript and printed form; handwriting probably of A. Miles; three pages; JS Collection, CHL.
Includes address, postal markings, and docket.*

Bifolium measuring 9⅞ × 8⅛ inches (25 × 21 cm) when folded. The upper left corner of the third
page is embossed with an oval paper-mill insignia containing a bird with a parcel hanging from its
neck. Above the bird are the words "JOHN BUTLER | HARTFORD CT". Below the bird are two
leafy branches that are crossed. The first and second pages are inscribed; the third contains a printed
advertisement for the Western Bank Note Engraving Company of Cincinnati, Ohio. The letter
included two enclosures of sample banknotes.

The letter was folded in two patterns. First, the document was trifolded in letter style, addressed,
and sealed with two red adhesive wafers, partially extant. Second, the letter was folded in a four-panel
roll fold for filing and was docketed in red ink by Leo Hawkins: "Mch 21. 1837 | A. Miles to | Joseph
Smith".[247] The docket indicates the letter was in institutional custody no later than the mid-1850s
(likely earlier). The letter first appeared in the Church Historian's Office inventory about 1904.

Historical Introduction

The 21 March 1837 letter featured here was sent to JS by one A. Miles, a business agent
for the Western Bank Note Engraving Company in Cincinnati, Ohio. The letter consisted
of a handwritten message from Miles soliciting engraving orders, a printed business notice
from the company, and sample banks notes. Miles likely contacted JS because of his position as an officer of the Kirtland Safety Society.[248]

The Western Bank Note Engraving Company was started by two engravers, William
Woodruff and Zelotus H. Mason, probably around 1836.[249] They were working to establish
a clientele for their new business by January 1837, when they printed a notice announcing

---

247. "Letters to and from the Prophet," ca. 1904, Historian's Office, Catalogs and Inventories, 1846–
1904, CHL.

248. See Introduction to Part 5: 5 Oct. 1836–10 Apr. 1837, pp. 285–286 herein.

249. Woodruff and Mason had created their partnership by the end of 1836. Woodruff was born in
Philadelphia around 1797. He trained under the respected engraver George Murray and worked
in Philadelphia from 1817 to 1824. He moved to Ohio and was working as an engraver in Cincinnati by
1825. Little is known about Mason. By 1839, Woodruff had a new partner, a Mr. Hammond. (See "Western
Bank Note Co.," *Ohio State Journal and Columbus Gazette*, 24 Jan. 1837, [1]; "William Woodruff," in U.S.
Customs Service, *Proof of Citizenship . . . for the Port of Philadelphia, Pennsylvania, 1792–1875*, Record
Group 36, microfilm, National Archives and Records Administration, Washington DC; Stauffer, *American
Engravers upon Copper and Steel*, 295; Hall, *Cincinnati Directory for 1825*, 107; and Bank Notes and Stock
Certificates, Ohio Obsolete Paper Money Collection, Western Reserve Historical Society, Cleveland.)

their services in at least one Ohio newspaper.[250] Their efforts to find business may have been made more difficult by the fact that the Ohio legislature granted no new bank charters in the legislative sessions from 1836 to 1838, even though many representatives petitioned for banks in these sessions.[251]

The Kirtland Safety Society had already commissioned the firm of Underwood, Bald, Spencer & Hufty to engrave notes for their institution. These notes bore the institution's original name, the Kirtland Safety Society Bank.[252] It appears that Miles or the engravers he worked for, Woodruff and Mason, learned of the society's January 1837 restructuring and sent enclosures of examples for engravings with the company's new name, the Kirtland Safety Society Anti-Banking Company, likely hoping the Safety Society would purchase new engravings from them.[253] However, there is no record of further communication between JS and Miles.

Document Transcript

/[254]Brunswick Medina Co
March 21. 1837

Dear Sir

I have been appointed by Mess[r] [William] Woodruff & [Zelotus] Mason Agent for this section of the state— should you wish any Bank note Engraving executed— you will please forward me your orders & it shall be done to your satisfaction

Very Respectfully
Your obt servt
A Miles

Joseph Smith Esq[r]
Kirtland [p. [1]]

~~Hosmer Curtis Esqr.~~[255]
~~Columbus~~
~~Ohio~~ [p. [2]]

---

250. "Western Bank Note Co.," *Ohio State Journal and Columbus Gazette*, 24 Jan. 1837, [1]. The note was prepared in December.

251. Huntington, "History of Banking and Currency in Ohio before the Civil War," 377; "Ohio Legislature," *Ohio State Journal and Columbus Gazette*, Dec. 1836–Apr. 1837.

252. See Historical Introduction to Kirtland Safety Society Notes, 4 Jan.–9 Mar. 1837, pp. 331–332 herein.

253. See Introduction to Part 5: 5 Oct. 1836–10 Apr. 1837, p. 286 herein; and Articles of Agreement for the Kirtland Safety Society Anti-Banking Company, 2 Jan. 1837, p. 324 herein.

254. TEXT: Handwriting—probably of A. Miles—begins.

255. Miles appears to have originally addressed the business announcement to a Hosmer Curtis in Columbus, Ohio. Instead of sending the notice to Curtis, Miles crossed out his name and used the reverse side of the paper to address the notice to JS.

/[256]WESTERN BANK NOTE ENGRAVING COMPANY.
WOODRUFF & MASON,

CINCINNATI, OHIO.

The subscribers having established themselves in Cincinnati for the purpose
of executing

BANK NOTE ENGRAVING AND PRINTING,

respectfully solicit any Orders in their line that may be agreeable to your
Institution to favor them with.

It may be necessary only to say in reference to their respective qualifica-
tions, that WILLIAM WOODRUFF was a pupil of the celebrated GEORGE
MURRAY,[257] of the firm of MURRAY, DRAPER, FAIRMAN & Co., and during a
term of many years, devoted his time principally to the execution of Bank
Notes—of which the West received a considerable portion of his labors.

In reference to Z. H. MASON, it is only necessary to say, that the beautiful
specimens of Die work with which many of the latest notes abound, are the
production of that gentleman.

Believing that an establishment, located in the West, would afford conve-
niences to the Banking Institutions of the country—which has not hitherto
existed—we have undertaken the above business, relying upon our own merits
for success.

Having been engaged for the last year in making new Dies,[258] Vignettes, &c.
we now prepared to furnish Notes in a very superior style, and on short notice.

☞ Bank Note Paper, of the best quality, always kept on hand.

Believing that the above information would not be unacceptable in the
distribution of your Orders,

The subscribers respectfully remain

Your obedient servants,
WM. WOODRUFF,
ZELOTUS H. MASON.

CINCINNATI, JANUARY, 1837.

---

256. TEXT: Handwriting ends; printed form begins.

257. George Murray was a well-known engraver, a native of Scotland who studied engraving in
London and moved to Philadelphia in 1800. In 1810–1811, he formed the engraving firm Murray, Draper,
Fairman & Co., a company that gained the reputation of being the finest banknote engravers in the
United States. He was responsible for training many young engravers who worked as his apprentices. He
died in Philadelphia in 1822. (Stauffer, *American Engravers upon Copper and Steel*, 186–187; Scharf and
Wescott, *History of Philadelphia*, 2:1057–1059.)

258. Metal dies created intricate designs, often geometric, that distinguished the notes of different
banks and made them harder to counterfeit.

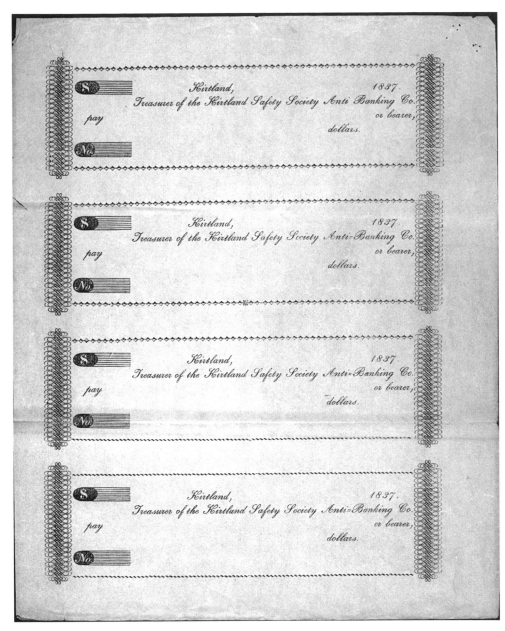

Sample Kirtland Safety Society notes from the Western Bank Note Engraving Company. 1837. Enclosed in his March 1837 letter to Joseph Smith, A. Miles included samples of the engraving company's work. Miles's letter mentioned two specimens; these were likely sheets of the sample banknotes shown here and sheets of printed promissory notes. The name of the Safety Society appears in these notes in its post-January 1837 form—the "Kirtland Safety Society Anti-Banking Co." Although never used as banknotes, the paper was retained and later used to record a discourse given by Joseph Smith on 5 October 1840. Sample Kirtland Safety Society Notes, JS Papers Holding Collection, Church History Library, Salt Lake City.

/²⁵⁹Enclosed you have 2 samples as specemines of their work²⁶⁰

A M [p. [3]]

10

Brunswick Ohio
March 22
/²⁶¹Joseph Smith Esqure
Kirtland
Geauga Co
Ohio

———— ↄↄ ————

Discourse, 6 April 1837

Source Note

JS, Discourse, [Kirtland Township, Geauga Co., OH], 6 Apr. 1837. Featured version published in "Anniversary of the Church of Latter Day Saints," Latter Day Saints' Messenger and Advocate, *Apr. 1837, 3:487–488. For more information on* Latter Day Saints' Messenger and Advocate, *see Source Notes for Multiple-Entry Documents, p. 527 herein.*

Historical Introduction

On 6 April 1837, the seventh anniversary of the organization of the church, the presidency, priesthood quorums, and other priesthood holders gathered in the House of the Lord in Kirtland, Ohio, for a solemn assembly. This gathering occurred just over a year after the solemn assembly that followed the dedication of the House of the Lord in March 1836.²⁶²

On the morning of the 1837 solemn assembly, each priesthood quorum met in the House of the Lord to perform the ordinance of washing of feet and to prepare "to receive instruction from the Presidents of the church."²⁶³ The First Presidency met separately with the Quorum of the Seventy in the upper room of the temple to confirm and bless new members of the Seventy, who had been anointed prior to the solemn assembly.²⁶⁴ They also met to address questions of authority and to correct inconsistencies in who had

---

259. TEXT: Printed form ends; handwriting—probably of A. Miles—begins.

260. The enclosures were separated from the letter but appear to have been retained by JS. Sheets of uncut banknotes bearing the phrase "Treasurer of the Kirtland Safety Society Anti=Banking Co.," along with sheets of printed promissory notes including "Kirtland" and "1837," were used to record a JS sermon on the priesthood in 1840 and may be the enclosures sent with this letter. (Sample Kirtland Safety Society Notes, JS Papers Holding Collection, CHL.)

261. TEXT: Handwriting—probably of A. Miles—ends; unidentified begins.

262. Minutes, 30 Mar. 1836, pp. 216–221 herein.

263. "Anniversary of the Church of Latter Day Saints," *LDS Messenger and Advocate,* Apr. 1837, 3:486.

264. Record of Seventies, bk. A, 17.

been called as quorum presidents. Previously, some presidents of the Seventy had been called from among the high priests, but according to minutes of the meeting, "It was decided by President Joseph Smith, that the seventies were not High priests as they had been previously taught."[265] Reminiscent accounts by Joseph Young and Zebedee Coltrin noted that there was tension between the quorums over which had authority over the other.[266] These concerns resulted in the removal and replacement of some of the presidents of the Seventy. It appeared that six of the seven presidents of the Seventy (the exception being Joseph Young) had already been ordained as high priests when they were appointed presidents of the Seventy and had not been chosen from the Quorum of the Seventy as set out in the 1835 "Instruction on Priesthood."[267] Warren A. Cowdery noted that the practice of appointing high priests as leaders of the Seventy "was declared to be wrong, and not according to the order of heaven."[268] To resolve the matter, the presidents who were thought to have been ordained high priests were removed as presidents of the Seventy and new men were appointed from the Quorum of the Seventy to serve as quorum presidents.[269] The five former presidents who were at the meeting, as well as other seventies who had been ordained high priests, were then asked to join the high priests quorum.[270]

After all the priesthood quorums gathered for instruction, they were addressed by members of the church presidency—JS, Hyrum Smith, Oliver Cowdery, and Sidney Rigdon. JS's discourse, featured here, is extracted from Warren A. Cowdery's synopsis of the proceedings of the solemn assembly. In his address, JS discussed the duties and roles

---

265. Record of Seventies, bk. A, 9, 18. Elias Smith prepared these meeting minutes using the journal of Hazen Aldrich. Wilford Woodruff wrote that a reorganization of the leadership of the Seventy was required because of the "difference in the authority and office of the quorums of high Priesthood & Seventies." (Woodruff, Journal, 6 Apr. 1837.)

266. Young and Coltrin noted that members of each quorum argued that theirs held greater authority. Young wrote in 1878 that the debate developed "with so much warmth that it amounted to jealousy." Coltrin's account, recorded by L. John Nuttall in 1879, specified that the debate began between Benjamin Winchester and Jared Carter: "Bro. W[inchester] A Seventy and Bro Jared [Carter] a High Priest got to contending which held the highest office. Carter was rebuking him on account of his folly, which he said he had not right to do. as he held a higher Priesthood than he did. and Jared contended that he didn't because [he] was a High Priest." Coltrin wrote that the debate came to the attention of Joseph Smith Sr., who then informed JS. (Young, *History of the Organization of the Seventies*, 4–5; Nuttall, Diary, 31 May 1879.)

267. Instruction on Priesthood, between ca. 1 Mar. and ca. 4 May 1835, in *JSP*, D4:321 [D&C 107:93].

268. "Anniversary of the Church of Latter Day Saints," *LDS Messenger and Advocate*, Apr. 1837, 3:486.

269. The six men who were removed as presidents of the Seventy were Hazen Aldrich, Leonard Rich, Zebedee Coltrin, Lyman Sherman, Sylvester Smith, and Levi Hancock. The six men appointed to fill the positions were James Foster, Josiah Butterfield, John Gould, John Gaylord, Daniel S. Miles, and Salmon Gee. (Young, *History of the Organization of the Seventies*, 5.)

270. Levi Hancock, who was removed at this meeting and replaced by John Gould, was not in Kirtland at the time of the meeting. When Hancock returned to Kirtland, he informed church leaders that he had not been ordained a high priest and should not have been removed from his position. It was decided that Hancock should retain his position as a president of the Seventy, and John Gould was removed. (Minutes, 3 Sept. 1837, p. 425 herein.)

of each of the priesthood quorums and explained the "grades of the different quorums" without clarifying which quorum had the higher authority.[271]

After JS finished speaking on the topic of priesthood, he spoke on the temporal affairs of the church. He informed the assembled priesthood holders that the city of Kirtland must be developed and that the Saints should gather there and purchase land intended for them. Hyrum Smith and Sidney Rigdon also spoke in the solemn assembly regarding the church's financial situation.[272] Hyrum chastised members who were giving new arrivals unauthorized advice about purchasing land; their actions contradicted guidelines established by church leaders the previous December to govern Saints wanting to move to Kirtland.[273] He also rebuked those members of the church who were taking the money of newly arrived Saints rather than directing them to purchase land from church leaders, who had gone into considerable debt to acquire property for church settlement.[274] Hyrum also told members to support the Kirtland Safety Society for the benefit of the church and its members.[275] In his remarks, Rigdon named the three most significant debts of the church, identifying $6,000 related to the Saints being driven from Jackson County, Missouri; $13,000 for building the House of the Lord in Kirtland; and an unspecified amount for land purchases in Kirtland.[276] Building on JS's earlier comments, Rigdon emphasized the principle of gathering and instructed the elders to tell church members that there was "a place *for them*" in Kirtland and that "it is the will of God that they should come."[277]

Document Transcript

Joseph Smith jr. rose and spoke on the subject of the Priesthood. The Melchisedec High priesthood, he said was no other then the priesthood of the Son of God.[278] There are certain ordinances which belong to the priesthood, and certain results flow from it.

The presidents, or presidency are over the church, and revelations of the mind and will of God to the church are to come through the presidency. This

---

271. "Anniversary of the Church of Latter Day Saints," *LDS Messenger and Advocate,* Apr. 1837, 3:486.

272. In contrast to the other members of the presidency, Oliver Cowdery spoke on proselytizing and teaching. ("Anniversary of the Church of Latter Day Saints," *LDS Messenger and Advocate,* Apr. 1837, 3:488; Woodruff, Journal, 6 Apr. 1837.)

273. Minutes, 22 Dec. 1836, p. 323 herein.

274. "Anniversary of the Church of Latter Day Saints," *LDS Messenger and Advocate,* Apr. 1837, 3:488; Minutes, 22 Dec. 1836, pp. 321–323 herein.

275. Woodruff, Journal, 6 Apr. 1837.

276. "Anniversary of the Church of Latter Day Saints," *LDS Messenger and Advocate,* Apr. 1837, 3:488. The losses for Jackson County were likely much higher than Rigdon's figure; on the amount of debt for the House of the Lord, see 199n120 herein; and Historical Introduction to Mortgage to Mead, Stafford & Co., 11 July 1837, p. 405 herein; for more information on the land purchases in Kirtland, see Historical Introduction to Mortgage to Peter French, 5 Oct. 1836, pp. 294–295 herein.

277. "Anniversary of the Church of Latter Day Saints," *LDS Messenger and Advocate,* Apr. 1837, 3:489, italics in original.

278. See Instruction on Priesthood, between ca. 1 Mar. and ca. 4 May 1835, in *JSP,* D4:312 [D&C 107:3].

is the order of heaven and the power and privilege of this priesthood.[279] It is also the privilege of any officer in this church, to obtain revelations so far as relates to his particular calling or duty in the church. All are bound by the principles of virtue and happiness, but one great privilege of this priesthood is to obtain revelations, as before observed, of the mind and will of God. It is also the privilege of the Melchisedec priesthood, to reprove, rebuke and admonish, as well as to receive revelations.[280]

He here remarked something concerning the will of God, and said, that what God commanded, the one half of the church would condemn.— A high Priest, is a member of the same Melchisedec priesthood, with the presidency, but not of the same power or authority in the church.[281] The seventies are also members of the same priesthood, are a sort of travelling council, or priesthood, and may preside over a church or churches until a high priest can be had.[282] The seventies are to be taken from the quorum of elders and are not to be high priests. They are subject to the direction and dictation of the twelve, who have the keys of the ministry.[283] All are to preach the gospel, by the power and influence of the Holy Ghost, and no man, said he, can preach the gospel without the Holy Ghost.[284]

The Bishop was a high priest, and necessarily so, because he is to preside over that particular branch of the church affairs that are denominated the lesser priesthood, and because we have no direct lineal descendent of Aaron to whom it would of right belong.[285] He remarked that this was the same, or a branch of the same priesthood; and illustrated his position by the figure of the human body, which has dfferent members, which have different offices to perform: all are necessary in their place, and the body is not complete without all the members.[286] From a view of the requirements of the servants of God to preach the gospel, he remarked that few were qualified even to be priests, and if a priest understood his duty, his calling and ministry and preached by

---

279. See Instruction on Priesthood, between ca. 1 Mar. and ca. 4 May 1835, in *JSP*, D4:313, 321 [D&C 107:9–10, 91–92].

280. See Instruction on Priesthood, between ca. 1 Mar. and ca. 4 May 1835, in *JSP*, D4:314 [D&C 107:18–19].

281. See Instruction on Priesthood, between ca. 1 Mar. and ca. 4 May 1835, in *JSP*, D4:312–313 [D&C 107:8–14].

282. See Instruction on Priesthood, between ca. 1 Mar. and ca. 4 May 1835, in *JSP*, D4:314 [D&C 107:25–26].

283. See Instruction on Priesthood, between ca. 1 Mar. and ca. 4 May 1835, in *JSP*, D4:315 [D&C 107:33–35].

284. See Revelation, 9 Feb. 1831, in *JSP*, D1:251 [D&C 42:16–17].

285. See Instruction on Priesthood, between ca. 1 Mar. and ca. 4 May 1835, in *JSP*, D4:319 [D&C 107:69–76].

286. See 1 Corinthians 12:12, 14, 20.

the Holy Ghost, his enjoyment is as great as if he were one of the presidency; and his services are necessary in the body, as are also those of teachers and deacons. Therefore in viewing the church as whole, we may strictly denominate it one priesthood.

He remarked that he rebuked and admonished his brethren frequently, and that because he loved them; not because he wished to incur their displeasure or mar their happiness.[287]

Such a course of conduct was not calculated to gain the good will of all, but rather the ill will of many, and thereby the situation in which he stood was an important one. So you see, brethren the higher the authority, the greater the difficulty of the station. But these rebukes and admonitions became nccssary from the perverseness of brethren, for their temporal as well as spiritual welfare. They actually constituted a part of the duties of his station and calling.

Others had other duties to perform that were important and far less enviable, and might be just as good, like the feet or hands in their relation to the human body, neither could claim priority, or say to the other I have no need of you.[288] After all that has been said the greatest duty and the most important is, to preach the gospel.

He then alluded to the temporal affairs of the church in this place, stating the causes of the embarrassments of a pecuniary nature that were now pressing upon the heads of the church. He observed they began poor, were needy, destitute, and were truly afflicted by their enemies; yet the Lord commanded them to go forth and preach the [p. 487] gospel, to sacirfice their time, their talents, their good name and jeopardize their lives, and in addition to this, they were to build a house for the Lord, and prepare for the gathering of the saints.[289]

Thus it was easy to see this must involve them. They had no temporal means in the beginning commensurate with such an undertaking, but this work must be done, this place had to be built up.[290] He further remarked that

---

287. During fall and winter 1835, JS rebuked several church members in Kirtland, correcting their errors in an effort to promote unity and order prior to the dedication of the House of the Lord and the promised endowment of power. (See Revelation, 1 Nov. 1835, pp. 29–30 herein; Revelation, 8 Nov. 1835, pp. 38–39 herein; Historical Introduction to Letter from William Smith, 18 Dec. 1835, pp. 110–113 herein; and JS, Journal, 8 Nov. 1835, in *JSP*, J1:85–86.)

288. See 1 Corinthians 12:15, 21.

289. JS and other church leaders hoped that building the city of Kirtland and gathering the Saints and their resources there might aid them in repaying debts. In this 6 April meeting, JS, Hyrum Smith, and Sidney Rigdon each urged church members to come to Kirtland and to purchase land that had already been obtained by church leaders. (See Historical Introduction to Constitution of the Kirtland Safety Society Bank, 2 Nov. 1836, p. 300 herein.)

290. At a previous meeting, Frederick G. Williams expressed similar sentiments about the impoverished beginning of the church and the many undertakings that involved church leaders in amassing large debts. (Minutes, 16 June 1836, p. 250 herein.)

it must yet be built up, that more houses must be built. He observed that large contracts had been entered into for land on all sides where our enemies had signed away their right.[291] We are indebted to them to be sure, but our brethren abroad have only to come with their money, take these eontracts [contracts], relieve their brethren of the pecuniary embarrassments under which they now labor, and procure for themselves a peaceable place of rest among us. He then closed at about 4 P. M. by uttering a prophesy saying this place must be built up, and would be built up, and that every brother that would take hold and help secure and discharge those contracts that had been made, should be rich.

—————— ✑ ——————

Deed to William Marks, 10 April 1837

Source Note

JS and Emma Smith, Deed for property in Kirtland Township, Geauga Co., OH, to William Marks, 10 Apr. 1837; signed by JS and Emma Smith; witnessed by Frederick G. Williams and James Emmett; certified by Frederick G. Williams. Featured version copied in Geauga County Deed Record, vol. 23, pp. 536–537; handwriting of Ralph Cowles; Geauga County Archives and Records Center, Chardon, OH. Transcription from a digital color image made of original in 2011.

Volume measuring 16½ × 11¾ × 3¼ inches (42 × 30 × 8 cm) and including 618 pages, plus 17 pages of an index of grantors and grantees. At an unknown time, the original cover and binding were replaced with a maroon leather binding, then later covered with a cream canvas cover with maroon leather corners. The volume contains 319 leaves measuring 15⅝ × 10 inches (40 × 25 cm). In the mid- to late nineteenth century, a page-for-page transcript of the volume was created; the transcript is also housed at the Geauga County Archives and Records Center.

This volume was in the possession of the Geauga County Recorder from its creation until 1996, when it was transferred to the newly organized Geauga County Archives and Records Center. Includes notations, redactions, and archival marking.

---

291. It is not clear to whom JS referred when he mentioned enemies, though he and other church members bought land in Kirtland from individuals who were antagonistic toward him or the church. In selling and transferring the titles of the land, they would have signed away their rights to the land to the church leaders who purchased it. Although no extant deeds document the land purchases, church leaders apparently arranged to buy land from Timothy Martindale and Christopher Crary. Christopher Crary's brother, Oliver A. Crary, and Martindale were part of the 1834 committee to investigate the validity of the Book of Mormon and try to "avert the evils" of JS's teachings. The committee provided financial support for Doctor Philastus Hurlbut to travel to the eastern states and collect affidavits concerning JS and the Book of Mormon. (Crary, *Pioneer and Personal Reminiscences,* 21; Transcript of Proceedings, 5 June 1837, Martindale v. JS, Whitney, Cahoon, and Johnson [Geauga Co. C.P. 1837], Geauga Co., OH, Court of Common Pleas, Record Book U, pp. 106–107, Geauga County Archives and Records Center, Chardon, OH; "To the Public," *Painesville [OH] Telegraph,* 31 Jan. 1834, [3]; for more on the hundreds of acres of land JS purchased in Kirtland between September and November 1836, see Historical Introduction to Mortgage to Peter French, 5 Oct. 1836, pp. 294–295 herein; and Historical Introduction to Letter from Newel K. Whitney, 20 Apr. 1837, pp. 367–368 herein.)

Historical Introduction

On 7 and 10 April 1837, JS and Emma Smith transferred a significant amount of land to William Marks in six different land transactions.[292] The deed featured here, for land on which the House of the Lord in Kirtland had been built, was one of these six transactions and is representative of the other deeds transferring land to Marks.[293] Even though each of the deeds between JS and Marks listed a precise monetary amount, it is possible that money was not exchanged and that JS instead transferred the titles for the land to Marks without payment.

The land sold in the featured deed was originally purchased from Peter French on behalf of the church in 1833, and a revelation on 23 April 1834 gave John Johnson stewardship over a portion of the land. Excluded from Johnson's stewardship was the land for the House of the Lord, which the 23 April 1834 revelation stipulated should be given to JS.[294] As a result, Johnson deeded the land to JS on 5 May 1834.[295] However, the 1834 deed includes a later note that a new deed was created in January 1837, again transferring the land from Johnson to JS, because the 1834 deed "was supposed to be illegal."[296] The new deed in 1837 was likely required because Johnson did not hold the title to the land in 1834, although he may have thought he did; he went on to acquire the title from Newel K. Whitney in 1836. A new deed was also needed because the 1834 deed had not excluded a portion of the lot owned by the Methodist Episcopal Church. The 1837 deed to JS was careful to omit this portion specifically.[297]

The reason for JS's sale or transfer of this land to Marks in April 1837 is not certain, but JS may have been trying to protect the House of the Lord from being sold to pay his debts or the debts of other church members.[298] In June and October 1836, mercantile partnerships

---

292. On women's dower rights and their involvement in real estate transactions, see 298n71 herein. Collectively, the land amounted to around 146 acres. Two of the six transactions were quitclaim deeds to properties, which meant that Marks was given only any interest and investment JS had in the original land purchase and could not rent or sell the property on his own since others were named on the original deed. The other land sold to Marks included property JS had purchased in fall 1836. (See JS to William Marks, Deed, Geauga Co., OH, 7 Apr. 1837; JS to William Marks, Deed, Geauga Co., OH, 10 Apr. 1837; JS to William Marks, Deed, Geauga Co., OH, 10 Apr. 1837; JS to William Marks, Deed, Geauga Co., OH, 10 Apr. 1837; JS to William Marks, Deed, Geauga Co., OH, 10 Apr. 1837, Geauga County Deed Record, vol. 23, pp. 536–539; vol. 24, p. 189, Geauga County Archives and Records Center, Chardon, OH.)

293. All six deeds will be published on the Joseph Smith Papers website, josephsmithpapers.org.

294. Revelation, 23 Apr. 1834, in *JSP*, D4:27 [D&C 104:34].

295. See Historical Introduction to Deed from John and Alice Jacobs Johnson, 5 May 1834, in *JSP*, D4:44–46.

296. John Johnson to JS, Deed, 5 May 1834, [2], Lyman Cowdery Papers, CHL.

297. Newel K. Whitney to John Johnson, Deed, Geauga Co., OH, 23 Sept. 1836, Geauga County Deed Record, vol. 22, pp. 497–498, Geauga County Archives and Records Center, Chardon, OH; Historical Introduction to Deed from John and Alice Jacobs Johnson, 5 May 1834, in *JSP*, D4:44–46; Geauga Co., OH, Deed Records, 1795–1921, vol. 24, p. 100, 4 Jan. 1837, microfilm 20,240, U.S. and Canada Record Collection, FHL.

298. Marks was likely functioning as an agent for JS by holding this land for him. Ownership of the church's Kirtland printing office and the church's newspaper *Messenger and Advocate* were also transferred to Marks in April 1837. Marks was later appointed as an agent for Kirtland bishop Newel K. Whitney in

formed by church leaders in Kirtland had purchased goods in New York, and promissory notes made out by the firms of Rigdon, Smith & Cowdery and Cahoon, Carter & Co. were due in April 1837. JS was liable for these debts, which the partners may have not been able to pay.[299] According to records of later litigation, the firms defaulted on some of these notes.[300] JS may have been concerned that as a result of litigation on these debts, important land—such as the land on which the House of the Lord was built—might be taken from him. JS faced lawsuits related to unpaid promissory notes and other debts throughout 1837, and judgments for such trials often resulted in the sheriff seizing an individual's land or other assets and then selling them at auction.[301] The House of the Lord was the largest asset held by the church and represented a significant investment; tens of thousands of dollars had gone into building, finishing, and furnishing the edifice.[302] Had the land or building been seized for debts, it would have been a severe blow to the church, both financially and spiritually.

On 11 July 1837, Marks transferred the title to the land he had received from JS to the mercantile firm of Mead, Stafford & Co. Marks deeded the land as part of an agreement in which JS, Sidney Rigdon, Oliver Cowdery, Hyrum Smith, Reynolds Cahoon, and Jared Carter mortgaged the House of the Lord to the firm.[303]

Document Transcript

Joseph Smith Jr. To William Marks

To all people to whom these p[r]esents shall come Greeting. Know Ye that we Joseph Smith Jr and Emma Smith wife of said Joseph Smith Jr. of the Township of Kirtland County of Geauga and State of Ohio. for the consideration of Five hundred dollars received to our full satisfaction of William Marks of the Town of Kirtland County of Geauga and State of Ohio do give grant bargain sell and confirm unto the said William Marks the following described

---

September 1837, and Marks may have been acting in a similar capacity in this instance. ("Notice," *LDS Messenger and Advocate,* Apr. 1837, 3:496; Minutes, 17 Sept. 1837–A, pp. 442–443 herein.)

299. Invoices for goods bought from several New York merchants in October 1836 have postscripts that record that they received promissory notes payable in six months. Other invoices from the same purchasing trip do not include information on the form of payment, but these may have also been due in April. (See Winthrop Eaton to JS and Oliver Cowdery, Invoice, New York City, 11 Oct. 1836, JS Office Papers, CHL; Keeler, McNeil & Co. to Sidney Rigdon, JS, and Oliver Cowdery, Invoice, New York City, 11 Oct. 1836, JS Office Papers, CHL; and Jesse Delano, Bill, 15 Oct. 1836, JS Office Papers, CHL.)

300. Transcript of Proceedings, 24 Oct. 1837, Eaton v. JS and Cowdery [Geauga Co. C.P. 1837]; Transcript of Proceedings, 24 Oct. 1837, Newbould v. Rigdon et al. [Geauga Co. C.P. 1837], Geauga Co., OH, Court of Common Pleas, Record Book U, pp. 277–278, 351–353, Geauga County Archives and Records Center, Chardon, OH.

301. "Sheriff's Sale," *Painesville (OH) Telegraph,* 22 Feb. 1838, [3]; Case Costs, 24 Oct. 1837, Rounds v. JS [Geauga Co. C.P. 1837]; Case Costs, 24 Oct. 1837, Rounds v. Rigdon [Geauga Co. C.P. 1837], Execution Docket Book G, pp. 105–106, Geauga County Archives and Records Center, Chardon, OH; see also Madsen, "Tabulating the Impact of Litigation on the Kirtland Economy," 232–235.

302. See 199n120 herein.

303. Mortgage to Mead, Stafford & Co., 11 July 1837, pp. 404–410 herein.

Tract or Lot of land situate in Kirtland Township N⁰· 9 in the 9ᵗʰ· Range of townships in the Connecticut Western Reserve in the State of Ohio and which is also in the County of Geauga and is known as part of Lot N⁰· 30 and is bounded as follows to wit [p. 536] on the South by land formerly owned by Isaac Moore. Beginning near the northeast corner of said Moores land in the centre of the Road leading from Kirtland flats to Chester and running west on the north line of said land twenty two rods, thence north seventeen Rods to a Stake marked N⁰· 1. thence East to the west line of the lot owned by the Methodist Episcopal Society on which their meeting house Stands, thence South to the Southwest corner of said Societies Lot, thence East to the centre of the centre of the Road before mentioned thence Southwesterly to the place of beginning, containing One Acre and one hundred and fifty four ~~rods~~ and a half ⟨rods⟩. Reserving the market house occupied by Whitmer, Rich & C⁰ which stands on the above described lot of land subject to all highways now laid out. Be the same more or less. To have and to hold the above granted and bargained premises with the appurtenances thereof unto the said William Marks heirs and assigns forever to their own proper use and behoof. And also I the said Joseph Smith Jr. do for myself my heirs executors and administrators, covenant with the said William Marks his heirs and assigns that at and until the ensealing of these presents I was well seized of these premises and as a good indefeasible estate in fee simple and have good right to bargain and sell the same in manner and form as is above written and the same is free from all incumbrances whatsoever And furthermore I the said Joseph Smith Jr. do by these presents bind myself and my heirs forever to Warrant and defend the above granted and bargained premises to him the said William Marks and to his heirs and assigns, against all lawful claims and demands whatsoever. And I the said Emma Smith do hereby remise, release and forever quit claim unto the said William Marks his heirs and assigns all my right and title of dower in and to the above described premises— In witness whereof we have hereunto set our hands and seals this tenth day of April A.D. One thousand Eight hundred and thirty-seven.

Joseph Smith Jr. Seal[304]

Emma Smith Seal

Signed Sealed acknowledged and delivered in presence of F[rederick] G Williams James Em[m]ett

The State of Ohio Geauga County ss.

Personally appeared Joseph Smith Jr & Emma Smith to me personally known as the signers and sealers of the above instrument and acknowledged

---

304. TEXT: Each instance of "Seal" is enclosed in a hand-drawn representation of a seal.

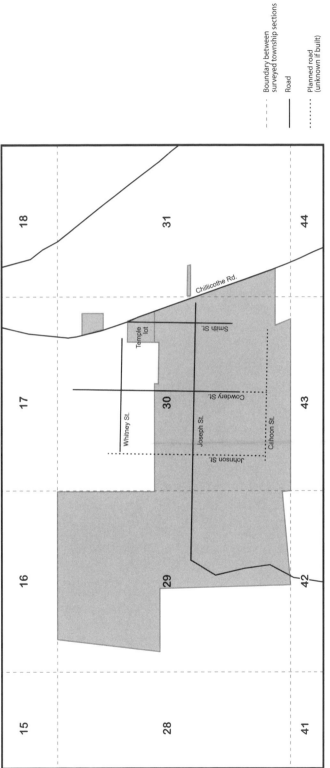

Selected lands transferred to William Marks, Kirtland, Ohio, 7 and 10 April 1837. In early April 1837, Joseph and Emma Smith transferred several parcels of land in Kirtland to William Marks. These transfers included some church properties that Joseph Smith had purchased in the fall of 1836, as well as the lot on which the House of the Lord was built, the former Frederick G. Williams farm, and the Peter French farm. Marks returned much of this land to Joseph Smith in 1841 after Smith was appointed trustee-in-trust for the church.

Boundary between surveyed township sections

Road

Planned road (unknown if built)

that they did voluntarily sign, ⟨&⟩ seal the same and that the same is their free
act and will. And I having fully made known and explained to the said Emma
Smith the contents of the above deed and having likewise examined her separate & apart from her said husband she declared that she did of her own free
will and accord voluntarily sign seal acknowledge and as her free act and deed,
deliver the same without the force coercion or compulsion of her said husband, and that she is still satisfied ~~therewith~~ ⟨the same⟩— Kirtland 10th. April
AD 1837 F. G. Williams Justice of the peace seal

Received 3rd. and Recorded 12th. June AD 1837 Ralph Cowles=Recorder

PART 6: 20 APRIL–
14 SEPTEMBER 1837

The documents created from mid-April to mid-September 1837 mark a turbulent period for JS and the church in Kirtland, Ohio. Economic concerns, intensified by the national financial panic of 1837, exacerbated existing dissatisfaction with JS's leadership, and in May 1837, dissenters—including some prominent church members—accused the church president of dishonesty and misconduct and challenged his ecclesiastical authority.

Discontent with the First Presidency, and especially with JS, began early in 1837.[1] JS's supporters gave discourses in January warning church members not to "murmer" against the church president, but during JS's absence from Kirtland on business in February, Wilford Woodruff reported, "many were stir'd up in their hearts & some were against him." Shortly after his return, JS gave a discourse silencing "the complainers," who according to Woodruff "saw that he stood in the power of a Prophet."[2]

Expressions of dissatisfaction increased, however, despite another discourse JS gave in April warning against dissension. The reasons for this opposition were not specified in contemporary documents.[3] On 23 May, Parley P. Pratt wrote a letter to JS accusing him of extortion and lying and censuring him for allegedly using his influence as the church president for his own benefit. In Pratt's estimation, JS had led the church into unfair financial practices, such as speculation.[4] Woodruff noted that during this period "many and some in high places had risen up against Joseph" and "were striving to overthrow his influence & cast him down." Then, at a tense meeting on Sunday, 28 May, JS and Sidney Rigdon spoke in defense of JS's actions. After their remarks Warren Parrish, formerly JS's scribe, rose to speak, and in Woodruff's words, "stretched out his puny arm and proclaimed against Joseph."[5] The Kirtland high council met the next day to address the concerns of a group of elders, headed by Abel Lamb, regarding what they saw as inappropriate behavior by five prominent church

---

1. In his reminiscent history, Brigham Young recounted that dissenters came together to depose JS as church president and replace him with David Whitmer. It is not clear when this took place, though it may have occurred as early as February 1837. (Historian's Office, Brigham Young History Drafts, 14; Esplin, "Emergence of Brigham Young," 235.)

2. Woodruff, Journal, 10 and 15 Jan. 1837; 19 Feb. 1837; Kirtland Elders Quorum, "Record," 18 Jan. 1837.

3. Woodruff, Journal, 9 Apr. 1837. For an overview of the different reasons for dissent in 1837, see Esplin, "Emergence of Brigham Young," 235–238.

4. Letter from Parley P. Pratt, 23 May 1837, pp. 386–391 herein.

5. Woodruff, Journal, 28 May 1837; Mary Fielding, Kirtland, OH, to Mercy Fielding, [Upper Canada], ca. June 1837, Mary Fielding Smith, Collection, CHL.

Mary Fielding. Circa 1844. Mary Fielding arrived in Kirtland from Canada in May 1837. In Kirtland, Fielding had direct interaction with Joseph Smith and other prominent church members. She also recorded discourses from various individuals, including one by Parley P. Pratt in which he spoke against Joseph Smith. Fielding's letters to her sister Mercy are a vital source of information on the viability of the Kirtland Safety Society and the events unfolding in Kirtland in the unsettled summer and fall months of 1837. Her various accounts provide rich detail for an otherwise sparsely documented period in Mormon history. Mary Fielding married Joseph Smith's brother Hyrum Smith on 24 December 1837. (Courtesy Don C. Corbett Family Organization. Portrait by Sutcliffe Maudsley.)

leaders.[6] On the same day, with encouragement from Parrish, apostles Luke Johnson, Lyman Johnson, and Orson Pratt made formal charges against members of the church presidency, including JS, whom Pratt and Lyman Johnson accused of lying, extortion, and disrespect.[7]

For dissenters, temporal difficulties raised questions about JS's prophetic authority. As the Latter-day Saints faced financial losses, some were troubled by the fact that JS as prophet had encouraged investment and put his confidence in developing what turned out to be a crumbling economy.[8] In early June, JS became gravely ill, and some church members feared he would not survive.[9] Parrish characterized JS's illness as divine punishment for transgression and for teaching "things contrary to godliness."[10] In mid-June, Parley P. Pratt gave a Sunday morning discourse in Kirtland in which, according to Mary Fielding, he sought "to show that nearly all the Church had departed from God and that Brother J.S had committed great sins."[11] Also in June 1837 John F. Boynton called JS a "fallen prophet," a charge that would be repeated by dissenters throughout 1837 and 1838.[12] On 23 July JS dictated a revelation that directed Thomas B. Marsh, the leader of the Quorum of the Twelve, to rebuke those still opposing JS.[13] By the end of July, the dissent seemed to be waning.

Still, financial concerns remained. JS and his partners faced frequent litigation for their outstanding debts.[14] In July JS, Sidney Rigdon, Oliver Cowdery, Reynolds Cahoon, Jared Carter, and Hyrum Smith mortgaged the Kirtland temple to Mead, Stafford & Co. to offset their mercantile debts with the firm.[15] With the help of Painesville, Ohio, lawyer William L. Perkins, the firms of Rigdon, Smith & Cowdery and Cahoon, Carter & Co. also renegotiated their outstanding debts with five other New York merchants in September.[16]

------

6. Minute Book 1, 29 May 1837; Letter from Abel Lamb and Others, ca. 28 May 1837, p. 393 herein.

7. Charges against JS Preferred to Bishop's Council, 29 May 1837, p. 397 herein; Complaints against Joseph Smith Sr. and Sidney Rigdon to the Bishop's Council, 29 May 1837, Newel K. Whitney, Papers, BYU.

8. See, for example, Minutes, 3 Sept. 1837, pp. 420–425 herein; and Warren Parrish, Kirtland, OH, 5 Feb. 1838, Letter to the Editor, *Painesville (OH) Republican,* 15 Feb. 1838, [3].

9. JS History, vol. B-1, 762; Mary Fielding, Kirtland, OH, to Mercy Fielding, [Upper Canada], ca. June 1837, Mary Fielding Smith, Collection, CHL.

10. JS History, vol. B-1, 763; Warren Parrish, Kirtland, OH, 5 Feb. 1838, Letter to the Editor, *Painesville (OH) Republican,* 15 Feb. 1838, [3].

11. Mary Fielding, Kirtland, OH, to Mercy Fielding, [Upper Canada], ca. June 1837, Mary Fielding Smith, Collection, CHL.

12. Heber C. Kimball wrote that as he was preparing to leave for England, Boynton told him he was a "fool as to go at the call of the fallen prophet, Joseph Smith." Parrish and other dissenters also later characterized JS as a false prophet. (Kimball, "History," 55; Warren Parrish, Kirtland, OH, 5 Feb. 1838, Letter to the Editor, *Painesville [OH] Republican,* 15 Feb. 1838, [3]; Thomas B. Marsh, Independence, MO, to Wilford Woodruff, Scarborough, ME, ca. Apr. 1838, in *Elders' Journal,* July 1838, 36.)

13. Revelation, 23 July 1837, pp. 410–417 herein [D&C 112].

14. For more on spring 1837 debts, see Historical Introduction to Letter from Emma Smith, 3 May 1837, pp. 373–374 herein; and Historical Introduction to Notes Receivable from Chester Store, 22 May 1837, pp. 382–384 herein.

15. See Historical Introduction to Mortgage to Mead, Stafford & Co., 11 July 1837, p. 405 herein.

16. See Historical Introduction to Power of Attorney to Oliver Granger, 27 Sept. 1837, p. 459 herein; and 438n366 herein.

By summer 1837, the survival of the Kirtland Safety Society had become doubtful, and the situation was further hindered by the discord within the church. Mary Fielding recorded concerns she had heard from JS: "So many of the Bank directors are become unfaithful that Brother J.S says he does not know that it will rise again. he says it can never [get] on while some pull one way and some another it requires the united efforts of all and when this will be the case the Lord only knows."[17] Possibly in early June, and certainly before 7 July, JS and Rigdon resigned as the officers of the Kirtland Safety Society and were replaced by Warren Parrish and Frederick G. Williams. The Kirtland Safety Society closed sometime during the summer, likely between the end of July and the end of August. The last entry in the society's stock ledger is dated 19 June 1837, and the last date on extant notes is 20 July 1837.[18] In the August issue of the *Messenger and Advocate,* JS published a notice cautioning the public against using the notes of the Kirtland Safety Society,[19] and in December 1837 the society was included in the Cleveland *Daily Herald and Gazette*'s list of closed or bankrupt banking institutions.[20]

Part 6 of this volume also relates events beyond Kirtland. Despite dissension and economic fears in the summer of 1837, proselytizing continued and even expanded, with Wilford Woodruff and Jonathan H. Hale leaving for the "eastern country" on 31 May and Heber C. Kimball being called to lead the first transatlantic mission to England in June 1837.[21] Saints in Missouri who were forced to leave Clay County in the summer of 1836 moved to the new town of Far West, which by July 1837 had grown considerably and now had a population of fifteen hundred, most of whom were church members.[22]

— ❧ —

Letter from Newel K. Whitney, 20 April 1837

Source Note

Newel K. Whitney, Letter, Kirtland Township, Geauga Co., OH, to JS and Sidney Rigdon, Palmyra, Wayne Co., NY, 20 Apr. 1837. Featured version copied [between ca. 27 June and ca. 5 Aug. 1839] in JS

---

17. Mary Fielding, Kirtland, OH, to Mercy Fielding, [Upper Canada], ca. June 1837, Mary Fielding Smith, Collection, CHL. It is not clear if the accusation of unfaithfulness described by Fielding was intended to apply to dissenters who were acting against JS and the church, to individuals practicing dishonest lending and speculation, or to both.

18. Historical Introduction to Notice, ca. Late Aug. 1837, p. 418 herein; Kirtland Safety Society, Stock Ledger, 36, 228; Nyholm, *Mormon Currency,* 45.

19. Notice, ca. Late Aug. 1837, pp. 418–420 herein.

20. "Broken Banks and Fraudulent Institutions," *Daily Herald and Gazette* (Cleveland, OH), 4 Dec. 1837, [1].

21. See Historical Introduction to Letter from Wilford Woodruff and Jonathan H. Hale, 18 Sept. 1837, pp. 447–450 herein; and Historical Introduction to Recommendation for Heber C. Kimball, between 2 and 13 June 1837, pp. 398–400 herein. Heber C. Kimball, Orson Hyde, Willard Richards, Joseph Fielding, Isaac Russell, John Goodson, and John Snider, at JS's direction, left for England in summer 1837. The group secured passage to Liverpool, arriving there by 19 July 1837. (Historical Introduction to Recommendation for Heber C. Kimball, between 2 and 13 June 1837, p. 400 herein.)

22. Letter from William W. Phelps, 7 July 1837, p. 402 herein.

Letterbook 2, pp. 61–62; handwriting of James Mulholland; JS Collection, CHL. For more information on JS Letterbook 2, see Source Notes for Multiple-Entry Documents, p. 526 herein.

Historical Introduction

On 13 April 1837 Grandison Newell filed a complaint with justice of the peace Edward Flint, alleging that JS tried to have him killed.[23] With such an allegation, Newell incited public opinion against JS, and according to Wilford Woodruff, JS's "life was so beset & sought for by wicked and ungodly men for the testimony of Jesus, that he was under the necessity of fleeing from his house & home."[24] JS and Sidney Rigdon left Kirtland by 13 April, their departure so sudden that JS could not officiate at the weddings of Wilford Woodruff to Phebe Carter and Jonathan Holmes to Marietta Carter on 13 April, as he had planned.[25]

On 20 April 1837, Newel K. Whitney wrote the letter featured here to JS and Rigdon, addressing it to Martin Harris's farm in Palmyra, New York, where they apparently planned to travel.[26] In the letter, Whitney apprised them of developments in two legal matters that involved JS: the criminal case brought against JS based on Newell's complaint, and a lawsuit filed against JS and others by Kirtland landowner Timothy Martindale for an unpaid debt. Whitney had discussed the cases with Lucius Bierce, a prominent lawyer in Ravenna, Ohio, and conveyed his advice to JS and Rigdon.

JS appears to have been absent from Kirtland from 13 April until 19 May 1837, and his location during most of this time is unknown.[27] Although he and Rigdon intended to travel to New York and may have done so, they were present in Painesville, Ohio, on 25 April, when a local sheriff, Abel Kimball, served them with a writ to appear in court. The writ stemmed

---

23. Transcript of Proceedings, 5 June 1837, State of Ohio on Complaint of Newell v. JS [Geauga Co. C.P. 1837], Geauga Co., OH, Court of Common Pleas, Record Book T, pp. 52–53, Geauga County Archives and Records Center, Chardon, OH. Grandison Newell had persecuted JS and other church members for several years. In 1837 he focused much of his opposition on the institution of the Kirtland Safety Society. (See Introduction to Part 5: 5 Oct. 1836–10 Apr. 1837, p. 287 herein.)

24. Woodruff, Journal, 13 Apr. 1837; see also "The Humbug Ended," *Painesville (OH) Republican,* 15 June 1837, [2].

25. Woodruff, Journal, 13 Apr. 1837. The trial record from Justice Flint indicates that a warrant was issued for JS on 13 April and that it was returned by the constable George Lockwood. Unlike other trial records, Flint does not mention if JS was arrested by Lockwood and released on a bail bond. Flint's transcript only indicates that after the warrant was returned JS appeared before the justice court in Painesville, Ohio, on 30 May to be tried on Newell's complaint. (Transcript of Proceedings, 5 June 1837, State of Ohio on Complaint of Newell v. JS [Geauga Co. C.P. 1837], Geauga Co., OH, Court of Common Pleas, Record Book T, pp. 52–53, Geauga County Archives and Records Center, Chardon, OH.)

26. Martin Harris may have had residences in both Palmyra and Kirtland at this time. After separating from his first wife in the early 1830s, he married Caroline Young in late 1836 or early 1837 in Kirtland and may have established a home there as early as November 1836, while retaining his Palmyra farm. (Geauga Co., OH, Probate Court, Marriage Records, 1806–1920, 1 Nov. 1836, microfilm 873,464, U.S. and Canada Record Collection, FHL.)

27. Though JS may have returned to Kirtland as early as 10 May—the date Brigham Young's account book contains an entry for JS—it is not clear that he was present in the immediate area until 19 May 1837, when he made a transaction at the store in Chester, Ohio. (Young, Account Book, [35]; "Bill of Goods Taken from the Chester Store," 19–24 May 1837, JS Office Papers, CHL.)

from a lawsuit filed by New York merchant John A. Newbould for an unpaid debt owed by the mercantile firm of Rigdon, Smith & Cowdery, dated 17 June 1836. Kimball accepted a bail bond on behalf of JS and Rigdon after William Smith, Roger Orton, Reynolds Cahoon, and "G. Bishop" (probably church member Francis Gladden Bishop) acted as sureties that the men would be present for the trial on the Newbould debt on 5 June 1837.[28] On 30 May, JS appeared before Justice of the Peace Flint in a preliminary hearing on Grandison Newell's complaint; a continuance was granted and the trial was delayed until June.[29]

The other legal matter discussed in Whitney's letter to JS and Rigdon was a lawsuit Timothy Martindale brought against JS and others for defaulting on a promissory note. The $5,000 note—signed on 11 October 1836 by JS, Newel K. Whitney, Reynolds Cahoon, and John Johnson—had been due on 1 January 1837 and seems to have been payment for land the men intended to purchase from Martindale.[30] On 16 February 1837, Martindale's lawyer, Reuben Hitchcock, brought the case to the Geauga County Court of Common Pleas.[31] In conjunction with the writs issued by the court, sheriff Abel Kimball arrested JS, Whitney, Cahoon, and Johnson on 22 February. Kimball accepted the four men's bail bond, with Warren Parrish, Hyrum Smith, Oliver Cowdery, and Vinson Knight acting as sureties, and released the men. On 21 March, Edmund Bosley and Roger Orton promised their goods and property as additional security for the payment of the note.[32]

JS and Rigdon may have traveled to Palmyra in April 1837 in order to obtain money from Martin Harris to pay for the Martindale purchase. It is not clear if JS and Rigdon were at Harris's Palmyra farm when they received the letter or if they received it at some other time during their spring 1837 travels. On 24 April, four days after this letter was written, Martindale's lawyer filed a declaration with the court reviewing the debt and renewing litigation against JS, Whitney, Cahoon, and Johnson.[33] Sometime between 24 April and 5 June, the two parties settled the matter outside of court.[34] Since no land deeds exist

28. Transcript of Proceedings, 24 Oct. 1837, Newbould v. Rigdon, JS, and Cowdery [Geauga Co. C.P. 1837], Geauga Co., OH, Court of Common Pleas, Record Book U, pp. 351–353, Geauga County Courthouse, Chardon, OH.

29. JS's trial on the allegation of conspiring to have Newell killed was heard first by the justice court in Painesville and then by the Geauga County Court of Common Pleas. Judge Van R. Humphrey of the court of common pleas dismissed the charges against JS. (Transcript of Proceedings, 5 June 1837, State of Ohio on Complaint of Newell v. JS [Geauga Co. C.P. 1837], Geauga Co., OH, Court of Common Pleas, Record Book T, pp. 52–53, Geauga County Archives and Records Center, Chardon, OH; "The Humbug Ended," *Painesville [OH] Republican,* 15 June 1837, [2].)

30. No deeds transferring property from Martindale to any of the four men are found in the Geauga County deed records. It is likely that the men attempted to buy the farm from Martindale but were unable to fulfill the payments.

31. Transcript of Proceedings, 5 June 1837, Martindale v. JS et al. [Geauga Co. C.P. 1837], Geauga Co., OH, Court of Common Pleas, Record Book U, pp. 106–107, Geauga County Courthouse, Chardon, OH.

32. Transcript of Proceedings, 5 June 1837, Martindale v. JS et al. [Geauga Co. C.P. 1837], Geauga Co., OH, Court of Common Pleas, Record Book U, pp. 106–107, Geauga County Courthouse, Chardon, OH.

33. Transcript of Proceedings, 5 June 1837, Martindale v. JS et al. [Geauga Co. C.P. 1837], Geauga Co., OH, Court of Common Pleas, Record Book U, pp. 107–108, Geauga County Courthouse, Chardon, OH.

34. Record of Judgment, 5 June 1837, Martindale v. JS et al. [Geauga Co. C.P. 1837], Geauga Co., OH, Court of Common Pleas, Journal Book N, p. 189, Geauga County Archives and Record Center, Chardon, OH.

transferring title from Martindale to any of the men involved in the earlier land transaction, the settlement likely included ownership of the farm reverting to Martindale, which Whitney's letter mentioned might be required.[35]

Document Transcript

Kirtland 20th April 1837

Brother Joseph & Sidney [Rigdon]

Your families are all well as usual and in good spirits— Mr Burse [Lucius Bierce][36] of Ravenna came here day before yesterday & after counseling together he thought best to defer doing any thing with Clarke[37] & others for the present, but let them go on as they could do nothing— the enemy[38] have learned that we have the advantage of them, and seem to be startled and Davis & Denton say they will rot in prison before they will testify in Court.[39] The fact is Clarke and others have learned that they have said too much for their

---

35. This was a common scenario when individuals who contracted to purchase land defaulted on their promissory notes or were otherwise unable to fulfill their financial obligations. (See, for example, Ames, Autobiography and Journal, [13].)

36. Lucius Verus Bierce was the prosecuting attorney for Portage County, Ohio, from 1829 to 1839. He lived in Ravenna, Ohio, until 1851, when he moved to Akron, Ohio. He may have offered JS and Newel K. Whitney legal advice regarding the charges filed by Grandison Newell. JS had a respectful relationship with Bierce dating back to their first meeting in April 1834. (*History of Portage County, Ohio*, 337, 339; JS, Journal, 2–5 Apr. 1834, in JSP, J1:37.)

37. This was likely Quartus Clarke, a miller in Kirtland who was antagonistic toward JS and the church. He was a witness in the trial *State of Ohio on Complaint of Grandison Newell v. JS*. In a letter to her sister Mercy, Mary Fielding also mentioned a Mr. Clarke who was cursed by JS for his refusal to sell his mill to the church. (Transcript of Proceedings, 5 June 1837, State of Ohio on Complaint of Newell v. JS [Geauga Co. C.P. 1837], Geauga Co., OH, Court of Common Pleas, Record Book T, pp. 52–53, Geauga County Archives and Records Center, Chardon, OH; Guinn, *Historical and Biographical Record of Southern California*, 444; Mary Fielding, [Kirtland, OH], to Mercy Fielding, [Upper Canada], ca. June 1837, Mary Fielding Smith, Collection, CHL.)

38. An unnamed enemy was also mentioned in Wilford Woodruff's journal and in Emma Smith's letters to JS. Although they do not identify the enemy who apparently wished to harm JS, it likely included Newell and his associates. (Woodruff, Journal, 13 Apr. 1837; Letter from Emma Smith, 25 Apr. 1837, p. 371 herein; Letter from Emma Smith, 3 May 1837, p. 375 herein; "The Humbug Ended," *Painesville [OH] Republican*, 15 June 1837, [2].)

39. In a May letter to Sidney Rigdon printed in the *Painesville Telegraph*, Grandison Newell claimed that two church members living in Kirtland, whom he later identified only by their surnames of Denton and Davis, were his would-be assassins. Newell likely referred to Solomon W. Denton, who was called as a witness in the trial. The identity of Davis is less certain. It may have been a reference to Marvel C. Davis, who was also listed as a witness in the trial record, although there is no indication that he testified. Both Solomon Denton and Marvel Davis had connections to the church, but Denton had been excommunicated two or three months before the June trial and Davis was disaffected at the time of the trial. ("To Sidney Rigdon—Letter No. 2," *Painesville [OH] Telegraph*, 26 May 1837, [3]; Grandison Newell, Letter to the Editor, *Painesville Telegraph*, 30 June 1837, [3]; Transcript of Proceedings, 5 June 1837, State of Ohio on Complaint of Newell v. JS [Geauga Co. C.P. 1837], Geauga Co., OH, Court of Common Pleas, Record Book T, pp. 52–53, Geauga County Courthouse, Chardon, OH.)

own good, and they feel more quiet than they did & the excitement got up by them runs low, in consequence of which Br Hyrum [Smith] says to me this morning write Joseph & Sidney to come home as soon as they please they need have any fears on account of the enemy at all——

Brother Hyrum, [Reynolds] Cahoon, & myself went and saw [Timothy] Martindale yesterday who says he will not settle otherwise than we pay him $2500 pay cost of Court & he keep the farm, or he will leave it to men to say how much we shall give him.[40] Esqr Burse thinks if we leave it to the Court to decide, Martindale will recover the 5000 $ therefore Hyrum thinks [p. 61] best to pay the 2^d payment if possible say 6500 $ certainly as soon as the 10th day of May as the farm is worth considirable to raise grain on this season &c. if any thing is done it must be done soon & if you can get the money (say 6500 $) deposit it in Bank and send a check or something that ~~will~~ we can sell to Geauga Bank we want you to write us immediately that we may know your feelings—

in haste but yours truly N K W [Newel K. Whitney]

P.S. Brother Hyrum just called on me and says he yet has doubts as to its being perfectly safe for you to come back immediately in consequence of some reports he has heard this morning & he thinks best you should learn of the Lord as to returning, but send us all the money possible to pay for farms &c as it is supposed to be important that we keep all the land we can.—

Br Marten [Martin Harris] If Sidney & Joseph have left your place please forward this to them immediately.

N K W

Mr Martin Harris
Palmyra
Wayne County N.Y.

——— ✒ ———

Letter from Emma Smith, 25 April 1837

Source Note

Emma Smith, Letter, Kirtland Township, Geauga Co., OH, to JS, 25 Apr. 1837. Featured version copied [between ca. 29 May and ca. 27 June 1839] in JS Letterbook 2, p. 35; handwriting of James Mulholland; JS Collection, CHL. For more information on JS Letterbook 2, see Source Notes for Multiple-Entry Documents, p. 526 herein.

---

40. The suit Martindale was pursuing against JS, Newel K. Whitney, Reynolds Cahoon, and John Johnson for their defaulted promissory of $5,000 had reached $7,500 in principal, damages, and interest by April 1837. (See Transcript of Proceedings, 5 June 1837, Martindale v. JS et al. [Geauga Co. C.P. 1837], Geauga Co., OH, Court of Common Pleas, Record Book U, pp. 106–107, Geauga County Courthouse, Chardon, OH.)

Historical Introduction

Emma Smith wrote the letter featured here in reply to a letter she had received from JS, which is no longer extant. JS and Sidney Rigdon left Kirtland, Ohio, earlier that month and remained absent from Kirtland for much of April and May because of threats made against JS's life. JS's location during his time away is unknown, but on 25 April—the same day Emma wrote this letter—he was arrested and released by Geauga County sheriff Abel Kimball in relation to a lawsuit for unpaid business debt.[41]

In the letter, Emma informed JS of the family's welfare, noting her and their children's unease at his absence. She also referred to tensions in Kirtland and a lack of faith among some church members, writing, "If I had no more confidence than some I could name, I should be a sad case indeed." This is one of the earliest indications of unrest among the Kirtland Saints in the spring of 1837; the turmoil would develop over the next few months into direct opposition against JS.[42]

Document Transcript

Dear Husband

Your letter was welcomed both by friends and foes, we were glad enough to hear that you was well, and our enemies[43] think they have almost found you, by seeing where the letters were mailed. We are all well as usual except Mother[44] is not quite as well as common. Our family is small and yet I have a great deal of business to see to, Brother Tenny[45] has not moved yet, and he does not know when he will, we have taken possession of all the room we could get.

I have got all the money that I have had any chance to, and as many goods as I could well, I have not got much at Chester,[46] no money at all, there is so

---

41. Transcript of Proceedings, 24 Oct. 1837, Newbould v. Rigdon et al. [Geauga Co. C.P. 1837], Geauga Co., OH, Court of Common Pleas, Record Book U, pp. 351–353, Geauga County Archives and Records Center, Chardon, OH; see also Historical Introduction to Letter from Newel K. Whitney, 20 Apr. 1837, pp. 367–368 herein.

42. For more on the growing dissent, see Historical Introduction to Letter from Parley P. Pratt, 23 May 1837, pp. 387–388 herein; Historical Introduction to Charges against JS Preferred to Bishop's Council, 29 May 1837, pp. 394–397 herein; and Historical Introduction to Letter from Abel Lamb and Others, ca. 28 May 1837, pp. 392–393 herein.

43. On these unspecified enemies, see 369n38 herein.

44. Lucy Mack Smith, JS's mother.

45. "Brother Tenny" might be William Tenney Jr. or his father, William Tenney Sr., both of whom were living in Kirtland in 1836. According to biographies of William Tenney Jr. and Eliza Webb Tenney compiled by one of their descendants, the couple purchased a house and lot from Jared Carter in late 1835 that was near JS's home. Emma's reference to more space may refer to trying to acquire land from the Tenneys. It is also possible that one of the Tenneys was boarding in JS and Emma's home north of the House of the Lord and that they were trying to reclaim the space. (Kirtland Elders Quorum, "Record," 30 Jan. and 29 Apr. 1836; *The Twelve Apostles* [Kirtland, OH: ca. Apr. 1836], copy at CHL; Morris, "William Tenney and Eliza L. Webb.")

46. JS and Sidney Rigdon jointly owned and operated a store in Chester, Ohio, under the mercantile firm of Rigdon, Smith & Co. Goods for this store were purchased in Buffalo, New York, in June 1836 and

many a watching that place that there is no prospect of my getting any thing of consequence there.[47]

Brother Knights[48] will tell you better about the business than I can write, as there is but a moment for me to improve. I cannot tell you my feelings when I found I could not see you before you left,[49] yet I expect you can realize them, the children[50] feel very anxious about you because they dont know where you have gone; I verily feel that if I had no more confidence in God than some I could name, I should be in a sad case indeed but I still believe that if we humble ourselves, and are ⟨as⟩ faithful as we can be we shall be delivered from every snare that may be laid for our feet, and our lives and property will be saved and we redeemed from all unreasonable encumbrances.

My time is out, I pray that God will keep you in purity and safety till we all meet again.

Emma Smith

Kirtland April 25th.
M[r] Joseph Smith Jr

———— ✑ ————

Letter from Emma Smith, 3 May 1837

Source Note

Emma Smith, Letter, Kirtland Township, Geauga Co., OH, to JS, 3 May 1837. Featured version copied [between ca. 29 May and ca. 27 June 1839] in JS Letterbook 2, pp. 35–36; handwriting of James Mulholland;

New York City in October 1836. (See Rigdon, Smith & Co., Store Ledger, Sept. 1836–May 1837, in JS Letterbook 2; Invoices for Buffalo Merchandise, 15–27 June 1836, JS Office Papers, CHL; and Invoices for New York City Merchandise, 8–15 Oct. 1836, JS Office Papers, CHL.)

47. The surveillance likely related to the "enemies" mentioned earlier in the letter. The ledger book for the Chester store records reduced business in spring 1837. The store was probably suffering from a combination of debt, collection actions resulting from litigation, opposition from Chester residents, and the effects of the financial panic in April and May 1837. (Rigdon, Smith & Co., Store Ledger, Sept. 1836–May 1837, in JS Letterbook 2; Letter from Orson Hyde, 15 Dec. 1835, pp. 104–109 herein; see also Historical Introduction to Notes Receivable from Chester Store, 22 May 1837, pp. 382–384 herein.)

48. Vinson Knight may have been the courier who delivered Emma Smith's letter to JS and apprised him of business matters in Kirtland and Chester. Knight served as a clerk for the store run by the firm H. Smith & Co. in Kirtland, and he may have worked in the Chester store as well. He was also a counselor to Bishop Newel K. Whitney. (H. Smith & Co., Store Daybook, July–Nov. 1836, in Belnap, Account Book, CHL; Minutes, 13 Jan. 1836, p. 140 herein.)

49. Emma was likely referencing JS's abrupt departure on 13 April. (See Historical Introduction to Letter from Newel K. Whitney, 20 Apr. 1837, p. 367 herein.)

50. The children of JS and Emma Smith at this time included Julia Murdock Smith, then almost six years old; Joseph Smith III, four years old; and Frederick Granger Williams Smith, who was almost one year old.

JS Collection, CHL. For more information on JS Letterbook 2, see Source Notes for Multiple-Entry Documents, p. 526 herein.

Historical Introduction

Emma Smith wrote this letter, dated 3 May 1837, to her husband while he was absent from Kirtland, Ohio. JS's location during the latter part of April and for much of May 1837 remains unknown.[51] In a previous letter to JS, dated 25 April 1837, Emma discussed her efforts to obtain goods and money, as well as the difficulty she faced at JS's mercantile store in Chester, Ohio.[52] In this 3 May letter she described how the family's financial situation had worsened, as money and goods she had expected to receive were not available and creditors were demanding repayment. Because of coverture laws, Emma Smith had no legal identity of her own, no legal right to JS's goods or property, and no ability to intervene with his creditors.[53] JS was liable not only for his own debts but also for those of his business partners and any individuals for whom he had acted as surety, or guarantor on a loan. Emma specifically noted here that the partnerships in which JS was involved were causing financial problems for their family.[54] Beginning in spring 1837, JS faced litigation on his and others' outstanding debts. Emma may have been referring to these debts, some of which were being pursued in court at the time, when she wrote that creditors claimed "an unaccountable right to every particle of property or money that they could lay their hands on" and that she felt everyone else had a "better right to all that is called yours than I have."[55]

---

51. When the letter was copied into JS's second letterbook by scribe James Mulholland, no mailing information was included. The "Brother Robinson" mentioned at the conclusion of the letter may have acted as a courier and personally delivered the letter to JS. For more information about JS's absence from Kirtland, see Letter from Newel K. Whitney, 20 Apr. 1837, pp. 366–370 herein.

52. See Letter from Emma Smith, 25 Apr. 1837, pp. 370–372 herein. The store in Chester was run by the mercantile firm of Rigdon, Smith & Co. The store appears to have closed in late May 1837. (See Rigdon, Smith & Co., Store Ledger, Sept. 1836–May 1837, in JS Letterbook 2.)

53. For more on coverture laws, see Historical Introduction to Deed to Caroline Grant Smith, 11 Dec. 1836, pp. 318–319 herein.

54. JS appears to have partnered with Sidney Rigdon and Oliver Cowdery in the printing firm of O. Cowdery & Co. in Kirtland, which purchased the church's printing office after the firm of F. G. Williams & Co. was dissolved in June 1836. When Cowdery became a bank director and vice president of the Bank of Monroe, he dissolved the firm of O. Cowdery & Co., and in February 1837 JS and Rigdon formed a firm named Smith & Rigdon. JS, Rigdon, and Cowdery were also involved in mercantile ventures, using the firm names of Rigdon, Smith & Cowdery; Rigdon, Smith & Co.; and Smith & Cowdery. ("Notice," *LDS Messenger and Advocate,* June 1836, 2:329; "Notice," *LDS Messenger and Advocate,* Feb. 1837, 3:458; Invoices, June and Oct. 1836, JS Office Papers, CHL.)

55. By April 1837 lawsuits had begun on at least five different cases on debts for which JS was liable. (See Transcript of Proceedings, 5 June 1837, Martindale v. JS et al. [Geauga Co. C.P. 1837], Record Book U, pp. 106–108; Transcript of Proceedings, 5 June 1837, Holmes v. Dayton et al. [Geauga Co. C.P. 1837], Record Book U, pp. 86–87; Transcript of Proceedings, 5 June 1837, Patterson and Patterson v. Cahoon et al. [Geauga Co. C.P. 1837], Record Book U, pp. 126–128; Transcript of Proceedings, 5 June 1837, Kelley v. Rigdon et al. [Geauga Co. C.P. 1837], Record Book U, pp. 97–101; Transcript of Proceedings, 5 June 1837, Bank of Geauga v. JS et al. [Geauga Co. C.P. 1837], Record Book U, pp. 67–69, Geauga County Archives and Records Center, Chardon, OH.)

Emma told JS she was resolved to do what she could to ensure that any subsequent transactions benefited JS and their family. She also wrote that the situation would be improved if JS returned and addressed the matters she could not. It was perhaps this need for someone to act in financial matters that prompted Emma's postscript about giving power of attorney to Vinson Knight, who served as clerk for the H. Smith & Co. store in Kirtland and as counselor to Bishop Newel K. Whitney.[56] Emma may also have thought if JS returned, he could relieve tensions that were growing among church members and counter a group of dissenters that was forming in his absence. Members of this group, including Warren Parrish, Lyman Johnson, Orson Pratt, and others, confronted JS in May after he returned to Kirtland.[57]

Document Transcript

Kirtland May 3rd 1837

Ever affectionate husband, myself and the children are well Father and Mother are not very well, tho not dangerous.[58] I do not know what to tell you, not having but a few minutes to write, the situation of your business is such as is very difficult for me to do any thing of any consequence, partnership matters give every body such an unaccountable right to every particle of property or money that they can lay their hands on,[59] that there is no prospect of my getting one dollar of current money[60] or even get the grain you left for our bread, as I sent to the French place[61] for that wheat and brother

---

56. See 372n48 herein.

57. See Charges against JS Preferred to Bishop's Council, 29 May 1837, p. 397 herein; and Letter from Abel Lamb and Others, ca. 28 May 1837, p. 393 herein.

58. Joseph Smith Sr. and Lucy Mack Smith had been living with JS and Emma in their home north of the House of the Lord since December 1835. (JS, Journal, 17 and 29 Dec. 1835, in *JSP*, J1:128–129, 139.)

59. Legal judgments that involved the collection of money from debtors usually stipulated the seizure of the debtor's goods or property. The sheriff was responsible for executing the seizure and auctioning off the goods or property to satisfy the amount stipulated in the judgment. Although Emma did not reference a particular debt or judgment, her statement here suggests that creditors were coming after JS's property and other assets to satisfy outstanding debts. (An Act Regulating Judgments and Executions [1 Mar. 1831], *Statutes of the State of Ohio* [1841], 467–473, secs. 1–5, 9; Record of Judgment, 5 June 1837, Patterson and Patterson v. Cahoon et al. [Geauga Co. C.P. 1837], Common Pleas, Journal Book N, p. 190, Geauga County Archives and Records Center, Chardon, OH; Case Costs, 5 June 1837–23 Nov. 1843, Patterson and Patterson v. Cahoon et al. [Geauga Co. C.P. 1838], Execution Docket G, p. 54, Geauga Co. Courthouse, Chardon, OH.)

60. Current money meant paper currency issued by a bank or other financial institution and circulating at face value.

61. "The French place" likely refers to the Peter French farm bought by the church in 1833 or possibly to another farm or business owned by French, a significant landowner in Kirtland who had sold hundreds of acres of land to JS and the church in 1833 and 1836. (Geauga Co., OH, Deed Records, 1795–1921, vol. 17, pp. 38–39, 359–360, 10 Apr. 1833; vol. 17, pp. 360–361, 17 June 1833, microfilm 20,237, U.S. and Canada Record Collection, FHL; William Miller et al. to Peter French, Deed, Kirtland, OH, Geauga Co. Deed Record, vol. 22, pp. 383–384, 5 Oct. 1836, Geauga County Archives and Records Center, Chardon, OH.)

Strong[62] says that he shall let us only have ten bushel, he has sold the hay and keeps the money. Dr [Warren A.] Cowdery tells me he can't get money to pay the postage of the office. I spoke to Parish [Warren Parrish] about ~~the~~ money, and he appeared rather indifferent [p. 35] and stiff,[63] and only observed that it was the opinion of the people, that Sharp[64] did not intend ever to pay that money. brother Parish has been very anxious ~~to~~ for some time ~~past~~ to get the little mare, and I do not know but it would be your will to have him have her, but I have been so treated that I have come to the determination not to let any man or woman have any thing whatever without being well assured, that it goes to your own advantage, but it is impossible for me to do any thing, as long as every body has so much better right to all that is called yours than I have.

Brother Holmes[65] went directly to keeping house. Brother Tenny[66] has not moved yet nor does not act much like it. I do not know every thing by considerable, but it is my anxiety for your company at home, or else it is realy so that your matters ~~would~~ and things would be much bettered by your presence just as soon as consistant, it is impossible for me to write what I wish you to know.

If you should write after you get this, I want you to let me know as much as possible about the situation of your business, that if possible I can benefit by the information;[67] And speak some word of encouragement to Hervey

---

62. Probably Ezra Strong, the only known church member in Kirtland with that surname. (Backman, *Profile*, 69.)

63. Warren Parrish was a clerk for the Kirtland Safety Society in 1836–1837. He also served as JS's scribe in 1835 and 1836 and became a scribe for the First Presidency in January 1836. His indifference toward Emma's financial situation may have been related to his discontent with JS. Parrish was a leader of the dissenters who at the end of May 1837 accused JS of lying and expressed doubts about his leadership and status as a prophet. (Kirtland Safety Society, Stock Ledger, 1836–1837, in Collection of Manuscripts about Mormons, Chicago History Museum; JS, Journal, 29 Oct. 1835, in *JSP*, J1:76; Partridge, Journal, 21 Jan. 1836; Historical Introduction to Charges against JS Preferred to Bishop's Council, 29 May 1837, pp. 394–397 herein.)

64. Possibly H. A. Sharp from Willoughby, Ohio. Sharp was listed as a subscriber to the Kirtland Safety Society in the March issue of the *Messenger and Advocate* and named on the society's petition for a bank charter presented in the Ohio Senate 10 February 1837. He does not appear to have been a member of the church. ("Minutes of a Meeting," *LDS Messenger and Advocate*, Mar. 1837, 3:476–477; *Journal of the Senate of the State of Ohio*, 365.)

65. Possibly Jonathan Harriman Holmes, who married Marietta Carter on 13 April 1837 and probably transitioned from boarding to keeping a house of his own. (Woodruff, Journal, 13 Apr. 1837; Geauga Co., OH, Probate Court, Marriage Records, 1806–1920, vol. C, pp. 215, 220, microfilm 873,461, U.S. and Canada Record Collection, FHL.)

66. Possibly William Tenney Jr. or William Tenney Sr. (See Letter from Emma Smith, 25 Apr. 1837, p. 371 herein.)

67. Emma may here be asking for additional information about JS's financial affairs in Kirtland or about any business JS and Sidney Rigdon were pursuing while away from Kirtland. The men planned to meet with Martin Harris in Palmyra, New York, and may have tried to obtain money or other resources

[Lyman Hervy Cowdery],[68] for he is very faithful not only in business, but in taking up his cross in the family.

There was a young man came with Brother Baldwin[69] and Father's folks took him in while br B was gone and he is here ⟨yet and is⟩ very sick with the measles which makes much confusion and trouble for me, and is also a subject of much fear and anxiety unto me, as you know that neither of your little ~~one~~ boys have ever had them,[70] I wish it could be possible for you to be at home when they are sick, you must remember them for they all remember you, and I could hardly pacify Julia and Joseph when they found ou[t] you was not coming home soon.

Br Robinson[71] must the rest as he is waiting so adieu my Dear—Joseph.

Emma.

P.S

If you should give anyone a power of attorney, you had better give it to brother [Vinson] Knight, as he is the only man that has not manifested a spirit of indifference to your temporal interest. I mean the only one I have had occasion to say muct [much] to about your business. You may be astonished because I have not accepted some but when I see you I will tell you the reason—, be assured I shall do the best I can in all things, and I hope that we shall be so humble and pure before God that he will set us at liberty to be our own masters in a few things at least, Yours for ever.

Emma

Joseph Smith Jr [p. 36]

———— ☙ ————

from him to help with JS's debts or the financially precarious Kirtland Safety Society. (See Letter from Newel K. Whitney, 20 Apr. 1837, pp. 369–370 herein; and Historical Introduction to Power of Attorney to Oliver Granger, 27 Sept. 1837, pp. 457–459 herein.)

68. Lyman Hervy Cowdery, the son of Warren A. Cowdery, had been indentured to JS in November 1836. (See Historical Introduction to Indenture from Warren A. Cowdery, 23 Nov. 1836, pp. 313–316 herein.)

69. Three men with the surname Baldwin may have been living in Kirtland in 1837: Blake Baldwin, Charles N. Baldwin, and Nathan B. Baldwin. It is not clear which of the men Emma was referring to here. (Backman, *Profile*, 4.)

70. Neither Joseph III, born in 1832, nor Frederick, born in 1836, had contracted measles. Measles, a highly infectious disease, was a leading cause of death for children five years old and younger in the nineteenth century. In 1832, Joseph and Julia Murdock, the twins Emma and JS adopted, contracted measles, leading to little Joseph's death. (Hardy, *Epidemic Streets,* 28.)

71. Probably George W. Robinson, who was Sidney Rigdon's son-in-law and may have acted as a courier taking letters to JS and Rigdon.

Map of Kirtland City, between circa 6 April and 18 May 1837

Source Note

Map of Kirtland City, Geauga Co., OH, [between ca. 6 Apr. and 18 May 1837]. Featured version copied 24 May 1837 onto oversized page that was tipped into Geauga County Deed Record, vol. 24, p. 99; cartography in handwriting of Willard Beals; surrounding text in handwriting of Ralph Cowles; Geauga County Archives and Records Center, Chardon, OH. Transcription from a digital color image made of original in 2011. For more information on Geauga County Deed Record, Volume 24, see Source Notes for Multiple-Entry Documents, p. 521 herein.

Single page, measuring 28⅜ × 21¼ inches (72 × 54 cm). Horizontal lines (three above the map and fourteen below) were inscribed in graphite. The top and bottom recto edges were folded inward into a gate fold. Then, the map was folded in half and adhered to the gutter edge of Geauga County Deed Record, vol. 24, p. 99. Tears at the folds have resulted in missing text. Due to preservation concerns, this fragile map was removed from the volume after 1997 and was conserved. The map was pasted onto cream-colored cardstock. The cardstock verso was later reinforced with nine letter-size pages of white cardstock and placed between sheets of Mylar and sealed with double-sided tape. This document remained in the possession of the Geauga County Recorder's Office from its recording date until 1997, when volume 24 of Geauga County Deed Record was transferred to the Geauga County Archives and Records Center.

Historical Introduction

An official map of Kirtland, Ohio, was created in spring 1837, during a time of development and population growth. The map drew on similar past efforts. In mid-1833, JS directed the church's first efforts at city planning in Kirtland.[72] In accordance with a 2 August 1833 revelation calling for the laying out of the city of Kirtland, Frederick G. Williams drew a plat that reenvisioned the town with the House of the Lord in the center block, serving as the city's sacred focal point, and twenty half-acre lots in each of the forty-eight surrounding blocks. That 1833 plat was maintained by Kirtland bishop Newel K. Whitney to track the land sold or allotted to individual church members.[73]

Town planning and land apportionment and acquisition continued in Kirtland in the years following. In late October 1835, JS "made some observations" to his scribe Warren Parrish "concerning the plan of the City which is to be built up hereafter on this ground consecrated for a stake of Zion."[74] Though contemporary records shed no light on JS's observations at that time, by fall and winter 1836 he and other church leaders had purchased a substantial amount of land in and around Kirtland. In addition, land purchased for the

---

72. JS and other church leaders first began planning for the city of Zion in June 1833 in connection with plans to build temples in both Kirtland and Jackson County, Missouri. In August 1833, church leaders made plans for urban development in Kirtland, at about the same time church leaders revised the first city of Zion plat. (See Plat of the City of Zion, ca. Early June–25 June 1833, in *JSP*, D3:121–131; and Plat of Kirtland, OH, not before 2 Aug. 1833, in *JSP*, D3:208–221.)

73. See Revelation, 2 Aug. 1833–B, in *JSP*, D3:205–206 [D&C 94:1–9]; and Plat of Kirtland, OH, not before 2 Aug. 1833, in *JSP*, D3:208–221.

74. JS, Journal, 29 Oct. 1835, in *JSP*, J1:76.

church in Kirtland had been divided into smaller allotments that could be sold to the growing number of church members.[75]

As the Kirtland population grew, so did the need to regulate land sales and allotments. In April 1837 JS and other Kirtland landowners approached Willard Beals, a Geauga County surveyor from Troy Township, about drawing an official map of Kirtland that would be recognized by Geauga County officials in land transactions.[76] The process to create a new survey of Kirtland may also have been part of church leaders' plan for developing the city. According to Wilford Woodruff, on 6 April JS "presented us in some degree the plot of the city of Kirtland (which is the strong hold of the daughter of Zion) as it was given him by vision, it was great marvelous & glorious. the city extended to the east, west, North, & South, Steam boats will come puffing into the city our Goods will be conveyed upon railroads from Kirtland to many places & probably to Zion. houses of worship would be reared unto the most high beautiful streets was to be made for the Saints to walk in Kings of the earth would come to behold the glory thereof & many glorious things not now to be named would be bestowed upon the Saints, but all these thing are better imagined than spoken by the Children of Jacob."[77]

In April, likely in response to JS's visionary description of Kirtland, Beals was commissioned to perform the survey and draw the map. He completed the survey and submitted his map to the county recorder, Ralph Cowles, on 18 May 1837. Sixty-eight landowners in Kirtland, including JS, approved the survey and acknowledged its accuracy before it was filed with the county. Beals earned $576.75 for his work, which included six days of surveying the land and the drawing of the map.[78] Shortly after Beals created the map, the block and lot numbers associated with it began appearing in land and tax records.[79]

Although it is not known if JS was directly involved in creating this map, he was one of the landowners who initiated its creation and paid Beals for the work, and the receipt suggests he played a leading role: "Joseph Smith jr Sidney Rigdon & others to W.W. Beals To making official Map of the City of Kirtland containing 4494 Lots."[80] The map resembles the earlier Kirtland city plat and the plat of the City of Zion, suggesting that Beals had access to these church documents or that he worked directly with JS and other church leaders while drafting. The Beals map, like earlier city plats that JS oversaw, highlights the centrality of the temple in Kirtland. City life was to continue to revolve around the House of the Lord, with six lots set aside in the city's central block for that edifice. In addition to the central

---

75. See Historical Introduction to Mortgage to Peter French, 5 Oct. 1836, pp. 294–295 herein.

76. *Pioneer and General History of Geauga County,* 70–71. Hyrum Smith discussed the Saints' intent to further develop Kirtland and the pressing need for town lots in a letter to Charles C. Rich in February 1837. (Hyrum Smith, Kirtland, OH, to Charles C. Rich, [Pleasant Grove, IL], 5 Feb. 1837, Charles C. Rich, Collection, CHL.)

77. Woodruff, Journal, 6 Apr. 1837.

78. Willard Beals, Account and Receipt, Kirtland, OH, 18 Sept. 1838, JS Collection, CHL.

79. Newel K. Whitney began a list to monitor and track the transfer of lot assignments from the 1833 plat to lots represented on the new Beals plat. ("List of Town Lots Sold by Johnson and Whitney," [Kirtland, OH], no date, Newel K. Whitney, Papers, BYU; see also Oliver and Elizabeth Cowdery to John Johnson, Deed, 27 May 1837, Geauga Co., OH, Deed Records, 1795–1921, vol. 24, p. 374, microfilm 20,240, U.S. and Canada Record Collection, FHL.)

80. Willard Beals, Account and Receipt, Kirtland, OH, 18 Sept. 1838, JS Collection, CHL.

block, plotting 224 residential blocks with twenty lots in each is also similar to the earlier design and reflects how JS and church leaders configured lots at that time. This map, much like the church's earlier city-planning maps, does not take into account the area topography and omits the Chagrin River and the major roads that ran through the town. The streets on the new map are laid out like those in the earlier Kirtland plat, though in that plat they are unnamed and in Beals's map featured here they are named after church leaders or members. There are 225 blocks arranged in a fifteen-by-fifteen-block pattern. The blocks are numbered in a serpentine pattern, beginning with block 1 in the northeast corner and ending with 225 in the southwest corner. That is, blocks 1–15 run north to south along the easternmost column, and then 16–30 run south to north in the next column, and so on. Each block is divided into twenty lots, organized in two rows of ten lots. The center block, 113, has only fourteen lots designated. Where the easternmost six lots would be is an open space, the north third of which is taken up by a drawing of the House of the Lord.

There are two contemporaneous versions of this map. The one featured here is the official version as delivered to and recorded by the county recorder. A copy made by Beals for church leaders is now at the Church History Library.[81] The two versions are nearly identical, except that the official version contains an explanatory addendum stating that the landowners had approved the plat map. Damage to and subsequent conservation work done on the featured copy rendered some words and characters illegible; footnotes and brackets below compare the text to the copy held at the Church History Library.

Document Transcript

A Map of Kirtland City

Situate in the Township of Kirtland Geauga County and State of Ohio. Surveyed into 225 blocks 40 Rods square each excepting the centre tier running N. & S. which is 43 Rods E & W. & the tier E. of the centre is 41 Rods E & W. with Streets crossing each other at right angles 4 Rods in width and running Magnetically N & S. E & W. Each block (excepting what is before excepted) are divided into 20 equal lots containing half an acre each— Numbered as will appear by the Map——

[Stylized arrow in top left of map, indicating up is north]

Streets Running North to South

Parris[82] Street
Christian Street
Martin Street
Carlos Street

Streets Running West to East

Peter Street
John Street
Luke Street
[Lyman Street][83]

---

81. Plat of Kirtland, OH, ca. 1837, CHL.
82. The CHL copy has "Parrish." (Plat of Kirtland, OH, ca. 1837, CHL.)
83. TEXT: [*page torn*]. Text supplied based on CHL copy. (Plat of Kirtland, OH, ca. 1837, CHL.)

Map of Kirtland. Geauga County Deed Record, vol. 24, p. 99, Geauga County Archives and Records Center, Chardon, OH.

Williams Street	Gilbert Street
Samuel Street	Whitmer Street
Johnson Street	Hiram Street
Cowdery Street	Whitney Street
Smith Street	Joseph Street
Rigdon Street	Cahoon Street
Williams Street	Carter Street
Orton Street	Kimball Street
Carle[84] Street	Boyan◊on Street[85]
Morley Street	Pratt Street
Partridge Street	Hyde Street
Phelps Street	Harris Street

[*Drawing of 225 numbered blocks in 15 rows and 15 columns. The center block, numbered 113, has a drawing of the House of the Lord taking up the north third.*]

The ground on which the Stone Meeting house[86] stands is 40 Rods front on Smith Street and 15 Rods on Whitney and Joseph Streets. The N. side of said building is just 4 Rods South of S. line of Whitney Street and parallel, there[with, the E. an]d[87] exactly 3 Rods W. of the W. line of [Smith S]treet—:[88] All the Lots lying lengthwise on the W. side of Smith Street ⟨and [a]djoining the same⟩ are 7 Rods by 20 all the other way 4 by 23. all on the E side of said ⟨Street⟩ lengthwise 5 Rods by 20. the other way 4 [by tw]enty one.[89] all others 4 by 20 Rods— The above Surveyed and certified by Willard W. Beals Surveyor for Geauga County. In the Year A.D. 1837—

Be it remembered that in this the month of April One thousand Eight hundred and thirty seven. Pe[rsona]lly[90] appeared the Persons whose names are below inserted personally known to me as part owners of the Kirtland City plat ⟨and acknowledged that the plat⟩ drawn and presented by Willard W Beals. County Surveyor, to be their free [w]ill,[91] and that they are still satisfied therewith F[rederick] G. Williams Justice of the Peace Seal[92] Arnold Healey,

---

84. The CHL copy has "Correl," probably intended as "Corrill." (Plat of Kirtland, OH, ca. 1837, CHL.)

85. The CHL copy has "Boynton Street." (Plat of Kirtland, OH, ca. 1837, CHL.)

86. "Stone Meeting house" is another name for the House of the Lord, or temple, in Kirtland.

87. TEXT: "there[*page torn*]d". In this instance of page damage and others in the paragraph, text is supplied based on the CHL copy of the plat. (Plat of Kirtland, OH, ca. 1837, CHL.)

88. TEXT: "[*page torn*]treet—:".

89. TEXT: "[*page torn*]enty one."

90. TEXT: "Pe[*page torn*]lly".

91. TEXT: "[*page torn*]ill,".

92. TEXT: "Seal" is enclosed in a hand-drawn representation of a seal.

Israel Knap, W^m McClary, John Johnson, John Isham, Harlow Redfield Nathl.
Milliken. Emma Smith Eliza R. Snow, Levi Osgood, Nancy Richardson
John P. Green[e] Stary [Sterry] Fisk Andrew L. Allen, Edmund Bosley, Ira
Ames, Reuben Field, Wm Aldrich, John Morton, Zemira Draper, Artemus
Millet, Zebede[e] Coltrin Sylvester Smith, Wm W. Spencer Willard Woodstock,
Reynolds Cahoon, Raymond Clark, Wm Tinney ⟨Jr.⟩ John Tanner, Wm Draper.
Jr, Samuel Newcomb. Blake Baldwin, Sabra Granger, Hiram Dayton
Alexander Badlam [Sr.], Solomon Freeman, Hyram [Hyrum] Smith Peter
Shirts Erastus Babbit[t] Russel Potter, Reuben McBride ~~Reuben~~ W^m. Felshaw.
Melvin Wolbour, Wm Gould. James Foster Symon Dyke. Bachis [Bechias]
Dustin Roger Orton Edmund Durfee Nathan Cheene [Cheney] Jacob
Bump Hezekiah Fisk, Oliver Olney, Warren Smith, David Clough, Cyrus
Smalling, Oliver Cow[de]ry[93] John [F.] Boynton, Heber [C.] Kimball, John
Gaylord, Ebenezer Jennings, Isaac H. Bishop, John B. Carpenter Joseph
Smith S[r]., Joseph Smith Jr., Sidney Rigdon, Ira Bond, Albert Miner,
        Received 18th. & Recorded 24th. May AD 1837—. Ralph Cowles Recorder.[94]

———— ❧ ————

Notes Receivable from Chester Store, 22 May 1837

Source Note

Chester Store, Notes Receivable, Chester, Meigs Co., OH, to JS, Kirtland Township, Geauga Co., OH, 22 May 1837; handwriting of Sylvester Smith; two pages; JS Collection, CHL. Includes docket.

One leaf, measuring 10 × 7⅞ inches (25 × 20 cm). The paper is purple-gray, with two vertical ledger lines inscribed in graphite on the right side of the recto. The top, bottom, and right edges of the recto have the square cut of manufactured paper; the left edge was torn. The left side of the recto was folded inward, and then the leaf was trifolded and docketed. There is marked soiling and soot at the folds. Exposure to the elements has turned large segments of the leaf a creamy yellow.

The provenance of this document is unknown; however, given the pattern of extant documents from the Kirtland, Ohio, era in possession of the Church History Library, this document was probably bundled and stored with other loose Kirtland financial material and was likely in continuous institutional custody.

Historical Introduction

By September 1836, JS and Sidney Rigdon formed a mercantile partnership, Rigdon, Smith & Co., which began operating a dry goods store in Chester, Ohio, about six miles south of Kirtland Township, Ohio.[95] Goods for the store were purchased, often in bulk,

---

93. TEXT: "Cow[*hole in page*]ry".

94. Ralph Cowles served as county recorder from 2 November 1835 to 4 November 1838. (*Pioneer and General History of Geauga County,* 69.)

95. Rigdon, Smith & Co., Store Ledger, Sept. 1836–May 1837, in JS Letterbook 2, p. [1]; "Mormonism

from wholesale merchants in New York.[96] Several church members and other residents in the Kirtland area had accounts in the store ledger, indicating they purchased goods on credit with the promise of later payment.

Although the extant Chester store ledger shows consistent business from September 1836 to March 1837, the period from April to May 1837 shows a significant decrease in mercantile activity, with no new purchases recorded after 19 May.[97] The store may have experienced economic pressure resulting from the national financial panic of May 1837 or from outstanding debts.[98] The store may also have faced reduced business caused by opposition to JS and the church.[99] Emma Smith wrote to JS on 3 May that the Chester store was being watched, possibly by the same people threatening JS's life in April 1837.[100] Such opposition could have affected business at the Chester store, since church members appear to have been the majority of the store's customers.

JS was absent from Kirtland in spring 1837 because of threats of violence, but he likely returned in mid-May, and he made at least two trips to the mercantile store in Chester between 19 and 24 May.[101] On 22 May, JS charged several hundred dollars' worth of household goods, tools, fabric, and books to his account and removed them from the store. He also gathered twenty-seven promissory notes from the Chester store, as recorded on the list featured here. These notes had been given to JS and the other store owners to pay for purchased goods, and JS likely took them from the store with the intention of collecting on the notes.

---

in Ohio," *Aurora* (New Lisbon, OH), 19 Jan. 1837, [3]. This was one of a few stores opened in the Kirtland area between 1835 and 1836. Reynolds Cahoon, Jared Carter, and Hyrum Smith started a store, sometimes referred to as the "Committee Store," under the mercantile firm of Cahoon, Carter & Co. in June 1835. John F. Boynton and Lyman Johnson began their own dry goods store by 1837. (Advertisement, *Northern Times*, 9 Oct. 1835, [4]; Pratt, Account Book and Autobiography, Oct. 1836–Jan. 1837; Cowdery, Docket Book, 86, 98, 219, 224.)

96. These goods included items ranging from pocketknives and washboards to shoes, fabric, and books. Some of these goods were likely purchased wholesale from merchants in New York City and Buffalo, New York. Receipts and invoices for the mercantile firms of Rigdon, Smith & Co; Cahoon, Carter & Co.; and H. Smith & Co. document purchasing agents' trips to Buffalo in June 1836 and New York City in October 1836 to obtain goods for the stores in Kirtland and Chester. (Buffalo and New York City Invoices, June and Oct. 1836, JS Office Papers, CHL.)

97. Rigdon, Smith & Co., Store Ledger, Sept. 1836–May 1837, in JS Letterbook 2, p. 79.

98. See Introduction to Part 5: 5 Oct. 1836–10 Apr. 1837, pp. 285–294 herein; and "Joseph Smith Documents from October 1835 through January 1838," pp. xxvii–xxxii herein.

99. Historical Introduction to Letter from Newel K. Whitney, 20 Apr. 1837, pp. 367–369 herein.

100. Letter from Emma Smith, 3 May 1837, pp. 372–376 herein. Emma Smith, Newel K. Whitney, and Wilford Woodruff each mentioned unidentified enemies threatening JS's life in April and May 1837. (See Letter from Newel K. Whitney, 20 Apr. 1837, p. 369 herein; Letter from Emma Smith, 25 Apr. 1837, p. 371 herein; and Woodruff, Journal, 13 Apr. 1837; see also Introduction to Part 6: 20 Apr.–14 Sept. 1837, pp. 363–366 herein.)

101. For more on JS's absence from Kirtland, see Historical Introduction to Letter from Newel K. Whitney, 20 Apr. 1837, pp. 367–368 herein. According to extant records, JS took out two bills of goods from the Chester store during this six-day period. One is dated 22 May, the same day he made the list of promissory notes, and the other includes three different dates: 19 May, 22 May, and 24 May. ("Bill of Goods Taken from the Chester Store," 20 May 1837, JS Collection, CHL; "Bill of Goods Taken from the Chester Store," 19–24 May 1837, JS Office Papers, CHL.)

Since these promissory notes were used to pay the store owners, they were categorized as "receivable," meaning that the store owners could collect the promised payments. Because the notes were payable to the store owners, the owners could treat them as assets.[102] At least eighteen of the twenty-two individuals identified in the list of promissory notes were members of the church.[103] Only four of the individuals named in the list are included in the extant store ledger, indicating they had accounts with the store and had purchased goods on credit.[104] The other eighteen individuals may have had accounts in a nonextant ledger book, or they may have paid for goods with a promissory note to begin with, rather than purchasing on store credit.[105]

The majority of store accounts in the extant ledger were settled in late May. The settling of accounts, along with the lack of purchases after 19 May and JS's removal of goods and promissory notes, suggests that the store closed at the end of May. Accounts remaining unpaid after May were settled in late June and July by promissory notes paid to Alexander Badlam and Sidney Rigdon.[106] The fact that none of these payments involved JS may indicate that in removing the goods and notes from the Chester store in late May 1837 he dissolved the partnership of Rigdon, Smith & Co. and took all or part of what was owed him as an investor and partner in the firm.

The list of notes is in the handwriting of Sylvester Smith, who may have been a clerk at the Chester store.

Document Transcript

	$	c[en]t
A list of Notes		
taken from the Chester store May 22. 1837		
" J[ohn] B. Carpenter $52.00. = d[itt]o[107] $44.20. = ———	96	20
" Edson Barn[e]y.s $58.43.[108] = do 50.63. = do 5.51. =	114	57

---

102. Coffin, *Progressive Exercises in Book Keeping*, 60; "Receivable," in *Oxford English Dictionary*, 8:231.

103. Three of the individuals named in the list have not been identified: E. Bevin, G. Kirkndall, and G. Coates. Samuel McBride may have been a relation of church member Reuben McBride, but no documentation indicates whether he too was a Mormon.

104. These were Sidney Rigdon, Samuel Smith, Alexander Badlam, and Edson Barney. (Rigdon, Smith & Co., Store Ledger, Sept. 1836–May 1837, in JS Letterbook 2, pp. 5, 21, 31, 50.)

105. There is also a possibility that individuals buying goods from the store paid using promissory notes from other individuals. Promissory notes were negotiable and could be transferred from one person to another until paid. As specie and credible currency became scarcer in the Panic of 1837, and as skepticism increased toward the notes of the Kirtland Safety Society, promissory notes would have served as a replacement for other circulating mediums.

106. Rigdon, Smith & Co., Store Ledger, Sept. 1836–May 1837, in JS Letterbook 2, pp. 31, 52, 56, 69.

107. The "d[itt]o" used here indicates that the second amount listed in that row was another promissory note from the same individual.

108. The account for Edson Barney in the Chester store ledger lists a credit on the account in the amount of $58.43, paid for goods purchased 16 January 1837, but does not specify how or when the payment was made. (Rigdon, Smith & Co., Store Ledger, Sept. 1836–May 1837, in JS Letterbook 2, p. 50.)

" Reuben McBride 25.16 26.75. = Samuel McBride $4.25 6.16   29[109] 20

                                                                 32   94

" L. Boothe [Lorenzo Booth] $24.74. = do $16.21. = ——   30   95

" Arvin A. Avory [Avery] $3.00 4.69. = do $6.63.——   19   63

                                                                 11   32

" Daniel Wood $5.75. = A[braham] Wood $2.43 = —   8   18

" E. Bevin $13.52. = H[iram] Stratton $4.92. =   18   44

" S[idney] Rigdon $50.00.[110] = S[amuel] H. Smith   301   53
$251.53.[111] =

" Horace Burgess $11.00. = do $3.82 = ——   14   82

" C[ornelius] P. Lott $8.08. = S[almon] Gee 6.37. = ——   14   45

" G. Kirkndall $6.00. = A. Badlem [Alexander Badlam Sr.][112]   71   12
$65.12.——

" W^m. Draper J[r.] $13.49. = H[arvey] Stanley $15.47. =   28   96

" L. Fisk[113] $2.13. = N[athan] Haskins 11.95. =   20   20
G. Cortes [Coates] $6.12

                                         Amt. $763   68
                                                 [p. [1]]

List of notes taken from the Chester Store by J. Smith Jr—
$763.68 [p. [2]]

---

109. TEXT: "29" written over "39" and then canceled by implication when revised to "32".

110. Rigdon was a partner in the firm running the Chester store. His account in the ledger lists $408.15 in goods purchased on credit from 28 September 1836 to April 1837. It is likely that his partnership allowed him to receive more store credit than was extended to others. The $50 note listed here does not appear in the ledger book, and no payments are recorded for his account. (Rigdon, Smith & Co., Store Ledger, Sept. 1836–May 1837, in JS Letterbook 2, p. 5.)

111. The store ledger account for Samuel Smith records goods purchased to the amount of $251.53 on 21 November and 26 December, payments on the account totaling $253.33, and a note that indicates the account was settled on 3 March 1837, likely by the promissory note listed here. (Rigdon, Smith & Co., Store Ledger, Sept. 1836–May 1837, in JS Letterbook 2, p. 21.)

112. Alexander Badlam's account in the Chester store ledger records a charge of $84.40 and a credit of $50. Badlam's account was settled by a note on 17 April 1837. It is not clear if the note in this list is the same as the one that settled the account or not. Within the ledger, Badlam was also listed as the individual receiving payments settling several store accounts on 23 June 1837. This may indicate that Badlam was working as an agent for the mercantile firm of Rigdon, Smith & Co. and may have helped resolve outstanding debts after May 1837. (Rigdon, Smith & Co., Store Ledger, Sept. 1836–May 1837, in JS Letterbook 2, pp. 31, 52, 56, 69.)

113. Possibly Hezekiah, Alfred, or Sterry Fisk. (Backman, *Profile*, 25.)

Letter from Parley P. Pratt, 23 May 1837

Source Note

Parley P. Pratt, Letter, Kirtland Township, Geauga Co., OH, to JS, Kirtland Township, Geauga Co., OH, 23 May 1837. Featured version published in "Parley P. Pratt's Letter," Naked Truths about Mormonism, *Apr. 1888, p. 4.*

The newspaper *Naked Truths about Mormonism* was published in Oakland, California, by Arthur B. Deming & Co. The featured text comes from vol. 1, no. 2, which is four pages on two conjoined leaves measuring 23½ × 18 inches (60 × 46 cm). Each leaf contains seven columns, with each column measuring 17¼ × 2¼ inches (44 × 6 cm). The featured letter begins in the second column of page 4 and ends in the third column.

Historical Introduction

Parley P. Pratt wrote the letter featured here to JS in desperation over financial matters in Kirtland, Ohio. Pratt even stood to lose his house. JS had purchased a large amount of land in Kirtland for the use of church members in 1836 and early 1837,[114] a period when land costs increased significantly in Kirtland due to both population growth and inflation.[115] At some point, likely in late 1836 or early 1837, Pratt arranged to purchase three lots of land for $2,000 from JS, and he provided JS with a financial instrument, probably a promissory note, for that amount. In May 1837, when Pratt found himself unable to fulfill this financial obligation, the Kirtland Safety Society demanded he forfeit his property.[116]

In April, a month after the death of his first wife, Thankful Halsey Pratt, Parley Pratt traveled to Canada and began making plans for a mission to England.[117] When this news reached Pratt's fellow apostles Thomas B. Marsh and David W. Patten in Far West, Missouri, they wrote Pratt and insisted that the Twelve Apostles must be united under Marsh's leadership. They asked that he delay plans for a foreign mission and requested that he travel to Kirtland for a meeting of the Quorum of the Twelve in late July.[118] Pratt followed their direction and returned to Kirtland in early May, bringing with him Canadian convert Mary Ann Frost Stearns, whom he married in Kirtland on 14 May.[119]

---

114. See Historical Introduction to Mortgage to Peter French, 5 Oct. 1836, pp. 294–295 herein.

115. Editorial, *LDS Messenger and Advocate,* June 1837, 3:521; Backman, *Heavens Resound,* 139–140; see also Historical Introduction to Minutes, 22 Dec. 1836, pp. 321–322 herein; Historical Introduction to Notice, ca. Late Aug. 1837, pp. 418–420 herein; and Historical Introduction to Mortgage to Peter French, 5 Oct. 1836, pp. 294–295 herein.

116. No deeds confirm JS's or Pratt's involvement in the transaction, probably because Pratt never acquired a deed for the lots, being unable to pay for the land.

117. Pratt, *Autobiography,* 181–183.

118. Thomas B. Marsh and David W. Patten, Far West, MO, to Parley P. Pratt, Toronto, Upper Canada, 10 May 1837, in JS Letterbook 2, pp. 62–63.

119. Geauga Co., OH, Probate Court, Marriage Records, 1806–1920, vol. C, p. 220, 14 May 1837, microfilm 873,464, U.S. and Canada Record Collection, FHL.

Like Pratt, JS was absent from Kirtland for much of April and returned in May 1837. After returning, JS gathered money and other assets in order to pay debts.[120] Around 22 May he apparently transferred Pratt's promissory note for $2,000 to the Kirtland Safety Society, which thus became responsible for collecting on Pratt's debt. Pratt noted in his letter that although he had offered to return the land, Sidney Rigdon, secretary for the Safety Society, required Pratt's home as well as the lot on which it was located.[121] This was not the situation Pratt expected. In his letter, Pratt reminded JS that he had promised Pratt that he "should not be ingured" by the transaction, and Pratt likely saw the financial losses as a betrayal by men he considered his spiritual leaders. According to the letter, other individuals were bound with Pratt for the debt, presumably because they had acted as co-financers in purchasing the land or as sureties on a promissory note.

Fearing the financial ruin of losing his house and land, Pratt wrote this letter to JS, threatening to bring charges against him for extortion, covetousness, and taking advantage through religious influence. Pratt never formally made these charges; however, his brother Orson Pratt and fellow apostle Lyman Johnson brought similar charges against JS six days later, on 29 May.[122] On that same day, Parley P. Pratt and four other prominent men in the church were called before the high council for actions "injurious to the church of God."[123] Pratt's discontent with JS over financial matters continued into June 1837, when he gave a discourse criticizing JS and the church before leaving for Missouri.[124] While traveling, he met Marsh, Patten, and William Smith, who were heading to Kirtland. Marsh persuaded Pratt to return with them.[125] Once he arrived in Kirtland, Pratt reconciled himself with JS. According to Pratt's autobiography, "I went to brother Joseph Smith in tears, and, with a broken heart and contrite spirit, confessed wherein I had erred in spirit, murmured, or done

---

120. By May 1837, JS faced lawsuits on debts relating to land purchased from Timothy Martindale, money borrowed from the Bank of Geauga, goods purchased from the New York firm of Patterson & Patterson, and promissory notes given to Ezra Holmes and Hezekiah Kelley. (Transcript of Proceedings, 5 June 1837, Martindale v. JS et al. [Geauga Co. C.P. 1837]; Transcript of Proceedings, 5 June 1837, Bank of Geauga v. JS et al. [Geauga Co. C.P. 1837]; Transcript of Proceedings, 5 June 1837, Holmes v. Dayton et al. [Geauga Co. C.P. 1837]; Transcript of Proceedings, 5 June 1837, Kelley v. Rigdon et al. [Geauga Co. C.P. 1837], Record Book U, pp. 67–69, 86–87, 97–101, 106–108, Geauga County Archives and Records Center, Chardon, OH. For information on JS's absence from Kirtland in April, see Letter from Newel K. Whitney, 20 Apr. 1837, pp. 366–370 herein; and Notes Receivable from Chester Store, 22 May 1837, pp. 382–385 herein.)

121. The return of land that had been mortgaged or paid through promissory notes was a common settlement when the purchaser could not pay the promised amount. However, in such a case the Kirtland Safety Society would have lost money on the transaction. By requiring Pratt's home—his improvement on the land—the society would make a small profit. For his part, Pratt requested the seventy-five dollars he had paid on the land transaction. Previous payments would not generally be returned but considered the loss of the purchaser. For similar resolutions of failed transactions, see Historical Introduction to Letter from Newel K. Whitney, 20 Apr. 1837, pp. 367–369 herein; and Ames, Autobiography and Journal, [11]–[12].

122. Charges against JS Preferred to Bishop's Council, 29 May 1837, p. 397 herein.

123. Letter from Abel Lamb and Others, ca. 28 May 1837, p. 393 herein.

124. Mary Fielding, Kirtland, OH, to Mercy Fielding, [Upper Canada], ca. June 1837, Mary Fielding Smith, Collection, CHL.

125. John Smith, Kirtland, OH, to George A. Smith, West Township, Columbiana Co., OH, 28 July 1837, George Albert Smith, Papers, CHL; Mary Fielding, Kirtland, OH, to Mercy Fielding, [Upper Canada], ca. June 1837, Mary Fielding Smith, Collection, CHL.

or said amiss. He frankly forgave me, prayed for me and blessed me."[126] Pratt also made an acknowledgment of his faults in a Sunday meeting in Kirtland on 9 July, before setting off with his family to proselytize in New York.[127]

In early 1838, Warren Parrish, a leader of the dissenters opposed to JS's leadership, sent Pratt's 23 May 1837 letter along with one of his own to *Zion's Watchman,* a publication of the New York Wesleyan Society edited by LaRoy Sunderland and Timothy Merritt.[128] Parrish's letter strongly condemned both JS and Rigdon, and the editors of *Zion's Watchman* printed Pratt's and Parrish's letters in the 24 March 1838 issue.[129] Pratt responded to the *Zion's Watchman* publication in a letter printed in the August 1838 issue of the Mormon newspaper *Elders' Journal.* Pratt acknowledged he was the author of the letter, which he said he wrote intending to injure the feelings of JS and Rigdon. Pratt noted that he wrote it "in great severity and harshness" as a "private admonition," not intended for public distribution. He further wrote that JS, like other men, was still "liable to errors, and nistakes [mistakes]," and he said he regretted writing the letter and had asked JS and Rigdon for their forgiveness. Pratt concluded his letter in the *Elders' Journal* stating, "From 1830 until now, I have had full confidence in the book of Mormon, the Revelations of God to Joseph Smith Jr., and I still esteem both him and President Rigdon, as men of the highest integrity, the most exalted principles of virtue and honor."[130]

Later that year, Richard Livesey, a Methodist Episcopal minister in England, included both Pratt's and Parrish's letters from *Zion's Watchman* in his pamphlet *An Exposure of Mormonism.*[131] Pratt learned of this reprinting while in England proselytizing, and he responded with a pamphlet of his own defending himself and the church.[132] Another version of the letter exists independent of the *Zion's Watchman* publication; it was printed in the 1888 publication *Naked Truths about Mormonism,* edited by Arthur Deming.[133] This appears to be more complete than the earlier printing, as Deming wrote that the copy of the letter he printed in *Naked Truths about Mormonism* was "an exact copy of the original" found in the holdings of the Lake County Historical Society.[134]

---

126. Pratt, *Autobiography,* 183–184.

127. Mary Fielding, Kirtland, OH, to Mercy Fielding Thompson, [Upper Canada], 8 July 1837, Mary Fielding Smith, Collection, CHL; Pratt, *Autobiography,* 184.

128. It is not clear how Parrish acquired a copy of Pratt's letter. Even though Pratt later stated it was not intended for publication, he may have circulated it among those individuals in Kirtland who shared his frustrations with JS and Rigdon in the summer of 1837. The letter Parrish sent to *Zion's Watchman* first appeared as a letter to the editor of the *Painesville (Ohio) Republican,* an original copy of which has not been located. (Parley P. Pratt, Kirtland, OH, to JS, 23 May 1837, in *Zion's Watchman,* 24 Mar. 1838, 46; "To the Public," *Elders' Journal,* Aug. 1838, 50–51.)

129. "Mormonism," *Zion's Watchman,* 24 Mar. 1838, 46.

130. "To the Public," *Elders' Journal,* Aug. 1838, 50–51.

131. Richard Livesey, *Exposure of Mormonism* (Preston: J. Livesey, 1838).

132. Pratt, *Reply,* 7.

133. "Parley P. Pratt's Letter," *Naked Truths about Mormonism* (Oakland, CA), Apr. 1888, 4.

134. Arthur Deming, Preface to "Parley P. Pratt's Letter," *Naked Truths about Mormonism* (Oakland, CA), Apr. 1888, 4. A "Lake County Library and Historical Society" was founded in June 1876, but that organization, long discontinued, has no relation to the present-day Lake County Historical Society, which

Pratt's original letter has not been located. Pratt claimed that the letter as published in *Zion's Watchman* was "not a true copy" but had been "altered, so as to convey a different idea from the original."[135] The version printed in *Zion's Watchman* appears to have been edited for spelling and punctuation, and it also contained some alterations to the text, most notably the omission of a postscript in which Pratt confirmed his belief in the Book of Mormon and the Doctrine and Covenants.[136] Deming's version includes the omitted postscript and what may be original spelling and punctuation errors. It appears to be the most complete extant version of the letter and is therefore the version featured here, but in the absence of the original, there is no way to be certain it is an exact copy as Deming affirmed. Substantive differences between Deming's 1888 copy and the 1838 *Zion's Watchman* version are annotated below.

Document Transcript

KIRTLAND, May 23, 1837.[137]

PRES'T J SMITH JR *Deare Brother* as it is dificult to obtain a personal interview with you at all times By reason of the multitude of Buisiness in which you are engaged you will Excuse my saying In writing what I would otherwise say By word of mouth.

Haveing Long Pondered the Path in which we as a people have been led in regard to our temporal management, I have at Length Become fully convinced that the whole scene[138] of Speculation in which we have Been Engaged is of the Devel; I allude to the covetous Extortionary Speculating Spirit which has reigned in this place for the Last season;[139] which Has given rise to Lying deceiveing and

---

was started in 1936 and has no record of the letter being in their collection. (*History of Geauga and Lake Counties*, 43.)

135. "To the Public," *Elders' Journal*, Aug. 1838, 50.

136. It is not clear who was involved in making these changes. Parrish may have altered the letter before sending it, or the editors of *Zion's Watchman* may have imposed changes to conform with standardized spelling in their publication. Sunderland and Merritt may also have decided to omit the postscript because of its affirmation of the Book of Mormon.

137. TEXT: Between the date and the body of the letter is a paragraph by Deming: "The following letter is an exact copy of the original, which is in the possession of the Lake County Historical Society at Painesville, Ohio. P. P. Pratt was a brother of Orson, and was killed in the Indian Territory in 1857 by a man whose wife he had seduced." For information on Pratt's murder by Hector McLean, former husband of Eleanor Jane McComb McLean Pratt, one of Parley P. Pratt's plural wives, see Givens and Grow, *Apostle Paul of Mormonism*, 361–383.

138. The *Zion's Watchman* instead has "scheme." ("Mormonism," *Zion's Watchman*, 24 Mar. 1838, 46.)

139. Engaging in uncertain land investments in hopes of making a profit was a reality for most of the western frontier, including Ohio in the mid-1830s. Church members were involved in frequent land transactions, some of which were likely risky investments made to turn a profit. Warren A. Cowdery's May 1837 editorial in the *Messenger and Advocate* detailed speculation and inflation in Kirtland: "Real estate rose from one to eight hundred per cent and in many cases more. Men who were not thought worth fifty or an hundred dollars became purchasers to the amount of thousands. Notes, (some cash,) deeds, and mortgages passed and repassed, till all, or nearly all, vainly supposed they had become wealthy." In

takeing the advantage of ones Nabour [neighbor][140] and In Short to Every Eavle [evil] work:

And Being as fully convinced that you and President [Sidney] Rigdon; Both By presept and Example have Been the principle means In Leading this people astray in these particulars and haveing myself Been Led astray and Caught in the same snare By your Example and By false Prophesying and preaching from your mouths; yea haveing done many things Rong [wrong] and plunged myself and family and others well nigh in to distruction, I have awoke to an awful sense of my situation and now resolve to retrace my steps, and to get out of the snare and make restitution as far as I can And now Dear Brother If you are still determined to persue this wicked course untill your self and the Church shall sink down to hell;[141] I Beseach you at least to have mercy on me and my family and others who are Bound with me for those certain 3 lots which you sold to me at the Extortionary price of $2;000 which never cost you $1:00;[142] for if It stands against me it will rewin [ruin] Myself and a helpless family as well as those Bound with me for yesterday Pres't Rigdon came to me and Informed me that you had drawn the money from the

---

April 1837, JS, Hyrum Smith, and Sidney Rigdon each emphasized the need for church members outside of Kirtland to move there and buy the lands for which JS and other church members had gone into debt to acquire for the Saints. Since no records indicate the amounts for which this land was sold, it is impossible to know if the prices were significantly inflated. (Editorial, *LDS Messenger and Advocate,* June 1837, 3:520–522; Historical Introduction to Mortgage to Peter French, 5 Oct. 1836, pp. 294–295 herein; Discourse, 6 Apr. 1837, pp. 356–357 herein. For accounts of speculation occurring among church members in this period, see JS History, vol. B-1, 761; Kimball, "History," 77–78; Fielding, Journal, 12–13; and Cyrus Smalling, Letter, Kirtland, OH, 10 Mar. 1841, in "Banking and Financiering at Kirtland," 669.)

140. Referencing how the spirit of speculation had led members to exploit their neighbors, in a May 1837 editorial, Warren A. Cowdery warned new arrivals in Kirtland to beware of those who would take advantage of their inexperience to sell them land at much higher rates. (Editorial, *LDS Messenger and Advocate,* May 1837, 3:505–506.)

141. The word "hell" is italicized in *Zion's Watchman.* ("Mormonism," *Zion's Watchman,* 24 Mar. 1838, 46.)

142. In *Zion's Watchman* this amount is written as $100. Pratt considered JS's treatment of him to be extortion because JS had originally paid much less for the land. The exact lots mentioned by Pratt are not known, but if these were lands for which JS had received the title from Fredrick G. Williams or John Johnson, JS may have paid very little. However, if they were sections of land from more recent purchases, JS may have still been paying off the high costs of land and may not have inflated the price as significantly as Pratt claimed. During the height of land transactions in late 1836 and early 1837, the price of lots around the House of the Lord in Kirtland were driven up by demand, and JS may have asked $2,000 for the property due to the inflated land values. The deeds for the three lots mentioned here were not recorded in the deed books for Geauga County. The land transaction may have been voided when Pratt was unable to pay his obligations on the land. ("Mormonism," *Zion's Watchman,* 24 Mar. 1838, 46; Historical Introduction to Revelation, 23 Apr. 1834, in *JSP,* D4:19–22; Balance of Account, 23 Apr. 1834, in *JSP,* D4:31–33; Hyrum Smith, Kirtland, OH, to Charles C. Rich, [Pleasant Grove, IL], 5 Feb. 1837, Charles C. Rich, Collection, CHL; see also Historical Introduction to Notice, ca. Late Aug. 1837, pp. 418–420 herein.)

Bank[143] on the obligation you hold against me[144] and that you had Left it to the mercy of the Bank and could not help what ever course they might take to collect it: notwithstanding the most sacred promise[145] on your part that I should not Be ingured [injured] By giveing these writings;[146] I offered him the 3 lots for the writings But he wanted my house and home also; now deare Brother will you take those Lots and give me up the writings and pay me the seventy-five dollars which I paid you on the same or will you taake the advantage of your Nabour Because he is in your Power if you will receive this admonition from one who Loves your Soul and repent of your Extortion and covetiousness in this thing, and make restitution you have my fellowship and Esteem as far as it respects our dealings Between ourselves; But if not I Shall Be under the painful necessity of prefering charges against you, for Extortion, covetousness, and takeing advantage of your Brother By an undue religious influence[147] for it is this kind of influence which Led us to make such kind of trades, in this society, such as saying it was the will of God that Lands Should Bear such a price and many other Prophesyings Preachings and Statements of a like nature.

Yours with respect,

P[arley] P PRATT.

P. S. Do not suppose for a moment that I Lack any Confidence in the Book of Mormons or Doctrine and Covenants Nay It is my firm belief in those Records that hinders my Belief In the course we have Been Led of Late.[148]

——— ❧ ———

Letter from Abel Lamb and Others, circa 28 May 1837

Source Note

Abel Lamb, Nathan Haskins, Harlow Redfield, Artemus Millet, and Isaac Rogers, Letter, Kirtland Township, Geauga Co., OH, to "the Presidency of the Church of the Latter Day Saints" [JS, Sidney Rigdon, Frederick G. Williams, Oliver Cowdery, Joseph Smith Sr., and Hyrum Smith], Kirtland Township, Geauga Co., OH, ca. 28 May 1837. Featured version copied [ca. 29 May 1837] in Minute Book 1, pp. 226–227; handwriting of Marcellus Cowdery; CHL. For more information on Minute Book 1, see Source Notes for Multiple-Entry Documents, p. 527 herein.

---

143. The Kirtland Safety Society.

144. This likely refers to a promissory note or something similar Pratt gave JS for the debt on the land.

145. In *Zion's Watchman*, this is rendered as "SACRED PROMISES." ("Mormonism," *Zion's Watchman*, 24 Mar. 1838, 46.)

146. "These writings" refer to promissory notes or other financial obligations held by JS.

147. Charges such as those Pratt refers to here against a member of the First Presidency would have been addressed not to the high council but to the bishop's council for possible action.

148. This postscript was not printed in the *Zion's Watchman* version of the letter. ("Mormonism," *Zion's Watchman*, 24 Mar. 1838, 46.)

Historical Introduction

Elders Abel Lamb, Nathan Haskins, Harlow Redfield, Artemus Millet, and Isaac Rogers signed the letter featured here asking the church presidency to investigate the behavior of five prominent men in the church: Missouri church president David Whitmer, First Presidency member Frederick G. Williams, apostles Lyman Johnson and Parley P. Pratt, and Warren Parrish, a seventy who had also served as JS's personal scribe. Before this meeting, Parrish, Pratt, Johnson, and others had spoken against JS, criticizing his leadership and accusing him of lying, extortion, and other actions unbecoming of a president of the church.[149] Lamb and the four other elders likely wrote the letter on 28 May 1837, the day before the Kirtland, Ohio, high council convened to address the concerns it raised.[150]

Opposition against the First Presidency, and especially JS, began in early 1837.[151] Vague dissatisfaction coalesced into specific accusations by the end of May, when Parley P. Pratt denounced JS for lying and extortion.[152] Then on Sunday, 28 May, about the time this letter was signed, Warren Parrish "proclaimed against" JS during Sabbath worship in the House of the Lord.[153] Although the events of 28 May might have prompted Lamb and the others to call for an investigation, at least some of the five men named in the letter had previously expressed their dissatisfaction with JS, as already noted.

The letter calling for an investigation was brought before the Kirtland high council on 29 May. After the letter was read, Parrish stated that it "was not in accordance with the copy" he and presumably the others had received. Parrish did not indicate what differences existed between the two copies, and no other versions of the letter are now extant. In the course of the 29 May meeting, both Williams and Whitmer objected to being tried by the high council, since an 1831 revelation had specified that members of the church presidency were to be tried by the bishop and his council.[154] Sidney Rigdon, who was presiding at the meeting, submitted this jurisdictional question to the high council, who decided that they could not try Williams and Whitmer and discharged them. The council then adjourned for an hour. After they reassembled in the afternoon with Rigdon and Oliver Cowdery presiding, Parley P. Pratt objected to being tried by Rigdon or JS, since both had previously made known their disapproval of his actions. After a discussion of who should appropriately lead the meeting,

---

149. Woodruff, Journal, 28 May 1837; Mary Fielding, Kirtland, OH, to Mercy Fielding, [Upper Canada], ca. June 1837, Mary Fielding Smith, Collection, CHL; Historical Introduction to Letter from Parley P. Pratt, 23 May 1837, pp. 386–389 herein.

150. Minute Book 1, 29 May 1837. Lamb was appointed to serve on a vigilance committee in a Kirtland elders quorum meeting on 17 February 1837 and may have drafted the letter featured here in connection with his service in this position. The purpose of the committee may have been to watch for dissension or other improprieties, but the records of the Kirtland elders quorum provide no specific focus for the committee. Abel Lamb, Peter Shirts, and Joshua Holman are the only elders appointed in the quorum record, but the committee may have included other elders in Kirtland. (Kirtland Elders Quorum, "Record," 17 Feb. 1837.)

151. See Introduction to Part 5: 5 Oct. 1836–10 Apr. 1837, pp. 287–294 herein.

152. Letter from Parley P. Pratt, 23 May 1837, pp. 386–391 herein.

153. Woodruff, Journal, 28 May 1837; Mary Fielding, Kirtland, OH, to Mercy Fielding, [Upper Canada], ca. June 1837, Mary Fielding Smith, Collection, CHL.

154. Minute Book 1, 29 May 1837; Revelation, 11 Nov. 1831–B, in *JSP*, D2:134 [D&C 107:82–84].

Rigdon recused himself. The high council attempted to find another member of the presidency to preside, but Cowdery stated that he was also "unfit to judge in the case," since he had likewise expressed his opinion of Pratt earlier. Williams, who had been implicated in the letter from Lamb and the other elders, said he was also unwilling to preside. Without someone to chair the meeting, "the council and assembly then dispersed in confusion."[155] Woodruff, who was at the meeting, noted that "the council closed without transacting business."[156] No extant accounts indicate whether or not these charges were considered again by the Kirtland high council or by the bishop's council.

By September 1837, those individuals who refused to accept JS's direction and confess their errors were removed from their leadership positions in the church. Of the five men named in the letter here, only Lyman Johnson was objected to at a meeting in Kirtland on 3 September.[157]

Document Transcript

To the Presidency of the Church of the Latter Day Saints.—

We the undersigned feeling ourselves aggrieved with the conduct of Presidents David Whitmer and F[rederick] G Williams and also with Elders Lyman Johnson ~~and~~ Parley P Pratt and Warren Parrish, believing that their course for some time past has been injurious to the church of God in which they are high officers. We therefore desire that the high council should be assembled and we should have [p. 226] an investigation of their behavior, believing it to be unworthy of their high calling all of which we respectfully submit.

Kirtland May 1837.

Abel Lamb
Nathan Haskins
Harlow Redfield
Artemas [Artemus] Millet
Isaac Rogers.

——— ❧ ———

Charges against Joseph Smith Preferred to Bishop's Council, 29 May 1837

Source Note

Lyman Johnson and Orson Pratt, Charges against JS Preferred to "the Bishop & his council in Kirtland," Kirtland Township, Geauga Co., OH, 29 May 1837; handwriting of Warren Parrish; signatures of Orson Pratt and probably Lyman Johnson; one page; Newel K. Whitney, Papers, BYU. Includes archival marking.

---

155. Minute Book 1, 29 May 1837.
156. Woodruff, Journal, 29 May 1837.
157. Minutes, 3 Sept. 1837, p. 423 herein.

One leaf, measuring 4⅞ × 7¾ inches (12 × 20 cm). The leaf is ruled with eleven blue-green lines (now faded) on the recto and has an unlined verso. The lines incline toward the right side of the page and end 1⅞ inches (5 cm) from the bottom. The left and bottom edges of the recto have the square cut of manufactured paper. The top and right edges were possibly torn. The leaf was folded twice.

This manuscript, along with many other personal and institutional documents kept by Newel K. Whitney, was inherited by his daughter Mary Jane Whitney, who married Isaac Groo. This collection was passed down in the Groo family and donated by members of the family to the Harold B. Lee Library at Brigham Young University between 1969 and 1974.[158]

Historical Introduction

On Monday, 29 May 1837, Lyman Johnson and Orson Pratt, both of whom were members of the Quorum of the Twelve Apostles, signed charges accusing JS of lying, extortion, and speaking disrespectfully of church members. The charges were written by Warren Parrish and were addressed to Bishop Newel K. Whitney and his council, following the direction given in an 1831 revelation that "inasmuch as the president of the high priesthood shall transgress he shall be had in remembrance before the common court of the church"— that is, the bishop's court.[159] These charges may relate to earlier accusations Orson Pratt's brother Parley P. Pratt made against JS in a letter written on 23 May. They may also have resulted from Johnson and other members of the Twelve earlier being charged with creating divisions within the church in Kirtland, Ohio.[160]

A handful of prominent church members had spoken against JS by the end of May 1837. Parley P. Pratt, Parrish, and other dissenters referenced JS's involvement in financial affairs, such as land transactions and the Kirtland Safety Society, in their objections to his leadership. Temporal concerns were likely also a factor in Johnson's and Orson Pratt's dissatisfaction with JS, and they may have blamed him for their recent financial reversals. The previous fall, after returning to Kirtland from proselytizing in Canada and New York, Orson Pratt began selling stoves and ironware, while Johnson had started a dry goods store with John F. Boynton, another member of the Twelve.[161] According to reminiscent accounts, Johnson and Boynton financed their mercantile efforts by buying a large amount of goods on credit and borrowing money from church members in the Boston area.[162] When the nationwide financial panic of 1837 brought economic decline and demands by creditors for repayment, Johnson, Boynton, and Pratt may have felt JS was responsible for their financial

---

158. Andrus and Fuller, *Register of the Newel Kimball Whitney Papers,* 5–6.

159. Revelation, 11 Nov. 1831–B, in *JSP,* D2:135 [D&C 107:82]. The issue of which council had the authority to try a member of the First Presidency was also debated in the high council meeting held the same day Johnson and Pratt wrote their charges against JS. (Historical Introduction to Letter from Abel Lamb and Others, ca. 28 May 1837, pp. 392–393 herein.)

160. Letter from Parley P. Pratt, 23 May 1837, pp. 386–391 herein; Thomas B. Marsh and David W. Patten, Far West, MO, to Parley P. Pratt, Toronto, Upper Canada, 10 May 1837, in JS Letterbook 2, pp. 62–63.

161. Contemporary records show that the Boynton & Johnson store was operating by November 1836 and closed by September 1837. Pratt's account book indicates that he often did business with the firm of Boynton & Johnson. (Pratt, Account Book and Autobiography, Oct. 1836–Jan. 1837, pp. 4–7, 9–10; Cowdery, Docket Book, 86, 98, 219, 224; see also Introduction to Part 5: 5 Oct. 1836–10 Apr. 1837, pp. 285–294 herein.)

162. Ames, Autobiography and Journal, [13]; Kimball, "History," 77–78.

troubles, since he had encouraged the Saints to develop Kirtland and they had consequently expected success in their commercial ventures. Describing the changes in Kirtland, Warren A. Cowdery contrasted the activity and industry of 1836, which brought "buyonant hope, lively anticipation and a firm confidence that our days of pinching adversity had passed by," with a "desponding gloom" in the summer of 1837, brought on by the "derangement of the currency, the loss of credit, the want of confidence" in the economy, and overextension of credit.[163]

The Kirtland Safety Society also caused financial concerns and uncertainty for Kirtland church members. By May 1837, amid the Panic of 1837, the society had produced none of the profits anticipated by its stockholders. In May and June, many of those stockholders transferred their stock shares or withdrew the money they had paid to the bank for stock, signaling their lack of confidence in the institution.[164] Although neither Johnson nor Orson Pratt were themselves stockholders in the Safety Society, they had personal and family connections to it, and its instability likely influenced their signing of the complaint featured here. Lyman Johnson had taken out loans from the institution, and his father, John Johnson, was one of the largest shareholders, owning three thousand shares of stock, and he had paid around six hundred dollars on his shares.[165] On 20 May, John Johnson and Lyman's sister Emily Johnson withdrew their money from the Safety Society. Orson Pratt's brother Parley P. Pratt likewise cut ties with the institution, selling his shares of stock to Lorenzo Young on 10 June 1837.[166]

As the Kirtland economy foundered, dissent among church members increased. On 23 May 1837 Parley P. Pratt accused JS of extortion and other dishonest business practices as Pratt's debts for land came due.[167] Lyman Johnson and Orson Pratt echoed these grievances in their 29 May complaint. The day before this complaint was signed, Sunday, 28 May, Wilford Woodruff described a "thick cloud of darkness" hanging over Kirtland and a meeting in the House of the Lord that ended with Warren Parrish speaking against JS.[168]

Parrish, who wrote out the charges against JS featured here, appears to have acted as a leader of those opposed to JS.[169] He may have been the one to instigate the charges against JS as well as charges brought the same day against two other members of the church presidency, Sidney Rigdon and Joseph Smith Sr.[170] Different individuals signed each complaint:

163. Editorial, *LDS Messenger and Advocate,* June 1837, 520–521.

164. On 22 May 1837, Wilford Woodruff, William F. Cahoon, and Sabra Granger each withdrew the same amount of money they had paid the society on their shares of stock. (Kirtland Safety Society, Stock Ledger, 45, 55, 219.)

165. Kirtland Safety Society, Discount and Loan Papers, JS Office Papers, CHL; Kirtland Safety Society, Stock Ledger, 151–152, 227–228.

166. Kirtland Safety Society, Stock Ledger, 47–48, 151, 227.

167. Letter from Parley P. Pratt, 23 May 1837, pp. 386–391 herein.

168. Woodruff, Journal, 28 May 1837; Mary Fielding, Kirtland, OH, to Mercy Fielding, [Upper Canada], ca. June 1837, Mary Fielding Smith, Collection, CHL; Historical Introduction to Letter from Abel Lamb and Others, ca. 28 May, pp. 392–393 herein.

169. Vilate Murray Kimball, for instance, wrote in a letter to Heber C. Kimball that Parrish was "the most rebelous" of the dissenters. (Vilate Murray Kimball, Kirtland Mills, OH, to Heber C. Kimball, Preston, England, 12 Sept. 1837, Heber C. Kimball, Collection, CHL.)

170. All three charges are in Warren Parrish's handwriting and are on a similar type of paper. (See Ecclesiastical Records, 1839–1846, Ohio Period, 29 May 1837, Newel K. Whitney, Papers, BYU.)

Charges against Joseph Smith. 29 May 1837. In spring 1837, dissent by church members against Joseph Smith reached its height, and Joseph Smith was formally charged with extortion, lying, and speaking disrespectfully of some of the brethren in the church leadership. The charges were written by Warren Parrish, leader of the dissenting Saints, and signed by Lyman Johnson and Orson Pratt, both of whom were members of the Quorum of the Twelve Apostles. Charges against Joseph Smith Preferred to Bishop's Council, 29 May 1837, Newel K. Whitney, Papers, L. Tom Perry Special Collections, Harold B. Lee Library, Brigham Young University, Provo, UT.

the charges against JS featured here were signed by Lyman Johnson and Orson Pratt, Parrish himself signed charges against Rigdon, and Luke Johnson signed the charges against Joseph Smith Sr. No extant documents record whether or not Kirtland bishop Newel K. Whitney acted on these charges, nor is it known if a council was convened to try JS or the others.

Document Transcript

To the Bishop & his council in Kirtland the Stake of Zion

We prefer the following charges against Pres. Joseph Smith Jr. viz. for lying & ~~misrepresenting~~ misrepresentation— also for extortion—[171] and for— speaking disrespectfully against his brethren behind their backs.—[172]

[173]Lyman. E. Johnson

Orson Pratt

Kirtland May 29th 1837

———— ❧ ————

Recommendation for Heber C. Kimball,
between 2 and 13 June 1837

Source Note

JS, Sidney Rigdon, and Hyrum Smith, Recommendation, for Heber C. Kimball, Kirtland Township, Geauga Co., OH, [between 2 and 13 June 1837]; handwriting of Orson Hyde; signatures of JS, Sidney Rigdon, and Hyrum Smith; one page; CHL. Includes docket.

Bifolium measuring 12½ × 8 inches (32 × 20 cm) when folded. The document has the square cut of manufactured paper and is ruled with thirty-nine blue-green lines, now faded. Pages 2 and 3 are blank. The recommendation was folded in two patterns. The first pattern is a double trifold in letter style; the document was then docketed by Orson Hyde and sealed with an adhesive wafer, which is now missing. In the second pattern, the recommendation in its folded state was folded in half. Sun exposure darkened the recto, and there is marked tearing at the folds.

Theresa R. Werner gave this recommendation to the Deseret Museum in 1912.[174] When the Deseret Museum closed its doors in July 1918, the holdings of the museum were dispersed among several repositories, including the LDS Church Museum (now Church History Museum) in Salt Lake City, Utah.[175] The recommendation was subsequently transferred to the Church Historian's Office.

---

171. See Historical Introduction to Letter from Parley P. Pratt, 23 May 1837, pp. 386–389 herein.

172. Lyman Johnson and Orson Pratt may be referring here to comments by JS and Sidney Rigdon about Parley P. Pratt and the letters he had written. In the high council meeting held the same day this complaint was signed, Parley objected to having JS or Rigdon involved with his case "in consequence of their having previously expressed their opinion against him." In that meeting, Rigdon confirmed that "he felt and said that Eld. Pratt has done wrong and that he still thought so." (Minute Book 1, 29 May 1837.)

173. TEXT: Likely signature of Lyman Johnson; signature of Orson Pratt.

174. Deseret Museum Catalog, 1891–1917, 331; "Deseret Museum's Riches Augmented," *Salt Lake Tribune*, 27 Nov. 1912, 16.

175. Eubanks, "The Deseret Museum," 374–375.

Historical Introduction

In June 1837, JS and the presidency of the church set apart the first contingent of missionaries assigned to preach in England, signaling the church's first foray into Europe. Heber C. Kimball of the Quorum of the Twelve Apostles was chosen to lead a group of men that eventually included fellow apostle Orson Hyde, Willard Richards, and four Canadian converts with English heritage. Sometime between 2 and 13 June 1837, Kimball was issued the following recommendation, labeled by a scribe as "letter of commendation," which appointed him to preach in that nation.

Though the church's earliest missionary efforts focused on the United States and Upper Canada, JS envisioned missionaries preaching well beyond the borders of these countries. On 3 November 1831, JS dictated a revelation that commanded the church to "send forth the Elders . . . unto the nations which are afar off unto the ilands of the sea send forth unto foreign lands."[176] After the Twelve Apostles were selected in February 1835, JS directed quorum members to "travel and preach among the Gentiles" and instructed them that they held "the keys of this ministry, to unlock the door of the kingdom of heaven unto all nations, and to preach the Gospel to every creature."[177] In January 1836, Warren Parrish recorded JS's account of a vision in which he "saw the 12, apostles of the Lamb, who are now upon the earth . . . in foreign lands."[178]

JS and other church leaders came to see England as the first logical extension of missionary efforts overseas, in part because of the conversion of English immigrants in Upper Canada. While in the House of the Lord on 8 February 1836, apostle William Smith reported seeing "a vision of the Twelve & Seven in council together in old England & prophecied that a great work would be done by them in the old countries & God was already beginning to work in the hearts of the p[e]ople."[179] In his autobiography, Parley P. Pratt recalled that in 1836, Heber C. Kimball gave him a blessing in which he prophesied that Pratt would preach in Toronto, Canada, and there find "a people prepared for the fulness of the gospel." Kimball's blessing predicted that many would join the church because of Pratt's efforts, and "from the things growing out of this mission, shall the fulness of the gospel spread into England, and cause a great work to be done in that land."[180] Shortly after the dedication of the House of the Lord in late March 1836, Pratt set off for Toronto. From April to September 1836, he preached in Upper Canada and baptized many people, among whom were several recent immigrants from England, including Joseph, Mary, and Mercy Fielding and John and Leonora Taylor.[181]

---

176. Revelation, 3 Nov. 1831, in *JSP*, D2:117 [D&C 133:8].

177. Minutes and Discourses, 27 Feb. 1835–A, in *JSP*, D4:254. Following this admonition, the Twelve preached and conducted church conferences in New York, New England, and Upper Canada during summer 1835. When the apostles were ordained and blessed in February 1835, many of those blessings included direction for the apostles to preach to people in "all nations, kingdoms and tongues." Heber C. Kimball's blessing specifically stated that "many millions may be converted by his instrumentality." (Esplin and Nielsen, "Record of the Twelve, 1835," 4–52; Minutes and Blessings, 14–15 Feb. 1835, in *JSP*, D4:230, 229.)

178. Visions, 21 Jan. 1836 [D&C 137], p. 159 herein.

179. JS, Journal, 6 Feb. 1836, in *JSP*, J1:182.

180. Pratt, *Autobiography*, 141–142.

181. Pratt, *Autobiography*, 164–165. Other Canadian converts included Isaac Russell, John Goodson,

By 1837, there appears to have been an expectation among some members of the Twelve that a mission to England was imminent. Parley P. Pratt had asserted that the church "shall soon take our several journeys to Europe, Asia, Africa, and the Islands of the sea."[182] In late March or early April 1837, Pratt returned to visit recently baptized church members in Canada. According to Joseph Fielding's account, "Word came from the Church in Kirtland, by Elder Parley P. Pratt, that the way was opened for them to go to other nations and it was determined that some should go to England as soon as possible." In his autobiography, Pratt recalled that at this time, "Several of the Canadian Elders felt a desire to go on a mission to their friends in that country."[183] Upon hearing that Pratt had left Kirtland for Canada and "intended to leave there soon for England," Thomas B. Marsh and David W. Patten, the two senior members of the Quorum of the Twelve Apostles, hastily wrote to Pratt on 10 May 1837. Marsh and Patten implored him to delay his journey until the quorum could meet together to address the difficulties among them and to coordinate a mission to England.[184] Pratt returned to Kirtland in mid-May, but he did not participate in the first mission to England.[185]

Sometime between 1 and 4 June 1837, JS approached Heber C. Kimball in the House of the Lord and informed him that he had received a revelation that Kimball should "gow to England to open the dore of procklamation to that nation and to he[e]d the same."[186] Kimball later wrote, "[I] believed the time would soon come when I should take leave of my own country and lift up my voice to other nations, yet, it never occurred to my mind, that I should be one of the first, commissioned to preach . . . on the shores of Europe."[187] According to his journal, Kimball then met JS, Sidney Rigdon, and Hyrum Smith at a conference at Rigdon's house, where the presidency "lade thare hand[s] on my

---

and John Snider, who, like Joseph Fielding, would later proselytize in England with Kimball. (Givens and Grow, *Apostle Paul of Mormonism*, 92; JS, Journal, 26 Mar. 1842, 23 Jan. 1843, in *JSP*, J2:47, 249.)

182. Pratt, "An Epistle Written by an Elder of the Church," 1, 6.

183. Fielding, Journal, CHL; Pratt, *Autobiography*, 183. Many Canadian converts had written enthusiastic letters to friends and relatives in England about their newfound faith. Joseph Fielding wrote several letters to his brother, Reverend James Fielding, who, in turn, read Joseph's letters to his congregation. Though James Fielding did not convert to Mormonism, several members of his congregation were baptized shortly after Joseph Fielding and others arrived in July 1837. John Taylor also communicated with a clergyman friend in England prior to his leaving for England in 1839. (Fielding, Journal, 9, 16; Joseph Fielding, Preston, England, to Mary Fielding and Mercy Fielding, [Kirtland, OH], 2 Oct. 1836, Mary Fielding Smith, Collection, CHL; John Taylor, Toronto, Upper Canada, to "Rev. and Dear Sir," [England], 3 May 1837, in *LDS Messenger and Advocate*, June 1837, 3:513–516.)

184. Thomas B. Marsh and David W. Patten, Far West, MO, to Parley P. Pratt, Toronto, Upper Canada, 10 May 1837, JS Letterbook 2, pp. 62–63. For more on the disaffection of some members of the Quorum of the Twelve Apostles, see Introduction to Part 6: 20 Apr.–14 Sept. 1837, pp. 363–366 herein.

185. After returning from Canada, Pratt wrote an angry letter to JS in which he accused him of fostering a spirit of financial speculation and selling land at inflated prices. (Letter from Parley P. Pratt, 23 May 1837, pp. 386–391 herein).

186. Heber C. Kimball, 1837–1838 Journal, 3–4, CHL. Kimball's journal dates this conversation to 4 June; in a reminiscent account published in 1858, Kimball wrote that the conversation occurred "about the first day of June." (Kimball, "Synopsis of the History of Heber Chase Kimball," *Deseret News*, 14 Apr. 1858, 33.)

187. Kimball, "Journal and Record of Heber Chase Kimball," 87.

head and set me a part for this mission and dedicated me to the Lord."[188] Orson Hyde entered the room as Kimball was being set apart and expressed a strong desire to accompany his fellow apostle to England; both he and Joseph Fielding (who had recently come to Kirtland from Canada) were then set apart.[189] Willard Richards, who returned from a mission to the East on 11 June, was set apart the next day to accompany the others and also received a recommendation, which closely resembles the recommendation featured here.[190]

Kimball, Hyde, Richards, and Fielding left Kirtland on 13 June 1837 and arrived in New York City on 21 June. In New York City they met up with Canadian converts Isaac Russell, John Goodson, and John Snider. The group sailed from New York harbor on 1 July 1837 and arrived in Liverpool, England, roughly nineteen days later.[191]

Document Transcript

At a Conference of the Elders and heads of the Church of "Latter Day Saints" held in Kirtland, Geauga County, Ohio, on the Second day of June[192] in the year of Our Lord, One Thousand Eight Hundred and Thirty Seven, Elder Heber C. Kimball, the Bearer of this, was unanimously appointed, set apart and ordained to go on a mission to England to proclaim the Gospel of Jesus Christ to the people of that Nation as it is believed and practised by us.

From the long acquaintance which we have had with, this, our worthy Brother, his integrity and zeal in the cause of truth, we do most cheerfully and confidently reccommend him to all candid and upright people as a servant of God and a faithful minister of Jesus Christ.

We do furthermore beseech all people who have an opportunity of hearing, this, our brother declare the doctrine believed by us, to listen with attention to the words of his mouth.

---

188. Heber C. Kimball, 1837–1838 Journal, 3–4, CHL.

189. Kimball, "Journal and Record of Heber Chase Kimball," 88–89. According to Kimball's journal, Isaac Russell, John Goodson, and John Snider were also set apart on this day, though they were not in Kirtland at the time. (Fielding, Journal, 9, 16; Heber C. Kimball, 1837–1838 Journal, 3–4, CHL.)

190. Richards, Journal, 11 June 1837; Willard Richards, Recommendation, ca. 11–13 June 1837, JS Collection, CHL; on Richards's previous mission, see Historical Introduction to Power of Attorney to Oliver Granger, 27 Sept. 1837, pp. 458–459 herein.

191. Heber C. Kimball, 1837–1838 Journal, 7–11, CHL; Kimball, "Journal and Record of Heber Chase Kimball," 87–94.

192. There is no other record of a formal meeting being held in Kirtland on 2 June 1837. This may refer to what Kimball later described as a "confrence at Elders Rigdons" where JS, Rigdon, and Hyrum Smith set Kimball apart for the mission. The journal indicates that the conference occurred on the same day JS informed Kimball of the mission to England. (Heber C. Kimball, 1837–1838 Journal, 3–4, CHL; Heber C. Kimball, "Synopsis of the History of Heber Chase Kimball," *Deseret News,* 14 Apr. 1858, 33.)

¹⁹³**J Smith Jr**
Sidney Rigdon ⎫ Presideing Elders of the Church of
Hyrum Smith ⎬ Latter Day Saints

[p. [1]]

Letter of Commendation Given to Heber C Kimball

———— ᴄᴩ ————

Letter from William W. Phelps, 7 July 1837

Source Note

William W. Phelps, Letter, Far West, Caldwell Co., MO, to JS, [Kirtland Township, Geauga Co., OH], 7 July 1837. Featured version published in "Communications," Latter Day Saints' Messenger and Advocate, *July 1837, 3:529. For more information on* Latter Day Saints' Messenger and Advocate, *see Source Notes for Multiple-Entry Documents, p. 527 herein.*

Historical Introduction

In August 1836, William W. Phelps and John Whitmer, the two counselors to David Whitmer in the Missouri church presidency, purchased a one-mile-square plot of land, or 640 acres, near Shoal Creek, as the town site for Far West. They anticipated it would become a gathering place for the Latter-day Saints, and they hoped it would serve as the government seat of the proposed Caldwell County, intended for Mormon settlement. Some Missourians saw such a county as the solution to their Mormon problem; they sought to avoid conflicts similar to those they had previously encountered in Jackson and Clay counties by creating a separate county for Mormons. As Latter-day Saint David Pettegrew recounted, "They came to the conclusion to give us Caldwell County and that we should live there by Ourselves."[194] In late 1836, Alexander Doniphan helped steer a bill through the Missouri legislature that created Caldwell and Daviess counties.[195] William W. Phelps wrote

---

193. TEXT: Signatures of JS, Sidney Rigdon, and Hyrum Smith.

194. Pettegrew, "History," 26. A later history likened the creation of Caldwell County as a new geopolitical jurisdiction on which to place Mormons to reservations created for American Indians. Segregating the Mormons worked, according to the later history, and trouble only erupted when they left county boundaries. ("Mormonism," *Kansas City Daily Journal,* 12 June 1881, 1; Stevens, *Centennial History of Missouri,* 108.)

195. Minute Book 2, 25 July 1836; "History of Thomas Baldwin Marsh," 5 [draft 4], Historian's Office, Histories of the Twelve, 1856–1858, 1861, CHL; *Laws of the State of Missouri,* 38–42, 46–47, 155, 188, 204; *Journal of the House of Representatives* [1835], 86, 188, 219; *History of Caldwell and Livingston Counties, Missouri,* 103–105. Latter-day Saints purchased land in the area beginning in spring 1836; for example, land was purchased for Hyrum Smith in May, June, September, and November; and for JS and Oliver Cowdery in June and September. By the end of September 1836, William W. Phelps and John Whitmer had purchased a total of 1,000 acres of land in what would become Caldwell County, including the 640 acres designated as the town plot. (Application for Land Patent, 22 June 1836, pp. 253–258 herein; Johnson and Romig, *Index to Early Caldwell County,* 47, 144–145, 202, 232–233.)

the letter featured here in July 1837 to inform JS of the progress in founding and developing the new community of Far West.

Mormons had begun settling in Far West and nearby areas in September and October 1836, and the population grew rapidly. In an October 1836 letter, Ambrose Palmer and Thomas Gordon wrote that "settlement is increasing very fast" and that "several hundred families" lived in the area.[196] By April 1837, Whitmer and Phelps had created a plat for the town and selected a location for a temple to be built there; the plat was eventually accepted by the Missouri high council, though not without controversy. The high council felt Whitmer and Phelps had gone beyond their authority in planning the town, and they objected to the two men profiting from the sale of land. It was decided that the bishop, Edward Partridge, should take responsibility for the plat and for the distribution of lands in Far West.[197] After the high council addressed the controversy, plans to build a temple moved forward. As Phelps reported in this letter, in early July they held a groundbreaking ceremony for the new House of the Lord.

Phelps's letter was printed in the July issue of the *Latter Day Saints' Messenger and Advocate*. The newspaper's printers typeset the date of the letter as 7 May 1837, but that was a mistake; the content of the letter itself indicates a July 1837 context. The church newspaper corrected its mistake in the August 1837 issue, giving the accurate date of 7 July 1837.[198]

Document Transcript

FAR WEST. May [July] 7, 1837.

DEAR BROTHER IN THE LORD,

Permit me to drop you a few lines to show you our progress temporally and spiritually. A multiplicity of business has prevented me from writing much the year past, but the greatness of our doings and the importance of the occasion require a recital to you for your consolation.— Monday the 3d of July, was a great and glorious day in Far West; more than fifteen hundred saints assembled in this place, and, at 1/2 past 8 in the morning, after a prayer, singing, and an address, proceeded to break the ground for the Lord's House;[199]

---

196. "Interesting Letter," *LDS Messenger and Advocate,* Dec. 1836, 3:428–429.

197. Minute Book 2, 7 Apr. 1837; "Description of Far West Plat," 1837, copy, Brigham Young University and Church History and Doctrine Department, Church History Project Collection, CHL; Johnson and Romig, *Index to Early Caldwell County,* xiii; Edward Partridge to John Whitmer and William W. Phelps, Bond, 17 May 1837, John Whitmer Family Papers, CHL; Edward Partridge and Lydia Clisbee Partridge to John Whitmer and William W. Phelps, Mortgage, 17 May 1837, John Whitmer Family Papers, CHL.

198. "Erratum," *LDS Messenger and Advocate,* Aug. 1837, 3:560.

199. David Whitmer, John Whitmer, and William W. Phelps, the Missouri presidency, met with other church leaders and Saints in Far West on 15 November 1836. At that meeting they selected "Jacob Whitmer, Elisha H. Groves, and George M. Hinkle for a building committee to assist the Presidency to build the house of the Lord in said City." On 7 April 1837, a council consisting of the Missouri presidency, high council, and bishopric accepted that committee to build the House of the Lord and appointed the

the day was beautiful, the Spirit of the Lord was with us, a cellar for this great edifice, 110 long by 80 broad was nearly finished: on Tuesday the fourth, we had a large meeting and several of the Missourians were baptized: Our meetings, held in the open prairie, or, in fact larger than they were in Kirtland when I was there. We have more or less to bless, confirm and, baptize every Sabbath.

This same day our school section was sold at auction, and although entirely a prairie, it brought, on a years credit, from 3 ½ to $10,20 an acre, making our first school fund $5070!![200] Land can not be had round town now much less than $10 per acre.

Our numbers increase daily, and, notwithstanding the season has been cold and backward, no one has lacked a meal, or went hungry. Provisions to be sure have risen, but not as high as our accounts say they are abroad.

Public notice has been given by the *mob* in Davi[es]s county, north of us, for the Mormons to leave that county by the first of August, and go into Caldwell.[201] Our enemies will not slumber, till Satan knows the bigness of his lot.

Our town gains some, we have about one hundred buildings, 8 of which are stores. If the brethren abroad are wise, and will come on with means, and help enter the land and populate the Co. and build the Lord's House, we shall soon have one of the most precious spots on the Globe. God grant that it may be so. Of late we receive but little news from you: and we think much of that is exaggerated.

As ever,

W[illiam] W. PHELPS.

---

presidency "to superintend the building of the House of the Lord in this City Far West and receive Revelations Visions &c concerning said house." Some questioned the propriety of locating a place for a temple, breaking ground on the site, and receiving revelations for the House of the Lord without the approval of JS and the church presidency. The matter was ultimately resolved in November 1837. (Minute Book 2, 15 Nov. 1836 and 7 Apr. 1837; Revelation, 4 Sept. 1837, pp. 431–433 herein; Minutes, 6 Nov. 1837, pp. 464–468 herein; Minutes, 10 Nov. 1837, pp. 472–476 herein.)

200. Early Missouri settlers regarded prairie lands as less fertile, and therefore less valuable, than wooded land near the rivers. The land to which Phelps refers was the section designated as "school land" in the township in which Far West was located. When offering federal lands for sale, the federal government gave states the land in each sixteenth section of every surveyed township to benefit public education in the various counties. The proceeds from its sale were to support public education locally. In Far West, section 16 was located a half-mile west of the town center. (Johnson and Romig, *Index to Early Caldwell County Land Records,* 11; An Act Concerning the Lands to Be Granted to the State of Missouri, for the Purposes of Education, and Other Public Uses [3 Mar. 1823], *Public Statutes at Large,* 17th Cong., 2nd Sess., chap. 69, p. 787.)

201. James B. Turner of Daviess County, Missouri, wrote a notice in summer 1837 that Mormons settling north of Grand River would be driven out. William Bowman, John Brassfield, and Adam Black were among a self-described "mob party" that "went to see the mormons" sometime that summer and demanded that they leave. (Johnson, *Mormon Redress Petitions,* 746–749.)

N. B. Please say in your Messenger: "A Post office has been established at *Far West*, Caldwell County, Missouri.[202] Our brethren will now have a chance to write to their friends."

———— ❧ ————

Mortgage to Mead, Stafford & Co., 11 July 1837

Source Note

JS, Sidney Rigdon, Oliver Cowdery, Hyrum Smith, Reynolds Cahoon, and Jared Carter, Mortgage for property in Kirtland Township, Geauga Co., OH, to Zalmon H. Mead, Robert Mead, and Jonas Stafford of Mead, Stafford & Co., 11 July 1837; handwriting of Reuben Hitchcock and Ralph Cowles; signatures of JS, Sidney Rigdon, Hyrum Smith, Reynolds Cahoon, Jared Carter, and Oliver Cowdery; three pages; Hiram Kimball Collection, CHL. Includes seals and dockets.

Two leaves, each measuring 12⅜ × 7⅞ inches (31 × 20 cm). Both leaves contain thirty-eight lines, now faded. A handwritten seal follows each of the signatures. Different ink flow beginning at the signatures indicates the document may have been composed in more than one session. Four adhesive wafer halves attach the leaves together at the top. The document was folded in a parallel fold twice and docketed three times by Ralph Cowles. The document was subsequently folded in half again. Complete tears at the folds were conserved in 2013.

This manuscript, along with other personal and institutional papers Oliver Granger kept, were inherited by Hiram Kimball, husband of Granger's daughter Sarah Granger Kimball. Hiram Kimball's papers and other manuscripts were in the possession of Preston W. Kimball, a descendant of Hiram's brother Phineas, until they were given to LeRoy L. Kimball (no relation), founder of Nauvoo Restoration, Inc. The Hiram Kimball Collection was donated to the Church History Library in 2013.[203]

Historical Introduction

On 11 July 1837, JS, Sidney Rigdon, Hyrum Smith, Reynolds Cahoon, Jared Carter, and Oliver Cowdery signed the agreement featured here, mortgaging the House of the Lord in Kirtland, Ohio, to Zalmon H. Mead, Jonas Stafford, and Robert W. Mead, the principals of the New York mercantile firm Mead, Stafford & Co.[204] JS and his associates had previously done business with Mead, Stafford & Co. in October 1836, when their own mercantile firms—Rigdon, Smith & Cowdery and Cahoon, Carter & Co.—purchased goods in New York City to be sold in their stores in and around Kirtland.[205]

---

202. This information had been published in an earlier correspondence in the *Messenger and Advocate*. (See "From Our Elders and Correspondents Abroad," *LDS Messenger and Advocate*, June 1837, 3:519.)

203. Hiram Kimball Collection, 1830–1910, CHL.

204. Mead, Stafford & Co. was a wholesale grocery and commission business composed of Jonas Stafford and brothers Zalmon and Robert Mead. The firm was in operation from 1834 to 1839. In 1839, Jonas Stafford left the partnership, and Zalmon and Robert formed a new firm named Z. & R. Mead, which they ran from 1839 to 1841. (Mead, *History and Genealogy of the Mead Family,* 377; "Co-Partnership Notice," *New-York Commercial Advertiser,* 4 Feb. 1839, [4]; Longworth, *Longworth's American Almanac* [1834], 543; [1837], 429; [1839], 455; [1841], 490.)

205. Mead, Stafford & Co. to Rigdon, Smith & Cowdery, Invoice, New York City, 8 Oct. 1836, JS Office Papers, CHL; Mead, Stafford & Co. to Cahoon, Carter & Co., Invoice, New York City, 8 Oct. 1836,

The 11 July 1837 mortgage was written by Painesville, Ohio, lawyer Reuben Hitchcock, who was likely acting on behalf of Mead, Stafford & Co.[206] Earlier mortgage agreements involving JS had been large land purchases and had given JS and his cofinancers access to the land before they had completed payments on it.[207] In the case of the agreement featured here, the House of the Lord, or temple, was mortgaged to Mead, Stafford & Co., but JS and the church retained use of the building as they paid off the mortgage. The land on which the House of the Lord was built was also involved in the mortgage agreement, but because JS had transferred the title from himself to William Marks in April 1837, a separate deed was made on 11 July 1837 to convey the land title from Marks to Mead, Stafford & Co. The terms of that deed were dependent on the mortgage agreement featured here.[208]

As part of the mortgage agreement, JS and his five cosigners sold the Kirtland temple to Mead, Stafford & Co., who held it as collateral for the debts owed the company. In order to pay off the debt and regain the title to the House of the Lord, JS and the five other men signed three promissory notes, due annually to Mead, Stafford & Co. on 8 July from 1838 to 1840 and amounting to $4,393.77, not including interest.[209] The sum of the promissory notes specified in the assignment was not equivalent to the original $4,500 that the firm agreed to provide JS and his five cosigners, but the addition of interest would have increased the amount due on the promissory notes beyond the $4,500.[210] According to the agreement, if JS and his associates paid these three notes, the sale and

---

JS Office Papers, CHL; Mead, Stafford & Co. to H. Smith & Co., Invoice, New York City, 8 Oct. 1836, JS Office Papers, CHL.

206. Reuben Hitchcock was born in 1806 to Peter Hitchcock and Nabbie Cook. He moved to Painesville, Geauga County, Ohio, and was admitted to the Ohio bar around 1831. He served as the prosecuting attorney in Geauga County in 1835 and 1838–1839 and was involved in legal proceedings against JS during that time. On 11 July 1837, Hitchcock and Eli T. Wilder began advertising their partnership in a legal practice. (*History of Geauga and Lake Counties,* 23, 61–62; "Death of Judge Reuben Hitchcock of Painesville," *Painesville [OH] Telegraph,* 13 Dec. 1883, [3]; "Law Notice," *Painesville Telegraph,* 21 July 1837, [2].)

207. For a contemporary definition of mortgages and an earlier JS mortgage, see Historical Introduction to Mortgage to Peter French, 5 Oct. 1836, pp. 294–295 herein.

208. Geauga Co., OH, Deed Records, 1795–1921, vol. 24, pp. 211–213, 11 July 1837, microfilm 20,240, U.S. and Canada Record Collection, FHL; see also Historical Introduction to Deed to William Marks, 10 Apr. 1837, pp. 358–359 herein. Marks's willingness to sell the title to Mead, Stafford & Co. suggests that in April 1837 he was likely acting as an agent for JS and holding the right to the land rather than purchasing the land for his own use. The printing office and the church newspaper it printed, the *Latter Day Saints' Messenger and Advocate,* were also transferred to Marks, as JS and Rigdon's agent, in April 1837. (See Historical Introduction to Deed to William Marks, 10 Apr. 1837, pp. 358–359 herein; and "Notice," *LDS Messenger and Advocate,* Apr. 1837, 3:496.)

209. Two of the promissory notes are extant and are held in private possession. Photographs of the notes show no endorsements or cancellations to indicate any payments were made. The note due on 8 July 1839 has court information recorded on the back of the note relating to possible litigation in 1841 and 1849.

210. According to debts recorded in Willard Richards's 1837 journal, the three firms owed Mead, Stafford & Co. at least $3,761.90 by March 1837. An additional debt listed in the journal, for $404.47, is not attributed to a specific firm but could account for additional debts to Mead, Stafford & Co., which would bring the total owed to $4,166.37. If Mead, Stafford & Co. forgave a general amount rather than a specific debt, they would be making a profit from the three promissory notes rather than agreeing to a deficit. (Richards, Journal, 1837; Geauga Co., OH, Deed Records, 1795–1921, vol. 24, pp. 211–214, 11 July 1837, microfilm 20,240, U.S. and Canada Record Collection, FHL.)

Mortgage to Mead, Stafford & Co. 11 July 1837. To offset debts owed by their mercantile firms, Joseph Smith, Sidney Rigdon, Oliver Cowdery, Reynolds Cahoon, Jared Carter, and Hyrum Smith signed an agreement on 11 July 1837 mortgaging the House of the Lord in Kirtland, Ohio, to the New York mercantile firm Mead, Stafford & Co. Using their greatest asset, the object of the past four years of labor and the spiritual core of the Latter-day Saint community, as collateral demonstrated the desperate financial situation in which Joseph Smith and other church leaders found themselves. Handwriting of Reuben Hitchcock with original signatures. Mortgage to Mead, Stafford & Co., 11 July 1837, Hiram Kimball Collection, Church History Library, Salt Lake City.

assignment of the House of the Lord and the land it was built on would become void. If they failed to pay the three promissory notes, then Mead, Stafford & Co. could take possession of the edifice and everything therein after 8 July 1840.

The first promissory note, which was due on 8 July 1838, appears to have not been paid. This meant that Mead, Stafford & Co. could bring a lawsuit against JS and the other men on the outstanding debt.[211] The firm did not do so, however, and Oliver Granger in his role as an agent for the church continued trying to resolve the debt. According to a May 1841 letter from JS to Granger, the mortgage for the Kirtland House of the Lord appeared to have been resolved by that time.[212]

Document Transcript

/[213]Know all men by these presents, that we Joseph Smith junior Sidney Rigdon, Oliver Cowdery, Hyram [Hyrum] Smith, Reynolds Cahoon, and Jared Carter of Kirtland, County of Geauga and State of Ohio, in consideration of the sum of four thousand five hundred Dollars received to our full satisfaction of Zalmon H. Mead, Jonas Stafford, and Robert W. Mead merchants of the City of New York trading under the name and firm of Mead Stafford & Co, do hereby bargain, sell, assign and transfer to the said Zalmon H. Mead, Jonas Stafford, and Robert W. Mead merchants of the City of New York trading under the name and firm of Mead Stafford & Co as aforesaid, their heirs and assigns, all the right, title, and interest, which we, or either, or any of us leave in and to the Stone temple ~~in~~ situate in Kirtland aforesaid, called also the "Chapel house" and in and to the land on which the same is situate, ~~and~~ including and hereby expressly selling and conveying to the said Zalmon H. Mead, Jonas Stafford, and Robert W. Mead their heirs and assigns all the right, title, and interest which we or either of us have in and to any and all furniture used in and about said house, and in and to all ancient curiosities, writings paintings ~~or~~ & sculpture, therein contained

211. Two bills sent to JS in 1838, one from the legal partnership of Perkins & Osborn and another by Hitchcock & Wilder, provide evidence of a possible lawsuit. The promissory notes to Mead, Stafford & Co. are listed as outstanding debts. One of the bills states that "no suit had been brought." (Perkins & Osborn to JS and Others, Bill, ca. 29 Oct. 1838; Hitchcock & Wilder to JS and Sidney Rigdon, Bill, between 9 July and 5 Nov. 1838, JS Collection, CHL.)

212. JS, Nauvoo, IL, to Oliver Granger, 4 May 1841, copy, JS Collection, CHL. In October 1843, when JS compiled his outstanding debts in order to file for bankruptcy in Illinois, he did not include the promissory notes given to Mead, Stafford & Co., suggesting he considered the debt paid. However, the verso of one of the promissory notes due in 1838 and 1839 bears court filing notations dated April 1849, which suggests it was brought as evidence of an outstanding debt against JS's estate. (William Marks to JS, Deed, 11 Feb. 1841; JS, "Schedule of Debts," ca. 4–6 Oct. 1843, CCLA; JS and Others to Mead, Stafford & Co., Promissory Note, 11 July 1837, copy, CHL.)

213. TEXT: Reuben Hitchcock handwriting begins.

and an kept,²¹⁴ and including also, and hereby expressly ~~understood~~ selling and conveying to said Zalmon ꝑ H. Mead, Jonas Stafford, and Robert W. Mead ⟨any and⟩ all the debts in any manner due and owing to us or either or any of us for services renderd, materials furnished, or advances of money or other property made for the building & ⟨furnishing⟩ of said house, and particularly a debt of about ~~six~~ ⟨sixteen⟩ thousand Dollars due said Hyram Smith, Reynolds Cahoon, and Jared Carter for advances made towards the building & furnishing of said house— To have and to hold all the premises aforesaid to the said Zalmon H. Mead, Jonas Stafford, and Robert W. Mead, their heirs or assigns forever ⟨to their own proper use & behoof forever—⟩ ~~On the~~

The condition of the above instrument is such that whereas we the said Joseph Smith junior, Sidney Rigdon, Oliver Cowdery, Hyram Smith, Reynolds Cahoon, and Jared ⟨Carter⟩ have this day executed and delivered to the said Zalmon ꝑ²¹⁵ H. Mead, Jonas Stafford, and Robert W. Mead our three joint and several promissory notes all duly executed by us and all bearing even date herewith [p. [1]] and all payable to said Zalmon ~~W~~ H. Mead, Jonas Stafford and Robert W. Mead (by the name & description of their said firm of Mead Stafford & Co) or order, one for the sum of thirteen hundred and seventy seven dollars and one cent due on the eighhth day of July AD ~~1837~~ 1838, one for the sum of fourteen hundred and sixty four Dollars and fifty four cents due on the eighth day of July AD 1839, and one other for the sum of fifteen hundred and fifty two Dollars and twenty two cents due on the eighth day of July AD 1840, now if we the said Joseph Smith junior, Sidney Rigdon, Oliver Cowdery, Hyram Smith, Reynolds Cahoon, and Jared Carter, or either ⟨of us⟩ shall well and truly pay the aforesaid notes according to the tenor and effect thereof ~~to~~ at the time the same become due, to the said Zalmon ꝑ H. Mead, Jonas Stafford, and Robert W. Mead, their heirs, executors, administrators or assigns, then the above ~~obliga~~ sale and assignment to be void, otherwise to remain in full force and virtue in law; and it is further ⟨expressly⟩ understood that the said Zalmon Є H. Mead, Jonas Stafford, and Robert [W.] Mead²¹⁶ are not to take possession of, or dispose of the property above described until the said eighth day of July AD 1840 when said last mentioned

---

214. The ancient curiosities and writings likely included the Egyptian mummies and papyri. The mummies were displayed in the upper rooms of the Kirtland House of the Lord for a time. Although the mortgage agreement initially included the Egyptian artifacts, an addendum signed by JS, found at the end of this featured text, excluded them from the mortgage. (Woodruff, Journal, 25 Nov. 1836; for more on the Egyptian artifacts, see Book of Abraham Manuscript, ca. Early July–ca. Nov. 1835–A [Abraham 1:4–2:6], pp. 69–80 herein.)

215. TEXT: Or "Є".

216. TEXT: "Robert [*page torn*] Mead".

note becomes due, provided however & it[217] is expressly stipulated, that in case we the said Joseph Smith junior, Sidney Rigdon, Oliver Cowdery, Hyram Smith, Reynolds Cahoon, ~~or~~ & Jared Carter, or either, or any of us shall ⟨at any time⟩ attempt to remove, or sell, or dispose of any of the property aforesaid, then it shall be competent for the said Zalmon C[218] H. Mead, Jonas Stafford, and Robert W. Mead, ~~forthwith~~ a[n]d[219] they are hereby authorized & empowered forthwith to take possession of, and sell, ~~and~~ convey and dispose of all ~~the~~ and singular the property rights and credits aforesaid, in such manner, and to such persons, and on such terms as they shall see fit— In witness whereof, we have hereunto set our hands and seals this eleventh day of July AD 1837—

[220]**Joseph Smith Jr** Seal[221] [p. [2]]

Sidney Rigdon Seal

Hyrum Smith Seal

Reynolds Cahoon Seal

Jared Carter Seal

Oliver Cowdery Seal [*6 lines blank*]

The mummies and ancient ~~mummies~~ ⟨writings⟩ now in said temple are ~~now~~ excepted from the above assignment because they are not owned by me or any of the other makers of the foregoing instrument—[222]

Kirtland July 11th 1837—

Joseph Smith Jr S[eal][223] [*5 lines blank*]

Whereas there is a doubt whether by the terms of the above assignment, the said makers of said assignment are ⟨not⟩ precluded from giving to any other

---

217. TEXT: Possibly "is it".

218. TEXT: Or "P".

219. TEXT: "a[*page torn*]d".

220. TEXT: Signatures of JS, Sidney Rigdon, Hyrum Smith, Reynolds Cahoon, Jared Carter, and Oliver Cowdery.

221. TEXT: Each "Seal" is enclosed in a hand-drawn representation of a seal. Handwriting of Reuben Hitchcock.

222. This addendum to the mortgage agreement was also written by Reuben Hitchcock on 11 July. The addendum may have been added because JS's ownership of the Egyptian artifacts was uncertain; at this time he may have been a partial owner or transferred his ownership to someone else. When the mummies were initially purchased from Michael Chandler, Joseph Coe provided promissory notes in his name to Chandler for $2,400. A later agreement, not extant, stipulated that an S. Andrews and JS would provide $800 each to Coe to offset the amount he paid Chandler. In 1844, Coe claimed that JS had not fully paid his portion of the contract and that he was owed an additional $100 by JS. In reply, JS stated that he had paid the $800 as agreed but did not indicate when. (Joseph Coe, Kirtland, OH, to JS, Nauvoo, IL, 1 Jan. 1844, JS Collection, CHL; JS, Nauvoo, IL, to Joseph Coe, Kirtland, OH, 18 Jan. 1844, copy, JS Collection, CHL.)

223. TEXT: Original signature of JS. "S" is enclosed in a hand-drawn representation of a seal. Handwriting of Reuben Hitchcock.

person or persons a mortgage on the above premises, we hereby declare that it is not ~~our~~ the intention of the above consignment that any mortgage ~~of~~ given by said makers on the same property shall ~~not~~ be construed as a sale or disposition of said property so as to authorize us to take possession of and sell, dispose of & convey the same, prior to said eighth day of July AD ~~1837~~ 1840, but we do not hereby waive any legal preference which the above sale & assignment gives us ~~over~~ to any subsequent mortgages of the same property— Kirtland July 11th 1837—

/[224]Mead Stafford & Co [p. [3]]

/[225]Joseph Smith Jr. & Others
To
Mead Stafford & Cº

Assignment

Recd July 14th. 1837 at 9 O.Clock PM & Recorded July 20th. AD 1837 in Geauga County Records Book 'X" pages 213 & 214
Ralph Cowles— Recorder
F 7 —

———— ℰℐ ————

Revelation, 23 July 1837 [D&C 112]

Source Note

Revelation, Kirtland Township, Geauga Co., OH, 23 July 1837. Featured version copied [ca. 30 Aug. 1838] in JS, Journal, Mar.–Sept. 1838, pp. 72–74; handwriting of James Mulholland; CHL. For more information on JS, Journal, Mar.–Sept. 1838, see Source Notes for Multiple-Entry Documents, p. 525 herein.

Historical Introduction

On 23 July 1837, JS dictated the revelation featured here to Thomas B. Marsh, the president of the Quorum of the Twelve Apostles. It contained directions for Marsh personally as well as for the Twelve generally.

Apostles Marsh, David W. Patten, and William Smith traveled from Far West, Missouri, to Kirtland, Ohio, in the summer of 1837 to address quorum members' dissent against JS and seek to unify the Twelve.[226] To these ends, Marsh and Patten called for a

---

224. TEXT: Reuben Hitchcock handwriting ends; unidentified scribe begins. The fact that this signature for Mead, Stafford & Co. appears in different handwriting than the rest of the document suggests that there was a representative of the firm present to sign the agreement on 11 July 1837. In contrast to other signatures, no seal is included.

225. TEXT: Unidentified handwriting ends; Ralph Cowles begins.

226. Mary Fielding, Kirtland, OH, to Mercy Fielding Thompson, [Upper Canada], 8 July 1837, Mary Fielding Smith, Collection, CHL; Julia and Mary Jane Smith, Kirtland, OH, to Elias Smith,

council meeting of the entire Quorum of the Twelve on 24 July 1837.[227] Marsh, Patten, and Smith arrived in Kirtland by 8 July, but they found that JS and the church presidency had sent two of the Twelve, Heber C. Kimball and Orson Hyde, to proselytize in England in mid-June.[228] Marsh saw it as his responsibility to direct members of the Twelve to preach in foreign lands—he had corrected Parley P. Pratt for planning to undertake a mission to England in May—and he may have harbored some frustration that he was not consulted regarding the mission.[229] The 23 July revelation assured Marsh that he was chosen to lead the Twelve and to spread the gospel "abroad among all nations" but made it clear that he should do so under the direction of the First Presidency.

The revelation also addressed dissent, which had intensified among some church members in mid-1837.[230] It troubled Marsh that several of the Twelve had been involved in the discord. By early May, he and Patten had heard rumors in Far West that apostles John F. Boynton and Luke and Lyman Johnson were speaking out in opposition to JS and other leaders.[231] Lyman Johnson, Orson Pratt, and Luke Johnson had preferred charges against JS and his father in late May.[232] In June, Parley P. Pratt had preached against JS before leaving for Missouri.[233] Reflecting in January 1838 on growing unrest, Vilate Murray Kimball wrote in a letter to her husband, Heber, that she felt the dissenters had valid reasons for their frustrations but that they had nonetheless pursued an improper course of action: "Now after all that I have said about this decenting party, there is some of them, that I love, and have great feeling, and pity for them; I know they have ben tryed to the very quick; and what greaves me the most of all is, that many things which they tell, I have no doubt but what are too true. Still I do not think they are justifyable in the course they have taken."[234]

Aug. 1837, Elias Smith Correspondence, CHL; Thomas B. Marsh, Far West, MO, to Wilford Woodruff, Vinalhaven, ME, 30 Apr. 1838, Wilford Woodruff, Journals and Papers, CHL.

227. Thomas B. Marsh and David W. Patten, Far West, MO, to Parley P. Pratt, Toronto, Upper Canada, 10 May 1837, in JS Letterbook 2, pp. 62–63.

228. M. Fielding to M. Thompson, 8 July 1837; see also Historical Introduction to Recommendation for Heber C. Kimball, between 2 and 13 June 1837, pp. 398–400 herein.

229. Marsh told Pratt that he (Marsh) had been "anointed" to counsel the Twelve regarding the introduction of the gospel into other countries. When this anointing took place is unclear, but it may have occurred when Marsh was ordained one of the Twelve Apostles on 26 April 1835 or before the first mission of the Twelve in May 1835. Marsh may have been referencing the blessing and anointing he received on 22 January 1836, when JS's journal records, "I . . . sealed such blessings upon him as the Lord put into my heart." (Thomas B. Marsh and David W. Patten, Far West, MO, to Parley P. Pratt, Toronto, Upper Canada, 10 May 1837, in JS Letterbook 2, pp. 62–63; Minutes, 26 Apr. 1835, in *JSP,* D4:293–295; JS, Journal, 22 Jan. 1836, in *JSP,* J1:171.)

230. See Letter from Parley P. Pratt, 23 May 1837, pp. 386–391 herein; Letter from Abel Lamb and Others, ca. 28 May 1837, pp. 391–393 herein; and Charges against JS Preferred to Bishop's Council, 29 May 1837, pp. 393–397 herein.

231. Thomas B. Marsh and David W. Patten, Far West, MO, to Parley P. Pratt, Toronto, Upper Canada, 10 May 1837, in JS Letterbook 2, pp. 62–63; see also Minute Book 1, 21 Feb. 1836.

232. Charges against JS Preferred to Bishop's Council, 29 May 1837, pp. 393–397 herein.

233. Mary Fielding, Kirtland, OH, to Mercy Fielding, [Upper Canada], ca. June 1837, Mary Fielding Smith, Collection, CHL; Letter from Parley P. Pratt, 23 May 1837, pp. 386–391 herein.

234. Vilate Murray Kimball, Kirtland, OH, to Heber C. Kimball, Preston, England, 19–24 Jan. 1838, Heber C. Kimball, Collection, CHL.

As they traveled to Kirtland, Marsh, Patten, and William Smith met Parley P. Pratt near Columbus, Ohio. Marsh convinced Pratt to return with them to Kirtland, and soon after they arrived, Marsh began working to reconcile the dissenting apostles. In an 8 July letter, Mary Fielding wrote that Marsh had told her he believed "the difficultys between the Presidency & the twelve will very shortly be settled."[235] Although several members of the Twelve were probably still disaffected from JS at the time of the 23 July revelation, other members of the quorum had begun to resolve their differences with him.[236] In early June, when preparations were made for Heber C. Kimball to travel to England, Orson Hyde's perspective changed; he acknowledged his faults and was set apart to accompany Kimball.[237] In July, both Parley P. and Orson Pratt made public confessions before leaving Kirtland to preach in the eastern United States.[238] After his return to Kirtland from Missouri, William Smith "made a confession for past sins and expressed a determination to pursue a different course."[239] Marsh appears to have been influential in bringing about at least Parley P. Pratt's confession, and the 23 July revelation directed Marsh to continue his efforts to admonish the Twelve and instruct them to "rebel not against my servant Joseph."

The original manuscript of the revelation, as written by Marsh, has not been found, but several copies are extant. The earliest extant version was copied by Vilate Kimball into a 6 September letter she sent to her husband, Heber. Vilate wrote that she had copied the revelation from "Elder Marshs book as he wrote it from Josephs mouth." She also provided additional details regarding the revelation, which Marsh had discussed with her. According to Vilate, JS had told Marsh at the time of the revelation that "the do[o]r of proclamation could not be effectually opened" until Marsh went to England or sent someone he had ordained for that purpose, but JS had instructed him not to include this in his transcript of the 23 July revelation.[240] Heber, who was now in England proselytizing, responded to Marsh's claims by telling Vilate that JS had told him it was "all right to prepare the way for brother Marsh, as john was the fore Runner of Christ to prepare before him and to baptise," and that despite what Marsh thought—that the missionaries would have little success without his direction—those preaching in England had already baptized many people in their short time there.[241] Unfortunately, a page has been lost from Vilate's 6 September letter and her copy of the revelation is incomplete.

The copy of the revelation featured here is another of the earliest complete copies. It was recorded in JS's journal by James Mulholland between August and September 1838

---

235. M. Fielding to M. Thompson, 8 July 1837.

236. One member of the Twelve, William E. McLellin, had been disaffected from the church earlier, in August 1836, and his whereabouts and involvement with the dissenters are unknown. (Porter, "Odyssey of William Earl McLellin," 322.)

237. JS History, vol. B-1, 761; Kimball, "History," 88.

238. M. Fielding to M. Thompson, 8 July 1837.

239. Julia Smith and Mary Jane Smith, Kirtland, OH, to Elias Smith, Aug. 1837, Elias Smith Correspondence, CHL. It is not clear if William had participated in the dissent or if his confession referred to other incidents.

240. Vilate Murray Kimball, Kirtland, OH, to Heber C. Kimball, Preston, England, 6 Sept. 1837, copy, Heber C. Kimball Correspondence, CHL.

241. Heber C. Kimball, Preston, England, to Vilate Murray Kimball, Kirtland, OH, 12 Nov. 1837, copy, Heber C. Kimball Correspondence, CHL.

Vilate Murray Kimball. 1866. A resident of Kirtland, Ohio, since 1833, Vilate Kimball participated in, observed, and recorded events pertinent to the church's early history. In 1837 and early 1838, Vilate wrote a series of letters to her husband, Heber C. Kimball, describing the difficulties taking place within the church in Kirtland while he was traveling to and proselytizing in England. Her letters provide a window to better understand dissent against Joseph Smith. Though partially missing and therefore not featured in this volume, the earliest extant copy of Joseph Smith's 23 July 1837 revelation is in Vilate Kimball's handwriting. (Church History Library, Salt Lake City. Photograph by studio of Savage and Ottinger.)

in Missouri and is preceded by a notation that reads, "The above revelation was given in Kirtland, and was not here in time to insert in its proper sequence."[242] Another early copy is held by the Community of Christ Library-Archives and was written by an unidentified scribe between 1837 and 1838. Although it may be an earlier text than the copy in JS's 1838 journal, this version has no verifiable provenance.[243] A third copy, written by Frederick G. Williams, has textual indicators that suggest it too was one of the earlier versions and was copied by 1838.[244] Significant differences between the early versions are noted below.

Later, in connection with their mission to Britain, several church apostles also made personal copies of this revelation. Wilford Woodruff inscribed the revelation into his "Book of Revelations" before leaving Illinois in August 1839, Willard Richards copied it into his "Pocket Companion" between 13 January 1840 and 20 April 1841, Brigham Young wrote a copy in his journal between April and September 1839, and Heber C. Kimball copied it from Vilate Kimball's 6 September 1837 letter into his journal between March 1841 and March 1842.[245] Other extant copies include one by William W. Phelps, who wrote a copy on loose-leaf pages, likely after November 1842.[246] Willard Richards copied the revelation into JS's history between January and March 1844, and the revelation was included in the 1844 edition of the Doctrine and Covenants as section 104.[247]

Document Transcript

A Revelation given Kirtland July 23[rd.] 1837.

The word of the Lord unto Thomas, B. Marsh concerning the twelve Apostles of the Lamb.[248]

Verily thus saith the Lord unto you my servant Thomas, I have heard thy prayers and thine alms have come up as a memorial before me[249] in behalf of those thy brethren who were chosen to bear testimony of my name and to send it abroad among all nations, kindreds, tongues and people and ordained through the instrumentality of my servants.[250]

---

242. Revelation, 23 July 1837, in *JSP*, J1:306–308 [D&C 112].

243. "Kirtland Geauga Co Ohio July 23 1837 the word of the lord unto Thomas B. Marsh concerning the Twelve," CCLA. This copy was written on three loose-leaf pages and was put with John Whitmer's history at some point.

244. Revelation, 23 July 1837, Revelations Collection, CHL [D&C 112].

245. Woodruff, "Book of Revelations," 11–19; Richards, "Pocket Companion," 4–9; Young, Journal, 1837–1845, 107–112; Kimball, Journal, 1840–1845, 62–72.

246. Revelation, 23 July 1837, Revelations Collection, CHL [D&C 112].

247. JS History, vol. B-1, 765–767; Doctrine and Covenants 104, 1844 ed. [D&C 112].

248. Neither Frederick G. Williams's copy nor the Community of Christ copy includes the clause "Apostles of the Lamb." (Revelation, 23 July 1837, Revelations Collection, CHL [D&C 112]; "Kirtland Geauga Co Ohio July 23 1837 the word of the lord," CCLA.)

249. See Acts 10:4.

250. This refers to the Quorum of the Twelve and their calling to "travel from nation to nation." (Minute Book 1, 21 Feb. 1835.)

Verily I say unto you there have been some few things in thine heart and with thee, with which I the Lord was not well pleased; nevertheless inasmuch as thou hast abased thyself thou shalt be exalted:[251] therefore all thy sins are forgiven thee. Let thy heart be of good cheer[252] before my face, and thou shalt bear record of my name, not only unto the Gentiles, but also unto the Jews; and thou shalt send forth my word unto the ends of the earth.

Contend thou therefore morning by morning, and day after day let thy warning voice go forth;[253] and when the night cometh let not the inhabitants of the earth slumber because of thy speech. Let thy habitation be known in Zion, and remove not thy house, for I the Lord have a great work for ~~you~~ ⟨thee⟩ to do, in publishing my name among the children of men, therefore gird up your loins for the work. Let your feet be shod[254] also for thou art chosen, and thy path lyeth among the mountains and among many nations, and by thy word many high ones shall be brought low; and by thy word many low ones shall be exalted,[255] thy voice shall be a rebuke[256] unto the transgressor, and at thy rebuke let the tongue of the slanderer cease its perverseness. Be thou humble and the Lord thy God shall lead thee[257] by the hand and give thee an answer to thy prayers, I know thy heart and have heard thy prayers concerning thy brethren. Be not partial towards them in love above many others, but let your love[258] be for them as for yourself, and let your love abound unto all men and unto all who love my name. And pray for your brethren of the twelve. Admonish[259] them sharply for my name's sake, and let them be admonished[260] for all their sins, and be ye faithful before me unto my name; and after their temptations and much tribulation[261] behold I the Lord will feel after them, and if they harden not their hearts and stiffen not their necks against me they shall be converted and I will heal them.[262]

Now I say unto you, and what I say [p. 72] unto you, I say unto all the twelve. Arise and gird up your loins, take up your cross,[263] follow me, and feed

---

251. See Matthew 23:12; and Luke 14:11.

252. See Matthew 9:2; and John 16:33.

253. See Book of Mormon, 1830 ed., 563 [Ether 12:3].

254. See Ephesians 6:15; and Revelation, ca. Aug. 1835, in *JSP*, D4:412 [D&C 27:16].

255. See Ezekiel 17:24; Matthew 23:12; and Book of Mormon, 1830 ed., 98 [2 Nephi 20:33].

256. See 2 Timothy 4:2.

257. See Isaiah 57:18.

258. See Matthew 5:43–48.

259. See Romans 15:14.

260. The Community of Christ copy has a canceled "sharpely" after "admonished."

261. See John 16:33; Revelation 7:14; and Revelation, 24 Feb. 1834, in *JSP*, D3:460 [D&C 103:12].

262. See John 12:40.

263. See Book of Mormon, 1830 ed., 481 [3 Nephi 12:30]; and Revelation, Apr. 1830–E, in *JSP*, D1:136 [D&C 23:6–7].

my sheep.[264] Exalt not yourselves; rebel not against my servant Joseph for Verily I say unto you I am with him and my hand shall be over him; and the keys[265] which I have given him, and also to youward shall not be taken from him untill I come.

Verily I say unto you my servant Thomas, thou art the man whom I have chosen to hold the keys of my kingdom (as pertaining to the twelve) abroad among all nations, that thou mayest be ~~thy~~ my servant to unlock the door of the kingdom in all places where my servant Joseph, and my servant Sidney [Rigdon], and my servant Hyrum [Smith], cannot come, for on them have I laid the burden of all the Churches for a little season: wherefore whithersoever they shall send you, go ye, and I will be with you and in whatsoever place ye shall proclaim my name an effectual door shall be opened unto you[266] that they may receive my word. Whosoever receiveth my word receiveth me, and whosoever receiveth me receiveth those (the first presidency) whom I have sent, whom I have made counsellors for my name's sake unto you. And again I say unto you, that whosoever ye shall send in my name, by the voice of your brethren the twelve, duly recommended and authorized by you, shall have power to open the door of my kingdom unto any nation whithersoever ye shall send them, inasmuch as they shall[267] humble themselves before me and abide in my word, and hearken to the voice of my spirit.

Verily verily! I say unto you, darkness covereth the earth and gross darkness the ~~people~~ minds of the people,[268] and all flesh has become corrupt before my face![269] Behold vengeance cometh speedily upon the inhabitants of the earth. A day of wrath! A day of burning! A day of desolation! Of weeping! Of mourning and of lamentation! And as a whirlwind it shall come upon all the face of the earth saith the Lord. And upon my house shall it begin and from my house shall it go forth saith the Lord. First among[270] those among you saith

---

264. See John 21:16–17.

265. See Revelation, Sept. 1830, in *JSP*, D1:183–186 [D&C 28]; Revelation, 30 Oct. 1831, in *JSP*, D2:93 [D&C 65:2]; and Revelation, between ca. 8 and ca. 24 Mar. 1832, in *JSP*, D2:221–222.

266. See 1 Corinthians 16:9.

267. The Community of Christ copy and the Vilate Kimball copy do not include "shall." ("Kirtland Geauga Co Ohio July 23 1837 the word of the lord," CCLA; V. M. Kimball to H. C. Kimball, 6 Sept. 1837.)

268. See Isaiah 60:2.

269. See Revelation, 2 Jan. 1831, in *JSP*, D1:231 [D&C 38:5–8].

270. Both the Community of Christ copy and the Vilate Kimball copy have "upon" in place of "among." The William W. Phelps copy has "among" crossed out and "upon" inserted. ("Kirtland Geauga Co Ohio July 23 1837 the word of the lord," CCLA; V. M. Kimball to H. C. Kimball, 6 Sept. 1837; Revelation, 23 July 1837, Revelations Collection, CHL [D&C 112].)

the Lord; who have professed to know my name and have not known me[271] and have blasphemed against me in the midst of my house saith the Lord[272]

Therefore see to it that you trouble not yourselves concerning the affairs of my Church in this place saith the Lord, but purify your hearts before me, and then go ye into[273] all the world and preach my gospel unto every creature who have not[274] received it and he that believeth and is baptized shall be saved, and he that believeth not, and is not baptized [p. 73] shall be damned.[275] For unto you (the twelve) and those (the first presidency) who are appointed with you to be your counsellors and your leaders,[276] is the power[277] of this priesthood given for the last days and for the last time, in the which is the dispensation of the fulness of times:[278] which power you hold in connection with all those who have received a dispensation at any time from the beginning of the creation, for verily I say unto you the keys of the dispensation which ye have received have came down from the fathers;[279] and last of all being sent down from heaven unto you. Verily I say unto you, Behold how great is your calling.

Cleanse your hearts and your garments, lest the blood of this generation[280] be required at your hands. Be faithful untill I come for I come quickly and my reward is with me to recompense every man according as his work shall be![281] I am Alpha and Omega. Amen.

——————— ∽ ———————

271. See Revelation, 4 Feb. 1831, in *JSP*, D1:243 [D&C 41:1].

272. This may be a reference to dissenters, such as Warren Parrish, who spoke against JS in the House of the Lord in mid-June 1837. (See Woodruff, Journal, 28 May 1837; and Historical Introduction to Letter from Abel Lamb and Others, ca. 28 May 1837, pp. 392–393 herein.)

273. In the Community of Christ copy the word "forth" was canceled and "ye into" written over it. ("Kirtland Geauga Co Ohio July 23 1837 the word of the lord," CCLA.)

274. The Community of Christ copy does not include this "not" (presumably a scribal error). ("Kirtland Geauga Co Ohio July 23 1837 the word of the lord," CCLA.)

275. See Mark 16:15.

276. The copies written by Willard Richards and William W. Phelps replace "leaders" with "teacher." (Richards, "Pocket Companion," 4–9; Revelation, 23 July 1837, Revelations Collection, CHL [D&C 112].)

277. The Community of Christ copy has "prayer" in place of "power." ("Kirtland Geauga Co Ohio July 23 1837 the word of the lord," CCLA.)

278. See Ephesians 1:10; and Revelation, ca. Aug. 1835, in *JSP*, D4:411–412 [D&C 27:13].

279. See Abraham 1:3.

280. See Revelation, 27–28 Dec. 1832, in *JSP*, D2:341–342 [D&C 88:75, 85].

281. See Revelation 22:12; and Revelation, 10 June 1831, in *JSP*, D1:336 [D&C 54:10].

Notice, circa Late August 1837

Source Note

JS, Notice, Kirtland Township, Geauga Co., OH, ca. late Aug. 1837. Featured version published in "Caution," Latter Day Saints' Messenger and Advocate, *Aug. 1837, 3:560. For more information on* Latter Day Saints' Messenger and Advocate, *see Source Notes for Multiple-Entry Documents, p. 527 herein.*

Historical Introduction

JS wrote the notice featured here in late August after returning to Kirtland, Ohio, from a trip to Canada.[282] The notice, printed in the August issue of the *Latter Day Saints' Messenger and Advocate,* warned the public against using or accepting the notes of the Kirtland Safety Society.

Prior to his travels, JS actively distanced himself from the Kirtland Safety Society in June and July 1837. On 8 June, he sold his shares of stock in the society to Oliver Granger and Jared Carter.[283] In addition, sometime before 7 July he and Sidney Rigdon resigned their respective positions as the treasurer and secretary of the Kirtland Safety Society.[284] Their resignations officially ended their leadership of the society but did not signal the close of the institution. The Safety Society's directors elected new officers, Fredrick G. Williams and Warren Parrish, and the society continued to function.[285] Its already tenuous credibility, however, was further marred by the new officers' decision to issue more loans, increasing the number of notes the society had in circulation.[286] The

---

282. JS, Sidney Rigdon, and Thomas B. Marsh began their trip to Canada on 27 July but were detained in Painesville, Ohio, by several lawsuits involving JS in the Geauga County Court of Common Pleas. They started again the evening of 28 July and arrived in Buffalo by 30 July. JS's history records that he spent most of August in Canada and returned to Kirtland "about the last of August." (JS History, vol. B-1, 767, 770, addenda, 6.)

283. By transferring or selling stock, individuals could discontinue their membership in and financial support of the Safety Society. The 8 June transaction appears to be the earliest instance of Oliver Granger acting in the capacity of an agent for JS. Granger was given a financial power of attorney for JS and Sidney Rigdon in September 1837. He was made an official agent of the church in May 1839. (Power of Attorney to Oliver Granger, 27 Sept. 1837, p. 460 herein; JS Authorization for Oliver Granger, 6 May 1839, CHL; JS and Others, Commerce, IL, Letter of Recommendation for Oliver Granger, 13 May 1839, in JS Letterbook 2, pp. 45–46.)

284. In a July 1837 editorial, Warren A. Cowdery suggested that JS's and Sidney Rigdon's resignations occurred around the same time as the transfer of their stock. According to the society's stock ledger, JS transferred his stock on 8 June, but there is no record of Rigdon transferring his stock. JS's history recounts that he resigned as an officer of the society before 7 July 1837. It is likely that the officers stepped down soon after they sold their stock, but they may have had to wait until the directors could meet and elect new officers before they could remove themselves from their positions. ("Argument to Argument Where I Find It," *Elders' Journal,* Aug. 1838, 55–60; Warren A. Cowdery, Editorial, *LDS Messenger and Advocate,* July 1837, 3:535–541; Kirtland Safety Society, Stock Ledger, 1–2, 273; JS History, vol. B-1, 764.)

285. An editorial in the July 1838 *Elders' Journal* mentions that Williams and Parrish were elected to replace JS and Rigdon but does not indicate when this election took place. ("Argument to Argument Where I Find It," *Elders' Journal,* Aug. 1838, 58.)

286. "Look Out," *Daily Herald and Gazette* (Cleveland, OH), 8 July 1837, [3].

society probably still held some specie to back its notes, but it had lost what little public confidence remained; in May and June, stockholders withdrew their funds and unloaded their stock.[287] The society's further-diminished specie reserves were likely not enough to provide any security for the number of notes already in circulation. By issuing additional loans, Williams and Parrish may have hoped to improve the Safety Society's funding, but their decision resulted in steeper discounts for the redemption of Safety Society notes at any banks still willing to accept them.

Faced with the resignation of JS and Rigdon, the unsound practices of Williams and Parrish, and the financial tensions throughout the United States, some Latter-day Saints felt there should be further separation between the church and the Kirtland Safety Society.[288] In a meeting of the Quorum of the Seventy in Kirtland held 30 July 1837, a suggestion was made, possibly by John Gould, that members of the church should no longer use society notes to meet their financial obligations outside of Kirtland.[289] The members of the Seventy present at that meeting voted "that none of the corum should hereafter be allowed to deal or trade in any manner Kirtland Money away from this place" and that "the above transactions be published in the messenger & advocate."[290] They appointed John Gould, Joseph Young, and Sylvester B. Stoddard to compose the message. On 6 August, the Seventy revisited the resolution and, after some deliberation, voted to "submit the above named resolutions to the inspection of the first Presidency of the church for their approval or disapproval," along with the suggestion that if the First Presidency approved of the resolution, it should be printed in the *Messenger and Advocate*.[291] No statement from the Seventy, however, appeared in the church's newspaper.

While such expressions of doubt may have influenced JS to write this notice, his warning goes beyond the suggestion of the Quorum of the Seventy. Instead, JS warned more broadly against any use or acceptance of the notes of the Kirtland Safety Society, and he cautioned the public that unscrupulous individuals were dealing in the severely devalued notes. He may have been particularly anxious to dissuade church members who

---

287. On 20 May John Johnson and his daughter Emily Johnson withdrew the money they had paid the society for their shares of stock; Wilford Woodruff, William F. Cahoon, and Sabra Granger followed suit on 22 May 1837. JS, eight members of his family, and nineteen other stockholders sold their stock to Oliver Granger and Jared Carter between 8 and 20 June 1837. (Kirtland Safety Society, Stock Ledger, 13–16, 23–24, 45, 47–50, 53–55, 61–64, 87–88, 107–108, 115–120, 149–151, 177–178, 181–182, 187–188, 193–196, 201–202, 207–208, 219, 227, 237–238, 261–262, 265–266, 273–274; see also Introduction to Part 6: 20 Apr.–14 Sept. 1837, pp. 363–366 herein.)

288. See Introduction to Part 5: 5 Oct. 1836–10 Apr. 1837, pp. 285–293 herein; and Introduction to Part 6: 20 Apr.–14 Sept. 1837, pp. 363–366 herein.

289. The Record of the Seventy does not name the individual responsible for the suggestion. Nathan Tanner's reminiscent account of the meeting attributes the idea to John Gould. Tanner also suggests that Gould's idea included disfellowshipping those who continued to circulate the notes. Tanner claimed that when a vote was called he was the sole opposing vote and that his opposition led Joseph Young to dismiss the resolution. In contrast, the Record of the Seventy indicates that the resolution was accepted and forwarded to the First Presidency. (Tanner, Address, [21]–[23]; Record of Seventies, bk. A, 31–33.)

290. Record of Seventies, bk. A, 32.

291. Record of Seventies, bk. A, 33.

were acquiring devalued notes in an effort to aid JS and Rigdon, who were thought to be responsible for repaying the notes they had signed.[292]

Document Transcript

CAUTION.

To the brethren and friends of the church of Latter Day Saints, I am disposed to say a word relative to the bills of the Kirtland Safety Society Bank. I hereby warn them to beware of speculators, renegadoes[293] and gamblers,[294] who are duping the unsuspecting and the unwary, by palming upon them, those bills, which are of no worth, here. I discountenance and disapprove of any and all such practices. I know them to be detrimental to the best interests of society, as well as to the principles of religion.

JOSEPH SMITH Jun,

———— ❧ ————

Minutes, 3 September 1837

Source Note

Minutes, Kirtland Township, Geauga Co., OH, 3 Sept. 1837. Featured version copied [ca. mid-Sept. 1837] in Minute Book 1, pp. 234–238; handwriting of George W. Robinson; CHL. For more information on Minute Book 1, see Source Notes for Multiple-Entry Documents, p. 527 herein.

Historical Introduction

JS presided over a conference on 3 September 1837, later referred to as a "re-organization of the Church" in Kirtland, Ohio, at which several men were removed and replaced as church leaders, including eight members of the high council and one of the presidents of the Quorum of the Seventy.[295] In addition, the conference objected to and disfellowshipped three members

---

292. Nathan Tanner recounted that he and other church members traded their goods for the devalued currency in order to remove it from circulation and thereby relieve JS and Rigdon of the burden of redeeming the notes of the Kirtland Safety Society. Entries in the society's stock ledger also suggest church members who were not stockholders were helping to buy up "Kirtland Funds." (Tanner, Address, [24]; Kirtland Safety Society, Stock Ledger, 130, 180.)

293. "An apostate from the faith; a deserter; a vagabond." ("Renegade," in *American Dictionary*.)

294. The fact that disreputable individuals were using the notes of the Kirtland Safety Society in fraudulent schemes is demonstrated by warnings printed in Cleveland newspapers, which mentioned that gamblers and other criminals were trading in Kirtland Safety Society notes. The prevalence of unscrupulous uses for Safety Society notes was also allegedly connected to Warren Parrish, who was elected as the society's cashier in July 1837 and was later accused of counterfeiting and embezzling. (See "Arrests," *Daily Herald and Gazette* [Cleveland, OH], 10 Aug. 1837, [3]; "More Suspensions," *Daily Herald and Gazette*, 28 Aug. 1837, [3]; "Beware of the Swindler!," *Huron Reflector* [Norwalk, OH], 27 Mar. 1838, [4]; "Argument to Argument Where I Find It," *Elders' Journal*, Aug. 1838, 58.)

295. Minutes, 7 Nov. 1837, p. 469 herein.

of the Quorum of the Twelve and added John Smith as an assistant counselor in the church presidency. This reorganization was undertaken to address the continuing opposition by some church leaders, including the three disfellowshipped members of the Twelve, and to reassert JS's authority as president of the church.

Dissent among church members that had intensified in May seemed to be diminishing by July. Thomas B. Marsh, leader of the Twelve Apostles, had helped reconcile most of the Twelve who had become disaffected.[296] JS, Sidney Rigdon, Marsh, and others had left in late July to meet with the Saints in Canada, and they returned in late August. Mary Fielding, writing in late August or early September, told her sister Mercy Fielding Thompson that the Saints in Kirtland "have had a terrible stir with W[arren] Parish" and that they were "not yet able to tell where it will end."[297] Yet even the rebellious Parrish had reconciled with JS. Vilate Murray Kimball noted that Parrish was restored to fellowship before the 3 September meeting, and she remarked, "I never saw him so humble as he is now." Kimball wrote further that the general climate of dissension was improving: "There has ben serious difficulties in the church here of late, Satan has led many of our brethren captive at his will. but thanks be to God the most of them are now striveing to humble them selves."[298] Despite the reconciliations that had occurred, though, a few prominent church members had still not resolved their differences with JS.

The 3 September 1837 conference was held in the Kirtland House of the Lord.[299] It lasted most of the day, beginning at nine o'clock in the morning, adjourning for an hour at one in the afternoon, and then reconvening at two o'clock. JS and Sidney Rigdon presented the various church leaders, including themselves, for a vote and requested that the assembled church members decide whether each individual should retain his position in the church. JS was the first to be presented to the congregation and he was unanimously accepted, thereby reaffirming his authority and leadership as church president. Of the men removed from their positions in the several quorums, some had moved away and one, Orson Johnson, had been excommunicated. The three men removed from the Kirtland high council—Martin Harris, Joseph Coe, and John Johnson—appear to have lost their positions because they were involved with dissenters.

The congregation, including other members of the Quorum of the Twelve Apostles, objected to apostles John F. Boynton, Luke Johnson, and Lyman Johnson remaining in the quorum; however, the men were not officially removed from their positions or replaced at this meeting. According to Vilate Kimball, who was present, the "case was then poot over until another time." A few days later, Marsh visited Kimball—whose husband, apostle

---

296. For a more detailed account of dissent and disaffection in spring and summer 1837, see Introduction to Part 6: 20 Apr.–14 Sept. 1837, pp. 363–366 herein; and Historical Introduction to Revelation, 23 July 1837 [D&C 112], pp. 410–412 herein.

297. Mary Fielding, Kirtland, OH, to Mercy Fielding Thompson, Upper Canada, [ca. Aug.–Sept. 1837], Mary Fielding Smith, Collection, CHL.

298. Vilate Murray Kimball, Kirtland, OH, to Heber C. Kimball, Preston, England, ca. 10 Sept. 1837, Heber C. Kimball, Collection, CHL.

299. In a reminiscent account of the conference Brigham Young described his efforts to encourage faithful church members to come early and fill the House of the Lord before the meeting. (Historian's Office, Brigham Young History Drafts, 15.)

Heber C. Kimball, was proselytizing in England—and told her about a private meeting at which he and JS met with Lyman Johnson, John F. Boynton, and possibly other dissenters. Marsh informed Vilate Kimball that "they had all become reconciled to each other" and that Lyman Johnson and Boynton "would come forward next Sunday and make their confession to the church." Luke Johnson had not yet returned to Kirtland from Missouri, but Marsh said "he thought there would be no difficulty with him when he come to find the rest all united." Kimball added, "I feel to rejoice this day for the prospect before us. I came from meeting last Sabbath with a heavy heart; I cannot bare a thought that one of the twelve should lose their standing. many thought they would. but thanks be to God I know he will hear and answer prayer."[300] Luke Johnson returned during the week, and the following Sunday, 10 September, all three men publicly offered "confession to the Church" and were accepted back into full fellowship. The congregation then unanimously voted in favor of their retaining their positions in the Quorum of the Twelve.[301]

George W. Robinson took the minutes for the conference and recorded them into Minute Book 1, the text featured here. He also copied them into a 4 September letter addressed to John Corrill and other church leaders in Missouri.[302] Significant differences between the two sets of minutes are noted below.

Document Transcript

Sunday 4th 3rd Sept 1837 Minutes of a conference assembled in the house of the Lord, in committee of the whole[303] at 9 O clock A. M. G[eorge] W. Robinson was requested by Joseph Smith Jr to take the proceedings of this meeting, The meeting was opened by prayer by S[idney] Rigdon who then introduced Joseph Smith Jr to the congregation to know if he should still act as their Pres. as the presiding officer of the church,[304] was chosen by a unanimous vois [voice] of the same. Pres. Smith then introduced Sidney Rigdon & Frederick G. Williams for councillors to Pres. Smith and together with him to constitute the three first presidents of the church, carried by a unanimous vote, Pres. Smith then introduced O[liver] Cowdery J[oseph] Smith Sen. Hyrum Smith, [p. 234] & John Smith for assistant councillors[305] & carried by

---

300. V. Kimball to H. Kimball, ca. 10 Sept. 1837; see also Minute Book 1, 10 Sept. 1837.

301. Minute Book 1, 10 Sept. 1837; V. Kimball to H. Kimball, ca. 10 Sept. 1837.

302. Letter to John Corrill and the Church in Missouri, 4 Sept. 1837, pp. 428–430 herein.

303. This is one of the earliest uses of the phrase "committee of the whole" to reference the church. In the 7 November 1837 reorganizational meeting in Far West, Missouri, both the men and women in the congregation were asked to vote on leadership positions. That may have been the case at this conference as well, though the minutes do not specify. (Minutes, 7 Nov. 1837, pp. 469–471 herein.)

304. The 4 September copy of the minutes replaces this section with the following: "S[idney] Rigdon then presented Joseph Smith Jr to the Church to know if they still looked upon & would still receive & uphold him as the Prest. of the whole Church." (Letter to John Corrill and the Church in Missouri, 4 Sept. 1837, p. 428 herein.)

305. The titles "assistant counselor" and "assistant president" seem to have been used synonymously. Oliver Cowdery, Joseph Smith Sr., and Hyrum Smith were ordained as assistant presidents on 5 and

a unanimous voice of the church these last four are allso, together with the first three to be concidered the heads of the Church Voted that N[ewel] K Whitney continue to act as Bishop of this church in Kirtland Voted that R[eynolds] Cahoon & Vinsan [Vinson] Knight be councillors to the Bishop, The question was then asked the church if the Twelve apostles should hold their office of Apostleship They were named by the President individually Voted that Thomas. B. Marsh David W. Patten Brigham Young Heber. C. Kimble [Kimball] Orson Hyde P. P. Prath [Parley P. Pratt] Orson Pratt William Smith Wm E. McLellin should retain their office of apostleship;[306] Luke Johnson, Lyman Johnson John F Boyngton [Boynton], were rejected[307] from serving in that office Privilege was given to those that were rejected of making their confession if they had any to make. Elder Boyngton which was the onley one present at the time arose and parsailly [partially] confessed his sins and partly justifying his conduct by reason of the failure of the bank, his acknowledgments appeared not to be satisfactory, his conduct was strongly protested against, by Elder Brigham Young in a plain and energetick manner stating various reasons why he could not receive him into fellowship untill a hearty repentance[308] was manifested, ~~the~~ Elder ⟨Young⟩ was followed by Elder Marsh who acquiesed in testimony, and allso disfellowshiped the conduct of Elder Boyngton [p. 235]

President Rigdon then arose, & made an address of conciderable length, showing the starting point or cause of all the difficulty of Elders Boyngton & Johnson, he allso cautioned all the Elders, concrning leaving their calling to persue any occupation derogatory to that calling,[309] assuring them that if

---

6 December 1834 and had been serving in that capacity since that time. Before this 3 September meeting, John Smith had acted as the president of the Kirtland high council. In the meeting, JS appointed him an assistant counselor and member of the presidency of the church. (Account of Meetings, Revelation, and Blessing, 5–6 Dec. 1834, in *JSP*, D4:194, 200.)

306. Despite their earlier discontent, both Parley P. Pratt and Orson Pratt had reconciled their differences with JS by this time and were in full fellowship and proselytizing in New York. Orson Hyde, who may have had some involvement with dissenters, had repented before leaving to preach in England with Heber C. Kimball. Although William E. McLellin was elected here, he was absent from Kirtland and would later claim that he was disaffected from the church at this time. (Julia Smith and Mary Jane Smith, Kirtland, OH, to Elias Smith, Shinnston, VA, Aug. 1837, Elias Smith Correspondence, CHL; V. Kimball to H. Kimball, ca. 10 Sept. 1837; see also Historical Introduction to Revelation, 23 July 1837 [D&C 112], pp. 410–414 herein.)

307. The 4 September copy of the minutes adds "& cut off" after "rejected." (Letter to John Corrill and the Church in Missouri, 4 Sept. 1837, p. 428 herein.)

308. The 4 September copy adds "conffession" to Young's requirements for Boynton being received back into fellowship. (Letter to John Corrill and the Church in Missouri, 4 Sept. 1837, p. 429 herein.)

309. Rigdon may be referring to the mercantile store run by Boynton and Lyman Johnson as an "occupation derogatory" to their calling in the Twelve. According to Heber C. Kimball and Ira Ames, Boynton and Johnson borrowed "considerable money" from Saints in Boston including Polly Vose, and

persued, God would let them run themselves into difficulties, that he may stop them in their career, that salvation may come unto them,[310] Elder Boyngton then arose and still attributed his difficulties & conduct to the failure of the bank, stating that the bank he understood was instituted by the will & revilations of God, & he had been told that it never would fail let men do what they pleased,[311] Pres. Smith then arose, and stated that if this had been published, it was without authority, at least from him, he stated that he allways said that unless the institution was conducted upon righteous principles it could not stand,[312] The church was then called upon to know whether they were sattisfied with the confession of Elder Boyngton, Voted in the negative Adjourned for one hour.

Congregation assembled at 2 O clock P.M. & called to order by the Pres. & meeting opened by prayer, by Elder [Henry G.] Sherwood, the Pres. then arose and said he should next call upon the church to know if they were satisfied with the high Council & next proceeded to name them individually [p. 236] John Johnson, Joseph Coe, Martin Harris,[313] & Joseph Kingsbury, were objected to,[314] allso John P. Green[e], but his case was put over till he should be present,

purchased thousands of dollars' worth of goods for their Kirtland store, which they were never able to repay. (Kimball, "History," [48]; Ames, Autobiography and Journal, [13].)

310. The synopsis of Rigdon's address is not included in the 4 September copy of the minutes. (Letter to John Corrill and the Church in Missouri, 4 Sept. 1837, pp. 428–429 herein.)

311. Disparaging newspaper articles printed in 1837 and Warren Parrish writing in 1838 echoed the claim that the society had been established by revelation and, therefore, should have been incapable of failure. Dissenters and detractors used the failure of the society to further question JS's prophetic role. ("How Have the Mighty Fallen!!," *Western Reserve Chronicle* [Warren, OH], 7 Feb. 1837, [3]; "About Matters in Kirtland," *Ohio Observer* [Hudson], 2 Mar. 1837, [2]; Warren Parrish, Kirtland, OH, 5 Feb. 1838, Letter to the Editor, *Painesville [OH] Republican*, 15 Feb. 1838, [3].)

312. In contrast to Boynton's insistence, other extant statements from JS about the bank are more conditional. Wilford Woodruff wrote on 6 January 1837 that JS told him and others assembled in the Safety Society office that he "had receieved that morning the Word of the Lord upon the Subject of the Kirtland Safety Society." According to Woodruff, "He did not tell us at that time what the Lord said upon the subject but remarked that if we would give heed to the Commandments the Lord had given this morning all would be well." Mary Fielding wrote in June 1837 that "so many of the Bank directors are become unfaithful that Brother J. S says he does not know that it will rise again." (Woodruff, Journal, 6 Jan. 1837; Mary Fielding, Kirtland, OH, to Mercy Fielding, [Upper Canada], ca. June 1837, Mary Fielding Smith, Collection, CHL.)

313. According to Vilate Kimball, Martin Harris was so angered by the congregation's decision to remove him from his position as a member of the Kirtland high council that he left the meeting. (V. Kimball to H. Kimball, ca. 10 Sept. 1837.)

314. John Johnson, Joseph Coe, and Martin Harris were likely among the dissenters in summer 1837. Coe and Harris were identified by John Smith as leaders of the dissenters and were excommunicated by the Kirtland high council in December 1837. Joseph Kingsbury was not identified in extant sources as a dissenter, but he may have been disaffected at this time. (John Smith and Clarissa Lyman Smith, Kirtland, OH, to George A. Smith, Shinnston, VA, 1 Jan. 1838, George Albert Smith, Papers, CHL.)

Noah Packard Jared Carter & Samuel H Smith were voted to stand in their office previously confered upon them. Samuel James[315] was dropped from the council in consequence of his being absent and his situation such that he could not attend to the duties of the office. Oliver Granger, Henry G. Sherwood, William Marks, Mahu [Mayhew] Hillman, Harlow Redfield, Asa[h]el Smith, Phineas Richards, & David Dort, were chosen to fill the place of those objected to, and the seats in the council which were vacated by reason of Thomas Grover having moved to the west[316] John Smith having been chosen one of the Presidents of the church, & Orson Johnson being excluded from the Church, all having belonged to the high council,[317] The Pres. then called upon the church to know if the new Presidents of the Seventies should stand in their calling.[318] Voted that John Gaylord, James Foster, Salmon Gee, Daniel S. Miles, Joseph Young, Josiah Butterfield, should retain their office, John Gould, was objected to and on learning that Levi Handcox [Hancock] one of the former presidents of the Seventies was not an high priest, he was chosen in the place of John Gould.[319] The Pres then arose & made some remarks concerning the former presidents of the Seventies, their calling the authority of the priesthood &.c.

Voted that the old or former presidents [p. 237] of the Seventies, be refered to the quorum of high priests, those which were previously ordained to the high priesthood.[320]

Closed by Singing an hymn & a short prayer by Pres. Smith

G. W. Robinson <u>Clerk</u>

———— ☙ ————

315. Samuel James was proselytizing in Virginia in August 1837. ("Minutes of a Conference," *LDS Messenger and Advocate,* Sept. 1837, 3:574–575.)

316. Thomas Grover and his family had moved to Far West, Missouri. (Minute Book 2, 1 Aug. 1837.)

317. The removal of Thomas Grover, John Smith, and Orson Johnson from the Kirtland high council is not included in the 4 September copy of the minutes, where only the individuals replacing them are named. (Letter to John Corrill and the Church in Missouri, 4 Sept. 1837, p. 429 herein.)

318. For more on earlier reorganizations of the presidents of the Quorum of the Seventy, see Historical Introduction to Discourse, 6 Apr. 1837, pp. 352–354 herein.

319. In April 1837, when the presidents of the Quorum of the Seventy were reorganized, Levi Hancock, one of the presidents, was absent from Kirtland. In that meeting, John Gould and others were appointed to become presidents of the Seventy in place of earlier presidents who had been ordained high priests. However, Hancock had not been ordained a high priest like the other men removed as presidents and should have retained his position. It is not clear from the extant records whether the objection to Gould was raised because the position he held was rightly Hancock's or because the congregation felt he should be removed for other reasons. (See Historical Introduction to Discourse, 6 Apr. 1837, pp. 352–357 herein.)

320. The 4 September copy of the minutes included an additional section at the end which reads: "And also that if any of the members of the quorum of the seventies should be dissattisfied & would not submit to the Present order, and receive these last Presidents that they Should have power to demand their Lisence & they should no longer be concidered members of the church." (Letter to John Corrill and the Church in Missouri, 4 Sept. 1837, pp. 429–430 herein.)

Letter to John Corrill and the Church in Missouri, 4 September 1837

Source Note

JS, Letter, Kirtland Township, Geauga Co., OH, to John Corrill and the church in Missouri, [Far West, Caldwell Co., MO], 4 Sept. 1837. Featured version copied [between 13 and 29 Mar. 1838] in JS, Journal, Mar.–Sept. 1838, pp. 18–23; handwriting of George W. Robinson; CHL. For more information on JS, Journal, Mar.–Sept. 1838, see Source Notes for Multiple-Entry Documents, p. 525 herein.

Historical Introduction

On 3 September 1837, after months of determined and outspoken opposition against him, JS convened a conference of the church in Kirtland, Ohio, at which he was sustained as president of the Church of the Latter Day Saints. Many other church leaders were also supported by the congregation, including Oliver Cowdery, who was unanimously sustained as one of four assistant counselors to JS despite having "been in transgression." Other church leaders were rejected, including three dissenting apostles and others deemed to be guilty of misbehavior.[321]

The day after the conference, JS sent to John Corrill and the Saints in Missouri the letter featured here, which included a copy of the conference minutes. In directing his letter to Corrill, who had been a member of the Missouri bishopric and was the church's agent in the West,[322] and to Missouri church members generally, JS bypassed the Missouri presidency, some of whom were in Kirtland at the time. In sending an open letter to church members in Missouri, JS may have been seeking to encourage them to push for regulation of the church there, much like the reorganization he had overseen in Kirtland the previous day. Following the minutes, JS added a note regarding the wrongdoings of various individuals, including Oliver Cowdery and Missouri president David Whitmer. Though Cowdery had retained his church position, JS advised the church members in Missouri that unless he changed his attitude and more diligently fulfilled his obligations in the presidency, he should be removed from office. JS also warned about Whitmer, Leonard Rich, and others who he said "have been in transgression."[323] JS may have wanted the Missouri church members to have this information prior to the arrival of Whitmer and Cowdery, who soon left Kirtland for Far West.[324]

JS sent the letter to Missouri with Thomas B. Marsh, who departed for Far West in company with Hyrum Smith shortly after 4 September 1837. The two men arrived at their

---

321. Minutes, 3 Sept. 1837, pp. 420–425 herein. For more on the opposition to JS, see Historical Introduction to Letter from Parley P. Pratt, 23 May 1837, pp. 386–389 herein; Historical Introduction to Letter from Abel Lamb and Others, ca. 28 May 1837, pp. 392–393 herein; Historical Introduction to Charges against JS Preferred to Bishop's Council, 29 May 1837, pp. 394–397 herein; Revelation, 23 July 1837, pp. 410–417 herein [D&C 112]; and Esplin, "Emergence of Brigham Young," 295–299.

322. JS was likely not aware that on 1 August 1837, Missouri church leaders voted to replace Corrill in the Missouri bishopric. (Minute Book 2, 1 Aug. 1837.)

323. See Minutes, 3 Sept. 1837, pp. 420–425 herein.

324. See Minutes, 17 Sept. 1837–A, pp. 442–443 herein; and Vilate Murray Kimball, Kirtland, OH, to Heber C. Kimball, Preston, England, ca. 10 Sept. 1837, Heber C. Kimball, Collection, CHL.

destination in October.[325] JS himself arrived in Missouri by early November and presided over meetings to further reorganize church leadership, settle differences within the church, and organize new stakes of Zion in Missouri.[326] At a 7 November 1837 conference held in Far West for the purpose of sustaining church leaders, Cowdery served as clerk but was not sustained to his former office as JS's counselor, perhaps because of the unnamed offenses alluded to in this letter.[327]

George W. Robinson copied the letter into JS's journal sometime in mid-March 1838, at the time he copied in a series of document transcripts and summaries pertaining to JS's efforts to set church leadership in order and replace dissenting leaders.[328]

Document Transcript

Sept 4ᵗʰ A.D. 1837

Kirtland Geauga Co. Ohio

Joseph Smith Jʳ. Presᵗ of the Church ⟨of Christ⟩ of Latter Day Saints in all the world[329]

To John Corroll [Corrill] & the whole Church in Zion [p. 18] Sendeth greeting, Blessed be the God ~~of~~ and father of our Lord Jesus Christ Who has blessed you with many blessings in Christ, And who has delivered you many times from the hands of your enimies And planted you many times in an heavenly or holy place, My respects & love to you all, and my blessings upon all the faithfull & true harted in the new & everlasting covenant & for as much as I have desired for a long time to see your faces, & converse with you & instruct you in those things which have been revealed to Me partaining to the Kingdom of God in the last days, I now write unto you offering an appolegy [apology], My being bound with bonds of affliction by the workers of iniquity and by the labours of the Church endeaveroung in all things to do the will of God, for the salvation of the Church both in temporal as well as spiritual things.[330] Bretheren we have

---

325. JS, Journal, 18, in *JSP,* J1:240; Thomas B. Marsh to Wilford Woodruff, in *Elders' Journal,* July 1838, 36–37; "T B Marsh," [2], Historian's Office, Histories of the Twelve, 1856–1858, 1861, CHL.

326. See Minutes, 17 Sept. 1837–B, pp. 444–446 herein; Minutes, 6 Nov. 1837, pp. 464–468 herein; and Minutes, 7 Nov. 1837, pp. 468–472 herein.

327. Minutes, 7 Nov. 1837, p. 469 herein. It is possible that these unnamed transgressions were discussed at a 6 November 1837 meeting in Far West, Missouri. (See Minutes, 6 Nov. 1837, pp. 464–468 herein.)

328. See JS, Journal, 4 Sept. 1837, in *JSP,* J1:240–244.

329. The title of president of the church "in all the world" emphasized JS's authority over the church in Missouri and its presidency. George W. Robinson copied this letter into JS's journal in mid-March 1838, after a 7 November 1837 conference held in Far West, Missouri, upheld JS as "the first President of the whole Church, to preside over the Same," in essence repeating the action that Kirtland church members took in unanimously sustaining JS as the "presiding officer of the church" at the 3 September 1837 conference. (JS, Journal, 18–23, in *JSP,* J1:240–244; Minutes, 7 Nov. 1837, p. 469 herein; Minutes, 3 Sept. 1837, p. 422 herein.)

330. JS's vision of a Zion that included both temporal and spiritual aspects drew increasing criticism as 1837 wore on. (See Introduction to Part 6: 20 Apr.–14 Sept. 1837, pp. 363–366 herein; Historical Introduction

waided through a scene of affliction and sorrow thus far for the will of God, that language is inadequate to describe pray yea therefore with more earnestness for our redemption, You have undoubtedly been informed by letter & otherwise of our difficulties in Kirtland which are now about being settled and that you may have a knowledge of the same I subscribe to you the following minuits of the comittee, of the whole Church of Kirtland the authorities &.c. refering you to my brother Hyrum [Smith] & br. T[homas] B. Marsh for further particulars also that you [p. 19] may know how to proceed to set in order & regulate the affairs of the Church in zion whenever they become disorganized The minuits are as follows;[331]

Minuits of a Conference assembled in committee of the whole Church on the 3ʳᵈ· of Sept. 1837 9 o clock A.M. G[eorge] W. Robinson was called upon to take the minuits of the conference, S[idney] Rigdon then presented Joseph Smith Jr to the Church to know if they still looked upon & would still receive & uphold him as the Presᵗ· of the whole Church And the vote was unanymous in the affirmative: Prsᵗ· Smith then presented S. Rigdon & F[rederick] G. Williams for his councilors and to constitute with himself the three first Presᵗ· of the Church. Vote unanymous in the affirmative, Presᵗ· Smith then introduced O[liver] Cowdery, J[oseph] Smith Sen. Hiram Smith & John Smith for assistant Councilors. These last four together with the three first are to be concidred [considered] the heads of the Church, Carried unanymously. Voted that N. K. Whitny [Newel K. Whitney] hold his office as Bishop & continue to act as such in Kirtland & that R[eynolds] Cahoon & V[inson] Knight continue to act as councilors to the Bishop The Twelve Apostles were then presented one by one When T. B. Marsh D[avid] W. Patten B[righam] Young H. C. Kimble [Heber C. Kimball] O[rson] Hyde P[arley] P. Pratt O. Prat [Orson Pratt] Wᵐ Smith Wᵐ E MᶜLellin, were received unanymously in their Apostleship Luke & Lyman Johnson & J[ohn] F. Boynton were rejected & cut off though privileged with conffesing and making sattisfaction, Elder Boynton (which was the only one present at the

---

to Letter from Parley P. Pratt, 23 May 1837, pp. 386–389 herein; Historical Introduction to Letter from Abel Lamb and Others, ca. 28 May 1837, pp. 392–393 herein; Historical Introduction to Charges against JS Preferred to Bishop's Council, 29 May 1837, pp. 394–397 herein; and Revelation, 23 July 1837, pp. 410–417 herein [D&C 112].)

331. What follows is a later version of the official minutes of the conference found in Minute Book 1. For the complete text of the official version and annotation of these 3 September 1837 minutes, including significant differences between the two sets of minutes, see Minutes, 3 Sept. 1837, pp. 420–425 herein.

time) arose and endeavoured to confess, Justifying himself ~~in~~ ⟨on⟩ ⟨in⟩ his former conduct by reason of the failure of the Bank &c his conduct was strongly protested by Elder [p. 20] Brigham Young in a plain and energetic manner, Stating verious reasons why he would or could not receive him into fellowship until a hearty conffession and repentance was manifested, He was followed by Elder Marsh who acquiesed in testimo[n]y & resolutions Elder Boynton again arose & still attributed his difficulties to the failure of the Bank, stating that he had understood the Bank was instituted by the will of God, and he had been told that it never should fail let men do what they would Pres⁼ Smith then arose and stated that if this had been declared, no one had authority from him for so doing, For he had allways said unless the institution was conducted on richeous [righteous] principals it would not stand, A Vote was then taken to know if the congregation was sattisfied with Boyntons confession Voted in the negative Conf— Adjourened for one hour———

Conferance assembled at 2 o clock P M. Op[e]ned by reading singing & prayer, The Pres⁼ then arose & said he would call upon the church to know if they were sattisfied with their High Council and should proceed to name them individualy John Johnson Joseph Coe Joseph Kingsbury & Martin ⟨*⟩³³² Harris wire [were] objected to, also John P Green[e] but this case put over untill he should be present, Noah Packard Jared Carter Samuel H Smith, These were voted to retain their office Oliver Granger Henry G. Sherwood Wᵐ Marks Mahue [Mayhew] Hillman Harlow Readfield [Redfield] Asa[h]el Smith Phinehas [Phineas] Richards & David Dort were chosen to fill the place of those objected to, The Pres⁼ then called upon the congregation to know if the recent appointed presidents of the seventies should stand in their calling Voted that John Gaylord James Foster Salmon Gee Daniel S Miles Joseph Youngs [Young] Josiah Butterfield [p. 21] & Levi Handcock [Hancock] should retain ~~his~~ ⟨their⟩ office as Pres⁼ˢ of the Seventies John Gould was objected. The Pres then arose and made some remarks concerning the formers Pres⁼ˢ of the Seventies, the callings and authorities of their Priesthood &c. &c. Voted that the old Presidents of the seventies be refered to the quorum of High Priests, And also that ~~of~~ if any of the members of the quorum of the seventies should be dissattisfied &

---

332. TEXT: The asterisk, inscribed in the margin next to Harris's name, references a note reading "over *" that appears at the foot of manuscript page 22. This "over" footnote refers the reader to the top of manuscript page 23, which adds part of a mistakenly passed-over section of minutes.

would not submit to the Present order, and receive these last Presidents that they Should have power to demand their Lisence & they should no longer be concidered members of the church

Conferance Closed by Prayer by the President

~~Joseph Smith Jr Pres~~ᵗ   ~~George W. Robinson Clerk~~
G W Robinson Clk   Joseph Smith Jr Presᵗ

Dear Brotheren

Oliver Cowdery has been in transgression, but as he is now chosen as one of the Presidents or councilors I trust that he will yet humble himself & magnify his calling but if he should not, the church will soon be under the necessaty of raising their hands against him[333] Therefore pray for him, David Whitmer[334] Leonard Rich[335] & others have been in transgression[336] but we hope that they may be humble & ere long make sattisfaction to the Church otherwise they cannot retain their standing, Therefore we say unto you beware of all disaffected Characters for they come not to build up but to destroy & scatter abroad,[337]

---

333. It is not clear what specific misdeed this refers to. In April 1838 Cowdery was brought before the Missouri high council on a variety of charges and was excommunicated from the church. It is likely that there is a connection between this mention of transgression and at least one of those charges. (See Oliver Cowdery, Far West, MO, to Warren A. Cowdery, 21 Jan. 1838; Oliver Cowdery, Far West, MO, to Warren A. Cowdery and Lyman Cowdery, [Kirtland, OH], 4 Feb. 1838, in Cowdery, Letterbook, 80–86; Fullmer, *Autobiography,* [1]; and Synopsis of Oliver Cowdery Trial, 12 Apr. 1838, in *JSP,* J1:251–254.)

334. David Whitmer's name is included among the dissenters in a late May 1837 complaint by Abel Lamb and others. According to that complaint, Whitmer and others had pursued a "course for some time past" that had been "injurious to the church of God." Whitmer, like Oliver Cowdery, was preparing to leave Kirtland to return to Missouri in early September 1837. Whitmer's standing as president of the church in Missouri was called into question by Thomas B. Marsh on 7 November 1837. Whitmer had been proposed by some to replace JS as church president in February 1837 and was later excommunicated after charges were brought against him for, among other matters, "uniting with and possesing the same spirit of the desenters." (Letter from Abel Lamb and Others, ca. 28 May 1837, p. 393 herein; Minutes, 7 Nov. 1837, p. 470 herein; Woodruff, Journal, 19 Feb. 1837; Synopsis of David Whitmer and Lyman Johnson Trials, 13 Apr. 1838, in *JSP,* J1:256; Minute Book 2, 15 Mar. 1838.)

335. Leonard Rich was among the church dissenters who signed Warren Parrish's inflammatory 5 February 1838 letter to the editor of the *Painesville Republican.* (Warren Parrish, Kirtland, OH, 5 Feb. 1838, Letter to the Editor, *Painesville [OH] Republican,* 15 Feb. 1838, [3]; see also "Mormonism," *Zion's Watchman,* 24 Mar. 1838, 46.)

336. There was great division within the church in Kirtland throughout 1837, with many accusing JS of poor leadership and improper conduct. According to Wilford Woodruff, the "spirits of murmering, complaining, & of mutiny" had been brewing "untill many & some in high places had risen up against" JS and were "striving to overthrow his influence & cast him down." (Woodruff, Journal, 28 May 1837; see also Introduction to Part 6: 20 Apr.–14 Sept. 1837, pp. 363–366 herein; and Historical Introduction to Letter from Abel Lamb and Others, ca. 28 May 1837, pp. 392–393 herein.)

337. Soon after the 3 September 1837 conference, Cowdery and Whitmer left Kirtland. Both arrived in Missouri weeks before JS and Sidney Rigdon, and both were in attendance at the 7 November 1837

Though we or an Angel from Heaven preach any other Gospel or introduce [any other?] order of things ⟨than⟩ those things which ye have received and are authorized to received from the first Presidency let him be accursed,[338] May God Almighty Bless you all & keep you unto the coming & kingdom of our Lord and Savior Jesus Christ; Yours in the Bonds of the new ⟨covenent⟩— J. Smith, Jr.

<u>over</u> * [p. 22]

Samu[e]l James was objected to by reason of his absence on a mission and circumstances such that it is impossible for him to attend to the duties of this office

<u>J. Smith J^r Pres^t</u>   <u>George W Robinson ⟨Clerk</u>

————— ℯↄ —————

Revelation, 4 September 1837

Source Note

Revelation, Kirtland Township, Geauga Co., OH, 4 Sept. 1837. Featured version copied [between 13 and 29 Mar. 1838] in JS, Journal, Mar.–Sept. 1838, p. 23; handwriting of George W. Robinson; CHL. For more information on JS, Journal, Mar.–Sept. 1838, see Source Notes for Multiple-Entry Documents, p. 525 herein.

Historical Introduction

JS dictated a revelation on 4 September 1837 making it known that John Whitmer and William W. Phelps had transgressed in some unspecified manner. One plausible reason for this divine rebuke was the two church leaders' handling of property in Missouri.

In August 1836, William Phelps and John Whitmer selected a 640-acre site for the new gathering place for the Saints in Missouri. The site, known as Far West, was located in what would become Caldwell County. Using funds obtained from Saints in Kentucky and Tennessee, Phelps and Whitmer purchased an additional 1,240 acres between early November 1836 and the end of January 1837 and pushed forward an ambitious plan for building Far West, including laying out the city plat and making plans to build a House of the Lord.[339] They did so without consulting the church presidency—or even the other local religious authorities, such as the bishopric and high council—which caused concern among

---

conference in Missouri. (Minutes, 17 Sept. 1837–A, pp. 442–443 herein; Minutes, 7 Nov. 1837, pp. 468–472 herein.)

338. See Galatians 1:8.

339. For more on the creation of Caldwell County and the founding of Far West, Missouri, see Application for Land Patent, 22 June 1836, pp. 253–258 herein; and Letter from William W. Phelps, 7 July 1837, pp. 401–404 herein; see also "Description of Far West Plat," 1837, copy, Brigham Young University and Church History and Doctrine Department, Church History Project Collection, CHL.

the Missouri high counselors.[340] In a letter written the next year, Thomas B. Marsh recalled what he saw as misdeeds by Phelps and Whitmer. He wrote:

> But these men, instead of laying out the money for the benefit of *poor bleeding Zion*, purchased land for their own emolument. They generally did their business, independently of the aid, or counsel of either the Bishop, or High Council. This gave some uneasiness to the two authorities of Zion: not only because they purchased land with church funds, in their own name, for their own aggrandizement, but because they selected the place for the city Far West, and appointed the spot for the house of the Lord to be built on, drew the plan of said house, and appointed and ordained a committee to build the same, without seeking counsel, at the hand of either Bishop, High Council, or First Presidency; when it was well understood that these authorities were appointed for the purpose of counseling on all important matters pertaining to the Saints of God. These two presidents also managed to get the town plot into their own hands, that they might reap the avails arising from the sales of the lots.[341]

In response to such concerns, the Missouri high council met on 3 April 1837 and determined that they should speak with Phelps and Whitmer. This meeting occurred on 7 April, and the church leaders in Far West who attended unanimously agreed that the city plat of Far West would remain as it was originally drafted by Phelps and Whitmer. The Missouri leaders also voted that the price and sale of town lots "be left with the Judgment of the wise men," including Phelps, Whitmer, Edward Partridge, and Partridge's counselors in the Missouri bishopric.[342] According to Marsh, "During this labor the two presidents acknowledged they were wrong, and they, to all appearance, willingly suffered themselves to be corrected by the Council."[343] Despite the earlier disagreement and this reproof, Phelps and Whitmer were appointed as those who would "superintend the building of the house of the Lord in this City Far West and receive Revelations Visions &c concerning said house."[344]

Though the Missouri high council and bishopric came to an agreement with Phelps and Whitmer on the land issues and the House of the Lord,[345] problems involving Phelps and Whitmer resurfaced. By early November 1837, two months after this revelation, JS arrived in Far West and held a conference to set the church in order. At a 6 November meeting, Phelps and Whitmer made remarks in an extensive discussion of "the previous

---

340. Murdock, Journal, 27–30 July 1836.

341. Thomas B. Marsh to Wilford Woodruff, in *Elders' Journal,* July 1838, 36–38, italics in original.

342. Minute Book 2, 3 and 7 Apr. 1837.

343. Thomas B. Marsh to Wilford Woodruff, in *Elders' Journal,* July 1838, 36–38.

344. Minute Book 2, 7 Apr. 1837.

345. The agreement involved Phelps and Whitmer deeding the Far West plat to Edward Partridge. The Missouri bishop then mortgaged the plat to Phelps and Whitmer, bonding himself to pay them $3,450 within the next two years. (Edward Partridge to John Whitmer and William W. Phelps, Bond, 17 May 1837, John Whitmer Family Papers, CHL; Edward Partridge and Lydia Clisbee Partridge to John Whitmer and William W. Phelps, Mortgage, 17 May 1837, John Whitmer Family Papers, CHL; Minutes, 6 Nov. 1837, p. 467 herein.)

disposition of the Town plot and the purchase of land &c." Again the matter seemed settled, but controversy emerged once more in the November 1837 meetings because Phelps and Whitmer had retained the money received from the sale of land rather than giving that money to Partridge for the use of the church. Discontent over this matter lingered into February 1838 when Phelps and Whitmer were charged with improperly using "monies which were loaned for the Church."[346]

A copy of this revelation was likely carried to Missouri by Thomas B. Marsh, who was also charged with carrying JS's 4 September 1837 letter to the church in Missouri.[347] George W. Robinson copied this revelation into JS's journal sometime in mid-March 1838. It was one of a series of document copies and summaries Robinson penned at this time, all of which pertained to JS's ongoing efforts to set church leadership in order and replace several church leaders.[348]

Document Transcript

Revelation to Joseph Smith Jr Given in Kirtland Geauga Co. Ohio Sept 4th 1837
    Making known the transgression of John Whitmer W[illiam] W. Phelps
    Verily thus saith the Lord unto you my Servent Joseph. My Servents John Whitmer & William W Phelps have done those things which are not pleasing in my sight Therefore if they repent not they shall be removed out of their places Amen—

                                                                    J Smith Jr

———— ⁊ ————

Power of Attorney to Hyrum Smith, 5 September 1837

Source Note

JS and Emma Smith, Power of Attorney, to Hyrum Smith, Kirtland Township, Geauga Co., OH, 5 Sept. 1837; handwriting of Oliver Cowdery; signatures of JS and Emma Smith; witnessed by John Long and Samuel Squire; certified by Charles H. Foot, Chardon, OH, 5 Sept. 1837, and John Cleminson, Caldwell Co., MO, 14 Oct. 1837; two pages; JS Collection, CHL. Includes dockets.

Single leaf, measuring 12⅜ × 7⅞ inches (31 × 20 cm). This document has three vertical folds and contains seals that read, "Common Pleas of the County of Geauga" and "Seal of Caldwell County". On the top fourth of the recto is a filing notation in Oliver Cowdery's handwriting that reads, "Joseph Smith Jr | and wife | to | Hyrum Smith | letter of Attorney". The provenance of this document is unknown; it is assumed that the document has remained in continuous institutional custody since its creation.

---

346. Minutes, 6 Nov. 1837, p. 467 herein; Minutes, 10 Nov. 1837, p. 475 herein; Minute Book 2, 5–9 Feb. 1838, pp. 97–98.

347. See Letter to John Corrill and the Church in Missouri, 4 Sept. 1837, pp. 426–431 herein; and Thomas B. Marsh to Wilford Woodruff, in *Elders' Journal,* July 1838, 36–37.

348. Letter to John Corrill and the Church in Missouri, 4 Sept. 1837, in *JSP,* J1:240–244.

Historical Introduction

On 5 September 1837, Oliver Cowdery wrote this power of attorney for JS and Emma Smith, designating Hyrum Smith as their agent to sell or transfer the titles of land purchased in their name in Missouri. The same day, Cowdery drafted another power of attorney for himself and his wife, Elizabeth Ann Whitmer Cowdery, which authorized Hyrum Smith to sell their Missouri land as well. The two powers of attorney were certified and sealed by Charles Foot, deputy clerk of Geauga County, Ohio.[349]

Both JS and Cowdery purchased land in Missouri through designated agents in the summer of 1836. In what became Caldwell County, this involved buying land from the federal government, which required an application for a land patent and a nonrefundable payment. The earliest applications filed on behalf of JS and Cowdery were submitted on 22 June 1836.[350] This land was then apparently sold to church members who moved to the area around what became Far West, Missouri, likely beginning in July 1836 with the removal of members from Clay County.[351] Because the land had been purchased in JS's and Cowdery's names, the title to the land could be conveyed only by them or their agents. These powers of attorney were timely. In late August 1837, John Whitmer wrote a letter from Far West to David Whitmer and Oliver Cowdery addressing these concerns. His letter, which would not have reached Kirtland by the time the powers of attorney were created, specifically mentioned the need for land titles to be transferred. Whitmer wrote that some church members were "becoming impatient" and wanted "a title for their land which is to come from yourself and J. Smith Jr."[352] He recommended that they send someone with a power of attorney to transfer the titles to their new owners in order to avoid litigation on the matter.

Hyrum Smith left Kirtland for Far West sometime before 11 September, accompanied by Thomas B. Marsh and David W. Patten.[353] The men arrived in Far West by mid-October, when Hyrum Smith took the powers of attorney to Caldwell County clerk John Cleminson to be recorded. Cleminson copied the text of the power of attorney featured here on 16 October 1837 and added a filing notation to the original power of attorney indicating a copy of the text was in "Book A." He then returned the original to Hyrum Smith for his use.[354] With the powers of attorney recognized and sealed by officials in both Geauga County, Ohio, and Caldwell County, Missouri, Smith was authorized to act as the agent for

---

349. Oliver Cowdery and Elizabeth Ann Cowdery, to Hyrum Smith, Power of Attorney, 5 Sept. 1837, Kirtland, OH, Hyrum Smith, Papers, CHL; Johnson and Romig, *Index to Early Caldwell County,* 47; Land Patents for Oliver Cowdery, Caldwell Co., MO, nos. 7869, 7870–7872, 8666, 8785, General Land Office Records, Bureau of Land Management, U.S. Department of the Interior.

350. Application for Land Patent, 22 June 1836, pp. 253–258 herein.

351. See Letter to William W. Phelps and Others, 25 July 1836, pp. 268–271 herein; and Letter to John Thornton and Others, 25 July 1836, pp. 258–268 herein.

352. John Whitmer, Far West, MO, to Oliver Cowdery and David Whitmer, Kirtland Mills, OH, 29 Aug. 1837, Western Americana Collection, Beinecke Rare Book and Manuscript Library, Yale University.

353. Vilate Murray Kimball, Kirtland, OH, to Heber C. Kimball, Preston, England, ca. 10 Sept. 1837, Heber C. Kimball, Collection, CHL.

354. On the process for filing and recording documents with government offices, see An Act to Provide for the Filing and Reporting the Decisions of the Supreme Court [20 Mar. 1835], *Revised Statutes of the State of Missouri* [1835], 217–219.

Power of Attorney. 5 September 1837. Oliver Cowdery wrote the initial power of attorney that authorized Hyrum Smith to act in the names of Joseph and Emma Smith while conducting their business in the state of Missouri. Subsequent entries on this document were written by court clerks in Geauga County, Ohio, and Caldwell County, Missouri. This document features the signatures of both Joseph and Emma Smith and is stamped with the seals from the courts of both Geauga and Caldwell counties, indicating that it was a legally recognized document in both Ohio and Missouri. Handwriting of Oliver Cowdery. Power of Attorney, 5 Sept. 1837, JS Collection, Church History Library, Salt Lake City. (Photograph by Welden C. Andersen.)

JS and Emma Smith and the Cowderys and conduct necessary business on their behalf. There is only one known land record indicating Hyrum Smith's actions in Missouri: he signed a deed selling land owned by JS and Emma in Caldwell County to George Beebe on 17 October 1837.[355]

Document Transcript

/[356]Know all men by these presents, that we, Joseph Smith, jr. and Emma Smith, wife of the said Joseph Smith, jr. of Kirtland, Geauga County, Ohio, do hereby constitute and appoint Hyrum Smith, of the place aforesaid, our attorney, for us and in our names to bargain, sell and convey, in fee simple, by deed of general warranty, for such price, upon such terms of credit, and to such person or persons, as he shall think fit, the whole or any part of land owned by us in Caldwell or Davi[es]s Counties,[357] in the State of Missouri. Hereby ratifying and confirming all such bargains, receipts for purchase money, agreements, and deeds as shall be made, executed, or acknowledged, in the premises, by our said attorney, the same as if we were personally present and ⟨did⟩ the same. In witness whereof we have hereunto set our hand and seals, this fifth day of September, in the year of our Lord, one thousand eight hundred and thirty seven.

[358]**J Smith Jr** Seal[359]

Emma Smith Seal

In the twelfth line from the top the word "did" is interlined before signing.

In the presence of

[360]John Ł Long

Saml Squire

/[361]The State of Ohio ⎫

    Geauga County ss. ⎭

Chardon Sept. 5. 1837.

---

355. JS and Emma Smith by Hyrum Smith to George Beebe, Deed, 17 Oct. 1837, Historical Department, Nineteenth-Century Legal Documents Collection, CHL.

356. TEXT: Oliver Cowdery handwriting begins.

357. According to the extant land records, agents acting on behalf of JS applied and paid for land patents for around 560 acres in what became Caldwell County, Missouri, in June and September 1836. Land claimed for JS in Daviess County is not documented but may have involved preemption claims since Daviess had not been surveyed. (Application for Land Patent, 22 June 1836, pp. 253–258 herein; Johnson and Romig, *Index to Early Caldwell County*, 202; Walker, "Mormon Land Rights," 4–55.)

358. TEXT: Signatures of JS and Emma Smith.

359. TEXT: Each instance of "Seal" is enclosed in a hand-drawn representation of a seal.

360. TEXT: Signatures of John Long and Samuel Squire.

361. TEXT: Oliver Cowdery handwriting ends; Charles H. Foot begins.

Personally appeared ⟨before me⟩ Joseph Smith Jr. and Emma Smith wife of the said Joseph Jr. and severally acknowledged the executing of the foregoing instrument to be their free act and deed— for the purposes therein stated— I further certify that I did examine the said Emma separate and apart from her said husband, and upon such examination she did declare that she did sign and seal the same as her own free act and deed and that she is still satisfied therewith.

In testimony whereof I hereunto sign my name and affix the seal of the Court of Common Pleas for said County at Chardon, the day and year above written

C[harles] H. Foot[362] Deputy Clerk of the Court of Common Pleas for said
County [p. [1]]

/[363]State of Missouri ⎱ Ss
County of Caldwell ⎰

I, John Cleminson clerk of the circuit court and Exofficio Recorder within and for the county aforesaid do certify that the written Letter of Attorney from Joseph Smith J[r.] to Hyrum Smith was filed[364] in my office October 16th 1837 and recorded in book A page 36

In testimony of which I have hereunto set my hand and affixed the seal of said office the day and year above written

John Cleminson Clerk & Exofficio Recorder [p. [2]]

———— ဢ ————

Promissory Note to Jason Brunell, 14 September 1837

Source Note

JS, Promissory Note, to Jacinth Buenell [Jason Brunell], Kirtland Township, Geauga Co., OH, 14 Sept. 1837; handwriting of JS; notations of payment in handwriting of Newel K. Whitney, Willard Richards, William Clayton, Brigham Young, and two unidentified scribes; two pages; JS Collection, CHL.

One leaf, measuring 4½ × 8¼ inches (11 × 21 cm). The top edge of the recto has the square cut of manufactured paper; the bottom, left, and right edges of the recto were cut. The note was folded in half and then folded twice in a parallel fold. Details of efforts to pay the note are found in subsequent notations on the verso by unidentified scribes, Newel K. Whitney, Willard Richards, and William Clayton. JS's signature was removed from the note, either to indicate payment when Brigham Young noted on the recto that the note was paid in full or later by a signature collector. The leaf contains

---

362. Charles H. Foot resided at Chardon, Ohio, the Geauga County seat, where he was "engaged for many years as deputy to Mr. D.D. Aikens' county clerk's office." (*History of Geauga and Lake Counties,* 127.)
363. TEXT: Charles H. Foot handwriting ends; John Cleminson begins.
364. The filing mentioned here likely refers to this filing notation made by Cleminson on 16 October. No records indicate that a duplicate of the original power of attorney was made.

marked staining, soiling at the folds, and fly specks. Payment notations by Willard Richards, William Clayton, and Brigham Young indicate continuous institutional custody.

Historical Introduction

On 14 September 1837, JS wrote this promissory note, thereby committing to pay Jason Brunell[365] five hundred dollars with interest by 20 January 1838. Given the scarcity of currency and JS's many financial obligations, it is likely that he borrowed money from Brunell to pay debts.[366] This is one of two notes JS gave to Brunell in fall 1837; the second note is not extant.[367]

Brunell was a member of the church from York County, Upper Canada, who moved to Kirtland, Ohio, with his family between August 1837 and March 1838.[368] During the summer of 1837, Brunell made more than one trip between Kirtland and Upper Canada. Mary Fielding, in a June 1837 letter to her sister Mercy, mentioned that Brunell personally delivered a note from Mercy, then living in Upper Canada (probably in Ontario County).[369] A month later, Mary Fielding recorded that Brunell departed Kirtland for Canada in late

---

365. Brunell's given name and surname were recorded with variant spellings in contemporary records. By the 1840s in Nauvoo, Illinois, the spelling Brunell became more standard.

366. On 1 September 1837, the mercantile firms of Rigdon, Smith & Cowdery and Cahoon, Carter & Co. renegotiated their existing debts to several New York mercantile firms, creating new promissory notes to pay outstanding debts with the firms. (JS, Sidney Rigdon, and Oliver Cowdery to Holbrook & Firme [Ferme], Promissory Note, Kirtland, OH, 1 Sept. 1837, Ohio Historical Society, Columbus, OH; JS, Sidney Rigdon, and Oliver Cowdery to Holbrook & Firme [Ferme], Promissory Note, Kirtland, OH, 1 Sept. 1837, BYU; Hyrum Smith, Reynolds Cahoon, and Jared Carter to Halsted, Haines & Co., Promissory Note, 1 Sept. 1837, private possession, copy at CHL; Hyrum Smith et al. to Halsted, Haines & Co., Promissory Note, 1 Sept. 1837, Brigham Young Office Files, CHL; Hyrum Smith et al. to Mead & Betts, Promissory Note, 1 Sept. 1837, Mead & Betts v. Estate of JS, Illinois State Historical Society, Circuit Court Case Files, CHL; see also Perkins & Osborn, Account Statement, ca. 29 Oct. 1838, JS Office Papers, CHL.)

367. A second note for $372 was due 10 January 1838 and was likely created around this same time. Although not extant, the note was listed in the estate records after Brunell's death in 1841. Those records indicate that the note was paid for with land in Nauvoo. (Adams Co., IL, Estate Records, ca. 1832–1938, box 4, microfilm 933,883, U.S. and Canada Record Collection, FHL.)

368. Jason Brunell was born in Upper Canada (now Ontario) around 1800. He married Susan Lamoreaux in 1824 in York, Upper Canada. He likely joined the church in 1836 at the same time as his wife and her parents, John and Abigail Lamoreaux. In April 1837, Brunell sent $200 with Parley P. Pratt, who had been proselytizing in Upper Canada, to pay for land purchased by the church in Kirtland. Brunell was in York, Upper Canada, on 26 April 1837 when he gave the money to Pratt. He traveled to Kirtland in June 1837 and returned to Upper Canada by July 1837, possibly to bring his family to Kirtland. He signed the Kirtland Camp constitution on 13 March 1838 and recorded seven members of his family participating in the Kirtland Camp, indicating that he had moved his family to Kirtland by March 1838. (Jenkins, *Richmond Hill, Ontario;* Pratt, *Autobiography,* 168–169; Jason Brunell, Receipt, York, Upper Canada, 26 Apr. 1837, JS Office Papers, CHL; Mary Fielding, Kirtland, OH, to Mercy Fielding, [Upper Canada], ca. June 1837, Mary Fielding Smith, Collection, CHL; Mary Fielding, Kirtland, OH, to Mercy Fielding Thompson, [Upper Canada], 8 July 1837, Mary Fielding Smith, Collection, CHL; Kirtland Camp, Journal, [2].)

369. Mary Fielding, Kirtland, OH, to Mercy Fielding, [Upper Canada], ca. June 1837, Mary Fielding Smith, Collection, CHL.

June or early July 1837.[370] He had returned to Kirtland by 3 August 1837, when he bought land there, and he may have remained in Kirtland from that time to mid-September, when this promissory note was created.[371]

The note was paid by April 1842. According to payment records on the back of the note, a portion was paid with a section of land in Nauvoo. The note was canceled by Brigham Young, indicating it had been paid and was no longer a transferable financial obligation. Notations on the back of the promissory note indicate it was fully paid by April 1842.

Document Transcript

[372]**Kirtland Sept 14th 1837**

For Value Recieved I promice to pay Jacinth Beunell [Jason Brunell] five hundred dollers by the twentieth of Jenuary next with use[373]

J[oseph Smith Jr.][374]

[375]Received payment in full.

B[righam] Young[376] [p. [1]]

[377]Recd this 3rd Day October 1840 on the within fifteen Dollars

[378]Recd this 5th of October 1840 on the within ~~sixteen~~ ⟨nine⟩ Dollars

[379]Rec^d 23^{d.} July 1841 at Nauvoo Ill. One Hundred and four dollars in Goods & cash on the within

[380][*3 illegible words*] 1842 Received on the within Ten dollars

[381]Received [*illegible*] 12 one buggy. per hand.

---

370. Mary Fielding, Kirtland, OH, to Mercy Fielding Thompson, [Upper Canada], 8 July 1837, Mary Fielding Smith, Collection, CHL.

371. Geauga Co., OH, Deed Records, 1795–1921, vol. 24, p. 482, 3 Aug. 1837, microfilm 20,240, U.S. and Canada Record Collection, FHL.

372. TEXT: JS handwriting begins.

373. That is, interest.

374. TEXT: JS's signature was cut out of the document, which may have served to cancel the note. However, it is unclear if this was done contemporaneously to void the note or years later by a signature collector.

375. TEXT: JS handwriting ends; Brigham Young begins.

376. TEXT: Note of payment—possibly paid by Young himself—written vertically over text, canceling the note. Eight payments, beginning October 1840, were recorded on the back of the note. Different individuals, including Jared Carter and Brigham Young, appear to have contributed to the effort to pay off JS's debt, which was due in January 1838. Since the back of the note does not contain any signatures of endorsement, it appears the note was never transferred from Brunell, who died in 1841, or his family thereafter, meaning he or his family likely collected these payments.

377. TEXT: Brigham Young handwriting ends; first unidentified scribe begins.

378. TEXT: First unidentified scribe handwriting ends; second unidentified scribe begins.

379. TEXT: Second unidentified scribe handwriting ends; Newel K. Whitney begins.

380. TEXT: Newel K. Whitney handwriting ends; Willard Richards begins.

381. TEXT: Willard Richards handwriting continues, though written at a later time than the previous line. Text from this point forward written vertically across preceding text.

Jared Carte[r][382] Law of the Lord page 79.[383] value eighty d[ol]lars. on the within.—

[384]Rceived Feb ◊◊th A. Bond for a Lot west of John Ha◊◊is in Kimballs additin value. $75.◊◊—

/[385]Received [on] the within March 30th· 1842 one hundre[d] and ninety dollars & fifty four cents.

[386]April 11th· [184]2 Received on the within one hundr[ed] and fourteen dollars and thirty five [ce]nts [p. [2]]

---

382. TEXT: Cut-out signature on opposite side of page results in missing text. From this point forward, text is supplied based on context.

383. The Nauvoo-era "Book of the Law of the Lord" records a tithing payment by Jared Carter for one buggy valued at eighty dollars. That inscription was crossed out, suggesting that although the buggy may have initially been intended as a tithing payment, it was instead applied to the debt on this promissory note. (Book of the Law of the Lord, 79.)

384. TEXT: Willard Richards handwriting continues, written still later.

385. TEXT: Willard Richards handwriting ends; William Clayton begins.

386. TEXT: Handwriting of William Clayton continues, though written at a later time.

PART 7: 17 SEPTEMBER 1837– 21 JANUARY 1838

Documents from 17 September 1837 to 21 January 1838 reflect profound changes in JS's life, including the excommunication of several dissenting church members—many of whom had been close friends—and the relocation of JS and his family from Kirtland, Ohio, to Far West, Missouri.

In September, JS and associates began work on a new publication called the *Elders' Journal*.[1] Late that same month, JS and other Kirtland church leaders left to travel to Far West, Missouri. They arrived by early November and attended to various matters of church business, including the reorganization of church leadership positions at a 7 November 1837 meeting, similar to what occurred in Ohio during the 3 September 1837 conference. The Missouri conference included a change in the First Presidency, with Hyrum Smith replacing Frederick G. Williams as second counselor to JS.[2] Other concerns were discussed at these early November meetings, including land purchases in Missouri and the need to have adequate space for new arrivals there. The next month, in an editorial in the *Elders' Journal,* JS expressed his intention to move his family to Far West and encouraged Saints in Kirtland to also make preparations to gather with the Saints in Missouri.[3]

JS and his party returned to Kirtland in early December to find that dissent had revived. Divisions in Kirtland became more pronounced in January 1838 as dissidents, excommunicated church members, and others made threats against the lives of JS and other church leaders.[4] In addition, JS and Sidney Rigdon faced litigation brought by their opponents, which meant their property might be seized and auctioned by the local sheriff.[5] On 12 January 1838, JS dictated three revelations that established rules to deter attempts at undermining the First Presidency's authority and to limit the influence of dissenters.[6] One of the revelations

---

1. See Historical Introduction to Selections from *Elders' Journal,* Oct. 1837, pp. 460–462 herein.

2. Minutes, 7 Nov. 1837, pp. 468–472 herein; see also Minutes, 3 Sept. 1837, pp. 420–425 herein.

3. Minutes, 10 Nov. 1837, pp. 472–476 herein; Travel Account and Questions, Nov. 1837, pp. 481–482 herein.

4. JS History, vol. B-1, 780; Hepzibah Richards, Kirtland, OH, to Willard Richards, Liverpool, England, 18 Jan. 1838, Willard Richards, Journals and Papers, CHL.

5. See Historical Introduction to Agreement, 4 Jan. 1838, pp. 489–491 herein.

6. See Historical Introduction to Revelation, 12 Jan. 1838–A, pp. 495–496 herein; Historical Introduction to Revelation, 12 Jan. 1838–B, pp. 498–499 herein; and Historical Introduction to Revelation, 12 Jan. 1838–C, pp. 500–501 herein.

also directed the First Presidency to leave Kirtland with their families "as soon as it is practicable" and commanded all their "faithfull friends" to likewise depart for Missouri.[7] JS and Rigdon left Kirtland the evening of 12 January and were later joined by their families in Norton, Ohio; the group started for Missouri by 16 January.[8] The leaders of the dissenters in Kirtland, now excommunicated from the church, took steps to organize their own church, which they called the Church of Christ. Identifying themselves as the "old standard" and arguing that the church under JS had been led astray and now required reform, the dissenters formally incorporated their church in the state of Ohio on 18 January, solidifying the separation between themselves and the Church of the Latter Day Saints.[9]

———— ☙ ————

Minutes, 17 September 1837–A

Source Note

Minutes, Kirtland Township, Geauga Co., OH, 17 Sept. 1837. Featured version copied [ca. 17 Sept. 1837] in Minute Book 1, p. 242; handwriting of George W. Robinson; CHL. For more information on Minute Book 1, see Source Notes for Multiple-Entry Documents, p. 527 herein.

Historical Introduction

JS and Sidney Rigdon, members of the church's First Presidency, presided over and participated in a Sunday meeting on 17 September 1837 in the House of the Lord in Kirtland, Ohio, during which William Marks and George W. Robinson received new assignments. After Kirtland bishop Newel K. Whitney nominated Marks to become the agent to the bishop, Marks was unanimously sustained by the members in attendance.[10] Marks appears to have acted as an agent for JS and Rigdon beginning in April 1837, and this appointment may have been an extension of that role.[11] He formally accepted the position in an evening meeting of the elders of the church on 17 September.[12]

---

7. Revelation, 12 Jan. 1838–C, pp. 501–502 herein.

8. JS History, vol. B-1, 780. JS, his family, and others who were traveling with them arrived in Far West on 14 March 1838. (JS, Journal, Mar.–Sept. 1838, 16, in *JSP,* J1:237.)

9. Thomas B. Marsh, [Far West, MO], to Wilford Woodruff, in *Elders' Journal,* July 1838, 36–37; Geauga Co., OH, Witness Docket, 1831–1835, 18 Jan. 1838, Geauga County Archives and Records Center, Chardon, OH.

10. Whitney's request for an agent and Marks's appointment were printed in minutes in the *Elders' Journal* summarizing events that occurred on 17 September. (Minutes, *Elders' Journal,* Nov. 1837, 17.)

11. In April 1837, JS and Rigdon each transferred land to Marks, and in May 1837 they transferred ownership of the *Latter Day Saints' Messenger and Advocate* and the church's Kirtland printing office to Marks. It is not clear whether any money was exchanged in these transactions, but Marks's willingness to transfer his right to land involved in the mortgage of the House of the Lord to Mead, Stafford & Co. suggests he was likely holding this land as an agent. (Deed to William Marks, 10 Apr. 1837, pp. 357–362 herein; Sidney Rigdon to William Marks, Geauga County Deed Record, vol. 23, p. 535, Geauga County Archives and Records Center, Chardon, OH; "Notice," *LDS Messenger and Advocate,* May 1837, 3:512; Mortgage to Mead, Stafford & Co., 11 July 1837, pp. 404–410 herein.)

12. Minutes, 17 Sept. 1837–B, pp. 445–446 herein.

After Marks was sustained, Sidney Rigdon spoke of the need to appoint a new general recorder and clerk for the church since Oliver Cowdery, who had previously acted in this position, had recently moved to Far West, Missouri.[13] Rigdon nominated one of his sons-in-law, George W. Robinson, for the office, and the assembled church members unanimously elected him. Robinson appears to have promptly undertaken his new office; he recorded the minutes featured here, acknowledging his position as "Clerk of the Church."

Document Transcript

Sunday 17ᵗʰ Sept. 1837 In an assembly of the Saints in the house of the Lord, the following business was transacted by the Church, N[ewel] K. Whitney the Bishop of the Church in Kirtland, stated to the Saints that the time had now arraved when it was necessary for him to have an agent, agreeable to the provisions made for him in the revelations,[14] he proceded to nominate Elder William Marks, and then Called upon the Church to know if it was their minds that Elder Marks Should officiate as Agent to the Bishop, Voted in the affirmative. by the unanimous voice of the Church,

Pres. [Sidney] Rigdon then stated that it was necessary that the Church should have a general recorder & Clerk, to fill the place of O[liver] Cowdery who had lately removed to the west, George W. Robinson was nominated & elected by a unanimous voice of the Church, to act in that office as general Clerk & recorder of the whole Church. Pres. Rigdon made some remarks upon the duties responsibility &c. of the Bishop his Agent & Councilors, & the nesessity of their standing forth immediately to degnify their office, After some remarks by Presidents Smith & Rigdon and others upon the disipline of Children, &c. the administration of the Lords Supper being attended to, the meeting Closed by a benediction from the Bishop.——

G.W. Robinson.} Clerk of the— <u>Church</u> [p. 242]

---

13. Oliver Cowdery left Kirtland with his family to travel to Far West shortly after 15 September 1837, the date of his last docket entry as a Kirtland justice of the peace. (Cowdery, Docket Book, 14 June–15 Sept. 1837.)

14. JS revelations in 1832 and 1833 had directed Newel K. Whitney to obtain an agent. The timing of Marks's appointment may be related to Whitney's need for additional help with the financial matters of the Kirtland church or to church leaders' decision to appoint additional stakes of Zion and relocate the majority of Kirtland Saints to Missouri. (See Revelation, 22–23 Sept. 1832, in *JSP*, D2:303 [D&C 84:112–113]; and Revelation, 8 Mar. 1833, in *JSP*, D3:30 [D&C 90:22–23].)

Minutes, 17 September 1837–B

Source Note

Minutes, Kirtland Township, Geauga Co., OH, 17 Sept. 1837. Featured version copied [ca. 17 Sept. 1837] in Minute Book 1, pp. 243–245; handwriting of George W. Robinson; CHL. For more information on Minute Book 1, see Source Notes for Multiple-Entry Documents, p. 527 herein.

Historical Introduction

On the evening of 17 September 1837, the elders of the church in Kirtland, Ohio, met in the House of the Lord. JS began the meeting with a discourse on the gathering of the Saints. According to Mary Fielding, whom JS visited after this meeting, "Some important things were shown to Bro. Jos^ph in vision . . . relitive to the enlargment of our Borders." This expansion was "necessary for the Inhabitants of Zion both here and in the West are crying the Citys are too strait for us give place that we may dwell the people are crouding in from all parts."[15] Sidney Rigdon likewise said that the Saints "will gather" and that "Earth and hell combind cannot hinder them for gather they will hence the necessaty of planting new stakes."[16] The conference then authorized JS and Rigdon to appoint additional stakes of Zion, since the present areas appointed for the Saints, in both Ohio and Missouri, were "crowded to overflowing" and would not have room for the additional church members intending to gather. The measure was unanimously approved by a vote of the assembled elders.

JS then asked the elders for volunteers to leave Kirtland and preach. The 109 elders who indicated their willingness to travel were divided into eight companies, with about thirteen men in each, and were assigned a direction in which to travel. Although it had been common for the elders to return from their travels and remain at home in the winter months, Marcellus Cowdery informed George A. Smith that this was not the case that winter: "Brother Joseph & Sidney say that the Elders must be out all winter this year, no compulsion you know, but this is the word to the Elders, and great promises to those who go and are faithful."[17] Although Cowdery intended to fulfill his mission, as others certainly did, extant documentation does not provide adequate details regarding the outcome of his planned missionary endeavor.

The day following this conference, Kirtland bishop Newel K. Whitney and his counselors, Reynolds Cahoon and Vinson Knight, printed a broadside containing a memorial addressed to "the Saints scattered abroad." The memorial informed church members outside Kirtland and northwest Missouri of the decision to appoint further stakes of Zion and appealed to the Saints to donate money to relieve the debts of church leaders in Kirtland and help build Zion. Whitney and his counselors also urged every individual

---

15. Mary Fielding, Kirtland, OH, to Mercy Fielding Thompson and Robert Thompson, Churchville, Upper Canada, 7 Oct. 1837, Mary Fielding Smith, Collection, CHL.

16. Mary Fielding, Kirtland, OH, to Mercy Fielding Thompson and Robert Thompson, Churchville, Upper Canada, 7 Oct. 1837, Mary Fielding Smith, Collection, CHL, underlining in original.

17. John Smith and Marcellus Cowdery, Kirtland, OH, to George A. Smith, Shinnston, VA, 26 Sept. 1837, George Albert Smith, Papers, CHL.

to "give heed the very instant that they embrace the gospel, and exert themselves with energy to send on means to build up Zion: for our God bids us to haste the building of the city, saying, the time has come when the city must be pushed forward with unceasing exertions."[18]

Ten days after the conference, JS and Rigdon left for Missouri to set the church there in order, locate new stakes of Zion, and conduct other church business.[19] They and their companions arrived in Far West, Missouri, by early November and there appointed a committee to locate areas for new settlements.[20]

Document Transcript

⟨Sunday Evening Sept. the ~~12th~~ 17th 1837⟩

Minuits of a conference of Elders held in the house of the Lord this evening Pres. Joseph Smith Jr presided, the conferance was op[e]ned by prayer by Pres. ⟨S[idney]⟩ Rigdon after which the conferance was addressed ~~by~~ from the Chair, on the subject of the gathering of the Saints in the last days and the duties of the of the different quorums relations thereto,[21] It appeared manifest to the conference that the places appointed for the gathering of the saints ⟨were⟩ at this time crowded to overflowing & that it was necessary that there be more Stakes of Zion appointed in order that the poor might have a place to gather to, wherefore it was moved seconded & carried by vote of the whole that Presidents J Smith Jr & S. Rigdon be requested by this conference to go & appoint other Stakes or places of gathering[22] and that they receive a certificate of this their appointment signed by the Clerk of the Church,[23] Elder William Marks who

---

18. *To the Saints Scattered Abroad, the Bishop and His Counselors of Kirtland Send Greeting* [Kirtland, OH: 18 Sept. 1837], CHL. The memorial was also printed in the September issue of the *Messenger and Advocate*. (Newel K. Whitney et al., Kirtland, OH, to "the Saints Scattered Abroad," *LDS Messenger and Advocate,* Sept. 1837, 3:561–564.)

19. Travel Account and Questions, Nov. 1837, pp. 480–482 herein.

20. Minutes, 10 Nov. 1837, p. 475 herein.

21. On 6 April 1837, Sidney Rigdon stated that the gathering of the Saints was "the object of this mission & ministry" and that "the preaching of the gospel was the first thing," since "nothing can effect the gathering of the Saints but that." Rigdon further informed the elders that they should instruct those who joined the church to gather at the appointed places for the Saints, including Kirtland. ("Anniversary of the Church of Latter Day Saints," *LDS Messenger and Advocate,* Apr. 1837, 3:488–489.)

22. Marcellus Cowdery, in a letter to George A. Smith in late September, wrote, "Brother Joseph & Sidney expect to start soon to appoint 11 or 12 new Stakes of Zion" in Missouri. Mary Fielding in a 7 October letter also noted that after JS and Rigdon established new stakes in Kirtland before they left, they would go to Missouri to "set in order the Church in the West" and there establish "11 new Stakes before they return." (John Smith and Marcellus Cowdery, Kirtland, OH, to George A. Smith, Shinnston, VA, 26 Sept. 1837, George Albert Smith, Papers, CHL, underlining in original; Mary Fielding, Kirtland, OH, to Mercy Fielding Thompson and Robert Thompson, Churchville, Upper Canada, 7 Oct. 1837, Mary Fielding Smith, Collection, CHL.)

23. The clerk and general recorder of the church was George W. Robinson, who had been appointed at an earlier meeting on 17 September 1837. (Minutes, 17 Sept. 1837–A, p. 443 herein.)

had been appointed, in the after part of the day to be the Bishops Agent[24] was called upon to know if he would accept the appointment he arose and said that he would comply with the request of the Church & the Lord being his helper he would discharge the duties thereof to the best of his abilities, After which the Elders present who were in a situation to travel were called upon [p. 243] to number themselves, begining on the South Side of the house, & so pass to the north, it appeared that there were one hundred & nine Elders present who wished to travel, they were then divided into eight companies in the following manner, Beginning with No 1 to No 13 formed the first company They were appointed to travel East, The next company was from 13 to 26 They were appointed to travel South East, The next was from 26 to 39 They were appointed to travel South, The next from 39 to 52 They were to travel South west, The next from 52 to 65 They were to go directly West The next from 65 to 78 Their course was North west, The next from 78 to 91 They were to travel North, The next from 91 to 104 They were to travel North East It appeared after this division that there 5 left Nos 105,-6-7-8 and 9 No 105 was appointed to travel with the company that go South East, 106 with the Com'y South, 107 to travel with the South Com'y, 108 with the East Company, ⟨&⟩ 109 North. It was farther appointed that those who might desire to travel a different course from the one which was appointed to the division to which They belonged, might have the privilege of changing with one of another division. And lastly it was appointed that the different divisions appoint a meeting for themselves to make [p. 244] such arrangments as they shall think proper in relation to their journying and after prayer by President S. Rigdon the conference adjourned

G[eorge] W. Robinson. Clerk of— Church

Letter from Wilford Woodruff and Jonathan H. Hale, 18 September 1837

Source Note

Wilford Woodruff and Jonathan H. Hale, Letter, Vinalhaven, Fox Islands, Hancock Co., ME, to JS and "the Church of Latter Day Saints," Kirtland Township, Geauga Co., OH, 18 Sept. 1837. Featured version published in "To Joseph Smith Jr. and the Church of Latter Day Saints," Elders' Journal of the Church of Latter Day Saints, Oct. 1837, 1–3. For more information on Elders' Journal of the Church of Latter Day Saints, see Source Notes for Multiple-Entry Documents, p. 521 herein.

---

24. See Minutes, 17 Sept. 1837–A, p. 443 herein.

Historical Introduction

On 31 May 1837, Wilford Woodruff, Jonathan H. Hale, and Milton Holmes, all members of the Quorum of the Seventy, departed Kirtland, Ohio, to preach in "the eastern country."[25] Over the next three and a half months, the men proselytized in communities in New York, Upper Canada, Connecticut, Massachusetts, New Hampshire, and Maine.[26] Then in late August, Woodruff and Hale made their way to the Fox Islands, an archipelago off the coast of southern Maine, where they preached, baptized, and eventually established a small branch of the church. On 18 September 1837, the pair sent a letter to JS and the church reporting on their travels and missionary efforts. The letter was published in the October 1837 issue of the *Elders' Journal*.

Woodruff, Hale, and Holmes set off for their eastern mission amid social and economic turmoil in Kirtland and two weeks before apostle Heber C. Kimball and others departed on a mission to England.[27] In a reminiscent account published two decades later, Woodruff recalled that he had "felt impressed to go out upon a mission; the Spirit was upon me, and lead me to go to Fox Islands; it was a country I had never visited. I named my feelings upon the subject to Elders Kimball, [Sidney] Rigdon and others; they encouraged me to go."[28] Woodruff's desire to preach in the Fox Islands may have been related to an ordination blessing given to him by Zebedee Coltrin in January 1837, in which Woodruff was told that he would preach "to the inhabitants upon the Islands of the Sea."[29] Woodruff recounted that he handpicked Hale to accompany him.[30] Unlike Woodruff, Hale—who was baptized in 1834 and had presided over a branch of the church in Dover, New Hampshire—had firsthand knowledge of the Fox Islands.[31]

The missionaries' indirect course to Maine was likely influenced by their desire to preach to and visit with family members scattered throughout the region. As they trekked across New York in early June, for example, Woodruff stopped in his former home of Richland, where he reunited with his two older brothers, Azmon and Thompson.[32] While preaching near his childhood home in Farmington, Connecticut, Woodruff visited his

---

25. Woodruff, Journal, 30–31 May 1837.

26. Holmes traveled with Woodruff and Hale as far as Connecticut before joining another companion to preach in a different region. He later rejoined Woodruff and Hale near his hometown of Rowley, Massachusetts. (Alexander, *Things in Heaven and Earth*, 57–58, 66; Woodruff, Journal, 23 July 1837.)

27. Letter from Abel Lamb and Others, ca. 28 May 1837, pp. 391–393 herein; Recommendation for Heber C. Kimball, between 2 and 13 June 1837, pp. 397–401 herein.

28. "History of Wilford Woodruff," *Deseret News,* 14 July 1858, 86.

29. Woodruff, Journal, 3 Jan. 1837.

30. Wilford Woodruff, "Discourse," 19 Oct. 1896, *Deseret Weekly,* 7 Nov. 1896, 643.

31. An entry in Hale's journal briefly refers to a trip he made to the Fox Islands in September 1834 to purchase a "vessel load of sheep." (Hale, Reminiscences and Journal, 3.)

32. Woodruff had been largely estranged from his brother Azmon since he left New York to participate in the Camp of Israel expedition in 1834. Azmon had been baptized but left the church shortly after Wilford departed for Missouri. The brothers exchanged letters in the years to follow, but Wilford's enthusiasm for and devotion to his new faith appears to have only widened the gulf between them. When he arrived in Richland around 4 June 1837, he noted in his journal that he "found sumthing of a colness manifest toward me and my brethren because of our religion from my Brothers household especially from Elizabeth my Brothers wife." Though Wilford was invited to eat with Azmon and his family, he was not

younger sister, Eunice, and his father, Aphek; he also baptized members of his extended family.[33] In July, Hale and Woodruff preached near Hale's childhood home of Bradford, Massachusetts, where Hale visited with members of his extended family; Milton Holmes was also from the area and visited family there.[34] Phebe Carter Woodruff, who had married Wilford in April 1837, joined the missionaries in Bradford as well, and in early August she accompanied her husband to her hometown of Scarborough, Maine, where Woodruff preached and spent two weeks becoming acquainted with his new bride's family.[35]

The letter to JS and the church briefly summarized the missionaries' three-month journey to Maine, but most of the communication was devoted to Woodruff and Hale's activities on the Fox Islands. Rising from southern Maine's Penobscot Bay, the Fox Island archipelago—comprising two larger islands and dozens of smaller islets—is situated twelve miles off the coast of Rockland. North Fox Island, known today as North Haven, exhibits a relatively flat topography that during the mid-1830s was sparsely wooded and largely dominated by open pastures and farmland. Characterized by its granite-covered hills, rocky shoreline, and woods of pine, fir, and spruce, South Fox Island (or Vinalhaven today) was not as suitable for agriculture; early nineteenth-century residents of this island instead made a living through logging, shipbuilding, and fishing. During Woodruff and Hale's time there, the islands were collectively known as Vinalhaven Township.[36]

On 18 August, Woodruff and Hale departed Scarborough, Maine, "for the purpose of visiting the Islands of the Sea." After obtaining passage on a small sloop that launched from Owls Head, near Rockland, on 19 August, they arrived on the north island at two o'clock the next morning.[37] Later that day, the two men attended a Sunday service at the island's lone Baptist church, where they became acquainted with the minister, Gideon Newton.[38] Newton initially welcomed the two preachers into his home and allowed them to use the meetinghouse to preach their message.[39] Woodruff and Hale preached in various locations during their first two weeks on the north island, including in the Baptist meetinghouse,

---

invited to stay with them, so he boarded with a former neighbor. (Alexander, *Things in Heaven and Earth,* 32–33, 56–57; Woodruff, Journal, 31 Dec. 1833 and 4 June 1837.)

33. Woodruff, Journal, 28 June–12 July 1837.

34. In the nine days he preached near Bradford (today part of Groveland and Haverhill) in July, Hale met with his sisters, his mother, his cousins, and the family of his wife, Olive Boynton Hale. Hale's journal entries do not indicate whether any of them joined the church during the 1837 mission. (Hale, Reminiscences and Journal, 23–25.)

35. Hale, Reminiscences and Journal, 25–27. On 13 April 1837 in Kirtland, Frederick G. Williams married Woodruff and Phebe Carter, a twenty-eight-year-old convert. (Woodruff, Journal, 13 Apr. 1837; Crocheron, *Representative Women of Deseret,* 35–36.)

36. *Brief Historical Sketch of the Town of Vinalhaven,* 12–13, 28; Coolidge and Mansfield, *History and Description of New England,* 236, 334.

37. Woodruff, Journal, 18 Aug. 1837.

38. Hale, Reminiscences and Journal, 28–29; Woodruff, Journal, 18 Aug. 1837. Hale observed that "the people on the North Island are mostly Baptist Calvinist order the south island are mostly Methodist." (Hale, Reminiscences and Journal, 29.)

39. Hale, Reminiscences and Journal, 28–29; Woodruff, Journal, 20 Aug. 1837; "History of Wilford Woodruff," *Deseret News,* 21 July 1858, 89.

Nathaniel Dyer farm, Fox Islands, Maine. Circa 1900. Wilford Woodruff and Jonathan H. Hale arrived on North Fox Island, Maine, in the early-morning hours of 20 August 1837. The two men made their way "over the rocks and through the cedars" until they came upon the Dyer residence (Woodruff, *Leaves from My Journal,* 31). The home can be seen on the left side of the photograph, which was taken looking south from North Haven across the Fox Islands thoroughfare to Vinalhaven. (Courtesy North Haven Historical Society, North Haven, ME.)

local schoolhouses, and private residences, and they apparently gained influence among the local inhabitants.[40] As the island's residents began to embrace their message, however, Newton's attitude toward Woodruff and Hale soured. According to the missionaries' journals, the minister's congregation shrunk substantially by late August, and he organized a campaign to stem the Mormon preachers' influence in the islands.[41] In early September, Newton enlisted the help of the south island's Methodist minister, a Mr. Douglass, to, as Woodruff put it, "come over and help him put down 'Mormonism.'"[42] Newton later traveled to the mainland to recruit two more ministers to aid in that endeavor.[43] In a letter printed in a local Baptist publication, Newton recounted that the ministers then held a series of revival meetings on the north island, during which some of the residents "who stood aloof from hearing the Mormons" eventually "obtained a hope" and were baptized into the Baptist congregation.[44]

Despite this opposition, Woodruff and Hale continued to preach and baptize on both the north and the south island. The men addressed a large congregation on the north island in early September, after which Justus Eames and his wife, Betsy, became the first residents of Vinalhaven to be baptized into the church. On 4 September, the two missionaries boarded a sailboat, crossed the narrow channel separating the two largest islands, and preached to an attentive crowd in one of the local schoolhouses.[45] Woodruff and Hale preached to audiences on the south island for five days before returning to the north island. According to their journals, the pair had preached twenty-five sermons on the Fox Islands by 10 September.[46] In response to the impassioned speech that the Methodist preacher Douglass gave on the north island on 11 September, Woodruff prepared and delivered a two-and-a-half-hour sermon at the Baptist church, attended by a large congregation of people from both islands. In just over one week, 10–17 September, Woodruff and Hale led six more of the islands' residents "into the waters of Baptism."[47]

---

40. Woodruff, Journal, 20 Aug.–3 Sept. 1837; Hale, Reminiscences and Journal, 28–35. In a letter printed in *Zion's Advocate,* Newton stated, "The novelty of their [Woodruff and Hale's] sentiments led many to hear them." (Gideon Newton, "Revivals," *Zion's Advocate,* 25 Oct. 1837, 170.)

41. Woodruff, Journal, 27 Aug. 1837. In an 1880s account of the mission, Woodruff observed that Newton attended a dozen of their meetings before he "made up his mind, contrary to the dictation of the Spirit of God to him, to reject the testimony, and come out against me." (Woodruff, *Leaves from My Journal,* 33.)

42. Woodruff, *Leaves from My Journal,* 34.

43. Woodruff, Journal, 19 Sept. 1837. One of the ministers was Reverend Amariah Kalloch, the first pastor of First Baptist Church in Rockland, Maine. (Eaton, *History of Thomaston, Rockland, and South Thomaston, Maine,* 374–375.)

44. Gideon Newton, "Revivals," *Zion's Advocate,* 25 Oct. 1837, 170. In a 20 November 1837 letter to Don Carlos Smith, Woodruff countered Newton's account of the revival meetings, asserting that the Baptist minister gained only two converts: "his own son and daughter." (Wilford Woodruff, Vinalhaven, ME, to Don Carlos Smith, Kirtland, OH, 20 Nov. 1837, in *Elders' Journal,* Nov. 1837, 17–19.)

45. Woodruff, Journal, 3–4 Sept. 1837; Hale, Reminiscences and Journal, 34–35.

46. Woodruff, Journal, 4–10 Sept. 1837; Hale, Reminiscences and Journal, 35.

47. The six other converts were Ebenezer Eames, Melannar Eames, Cyrus Sterrett, Phebe Sterrett, Abigail Farnham, and Eliza Luce. On 1 October, Woodruff and Hale organized the first branch of the church in Vinalhaven, comprising twelve members. (Woodruff, Journal, 10, 12, and 17 Sept. 1837; 1 Oct. 1837; Hale, Reminiscences and Journal, 35, 37, 40–42.)

Document Transcript

North Lat, 44. Long. 69, 10. Vinalhaven, Fox Islands, Monday, Sept. 18th, 1837.
To Joseph Smith Jr. and the church of Latter Day Saints in
Kirtland greeting:

Dear Saints of God, whom we love of a truth for the truth' sake that
dwelleth in you, and we pray God that it may abide with you forever: As we
are called to stand upon the Islands of the sea,[48] in defence of the truth and for
the word of God the testimony of Jesus Christ. We are under the necessity
of making use of our pen, to give you an account of our labors in the ministry
since we left Kirtland, as we cannot at present speak to you face to face. We
left Kirtland May 31st, and took Steamboat at Fairport[49] in company with
Elder Milton Holmes, to go forth to labor in the vineyard as the Lord should
direct.— After calling on the Saints in Jefferson Co. N. Y.[50] we arrived at
Sackett's Harbour and took Steamboat on the 6th of June for Upper Canada
and on the 8th arived at Brother Artemus Judd's.[51] And on the 10th, had the
happy privilege of setting in conference with John E. Page, James Blakeslee,
and a number other elders, and a large congregation of Saints. And we were
blessed with a very interesting time. After spending several days with them we
took the parting hand with these beloved friends and proceeded on our journey for the East in company with elder John Goodson, and others bound for
England.[52] We took the parting hand with them at Schenectady,[53] and arrived
at the Caanan church in Connecticut, visited the church a few days. Here

---

48. See Testimony, ca. 2 Nov. 1831, in *JSP*, D2:110–114; and Revelation, 3 Nov. 1831, in *JSP*, D2:117
[D&C 133:8].

49. Aboard the steamboat *Sandusky*, the group crossed Lake Erie and arrived in Buffalo, New York, at
six in the morning on 1 June 1837. (Woodruff, Journal, 31 May and 1 June 1837.)

50. The missionaries traveled on a canal boat from Buffalo to Syracuse, New York, between 1 and 3 June
1837; Hale spent two days in Syracuse, while Woodruff apparently walked forty miles north to visit family
in Richland, New York. Woodruff and Hale likely met somewhere near Ellisburg, Jefferson County, New
York, on 5 June. (Woodruff, Journal, 1–5 June 1837; Hale, Reminiscences and Journal, 9.)

51. Judd lived in Bastard Township, today part of Rideau Lakes, Ontario, Canada, located approximately thirty miles northeast of Kingston, Ontario, Canada. (Woodruff, Journal, 8 June 1837; Hale,
Reminiscences and Journal, 9.)

52. John Goodson, Isaac Russell, and John Snider—all recent converts—were headed for New York
City to rendezvous with Heber C. Kimball in preparation for the impending mission to England.
Woodruff, Hale, Holmes, Goodson, and Snider trekked thirty miles from Bastard Township to Leeds
Township on 12 June; on 13 June, they walked twenty-six miles to Kingston. (Woodruff, Journal,
12–13 June 1837; Hale, Reminiscences and Journal, 11–12; Recommendation for Heber C. Kimball,
between 2 and 13 June 1837, pp. 397–401 herein.)

53. From Kingston, the six men (Woodruff, Hale, Holmes, Goodson, and Snider, now joined by Isaac
Russell) took a steamboat across Lake Ontario to Oswego, New York, and then a canal boat to Syracuse
on 14 June 1837; they then took another canal boat to Utica on 15 June and arrived in Schenectady at eight
o'clock in the evening on 16 June. (Hale, Reminiscences and Journal, 12–13; Woodruff, Journal, 6–16 June

elder M. Holmes took his departure for Mass. and we went to Colebrook, visited different parts of the town and held eight meetings, from thence to Canton and held a meeting in the village hall in Collinsville.— As we commenced speaking several began to beat their drums at the doors which made much confusion.[54] This is the only disturbance we have had since we left Kirtland. We next visited Avon, where we held four meetings and many came out to hear and manifested a spirit of inquiry. And elder [Wilford] Woodruff had the privilege of leading three of his kinfolk into the waters of baptism.[55] And had not the Spirit called us away to perform a greater work, we should have had no difficulty in establishing a branch of the church in that place. A family where we tarried but one night, and taught them the things of the kingdom, believed our testimony, and after our departure, two of the household followed us 15 miles to receive baptism at our hands, but we were gone, and they truly believed it to be a day of warning and not of many words.[56] We also visited Farmington[57] and held one meeting in the Methodist meeting house, and preached to an attentive congregation who wished to hear more concerning the great work of God. We left Farmington on the 20 of July, for Mass.[58] and after visiting the Bradford church, and after preaching several times with them, we proceeded on our journey to Saco, Maine, where we spent several days with the church and friends.[59] But duty urging us forward to lift

---

1837.) From Schenectady, Woodruff, Hale, and Holmes traveled for approximately seventy miles on foot to Canaan. (Hale, Reminiscences and Journal, 13.)

54. This likely refers to a 10 July conflict, instigated by a Presbyterian priest whom Hale had met earlier that day, that occurred near Collinsville, Connecticut. While Woodruff preached in the village hall, the priest (named by Woodruff as "Vanarsdalen") and presumably others began beating drums outside. The priest later entered the hall, loudly disputed the missionaries' teachings, and questioned their authority to preach, asserting that "no man had a right to preach the gospel unless he had a collegiate education." Woodruff reportedly responded, "I would admit that point when he would tell me at what college Jesus Christ and his apostles obtained their education." ("History of Wilford Woodruff," *Deseret News,* 21 July 1858, 89; Hale, Reminiscences and Journal, 20–21; Woodruff, Journal, 11 July 1837.)

55. Woodruff and Hale traveled to Avon, Connecticut, on 5 July 1837. During their stay in the area, which lasted until 18 July, Woodruff visited his father, stepmother, uncles, and other family friends. There he baptized his uncle Ozem, his aunt Hannah, and his cousin John Woodruff. (Woodruff, Journal, 5–18 July 1837; Hale, Reminiscences and Journal, 19–21.)

56. See Revelation, 30 Aug. 1831, in *JSP,* D2:54 [D&C 63:58].

57. Phebe Woodruff joined Wilford in Farmington on 16 July. (Woodruff, Journal, 16 July 1837.)

58. Hale's journal indicates that he left for Worcester, Massachusetts, on 19 July. He left Worcester on 21 July and took a stage to Lowell; the next day, he moved on to New Rowley. Wilford and Phebe rode a stagecoach to nearby Hartford, Connecticut, on 20 July. Wilford apparently sent Phebe on to Maine on 21 July, while he walked nearly one hundred miles to Lowell, Massachusetts; he met Hale in New Rowley (near Haverhill, Massachusetts) on 23 July. (Woodruff, Journal, 19–23 July 1835; Hale, Reminiscences and Journal, 23.)

59. Woodruff and Hale remained in the Haverhill area until 1 August; on that day, they departed for Dover, New Hampshire, and arrived in Saco on 5 August. In Saco, they stayed with Edward Milliken and

the warning voice to those that had not heard the sound of the gospel, we then went to the city of Portland.[60] We there took the Steamer Bangor on the 19 of August, to speed us on our way to the Islands of the sea, they landed us at Owls head[61] at the setting of the sun: But how to get conveyance to the Islands we knew not, we retired to a grove and offered up our thanks unto God for his mercies and asked him to open our way before us; we returned to the Inn and soon found some men that were going near the Islands that night, they said they would land us if we chose to take passage with them.[62] We accordingly went on board, they hoisted sail and landed us on North Fox Island, Vinalhaven, at 2 o'clock Sunday morning, August 20th. It was with peculiar feelings and sensations that we began to walk forth upon one of the Islands of the sea which was wrapped in the sable shades of night, whose waters had never covered a soul for the remission of their sins after the order of the gospel, and which soil had never before been pressed by the foot steps of an elder of Israel. We were strangers, pilgrims, and almost pennyless. But we had [p. [1]] come on the Lords business, we believed him faithful that had promised, and we felt willing to trust in his name, we soon came to a house, where we were received and we retired to rest.[63] We arose in the morning made ourselves known as servants of the Lord, we inquired if there was any religion or priests on the Island; we were informed that there was a Baptist priest, a small church and a meeting house at the center of the Island.[64] The town of Vinalhaven includes both North and South Fox Islands: Pop. 1800. The inhabitants are generally wealthy, intelligent, industrious, generous and hospitable to strangers. North Island is 9 miles long, and 2 wide, pop. 800. South Island is 10 miles long, and 5 wide, pop. 1000 &c. As it was Sabbath morning there was to be preaching in the meeting house, we concluded to attend considering it a

---

visited with the family of Milton Holmes. Phebe Woodruff met Wilford in Saco, and the couple proceeded to Scarborough with Hale on 8 August. Woodruff and Hale spent the next week conducting church business in the area; Woodruff also devoted some time to getting to know his in-laws, whom he had not met previously. (Hale, Reminiscences and Journal, 20–27; Woodruff, Journal, 1–18 Aug. 1835.)

60. Hale walked to Portland to visit with his uncle Samuel Hale on 16 August; on 18 August, he briefly returned to Scarborough and then went with Woodruff to Portland. (Hale, Reminiscences and Journal, 27; Woodruff, Journal, 18 Aug. 1837.)

61. Owls Head (then part of the town of Thomaston) is a peninsula on Penobscot Bay with a harbor, roughly five miles southeast of Rockland.

62. Hale's journal indicates that they "set sail in a small boat in company with 5 other men that ware going East." (Hale, Reminiscences and Journal, 28.)

63. After arriving on the island, the two men called on Nathaniel Dyer, who "arose from his bed and let us into his house gave us a bed & in the morning gave us some Brakefast & bid us welcome." (Hale, Reminiscences and Journal, 28.)

64. The Baptist church mentioned by Woodruff stands near the intersection of what are now Crabtree Point Road and School Road, overlooking Pulpit Harbor on North Haven, Maine.

proper place to introduce the gospel. When we arived at the place, meeting had commenced, the deacon came to the door and we informed him that we were servants of the Lord, that we had a message for the people and wished to be heard, the deacon informed the priest[65] that we were preachers of the gospel. He invited us into the stand and gave out an appointment for us at 5 o'clock P. M. After the priest had closed his discourse he invited us to his house during the intermission. We presented him the book of Mormon, he appeared friendly and said he should like to read it. We met according to appointment and preached to them the first principles of the gospel. We then gave out appointments for the four following evenings to be held at the several school houses on the Island. The people came out in great numbers and heard with attention and manifested much anxiety, and in fourteen days we held nineteen meetings. The Baptist priest became alarmed seeing that his craft was in danger; and fearing that if he held his peace all Fox Islands would believe on our words, accordingly he strove to use his influence against us, but without effect as you may judge on learning the fact that on Sunday the 27th while we met with a congregation, he had not so much as one to meet with him at his usual place of worship, for the excitement was so great that the members of his church and deacon, were attending our meetings and inviting us to visit them, and inquiring into these things. The Lord clothed us with his Spirit and we were enabled to stand up and boldly declare those things that are commanded us.— And the sound thereof soon reached the neighboring Islands and some of the inhabitants soon hoisted their sails to convey them over the waters to hear the tidings for themselves. On Sunday the 3rd of Sept. we preached to a large congregation assembled together from these Islands, at the close of our meeting we opened a door for baptism, and a respectable sea captain and his wife offered themselves as candidates, we then assembled where there was much water and after offering up our prayers unto God, we then lead them down into the sea and baptized them and we returned rejoicing.[66] On Monday following we visited the South Island to set before them the truths of the everlasting gospel. We held five meetings, the people came out by hundreds, to hear and filled the school houses to overflowing.

Notwithstanding the anxiety of the people to hear more upon this important subject, yet we were under the necessity of returning to the North Island, to attend an appointment on Sunday, accordingly we met and preached to the

---

65. The priest referred to here was Gideon J. Newton, pastor of the Baptist church on the north island.

66. Hale's 3 September journal entry reads, "After meeting I Baptised Capt Justus Eames aged 48 and his wife Betsy Eames these are the first I ever Baptised I must say this was a rejoicing time to us and also to them, as I suppose they are the first that has been Baptised into the new and everlasting covenant on the Islands of the sea." (Hale, Reminiscences and Journal, 34–35.)

people and opened a door for baptism and another sea Captain and a young lady came forward and we repaired to the sea shore and baptized them,[67] and on Tuesday following, we administered the ordinance of baptism unto three others.[68]

A Methodist priest on the South Island fearing whereunto these things would grow, came over to the Island where we were baptizing and made friends with the Baptist priest (like Herod and Pilate) and called a meeting, we attended.[69] The Methodist priest arose and commenced warm hostilities against the book of Mormon, and our principles, we took minutes of his discourse that we might be correct in answering him. As he could not bring proof from the word of God against our principles, and in order to make an impression upon the minds of his hearers against the work; he took the book of Mormon in his hand, and with an out stretched arm declared that he feared none of the judgments of God that would come upon him for rejecting that book as the word of God.[70] When [p. 2] he closed his meeting we arose and rectified some of his wide mistakes in his presence before the congregation, and informed the people if they would meet next Sabbath at the meeting house we would answer every objection that had been presented against the book of Mormon and our principles during the meeting. And last Sabbath we met a congregation of several hundred at the meeting house, assembled together from the different Islands, and we arose in their midst, and redeemed our pledge by answering every objection that had been brought against the book of Mormon, or our principles.— After meeting we repaired to the water and again administered the ordinance of baptism.[71] The Baptist priest is no less busy than his Methodist brother, for while one is in the pulpit declaring to the people, that the principles of the book of Mormon are saping the very foundation of our churches and holy religion; the other is gone over to the main land calling

---

67. On 10 September, Woodruff recorded in his journal, "After meeting I opened a door for baptism, when another Sea Captain offered himself as a candidate, by the name of Ebenezar Eames he was a brother to Capt. Justus Eames . . . a young Lady also offered herself for Baptism." Hale's journal entry for the same day clarifies that the young woman's name was Melannar Eames. A Justus Ames and an Ebenezer Ames Jr. appear in an 1830 census of the island. (Woodruff, Journal, 10 Sept. 1837; Hale, Reminiscences and Journal, 39; 1830 U.S. Census, Vinalhaven, Hancock Co., ME, 82.)

68. On 12 September, Cyrus Sterrett, Phebe Sterrett, and Abigail Farnham were baptized. (Woodruff, Journal, 12 Sept. 1837; Hale, Reminiscences and Journal, [40]–[41].)

69. Woodruff and Hale referred to this Methodist priest simply as "Mr. Douglass." In an 1858 account, Woodruff noted that Gideon Newton "had been long at variance with Mr. Douglass, but they became very friendly and united in a war against us." (Woodruff, Journal, 11 Sept. 1837; Hale, Reminiscences and Journal, 40; "History of Wilford Woodruff," *Deseret News,* 21 July 1858, 89.)

70. For more detailed accounts of this encounter with Gideon Newton, see Woodruff, Journal, 11 Sept. 1837; and Hale, Reminiscences and Journal, 40.

71. Eliza G. Luce was baptized on 17 September 1837. (Hale, Reminiscences and Journal, [42].)

upon his Baptist brethren, saying come over and help us lest we fall. But cursed is man that trusteth in man or maketh flesh his arm saith the Lord God. O ye priests of Baal[72] your cry is in vain, the God of Israel has set his hand the second time to recover his people. The stone has began to roll, and will soon become a mountain and fill the whole earth.[73] The Lord is calling his church out of the wilderness, with her gifts and graces and restoring her judges as at the first.[74] God hath chosen the weak things of this world to confound the wise, and with them he will rend your kingdoms, that the wisdom of your wise men may perish, and the understanding of your prudent men may be hid.[75] The cry of the Saints is ascending into the ears of the Lord of Sabaoth for Ephraim.—[76] The horns of Joseph are begining to push the people together.[77] The apostles of the Lamb of God are bearing the keys of his kingdom on the shores of Europe.[78] Yea and the mighty Captains of the ships at sea, are receiving the gospel of Jesus Christ; and enjoying its power, and the call of many from distant Islands, has already entered our ears; O come and preach to us, we have sent a book of Mormon over the billows of the great deep, to teach those that are at sea. And the word and work are propelled by the arm of JEHOVAH. And the weapon that is formed against Zion shall soon be broken.[79] And he that raises his puny arm against it, is fighting against God and shall soon mourn because of his loss. We say these things are true as God liveth, and the Spirit beareth record and the record is true, and vengeance will be speedily executed upon an evil work in these last days, therefore, O Babylon thy fall is sure.[80]

Although we have not baptized but few on these Islands, yet there is hundreds believing and many are almost ready to enter into the kingdom, the calls are numerous from the neighboring Islands,[81] and also from the main land, for us to come and preach unto them, and tell them words whereby they may be saved from the pending judgments that await the world. There are

---

72. See 1 Kings 18:21–40.

73. See Daniel 2:34–35; and Revelation, 30 Oct. 1831, in *JSP,* D2:92–94 [D&C 65].

74. See Isaiah 1:26.

75. See 1 Corinthians 1:27; Isaiah 29:14; and Vision, 16 Feb. 1832, in *JSP,* D2:184 [D&C 76:9].

76. See James 5:4.

77. See Deuteronomy 33:16–17.

78. On the Twelve's mission to England, see Historical Introduction to Recommendation for Heber C. Kimball, between 2 and 13 June 1837, pp. 398–400 herein.

79. See Isaiah 54:17 (also in Book of Mormon, 1830 ed., 502 [3 Nephi 22:17]); and Minutes and Prayer of Dedication, 27 Mar. 1837, p. 202 herein [D&C 109:25].

80. See Jeremiah 51; and Revelation 18:2.

81. In November 1837, Woodruff spent a day and a half on the nearby Isle au Haut (sometimes referred to as Isle of Holt), population 315. There he preached and sold a copy of the Book of Mormon. (Woodruff, Journal, 15 Nov. 1837; 1830 U.S. Census, Isle au Haut, Hancock Co., ME.)

fifteen or twenty neighboring Islands that are inhabited, some of them contain a population of several thousand.[82] And while the fields are white, we view the harvest great in this country: and the laborers few.[83] And while we are faithfully laboring day and night for the salvation of his people; we ask an interest in your prayers, O ye Saints of the most high God. O ye elders of Israel will ye not go forth into the vineyard and help wind up the scene of this generation which sits in darkness and in the shadow of death. O ye ministers of our God, if we altogether hold our peace at this time, shall we not suffer loss when the Lord raises up deliverance unto Israel. But for Zion's sake let us not hold our peace, and for Jerusalem's sake let us not rest until the light thereof go forth as brightness and salvation as a lamp that burneth.[84]

That we all may keep the patience and faith of the Saints and see that no man take our crown, is the prayer of your brethren in the Lord Jesus.[85]

WILLFORD WOODRUFF,
JOHNATHAN [Jonathan] H. HALE.

————— ⁊ —————

Power of Attorney to Oliver Granger, 27 September 1837

Source Note

Sidney Rigdon and JS, Power of Attorney, to Oliver Granger, Kirtland Township, Geauga Co., OH, 27 Sept. 1837; handwriting of Sidney Rigdon; signatures of Sidney Rigdon and JS; one page; JS Collection, CHL. Includes dockets.

One leaf, measuring 10 × 7⅞ inches (25 × 20 cm). The top, bottom, and right edges of the recto have the square cut of manufactured paper. The left edge of the recto is torn and contains remnants of the second leaf of a bifolium; that leaf is not extant. Compression marks from the nib of a steel pen are concentrated in two small areas of the upper right of the recto. The document was folded into a roll fold and docketed twice. The first docket, in unidentified handwriting, reads, "O. Cowdery | comp◊◊d"; the second docket by Leo Hawkins reads, "Sept 27. 1837". The document was folded again, creating a second fold pattern. The upper left of the recto is torn. The docket by Hawkins suggests this document was in the Church Historian's Office collection no later than the mid-1850s.

Historical Introduction

On 27 September 1837 JS and Sidney Rigdon signed this power of attorney, designating Oliver Granger their agent and charging him to settle their business with New York

---

82. Apart from Vinalhaven's approximately 1,800 residents, over 6,000 people lived on the numerous islands of Penobscot, Jericho, Blue Hill, and Frenchman bays. In 1830, the most populous islands, in order, were Mount Desert Island, Deer Isle, the north and south islands of Vinalhaven, Islesboro Island, Isle au Haut, and Swans Island. (1830 U.S. Census, Hancock Co. and Waldo Co., ME.)

83. See John 4:35; Matthew 9:37; and Revelation, Feb. 1829, in *JSP*, D1:9–13 [D&C 4].

84. See Isaiah 62:1.

85. See Revelation 3:11.

merchant Jonathan F. Scribner.[86] The business matters probably related to the nearly $1,800 JS and Rigdon owed to Scribner, a debt that originated in purchases made on credit by the firm of Rigdon, Smith & Cowdery from Scribner's hardware store in Buffalo, New York, on 16 June 1836, with payment due on 16 October.[87] Purchasing agents for the firm, probably Oliver Cowdery and Hyrum Smith, traveled to New York again in October 1836 to purchase additional goods, including lead piping.[88]

The power of attorney suggests that Scribner had been paid using Kirtland Safety Society notes by one of the Kirtland area mercantile firms, either Rigdon, Smith & Cowdery or Cahoon, Carter & Co.[89] This payment would have probably happened in spring 1837 when JS sent Brigham Young and Willard Richards on a "special Business Mission" to the East. Their mission seems to have consisted of contacting New York merchants about Kirtland debts and possibly raising money from church members in the state.[90] In April 1837, Richards and Young met with Scribner in Troy, New York, and may have renegotiated the debts or paid Scribner using notes of the Kirtland Safety Society.[91] If Scribner was paid with Safety Society notes, they would have been worth significantly less after discounting than their face value and would not have been adequate to cover the

---

86. According to store invoices, Scribner was an "Importer and Wholesale and Retail Dealer in Fancy and Staple Hardware" in Buffalo, New York. By 1837, Scribner appears to have been living in Troy, New York, which was around three hundred miles from Buffalo. (Jonathan F. Scribner to Rigdon, Smith & Cowdery, Invoice, Buffalo, NY, 16 June 1836, JS Office Papers, CHL; *Directory for the City of Buffalo* [1836], 133; *Directory for the City of Buffalo* [1837], 119.)

87. Jonathan F. Scribner to Rigdon, Smith & Cowdery, Invoice, Buffalo, NY, 16 June 1836, JS Office Papers, CHL. The firm of Rigdon, Smith & Cowdery may also have borrowed money from Scribner. Both invoices indicate a due date of 16 October 1836. Scribner assessed interest in December 1836, and the records of Scribner's attorneys list 15 December as the date the bill was due. The December due date may have been a renegotiated payment or a second due date after the first note had been defaulted on. (Transcript of Proceedings, 20 Oct. 1840, Scribner v. Rigdon et al. [Geauga Co. C.P. 1840], Geauga Co., OH, Court of Common Pleas, Record Book X, pp. 530–532, Geauga County Archives and Records Center, Chardon, OH; Jonathan F. Scribner, Statement, ca. Apr. 1838, JS Office Papers, CHL.)

88. Jonathan F. Scribner, Statement, ca. Apr. 1838, JS Office Papers, CHL. Two reminiscent accounts identify Oliver Cowdery and Hyrum Smith as the men who traveled to New York to purchase merchandise in 1836, but the date of their trip is not specified. (Ames, Autobiography and Journal, [12]; "Banking and Financiering at Kirtland," 609.)

89. The Kirtland mercantile firm of Cahoon, Carter & Co. was also in debt to Scribner in 1837 and may have been the firm that paid him in notes of the Kirtland Safety Society. In this case, JS and Rigdon were likely settling business matters as former officers of the society responsible for redeeming the notes they signed for the society. (Jonathan F. Scribner to Cahoon, Carter & Co., Invoice, Buffalo, NY, 16 June 1836, JS Office Papers, CHL.)

90. JS History, vol. B-1, 762; Richards, Journal, Apr. and 12 June 1837. Richards recorded the names and addresses of several New York merchants to whom Kirtland mercantile firms—including Rigdon, Smith & Cowdery and Cahoon, Carter & Co.—owed money for goods bought on credit. It is unclear if the information regarding the various mercantile firms was written before, during, or after the trip to New York.

91. The first trip to Troy in Richards's journal was recorded on 19 April 1837 and includes Scribner's name next to the date. The second trip, on 26 April, involved both Richards and Young. Richards's journal notes that they "Saw Mr. Scribner" in Troy. The following day Young left to return to Kirtland and Richards returned to his family's home in Richmond, Massachusetts. (Richards, Journal, Mar.–July 1837, [13], [14].)

money he was owed.[92] In fact, Scribner may not have been able to redeem the society's notes with any New York banks, given the financial panic and specie suspension that began in May 1837.[93] If this was the case, Scribner's inability to redeem the notes at their face value likely led to the situation that Granger was empowered to handle.

On 1 September 1837, with the assistance of Painesville, Ohio, lawyer William Perkins, members of the firms Rigdon, Smith & Cowdery and Cahoon, Carter & Co. renegotiated promissory notes with four New York mercantile firms, including Holbrook & Ferme and Halsted, Haines & Co.[94] On 26 September, the day before this power of attorney was signed, JS and Rigdon also revised their debts with the firm of Bailey, Keeler & Remsen and signed three new promissory notes.[95] JS and Rigdon may have made Granger their agent to renegotiate their debt with Scribner in a similar manner. On 26 October 1837, however, Scribner had a writ of summons issued against JS, Rigdon, and Cowdery in the Geauga County Court of Common Pleas to reclaim his money, indicating that Granger had not been successful in making satisfactory arrangements with the hardware store owner. Writs were also issued against Reynolds Cahoon, Jared Carter, and Hyrum Smith as Scribner pursued litigation in a separate case against the Kirtland mercantile firm of Cahoon, Carter & Co. for defaulted promissory notes.[96] Both sets of charges were ruled nonsuits, meaning the cases were terminated, in 1840. In the case of *Scribner v. Rigdon, Smith & Cowdery,* the termination resulted from Scribner or his representative failing to appear in court on three occasions, suggesting he abandoned his efforts to collect the debt or lacked the evidence necessary to pursue the case. In the case of *Scribner v. Cahoon, Carter & Co.,* both parties failed to appear in court and the judge required Cahoon and Hyrum Smith to pay $957 to Scribner.[97]

----

92. Transcript of Proceedings, 20 Oct. 1840, Scribner v. Rigdon et al. [Geauga Co. C.P. 1840], Geauga Co., OH, Court of Common Pleas, Record Book X, pp. 530–532, Geauga County Archives and Records Center, Chardon, OH.

93. See Introduction to Part 5: 5 Oct. 1836–10 Apr. 1837, pp. 287–293 herein.

94. JS, Sidney Rigdon, and Oliver Cowdery to Holbrook and Firme [Ferme], Promissory Note, Kirtland, OH, 1 Sept. 1837, Joseph Smith Papers, Ohio Historical Society, Columbus, OH; JS, Sidney Rigdon, and Oliver Cowdery to Holbrook & Firme [Ferme], Promissory Note, Kirtland, OH, 1 Sept. 1837, BYU; Hyrum Smith, Reynolds Cahoon, and Jared Carter to Halsted, Haines & Co., Promissory Note, Kirtland, OH, 1 Sept. 1837, private possession, copy at CHL; Hyrum Smith et al. to Halsted, Haines & Co., Promissory Note, 1 Sept. 1837, Brigham Young Office Files, CHL; Hyrum Smith et al. to Mead & Betts, Promissory Note, 1 Sept. 1837, Mead & Betts v. Estate of JS, Illinois State Historical Society, Circuit Court Case Files, CHL; see also Perkins & Osborn, Account Statement, ca. 29 Oct. 1838, JS Office Papers, CHL.

95. JS et al. to Bailey, Keeler, & Remsen, Promissory Notes, 26 Sept. 1837, Lord Sterling Papers, Lake County Historical Society, Painesville, OH.

96. Transcript of Proceedings, 20 Oct. 1840, Scribner v. Rigdon et al. [Geauga Co. C.P. 1840], Geauga Co., OH, Court of Common Pleas, Record Book X, pp. 530–532, Geauga County Archives and Records Center, Chardon, OH; Transcript of Proceedings, 3 Apr. 1838, Scribner v. Cahoon, Carter & Co. [Geauga Co. C.P. 1838], Geauga Co., OH, Court of Common Pleas, Record Book U, pp. 584–585, Geauga County Archives and Records Center, Chardon, OH.

97. Transcript of Proceedings, 20 Oct. 1840, Scribner v. Rigdon et al. [Geauga Co. C.P. 1840], Geauga Co., OH, Court of Common Pleas, Record Book X, pp. 530–532; Transcript of Proceedings, 3 Apr. 1838, Scribner v. Cahoon, Carter & Co. [Geauga Co. C.P. 1838], Geauga Co., OH, Court of Common Pleas, Record Book U, pp. 584–585, Geauga County Archives and Records Center, Chardon, OH.

Document Transcript

Kirtland Ohio Sep 27— 1837

Know all men by these presents that we Joseph Smith Jr and Sidney Rigdon do hereby appoint and constitute Oliver Granger our proper agent and attorney to act in our name to all intents and purposes as we ourselves could do if we were personally present: to manage conduct and bring to settlement a business which we have with J[onathan] F Scribner of Tory [Troy] city in the State of New york in relation to the paper of Kirtland safety society

Given under our ⟨hand⟩ at Kirtland Geauga County Ohio the day and date above written

Sidney Rigdon
Joseph Smith Jr

——— ᘓ ———

Selections from *Elders' Journal,* October 1837

Source Note

Selections from Elders' Journal of the Church of Latter Day Saints, *Kirtland Township, Geauga Co., OH, Oct. 1837, 3–4, 15. For more information on* Elders' Journal of the Church of Latter Day Saints, *see Source Notes for Multiple-Entry Documents, p. 521 herein.*

Historical Introduction

In the August 1837 issue of the *Latter Day Saints' Messenger and Advocate,* a prospectus announced that a new publication, the *Elders' Journal of the Church of Latter Day Saints,* would replace the *Messenger and Advocate* as the church's newspaper. The prospectus, written by Sidney Rigdon, informed readers that JS would act as editor for the new Kirtland, Ohio, periodical, which was owned by Thomas B. Marsh of the Quorum of the Twelve Apostles.[98] The first issue of the *Elders' Journal* likely appeared sometime in mid- to late October. Included were the two short editorial passages featured here. One of the passages briefly addresses Heber C. Kimball's experiences in England; the other discusses the new paper's circulation.

---

98. Sidney Rigdon, *Elders' Journal* Prospectus, *LDS Messenger and Advocate,* Aug. 1837, 3:545–547; also reprinted as Sidney Rigdon, *Elders' Journal* Prospectus, *LDS Messenger and Advocate,* Sept. 1837, 3:571–574. Marsh had worked at a Boston type foundry for several years in the 1820s. He then acted as proprietor of the Kirtland-era *Elders' Journal* while living in Missouri. Publishers of the new newspaper apparently rented the Kirtland printing office and press from William Marks. According to a statement in the April *Messenger and Advocate,* JS and Sidney Rigdon transferred ownership of the printing office and its contents to Marks in April 1837, though they apparently acted as his agents following the transfer. ("T B Marsh," [1], Historian's Office, Histories of the Twelve, 1856–1858, 1861, CHL; Masthead, *LDS Messenger and Advocate,* Apr. 1837, 3:496; Sidney Rigdon, *Elders' Journal* Prospectus, *LDS Messenger and Advocate,* Aug. 1837, 3:545–547; *Elders' Journal,* Oct. 1837.)

By establishing the new periodical, church leaders were trying to steer the church's monthly publication toward a focus on missionary labors. After taking over as editor of the *Messenger and Advocate* in February 1837, Warren A. Cowdery printed lengthy editorials and articles on history and philosophy, devoting less space to missionary work.[99] By September 1837, the *Messenger and Advocate* had finished its volume run, and a "large body of the elders of the church" established the *Elders' Journal* as a new monthly publication.[100] In the August prospectus, Rigdon called attention to the intended focus on missionary efforts in the United States and England, writing that the new paper was to be "a vehicle of communication for all the elders of the church . . . through which they can communicate to others, all things pertaining to their mission." By featuring letters from missionaries, the paper would also inform church members of "the progress of the work."[101]

Assuming editorial control of a new church publication was one of the ways in which JS and other church leaders could limit dissent in Kirtland.[102] During his time as editor, Warren A. Cowdery had occasionally used the columns of the *Messenger and Advocate* to criticize JS. In a July 1837 editorial, Cowdery asserted: "Whenever a people have unlimited confidence in a civil or eclesiastical rule or rulers, who are but men like themselves, and begin to think they can do no wrong, they increase their tyrany, and oppression. . . . Who does not see a principle of popery and religious tyrany involved in such and order of things?"[103] Cowdery's editorial echoed the sentiment of other church dissenters who had in previous months expressed similar dissatisfaction with JS's leadership and his control over spiritual and temporal matters.[104] Several months later, JS informed readers

---

99. See *LDS Messenger and Advocate,* Feb.–July 1837, 3:449–544. The March 1837 issue of the *Messenger and Advocate,* for example, included a two-page article on the philosophy of religion, one page on the history of ancient Egypt, and several other articles with titles such as "The Causes of Human Misery," "Philosophy and Consistency," and "Duties of Masters and Apprentices." (*LDS Messenger and Advocate,* Mar. 1837, 3:472–474.)

100. Sidney Rigdon, *Elders' Journal* Prospectus, *LDS Messenger and Advocate,* Aug. 1837, 3:545; "Notice," *LDS Messenger and Advocate,* Apr. 1837, 3:496. JS and other leaders may have seen October as a logical time to make this transition, given that the third volume of the *Messenger and Advocate* was coming to a close in September. The first volume (twelve issues in total) had run from October 1834 to September 1835, the second from October 1835 to September 1836, and the third from October 1836 to September 1837. ("Address," *LDS Messenger and Advocate,* Oct. 1834, 1:1; Sidney Rigdon, *Elders' Journal* Prospectus, *LDS Messenger and Advocate,* Sept. 1837, 3:571.)

101. Sidney Rigdon, *Elders' Journal* Prospectus, *LDS Messenger and Advocate,* Aug. 1837, 3:545–547. The prospectus further asserted that the new periodical would be a vehicle to "transmit to succeeding generations an account of their religion, and a history of their travels, and of the reception which they met with in the nations." The October and November 1837 issues of the *Elders' Journal* did in fact consist primarily of such communications. (*Elders' Journal,* Oct. 1837, 1–16; *Elders' Journal,* Nov. 1837, 17–32.)

102. Around the same time the *Elders' Journal* prospectus appeared in the *Messenger and Advocate,* several church leaders were removed from their positions by a conference of church members for dissenting against JS and the church. In a 4 September letter addressed to John Corrill and the church in Missouri, JS also singled out particular church leaders who he asserted had been in "transgression." (Minutes, 3 Sept. 1837, pp. 423–425 herein; Letter to John Corrill and the Church in Missouri, 4 Sept. 1837, p. 430 herein.)

103. Editorial, *LDS Messenger and Advocate,* July 1837, 3:538.

104. See Letter from Parley P. Pratt, 23 May 1837, pp. 386–391 herein; and Charges against JS Preferred to Bishop's Council, 29 May 1837, pp. 393–397 herein.

of the *Elders' Journal* that the new paper would "pursue a different course from that of our predecessor in the editorial department." He continued, "We will endeavor not to scandalize our own citizens, especially when there is no foundation in truth for so doing."[105]

Although JS was listed as editor of the *Elders' Journal,* his role in editing the subject matter in the October 1837 issue is unclear, since he was away from Kirtland from 27 September until approximately 10 December.[106] It is possible that he edited some content before leaving Kirtland, but it is more likely that his younger brother Don Carlos Smith, who was acting temporarily as editor in his absence, authored the featured sections.[107] Because JS was ultimately responsible for the content of the *Elders' Journal* and did in fact author editorials in subsequent issues of the paper, the selections below are featured as JS documents.[108]

The first editorial passage in the October *Elders' Journal* introduced a letter from Heber C. Kimball to his wife, Vilate Murray Kimball.[109] At this time, Heber was in England on the church's first transatlantic mission.[110] Writing from the city of Preston on 2 September, he described the elders' experiences overseas. Though some ministers closed their doors to them, Kimball informed his wife that the elders were "baptizing almost every day."[111]

Document Transcript

Our readers will notice that the following from elder [Heber C.] Kimball was intended for a private letter to his wife, consequently it was not expected by him to be placed before the public; but as Elder Kimball is like ourselves, a man that delights in plainness, and is not skilled in the art of daubing with untempered morter;[112] we have taken the liberty to give it publicity almost

---

105. Selections from *Elders' Journal,* Nov. 1837, p. 486 herein.

106. JS to "the Saints Scattered Abroad," in *Elders' Journal,* Nov. 1837, 27; Thomas B. Marsh to Wilford Woodruff, in *Elder's Journal,* July 1838, 37; Vilate Murray Kimball, Kirtland, OH, to Heber C. Kimball, Preston, England, 19–24 Jan. 1838, Heber C. Kimball, Collection, CHL.

107. An addendum to a 7 August 1841 entry in JS's history indicates, "On the commencement of the publication of the Elders Journal in Kirtland, he [Don Carlos Smith] took the control of the establishment until the office was destroyed by fire in December 1837." (JS History, vol. C-1, addenda, 12.)

108. See Travel Account and Questions, Nov. 1837, pp. 478–484 herein. The complete issues of the *Elders' Journal* are available on the Joseph Smith Papers website.

109. In the newspaper's prospectus, Sidney Rigdon explained the rationale for highlighting letters such as this. "Since our missionaries started for England," he noted, "how many deep anxieties are felt in the minds of many, that they never felt before, to know how they will be received, and what will be the success of their mission." Rigdon concluded, "How grateful then would a letter be from any of them, making its appearance in the Journal, by this means satisfying the desires of all at once, which could not be done in any other way, but by great expense and great waste of time." (Sidney Rigdon, *Elders' Journal* Prospectus, *LDS Messenger and Advocate,* Sept. 1837, 3:573.)

110. See Historical Introduction to Recommendation for Heber C. Kimball, between 2 and 13 June 1837, pp. 398–400 herein.

111. Kimball specified that fifty-five people had been baptized by 2 September 1837. (Heber C. Kimball, Preston, England, to Vilate Murray Kimball, Kirtland, OH, 2 Sept. 1837, in *Elders' Journal,* Oct. 1837, 4–7.)

112. See Ezekiel 13:10–15.

en[p. 3]tire, that the saints may have the long desired information, that the standard of truth is hoisted on the Eastern continent,[113] and hundreds are already enlisting under the blood stained banner of Immanuel, even him who once trod in the same path that our beloved brethren who are laboring in England are now pursuing, i. e. "and the poor have the gospel preached to them."— *Mat.* 11:5. We feel thankful in very deed that God *is* no respecter of persons.[114]—Ed.

[. . .] [p. 4] [. . .]

———— ∽ ————

Editorial Note

In a second passage, the editor asked readers of the church publication to forward subscription money, reminding them of the printing office's precarious financial situation.[115]

———— ∽ ————

We are in hopes that our patrons from seeing the Journal, close at the heels of the Messenger and Advocate,[116] will take courage and forward us the *ready*;[117] for they may be assured that if there is no lack on their part, that the Journal shall at all times be forth coming in its *season* without delay, and by so doing our readers can get the news before it gets *cold*.

When our patrons are aware of the fact, that on the old subscription, out of about 1500 subscribers, there is now between 800 and $1000 behind, they will not blame our predecessors for being in the *drag*[118]—a word to the wise is sufficient.

[. . .] [p. 15]

———— ∽ ————

---

113. That is, Europe.

114. See Acts 10:34.

115. An annual subscription to the paper cost one dollar. (Masthead, *Elders' Journal,* Oct. 1837, 16.)

116. Sidney Rigdon had earlier explained to patrons that the first issue of the *Elders' Journal* would be printed in October and would be "forwarded to the subscribers of the Messenger and Advocate, unless they say to the contrary." (Sidney Rigdon, *Elders' Journal* Prospectus, *LDS Messenger and Advocate,* Sept. 1837, 3:574.)

117. In other words, ready money, or "immediate payment in coin for anything bought." ("Ready Money," in *Oxford English Dictionary,* 8:200.)

118. "In the drag" is likely a reference to the publishers of the *Messenger and Advocate* being in debt because subscribers had not paid their subscriptions; it may also be a reference to the publishers producing issues late.

Minutes, 6 November 1837

Source Note

Minutes, Far West, Caldwell Co., MO, 6 Nov. 1837. Featured version copied [between ca. 6 Apr. and 19 June 1838] in Minute Book 2, pp. 80–82; handwriting of Ebenezer Robinson; CHL. For more information on Minute Book 2, see Source Notes for Multiple-Entry Documents, p. 529 herein.

Historical Introduction

In fall 1837, JS, Sidney Rigdon, Hyrum Smith, and members of the Quorum of the Twelve Apostles traveled to Far West, Missouri, to address issues the church faced relating to settlement and church authority. On 6 November 1837, they met in Far West with the Missouri high council and a group of elders to discuss those matters.

Hyrum Smith and apostles Thomas B. Marsh and David W. Patten had traveled from Kirtland, Ohio, in early September. JS, Sidney Rigdon, William Smith, and Vinson Knight left Kirtland on 27 September and spent several weeks on their journey west holding meetings in Ohio, Indiana, and Missouri before arriving in Far West by early November.[119] This was JS's and Rigdon's first visit to Far West, which had been a growing Latter-day Saint community since the Saints began settling there in fall 1836.[120] JS and Rigdon's fall 1837 trip was motivated in part by the need for more locations for church members to gather in Missouri. A 17 September conference of elders in Kirtland had appointed JS and Rigdon to establish new areas since "the places appointed for the gathering of the saints were at this time crowded to overflowing." The elders agreed "that it was necessary that there be more Stakes of Zion appointed in order that the poor might have a place to gather to."[121] An 18 September memorial from Kirtland bishop Newel K. Whitney and his counselors also emphasized the need for more places for the Saints to gather.[122] The 6 November meeting minutes featured here indicate that the church leaders unanimously approved decreasing lot sizes in Far West, perhaps in an effort to provide more lots for church members moving to Missouri. The assembled leaders also decided that there was sufficient room in that part of Missouri to accommodate church members who would continue to arrive there. At a meeting held a few days later, on 10 November, men ordained to the priesthood voted to expand the town's boundaries from one to four square miles, and a committee was assigned to locate sites for additional settlements.[123]

Another decision at the 6 November meeting related to the temple in Far West. According to a letter written by Thomas B. Marsh, in 1836 William W. Phelps and John Whitmer had

---

119. Selections from *Elders' Journal,* Nov. 1837, p. 487 herein; Travel Account and Questions, *Elders' Journal,* Nov. 1837, pp. 478–484 herein.

120. See Historical Introduction to Letter from William W. Phelps, 7 July 1837, pp. 401–402 herein.

121. Minutes, 17 Sept. 1837–B, p. 445 herein. "Crowded to overflowing" may have indicated that the land the Saints had purchased was fully occupied, not that there was no room for additional settlement in the vicinity.

122. *To the Saints Scattered Abroad, the Bishop and His Counselors of Kirtland Send Greeting* [Kirtland, OH: 18 Sept. 1837], CHL.

123. Minutes, 10 Nov. 1837, p. 475 herein; Selections from *Elders' Journal,* Nov. 1837, p. 487 herein.

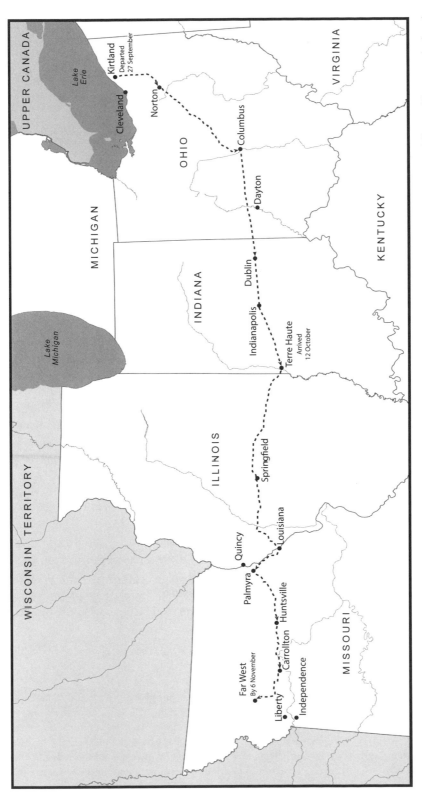

Trip to Far West, Missouri, September–November 1837. Joseph Smith and other church leaders traveled to Far West, Missouri, in fall 1837. They preached and held meetings along the way, and in early November they arrived in Far West, where they conducted a series of meetings with Missouri leaders and members to address issues related to resettlement and church authority.

"appointed the spot for the house of the Lord to be built" and "drew the plan of said house" without consulting the bishop, high council, or First Presidency.[124] In November 1836, Whitmer and Phelps appointed a building committee for the temple, again without the permission or counsel of other Missouri church leaders. The two men were brought before the Far West high council in early April 1837 to explain why they had taken these steps without consultation and why they had kept the profits from land sales.[125] After investigating the subject, the high council resolved that the original building committee would retain their positions and that Missouri church president David Whitmer and his counselors John Whitmer and Phelps "be appointed to superintend the building of the house of the Lord" and "receive Revelations Visions &c concerning said house."[126] John Whitmer and Phelps were required to transfer the land they held privately to Missouri bishop Edward Partridge, who was to oversee the sale of land for the benefit of the church.[127] Ground was broken for the Far West House of the Lord on 3 July 1837, and Phelps expressed his hope that Saints moving there would help fund the building efforts.[128] In August 1837 the Missouri presidency and high council unanimously agreed to "go on moderately and build a house unto the name of the Lord in this place. (Far West) as we have means." As part of this decision, they made Partridge treasurer, to receive donations and subscriptions for the House of the Lord.[129] Though church leaders apparently continued to collect money for the House of the Lord into fall 1837, plans to build the Far West temple were suspended in this 6 November meeting until revelation directed otherwise.

After returning to Kirtland on 10 December 1837, JS wrote an editorial for the *Elders' Journal* describing his travels and the events that had occurred in Far West while he was there in early November. In describing this meeting, JS stated that a committee of four men—Oliver Cowdery, David Whitmer, John Corrill, and Lyman Wight—had been appointed to locate new stakes and instruct the Saints where they should settle, but the committee is not mentioned in the minutes featured here.[130]

Document Transcript

Far West Mo. Nov. 6. 1837.

A number of members of the Church of the Latter Day Saints met to take into consideration some of the affairs of said Church; consisting of the Presidency of the Church here, and President J. Smith jr. Sidney Rigdon & Hyrum Smith.

---

124. Thomas B. Marsh to Wilford Woodruff, in *Elders' Journal*, July 1838, 36–38.

125. Minute Book 2, 3–7 Apr. 1837.

126. Minute Book 2, 7 Apr. 1837.

127. Historical Introduction to Revelation, 4 Sept. 1837, pp. 431–433 herein.

128. Letter from William W. Phelps, 7 July 1837, pp. 402–403 herein.

129. Minute Book 2, 5 Aug. 1837.

130. When the committee reported to the Far West high council in December, the committee members had changed from those originally named by JS. David W. Patten and Frederick G. Williams had joined the committee, and David Whitmer and John Corrill were no longer on the committee. (Minute Book 2, 7 Dec. 1837.)

With Elders T[homas] B. Marsh, Wm. E. Mc.lellin, L[yman] E. Johnson, [p. 80] Wm. Smith & Vinson Knight (from Ohio.) The High Counsellors of the church here, and some other Elders.

Opened by prayer by W[illiam] W. Phelps—

Several topics were discussed, where[131] it was unanimously voted, that it be reccommended to the proprietors of the Corporation of Far West, to petition the Trustees of said corporation, to alter the streets or lessen them so as to make each block contain four acres of ground and each block be divided into four lots.[132]

Secondly:

Voted unanimously, that it is the opinion of this Council, that there— is sufficient room in this country, for the Churches to continue gathering from abroad.

Third

Voted unanimously, that the building of the house of the Lord in this place be postponed till the Lord shall reveal it to be his will to be commenced.[133]

On motion of S. Rigdon the meeting was adjourned until early candle-light.

Council met according to adjournment.

Remarks by John Corrill, Isaac Morley, W. W. Phelps and John Whitmer, and Edward Partridge, Thomas Grover, John Murdock, Wm. Smith, T. B Marsh, Hyrum Smith, Joseph Smith jr. Sidney Rigdon, upo[n] the previous disposition of the Town plot and the purchase of land &c. &c.[134]

All difficulties were satisfactorily settled except a matter between J. Smith jr. Oliver Cowdery and T. B. Marsh, which was refered to themselves with the

---

131. TEXT: Or "when".

132. This standardization of street widths and block sizes may relate to earlier decisions by the Far West high council to allow for alleys to be made within the different blocks. (See Minute Book 2, 7 Apr. 1837.)

133. A JS revelation dated 26 April 1838 directed that a House of the Lord be built in Far West. The cornerstone for the House of the Lord was laid on 4 July 1838, as the 26 April revelation instructed the Saints. (See Revelation, 26 Apr. 1838, in JS, Journal, 26 Apr. 1838, in *JSP*, J1:258–260 [D&C 115].)

134. Whitmer and Phelps purchased the land for Far West in their own names and profited by selling the land to arriving Saints and retaining that money rather than turning it over to the bishop for the use and benefit of the church. The sale of land, creation of a town plat, and decision to begin building a House of the Lord in Far West were done independent of Bishop Edward Partridge, the Far West high council, and other church leaders. An investigation into the actions of Phelps and Whitmer was conducted by the Far West high council in April 1837. JS may have learned of these charges when Thomas B. Marsh and David W. Patten visited Kirtland in July 1837. JS, Marsh, or Patten may have again raised their concerns about the matter after they arrived in Far West in fall 1837. On 7 November, Marsh objected to Whitmer and Phelps retaining their positions as counselors to Missouri church president David Whitmer. (See Minute Book 2, 3–7 Apr. 1837; and Minutes, 7 Nov. 1837, p. 470 herein.)

agreement [p. 81] that their settlement of the affair should be sufficient for the Council.[135]

W. W. Phelps
President.

Attest.
Oliver Cowdery, Clerk.

———— ✌ ————

Minutes, 7 November 1837

Source Note

Minutes, Far West, Caldwell Co., MO, 7 Nov. 1837. Featured version copied [between ca. 6 Apr. and 19 June 1838] in Minute Book 2, pp. 82–85; handwriting of Ebenezer Robinson; CHL. For more information on Minute Book 2, see Source Notes for Multiple-Entry Documents, p. 529 herein.

Historical Introduction

On 7 November 1837 church members in Far West, Missouri, gathered to vote on church leaders and conduct other matters of church business. A similar meeting had been held in Kirtland, Ohio, on 3 September 1837, during which several men were removed and replaced as church leaders. In his remarks on 7 November, Sidney Rigdon discussed the 3 September reorganization of the church, after which moderator Thomas B. Marsh read the minutes of that meeting to the congregation.[136]

In a departure from earlier church voting practices, which usually included only men who had been ordained to the priesthood, all those in attendance were asked to vote, including women and unordained men. Some members of the assembled congregation objected to several individuals, including Frederick G. Williams, David Whitmer, John Whitmer, and William W. Phelps, who held leadership positions within the church. Ultimately, however, only Williams was removed from his position, as a counselor to JS in the First Presidency; Hyrum Smith was unanimously approved to replace him. Despite some objections raised against two members of the Far West high council, other church leaders were unanimously chosen to retain their current positions, including the members of the Twelve who had been objected to in Kirtland on 3 September.[137]

---

135. For more on this unsettled matter, see Historical Introduction to Letter from Oliver Cowdery, 21 Jan. 1838, pp. 502–504 herein; Oliver Cowdery, Far West, MO, to Warren A. Cowdery, 21 Jan. 1838, in Cowdery, Letterbook, 81; Minute Book 2, 12 Apr. 1838; and Synopsis of Oliver Cowdery Trial, 12 Apr. 1838, in *JSP*, J1:251–255.

136. Minutes, 3 Sept. 1837, pp. 422–425 herein.

137. Minutes, 3 Sept. 1837, p. 423 herein. Although they had been sustained in Kirtland on 3 September 1837, Oliver Cowdery, Joseph Smith Sr., and John Smith were not presented to the Far West congregation on 7 November for a vote on their positions as assistant presidents or assistant counselors in the church presidency. Nonetheless, the three men appear to have retained their positions at this time. (Minute Book 1, 7 and 30 Nov. 1837; Minute Book 2, 12 Apr. 1838; "Conference Minutes," *Elders' Journal*, Aug. 1838, 61.)

Document Transcript

Far West. Mo. Tuesday Nov 7 1837

At a general assembly of the Church of Latter Day Saints, assembled at Far, West, to take into consideration and transact the business of said Church. Elder Thomas B. Marsh was chosen Moderator and Oliver Cowdery Clerk.

After singing, the Moderator addressed the throne of grace[138] in prayer, after which Prest. Sidney Rigdon explained the object of the meeting, giving a relation of the recent re-organization of the Church in Kirtland; the minutes of said meeting were read by the Moderator,[139] who also nominated Joseph Smith jr. the first President of the whole Church, to preside over the Same. All were requested, (males and females,) to vote—who was unanimously chosen. He then made a few remarks, accepting the appointment requesting the prayers of the Church in his behalf.

President Smith then nominated Pres't. Sidney Rigdon to be one of his Counsellors—who was unanimously chosen.

He then nominated Frederick G Williams to be his next councillor who was objected to by Elder Lyman Wight in a few remarks refering to a certain letter[140] written to this place by the said Frederick G Williams Also Elder Marsh objected to Prest Williams Elder James Emmet[t] also objected to Pres't Williams[141] [p. 82]

Bishop Edward Partridge said he seconded Pres't. William's nomination and should vote for him; and as to said letter, he had heard it, and saw nothing so criminal in it.

President David Whitmer also made a few remarks in Pres't. Williams' favor.

Elder Marsh made further remarks.

Elder Thomas Grover also objected to Pres't. Williams.

Pres't S. Rigdon then nominated Pres't. Hyrum Smith to take Pres't. Williams' place. He then called for a vote in favor of Pres't. Williams' who was

---

138. See Hebrews 4:16.

139. See Minutes, 3 Sept. 1837, pp. 422–425 herein.

140. The letter referenced by Lyman Wight and Edward Partridge is not extant.

141. The reasons for objecting to Frederick G. Williams were not specified. In late May 1837, Abel Lamb and others mentioned Williams as one whose conduct had been "injurious to the church of God." Williams's sentiments may have been in line with other dissenters in Kirtland during the spring and summer of 1837, though he was sustained as a counselor in the First Presidency at the 3 September meeting. (Letter from Abel Lamb and Others, ca. 28 May 1837, p. 393 herein; Minutes, 3 Sept. 1837, p. 422 herein.)

rejected.[142] He then called for a vote in favor of Pres't. Hyrum Smith, which was carried unanimous.

Some few remarks were made by Pres'ts. David Whitmer and S. Rigdon.

David Whitmer was then nominated as the first President of this branch of the Church, and was objected to by Elder Marsh.[143] Bishop Partridge said he should vote for Prs't. Whitmer— also Elder King Follet[t].

Elder Caleb Baldwin spake against pres't. Whitmer: also Elder Seymour Brunsen [Brunson].

Elder Elisha H. Groves spake in favor of Pres't. Whitmer. Further remarks from Elder [William E.] Mc.lellin, by request of Pres't. Whitmer, who made satisfaction for him. Remarks from Pres't. Joseph Smith jr. who called for an expression,[144] which was carried by almost a unanimous vote.

Pres't. Joseph Smith, jr. then nominated John Whitmer for an assistant President, who was objected, to and Elder Marsh spake in opposition to him, and read a list of charges from a written document against [p. 83] him, and Pres't. [William W.] Phelps.[145] Pres't. John Whitmer then spake a few words by way of confession, and was followed by Elder Isaac Morley.

The vote was called and carried unanimously. The meeting adjourned for one hour.

Meeting convened according to adjournment, a hymn was sung and a prayer offered up by the Moderator. Wm. W. Phelps was nominated for an assistant President, for this Church, by Pres't. Joseph Smith jr. He rose and made certain remarks on the subject of the charges refered to above, by way of confession also. when the vote was put by Pres't. S. Rigdon, and passed unanimous.

---

142. The subject of Williams's standing was again brought before church members in Kirtland at a general assembly on 17 December 1837. Nothing was done at that meeting to "reinstate Frederick G. Williams in the First Presidency." (George W. Robinson, Kirtland, OH, to Thomas B. Marsh, Far West, MO, 10 Jan. 1838, CHL; Williams, *Life of Dr. Frederick G. Williams,* 528–531.)

143. The reasons for objecting to David Whitmer were not specified at this time. Thomas B. Marsh later wrote that the "church has had much sorrow . . . on account of the unfaithfulness" of Whitmer and others. For more on the issues with David Whitmer, see 430n334 herein. (Thomas B. Marsh to Wilford Woodruff, in *Elders' Journal,* July 1838, 38.)

144. The word "expression" here may mean "expression in support of."

145. The document is not extant. While the charges read by Marsh are not specified, they may have been related to allegations of earlier mismanagement of affairs in Far West by John Whitmer and Phelps. Marsh borrowed money from Saints in Tennessee and Kentucky in summer 1836, which was then used by Whitmer and Phelps to purchase land in Caldwell County. Marsh may have personally borrowed the money, and thus been liable for its repayment, or he may have felt a responsibility for the money to be used solely for the benefit of Zion and then repaid to the Kentucky and Tennessee Saints. Although the council ruled that Whitmer and Phelps were to transfer the original town plat and a portion of common land to Bishop Edward Partridge, the two men remained involved with selling land in Far West. ("History of Thomas Baldwin Marsh," 5 [draft 4], Historian's Office, Histories of the Twelve, 1856–1858, 1861, CHL; Minute Book 2, 68–73; Historical Introduction to Revelation, 4 Sept. 1837, pp. 431–433 herein.)

Elder John Murdock, Solomon Hancock, Elias Higbee, Calvin Bebee [Beebe], George Moery [Morey], Thomas Grover, and Simeon Carter, were unanimously chosen high counsellors, and Lyman Wight was objected by John Anderson, who went aside to converse. Newel Knight was unanimously chosen. George M. Hinkle was nominated and was objected by Elder James Emmet, because he was too noisy— By King Follet because of his military office,[146] and by James Durfee because he was a merchant— Elder H. made a few remarks, the vote was called and was unanimous. Levi Jackman and Elisha H. Groves were unanimously chosen. John Anderson then took the stand and made his objections to Lyman Wight, after which Elder Wight also spake the vote was called and he unanimously chosen.

The twelve were then called viz: Thomas B. Marsh, David W. Patten, Brigham Young, Heber C. Kimball, Orson Hyde, Wm. E. Mc.Lellin, Parley P. Pratt, William Smith, Luke Johnson, Orson Pratt, John F. Boynton and Lyman E. Johnson.[147] [p. 84] and were unanimously chosen.

Bishop Edward Partridge was then nominated to still act as Bishop, and was unanimously chosen. Who then nominated Isaac Morly and Titus Billings for his counsellors who were unanimously chosen.[148]

Elder Isaac Morley was then unanimously appointed Patriarch of this Branch of the Church.

Elder John Corrill was chosen to be keeper of the Lord's Storehouse.[149]

Elder Isaac Morley was ⟨then⟩ ordained to the office of Patriarch under the hands of Pres'ts. Joseph Smith, jr. Sidney Rigdon and Hyrum Smith.[150]

---

146. TEXT: The text from this point forward was written at a later time. Hinkle was a commissioned colonel in the Missouri state militia. (*Document Containing the Correspondence,* 34, 73–74, 100; Baugh, *Call to Arms,* 101–102.)

147. At the 3 September 1837 meeting in Kirtland, the congregation voted to reject Luke Johnson, Lyman Johnson, and John F. Boynton as members of the Quorum of the Twelve. Unlike other men who were removed from their church positions at that meeting, the three members of the Twelve were not replaced on 3 September. A week later, each of the men confessed his errors and was restored to full fellowship in the church as well as his position within the Twelve, as their inclusion in the voting on 7 November suggests. (Minutes, 3 Sept. 1837, pp. 423–425 herein.)

148. Isaac Morley had served as a counselor to Partridge since June 1831. Titus Billings was voted to replace John Corrill as a "Bishop's Counsellor" at a general meeting of Missouri church leaders on 1 August 1837. This vote confirmed the Missouri leaders' earlier decision. Corrill had served as a counselor since June 1831. (Minutes, ca. 3–4 June 1831, in *JSP,* D1:326–327; Minute Book 2, 1 Aug. 1837.)

149. Corrill had been nominated by the Missouri presidency and voted to be "an agent to the Church and Keeper of the Lords' store House" at a Far West high council meeting on 22 May 1837. (Minutes, ca. 3–4 June 1831, in *JSP,* D1:326–327; Minute Book 2, 3 June 1831 and 22 May 1837.)

150. Morley was the first ordained patriarch for the church in Missouri and the second ordained patriarch in the church. Joseph Smith Sr. continued to serve in his role as church patriarch in Kirtland at this time.

[151]The congregation then after a few remarks from Pres't. Rigdon, unanimously voted not to support Stores and Shops selling spirituous liquors, Tea, Coffee or Tobacco.[152]

A vote was called on the the subject of the Presidents of the Seventies—and those who have been recently appointed to that office, were unanimously received.[153]

The congregation then united with Pres't. Rigdon, who, in the closing prayer, called upon the Lord to dedicate this land for the gathering of the Saints, and their inheritances.[154]

Thomas B. Marsh, Moderator.

Attest.
Oliver Cowdery Clerk [p. 85]

———— ✧ ————

Minutes, 10 November 1837

Source Note

Minutes, Far West, Caldwell Co., MO, 10 Nov. 1837. Featured version copied [between ca. 6 Apr. and 19 June 1838] in Minute Book 2, p. 86; handwriting of Ebenezer Robinson; CHL. For more information on Minute Book 2, see Source Notes for Multiple-Entry Documents, p. 529 herein.

Historical Introduction

On 10 November 1837, priesthood officers met in Far West, Missouri, to receive instruction from JS and Sidney Rigdon regarding the acquisition of additional church lands, the expansion of the city of Far West, and other church matters. A central topic of the meeting was the gathering of the Saints and the need for establishing additional Latter-day

---

151. TEXT: The text from this point forward was written at a still later time.

152. Strict adherence to the church's dietary code known as the "Word of Wisdom" was not universally practiced at this time. In undated minutes, possibly circa May 1837, the Far West high council had resolved to withdraw fellowship from "any ordained member who will or docs not observe the word of <u>Wisdom</u> <u>according</u> <u>to</u> <u>its</u> <u>litteral</u> <u>reading.</u>" In June 1837 the high council resolved not to uphold any man associated with the business of selling alcohol in Far West, but it did not limit personal use. Failure to observe the Word of Wisdom was one of the charges brought against David Whitmer when he was tried and excommunicated in 1838. (Historical Introduction to Revelation, 27 Feb. 1833, in *JSP,* D3:15–16; Minute Book 2, p. 71, underlining in original; 11 June 1837; 13 Apr. 1838; JS History, vol. B-1, 761–762; Synopsis of David Whitmer Trial, 13 Apr. 1838, in *JSP,* J1:256.)

153. For more on the reorganization of the presidents of the Quorum of the Seventy, see Historical Introduction to Discourse, 6 Apr. 1837, pp. 352–353 herein; and Minutes, 3 Sept. 1837, pp. 420–422 herein.

154. For more on discussions of the gathering of the Saints to Missouri, see Historical Introduction to Minutes, 6 Nov. 1837, pp. 464–466 herein; and Historical Introduction to Minutes, 10 Nov. 1837, pp. 472–475 herein.

Saint settlements, or new stakes of Zion. Finding locations for those settlements was one of JS's and Rigdon's reasons for traveling to Far West.

At the beginning of the meeting, Rigdon read a memorial issued by Kirtland, Ohio, bishop Newel K. Whitney and his counselors on 18 September, which discussed recent struggles in Kirtland, the gathering of the Saints, and the decision made on 17 September to create additional stakes of Zion.[155] Rigdon then spoke on taking appropriate steps to create more cities and provide remuneration for those who were purchasing lands for church members. Conflicts had arisen in obtaining land for the church in Caldwell County, Missouri, when John Whitmer and William W. Phelps made decisions regarding land purchases and building sites without consulting other church leaders. The two also faced criticism for using funds raised for the redemption of Zion to purchase the land in their own names and then keeping the profits rather than providing those funds to Missouri bishop Edward Partridge.[156] As JS and Rigdon prepared to organize more areas for church members to settle, Rigdon's instructions were intended to ensure that those involved in purchasing land would be repaid and that the land and the proceeds from land sales would be used for the benefit of the church and community and not for the profit of individual church members.

The 10 November meeting also focused on the church elders' proselytizing efforts. Rigdon introduced to the Saints in Missouri the church's newly published newspaper, the *Elders' Journal,* of which JS served as editor.[157] According to its prospectus, the paper was intended to "be a vehicle of communication for all the elders of the church of Latter Day Saints, through which they can communicate to others, all things pertaining to their mission, and calling as servants of the living God."[158] Later in the meeting, the assembled men were asked to volunteer if they were able to travel and preach, a request similar to one delivered in an elders' meeting held in Kirtland on 17 September 1837. The twenty-three men who volunteered at this 10 November meeting may have received instructions akin to those given to the Kirtland elders regarding where they should travel, but Oliver Cowdery did not record any such directions in the meeting minutes.[159]

Before leaving Far West to return to Kirtland, JS and Rigdon conferred with church leaders in Missouri and determined that there was room in the vicinity of Far West in Caldwell County to accommodate the church members planning to settle there.[160] Accordingly, the Far West high council and the church's First Presidency voted that "other Stakes be appointed in the regions round about, therefore a committee was appointed to locate the same; consisting of Oliver Cowdery, David Whitmer, John Corril[l], and

---

155. This memorial was printed as a broadside and was also included in the September issue of the *Latter Day Saints' Messenger and Advocate.* (*To the Saints Scattered Abroad, the Bishop and His Counselors of Kirtland Send Greeting* [Kirtland, OH: 18 Sept. 1837], CHL; Newel K. Whitney et al., Kirtland, OH, to "the Saints Scattered Abroad," 18 Sept. 1837, in *LDS Messenger and Advocate,* Sept. 1837, 3:561–564.)

156. "T. B. Marsh," [2], Historian's Office, Histories of the Twelve, 1856–1858, 1861, CHL; Minute Book 2, pp. 68–73. For more on charges against Whitmer and Phelps, see Historical Introduction to Revelation, 4 Sept. 1837, pp. 431–433 herein.

157. See Selections from *Elders' Journal,* Oct. 1837, pp. 460–463 herein.

158. Sidney Rigdon, *Elders' Journal* Prospectus, *LDS Messenger and Advocate,* Aug. 1837, 3:545.

159. See Minutes, 17 Sept. 1837–B, pp. 445–446 herein.

160. Travel Account and Questions, Nov. 1837, pp. 480–481 herein; Minutes, 6 Nov. 1837, p. 467 herein.

KIRTLAND, OHIO, SEPTEMBER 18th, 1837.

To the Saints scattered abroad, the Bishop and his Counselors of Kirtland send greeting.

WHEREAS the church in Kirtland has taken into consideration the affairs of the Latter Day Saints in general, having opportunities of making themselves acquainted with the situation of the Saints throughout the continent, together, with the very flattering prospects of the prosperity of the cause of God in our land. And also of the peculiar condition of the city of Kirtland, which is a kind of first fruits of the cities, which the Lord has began to build unto himself in these last days. It has been deemed of great importance to the prosperity of the cause of truth in general, that the Bishop and his counselors send abroad this their memorial to all the saints throughout the land, as well as to all well-wishers to the cause of Zion, in this our most happy country.

It is a fact well known, that the saints in the city of Kirtland have been called to endure a great fight of affliction for the truth's sake; and to bear a heavy burden in order that the foundation of the kingdom of God might be laid on a sure and certain basis, so that the prophetic vision of Daniel might most certainly be fulfilled. That this kingdom might break in pieces all other kingdoms, and stand forever.

The exertions of the enemy to prevent this have been very great, and through their great exertions, they have given to the saints great trouble, and caused them much expense. In addition to this, they have had to publish the word of the Lord, which has been attended with great expense: these together with building the house of the Lord, have embarrassed them very much; for when subscriptions failed, they went on and accomplished the work of building the house themselves, plighting all that they had, property, credit, and character, and by these means accomplished this great work which is the wonder and admiration of the world.

This they have done in faith believing that as the multitude of saints increased, that their liberality would abound towards those who regarding nothing but the salvation of the world, have thus exposed themselves to ruin, in order that the work of the gathering might not fail.

And besides all this, there have been a large number of poor who have had to receive assistance from the donations of the church, which have tended to increase its embarrassments. And now so numerous are the saints grown, that it is impracticable for them all to gather to the places which are now appointed for this purpose.

The church of Kirtland has, therefore, required at the hand of our beloved brethren Joseph Smith jun. and Sidney Rigdon; (men who have not thought their lives dear unto them, in order that the cause of God might be established,) Presidents, whom God has appointed to preside over the whole church, and the persons to whom this work belongs, that they should go forth, and lay off other stakes of Zion or places of gathering, so that the poor may have a place of refuge, or places of refuge, in the day of tribulation which is coming swiftly on the earth.

All these things will be attended with expense.

Feeling ourselves under great responsibility by virtue of our office and calling in the church of God, we present this our memorial to all the saints, making a most solemn appeal to the feelings, benevolence, and philanthropy, of all the saints into whose hands this our memorial comes, in faith and confidence, that this appeal will not be made in vain.

It is the fixed purpose of our God, and has been so from the beginning, as appears by the testimony of the ancient prophets, that the great work of the last days was to be accomplished by the tithing of his saints. The saints were required to bring their tithes into the store house, and after that, not before, they were to look for a blessing that there should not be room enough to receive it. See Malachi 3rd chapter 10th verse.

Our appeal then to the saints is founded on the best of testimony, that which no saint will feel to gainsay, but rejoice to obey. The saint of God will rejoice in all that the Lord does, and in doing all that the Lord requires.

The sacrafice of righteousness which the Lord requires will be offered with a willing heart, and ready mind, and with great joy, because they are counted worthy to offer up cacrifice for his name.

In making this appeal to the benevolence of the saints of God, we do not only take into consideration the situation of the poor, the embarrassments of the stake of Kirtland; but also their own interest; for every saint has an equal interest in building up of the Zion of our God; for it is after the Lord has built up Zion, that he will appear in his glory.—Psalms 102:16. We all look for the appearing of the great God, and our Savior Jesus Christ; but we shall look in vain, until Zion is built; for Zion is to be the dwelling place of our God when he comes.—Joel 3:21. Any one who will read this chapter with attention, will see that it treats of the last days, and of the Zion of the last days.

How then is the Lord to dwell in Zion, if Zion is not built up? This question we leave the saints to answer.—The salvation of the saints one and all depends on the building up of Zion; for without this there is no salvation; for deliverence in the last days is found in Zion, and in Jerusalem, and in the remnant whom the Lord our God shall call, or in other words, in the stakes which he shall appoint.—Joel 2:32.

It is in Zion where the Lord is to create upon every dwelling place, and upon her assemblies, a cloud and a smoke by day, and the shining of a flaming fire by night. It is upon the glory of Zion, that there will be a defense. It is in Zion that there shall be a tabernacle for a shadow in the day time from the heat, and for a place of refuge, and for a covert from storm and from rain, Isaiah 4:5,6. It is upon the walls of Zion, where the watchman shall see eye to eye Isaiah 52:8.

Whatever is glorious.—Whatever is desirable.—Whatever pertains to salvation, either temporal or spiritual. Our hopes, our expectations, our glory and our reward, all depend on our building up Zion according to the testimony of the prophets. For unless Zion is built: our hopes perish, our expectations fail, our prospects are blasted, our salvation withers, and God will come and smite the whole earth with a curse.

Hear then O ye saints of the last days! and let this our appeal have a favorable reception among you. Let every saint consider well the nature of his calling in the last days, and the great responsibility which rests upon him or her, as one to whom God has revealed his will, and make haste not only to the relief of Kirtland, but also to the building up of Zion.

Let every man, and every woman, give heed to the very instant that they embrace the gospel, and exert themselves with energy to send on means to build up Zion: for our God bids us to haste the building of the city, saying, the time has come when the city must be pushed forward with unceasing exertions; for, behold, the day of calamity draweth nigh, and unless the saints speed the building of the city, they will not escape. Be admonished then O ye saints! and let not covetousness, which is idolatry, nor worldly ambition hinder you; but gather up your gold and your silver, and all the means you have, and send on to the saints who are engaged in this great work of building the zion of our God, that there may be a place of refuge for you, and for your children in the day of God's vengeance, when he shall come down on Idumea, or the world, in his fury, and stamp them down in his wrath, and none shall escape, but the inhabitants of zion.

What we say unto one, we say unto all, haste—haste—and delay not; for the hour of desolation does not linger, and with all the power that the saints have, and with all the diligence they can use, they will scarcely escape.

The time is not far distant, when some of those who now deride and mock the saints for devoting their all to build up the zion of God, will bless their name, for having provided a city of refuge, for them and their children, regardless of the ravings of ungodly priests, and the mockings of a stupid and ignorant people.

In the confidence which we have in the good sense and righteous principles of the multitude of the saints, we send this our memorial in the name of our master Jesus; believing that this appeal will be received with great kindness, and will be attended to with untiring perseverance, until the object for which it has been sent shall be accomplished.

And may the God of all grace, pour out his richest blessings on your heads, and crown you with abundance, that the zion of our God may flourish, and cease not, until the righteousness thereof shall go forth as the light, and the salvation thereof as a lamp which burneth, is the prayer of your brethren in Christ Jesus.

N. K. WHITNEY,
R. CAHOON,
V. KNIGHT,

Memorial, 18 September 1837. Newel K. Whitney, bishop of Kirtland, Ohio, and his counselors, Reynolds Cahoon and Vinson Knight, had this broadside printed to send to the far-flung branches of the church. The memorial gives insight into the direction of the church in the months before tension increased in Kirtland and Joseph Smith relocated to Missouri. The Kirtland bishopric requested that the Saints abroad donate money to relieve the debts of church leaders and to help build Zion. Whitney and his counselors also notified church members of the decision to find locations for new stakes of Zion "so that the poor may have a place of refuge, or places of refuge, in the day of tribulation which is coming swiftly on the earth." Sidney Rigdon read this memorial to priesthood officers in Far West, Missouri, on 10 November 1837. *To the Saints Scattered Abroad, the Bishop and His Counselors of Kirtland Send Greeting* [Kirtland, OH: 18 Sept. 1837], Church History Library, Salt Lake City.

Lyman Wight." Members of that committee promptly began surveying land in northwest Missouri for these new stakes of Zion.[161]

Document Transcript

Far West. Tuesday, Nov. 10. 1837.

At a general meeting of the ordained members of the Church of Latter Day Saints in this place, Elder Thomas B. Marsh opened the meeting by prayer, and Pres't. S[idney] Rigdon read the memorial of the Bishop of Kirtland, and his counsellors, to the churches abroad of Sept. 18th. 1837. He then laid before the meeting the subject of laying off Cities, of consecrating for public purposes, and for remunerating those who appoint and lay them off, &c. When it was unanimously voted that all city plotts hereafter laid off, after remunerating those for their labors who may be engaged in appointing and laying off the same, shall be consecrated for the public benefit of the church— for building houses for public worship, or such other purposes as the church shall say.

President Rigdon then read the prospectus of the "Elders' Journal,"— which was unanimously received. It was then also unanimously voted that the persons present use their exertions to support said paper.[162]

It was then voted that the town of Far West be enlarged so that it contain four sections— that is, two miles square.

Voted, that Bishop Edward Partridge and his counsellors be appointed a committee to appraise the land adjacent to the present Town Plott, see that it is enlarged according to the above vote,[163] provided the present holders of the lands will take such a price for the same, as the above appraisers shall think worth, and that the same be then disposed of as is voted above.

A call was then made for those whose circumstances were such as to permit, to go out to preach, to present themselves. These were twenty-three who arose.

---

161. JS also noted that the members of this committee "started on their mission before we left." By December 1837 the committee included Cowdery, Wight, David W. Patten, and Frederick G. Williams. Cowdery reported his efforts to survey land and determine new locations for the Saints in a 21 January 1838 letter. (Travel Account and Questions, Nov. 1837, p. 481 herein; Minute Book 2, 6–7 Dec. 1837; Letter from Oliver Cowdery, 21 Jan. 1838, pp. 504–505 herein.)

162. The same request for support is found in the prospectus for the *Elders' Journal*. Rigdon may have emphasized the need for support because of the debts of the printing office, many of which were the result of subscribers of the *Messenger and Advocate* failing to make payments. (Sidney Rigdon, *Elders' Journal* Prospectus, *LDS Messenger and Advocate*, Sept. 1837, 3:573; Selections from *Elders' Journal*, Oct. 1837, p. 463 herein; Selections from *Elders' Journal*, Nov. 1837, p. 488 herein.)

163. The original town plot purchased by John Whitmer and William W. Phelps was one square mile and was divided into 121 blocks of land. Phelps and Whitmer signed and acknowledged a plat for the town plot before Elias Higbee, a justice of the Caldwell County court, on 13 April 1837. (See "Description of Far West Plat," copy, Brigham Young University and Church History and Doctrine Department, Church History Project Collection, CHL; and Cannon and Cook, *Far West Record*, 121.)

Sylvester H. Earl, Henry Jackson, Harrison Sagers and John W. Clark, were ordained Elders, and William J. Lemans was ordained a Priest.

President Rigdon then closed the meeting by prayer.

Oliver Cowdery Clerk—. [p. 86]

───── ✑ ─────

Letter from Benjamin Benson, 12 November 1837

Source Note

Benjamin Benson, Letter, [Far West, Caldwell Co., MO], to JS, Far West, Caldwell Co., MO, 12 Nov. 1837. Featured version copied [between ca. 27 June and ca. 5 Aug. 1839] in JS Letterbook 2, p. 51; handwriting of James Mulholland; JS Collection, CHL. For more information on JS Letterbook 2, see Source Notes for Multiple-Entry Documents, p. 526 herein.

Historical Introduction

During his fall 1837 visit to Far West, Missouri, JS spoke with Missouri church member Benjamin Benson on the evening of 11 November.[164] At JS's request, Benson wrote a letter the next day recounting a "dream or vision" he had shared with JS the previous night. The original letter is not extant, but James Mulholland copied Benson's letter into JS's second letterbook in 1839.

The account of his dream reveals that, like many of his era, Benson was concerned about the origins of American Indians and the validity of the Bible's account of human origins.[165] Benson had prayed to learn whether Indians had been placed on the American continent at the creation of the world or had descended from Adam, as he understood the Bible taught. The dream he related to JS occurred forty-two years earlier, in 1795, when he was twenty-two years old. In Benson's account of the dream, an angel took him to a specific place where a record was deposited. There the angel showed him a book, which was to come forth at a later time, that contained a record of a people from Jerusalem, who were the forefathers of the American Indians. Benson also saw in his dream a man who would bring forth that book. In the letter, Benson mentions the "Book [of] Ether" from the Book of Mormon, which along with other details indicates he likely felt that the book in the dream was the Book of Mormon and that the man bringing forth the book in his vision was JS.

───────────────

164. Benson was born on 3 August 1773 in New York to Stutson Benson and Bathsheba Lewis. Benjamin was living in Pompey, New York, by 1795; his brother Peter moved there in 1793. Benjamin married Keziah Messenger in 1795 and moved to Indiana by 1820. Benjamin joined the church in Indiana in 1832 and sold his land in Indiana in October of that year. By 1837 he appears to have moved his family to Missouri. (Benson, *Benson Family Records*, 23–24, 34–35; Inez Benson Russell, "Third Edition—Benson History," microfilm 908,999, U.S. and Canada Record Collection, FHL; *Re-union of the Sons and Daughters of the Old Town of Pompey*, 270; 1820 U.S. Census, Charlestown, Clark Co., IN, 19; Tippecanoe Co., IN, Deed Records, 1828–1866, vol. D, p. 367, microfilm 854,177, U.S. and Canada Record Collection, FHL.)

165. Livingstone, *Adam's Ancestors*, 109–136; Berkhofer, *White Man's Indian*, 33–69.

Document Transcript

Dear Brother in the Lord, Having reflected on the short interview we had last evening respecting the dream (or vision as you may think proper to term it) and as you stated several times that you should like to have it wrote so that you could take it home with you to Kirtland, I therefore consent to give a statement in as short ⟨a⟩ manner as I can, without going into every minute circumstance. To wit.—

In the year 1795, I then being in the Town of Pompey, County of Onondagua and State of New York; I then being 22 years old; seeing and viewing the ancient Indian Forts[166] and trates thereof through that part of the Country; my mind was anxiously led to contemplate and reflect on where ~~these~~ those Indians came from, or from what race of People they sprang from, and oftentimes heard it stated that these Indians were natives of this Continent, and that they were created and placed here at the creation of the world.[167] Then said I the Bible cannot be true, ~~part of~~ for it (The Bible) says that all the human family sprang from Adam &c, and that ~~all~~ at the time of the flood, the whole earth was covered with water, and that all flesh died, except what were in the ark with Noah, then with things taking place, and I firmly believing that the Bible was true, my heart's desire was to God in solemn prayer to know where and what race of people these Indians sprang from, It was made known (whether by dream or vision I will leave that for you, to judge) An angel as I thought came to me and said, Come along with me and I was immediately on a beast like a horse, and the angel at my left hand with his feet about the same height that my

---

166. Benson may have been referring to the fortified villages or traditional longhouses built by the Oneida and Onondaga tribes of the Iroquois Six Nations in central New York. He also may have seen forts built during the French and Indian War, some of which were constructed on the ruins of American Indian villages. The forts described by Benson also may have had connections to other indigenous people. Contemporary accounts identified several mounds in western New York and associated these mounds and their fortifications with an ancient moundbuilding people. (Hauptman, *Conspiracy of Interests,* 27–33, 78, 107; Hamilton, *French and Indian Wars,* 161–184, 239–249; Vogel, *Indian Origins and the Book of Mormon,* 24–30.)

167. The theory of polygenism, or different origins for different races, emerged in European scholarly thought in the sixteenth century. As Europeans encountered new cultures and races, polygenism attempted to explain their origins. Discussions of this theory were particularly widespread in the eighteenth and nineteenth centuries as Enlightenment thought led to the development of racial science and the categorization and ranking of different races. Some scholars tried to make the Bible compatible with polygenism, creating theories of multiple or simultaneous creations besides the creation of Adam. Polygenism and its underlying racial concerns are found throughout nineteenth-century popular and religious literature. For many nineteenth-century Christians, the theory was a direct challenge to Christianity's single biblical creation and the religious requirement of redemption after the fall of Adam and Eve. JS, like other Christians of his day, emphasized the single creation found in the Bible and humanity's common descent from Adam and Eve. (Kidd, *Forging of Races,* 121–167; Livingstone, *Adam's Ancestors,* 169–201; Reeve, *Religion of a Different Color,* 131.)

feet were as I sat on the horse, and in this position was conveyed to near the place where the record was deposited and he said stop here, and the angel went about 4 or 5 Rods and took in his hand a book, and on his return to where I stood, as I thought there were many stood with me; One said, what book is that? and the answer was, it is a bible a bible, the word of God, a record of a people that came from Jerusalem, the fore fathers of these Indians, And it also contains a record of a people that came from the Tower of Babel at the time the Lord confounded the language and scattered the people into all the world, and it the Book Ether;[168] and then with great anxiety of heart I asked if I might have the book, and answer was that it was not the Lords time then, but it should come, "and you shall see it," and then said look, and as I looked, I beheld a man standing as I thought at a distance of two hundred yards, and the angel said "there is the Man that the Lord hath appointed &c, and he is not yet born.["] I have related it in short, as I have not time now to give a full detail of all that I had a view of. Yours with respect.

Benjamin Benson

November 12ᵗʰ 1837
Joseph Smith Jʳ· Far West.

N. B At some further time if the Lord will I will be more full if you should wish it. I shall direct this to you as a letter and you cannot act your Judgement in either keeping it to yourself or publishing it by making use of my name.[169] [p. 51]

———— ❧ ————

Travel Account and Questions, November 1837

Source Note

JS, Travel Account and Questions, Kirtland Township, Geauga Co., OH, Nov. 1837. Featured version published in Elders' Journal of the Church of Latter Day Saints, *Nov. 1837, 27–29. For more information on* Elders' Journal of the Church of Latter Day Saints, *see Source Notes for Multiple-Entry Documents, p. 521 herein.*

Historical Introduction

In late September 1837, JS and several other church leaders traveled to Far West, Missouri, to reorganize church leadership and to establish "places of gathering for the Saints." After returning to Kirtland on 10 December, JS published an account of his travels

---

168. See Book of Mormon, 1830 ed., 539 [Ether 1:33–35]; and Title Page of the Book of Mormon, ca. Early June 1829, in *JSP*, D1:65.

169. The letter was not published in either the *Elders' Journal* or the church's later publication, *Times and Seasons*.

from Ohio, through Indiana, and to Missouri, as well as a summary of various meetings held in Far West, in the church's recently inaugurated periodical, *Elders' Journal*.[170] In addition, JS included a list of twenty questions concerning his history and the church's beliefs and practices. The questions and travel account were published in the November issue of the *Elders' Journal*, which was likely printed shortly after JS's return to Kirtland.[171]

JS, Sidney Rigdon, William Smith, and Vinson Knight set out for Missouri on 27 September 1837.[172] Traveling southwest from Kirtland to Norton, Ohio, the men proceeded west along the National Road through central Ohio and Indiana before arriving at Terre Haute, Indiana, on 12 October; the party later proceeded west through Huntsville and Carrollton, Missouri, reaching Far West sometime before 6 November.[173] Shortly after his arrival in Far West, JS participated in a series of meetings at which those assembled sustained—or in the case of Frederick G. Williams, did not sustain—church leaders and discussed the gathering of church members to that place.[174] At the meetings, it was determined that there were sufficient resources in the area to support additional members of the church, and they appointed Oliver Cowdery, David Whitmer, John Corrill, and Lyman Wight to find locations for other stakes of Zion in the surrounding region.[175] In the article featured here, JS encouraged church members to "make all possible exertions to gather themselves together" in Missouri; he also informed readers that he and other church leaders would be relocating their families there "as soon as our circumstances will admit."

In addition to summarizing his journey to Far West and the administrative decisions made there, JS enumerated a series of questions that he said were "daily and hourly asked by all classes of people whilst we are traveling." Though the specific circumstances that prompted such questions are unclear, many of the queries were related to longstanding misconceptions about church doctrine and JS's past. Avowedly anti-Mormon publications had long influenced how the public viewed JS and the church. Eber D. Howe's *Mormonism Unvailed,* which had been published three years prior in Painesville, Ohio, had shaped some of the public discourse surrounding JS and the church.[176] Although JS stated his

---

170. Historical Introduction to Selections from *Elders' Journal,* Oct. 1837, pp. 460–462 herein.

171. Vilate Murray Kimball, Kirtland, OH, to Heber C. Kimball, Preston, England, 19–24 Jan. 1838, Heber C. Kimball, Collection, CHL; Thomas B. Marsh, Far West, MO, to Wilford Woodruff, [ca. Apr. 1838], in *Elders' Journal,* July 1838, 36–38.

172. Minutes, *Elders' Journal,* Nov. 1837, 17; Minutes, 17 Sept. 1837–A, p. 443 herein; Minutes, 17 Sept. 1837–B, pp. 445–446 herein.

173. Sidney Rigdon, Terre Haute, IN, to Don Carlos Smith, [Kirtland, OH], 13 Oct. 1837, in *Elders' Journal,* Oct. 1837, 7–8; Minutes, 6 Nov. 1837, pp. 464–468 herein.

174. JS's editorial in the November *Elders' Journal* may have included information from more than one meeting in Far West, but it certainly incorporated information from Minutes, 6 Nov. 1837, pp. 464–468 herein.

175. Though JS's report names the members of the committee and indicates when they began their work, the composition of the committee subsequently changed. In minutes of a 7 December 1837 meeting held in Far West, Cowdery, Wight, and David W. Patten are noted as being members of the committee, while Whitmer and Corrill are not mentioned. Frederick G. Williams was added to the committee on that day. (Minute Book 2, 7 Dec. 1837.)

176. Written to convince the public that JS was an imposter and to warn "those who are yet liable . . . to be enclosed within its [Mormonism's] fetters," Howe's book featured a series of affidavits collected by

intention to answer the questions in the next issue of the *Elders' Journal,* JS's departure from Ohio and the seizure and burning of the Kirtland printing office in January 1838 delayed the publication of these answers until the paper resumed printing in Far West, Missouri, in July 1838.[177]

As editor of the *Elders' Journal,* JS may have been involved in writing the other editorials found in the November 1837 issue. Those editorials are featured in Selections from *Elders' Journal,* November 1837, pp. 484–489 herein.

Document Transcript

Be it known unto the Saints scattered abroad greeting:

That myself together with my beloved brother Sidney Rigdon, having been appointed by a general conference of elders held in Kirtland in the house of the Lord on the 18th of Sept.[178] for the purpose of establishing places of gathering for the Saints &c. we therefore would inform our readers that we started from Kirtland in company with V[inson] Knight and Wm. Smith on the 27th of Sept. last, for the purpose of vislting [visiting] the Far West, and also to discover situations suitable for the location of the Saints who are gathering for a refuge and safety, in the day of the wrath of God which is soon to burst upon the head of this generation, according to the testimony of the prophets; who speak expressly concerning the last days: We had a prosperous and a speedy journey; we held one meeting in Norton township Ohio, and three in Doublin, Ia. [Dublin, Indiana] one between Doublin and Ter[r]e Haute, Ia. two in Tere Haute, one in Palmyra, Mo. 2 in Huntsville, one in Carlton;[179] all of which were tended with good success and generally allayed

---

Doctor Philastus Hurlbut from individuals who claimed to have been acquainted with JS and his family when they lived in New York. Following its publication, JS defended his and his family's reputations, stating that he had never "been guilty of wronging or injuring any man or society of men" and that he was only guilty of having, in his youth, "a light, and too often, vain mind." Howe's book received a favorable review in Alexander Campbell's *Millennial Harbinger* and was available for purchase throughout Ohio, western New York, and Pennsylvania. (Howe, *Mormonism Unvailed,* ix; JS to Oliver Cowdery, *LDS Messenger and Advocate,* Dec. 1834, 1:40; "Mormonism Unveiled," *Millennial Harbinger,* Jan. 1835, 44–45; "Mormonism Unveiled," *Fredonia [NY] Censor,* 25 Mar. 1835, [3]; News Item, *Naked Truths about Mormonism* [Oakland, CA], Apr. 1888, 4.)

177. See Questions and Answers, *Elders' Journal,* July 1838, 42–44. In late December 1837 or early January 1838, the Geauga County sheriff seized the printing office, along with its contents, in response to a legal judgment rendered against JS. The office was destroyed by fire on 16 January 1838. ("Sheriff Sale," *Painesville [OH] Telegraph,* 5 Jan. 1838, [3]; Hepzibah Richards, Kirtland, OH, to Willard Richards, Bedford, England, 18–19 Jan. 1838, Willard Richards, Journals and Papers, CHL; John Smith, Kirtland, OH, to George A. Smith, Shinnston, VA, 15–17 Jan. 1838, George Albert Smith, Papers, CHL.)

178. Meeting minutes indicate that the conference was actually held on 17 September 1837. (Minutes, *Elders' Journal,* Nov. 1837, 17; Minutes, 17 Sept. 1837–A, p. 443 herein; Minutes, 17 Sept. 1837–B, p. 445 herein.)

179. Likely the city of Carrollton, Carroll County, Missouri.

the prejudice and feeling of the people, as we judge from the treatment we received, being kindly and hospitably entertained. On our arrival at the city of Far West, we [p. 27] found the church of Latter Day Saints in that place in as prosperous a condition as we could have expected, and as we believe enjoying a goodly portion of the Spirit of God, to the joy and satisfaction of our hearts.

The High council was immediately called and many difficulties adjusted,[180] and the object of our mission was laid before them, after which the subject of the propriety of the Saints, gathering to the city of Far West, was taken into consider[a]tion, after a lengthy discussion upon the subject, it was voted, that the work of the gathering to that place be continued, and that there is a plenty of provisions in the upper counties for the support of that place, and also the emigration of the Saints; also voted that other Stakes be appointed in the regions round about, therefore a committee was appointed to locate the same; consisting of Oliver Cowdery, David Whitmer, John Corril[l], and Lyman Wight; who started on their mission before we left.

It was also voted that the Saints be directed to those men for instruction concerning those places; and it may be expected that all the information necessary will be had from them concerning the location of those places, roads &c. Now we would recommend to the Saints scattered abroad, that they make all possible exertions to gather themselves together unto those places; as peace, verily thus saith the Lord, peace shall soon be taken from the earth,[181] and it has already began to be taken; for a lying spirit has gone out upon all the face of the earth and shall perplex the nations, and shall stur them up to anger against one another: for behold saith the Lord, very fierce and very terrible war is near at hand, even at your doors, therefore make haste saith the Lord O ye my people, and gather yourselres together and be at peace among yourselves, or there shall be no saf[e]ty for you.

We furthermore say to those who wish to stop short of the city of Far West, to call on us and get information concerning those places of gathering: We would say to the Saints it is now a day of warning and not of many words;[182] therefore, a word to the wise is sufficent. We exhort you to remember the words of the prophet Malichi which says, bring ye all the tithes into the store house that there may be meet in mine house, and prove me herewith saith the Lord of hosts, if I will not open you the windows of heaven and pour you

---

180. This statement likely refers to a number of difficulties discussed in meetings held on 6 November 1837. (Minutes, 6 Nov. 1837, pp. 464–468 herein.)

181. See Revelation 6:4; and Revelation, 1 Nov. 1831–B, in *JSP*, D2:107 [D&C 1:35].

182. See Revelation, 30 Aug. 1831, in *JSP*, D2:54 [D&C 63:58].

out a blessing, that there shall not be room enough to receive it, and I will rebuke the devourer for your sake, and he shall not destroy the fruits of your ground, neither shall your vine cast her fruit before the time in the field, saith the Lord of hosts, and all nations shall call you blessed for ye shall be a delightsome land satth [saith] the Lord of hosts.[183] We would also say to the Saints, that we were much pleased with the location of the Far West, and also the society of that place; and we purpose of locating our families in that place as soon as our circumstances will admit.[184]

We shall be under the necessity of observing brevity in this our communication for want of room to publish it, and we shall close after naming a few questions which are daily and hourly asked by all classes of people whilst we are traveling, and will answer them in our next.[185]

Firstly, Do you believe the bible?

2nd, Wherein do you differ from other denominations?

3rd, Will every body be damned but Mormons?

4th, How and where did you obtain the book of Mormon?

5th, Do you believe Jo Smith to be a prophet?

6th, Do the Mormons believe in having all things common?[186]

7th, Do the Momons believe in having more wives than one?[187]

---

183. See Malachi 3:10–12.

184. It is unknown precisely when JS intended to relocate his family to Missouri. On 12 January 1838, JS dictated a revelation that instructed the presidency to "take their families as soon as it is practicable . . . and move on to the west"; the revelation also encouraged faithful members to "arise with their families also and get out of this place [Kirtland, Ohio] and gather themselves together unto Zion." (Revelation, 12 Jan. 1838–C, pp. 501–502 herein.)

185. Some of the questions posed to JS appear to be rhetorical ("Does not Jo Smith pretend to be Jesus Christ?"), while others are broader doctrinal questions ("Wherein do you differ from other denominations?"). Where a question is sufficiently narrow, annotation provides specific historical sources or contexts that likely informed the question. JS answered the questions in the July 1838 issue of the *Elders' Journal*. (Questions and Answers, *Elders' Journal*, July 1838, 42–44.)

186. This question likely arose from the church's early practice of "consecration." In February 1831, a JS revelation outlined the "Laws of the Church of Christ," which included the principle of consecration, or donation, of personal and real property to the church. Latter-day Saints who consecrated their property were to receive in turn a "stewardship" over property that was deeded to them by the church to meet their needs. This program was practiced irregularly among church members in the 1830s. Although Latter-day Saints maintained that this system did not constitute a "common stock" arrangement, where property was owned jointly, allegations persisted in the 1830s that the church members held "all things 'in common.'" While there were common properties held in the name of the church, "stewardships" or inheritances were deeded to individuals and held in their private names. (Revelation, 9 Feb. 1831, in *JSP*, D1:245–256 [D&C 42:1–72]; Revelation, 20 May 1831, in *JSP*, D1:314–317 [D&C 51:4–5]; JS, Journal, 30 Oct. 1835, in *JSP*, J1:79; JS History, vol. A-1, 93; Howe, *Mormonism Unvailed*, 120–121, 125–126.)

187. According to a circa August 1835 "Statement on Marriage," the church had been accused of "the crime of fornication, and polygamy," though the specific source of the allegations is unknown. (Statement on Marriage, ca. Aug. 1835, in *JSP*, D4:477.)

8th, Can they riase the dead?[188] [p. 28]

9th, What signs does Jo Smith give to establish his divine mission?

10th, Was not Jo Smith a money digger?[189]

11th, Did he not Steal his wife?[190]

12th, Do the people have to give up their money when they join his church?

13th, Are the Mormons Abolitionists?[191]

14th, Do they not stur up the Indians to war and to commit depredations?[192]

15th, Do the Mormons baptize in the name of Jo Smith?

16th, If the Mormon doctrine is true, what have become of all that have died since the days of the apostles?

17th Does not Jo Smith pretend to be Jesus Christ?

---

188. In an 1893 reminiscent account, prominent Missouri resident Alexander Majors wrote that church members in Jackson County "claimed they could raise the dead." (Ingraham, *Seventy Years on the Frontier,* 44.)

189. JS's reputation as a treasure seer, or someone who used a seer stone to locate gold or other valuable objects buried in the earth, likely prompted this question. (Historical Introduction to Agreement of Josiah Stowell and Others, 1 Nov. 1825, in *JSP,* D1:345–350; Isaac Hale, Affidavit, Harmony, PA, 20 Mar. 1834, in "Mormonism," *Susquehanna Register, and Northern Pennsylvanian* [Montrose, PA], 1 May 1834, [1]; Howe, *Mormonism Unvailed,* 234.)

190. This query may have arisen from statements made by Emma Smith's father, Isaac Hale, as well as an affidavit published in *Mormonism Unvailed.* Twenty-two-year-old Emma Hale married JS in January 1827. Isaac Hale opposed the union and alleged in 1834 that JS had "carried off my daughter" and married her "without my approbation or consent." (Isaac Hale, Affidavit, Harmony, PA, 20 Mar. 1834, in "Mormonism," *Susquehanna Register, and Northern Pennsylvanian* [Montrose, PA], 1 May 1834, [1]; Howe, *Mormonism Unvailed,* 232–237.)

191. On this issue, see Historical Introduction to Letter to Oliver Cowdery, ca. 9 Apr. 1836, pp. 231–243 herein.

192. This question may have been informed by allegations that, as early as 1831, Latter-day Saint missionaries were seeking to convert American Indians and incite them to attack non-Mormons. These claims were based on interpretations of Book of Mormon prophecies stating that converted Indians would be—echoing language from the biblical book of Micah—"as a young lion among the flocks of sheep, who, if he goeth through, both treadeth down and teareth in pieces, and none can deliver."[a] In 1832, fearing that non-Mormons would believe that the Latter-day Saints were "putting up the Indians to slay" whites—thereby endangering "the lives of the Saints evry where"—JS cautioned church members against discussing these prophecies.[b] Fears that the Saints were "tampering" with American Indians contributed to opposition of Mormon settlements in Jackson County in 1833 and Clay County in 1836, leading church leaders to deny having any connection with the Indians and to state that the Saints feared "the barbarous cruelty of rude savages" like other frontier whites.[c] Similar allegations were made in Eber D. Howe's 1834 book *Mormonism Unvailed.*[d] (a. "Mormonism—No. VI," *Ohio Star* [Ravenna], 17 Nov. 1831, [3]; Book of Mormon, 1830 ed., 496–497, 500 [3 Nephi 20:15–16; 21:11–12]; Micah 5:8. b. Letter to William W. Phelps, 31 July 1832, in *JSP,* D2:266. c. Isaac McCoy, "The Disturbances in Jackson County," *Missouri Republican* [St. Louis], 20 Dec. 1833, [2]–[3]; "Public Meeting," *LDS Messenger and Advocate,* Aug. 1836, 2:359–360; Letter to John Thornton and Others, 25 July 1836, pp. 263–264 herein. d. Howe, *Mormonism Unvailed,* 145–146, 196–197.)

18th, Is there any thing in the bible that liscences you to believe in revelation now days?[193]

19th, Is not the canon of the scriptures full?

20th, What are the fundamental principles of your religion?

The above questions are as many as we probably shall have room to answer in our next article, though many more may hereafter be asked and answered as circumstances will permit.

—————— ☙ ——————

Selections from *Elders' Journal,* November 1837

Source Note

Selections from Elders' Journal of the Church of Latter Day Saints, *Kirtland Township, Geauga Co., OH, Nov. 1837, 17, 19, 27, 29, 31, 32. For more information on* Elders' Journal of the Church of Latter Day Saints, *see Source Notes for Multiple-Entry Documents, p. 521 herein.*

Historical Introduction

In November 1837, the second issue of the church's new periodical, *Elders' Journal of the Church of Latter Day Saints,* was published in Kirtland, Ohio. The paper was first published in October 1837 as an instrument for the elders of the church to "communicate to others, all things pertaining to their mission, and calling as servants of the living God, and messengers of righteousness to the nations among whom they are sent."[194] As editor of the *Elders' Journal,* JS was ultimately responsible for its content, including editorial selections in the November issue that introduced conference minutes, prefaced a letter from Orson Hyde in England, articulated an editorial philosophy, and implored subscribers to remit payment for their subscriptions. Though JS authored an account of his trip to Missouri and an attending list of questions, the extent of his involvement in writing the other editorial pieces is unclear.[195] Given that he did not return to Kirtland from Far West, Missouri, until 10 December 1837, the November issue was likely not published until after that date.[196]

---

193. JS had previously defended the idea of modern-day revelation in an 1833 letter to his uncle Silas Smith and in a circa March 1834 letter to the church. The latter was published in *The Evening and the Morning Star* in March 1834. (Historical Introduction to Letter to Silas Smith, 26 Sept. 1833, in *JSP,* D3:301–303; Letter to the Church, ca. Mar. 1824, in *JSP,* D3:475–476.)

194. Sidney Rigdon, *Elders' Journal* Prospectus, *LDS Messenger and Advocate,* Aug. 1837, 3:545.

195. See Travel Account and Questions, Nov. 1837, pp. 478–484 herein. For more on JS's role in editing content in the October and November issues of the *Elders' Journal,* see Historical Introduction to Selections from *Elders' Journal,* Oct. 1837, pp. 461–462 herein. The complete issues of the *Elders' Journal* are available on the Joseph Smith Papers website.

196. Vilate Murray Kimball, Kirtland, OH, to Heber C. Kimball, Preston, England, 19–24 Jan. 1838, Heber C. Kimball, Collection, CHL; Thomas B. Marsh to Wilford Woodruff, in *Elders' Journal,* July 1838, 36–38.

The first editorial passage from the November *Elders' Journal* introduces minutes of a church assembly held in Kirtland on 17 September 1837 to discuss the building up of Zion.[197] The following day, Bishop Newel K. Whitney and his counselors issued a memorial to members of the church to "exert themselves with energy to send on means to build up Zion." The appeal was distributed as a broadside and reprinted in the September 1837 issue of the *Latter Day Saints' Messenger and Advocate*.[198]

Document Transcript

The following conference minutes should have been published in the Sept. No.[199] with the Bishop's Appeal or Memmorial, but through a press of business it has been overlooked and not handed to us until now, however, we feel in hopes that it will serve to call the attention of our readers (those that have the last No. of the Messenger) to the second *candid* perusal of the Appeal.[200] —ED.

[. . .] [p. 17] [. . .]

——————— ☙ ———————

Editorial Note

Another editorial passage served as a short preface to a letter from apostle Orson Hyde to his wife, Marinda Nancy Johnson Hyde. Along with Heber C. Kimball, Willard Richards, Joseph Fielding, Isaac Russell, John Goodson, and John Snider, Orson Hyde had arrived in England around 18 July 1837.[201] In his letter, written on 14 September from the city of Preston, Hyde described the proselytizing experiences of the Mormon elders in England, including a candid description of the poverty faced by those to whom they preached.[202] The publication of such correspondence embodied the paper's objective of "making known the progress of the work" in the United States and abroad.[203]

——————— ☙ ———————

197. See Minutes, 17 Sept. 1837–A, p. 443 herein; and Minutes, 17 Sept. 1837–B, pp. 445–446 herein.

198. *To the Saints Scattered Abroad, the Bishop and His Counselors of Kirtland Send Greeting* [Kirtland, OH: 18 Sept. 1837], CHL; Newel K. Whitney et al., Kirtland, OH, to "the Saints Scattered Abroad," in *LDS Messenger and Advocate,* Sept. 1837, 3:561–563.

199. That is, the September issue of the *Messenger and Advocate*.

200. See Newel K. Whitney et al., Kirtland, OH, to "the Saints Scattered Abroad," in *LDS Messenger and Advocate,* Sept. 1837, 3:561–563.

201. See Historical Introduction to Recommendation for Heber C. Kimball, between 2 and 13 June 1837, pp. 398–400 herein; and Historical Introduction to Selections from *Elders' Journal,* Oct. 1837, p. 462 herein.

202. Orson Hyde, Preston, England, to Marinda Johnson Hyde, [Kirtland, OH], 14 Sept. 1837, in *Elders' Journal,* Nov. 1837, 19–22.

203. Sidney Rigdon, *Elders' Journal* Prospectus, *LDS Messenger and Advocate,* Aug. 1837, 3:545.

We are aware that it is not expected by the elders of the church of Latter Day Saints, that their private epistles will be spread before the public, especially when addressed to their wives; & the apology we have to offer for so doing at this time is, that our columes could not be devoted to a better use, than they are with the following epistle from our beloved Bro. O[rson] Hyde. Although it is but ten days later than that of elder [Heber C.] Kimball's, published in the Oct. No.[204] yet, we think it will be a sweet morsel to every Saint, and will serve as a stimulative to the ministers of our God,[205] that their exertions in the proclatmaion [proclamation] of the gospel may be untiring, until the uttermost corners of the earth shall be made to tremble with the sound of their voices, and the Israel of God be gathered out against the day of disolution, which is speedily to come upon the earth, if the ancient prophets have not prophesied falsely.

—ED.

[. . .] [p. 19] [. . .]

Editorial Note

This third passage of editorial content in the November 1837 issue of the *Elders' Journal* commented pointedly on the editorial style of the *Messenger and Advocate*'s editor, Warren A. Cowdery, who had printed lengthy articles on history and philosophy, devoting less space to missionary work. In July 1837, Cowdery had also written a piece critical of JS and the direction of church affairs in Kirtland.[206]

We would say to the patrons of the Journal, that we calculate to pursue a different course from that of our predecessor in the editorial department.— We will endeavor not to scandalize our own citizens, especially when there is no foundation in truth for so doing; we consider that when a man scandalizes his neighbor, it follows of course that he designs to cover his own iniquity: we consider him who puts his foot upon the neck of his benefactor, an object of pitty rather than revenge, for in so doing he not only shows the contraction of his own mind but the wickedness of his heart also.

204. Heber C. Kimball, Preston, England, to Vilate Murray Kimball, [Kirtland, OH], 2 Sept. 1837, in *Elders' Journal,* Oct. 1837, 4–7.

205. Reporting that between one hundred and two hundred people had been baptized since the arrival of the Mormon elders, Hyde confided to his wife, "I can truly say that I never before preached with that power and Spirit that I have since I come to this place." (Orson Hyde, Preston, England, to Marinda Johnson Hyde, [Kirtland, OH], 14 Sept. 1837, in *Elders' Journal,* Nov. 1837, 19–22.)

206. Editorial, *LDS Messenger and Advocate,* July 1837, 3:538. For more background on Warren A. Cowdery and his editorial practices, see Historical Introduction to Selections from *Elders' Journal,* Oct. 1837, pp. 461–462 herein.

And as there are shaving shops[207] in the world, we would caution the subscribers of the Star[208] and Messenger and Advocate to send their subscriptions agreeable to the notice given in this number,[209] and furthermore those who have had deal with the office, or bindery,[210] those who have books or other articles at this office will please hand or send the money to the persons named in the above alluded notice, also all applications for books or back Nos. of the Star and Messenger and Advocate, and for books to be rebound &c. &c. &c. to be made to the same persons, who will wait upon them with pleasure. The reason of this notice is, that our subscribers as well as ourselves may not suffer loss. O confidence where hast thou fled! Whither art thou gone? Art thou in search of *lucre*, is it *he* which has destroyed thee?

[. . .] [p. 27] [. . .]

Editorial Note

The following notice introduced minutes of a general assembly held in Far West, Missouri, on 7 November 1837. After departing Kirtland in late September and proselytizing in towns in Ohio, Indiana, and Missouri, JS and several other leaders arrived in Far West by 6 November.[211] On 7 November, an assembly of members voted on the organization of church leaders and conducted other matters of church business.[212]

In consequence of the delay of this No. which was occasioned by the preasure of times operating against us, so that paper was not to be obtained in season for its is[s]ue, we are enabled to lay before our readers a few items of the proceedings of our brethren in the Far West during our visit to that place; which we trust will satisfy for the delay.

[. . .] [p. 29] [. . .]

---

207. A "shaving shop" is a nineteenth-century idiom for a banking company or money broker that would "purchase notes at more than legal interest" or "resort to any means to obtain a large discount." (Bartlett, *Dictionary of Americanisms,* 295; "Shaver," in *American Dictionary.*)

208. The church's Kirtland printing office produced reprints of *The Evening and the Morning Star* between January 1835 and October 1836; it began selling bound copies of the *Star* by January 1837. (Crawley, *Descriptive Bibliography,* 1:50; Advertisement, *LDS Messenger and Advocate,* Jan. 1837, 3:448.)

209. According to the October issue of the *Elders' Journal,* subscribers of the *Messenger and Advocate* were $800 to $1,000 in arrears. (Notice, *Elders' Journal,* Oct. 1837, 15.)

210. Contemporary sources first mention the church's effort to establish a bookbindery in Kirtland in November 1835; it was functioning in the printing office sometime before January 1837. Bound books included compiled copies of the *Evening and Morning Star* and the *Messenger and Advocate.* (Revelation, 2 Nov. 1835, pp. 30–32 herein; Advertisement, *LDS Messenger and Advocate,* Jan. 1837, 3:448.)

211. Historical Introduction to Travel Account and Questions, Nov. 1837, pp. 478–480 herein.

212. Minutes, 7 Nov. 1837, pp. 468–472 herein.

Editorial Note

Another editorial note appealed to subscribers of both the defunct *Messenger and Advocate* and the *Elders' Journal* to send in their subscription money. In late 1837, the church faced a difficult financial situation, including debts resulting from the construction of the House of the Lord and the church's various publishing endeavors.[213]

———— ❧ ————

NOTICE.

The subscribers for the Messenger and Advocate, are propably aware, that much of their subscription is yet in the rear; the office being changed into the hands of others, and the debts of the same pressing hard upon the former proprietors:[214] it therefore becomes necessary to urge mildly the patrons of this office, to send up their subscriptions as soon as possible. and this will relieve those debts, and help forward the Journal in its season. It is also necessary that those who wish to continue on with the Journal, for them to forward their money, in order that their names may be entered on the Journal book. The books of the Evening and Morning Star, and Messenger and Advocate are in the hands of Wm. Marks and G[eorge] W. Robinson,[215] consequently those indebted for the same, (Star and Messenger,) will please send their subscription to them.

All letters subscribed Marks and Robinson, and *Post paid.*—Ed.

[. . .] [p. 31] [. . .]

———— ❧ ————

Editorial Note

A final editorial passage looked ahead to content in the next issue. However, the November issue represented the last installment of the *Elders' Journal* printed in Kirtland; the paper resumed publication in Far West, Missouri, in July 1838.[216]

---

213. Newel K. Whitney et al., Kirtland, OH, to "the Saints Scattered Abroad," in *LDS Messenger and Advocate,* Sept. 1837, 3:561–563; Historical Introduction to Discourse, 6 Apr. 1837, p. 354 herein.

214. JS and Sidney Rigdon purchased the printing office from Oliver Cowdery on 1 February 1837. The paper was transferred to William Marks in April 1837, with JS and Rigdon acting as Marks's agents. ("Notice," *LDS Messenger and Advocate,* Feb. 1837, 3:458–459; Masthead, *LDS Messenger and Advocate,* Apr. 1837, 3:496.)

215. Robinson's involvement with the printing office is unknown. He had been elected general clerk and recorder on 17 September 1837 in place of Oliver Cowdery, who had moved to Missouri. (Minutes, 17 Sept. 1837–A, p. 443 herein.)

216. In late December 1837 or early January 1838, the Geauga County sheriff seized the printing office, along with its contents, in response to a legal judgment rendered against JS. The office was destroyed by fire on 16 January 1838. The *Elders' Journal* resumed publication on another press in Far West in July 1838. ("Sheriff Sale," *Painesville [OH] Telegraph,* 5 Jan. 1838, [3]; Hepzibah Richards, Kirtland, OH, to Willard Richards, Bedford, England, 18–19 Jan. 1838, Willard Richards, Journals and Papers, CHL; John Smith,

For the want of room we have been under the necessity of leaving out the Obituary[217] of our friends, and also several communications, which will probably appear in our next.—ED.

[. . .] [p. 32]

——————— ꝏ ———————

Agreement, 4 January 1838

Source Note

JS, Agreement, Kirtland Township, Geauga Co., OH, 4 Jan. 1838; handwriting of two unidentified scribes (probably John P. Markell and Nicholas Markell); signature of JS; attested by John P. Markell and Nicholas Markell; one page; CHL. Includes docket.

One leaf, measuring 9½ × 7⅞ inches (24 × 20 cm). The agreement was folded in two patterns. In the first, the agreement was folded twice in a parallel fold and was then docketed. In the second, which retained the first folding pattern, the document was again folded twice in a parallel fold, with the docket remaining visible. The docket in unidentified handwriting (probably John P. Markell) reads: "Articcle of Agreemen[t] | Between Joseph | Smith Jun and | Joseph Smith Sen". The top panel of the agreement was lost due to wear and weakening of a fold. Remaining folds are partially broken. The agreement has undergone conservation. The conservation technique used, the "Barrow method," was a common preservation practice in libraries and archives from the 1930s to the mid-1970s.[218] The Church History Library acquired this document from a private collector in 2010.

Historical Introduction

On 4 January 1838, Nicholas Markell of Kirtland, Ohio, wrote an agreement releasing his claim to a "box and records" that had been seized from JS by legal action. In the same document, JS entered into an agreement with an individual, likely Joseph Smith Sr., to whom he transferred "two undivided thirds of records and box Exclusive of the mummies." The top quarter of the document, including part of the agreement, is no longer extant, and the nature of the arrangement is not fully understood. It is likely, however, that the "records" named were the Egyptian papyri JS had obtained from Michael Chandler in July 1835 and that the agreement pertained to a legal judgment for an unidentified lawsuit, probably rendered against JS in 1837, that resulted in the seizure of his personal property.[219]

Kirtland, OH, to George A. Smith, Shinnston, VA, 15–17 Jan. 1838, George Albert Smith, Papers, CHL; Oliver Cowdery, Far West, MO, to Warren A. Cowdery and Lyman Cowdery, Kirtland, OH, 4 Feb. 1838, in Cowdery, Letterbook, 83–86; Oliver Cowdery, Far West, MO, to Warren A. Cowdery and Lyman Cowdery, Kirtland, OH, [after 10 Mar. 1838], in Cowdery, Letterbook, 92; Minute Book 2, 12 and 21 Apr. 1838.)

217. TEXT: "Obituary" is set in a larger, heavier typeface.

218. Church, "William J. Barrow," 152; Ellis, *Historical Perspectives in the Conservation of Works of Art on Paper*, 263.

219. For more information on Chandler and the Egyptian artifacts, see Introduction to Part 1: 2 Oct.–1 Dec. 1835, pp. 4–6 herein; for information on legal judgments and the seizure of property, see Historical Introduction to Letter from Emma Smith, 3 May 1837, pp. 373–374 herein.

After returning to Kirtland from Missouri on 10 December 1837, JS and the church endured another round of ecclesiastical, financial, and legal challenges both from church
members and from others in the community. During JS's two-and-a-half-month absence,
dissenters in Kirtland denounced him and the church; in late December, twenty-eight
people associated with this group were excommunicated.[220] Following his return, JS and
other church leaders who had partnered with him in business affairs faced new and ongoing
litigation, including various legal charges related to outstanding debts.[221] As a result of these
legal proceedings, the assets of JS and other church leaders, including the contents of the
church's printing office and at least some of the Egyptian documents, were seized.[222] Vilate
Murray Kimball chronicled some of these events in a January letter to her husband, Heber,
who was then proselytizing in England. Referring to lawsuits filed by Samuel Rounds,
Kimball reported that "as soon as Presidents Smith and Rigdon got home from the west, they
were called upon to pay a fine of one thousand dollars each, for puting out Kirtland money.
They were strip[p]ed of every thing; even to food and ra[i]ment." According to Kimball, other
church members had also been "strip[p]ed of all their loos property for debt."[223] In a reminiscent account written in 1844–1845, Lucy Mack Smith recalled that some of the church's dissenters began suing JS, "and with this pretense they siezed upon every piece of property which
they could have least pretext to lay hold upon." Smith continued, "They determined to get
possession of some Mum[m]ies and the records which attended them and . . . accordingly
they levied an execution upon them claiming that they belonged to Joseph and he was owing
them a debt of 50 dollars."[224] These dissenters seem to have temporarily procured at least some
of the Egyptian records. In an 18–19 January letter to her brother Willard, Hepzibah Richards
indicated that along with the printing office—which had been attached on a judgment and
sold at an auction on 15 January—the "Mummies and records have been attached— mummies sold— Records missing."[225]

Though a legal judgment was apparently used to obtain the Egyptian records,
the featured agreement suggests that the records eventually ended up in the hands
of Nicholas Markell. Nicholas, John, and James Markell—all signatories to the agreement—were sons of Peter and Elizabeth Koch Markell, members of one of Kirtland's

220. Thomas B. Marsh, Far West, MO, to Wilford Woodruff, Vinalhaven, ME, ca. 18 June 1838,
Wilford Woodruff, Journals and Papers, CHL; John Smith and Clarissa Lyman Smith, Kirtland, OH, to
George A. Smith, Shinnston, VA, 1 Jan. 1838, George Albert Smith, Papers, CHL; Historical Introduction
to Revelation, 12 Jan. 1838–A, pp. 495–496 herein.

221. For a list of cases brought before the Geauga County Court of Common Pleas, see Madsen,
"Tabulating the Impact of Litigation on the Kirtland Economy," 234. For cases brought before the justice
court in Geauga County, see Cowdery, Docket Book, 269, 280–282, 293.

222. "Sheriff Sale," *Painesville (OH) Telegraph*, 5 Jan. 1838, [3]; Lucy Mack Smith, History, 1844–
1845, bk. 14, [11].

223. Vilate Murray Kimball, Kirtland, OH, to Heber C. Kimball, Preston, England, 19–24 Jan.
1838, Heber C. Kimball, Collection, CHL. On the Samuel Rounds case, see Introduction to Part 5: 5 Oct.
1836–10 Apr. 1837, pp. 292–293 herein.

224. Lucy Mack Smith, History, 1844–1845, bk. 14, [11].

225. Hepzibah Richards, Kirtland, OH, to Willard Richards, Bedford, England, 18–19 Jan. 1838,
Willard Richards, Journals and Papers, CHL.

pioneering families.[226] Contemporary documents offer no clues as to what may have motivated Nicholas Markell to procure the Egyptian records and subsequently return them to JS.[227] Ultimately, according to an 1844–1845 statement by Lucy Mack Smith, "By various statagems we kept them [the Mummies and records] out of the hands of the rabble who were joined with the appostates in devising every invention to get these things into their possession."[228]

In the top half of the agreement—a significant portion of which is missing—JS transferred the Egyptian records to another individual on the same day. The docketing, recorded on the other side of the agreement, suggests that JS conveyed the papyri to his father, Joseph Smith Sr.[229] Both sections of the 4 January agreement, as well as the docketing, are written in the same unidentified hand.

Document Transcript

[*Portion of page missing*]

/[230]I conv[e]y the two undivided thirds of records ~~exclusive of~~ and box Exclusive of the mummies[231]

---

226. Peter Markell and Elizabeth Koch were married in 1792 and resided in Palatine, Montgomery County, New York, before moving to Ohio sometime between October 1817 and mid-1819. The Markells had ten children. (Vosburgh, *Records of the Reformed Dutch Church of Stone Arabia*, 2:152; Kirtland Township Trustees' Minutes and Poll Book, 1817–1838, p. 18, in Kirtland, Lake Co., OH, Minutes, microfilm 877,763, U.S. and Canada Record Collection, FHL; *Record of the Revolutionary Soldiers Buried in Lake County, Ohio*, 36–37.)

227. A letter written by a Markell descendant more than 130 years later provides information that may contextualize the 1838 agreement. Writing in the early 1970s to Jay Todd, author of *The Saga of the Book of Abraham,* John P. Markell's great-granddaughter Hazel B. Roese asserted that the Markell family were "very close friends of Joseph Smith." Roese stated that someone related to Joseph Coe, who had originally helped purchase the Egyptian artifacts in 1835 and was excommunicated with other dissenters in December 1837, had obtained the Egyptian papyri but that the Markells "were foxey enough to conn this fellow out" of them. "It seems he [Coe] owed Judge [John P.] Markell some money," indicated Roese, "and Uncle James was deputized to help retrieve the records." In her letter, Roese suggested that she had read this information and heard the story from her grandfather Patrick Henry Booth (husband of John P. Markell's daughter Laura Ann Markell). (Hazel B. Roese, Ferndale, MI, to Jay Todd, Salt Lake City, UT, ca. 1970, photocopy, H. Donl Peterson Research Collection on the Book of Abraham Papyri, BYU; Joseph Coe, Kirtland, OH, to JS, Nauvoo, IL, 1 Jan. 1844, JS Collection, CHL; John Smith and Clarissa Lyman Smith, Kirtland, OH, to George A. Smith, Shinnston, VA, 1 Jan. 1838, George Albert Smith, Papers, CHL.)

228. Lucy Mack Smith, History, 1844–1845, bk. 14, [11].

229. In an 1855 reminiscent account, William Huntington recorded that Joseph Smith Sr. hid in Huntington's home during the winter of 1838; he also wrote, "In my house the mummies and Egyptian records were hid to keep from sworn destruction by apostates." (Huntington, "History of William Huntington," 13.)

230. TEXT: Unidentified handwriting—probably John Markell—begins.

231. During the summer of 1835, JS and other local investors purchased four mummies, along with Egyptian records written on papyrus, from Michael Chandler. The mummies had been housed or displayed at various times in the home of Frederick G. Williams, the John Johnson inn, and the House of the Lord in Kirtland. (See Historical Introduction to Book of Abraham Manuscript, ca. Early July–ca. Nov. 1835–A [Abraham 1:4–2:6], pp. 71–77 herein; Historical Introduction to Egyptian Alphabet,

Kirtland January 4th. 1838

²³²**Joseph Smith Jr**

Attest—

John P Markell²³³

²³⁴Nicholas Markell²³⁵

I do hereby relinquish on the box and records which James Markell[236]
Constable has Levied in my favor as the property of J. Smith Jr. and my claim on
the same

/[237]Kirtland Jan;[238] the th4 1838

Nicholas Marke[ll]

/[239]Attest

John P Markell

———— ∾ ————

Letter and Revelation to Edward Partridge,
7 January 1838

Source Note

*JS, Letter and Revelation, [Kirtland Township, Geauga Co., OH], to Edward Partridge, [Far West,
Caldwell Co., MO], 7 Jan. 1838. Featured version copied [ca. Jan. 1878] in Edward Partridge Jr., Genealogical
Record, 52; handwriting of Edward Partridge Jr.; CHL.*

---

ca. Early July–ca. Nov. 1835–A, pp. 81–83 herein; JS, Journal, 24 Oct. 1835; 17 Nov. 1835; 17 Feb. 1836, in
JSP, J1:73, 105, 186; and Woodruff, Journal, 25 Nov. 1836.)

232. TEXT: Signature of JS.

233. John Markell, who acted as a witness in both agreements, previously served as a town constable
and elector. (Kirtland Township Trustees' Minutes and Poll Book, 1817–1838, pp. 36–39, 63, in Kirtland,
Lake Co., OH, Minutes, microfilm 877,763, U.S. and Canada Record Collection, FHL; see also Obituary
for John P. Markell, *Painesville [OH] Telegraph*, 24 Feb. 1881, [3].)

234. TEXT: Signature probably of Nicholas Markell.

235. Little is known about Nicholas Markell's activities in 1837, but he later served as a town juror and
overseer of the poor in Kirtland during the early 1840s. (Kirtland Township Trustees' Minutes and Poll
Book, 1838–1846, pp. 52, 81–83, in Kirtland, Lake Co., OH, Minutes, microfilm 877,763, U.S. and Canada
Record Collection, FHL; see also Obituary for Nicholas Markell, *Painesville [OH] Telegraph*, 10 Sept. 1885,
[3].)

236. James Markell was appointed as a constable in April 1837. Along with Luke Johnson, also a constable, Markell was assigned to serve executions on judgments rendered against JS and other church leaders
on actions of debt in the Geauga County justice court in December 1837 and January 1838. (Kirtland
Township Trustees' Minutes and Poll Book, 1817–1838, p. 159, in Kirtland, Lake Co., OH, Minutes, microfilm 877,763, U.S. and Canada Record Collection, FHL; Cowdery, Docket Book, 254–269, 293.)

237. TEXT: Unidentified handwriting—probably John Markell—ends; unidentified—probably
Nicholas Markell—begins.

238. TEXT: Or "Jany".

239. TEXT: Unidentified handwriting—probably Nicholas Markell—ends; unidentified—probably
John Markell—begins.

Book measuring 13 × 8⅝ × 1½ inches (33 × 22 × 4 cm). Record contains 120 pages. The text block consists of 215 leaves (430 pages) measuring 12½ × 7⅞ inches (32 × 20 cm) each. Spine has "RECORDS" in gold lettering. A penciled inscription at the top corner of the front flyleaf lists the price of the book: "$3[.]45". The flyleaf also contains notations by George A. Partridge, former president of the Partridge Family Association.

Edward Partridge Jr. used the first sixty pages of the book "to write a few items and facts with regard to the life of my father," Edward Partridge.[240] Subsequent pages contain family genealogical information inscribed by Edward Partridge Jr. and several unidentified scribes. Page 429 contains the testimony of Partridge's mother, Lydia Clisbee Partridge.

The Historian's Office received this genealogical record in 1925 from George A. Partridge.[241] It includes archival stickers and marking.

Historical Introduction

As the church's first bishop, Edward Partridge played a significant role in building up and leading the church in Missouri.[242] Along with the other Missouri Saints, Partridge was driven from Jackson County amid mob violence in 1833. By fall 1836, he and many other church members had migrated from temporary exile in Clay County to what would become Caldwell County.[243] As bishop in Far West, Partridge performed important administrative and financial duties, including acquiring and managing church lands and properties and raising revenue to build up the church in Missouri.[244]

In early November 1837, JS and other church leaders visited the burgeoning settlement of Far West, where they regulated church affairs and discussed the creation of new stakes of Zion.[245] After returning to Kirtland, Ohio, in early December, JS faced renewed opposition from a vocal group of dissenters who denounced him and his supporters.[246] It was in these circumstances, five days before relocating to Missouri, that JS sent the letter and revelation featured here to Partridge in Far West. Portions of the letter were apparently read aloud at a general assembly held in Far West on 5 February 1838, in which church members voted to reject the Missouri church presidency.[247]

---

240. Partridge, Genealogical Record, 1.

241. Partridge, Genealogical Record, [i].

242. Revelation, 4 Feb. 1831, in *JSP*, D1:241–245 [D&C 41]; Revelation, 20 May 1831, in *JSP*, D1:314–317 [D&C 51]; Revelation, 20 July 1831, in *JSP*, D2:5–12 [D&C 57]; Letter from Oliver Cowdery, 28 Jan. 1832, in *JSP*, D2:163–179.

243. Edward Partridge, Affidavit, Quincy, IL, 15 May 1839, Edward Partridge, Papers, CHL. Partridge, along with William W. Phelps, John Whitmer, and John Corrill, began scouting out land north of Clay County in May 1836. On 29 December 1836, the Missouri legislature officially organized Caldwell County. (Partridge, Journal, [46]–[48]; "2d Series—Letter No. I," *LDS Messenger and Advocate,* July 1836, 2:340–341; Application for Land Patent, 22 June 1836, pp. 253–258 herein; An Act to Organize the Counties of Caldwell and Daviess [29 Dec. 1836], *Laws of the State of Missouri* [1836], 46–47.)

244. In addition to obtaining and managing land in Far West, during fall and winter 1837 Partridge was assigned to collect donations for the construction of a new House of the Lord and raise revenue through a voluntary tithe to "assist the poor" and "compensate the Servents of the Lord for their services in attending to the business of the church." (Minute Book 2, 25 July 1836; 7 Apr. 1837; 11 June 1837; 5 Aug. 1837; 7 Dec. 1837.)

245. Minutes, 6 Nov. 1837, pp. 464–468 herein; Minutes, 7 Nov. 1837, pp. 468–472 herein.

246. Historical Introduction to Revelation, 12 Jan. 1838–A, pp. 495–496 herein.

247. Minute Book 2, 5 Feb. 1838.

JS's original letter including the revelation to Partridge is no longer extant. Approximately forty years after the letter was created, Edward Partridge Jr. copied a portion of the letter—primarily consisting of the text of the revelation—into the Partridge family genealogical record, prefaced by the words, "The following is an extract of a letter from the Prophet."[248] This is the copy featured here. The Church History Library retains another, virtually identical copy of the revelation in Partridge Sr.'s handwriting.[249] That copy does not include portions of the original letter from JS; therefore, the copy featured here more closely resembles the original text that Partridge received in early 1838.

Document Transcript

Kirtland, Jan. 7th 1838

Brother [Edward] Partridge, Thus saith the Lord, my servant Edward and his house[250] shall be numbered with the blessed and Abraham their father, and his name shall be had in sacred rem[em]brance. And again thus saith the Lord, let my people be aware of dissensions[251] among them lest the enemy have power ⟨over⟩ them, Awake my shepherds and warn my people! for behold the wolf cometh to destroy them![252] receive him not. Now I would inform you that my health is good and also that of my family, and it is my earnest prayer to God that health, peace, and pleanty may crown your board and blessings of Heaven rest upon the head of him in whom the Lord hath said there is no guile.[253]

———— ✒ ————

Revelation, 12 January 1838–A

Source Note

Revelation, Kirtland Township, Geauga Co., OH, 12 Jan. 1838. Featured version copied [ca. 12 Jan. 1838]; handwriting of George W. Robinson; three pages; Revelations Collection, CHL. Includes docket.

---

248. Partridge, Genealogical Record, 52. Edward Partridge Jr. was the youngest child of Edward and Lydia Clisbee Partridge. He was born in Independence, Missouri, on 25 July 1833 and died in Provo, Utah, on 17 November 1900. (Partridge, Genealogical Record, 64; Obituary for Edward Partridge Jr., *Deseret News,* 17 Nov. 1900, 6.)

249. Revelation, 7 Jan. 1838, in Revelations Collection, CHL.

250. Partridge married Lydia Clisbee on 22 April 1819; by 1838, the couple had six children. (Partridge, Genealogical Record, 64.)

251. The word "dissentiors," rather than "dissensions," appears in the other copy of the revelation housed at the Church History Library. (Revelation, 7 Jan. 1838, in Revelations Collection, CHL.)

252. During a meeting in Far West at which this revelation was read, David W. Patten interpreted "the wolf" as a reference to the "dissenters in Kirtland." Referring to dissenters in a 4 September 1837 letter, JS had counseled church members in Missouri to "beware of all disaffected Characters for they come not to build up but to destroy & scatter abroad." (Minute Book 2, 5 Feb. 1838; Letter to John Corrill and the Church in Missouri, 4 Sept. 1837, p. 430 herein.)

253. A 4 February 1831 revelation described Partridge as a man whose "heart is pure before me for he is like unto Nathaniel of old in whome there is no guile." (Revelation, 4 Feb. 1831, in *JSP,* D1:245 [D&C 41:11].)

Bifolium, each page measuring 10 × 8 inches (25 × 20 cm). This document contains two horizontal folds, and the torn right edges of the rectos have undergone conservation work. There are splotches of ink on the paper, and the following docket is on the verso of the second leaf: "Revelation given at Kirtland Jan 12—1838". The document contains docketing and other wear that are similar to those on other documents that have been in the custody of the church since the Kirtland, Ohio, era, indicating that this document has likely been in continuous institutional custody since the time of its creation.

Historical Introduction

On 12 January 1838, just before leaving Kirtland, Ohio, to move to Missouri, JS dictated three revelations.[254] The revelation featured here includes questions and answers about the procedure for holding an ecclesiastical disciplinary hearing to try the members of the First Presidency for transgression. The questions asked seem to be seeking clarification on an earlier revelation instructing that if a church president transgressed, he should be brought "before the common council of the church, who shall be assisted by twelve counsellors of the high priesthood; and their decision upon his head shall be an end of controversy concerning him."[255] These questions were especially pressing because dissenting church members, whose number increased in December 1837 and January 1838, desired to remove JS, Sidney Rigdon, and Hyrum Smith as the presidents of the church.

In late May 1837 dissenters brought charges against JS, but no records indicate that a disciplinary hearing was held to investigate the charges.[256] Although dissent among church members apparently decreased by mid-September 1837, opposition against the First Presidency returned by December.[257] Vilate Murray Kimball wrote that while JS and other church leaders were away visiting Missouri in late 1837, "quite a large party decented from the church; being dissatisfied with the late reorganization of the church, and with the heads of the church alltogether, and all who uphold them."[258] This renewed dissension led the Kirtland high council to excommunicate twenty-eight individuals, including some of the leading dissenters: Warren Parrish, Joseph Coe, Luke Johnson, Martin Harris, and John F. Boynton.[259] Thomas B. Marsh wrote that Parrish, Boynton, Coe, and others had

---

254. See also Revelation, 12 Jan. 1838–B, pp. 498–499 herein; and Revelation, 12 Jan. 1838–C, pp. 500–502 herein.

255. Instruction on Priesthood, between ca. 1 Mar. and ca. 4 May 1835, in *JSP*, D4:320 [D&C 107:82–84].

256. See Historical Introduction to Charges against JS Preferred to Bishop's Council, 29 May 1837, pp. 394–397 herein.

257. Thomas B. Marsh, writing in Missouri in 1838, noted that all dissension and difficulties between JS and the dissenters appeared to be settled before he, JS, and other church leaders left Kirtland in late September to travel to Far West. (Thomas B. Marsh, Far West, MO, to Wilford Woodruff, Vinalhaven, ME, ca. 18 June 1838, Wilford Woodruff, Journals and Papers, CHL; see also John Smith and Clarissa Lyman Smith, Kirtland, OH, to George A. Smith, Shinnston, VA, 1 Jan. 1838, George Albert Smith, Papers, CHL.)

258. Vilate Murray Kimball, Kirtland, OH, to Heber C. Kimball, Preston, England, 19–24 Jan. 1838, Heber C. Kimball, Collection, CHL; for information on the church reorganization alluded to here, see Minutes, 3 Sept. 1837, pp. 420–425 herein; and Minutes, 7 Nov. 1837, pp. 469–471 herein.

259. Vilate Murray Kimball, Kirtland, OH, to Heber C. Kimball, Preston, England, 19–24 Jan. 1838, Heber C. Kimball, Collection, CHL; Thomas B. Marsh, Far West, MO, to Wilford Woodruff, Vinalhaven, ME, ca. 18 June 1838, Wilford Woodruff, Journals and Papers, CHL; John Smith and

"united togeather" with the intention of overthrowing the church and had denounced JS and his followers as heretics.[260] Vilate Murray Kimball added that "the tenor of their [the dissenters'] worship, is to expose the iniquitys of this church, they say when they have done that; they calculate to preach the Gospel. (but I think they will be illy prepared to do it) they profess to believe in the book of Mormon, and [the Doctrine and] Covenants. but in works deny them."[261] As unrest increased, additional church members became disaffected and questioned the actions of the First Presidency; the dissenters may have demanded that the First Presidency be tried in a disciplinary hearing for their actions.

A main point of concern addressed by the 12 January revelation featured here was whether a verdict made in one stake of Zion, like Kirtland, extended to the rest of the church. With ebbing support and many in Kirtland doubting the First Presidency, JS worried that opposition in Kirtland, or perhaps in any church branch, might have broader ramifications for the church as a whole. This revelation directed that a disciplinary hearing for the First Presidency be restricted to Missouri, as the center place of Zion. After the initial disciplinary hearing, a stake of Zion could hold its own disciplinary hearing for the First Presidency, but the decision of that stake's council would not apply to other stakes of the church without a majority approval. The revelation also required three witnesses in good standing to bring charges against the presidency and a majority vote to accept the decision of the council.

The text of the revelation featured here was written on loose sheets of paper, and textual analysis indicates it is likely the original text, written down as JS dictated the words. This revelation and the other two revelations dictated on 12 January 1838 were copied into JS's journal in July 1838 when the revelations were read to the Saints in Far West, Missouri.[262] The revelation was also copied into the Book of the Law of the Lord—a record book used in Nauvoo to preserve revelation transcripts, donation records, and JS journal entries—by Robert B. Thompson in 1841.[263] Significant differences between the versions of the revelation are noted.

Document Transcript

Kirtland Ohio Jan. 12th 1838

In the presence of Joseph Smith Jr Sidney Rigdon Vinson Knight & G[eorge] W. Robinson at the French Farm,[264] The following inquiry was made of the Lord

---

Clarissa Lyman Smith, Kirtland, OH, to George A. Smith, Shinnston, VA, 1 Jan. 1838, George Albert Smith, Papers, CHL. John Smith also named Cyrus Smalling as a leader of the dissenters.

260. Marsh himself did not witness the increased dissent in winter 1837–1838 but had heard accounts from JS and other Kirtland Saints, which he related to Wilford Woodruff. (Thomas B. Marsh, Far West, MO, to Wilford Woodruff, Vinalhaven, ME, ca. 18 June 1838, Wilford Woodruff, Journals and Papers, CHL.)

261. Vilate Murray Kimball, Kirtland, OH, to Heber C. Kimball, Preston, England, 19–24 Jan. 1838, Heber C. Kimball, Collection, CHL.

262. See JS, Journal, 8 July 1838, in *JSP*, J1:281–284.

263. Revelation, 12 Jan. 1838–A, in Book of the Law of the Lord, 17.

264. The land known as the French farm was purchased by the church from Peter French in April 1833. The land was subdivided into lots, which included the lots for the Kirtland House of the Lord as well as the

A question asked of the Lord concerning the trying of the first Presidency of the Church of Latter Day Saints for transgression according to the item of Law found in third sec of the Book of covenants 37 verse[265] Whether the decision of such an council of one stake shall be conclusive for Zion and all the Stake——

Answer} Thus saith the Lord the time has now come when a decision of such an council would not answer for Zion and all her stakes[266]——

What will answer for Zion and all her Stakes[267]

Answer; Thus saith the Lord let the first presidency of my Church be held in full fellowship in Zion and all her stakes until they shall be found transgressors by such an high council—— [p. [1]] as is named in the 3rd sec. 37 verse of the Book of Covenants, in Zion by 3 witnesses standing against Each member of said presidency and said witnesses shall be of long and faithful standing and such also as cannot be impeached by other witnesses before said council and when a desision is had by such an council in Zion it shall only be for Zion it shall not answer for her stakes but if said desision be acknowleged by the Council of her stakes then it shall answer for her stakes ⟨But if it is not acknowleged by the Stakes then such ⟨stakes⟩ may have the privilege of hearing for themselves⟩ or if said decision shall be acknowleged by a majority of her stakes then it shall ⟨answer⟩ for ⟨all⟩ her stakes And again the presidency of said Church may be tried by the ⟨voice⟩ of the whole body of ⟨the Church of⟩ Zion, and the ~~whole body~~ ⟨voice of a majority⟩ of all her stakes,[268] And again except a majority is had by the voice of the Church of Zion, and the majority of her stakes, the charges will be considered not sustained, and in order to sustain such charge or charges before said Church ⟨of Zion⟩ or her stakes [p. [2]] Such witnesses must be had as is

---

homes of JS and Emma Smith and several other church members. (Geauga Co., OH, Deed Records, 1795–1921, vol. 17, pp. 38–39, 359–360, 10 Apr. 1833; vol. 17, pp. 360–361, 17 June 1833, microfilm 20,237, U.S. and Canada Record Collection, FHL; Minutes, 23 Mar. 1833–A, in *JSP*, D3:47–50; Minutes, 23 Mar. 1833–B, in *JSP*, D3:54; Revelation, 23 Apr. 1834, in *JSP*, D4:19–31 [D&C 104].)

265. Instruction on Priesthood, between ca. 1 Mar. and ca. 4 May 1835, in *JSP*, D4:320 [D&C 107:82–84]. "Book of covenants" is a reference to the 1835 edition of the Doctrine and Covenants.

266. This answer, that the decision of one council cannot represent the whole church, is not included in the copies of the revelation found in JS's journal or in the Book of the Law of the Lord. (See JS, Journal, 8 July 1838, in *JSP*, J1:281–284; and Revelation, 12 Jan. 1838–A, in Book of the Law of the Lord, 17.)

267. This question is not included in the copies of the revelation found in JS's journal or in the Book of the Law of the Lord. (See JS, Journal, 8 July 1838, in *JSP*, J1:281–284; and Revelation, 12 Jan. 1838–A, in Book of the Law of the Lord, 17.)

268. The voice of the church mentioned here may mean all members, as it did in the election of church leaders in Kirtland on 3 September 1837 and in Far West on 7 November 1837. (See Historical Introduction to Minutes, 3 Sept. 1837, pp. 420–422 herein; and Historical Introduction to Minutes, 7 Nov. 1837, p. 468 herein.)

named above, That is three witnesses ◊◊ Each president[269] that is of long &
faithfull sta[nd]ing[270] that can[not] be impeached by other wi[tnesses] before
[the] Church of Zion or her stakes, and all this saith the Lord, because of wicked
and aspiring men,[271] let all your doing be in meekness and humility before me
even so Amen [p. [3]]

———— ✧ ————

Revelation, 12 January 1838–B

Source Note

*Revelation, Kirtland Township, Geauga Co., OH, 12 Jan. 1838. Featured version copied [ca. 12 Jan. 1838];
handwriting of George W. Robinson; one page; Revelations Collection, CHL. Includes docket.*

Bifolium, each page measuring 10 × 8 inches (25 × 20 cm). This document contains two horizontal
folds, and tears along the folds have undergone conservation work. The docket on the verso of the sec-
ond leaf reads, "Revelation | To The Presidency | Jan 12th, 1838". The document contains docketing and
other wear that are similar to those on other documents that have been in the custody of the church
since the Kirtland, Ohio, era, indicating that this document has likely been in continuous institutional
custody since the time of its creation.

Historical Introduction

On 12 January 1838, before departing Kirtland, Ohio, to move to Missouri, JS dictated a revelation that answered two questions about establishing new stakes of Zion—
that is, new Latter-day Saint communities. Church leaders had been concerned about
creating new settlements in Missouri for several months, and by fall 1837 they had determined that additional stakes were needed to accommodate the growth of the church and
the Kirtland church members who intended to move there. In a 17 September elders conference, JS and Sidney Rigdon were commissioned to designate locations for additional
stakes.[272] By early November JS and Rigdon had arrived in Far West, Missouri, and appointed Far West specifically and Caldwell County generally as the site for the continued
gathering of church members. They also instructed the Saints in Far West concerning the

---

269. The copy of this revelation in JS's journal reads "that is the witnesses to each President." (JS,
Journal, 8 July 1838, in *JSP*, J1:282.)

270. TEXT: Page damage renders several words on this page wholly or partly illegible. Text is supplied based on the copy of the revelation in JS, Journal, 8 July 1838, in *JSP*, J1:282.

271. This is likely a reference to the dissenters and excommunicated church members in Kirtland.
According to Vilate Murray Kimball, in January 1838 the dissenters had joined with other individuals who
opposed JS or the church. She wrote that the dissenters "join with those that had previously left the
church and openly profess infidelity" and "they are united with the worlds people, and those of our greatest enemies; Mr. Newel [Grandison Newell] not excepted, he attends their meetings, and it is said they
have has privet councils togather." (Vilate Murray Kimball, Kirtland, OH, to Heber C. Kimball, Preston,
England, 19–24 Jan. 1838, Heber C. Kimball, Collection, CHL.)

272. Historical Introduction to Minutes, 17 Sept. 1837–B, pp. 444–445 herein.

creation of new stakes.[273] In a 10 November 1837 meeting, Rigdon outlined the procedure for acquiring and paying for land to be used for the gathering of the Saints.[274] Before leaving Missouri, JS and Rigdon also formed a committee to scout for additional areas in which the Saints could gather.[275]

Despite the earlier instructions about new settlements, the 12 January revelation mandated that only the First Presidency was authorized to appoint and dedicate a stake of Zion.[276] The revelation also required branch members to acknowledge by vote the authority of the First Presidency before their branch could be considered a stake of Zion. Requiring the members of prospective stakes to accept the leadership of the presidency and specifying that only the First Presidency could designate new stakes ensured that no ad hoc stakes could be created by dissenting members.

This revelation and the other two revelations dictated on 12 January 1838 were read to the church in Far West on 8 July 1838 and copied into JS's journal around that time.[277] The text of the revelation featured here was written on a loose sheet of paper, and textual analysis indicates it is likely the original text, written down as JS dictated the words. The revelation was also copied into the Book of the Law of the Lord by Robert B. Thompson in 1841.[278] There are no substantive differences between the versions.

Document Transcript

Kirtland Jan 12th 1838

Can the first any branch of the Church of Latter Day Saints be concidered a stake of Zion utill [until] they have acknowleged the authority of the first Presidensy, by a vote of said Church,

Thus saith the Lord verly I say unto you nay

How then

Answer. No stake shall be appointed except by the first presidency and this Presidency be acknowleged by the voice of the same, otherwise it shall not be counted as a stake of Zion, And again except it be dedicated by this Presidency it cannot be acknowleged as a stake of Zion, For unto this end, have I appointed them, in laying the foundation of and establishing my Kingdom

———— ⁊ ————

273. Historical Introduction to Minutes, 6 Nov. 1837, pp. 464–466 herein; Minutes, 7 Nov. 1837, p. 469 herein.

274. Minutes, 10 Nov. 1837, p. 475 herein.

275. Historical Introduction to Minutes, 10 Nov. 1837, pp. 472–476 herein.

276. The instructions contained in this revelation were repeated in a September 1838 letter written by JS and Sidney Rigdon to Stephen Post, which specified that all new stakes were to be "appointed, dedicated, and set apart, by the first presidency." (JS and Sidney Rigdon, Far West, MO, to Stephen Post, Bloomfield Township, PA, 17 Sept. 1838, Stephen Post, Papers, CHL.)

277. See JS, Journal, 8 July 1838, in *JSP*, J1:281–284.

278. See Revelation, 12 Jan. 1838–B, in Book of the Law of the Lord, 18.

Revelation, 12 January 1838–C

Source Note

Revelation, Kirtland Township, Geauga Co., OH, 12 Jan. 1838. Featured version copied [ca. 12 Jan. 1838]; handwriting of George W. Robinson; one page; Revelations Collection, CHL. Includes docket.

Bifolium, each page measuring 10 × 8 inches (25 × 20 cm). This document contains two horizontal folds, and tears along the folds and edges have undergone conservation work. The docket on the verso of the second leaf reads, "Revelation | To The Presidency | Jan 12th, 1838". The document contains docketing and other wear that are similar to those on other documents that have been in the custody of the church since the Kirtland, Ohio, era, indicating that this document has likely been in continuous institutional custody since the time of its creation.

Historical Introduction

This revelation directed the First Presidency to leave Kirtland, Ohio, with their families and move to Far West, Missouri, "as soon as it is praticable." The members of the First Presidency had already contemplated such a move; in the November issue of the *Elders' Journal,* JS wrote that his family would relocate to Far West "as soon as our circumstances will admit."[279] John Smith similarly wrote in a 1 January 1838 letter that JS, Sidney Rigdon, and Hyrum Smith "mean to go to the west as soon as they can Settle their affairs here."[280]

A central factor in JS's departure from Kirtland was the conflict that had recently intensified there. In late December 1837 the Kirtland high council excommunicated twenty-eight dissenters, who then came together in early January 1838 to form their own church.[281] The dissenters claimed that JS was a fallen prophet who had led the church astray and that his followers were heretics.[282] Their fervor led to threats of violence, and on 22 December 1837 Brigham Young left Kirtland to evade former church members who were threatening his life. According to JS's history, the dissenters were incensed with Young "because he would proclaim publicly and privately that he knew by the power of the holy Ghost that I was a prophet of the most high God, that I had not transgressed and fallen as the apostates declared."[283] Hepzibah Richards wrote on 18 January 1838 that "we do not dare to have Cousin B[righam] return to this place."[284]

---

279. Travel Account and Questions, Nov. 1837, p. 482 herein.

280. John Smith and Clarissa Lyman Smith, Kirtland, OH, to George A. Smith, Shinnston, VA, 1 Jan. 1838, George Albert Smith, Papers, CHL.

281. John Smith and Clarissa Lyman Smith, Kirtland, OH, to George A. Smith, Shinnston, VA, 1 Jan. 1838, George Albert Smith, Papers, CHL; Thomas B. Marsh, Far West, MO, to Wilford Woodruff, Vinalhaven, ME, ca. 18 June 1838, Wilford Woodruff, Journals and Papers, CHL; see also Historical Introduction to Revelation, 12 Jan. 1838–A, pp. 495–496 herein; and Introduction to Part 5: 5 Oct. 1836–10 Apr. 1837, pp. 292–293 herein.

282. Vilate Murray Kimball, Kirtland, OH, to Heber C. Kimball, Preston, England, 19–24 Jan. 1838, Heber C. Kimball, Collection, CHL; Thomas B. Marsh, Far West, MO, to Wilford Woodruff, Vinalhaven, ME, ca. 18 June 1838, Wilford Woodruff, Journals and Papers, CHL.

283. JS History, vol. B-1, addenda, 6nT.

284. Hepzibah Richards, Kirtland, OH, to Willard Richards, Bedford, England, 18–19 Jan. 1838, Willard Richards, Journals and Papers, CHL.

Like Young, JS and Rigdon were in danger in Kirtland. Fearing mob violence and facing arrest for debts and spurious legal claims made by dissenters and other enemies, they heeded the direction of this revelation and left Kirtland the same day, on the evening of 12 January.[285] JS and Rigdon arrived in Norton, Ohio, on 13 January and waited there until 16 January, when their families arrived and they began their journey to Missouri. The third member of the First Presidency, Hyrum Smith, did not leave Kirtland until March 1838;[286] he may have delayed his departure because he had just married Mary Fielding on 24 December 1837 in Kirtland.[287] Hyrum also may have remained to aid the new church leadership in Kirtland after the departure of JS and Rigdon. He played a vital role later in 1838 when he helped organize the Kirtland Camp, the largest body of church emigrants to Missouri.[288]

The text of the revelation featured here was written on a loose sheet of paper, and textual analysis indicates it is likely the original text, written down as JS dictated the words. This revelation and Revelation, 12 January 1838–B are copied on the same sheet of paper. The three revelations dictated on 12 January 1838 were copied into JS's journal in July 1838, when the revelations were read to the Saints in Far West.[289] There are no substantive differences between the versions.

Document Transcript

Thus saith the Lord Let the presidency of my Church take their families as soon as it is praticable and a door is open for them and move on to the west as fast as the way is made plain before their faces and let their hearts be comforted for I will be with them

Verily I say unto you the time [has][290] come that your laibours are finished in this place, for a season, Therefore arise and get yourselves on to a land which

---

285. JS History, vol. B-1, 780. Hepzibah Richards noted that if JS and Rigdon had remained in Kirtland that it was "thought the lives of the presidents would have been taken" in a confrontation over the printing office that erupted on 15 January. (Hepzibah Richards, [Kirtland, OH], to William Richards, 22 Jan. 1838, in Historical Department, Journal History of the Church, 22 Jan. 1838. For more on the threats of arrest, see Lucy Mack Smith, History, 1844–1845, bk. 14, [11]–[12]; "History of Luke Johnson," 6, in Historian's Office, Histories of the Twelve, 1856–1858, 1861, CHL; and Adams, "Grandison Newell's Obsession," 179–184.)

286. Hyrum Smith was still in Kirtland on 17 March but left sometime that month. He and his family arrived in Far West in late May 1838. (Kirtland Camp, Journal, 17 Mar. 1838; Hyrum Smith, Commerce, IL, to "the Saints Scattered Abroad," Dec. 1839, in *Times and Seasons,* Dec. 1839, 1:21.)

287. Hyrum's first wife, Jerusha Barden Smith, had died in childbirth on 13 October 1837. (Hyrum Smith Family Bible; Geauga Co., OH, Probate Court, Marriage Records, vol. C, p. 262, microfilm 873,461, U.S. and Canada Record Collection, FHL.)

288. Kirtland Camp, Journal, 6 Mar. 1838.

289. See JS, Journal, 8 July 1838, in *JSP,* J1:281–284; Revelation, 12 Jan. 1838–A, pp. 494–498 herein; and Revelation, 12 Jan. 1838–B, pp. 498–499 herein.

290. TEXT: "[*Page damaged*]". Text supplied based on the copy of the revelation in JS, Journal, 8 July 1838, in *JSP,* J1:238.

I shall show unto you even a land flowing with milk and honey[291] you are clean from the blood of this people and wo unto those who have become your enimies[292] who ⟨have⟩ professed my name saith the Lord, for their judgement lingereth not and their damnation slumbereth not, let all your faithfull friends arise with their families also and get out of this place and gather themselves together unto Zion[293] and be at peace among yourselves O ye inhabitants of Zion or there shall be no saf[e]ty for you[294]

——————— ☙ ———————

Letter from Oliver Cowdery, 21 January 1838

Source Note

Oliver Cowdery, Letter, Far West, Caldwell Co., MO, to JS, [Kirtland Township, Geauga Co., OH], 21 Jan. 1838. Featured version copied [ca. 21 Jan. 1838] in Oliver Cowdery, Letterbook, [80]; handwriting of Warren F. Cowdery; Huntington Library, San Marino, CA. For more information on Oliver Cowdery, Letterbook, see Source Notes for Multiple-Entry Documents, p. 531 herein.

Historical Introduction

On 21 January 1838, Oliver Cowdery penned a terse letter to JS in which he reported his efforts to explore and survey land north of Far West, Missouri, as well as his subsequent illness. In the letter's concluding sentence, Cowdery accused JS, his longtime friend, of telling church members in Kirtland, Ohio, that Cowdery had confessed to lying about him. Cowdery was almost certainly referring to a dispute the two men had regarding JS's relationship with Fanny Alger, a young woman who had worked in the Smith household. Cowdery viewed JS's relationship with Alger as adulterous, while other church members,

---

291. See Exodus 3:8. This language was used in earlier revelations to describe Zion in Missouri. (Revelation, 2 Jan. 1831, in *JSP*, D1:231–232 [D&C 38:18–20]; Revelation, 20 July 1831, in *JSP*, D2:7–11 [D&C 57:1–5].)

292. For more information on those individuals identified as dissenters in contemporary records, see Historical Introduction to Revelation, 12 Jan. 1838–A, pp. 495–496 herein; and Introduction to Part 5: 5 Oct. 1836–10 Apr. 1837, pp. 287–288 herein.

293. Writing to her husband in January 1838, Vilate Murray Kimball noted, "The Presidency have advised the wives of the Elders to write to their husbands to come home as soon as posable, and get there families out of this place." In a January 1838 letter John Smith wrote that "it seems to be the will of the Lord that those who came here first and have Done their Duty to their friend abroad Should go to the west with their families as soon as is convenient." Receiving news of the events in Kirtland in March 1838, Wilford Woodruff wrote in his journal that "Joseph & Sidney had gone to the far west with their family & the faithful are to follow them for Kirtland will be scorged." (Vilate Murray Kimball, Kirtland, OH, to Heber C. Kimball, Preston, England, 19–24 Jan. 1838, Heber C. Kimball, Collection, CHL; John Smith and Don Carlos Smith, Kirtland, OH, to George A. Smith, 15–18 Jan. 1838, George Albert Smith, Papers, CHL; Woodruff, Journal, 8 Mar. 1838.)

294. The copy of this 12 January revelation in JS's journal adds "Even so Amen" to the end of the revelation. (JS, Journal, 8 July 1838, in *JSP*, J1:284.)

including members of Alger's extended family, later stated that JS had married Alger as his first plural wife.[295]

Though Cowdery was once one of JS's closest associates, his relationship with JS began to deteriorate sometime during fall 1837. On 4 September 1837, a day after Cowdery was unanimously sustained by the Kirtland Saints as an assistant counselor in the church presidency, JS dictated a letter to Missouri church officials informing them that Cowdery was in "transgression" and that if he did not humble himself, "the church will soon be under the necessaty of raising their hands against him."[296] Soon after Cowdery left Kirtland to relocate to Missouri,[297] several apostles and members of the presidency, including JS, traveled to Far West, where they convened a series of meetings in early November. The minutes of a 6 November meeting indicate that "all difficulties were satisfactorily settled except a matter between J. Smith jr. Oliver Cowdery and T[homas] B. Marsh, which was refered to themselves."[298] The record of the meeting does not note the nature of the disagreement, but it likely related to what others interpreted as an insinuation by Cowdery that JS had engaged in an extramarital relationship with Alger.[299] A day after this 6 November meeting, during a general assembly in which church leaders were presented for a sustaining vote, Cowdery was not nominated as an assistant counselor to JS.[300] Though Cowdery later asserted that he and JS settled their differences amicably before JS returned to Kirtland, Cowdery's influence within the presidency was clearly diminishing.[301]

Despite this development, Cowdery continued to play a role in Missouri church affairs.[302] During the 7 November general assembly, Cowdery and three other men were appointed to

---

295. Minute Book 2, 12 Apr. 1838; Benjamin F. Johnson to George F. Gibbs, Salt Lake City, UT, 1903, pp. 25–27, Benjamin Franklin Johnson, Papers, CHL; Hancock, "Autobiography of Levi Ward Hancock," 61–65; Eliza Churchill Webb, Lockport, NY, to Mary Bond, 24 Apr. 1876, Myron H. Bond Folder, Biographical Folder Collection, CCLA; Hawley, "Life of John Hawley," 97. JS taught and authorized the practice of plural marriage for Latter-day Saints in Nauvoo in the early 1840s. (See "Nauvoo Journals, December 1841–April 1843," in *JSP*, J2:xxiv-xxx.)

296. Letter to John Corrill and the Church in Missouri, 4 Sept. 1837, pp. 426–431 herein.

297. Cowdery left Kirtland about 16 September 1837 and arrived in Far West on 20 October 1837. (Cowdery, Docket Book, 227; Minutes, 17 Sept. 1837–A, p. 443 herein; Whitmer, Daybook, 20 Oct. 1837.)

298. Minutes, 6 Nov. 1837, p. 467 herein.

299. During Oliver Cowdery's April 1838 trial in Far West, several witnesses testified that Cowdery had insinuated to them during fall 1837 that JS had been "guilty of adultery." In a 21 January letter to Warren A. Cowdery, Oliver stated that when JS was in Far West, the two men had conversed about JS's relationship with Fanny Alger. Oliver Cowdery informed his brother, "I strictly declared that I had never deviated from the truth in the matter, and as I supposed was admitted by himself [JS]." (Minute Book 2, 12 Apr. 1838; Oliver Cowdery, Far West, MO, to Warren A. Cowdery, 21 Jan. 1838, in Cowdery, Letterbook, 81.)

300. Minutes, 7 Nov. 1837, pp. 469–471 herein.

301. Cowdery told his brother that just before JS left Missouri, "he [JS] wanted to drop every past thing, in which had been a difficulty or difference—he called witnesses to the fact, gave me his hand in their presence, and I might have supposed of an honest man, calculated to say nothing of former matters." (O. Cowdery to W. Cowdery, 21 Jan. 1838, 81.)

302. On 6 December 1837, Cowdery was appointed "recording Clerk" for priesthood licenses, "standing Clerk" for the high council, and recorder of patriarchal blessings in Far West. (Minute Book 2, 6–7 Dec. 1837.)

locate land nearby for additional Mormon settlements.[303] As the featured text indicates, Cowdery and the other members of the committee explored and surveyed lands north of Far West for approximately three weeks before Cowdery returned to Far West in early December. At some point during this expedition, or shortly after returning home, Cowdery became ill and was confined to his bed.[304]

In December and January, Cowdery received information about the events unfolding in Kirtland through a series of letters written by his brothers, Warren A. and Lyman Cowdery.[305] In at least one of these letters, the brothers asked Oliver about a statement he had allegedly made regarding JS's relationship with Fanny Alger. On 21 January Oliver Cowdery wrote a response to Warren, prefacing it by inserting an "exact copy" of the letter to JS featured here. In addition to providing further information about his expedition north, his poor health, and his growing disaffection from JS and the church, Cowdery affirmed in the letter to his brother that he had "never confessed intimated or admitted that I ever willfully lied" about JS and Alger's relationship. Further indicating his estrangement from JS, Cowdery also informed his brother that when JS and Sidney Rigdon came to live in Far West, Cowdery would travel north again and "endeavor to seek a location for myself & friends some where else."[306]

Cowdery's 21 January letter to JS is extant only because he included it in the letter written to Warren that same day. The letter has not been located in any collection of JS's papers, and it is unclear whether JS received it; he had departed Kirtland on 12 January. Warren F. Cowdery, son of Warren A. Cowdery, likely copied the original letter into Oliver Cowdery's letterbook shortly after 21 January 1838.

Document Transcript

Sir.—

Far West Mo. Jany. 21$^{st.}$ 1838.

Sir.— I should have written you long since but for ill health, I have anxiously waited to recover, that I might give you a full history of my excursion to ⟨the⟩ north[307] according to my promise; and were it not for the recent

---

303. David Whitmer, John Corrill, and Lyman Wight were the other members of the committee; the four men apparently embarked on their mission before JS departed for Kirtland. (Travel Account and Questions, Nov. 1837, p. 481 herein; for more on Missouri land transactions during this period, see Application for Land Patent, 22 June 1836, pp. 253–258 herein.)

304. O. Cowdery to W. Cowdery, 21 Jan. 1838, 82; Oliver Cowdery, Far West, MO, to Warren A. Cowdery and Lyman Cowdery, [Kirtland, OH], 4 Feb. 1838, in Cowdery, Letterbook, 83.

305. In a letter written to Warren on 21 January and another written to Warren and Lyman on 4 February, Oliver referred to several letters written by the brothers dated 10, 18, and 24 December 1837 and 8 January 1838. (O. Cowdery to W. Cowdery, 21 Jan. 1838, 81–82; O. Cowdery to W. Cowdery and L. Cowdery, 4 Feb. 1838, 83.)

306. O. Cowdery to W. Cowdery, 21 Jan. 1838, 80–83.

307. In his 21 January letter to his brother Warren, Oliver reported, "I am delighted with the county north (Daviess) and now think we shall all find it to our interest to locate there. . . . The timber is better and more plenty, beside Grand River which is navigable for Steam Boats, passes through its centre." (O. Cowdery to W. Cowdery, 21 Jan. 1838, 82.)

intelligence from Kirtland,[308] which gives me so much surprise, should still defer— you will be able to judge from the formation of my letter how week and infirm are my nerves. I have been sick six weeks, and a large part of the time confined to my room and bed.

I was absent, when north. some twenty days, and should not have returned then but for the failure of Col. [Lyman] Wight[309] to forward provisions as he agreed. I labored incessantly every day except one,—rain, snow or frost. I lay on the cold damp earth; had but little to eat, and that indifferent; but explored a great ~~any~~ and precious country. I ran many lines with compass and chain,[310] found a great many of the finest mill-Sites I have seen in the western country ⟨or world,⟩ and made between forty and fifty choice locations.

Notwithstanding the feeble sta[t]e of my health, I had previously made preparations, and yet expect to start to morrow morning (Monday) to view still east of where I previously went.

I learn from Kirtland, by the last letters,[311] that you have publickly said, that when you were here I confessed to you that I had willfully lied about you— this compels me to ask you to correct that statement, and give me an explanation—until which you and myself are two.

Oliver Cowdery

Mr. Joseph Smith Jr [p. [80]]

---

308. O. Cowdery to W. Cowdery, 21 Jan. 1838, 80–83; O. Cowdery to W. Cowdery and L. Cowdery, 4 Feb. 1838, 83–86.

309. Lyman Wight was elected colonel of the Caldwell County militia in August 1837; in December 1837, he was appointed as a member of the "committee sent to explore the north country," along with Oliver Cowdery, David W. Patten, and Frederick G. Williams. Describing this time period in a letter sent to Wilford Woodruff in 1857, Wight reported attending to "temperal business" related to a "large flood of emigration" to Caldwell County and preaching in surrounding communities before relocating to what would later be referred to as Adam-ondi-Ahman, in Daviess County, Missouri, in early February 1838. (Lyman Wight, Journal, in *History of the Reorganized Church,* 2:114; Minute Book 2, 6–7 Dec. 1837, p. [92]; Lyman Wight, Mountain Valley, TX, to Wilford Woodruff, 24 Aug. 1857, p. 9, Historian's Office, Histories of the Twelve, 1856–1858, 1861, CHL.)

310. A compass and chain were tools commonly used to survey land. (Gummere, *Treatise on Surveying,* 81–82; Bourne, *Surveyor's Pocket-Book,* 41–42.)

311. Warren and Lyman Cowdery had inquired "concerning the Stated confession made to Mr. Smith." (O. Cowdery to W. Cowdery, 21 Jan. 1838, 81, underlining in original.)

APPENDIX: BLESSINGS TO DON CARLOS SMITH, OLIVER COWDERY, FREDERICK G. WILLIAMS, AND SIDNEY RIGDON, 1–2 OCTOBER 1835

Historical Introduction

In November and December 1833, JS pronounced blessings on Frederick G. Williams, Sidney Rigdon, Oliver Cowdery, and some of his own family members.[1] In October 1835, the blessings to Don Carlos Smith, Cowdery, Williams, and Rigdon were recorded in Patriarchal Blessing Book 1 with extensive modifications. Because JS's role in producing the altered 1835 texts is unclear, they are presented as an appendix rather than being included in the body of the volume itself.

The manner in which JS originally gave these blessings is likewise unclear. It is likely he dictated the blessings, though each individual recipient may not have been present, after which Cowdery and Williams recorded them in JS's journal in 1833.[2] Cowdery wrote that the blessings, as recorded in the patriarchal blessing book, contained "the words which fell from his [JS's] lips while the visions of the Almighty were open to his view."[3]

In September 1835, soon after being appointed church recorder, Cowdery made the first entries in Joseph Smith Sr.'s patriarchal blessing book.[4] Among those initial entries, Cowdery re-recorded JS's 1833 blessings in the patriarchal blessing book. This copying work occurred over several days in September and early October 1835.[5] At the time Cowdery recorded these blessings, he noted that they "were given by vision and the spirit of prophecy, on the 18th of December, 1833, and written by my own hand at the time."[6] Cowdery made an error and conflated the date of the earlier blessings with his own blessing from JS, which he received on 18 December 1833. Frederick G. Williams and Sidney Rigdon actually received their blessings in mid-November 1833; Cowdery had assisted in writing the blessings into JS's journal.[7] Don Carlos Smith is not named in blessings recorded in the November

---

1. Members of the Smith family who received blessings from JS in 1833 were Joseph Smith Sr., Lucy Mack Smith, Hyrum Smith, Samuel Smith, William Smith, and Don Carlos Smith. Don Carlos's blessing is presented here; for the text of the other blessings, as recorded in the Patriarchal Blessing Book in September 1835, see Blessings to Joseph Smith Sr. and Lucy Mack Smith, Hyrum Smith, Samuel Smith, and William Smith, Sept. 1835, in *JSP*, D4:485–494.

2. JS, Journal, 14–19 Nov. and 18 Dec. 1833, in *JSP*, J1:18–19, 21–24.

3. Patriarchal Blessings, 1:9.

4. On Cowdery's appointment as church recorder, see Minutes, 14 Sept. 1835, in *JSP*, D4:412–415.

5. Patriarchal Blessings, 1:11–13.

6. Patriarchal Blessings, 1:9.

7. JS, Journal, 14–19 Nov. 1833, in *JSP*, J1:18–19.

or December 1833 journal entries, but a few sentences concerning the Smith family in the 1833 blessings are included in the text of his 1835 patriarchal blessing.[8]

Comparing the blessings as recorded by Cowdery in 1835 in Patriarchal Blessing Book 1 with the 1833 versions in JS's journal shows that most sections of the 1835 texts are expansions of and alterations to the earlier blessing texts, while other passages correspond word for word. Nearly ninety percent of the text of JS's blessing to Don Carlos Smith is new or different from the earlier journal version, and an even greater portion of the blessing to Oliver Cowdery is new or altered. In the 1835 patriarchal blessing book, the texts of JS's blessings to Sidney Rigdon and Frederick G. Williams contain, respectively, sixty-six and seventy-nine percent new or different words from the journal versions. Each of the blessings includes several long passages that are the same in both versions, and those portions of the patriarchal blessing book texts seem to derive from the words of the blessings found in the journal. Some passages found in the journal are missing from the patriarchal blessing book, particularly in the Rigdon, Williams, and Cowdery blessings.

It is not clear when or by what means the blessings were expanded and altered. With only the journal text and no loose blessing texts extant, it is not possible to trace the origin of the additional or edited words that appear in the 1835 blessing texts. It is not clear if JS participated in the process of expanding or editing the text of the re-recorded 1833 blessings or if the project was Cowdery's alone. It is conceivable that after dictating the blessings in November and December 1833, JS at some point either dictated or wrote the expansions himself, but there is no evidence that he did.

The only evidence of JS working with Cowdery on blessings in September and October 1835 is for 22 September 1835, not in October when Cowdery inscribed these blessings into the patriarchal blessing book. On that September day JS pronounced blessings upon Missouri church leaders David Whitmer, John Whitmer, John Corrill, and William W. Phelps. JS's clerk, Warren Parrish, began a new JS journal on that day by writing, "This day Joseph Smith, jr. labored with Oliver Cowdery, in obtaining and writing blessings." To this JS added in his own hand, "This day Joseph Smith, Jr. was at home writing blessings for my most beloved Brotheren."[9] These entries provide the only extant evidence that JS was involved in giving, obtaining, or recording blessings of any kind in this period, and they likely refer not to work on 1833 blessings but to the process of JS and Cowdery preparing written blessings given orally at various times throughout that day to the four Missouri leaders. In the absence of a trained stenographer who could write the blessings as they were spoken, such oral blessings were apparently filled in after the fact based on incomplete notes and memory. In an 1835 letter to his wife, Lydia Clisbee Partridge, about the recording of his own recent patriarchal blessing from Joseph Smith Sr., Edward Partridge noted that the blessing was "not delivered and written sentence by sentence" but that Smith "delivered them as fast as he naturaly speaks." In the meantime, Partridge continued, "the heads were sketched down and they had to be filled out from memory."[10] It is likely that on

8. See JS, Journal, 18 Dec. 1833, in *JSP*, J1:21–24; and JS to Don Carlos Smith, Blessing, 18 Dec. 1833, in Patriarchal Blessings, 1:11.

9. JS, Journal, 22 Sept. 1835, in *JSP*, J1:61–62.

10. Edward Partridge, Kirtland, OH, to Lydia Clisbee Partridge, 2 Nov. 1835, in Partridge, Genealogical Record, 25.

22 September 1835, JS and Cowdery were similarly inscribing on loose sheets of paper the details of blessings that JS had delivered orally earlier that day. Cowdery then took those loose pages and recorded the blessings in the patriarchal blessing book on 3 October 1835.

Though it is possible that JS worked with Cowdery on the changes or instructed him to expand the blessings on his own, it seems more likely that Cowdery made the expansions without direction from JS. This would not have been the only occasion he did so: there is evidence that Cowdery altered at least one other blessing text—his own—when he recorded it in the volume.[11] Because Cowdery was acting in his role as church recorder when he recorded the blessings,[12] he may have felt authorized to "improve" the texts on occasion. However, Cowdery stated that the blessings as recorded in the patriarchal blessing book were "correct and according to the mind of the Lord," suggesting that he believed he was operating within his calling and that his work met the expectations of JS and of heaven.[13] This seems to be what he meant when he said that the words he recorded came from "the mouth of the Seer," rather than meaning that every word he wrote was congruent with the words JS spoke in 1833.[14]

Some of the material in the expansions seems to originate from 1835 sources. Joseph Smith Sr. and Lucy Mack Smith's blessing, for example, contains an explanation of Jesus Christ appearing to Adam and his sons in "the valley of Adam-ondi-ahman"—text that first appears in writing in the Instruction on Priesthood prepared sometime in late winter or spring 1835.[15] The inclusion of such material in the blessings may indicate that JS, Cowdery, and others considered the blessings subject to revision as they gained new understanding of church doctrine. JS and other church leaders believed that revelation texts could change based on new understanding, so it is possible that blessings were regarded in a similar way.[16]

In summary, there is no direct evidence that JS was involved in expanding and editing the 1833 blessings in September or October of 1835, and there are reasons to think he was not—but there remains a possibility that he, with Cowdery, authored the alterations to those blessings around the same time he bestowed blessings on John and David Whitmer, John Corrill, and William W. Phelps on 22 September 1835. The 1833 text of the blessings is reproduced in the first volume of the Journals series of *The Joseph Smith Papers,*

---

11. For example, when copying his own blessing, which was also given in December 1833, Cowdery omitted references to "two evils" that he was admonished to forsake. The omitted text appears in JS's journal under the 18 December 1833 entry. (JS to Oliver Cowdery, Blessing, [18 Dec. 1833], in Patriarchal Blessings, 1:12–13; JS, Journal, 18 Dec. 1833, in *JSP,* J1:21–23.)

12. Beyond the fact that Cowdery was the recorder and the blessing book was his responsibility, the fact that he charged Hyrum, Samuel, and William Smith money for recording their blessings underscores the official nature of his actions. The amount Cowdery charged was based on the number of words in the blessing. He routinely charged individuals ten cents per one hundred words. (Cowdery and Cowdery, Financial Account Books, 2–3.)

13. Patriarchal Blessings, 1:9; see also Blessing to David Whitmer, 22 Sept. 1835, in *JSP,* D4:428–430; Blessing to John Whitmer, 22 Sept. 1835, in *JSP,* D4:430–433; Blessing to John Corrill, 22 Sept. 1835, in *JSP,* D4:433–434; and Blessing to William W. Phelps, 22 Sept. 1835, in *JSP,* D4:435–436.

14. Patriarchal Blessings, 1:15.

15. Blessing to Joseph Smith Sr. and Lucy Mack Smith, ca. 15–28 Sept. 1835, in *JSP,* D4:488; Instruction on Priesthood, between ca. 1 Mar. and ca. 4 May 1835, in *JSP,* D4:317 [D&C 107:53–54].

16. See, for example, Minutes, 8 Nov. 1831, in *JSP,* D2:123; and Minutes, 30 Apr. 1832, in *JSP,* D2:239.

and the expanded 1835 texts are reproduced here.[17] Gray shading in the blessings indicates the parts that are the same in both versions, and footnotes provide text found in the journal version that is either missing or modified here. Because JS's role in the expansions is not clear, the blessings as recorded in Patriarchal Blessing Book 1 are included in the appendix rather than as featured texts.

———— ✌ ————

I. Blessing to Don Carlos Smith, 1 October 1835

Source Note

JS, Blessing, to Don Carlos Smith, Kirtland Township, Geauga, Co., OH, 1 Oct. 1835. Featured version copied [1 Oct. 1835] in Patriarchal Blessing Book 1, p. 11; handwriting of Oliver Cowdery; CHL. For more information on Patriarchal Blessing Book 1, see Source Notes for Multiple-Entry Documents, p. 532 herein.

Document Transcript

Blessed of the Lord is brother Carlos [Don Carlos Smith], for the Lord my God delighteth in him: He shall be made a polished shaft in the quiver[18] of the Almighty unto the confounding of thousands and tens of thousands of mine enemies; and he shall never want a friend. He shall dream dreams and see visions,[19] and the Spirit of the Lord shall dwell in him; and he shall be a chosen vessel of the Lord, for the spirit of prophecy shall be upon him: therefore, he shall never fail in his understanding, and by the help of his judgment he shall be as a choice seer in the house of the Lord. He shall also become a great lawyer, pertaining to the laws of God, and also pertaining to the laws of the land; for he shall have understanding in these things, and shall be called to stand in legislative bodies, and shall confront the errors of rulers and kings, to their face, and they shall reverence him because of the greatness of his understanding and his nobility of soul. He shall be taught of his God like unto Jacob in ancient days; for his God shall delight in him all the days of his life, which shall be many. It shall be his lot to stand among the nobles of the earth: and the burden of his influence, over the inhabitants of the earth, shall render him like unto an orchard in a fruitful season, as it is borne down with the abundance of fruit— so shall the weight of his influence be over the minds of those who know his name: for his name shall be magnified among men. Unto what shall I liken my

————————————

17. The earlier blessings to Sidney Rigdon and Frederick G. Williams are found in JS, Journal, 14–19 Nov. 1833, in *JSP*, J1:18–19. The blessing to Oliver Cowdery and the text from Don Carlos Smith's blessing are found in JS, Journal, 18 Dec. 1833, in *JSP*, J1:21–24.

18. See Isaiah 49:2.

19. See Joel 2:28.

brother Carlos? I will liken him unto a mighty river that is continually running into the fountain of the great deep—so shall the blessings of his labors be, a fountain of righteousness because of the greatness of his soul. And he shall be blessed upon the mountains of Zion with the fruit of the vine and with the fruit of the field, and shall be sustained with corn and oil,[20] and his heart shall be sustained with the good things of the earth: with houses and with lands, with chariots and with horses, with mules and with asses, with camels and with swift beasts, at home upon the mountains of Zion, and also abroad: among foreign nations shall the power of his wealth extend, even to kingdoms afar off. All these things shall come upon him and his seed after him to the latest generation. He shall be filled with the good things of the earth. He shall have power over the wicked and escape the hands of his enemies; for he shall prevail against them: and he shall have his right to the holy priesthood. All these blessings shall come upon him and his seed after him; for they shall be numerous, and shall rise up and call him blessed. And in addition to these he shall have a diligent mind, even to persevere in the time of trouble, and prevail. He shall inherit a crown of eternal life. Amen.

A prayer— O God, let the residue of my father's house, with the residue of those whom thou hast blessed, ever come up in remembrance before thee and stand virtuous and pure in thy presence, that thou mayest save them from the hand of the oppressor, and establish their feet upon the rock of ages, that they may have place in thy house and be saved in thy kingdom, even where God and Christ is: and let all these things be as I have said, for Christ's sake. Amen.

Oliver Cowdery, <u>Clerk and Recorder</u>.

Given in Kirtland, Geauga County, Ohio, December 18th, 1833, and recorded in this book by me, October 1, 1835.

Oliver Cowdery. [p. 11]

———— ✢ ————

II. Blessing to Oliver Cowdery, 2 October 1835

Source Note

JS, Blessing, to Oliver Cowdery, Kirtland Township, Geauga Co., OH, 2 Oct. 1835. Featured version copied [2 Oct. 1835] in Patriarchal Blessing Book 1, p. 12; handwriting of Oliver Cowdery; CHL. For more information on Patriarchal Blessing Book 1, see Source Notes for Multiple-Entry Documents, p. 532 herein.

---

20. See Joel 2:19.

Document Transcript

Blessed of the Lord is Brother ~~Oliver~~ [Cowdery]²¹ for he shall be made like unto the bow which the Lord hath set in the heavens: he shall be a sign unto the nations, and shall be an instrument in lifting up an ensign unto them. Behold, he is blessed of the Lord for his constancy and steadfastness ~~and~~ ⟨in the⟩ work of the Lord: wherefore, he shall be blessed in his generations,²² and they shall never be cut off; and he shall be helped out of all his troubles²³ because he shall keep the commandments of the Lord and hearken unto all his counsels.²⁴ He shall be blessed with the blessings of the lasting hills: with blessings from above and with blessings that couch beneath; even the hidden things of the ancient mountains: even the records that have been hid from ⟨the first ages, from⟩ generation to generation shall he be an instrument in the hands of his God, with his brother Joseph, of translating and bringing forth to the house of Israel.²⁵ And blessed upon the mountains shall his feet be, for he shall publish peace and salvation among all the Gentile nations, and lo, lo, among the Jews,²⁶ also: and his name shall be had in remembrance among all nations, and it shall be said of him, This man is blessed of the Lord, for he went out in search of the promised land, like Abraham of old, not knowing whither he went, and the right hand of his God did protect him that he did not stop till his feet stood thereon: therefore, for this he is blessed and his posterity after him; and when men bless in Israel they shall bless, saying, The Lord bless thee as he did his servant ~~Oliver~~ who sought diligently for the promised land, whereon the city of Zion should stand:²⁷ the Lord bring peace and blessings upon thy house as he has upon the house of this man; for inasmuch as he has done like Abraham, in this thing, the blessings of his father Abraham shall come upon him. Thus shall his name remain a blessing. And he shall yet do the work of an evangelist in his day; and Zion shall rejoice for the multitudes that ⟨shall⟩ flow unto her because of him. And he shall be

---

21. Here the blessing in JS's journal has the following: "nevertheless there are are two evils in him that he must needs forsake or he cannot altogeth[er] escape the buffettings of the advers[ar]y if he shall forsak these evils he shall be forgiven." (JS, Journal, 18 Dec. 1833, in *JSP*, J1:21–23.)

22. The blessing found in JS's journal has "generation." (JS, Journal, 18 Dec. 1833, in *JSP*, J1:23.)

23. The blessing found in JS's journal has "many troubles." (JS, Journal, 18 Dec. 1833, in *JSP*, J1:23.)

24. The journal puts this last phrase as the conditional: "and if he keep the commandments and harken unto the council of the Lord his rest shall be glorious." (JS, Journal, 18 Dec. 1833, in *JSP*, J1:23.)

25. See Revelation, Apr. 1829–A in *JSP*, D1:37 [D&C 6:27]; and Revelation, Apr. 1829–B, in *JSP*, D1:46 [D&C 8:1].

26. See Revelation, 6 Apr. 1830, in *JSP*, D1:130 [D&C 21:12]. Oliver Cowdery never preached to the Jews as a people, but he was the first missionary called to the American Indians, whom early Latter-day Saints associated with the Lamanites of the Book of Mormon. The Lamanites were sometimes referred to as Jews in JS's revelations. (See Revelation, ca. Summer 1829, in *JSP*, D1:91 [D&C 19:27]; and Revelation, 20 July 1831, in *JSP*, D2:8 [D&C 57:4].)

27. See Covenant of Oliver Cowdery and Others, 17 Oct. 1830, in *JSP*, D1:202–205.

kept under the shadow of the wing of the Almighty, and he made a polished shaft in his quiver, and lead forth by his mighty hand. He shall sit in the council of the patriarchs, with his brother Joseph, and with him have part in the keys of that ministry when the Ancient of Days shall come.[28] Behold, there is no end to the blessings and glories that shall come upon my brother ~~Oliver~~ yet in his days; for he shall have part with me in the keys of the kingdom of the last days, and we shall judge this generation by our testimony: and the keys shall never be taken from us, but shall rest with us for an everlasting briesthood [priesthood], forever and ever.[29] Behold, he shall be a choice lawyer in Israel, both pertaining to the law of God and also the law of ~~the land~~ ⟨man;⟩ for he shall have understanding in these matters. He shall be equal in the councils of Israel, for he shall sit in the great assemblys of the house of Jacob, and by his understanding shall they be benefited. He shall also stand in the councils of nations and states, and his voice shall be heard ~~among~~ ⟨in the midst of⟩ the most renowned among the statesmen of the world, and by his superior intelligence and great wisdom convince them of their errors: thus shall he be reverenced; for he shall be had in repute even by governors and kings, and stand in the legislatures of nations. And because of the liberality of his soul shall the poor be benefitted, and their blessings shall rest upon his head. Though his heart shall desire, above all things, to see the law of God fulfilled, yet because he is ever filled with charity he shall be quick to forgive the transgressor, when he repents. He shall be blessed with an abundance of the good things of this earth, even with houses and with lands, and in the fruit of the vine, the fruit of the olive and the fruit of the field, and in the abundance of cattle, and of horses, and of asses and of she asses, of sheep, and of goats, of camels, dromedaries, and all swift beasts, and of chariots in abundance, ⟨with gold and with silver, with diamonds and all precious stones, with brass and with iron, and with the choice platina;⟩ and of blessings at home and abroad, and of blessings pertaining to right among the nobles of the earth, in palaces of governors and kings, and in foreign nations, and in kingdoms afar off unto the utmost parts of the earth, and they shall acknowledge his right and his authority. So shall the blessings come upon my brother ~~Oliver~~ and upon his seed after him, from generation to generation, unto the latest posterity. These blessings shall come upon him according to the blessings of the prophecy of Joseph, in ancient days, which he said should come upon the Seer of the last days and the Scribe that should sit with him, and that should be ordained with him, by the hand of the angel in the bush, unto the lesser priesthood, and after receive the holy priesthood under

---

28. See Revelation, ca. Aug. 1835, in *JSP*, D4:411 [D&C 27].
29. See Revelation, 8 Mar. 1833, in *JSP*, D3:27 [D&C 90:3].

the hands of they who had been held in reserve for a long season, even those who received it under the hand of the Messiah, while he should dwell in the flesh, upon the earth, and should receive the blessings with him, even the Seer of the God of Abraham, Isaac and Jacob, saith he, even Joseph of old,[30] by his hand, even God. And he shall inherit a crown of eternal life, at the end; and while in the flesh shall stand up in Zion and assist to crown the tribes of Jacob; even so. Amen.

Oliver Cowdery, <u>Clerk and Recorder</u>.

Given December 18th, 1833, and recorded in this book October 2, 1835. [p. 12]

——— ∾ ———

III. Blessing to Frederick G. Williams, 2 October 1835

Source Note

JS, Blessing, to Frederick G. Williams, Kirtland Township, Geauga Co., OH, 2 Oct. 1835. Featured version copied [2 Oct. 1835] in Patriarchal Blessing Book 1, p. 13; handwriting of Oliver Cowdery; CHL. For more information on Patriarchal Blessing Book 1, see Source Notes for Multiple-Entry Documents, p. 532 herein.

Document Transcript

[31]Blessed be brother Frederick [G. Williams], for he shall never want a friend, and his generation after him shall flourish: The Lord hath appointed him an inheritance in the land of Zion. Yea, and his head shall blossom with old age, and he shall be as an olive branch that is bowed down with fruit. And he shall be blessed with the abundance of the good things of the earth because of the liberality of his soul, even with the precious things that couch beneath; even with gold and with silver in abundance, and with antiquities of every kind: with precious stones, and with platina; with houses and with lands, and

---

30. In Oliver Cowdery's introductory comments to the blessings he copied into the Patriarchal Blessing Book in 1835, he provided an important narrative of the restoration of authority. There he wrote: "Therefore, we repaired to the woods, even as our father Joseph said we should, that is to the bush, and called upon the name of the Lord, and he answered us out of the heavens, and while we were in the heavenly vision the angel came down and bestowed upon us this priesthood; and then, as I have said, we repaired to the water and were baptized." Both Cowdery's narrative and JS's blessing as recorded by Cowdery refer to a prophecy by the biblical Joseph of Egypt, resembling the prophecy retold by Lehi in 2 Nephi chapter 3 but given with more detail here. (Patriarchal Blessings, 1:8–9.)

31. Frederick G. Williams's blessing in JS's journal begins with the following: "Brother Frederick is one of those men in whom I place the greatest confidence and trust for I have found him ever full of love and Brotherly kindness he is not a man of many words but is ever wining because of his constant mind he shall ever have place in my heart and is ever intitled to my confidence He is perfectly honest and upright, and seeks with all his heart to magnify his presidency in the church of ch[r]ist, but fails in many instances, in consequence of a want of confidence in himself: God grant that he may overcome all evil." (JS, Journal, 14–19 Nov. 1833, in *JSP*, J1:19.)

with cattle, with charriots and with horses, and asses and with she asses, with mules and camels, and dromedaries, and all swift beasts, at home and abroad, among governors, rulers and kings, and nations afar off: and all these because of the liberality of his soul, always abounding unto the poor. Therefore, the hand of his God shall be over him and his seed after him, from generation to generation. And his head shall blossom and be as white as the pure wool[32]— and his rest shall be glorious:[33] He shall be caught up to meet the Lord in the cloud,[34] and ever be with the Lord. Amen.

Oliver Cowdery, <u>Clerk and Recorder</u>.
Recorded in this book, October 2, 1835.

IV. Blessing to Sidney Rigdon, 2 October 1835

Source Note

JS, Blessing, to Sidney Rigdon, Kirtland Township, Geauga Co., OH, 2 Oct. 1835. Featured version copied [2 Oct. 1835] in Patriarchal Blessing Book 1, p. 13; handwriting of Oliver Cowdery; CHL. For more information on Patriarchal Blessing Book 1, see Source Notes for Multiple-Entry Documents, p. 532 herein.

Document Transcript

[35]Blessed of the Lord is brother Sidney [Rigdon]: notwithstanding he shall be high and lifted up, yet he will humble himself[36] like an ass that coucheth beneath his burden,[37] that learneth his master's will by the stroke of the rod, thus saith the Lord. Yet the Lord will have mercy on him, and he shall bring

---

32. See Daniel 7:9; and Revelation 1:14.

33. See Isaiah 11:10.

34. See 1 Thessalonians 4:17.

35. Sidney Rigdon's blessing in JS's journal is prefaced with the following: "Brother Sidney is a man whom I love but is not capab[le] of that pure and stedfast love for those who are his benefactors as should possess the breast of a Presedent of the chu[r]ch of Christ this with some other little things such as a selfish and indipendance of mind which to[o] often manifest distroys the confidence of those who would lay down their lives for him but notwithstanding these things he is a very great and good man a man of great power of words and can gain the friendship of his hearrers very quick he is a man whom god will uphold if he will continue faithful to his calling O God grant that he may for the Lords sake Amen the man who willeth to do well we should extall his virtues and speak not of his faults behind his back a man who willfuly turneth away from his friend without a cause is not easily forgiven. the kindness of a man should never be forgotten that person who never forsaketh his trust should ever have the highest place for regard in our hearts and our love should never fail but increase more and more and this my disposition and sentiment &c Amen." (JS, Journal, 14–19 Nov. 1833, in *JSP,* J1:18–19.)

36. For "humble himself," the blessing in JS's journal has "bow down under the yoke." (JS, Journal, 14–19 Nov. 1833, in *JSP,* J1:19.)

37. See Genesis 49:14.

forth much fruit, even as the vine of the choice grape,[38] before the time of the gleaning of the vintage,[39] and the Lord shall make his heart merry as with sweet wine because of him who putteth forth his hand and and lifteth him up out of deep mire[40] and pointeth him out the way and guideth his feet when he stumbles, and humbleth him in his pride. Blessed are his generations: nevertheless, one shall hunt after them as a̶s̶ a man hunteth after an ass that is strayed in the wilderness and straitway findeth him and bringeth him into the fold: and thus shall the Lord watch over his generations that they may be saved. A spokesman unto the Lord shall he be all the days of his life;[41] and it shall come to pass that he shall hold the rod as of Aaron,[42] in his right hand. He shall be called blessed, and his name shall be held sacred among all nations. He shall be called to stand before k̶i̶n̶g̶s̶ ⟨governors⟩ and rulers, and among the nobles and the great ones of the earth: and there shall be no greater, in this generation, for the Lord shall reveal unto the Seer of Israel, and he shall declare it.[43] And his testimony shall be borne off triumphantly victorious. He shall put to flight and to shame his enemies, who have endeavored to hold him in bondage: he shall live to see them wasted out of the earth, and he shall walk proudly upon t̶h̶e̶i̶r̶ places of their dead.[44] He shall never be disgraced in his generations, but they shall rise up and do honor to his name; and his name shall be had among them as a sweet memorial, from generation to generation, forever. And it shall come to pass that he shall sit in council with the Ancient of Days.[45] He shall see with his eyes, and hear with his ears, and handle with his hands of t̶h̶i̶s̶ ⟨the⟩ word of life, and shall say, I am satisfied, my soul doth magnify God.[46] Great and numberless are the multiplicity of blessings which shall be poured out upon the head of brother Sidney. He shall have abundance of the good things of this earth, because of the nobility of his soul, and his liberality to the poor. He shall not decrease, but increase an hundred fold,[47] in houses and in lands, and in the increase of his fields, and of all that

---

38. The blessing in JS's journal also has here "when her clusters are is ripe." (JS, Journal, 14–19 Nov. 1833, in *JSP*, J1:19.)

39. See Isaiah 24:13.

40. See Psalm 69:2, 14.

41. See Revelation, 12 Oct. 1833, in *JSP*, D3:324–325 [D&C 100:9–11].

42. See Numbers 17:6–8.

43. See Revelation, 7 Dec. 1830, in *JSP*, D1:223 [D&C 35:23].

44. See Malachi 4:1–3.

45. See Revelation, ca. Aug. 1835, in *JSP*, D4:411 [D&C 27].

46. See Luke 1:46.

47. See Revelation, 1 Mar. 1832, in *JSP*, D2:200 [D&C 78:19]; and Revelation, 6 Aug. 1833, in *JSP*, D3:226 [D&C 98:25].

he hath: And his mind shall never fail, neither his understanding unto the end; even so. Amen.

Oliver Cowdery, <u>clerk and Recorder</u>.

Given December 18, 1833, and recorded in this book October 2, 1835.

REFERENCE
MATERIAL

Source Notes for Multiple-Entry Documents

Many of the texts featured in this volume are drawn from early church record books and other sources that consist of or include multiple individual texts. The following notes provide bibliographical and physical descriptions of such sources, as well as information on provenance and custodial history. Providing this information for these multiple-entry sources here reduces repetition in the source notes that appear throughout the main body of the volume. Images of many of these sources are available at josephsmithpapers.org. Information specific to the individual texts featured in the main body of the volume can be found in the source notes and historical introductions preceding them.

Elders' Journal of the Church of Latter Day Saints, Volume 1, 1837–1838

Elders' Journal of the Church of Latter Day Saints *(Kirtland, Geauga Co., OH, and Far West, Caldwell Co., MO), vol. 1, nos. 1–2, Oct.–Nov. 1837, and nos. 3–4, July–Aug. 1838; nos. 1–2 edited by JS (in Kirtland) and nos. 3–4 edited by JS (in Far West).*

Each monthly issue featured sixteen octavo pages that measured 10⅛ × 6⅛ inches (26 × 16 cm). Each page was printed in two columns, with each column 2⅛ inches (5 cm) wide.

The copy used for transcription was bound at a later, unknown date. The hardcover copy measures 10½ × 6¾ inches (27 × 17 cm). It includes marginalia and archival notations and is held at the CHL; the provenance for this volume is not known.

Elders' Journal of the Church of Latter Day Saints, volume 1, is the source for four featured texts in this volume.

Geauga County Deed Record, Volume 24

Geauga Co., OH, Recorder, Deed Record, vol. 24, 22 Feb.–27 Nov. 1837; handwriting of Ralph Cowles, William Kerr, John French, and unidentified scribes; 620 pages, plus 16 pages of an index of grantors and grantees; Geauga County Archives and Records Center, Chardon, OH. Includes tipped-in documents, redactions, use marks, and archival marking.

Volume measuring 16½ × 11 × 2¾ inches (42 × 28 × 7 cm). At an unknown time, the original cover and binding were replaced with a gray canvas cover and metal-hinged spine. The leaves measure 16 × 10 inches (40½ × 25½ cm). After 1996, the map tipped in to page 99 was removed and filed separately because of preservation concerns. Page 99 is completely loose from the volume.

This volume was in the possession of the Geauga County Recorder from its creation until 1996, when it was transferred to the newly organized Geauga County Archives and Records Center.

Geauga County Deed Record, volume 24, is the source for two featured texts in this volume.

John Whitmer, History, 1831–circa 1847

John Whitmer, History, 1831–ca. 1847, as found in "The Book of John, Whitmer kept by Comma[n]d," ca. 1838–ca. 1847; handwriting of John Whitmer; ninety-six pages (two additional leaves missing); CCLA. Includes redactions, editing marks, and archival marking.

John Whitmer inscribed his history into a blank book containing leaves ruled with thirty-four blue-green horizontal lines (now faded). Evidence suggests there were originally twelve gatherings of twelve leaves (twenty-four pages) each. The entire fifth gathering is missing from the current volume, and one extra leaf not part of the original text block was inserted between the fourth and sixth gatherings, making 133 interior leaves in the current volume. The text block was sewn all along on recessed cords. The blank leaves measure 12¼ × 7⅞ inches (31 × 20 cm); the inscribed leaves are slightly smaller in width, having been trimmed about ⅛ inch (0.3 cm) during conservation work. The volume was constructed with front and back covers of pasteboard and likely had a hollow-back spine and quarter-leather binding. The outside covers are adorned in shell marbled paper, with a gray-green body and veins of blue and red. The complete volume currently measures 12½ × 8⅛ × 1 inches (32 × 21 × 3 cm).

Details of the original state of the volume are impossible to determine because of conservation work done in the second half of the twentieth century. Initially the inscribed leaves were removed from the original boards and from the intact blank leaves of the volume and rebound separately in a modern comb binding. These inscribed leaves were later removed from this binding, reinforced along the bound edge with paper, laminated with thin paper, and bound in a modern case binding. A third conservation effort reversed the earlier work by removing the laminated material and reattaching the inscribed leaves to the blank leaves and the original boards.

The final leaf of the fourth gathering contains manuscript pages 95 and 96. The next two leaves, containing manuscript pages 97–100, are missing. They were removed before 1893, when Andrew Jenson, a representative of the Church Historian's Office in Salt Lake City, inspected the volume and noted that it was missing two leaves at that point. Evidence indicates that the remaining leaves of the fifth gathering were intact but blank when Jenson inspected the volume in 1893, suggesting they were discarded during the first conservation effort in the twentieth century. The first blank leaf following manuscript page 96 does not match the texture or form of the other blank leaves, but it does bear a slight water stain matching staining found on almost all leaves within the book. It may be an extra flyleaf from either the front or back of the volume inserted after page 96, or it may be paper from a different source; in either case, it was inserted early enough to be stained with the rest of the volume. The endpapers are original and currently consist of pastedowns and single flyleaves in the front and back of the volume.

An unidentified scribe, most likely working in the nineteenth century, wrote "Church History" on the top of the front cover. A green adhesive label is affixed to the front cover. At some point, someone attempted to remove the label but succeeded in removing only portions of it. The only writing visible on the label is "HURC", a remnant of the word "CHURCH". The current spine of the volume was added during conservation work, and thus it is unknown whether the original spine bore a title. The recto of the front flyleaf contains several redactions or archival markings in graphite in an unknown hand: "John Whitmer | written | 1835–1838 | after 1860" and "MS History of church | 1830–1838". The verso is blank, aside from offsetting from the first interior page and a stamped "1072" near the bottom. Whitmer inscribed his history from page 1 through the bottom of page 96, at which point the narrative ends midsentence, suggesting it originally continued onto the next page. When Andrew Jenson saw the book in 1893 while visiting Missouri to gather historical information, he made a handwritten copy of the volume and provided a physical description. He wrote that "four pages or two leaves have been torn off the book, which is seen from fragments of the leaves remaining." He also noted that "the next page left intact is 101. No other writing, however, appears on this page or on any of the succeeding pages."[1] Jenson's earlier draft stated that the page "is numbered 101."[2] If this was the case, then the page numbered 101 was part of the fifth gathering and is now missing. At some point, likely during the early twentieth century, the leaf containing pages 95 and 96 was repaired with adhesive tape; the tape was removed during a later conservation effort.[3] Redactions were made by John Whitmer himself, and subsequent editing marks were made that correspond to the early twentieth-century publication of Whitmer's history by the Reorganized Church of Jesus Christ of Latter Day Saints (RLDS church).[4]

Following his excommunication in 1838, John Whitmer apparently retained possession of the history. In a January 1844 offer to sell his history to the church, Whitmer wrote that the "church history" was "at my controll but not in my Possession."[5] Willard Richards declined the offer,[6] and Whitmer certainly had the "Book of John Whitmer" after January 1844, because he updated the volume after JS's death.

It appears Whitmer retained his papers until his death in July 1878, after which his widow, Sarah Maria Jackson Whitmer, sent the "Book of John Whitmer" (though apparently not any earlier notes or drafts) and other papers to Richmond, Missouri, where Whitmer's brother David resided.[7] David Whitmer had possession of the volume in the 1880s, before his death in 1888.[8] In 1893, when Andrew Jenson inspected and copied the "Book of John Whitmer," it was in the possession of David J. Whitmer, David Whitmer's son. Following David J. Whitmer's death, his nephew George Schweich, a grandson of David Whitmer, took possession of the material, along with the Book of

---

1. Whitmer, "The Book of John Whitmer," Andrew Jenson typescript, ca. Mar. 1894, 68.

2. Whitmer, "The Book of John Whitmer," Andrew Jenson manuscript copy, ca. Sept. 1893, 85.

3. The leaf currently bears remnants of this tape. A microfilm made of the manuscript in 1974 shows clear evidence of the tape. (Whitmer, "The Book of John Whitmer," microfilm, Oct. 1974, Research Library and Archives, Reorganized Church of Jesus Christ of Latter Day Saints, Independence, MO, copy at CHL.)

4. "Church History," *Journal of History,* Jan. 1908, 43–63; Apr. 1908, 135–150; July 1908, 292–305.

5. John Whitmer, Far West, MO, to William W. Phelps, Nauvoo, IL, 8 Jan. 1844, JS, Office Papers, CHL.

6. Willard Richards, Nauvoo, IL, to John Whitmer, Far West, MO, 23 Feb. 1844, copy, Willard Richards, Papers, CHL.

7. Whitmer, "The Book of John Whitmer," Andrew Jenson typescript, ca. Mar. 1894, [69]; "Report of Elders Orson Pratt and Joseph F. Smith," *Deseret News,* 27 Nov. 1878, 674–675; 4 Dec. 1878, 690.

8. "Revelation Revisers," *Missouri Republican* (St. Louis), 16 July 1884, [7]; see also "The Book of Mormon," *Chicago Tribune,* 17 Dec. 1885, 3.

Mormon printer's manuscript and other early Latter-day Saint manuscripts.[9] By 1902, the First Presidency of the RLDS church approved the purchase of papers owned by Schweich, including the "Book of John Whitmer," the Book of Mormon printer's manuscript, and several leaves that had been separated from Revelation Book 1.[10] The RLDS church, later renamed the Community of Christ, has maintained custody of the Whitmer history since that time.

John Whitmer, History, is the source for one featured text in this volume.

JS, Journal, 1835–1836

JS, "Sketch Book for the use of Joseph Smith, jr.," Journal, Sept. 1835–Apr. 1836; handwriting of Warren Parrish, an unidentified scribe, Sylvester Smith, Frederick G. Williams, Warren Cowdery, JS, and Oliver Cowdery; 195 pages; JS Collection, CHL. Includes redactions and archival marking.

The text block consists of 114 leaves—including single flyleaves and pastedowns in the front and back—measuring 12¼ × 8 inches (31 × 20 cm). The 110 interior leaves are ledger paper with thirty-four lines in faint—and now faded—black ink that has turned brown. There are nine gatherings of various sizes—each gathering with about a dozen leaves. The text block is sewn all along over cloth tapes. The front and back covers of the journal are pasteboard. The ledger has a tight-back case binding with a brown calfskin quarter-leather binding. The outside covers are adorned in shell marbled paper, with dark green body and veins of light green. The bound volume measures 12⅜ × 8¼ inches (31 × 21 cm) and is 13/16 inches (2 cm) thick. One cover of the book is labeled "Repentence." in black ink. The first page of ledger paper under that cover contains eight lines of references to the book of Genesis under the heading "Scriptures relating to Repentince". The spine has "No 8" inscribed upside up when the book is standing upright for this side. When the volume is turned upside down and flipped front to back, the other cover is titled "Sabbath Day", with "No 9" written beneath in black ink. The first page of ledger paper under that cover contains two lines of references to the book of Genesis under the heading "Scriptures relating to the Sabbath day". Thus the book was used to simultaneously house two volumes of topical notes on biblical passages. This book was apparently part of a larger series that included at least two other extant volumes—one bearing "Faith" and "10" on the cover, and the other bearing "Second Comeing of Christ" and "No 3" on one cover and "Gift of the Holy Ghost" on the other cover.[11] In late 1835, JS and scribes began using the book to

---

9. Andrew Jenson et al., "Historical Landmarks," *Deseret Evening News,* 26 Sept. 1888, 7; T. E. Lloyd, "The Carroll-Lloyd Expose," *Zion's Ensign,* 15 July 1893, 6; "The Book of Mormon," *New York Times,* 21 Sept. 1899, 9; George Schweich, Richmond, MO, to O. R. Beardsley, 17 Jan. 1900, Miscellanea, Marie Eccles-Caine Archives of Intermountain Americana, Utah State University Special Collections, Logan; Walter W. Smith, Independence, MO, to S. A. Burgess, Independence, MO, 15 Apr. 1926, J. F. Curtis Papers, CCLA; see also Heman C. Smith, Lamoni, IA, to George Schweich, 20 July 1896, CCLA.

10. "Minutes of First Presidency," 24 Apr. 1902, CCLA; Walter W. Smith, Independence, MO, to the RLDS First Presidency, Independence, MO, 14 Sept. 1925, Whitmer Papers, CCLA; see also Source Note for Revelation Book 1, in *JSP,* MRB:4.

11. "Grammar & A[l]phabet of the Egyptian Language," Kirtland Egyptian Papers, ca. 1835–1836, CHL; Kirtland Elders Quorum, "Record."

record his journal for 1835–1836, which begins on the recto of the second leaf of ledger paper. Warren Parrish added the title "Sketch Book" to the cover, beneath "Repentence."

The entire journal is inscribed in black ink that later turned brown. Pages 25, 51, 77, 103, 129, and 154 bear the marks of adhesive wafers that were probably used to attach manuscripts until they were copied into the journal. The journal was used in Nauvoo, Illinois, in 1843 as a major source in composing JS's multivolume manuscript history of the church. At this time, redactions were made in ink and in graphite pencil, and use marks were made in graphite. Also, apparently in Nauvoo, the cover of the journal side of the book was marked with a "D" and then with a larger, stylized "D". At some point a white paper spine label was added with "1835–6 ⟨Kirtland⟩ JOURNAL" hand printed or stenciled in black ink that later turned brown. The insertion "Kirtland" is written in graphite. Also, in the "Repentence" side of the volume, the rectos of the third through eighth leaves of ledger paper are numbered on the upper right-hand corners as 195, 197, 199, 201, 203, and 205—all written in graphite and apparently redactions. Except with regard to the title "Sketch Book", none of the authors of the inscriptions mentioned previously have been identified. This volume is listed in Nauvoo and early Utah inventories of church records, indicating continuous custody.[12]

JS, Journal, 1835–1836, is the source for twenty-six featured texts in this volume.

JS, Journal, March–September 1838

JS, "The Scriptory Book—of Joseph Smith Jr.—President of The Church of <u>Jesus Christ</u>, of Latterday Saints In all the World," Journal, Mar.–Sept. 1838; handwriting of George W. Robinson and James Mulholland; sixty-nine pages; in "General," Record Book, 1838, verso of Patriarchal Blessings, vol. 5, CHL. Includes redactions and archival marking.

JS's "Scriptory Book" is recorded on pages 15 to 83 of a large record book entitled "General" that also includes a list of church members in Caldwell County, Missouri (pages 2–14), a copy of JS's 16 December 1838 letter from the jail in Liberty, Missouri (pages 101–108), and an aborted record partially entitled "Recor" in unidentified handwriting (page 110). The book, which measures 13 × 8¼ × 1¾ inches (33 × 21 × 4 cm), has 182 leaves of ledger paper sized 12½ × 7¾ inches (32 × 20 cm) with thirty-seven lines in blue ink per page. There are eighteen gatherings of various sizes, each of about a dozen leaves. The text block is sewn all along over three vellum tapes. The heavy pink endpapers each consist of a pastedown and two flyleaves pasted together. The text block edges are stained green. The volume has a hardbound ledger-style binding with a hollow-back spine and glued-on, blue-striped cloth headbands. It is bound in brown split-calfskin leather with blind-tooled decoration around the outside border and along the turned-in edges of the leather on the inside covers. At some point, the letter "G" was hand printed in ink on the front cover. The original leather cover over the spine—which appears to have been intentionally removed—may have borne a title or filing notation.

The journal is inscribed in black ink that later turned brown and is almost entirely in the handwriting of George W. Robinson. James Mulholland's handwriting appears in a copy of

---

12. "Schedule of Church Records. Nauvoo 1846," [1]; "Historian's Office Catalogue 1858," 1, Historian's Office, Catalogs and Inventories, 1846–1904, CHL; Johnson, *Register of the Joseph Smith Collection,* 7.

the 23 July 1837 revelation for Thomas B. Marsh (D&C 112) on pages 72–74. Running heads added by Robinson throughout the journal indicate the months of the entries on the page. The volume was later used in Nauvoo, Illinois, as a source for JS's multivolume manuscript history of the church. During the preparation of the history, redactions and use marks were made in graphite. Redactions in graphite and ink may have been made at other times as well. In 1845, the book was turned over so that the back cover became the front and the last page became the first. This side of the book was used to record patriarchal blessings. The original spine may have been removed at this time. The spine is now labeled with a number "5", designating its volume number in a series of books of patriarchal blessings.

The volume is listed in inventories of church records in Nauvoo and early Utah, indicating continuous institutional custody.[13] At some point, the leaf containing pages 54 and 55 was torn from the journal. This removed leaf—which contains, among other writings, the earliest extant text of an 8 July 1838 revelation for the Quorum of the Twelve (D&C 118)— was for a time kept in Revelation Book 2.[14] It is now part of the Revelations Collection at the Church History Library.

JS, Journal, March–September 1838, is the source for three featured texts in this volume.

JS Letterbook 2, 1839–1843

JS Letterbook 2, [1839–ca. summer 1843]; handwriting of Howard Coray, James Mulholland, Robert B. Thompson, Willard Richards, John Fullmer, William Clayton, and George Walker; 271 pages, including twenty-six pages of an index; JS Collection, CHL.

This letterbook was inscribed in a large-size, commercially produced ledger book measuring 14¼ × 9½ × 1¾ inches (36 × 24 × 4 cm) with leather-covered boards. It contains 238 leaves. The leaves, which measure 13½ × 8⅞ inches (34 × 23 cm), are vertically ruled with eight single red lines and three interspersed double red lines and horizontally ruled with thirty-nine blue lines and one double red line at the top or bottom of the page depending on how the ledger book was turned. The book was originally used as a financial ledger book for Rigdon, Smith & Co., beginning in September 1836; eighty-three pages of financial entries were inscribed. In April 1839, the book was inverted, and what would have been the back of the book for the financial firm became the front of a letterbook. A title is inscribed on the blank leaf before the letterbook that reads "Copies of Letters, &c. &c. 1839 AD." Following the title page, there are 245 pages of inscribed letters. There is a mix of contemporaneous letters, earlier letters, church records, and church business records. The first fifty-one pages of Letterbook 2 contain letters on the 1838 Missouri difficulties, and many of them appear to be copies of letters that JS or others received while in jail in Liberty, Missouri, in winter 1838–1839. These pages also feature copies of letters sent to and from church leaders in Quincy and Commerce, Illinois, in spring and early summer 1839; JS's journal provides evidence that he was "employed

---

13. Historian's Office, "Schedule of Church Records"; "Historian's Office Catalogue," [2]; "Index of Records and Journals," [12], Historian's Office, Catalogs and Inventories, 1846–1904, CHL; JS, Journal, Mar.–Sept. 1838, microfilm, JS Collection, CHL.

14. Best, "Register of the Revelations Collection," 19.

dictating letters and attending to the various business of the Church" during this time,[15] indicating that this volume was an active letterbook, with letters being contemporaneously copied into it. On page 52, following a 27 June 1839 letter and a 12 November 1837 letter, the copies of much earlier letters began to be inscribed; these letters include a letter originally written on 29 July 1833 by John Whitmer with a postscript by William W. Phelps to Oliver Cowdery and JS, which is followed by a letter from JS to Emma Smith dated 4 June 1834 and a 17 June 1829 letter from Jesse Smith to Hyrum Smith. Copying these documents may have coincided with the writing of JS's history or with the writing of the history of the difficulties in Missouri per JS's instructions in March 1839.[16] The active recording of contemporaneous letters continued after these few earlier letters until February 1843.

JS Letterbook 2 is the source for four featured texts in this volume.

Latter Day Saints' Messenger and Advocate, Volumes 1–3, 1834–1837

Latter Day Saints' Messenger and Advocate *(Kirtland, Geauga Co., OH), vol. 1, no. 12, Sept. 1835; edited by John Whitmer (in Kirtland); vol. 2, nos. 1–6, Oct. 1835–Mar. 1836, and nos. 7–12, Apr.–Sept. 1836; nos. 1–6 edited by John Whitmer (in Kirtland) and nos. 7–12 edited by Oliver Cowdery (in Kirtland); vol. 3, nos. 1–4, Oct. 1836–Feb. 1837, and nos. 5–12, Mar.–Sept. 1837; nos. 1–4 edited by Oliver Cowdery (in Kirtland) and nos. 5–12 edited by Warren Cowdery (in Kirtland).*

Each monthly issue featured sixteen octavo pages that measured 8½ × 5⁷⁄₁₆ inches (22 × 14 cm). Each page was printed in two columns. Currently bound in a volume at CHL.

The *Latter Day Saints' Messenger and Advocate* is the source for fourteen featured texts in this volume.

Minute Book 1, 1832–1837

Minute Book 1, *[ca. 3 Dec. 1832–ca. 30 Nov. 1837]; handwriting of Warren Cowdery, Frederick G. Williams, Orson Hyde, Marcellus F. Cowdery, George W. Robinson, Phineas Richards, and Harlow Redfield; 259 pages; CHL. Includes dockets, redactions, copy notes, use marks, and archival stamping and marking.*

Medium-size blank book. The paper, which is ruled with thirty-four blue-green horizontal lines (now faded), measures 12 × 7½ inches (30 × 19 cm). The book originally contained 149 leaves (now 143 leaves), consisting of twelve gatherings of twelve leaves each, two front flyleaves, and three back flyleaves. The text block is sewn all along over recessed cords. The front and back covers of the volume are pasteboard. The book has a tight-back case binding with a brown calfskin quarter-leather binding, the bound volume measuring 12⅜ × 7¾ × 1 inches (31 × 20 × 3 cm). The outside covers are adorned with shell marbled paper, with a red, green, and black body and veins of black. The back pastedown bears the inscriptions "c", "c/i", and "pep"—possibly original merchandising notes.

---

15. JS, Journal, 20–24 May 1839, in *JSP*, J1:339.
16. See JS, Journal, 11 June; 3 and 4–5 July 1839, in *JSP*, J1:340, 345.

A single leaf—the conjugate of the leaf bearing pages 15 and 16—was removed from the first gathering of the book, but this occurred before the adjacent leaves were inscribed or paginated. Page 1 is the first lined page. Minutes were inscribed in the book on pages 1–219 and 226–265. Pages 220–225 were left blank, except for their page numbers. Following page 265, the remaining twenty-one pages and the three back flyleaves were left blank. At some point, Frederick G. Williams began a table of contents, which was continued by Warren Cowdery but never completed; this table of contents is inscribed on all four pages of the two front flyleaves. The minute book was kept with quill pens. The entries and pagination were inscribed in ink that is now brown. Pages 39–55 include entry-dividing lines inscribed in red ink. There is also residue from an adhesive wafer on pages 156 and 157, indicating a sheet of paper was attached there at one time.

At some point, probably in the early 1840s, the front cover of the volume was labeled "Conference | A" in black ink. The "A" is written in a formal style that matches the covers of other early manuscript books in the Church History Library's holdings. Copy notes and use marks, inscribed in graphite, were made by later scribes who used the minute book when compiling JS's 1838–1856 history. At some point, probably in Utah, a white paper label was pasted on the spine; the label is now only partially extant, with the remaining inscription illegible. Another white paper label, also only partially extant, was pasted over this. It reads: "Kirtland Coun". The rest of the label, which would have included approximately two more words, is missing. The pastedown on the inside of the book's front cover bears an archival identification number inscribed in black ink and a more recent Historian's Office library sticker. The spine also bears a more recent sticker with an identification number. Ink has bled through on several of the pages. The book has also suffered some wear and staining in the front and back.

The volume is listed in the 1846 Historian's Office inventory as "Book of Conference A"[17] and referred to as a Kirtland high council record in subsequent Historian's Office inventories from the 1850s.[18] In 1988, the Church History Department transferred Minute Book 1 to the First Presidency's Office.[19] The minute book was transferred to the Church History Library in 2009.[20] Archival records and the markings mentioned above indicate continuous institutional custody.

Sixteen different clerks took down the original minutes that were later copied into Minute Book 1, which was begun as part of a new effort in more permanent church record keeping. It appears that the book was begun in early December 1832, about two weeks after JS began his own personal journal and apparently began keeping a letterbook in which to copy outgoing correspondence. Frederick G. Williams began the minute book, which was later continued by Warren Cowdery and others in Ohio. Entries in the minute book are occasionally out of chronological order. Minutes of meetings held between April and August 1834

---

17. "Schedule of Church Records. Nauvoo 1846," [1], Historian's Office, Catalogs and Inventories, 1846–1904, CHL.

18. "Inventory. Historian's Office. 4th April 1855," [1]; "Inventory. Historian's Office. G. S. L. City April 1. 1857," [1]; "Historian's Office Inventory G. S. L. March 19. 1858," [1], Historian's Office, Catalogs and Inventories, 1846–1904, CHL.

19. Letter of Transfer, Salt Lake City, UT, 13 Dec. 1988, CHL.

20. Letter of Transfer, Salt Lake City, UT, 15 Dec. 2009, CHL.

were recorded by Orson Hyde, likely not long after the meetings were held. Those from August 1834–September 1835 were not recorded before 25 February 1836, the date that Warren Cowdery, who entered these minutes into Minute Book 1, arrived in Kirtland, Ohio, where the minute book was kept.[21] Cowdery served as a scribe at the dedication of the Kirtland House of the Lord on 27 March 1836 and also began recording entries into JS's journal in early April.[22] His work on Minute Book 1 likely occurred around this same time.

Minute Book 1 is the source for twenty-six featured texts in this volume.

Minute Book 2, 1838, 1842, 1844

Zion (Missouri) High Council and Nauvoo Stake High Council, "The Conference Minutes, and Record Book, of Christ's Church of Latter Day Saints," Minute Book 2, 6 Apr. 1838–[ca. June 1838], [ca. Oct. 1842], [ca. June 1844]; handwriting of Ebenezer Robinson, Hosea Stout, Levi Richards, Joseph M. Cole, and an unidentified scribe; 178 pages, as well as indexing in tabbed pages at beginning of book; CHL. Includes tables, redactions, use marks, and archival marking.

The second of two texts inscribed in a ledger book. The paper, which is ruled both horizontally and vertically, measures 12½ × 7¾ inches (32 × 20 cm). The book contains 276 leaves, including the flyleaves in the front and back of the book. The bound book, which features a brown suede cover, measures 13 × 8½ × 1¾ inches (33 × 22 × 4 cm). The spine has a pasted red label with "LEDGER" in gold lettering. Following the four front flyleaves, the first twenty-four pages are tabbed index pages. The next seventy-three pages were used by Warren Parrish for various financial accounts he kept prior to his move to Kirtland, Ohio. Following a blank page, Minute Book 2 fills the next 187 pages, although there are some blank pages within and at the end of this record. The portion of the ledger in which Minute Book 2 is inscribed has its own pagination, all apparently done by Hosea Stout. Ebenezer Robinson's handwriting appears on the title page (the recto of the leaf preceding page 1) and on pages 1–37, 41–42, 44–52, and 55–93. Pages 38–40 are blank. Levi Richards's handwriting appears on pages 43 and 52–55. There is also unidentified handwriting in the middle of page 87. The inscription ends with minutes of the Nauvoo, Illinois, stake high council meetings held 1 and 15 June 1844, recorded by Joseph M. Cole on pages 178–185. The minutes were recorded with a quill pen, and all are in brown ink, except for some blue ink on pages 179–181. The remaining 251 pages of the book are blank. There were originally four back flyleaves; only two remain, and they are blank.

Minute Book 2 includes several redactions made in graphite, as well as some marking in blue pencil. At some point, the leather cover was decorated with blind tooling, and a paper sticker was pasted on the spine with "CONFERENCE MINUTES AND HIGH COUNCIL RECORDS OF FAR WEST" inscribed in unidentified handwriting. This sticker resembles several other such stickers found on early church record books.

The volume may have been included in the Nauvoo exodus inventory as part of "Records of High Council."[23] It is listed in mid- and late nineteenth-century inventories

---

21. Cowdery, Diary, 25 Feb. 1836.

22. JS, Journal, 27 Mar. 1836, in *JSP*, J1:201; Historical Introduction to JS, Journal, 1835–1836, in *JSP*, J1:56.

23. "Schedule of Church Records. Nauvoo 1846," Historian's Office, Catalogs and Inventories, 1846–1904, CHL.

of the Historian's Office in Salt Lake City.[24] The Genealogical Society of Utah made a microfilm copy of the volume in 1954.[25] Church historian Joseph Fielding Smith took the volume with him to the Office of the First Presidency when he became church president in 1970 and kept it in his safe.[26] The book was returned to the Church History Department in 2008.[27] These archival records and archival marking on the book indicate continuous institutional custody.

Minute Book 2 includes minutes of the first church conferences held in New York in 1830 and in Ohio in 1831. The bulk of the minutes, however, are from meetings held in Missouri in Jackson, Clay, and Caldwell counties during the 1830s. The record also includes minutes of meetings held in Indiana and Illinois. JS was present at New York and Ohio meetings and was present at Missouri meetings when he visited there and after moving there in March 1838. This record of minutes concludes in 1839, with the exception of minutes for two high council meetings held in Nauvoo in 1844.

The minutes inscribed in Minute Book 2 are copies—most likely copies of copies. The original minutes of these early church conferences, councils, and other meetings were taken by John Whitmer and several other men who acted as clerks. Whitmer, who lived in Missouri and was the appointed church historian, may have collected and kept the minutes that he and other clerks had taken down. Ebenezer Robinson, who began functioning as the clerk of the Zion (Missouri) high council in Far West on 3 March 1838, was formally appointed to that position on 6 April 1838.[28] Immediately following his appointment, Robinson attempted to procure the records of the church in Far West from Whitmer, but Whitmer refused to relinquish them. In response, JS and Sidney Rigdon wrote a letter on 9 April 1838 demanding that Whitmer surrender his notes for the history he had been appointed to keep for the church.[29] Half a century later, Robinson recounted that although Whitmer ignored this demand to give up his historical notes, a "record" was obtained from Whitmer and brought to Robinson's house, and Robinson "copied the entire record into another book, assisted a part of the time, by Dr. Levi Richards."[30] That Robinson copied the record into "another book" seems to imply that Whitmer's record was also kept in a record book. That Minute Book 2 is dated 6 April 1838 (when Robinson was appointed clerk), begins in Robinson's handwriting, and includes handwriting from Richards indicates that it is the copy of the early min-

---

24. See "Inventory. Historians Office. G. S. L. City April 1. 1857," [1]; "Index of Records and Journals in the Historian's Office 1878," [4], Historian's Office, Catalogs and Inventories, 1846–1904, CHL.

25. Minute Book 2, microfilm, 2 Nov. 1954, CHL.

26. "Inventory of President Joseph Fielding Smith's Safe," 23 May 1970, First Presidency, General Administration Files, CHL; Francis M. Gibbons to Earl E. Olson, 1 Nov. 1974, CHL; see also Cannon and Cook, *Far West Record,* v. The volume, however, was made available for microfilming in 1974 and for scanned images in 2006. (Microfilm Operator's Report, 2 Nov. 1974, Case File for Minute Book 2, CHL; Minute Book 2, microfilm, 1 Nov. 1974, CHL; Minute Book 2, CD, 2006, CHL; see also the full bibliographic record for Minute Book 2 in the CHL catalog.)

27. Church History Department Correspondence, 17 Oct. 2008, in Case File for Minute Book 2, CHL.

28. Minute Book 2, 3 Mar. and 6 Apr. 1838.

29. This letter was attested by Robinson. (JS and Sidney Rigdon, Far West, MO, to John Whitmer, 9 Apr. 1838, in *JSP,* J1:249–250.)

30. Ebenezer Robinson, "Items of Personal History of the Editor," *Return,* Sept. 1889, 133.

utes of the church that Robinson made from Whitmer's record. Robinson titled his copy of the record book "The Conference Minutes, and Record Book, of Christ's Church of Latter Day Saints." The minute book has been more commonly known by the shorter and less formal name "Far West Record."[31] Because of its importance in the 1830s and the frequency with which it is cited in the annotation of *The Joseph Smith Papers,* it has been designated with the short citation "Minute Book 2."

The minutes of the church's January 1831 conference, as recorded on page 2 of Minute Book 2, include a reference to a revelation recorded on page 80 of the "Book of Commandments." This indicates that Whitmer's record was a copy of the original minutes and was likely made sometime between 1833 and 1835 after printing of the Book of Commandments had begun and before the Doctrine and Covenants was published. If Whitmer had begun making his copy of the minutes after the publication of the Doctrine and Covenants, he would have been much more likely to reference that book than the unfinished printing of the Book of Commandments.[32] That Robinson made a copy of the minutes, rather than continuing Whitmer's record, suggests that Whitmer's record was returned to him. Whitmer left Far West on 19 June 1838.[33] He remained in Missouri and never reestablished ties with the church in Illinois.[34] Robinson, therefore, apparently finished copying Whitmer's record of minutes by 19 June, when Whitmer separated from the body of the Saints. In the lists of conference and council participants found in some of the minutes, some names are followed by parenthetical remarks regarding their excommunication or their disciplinary status. These parenthetical notes were evidently added by Whitmer when he copied the originals and were then copied from Whitmer's record by Robinson.

Minute Book 2 is the source for three featured texts in this volume.

Oliver Cowdery, Letterbook, 1833–1838

Oliver Cowdery, Letterbook, [ca. 30 Oct. 1833–ca. 24 Feb. 1838]; handwriting of Thomas Burdick, J. M. Carrel, and Warren F. Cowdery; ninety-six pages; Henry E. Huntington Library, San Marino, CA.

---

31. The book was referred to as "Far West record Book A" in JS's March–September 1838 journal and was listed as "Far West Record" in mid-nineteenth-century archival records of the Church Historian's Office. A transcript of the minute book was also published under that name: Donald Q. Cannon and Lyndon W. Cook, eds., *Far West Record: Minutes of the Church of Jesus Christ of Latter-day Saints, 1830–1844* (Salt Lake City: Deseret Book, 1983). (JS, Journal, 13 Apr. 1838, in *JSP,* J1:256; "Historian's Office Inventory G. S. L. City March 19. 1858," [1], Historian's Office, Catalogs and Inventories, 1846–1904, CHL.)

32. Whitmer could not have copied these minutes before January 1833, the earliest that the third gathering of the Book of Commandments (which included page 80) could have been printed, and would likely not have copied them after mid-September 1835, when the referenced revelation was available in the published Doctrine and Covenants. (*JSP,* R2:9n35; William W. Phelps, Kirtland, OH, to Sally Waterman Phelps, Liberty, MO, 16–18 Sept. 1835, private possession, copy at CHL.)

33. Whitmer, Daybook, 19 June 1838; Whitmer, History, 87–88, in *JSP,* H2:98–99; see also Minute Book 2, 10 Mar. 1838.

34. Jenson, *LDS Biographical Encyclopedia,* 1:251–252.

This letterbook is unbound, consisting of four gatherings of twelve leaves each plus an additional three leaves. All of the leaves together measure 12½ × 7⅞ × ¼ inches (32 × 20 × 1 cm).

The Huntington Library purchased the letterbook from Carl C. Curtis on 21 November 1931. Curtis was the nephew of Warren F. Cowdery, the last scribe in the letterbook; he was living in Pasadena, California, in 1931.[35]

Oliver Cowdery, Letterbook, is the source for two featured texts in this volume.

Patriarchal Blessing Book 1

Joseph Smith Sr., Patriarchal Blessing Book 1, [Dec. 1834–ca. Spring 1868]; handwriting of Oliver Cowdery, Warren Cowdery, George W. Robinson, Willard Richards, Thomas Bullock, Wilford Woodruff, George A. Smith, Robert L. Campbell, John L. Smith, Richard Bentley, and James C. Snow; 144 pages, plus 52 pages of index; Patriarchal Blessings, CHL. Includes tipped in documents, redactions, use marks, and archival marking.

Patriarchal Blessing Book 1 is a commercially produced ledger measuring 17 × 10⅞ × 1¼ inches (43 × 28 × 3 cm) with tan leather-covered boards. The volume contains ninety-eight leaves measuring 16⅜ × 10½ inches (42 × 27 cm).

The ledger's front page contains the title "The Book of Patriarchal Blessings 1834." Robert L. Campbell recorded in the front of the volume "A History of this Record," which was written in 1859 by church historians George A. Smith and Wilford Woodruff. That history explains the provenance of the ledger, which was stolen on a couple of occasions, before Benjamin F. Johnson obtained it and delivered it to George A. Smith in January 1859. The ledger was re-bound at least once. In a 7 October 1835 notation in Patriarchal Blessing Book 1, Oliver Cowdery indicated that it would be impossible to collect all blessings given by Joseph Smith Sr., leaving the volume incomplete.[36]

The first patriarchal blessings recorded in the ledger are those Joseph Smith Sr. gave to his children and their spouses on 9 December 1834 at a special feast.[37] Cowdery began serving as the primary scribe for Patriarchal Blessing Book 1 probably sometime in September 1835 when he was appointed church recorder, and he likely recorded these blessings around that same time.[38] Cowdery served as the primary scribe for Patriarchal Blessing Book 1 until April 1836 when his brother Warren, the assistant recorder, took over scribal duties. A variety of clerks inscribed the text of loose blessings into the ledger in and after 1837; active recording of Joseph Smith Sr.'s blessings to individuals continued until April 1868.

Patriarchal Blessing Book 1 is the source for the four texts in the appendix.

---

35. See the full bibliographic entry for Letterbook, Docket, and Correspondence of Oliver Cowdery, 1833–1894, in the Huntington Library catalog; 1930 U.S. Census, Pasadena, Los Angeles Co., CA, 102; and 1940 U.S. Census, Pasadena, Los Angeles Co., CA, 8775.

36. Patriarchal Blessings, 1:16; Cowdery, "Account Book of Writing," 1; Minutes, 14 Sept. 1835, in *JSP,* D4:412–415.

37. See Historical Introduction to Blessing from Joseph Smith Sr., 9 Dec. 1834, in *JSP,* D4:200–202.

38. Minutes, 14 Sept. 1835, in *JSP,* D4:414.

Chronology for October 1835–January 1838

This brief chronology is designed as a reference tool for situating any particular document or group of documents among the more significant events of JS's life. It includes important journeys, selected revelations, developments in ecclesiastical organization, and other significant incidents. Readers wishing to conduct further research into events in JS's life may consult the documented chronology posted on the Joseph Smith Papers website, josephsmithpapers.org.

1835

Fall		JS worked periodically on Book of Abraham translation; he and associates produced several manuscripts related to the Egyptian papyri, including an Egyptian alphabet, Kirtland, Ohio.
October	4–5	JS and John Corrill traveled to Perry, Ohio.
	6–11	JS attended father, Joseph Smith Sr., during serious illness, Kirtland.
	29	JS hired Warren Parrish as a scribe, Kirtland.
November	2	JS and several others attended medical lecture by Daniel Peixotto at Willoughby Medical College, Willoughby, Ohio.
	3	JS organized 1835–1836 session of the Elders School, Kirtland.
	9–11	JS hosted and ultimately denounced Robert Matthews, commonly known as the Prophet Mathias, to whom he recounted his first vision of Deity, other divine visitations, and establishment of the church, Kirtland.
	12	JS instructed apostles regarding ordinance of washing of feet and forthcoming endowment, Kirtland.
	14–17	JS hosted a visitor, Erastus Holmes, to whom he recounted his divine visitations and the "rise and progress of the church," Kirtland.
	20	Upon returning from New York City, Oliver Cowdery presented Hebrew study materials to JS, Kirtland.
	24	JS solemnized his first recorded wedding, marrying Newel Knight and Lydia Goldthwaite Bailey, Kirtland.
December	16	Argument between JS and brother William Smith during session of Kirtland debating school erupted into physical fight, injuring JS.
	ca. 17–29	JS's parents, Joseph Smith Sr. and Lucy Mack Smith, moved into his home, Kirtland.
	26	Revelation directed to Lyman Sherman, who had requested that the Lord "make known [his] duty," Kirtland.

1836

January	1	JS reconciled with brother William, Kirtland.
	4	JS organized school for study of Hebrew language, Kirtland.
	7, 9	JS attended feast for the poor and disabled at home of Newel K. Whitney, Kirtland.
	13	JS presided over meeting of church leaders in which Kirtland bishop's council and high councils of Kirtland and Missouri were fully organized, Kirtland.
	21	JS administered and received ritual washings and anointings with priesthood leaders and experienced vision of celestial kingdom, Kirtland.
	26	First day of formal instruction by Joshua Seixas at Hebrew School, Kirtland.
March	13	Church presidency and some members of the Quorum of the Twelve resolved to relocate to Missouri by 15 May 1837, Kirtland.
	27	JS dedicated House of the Lord, Kirtland.
	29	JS administered and received ritual washing of feet with priesthood leaders in House of the Lord, Kirtland.
	30	Solemn assembly held in House of the Lord, Kirtland.
	31	JS repeated temple dedication ceremonies for those who could not attend 27 March session, Kirtland.
April	early	Warren A. Cowdery began work as JS's clerk, including acting as scribe for JS's history, Kirtland.
	2	In Kirtland, JS and Oliver Cowdery appointed to raise money to purchase land in Zion.
	3	In House of the Lord, JS and Oliver Cowdery experienced vision of Jesus Christ, who accepted the building; also visions of Moses, Elias, and Elijah conveying divine authority, Kirtland.
May	17	JS escorted grandmother Mary Duty Smith from Fairport Harbor, Ohio, to Kirtland.
	27	Mary Duty Smith passed away, Kirtland.
June	20	Frederick Granger Williams Smith born to JS and Emma Smith, Kirtland.
	22	JS purchased land from federal government in what would become Caldwell County, with John Corrill acting as agent, Lexington, Missouri.
	29	Ad hoc committee of citizens in Clay County, Missouri, demanded that Latter-day Saints stop immigrating to the county and that those without substantial farms leave after fall harvest.
July	1	Church leaders in Missouri agreed to demands of citizens' committee to leave Clay County.

	25	JS and associates departed Kirtland on journey to New York and New England.
August	5	JS and others rented a house and stayed for about three weeks, Salem, Massachusetts.
	6	Revelation regarding journey to New England and debts, Salem.
	8	Church funds used to purchase land for future site of Far West from federal government, Lexington.
September	mid	JS returned to Kirtland from journey to New York and New England.
October	5	JS and others purchased 239 acres of land from Peter French, who had previously sold the church land on which temple was built, Kirtland.
November	2	Stockholders of Kirtland Safety Society Bank ratified its constitution; JS elected as cashier, Kirtland.
December	29	Missouri governor Lilburn W. Boggs signed bill creating Caldwell County for Mormon settlement, Jefferson City, Missouri.

1837

January	2	In absence of bank charter, stockholders reorganized Kirtland Safety Society Bank as Kirtland Safety Society Anti-Banking Company and drafted new articles of agreement, Kirtland.
	early	Kirtland Safety Society Anti-Banking Company opened for business and began issuing notes, Kirtland.
February ca. early		JS traveled to Monroe, Michigan, to transact business related to recent investment in Bank of Monroe.
	9	Samuel Rounds brought charges against JS and others for issuing banknotes without state charter, Kirtland.
	10	Petition for bank charter for Kirtland Safety Society Bank rejected by state senate, Columbus, Ohio.
	19	JS spoke in temple denouncing dissenters, Kirtland.
April	5	Missouri high council confronted John Whitmer and William W. Phelps concerning business conduct, Far West, Caldwell County, Missouri.
	6	JS held solemn assembly in House of the Lord on anniversary of church's organization, Kirtland.
	7–10	JS transferred significant amount of land in Kirtland, including land on which temple stood, to William Marks.
	13	Grandison Newell alleged JS hired men to kill him; warrant issued for JS's arrest, Painesville, Ohio.
		JS departed from Kirtland; whereabouts in following days unknown.
	25	JS and Sidney Rigdon arrested in connection with lawsuit filed by John Newbould, Painesville.

May	19	JS returned to Kirtland after several weeks of absence.
	19–24	JS traveled between Kirtland and Chester, Ohio, to collect promissory notes and dry goods from Rigdon, Smith & Co. store, which had likely closed earlier in month.
	28	At church meeting, JS and others defended his leadership against accusations of dissenters, after which Warren Parrish denounced JS, Kirtland.
	ca. 28	Abel Lamb and others petitioned church presidency to investigate behavior of David Whitmer, Frederick G. Williams, Lyman Johnson, Parley P. Pratt, and Warren Parrish, Kirtland.
	29	Orson Pratt and Lyman Johnson charged JS with lying, extortion, and speaking disrespectfully, Kirtland.
June	ca. 1–4	JS appointed first missionaries to England, including apostles Heber C. Kimball and Orson Hyde, Kirtland.
	5	Charges brought against JS by Grandison Newell dismissed, Chardon, Ohio.
	8	JS sold his stock and withdrew from Kirtland Safety Society, Kirtland.
	13	Heber C. Kimball, Orson Hyde, Willard Richards, and Joseph Fielding departed Kirtland on mission to England.
	mid	JS suffered onset of severe illness, Kirtland.
July	by 7	JS and Sidney Rigdon resigned as officers of Kirtland Safety Society; the society's directors elected Warren Parrish and Frederick G. Williams to replace them, Kirtland.
	11	JS and others mortgaged House of the Lord to New York mercantile firm Mead, Stafford & Co., Kirtland.
	ca. 19	Heber C. Kimball and other missionaries arrived in Liverpool, England.
	23	Revelation on duties of Quorum of the Twelve and quorum president, Thomas B. Marsh, Kirtland.
	28	JS departed Kirtland to visit Latter-day Saints in Upper Canada.
August	ca. 27	JS returned to Kirtland from journey to Upper Canada.
	ca. late	JS issued notice printed in *LDS Messenger and Advocate* warning the public against using or accepting notes of Kirtland Safety Society, Kirtland.
September	1	JS and others renegotiated debts with four New York mercantile firms through Painesville attorney William Perkins, Kirtland.
	3	JS presided over conference at which objections were raised against several church leaders for dissent, and apostles Luke Johnson, Lyman Johnson, and John F. Boynton were disfellowshipped, Kirtland.
	5	In Kirtland, JS designated Hyrum Smith as agent to sell or transfer land JS owned in Missouri.

10   JS presided over conference at which apostles Luke Johnson, Lyman Johnson, and John F. Boynton confessed errors and were received back into church fellowship, Kirtland.

17   George W. Robinson appointed general church clerk and recorder, Kirtland.

27   JS and others departed Kirtland for northwest Missouri to attend to church business and identify places for Latter-day Saints to settle.

October   24   JS tried in absentia in county court in lawsuit *Rounds v. JS;* he was found guilty and fined $1,000, Chardon.

late   First issue of *Elders' Journal,* a new church periodical edited by JS, published, Kirtland.

November   7   JS held church conference at which Frederick G. Williams was removed from church presidency and Hyrum Smith appointed in his place, Far West.

December   ca. 10   JS returned from Missouri and faced renewed dissent, Kirtland.

late   High council excommunicated twenty-eight dissenters, including Martin Harris, Warren Parrish, and apostles Luke Johnson and John F. Boynton, Kirtland.

1838

January   early   JS continued to face new and ongoing litigation; in relation to court judgment, JS's assets, including Egyptian mummies and records, were seized and auctioned off; lives of church presidency threatened by dissenters, Kirtland.

12   JS dictated three revelations, one of which directed church presidency to leave Kirtland; JS and Sidney Rigdon departed Kirtland to relocate to Far West; later joined by families.

15   Kirtland church printing office destroyed by arsonist, Kirtland.

March   14   JS and others arrived at Far West.

Geographical Directory

This directory provides geographical descriptions of most of the places mentioned in this volume of *The Joseph Smith Papers*. It includes villages and towns, townships, counties and states, and waterways.

Each place is listed with a complete political location. Many entries also include information such as municipal history, population, and distinctive natural environments, as well as details more particular to the significance of the place within JS's documents dated between October 1835 and January 1838. Unless otherwise noted, all places were within the United States of America during this time period. Spellings of the time period have been used for proper nouns. In the state of New York, the terms *town* and *township* were used interchangeably during JS's lifetime; this geographical directory uses the term *township*. "LDS church" refers to the church established by JS in 1830 and later known as the Church of Jesus Christ of Latter-day Saints.

Map coordinates refer to the maps found on pages 550–557. Readers wishing to conduct further research may consult the documented Geographical Directory posted on the Joseph Smith Papers website, josephsmithpapers.org.

Akron, Portage County, Ohio. Map 1: B-4; Map 3: B-4, F-1. Post town located about thirty-five miles southeast of Cleveland. Laid out, by 1825. Population in 1830 about 350; in 1836 about 1,600; and in 1840 about 1,700. Located at intersection of Ohio Canal and Pennsylvania and Ohio Canal. First branch of LDS church established in town, by 1841.

Avon Township, Livingston County, New York. Map 1: B-5. Area settled, 1785. Formed as Hartford, Jan. 1789; name changed to Avon, 1808. Located in west-central New York on Genesee River, eighteen miles southwest of Rochester. Included village of Avon. Population in 1835 about 2,800. Population in 1840 about 3,000. JS presided over conference of elders at home of Alvah Beman in township, 17 Mar. 1834.

Bank of Geauga, Painesville Township, Geauga County (now in Lake County), Ohio. Not mapped. Organized, Oct. 1831, with capital stock of $100,000. Originally located on first floor of building at corner of Main and State streets in Painesville village. Made loan to JS, Dec. 1835. New building completed, 1836.

Boston, Suffolk County, Massachusetts. Map 1: B-6. Capital city located on eastern seaboard of Massachusetts at mouth of Charles River. Founded by English Puritans, 1630; received city charter, 1822. Population in 1820 about 43,000; in 1830 about 61,000; and in 1840 about 93,000. JS's ancestor Robert Smith emigrated from Europe through Boston, 1638. Samuel Smith and Orson Hyde commenced Mormon missionary work in Boston, June 1832; JS and Newel K. Whitney visited city, Oct. 1832. Brigham Young and Joseph Young visited Boston, Aug. 1836, and baptized seventeen people. Eight members of Quorum of the Twelve held conference in Boston, Sept. 1841. By 1843, fourteen branches of LDS church had been established in area. Brigham Young and others spoke in Boston about JS's death, 18 July 1844.

Caldwell County, Missouri. MAP 4: B-4. Located in northwest Missouri. Settled by whites, by 1831. Described as being "one-third timber and two-thirds prairie" in 1836. Created specifically for Latter-day Saints by Missouri state legislature, 29 Dec. 1836, in attempt to solve "Mormon problem." Major Mormon immigration followed. Population by summer 1838 about 5,000. Population by 1840 about 1,500. Included at least nineteen Mormon settlements. Expansion of Mormon settlement beyond county borders resulted in conflict and violence between Saints and other Missourians. Governor Lilburn W. Boggs ordered that Saints be exterminated or driven from state, 27 Oct. 1838. State militia arrested and imprisoned JS and other Mormon leaders and expelled remaining Saints from state. Almost all Caldwell Co. Saints evacuated, by spring 1839.

Chardon Township, Geauga County, Ohio. MAP 1: B-4; MAP 3: E-2. Located eight miles south of Lake Erie and immediately east of Kirtland Township. Settled by 1812. Included village of Chardon. Population of township in 1820 about 430; in 1830 about 880; and in 1840 about 1,100. Two of JS's sisters resided in township. JS participated in at least twenty legal proceedings in courthouse and preached frequently in branch of LDS church in township. Chardon Saints obtained permission to travel to Missouri, summer 1831. Latter-day Saints in Kirtland often traveled to Chardon for legal and other business.

Chester Township, Geauga County, Ohio. MAP 3: F-1. Surveyed 1796 and 1801. Area settled, 1801–1802. Initially called Wooster. Name changed to Chester and officially incorporated as township, 1816. Population in 1830 about 550. Population in 1840 about 960. JS purchased land for store in Chester, 1836–1837. Kirtland Camp of over 500 Saints traveled from Kirtland, Ohio, to Chester en route to join JS and Saints in northern Missouri, 6 July 1838.

Cincinnati, Hamilton County, Ohio. MAP 1: C-4; MAP 3: D-1. Area settled largely by emigrants from New England and New Jersey, by 1788. Village founded and surveyed adjacent to site of Fort Washington, 1789. First seat of legislature of Northwest Territory, 1790. Incorporated as city, 1819. Developed rapidly as shipping center after opening of Ohio and Erie Canal, 1832. Seventh most populous city in U.S., by 1833. Port of entry and county seat. Population in 1820 about 9,600; in 1830 about 25,000; and in 1840 about 46,000. Four missionaries to American Indians preached here en route from Kirtland to Missouri, by Jan. 1831. JS visited city, June 1831, meeting with Campbellite minister Walter Scott. JS revelations directed him, Sidney Rigdon, and Oliver Cowdery to preach in city while traveling from Independence, Missouri, to Kirtland, Ohio, Aug. 1831. Lyman Wight baptized nearly one hundred people and formed first branch of LDS church in city, 1833. Second branch formed, 1840, by John E. Page and Orson Hyde. Hyde departed city for Jerusalem to dedicate Palestine, at JS's direction, for return of Jews. Third edition of Book of Mormon printed in city, 1840. Brigham Young, Heber C. Kimball, and Lyman Wight held conference in city, 27 May 1844.

Clay County, Missouri. MAP 4: C-3. Settled ca. 1800. Organized from Ray Co., 1822. Original size diminished when land was taken to create several surrounding counties. Liberty designated county seat, 1822. Population in 1830 about 5,000; in 1836 about 8,500; and in 1840 about 8,300. Refuge for Latter-day Saints expelled from Jackson Co., 1833. LDS population in 1834 about 900. Citizens demanded Saints leave, summer 1836. Most Saints immigrated to newly formed Caldwell County, by 1838. During Mormon-Missouri conflict in Caldwell

County, militia from Clay County assembled to combat Mormons, but did not fight. JS imprisoned in jail at Liberty, winter 1838–1839.

Clinton County, Missouri. Map 4: B-3. Located in northwestern part of state. Adjacent counties include Ray and Clay. Organized 1833. Plattsburg designated county seat. Population in 1840 about 2,700. Contained some small Mormon settlements, 1830s. During Mormon-Missouri conflict, furnished several militia companies that assisted in expelling Saints from Far West, Missouri.

Commercial Bank of Lake Erie, Cleveland Township, Cuyahoga County, Ohio. Not mapped. First bank in Cleveland; chartered 1816. Failed, 1820, after Panic of 1819; revived 1832. During Panic of 1837, faltered but did not fail. Charter not renewed by state legislature, 1842. Bank closed and all assets distributed, by 1845. In Jan. 1837, loaned $1,200 to agents of Kirtland Safety Society, likely JS and Sidney Rigdon.

Connecticut Western Reserve. Not mapped. Also known as New Connecticut or Connecticut Reserve. Approximately three million acres in northeastern part of present-day Ohio. Claimed as part of Connecticut, 1786. Connecticut granted jurisdiction of reserve to U.S. government, 1800. Population in 1820 about 57,000. In 1829, included eight counties: Huron, Lorain, Medina, Cuyahoga, Geauga, Portage, Trumbull, and Ashtabula. Many Saints gathered in region, 1830s. JS lived within reserve's boundaries, 1831–1838, in Kirtland and Hiram, Ohio.

Daviess County, Missouri. Map 4: B-4. Area in northwest Missouri settled by European Americans, 1830. Sparsely inhabited until 1838. Created from Ray Co., Dec. 1836, in attempt to resolve conflicts related to Mormon settlement in that region. County is transected diagonally from northwest to southeast by Grand River, a principal tributary of Missouri River. Described as "equally divided between gently rolling prairie and fine timber lands." Small number of Mormons had settled in Daviess Co. by 1837. JS led expedition into county to survey possible future settlements for Latter-day Saints, May 1838. Significant Mormon settlements in Daviess Co. were Adam-ondi-Ahman, Marrowbone, Honey Creek, and Lick Fork. As Mormon population grew, so did antagonism of neighboring Missourians who feared Saints would soon dominate county government. On election day, candidate William Peniston denounced right of Saints to vote, and violence erupted on 6 Aug. 1838. JS and others soon arrived to help Saints. Vigilantes from neighboring counties joined Daviess Co. residents to harass and intimidate Saints. Anticipating attack, Saints made preemptive strike, plundering and burning property in Millport, Gallatin, and Grindstone Fork settlements known to harbor vigilantes. Responding to reports of Mormon depredations, Missouri governor Lilburn W. Boggs ordered state militia to area and issued new order to exterminate Saints or drive them from state, Oct. 1838. Ultimatum was given, essentially compelling all Saints to leave county, early Nov. 1838. Many moved to Caldwell Co., where they stayed until moving to Illinois and Iowa Territory, winter–spring 1839. Population of Daviess Co. in 1840 about 2,800. JS last traveled to Daviess Co., early Apr. 1839, while a prisoner of state.

Elders School, Kirtland Township, Geauga County (now in Lake County), Ohio. Not mapped. Initially held in lower floor of schoolhouse. Moved to third floor of House of the Lord, in room adjoining westernmost room where Hebrew School met, 18 Jan. 1836. See also "Schoolhouse, Kirtland" and "House of the Lord, Kirtland."

England. Map 1: D-6. Island nation consisting of southern portion of Great Britain and surrounding smaller islands. Bounded on north by Scotland and on west by Wales. Became province of Roman Empire, first century. Ruled by Romans, through 447. Ruled by Picts, Scots, and Saxons, through 860. Ruled by Danes, through 1066. Conquered by William of Normandy, in 1066, and subsequently ruled almost exclusively by successive line of kings and queens. Magna Carta provided citizens with foundation for political and personal liberty, 1215. First parliament convened, 1295. Capital city, London. Ruled by Queen Victoria, 1837–1901. Nation consisted of forty counties, 1843. Population in 1801 about 8,300,000; in 1831 about 13,000,000; and in 1841 about 15,000,000. JS appointed first Latter-day Saint missionaries to go to England, early June 1837; seven elders arrived in Liverpool, 19 July 1837. By Apr. 1838, about 1,500 people in England had joined LDS church. Latter-day Saint population in Apr. 1841 about 5,800.

Fairport (now Fairport Harbor), Painesville Township, Geauga County (now in Lake County), Ohio. Map 3: E-1. Situated on southern shore of Lake Erie; area originally called Grandon; settled 1803. Located twelve miles northeast of Kirtland. Harbor established at mouth of Grand River, by 1812. Harbor became significant port. Name officially changed to Fairport, 14 Mar. 1836. Port used by early LDS converts immigrating to Kirtland area, by May 1831, and by departing and returning missionaries.

Far West, Rockford Township (now in Mirabile Township), Caldwell County, Missouri. Map 1: C-2 Map 4: B-4. Originally called Shoal Creek. Located fifty-five miles northeast of Independence. Surveyed 1823; first settled by whites, 1831. Site purchased, 8 Aug. 1836, before Caldwell Co. was organized for Latter-day Saints in Missouri. William W. Phelps and John Whitmer held one square mile of land in trust for LDS church. Site described as "high rolling prairie" between Shoal and Goose creeks, and the homes as "very scattering, and small, being chiefly built of hewed logs." During Mormon period, population estimated at 3,000 to 5,000. JS moved to Far West, Mar. 1838. By 1838, town featured 150 houses, four dry-goods stores, three family groceries, six blacksmith shops, two hotels, a printing office (where *Elders' Journal* was printed), and at least two schoolhouses. Saints laid cornerstones for planned temple, 4 July 1838. Four days later, JS dictated revelation directing ordination of apostles and preaching by Quorum of the Twelve "over the great waters." Became church headquarters and center of Mormon activity in Missouri. JS dictated seven revelations in area. JS arrested with other church leaders just outside of Far West, late Oct.–early Nov. 1838, following Missouri governor Lilburn W. Boggs's executive order to exterminate Saints or drive them from state. Saints expelled from state into Iowa Territory and western Illinois.

Fox Islands, Hancock County (now Knox County), Maine. Map 1: A-6. Archipelago featuring two large islands about twelve miles east of central Maine in Penobscot Bay. English ship captain Martin Pring named islands after indigenous silver-gray foxes, 1603. Established as part of Massachusetts Bay Colony, by 1658. First permanent English settlement established on islands, ca. 1765. Town of Vinalhaven, named for Boston attorney John Vinal, established on both islands; incorporated 25 June 1789; population in 1830 about 1,800 and in 1840 about 2,000. Maine, including Fox Islands, granted statehood, 1820. Quarrying of high-quality granite began on south island, 1826. North island officially set off as separate town, 1846; name changed to North Haven, 1847. Thereafter,

Vinalhaven referred to south island only. First Latter-day Saint missionaries preached on islands, beginning 20 Aug. 1837. By winter 1837–1838, branches of LDS church established on both islands, with about 100 members.

Freedom Township, Cattaraugus County, New York. Map 1: B-5. Area settled, 1811. Township created, 1820. Population in 1835 and 1840 about 1,800. Included Freedom village, which had about fifteen dwellings in 1836. Branch of LDS church organized in township, 1834. Warren Cowdery appointed to preside in area. JS preached and recruited participants for Camp of Israel expedition, 1834. Members of Quorum of the Twelve preached here, 1835. Freedom branch had 70 members, 1835.

Geauga County, Ohio. Map 3: B-4. Located in northeastern Ohio, south of Lake Erie. Rivers in area include Grand, Chagrin, and Cuyahoga. Settled mostly by New Englanders, beginning 1798. Formed from Trumbull Co., 1 Mar. 1806. Chardon established as county seat, 1808. Population in 1830 about 16,000. Later formation of new counties, including Ashtabula, Cuyahoga, and Lake, considerably reduced original boundaries. Lake Co. formed from Geauga Co.'s seven northern townships, including Kirtland, 1840. JS moved to Geauga Co., Feb. 1831. See also "Kirtland Township."

House of the Lord, Kirtland Township, Geauga County (now in Lake County), Ohio. Map 5: D-2; Map 6: D-2. JS revelation, dated Jan. 1831, directed Latter-day Saints to migrate to Ohio, where they would "be endowed with power from on high." In Dec. 1832, JS revelation directed Saints to "establish . . . an house of God." JS revelation, dated 1 June 1833, chastened Saints for not building house. Cornerstone laid, 23 July 1833, and temple completed, Mar. 1836. Had three stories with large rooms for assemblies on first two floors and five rooms or offices on attic floor. Included variety of pulpits in tiers at either end of assembly rooms for various priesthood offices. Used for variety of purposes, both before and after dedication, including confirmations, ordinations, quorum organizations, anointings, Elders School, and Hebrew School. Temple dedicated, 27 Mar. 1836 and again 31 Mar. 1836. Long-anticipated solemn assembly held, 30 Mar. 1836. In temple, 3 Apr. 1836, JS and Oliver Cowdery reported receiving priesthood "keys," or authority, from Old Testament prophets Moses, Elias, and Elijah and reported seeing Jesus Christ.

Jackson County, Missouri. Map 4: D-3. Settled at Fort Osage, 1808. County created, 16 Feb. 1825; organized 1826. Named after U.S. president Andrew Jackson. Featured fertile lands along Missouri River and was Santa Fe Trail departure point, which attracted immigrants to area. Area of county reduced considerably in 1833 by creation of Van Buren and Bates counties from southern portion. Population in 1830 about 2,800; in 1836 about 4,500; and in 1840 about 7,600. JS appointed missionaries to proselytize among American Indians west of Independence, fall 1830. Saints began settling in county, July 1831. JS revelation, dated 20 July 1831, designated area near Independence as "city of Zion" for gathering of Saints and building of temple. Saints were instructed to buy land from temple site to western border of county. Saints began settling in Independence and Kaw Township. Mormon population by 1832 about 850. Mormon population by summer 1833 about 1,000. As increasing numbers of Saints entered Missouri, mob violence by earlier settlers erupted, July 1833. Saints expelled from county into Clay and other counties, Nov. 1833. Efforts to seek justice through courts were unsuccessful. JS led Camp of Israel expedition to western Missouri in failed effort to recover Mormon lands in Jackson Co., summer 1834.

Jefferson County, New York. NOT MAPPED. Created 1805. Population in 1830 about 48,000. Latter-day Saints proselytized in county, 1830s.

Kirtland Safety Society office, Kirtland Township, Geauga County (now in Lake County), Ohio. MAP 6: D-3. Also known as "banking house" and "Mormon Bank." Likely located south of and adjacent to House of the Lord on west side of Chillicothe Road. Housed offices of Kirtland Safety Society Anti-Banking Company. Institution failed, by late summer 1837, after failure to obtain state charter, negative publicity, and other problems.

Kirtland Township, Geauga County (now in Lake County), Ohio. MAP 1: B-4; MAP 3: B-4. Located ten miles south of Lake Erie. Settled by 1811. Organized by 1818. Population in 1830 about 55 Latter-day Saints and 1,000 others; in 1838 about 2,000 Saints and 1,200 others; in 1839 about 100 Saints and 1,500 others. Mormon missionaries visited township, early Nov. 1830; many residents joined LDS church. JS and New York Saints migrated to Kirtland, 1831. Organized as "stake of Zion," with presidency and high council, 17 Feb. 1834. House of the Lord built, 1833–1836. JS and other Saints participated in School of the Prophets as well as other schools devoted to wide variety of subjects, including Hebrew. Latter-day Saint press in Kirtland published newspapers, hymnal, second edition of Book of Mormon, and Doctrine and Covenants. While in township, JS obtained several ancient Egyptian mummies and papyrus scrolls; part of JS translation of some scrolls later published as Book of Abraham. JS also dictated at least forty-six revelations in township. JS appointed Heber C. Kimball to lead group of elders from Kirtland to serve first mission to England, 1837. Rapid immigration of Saints posed difficulty for both Saints and other residents. With increased demand for land in Kirtland, prices rose. Need for capital led to establishment of Kirtland Safety Society, but failure to obtain state charter, negative publicity, and other problems led to failure of financial institution, 1837. Under threats from dissidents and outside antagonists, JS and other church leaders fled township, early 1838. Many loyal Saints followed. Kirtland stake reorganized with 300 to 400 members, 1841. Acting on directive from JS, organized effort to leave Kirtland was again made in 1843, but many Saints remained through 1845. After death of JS and departure of most Saints, schismatic activity became prevalent in Kirtland.

Missouri. MAP 1: C-2; MAP 2: C-4. Area acquired by U.S. in Louisiana Purchase, 1803, and established as territory, 1812. Missouri Compromise, 1820, admitted Missouri as slave state, 1821. Population in 1830 about 140,000; in 1836 about 240,000; and in 1840 about 380,000. Mormon missionaries preached to American Indians just west of Missouri border, early 1831. JS revelation, dated 20 July 1831, designated Missouri as "land of promise" and location of "city of Zion." Saints began immigrating to Jackson Co., summer 1831. Many Missouri immigrants came from southern states while most Saints came from northeastern states. Regional and cultural differences, as well as religious and ideological differences, caused tension and eventual violence. Saints expelled from Jackson Co. into Clay and other counties, 1833. Clay Co. citizens demanded Saints leave county, 1836. Missouri state legislature consequently created Caldwell Co. specifically for Saints. JS moved to Far West in Caldwell Co., Mar. 1838. Saints' settlement expanded northward into Daviess Co. and eastward into Carroll Co., 1838. Conflict in these counties escalated quickly. Missouri governor Lilburn W. Boggs issued order to exterminate Saints or drive them from state, 27 Oct. 1838. JS and others taken prisoner by Missouri militia, 31 Oct. 1838, and incarcerated through winter in jail at Liberty while approximately 12,000 Saints evacuated eastward into Illinois. JS allowed to escape, Apr. 1839. Missouri officials continued attempts to extradite, arrest, or kidnap JS, 1841–1843.

N. K. Whitney & Co. white store, Kirtland Township, Geauga County (now in Lake County), Ohio. Map 5: C-3; Map 6: C-3. In Apr. 1826, Whitney purchased quarter-acre lot on northeast corner of Chardon and Chillicothe roads and built two-story, 1,500-square-foot white store. Mercantile store also functioned as Kirtland Mills post office. Whitney met JS at store, 4 Feb. 1831. Whitney and new partner A. Sidney Gilbert maintained relatively large inventory for northeastern Ohio. White store also helped supply Gilbert and Whitney's store in Independence, Missouri. JS revelations, 1831–1832, specified that store should also serve as bishop's storehouse for provisioning poor. In 1832, Whitney family began remodeling store to provide living space for JS and family, who lived there 12 Sept. 1832–ca. Feb. 1834. Upper room in southeast corner functioned as administrative and translation site. Upper room in northeast corner, built at JS's request, served as council room and location of School of the Prophets. In these rooms, JS dictated numerous revelations, including one on health code; gave preparatory instruction for missionaries; and worked on translation of Bible. Store ceased operation as N. K. Whitney & Co., 4 Aug. 1838.

New York. Map 1: B-5; Map 2: A-6. Located in northeast region of U.S. Area settled by Dutch traders, 1620s; later governed by Britain, 1664–1776. Admitted to U.S. as state, 1788. Population in 1810 about 1,000,000; in 1820 about 1,400,000; in 1830 about 1,900,000; and in 1840 about 2,400,000. New York City was major port of European trade and immigration. Canals, particularly Erie Canal (completed 1825), further escalated inland mercantilism. Joseph Sr. and Lucy Mack Smith family lived in Palmyra and Manchester areas, 1817–1830. Western New York known as "burned-over district" during JS's early life because of numerous religious revivals. JS married Emma Hale in South Bainbridge (now Afton), 1827. Book of Mormon published in Palmyra, 1830. LDS church organized in Fayette, 1830. In 1830, three main branches of church located in townships of Fayette, Manchester, and Colesville. JS and most Latter-day Saint residents emigrated to Ohio, 1831. JS traveled through New York, 1832, 1833, 1834, 1836, and 1837. JS dictated dozens of revelations in New York. Several Mormon congregations established in New York, 1830s and 1840s.

Ohio. Map 1: B-4; Map 2: B-5; Map 3. French explored area, 1669. British took possession following French and Indian War, 1763. Ceded to U.S., 1783. First permanent white settlement established, 1788. Northeastern portion maintained as part of Connecticut, 1786, and called Connecticut Western Reserve. Connecticut granted jurisdiction of Western Reserve to U.S. Government, 1800. All of Ohio area partitioned from Northwest Territory and admitted to U.S. as state, 1803. State bordered by Lake Erie on north and Ohio River on south. Population in 1820 about 580,000; in 1830 about 940,000; and in 1840 about 1,500,000. Mormon missionaries preached in northeastern Ohio, Oct. 1830. Reformed Baptist preacher Sidney Rigdon and many of his congregants in state joined LDS church, late 1830. JS revelation, dated 30 Dec. 1830, directed church members in New York to migrate to Ohio. JS lived in Kirtland and Hiram, 1831–1838. JS dictated at least sixty-five revelations in state. JS and most loyal Ohio Saints migrated to Missouri, 1838. However, some Saints remained, and Ohio became location of schismatic activity after death of JS.

Onondaga County, New York. NOT MAPPED. Located in central New York. Formed from part of Herkimer Co., 1794. Syracuse established as county seat, ca. 1829. Population in 1830 about 59,000. Population in 1840 about 68,000.

Palmyra, Palmyra Township, Wayne County, New York. MAP 1: B-5. Known as Swift's Landing and Tolland before being renamed Palmyra, 1796. Incorporated, Mar. 1827, two years after completion of adjacent Erie Canal. Population in 1820 about 3,700. Joseph Sr. and Lucy Mack Smith family lived in village briefly, beginning 1817. First edition of Book of Mormon printed at E. B. Grandin printing office in village, 1829–1830.

Portage County, Ohio. MAP 3: B-4. Located in northeastern Ohio. Settled by 1799. Established June 1807. Bordered by Geauga Co. on north. Pennsylvania and Ohio Canal ran through county; completed 1825. Population in 1830 about 19,000. Population in 1840 about 23,000. Included Portage and Hiram townships, where JS and family lived, 1831–1832. Also included Hudson (now in Summit Co.), location of Western Reserve College, where Joshua Seixas taught. About one hundred Saints left Portage Co. for Jackson Co., Missouri, 2 May 1832.

Printing office, Kirtland Township, Geauga County (now in Lake County), Ohio. MAP 5: D-2; MAP 6: D-2. Following destruction of church printing office in Independence, Missouri, July 1833, JS and other church leaders determined to set up new printing office in Kirtland under firm name F. G. Williams & Co. Oliver Cowdery purchased new printing press in New York, Oct. 1833, and Kirtland printing office was opened and dedicated in John Johnson inn, Dec. 1833. JS revelation, dated 23 Apr. 1834, gave Williams and Cowdery joint stewardship of office. Publication of Missouri newspaper *The Evening and the Morning Star* soon resumed. In Dec. 1834, printing office was moved to second story of newly built schoolhouse, immediately west of temple lot. Press later launched new periodical, *Latter Day Saints' Messenger and Advocate* (Oct. 1834–Sept. 1837), followed by *Elders' Journal* (Oct.–Nov. 1837). Also published local political paper *Northern Times* (Feb. 1835–ca. Feb. 1836), first LDS church hymnal, first edition of Doctrine and Covenants (1835), and second edition of Book of Mormon (1837). Printing office destroyed when schoolhouse was torched by arsonist, 16 Jan. 1838.

Ray County, Missouri. MAP 4: C-4. Located in northwestern Missouri. Area settled, 1815. Created from Howard Co., 1820. Initially included all state land north of Missouri River and west of Grand River. Population in 1830 about 2,700; in 1836 about 6,600; and in 1840 about 6,600. Latter-day Saints who were driven from homes in Jackson Co., Missouri, 1833, moved northward across Missouri River and took refuge in Ray and other counties. Camp of Israel passed through Ray Co., June 1834. Missouri legislature created Caldwell and Daviess counties from Ray Co., 29 Dec. 1836. In attempt to rescue LDS prisoners, Caldwell Co. militia contended with Ray Co. militia at Crooked River in unorganized territory attached to Ray Co., 25 Oct. 1838. JS and about sixty other LDS men were incarcerated in Richmond, Ray Co., jails to await hearings on charges related to Mormon-Missouri conflict, Nov. 1838.

Saco, York County, Maine. MAP 1: A-6. Originally part of Massachusetts; land grant established by Plymouth Company, 1630. Settled 1631. Organized and named Saco, 1653. Boundary surveyed, 1659. Incorporated as town and named Pepperellborough, 1762. Renamed

Saco by Massachusetts state legislature, 1805. Became part of Maine upon state's formation, 1820. Population in 1820 about 2,500; in 1830 about 3,200; and in 1840 about 4,400. First LDS missionaries, Orson Hyde and Samuel Smith, preached in town, Sept.–Nov. 1832. First convert baptized in Saco, 31 Oct. 1832. Branch of LDS church established in town, 1832. Wilford Woodruff and Jonathan H. Hale preached in town, summer 1837, en route to Fox Islands.

Salem, Essex County, Massachusetts. Map 1: B-6. Port city located northeast of Boston. Population in 1830 about 14,000. Population in 1840 about 15,000. JS visited city as a young boy while recovering from leg surgery to remove diseased bone. JS, Hyrum Smith, Oliver Cowdery, and Sidney Rigdon visited city, Aug. 1836. JS dictated revelation in city, 6 Aug. 1836.

Schoolhouse, Kirtland Township, Geauga County (now in Lake County), Ohio. Map 5: D-2; Map 6: D-2. Two-story structure measuring thirty by thirty-eight feet, built during fall and winter of 1834. Located immediately west of temple lot on Whitney Street (now Maple Street) in Kirtland. School of the Elders met here from winter 1834–1835 to Jan. 1836. Ground floor was used as schoolroom and meetinghouse prior to completion of temple. JS frequently preached here. First members of Quorum of the Twelve were appointed and ordained on ground floor of schoolhouse, Feb. 1835. Second floor housed printing office and office for church presidency. Third-floor attic or loft was also used for meetings (sometimes called "council room") and was site of first administration of ritual washings and anointings prior to dedication of temple. Building seized and sold at public auction, 15 Jan. 1838, in order to pay fine charged to JS and Sidney Rigdon in lawsuit encouraged by Grandison Newell. Destroyed by fire during night following auction. Disaffected members of LDS church accused Saints of burning building, while many Saints felt that auction would not legally stand and that dissenters had burned building to prevent church from recovering it. LDS member Benjamin F. Johnson later recounted that his brother-in-law Lyman Sherman had burned building in order to prevent enemies of church from gaining access to printing press. See also "Printing office, Kirtland."

Seneca County, New York. Not mapped. Created from Cayuga Co., Mar. 1804. Most of western and eastern boundaries formed by Seneca and Cayuga lakes, respectively. Area first settled at Seneca Falls, 1787. Population in 1830 about 21,000. Population in 1840 about 25,000. Many people in area were receptive to JS and were baptized into LDS church. Fayette Township was significant Mormon settlement where many key events in early Mormon history occurred.

Shoal Creek, Missouri. Map 4: B-5. Stream that flows eastward for about forty-five miles from east central Clinton Co. through Caldwell Co. to confluence with Grand River in central Livingston Co. Thousands of Saints moved from Clay Co. to sites along Shoal Creek in Caldwell Co., beginning summer 1836. Stream powered numerous mills within county, including those at Whitney's Mill, Far West, and Hawn's Mill settlements. JS and family arrived in area from Ohio, 14 Mar. 1838. JS reported attempt on his life while watering horse at Shoal Creek.

Terre Haute, Harrison Township, Vigo County, Indiana. Map 1: C-3. Situated high on east bank of Wabash River. French settlement, 1720–1763; name is French for "high land." Founded as Fort Harrison, 1811. Laid out and incorporated, 1816. Seat of Vigo Co. Population in 1830 about 600; in 1837 about 1,100; and in 1840 about 2,000. JS and Sidney Rigdon held meetings in town en route to Far West, Missouri, Nov. 1837. JS's brother Don Carlos wrote him from near Terre Haute, 6 July 1838, citing ongoing difficulties of Smith family's relocation from Kirtland, Ohio, to Caldwell Co., Missouri.

Toronto, York County (now Metropolitan Toronto, Ontario), Upper Canada. MAP 1: B-4. Situated on northwest shore of Lake Ontario. Capital of Upper Canada. Founded as York, 1794. Incorporated as city and changed name to Toronto, 1834. Population in 1830 about 2,900. Population in 1842 about 15,000. In 1836, Parley P. Pratt served mission to city and converted several people, including John Taylor. JS visited city, Aug. 1837.

Upper Canada. MAP 1: A-4; MAP 2: A-5; MAP 3: A-2. British colony of Canada divided into Upper Canada and Lower Canada, 1791; reunited 1841. Upper Canada's boundaries corresponded roughly to portion of present-day Ontario south of Hudson Bay watershed. Population in 1840 about 430,000. Immigrants mainly from England, Scotland, and U.S. Principally Protestant. JS proselytized in Upper Canada, Oct. 1833.

Wayne County, New York. NOT MAPPED. First permanent white settlement established, Mar. 1789. Created from Ontario and Seneca counties, 11 Apr. 1823. Bounded on north by Lake Ontario. County seat, Lyons. Erie Canal completed through southern portion of county, near Palmyra, by 1825. Population in 1820 about 20,000. Population in 1830 about 34,000. Locations of important activities and events in early Mormon history in county include townships of Palmyra, Arcadia, and Lyons.

Willoughby, Willoughby Township, Cuyahoga (now in Lake) County, Ohio. MAP 3: E-1. Village located in northeastern Ohio at mouth of Chagrin River, about three miles northwest of Kirtland, Ohio, and four miles from Lake Erie. Area settled, 1797. Township formerly named Charlton, then Chagrin. Became home of Willoughby Medical College, 1834, after which both village and township were renamed Willoughby. Became part of Lake Co., Mar. 1840. Incorporated as village, 1853. Population in 1835 about 750. Population in 1840 about 1,900. Described in 1843 as having two churches, nine stores, one mill, and two tanneries, in addition to college. JS and wife Emma purchased goods in Willoughby, 12 Oct. 1835, and visited Shadrach Roundy near there, later that month. JS, accompanied by other church officers, attended lecture at Willoughby College, 2 Nov. 1835.

Wisconsin Territory. MAP 1: B-2; MAP 2: A-4. Area settled by French, before 1700. Became part of U.S. by Treaty of Paris, 1783. Territory officially formed, 1836, with Belmont established as capital. Capital moved to present-day Burlington, Iowa, 1837. Territory initially included all or part of present-day states of Wisconsin, Minnesota, Iowa, North Dakota, and South Dakota. Reduced to areas east of Mississippi River by creation of Iowa Territory, and capital moved to Madison, 1838. Admitted to U.S. as state, 1848. Population in 1838 about 18,000. Population in 1840 about 31,000. Population in 1847 about 210,000. Mormons resided in Wisconsin, by 1835. JS letters, dated 1836, mentioned possible exploration of and migration to territory. By 1838, branch of LDS church established in Burlington area, with around 100 members. Twelve Apostles met in Nauvoo, 29 May 1843, and sent missionaries to Wisconsin. Lumbering operation near Black River provided timber for construction of Nauvoo House and Nauvoo temple, 1841–1845. Seven LDS branches functioned in territory, 1844. Following JS's death, many Wisconsin members joined westward migration of Saints. Lyman Wight led 150 Saints from Wisconsin branches to settle in Republic of Texas, fall 1845.

Zion. NOT MAPPED. JS revelation, dated 20 July 1831, designated Missouri as "land of promise" for gathering of Saints and place for "city of Zion," with Independence area as "center place" of Zion. Latter-day Saint settlements elsewhere, such as in Kirtland, Ohio, became known as "stakes" of Zion. About 1,200 Saints gathered in Jackson Co., but were expelled by other residents, 1833. After Saints settled in other counties, such as Clay and Caldwell, JS and church members continued to refer to main body of Saints in Missouri as Zion but still considered Independence to be center place and planned to return. JS dictated several revelations about "redeeming Zion" and recovering their lands in Jackson Co. In 1840, after Saints had left Missouri and settled in Nauvoo, Illinois, JS declared that Zion referred to all of North and South America and anywhere Saints gathered.

Maps

The following maps show nearly every town and city mentioned in this volume of *The Joseph Smith Papers,* along with other significant features and boundaries, as they existed during the period indicated on each map.

To locate a particular place on these maps, consult the Geographical Directory in this volume. The directory provides grid coordinates and other information for each place.

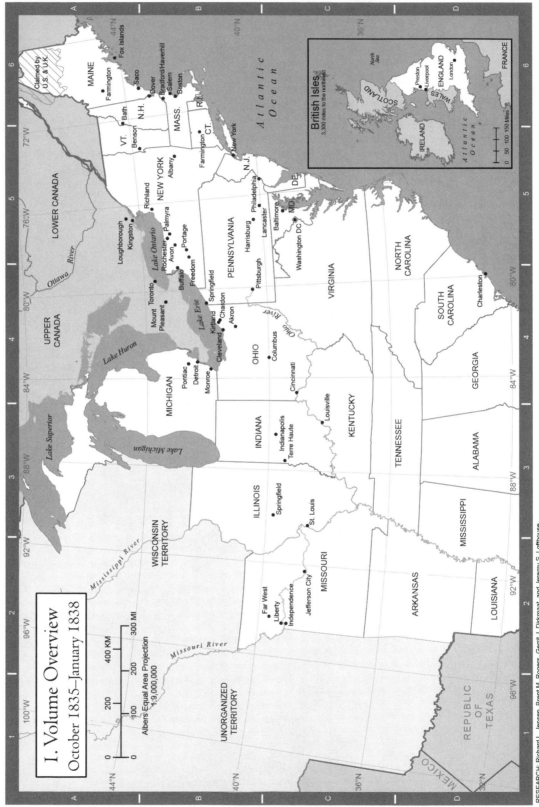

I. Volume Overview
October 1835–January 1838

Albers Equal Area Projection
1:9,000,000

British Isles
3,300 miles to the northeast

RESEARCH: Richard L. Jensen, Brent M. Rogers, Gerrit J. Dirkmaat, and Jeremy S. Lofthouse
CARTOGRAPHY: Blake A. Baker

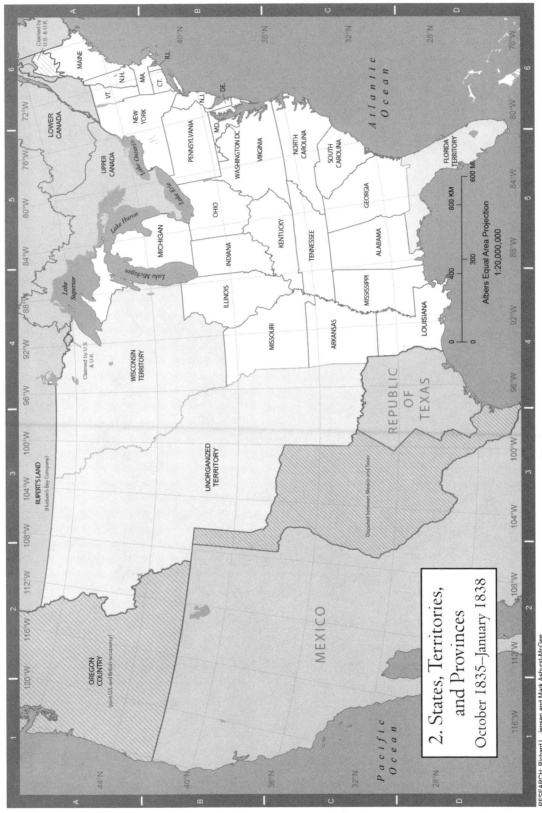

2. States, Territories, and Provinces
October 1835–January 1838

Albers Equal Area Projection
1:20,000,000

RESEARCH: Richard L. Jensen and Mark Ashurst-McGee
CARTOGRAPHY: Blake A. Baker

552

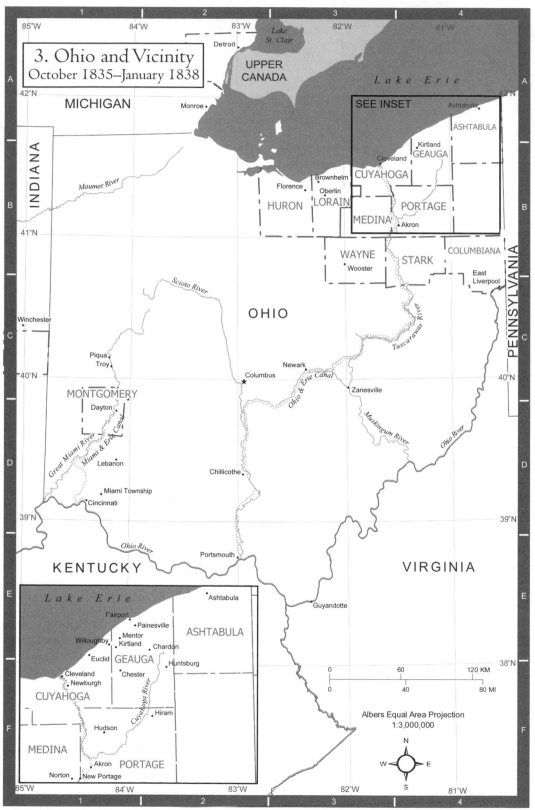

3. Ohio and Vicinity
October 1835–January 1838

MICHIGAN

INDIANA

Maumee River

Detroit

Lake
St. Clair

**UPPER
CANADA**

Lake Erie

Monroe

SEE INSET

Ashtabula

ASHTABULA

Kirtland
GEAUGA

Cleveland

CUYAHOGA

Florence

Brownhelm

Oberlin

HURON

LORAIN

MEDINA

PORTAGE

Akron

WAYNE

STARK

COLUMBIANA

Wooster

East
Liverpool

Scioto River

OHIO

Tuscarawas River

Winchester

Piqua
Troy

Newark

PENNSYLVANIA

Columbus

Ohio & Erie Canal

Zanesville

MONTGOMERY

Dayton

Muskingum River

Great Miami River

Miami & Erie Canal

Lebanon

Chillicothe

Miami Township

Ohio River

Cincinnati

KENTUCKY

Ohio River

Portsmouth

Guyandotte

VIRGINIA

Lake Erie

Ashtabula

Fairport

Painesville

Willoughby

Mentor
Kirtland

Chardon

ASHTABULA

Euclid

GEAUGA

Huntsburg

Cleveland

Chester

Newburgh

Cuyahoga River

CUYAHOGA

Hiram

Hudson

MEDINA

Akron

PORTAGE

Norton

New Portage

0   60   120 KM
0   40   80 MI

Albers Equal Area Projection
1:3,000,000

N
W   E
S

RESEARCH: Matthew C. Godfrey, Mark Ashurst-McGee, Brent M. Rogers, Gerrit J. Dirkmaat, and Jeremy S. Lofthouse
CARTOGRAPHY: Blake A. Baker and Heidi Springsteed

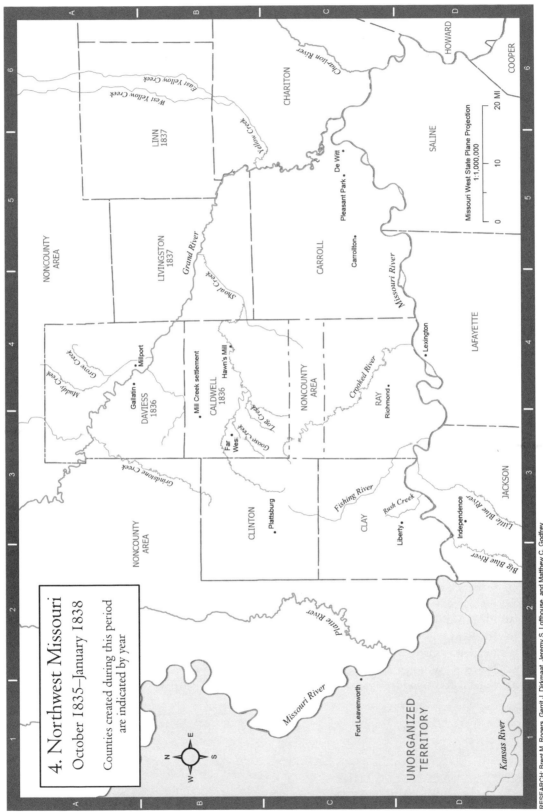

4. Northwest Missouri
October 1835–January 1838

Counties created during this period
are indicated by year

RESEARCH: Brent M. Rogers, Gerrit J. Dirkmaat, Jeremy S. Lofthouse, and Matthew C. Godfrey
CARTOGRAPHY: Blake A. Baker

Portion of Kirtland Township, Ohio
31 December 1835

Selected Structures

A. Loud-Lyman gristmill
B. Loud-Lyman sawmill
C. Milldam
D. Newel K. and Elizabeth Ann Whitney house
E. N. K. Whitney & Co. red store
F. N. K. Whitney & Co. white store
G. Tannery
H. Bark mill
I. Tannery vats
J. John Johnson inn
K. Distillery
L. Sawmill
M. Ashery
N. Schoolhouse on the flats
O. Joseph Smith Jr. and Emma Smith house
P. Joseph Smith Sr. and Lucy Mack Smith house
Q. Methodist Episcopal church
R. John Johnson Sr. and Elsa Johnson house
S. Schoolhouse/printing office
T. House of the Lord (temple)
U. Sidney and Phoebe Rigdon house

Selected Properties and Owners

1. N. K. Whitney & Co.
2. N. K. Whitney & Co.
3. N. K. Whitney & Co.
4. Austin Loud and Azariah Lyman
5. Austin Loud and Azariah Lyman
6. Austin Loud
7. Frederick G. Williams
8. Frederick G. Williams
9. Elijah Smith
10. Ira Bond
11. Azariah Lyman
12. Newel K. Whitney
13. Martha Raymond Parrish
14. Newel K. Whitney
15. Sidney Rigdon
16. Samuel Smith
17. Elijah Smith
18. N. K. Whitney & Co.
19. N. K. Whitney & Co.
20. Newel K. Whitney
21. Ira Bond
22. Leonard Rich
23. Joseph Smith Jr.
24. Newel K. Whitney
25. Oliver Cowdery
26. Newel K. Whitney
27. Oliver Cowdery
28. Joseph Smith Jr.
29. Sidney Rigdon
30. Edmund Bosley
31. Edmund Bosley
32. Joseph Smith Jr.
33. Isaac Hill

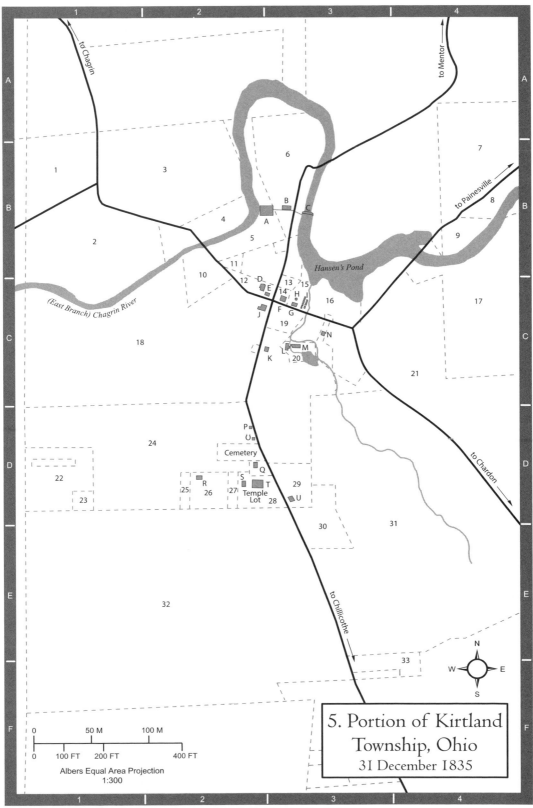

1

2

3

4

to Chagrin

to Mentor

A

A

7

1

3

6

to Painesville

8

B

B

4

A B C

5

9

11

Hansen's Pond

10

12 D

E 13 15

16

17

(East Branch) Chagrin River

14 H

F G I

J

19

N

C

C

18

L M

K

20

21

P

U

24

Cemetery

D

D

Q

22

S

R

T

29

to Chardon

23

25 26 27

Temple

U

Lot 28

30

31

32

E

E

to Chillicothe

N

W E

33

S

0   50 M   100 M

F

F

0   100 FT   200 FT   400 FT

5. Portion of Kirtland
Township, Ohio
31 December 1835

Albers Equal Area Projection
1:300

1

2

3

4

RESEARCH: Mark Staker, Lyle Briggs, Lissa Thompson, Jeremy S. Lofthouse, Gerrit J. Dirkmaat, and Brent M. Rogers
CARTOGRAPHY: Brice Lucas and Blake A. Baker

Kirtland Township with Plots
January 1838

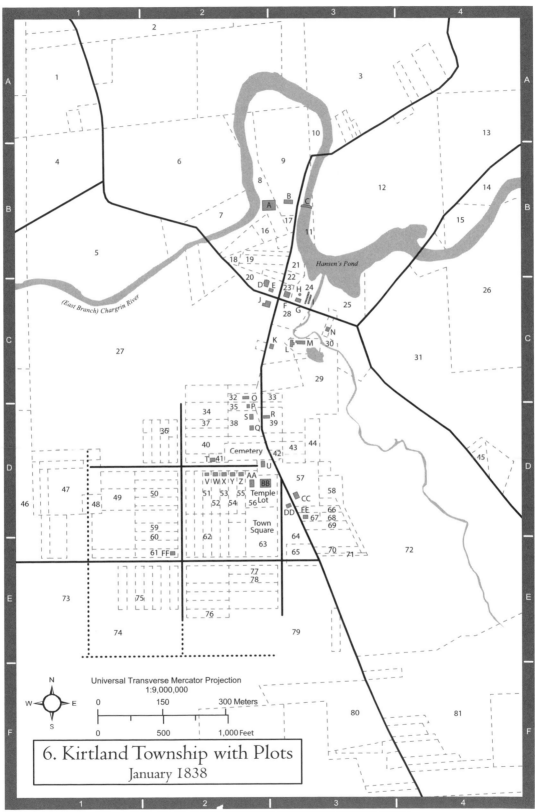

6. Kirtland Township with Plots
January 1838

Universal Transverse Mercator Projection
1:9,000,000

0   150   300 Meters

0   500   1,000 Feet

(East Branch) Chargrin River

Hansen's Pond

Cemetery

Temple Lot

Town Square

RESEARCH: Mark L. Staker, Matthew C. Godfrey, Mark Ashurst-McGee, Brent M. Rogers, Gerrit J. Dirkmaat, and Jeremy S. Lofthouse
CARTOGRAPHY: Blake A. Baker

GRANDPARENTS	PARENTS, AUNTS, AND UNCLES	BROTHERS AND SISTERS	CHILDREN
	Jesse Smith (1768–1853) *Hannah Peabody*	unnamed son (ca. 1796–ca. 1796)	**unnamed son** (1828–1828)
	Priscilla Smith (1769–1860) *John Curtis Waller*	Alvin Smith (1798–1823) *unmarried*	**unnamed daughter** (1831–1831)
	Joseph Smith Sr. (1771–1840) *Lucy Mack*	Hyrum Smith (1800–1844) *Jerusha Barden* *Mary Fielding*	**unnamed son** (1831–1831)
	Asahel Smith (1773–1848) *Elizabeth Schellenger*	Sophronia Smith (1803–1876) *Calvin W. Stoddard* *William McCleary*	**Julia M. Smith** (adopted 1831) (1831–1880) *Elisha Dixon* *John Jackson Middleton*
	Mary Smith (1775–ca. 1844) *Isaac Pierce*	**Joseph Smith Jr.** (1805–1844) *Emma Hale*	**Joseph Murdock Smith** (adopted 1831) (1831–1832)
Asael Smith (1743/4–1830)	Samuel Smith (1777–1830) *Frances or Fanny Wilcox*	Samuel Harrison Smith (1808–1844) *Mary Bailey* *Levira Clark*	**Joseph Smith III** (1832–1914) *Emmeline Griswold* *Bertha Madison* *Ada Rachel Clark*
Mary Duty (1743–1836)	Silas Smith (1779–1839) *Ruth Stevens* *Mary Aikens*	Ephraim Smith (1810–1810)	**Frederick Granger Williams Smith** (1836–1862) *Anna Marie Jones*
	John Smith (1781–1854) *Clarissa Lyman*	William B. Smith (1811–1893) *Caroline Amanda Grant* *Mary Jane Rollins* *Roxey Ann Grant* *Eliza Elsie Sanborn* *Rosanna Jewitt Surprise*	**Alexander Hale Smith** (1838–1909) *Elizabeth Agnes Kendall*
	Susanna Smith (1783–1849) *unmarried*	Katharine Smith (1813–1900) *Wilkins Jenkins Salisbury* *Joseph Younger*	**Don Carlos Smith** (1840–1841)
	Stephen Smith (1785–1802) *unmarried*	Don Carlos Smith (1816–1841) *Agnes Moulton Coolbrith*	**unnamed son** (1842–1842)
	Sarah Smith (1789–1824) *Joseph Sanford*	Lucy Smith (1821–1882) *Arthur Millikin*	**David Hyrum Smith** (1844–1904) *Clara Charlotte Hartshorn*
	Jason Mack (ca. 1760–1841) *unknown wife*		
	Lovisa Mack (ca. 1761–1794) *Joseph Tuttle*		
	Lovina Mack (ca. 1762–ca. 1794) *unmarried?*		
Solomon Mack Sr. (1732–1820)	Lydia Mack (ca. 1763–1826) *Samuel Bill*		
Lydia Gates (1732–ca. 1818)	Stephen Mack (1766–1826) *Temperance Bond*		
	Daniel Gates Mack (ca. 1770–by 1841) *Sally Ball*		
	Solomon Mack Jr. (1773–1851) *Esther Hayward* *Hulda Hayward Whipple* *Betsy Way Alexander*		
	Lucy Mack (1775–1856) *Joseph Smith Sr.*		

Pedigree Chart

The names of persons in JS's direct line are rendered in boldface type. Names of other genetic family members are rendered in roman type. Names of spouses are rendered in italic type. The plural wives of JS and his brothers Hyrum and William Smith are not listed here. A list of JS's plural wives will appear on the Joseph Smith Papers website. Further information about many of the people listed here can be found in the Biographical Directory. Readers wishing to conduct further research may consult the documented pedigree chart posted on the Joseph Smith Papers website.

Biographical Directory

This register contains brief biographical sketches for most of the persons mentioned in this volume. These persons include church leaders, members of JS's family, people JS encountered on his travels, his acquaintances, and other figures from the earliest decades of the Latter-day Saint movement. Plural wives of JS and others are not listed here. A list of JS's plural wives will appear on the Joseph Smith Papers website.

The biographical entries identify persons by complete name (correctly spelled), birth and death dates, and additional information, such as parentage and birth place, migrations and places of residence, dates of marriage and names of spouses, occupation, denominational affiliation, religious and civic positions, and place of death. Occupations listed in an entry may not be comprehensive. Key figures with major significance to JS's activities receive the fullest biographical sketches. Others receive much briefer descriptions, often with less data than is available. Because unverified and sometimes incorrect data has been recirculated for decades, professional genealogists on the staff of the Joseph Smith Papers Project have utilized original sources whenever possible.

Entries for women are generally listed under their final married names, with appropriate cross-references under maiden names or earlier married names. Partial names in the text are not included in this directory when research could not determine the full name. In some cases, a footnote in the text provides possible identifications. The index found in this volume can often lead the reader to helpful information.

Locations that are noted include city or town, county, and state, when identified, for the first mention of a locale in each sketch. The counties and states of a handful of well-known cities have been omitted. "LDS church" refers to the church established by JS in 1830 and later known as the Church of Jesus Christ of Latter-day Saints. "RLDS church" refers to the church known originally as the New Organization and subsequently as the Reorganized Church of Jesus Christ of Latter Day Saints (1860–2001) and the Community of Christ (2001 to the present).

Even the fullest entries in this directory provide, of necessity, only a bare skeleton of a person's life. Readers wishing to conduct further research may consult the documented biographical directory posted on the Joseph Smith Papers website, josephsmithpapers.org.

Aiken, David Dickey (20 Sept. 1794–12 Dec. 1861), county clerk, associate judge, merchant. Born in New York. Baptized into Episcopalian church, 9 Aug. 1818, in New York. Married Laura Loomis. Moved to Brown, Stark Co., Ohio, by 1820; to Painesville, Geauga Co., Ohio; and to Chardon, Geauga Co., 1828. Served as county clerk, 1828–1842, in Geauga Co. Participated in legal case involving JS, Mar.–June 1837. Elected associate judge of Geauga Co. Court of Common Pleas, 1846. Moved back to Painesville, by 1850, where he died.

Angell, Truman Osborn (5 June 1810–16 Oct. 1887), carpenter, joiner, architect, farmer. Born at North Providence, Providence Co., Rhode Island. Son of James W. Angell and Phebe Morton. Joined Freewill Baptist Church, ca. 1829. Married Polly Johnson of Genesee Co., New York, 7 Oct. 1832. Baptized into LDS church, Jan. 1833, and ordained an elder five weeks later. Served mission with Joseph Holbrook to New York and Massachusetts, spring 1833. Moved to Lima, Livingston Co., New York, July 1833. Moved to Kirtland, Geauga Co., Ohio, fall 1835. Labored on Kirtland temple. Appointed member of Second Quorum of the Seventy, 1836. Stockholder in Kirtland Safety Society. Moved to Missouri, spring 1838; to Quincy, Adams Co., Illinois, winter 1838–1839; and to Nauvoo, Hancock Co., Illinois, 1841. Directed joiner work of Nauvoo temple under architect William Weeks. Migrated with family to Salt Lake Valley, 1848. Served as architect for LDS church, ca. 1848–1861. Began work on Salt Lake temple, 1853. Served mission to Europe to study architecture and preach, 1856. Again appointed church architect, 1867. Served as president of Fourteenth Quorum of the Seventy in Salt Lake City. Ordained a high priest and a patriarch, Feb. 1884. Died at Salt Lake City.

Babbitt, Almon Whiting (Oct. 1812–Sept. 1856), postmaster, editor, attorney. Born at Cheshire, Berkshire Co., Massachusetts. Son of Ira Babbitt and Nancy Crosier. Baptized into LDS church, ca. 1830. Located in Amherst, Lorain Co., Ohio, July 1831. Served mission to New York, fall 1831. Served mission to Pomfret, Chautauque Co., New York, fall 1833. Married Julia Ann Johnson, 23 Nov. 1833, in Kirtland, Geauga Co., Ohio. Participated in Camp of Israel expedition to Missouri, 1834. Appointed member of First Quorum of the Seventy, Feb. 1835. Disfellowshipped, Dec. 1835. Restored to fellowship, Jan. 1836. Served mission to Upper Canada, 1837–1838. Led company of Canadian Latter-day Saints to Missouri, 1838. Appointed to gather reports and publications circulated against LDS church, 4 May 1839, at Quincy, Adams Co., Illinois. Appointed president of Kirtland stake, 3 Oct. 1840, at Nauvoo, Hancock Co., Illinois. Disfellowshipped, 1840, 1841. Moved to Ramus (later Webster), Hancock Co. Restored to fellowship and appointed presiding elder of Ramus, 1843. Appointed commander of Ramus militia. Admitted to Council of Fifty, 26 Mar. 1844. Appointed by Council of Fifty to serve mission to France, May 1844; mission never fulfilled. Elected to represent Hancock Co. in Illinois legislature, Dec. 1844. Appointed one of five trustees responsible for financial and temporal affairs in Nauvoo, 1846. Appointed postmaster of Nauvoo, 1846. Participated in battle at Nauvoo and signed surrender treaty, Sept. 1846. Migrated to Salt Lake Valley, 1849. Elected delegate to U.S. Congress for provisional state of Deseret, 5 July 1849. Disfellowshipped, 1849, 1851. Appointed secretary of Utah Territory, 1852. Excommunicated, May 1854. Was killed at Ash Hollow, Garden Co., Nebraska Territory.

Beebe, Calvin (1 July 1800–17 July 1861), farmer, merchant, postmaster. Born in Paris, Oneida Co., New York. Son of Isaac Beebe and Olive Soule. Moved to Chardon, Geauga Co., Ohio, by 1820. Married Submit Rockwell Starr, 19 Nov. 1823. Baptized into LDS church. Ordained an elder, by June 1831. Moved to Jackson Co., Missouri, Sept. 1831. Served mission to Illinois, Indiana, Michigan Territory, and Ohio, 1832. Ordained a high priest by Oliver Cowdery, 5 Oct. 1832, in Independence, Jackson Co. Clerk of church conference held at Jackson Co., 26 Sept. 1833. Moved near Fishing River, Clay Co., Missouri, 1833. Member of Missouri high council, 1834. Appointed to serve mission to Kirtland, Geauga Co., Ohio, 1834. Moved to what became Caldwell Co., Missouri, ca. 1836; to Daviess Co., Missouri; to Clinton Co., Missouri, 1838; and to Montrose, Lee Co., Iowa

Territory, Mar. 1839. Excommunicated, 1841. Moved to Pottawattamie Co., Iowa, by 1850. Acting justice of the peace, 1857, at Mills Co., Iowa. Presided over branch of Alpheus Cutler's Church of Jesus Christ, 1859, at Farm Creek (later in Henderson), Mills Co. Appointed to high council of RLDS church, 6 Apr. 1860, in Amboy, Lee Co., Illinois. Moved to Mud Creek (later Anderson Township), Mills Co., by 1860. Moved to Farm Creek, by 1861.

Beman (Beaman), Alvah (22 May 1775–15 Nov. 1837), farmer. Born at New Marlboro, Berkshire Co., Massachusetts. Son of Reuben Beman and Mariam. Married Sarah (Sally) Burt, 18 Aug. 1796. Moved to what became Livonia, Ontario Co., New York, 1799. Moved to Avon, Livingston Co., New York, 1831. Among first to be acquainted with JS and his work at Palmyra, Wayne Co., New York. Assisted JS in concealing Book of Mormon plates from Palmyra mob and in fashioning box to contain plates. Baptized into LDS church. Moved to Kirtland, Geauga Co., Ohio, after Oct. 1835. Appointed to preside over elders quorum in Kirtland, 15 Jan. 1836. Died at Kirtland.

Billings, Titus (24 Mar. 1793–6 Feb. 1866), stonemason, carpenter, musician. Born in Greenfield, Hampshire Co., Massachusetts. Son of Ebenezer Billings and Esther Joyce. Moved to Mentor, Geauga Co., Ohio, by 1817. Married Diantha Morley, 16 Feb. 1817, in Geauga Co. Moved to Kirtland, Geauga Co., by 1820. Moved back to Mentor, 1827. Affiliated with Campbellite faith. Baptized into LDS church, 15 Nov. 1830, in Kirtland. Ordained a deacon, by Oct. 1831. Moved to Jackson Co., Missouri, 1832. Ordained an elder by Thomas B. Marsh, 10 Mar. 1832, in Jackson Co. Moved to Clay Co., Missouri, 1833. Moved back to Kirtland, ca. 1835. Labored on Kirtland temple. Moved to Caldwell Co., Missouri, by 1837. Ordained a high priest by Edward Partridge and Isaac Morley, 1 Aug. 1837, in Caldwell Co. Served as counselor to Bishop Edward Partridge, 1837–1840, in Missouri and Illinois. Fought in Battle of Crooked River, 1838. Moved to Lima, Adams Co., Illinois, 1838. Moved to Yelrome (Morley's Settlement, later in Tioga), Hancock Co., Illinois, 1839. Member of Yelrome high council, 1839–1845. Appointed colonel in Nauvoo Legion, 1841. Appointed warden of Department of Music for University of Nauvoo, 1842. Served mission to New England, 1842. Moved to Nauvoo, Hancock Co., 1845. Migrated to what became Utah Territory, 1848; settled in Sessions Settlement (later Bountiful, Davis Co.). Member of Salt Lake stake high council, 1849. Moved to Manti (later in Sanpete Co., Utah Territory), 1849. Counselor in Sanpete stake presidency, 1851. Moved to Provo, Utah Co., Utah Territory, ca. 1864. Died in Provo.

Bishop, Isaac H. (1804–24 Dec. 1854), carpenter. Born in New York. Son of Isaac Gates Bishop and Mary Hyde. Raised Methodist. Resided in Livonia, Ontario Co., New York, ca. 1809–1819. Moved to Gates, Genesee Co. (later in Monroe Co.), New York, by 1820. Married Harriet Phebe Osborn, 13 Dec. 1827. Moved to Brighton, Monroe Co., by 1830. Moved to Lima, Livingston Co., New York, by 1831. Baptized into LDS church, 1833. Moved to Kirtland, Geauga Co., Ohio, ca. June 1834. Ordained a seventy, by Apr. 1836. Appointed member of Kirtland high council, by May 1836. Received elder's license, 16 June 1836, in Kirtland. Stockholder in Kirtland Safety Society. Moved to Springfield, Sangamon Co., Illinois, by 1840. Member of stake presidency in Springfield. Ordained a high priest, by 6 Nov. 1847. Joined James Brewster's Church of Christ; later joined Austin Cowles's Church of Christ. Died in Sangamon Co.

Bond, Ira (19 Jan. 1798–30 Nov. 1887), farmer. Born at Caldwell, Essex Co., New Jersey. Son of Abner Bond and Mary Elizabeth Gould. Moved to Mendon, Monroe Co., New York, before 1830. Married Charlotte Wilcox in Honeoye Falls, Monroe Co. Baptized into LDS church by Joseph Young, 1833, at Mendon. Moved to Kirtland, Geauga Co., Ohio, 1834. Labored on Kirtland temple. Appointed to preside over Kirtland deacons quorum, 15 Jan. 1836. Affiliated with RLDS church. Died in Kirtland.

Bosley, Edmund (Edmond) (25 June 1776–15 Dec. 1846), miller. Born at Northumberland, Northumberland Co., Pennsylvania. Son of John P. Bosley and Hannah Bull. Married Ann Kelly of Northumberland Co. Lived at Livonia, Livingston Co., New York, 1792–1834. Moved to Kirtland, Geauga Co., Ohio, Mar. 1834. Stockholder in Kirtland Safety Society. Served as second counselor in Kirtland elders quorum, 1837. Moved to Missouri, by 1838. Located at Adams Co., Illinois, 1839. Ordained a high priest, 1844, at Nauvoo, Hancock Co., Illinois. Died at Winter Quarters, unorganized U.S. territory (now in Omaha, Douglas Co., Nebraska), during Mormon exodus to Salt Lake Valley.

Boynton, John Farnham (20 Sept. 1811–20 Oct. 1890), merchant, dentist, lecturer, scientist, inventor. Born at East Bradford (later Groveland), Essex Co., Massachusetts. Son of Eliphalet Boynton and Susanna Nichols. Baptized into LDS church by JS, Sept. 1832, at Kirtland, Geauga Co., Ohio. Ordained an elder by JS, 16 Nov. 1832. Served missions to Pennsylvania, 1832, with Zebedee Coltrin; to Maine, 1833–1834, with Evan Greene; and to Painesville, Geauga Co., Ohio, Nov. 1834, with William E. McLellin. Ordained member of Quorum of the Twelve, 15 Feb. 1835, in Kirtland. Served mission to eastern states and Canada with Quorum of the Twelve. Married first to Susannah (Susan) Lowell by JS, 20 Jan. 1836, at Kirtland. Dissented over JS's handling of temporal matters in Kirtland; disfellowshipped from Quorum of the Twelve, 3 Sept. 1837. Reinstated to church and membership in Quorum of the Twelve, 10 Sept. 1837. Excommunicated, 1837. Practiced dentistry in vicinity of Nauvoo, Hancock Co., Illinois, Sept. 1842. Settled at Syracuse, Onondaga Co., New York, ca. 1851. Wife died, 7 Aug. 1859. Married second Mary West Jenkins, Nov. 1865; separated, ca. 1869. Married third Caroline Foster Harriman, 20 Jan. 1883. Died at Syracuse.

Bump, Jacob (1791–by 10 Oct. 1865), brickmason, plasterer, carpenter, mechanic, farmer, craftsman. Born at Butternuts, Otsego Co., New York. Son of Asa Bump and Lydia Dandley. Married Abigail Pettingill, ca. 1811. Moved to Meadville, Crawford Co., Pennsylvania, by 1826. Baptized into LDS church, by 1833. Moved to Kirtland, Geauga Co., Ohio, by 1833. Participated in Camp of Israel expedition to Missouri, 1834. Labored on Kirtland temple, 1835. Joined dissenters in Kirtland to depose JS. Used influence with dissenters to prevent mob violence against Mormons leaving Kirtland, 1838. Appointed bishop in Kirtland stake of James J. Strang's Church of Jesus Christ of Latter Day Saints, 7 Aug. 1846. Broke with Strang and reconstituted Church of Christ with William E. McLellin, Jan. 1847. Still living at Kirtland, 1860.

Burdick, Thomas (17 Nov. 1795/1797–6 Nov. 1877), farmer, teacher, judge, postmaster, clerk, civil servant. Born at Canajoharie, Montgomery Co., New York. Son of Gideon Burdick and Catherine Robertson. Married Anna Higley, 1828, at Jamestown, Chautauque Co., New York. Baptized into LDS church and moved to Kirtland, Geauga Co., Ohio, by Aug. 1834. Ordained an elder, by Aug. 1834. Appointed church clerk to record membership licenses, 24 Feb. 1836. Appointed elders quorum treasurer, 9 Nov. 1836. Appointed member of Kirtland high council, 7 Nov. 1837. Appointed bishop of Kirtland, 22 May 1841. Moved to Burlington, Des Moines Co., Iowa Territory, 1845. Moved to what became Council Bluffs, Pottawattamie Co., Iowa Territory, 1846. Located at San Bernardino, San Bernardino Co., California, 1853. Settled at San Gabriel Township, Los Angeles Co., California, winter 1853–1854. Died at Los Angeles Co.

Butterfield, Josiah (13 Mar. 1795–3 Mar. 1871), farmer, stockman. Born at Dunstable, Middlesex Co., Massachusetts. Son of Abel Butterfield and Mercy Farnsworth. Married first Polly Moulton, 30 Oct. 1819. Moved to Buxton, York Co., Maine, 1820. Baptized into LDS church by John F. Boynton, 1 Oct. 1833, in Maine. Moved to Kirtland, Geauga Co., Ohio, ca. 1834. Served missions to Maine and Vermont, 1834, 1836. Received elder's license, 4 Apr. 1836; ordained a seventy, 1836. Stockholder in Kirtland Safety Society. Appointed a president of the Seventy, 6 Apr. 1837. Assisted in migration of Kirtland Camp to Missouri, 1838. Appointed member of committee on removal from Missouri under Brigham Young, 26 Jan. 1839. Following expulsion of Mormons from Missouri, settled at Bear Creek, Adams Co., Illinois, 1839. Excommunicated, 7 Oct. 1844; rebaptized into LDS church, by Jan. 1846. Married second Margaret Lawrence, by Jan. 1846. Married third Clarinda, by 1853, possibly in California. Moved to California, before 1854. Resided at Gilroy, Santa Clara Co., California, by June 1860. Baptized into RLDS church by Glaud Rodger, 1 May 1865, at Watsonville, Santa Cruz Co., California. By June 1870, moved to Watsonville, where he served as RLDS branch president. Died at Watsonville.

Cahoon, Reynolds (30 Apr. 1790–29 Apr. 1861), farmer, tanner, builder. Born at Cambridge, Washington Co., New York. Son of William Cahoon Jr. and Mehitable Hodges. Married Thirza Stiles, 11 Dec. 1810. Moved to northeastern Ohio, 1811. Located at Harpersfield, Ashtabula Co., Ohio. Served in War of 1812. Moved near Kirtland, Geauga Co., Ohio, 1825. Baptized into LDS church by Parley P. Pratt, Nov. 1830. Ordained an elder by Sidney Rigdon and a high priest by JS, 4 June 1831. Appointed to serve mission to Missouri, 6 June 1831. Appointed counselor to Bishop Newel K. Whitney at Kirtland, 10 Feb. 1832. Appointed to serve mission with David W. Patten to Warsaw, Wyoming Co., New York, 23 Mar. 1833. Member of committee to oversee building of Kirtland temple. Stockholder in Kirtland Safety Society. Member of Kirtland stake presidency. Moved to Missouri, June 1838. Appointed counselor to stake president at Adam-ondi-Ahman, Daviess Co., Missouri, 28 June 1838. Located in Iowa Territory following exodus from Missouri. Appointed counselor in Iowa stake, Lee Co., Iowa Territory, 1839. Appointed guard in Nauvoo Legion, Mar. 1841. Served on building committee for Nauvoo temple. Member of Nauvoo Masonic Lodge. Admitted to Council of Fifty, 11 Mar. 1844. Resided at Winter Quarters, unorganized U.S. territory (later in Omaha, Douglas Co., Nebraska), 1846. Migrated to Salt Lake Valley, 1848. Died in Salt Lake City.

Cahoon, William Farrington (7 Nov. 1813–6 Apr. 1893), shoemaker, carpenter, joiner. Born at Harpersfield, Ashtabula Co., Ohio. Son of Reynolds Cahoon and Thirza Stiles. Baptized into LDS church by Parley P. Pratt, 16 Oct. 1830, at Kirtland, Geauga Co., Ohio. Ordained a priest by Oliver Cowdery, 25 Oct. 1831, at Orange, Cuyahoga Co., Ohio. Served mission to Ohio, Pennsylvania, and New York, 1832–1833. Ordained an elder, 1833. Participated in Camp of Israel expedition to Missouri, 1834. Ordained a seventy, 28 Feb. 1835. Married to Nancy Miranda Gibbs by JS, 17 Jan. 1836, at Kirtland. Stockholder in

Kirtland Safety Society. Moved to Far West, Caldwell Co., Missouri, spring 1838. Moved to Adam-ondi-Ahman, Daviess Co., Missouri, fall 1838. Located at Montrose, Lee Co., Iowa Territory, fall 1839. Moved to Nauvoo, Hancock Co., Illinois, spring 1842. Migrated to Salt Lake Valley, 1849. Served in presiding council of Second Quorum of the Seventy. Died at Salt Lake City.

Carrico, Thomas, Jr. (20 Sept. 1801–22 Feb. 1882), shoemaker. Born at Beverly, Essex Co., Massachusetts. Son of Thomas Carrico and Deborah Wallis. Baptized into Unitarian church, 27 Sept. 1801, at Beverly. Married first Mary E. Raymond, 30 Aug. 1827, at Beverly. Wife died, 1833. Baptized into LDS church by John F. Boynton, 24 Mar. 1834, at New Rowley (later Georgetown), Essex Co. Moved to Kirtland, Geauga Co., Ohio, Aug. 1835. Married second to Elizabeth (Betsey) Baker by JS, 14 Jan. 1836, at Kirtland. Ordained a teacher, Feb. 1836, at Kirtland. Lived in Missouri and then settled at Nauvoo, Hancock Co., Illinois, Apr. 1842. Appointed counselor to Bishop Jonathan H. Hale at Nauvoo. Ordained a high priest, Sept. 1842, at Nauvoo. Later joined RLDS church. Moved to Galena, Jo Daviess Co., Illinois, by 1850; to Boyer, Harrison Co., Iowa, by 1860; and to Jefferson, Harrison Co., by 1870. Died near Logan, Harrison Co.

Carter, Jared (14 June 1801–6 July 1849). Born at Killingworth, Middlesex Co., Connecticut. Son of Gideon Carter and Johanna Sims. Moved to Benson, Rutland Co., Vermont, by 1810. Married Lydia Ames, 20 Sept. 1823, at Benson. Moved to Chenango, Broome Co., New York, by Jan. 1831. Baptized into LDS church by Hyrum Smith, 20 Feb. 1831, in Colesville, Broome Co. Moved with Colesville branch to Thompson, Geauga Co., Ohio, May 1831. Ordained a priest, June 1831. Ordained an elder, Sept. 1831. Appointed to serve missions to eastern U.S., 22 Sept. 1831 and 12 Mar. 1832. Left to serve mission to Michigan Territory, Dec. 1832. Appointed to serve mission to eastern U.S., Mar. 1833. Ordained a high priest, by May 1833. Appointed to obtain funds for Elders School, 4 May 1833. Member of Kirtland temple building committee, 1833. Appointed to first Kirtland high council, 17 Feb. 1834. Appointed to serve mission to Upper Canada, 20 Feb. 1834. Labored on Kirtland temple. Stockholder in Kirtland Safety Society. Appointed president of Kirtland high council, 9 Sept. 1837. Removed family to Far West, Caldwell Co., Missouri, 1837. Appointed member of Far West high council, 3 Mar. 1838. Prominent in Missouri Danite activities, 1838. Moved from Far West to Commerce (later Nauvoo), Hancock Co., Illinois, 1839. Member of Nauvoo Masonic Lodge. Affiliated with James J. Strang's Church of Jesus Christ of Latter Day Saints, 1846. Excommunicated from Strangite movement, 8 Nov. 1846. Returned to LDS church. By June 1849, moved to DeKalb Co., Illinois, where he died.

Carter, Simeon (7 June 1794–3 Feb. 1869), farmer. Born at Killingworth, Middlesex Co., Connecticut. Son of Gideon Carter and Johanna Sims. Moved to Benson, Rutland Co., Vermont, by 1810. Married Lydia Kenyon, 2 Dec. 1818, at Benson. Moved to Amherst, Lorain Co., Ohio, by 1830. Baptized into LDS church, Feb. 1831. Ordained an elder. Ordained a high priest by Lyman Wight, 4 June 1831. Appointed to serve mission to Missouri with Solomon Hancock, June 1831. President of branch at Big Blue River, Kaw Township, Jackson Co., Missouri, 1833. Member of Missouri high council, 1834–1838. Exiled from Missouri, 1838. Located at Lee Co., Iowa Territory, 1840. Served mission to England, 1846–1849. Arrived at Salt Lake Valley, 1849. Moved to Brigham City, Box Elder Co., Utah Territory, by 1860. Died at Brigham City.

Cleminson (Clemenson), John James (28 Dec. 1798–28 Nov. 1879), farmer, teacher, cabinet maker, carpenter, clerk. Born at Lancaster, Lancashire, England. Migrated to St. John's, New Brunswick (later in Canada), 1812. Moved to Louisville, Jefferson Co., Kentucky. Moved to Lexington, Lillard Co., Missouri, by 1823. Married Lydia Lightner, 5 Jan. 1823, at Lillard Co., Missouri. Baptized into LDS church and moved to Far West, Caldwell Co., Missouri, by 1837. Elected Caldwell Co. clerk and circuit clerk, 1837. Testified against JS at hearing in Richmond, Ray Co., Missouri, Nov. 1838. Moved to Rockport, Caldwell Co., by June 1840. Lived at Montrose, Lee Co., Iowa Territory, by Mar. 1842. Wrote to JS seeking reconciliation, May 1842. Ordained a high priest, by 31 Jan. 1846. Lived at San Diego Co., California, 1852. Moved to San Bernardino, Los Angeles Co., California, 1852. By June 1860, lived at El Monte, Los Angeles Co., where he died.

Coe, Joseph (12 Nov. 1784–17 Oct. 1854), farmer, clerk. Born at Cayuga Co., New York. Son of Joel Coe and Huldah Horton. Lived at Scipio, Cayuga Co., by 1800. Married first Pallas Wales, 12 Jan. 1816. Married second Sophia Harwood, ca. 1824. Moved to Macedon, Wayne Co., New York, by June 1830. Baptized into LDS church and ordained an elder, 1831. Moved to Kirtland, Geauga Co., Ohio, 1831. Served missions to New York and Missouri, 1831. Ordained a high priest by JS, 1 Oct. 1831, in Kirtland. Member of Kirtland high council, 1834–1837. Provided one-third of money for purchase of mummies and papyri associated with JS translation of Book of Abraham, 1835, at Kirtland. Excommunicated, Dec. 1838. Died at Kirtland.

Coltrin, Zebedee (7 Sept. 1804–21 July 1887). Born at Ovid, Seneca Co., New York. Son of John Coltrin and Sarah Graham. Member of Methodist church. Married first Julia Ann Jennings, Oct. 1828. Baptized into LDS church by Solomon Hancock, 9 Jan. 1831, at Strongsville, Cuyahoga Co., Ohio. Ordained an elder by John Whitmer, 21 Jan. 1831. Served mission to Missouri with Levi Hancock, summer 1831. Appointed to serve mission to Illinois, Indiana, Michigan, and Ohio, Jan. 1832. Ordained a high priest by Hyrum Smith and Reynolds Cahoon, 27 July 1832, at Kirtland, Geauga Co., Ohio. Attended organizational meeting of School of the Prophets, 22–23 Jan. 1833, in Kirtland. Appointed to serve mission with John Murdock to Thompson, Geauga Co., and eastern states, 23 Mar. 1833. Appointed to serve mission with Henry Harriman to Canada, 20 Feb. 1834. Participated in Camp of Israel expedition to Missouri, 1834. Appointed a president of First Quorum of the Seventy, 28 Feb. 1835, at Kirtland. Stockholder in Kirtland Safety Society. Reassigned from Seventy to high priests quorum, 6 Apr. 1837. Located at Commerce (later Nauvoo), Hancock Co., Illinois, 1839, but soon after moved to Kirtland. Wife died, 1841. Appointed second counselor to Almon W. Babbitt in Kirtland stake, 22 May 1841. Married second Mary Mott, 5 Feb. 1843. Received into Nauvoo stake high priests quorum, 4 June 1843. Migrated to Salt Lake Valley with Brigham Young pioneer company, 1847. Settled at Spanish Fork, Utah Co., Utah Territory, 1852. Died at Spanish Fork.

Corrill, John (17 Sept. 1794–26 Sept. 1842), surveyor, politician, author. Born at Worcester Co., Massachusetts. Married Margaret Lyndiff, ca. 1830. Lived at Harpersfield, Ashtabula Co., Ohio, 1830. Baptized into LDS church, 10 Jan. 1831, at Kirtland, Geauga Co., Ohio. Ordained an elder, Jan. 1831, at Kirtland. Served mission to New London, Huron Co., Ohio, 1831. Ordained a high priest by Lyman Wight, 4 June 1831, at Kirtland. Appointed second counselor to Bishop Edward Partridge. Moved to Jackson Co., Missouri. Presided over group of church members in Independence, Jackson Co., 1831–1833. Appointed one of ten high priests to watch over the ten Missouri branches, 11 Sept. 1833. In Nov. 1833, expelled from Jackson Co. and located at Clay Co., Missouri, where he continued as counselor to Bishop Partridge. Returned to Kirtland and labored on temple, 1834–1836. Returned to Missouri and became a founder of Far West, Missouri, after Mar. 1836. Appointed "Keeper of the Lord's store House," at Far West, 22 May 1837. Released as counselor to Bishop Partridge, Aug. 1837. Elected state representative from Caldwell Co., Missouri, 1838. Appointed church historian, 1838. Testified for state at JS's hearing in Richmond, Ray Co., Missouri, Nov. 1838. Moved to Illinois, 1839. Excommunicated, 17 Mar. 1839, at Quincy, Adams Co., Illinois. Published *A Brief History of the Church of Christ of Latter Day Saints, (Commonly Called Mormons)*, 1839. Died in Adams Co.

Cowdery, Oliver (3 Oct. 1806–3 Mar. 1850), clerk, teacher, justice of the peace, lawyer, newspaper editor. Born at Wells, Rutland Co., Vermont. Son of William Cowdery and Rebecca Fuller. Raised Congregationalist. Moved to western New York and clerked at a store, ca. 1825–1828. Taught term as local schoolmaster at Manchester, Ontario Co., New York, 1828–1829. Assisted JS as principal scribe in translation of Book of Mormon, 1829. With JS, baptized and received priesthood authority, 1829. Moved to Fayette, Seneca Co., New York, and was one of the Three Witnesses of the Book of Mormon, June 1829. Helped oversee printing of Book of Mormon by E. B. Grandin, 1829–1830. Among six original members of LDS church, 6 Apr. 1830. Served as church recorder, 1830, 1835–1837. Led missionaries through Ohio and to Missouri, 1830–1831. Ordained a high priest by Sidney Rigdon, 28 Aug. 1831. With John Whitmer, left Ohio to take revelations to Missouri for publication, Nov. 1831. Assisted William W. Phelps in conducting church's printing operations at Jackson Co., Missouri, 1832–1833. Married Elizabeth Ann Whitmer, 18 Dec. 1832, in Kaw Township, Jackson Co. Edited *The Evening and the Morning Star*, 1833. Moved to Kirtland, Geauga Co., Ohio, by Sept. 1833. Member of United Firm, Literary Firm, and Kirtland high council. Appointed assistant president of church, 5 Dec. 1834. Edited Kirtland continuation of *The Evening and the Morning Star*, 1833, and edited reprint under modified title *Evening and Morning Star*, 1835–1836. Edited *LDS Messenger and Advocate*, 1834–1835, 1836–1837, and *Northern Times*, 1835. Elected justice of the peace in Kirtland, 1837. Moved to Far West, Caldwell Co., Missouri, 1837. Excommunicated, 1838. Moved to Richmond, Ray Co., Missouri, summer 1838. Returned to Kirtland, 1838, and briefly practiced law. Moved to Tiffin, Seneca Co., Ohio, where he continued law practice and held political offices, 1840–1847. Attended Methodist Protestant Church at Tiffin. Moved to Elkhorn, Walworth Co., Wisconsin Territory, 1847. Ran unsuccessfully for Wisconsin State Assembly, 1848. Coeditor of *Walworth County Democrat*, 1848. Requested and received readmission to LDS church, 1848, at Kanesville (later Council Bluffs), Pottawattamie Co., Iowa. Died at Richmond, Ray Co., Missouri.

Cowdery, Warren A. (17 Oct. 1788–23 Feb. 1851), physician, druggist, farmer, editor. Born at Wells, Rutland Co., Vermont. Son of William Cowdery and Rebecca Fuller. Married Patience Simonds, 22 Sept. 1814, in Pawlet, Rutland Co. Moved to Freedom, Cattaraugus Co., New York, 1816. Became first town postmaster of Freedom, 1824. Baptized into LDS church, 1834. Appointed presiding elder of church at Freedom, 25 Nov. 1834. Moved to Kirtland, Geauga Co., Ohio, Feb. 1836. Involved in managing bookbindery and printing office in Kirtland. Assisted in writing dedicatory prayer delivered by JS in Kirtland temple, 1836. Editor of *LDS Messenger and Advocate* and clerk to JS, 1836–1837. Served on Kirtland high council, 1837. Became disaffected with church leadership, 1838. Served as justice of the peace, 1838–1840. Served as election judge in Kirtland, 1841–1842. In 1850, farmed at Kirtland. Died at Kirtland.

Cowdery, Warren Franklin (12 Sept. 1817–23 Oct. 1895), sawmill operator, businessman. Born in Livingston Co., New York. Son of Warren A. Cowdery and Patience Simonds. Stockholder in Kirtland Safety Society. Married Jane Pomeroy Reed, 22 Apr. 1847, in Wooster, Wayne Co., Ohio. Moved to Wheeling, Ohio Co., Virginia (later in West Virginia), by 1855; to Fairfield, Jefferson Co., Iowa, 1855; and to St. Louis, by 1887. Died in St. Louis.

Dort, David (6 Jan. 1793–10 Mar. 1841), farmer, miller. Born at Gilsum, Cheshire Co., New Hampshire. Son of John Dort and Elishaba Briggs. Married first JS's cousin Mary (Polly) Mack, 2 June 1813, at Gilsum. After Mary's death, married her sister Fanny Mack. Moved to Pontiac, Oakland Co., Michigan Territory. Baptized into LDS church, 1831. Participated in Camp of Israel expedition to Missouri, 1834. Member of high council in Kirtland, Geauga Co., Ohio, 1837. In 1838, moved to Far West, Caldwell Co., Missouri, where he served on high council. Located at Commerce (later Nauvoo), Hancock Co., Illinois, following exodus from Missouri, 1839, and became member of high council there. Died at Nauvoo.

Durfee, Edmund (3 Oct. 1788–15 Nov. 1845), farmer, miller. Born in Tiverton, Newport Co., Rhode Island. Son of Perry Durfee and Annie Salisbury. Moved with grandparents to Broadalbin, Montgomery Co., New York, 1801. Married Magdalena Pickle, ca. 1810. Moved to Lenox, Madison Co., New York, by 1811. Operated a mill in Lincoln, Madison Co., before 1815. Moved to Amboy, Oswego Co., New York, by 1822. Moved to Ruggles Township, Huron Co., Ohio, 1830. Member of Methodist church. Baptized into LDS church by Simeon Carter, 15 May 1831, in Ruggles Township; ordained an elder by Simeon Carter and Solomon Hancock shortly after. Ordained a high priest by Oliver Cowdery, 25 Oct. 1831, in Orange, Cuyahoga Co., Ohio. Appointed to serve mission to Chautauque Co., New York, Dec. 1831. Traveled to Jackson Co., Missouri, to build houses and plant grain, spring 1832. Served mission to eastern states, fall 1832. Moved to Kirtland, Geauga Co., Ohio, May 1833. Labored on Kirtland temple; one of twenty-four elders who laid temple cornerstone. Moved to Caldwell Co., Missouri, spring 1837, settling six miles south of Far West on Log Creek. Assisted with Mormon evacuation from Missouri, 29 Jan. 1839. Moved to Yelrome (Morley's Settlement, later in Tioga), Hancock Co., Illinois, ca. 1839. Appointed to high council of Lima branch, Adams Co., Illinois, June 1843. Killed in Green Plains, Hancock Co.

Elliott, David (18 Nov. 1799–2 Dec. 1855), blacksmith. Born at Charleston, Montgomery Co., New York. Son of Peter Elliott and Phebe Holley. Married first Almira Holliday of Solon, Cortland Co., New York, ca. 1821. Married second Margery Quick. Lived at Ithaca, Tompkins Co., New York, 1830. Baptized into LDS church, 2 Jan. 1831. Married third Mary Cahoon, 21 May 1831, at Kirtland, Geauga Co., Ohio. Appointed to go to Missouri, 31 Aug. 1831. Resided at Jackson Co., by July 1833. Participated in Camp of Israel expedition to Missouri, 1834. Ordained a seventy, 1835. Stockholder in Kirtland Safety

Society. Married fourth Miranda Pratt, 11 Mar. 1838, in Cuyahoga Co., Ohio. Moved to Missouri with Kirtland Camp, 1838. Following exodus from Missouri, settled at Springfield, Sangamon Co., Illinois. Married fifth Margaret Straway, 12 Mar. 1848, in Henry Co., Iowa. Lived at Mount Pleasant, Henry Co., 1850. Migrated to Salt Lake Valley, 1852. Died in Salt Lake City.

Emmett, James (22 Feb. 1803–28 Dec. 1852), farmer, policeman, explorer, miner. Born at Boone Co., Kentucky. Son of Silas Emmett and Elizabeth Trowbridge. Married Phebe Jane Simpson, 13 Apr. 1823. Baptized into LDS church, 1831, in Boone Co. Moved to Jackson Co., Missouri, by Apr. 1832. Ordained an elder, by Sept. 1834. Served mission to Illinois, Indiana, Kentucky, Ohio, and Missouri, 1835. Moved to Far West, Caldwell Co., Missouri, by 1837. Member of Far West high council, 1838. Moved to Adams Co., Illinois, 1839. Moved to Lee Co., Iowa Territory, by Apr. 1841. Appointed to Iowa stake high council, Lee Co., 24 Apr. 1841. Moved to Nauvoo, Hancock Co., Illinois, by Dec. 1843. Appointed to Nauvoo police force, 29 Dec. 1843. Appointed by JS to explore western U.S. and select new location for Latter-day Saints, 21 Feb. 1844. Admitted to Council of Fifty, 13 Mar. 1844; rejected from council, 4 Feb. 1845. Led advance party of Latter-day Saint settlers from vicinity of Nauvoo to vicinity of present-day Vermillion, Clay Co., South Dakota, 1845–1846. Moved to Waubonsie, Fremont Co., Iowa, by Apr. 1847. Migrated west, 1849. Resided at Tuolumne Co., California, by June 1850. Moved to San Bernardino, Los Angeles Co., California, where he died.

Foster, James (1 Apr. 1786–12 Dec. 1846). Born at Hillsborough, Hillsborough Co., New Hampshire. Moved to Vienna, Kennebec Co., Maine, by Feb, 1811. Married Abigail Glidden, 29 Feb. 1811, at Vienna. Moved to Lyons, Wayne Co., New York, by 1824. Baptized into LDS church, by 1834. Participated in Camp of Israel expedition to Missouri, 1834. Appointed a president of the Seventy, 6 Apr. 1837. One of leaders of Kirtland Camp migration to Missouri, 1838. After Latter-day Saints left Missouri, settled at Jacksonville, Morgan Co., Illinois. Buried at Jacksonville.

Gaylord, John C. (12 July 1797–17 July 1874), farmer, carpenter. Born at Luzerne Co., Pennsylvania. Son of Chauncey John Gaylord and Dorithy Taylor. Married first Elizabeth Terry of East Palmyra, Wayne Co., New York, Apr. 1820. Baptized into LDS church by Leonard Rich, 2 Aug. 1835, at Niagara, Niagara Co., New York. Moved to Kirtland, Geauga Co., Ohio, 1836. Ordained an elder. Stockholder in Kirtland Safety Society. Ordained a seventy by Hazen Aldrich, 20 Dec. 1836. Appointed a president of First Quorum of the Seventy, 6 Apr. 1837, at Kirtland. Excommunicated, 13 Jan. 1838, at Kirtland. Moved to Commerce (later Nauvoo), Hancock Co., Illinois, 1839. Rejoined LDS church, 5 Oct. 1839, at Nauvoo. Married second Elvira Edmonds, 31 Dec. 1840, in Walnut Grove, Knox Co., Illinois. Affiliated with James J. Strang at Voree, Walworth Co., Wisconsin. Received into RLDS church; appointed member of high council, 6 Apr. 1860. Died near Burlington, Racine Co., Wisconsin.

Gee, Salmon (16 Oct. 1792–13 Sept. 1845), farmer. Born at Lyme, New London Co., Connecticut. Son of Zopher Gee and Esther Beckwith. Moved to Lebanon, Warren Co., Ohio, by 1814. Married Sarah (Sally) Watson Crane, 15 Nov. 1814, at Ashtabula Co., Ohio. Baptized into LDS church by Zebedee Coltrin, July 1832, at Geauga Co., Ohio. Ordained an elder by Sidney Rigdon, 4 Feb. 1833. Moved to Kirtland, Geauga Co., Apr. 1834. Member of Second Quorum of the Seventy, 1836. Appointed a president of the Seventy, 6 Apr. 1837. Member of Kirtland high council under Almon W. Babbitt, 1841–1844. Moved to Ambrosia, Lee Co., Iowa Territory, 1844. Died at Ambrosia.

Gould, John (21 Dec. 1784–25 June 1855), pastor, farmer. Born in New Hampshire. Married first Oliva Swanson of Massachusetts. Resided at Portsmouth, Rockingham Co., New Hampshire, 1808. Lived in Vermont. Moved to northern Pennsylvania, 1817. Served as minister in Freewill Baptist Church, 1817–1832, in New York and Pennsylvania. Lived at Spafford, Onondaga Co., New York, 1830. Baptized into LDS church by Reynolds Cahoon, 16 Dec. 1832, in Chautauque Co., New York. Ordained an elder by David W. Patten, 17 Dec. 1832, in Chautauque Co. Moved to Kirtland, Geauga Co., Ohio, ca. 1833. Traveled from Kirtland with Orson Hyde to inform church leaders in Missouri of JS's instructions to obtain redress through legal channels for impending eviction from Jackson Co., Missouri, Aug. 1833. Assisted JS in recruiting volunteers for Camp of Israel expedition to Missouri, 1834. Attended church conference at Freedom, Cattaraugus Co., New York, 24–25 Jan. 1835. Member of Second Quorum of the Seventy, by Apr. 1836. Served as a president of the Seventy, 6 Apr.–3 Sept. 1837. In 1846, located in Knoxville, Knox Co., Illinois, where he affiliated with James J. Strang's Church of Jesus Christ of Latter Day Saints. Wife died, 2 Sept. 1847. Married second Delia Metcalf, 9 July 1848, at Knox Co. Died at Truro Township, Knox Co.

Granger, Oliver (7 Feb. 1794–23/25 Aug. 1841), sheriff, church agent. Born at Phelps, Ontario Co., New York. Son of Pierce Granger and Clarissa Trumble. Married Lydia Dibble, 8 Sept. 1813, at Phelps. Member of Methodist church and licensed exhorter. Sheriff of Ontario Co. and colonel in militia. Nearly blind from 1827 onward. Lived at Phelps, 1830. Baptized into LDS church and ordained an elder by Brigham and Joseph Young, ca. 1832–1833, at Sodus, Wayne Co., New York. Moved to Kirtland, Geauga Co., Ohio, 1833. Served mission to eastern states with Samuel Newcomb. Ordained a high priest, 29 Apr. 1836, at Kirtland. Served mission to New York with John P. Greene, spring 1836. Appointed to Kirtland high council, 8 Oct. 1837. Appointed to settle JS's business affairs in Kirtland, 1838. Left Kirtland for Far West, Caldwell Co., Missouri, June 1838, possibly to confer regarding JS's Kirtland business affairs. Directed in July 1838 revelation to move to Far West. Returned to Kirtland to settle his and JS's affairs and move family to Far West. Left Kirtland for Far West in Oct. 1838 with family, but turned back by mob in Missouri and returned to Kirtland. Following Mormon exodus from Missouri, moved from Kirtland to Commerce (later Nauvoo), Hancock Co., Illinois, spring 1839. Acted as agent in securing lands in Lee Co., Iowa Territory, 1839. Appointed to preside over church in Kirtland, 4 May 1839. Died at Kirtland.

Greene, Evan Melbourne (22 Dec. 1814–2 May 1882), schoolteacher, farmer, postmaster, politician, justice of the peace, judge. Born at Aurelius, Cayuga Co., New York. Son of John P. Greene and Rhoda Young. Baptized into LDS church, 1831/1832. Served mission to Maine, 1833, with John F. Boynton. Married Susan Kent, 1835. Moved to Kirtland, Geauga Co., Ohio, by 1836. Clerk of Kirtland elders quorum, 1836–1837. Moved to Pike Co., Illinois, by 1840. Ordained a high priest, by 1845. Moved to Kanesville, Pottawattamie Co., Iowa, ca. 1847. Postmaster at Kanesville and recorder and treasurer of Pottawattamie Co., beginning 1848. Migrated to Salt Lake Valley, 1852. Moved to Provo, Utah Co., Utah Territory,

1852. Served as mayor of Provo and member of Utah territorial legislature, 1852–1856. Moved to Grantsville, Tooele Co., Utah Territory, 1858; to area near Bear Lake, Owyhee Co., Idaho Territory, 1863; and to Smithfield, Cache Co., Utah Territory, 1865. Ordained a patriarch, 1873. Moved to Springdale, Washington Co., Utah Territory, 1875. Moved to Escalante, Iron Co., Utah Territory, 1879. Died at Clover Flat, Piute Co., Utah Territory.

Greene, John Portineus (3 Sept. 1793–10 Sept. 1844), farmer, shoemaker, printer, publisher. Born at Herkimer, Herkimer Co., New York. Son of John Coddington Greene and Anna Chapman. Married first Rhoda Young, 11 Feb. 1813. Moved to Aurelius, Cayuga Co., New York, 1814; to Brownsville, Ontario Co., New York, 1819; to Watertown, Jefferson Co., New York, 1821; and to Mentz, Cayuga Co., 1826. Member of Methodist Episcopal Church; later, member of Methodist Reformed Church. A founder of Methodist Protestant Church, 1828. Moved to Conesus, Livingston Co., New York, 1829. Moved to Mendon, Monroe Co., New York, by 1832. Baptized into LDS church by Eleazer Miller, Apr. 1832, at Mendon; ordained an elder by Miller shortly after. Organized branch of church at Warsaw, Genesee Co., New York, 1832. Moved to Kirtland, Geauga Co., Ohio, Oct. 1832. Appointed to preside over branch in Parkman, Geauga Co., spring 1833. Returned to Kirtland, fall 1833. Ordained a high priest and left to serve mission to eastern U.S., 16 Sept. 1833. Left to serve mission to western New York and Canada, 25 Feb. 1834. Served mission to eastern U.S., 1835. Appointed member of Kirtland high council, 13 Jan. 1836. Served mission to Ohio to raise funds for Kirtland temple, Mar. 1836. Left to serve mission to New York, 13 July 1836. Stockholder in Kirtland Safety Society. Left to serve mission to Canada, 16 Nov. 1837. Moved to Far West, Caldwell Co., Missouri, 1838. Member of Caldwell Co. militia. Participated in battle of Crooked River, near Ray Co., Missouri, 25 Oct. 1838. Moved to Quincy, Adams Co., Illinois, Nov. 1838. Served mission to Ohio, Pennsylvania, and New York, 1839. Moved to Nauvoo, Hancock Co., Illinois, spring 1840. Member of Nauvoo City Council, 1841–1843. Married second Mary Eliza Nelson, 6 Dec. 1841, in Nauvoo. Member of Nauvoo Masonic Lodge. Member of Nauvoo Legion, 1842. Served mission to Ohio and New York, Aug. 1842. Elected Nauvoo city marshal, Dec. 1843. Assessor and collector of Nauvoo Fourth Ward. Admitted to Council of Fifty, 26 Mar. 1844. Carried out orders of JS and city council to suppress *Nauvoo Expositor* press, 10 June 1844. Died at Nauvoo.

Grover, Thomas (22 July 1807–20 Feb. 1886), farmer, boat operator. Born at Whitehall, Washington Co., New York. Son of Thomas Grover and Polly Spaulding. Married first Caroline Whiting of Whitehall, 1828. Became a Methodist preacher, by 1834. Moved to Freedom, Cattaraugus Co., New York, by 1834. Baptized into LDS church by Warren A. Cowdery, Sept. 1834, at Freedom. Moved to Kirtland, Geauga Co., Ohio, 1835. Ordained an elder, 2 Jan. 1836. Appointed to Kirtland high council, 1836. Removed his family to Far West, Caldwell Co., Missouri, where he served on high council, 1837. Member of committee at Far West to supervise removal of Latter-day Saints from Missouri, Jan. 1839. Moved to Adams Co., Illinois, by 7 May 1839. Located at Commerce (later Nauvoo), Hancock Co., Illinois, 1839. Appointed to Commerce high council, 1839. Member of Nauvoo Legion, 1841. Married second Caroline Nickerson Hubbard, 20 Feb. 1841, in Nauvoo. Served three short missions during early 1840s. Moved to Winter Quarters, unorganized U.S. territory (later in Omaha, Douglas Co., Nebraska), winter 1846–1847. Migrated to Salt Lake Valley, Oct. 1847; settled at Deuel Creek (later in Centerville), Davis Co., Utah Territory. Collected tithing in California, winter 1848–1849. Moved to Farmington, Davis Co., 1849. Moved to Kanesville (later Council Bluffs), Pottawattamie Co., Iowa, 1850; returned to Farmington, 1853. Member of Davis Co. high council. Served in Utah territorial legislature. Probate judge in Davis Co. Served mission to eastern U.S., 1874–1875. Died at Farmington.

Groves, Elisha Hurd (5 Nov. 1797–29 Dec. 1867), farmer. Born in Madison Co., Kentucky. Son of John Groves and Mary Hurd. Moved to Indiana, 1819. Married first Sarah Hogue, ca. 1825, in Indiana. Member of Presbyterian church. Baptized into LDS church by Calvin Beebe, 1 Mar. 1832, in Greene Co., Indiana; ordained an elder by Peter Dustin and Calvin Beebe shortly after in Greene Co. Divorced wife, by 1833. Moved to Jackson Co., Missouri, 1833. Served mission to Illinois, 1833–1834. Joined Camp of Israel expedition at Salt River, Monroe Co., Missouri, 1834. Ordained a high priest, 10 Sept. 1834, in Clay Co., Missouri. Served mission to Illinois, 1834. Moved to Kirtland, Geauga Co., Ohio, 1835. Labored on Kirtland temple. Served mission in Ohio, 1835. Appointed to Missouri high council, 1836, in Kirtland. Married second Lucy Simmons, 19 Jan. 1836, in Kirtland. Moved to Clay Co., 1836. Served mission to Kentucky to raise funds for church purchase of lands, 1836. Moved to what became Caldwell Co., Missouri, 1836. Served mission to Ohio to raise funds for construction of temple at Far West, Caldwell Co., 1836–1837. Moved to Daviess Co., Missouri, by spring 1838. Moved to Caldwell Co., Nov. 1838. Moved to Columbus, Adams Co., Illinois, 1839. Served mission to northern Illinois, 1839. Served mission to Wisconsin, 1841. Moved to Nauvoo, Hancock Co., Illinois, 1842. Served multiple missions in Illinois, 1842–1844. Appointed to settle Mount Pisgah, Clarke Co., Iowa Territory, 1846. Moved to Winter Quarters, unorganized U.S. territory (later in Omaha, Douglas Co., Nebraska), 1846. Migrated to Salt Lake City, 1848. Appointed to settle Iron Co., Utah Territory, 1850. Appointed to settle Harmony (later in New Harmony), Washington Co., Utah Territory, 1853. Died in Washington Co.

Hale, Jonathan Harriman (1 Feb. 1800–4 Sept. 1846), butcher, school director, assessor. Born in Bradford, Essex Co., Massachusetts. Son of Soloman Hale and Martha Harriman. Married Olive Boynton, 5 Sept. 1825, in Bradford. Moved to Dover, Strafford Co., New Hampshire, between June 1830 and June 1834. Baptized into LDS church, 13 June 1834, in Dover. Ordained an elder by Gladden Bishop, Aug. 1834, in Dover. Presided over Dover branch, Aug. 1834–Sept. 1835. Moved to Kirtland, Geauga Co., Ohio, July 1836. Stockholder in Kirtland Safety Society. Ordained a seventy, by Hazen Aldrich, 3 Jan. 1837, in Kirtland. Served mission with Wilford Woodruff to Upper Canada and Fox Islands, Maine, 31 May 1837–29 Oct. 1837. Served mission with Amos B. Fuller to southern Ohio, 2 Jan.–Mar. 1838. Moved to Daviess Co., Missouri, July 1838. Resided at various church settlements in Missouri before being expelled and settling in Quincy, Adams Co., Illinois, 15 Feb. 1839. Served mission to Indiana and Kentucky, Dec. 1839–Feb. 1840. Moved to Commerce (later Nauvoo), Hancock Co., Illinois, Feb. 1840. Ordained a high priest, 6 Apr. 1841, in Nauvoo. Served as counselor to Bishop Newel K. Whitney, beginning Apr. 1841. Member of Nauvoo Legion. Served as bishop of Nauvoo Ninth Ward, beginning Aug. 1842. Appointed a city assessor and collector by Nauvoo City Council, 26 Nov. 1842. Appointed assistant temple recorder, 30 July 1843. Moved to what became Council Bluffs,

Pottawattamie Co., Iowa, 1846. Appointed to Council Bluffs high council, 1846. Died at Council Bluffs.

Hancock, Levi Ward (7 Apr. 1803–10 June 1882). Born at Springfield, Hampden Co., Massachusetts. Son of Thomas Hancock III and Amy Ward. Baptized into LDS church, 16 Nov. 1830, at Kirtland, Geauga Co., Ohio. Married Clarissa Reed, 20 Mar. 1831. Served mission to Missouri with Zebedee Coltrin, summer 1831. Appointed to serve mission to Missouri, Ohio, and Virginia, Jan. 1832. Attended organizational meeting of School of the Prophets, 22–23 Jan. 1833, in Kirtland. Participated in Camp of Israel expedition to Missouri, 1834. Ordained a seventy, 28 Feb. 1835; appointed a president of the Seventy shortly after. Moved to Missouri, 1838. Member of committee at Far West, Caldwell Co., Missouri, to supervise removal of Latter-day Saints from Missouri, Jan. 1839. Located at Commerce (later Nauvoo), Hancock Co., Illinois, 1839. Enlisted in Mormon Battalion at what became Council Bluffs, Pottawattamie Co., Iowa Territory; served 1846–1847. Only general authority of church on march; served as unofficial chaplain for battalion. Arrived in Salt Lake Valley, 1847. Member of Utah territorial legislature for three terms, beginning in 1851. Ordained a patriarch, 1872. Died at Washington, Washington Co., Utah Territory.

Hancock, Solomon (15 Aug. 1793/1794–2 Dec. 1847). Born at Springfield, Hampden Co., Massachusetts. Son of Thomas Hancock III and Amy Ward. Moved to Wolcott, Seneca Co., New York, by 1810. Joined Methodist church, 1814. Married first Alta Adams, 12 Mar. 1815. Moved to Columbia, Hamilton Co., Ohio, by 1823. Moved to Chagrin (later Willoughby), Cuyahoga Co., Ohio, by 1830. Baptized into LDS church, 16 Nov. 1830, in Ohio. Ordained an elder, by June 1831. Ordained a high priest by Lyman Wight, 4 June 1831, at Geauga Co., Ohio. Appointed to serve mission with Simeon Carter to Missouri, June 1831. Lived in Jackson Co., Missouri, by 1833. Appointed to Missouri high council, 1834. Served mission to eastern states, fall 1834. Wife died, 1836. Married second Phebe Adams, 28 June 1836. Moved to Caldwell Co., Missouri, by Dec. 1836. Exiled from Missouri, spring 1839; located at Adams Co., Illinois. Moved to Lima, Adams Co., 1841. Appointed member of Lima high council, 1843. Moved to Yelrome (Morley's Settlement, later in Tioga), Hancock Co., Illinois, ca. 1844, and presided over Yelrome branch of church. Died near what became Council Bluffs, Pottawattamie Co., Iowa.

Harris, Martin (18 May 1783–10 July 1875), farmer. Born at Easton, Albany Co., New York. Son of Nathan Harris and Rhoda Lapham. Moved with parents to area of Swift's Landing (later in Palmyra), Ontario Co., New York, 1793. Married first his first cousin Lucy Harris, 27 Mar. 1808, in Palmyra. Served in War of 1812 in New York militia. Became landowner of some 320 acres at Palmyra. Reportedly investigated Quakers, Universalists, Restorationists, Baptists, Methodists, and Presbyterians. Took transcript of Book of Mormon characters to Luther Bradish, Samuel Latham Mitchill, and Charles Anthon, Feb. 1828. Assisted JS as scribe during translation of first portion of Book of Mormon, ca. 12 Apr.–14 June 1828. One of the Three Witnesses of the Book of Mormon, June 1829. Separated from wife, after June 1830. Baptized into LDS church by Oliver Cowdery, 6 Apr. 1830. Ordained a priest, by 9 June 1830. Paid printing costs for publication of Book of Mormon through sale of 151 acres. Led members of Manchester, Ontario Co., branch from Palmyra to Kirtland, Geauga Co., Ohio, May 1831. Ordained a high priest by Lyman Wight, 4 June 1831, at Kirtland. Appointed to serve mission to Missouri, 6 June

1831. Appointed member of what became the Literary Firm, Nov. 1831. Appointed member of United Firm, Apr. 1832. Participated in Camp of Israel expedition to Missouri, 1834. Member of Kirtland high council, 1834. Married second Caroline Young, 1836/1837. Excommunicated, Dec. 1837. Rebaptized into LDS church, 1842, at Kirtland. Member of high council of James J. Strang's Church of Jesus Christ of Latter Day Saints at Kirtland, 7 Aug. 1846. Joined with William E. McLellin's religious movement, 1847. Initiated a new movement with William Smith and Chilton Daniels at Kirtland, likely 1855. Migrated to Salt Lake Valley, 1870. Rebaptized into LDS church, 1870. Died at Clarkston, Cache Co., Utah Territory.

Harris, Preserved (ca. 1785–18 Apr. 1867), farmer. Born at Easton, Albany Co., New York. Son of Nathan Harris and Rhoda Lapham. Moved with parents to area of Swift's Landing (later in Palmyra), Ontario Co., New York, 1793. Married Nancy Warren. One of five to whom JS gave Martin Harris permission to show 116 pages of Book of Mormon transcription, 1828. Baptized into LDS church, ca. 1831. Disfellowshipped, 16 June 1836. Located at Mentor, Lake Co., Ohio, 1840. Member of high council of James J. Strang's Church of Jesus Christ of Latter Day Saints at Kirtland, Lake Co., by Aug. 1846. Died at Mentor.

Haskins, Nathan (10 Mar. 1808–22 Mar. 1857), physician, farmer. Born in Granger, Allegany Co., New York. Married Almena Thompson. Baptized into LDS church, by July 1836. Moved to Kirtland, Geauga Co., Ohio, by July 1836. Received elder's certificate, 21 July 1836, in Kirtland. Stockholder in Kirtland Safety Society. Moved to Rockport, Caldwell Co., Missouri, by 1840; to Nauvoo, Hancock Co., Illinois, by 1842; and to Centerville, Allegany Co., by 1843. Served as president of church conference in Batavia, Genesee Co., New York, 2 Mar. 1844. Died in Centerville.

Hedlock, Reuben (1809–5 July 1869), printer, carpenter, journeyman. Born in U.S. Married first Susan Wheeler, 1827. Married second Lydia Fox. Baptized into LDS church, by 1836. Moved to Kirtland, Geauga Co., Ohio, and ordained an elder, by 1836. Appointed counselor to Alvah Beman in presidency of elders quorum in Kirtland, 25 Jan. 1836. Stockholder in Kirtland Safety Society. Appointed president of elders quorum, 27 Nov. 1837, after Beman's death. Moved to Missouri with Kirtland Camp, 1838; to Far West, Caldwell Co., Missouri, before 1839; and to Quincy, Adams Co., Illinois, Apr. 1839. Settled family in Commerce (later Nauvoo), Hancock Co., Illinois, Sept. 1839. Ordained a seventy, before 21 Sept. 1839. Left to serve mission to England, Sept. 1839; arrived in Liverpool, 6 Apr. 1840, and returned, Apr. 1841. Ordained a high priest, 3 Oct. 1841, in Nauvoo. Member of Nauvoo Masonic Lodge. Presided over British mission, Oct. 1843–Jan. 1845, Jan. 1846–July 1846. Disfellowshipped, 16 July 1846. Excommunicated, 17 Oct. 1846, at Manchester, Lancashire, England. Married third Mary A., by 1851. Lived in Marylebone, London, England, 1851, and in Croydon, Sussex Co., England, 1861. Died at Gravesend, Kent Co., England.

Higbee, Elias (23 Oct. 1795–8 June 1843), clerk, judge, surveyor. Born at Galloway, Gloucester Co., New Jersey. Son of Isaac Higbee and Sophia Somers. Moved to Clermont Co., Ohio, 1803. Married Sarah Elizabeth Ward, 10 Sept. 1818, in Tate Township, Clermont Co. Lived at Tate Township, 1820. Located at Fulton, Hamilton Co., Ohio, 1830. Baptized into LDS church, summer 1832, at Jackson Co., Missouri. Ordained an elder by Isaac Higbee, 20 Feb. 1833, at Cincinnati. Migrated to Jackson Co., Apr. 1833. Driven from Jackson Co. into Clay Co., Missouri, Nov. 1833. Ordained a high priest by Orson Pratt, 7 Aug. 1834, in Clay Co. Served mission to Missouri, Illinois, Indiana, and Ohio, 1835. Labored on Kirtland temple. Returned to Clay Co. Member of Missouri high council, 1836–1838. Moved to what became Caldwell Co., Missouri, spring 1836. Appointed a justice for Caldwell Co., 1837. Appointed president or presiding justice of Caldwell Co. court, Aug. 1838. With John Corrill, appointed church historian, 6 Apr. 1838, at Far West. Appointed captain general of the Danites, 1838. Participated in Battle of Crooked River, near Ray Co., Missouri, 25 Oct. 1838. Fled Missouri; located at Quincy, Adams Co., Illinois, 1839. Member of committee that investigated lands offered for sale by Isaac Galland, 1839. Settled at Commerce (later Nauvoo), Hancock Co., Illinois, 1839. Traveled to Washington DC with JS to seek redress for Missouri grievances, Oct. 1839–Mar. 1840. Appointed member of Nauvoo temple committee, 6 Oct. 1840. Appointed guard in Nauvoo Legion, Mar. 1841. Member of Nauvoo Masonic Lodge. Died at Nauvoo.

Hillman, Mayhew (Mahew) (4 Mar. 1793–2 Nov. 1839), farmer. Born at Chilmark, Dukes Co., Massachusetts. Son of Samson Hillman and Damaris Look. Married Sarah King, ca. 1818. Moved to Cambridge, Washington Co., New York, by Aug. 1820. Member of Freewill Baptist Church. Moved to Spafford, Onondaga Co., New York, 1823. Baptized into LDS church by Lyman E. Johnson, 10 Nov. 1832, at Spafford. Lived at Kirtland, Geauga Co., Ohio, 1833–1838. Ordained an elder, 29 Apr. 1836, in Kirtland. Stockholder in Kirtland Safety Society. Appointed to Kirtland high council, 3 Sept. 1837. Moved to western Missouri, 1838. Member of Adam-ondi-Ahman high council, 1838. Moved to Quincy, Adams Co., Illinois, spring 1839. Died at Commerce (later Nauvoo), Hancock Co., Illinois.

Hinkle, George M. (13 Nov. 1801–Nov. 1861), merchant, physician, publisher, minister, farmer. Born in Jefferson Co., Kentucky. Son of Michael Hinkle and Nancy Higgins. Married first Sarah Ann Starkey. Baptized into LDS church, 1832. Moved to Far West, Caldwell Co., Missouri. Served on Missouri high council, 1836–1838. Commissioned colonel in Missouri state militia. With John Murdock, purchased large number of lots for Mormon settlement in De Witt, Carroll Co., Missouri, 23 June 1838. During Missouri conflict in 1838, directed defense of De Witt and commanded Mormon militia defending Far West. While assisting in negotiation of truce between state militia and Latter-day Saints at Far West, surrendered church leaders to General Samuel D. Lucas. Excommunicated, 17 Mar. 1839, at Quincy, Adams Co., Illinois. Moved to Duncan Prairie, Mercer Co., Illinois, 1839. Organized religious society named The Church of Jesus Christ, the Bride, the Lamb's Wife, 24 June 1840, at Moscow, Muscatine Co., Iowa Territory. Affiliated briefly with Sidney Rigdon and Church of Christ, 1845. Moved to Iowa Territory, by Dec. 1845. Wife died, 1 Dec. 1845. Returned to Mercer Co., by June 1850. Married second Mary Loman Hartman. Moved to Decatur Co., Iowa, by 1852. Moved to Adair Co., Iowa. Served in Civil War, 1861. Died at Decatur, Decatur Co.

Hyde, Orson (8 Jan. 1805–28 Nov. 1878), laborer, clerk, storekeeper, teacher, editor, businessman, lawyer, judge. Born at Oxford, New Haven Co., Connecticut. Son of Nathan Hyde and Sally Thorpe. Moved to Derby, New Haven Co., 1812. Moved to Kirtland, Geauga Co., Ohio, 1819. Joined Methodist church, ca. 1827. Later affiliated with reformed

Baptists (later Disciples of Christ or Campbellites). Baptized into LDS church by Sidney Rigdon and ordained an elder by JS and Sidney Rigdon, Oct. 1831, at Kirtland. Ordained a high priest by Oliver Cowdery, 26 Oct. 1831. Appointed to serve mission to Ohio, Nov. 1831, in Orange, Cuyahoga Co., Ohio. Baptized many during proselytizing mission with Samuel Smith to eastern states, 1832. Attended organizational meeting of School of the Prophets, 22–23 Jan. 1833, in Kirtland. Appointed clerk to church presidency, 1833. Appointed to serve mission to Jackson Co., Missouri, summer 1833. Served mission to Pennsylvania and New York, winter and spring 1834. Member of Kirtland high council, 1834. Participated in Camp of Israel expedition to Missouri, 1834. Married to Marinda Nancy Johnson by Sidney Rigdon, 4 Sept. 1834, at Kirtland. Ordained member of Quorum of the Twelve by Oliver Cowdery, David Whitmer, and Martin Harris, 15 Feb. 1835, in Kirtland. Served mission to western New York and Upper Canada, 1836. Served mission to England with Heber C. Kimball, 1837–1838. Moved to Far West, Caldwell Co., Missouri, summer 1838. Sided with dissenters against JS, 1838. Lived in Missouri, winter 1838–1839. Removed from Quorum of the Twelve, 4 May 1839. Restored to Quorum of the Twelve, 27 June 1839, at Commerce (later Nauvoo), Hancock Co., Illinois. Served mission to Palestine to dedicate land for gathering of the Jews, 1840–1842. Member of Nauvoo Masonic Lodge, 1842. Member of Nauvoo City Council, 1843–1845. Admitted to Council of Fifty, 13 Mar. 1844. Presented petition from JS to U.S. Congress, 1844. Participated in plural marriage during JS's lifetime. Departed Nauvoo during exodus to the West, mid-May 1846. Served mission to Great Britain, 1846–1847. Presided over Latter-day Saints in Iowa before migrating to Utah Territory. Appointed president of Quorum of the Twelve, 1847. Published *Frontier Guardian* at Kanesville (later Council Bluffs), Pottawattamie Co., Iowa, 1849–1852. Appointed to preside over church east of Rocky Mountains, 20 Apr. 1851, at Kanesville. Migrated to Utah Territory, 1852. Appointed associate judge of U.S. Supreme Court for Utah Territory, 1852. Elected to Utah territorial legislature, 27 Nov. 1852, 1858. Presided over church in Carson Co., Utah Territory (later in Nevada Territory), 1855–1856. Served colonizing mission to Sanpete Co., Utah Territory, by 1860; presided as ecclesiastical authority there, beginning 1860. Died at Spring City, Sanpete Co.

Johnson, John (14 Apr. 1779–30 July 1843), farmer, innkeeper. Born at Chesterfield, Cheshire Co., New Hampshire. Son of Israel Johnson and Abigail Higgins. Married Alice (Elsa) Jacobs, 22 June 1800. Moved to Pomfret, Windsor Co., Vermont, ca. 1803. Settled at Hiram, Portage Co., Ohio, 1818. Associated with Methodist church. Baptized into LDS church, ca. 1831. JS lived at Johnson home, 1831–1832. Moved to Kirtland, Geauga Co., Ohio, 1833. Ordained an elder by JS, 17 Feb. 1833, in Kirtland. Ordained a high priest and appointed member of United Firm, 4 June 1833, in Kirtland. Provided funds to church for purchase of Peter French properties. Member of Kirtland high council, 1834–1837. Stockholder in Kirtland Safety Society. Disaffected from church, 1837–1838. Died at Kirtland.

Johnson, Luke (3 Nov. 1807–8 Dec. 1861), farmer, teacher, doctor. Born at Pomfret, Windsor Co., Vermont. Son of John Johnson and Alice (Elsa) Jacobs. Lived at Hiram, Portage Co., Ohio, when baptized into LDS church by JS, 10 May 1831. Ordained a priest by Christian Whitmer shortly after baptism. Ordained an elder, by Oct. 1831. Ordained a high priest by Oliver Cowdery, 25 Oct. 1831, at Orange, Cuyahoga Co., Ohio. Served missions to Ohio, Pennsylvania, Virginia, and Kentucky, 1831–1833. Married first Susan Harminda

Poteet, 1 Nov. 1833, in Cabell Co., Virginia (later in West Virginia). Appointed to high council, 17 Feb. 1834, at Kirtland, Geauga Co., Ohio. Participated in Camp of Israel expedition to Missouri, 1834. Member of Quorum of the Twelve, 1835–1837. Served mission to eastern states, 1835, and to New York and Upper Canada, 1836. Constable in Kirtland. Disfellowshipped, 3 Sept. 1837. Reinstated to church and membership in Quorum of the Twelve, 10 Sept. 1837. Excommunicated, 1838. Taught school in Virginia and also studied medicine, which he practiced at Kirtland. Rebaptized into LDS church by Orson Hyde, 8 Mar. 1846, at Nauvoo, Hancock Co., Illinois. Wife died, 1846. Married second America Morgan Clark, Mar. 1847. Member of Brigham Young pioneer company to Salt Lake Valley, 1847. Moved to St. John, Tooele Co., Utah Territory, 1858. Bishop at St. John. Died at Salt Lake City.

Johnson, Lyman Eugene (24 Oct. 1811–20 Dec. 1859), merchant, lawyer, hotelier. Born at Pomfret, Windsor Co., Vermont. Son of John Johnson and Alice (Elsa) Jacobs. Moved to Hiram, Portage Co., Ohio, Mar. 1818. Baptized into LDS church by Sidney Rigdon, Feb. 1831. Ordained an elder by Oliver Cowdery, 25 Oct. 1831, at Orange, Cuyahoga Co., Ohio. Ordained a high priest by Sidney Rigdon, 2 Nov. 1831. Served missions with Orson Pratt to eastern states and New England, 1832–1833, and to Upper Canada, 1834. Attended organizational meeting of School of the Prophets, 22–23 Jan. 1833, in Kirtland. Participated in Camp of Israel expedition to Missouri, 1834. Married Sarah Lang (Long), 4 Sept. 1834, in Geauga Co., Ohio. Member of Quorum of the Twelve, 1835–1838. Disfellowshipped, 3 Sept. 1837; restored to fellowship, 10 Sept. 1837. Migrated to Far West, Caldwell Co., Missouri. Excommunicated, 13 Apr. 1838. Member of Nauvoo Masonic Lodge, 1842. Lived in Iowa Territory, 1842. Practiced law at Davenport, Scott Co., Iowa Territory, and at Keokuk, Lee Co., Iowa Territory. Drowned near Prairie du Chien, Crawford Co., Wisconsin.

Johnson, Orson (15 June 1803–21 Mar. 1883), shoemaker, innkeeper, farmer. Born at Chesterfield, Cheshire Co., New Hampshire. Son of Thomas Johnson and Elizabeth (Betsey) Smith. Married first Nancy Mason, 24 Oct. 1827, at Bath, Grafton Co., New Hampshire. Baptized into LDS church by Orson Pratt and Lyman E. Johnson, 1832, in Bath. Attended church conference for elders near Big Blue River, Jackson Co., Missouri, 27 Sept. 1832. Moved to Kirtland, Geauga Co., Ohio. Member of Kirtland high council, 28 Aug. 1834. Excommunicated, by 3 Sept. 1837. Moved to Copperas, Peoria Co., Illinois, by June 1840. Married second Caroline M. C. Hassler, 22 May 1855, in Boston. Moved to Trivoli, Peoria Co., by June 1860; to Altona, Knox Co., Illinois, by June 1870; and to San Bernardino Co., California, after 1880. Died at San Bernardino Co.

Kimball, Heber Chase (14 June 1801–22 June 1868), blacksmith, potter. Born at Sheldon, Franklin Co., Vermont. Son of Solomon Farnham Kimball and Anna Spaulding. Married Vilate Murray, 22 Nov. 1822, at Mendon, Monroe Co., New York. Member of Baptist church at Mendon, 1831. Baptized into LDS church by Alpheus Gifford, 15 Apr. 1832, at Mendon. Ordained an elder by Joseph Young, 1832. Moved to Kirtland, Geauga Co., Ohio, 1833. Participated in Camp of Israel expedition to Missouri, 1834. Ordained member of Quorum of the Twelve by Oliver Cowdery, David Whitmer, and Martin Harris, 14 Feb. 1835, at Kirtland. Served mission to the East with Quorum of the Twelve, 1835. Served mission to eastern states, 1836. Stockholder in Kirtland Safety Society. Presided over first Latter-day Saint missionaries to British Isles, 1837–1838. Moved to Far West, Caldwell Co., Missouri, 1838. Worked closely with Brigham Young and others in supervising removal of Latter-day Saints from Missouri, 1838–1839. Present at Far West temple site, 26 Apr. 1839, when members of Quorum of the Twelve formally began their missionary assignment to British Isles. In removing from Missouri, initially located at Quincy, Adams Co., Illinois, and then at Commerce (later Nauvoo), Hancock Co., Illinois, May 1839. Served mission with Quorum of the Twelve to British Isles, 1839–1841. Member of Nauvoo City Council, 1841–1845. Member of Nauvoo Masonic Lodge. Participated in plural marriage during JS's lifetime. Served mission to eastern states, 1843. Labored on Nauvoo temple. Admitted to Council of Fifty, 11 Mar. 1844. Joined exodus from Illinois into Iowa Territory, Feb. 1846. Member of Brigham Young pioneer company to Salt Lake Valley; arrived July 1847. Sustained as first counselor to Brigham Young in First Presidency at what became Council Bluffs, Pottawattamie Co., Iowa, 27 Dec. 1847. Elected lieutenant governor in provisional state of Deseret. Served in Utah territorial legislature. Died at Salt Lake City.

Kingsbury, Joseph Corrodon (2 May 1812–15 Oct. 1898), mining superintendent, store clerk, teacher, farmer, ferry operator, tithing storehouse supervisor, Temple Square guide. Born at Enfield, Hartford Co., Connecticut. Son of Solomon Kingsbury and Bathsheba Amanda Pease. Moved from Enfield to Painesville, Geauga Co., Ohio, ca. Sept. 1812. Baptized into LDS church by Burr Riggs, 15 Jan. 1832. Ordained an elder, 23 July 1833, at Kirtland, Geauga Co. Served mission to eastern states, 1835. Ordained a high priest and appointed to Kirtland high council, 13 Jan. 1836. Married to Caroline Whitney by JS, 3 Feb. 1836, at Kirtland. Moved to Far West, Caldwell Co., Missouri, May–Sept. 1838. Joined exodus from Missouri, Jan. 1839, and finally located at Montrose, Lee Co., Iowa Territory. Appointed to Zarahemla high council, 24 Apr. 1841, at Montrose. Clerk in JS's red brick store in Nauvoo, Hancock Co., Illinois, 1841–1842. Wife died, Oct. 1842. Served mission to eastern states, 1843–1844. Entered Salt Lake Valley, Sept. 1847. Appointed bishop of Salt Lake City Second Ward, July 1851. Supervisor of tithing storehouse, 1865–1889. Ordained a patriarch, 25 Jan. 1883. Died at Salt Lake City.

Knight, Newel (13 Sept. 1800–11 Jan. 1847), miller, merchant. Born at Marlborough, Windham Co., Vermont. Son of Joseph Knight Sr. and Polly Peck. Moved to Jericho (later Bainbridge), Chenango Co., New York, ca. 1809. Moved to Windsor (later in Colesville), Broome Co., New York, 1811. Married first Sarah (Sally) Coburn, 7 June 1825. Became acquainted with JS when Knight's father hired JS, 1826. Baptized into LDS church by David Whitmer, last week of May 1830, in Seneca Co., New York. Ordained a priest, 26 Sept. 1830. President of Colesville branch of church; led Colesville branch from Broome Co. to Thompson, Geauga Co., Ohio, Apr.–May 1831. Ordained an elder, before June 1831. Moved again with Colesville branch to Kaw Township, Jackson Co., Missouri, July 1831. Ordained a high priest, by July 1832. Expelled from Jackson Co. and moved to Clay Co., Missouri, Nov. 1833. Appointed member of Missouri high council in Clay Co., July 1834. Wife died, Sept. 1834. Lived at Kirtland, Geauga Co., Ohio, spring 1835–spring 1836. Married second to Lydia Goldthwaite Bailey by JS, 24 Nov. 1835, at Kirtland. Lived at Clay Co., 1836. Member of high council at Far West, Caldwell Co., Missouri, 1837–1838. Left Missouri during exodus and moved to Commerce (later Nauvoo), Hancock Co., Illinois, 1839. Member of Commerce/Nauvoo high council, 1839–1845. Left Nauvoo, 1846. Died at Fort Ponca (later near Niobrara in present-day northern Nebraska).

Knight, Vinson (14 Mar. 1804–31 July 1842), farmer, druggist, school warden. Born at Norwich, Hampshire Co., Massachusetts. Son of Rudolphus Knight and Rispah (Rizpah) Lee. Married Martha McBride, July 1826. Moved to Perrysburg, Cattaraugus Co., New York, by 1830. Owned farm at Perrysburg when baptized into LDS church, spring 1834. Moved to Kirtland, Geauga Co., Ohio, by 24 June 1835. Ordained an elder, 2 Jan. 1836. Ordained a high priest and appointed counselor to Bishop Newel K. Whitney, 13 Jan. 1836, at Kirtland. Stockholder in Kirtland Safety Society. Appointed township clerk, 1837. Traveled with JS and others to Far West, Missouri, 1837. Located at Adam-ondi-Ahman, Daviess Co., Missouri, summer 1838. Appointed acting bishop at Adam-ondi-Ahman, 28 June 1838. Exiled from Missouri; located at Quincy, Adams Co., Illinois, 1839. Church land agent; with others purchased approximately 19,000 acres of Half-Breed Tract in Lee Co., Iowa Territory, from Isaac Galland, and about 190 acres in Hancock Co., Illinois, from Galland and Hugh White, 1839. Appointed bishop in Commerce (later Nauvoo), Hancock Co., 4 May 1839. Appointed bishop of Lower Ward at Commerce, 5 Oct. 1839. Instructed in JS revelation to buy stock for building Nauvoo House, 19 Jan. 1841. Appointed presiding bishop of church, 19 Jan. 1841. Member of Nauvoo City Council, 1841–1842. Served as warden of Nauvoo common schools and member of Nauvoo University building committee, 1841–1842. Appointed guard in Nauvoo Legion, Mar. 1841. Member of Nauvoo Masonic Lodge. Died at Nauvoo.

Marks, William (15 Nov. 1792–22 May 1872), farmer, printer, publisher, postmaster. Born at Rutland, Rutland Co., Vermont. Son of Cornell (Cornwall) Marks and Sarah Goodrich. Married first Rosannah R. Robinson, 2 May 1813. Lived at Portage, Allegany Co., New York, where he was baptized into LDS church, by Apr. 1835. Ordained a priest, by 3 Apr. 1835. Ordained an elder, by 3 June 1836. Moved to Kirtland, Geauga Co., Ohio, by Sept. 1837. Appointed member of Kirtland high council, 3 Sept. 1837, and agent to Bishop Newel K. Whitney, 17 Sept. 1837. President of Kirtland stake, 1838. While at Kirtland, appointed stake president at Far West, Caldwell Co., Missouri, 8 July 1838. Did not reach Far West before expulsion of Latter-day Saints from Missouri. Located with Latter-day Saints at Quincy, Adams Co., Illinois, 1839. Appointed president of stake in Commerce (later Nauvoo), Hancock Co., Illinois, 5 Oct. 1839. Instructed in JS revelation to buy stock for building Nauvoo House, 19 Jan. 1841. Nauvoo city alderman, 1841–1843. Appointed a regent of University of Nauvoo, 3 Feb. 1841. Appointed guard in Nauvoo Legion, Mar. 1841. Member of Nauvoo Masonic Lodge. Admitted to Council of Fifty, 19 Mar. 1844. Aligned himself with leadership claims of Sidney Rigdon following death of JS, 1844. Rejected from Council of Fifty, 4 Feb. 1845. Left Nauvoo, Mar. 1845. Counselor to James J. Strang, 6 Mar. 1846. Located at Shabbona, De Kalb Co., Illinois, by June 1850. Affiliated with Charles B. Thompson, 1852–1853, and John E. Page, 1855, in leadership of new religious movements. Baptized into RLDS church, 10 June 1859, at Amboy, Lee Co., Illinois. Ordained a counselor in RLDS church presidency, 8 Apr. 1863. Married second Julia A. Muir, 5 Sept. 1866, in Shabbona. Moved to Little Rock, Kendall Co., Illinois, by June 1870. Died at Plano, Kendall Co.

Marsh, Thomas Baldwin (1 Nov. 1800–Jan. 1866), farmer, hotel worker, waiter, horse groom, grocer, type foundry worker, teacher. Born at Acton, Middlesex Co., Massachusetts.

Son of James Marsh and Molly Law. Married first Elizabeth Godkin, 1 Nov. 1820, at New York City. Moved to Boston, 1822. Joined Methodist church at Boston. Migrated to Palmyra, Wayne Co., New York, by Sept. 1830. Baptized into LDS church by David Whitmer, 3 Sept. 1830, at Cayuga Lake, Seneca Co., New York. Ordained an elder by Oliver Cowdery, Sept. 1830. Moved to Kirtland, Geauga Co., Ohio, with Manchester, Ontario Co., New York, branch of church, May 1831. Ordained a high priest by Lyman Wight, 4 June 1831, at Kirtland. Served mission to Missouri, June 1831–Jan. 1832. Moved to Jackson Co., Missouri, 10 Nov. 1832. Appointed president of Big Blue River, Jackson Co., branch. Expelled from Jackson Co., 1833. Lived in Lafayette Co., Missouri, winter 1833–1834. Member of Clay Co., Missouri, high council, 1834. Ordained member of Quorum of the Twelve, 26 Apr. 1835, at Kirtland. Sustained as president of Quorum of the Twelve, 2 May 1835. Served mission with the Twelve to eastern states, 1835. President pro tempore of church in Far West, Caldwell Co., Missouri, 10 Feb. 1838. Withdrew from church at Far West, 22 Oct. 1838. Excommunicated in absentia, 17 Mar. 1839, at Quincy, Adams Co., Illinois. Moved to Clay Co. and Ray Co., Missouri, before settling in Bonne Femme, Howard Co., Missouri, by June 1840. Moved to Grundy Co., Missouri, by 1854. Wife died, 1854. Sought readmittance, Jan. 1857. Rebaptized into LDS church at Florence, Douglas Co., Nebraska, 16 July 1857. Married second Hannah Adams, 4 Oct. 1857. Migrated to Utah Territory, 1857. Settled at Spanish Fork, Utah Co., Utah Territory, where he taught school. Moved to Ogden, Weber Co., Utah Territory, latter part of 1862. Died at Ogden.

Matthews, Robert (1788–ca. 1841), carpenter, joiner, merchant, minister. Born at Cambridge, Washington Co., New York. Raised in Anti-Burgher Secession Church. Married Margaret Wright, 1813, at New York City. Adopted beliefs of Methodism and then Judaism. Moved to Albany, ca. 1825. Claimed to be God the Father reincarnated in body of Matthias, the ancient apostle. Prophesied destruction of Albany, 1830. Left Albany and his family to embark on apostolic preaching tour through eastern and southern U.S. Upon returning to New York, recruited local religious figures Elijah Pierson and Benjamin Folger. Committed to hospital for the insane at Bellevue, New York City, for a time. Little is known of Matthews after his 1835 visit with JS at Kirtland, Geauga Co., Ohio. Reported to have died in Iowa Territory.

McBride, Reuben (16 June 1803–26 Feb. 1891), farmer. Born at Chester, Washington Co., New York. Son of Daniel McBride and Abigail Mead. Married Mary Ann Anderson, 16 June 1833. Baptized into LDS church, 4 Mar. 1834, at Villanova, Chautauque Co., New York. Participated in Camp of Israel expedition to Missouri, 1834. Appointed member of Second Quorum of the Seventy, Feb. 1835. Lived at Kirtland, Geauga Co., Ohio, ca. 1836–1848. Appointed counselor in Kirtland bishopric, 22 May 1841. Migrated to Salt Lake Valley, 1850. Returned to Kirtland, 1851. Settled at Fillmore, Millard Co., Utah Territory, by 1853. Appointed to serve mission to Europe, 1857. Served mission to England, 1867. Member of Millard stake high council, 1877–1884. Died at Fillmore.

McLellin, William E. (18 Jan. 1806–14 Mar. 1883), schoolteacher, physician, publisher. Born at Smith Co., Tennessee. Son of Charles McLellin and Sarah (a Cherokee Indian). Married first Cynthia Ann, 30 July 1829. Wife died, by summer 1831. Baptized into LDS church by Hyrum Smith, 20 Aug. 1831, in Jackson Co., Missouri. Ordained an elder by Hyrum Smith and Edward Partridge, 24 Aug. 1831. Ordained a high priest by

Oliver Cowdery, 25 Oct. 1831. Served two short-term missions. Married second Emeline Miller, 26 Apr. 1832, at Portage Co., Ohio. Left Ohio for Independence, Jackson Co., Missouri, 2 May 1832. Excommunicated, 3 Dec. 1832. Apparently reinstated; served mission to Missouri and Illinois with Parley P. Pratt, Jan.–June 1833. Fled with fellow Latter-day Saints from Jackson Co. into Clay Co., Missouri, Nov. 1833. Proselytized in Indiana on way to Kirtland, Geauga Co., Ohio, 1834. Appointed instructor in Kirtland School, 19 Nov. 1834. Ordained member of Quorum of the Twelve, 15 Feb. 1835. Disfellowshipped over difficulties arising during eastern mission with Quorum of the Twelve; reinstated 26 Sept. 1835. Wrote letter of withdrawal from church, Aug. 1836. Again sustained to Quorum of the Twelve, 3 Sept. 1837, at Kirtland. In Far West, Caldwell Co., Missouri, commissioned captain in First Company, Fifty-Ninth Regiment, Second Brigade, Third Division of Missouri state militia, 22 Nov. 1837. Excommunicated, 1838. Associated with factions organized under leadership of George M. Hinkle, William Law, Sidney Rigdon, James J. Strang, David Whitmer, and Granville Hedrick. Broke with all organized religion, 1869. Died at Independence.

McWithy, Isaac (1778–4 May 1851), farmer. Born in New York. Married Hannah Taylor of Vermont. Moved to Covington, Genesee Co., New York, by 1820. Lived at Bennington, Genesee Co., with family of five, 1830. Ordained an elder, 15 Feb. 1833. Lived at Kirtland, Geauga Co., Ohio, 1835. Appointed to Missouri high council, 13 Jan. 1836, in Kirtland. Stockholder in Kirtland Safety Society. Died at Kirtland.

Miles, Daniel Sanborn (23 July 1772–12 Oct. 1845). Born at Sanbornton, Belknap Co., New Hampshire. Son of Josiah Miles and Marah Sanborn. Married Electa Chamberlin, 30 Sept. 1813. Moved to Bath, Grafton Co., New Hampshire, by 1820. Baptized into LDS church by Orson Pratt and Lyman E. Johnson, Apr. 1832, at Bath. Moved to Kirtland, Geauga Co., Ohio, 1836. Ordained an elder by Reuben Hedlock, 28 Feb. 1836, in Kirtland. Stockholder in Kirtland Safety Society. Ordained a seventy by Hazen Aldrich, 20 Dec. 1836. Appointed a president of the Seventy, 6 Apr. 1837. Arrived at Far West, Caldwell Co., Missouri, Mar. 1838. Early settler at Commerce (later Nauvoo), Hancock Co., Illinois. Died in Hancock Co.

Millet, Artemus (11 Sept. 1790–19 Nov. 1874), farmer, lumberman, merchant, builder, stonemason. Born at Westmoreland, Cheshire Co., New Hampshire. Son of Ebenezer Millet and Catherine Dryden. Moved to Stockbridge, Windsor Co., Vermont, fall 1800; to Shelburn, Chittendon Co., Vermont, 1809; and to Louisville, St. Lawrence Co., New York, 1810. Returned to Stockbridge, 1811. Married first Ruth Grannis of Milton, Chittenden Co., 17 May 1815. Moved near Plattsburg, Clinton Co., New York, 1815. Moved to Volney, Oswego Co., New York, fall 1816. Member of Methodist church. Moved to Long Island, Queens Co., New York, 1822. Moved to Ernestown (later in Lennox and Addington Co., Ontario), Upper Canada, 1824. Married second Susanna Peters, 15 Jan. 1832, in Ernestown. Baptized into LDS church by Brigham Young and confirmed by Joseph Young, Jan. 1833, at Loughborough, Frontenac Co., Midland District (later in Ontario), Upper Canada. In Oct. 1833, moved to Kirtland, Geauga Co., Ohio, where he supervised construction of temple. Ordained an elder and served mission to Highland Co., Ohio, 1836. Stockholder in Kirtland Safety Society. Moved back to Upper Canada, ca. 1837; returned to Ohio, 1841. Returned to body of church in Nauvoo, Hancock Co., Illinois, Apr. 1843. Married third Catherine Almira Prichard

Oaks, 20 Apr. 1843. Ordained a high priest by Noah Packard, 8 Oct. 1844, in Nauvoo. Left Nauvoo, summer 1846. Married fourth Triphenia Booth, Oct. 1847, in Iowa. Married fifth Nancy Lemaster, 11 Mar. 1849, in Kanesville (later Council Bluffs), Pottawattamie Co., Iowa. Moved to northern Missouri, 1849. Migrated to Utah Territory, Oct. 1850. Arrived at Manti, Sanpete Co., Utah Territory, to serve colonizing mission, 18 Nov. 1850. Appointed president of Manti high council, 30 Apr. 1851. Served colonizing missions to various locations in present-day southern Utah and Nevada. Died at Scipio, Millard Co., Utah Territory.

Milliken, Nathaniel (25 Dec. 1793–Aug. 1874), farmer, post office clerk. Born at Buxton, York Co., Maine. Son of Nathaniel Milliken and Mary Lord. Married first Mary Fairfield Hayes, 22 Apr. 1819. Baptized into LDS church, 1 Oct. 1833, at Buxton. Moved to Kirtland, Geauga Co., Ohio, ca. 1834. Appointed member of Second Quorum of the Seventy, Apr. 1836. Stockholder in Kirtland Safety Society. Excommunicated, by 7 Jan. 1838. Wife died, 1853. Married second Mary Beckwith, 26 Jan. 1862. Died at Kirtland.

Morey, George (30 Nov. 1803–15 Dec. 1875), farmer. Born at Pittstown, Rensselaer Co., New York. Son of William Morey and Anda Martin. Moved to Collinsville, Butler Co., Ohio, 1814. Married Sylvia Butterfield, 29 Oct. 1825, at Butler Co. Moved to Vermillion Co., Illinois, 1831. Baptized into LDS church, 1833. Located in Clay Co., Missouri, 1834; in Kirtland, Geauga Co., Ohio, 1835–1836; and in Far West, Caldwell Co., Missouri, by Aug. 1837. Member of Far West high council, 1837–1838. Participated in Battle of Crooked River, near Ray Co., Missouri, 25 Oct. 1838. Returned to Vermillion Co., by June 1840. Moved to Nauvoo, Hancock Co., Illinois, by 1841. Ordained a high priest, 1841. Constable in Nauvoo, 1841. Member of Nauvoo Legion. Supported Sidney Rigdon as successor to JS. Moved to Brown Co., Illinois, late 1844; to DeKalb Co., Illinois, 1849; and to Whiteside Co., Illinois, 1851. Settled at Hamilton Township, Decatur Co., Iowa, 1852. Presided over Little River branch of RLDS church, in Pleasanton, Decatur Co., 1859. Died near Pleasanton.

Morley, Isaac (11 Mar. 1786–24 June 1865), farmer, cooper, merchant, postmaster. Born at Montague, Hampshire Co., Massachusetts. Son of Thomas Morley and Editha (Edith) Marsh. Family affiliated with Presbyterian church. Moved to Kirtland, Geauga Co., Ohio, before 1812. Married Lucy Gunn, June 1812, at Montague; immediately returned to Kirtland. Served in War of 1812 as private and captain in Ohio militia. Elected trustee of Kirtland, 1818. Baptized into reformed Baptist (later Disciples of Christ or Campbellite) faith by Sidney Rigdon, 1828. Baptized into LDS church by Parley P. Pratt, 15 Nov. 1830. Saints migrating from New York settled on his farm at Kirtland, 1831. Ordained a high priest by Lyman Wight, 4 June 1831. Counselor to Bishop Edward Partridge at Kirtland, 1831, and in Missouri, 1831–1838. Lived at Independence, Jackson Co., Missouri, 1831. Appointed to set in order branches of church in Missouri, 3 Dec. 1832. Appointed bishop, 25 June 1833. Driven from Jackson Co. into Clay Co., Missouri, Nov. 1833. Member of Missouri high council, by 19 Dec. 1833. Served mission to eastern U.S. with Edward Partridge, June–Oct. 1835. Returned to Missouri and moved family to what became Far West, Caldwell Co., Missouri, Apr. 1836. Ordained a patriarch by JS, Sidney Rigdon, and Hyrum Smith, 7 Nov. 1837. Moved to Hancock Co., Illinois, 1839; founded Yelrome (Morley's Settlement, later in Tioga), where he served as bishop. Appointed president of stake at Lima, Adams Co., Illinois, 22 Oct. 1840. Member of Masonic lodge in Nauvoo, Hancock Co. Moved to Nauvoo, 1845. Admitted to

Council of Fifty, 11 Apr. 1845. Moved to Winter Quarters, unorganized U.S. territory (later in Omaha, Douglas Co., Nebraska), 1846. Migrated to Salt Lake Valley, 1848. Elected senator of provisional state of Deseret, 12 Mar. 1849. Led initial settlement of Latter-day Saints at Sanpete Valley, unorganized U.S. territory (later in Sanpete Co., Utah Territory), 28 Oct. 1849, and presided at Manti, Sanpete Co., 1849–1853. Member of Utah territorial legislature, 1851–1857. Died at Fairview, Sanpete Co.

Morton, John (31 Jan. 1790–1 Jan. 1858), carpenter, joiner. Born at Portsmouth, Rockingham Co., New Hampshire. Son of Isaac Morton and Anna Barber. Married Elizabeth Stimson, ca. 1812, at Batavia, Genesee Co., New York. Baptized into LDS church, by Jan. 1836. Appointed counselor in Kirtland, Geauga Co., Ohio, elders quorum, 28 Jan. 1836; served as president of that quorum, 1838–1840. Ordained a high priest, Nov. 1840. Died at Akron, Summit Co., Ohio.

Murdock, John (15 July 1792–23 Dec. 1871), farmer. Born at Kortright, Delaware Co., New York. Son of John Murdock Sr. and Eleanor Riggs. Joined Lutheran Dutch Church, ca. 1817, then Presbyterian Seceder Church shortly after. Moved to Orange, Cuyahoga Co., Ohio, ca. 1819. Baptized into Baptist church, at Orange. Married first Julia Clapp of Mentor, Geauga Co., Ohio, 14 Dec. 1823. Joined reformed Baptist (later Disciples of Christ or Campbellite) faith, ca. 1827. Baptized into LDS church by Parley P. Pratt, 5 Nov. 1830, at Kirtland, Geauga Co. Ordained an elder by Oliver Cowdery, 7 Nov. 1830, at Mayfield, Cuyahoga Co. Organized branches of church at Orange and Warrensville, Cuyahoga Co., 1831. Wife died following birth of twins, 30 Apr. 1831, at Warrensville. JS and Emma Smith adopted the twins, Joseph and Julia. Ordained a high priest by JS, 4 June 1831, at Kirtland. Left to serve mission to Missouri with Hyrum Smith, June 1831. Appointed to serve mission to Missouri, Ohio, and Virginia, Jan. 1832. Attended organizational meeting of School of the Prophets, 22–23 Jan. 1833, in Kirtland. Left to serve mission to eastern states with Zebedee Coltrin, Apr. 1833. Participated in Camp of Israel expedition to Missouri, 1834. Member of Missouri high council, 1834. Served mission to Vermont and New York, 1835–1836. Married second Amoranda Turner, 4 Feb. 1836; she died, 1837. Married third Electra Allen, 3 May 1838. With George M. Hinkle, purchased large number of lots for Mormon settlement in De Witt, Carroll Co., Missouri, 23 June 1838. Forced out of De Witt by vigilantes, 11 Oct. 1838; returned to Far West, 14 Oct. 1838. Left Far West for Quincy, Adams Co., Illinois, 4 Feb. 1839. Lived near Lima, Adams Co., 1839–1841. Moved to Nauvoo, Hancock Co., Illinois, spring 1841. Bishop of Nauvoo Fifth Ward, 1842–1844. Served mission to Indiana, Nov. 1844–Mar. 1845. Wife died, 1845. Married fourth Sarah Zufelt, 13 Mar. 1846, in Fulton Co., Illinois. Arrived in Salt Lake Valley, 24 Sept. 1847. Member of Salt Lake high council, ca. 1847–1849, and appointed bishop of Salt Lake City Fourteenth Ward, 1849. Served in Utah territorial legislature, 1849–1851. Served mission to Australia, 1851–1853. Moved to Lehi, Utah Co., Utah Territory, ca. 1854. Served as patriarch, Apr. 1854–Mar. 1867. Moved to Beaver, Beaver Co., Utah Territory, fall 1867. Died at Beaver.

Orton, Roger (ca. 1799–1851), miller. Son of Roger Orton and Esther Avery. Moved to Geneseo, Ontario Co., New York, by 1810. Married Clarissa Bicknell, ca. 1822. Baptized into LDS church. Ordained an elder, by 1834. Participated in Camp of Israel expedition to Missouri, 1834. Appointed to high council in Kirtland, Geauga Co., Ohio, and to First Quorum of Seventy, by 1835. Stockholder in Kirtland Safety Society. Excommunicated, 1837, at Kirtland; later restored to membership. Appointed a president of the Seventy, ca. 1844; never accepted, and appointment later rescinded. Moved to Des Moines Co., Iowa Territory, by 1840. Lived in Augusta, Des Moines Co., 1845. Moved to Lee Co., Iowa, by 1850. Died in Iowa.

Packard, Noah (7 May 1796–17 Feb. 1860), farmer, surveyor, miner. Born at Plainfield, Hampshire Co., Massachusetts. Son of Noah Packard and Molly Hamblin. Moved to Parkman, Geauga Co., Ohio, 1817. Married Sophia Bundy, 29 June 1820, at Parkman. Baptized into LDS church by Parley P. Pratt, June 1832, in Parkman. Ordained a priest by JS, 3 Dec. 1832, at Kirtland, Geauga Co. Appointed to serve mission to Parkman, 5 Dec. 1832. Left to serve mission to eastern U.S., 22 Apr. 1833. Ordained an elder by John Gould, 6 May 1833, at Westfield, Chautauque Co., New York. Appointed president of Parkman branch, 1833. Moved to Kirtland, 1835. Ordained a high priest, 13 Jan. 1836. Member of Kirtland high council, 1836. Stockholder in Kirtland Safety Society. Left Ohio for Missouri, late fall 1838, but instead spent winter at Wellsville, Columbiana Co., Ohio. Located at Quincy, Adams Co., Illinois, 1839. Moved to Commerce (later Nauvoo), Hancock Co., Illinois, 18 May 1839. Served as counselor in Nauvoo high priests quorum presidency under Don Carlos Smith and then George Miller, 1840–1846. Served missions to various U.S. states, 1841–1843, 1845. Agent for church to collect funds in Michigan for Nauvoo temple, 1845. Moved to Hazelgreen, Orren Co., Wisconsin, spring 1846. Migrated to Utah Territory, 18 Sept. 1850. In 1851, settled at Springville, Utah Co., Utah Territory, where he was appointed first counselor in branch presidency. Alderman in Springville city government. Died at Springville.

Parrish, Martha H. Raymond (1 Dec. 1804–1/14 July 1875). Born in Massachusetts. Married to Warren F. Parrish by JS, 3 Dec. 1835, at Kirtland, Geauga Co., Ohio. Lived at Chardon, Geauga Co., 1840; at Mendon, Monroe Co., New York, 1850; at Rockford, Winnebago Co., Illinois, 1860; and at Emporia, Lyon Co., Kansas, 1870. Died at Emporia.

Parrish, Warren Farr (10 Jan. 1803–3 Jan. 1877), clergyman, gardener. Born in New York. Son of John Parrish and Ruth Farr. Married first Elizabeth (Betsey) Patten of Westmoreland Co., New Hampshire, ca. 1822. Lived at Alexandria, Jefferson Co., New York, 1830. Purchased land at Chaumont, Lyme Township, Jefferson Co., 1831. Baptized by Brigham Young, 20 May 1833, at Theresa, Jefferson Co. Participated in Camp of Israel expedition to Missouri, 1834. Wife died of cholera at Rush Creek, Clay Co., Missouri, while accompanying him on expedition, 27 June 1834. Served mission to Missouri, Kentucky, and Tennessee with David W. Patten, 1834. Appointed member of First Quorum of the Seventy, 1835. Served mission to Kentucky and Tennessee with Wilford Woodruff, 1835. Worked as scribe for JS, 1835. Married second to Martha H. Raymond by JS, 3 Dec. 1835, at Kirtland, Geauga Co., Ohio. Served as clerk for Kirtland Safety Society, late 1836. Appointed treasurer of Kirtland Safety Society, by July 1837. Led movement of reformers opposed to JS. Lived at Chardon, Geauga Co., 1840. Baptist clergyman in Fox River area of Wisconsin/Illinois, 1844. Clergyman at Mendon, Monroe Co., New York, 1850. Lived at Rockford, Winnebago Co., Illinois, 1860. Lived at Emporia, Lyon Co., Kansas, 1870. Wife died, 1875. Died at Emporia.

Partridge, Edward (27 Aug. 1793–27 May 1840), hatter. Born at Pittsfield, Berkshire Co., Massachusetts. Son of William Partridge and Jemima Bidwell. Moved to Painesville,

Geauga Co., Ohio. Married Lydia Clisbee, 22 Aug. 1819, at Painesville. Initially a Universal Restorationist but adhered to reformed Baptist (later Disciples of Christ or Campbellite) faith when first contacted by Mormon missionaries in Nov. 1830. With Sidney Rigdon, visited JS at Fayette, Seneca Co., New York. Baptized into LDS church by JS, 11 Dec. 1830, in nearby Seneca River. Ordained an elder by Sidney Rigdon, by 15 Dec. 1830. Named first bishop in church, Feb. 1831, at Kirtland, Geauga Co. Ordained a high priest by Lyman Wight, 4 June 1831, at Kirtland. Accompanied JS to Missouri and appointed to oversee settlement of Saints in Missouri, summer 1831. Involved in administering stewardships of land under law of consecration. Appointed member of United Firm, Apr. 1832. Tarred and feathered during mob violence in Jackson Co., Missouri, July 1833. Fled with family to Clay Co., Missouri, Nov. 1833. Served as bishop in Clay Co. Served mission to Missouri, Illinois, Indiana, and Ohio, Jan.–Apr. 1835. Served mission to New York and New England, June–Oct. 1835. In fall 1836, forced to move from Clay Co. to what soon became Caldwell Co., Missouri, where he continued to serve as bishop. Jailed at Richmond, Ray Co., Missouri, fall 1838. Exiled from state, 1839. Appointed bishop of Upper Ward at Commerce (later Nauvoo), Hancock Co., Illinois, 1839. Died at Nauvoo.

Patten, David Wyman (14 Nov. 1799–25 Oct. 1838), farmer. Born in Vermont. Son of Benoni Patten and Edith Cole. Moved to Theresa, Oneida Co., New York, as a young child. Moved to Dundee, Monroe Co., Michigan Territory, as a youth. Married Phoebe Ann Babcock, 1828, in Dundee. Affiliated with the Methodists. Baptized into LDS church by his brother John Patten, 15 June 1832, at Fairplay, Greene Co., Indiana. Ordained an elder by Elisha H. Groves, 17 June 1832. Served mission to Michigan Territory, 1832. Ordained a high priest by Hyrum Smith, 2 Sept. 1832. Served mission to eastern states, 1832–1833. Moved family from Michigan Territory to Florence, Erie Co., Ohio, 1833. With William Pratt, carried dispatches from JS to church leaders in Clay Co., Missouri, Dec. 1833. Served mission to southern U.S. with Warren F. Parrish, 1834–1835. Ordained member of Quorum of the Twelve, 15 Feb. 1835, at Kirtland, Geauga Co., Ohio. Served mission to Tennessee, spring 1835. With the Twelve, served mission to eastern states, summer 1835. Moved from Kirtland to Far West, Missouri, 1836. Member of presidency pro tempore of church in Far West, 1838. Captain of local militia in Caldwell Co., Missouri. Mortally wounded during battle of Crooked River, near Ray Co., Missouri, 25 Oct. 1838. Died near Far West.

Phelps, William Wines (17 Feb. 1792–7 Mar. 1872), writer, teacher, printer, newspaper editor, publisher, postmaster, lawyer. Born at Hanover, Morris Co., New Jersey. Son of Enon Phelps and Mehitabel Goldsmith. Moved to Homer, Cortland Co., New York, 1800. Married Sally Waterman, 28 Apr. 1815, in Smyrna, Chenango Co., New York. Editor of *Western Courier*. Moved to Wooster, Wayne Co., Ohio, by 3 July 1819. Returned to Homer, by Nov. 1821. Moved to Trumansburg, Tompkins Co., New York, 1823. Edited Anti-Masonic newspaper *Lake Light*. Moved to Canandaigua, Ontario Co., New York, Apr. 1828, and there published Anti-Masonic newspaper *Ontario Phoenix*. Obtained copy of Book of Mormon, 1830. Met JS, 24 Dec. 1830. Migrated to Kirtland, Geauga Co., Ohio, 1831. Baptized into LDS church, 16 June 1831, at Kirtland. Ordained an elder by JS, June 1831, at Kirtland. Appointed church printer, 20 July 1831. Ordained a high priest by JS, 1 Oct. 1831. Appointed member of what became the Literary Firm, Nov. 1831. Moved to Jackson Co.,

Missouri, late 1831. Appointed member of United Firm, Apr. 1832. Became editor of *The Evening and the Morning Star* and *Upper Missouri Advertiser,* published 1832–1833 at Independence, Jackson Co. Published Book of Commandments, but most copies destroyed by mob when printing office was razed, 20 July 1833. Exiled from Jackson Co. to Clay Co., Missouri, Nov. 1833. Appointed counselor/assistant president to David Whitmer, president of church in Missouri, 3 July 1834. Returned to Kirtland and served as JS's scribe. Helped compile Doctrine and Covenants and first Latter-day Saint hymnal, 1835, at Kirtland. Prolific writer of hymns. Appointed to draft rules and regulations for Kirtland temple, 13 Jan. 1836. Returned from Kirtland to Clay Co., where he resumed duties with Missouri presidency, 1836. Appointed postmaster, 27 May 1837, at Far West, Caldwell Co., Missouri. Excommunicated, 10 Mar. 1838. Moved to Dayton, Montgomery Co., Ohio, before Mar. 1840. Reconciled with church; rebaptized into LDS church, late June 1840. Returned to Kirtland, by May 1841. Appointed to serve mission to eastern U.S., 23 May 1841. Appointed recorder of church licenses, 2 Oct. 1841, in Kirtland. Moved to Nauvoo, Hancock Co., Illinois, by Nov. 1842. Acted as clerk to JS and assisted John Taylor in editing *Times and Seasons* and *Nauvoo Neighbor.* Assisted Willard Richards in writing JS's history, by Jan. 1843. Elected fire warden, 11 Feb. 1843. Elected to Nauvoo City Council, early 1844. Admitted to Council of Fifty, 11 Mar. 1844. Migrated to Salt Lake Valley, 1848. Served as counselor to Parley P. Pratt on exploration mission to southern Utah Territory, Nov. 1849. Admitted to Utah territorial bar, 1851. Member of Utah territorial Legislative Assembly, 1851–1857. Died at Salt Lake City.

Pratt, Orson (19 Sept. 1811–3 Oct. 1881), farmer, writer, teacher, merchant, surveyor, editor, publisher. Born at Hartford, Washington Co., New York. Son of Jared Pratt and Charity Dickinson. Moved to New Lebanon, Columbia Co., New York, 1814; to Canaan, Columbia Co., fall 1823; to Hurl Gate, Queens Co., New York, spring 1825; and to New York City, spring 1826. Returned to Hurl Gate, fall 1826, and to Canaan, spring 1827. Moved to Lorain Co., Ohio, fall 1827; to Chagrin (later Willoughby), Cuyahoga Co., Ohio, spring 1828; and to Connecticut, fall 1828. Returned to Hurl Gate, winter 1828–1829, and to Canaan, spring 1829. Baptized into LDS church by Parley P. Pratt, 19 Sept. 1830, at Canaan. Ordained an elder by JS, 1 Dec. 1830, in Fayette, Seneca Co., New York, and appointed to serve mission to Colesville, Broome Co., New York. With Samuel Smith, traveled from New York to Kirtland, Geauga Co., Ohio; arrived, 27 Feb. 1831. Served mission to Missouri, summer 1831. Moved to Hiram, Portage Co., Ohio, Dec. 1831. Ordained a high priest by Sidney Rigdon, 2 Feb. 1832, in Hiram. Began mission with Lyman E. Johnson to the East from Kirtland, Feb. 1832. Participated in Camp of Israel expedition to Missouri, 1834. Ordained member of Quorum of the Twelve by David Whitmer and Oliver Cowdery, 26 Apr. 1835, at Kirtland. Married Sarah Marinda Bates, 4 July 1836, at Henderson, Jefferson Co., New York. Served mission to Upper Canada, 1836. Served mission to Great Britain with other members of Quorum of the Twelve, 1839–1841. Appointed assistant chaplain in Nauvoo Legion, 3 July 1841. Member of city council, 1841–1845, in Nauvoo, Hancock Co., Illinois. Member of Nauvoo Masonic Lodge. Excommunicated, 20 Aug. 1842, at Nauvoo. Rebaptized into LDS church, 20 Jan. 1843, and ordained to his former office in Quorum of the Twelve. Admitted to Council of Fifty, 11 Mar. 1844. Served mission to Washington DC and eastern U.S., 1844. Moved to what became Council Bluffs, Pottawattamie Co., Iowa Territory, 1846. Entered Salt Lake Valley with Mormon pioneers, 1847. Presided over church in Great Britain, 1848–1849, 1856–1857. Member of Utah territorial legislature. Appointed church historian, 1874. Died at Salt Lake City.

Pratt, Parley Parker (12 Apr. 1807–13 May 1857), farmer, editor, publisher, teacher, school administrator, legislator, explorer, author. Born at Burlington, Otsego Co., New York. Son of Jared Pratt and Charity Dickinson. Traveled west with brother William to acquire land, 1823. Affiliated with Baptist church at age eighteen. Lived in Ohio, 1826–1827. Married first Thankful Halsey, 9 Sept. 1827, at Canaan, Columbia Co., New York. Converted to reformed Baptist (later Disciples of Christ or Campbellite) faith by Sidney Rigdon, 1829. Baptized into LDS church and ordained an elder by Oliver Cowdery, 1 Sept. 1830, at Seneca Lake, Seneca Co., New York. Served mission to unorganized Indian Territory and Missouri with Oliver Cowdery and others, 1830–1831. En route, stopped at Kirtland, Geauga Co., Ohio, and vicinity; missionaries baptized some 130 individuals. Returned to Kirtland, 3 Apr. 1831. Ordained a high priest by Lyman Wight, 4 June 1831. Served mission to western U.S., 7 June 1831–May 1832. Moved to Jackson Co., Missouri, summer 1832. Appointed president of Elders School in Jackson Co. Left to serve mission to eastern U.S., Mar. 1834. Participated in Camp of Israel expedition to Missouri, 1834. Moved to Kirtland, Oct. 1834. Ordained member of Quorum of the Twelve by JS, David Whitmer, and Oliver Cowdery, 21 Feb. 1835. Served mission to eastern U.S., spring–28 Aug. 1835. Served mission to Canada, Apr.–June 1836. Stockholder in Kirtland Safety Society. Wife died, 25 Mar. 1837. Married second Mary Ann Frost Stearns, 14 May 1837, at Kirtland. Left to serve mission to New York City, July 1837. Moved to Far West, Caldwell Co., Missouri, Apr. 1838. Participated in battle of Crooked River, near Ray Co., Missouri, 25 Oct. 1838. Jailed at Richmond, Ray Co., and Columbia, Boone Co., Missouri, 1838–1839. Reunited with family, 11 July 1839, in Illinois. Served mission to England, 1839–1842. Edited first number of *LDS Millennial Star,* published in Manchester, England, 27 May 1840. President of British mission, 1841–1842. Arrived at Nauvoo, Hancock Co., Illinois, 7 Feb. 1843. Member of Nauvoo Masonic Lodge. Admitted to Council of Fifty, 11 Mar. 1844. Participated in plural marriage during JS's lifetime. Directed affairs of church in New York City, 1844–1845. Moved to what became Mount Pisgah, Clarke Co., Iowa Territory, 1846. Left to serve mission to England, 31 July 1846. Arrived at Winter Quarters, unorganized U.S. territory (later in Omaha, Douglas Co., Nebraska), 8 Apr. 1847. Arrived in Salt Lake Valley, 28 Sept. 1847. Led exploration party into southern Utah Territory, Nov. 1849–Feb. 1850. Served mission to Chile and California, 16 Mar. 1851–18 Oct. 1852. Served mission to eastern U.S., beginning Sept. 1856. Murdered at Van Buren, Crawford Co., Arkansas.

Redfield, Harlow (25 Sept. 1801–3 Aug. 1866), farmer. Born at Chestnut Hill, Killingworth Township, Middlesex Co., Connecticut. Son of Levi Redfield and Weltha Stevens. Christened member of First Congregational Church, 21 Jan. 1821. Married first Caroline Foster, 1824. Moved to Vermont, before 1830. Baptized into LDS church. Ordained a high priest, by 8 June 1833. Wife died, 26 Dec. 1834. Married second Alpha Foster, 11 Oct. 1835, in Killingworth Township. Moved to Kirtland, Geauga Co., Ohio, by 26 Dec. 1835. Received elder's license, 1 Apr. 1836. Stockholder in Kirtland Safety Society. Served as secretary of Kirtland high priests quorum, May 1837. Appointed to Kirtland high council, Sept. 1837. Moved to Far West, Caldwell Co., Missouri, May 1838. Member of Far West high council. Forced to flee Far West, Feb. 1839. Lived at Pittsfield, Pike Co., Illinois,

1840. Migrated to Utah Territory, Sept. 1850. Settled at Provo, Utah Co., Utah Territory. Elected alderman in Provo city government, Apr. 1851. Moved to Salt Lake City, by June 1860. Died at Salt Lake City.

Rich, Leonard (1800–1868), farmer. Born in New York. Married first Keziah. Lived at Warsaw, Genesee Co., New York, 1830. Participated in Camp of Israel expedition to Missouri, 1834. Served as a president of First Quorum of the Seventy, 1835–1837. Moved to Kirtland, Geauga Co., Ohio, by 1840. Sustained in Sidney Rigdon's Church of Christ as president of Quorum of the Seventy, 1845, at Pittsburgh. With William E. McLellin and Jacob Bump, organized the Church of Christ at Kirtland, Jan. 1847. Wife died, 1853. Married second Marina Bassett, 7 Mar. 1858, in Kirtland. Died at Kirtland.

Richards, Phineas Howe (15 Nov. 1788–25 Nov. 1874), cabinetmaker, joiner, carpenter, botanic physician. Born at Framingham, Middlesex Co., Massachusetts. Son of Joseph Richards and Rhoda Howe. Served as sergeant major during War of 1812. Married Wealthy Dewey, 24 Feb. 1818. Moved to Richmond, Berkshire Co., Massachusetts, 1818. Appointed Berkshire Co. coroner, 1825. Moved to Kirtland, Geauga Co., Ohio, May 1837. Baptized into LDS church by Brigham Young, 13 June 1837, at Kirtland. Ordained a high priest by JS, Joseph Smith Sr., and Sidney Rigdon, Sept. 1837. Appointed to Kirtland high council, 3 Sept. 1837. Began serving mission to eastern states, Nov. 1837. Moved to Nauvoo, Hancock Co., Illinois, 1843. Appointed to Nauvoo City Council, 29 Apr. 1844. Appointed to Nauvoo high council, 23 Nov. 1844. Member of Nauvoo Legion. Arrived in Salt Lake Valley with Willard Richards company, 19 Oct. 1848. Member of Salt Lake high council and of Utah territorial legislature. Served colonizing mission to Sanpete Co., Utah Territory, where he served as a bishop's counselor. Returned to Salt Lake City, where he died.

Rigdon, Sidney (19 Feb. 1793–14 July 1876), tanner, farmer, minister. Born at St. Clair, Allegheny Co., Pennsylvania. Son of William Rigdon and Nancy Gallaher. Joined United Baptists, ca. 1818. Preached at Warren, Trumbull Co., Ohio, and vicinity, 1819–1821. Married Phebe Brooks, 12 June 1820, at Warren. Minister of First Baptist Church of Pittsburgh, 1821–1824. Later joined reformed Baptist (later Disciples of Christ or Campbellite) movement and became influential preacher. Moved to Bainbridge, Geauga Co., Ohio, 1826. Moved to Mentor, Geauga Co., Ohio, 1827. Introduced to Mormonism by his former proselyte to reformed Baptist faith, Parley P. Pratt, who was en route with Oliver Cowdery and others on mission to unorganized Indian Territory. Baptized into LDS church by Oliver Cowdery, Nov. 1830. Scribe for JS, 1830. Ordained a high priest by Lyman Wight, 4 June 1831, in Kirtland, Geauga Co. Appointed to serve mission to Missouri, 6 June 1831. Moved to Hiram, Portage Co., Ohio, 1831. Appointed member of what became the Literary Firm, Nov. 1831. Counselor/assistant president in church presidency, 1832–1844. Appointed member of United Firm, Apr. 1832. Attended organizational meeting of School of the Prophets, 22–23 Jan. 1833, in Kirtland. Accompanied JS to Upper Canada on proselytizing mission and helped keep JS's diary during trip, 1833. Stockholder in Kirtland Safety Society. Arrived at Far West, Caldwell Co., Missouri, from Kirtland, 4 Apr. 1838. With JS in jail at Liberty, Clay Co., Missouri, Dec. 1838–Feb. 1839. After release, found refuge at Quincy, Adams Co., Illinois. Accompanied JS to Washington DC to seek redress for Missouri grievances, 1839–1840. Member of city council in Nauvoo, Hancock Co., Illinois, 1841. Appointed postmaster of Nauvoo, 24 Feb. 1841. Member of Nauvoo Masonic

Lodge. Admitted to Council of Fifty, 19 Mar. 1844. Claimed right to lead church after death of JS; excommunicated, 1844. Moved to Pittsburgh to lead schismatic Church of Jesus Christ of Latter Day Saints, 1844; name of church changed to Church of Christ, 1845. Rejected from Council of Fifty, 4 Feb. 1845. Located near Greencastle, Antrim Township, Franklin Co., Pennsylvania, May 1846. Removed to Friendship, Allegany Co., New York, where he died.

Robinson, Ebenezer (25 May 1816–11 Mar. 1891), printer, editor, publisher. Born at Floyd (near Rome), Oneida Co., New York. Son of Nathan Robinson and Mary Brown. Moved to Utica, Oneida Co., ca. 1831, and learned printing trade at *Utica Observer.* Moved to Ravenna, Portage Co., Ohio, Aug. 1833, and worked as compositor on the *Ohio Star.* Moved to Kirtland, Geauga Co., Ohio, May 1835, and worked in printing office. Baptized into LDS church by JS, 16 Oct. 1835. Married first Angelina (Angeline) Eliza Works, 13 Dec. 1835, at Kirtland. Ordained an elder, 29 Apr. 1836, and a seventy, 20 Dec. 1836. Served mission to Richland Co., Ohio, June–July 1836, and shortly after served mission to New York. Moved to Far West, Caldwell Co., Missouri, spring 1837. Assisted with publication of *Elders' Journal,* summer 1838. Recorder and clerk of Missouri high council and church clerk, 1838. Member of Far West high council, Dec. 1838. Justice of the peace, 1839. When driven from Missouri, moved to Quincy, Adams Co., Illinois, and worked on *Quincy Whig,* 1839. Became publisher, coeditor, and editor of *Times and Seasons,* 1839–1842, at Commerce (later Nauvoo), Hancock Co., Illinois. Member of Nauvoo Masonic Lodge. Justice of the peace in Hancock Co., by 1842. Served mission to New York, 1843. Moved to Pittsburgh, June 1844. Affiliated with Sidney Rigdon and served as his counselor. In May 1846, moved to Greencastle, Franklin Co., Pennsylvania, where he edited Rigdonite *Messenger and Advocate of the Church of Christ.* Moved to Decatur Co., Iowa, Apr. 1855. Baptized into RLDS church by William W. Blair, 29 Apr. 1863, at Pleasanton, Decatur Co. Wife died, 1880. Married second Martha A. Cunningham, 5 Feb. 1885. Affiliated with David Whitmer's Church of Christ, 1888. Edited Whitmerite periodical *The Return,* 1889–1891. Died at Davis City, Decatur Co.

Robinson, George W. (14 May 1814–10 Feb. 1878), clerk, postmaster, merchant, clothier, banker. Born at Pawlet, Rutland Co., Vermont. Baptized into LDS church and moved to Kirtland, Geauga Co., Ohio, by 1836. Clerk and recorder for Kirtland high council, beginning Jan. 1836. Stockholder in Kirtland Safety Society. Ordained a seventy, 20 Dec. 1836. Married Athalia Rigdon, oldest daughter of Sidney Rigdon, 13 Apr. 1837, in Kirtland. In Sept. 1837, appointed general church recorder to replace Oliver Cowdery. Moved to Far West, Caldwell Co., Missouri, 28 Mar. 1838. Sustained as general church recorder and clerk to First Presidency at Far West, Apr. 1838. Imprisoned with JS and other church leaders in Missouri, Nov. 1838. Moved to Quincy, Adams Co., Illinois, winter 1839. Moved to Commerce (later Nauvoo), Hancock Co., Illinois, before 1840. Appointed first postmaster in Nauvoo, Apr. 1840. Member of Nauvoo Masonic Lodge. Left LDS church, by July 1842. Moved to Cuba, Allegany Co., New York, by 1846. Affiliated with Sidney Rigdon's Church of Christ as an apostle. Moved to Friendship, Allegany Co., 1847. Charter member of Masonic lodge in that community. Founder and president of First National Bank, 1 Feb. 1864. Died at Friendship.

Seixas, Joshua (4 June 1802–1874), hebraist, textbook writer, teacher. Probably born at New York City. Son of Gershom Mendez Seixas and Hannah Manuel. Married Henrietta Raphael of Richmond, Henrico Co., Virginia. Taught Hebrew at New York and Charlestown,

Massachusetts. His work *Manual Hebrew Grammar for the Use of Beginners* was published at Andover, Essex Co., Massachusetts, 1833. Taught at Oberlin College, Ohio, 1835. Among his students was Lorenzo Snow, whose sister Eliza was a Latter-day Saint and lived in JS household at Kirtland, Geauga Co., Ohio. Taught private course in Hebrew for six weeks at Western Reserve College at Hudson, Portage Co., Ohio, Dec. 1835–23 Jan. 1836. On 26 Jan. 1836, arrived at Kirtland, where he taught Hebrew, 26 Jan.–29 Mar. 1836. Returned to New York, by 1838.

Sherman, Lyman Royal (22 May 1804–ca. 15 Feb. 1839). Born at Monkton, Addison Co., Vermont. Son of Elkanah Sherman and Asenath Hurlbut. Married Delcena Didamia Johnson, 16 Jan. 1829, at Pomfret, Chautauque Co., New York. Baptized into LDS church, Jan. 1832. Located at Kirtland, Geauga Co., Ohio, 1833. Participated in Camp of Israel expedition to Missouri, 1834. Appointed a president of First Quorum of the Seventy, 28 Feb. 1835. Issued elder's certificate, 30 Mar. 1836, at Kirtland. Ordained a high priest and appointed to Kirtland high council, 2 Oct. 1837. Moved to Far West, Caldwell Co., Missouri, by Oct. 1838. Appointed temporary member of Far West high council, 13 Dec. 1838. Appointed member of Quorum of the Twelve, 16 Jan. 1839, but died at Far West before notified and ordained.

Sherwood, Henry Garlick (20 Apr. 1785–24 Nov. 1867), surveyor. Born at Kingsbury, Washington Co., New York. Son of Newcomb Sherwood and a woman whose maiden name was Tolman (first name unidentified). Married first Jane J. McManagal (McMangle) of Glasgow, Lanark, Scotland, ca. 1824. Lived at Bolton, Warren Co., New York, 1830. Baptized into LDS church, by Aug. 1832. Ordained an elder by Jared and Simeon Carter, Aug. 1832. Moved to Kirtland, Geauga Co., Ohio, ca. 1834. Appointed to Kirtland high council, by 17 Aug. 1835. Married second Marcia Abbott of Windham Co., Vermont, ca. 1835. Served mission to Ohio, Kentucky, and Tennessee, 1836. Stockholder in Kirtland Safety Society. Migrated to Missouri; located at De Witt, Carroll Co., and then Daviess Co., 1838. Member of committee at Far West, Caldwell Co., Missouri, to supervise removal of Latter-day Saints from Missouri, Apr. 1839. Exiled from Missouri and located at Commerce (later Nauvoo), Hancock Co., Illinois, 1839. Member of Commerce high council, 6 Oct. 1839. Instructed in JS revelation to buy stock for building Nauvoo House, 19 Jan. 1841. Nauvoo city marshal, 1841–1843. Appointed guard in Nauvoo Legion, Mar. 1841. Member of Nauvoo Masonic Lodge. Member of Brigham Young pioneer company to Salt Lake Valley, 1847. Served colonizing mission to San Bernardino, Los Angeles Co., California, 1852. Returned to Utah Territory, 1855. Became disaffected with church and removed from high priests quorum, 27 Feb. 1856. Returned to San Bernardino, where he died.

Smith, Alvin (11 Feb. 1798–19 Nov. 1823), farmer, carpenter. Born at Tunbridge, Orange Co., Vermont. Son of Joseph Smith Sr. and Lucy Mack. Moved to Randolph, Orange Co., 1802; returned to Tunbridge, before May 1803. Moved to Royalton, Windsor Co., Vermont, 1804, and to Sharon, Windsor Co., by Aug. 1804; returned to Tunbridge, by Mar. 1808. Returned to Royalton, by Mar. 1810. Moved to Lebanon, Grafton Co., New Hampshire, 1811; to Norwich, Windsor Co., 1813; and to Palmyra, Ontario Co., New York, 1816–Jan. 1817. Played prominent role in family economy, working to pay for 99.5-acre farm at Farmington (later Manchester), Ontario Co., jointly articled for with his father, 1820. Supervised construction of Smiths' frame home in Manchester. Supporter of JS's claims of heavenly manifestations. Experienced severe stomach cramps, perhaps caused by appendicitis, 15 Nov. 1823; situation was apparently complicated by overdose of calomel. Died at Palmyra.

Smith, Asahel (21 May 1773–22 July 1848), farmer. Born at Windham, Rockingham Co., New Hampshire. Son of Asael Smith and Mary Duty. Moved to Dunbarton, Hillsborough Co., New Hampshire, 15 Apr. 1774; to Derryfield (later Manchester), Hillsborough Co., New Hampshire, 1778; and to Tunbridge, Orange Co., Vermont, 1791. Married Elizabeth Schellenger of Royalton, Windsor Co., Vermont, 21 Mar. 1802. Moved to Stockholm, St. Lawrence Co., New York, 1809. Baptized into LDS church by Lyman E. Johnson, June 1835, at Stockholm. Migrated to Kirtland, Geauga Co., Ohio, 1836. Appointed to Kirtland high council, 3 Sept. 1837. Moved to Iowa Territory, 1839. Appointed to Iowa stake high council, 5 Oct. 1839. Ordained a patriarch, 7 Oct. 1844, in Nauvoo, Hancock Co., Illinois. Died at Iowaville, Van Buren Co., Iowa.

Smith, Don Carlos (25 Mar. 1816–7 Aug. 1841), farmer, printer, editor. Born at Norwich, Windsor Co., Vermont. Son of Joseph Smith Sr. and Lucy Mack. Moved to Palmyra, Ontario Co., New York, 1816–Jan. 1817. Moved to Manchester, Ontario Co., 1825. Baptized into LDS church by David Whitmer, ca. 9 June 1830, at Seneca Lake, Seneca Co., New York. Accompanied his father on mission to Asael Smith family in St. Lawrence Co., New York, Aug. 1830. Lived at The Kingdom, unincorporated settlement near Waterloo, Seneca Co., Nov. 1830. Migrated to Kirtland, Geauga Co., Ohio, with Lucy Mack Smith company of Fayette, Seneca Co., branch of Latter-day Saints, May 1831. Employed by Kirtland printing shop under Oliver Cowdery, fall 1833. Married Agnes Moulton Coolbrith, 30 July 1835, at Kirtland. Ordained a high priest and appointed president of Kirtland high priests quorum, 15 Jan. 1836. Served mission to Pennsylvania and New York, 1836. Continued working in Kirtland printing shop, including involvement with *Elders' Journal.* Moved to New Portage, Medina Co., Ohio, Dec. 1837. Served mission to Virginia, Pennsylvania, and Ohio, spring 1838. Left Ohio for Far West, Caldwell Co., Missouri, May 1838. Served mission to Kentucky and Tennessee, 1838. Expelled from Far West, Feb. 1839; moved to Quincy, Adams Co., Illinois. Lived at Macomb, McDonough Co., Illinois, and then moved to Commerce (later Nauvoo), Hancock Co., Illinois, 1839. President of high priests in Commerce, 1839. Editor and publisher of *Times and Seasons,* with Ebenezer Robinson, 1839–1841, at Nauvoo. Elected member of Nauvoo City Council, 1 Feb. 1841. Appointed a regent of University of Nauvoo, 3 Feb. 1841. Elected brigadier general in Nauvoo Legion, 5 Feb. 1841. Died at Nauvoo.

Smith, Emma Hale (10 July 1804–30 Apr. 1879), scribe, editor, boardinghouse operator, clothier. Born at Willingborough Township (later in Harmony), Susquehanna Co., Pennsylvania. Daughter of Isaac Hale and Elizabeth Lewis. Member of Methodist church at Harmony (later in Oakland). Married first to JS by Zechariah Tarble, 18 Jan. 1827, at South Bainbridge (later Afton), Chenango Co., New York. Assisted JS as scribe during translation of Book of Mormon at Harmony, 1828, and joined him during completion of translation at Peter Whitmer Sr. farm, Fayette, Seneca Co., New York, summer 1829. Baptized into LDS church by Oliver Cowdery, 28 June 1830, at Colesville, Broome Co., New York. Migrated from New York to Kirtland, Geauga Co., Ohio, Jan.–Feb. 1831. Lived at John Johnson home at Hiram, Portage Co., Ohio, 1831–1832. Edited *A Collection of Sacred*

Hymns, for the Church of the Latter Day Saints, published 1835, at Kirtland. Stockholder in Kirtland Safety Society. Fled Ohio for Far West, Caldwell Co., Missouri, Jan.–Mar. 1838. Exiled from Missouri, Feb. 1839; located near Quincy, Adams Co., Illinois. Moved to Commerce (later Nauvoo), Hancock Co., Illinois, 10 May 1839. Appointed president of Female Relief Society in Nauvoo, 17 Mar. 1842. Husband murdered, 27 June 1844. Fled to Fulton, Fulton Co., Illinois, Sept. 1846–Feb. 1847, then returned to Nauvoo. Married second Lewis Crum Bidamon, 23 Dec. 1847, at Nauvoo. Affiliated with RLDS church, 1860. Died at Nauvoo.

Smith, Hyrum (9 Feb. 1800–27 June 1844), farmer, cooper. Born at Tunbridge, Orange Co., Vermont. Son of Joseph Smith Sr. and Lucy Mack. Moved to Randolph, Orange Co., 1802; to Tunbridge, before May 1803; to Royalton, Windsor Co., Vermont, 1804; to Sharon, Windsor Co., by Aug. 1804; to Tunbridge, by Mar. 1808; to Royalton, by Mar. 1810; to Lebanon, Grafton Co., New Hampshire, 1811; to Norwich, Windsor Co., 1813; and to Palmyra, Ontario Co., New York, 1816–Jan. 1817. Member of Western Presbyterian Church of Palmyra, early 1820s. Lived at Palmyra, 1817–1825. Lived at Manchester, Ontario Co., 1825–1826. Married first Jerusha Barden, 2 Nov. 1826, at Manchester. Returned to Palmyra, 1826. Baptized by JS, June 1829, at Seneca Lake, Seneca Co., New York. One of the Eight Witnesses of the Book of Mormon, June 1829. Assisted in arrangements for publication of Book of Mormon, 1829–1830, at Palmyra. Among six original members of LDS church, 6 Apr. 1830. Ordained a priest, 9 June 1830. Presided over branch of church at Colesville, Broome Co., New York, 1830–1831. Migrated to Kirtland, Geauga Co., Ohio, 1831. Ordained a high priest by JS, 4 June 1831. Left to serve mission to Missouri with John Murdock, June 1831. Appointed counselor to Bishop Newel K. Whitney, 10 Feb. 1832. Attended organizational meeting of School of the Prophets, 22–23 Jan. 1833, in Kirtland. Member of committee to supervise construction of Kirtland temple, 1833–1836. Participated in Camp of Israel expedition to Missouri, 1834. Appointed to Kirtland high council, 24 Sept. 1834. Ordained a member of presidency of the high priesthood, Dec. 1834. Stockholder in Kirtland Safety Society. Sustained as assistant counselor in presidency of church, 3 Sept. 1837. Wife died, 13 Oct. 1837. Appointed counselor in First Presidency, 7 Nov. 1837. Married second Mary Fielding, 24 Dec. 1837, at Kirtland. Migrated to Far West, Caldwell Co., Missouri, Mar.– May 1838. Imprisoned at Liberty, Clay Co., Missouri, with his brother JS, 1838–1839. Allowed to escape during change of venue, 16 Apr. 1839, en route from trial in Gallatin, Daviess Co., Missouri, to Columbia, Boone Co., Missouri. Arrived at Quincy, Adams Co., Illinois, 22 Apr. 1839. Moved to Commerce (later Nauvoo), Hancock Co., Illinois, 1839. Succeeded Joseph Smith Sr. as church patriarch, 1840. In JS revelation dated 19 Jan. 1841, instructed to buy stock for building Nauvoo House, appointed patriarch of church, released as counselor in First Presidency, and appointed a prophet, seer, and revelator in First Presidency; instructed to "act in concert" with JS, who would "show unto him the keys whereby he may ask and receive, and be crowned with the same blessing, and glory, and honor, and priesthood, and gifts of the priesthood, that once were put upon . . . Oliver Cowdery." Elected to Nauvoo City Council, 1 Feb. 1841. Appointed chaplain in Nauvoo Legion, Mar. 1841. Member of Nauvoo Masonic Lodge; elected Worshipful Master, 10 Nov. 1842. Vice mayor of Nauvoo, 1842–ca. 1843. Appointed to replace Elias Higbee as member of Nauvoo temple committee, 10 Oct. 1843. Admitted to Council of Fifty, 11 Mar. 1844. Participated in plural marriage during JS's lifetime. Murdered at Carthage, Hancock Co.

Smith, John (16 July 1781–23 May 1854), farmer. Born at Derryfield (later Manchester), Rockingham Co., New Hampshire. Son of Asael Smith and Mary Duty. Member of Congregational church. Appointed overseer of highways at Potsdam, St. Lawrence Co., New York, 1810. Married Clarissa Lyman, 11 Sept. 1815. Baptized into LDS church by Solomon Humphrey, 9 Jan. 1832. Confirmed and ordained an elder by Joseph Wakefield and Solomon Humphrey, 9 Jan. 1832. Moved to Kirtland, Geauga Co., Ohio, 1833. Ordained a high priest, June 1833. President of Kirtland high council. Served mission to eastern states with his brother Joseph Smith Sr., 1836. Stockholder in Kirtland Safety Society. Appointed assistant counselor in First Presidency, 1837; member of Kirtland stake presidency, 1838. Left Kirtland for Far West, Caldwell Co., Missouri, 5 Apr. 1838. Appointed president of stake in Adam-ondi-Ahman, Daviess Co., Missouri, 28 June 1838. Expelled from Missouri; arrived in Illinois, 28 Feb. 1839. Moved to Commerce (later Nauvoo), Hancock Co., Illinois, June 1839. Appointed president of stake in Lee Co., Iowa Territory, 5 Oct. 1839. Moved to Nashville, Lee Co., Oct. 1839. Member of Nauvoo Masonic Lodge. Appointed to preside at Macedonia (later Webster), Hancock Co., Illinois, 1843–1844. Ordained a patriarch, 10 Jan. 1844. Admitted to Council of Fifty, 26 Mar. 1844. Appointed Nauvoo stake president, 7 Oct. 1844. Joined westward exodus of Latter-day Saints into Iowa Territory, 9 Feb. 1846. Arrived in Salt Lake Valley, 23 Sept. 1847. Presided over Salt Lake stake, 1847–1848. Ordained patriarch of church, 1 Jan. 1849. Died at Salt Lake City.

Smith, Joseph, Sr. (12 July 1771–14 Sept. 1840), cooper, farmer, teacher, merchant. Born at Topsfield, Essex Co., Massachusetts. Son of Asael Smith and Mary Duty. Nominal member of Congregationalist church at Topsfield. Married to Lucy Mack by Seth Austin, 24 Jan. 1796, at Tunbridge, Orange Co., Vermont. Joined Universalist Society at Tunbridge, 1797. Entered mercantile business at Randolph, Orange Co., ca. 1802, and lost all in a ginseng root investment. Moved to Tunbridge, before May 1803; to Royalton, Windsor Co., Vermont, 1804; to Sharon, Windsor Co., by Aug. 1804; to Tunbridge, by Mar. 1808; to Royalton, by Mar. 1810; to Lebanon, Grafton Co., New Hampshire, 1811; to Norwich, Windsor Co., 1813; to Palmyra, Ontario Co., New York, 1816; and to Manchester, Ontario Co., 1825. One of the Eight Witnesses of the Book of Mormon, June 1829. Baptized into LDS church by Oliver Cowdery, 6 Apr. 1830, most likely at Seneca Lake, Seneca Co., New York. With his son Don Carlos, served mission to family of his father in St. Lawrence Co., New York, Aug. 1830. Lived at The Kingdom, unincorporated settlement near Waterloo, Seneca Co., Nov. 1830–1831. Moved to Kirtland, Geauga Co., Ohio, 1831. Ordained a high priest by Lyman Wight, 4 June 1831. Attended first meeting of School of the Prophets, 22–23 Jan. 1833, in Kirtland. Member of Kirtland high council, 1834. Ordained patriarch of church and assistant president, 6 Dec. 1834. Labored on Kirtland temple. Served mission to eastern states with his brother John Smith, 1836. Stockholder in Kirtland Safety Society. Sustained as assistant counselor in First Presidency, 1837. Left Ohio for Far West, Caldwell Co., Missouri, May 1838. Fled to Quincy, Adams Co., Illinois, Feb. 1839. Located at Commerce (later Nauvoo), Hancock Co., Illinois, spring 1839. Died at Nauvoo.

Smith, Lucy Mack (8 July 1775–14 May 1856), oilcloth painter, nurse, fund-raiser, author. Born at Gilsum, Cheshire Co., New Hampshire. Daughter of Solomon Mack Sr. and

Lydia Gates. Moved to Montague, Franklin Co., Massachusetts, 1779; to Tunbridge, Orange Co., Vermont, 1788; to Gilsum, 1792; and to Tunbridge, 1794. Married to Joseph Smith Sr. by Seth Austin, 24 Jan. 1796, at Tunbridge. Moved to Randolph, Orange Co., 1802; to Tunbridge, before May 1803; to Royalton, Windsor Co., Vermont, 1804; to Sharon, Windsor Co., by Aug. 1804; to Tunbridge, by Mar. 1808; to Royalton, by Mar. 1810; to Lebanon, Grafton Co., New Hampshire, 1811; to Norwich, Windsor Co., 1813; and to Palmyra, Ontario Co., New York, 1816–Jan. 1817. Member of Western Presbyterian Church of Palmyra, early 1820s. Moved to Manchester, Ontario Co., 1825. Baptized into LDS church, 6 Apr. 1830, most likely at Seneca Lake, Seneca Co., New York. Lived at The Kingdom, unincorporated settlement near Waterloo, Seneca Co., Nov. 1830–May 1831. Led company of approximately eighty Fayette, Seneca Co., branch members from Seneca Co. to Kirtland, Geauga Co., Ohio, May 1831. Stockholder in Kirtland Safety Society. Left Ohio for Far West, Caldwell Co., Missouri, May 1838. Fled to Quincy, Adams Co., Illinois, Feb. 1839. Located at Commerce (later Nauvoo), Hancock Co., Illinois, spring 1839. Husband died, 1840. Joined Female Relief Society, Mar. 1842, in Nauvoo. Lived with daughter Lucy Smith Millikin in Colchester, McDonough Co., Illinois, 1846–1852. Died in Nauvoo. Her narrative history of Smith family, published as *Biographical Sketches of Joseph Smith*, 1853, has been an invaluable resource for study of JS and early church.

Smith, Samuel Harrison (13 Mar. 1808–30 July 1844), farmer, logger, scribe, builder, tavern operator. Born at Tunbridge, Orange Co., Vermont. Son of Joseph Smith Sr. and Lucy Mack. Moved to Royalton, Windsor Co., Vermont, by Mar. 1810; to Lebanon, Grafton Co., New Hampshire, 1811; to Norwich, Windsor Co., 1813; and to Palmyra, Ontario Co., New York, 1816–Jan. 1817. Member of Western Presbyterian Church of Palmyra, early 1820s. Moved to Manchester, Ontario Co., 1825. Baptized by Oliver Cowdery, May 1829, at Harmony (later in Oakland), Susquehanna Co., Pennsylvania. One of the Eight Witnesses of the Book of Mormon, June 1829. Among six original members of LDS church, 6 Apr. 1830. Ordained an elder, 9 June 1830, at Fayette, Seneca Co., New York. Began mission to New York, 30 June 1830. Appointed to preach in Ohio, Dec. 1830. With Orson Pratt, journeyed from New York to Kirtland, Geauga Co., Ohio; arrived, 27 Feb. 1831. Ordained a high priest by Lyman Wight, 4 June 1831. Served mission to Missouri with Reynolds Cahoon, 1831. Served mission to eastern states with Orson Hyde, 1832. Attended organizational meeting of School of the Prophets, 22–23 Jan. 1833, in Kirtland. Appointed member of first Kirtland high council, 17 Feb. 1834. Married first Mary Bailey, 13 Aug. 1834, at Kirtland. Committee member and general agent for Literary Firm in Kirtland, 1835. Stockholder in Kirtland Safety Society. Appointed president of Kirtland high council, 2 Oct. 1837. Moved to Far West, Caldwell Co., Missouri, where he lived briefly before moving to Marrowbone, Daviess Co., Missouri, 1838. Participated in battle of Crooked River, near Ray Co., Missouri, 25 Oct. 1838. Among first Latter-day Saints to seek refuge at Quincy, Adams Co., Illinois, 1838. Hired to farm for George Miller near Macomb, McDonough Co., Illinois, Mar. 1839. Moved to Nauvoo, Hancock Co., Illinois, 1841. Wife died, Jan. 1841. Appointed a bishop at Nauvoo, 1841. Nauvoo city alderman, 1841–1842. Appointed guard in Nauvoo Legion, Mar. 1841. Married second Levira Clark, 30 May 1841, in Scott Co., Illinois. Appointed a regent of University of Nauvoo. Moved to Plymouth, Hancock Co., Jan. 1842. Member of Nauvoo Masonic Lodge. Member of Nauvoo City Council, 1842–1843. Died at Nauvoo.

Smith, Sylvester (25 Mar. 1806–22 Feb. 1880), farmer, carpenter, lawyer, realtor. Born at Tyringham, Berkshire Co., Massachusetts. Son of Chileab Smith and Nancy Marshall. Moved to Amherst, Lorain Co., Ohio, ca. 1815. Married Elizabeth Frank, 27 Dec. 1827, likely in Chautauque Co., New York. Baptized into LDS church and ordained an elder, by June 1831. Ordained a high priest by Oliver Cowdery, 25 Oct. 1831. Served mission to New England with Gideon Carter, 1832. Moved to Kirtland, Geauga Co., Ohio, by 1834. Member of Kirtland high council, 1834. Participated in Camp of Israel expedition to Missouri, 1834. Tried by Kirtland high council for making false charges against JS, confessed, and retained his membership, 1834. Appointed a president of First Quorum of the Seventy, 1835. Temporary scribe to JS during illness of Warren F. Parrish, 1836. Left church, by 1838. Moved to Council Bluffs, Pottawattamie Co., Iowa, 1853. Served as Pottawattamie Co. school fund commissioner and justice of the peace. Died at Council Bluffs.

Smith, William B. (13 Mar. 1811–13 Nov. 1893), farmer, newspaper editor. Born at Royalton, Windsor Co., Vermont. Son of Joseph Smith Sr. and Lucy Mack. Moved to Lebanon, Grafton Co., New Hampshire, 1811; to Norwich, Windsor Co., 1813; and to Palmyra, Ontario Co., New York, 1816–Jan. 1817. Moved to Manchester, Ontario Co., 1825. Baptized into LDS church by David Whitmer, ca. 9 June 1830, at Seneca Lake, Seneca Co., New York. Ordained a teacher, by 5 Oct. 1830. Lived at The Kingdom, unincorporated settlement near Waterloo, Seneca Co., Nov. 1830. Moved to Kirtland, Geauga Co., Ohio, May 1831. Ordained an elder by Lyman Johnson, 19 Dec. 1832, at Kirtland. Served mission to Erie Co., Pennsylvania, Dec. 1832. Attended organizational meeting of School of the Prophets, 22–23 Jan. 1833, in Kirtland. Married Caroline Amanda Grant, 14 Feb. 1833, likely in Erie Co. Ordained a high priest, 21 June 1833. Participated in Camp of Israel expedition to Missouri, 1834. Ordained member of Quorum of the Twelve, 15 Feb. 1835, at Kirtland. Left Ohio for Far West, Caldwell Co., Missouri, May 1838. Disfellowshipped, 4 May 1839. Restored to Quorum of the Twelve, 25 May 1839. Settled at Plymouth, Hancock Co., Illinois, ca. 1839, where he kept a tavern. Member of Masonic lodge in Nauvoo, Hancock Co. Member of Nauvoo City Council, 1842–1843. Editor of Nauvoo newspaper the *Wasp*, 1842. Represented Hancock Co. in Illinois House of Representatives, 1842–1843. Moved to Philadelphia to care for his sick wife, 1843. Admitted to Council of Fifty, 25 Apr. 1844. Participated in plural marriage during JS's lifetime. Moved to Nauvoo, 4 May 1845. Wife died, May 1845. Ordained patriarch of church, 24 May 1845. Married Mary Jane Rollins, 22 June 1845, at Nauvoo. Excommunicated, 12 Oct. 1845. Dropped from Council of Fifty, 11 Jan. 1846. Sustained James J. Strang as successor to JS, 1 Mar. 1846. Married Roxey Ann Grant, 19 May 1847, in Knox Co., Illinois. Ordained patriarch and apostle of Strang's Church of Jesus Christ of Latter Day Saints, 11 June 1846, at Voree, Walworth Co., Wisconsin Territory. Excommunicated from Strangite movement, 8 Oct. 1847. Affiliated briefly with Lyman Wight, 1849–1850. Initiated a new movement with Martin Harris and Chilton Daniels at Kirtland, likely 1855. Married Eliza Elsie Sanborn, 12 Nov. 1857, at Kirtland. Moved to Venango, Erie Co., Pennsylvania, by 1860, and to Elkader, Clayton Co., Iowa, shortly after. Enlisted in U.S. Army during Civil War and apparently adopted middle initial *B* at this time. Spent active duty time in Arkansas. Joined RLDS church, 1878. Wife died, Mar. 1889. Married Rosanna Jewitt Surprise, 21 Dec. 1889, at Clinton, Clinton Co., Iowa. Moved to Osterdock, Clayton Co., 1890. Died at Osterdock.

Strong, Ezra (26 June 1788–3 Apr. 1877), farmer. Born at Philipstown, Albany Co., New York. Son of Ezra Strong and Nancy Gates. Married Olive Lowell, 19 Nov. 1814. Moved to Erie Co., New York, by Jan. 1816. Moved to Sheldon, Genesee Co., New York, by June 1830. Baptized into LDS church and ordained a priest, by 1833. Moved to Rockport, Allen Co., Ohio, by Oct. 1834. Ordained a high priest at Kirtland, Geauga Co., Ohio, 1836. Stockholder in Kirtland Safety Society. Moved to Nauvoo, Hancock Co., Illinois, area by 1842. Migrated to Salt Lake Valley by 1850. Baptized into RLDS church, 12 Oct. 1862, at Santaquin, Utah Co., Utah Territory. Died at Woodland, Cowlitz Co., Washington Territory.

Thornton, John (24 Dec. 1786–24 Oct. 1847), ferry operator, military officer, judge, lawyer, politician. Born in Lancaster Co., Pennsylvania. Son of William Thornton Sr. and Sarah Jane Allison. Moved to Kentucky, ca. 1795. Studied law and admitted to bar. Moved to Old Franklin (near present-day Franklin, Howard Co., Missouri), 1816. Married Elizabeth Trigg, 10 Feb. 1820, in Old Franklin. Moved to area that became Clay Co., Missouri, 1820. Operated ferry in Jackson and Clay counties, Missouri. Represented Clay Co. in Missouri House of Representatives, ca. 1824–1832. Served as Speaker of the House, 1828–1830. Colonel in Clay Co. militia, 1834. Reelected to Missouri General Assembly, 1836. Died in Clay Co. Buried in Liberty, Clay Co.

Whitlock, Harvey Gilman (1809–after 1880), physician. Born in Massachusetts. Married Minerva Abbott, 21 Nov. 1830. Baptized into LDS church, 1831. Ordained an elder, by June 1831. Ordained a high priest, 4 June 1831. Served mission to Jackson Co., Missouri, with David Whitmer, 1831. In 1831, moved his household to Missouri, where he became member of Whitmer branch. Appointed to serve mission to Illinois, Indiana, Michigan, and Ohio, Jan. 1832. Expelled from Jackson Co., Missouri, 1833. Excommunicated, by 1835. Conference of church presidency recommended he be rebaptized and reordained, 30 Jan. 1836. Withdrew from church, 1838. Moved to Cedar Co., Iowa Territory, by 1840. Baptized into Sidney Rigdon's Church of Christ at West Buffalo, Scott Co., Iowa Territory, 1845. Migrated to Salt Lake Valley, by 1850. Rebaptized into LDS church, 1858. By 1860, moved to San Bernardino, San Bernardino Co., California, where he was baptized into RLDS church. President of Pacific Slope area of RLDS church, 1866. Excommunicated from RLDS church, 1868. Moved to Contra Costa Co., California, by 1870. Lived at Bishop Creek, Inyo Co., California, 1880. Likely died in California.

Whitmer, David (7 Jan. 1805–25 Jan. 1888), farmer, livery keeper. Born near Harrisburg, Dauphin Co., Pennsylvania. Son of Peter Whitmer Sr. and Mary Musselman. Raised Presbyterian. Moved to Ontario Co., New York, shortly after birth. Attended German Reformed Church. Arranged for completion of translation of Book of Mormon in his father's home, Fayette, Seneca Co., New York, June 1829. Baptized by JS, June 1829, in Seneca Lake, Seneca Co. One of the Three Witnesses of the Book of Mormon, 1829. Among six original members of church and ordained an elder, 6 Apr. 1830. Married Julia Ann Jolly, 9 Jan. 1831, at Seneca Co. Migrated from Fayette to Kirtland, Geauga Co., Ohio, 1831. Ordained a high priest by Oliver Cowdery, 25 Oct. 1831, at Orange, Cuyahoga Co., Ohio. Traveled to Jackson Co., Missouri, with Harvey G. Whitlock, 1831. Driven from Jackson Co. by vigilantes, Nov. 1833; located in Clay Co., Missouri. Appointed president of church in Missouri, 7 July 1834. Left for Kirtland, Sept. 1834. Stockholder in Kirtland Safety Society. Moved to Far West, Caldwell Co., Missouri, by 1837. Rejected as president in Missouri at meetings in

Far West, 5–9 Feb. 1838. Excommunicated, 13 Apr. 1838, at Far West. In 1838, moved to Clay Co. and then to Richmond, Ray Co., Missouri, where he operated a livery stable. Ordained by William E. McLellin to preside over McLellinite Church of Christ, 1847, but later rejected that movement. Elected mayor of Richmond, 1867–1868. Founded Church of Christ (Whitmerite), 1875. Later set forth his religious claims in *An Address to All Believers in Christ, by a Witness to the Divine Authenticity of the Book of Mormon,* published 1887. Died at Richmond.

Whitmer, John (27 Aug. 1802–11 July 1878), farmer, stock raiser, newspaper editor. Born in Pennsylvania. Son of Peter Whitmer Sr. and Mary Musselman. Member of German Reformed Church, Fayette, Seneca Co., New York. Baptized by Oliver Cowdery, June 1829, most likely in Seneca Lake, Seneca Co. Acted as scribe during translation of Book of Mormon at Whitmer home. One of the Eight Witnesses of the Book of Mormon, June 1829. Ordained an elder, by 9 June 1830. Copied revelations as scribe to JS, July 1830. Sent by JS to Kirtland, Geauga Co., Ohio, ca. Dec. 1830. Appointed church historian, ca. 8 Mar. 1831. Worked on a church history, 1831–ca. 1847. Ordained a high priest by Lyman Wight, 4 June 1831, at Kirtland. With Oliver Cowdery, left Ohio to take revelations to Missouri for publication, Nov. 1831. Appointed member of United Firm, Apr. 1832. Married to Sarah Maria Jackson by William W. Phelps, 10 Feb. 1833, at Kaw Township, Jackson Co., Missouri. Expelled from Jackson Co. into Clay Co., Missouri, Nov. 1833. Appointed an assistant to his brother David Whitmer in Missouri church presidency, July 1834. Editor of *LDS Messenger and Advocate,* Kirtland, 1835–1836. Lived in Clay Co., 1836. Helped establish Latter-day Saints at Far West, Caldwell Co., Missouri, 1836–1837. Excommunicated, 10 Mar. 1838, at Far West. Left Far West for Richmond, Ray Co., Missouri, June 1838. Returned to Far West after departure of Latter-day Saints. In Sept. 1847, met with his brother David Whitmer and William E. McLellin at Far West in an attempt to reconstitute Church of Christ under presidency of David Whitmer. Died at site of Far West.

Whitney, Newel Kimball (3/5 Feb. 1795–23 Sept. 1850), trader, merchant. Born at Marlborough, Windham Co., Vermont. Son of Samuel Whitney and Susanna Kimball. Moved to Fairfield, Herkimer Co., New York, 1803. Merchant at Plattsburg, Clinton Co., New York, 1814. Mercantile clerk for A. Sidney Gilbert at Painesville, Geauga Co., Ohio, ca. 1820. Opened store in Kirtland, Geauga Co., by 1822. Married Elizabeth Ann Smith, 20 Oct. 1822, in Geauga Co. Member of reformed Baptist (later Disciples of Christ or Campbellite) faith. Partner with A. Sidney Gilbert in N. K. Whitney & Co. store, by 1827. Baptized into LDS church by missionaries to unorganized Indian Territory, Nov. 1830. Appointed agent for church, 30 Aug. 1831. Ordained a high priest, by Dec. 1831. Appointed bishop at Kirtland, Dec. 1831. Traveled with JS to Missouri and then to New York City, Albany, and Boston, 1832. Appointed member of United Firm, Apr. 1832. Attended organizational meeting of School of the Prophets, 22–23 Jan. 1833, in Kirtland. En route to Missouri, fall 1838, when difficulties in that state were confirmed at St. Louis. Located his family temporarily at Carrollton, Greene Co., Illinois, and returned to Kirtland to conduct business. Moved family from Carrollton to Quincy, Adams Co., Illinois, and then to Commerce (later Nauvoo), Hancock Co., Illinois. Appointed bishop of Middle Ward at Commerce, Oct. 1839. Nauvoo city alderman, 1841–1843. Member of Nauvoo Masonic Lodge. Admitted to Council of Fifty, 11 Mar. 1844. Appointed trustee-in-trust for church following JS's death, Aug. 1844. Appointed "first bishop" of church, Oct. 1844. Joined exodus of Latter-day Saints into Iowa Territory and Winter Quarters, unorganized U.S. territory (later in Omaha, Douglas Co., Nebraska), 1846. Migrated to Salt Lake Valley, fall 1848. Bishop of Salt Lake City Eighteenth Ward, 1849. Elected treasurer and associate justice of provisional state of Deseret, 1849. Died at Salt Lake City.

Wight, Lyman (9 May 1796–31 Mar. 1858), farmer. Born at Fairfield, Herkimer Co., New York. Son of Levi Wight Jr. and Sarah Corbin. Served in War of 1812. Married Harriet Benton, 5 Jan. 1823, at Henrietta, Monroe Co., New York. Moved to Warrensville, Cuyahoga Co., Ohio, ca. 1826. Baptized into reformed Baptist (later Disciples of Christ or Campbellite) faith by Sidney Rigdon, May 1829. Moved to Isaac Morley homestead at Kirtland, Geauga Co., Ohio, and joined with other reformed Baptist families having all things in common, Feb. 1830. Lived at Mayfield, Cuyahoga Co., when baptized into LDS church in Chagrin River, 14 Nov. 1830, and confirmed by Oliver Cowdery at Kirtland, 18 Nov. 1830. Ordained an elder by Oliver Cowdery, 20 Nov. 1830. Ordained JS and Sidney Rigdon high priests, 4 June 1831. Ordained a high priest by JS, 4 June 1831. Served mission to Jackson Co., Missouri, via Detroit and Pontiac, Michigan Territory, June–Aug. 1831. Joined by family at Jackson Co., Sept. 1831; located at Prairie branch, Jackson Co. Appointed to serve mission to Missouri, Ohio, and Virginia, Jan. 1832. Moved to and presided over Big Blue settlement, Jackson Co. Driven from Jackson Co. into Clay Co., Missouri, Nov. 1833. Recruited volunteers for Camp of Israel expedition to Missouri, 1834. Member of Missouri high council, 1834. Moved to Caldwell Co., Missouri, 1837. Elected colonel at organization of Caldwell Co. militia, Aug. 1837. Moved to Adam-ondi-Ahman, Daviess Co., Missouri, 1838. Member of Adam-ondi-Ahman stake presidency, 1838. Prominent in Missouri Danite activities, 1838. Imprisoned with JS at Richmond, Ray Co., Missouri; Liberty, Clay Co.; and Gallatin, Daviess Co., 1838–1839. Allowed to escape Missouri imprisonment during change of venue to Columbia, Boone Co., Missouri. Moved to Quincy, Adams Co., Illinois, Apr. 1839. Counselor in Zarahemla stake presidency, Lee Co., Iowa Territory, Oct. 1839. Moved to Augusta, Des Moines Co., Iowa Territory, Nov. 1839. Trustee of Nauvoo House Association. Ordained member of Quorum of the Twelve, 8 Apr. 1841, at Nauvoo, Hancock Co., Illinois. Appointed aide-de-camp to major general in Nauvoo Legion, May 1841. Served fund-raising mission for Nauvoo House Association to Illinois, May–Sept. 1841. Served fund-raising mission for Nauvoo House Association to Illinois, Kentucky, Tennessee, Mississippi, and Louisiana, Jan.–Mar. 1842. Served mission to Tennessee, June–Aug. 1842. Member of Nauvoo City Council, 1841–1843. Member of Nauvoo Masonic Lodge. Served mission to New York and other eastern states, Sept. 1842–June 1843. Leader in procuring lumber for Nauvoo temple and Nauvoo House from pineries on Black River, Wisconsin Territory, 1843–1844. Added to Council of Fifty by JS, 18 Apr. 1844; formally admitted to council, 3 May 1844. Served mission to eastern states to campaign for JS as candidate for U.S. president, 1844. Returned to Wisconsin Territory, 1844–1845. Rejected from Council of Fifty, 4 Feb. 1845. Led company of some 150 Latter-day Saints from Wisconsin Territory to Republic of Texas, arriving in Nov. 1845. Moved to Zodiac, Gillespie Co., Texas, 1847. Excommunicated, 3 Dec. 1848. Died at Dexter, Medina Co., Texas, en route to Jackson Co., Missouri.

Williams, Frederick Granger (28 Oct. 1787–10 Oct. 1842), ship's pilot, teacher, physician, justice of the peace. Born at Suffield, Hartford Co., Connecticut. Son of William Wheeler Williams and Ruth Granger. Moved to Newburg, Cuyahoga Co., Ohio, 1799. Practiced Thomsonian botanical system of medicine as physician. Married Rebecca Swain, Dec. 1815. Lived at Warrensville, Cuyahoga Co., by 1816. Worshipped with Sidney Rigdon's reformed Baptist (later Disciples of Christ or Campbellite) congregation. Moved to Chardon, Geauga Co., Ohio, by 1828. Moved to Kirtland, Geauga Co., 1830. Baptized into LDS church and ordained an elder, Oct./Nov. 1830, by missionaries under leadership of Oliver Cowdery who were en route to Missouri and unorganized Indian Territory. Accompanied Cowdery to Missouri frontier on mission. Ordained a high priest, 25 Oct. 1831, at Orange, Cuyahoga Co., Ohio. Appointed clerk and scribe to JS, 20 July 1832. Attended organizational meeting of School of the Prophets, 22–23 Jan. 1833, in Kirtland. Member of United Firm, 1833. Assistant president/counselor in presidency of church, 1833–1837. Consecrated by deed to JS roughly 142 prime acres in Kirtland, 1834. Participated in Camp of Israel expedition to Missouri, 1834. Editor of *Northern Times* and member of publications committee that printed Doctrine and Covenants and Emma Smith's *A Collection of Sacred Hymns, for the Church of the Latter Day Saints* under auspices of firm F. G. Williams & Co., 1835. Helped organize and was a trustee of School of the Prophets. Elected justice of the peace, Kirtland, 1837. Officer in Kirtland Safety Society, 1837. Removed from church presidency, 7 Nov. 1837. Moved to Far West, Caldwell Co., Missouri, 1837. An 8 July 1838 JS revelation directed Williams be ordained an elder and preach abroad. Rebaptized into LDS church, by 5 Aug. 1838. Excommunicated, 17 Mar. 1839, at Quincy, Adams Co., Illinois. Restored to fellowship at Nauvoo, Hancock Co., Illinois, Apr. 1840. Died at Quincy.

Woodruff, Wilford (1 Mar. 1807–2 Sept. 1898), farmer, miller. Born at Farmington, Hartford Co., Connecticut. Son of Aphek Woodruff and Beulah Thompson. Moved to Richland, Oswego Co., New York, 1832. Baptized into LDS church by Zera Pulsipher, 31 Dec. 1833, near Richland. Ordained a teacher, 2 Jan. 1834, at Richland. Moved to Kirtland, Geauga Co., Ohio, Apr. 1834. Participated in Camp of Israel expedition to Missouri, 1834. Ordained a priest, 5 Nov. 1834. Served mission to Arkansas, Tennessee, and Kentucky, 1834–1836. Ordained an elder, 1835. Appointed member of the Seventy, 31 May 1836. Stockholder in Kirtland Safety Society. Married to Phebe Carter by Frederick G. Williams, 13 Apr. 1837, at Kirtland. Served missions to New England and Fox Islands off coast of Maine, 1837–1838. Ordained member of Quorum of the Twelve by Brigham Young, 26 Apr. 1839, at Far West, Caldwell Co., Missouri. Served mission to Great Britain, 1839–1841. Appointed assistant chaplain in Nauvoo Legion, 3 July 1841. Member of city council, 1841–1843, in Nauvoo, Hancock Co., Illinois. Member of Nauvoo Masonic Lodge. Served mission to eastern states to raise funds for building Nauvoo temple, 1843. Admitted to Council of Fifty, 13 Mar. 1844. Served mission to eastern states to campaign for JS as candidate for U.S. president, 1844. Presided over British mission, Aug. 1844–Apr. 1846. Member of Brigham Young pioneer company that journeyed to Salt Lake Valley, 1847. Served mission to eastern states, 1848–1850. Member of Utah territorial legislature. Appointed assistant church historian, 7 Apr. 1856. President of temple in St. George, Washington Co., Utah Territory, 1877. President of Quorum of the Twelve, 1880. Sustained as church historian and general church recorder, 1883. President of church, 7 Apr. 1889–2 Sept. 1898. Died at San Francisco.

Young, Brigham (1 June 1801–29 Aug. 1877), carpenter, painter, glazier, colonizer. Born at Whitingham, Windham Co., Vermont. Son of John Young and Abigail (Nabby) Howe. Brought up in Methodist household; later joined Methodist church. Moved to Sherburne, Chenango Co., New York, 1804. Married first Miriam Angeline Works of Aurelius, Cayuga Co., New York, 8 Oct. 1824. Lived at Mendon, Monroe Co., New York, when baptized into LDS church by Eleazer Miller, 9/15 Apr. 1832. Wife died, 8 Sept. 1832. Served missions to New York and Upper Canada, 1832–1833. Migrated to Kirtland, Geauga Co., Ohio, 1833. Labored on Kirtland temple. Married second Mary Ann Angell, 31 Mar. 1834, in Geauga Co. Participated in Camp of Israel expedition to Missouri, 1834. Ordained member of Quorum of the Twelve by Oliver Cowdery, David Whitmer, and Martin Harris, 14 Feb. 1835, at Kirtland. Served mission to New York and New England, 1835–1837. Stockholder in Kirtland Safety Society. Fled Kirtland, 22 Dec. 1837. Joined JS en route to Far West, Caldwell Co., Missouri; arrived, 14 Mar. 1838. Member of presidency pro tempore of church in Far West, 1838. Directed Mormon evacuation from Missouri. Forced to leave Far West; reached Quincy, Adams Co., Illinois, Feb. 1839. Served mission to England, 1839–1841, departing from Montrose, Lee Co., Iowa Territory. Appointed president of Quorum of the Twelve, 14 Apr. 1840. Arrived in Nauvoo, Hancock Co., Illinois, 1 July 1841. Appointed assistant chaplain in Nauvoo Legion, 3 July 1841. Member of Nauvoo City Council, 1841–1845. Member of Nauvoo Masonic Lodge. Participated in plural marriage during JS's lifetime. Officiator in proxy baptisms for the dead in Nauvoo, 1843. Admitted to Council of Fifty, 11 Mar. 1844. Served mission to campaign for JS as candidate for U.S. president, 1844. With the Twelve, sustained to administer affairs of church after JS's death, 8 Aug. 1844, at Nauvoo. Reorganized Council of Fifty, 4 Feb. 1845. Recognized as "President of the whole Church of Latter Day Saints" at conference in Nauvoo, 7 Apr. 1845. Directed Mormon migration from Nauvoo to Salt Lake Valley, 1846–1848. Reorganized First Presidency of church, Dec. 1847. Governor of Utah Territory, 1850–1857. Superintendent of Indian affairs for Utah Territory, 1851–1857. Directed establishment of hundreds of communities in western U.S. Died at Salt Lake City.

Young, Joseph (7 Apr. 1797–16 July 1881), farmer, painter, glazier. Born at Hopkinton, Middlesex Co., Massachusetts. Son of John Young and Abigail (Nabby) Howe. Moved to Auburn, Cayuga Co., New York, before 1830. Joined Methodist church, before Apr. 1832. Baptized into LDS church by Daniel Bowen, 6 Apr. 1832, at Columbia, Bradford Co., Pennsylvania. Ordained an elder by Ezra Landon, Apr. 1832. Served mission to New York, spring 1832. Served mission to Upper Canada, summer 1832. Moved to Kirtland, Geauga Co., Ohio, fall 1832. Served mission to Upper Canada, winter 1832–1833. Married Jane Adeline Bicknell, 18 Feb. 1834, at Geneseo, Livingston Co., New York. Participated in Camp of Israel expedition to Missouri, 1834. Ordained a seventy, 28 Feb. 1835, in Kirtland. Appointed a president of First Quorum of the Seventy, 1 Mar. 1835. Served missions to eastern states, 1835, 1836. Stockholder in Kirtland Safety Society. Moved from Kirtland to Missouri, July–Oct. 1838, and witnessed massacre at Hawn's Mill, Caldwell Co., Missouri. During exodus from Missouri, located temporarily at Quincy, Adams Co., Illinois. Moved to Nauvoo, Hancock Co., Illinois, 1840. Member of

Nauvoo Legion, 1842. Appointed "first president over all the quorums of the seventies" at conference in Nauvoo, Oct. 1844. Admitted to Council of Fifty, 1 Mar. 1845. Resided at Winter Quarters, unorganized U.S. territory (later in Omaha, Douglas Co., Nebraska), and at Carterville, Iowa, 1846–1850. Migrated to Utah Territory, Sept. 1850. Served in Utah territorial legislature. Served mission to British Isles, 1870. Died at Salt Lake City.

General Church Officers

The following charts list the general leadership of the Church of the Latter Day Saints between October 1835 and January 1838. Many of the charts reflect important changes to these organizations during the period covered in this volume. Readers wishing to conduct further research on specific groups or individuals may consult the annotated organizational charts posted on the Joseph Smith Papers website, josephsmithpapers.org, as well as the Biographical Directory in this volume.

Church Presidency

The general church presidency, or presidency of the high priesthood, was the presiding body of the church. JS was ordained president of the high priesthood on 25 January 1832; six weeks later, Jesse Gause and Sidney Rigdon were selected and ordained "councillers of the ministry of the presidency of th[e] high Pristhood." Following Gause's excommunication in December 1832, Frederick G. Williams was appointed to replace him. In an 18 March 1833 meeting, JS ordained Rigdon and Williams as "equal with him in holding the Keys of the Kingdom and also to the Presidency of the high Priest hood." On 5 and 6 December 1834, Oliver Cowdery, Hyrum Smith, and Joseph Smith Sr. were ordained as assistant presidents in the presidency of the high priesthood.

JS, Sidney Rigdon, Frederick G. Williams, Oliver Cowdery, Hyrum Smith, and Joseph Smith Sr. constituted the presidency of the high priesthood during the majority of the period covered in this volume. Even though Oliver Cowdery was ordained as the ranking assistant president to JS in December 1834, JS, Rigdon, and Williams were considered first presidents, constituting the First Presidency.

In a 7 November 1837 general assembly meeting held in Far West, Missouri, JS nominated Frederick G. Williams to continue as his counselor in the First Presidency, but the nomination was objected to by four men, including Thomas B. Marsh of the Quorum of the Twelve Apostles. After some discussion, Sidney Rigdon nominated Hyrum Smith to take Williams's place in the First Presidency, and those gathered at the meeting unanimously approved the nomination. The assistant counselors, who had been approved at a 3 September 1837 reorganization conference in Kirtland, Ohio, were not presented at this Far West meeting but retained their positions.

6 December 1834	16 January 1836	3 September 1837	7 November 1837
President	*President*	*First Presidency*	*First Presidency*
Joseph Smith Jr.	Joseph Smith Jr.	Joseph Smith Jr.	Joseph Smith Jr.
		Sidney Rigdon	Sidney Rigdon
Assistant Presidents	*Assistant Presidents*	Frederick G. Williams	Hyrum Smith
Oliver Cowdery	Sidney Rigdon		
Sidney Rigdon	Frederick G. Williams	*Assistant Counselors*	*Assistant Counselors*
Frederick G. Williams	Oliver Cowdery	Oliver Cowdery	Oliver Cowdery
Hyrum Smith	Hyrum Smith	Joseph Smith Sr.	Joseph Smith Sr.
Joseph Smith Sr.	Joseph Smith Sr.	Hyrum Smith	John Smith
		John Smith	

Quorum of the Twelve Apostles

The Quorum of the Twelve Apostles was organized on 14 February 1835. JS initially referred to the quorum as a "travelling high council" with responsibility to "preside over all the churches of the saints . . . where there is no presidency established." In a 16 January 1836 meeting, JS explained to quorum members that their authority in the church was "next to" the church presidency. The composition of the quorum remained the same until the end of December 1837, when John F. Boynton and Luke Johnson were excommunicated from the church. John Taylor and John E. Page were appointed to replace them shortly thereafter, though they were not officially ordained to the Quorum of the Twelve until December 1838. Quorum members are listed in order of seniority. For original quorum members, seniority was determined based on age; thereafter, new members were ordered based on ordination date. David W. Patten was actually a year older than Thomas B. Marsh, but Patten died in 1838 before the error was corrected.

14 February 1835	31 January 1838
Thomas B. Marsh	Thomas B. Marsh
David W. Patten	David W. Patten
Brigham Young	Brigham Young
Heber C. Kimball	Heber C. Kimball
Orson Hyde	Orson Hyde
William E. McLellin	William E. McLellin
Parley P. Pratt	Parley P. Pratt
Luke Johnson	William Smith
William Smith	Orson Pratt
Orson Pratt	Lyman Johnson
John F. Boynton	John Taylor
Lyman Johnson	John E. Page

Patriarch

Joseph Smith Sr. was ordained patriarch in December 1834 and began giving patriarchal blessings to members of the church that month.

December 1834
Joseph Smith Sr.

Presidents of the Seventy

In late February and early March 1835, JS and other church leaders appointed a number of men to serve as "seventies." JS's spring 1835 "Instruction on Priesthood" indicated, "The seventy are to act in the name of the Lord, under the direction of the twelve . . . in building up the church and regulating all the affairs of the same, in all nations"; the instruction also specified that the Quorum of the Seventy was "called to preach the gospel, and to be especial witnesses unto the Gentiles and in all the world."

Unlike other ecclesiastical organizations presided over by a president and two counselors, the Quorum of the Seventy was led by seven presidents. It appears that the first seven presidents were appointed between 28 February and 1 March 1835. In April 1837, JS determined that the practice of appointing high priests as leaders of the Seventy was "wrong, and not according to the order of heaven." Six of the seven presidents were asked to join the high priests quorum, and new presidents were appointed in their stead on 6 April 1837. One of the six removed, Levi Hancock, was in Missouri at the time, and when he returned to Kirtland, he informed church leaders that he had not in fact been a high priest and should not have been removed. As a result, John Gould was asked to join the high priests quorum and Levi Hancock was reinstated to his former position on 3 September 1837. On 13 January 1838, John Gaylord was excommunicated, along with several other members of the Quorum of the Seventy, for "rising up in rebellion against the church." Gaylord was removed as a president of the Seventy on 6 February 1838 and replaced by Henry Harriman.

28 February–1 March 1835	6 April 1837	3 September 1837	6 February 1838
Hazen Aldrich	John Gould	Levi Hancock	Levi Hancock
Joseph Young	Joseph Young	Joseph Young	Joseph Young
Leonard Rich	James Foster	James Foster	James Foster
Levi Hancock	Salmon Gee	Salmon Gee	Salmon Gee
Zebedee Coltrin	Daniel Miles	Daniel Miles	Daniel Miles
Lyman Sherman	Josiah Butterfield	Josiah Butterfield	Josiah Butterfield
Sylvester Smith	John Gaylord	John Gaylord	Henry Harriman

First Quorum of the Seventy

Between 28 February and 1 March 1835, JS and other church leaders appointed forty-four men to serve in the Quorum of the Seventy and designated seven of them as presidents of the quorum; the rest of the quorum was appointed during the next year. The first comprehensive list of quorum members appeared in a broadside published circa April 1836. All of the men appointed to the quorum had participated in the 1834 Camp of Israel expedition. During summer and fall 1835, many of the Seventy left Kirtland to preach in surrounding states. Though the composition of the quorum remained largely the same from early 1835 to early 1838, four members were moved to the high priests quorum and replaced in April 1837, and in 1837 and 1838, seven men were removed for apostasy and for "rising up in rebellion." On 6 February 1838, the presidents of the Seventy appointed new members of the First and Second Quorums of the Seventy to replace those who had been excommunicated.

The charts for the various Quorums of the Seventy list the members in alphabetical order, except that new members are listed in the place of the men they succeeded.

By circa April 1836	*6 February 1838*
Milo Andrus	Milo Andrus
Solomon Angell	Solomon Angell
Almon Babbitt	Almon Babbitt
Alexander Badlam Sr.	Alexander Badlam Sr.
Nathan Baldwin	Nathan Baldwin
Israel Barlow	Israel Barlow
Lorenzo Barnes	Lorenzo Barnes
Edson Barney	Edson Barney
Royal Barney Jr.	Royal Barney Jr.
Henry Beaman	Henry Beaman
Henry Benner	Henry Benner
Hiram Blackman	Hiram Blackman
Lorenzo Booth	Lorenzo Booth
George Brook	George Brook
Harry Brown	Harry Brown
Samuel Brown	Samuel Brown
Peter Buchanan	Peter Buchanan
Alden Burdick	Alden Burdick
Harrison Burgess	Harrison Burgess
William Cahoon	William Cahoon
Jacob Chapman	Jacob Chapman
Zerah Cole	Zerah Cole
Libbeus Coons	Libbeus Coons
David Elliott	David Elliott
David Evans	Sherman Gilbert
Edmond Fisher	Edmond Fisher
Levi Gifford	Levi Gifford
True Gliddon	True Gliddon
Jedediah M. Grant	Jedediah M. Grant
Michael Griffith	Michael Griffith
Joseph Hancock	Joseph Hancock
Jesse Harmon	Milton Holmes
Henry Harriman	Levi Nickerson
Nelson Higgins	Nelson Higgins
Jesse Huntsman	Wilford Woodruff
Elias Hutchings	Elias Hutchings
Heman Hyde	Heman Hyde
Charles Kelly	Charles Kelly
Amasa Lyman	Elias Wells
Moses Martin	Moses Martin
Joseph B. Noble	Joseph B. Noble
Roger Orton	Harrison Sagers
John Parker	John Parker
Warren Parrish	Justus Morse
William Pratt	William Pratt
Darwin Richardson	Darwin Richardson
Burr Riggs	Burr Riggs
Harpin Riggs	James Thompson
Lewis Robbins	Lewis Robbins
Wilkins Jenkins Salisbury	Reuben McBride
Henry Shibley	Henry Shibley
Cyrus Smalling	William Carpenter
George A. Smith	George A. Smith
Jaazeniah B. Smith	Jaazeniah B. Smith
Lyman Smith	Lyman Smith
Willard Snow	Willard Snow

By circa April 1836 (cont.)	6 February 1838 (cont.)
Zerubbabel Snow	Solon Foster
Harvey Stanley	Benjamin Winchester
Daniel Stevens	Daniel Stevens
Hiram Stratton	Elijah Fordham
Salmon Warner	Salmon Warner
Alexander Whiteside	Alexander Whiteside
Stephen Winchester	Stephen Winchester
Hiram Winters	Hiram Winters

Second Quorum of the Seventy

Shortly after calling the Twelve Apostles and designating men as seventies in February and March 1835, JS told a grand council of church officers, "If the first Seventy are all occupied, and there is a call for more laborers it will be the duty of the seven presidents of the first seventy to call and ordain other Seventy and send them forth to labor, in the vineyard until if need be they set a part apart seven times Seventy." At least one individual, Sherman Gilbert, was told in an August 1835 blessing that he would be "numbered with the 2d 70," but the Second Quorum of the Seventy was not officially organized until early February 1836. Its seventy members were selected primarily from the newly organized elders quorum. The quorum remained relatively stable through early 1838, with nearly three-quarters of members remaining the same. Four quorum members—John Gould, Salmon Gee, James Foster, and Josiah Butterfield—were selected as presidents of the Seventy on 6 April 1837. John E. Page was appointed to the Quorum of the Twelve Apostles in late December 1837. Also in late December 1837 or early January 1838, five men were removed for "rising up in rebellion," and seven members were moved to the First Quorum of the Seventy to replace those men who had moved to the high priests quorum or the presidency of the Seventy or who had been excommunicated. On 6 February 1838, the presidents of the Seventy appointed new members of the First and Second Quorums of the Seventy to replace those who had been removed.

8–11 February 1836	6 February 1838
Truman Angell	Truman Angell
Arvin Avery	Arvin Avery
Loren Babbit	Loren Babbit
Elias Benner	Elias Benner
Francis Gladden Bishop	Francis Gladden Bishop
Isaac Bishop	Frederick Vanleuven
Amasa Bonney	Amasa Bonney
William Bosley	William Bosley
Josiah Butterfield	David Clough
William Carpenter	Lorenzo Wells
Giles Cook	Alanson Pettingall
Jonathan Crosby	Jonathan Crosby
Robert Culvertson	Robert Culvertson
Marvel Davis	Stephen Shumway
James Dayley	James Dayley
Hiram Dayton	Hiram Dayton
Edmund Durfee	Edmund Durfee
Rufus Fisher	Rufus Fisher
King Follett	King Follett
Elijah Fordham	Jonathan H. Hale

8–11 February 1836 (cont.)	6 February 1838 (cont.)
James Foster	Gardner Snow
Solon Foster	Daniel Bowen
Thomas Gates	Garland Meeks
Salmon Gee	Benjamin Sweat
Sherman Gilbert	Jonathan Dunham
John Gould	Benjamin Webber
William Gould	William Gould
Joshua Grant	Joshua Grant
Selah Griffin	Selah Griffin
Jonathan Hampton	Jonathan Hampton
John Herritt	John Herritt
Jonathan Holmes	Jonathan Holmes
Milton Holmes	Melvin Wilber
Joel Johnson	Joel Johnson
Edmund Marvin	Edmund Marvin
Reuben McBride	Oliver Olney
Joel McWithy	Joel McWithy
William Miller	William Miller
Nathaniel Milliken	Dana Jacobs
Levi Nickerson	Otis Shumway
Ebenezer Page	Ebenezer Page
John E. Page	Duncan McArthur
William Perry	William Perry
Samuel Phelps	Samuel Phelps
Stephen Post	Stephen Post
Uriah Powel	Uriah Powel
Zerah Pulsipher	Zerah Pulsipher
Robert Rathbun	Robert Rathbun
William Redfield	William Redfield
Elijah Reed	Elijah Reed
Joseph Rose	Joseph Rose
Shadrach Roundy	Shadrach Roundy
Almon Sherman	Almon Sherman
Erastus Snow	Erastus Snow
Andrew Squires	Elias Smith
Stephen Starks	Stephen Starks
Arial Stephens	Arial Stephens
Dexter Stillman	Dexter Stillman
Nathan Tanner	Nathan Tanner
William Terney	William Terney
Charles Thompson	Charles Thompson
Chauncey Webb	Chauncey Webb
Edmund Webb	Edmund Webb
Henry Wilcox	Henry Wilcox
Daniel Wood	Daniel Wood
Levi Woodruff	Levi Woodruff
Wilford Woodruff	Sylvester Stoddard
Gad Yale	Gad Yale
John Young	John Young
Lorenzo Young	Lorenzo Young

Third Quorum of the Seventy

The first twenty-seven members of the Third Quorum of the Seventy were ordained on 20 December 1836; other members were ordained over the succeeding months. By 3 May 1837, approximately forty-nine men had been ordained to the quorum. Two members of the quorum, John Gaylord and Daniel Miles, were ordained to the presidency of the Seventy on 6 April 1837. Nine others were moved to the First or Second Quorums of the Seventy in 1837 or early 1838 to replace those men who had moved to other quorums or been excommunicated. Their replacements were not specified by February 1838 in extant records.

The table below lists known members of the Third Quorum of the Seventy during the period covered in this volume. Blank spaces in the second column reflect apparent vacancies in the quorum.

By 3 May 1837	*6 February 1838*
Elijah Able	Elijah Able
Blake Baldwin	Blake Baldwin
Daniel Bowen	
Benjamin Brown	Benjamin Brown
David Clough	
Jonathan Dunham	
Willard Fisher	Willard Fisher
Amos Fuller	Amos Fuller
John Gaylord	
Benjamin Gifford	Benjamin Gifford
John Goodson	John Goodson
Jonathan H. Hale	
Joel Haskins	Joel Haskins
Nathan Haskins	Nathan Haskins
James Holman	James Holman
Joshua Holman	Joshua Holman
William D. Huntington	William D. Huntington
Daniel Jackson	Daniel Jackson
Truman Jackson	Truman Jackson
Dana Jacobs	
Michael Jacobs	Michael Jacobs
Duncan McArthur	
Elam Meacham	Elam Meacham
Garland Meeks	
Daniel Miles	
John Olney	John Olney
Oliver Olney	
Amos Orton	
Alanson Pettingall	
William Presley	William Presley
Ebenezer Robinson	Ebenezer Robinson
George W. Robinson	George W. Robinson
Enoch Sanborn	Enoch Sanborn
Otis Shumway	
Stephen Shumway	
Elias Smith	
Abram Smoot	Abram Smoot
Gardner Snow	
James Snow	James Snow
Sylvester Stoddard	

By 3 May 1837 (cont.)	*6 February 1838 (cont.)*
Benjamin Sweat	
James Thompson	
Frederick Vanleuven	
Lorenzo Wells	
Charles Wightman	Charles Wightman
Melvin Wilber	
Levi Wilder	Levi Wilder
George Wilson	George Wilson
Benjamin Winchester	
Abraham Wood	Abraham Wood

Other Seventies (Quorum Unknown)

Church records document several other individuals who were appointed as seventies, but those records do not indicate the quorum to which they were assigned. Below is a list of those individuals, ordered by date of ordination.

March 1835–February 1838
Joseph Winchester
Benjamin Wilber
George Rose
David Nobleman
Jeremiah Willey
Henry Stevens
Dominicus Carter
Samuel Parker
Amos Jackson
Lewis Eager
Russell Potter
David Dixon
Benjamin Ellsworth
Cheney Van Buren

Church Officers in the Kirtland Stake

The following charts list local ecclesiastical leadership of the Church of the Latter Day Saints in the "stake of Zion" at Kirtland, Ohio, between October 1835 and January 1838. Many of the charts reflect important changes to these organizations during the period covered in this volume. Readers wishing to conduct further research on specific groups or individuals may consult the annotated organizational charts posted on the Joseph Smith Papers website, josephsmithpapers.org, as well as the Biographical Directory in this volume.

Presidency of the High Council

The Kirtland high council, consisting of a three-person presidency and twelve counselors, was organized on 17 February 1834. The council was responsible for conducting disciplinary proceedings, making administrative decisions, and "settleing important difficulties which might arise in the church, which could not be settled by the Church, or the bishop's council to the satisfaction of the parties." The presidency of the high council, organized on the same date, was composed of the church's general presidency, and its members did not change until late 1837. During a 7 November 1837 general assembly in Missouri, Frederick G. Williams was replaced by Hyrum Smith in the general church presidency; he presumably lost his place in the presidency of the high council at the same time. In mid-January 1838, JS and Sidney Rigdon departed Kirtland and relocated to Far West, Missouri. Around this time, William Marks, John Smith, and Reynolds Cahoon were appointed as the presidency of the high council in Kirtland.

17 February 1834	*31 January 1838*
Joseph Smith Jr.	William Marks
Sidney Rigdon	John Smith
Frederick G. Williams	Reynolds Cahoon

High Council

After it was organized on 17 February 1834, the Kirtland high council underwent two changes later that year: in August, Orson Johnson replaced John S. Carter, who had died during the Camp of Israel expedition, and in September, Hyrum Smith replaced Sylvester Smith, who faced discipline for misconduct in the Camp of Israel. On 13 January 1836, several members of the council—including Joseph Smith Sr., Oliver Cowdery, Orson Hyde, Luke Johnson, and Hyrum Smith—were "called to fill other offices" and thus replaced. Sometime before 21 January 1836, John Smith was appointed president of the Kirtland high council. Another major reorganization of the Kirtland high council occurred on 3 September 1837, when eight members were removed, some of whom had been associated with dissent.

17 February 1834	13 January 1836	3 September 1837	31 January 1838
Joseph Smith Sr.	Samuel James	Harlow Redfield	Harlow Redfield
John Smith	John Smith	Phineas Richards	Phineas Richards
Joseph Coe	Joseph Coe	Henry Sherwood	Henry Sherwood
John Johnson	John Johnson	Oliver Granger	Oliver Granger
Martin Harris	Martin Harris	William Marks	William Marks
John S. Carter	Orson Johnson	David Dort	David Dort
Jared Carter	Jared Carter	Jared Carter	Lyman Sherman
Oliver Cowdery	John P. Greene	John P. Greene	John P. Greene
Samuel Smith	Samuel Smith	Samuel Smith	
Orson Hyde	Joseph Kingsbury	Mayhew Hillman	Mayhew Hillman
Sylvester Smith	Noah Packard	Noah Packard	Noah Packard
Luke Johnson	Thomas Grover	Asahel Smith	Asahel Smith

Bishopric

A December 1831 revelation directed that Newel K. Whitney be appointed and ordained bishop of the church in Ohio; two months later, Hyrum Smith and Reynolds Cahoon were ordained as his counselors. Even though Hyrum Smith was ordained as an assistant president in the church presidency in December 1834, it appears he continued in his capacity as a counselor in the bishopric until January 1836, when Vinson Knight was appointed to replace him. Reynolds Cahoon, and possibly Vinson Knight, left Kirtland to move to Missouri sometime in January 1838. Whitney continued to act as bishop in Kirtland until he left for Missouri in fall 1838.

By 10 February 1832	13 January 1836	31 January 1838
Newel K. Whitney, bishop	Newel K. Whitney, bishop	Newel K. Whitney, bishop
Hyrum Smith	Reynolds Cahoon	
Reynolds Cahoon	Vinson Knight	

Quorum of High Priests and Quorum of Elders

Though the offices of elder and high priest had existed in the church since the early 1830s, the quorum of the elders and the quorum of the high priests were not officially organized in Kirtland until January 1836. During a 15 January 1836 grand council meeting in which church leaders "organized the authorities of the church," Don Carlos Smith was selected and ordained as president of the Kirtland high priests quorum; Alvah Beman was subsequently chosen and ordained as president of the elders quorum. Beman chose Reuben Hedlock and John Morton to be his first and second counselors during a meeting on 25 January 1836, after which he "organized the quorum according to age, and [took] their names." Don Carlos Smith's counselors were selected around the same time, though extant records do not reveal their identities. On 27 November 1837, Joseph Smith Sr. nominated Reuben Hedlock to preside over the elders quorum after Beman passed away. Presumably John Morton then became Hedlock's first counselor. Two days after Hedlock's appointment, Edmond Bosley was ordained as his second counselor.

Following the church presidency's departure from Kirtland in mid-January 1838, the elders quorum, led by Hedlock, Morton, and Bosley, remained in Kirtland and continued to meet regularly until at least mid-September 1841. Don Carlos Smith also remained in Kirtland until early May 1838.

Presidency of Quorum of High Priests	
By 28 January 1836	*31 January 1838*
Don Carlos Smith, president Unidentified counselors	Don Carlos Smith, president Unidentified counselors

Presidency of Quorum of Elders	
By 25 January 1836	*31 January 1838*
Alvah Beman, president Reuben Hedlock John Morton	Reuben Hedlock, president John Morton Edmund Bosley

Church Officers in Zion (Missouri)

The following charts list local ecclesiastical leadership of the Church of the Latter Day Saints in northwestern Missouri, or Zion, between October 1835 and January 1838. During the period covered by this chronology, the presiding officers of the church in Missouri moved from Clay County to Caldwell County. Many of the charts reflect important changes to these organizations during the period covered in this volume. Readers wishing to conduct further research on specific groups or individuals may consult the annotated organizational charts posted on the Joseph Smith Papers website, josephsmithpapers.org, as well as the Biographical Directory in this volume.

Presidency of the High Council

In July 1834, a meeting of high priests organized a high council in Missouri, designating David Whitmer, John Whitmer, and William W. Phelps as the presidency of that council and twelve men as counselors. The president of the high council, David Whitmer, was also designated the "President of the Church in Zion." The composition of the presidency remained the same until 1838. In January 1838, the high council members expressed concern with the actions of the presidency and ultimately determined that they could "no longer recieve them as presidents." During meetings of a general assembly held between 5 and 9 February, the presidency was rejected; a body composed of the high council and bishop's council then appointed apostles Thomas B. Marsh and David W. Patten as presidents pro tempore.

3 July 1834	*10 February 1838*
David Whitmer, president	Thomas B. Marsh, president pro tempore
William W. Phelps, assistant president	David W. Patten, president pro tempore
John Whitmer, assistant president	

High Council

The Missouri high council was organized in July 1834. Patterned after the Kirtland high council, the high council in Missouri was specifically responsible for the regulation of "all the affairs of Zion." On 6 January 1836, men were appointed to the council to replace Christian Whitmer, who had died, and those who had been ordained to the Quorum of the Twelve Apostles, including Parley P. Pratt, William E. McLellin, Orson Pratt, and Thomas B. Marsh. John Murdock was apparently made a president over the council sometime before 3 March 1836. On 1 August 1837, Thomas Grover replaced Jesse Hitchcock, who had been cut off from the high council the previous May; George Morey was also appointed to the council following the death of Peter Whitmer Jr. The members of the high council were presented at a church conference in Far West in November 1837, and all were approved to retain their position.

3 July 1834	*Circa 6 January 1836*	*7 November 1837*
Christian Whitmer	Peter Whitmer Jr.	George Morey
Newel Knight	Newel Knight	Newel Knight
Lyman Wight	Lyman Wight	Lyman Wight
Calvin Beebe	Calvin Beebe	Calvin Beebe
William E. McLellin	Jesse Hitchcock	Thomas Grover
Solomon Hancock	Solomon Hancock	Solomon Hancock
Thomas B. Marsh	Elias Higbee	Elias Higbee
Simeon Carter	Simeon Carter	Simeon Carter
Parley P. Pratt	Elisha Groves	Elisha Groves
Orson Pratt	George M. Hinkle	George M. Hinkle
John Murdock	John Murdock	John Murdock
Levi Jackman	Levi Jackman	Levi Jackman

Patriarch

Isaac Morley was ordained patriarch in Missouri on 7 November 1837.

7 November 1837
Isaac Morley

Bishopric

Edward Partridge was appointed as the church's first bishop in February 1831, and Isaac Morley and John Corrill were ordained assistants to the bishop in June 1831. After relocating to Missouri in summer 1831, all three members of the Missouri bishopric remained in their positions until late spring 1837. On 22 May 1837, John Corrill was nominated as "an agent to the Church and Keeper of the Lords', store House." On 1 August 1837, the Missouri presidency and high council voted "unanimously that Titus Billings be a Bishop's Counsellor instead of John Corrill." During a November 1837 reorganization of the church in Missouri, Partridge, Morley, and Billings were unanimously approved.

Summer 1831	*7 November 1837*
Edward Partridge, bishop	Edward Partridge, bishop
Isaac Morley	Isaac Morley
John Corrill	Titus Billings

Quorum of High Priests and Quorum of Elders

Though the offices of elder and high priest had existed in the church since the early 1830s, it appears that the quorum of the elders and the quorum of the high priests were not officially organized in Missouri until August 1837. During a 1 August meeting, the Missouri presidency "appointed the 15th inst. for the High Priests and Elders to meet and choose their respective Presidents." Sometime before 20 August 1837, Charles C. Rich was "duly elected a president of the High priesthood in Zion and was ordained to that office under the hand of John Whitmer and William W. Phelps presidents." During the same meeting, Harvey Green was elected "to the presidency of Elders in Caldwell Co. Mo." The high priests and elders quorums were organized shortly after that date. Both Rich and Green remained as the heads of their respective quorums through the end of the time period covered in this volume.

Presidency of Quorum of High Priests
Before 20 August 1837
Charles C. Rich, president

Presidency of Quorum of Elders
Before 20 August 1837
Harvey Green, president

Essay on Sources

The sources used in the annotation for this volume are drawn from a variety of genres, ranging from personal writings to official ecclesiastical records and published books. The volume's featured texts themselves constitute a significant collection of contemporary sources. Many of these documents are copies preserved in institutional records such as Minute Book 1 (1832–1837), Minute Book 2 (1838, 1842, 1844), Letterbook 2 (1839–1843), the *Latter Day Saints' Messenger and Advocate* (1834–1837), and the *Elders' Journal* (1837–1838). These records also provide contextual details for JS's papers and the history of the early Latter-day Saint church in general.[1]

Letters, minutes, and revelations compose nearly two-thirds of the documents in this volume. To preserve letters and minutes of church meetings, official church historians and clerks copied texts from loose sheets of paper into more permanent record books. Frederick G. Williams began compiling minutes from meetings in Kirtland, Ohio, into Minute Book 1 in late 1832. Minute Book 2, begun in 1838 and likely copied from an earlier compilation, contains minutes of church meetings in New York, Ohio, and Missouri. James Mulholland began copying surviving letters, including several from 1837, into Letterbook 2 beginning in 1838. Besides containing many JS documents, the minute books and letterbook are also a rich source of other documents that aid in understanding the Ohio and Missouri periods of Mormon history.

The other third of the volume comprises documents of various genres, with records related to ecclesiastical matters, legal involvement, and financial transactions. The financial documents range from land transactions and promissory notes to documents related to JS's involvement in banking as an officer of the Kirtland Safety Society. The Ohio legislative sources and collections of bank records held by the Western Reserve Historical Society in Cleveland, Ohio, also provide indispensable information relative to the Kirtland Safety Society. Likewise important are documents produced for the Kirtland Safety Society itself, including the stock ledger, discount and loan papers, and banknotes, which provide essential financial information on that institution and JS's involvement in it. Other contemporary financial sources include Newel K. Whitney's store records; the Rigdon, Smith & Co. store ledger; and account books kept by Frederick G. Williams, Orson Pratt, and Brigham Young. Records from the Geauga County, Ohio, Court of Common Pleas as well as Oliver Cowdery's docket book from his tenure as a justice of the peace in Kirtland furnish legal and financial context for the litigation JS faced beginning in early 1837. In addition to supplying some of the source texts for the volume, land deeds from Geauga County helped verify information regarding land transactions and places of residence. Local and federal government documents, such as legislative proceedings, statutes, county taxes, and censuses, were also consulted for contextual information.

---

1. For more information on the source texts included in this volume, see Source Notes for Multiple-Entry Documents, pp. 521–532 herein.

One unique genre related to *Documents, Volume 5* includes papers containing Egyptian characters. The larger body of JS's Egyptian-related documents can be viewed on the Joseph Smith Papers website. Additionally, the H. Donl Peterson Collection at Brigham Young University's L. Tom Perry Special Collections was an invaluable source for information on Michael Chandler and the Egyptian mummies and papyri that JS purchased.

While several JS revelations were dictated between October 1835 and January 1838, the majority of these were never canonized and were directed to individuals rather than to the church. Most of JS's revelations during this period were recorded in his 1835–1836 journal and were not inscribed in the revelation books, which had previously been used to compile revelations. These revelations were generally not disseminated. In contrast, the prayer of dedication for the Kirtland House of the Lord, a pivotal sacred text found in this volume, was printed as a broadside and published in the *Messenger and Advocate,* as well as copied into JS's journal.[2]

Other records from the period, such as journals and correspondence, help contextualize the documents between October 1835 and January 1838. Journals of JS's contemporaries provide helpful details regarding the church in this era. Among the most essential journals for understanding these years include those kept by Wilford Woodruff, Oliver Cowdery, Edward Partridge, Jonathan H. Hale, and Stephen Post. JS's own 1835–1836 journal records his efforts to complete the House of the Lord in Kirtland and prepare church leaders for the promised endowment of power. Unfortunately, no JS journal exists for the period from 4 April 1836 to 12 March 1838. Letters written by Oliver Cowdery, Mary Fielding, Vilate Murray Kimball, Thomas B. Marsh, John Smith, and Hepzibah Richards also contain key information for understanding the events in this volume.

Newspaper articles, editorials, correspondence, and other materials published in the church newspapers, namely the *Latter Day Saints' Messenger and Advocate* and the *Elders' Journal,* contribute additional context. Regional newspapers in Ohio and Missouri also included significant coverage of JS and the church, as did national newspapers and journals published in larger cities such as New York City, Boston, Philadelphia, and Washington DC. For example, articles and exhibit notices in newspapers in the eastern United States and Ohio were crucial for understanding the popular interest in Egyptian artifacts as well as re-creating Michael Chandler's travels. The collection of regional Ohio newspapers held by the Western Reserve Historical Society was particularly useful in gauging public knowledge of and reactions to the Kirtland Safety Society. These newspaper accounts often provide details not otherwise available and added important non-Mormon perspectives.

Legal, financial, and legislative papers were drawn upon when possible.

Sometimes, the only sources for a specific event in this volume's period are personal recollections, reminiscences, and autobiographies written several years or even decades later. Notable among these is JS's multivolume manuscript history, which was compiled by scribes who used JS's journal, institutional documents, and private papers to produce

---

2. Minutes and Prayer of Dedication, 27 Mar. 1836 [D&C 109], pp. 188–208 herein; JS, Journal, 27 Mar. 1836, in *JSP,* J1:204–211.

a documentary history of JS and the church.[3] Reminiscent accounts from Heber C. Kimball, Parley P. Pratt, Lucy Mack Smith, Ira Ames, and other church members also supply important details. The sources used to contextualize JS's 6 August 1836 revelation (D&C 111) are later reminiscences, most prominently Ebenezer Robinson's editorials in the *Return,* written a half-century after JS's stay in Salem, Massachusetts. Few contemporaneous documents related to JS's summer trip to the eastern United States in 1836 are extant, and current historiography is based almost solely on Robinson's account. In general, reminiscences and later recollections are helpful for filling gaps in the contemporaneous historical record. They have been used cautiously when necessary to annotate documents in this volume.

---

3. For more information on the manuscript of JS's history, see volume 1 of the Histories series.

Works Cited

This list of sources serves as a comprehensive guide to all sources cited in this volume (documentation supporting the reference material in the back of this volume may be found on the Joseph Smith Papers website, josephsmithpapers.org). Annotation has been documented with original sources where possible and practical. In entries for manuscript sources, dates identify when the manuscript was created, which is not necessarily the time period the manuscript covers. Newspaper entries are listed under the newspaper titles used during the time period covered by this volume. Newspaper entries also provide beginning and ending years for the publication. Since newspapers often changed names or editors over time, such dates typically approximate the years the paper was active under a particular editor; when it is impractical to provide beginning and ending publication dates by an editor's tenure, dates may be determined by major events in the paper's history, such as a merger with another sizable newspaper.

Some sources cited in this volume are referred to on first and subsequent occurrences by a conventional shortened citation. For convenience, some documents are referred to by editorial titles rather than by their original titles or by the titles given in the catalogs of their current repositories, in which case the list of works cited provides the editorial title followed by full bibliographic information.

Transcripts and images of a growing number of Joseph Smith's papers are available on the Joseph Smith Papers website.

Scriptural References

The annotation within volumes of *The Joseph Smith Papers* includes numerous references to works accepted as scripture by The Church of Jesus Christ of Latter-day Saints. The principal citations of Mormon scripture appearing in annotation are to JS-era published or manuscript versions. However, for reader convenience, these citations also include a bracketed reference to the current and widely available Latter-day Saint scriptural canon. Early extant copies of JS's revelations dictated during the period covered in this volume are transcribed in the main body of this volume. All versions of scripture cited in this volume, early or modern, are identified in the list of works cited.

The church's current scriptural canon consists of the King James (or Authorized) Version of the Bible (KJV), plus three other volumes: the Book of Mormon, the Doctrine and Covenants, and the Pearl of Great Price. The following paragraphs provide more detailed information about uniquely Mormon scriptures and how they are cited in this volume.

Book of Mormon. The first edition of the Book of Mormon was printed for JS in 1830. He oversaw the publication of subsequent editions in 1837 and 1840. The Book of Mormon, like the Bible, consists of a number of shorter books. However, the present volume cites early editions of the Book of Mormon by page numbers because these editions were not divided into numbered verses. The bracketed references to the modern (2013) Latter-day Saint edition of this work identify the book name with modern chapter and verse.

Doctrine and Covenants. JS authorized publication of early revelations beginning in 1832 in *The Evening and the Morning Star,* the church's first newspaper, and initiated the publication of a compilation of revelations, which first appeared in 1833 under the title Book of Commandments. Revised and expanded versions of this compilation were published in 1835 and 1844 under the title Doctrine and Covenants. Since JS's time, The Church of Jesus Christ of Latter-day Saints has continued to issue revised and expanded versions of the Doctrine and Covenants, as has the Community of Christ (formerly the Reorganized Church of Jesus Christ of Latter Day Saints). The bracketed references to the modern (2013) Latter-day Saint edition of the Doctrine and Covenants, which cite by section number and verse, use the abbreviation D&C in the place of Doctrine and Covenants. A table titled Corresponding Section Numbers in Editions of the Doctrine and Covenants, which appears after the list of works cited, aligns the corresponding section numbers of the three JS-era compilations and the current editions of the Doctrine and Covenants published by The Church of Jesus Christ of Latter-day Saints and by the Community of Christ.

Joseph Smith Bible revision. Beginning in June 1830, JS systematically reviewed the text of the KJV and made revisions and additions to it. JS largely completed the work in 1833, but only a few excerpts were published in his lifetime. The Reorganized Church of Jesus Christ of Latter Day Saints published the entire work in 1867 under the title Holy Scriptures and included excerpts from the writings of Moses in two sections of its Doctrine and Covenants. The Church of Jesus Christ of Latter-day Saints, which today officially refers to JS's Bible revisions as the Joseph Smith Translation, has never published the entire work, but two excerpts are canonized in the Pearl of Great Price and many other excerpts are included in the footnotes and appendix of the modern (2013) Latter-day Saint edition of the KJV. In the *Papers,* references to JS's Bible revision are cited to the original manuscripts, with a bracketed reference given where possible to the relevant book, chapter, and verse of the Joseph Smith Translation.

Pearl of Great Price. The Pearl of Great Price, a collection of miscellaneous writings that primarily originated with JS, was first published in 1851 and was canonized by The Church of Jesus Christ of Latter-day Saints in 1880. The modern (2013) edition of this work consists of the following: selections from the Book of Moses, an extract from JS's Bible revision manuscripts; the Book of Abraham, writings translated from papyri JS and others acquired in 1835 and first published in the *Times and Seasons* in 1842; Joseph Smith—Matthew, another extract from JS's Bible revision manuscripts; Joseph Smith—History, a selection from the history that JS began working on in 1838; and the Articles of Faith, a statement of beliefs included in a JS letter to Chicago newspaper editor John Wentworth and published in the *Times and Seasons* in 1842. Except in the case of Joseph Smith—History, citations in this volume to early versions of each of these works also include a bracketed reference to the corresponding chapter and verse in the modern Latter-day Saint canon. The Pearl of Great Price is not part of the canon of the Community of Christ. References to the history JS began work on in 1838 are cited to the original manuscript of that history (see entry on "JS History" in the list of works cited).

Court Abbreviations

Citations to legal cases in this volume usually reference the name of the case, the deciding court, and the year of the court's decision. Jurisdictions and court names used in legal citations are contemporary to the year of the cited case and do not necessarily correspond to modern courts or jurisdictions. The following abbreviations are used within this volume:

Geauga Co. C.P.	Geauga County, Ohio, Court of Common Pleas
J.P. Ct.	Justice of the Peace Court

Abbreviations for Frequently Cited Repositories

BYU	L. Tom Perry Special Collections, Harold B. Lee Library, Brigham Young University, Provo, Utah
CCLA	Community of Christ Library-Archives, Independence, Missouri
CHL	Church History Library, The Church of Jesus Christ of Latter-day Saints, Salt Lake City
FHL	Family History Library, The Church of Jesus Christ of Latter-day Saints, Salt Lake City

———— ⁊ ————

Abraham (book of). See *Pearl of Great Price.*

Acts of a General Nature, Enacted, Revised and Ordered to Be Reprinted, at the First Session of the Twenty-Ninth General Assembly of the State of Ohio. Columbus: Olmstead and Bailhache, 1831.

Acts of a General Nature Passed by the Forty Third General Assembly of the State of Ohio, Begun and Held in the City of Columbus, December 4, 1844, and in the Forty Third Year of Said State. Columbus: Samuel Medary, 1845.

Adams, Dale W. "Grandison Newell's Obsession." *Journal of Mormon History* 30, no. 1 (Spring 2004): 159–188.

Albany Evening Journal. Albany, NY. 1830–1867.

Alexander, Thomas G. *Things in Heaven and Earth: The Life and Times of Wilford Woodruff, a Mormon Prophet.* Salt Lake City: Signature Books, 1991.

Allen, Daniel. Reminiscences, ca. 1865. Typescript. CHL.

An American Dictionary of the English Language. . . . Edited by Noah Webster. New York: S. Converse, 1828.

Ames, Ira. Autobiography and Journal, 1858. CHL.

Andrus, Hyrum L., and Chris Fuller, comp. *Register of the Newel Kimball Whitney Papers.* Provo, UT: Division of Archives and Manuscripts, Harold B. Lee Library, Brigham Young University, 1978.

Angell, Truman O. Autobiography, 1884. CHL. Also available in Archie Leon Brown and Charlene L. Hathaway, *141 Years of Mormon Heritage: Rawsons, Browns, Angells—Pioneers* (Oakland, CA: By the authors, 1973), 119–135.

Aurora. New Lisbon, OH. 1835–1837.

Backman, Milton V., Jr. *The Heavens Resound: A History of the Latter-day Saints in Ohio, 1830–1838.* Salt Lake City: Deseret Book, 1983.

———, comp. *A Profile of Latter-day Saints of Kirtland, Ohio, and Members of Zion's Camp, 1830–1839: Vital Statistics and Sources.* 2nd ed. Provo, UT: Department of Church History and Doctrine and Religious Studies Center, Brigham Young University, 1983.

Baltimore Gazette and Daily Advertiser. Baltimore. 1825–1838.

"Banking and Financiering at Kirtland." *Magazine of Western History* 11, no. 6 (Apr. 1890): 668–670.

Bank of Geauga. Discount Book, 1832–1838. Lake County Historical Society, Painesville, OH.

Bank of Monroe. Account Statement, [Monroe, MI], for Kirtland Safety Society, ca. Apr. 1837. CHL.

Barnes, Lorenzo D. Reminiscences and Diaries, 1834–1839. CHL.

Bartlett, John Russell. *Dictionary of Americanisms. A Glossary of Words and Phrases. Usually Regarded as Peculiar to the United States.* New York: Bartlett and Welford, 1848.

Baugh, Alexander L. *A Call to Arms: The 1838 Mormon Defense of Northern Missouri.* Dissertations in Latter-day Saint History. Provo, UT: Joseph Fielding Smith Institute for Latter-day Saint History; BYU Studies, 2000.

Belnap, Gilbert. Account Book, 1836–1874. CHL.

Benjamin Brown Family Collection, 1835–1983. CHL.

Benson, Fred H., comp. *The Benson Family Records.* Syracuse, NY: Craftsman Press, 1920.

Berkhofer, Robert F., Jr. *The White Man's Indian: Images of the American Indian from Columbus to the Present.* New York: Knopf, 1978.

Berrett, LaMar C. "History of the Southern States Mission, 1831–1861." Master's thesis, Brigham Young University, 1960.

———, ed. *Sacred Places: A Comprehensive Guide to Early LDS Historical Sites.* 6 vols. Salt Lake City: Deseret Book, 1999–2007.

Best, Christy. "Register of the Revelations Collection in the Church Archives, the Church of Jesus Christ of Latter-day Saints," July 1893. CHL.

Bible. See *Holy Bible.*

Biographical and Historical Record of Ringgold and Decatur Counties, Iowa. Containing Portraits of all the Presidents of the United States from Washington to Cleveland, with Accompanying Biographies of Each; A Condensed History of the State of Iowa; Portraits and Biographies of the Governors of the Territory and State. . . . Chicago: Lewis Publishing, 1887.

Biographical Directory of the United States Congress, 1774–1989: The Continental Congress September 5, 1774, to October 21, 1788, and the Congress of the United States from the First through the One Hundredth Congress March 4, 1789, to January 3, 1898, Inclusive. Edited by Kathryn Allamong Jacob and Bruce A. Ragsdale. Washington DC: U.S. Government Printing Office, 1989.

Bode, Carl. *The American Lyceum: Town Meeting of the Mind.* New York: Oxford University Press, 1956.

Bodenhorn, Howard. "Bank Chartering and Political Corruption in Antebellum New York: Free Banking as Reform." In *Corruption and Reform: Lessons from America's Economic*

History, edited by Edward L. Glaeser and Claudia Goldin, 231–257. Chicago: University of Chicago Press, 2006.

———. *A History of Banking in Antebellum America: Financial Markets and Economic Development in an Era of Nation-Building.* New York: Cambridge University Press, 2000.

———. *State Banking in Early America: A New Economic History.* New York: Oxford University Press, 2003.

The Book of Abraham. See *Pearl of Great Price.*

Book of Abraham Manuscripts, ca. Early July–ca. Nov. 1835, ca. 1841–1842. CHL.

A Book of Commandments, for the Government of the Church of Christ, Organized according to Law, on the 6th of April, 1830. Zion [Independence], MO: W. W. Phelps, 1833. Also available in Robin Scott Jensen, Richard E. Turley Jr., and Riley M. Lorimer, eds., *Revelations and Translations, Volume 2: Published Revelations.* Vol. 2 of the Revelations and Translations series of *The Joseph Smith Papers,* edited by Dean C. Jessee, Ronald K. Esplin, and Richard Lyman Bushman (Salt Lake City: Church Historian's Press, 2011).

Book of Doctrine and Covenants: Carefully Selected from the Revelations of God, and Given in the Order of Their Dates. Independence, MO: Herald Publishing House, 2004.

The Book of Mormon: An Account Written by the Hand of Mormon, upon Plates Taken from the Plates of Nephi. Palmyra, NY: E. B. Grandin, 1830.

The Book of Mormon: Another Testament of Jesus Christ. Salt Lake City: The Church of Jesus Christ of Latter-day Saints, 2013.

The Book of Moses (selections from). See *Pearl of Great Price.*

The Book of the Law of the Lord, Record Book, 1841–1845. CHL.

Boston Daily Times. Boston. 1836–1837.

Bourne, A. *The Surveyor's Pocket-Book, Containing Brief Statements of Mathematical Principles, and Useful Results in Mechanical Philosophy.* Chillicothe, OH: I. N. Pumroy, 1834.

Bouvier, John. *A Law Dictionary, Adapted to the Constitution and Laws of the United States of America, and of the Several States of the American Union; with References to the Civil and Other Systems of Foreign Law.* 2 vols. Philadelphia: T. and J. W. Johnson, 1839.

———. *A Law Dictionary, Adapted to the Constitution and Laws of the United States of America, and of the Several States of the American Union; with References to the Civil and Other Systems of Foreign Law.* 2nd ed. 2 vols. Philadelphia: T. and J. W. Johnson, 1843.

———. *A Law Dictionary, Adapted to the Constitution and Laws of the United States of America, and of the Several States of the American Union; with References to the Civil and Other Systems of Foreign Law.* 2nd ed. 2 vols. Philadelphia: Deacon and Peterson, 1854.

Bradley, James L. *Zion's Camp 1834: Prelude to the Civil War.* Logan, UT: By the author, 1990.

Bradshaw, M. Scott. "Joseph Smith's Performance of Marriages in Ohio." *BYU Studies* 39, no. 4 (2000): 23–69.

Brewster, James Colin. *Very Important! To the Mormon Money Diggers*. Springfield, IL: No publisher, 1843.

A Brief Historical Sketch of the Town of Vinalhaven, from Its Earliest Known Settlement. Prepared by Order of the Town, on the Occasion of Its One Hundredth Anniversary. Rockland, ME: Free Press Office, 1889.

Brigham Young Office Files, 1832–1878. CHL.

Brigham Young University and Church History and Doctrine Department. Church History Project Collection, 1977–1981. CHL.

Brown, Samuel. "Joseph (Smith) in Egypt: Babel, Hieroglyphs, and the Pure Language of Eden." *Church History: Studies in Christianity and Culture* 78, no. 1 (Mar. 2009): 26–65.

Burgess, G. A., and J. T. Ward. *Free Baptist Cyclopaedia. Historical and Biographical. The Rise of the Freewill Baptist Connection and of Those General and Open Communion Baptist Which, Merging Together, Form One People. . . .* Chicago: Free Baptist Cyclopaedia, 1889.

Burgess, Harrison. Autobiography, ca. 1883. CHL. Also available as "Sketch of a Well-Spent Life," in *Labors in the Vineyard,* Faith-Promoting Series 12 (Salt Lake City: Juvenile Instructor Office, 1884), 65–74.

Burleigh, Nina. *Mirage: Napoleon's Scientists and the Unveiling of Egypt*. New York: Harper, 2007.

Bushman, Richard Lyman. "The Character of Joseph Smith." *BYU Studies* 42, no. 2 (2003): 23–34.

Butts, I. R. *The Business Man's Assistant, Part 1. Containing Useful Forms of Legal Instruments: Enlarged by the Addition of Forms of Acknowledgments, Agreements, Assignments, Awards, Bonds, Leases, Mortgages, Powers of Attorney, and Legal Opinions, Found in No Other Work. Adapted to the Wants of Business Men throughout the United States*. Boston: By the author, 1847.

Cahoon, Reynolds. Diaries, June 1831–Aug. 1832. CHL.

Cahoon, William F. Autobiography, 1878. CHL.

———. Autobiography and Family Records, 1891. CHL.

Campbell, Alexander. *Delusions. An Analysis of the Book of Mormon; with an Examination of Its Internal and External Evidences, and a Refutation of Its Pretences to Divine Authority*. Boston: Benjamin H. Greene, 1832.

Cannon, Donald Q. "Licensing in the Early Church." *BYU Studies* 22, no. 1 (Winter 1982): 96–105.

Cannon, Donald Q., and Lyndon W. Cook, eds. *Far West Record: Minutes of the Church of Jesus Christ of Latter-day Saints, 1830–1844*. Salt Lake City: Deseret Book, 1983.

Chardon Spectator and Geauga Gazette. Chardon, OH. 1833–1835.

Chicago Historical Society, Collection of Mormon Materials, 1836–1886. Microfilm. CHL.

Chicago Tribune. Chicago. 1847–.

Chitty, Joseph. *A Practical Treatise on Bills of Exchange, Checks on Bankers, Promissory Notes, Bankers' Cash Notes, and Bank Notes*. Springfield, IL: G. and C. Merriam, 1836.

Christian Palladium. Union Mills, NY. 1832–1839.

Christian Register and Boston Observer. Boston. 1835–1843.

Christian Watchman. Boston. 1821–1848.

Church, John. "William J. Barrow: A Remembrance and Appreciation." *American Archivist* 68, no. 1 (Spring/Summer 2005): 152–160.

Cincinnati Advertiser, and Ohio Phoenix. Cincinnati. 1829–1838.

Cleveland Advertiser. Cleveland. 1831–1837.

Cleveland Daily Gazette. Cleveland. 1836–1837.

Cleveland Weekly Advertiser. Cleveland. 1836–1840.

Cleveland Whig. Cleveland. 1834–1836.

Coffin, James H. *Progressive Exercises in Book Keeping, by Single and Double Entry.* Greenfield, MA: A. Phelps, 1836.

Coin and Currency Collection, no date. CHL.

Collection of Manuscripts about Mormons, 1832–1954. Chicago History Museum.

A Collection of Sacred Hymns, for the Church of the Latter Day Saints. Edited by Emma Smith. Kirtland, OH: F. G. Williams, 1835.

Coltrin, Zebedee. Diaries and Notebook, 1832–1834. CHL.

Commercial Bank of Lake Erie Records, 1816–1840. Western Reserve Historical Society, Cleveland.

The Constitution of the American Anti-Slavery Society: With the Declaration of the National Anti-Slavery Convention at Philadelphia, December, 1833, and the Address to the Public, Issued by the Executive Committee of the Society, in September, 1835. New York: American Anti-Slavery Society, 1838.

Cook, Lyndon W., and Milton V. Backman Jr., eds. *Kirtland Elders' Quorum Record, 1836–1841.* Provo, UT: Grandin Book, 1985.

Coolidge, A. J., and J. B. Mansfield. *A History and Description of New England, General and Local.* Vol. 1, *Maine, New Hampshire, and Vermont.* Boston: Austin J. Coolidge, 1859.

Coray, Martha Jane Knowlton. Notebook, ca. 1841–ca. 1850. BYU.

Corrill, John. *A Brief History of the Church of Christ of Latter Day Saints, (Commonly Called Mormons;) Including an Account of Their Doctrine and Discipline; with the Reasons of the Author for Leaving the Church.* St. Louis: By the author, 1839.

Cowdery, Lyman. Papers, 1834–1858. CHL.

Cowdery, Oliver. Diary, Jan.–Mar. 1836. CHL. Also available as Leonard J. Arrington, "Oliver Cowdery's Kirtland, Ohio, 'Sketch Book,'" *BYU Studies* 12, no. 4 (Summer 1972): 410–426.

———. Docket Book, June–Sept. 1837. Henry E. Huntington Library, San Marino, CA.

———. Letterbook, 1833–1838. Henry E. Huntington Library, San Marino, CA.

Cowdery, Warren A., and Oliver Cowdery. Financial Account Books, 1835–1836. CHL.

Crary, Christopher G. *Pioneer and Personal Reminiscences.* Marshalltown, IA: Marshall, 1893.

Crawley, Peter. *A Descriptive Bibliography of the Mormon Church.* 3 vols. Provo, UT: Religious Studies Center, Brigham Young University, 1997–2012.

Crocheron, Augusta Joyce. *Representative Women of Deseret, a Book of Biographical Sketches, to Accompany the Picture Bearing the Same Title.* Salt Lake City: J. C. Graham, 1884.

Crosby, Caroline Barnes. Reminiscences, no date. In Jonathan Crosby and Caroline Barnes Crosby Papers, 1848–1882. CHL.

Cutler, Carroll. *A History of Western Reserve College, during Its First Half Century, 1826–1876.* Cleveland: Crocker's Publishing House, 1876.

Daily Chronicle. Philadelphia. 1828–1834.

Daily Cleveland Herald. Cleveland. 1835–1837.

Daily Herald and Gazette. Cleveland. 1837–1839.

Daily Intelligencer. Philadelphia. 1832–1833.

Daily Missouri Republican. St. Louis. 1822–1869.

Daily Pittsburgh Gazette. Pittsburgh. 1833–1841.

D&C. See *Doctrine and Covenants of the Church of Jesus Christ of Latter-day Saints* (2013).

Description de l'Égypte, ou Recueil des observations et des recherches qui ont été faites en Égypte pendant l'expédition de l'armée française, publié par les ordres de Sa Majesté l'Empereur Napoléon le Grand. Paris: Imprimerie Impériale, 1809–1829.

"Description of Far West Plat," 1837. Brigham Young University and Church History and Doctrine Department, Church History Project Collection, 1977–1981. Photocopy. CHL. Original at State Historical Society of Missouri, Columbia.

Deseret Museum Catalog, 1891–1917. In Deseret Museum Records, 1875–1918. CHL.

Deseret News. Salt Lake City. 1850–.

Deseret Weekly. See *Deseret News.*

"Dewdney & Tremlett." Yoward/Logan, database no. 4206, Mills Archive. Accessed 24 Mar. 2016. https://millsarchive.org.

A Directory for the City of Buffalo; Containing the Names and Residence of the Heads of Families and Householders, in Said City, on the First of May, 1836. Buffalo, NY: Charles Faxon, 1836.

A Directory for the City of Buffalo; Containing the Names and Residence of the Heads of Families, Households, and Other Inhabitants, in Said City, on the 1st of May, 1837. Buffalo, NY: Sarah Crary, 1837.

Doctrine and Covenants, 2004 Community of Christ edition. See *Book of Doctrine and Covenants.*

Doctrine and Covenants of the Church of the Latter Day Saints: Carefully Selected from the Revelations of God. Compiled by Joseph Smith, Oliver Cowdery, Sidney Rigdon, and Frederick G. Williams. Kirtland, OH: F. G. Williams, 1835. Also available in Robin Scott Jensen, Richard E. Turley Jr., and Riley M. Lorimer, eds. *Revelations and Translations, Volume 2: Published Revelations.* Vol. 2 of the Revelations and Translations series of *The Joseph Smith Papers,* edited by Dean C. Jessee, Ronald K. Esplin, and Richard Lyman Bushman (Salt Lake City: Church Historian's Press, 2011).

The Doctrine and Covenants of the Church of Jesus Christ of Latter Day Saints; Carefully Selected from the Revelations of God. Compiled by Joseph Smith. 2nd ed. Nauvoo, IL: John Taylor, 1844. Selections also available in Robin Scott Jensen, Richard E. Turley Jr., and Riley M. Lorimer, eds. *Revelations and Translations, Volume 2: Published Revelations.* Vol. 2 of the Revelations and Translations series of *The Joseph Smith Papers,* edited by Dean C. Jessee, Ronald K. Esplin, and Richard Lyman Bushman (Salt Lake City: Church Historian's Press, 2011).

The Doctrine and Covenants of the Church of Jesus Christ of Latter-day Saints: Containing Revelations Given to Joseph Smith, the Prophet, with Some Additions by His Successors in the Presidency of the Church. Salt Lake City: The Church of Jesus Christ of Latter-day Saints, 2013.

Document Containing the Correspondence, Orders, &c., in relation to the Disturbances with the Mormons; and the Evidence Given before the Hon. Austin A. King, Judge of the Fifth Judicial Circuit of the State of Missouri, at the Court-House in Richmond, in a Criminal Court of Inquiry, Begun November 12, 1838, on the Trial of Joseph Smith, Jr., and Others, for High Treason and Other Crimes against the State. Fayette, MO: Boon's Lick Democrat, 1841.

Eastern Argus. Portland, ME. 1803–1863.

East India Marine Society Records, 1799–1972. Phillips Library, Peabody Essex Museum, Salem, MA.

Eaton, Cyrus. *History of Thomaston, Rockland, and South Thomaston, Maine, from Their First Exploration, A. D. 1605; with Family Genealogies.* Vol. 1. Hallowell: Masters Smith, 1865.

Elders' Journal of the Church of Latter Day Saints. Kirtland, OH, Oct.–Nov. 1837; Far West, MO, July–Aug. 1838.

"Elders License Elijah Abel Certificate." In James D. Wardle, Papers, 1812–2001. Special Collections, J. Willard Marriott Library, University of Utah, Salt Lake City.

Ellis, Margaret Holben. *Historical Perspectives in the Conservation of Works of Art on Paper.* Los Angeles: Getty Conservation Institute, 2014.

Encyclopedia Judaica. 2nd ed. Edited by Fred Skolnik and Michael Berenbaum. Vol. 18. Detroit: Macmillan Reference, 2007.

Esplin, Ronald K. "The Emergence of Brigham Young and the Twelve to Mormon Leadership, 1830–1841." PhD diss., Brigham Young University, 1981. Also available as *The Emergence of Brigham Young and the Twelve to Mormon Leadership, 1830–1841,* Dissertations in Latter-day Saint History (Provo, UT: Joseph Fielding Smith Institute for Latter-day Saint History; BYU Studies, 2006).

Esplin, Ronald K., and Sharon E. Nielsen. "The Record of the Twelve, 1835: The Quorum of the Twelve Apostles' Call and 1835 Mission." *BYU Studies* 51, no. 1 (2012): 4–52.

Essex Register. Salem, MA. 1807–1840.

Esshom, Frank. *Pioneers and Prominent Men of Utah. Comprising Photographs—Genealogies—Biographies. . . .* Salt Lake City: Utah Pioneers, 1913.

Eubanks, Lila Carpenter. "The Deseret Museum," *Utah Historical Quarterly* 50, no. 4 (Fall 1982): 361–376.

Evening and Morning Star. Edited reprint of *The Evening and the Morning Star.* Kirtland, OH. Jan. 1835–Oct. 1836.

The Evening and the Morning Star. Independence, MO, June 1832–July 1833; Kirtland, OH, Dec. 1833–Sept. 1834.

"Extracts from the Daily Journal of John Bus," Enclosure in F. C. Waite, Letter, Cleveland, OH, to Joseph L. Rubin, Washington DC, 19 Oct. 1933, Western Reserve Historical Society, Cleveland. Copy at CHL.

Faculty Minutes. Board of Trustees Records, 1833–1982, Record Group 1, Series 2. Oberlin College Archives, Oberlin, OH.

FamilySearch. https://familysearch.org.

Far West. Liberty, MO. Aug.–Oct. 1836.

Feldman, Stephen M. *Free Expression and Democracy in America: A History.* Chicago: University of Chicago Press, 2008.

F. G. Williams & Co. Account Book, 1833–1835. In Patience Cowdery, Diary, 1849–1851. CHL.

Fielding, Joseph. Journals, 1837–1859. CHL.

Find a Grave. http://findagrave.com.

Fletcher, Robert Samuel. *A History of Oberlin College from Its Foundation through the Civil War.* Vol. 1. Oberlin, OH: Oberlin College, 1943.

Force, Peter. *The National Calendar for MDCCCXXX. Vol. VIII.* Washington DC: By the author, 1830.

Fredonia Censor. Fredonia, NY. 1824–1932.

Friends' Weekly Intelligencer. Philadelphia. 1844–1853.

Fullmer, Desdemona Wadsworth. Autobiography, 7 June 1868. Desdemona Wadsworth Fullmer, Papers, 1868. CHL.

Gates, Susa Young [Homespun, pseud.]. *Lydia Knight's History.* Noble Women's Lives Series 1. Salt Lake City: Juvenile Instructor Office, 1883.

Gaustad, Edwin Scott. *A Religious History of America.* Rev. ed. San Francisco: Harper San Francisco, 1990.

Geauga County, OH. Common Pleas Court Marriage Licenses, 1835–1836. CHL.

Geauga County Archives and Records Center, Chardon, OH.

Geauga County Court of Common Pleas, Geauga County Archives and Records Center, Chardon, OH.

Geauga Gazette. Painesville, OH. 1828–1833.

General Land Office Records. Bureau of Land Management, U.S. Department of the Interior. Accessed 4 Aug. 2015. http://www.glorecords.blm.gov/.

Genovese, Eugene D. "Religion in the Collapse of the American Union." In *Religion and the American Civil War,* edited by Randall M. Miller, Harry S. Stout, and Charles Reagan Wilson, 74–88. New York: Oxford University Press, 1998.

Gibbons, Francis M. Letter to Earl E. Olson, 1 Nov. 1974. CHL.

Gilbert, Algernon Sidney. Notebook of Revelations, 1831–ca. 1833. Revelations Collection, 1831–ca. 1844, 1847, 1861, ca. 1876. CHL.

Givens, Terryl L., and Matthew J. Grow. *Parley P. Pratt: The Apostle Paul of Mormonism.* New York: Oxford University Press, 2011.

Godfrey, Kenneth W. "More Treasures Than One: Section 111." In *Hearken, O Ye People: Discourses on the Doctrine and Covenants.* Sperry Symposium 1984, 191–204. Sandy, UT: Randall Book, 1984.

Goldenberg, David M. *The Curse of Ham: Race and Slavery in Early Judaism, Christianity, and Islam.* Princeton, NJ: Princeton University Press, 2003.

Goldman, Shalom. *God's Sacred Tongue: Hebrew and the American Imagination.* Chapel Hill and London: University of North Carolina Press, 2004.

Golembe, Carter H. *State Banks and the Economic Development of the West 1830–44.* New York: Arno, 1978.

Gorn, Elliott J. "'Gouge and Bite, Pull Hair and Scratch': The Social Significance of Fighting in the Southern Backcountry." *American Historical Review* 90, no. 1 (Feb. 1985): 18–43.

Grandstaff, Mark R., and Milton V. Backman Jr. "The Social Origins of the Kirtland Mormons." *BYU Studies* 30, no. 2 (Spring 1990): 47–66.

Greene, Evan M. Diaries, 1833–1852. CHL.

Greenwood, Val D. *The Researcher's Guide to American Genealogy*. 3rd ed. Baltimore: Genealogical Publishing, 2000.

Greppo, J. G. H. *Essay on the Hieroglyphic System of M. Champollion, Jun. and on the Advantages Which It Offers to Sacred Criticism*. Translated by Isaac Stuart. Boston: Perkins and Marvin, 1830.

Grey, Matthew J. "'The Word of the Lord in the Original': Joseph Smith's Study of Hebrew in Kirtland." In *Approaching Antiquity: Joseph Smith and the Ancient World*, edited by Lincoln H. Blumell, Matthew J. Grey, and Andrew H. Hedges, 249–302. Provo, UT: Religious Studies Center, Brigham Young University; Salt Lake City: Deseret Book, 2015.

Grow, Matthew J. "'Clean from the Blood of This Generation': The Washing of Feet and the Latter-day Saints." In *Archive of Restoration Culture Summer Fellows' Papers, 2000–2002*, edited by Richard Lyman Bushman, 131–138. Provo, UT: Joseph Fielding Smith Institute for Latter-day Saint History, 2005.

Guinn, J. M. *Historical and Biographical Record of Southern California. Containing a History of Southern California from Its Earliest Settlement to the Opening Year of the Twentieth Century*. Chicago: Chapman, 1902.

Gummere, John. *A Treatise on Surveying, Containing the Theory and Practice: To Which Is Prefixed, a Perspicuous System of Plane Trigonometry*. 5th ed. Philadelphia: Kimber and Sharpless, 1828.

Gurley, Zenos. "Questions Asked of David Whitmer at His Home in Richmond, Ray County, Missouri," 1885. CHL.

Hale, Jonathan H. Reminiscences and Journals, 1837–1840. CHL.

Hall, Harvey. *The Cincinnati Directory, for 1825, Containing the Names of Its Citizens, Their Occupations, Places of Residence, and Places of Nativity; Alphabetically Arranged. With a Variety of Other Matter*. Cincinnati: Samuel J. Browne, 1825.

Haller, John S., Jr. *The People's Doctors: Samuel Thompson and the American Botanical Movement, 1790–1860*. Carbondale and Edwardsville: Southern Illinois University Press, 2000.

Hamilton, Edward Pierce. *The French and Indian Wars: The Story of Battles and Forts in the Wilderness*. Garden City, NY: Doubleday, 1962.

Hammond, Bray. *Banks and Politics in America from the Revolution to the Civil War*. Princeton, NJ: Princeton University Press, 1957.

Hampshire Gazette. Northampton, MA. 1820–1918.

Hancock, Levi. Autobiography, ca. 1854. CHL.

Hancock, Mosiah. "Autobiography of Levi Ward Hancock," ca. 1896. CHL.

Hardy, Anne. *The Epidemic Streets: Infectious Disease and the Rise of Preventive Medicine, 1856–1900*. Oxford: Clarendon Press, 1993.

Harper, Steven C. "'A Pentecost and Endowment Indeed': Six Eyewitness Accounts of the Kirtland Temple Experience." In *Opening the Heavens: Accounts of Divine Manifestations, 1820–1844,* edited by John W. Welch. Salt Lake City: Deseret Book; Provo, UT: Brigham Young University Press, 2005.

———. "Pentecost Continued: A Contemporaneous Account of the Kirtland Temple Dedication." *BYU Studies* 42, no. 2 (2003): 5–22.

Harris, Katherine. "Homesteading in Northeastern Colorado, 1873–1920: Sex Roles and Women's Experience." In *The Women's West*, edited by Susan Armitage and Elizabeth Jameson, 165–178. Norman: University of Oklahoma Press, 1987.

Hatch, Nathan O. "Mormon and Methodist: Popular Religion in the Crucible of the Free Market." *Journal of Mormon History* 20, no. 1 (Spring 1994): 24–44.

Hauglid, Brian M. *A Textual History of the Book of Abraham: Manuscripts and Editions.* Studies in the Book of Abraham, edited by John Gee and Brian M. Hauglid. Provo, UT: Neal A. Maxwell Institute for Religious Scholarship, Brigham Young University, 2010.

Hauptman, Laurence M. *Conspiracy of Interests: Iroquois Dispossession and the Rise of New York State.* Syracuse, NY: Syracuse University Press, 1999.

Hawkins, Kenneth. *Research in the Land Entry Files of the General Land Office: Record Group 49.* Reference Information Paper 114, rev. ed. Washington DC: National Archives and Records Administration, 2009.

Hawley, John. "The Life of John Hawley," ca. Jan. 1885. CCLA.

Hayden, Amos Sutton. *Early History of the Disciples in the Western Reserve, Ohio: With Biographical Sketches of the Principal Agents in Their Religious Movement.* Cincinnati: Chase and Hall, 1875.

Haynes, Stephen R. *Noah's Curse: The Biblical Justification of American Slavery.* New York: Oxford University Press, 2002.

Hays, Daniel Peixotto. "Daniel L. M. Peixotto, M. D." *Publications of the American Jewish Historical Society* 26 (1918): 219–230.

Hendricks, Drusilla. Reminiscences, ca. 1877. CHL.

Herndon, Ruth Wallis. "'Proper' Magistrates and Masters: Binding Out Poor Children in Southern New England, 1720–1820." In *Children Bound to Labor: The Pauper Apprentice System in Early America*, edited by Ruth Wallis Herndon and John E. Murray, 39–51. Ithaca, NY: Cornell University Press, 2009.

Herndon, Ruth Wallis, and John E. Murray, eds. "'A Proper and Instructive Education': Raising Children in Pauper Apprenticeship." In *Children Bound to Labor: The Pauper Apprentice System in Early America*, edited by Ruth Wallis Herndon and John E. Murray, 3–18. Ithaca, NY: Cornell University Press, 2009.

———. *Children Bound to Labor: The Pauper Apprentice System in Early America*. Ithaca, NY: Cornell University Press, 2009.

"Hieroglyphics," *North American Review* 32, no. 70 (Jan. 1831): 95–127.

Hill, Marvin S., C. Keith Rooker, and Larry T. Wimmer. *The Kirtland Economy Revisited: A Market Critique of Sectarian Economics.* Provo, UT: Brigham Young University Press, 1977.

Hindle, Steve, and Ruth Wallis Herndon. "Recreating Proper Families in England and North America." In *Children Bound to Labor: The Pauper Apprentice System in Early America*, edited by Ruth Wallis Herndon and John E. Murray, 19–38. Ithaca, NY: Cornell University Press, 2009.

Historian's Office. Brigham Young History Drafts, 1856–1858. CHL.

———. Catalogs and Inventories, 1846–1904. CHL.

———. Histories of the Twelve, 1856–1858, 1861. CHL.

———. Reports of Speeches, 1845–1855. CHL.

Historical Department. Journal History of the Church, 1896–2001. CHL.

———. Nineteenth-Century Legal Documents Collection, ca. 1835–1890. CHL.

History of Caldwell and Livingston Counties, Missouri, Written and Compiled from the Most Authentic Official and Private Sources. . . . St. Louis: National Historical Co., 1886.

History of Cattaraugus Co., New York. With Illustrations and Biographical Sketches of Some of Its Prominent Men and Pioneers. Philadelphia: L. H. Everts, 1879.

History of Clermont County, Ohio, with Illustrations and Biographical Sketches of Its Prominent Men and Pioneers. Philadelphia: Louis H. Everts, 1880.

History of Geauga and Lake Counties, Ohio, with Illustrations and Biographical Sketches of Its Pioneers and Most Prominent Men. Philadelphia: Williams Brothers, 1878.

The History of Jackson County, Missouri, Containing a History of the County, Its Cities, Towns, Etc. . . . Kansas City, MO: Union Historical, 1881.

History of Portage County, Ohio. Containing a History of the County, Its Townships, Towns, Villages, Schools, Churches, Industries, Etc.; Portraits of Early Settlers and Prominent Men; Biographies; History of the Northwest Territory; History of Ohio; Statistical and Miscellaneous Matter, Etc., Etc. Chicago: Warner, Beers, 1885.

The History of the Reorganized Church of Jesus Christ of Latter Day Saints. 4 vols. Lamoni, IA: 1896–1902. Reprint, Independence, MO: Herald Publishing House, [after 1976].

Holbrook, Joseph. Reminiscences, not before 1871. Private possession. Copy at CHL.

Holcomb, Henry. Papers, 1864–1919. Western Reserve Historical Society, Cleveland.

The Holy Bible, Containing the Old and New Testaments Translated Out of the Original Tongues: And with the Former Translations Diligently Compared and Revised, by His Majesty's Special Command. Authorized King James Version with Explanatory Notes and Cross References to the Standard Works of The Church of Jesus Christ of Latter-day Saints. Salt Lake City: The Church of Jesus Christ of Latter-day Saints, 2013.

Howe, Daniel Walker. *What Hath God Wrought: The Transformation of America, 1815–1848.* The Oxford History of the United States. New York: Oxford University Press, 2007.

Howe, Eber D. *Mormonism Unvailed; or, A Faithful Account of That Singular Imposition and Delusion, from Its Rise to the Present Time. With Sketches of the Characters of Its Propagators, and a Full Detail of the Manner in Which the Famous Golden Bible Was Brought before the World. To Which Are Added, Inquiries into the Probability That the Historical Part of the Said Bible Was Written by One Solomon Spalding, More Than Twenty Years Ago, and by Him Intended to Have Been Published as a Romance.* Painesville, OH: By the author, 1834.

H. Smith & Co. Daybook, July–Nov. 1836. In Gilbert Belnap, Account Book, 1836–1874. CHL.

Hughes, Richard T. "From Primitive Church to Civil Religion: The Millennial Odyssey of Alexander Campbell." *Journal of the American Academy of Religion* 44, no. 1 (Mar. 1976): 87–103.

Hume, Ivor Noël. *Belzoni: The Giant Archaeologists Love to Hate.* Charlottesville: University of Virginia Press, 2011.

Huntington, C. C. "A History of Banking and Currency in Ohio before the Civil War." *Ohio Archaeological and Historical Quarterly* 24, no. 3 (July 1915): 235–539.

Huntington, William. "A History of William Huntington Written by Himself and Transcribed by His Son O. B. Huntington," Jan. 1855. BYU.

Huron Reflector. Norwalk, OH. 1830–1852.

Illinois State Historical Society. Circuit Court Case Files, 1830–1900. Microfilm. CHL.

Independent Messenger. Boston. 1831–1839.

Ingraham, Prentiss, ed. *Seventy Years on the Frontier: Alexander Majors' Memoirs of a Lifetime on the Border.* Denver: Western Miner and Financier Publishers, 1893.

"Inventory of President Joseph Fielding Smith's Safe," 23 May 1970. First Presidency, General Administration Files, 1921–1972. CHL.

Jackman, Levi. Diary, 1835–1844. Microfilm. CHL.

Jackson, Kent P., ed. *Manuscript Found: The Complete Original "Spaulding Manuscript."* Provo, UT: Religious Studies Center, Brigham Young University, 1996.

James, Jane Manning. Autobiography, ca. 1902. CHL.

Jenkins, Reverend William. *Richmond Hill, Ontario: A Transcription of the Register of Marriages, 1819–1843.* Richmond Hill, Ontario: York Region Branch, Ontario Genealogical Society, 1999.

Jennings, Warren A. "Isaac McCoy and the Mormons." *Missouri Historical Review* 61, no. 1 (Oct. 1966): 62–82.

Jenson, Andrew. *Latter-day Saint Biographical Encyclopedia: A Compilation of Biographical Sketches of Prominent Men and Women in the Church of Jesus Christ of Latter-day Saints.* 4 vols. Salt Lake City: Andrew Jenson History Co., 1901–1936.

Jessee, Dean C. "Joseph Knight's Recollection of Early Mormon History." *BYU Studies* 17, no. 1 (Autumn 1976): 29–39.

———. "The Writing of Joseph Smith's History." *BYU Studies* 11, no. 4 (Summer 1971): 439–473.

John, Richard R. *Spreading the News: The American Postal System from Franklin to Morse.* Cambridge, MA: Harvard University Press, 1995.

Johnson, Benjamin Franklin. "A Life Review," after 1893. Benjamin Franklin Johnson, Papers, 1852–1911. CHL.

———. Papers, 1852–1923. CHL.

Johnson, Clark V., ed. *Mormon Redress Petitions: Documents of the 1833–1838 Missouri Conflict.* Religious Studies Center Monograph Series 16. Provo, UT: Religious Studies Center, Brigham Young University, 1992.

Johnson, Clark V., and Ronald E. Romig. *An Index to Early Caldwell County, Missouri, Land Records.* Rev. ed. Independence, MO: Missouri Mormon Frontier Foundation, 2002.

Johnson, Joel Hills. Autobiographical Sketch, ca. 1855–1859. Joel Hills Johnson, Papers, ca. 1835–1882. CHL.

———. Reminiscences and Journals, 1835–1882. Joel Hills Johnson, Papers, ca. 1835–1882. CHL.

Johnson, Paul E., and Sean Wilentz. *The Kingdom of Matthias.* New York: Oxford University Press, 1994.

John Whitmer Family Papers, 1837–1912. CHL.

Jones, Christopher C. "Mormonism in the Methodist Marketplace: James Covel and the Historical Background of Doctrine and Covenants 39–40." *BYU Studies* 51, no. 1 (2012): 67–98.

———. "'We Latter-day Saints Are Methodists': The Influence of Methodism on Early Mormon Religiosity." Master's thesis, Brigham Young University, 2009.

Jones, G. Lloyd. *The Discovery of Hebrew in Tudor England: A Third Language.* Manchester: Manchester University Press, 1983.

Joseph Smith Authorization for Oliver Granger. 6 May 1839. CHL.

Joseph Smith Papers, 1837–1838. Ohio Historical Society, Columbus, OH.

Joseph Smith Translation. See *Holy Bible.*

Journal of Discourses. 26 vols. Liverpool: F. D. Richards, 1855–1886.

Journal of History. Lamoni, IA, 1908–1920; Independence, MO, 1921–1925.

Journal of the House of Representatives of the United States: Being the First Session of the Twenty-Fourth Congress Begun and Held at the City of Washington, December 7, 1835, and in the Sixtieth Year of the Independence of the United States. Washington DC: Blair and Rives, 1835.

Journal of the House of Representatives of the United States: Being the Second Session of the Twenty-Eighth Congress; Begun and Held at the City of Washington, December 2, 1844, in the Sixty-Ninth Year of the Independence of the United States. Washington DC: Blair and Rives, 1844–1845.

Journal of the Senate of the State of Ohio; Being the First Session of the Thirty-Fifth General Assembly, Begun and Held in the City of Columbus, Monday Dec. 5, 1836 and in the Thirty-Fifth Year of Said State. Columbus, OH: James E. Gardiner, 1836.

JS. In addition to the entries that immediately follow, see entries under "Smith, Joseph."

JS Collection / Joseph Smith Collection, 1827–1846. CHL.

JS History / Smith, Joseph, et al. History, 1838–1856. Vols. A-1–F-1 (originals), A-2–E-2 (fair copies). CHL. The history for the period after 5 Aug. 1838 was composed after the death of Joseph Smith.

JS History, ca. Summer 1832 / Smith, Joseph. "A History of the Life of Joseph Smith Jr," ca. Summer 1832. In Joseph Smith, "Letterbook A," 1832–1835, 1–[6] (earliest numbering). JS Collection, CHL.

JS History, 1834–1836 / Smith, Joseph, et al. History, 1834–1836. In Joseph Smith et al., History, 1838–1856, vol. A-1, back of book (earliest numbering), 9–20, 46–187. CHL.

JS Letterbook 1 / Smith, Joseph. "Letter Book A," 1832–1835. JS Collection. CHL.

JS Letterbook 1, JS Collection. Microfilm, 12 Nov. 1968. CHL.

JS Letterbook 2 / Smith, Joseph. "Copies of Letters, &c. &c.," 1839–1843. JS Collection. CHL.

JS Office Papers / Joseph Smith Office Papers, ca. 1835–1845. CHL.

JS Papers Holding Collection, 1834–1846. CHL.

JSP, D1 / MacKay, Michael Hubbard, Gerrit J. Dirkmaat, Grant Underwood, Robert J. Woodford, and William G. Hartley, eds. *Documents, Volume 1: July 1828–June 1831.* Vol. 1 of the Documents series of *The Joseph Smith Papers,* edited by Dean C. Jessee, Ronald K. Esplin, Richard Lyman Bushman, and Matthew J. Grow. Salt Lake City: Church Historian's Press, 2013.

JSP, D2 / Godfrey, Matthew C., Mark Ashurst-McGee, Grant Underwood, Robert J. Woodford, and William G. Hartley, eds. *Documents, Volume 2: July 1831–January 1833.* Vol. 2 of the Documents series of *The Joseph Smith Papers,* edited by Dean C. Jessee, Ronald K. Esplin, Richard Lyman Bushman, and Matthew J. Grow. Salt Lake City: Church Historian's Press, 2013.

JSP, D3 / Dirkmaat, Gerrit J., Brent M. Rogers, Grant Underwood, Robert J. Woodford, and William G. Hartley, eds. *Documents, Volume 3: February 1833–March 1834.* Vol. 3 of the Documents series of *The Joseph Smith Papers,* edited by Ronald K. Esplin and Matthew J. Grow. Salt Lake City: Church Historian's Press, 2014.

JSP, D4 / Godfrey, Matthew C., Brenden W. Rensink, Alex D. Smith, Max H Parkin, and Alexander L. Baugh, eds. *Documents, Volume 4: April 1834–September 1835.* Vol. 4 of the Documents series of *The Joseph Smith Papers,* edited by Ronald K. Esplin, Matthew J. Grow, and Matthew C. Godfrey. Salt Lake City: Church Historian's Press, 2016.

JSP, H1 / Davidson, Karen Lynn, David J. Whittaker, Mark Ashurst-McGee, and Richard L. Jensen, eds. *Histories, Volume 1: Joseph Smith Histories, 1832–1844.* Vol. 1 of the Histories Series of *The Joseph Smith Papers,* edited by Dean C. Jessee, Ronald K. Esplin, and Richard Lyman Bushman. Salt Lake City: Church Historian's Press, 2012.

JSP, H2 / Davidson, Karen Lynn, Richard L. Jensen, and David J. Whittaker, eds. *Histories, Volume 2: Assigned Historical Writings, 1831–1847.* Vol. 2 of the Histories series of *The Joseph Smith Papers,* edited by Dean C. Jessee, Ronald K. Esplin, and Richard Lyman Bushman. Salt Lake City: Church Historian's Press, 2012.

JSP, J1 / Jessee, Dean C., Mark Ashurst-McGee, and Richard L. Jensen, eds. *Journals, Volume 1: 1832–1839.* Vol. 1 of the Journals series of *The Joseph Smith Papers,* edited by Dean C. Jessee, Ronald K. Esplin, and Richard Lyman Bushman. Salt Lake City: Church Historian's Press, 2008.

JSP, J2 / Hedges, Andrew H., Alex D. Smith, and Richard Lloyd Anderson, eds. *Journals, Volume 2: December 1841–April 1843.* Vol. 2 of the Journals series of *The Joseph Smith Papers,* edited by Dean C. Jessee, Ronald K. Esplin, and Richard Lyman Bushman. Salt Lake City: Church Historian's Press, 2011.

JSP, J3 / Hedges, Andrew H., Alex D. Smith, and Brent M. Rogers, eds. *Journals, Volume 3: May 1843–June 1844.* Vol. 3 of the Journals series of *The Joseph Smith Papers,* edited by Ronald K. Esplin and Matthew J. Grow. Salt Lake City: Church Historian's Press, 2015.

JSP, R2 / Jensen, Robin Scott, Richard E. Turley Jr., and Riley M. Lorimer, eds. *Revelations and Translations, Volume 2: Published Revelations.* Vol. 2 of the Revelations and

Translations series of *The Joseph Smith Papers,* edited by Dean C. Jessee, Ronald K. Esplin, and Richard Lyman Bushman. Salt Lake City: Church Historian's Press, 2011.

Kansas City Daily Journal. Kansas City, MO. 1878–1891.

Kennedy, J. H. *Early Days of Mormonism, Palmyra, Kirtland, and Nauvoo.* New York: Charles Scribner's Sons, 1888.

Kerber, Linda K. "A Constitutional Right to Be Treated Like American Ladies: Women and the Obligations of Citizenship." In *U.S. History as Women's History: New Feminist Essays,* edited by Linda K. Kerber, Alice Kessler-Harris, and Kathryn Kish Sklar, 17–35. Chapel Hill: University of North Carolina Press, 1995.

Kidd, Colin. *The Forging of Races: Race and Scripture in the Protestant Atlantic World, 1600–2000.* Cambridge: Cambridge University Press, 2006.

Kimball, Heber C. Collection, 1837–1898. CHL.

———. Correspondence, 1837–1864. Private possession. Copy at CHL.

———. "History of Heber Chase Kimball by His Own Dictation," ca. 1842–1856. Heber C. Kimball, Papers, 1837–1866. CHL.

———. Journals, 1837–1838, 1840–1845. Heber C. Kimball, Papers, 1837–1866. CHL.

———. "The Journal and Record of Heber Chase Kimball an Apostle of Jesus Christ of Latter Day Saints," ca. 1842–1858. Heber C. Kimball, Papers, 1837–1866. CHL.

Kimball, Hiram. Collection, 1830–1910. CHL.

Kirtland Camp. Journal, Mar.–Oct. 1838. CHL.

Kirtland Egyptian Papers, ca. 1835–1836. CHL.

Kirtland Elders' Certificates / Kirtland Elders Quorum. "Record of Certificates of Membership and Ordinations of the First Members and Elders of the Church of Jesus Christ of Latter Day Saints Dating from March 21st 1836 to June 18th 1838 Kirtland Geauga Co. Ohio," 1836–1838. CHL.

Kirtland Elders Quorum. "A Record of the First Quorurum of Elders Belonging to the Church of Christ: In Kirtland Geauga Co. Ohio," 1836–1838, 1840–1841. CCLA.

"Kirtland Geauga Co Ohio July 23 1837 the word of the lord unto Thomas B. Marsh concerning the Twelve." CCLA.

Kirtland High School Register, ca. 1836–1837. CHL.

Kirtland Safety Society. Stock Ledger, 1836–1837. Collection of Manuscripts about Mormons, 1832–1954, Chicago History Museum. Copy at CHL.

Kirtland Township Trustees' Minutes and Poll Book, 1817–1838. Lake County Historical Society, Painesville, OH.

Knight, Newel. Autobiographical Sketch, no date. CHL.

———. Autobiography and Journal, ca. 1846. CHL.

———. Autobiography, ca. 1871. CHL.

Lancaster Journal. Lancaster, PA. 1794–1839.

Lane, Samuel A. *Fifty Years and Over of Akron and Summit County.* Akron, OH: Beacon Job Department, 1892.

Latter Day Saints' Messenger and Advocate. Kirtland, OH. Oct. 1834–Sept. 1837.

Latter-day Saints' Millennial Star. Liverpool. 1840–1970.

Laws of a Public and General Nature of the State of Missouri, Passed between the Years 1824 and 1836, Not Published in the Digest of 1825, Nor in the Digest of 1835. Vol. 2. Jefferson City, MO: W. Lusk and Son, 1842.

Laws of the State of Missouri, Passed at the First Session of the Ninth General Assembly, Begun and Held at the City of Jefferson, on Monday, the Twenty-first Day of November, in the Year of Our Lord One Thousand Eight Hundred and Thirty-Six. 2nd ed. St. Louis: Chambers and Knapp, 1841.

Lemire, Elise. *"Miscegenation": Making Race in America.* Philadelphia: University of Pennsylvania Press, 2002.

Lepler, Jessica M. *The Many Panics of 1837: People, Politics and the Creation of a Transatlantic Financial Crisis.* Cambridge: Cambridge University Press, 2013.

Letter of Transfer, Salt Lake City, UT, 13 Dec. 1988. CHL.

Letter of Transfer, Salt Lake City, UT, 15 Dec. 2009. CHL.

Levi Richards Family Correspondence, 1827–1848. CHL.

Lewis, Wayne J. "Mormon Land Ownership as a Factor in Evaluating the Extent of Mormon Settlements and Influence in Missouri, 1831–1841." Master's thesis, Brigham Young University, 1981.

Liberator. Boston. 1831–1865.

Livesey, Richard. *An Exposure of Mormonism, Being a Statement of Facts relating to the Self-Styled "Latter Day Saints," and the Origin of the Book of Mormon.* Preston, England: J. Livesey, 1838.

Livingstone, David N. *Adam's Ancestors: Race, Religion, and the Politics of Human Origins.* Baltimore: Johns Hopkins University Press, 2008.

Longworth, Thomas. *Longworth's American Almanac, New-York Register and City Directory for 1829.* New York: By the author, 1829.

———. *Longworth's American Almanac, New-York Register, and City Directory, for the Fifty-Ninth Year of American Independence.* New York: By the author, 1834.

———. *Longworth's American Almanac, New-York Register, and City Directory, for the Sixty-Second Year. Of American Independence.* New York: By the author, 1837.

———. *Longworth's American Almanac, New-York Register, and City Directory, for the Sixty-Fourth Year of American Independence.* New York: By the author, 1839.

———. *Longworth's American Almanac, New-York Register, and City Directory, for the Sixty-Sixth Year of American Independence.* New York: By the author, 1841.

Lord Sterling Papers, 1835–1850. Lake County Historical Society, Painesville, OH.

Louisville Public Advertiser. Louisville, KY. 1834–1842.

Lyman, Amasa M. Journals, 1832–1877. Amasa M. Lyman Collection, 1832–1877. CHL.

Lyman, Eliza Maria Partridge. Journal, 1846–1885. CHL.

Madsen, Gordon A. "Tabulating the Impact of Litigation on the Kirtland Economy." In *Sustaining the Law: Joseph Smith's Legal Encounters*, edited by Gordon A. Madsen, Jeffrey N. Walker, and John W. Welch, 227–246. Provo, UT: BYU Studies, 2014.

Margo, Robert A. *Wages and Labor Markets in the United States, 1820–1860.* Chicago: University of Chicago Press, 2000.

Material Relating to Mormon Expulsion from Missouri, 1839–1843. Photocopy. CHL. Originals located in Record Group 233, Records of the United States House of Representatives, 1789–1900. National Archives and Records Administration, Washington DC.

McKee, Howard I. "The Platte Purchase." *Missouri Historical Review* 32 (Jan. 1938): 129–147.

McLellin, William E. Journals, July 1834–Apr. 1835; May–Sept. 1835; Apr.–June 1836. William E. McLellin, Papers, 1831–1836, 1877–1878. CHL. Also available as Jan Shipps and John W. Welch, eds., *The Journals of William E. McLellin, 1831–1836* (Provo, UT: BYU Studies; Urbana: University of Illinois Press, 1994).

Mead, Spencer P. *History and Genealogy of the Mead Family of Fairfield County, Connecticut, Eastern New York, Western Vermont and Western Pennsylvania from A.D. 1180 to 1900.* New York: Knickerbocker, 1901.

Mehling, Mary Bryant Alverson. *Cowdrey-Cowdery-Cowdray Genealogy: William Cowdery of Lynn, Massachusetts, 1630, and His Descendants.* [New York]: Frank Allaben, 1911.

Memorial of the General Assembly of Missouri, That the N. and N. W. Boundary May Be Enlarged, and a Mounted Force Granted for the Protection of the Frontier of the State, and Its Trade with Mexico and the Indians. S. Doc. No. 71, 21st Cong., 2nd Sess. (1831).

Millennial Harbinger. Bethany, VA. 1830–1870.

Millet, Artemus. Reminiscences, ca. 1855 and ca. 1872, as copied in 1936. CHL.

Minute Book 1 / "Conference A," 1832–1837. CHL.

Minute Book 2 / "The Conference Minutes and Record Book of Christ's Church of Latter Day Saints," 1838, 1842, 1844. CHL.

"Minutes of First Presidency, March 1898 to September 1907, Record No. 1." CCLA.

Missionary Reports, 1831–1900. CHL.

Missouri Republican. St. Louis. 1822–1919.

Morris, J. Brent. *Oberlin, Hotbed of Abolitionism: College, Community, and the Fight for Freedom and Equality in Antebellum America.* Chapel Hill: University of North Carolina Press, 2014.

Morris, Rod. "William Tenney and Eliza L. Webb." The Morris Clan. Accessed 9 June 2016. http://www.themorrisclan.com.

Morton, Samuel George. *Catalogue of Skulls of Man and the Inferior Animals in the Collection of Samuel George Morton, M. D., Penn. and Edinb.* Philadelphia: Merrihew and Thompson, 1849.

———. *Crania Aegyptiaca; or, Observations on Egyptian Ethnography, Derived from Anatomy, History and the Monuments.* 3rd ed. Philadelphia: John Penington; London: Madden, 1844.

———. *Crania Americana; or, A Comparative View of the Skills of Various Aboriginal Nations of North and South America: To Which Is Prefixed an Essay on the Varieties of the Human Species.* Philadelphia: J. Dobson; London: Simpkin, Marshall, 1839.

Moses (selections from the Book of). See *Pearl of Great Price.*

Murdock, John. Journal, ca. 1830–1859. CHL.

Myers, John L. "Antislavery Activities of Five Lane Seminary Boys in 1835–36." *Bulletin of the Historical and Philosophical Society of Ohio* 21, no. 2 (Apr. 1963): 95–111.

Naked Truths about Mormonism: Also a Journal for Important, Newly Apprehended Truths, and Miscellany. Oakland, CA. Jan. and Apr. 1888.

Nauvoo Ninth Ward High Priests Quorum. Minutes, Nov. 1844–Feb. 1845. CHL.

Neibaur, Alexander. Journal, 1841–1862. CHL.

New Testament Revision 1 / "A Translation of the New Testament Translated by the Power of God," 1831. CCLA. Also available in Scott H. Faulring, Kent P. Jackson, and Robert J. Matthews, eds. *Joseph Smith's New Translation of the Bible: Original Manuscripts* (Provo, UT: Religious Studies Center, Brigham Young University, 2004), 159–228.

New Testament Revision 2, part 2 / New Testament Revision Manuscript 2, part 2, 1831–1832. CCLA. The corresponding Bible marked with JS's revisions is at CCLA: *The Holy Bible, Containing the Old and New Testaments: Together with the Apocrypha. . . .* Cooperstown, NY: H. Phinney and E. Phinney, 1828. Also available in Scott H. Faulring, Kent P. Jackson, and Robert J. Matthews, eds., *Joseph Smith's New Translation of the Bible: Original Manuscripts* (Provo, UT: Religious Studies Center, Brigham Young University, 2004), 305–581.

New-York Commercial Advertiser. New York City. 1831–1889.

New York Herald. New York City. 1835–1924.

New York Journal of Commerce. New York City. 1827–1893.

New York Times. New York City. 1851–.

Nibley, Hugh. *The Message of the Joseph Smith Papyri: An Egyptian Document.* Vol. 16 of *The Collected Works of Hugh Nibley*, edited by John Gee and Michael D. Rhodes. Salt Lake City: Deseret Book; Provo, UT: Foundation for Ancient Research and Mormon Studies, Brigham Young University, 2005.

Noble, Mary A. Reminiscences, ca. 1836. In Joseph B. Noble, Reminiscences, ca. 1836. CHL.

Noll, Mark A. *The Civil War as a Theological Crisis.* Chapel Hill: University of North Carolina Press, 2006.

Northern Times. Kirtland, OH. 1835–[1836?].

Nuttall, L. John. Diary, 1876–1884. L. John Nuttall, Papers, 1857–1904. BYU.

Nyholm, Douglas A. *Mormon Currency, 1837–1937.* N.p.: By the author, 2010.

Ohio Anti-Slavery Society. *Narrative of the Late Riotous Proceedings against the Liberty of the Press, in Cincinnati. With Remarks and Historical Notices, Relating to Emancipation.* Cincinnati: No publisher, 1836.

Ohio Observer. Hudson. 1827–1855.

Ohio Obsolete Paper Money Collection. Western Reserve Historical Society, Cleveland.

Ohio Repository. Canton. 1830–1868.

Ohio Star. Ravenna. 1830–1854.

Ohio State Journal and Columbus Gazette. Columbus. 1825–1837.

Old Testament Revision 1 / "A Revelation Given to Joseph the Revelator June 1830," 1830–1831. CCLA. Also available in Scott H. Faulring, Kent P. Jackson, and Robert J. Matthews, eds., *Joseph Smith's New Translation of the Bible: Original Manuscripts* (Provo, UT: Religious Studies Center, Brigham Young University, 2004), 75–152.

Olney, Oliver H. *The Absurdities of Mormonism Portrayed*. Hancock Co., IL: No publisher, 1843.

Ontario Phoenix. Canandaigua, NY. 1828–1831.

The Oxford English Dictionary. Edited by James A. H. Murray, Henry Bradley, W. A. Craigie, and C. T. Onions. 12 vols. 1933. Reprint. Oxford: Oxford University Press, 1970.

Painesville Republican. Painesville, OH. 1836–1841.

Painesville Telegraph. Painesville, OH. 1831–1838.

Park, Benjamin E. "'Thou Wast Willing to Lay Down Thy Life for Thy Brethren': Zion's Blessings in the Early Church." *John Whitmer Historical Association Journal* 29 (2009): 27–37.

Parkin, Max H. "A History of the Latter-day Saints in Clay County, Missouri, from 1833 to 1837." PhD diss., Brigham Young University, 1976.

———. "Zion's Camp Cholera Victims Monument Dedication." *Missouri Mormon Frontier Foundation Newsletter* 15 (Fall 1997): 2–6.

Parkinson, Richard. With W. Diffie, M. Fischer, and R. S. Simpson. *Cracking Codes: The Rosetta Stone and Decipherment*. Berkeley: University of California Press, 1999.

Partridge, Edward. Journal, Jan. 1835–July 1836. In Edward Partridge, Papers, 1818–1839. CHL.

———. Miscellaneous Papers, ca. 1839–May 1840. CHL.

———. Papers, 1818–1839. CHL.

Partridge, Edward, Jr. Genealogical Record, 1878. CHL.

Patriarchal Blessings, 1833–. CHL.

Patten, David Wyman. Journal, 1832–1834. CHL.

Patterson, James. "Beaver County." In *An Illustrated History of the Commonwealth of Pennsylvania, Civil Political, and Military, from Its Earliest Settlement to the Present Time, including Historical Descriptions of Each County in the State, Their Towns, and Industrial Resources*, by William H. Egle, 340–360. Harrisburg, PA: De Witt C. Goodrich, 1876.

The Pearl of Great Price: A Selection from the Revelations, Translations, and Narrations of Joseph Smith, First Prophet, Seer, and Revelator to the Church of Jesus Christ of Latter-day Saints. Salt Lake City: The Church of Jesus Christ of Latter-day Saints, 2013.

Peterson, H. Donl. Research Collection on the Book of Abraham Papyri, 1964–1994. BYU.

———. *The Story of the Book of Abraham: Mummies, Manuscripts, and Mormonism*. Springville, UT: Cedar Fort, 2008.

Pettegrew, David. "A History of David Pettegrew," no date. David Pettegrew, Papers, 1840–1857. CHL.

Phelps, William W. "A Short History of W. W. Phelps' Stay in Missouri," 1864. In Information concerning Persons Driven from Jackson County, Missouri in 1833, 1863–1868. CHL.

———. Collection of Missouri Documents, 1833–1837. CHL.

———. Diary, 1835–1864. CHL.

———. Letter, Kirtland Mills, OH, to Sally Waterman Phelps, Liberty, MO, 16–18 Sept. 1835. Private possession. Copy at CHL.

———. Letter, Kirtland, OH, to Sally Waterman Phelps, [Liberty, MO], 27 Oct. 1835. In Historical Department, Journal History of the Church, 1896–2001. CHL.

———. Letter, Kirtland, OH, to Sally Waterman Phelps, [Liberty, MO], 14 Nov. 1835. In Historical Department, Journal History of the Church, 1896–2001. CHL.

———. Letters, 1835–1841. Microfilm. CHL.

———. Papers, 1835–1865. BYU.

Philadelphia Gazette and Universal Daily Advertiser. Philadelphia. 1833–1834.

Philanthropist. Cincinnati. 1836–1847.

Phillips, N. Taylor. "The Levy and Seixas Families of Newport and New York." In *Publications of the American Jewish Historical Society,* 4: 189–214. Baltimore: American Jewish Historical Society, 1896.

Pioneer and General History of Geauga County, with Sketches of Some of the Pioneers and Prominent Men. [Burton, OH]: Historical Society of Geauga County, 1880.

Plat of Kirtland, OH, ca. 1837. CHL.

Plewe, Brandon S., ed. *Mapping Mormonism: An Atlas of Latter-day Saint History.* Provo, UT: Brigham Young University Press, 2012.

Porter, Larry C. "The Odyssey of William Earl McLellin: Man of Diversity, 1806–83." In *The Journals of William E. McLellin, 1831–1836,* edited by Jan Shipps and John W. Welch, 291–378. Provo, UT: BYU Studies; Urbana: University of Illinois Press, 1994.

Portland Advertiser. Portland, ME. 1829–1841.

Post, Stephen. Journal, 1835–1839. Stephen Post, Papers, 1835–1921. CHL.

———. Papers, 1835–1921. CHL.

Potter, Paraclete. *Every Man His Own Lawyer; or, The Clerk and Magistrate's Assistance.* Poughkeepsie, NY: By the author, 1836.

Pratt, Orson. Account Book and Autobiography, 1833, 1836–1837. CHL.

Pratt, Parley P. "An Epistle Written by an Elder of the Church," ca. 1837. CHL.

———. *A Reply to Mr. Thomas Taylor's "Complete Failure," &c., and Mr. Richard Livesey's "Mormonism Exposed."* Manchester: R. Thomas, 1840.

———. *A Short Account of a Shameful Outrage, Committed by a Part of the Inhabitants of the Town of Mentor, upon the Person of Elder Parley P. Pratt, while Delivering a Public Discourse upon the Subject of the Gospel; April 7th 1835.* [Kirtland?]: [1835?].

———. *The Autobiography of Parley Parker Pratt, One of the Twelve Apostles of the Church of Jesus Christ of Latter-day Saints, Embracing His Life, Ministry and Travels, with Extracts, in Prose and Verse, from His Miscellaneous Writings.* Edited by Parley P. Pratt Jr. New York: Russell Brothers, 1874.

Prayer, at the Dedication of the Lord's House in Kirtland, Ohio, March 27, 1836—By Joseph Smith, Jr. President of the Church of the Latter Day Saints. Kirtland, OH: 1836.

Proceedings of the Ohio Anti-Slavery Convention. Held at Putnam, on the Twenty-Second, Twenty-Third, and Twenty-Fourth of April, 1835. N.p.: Beaumont and Wallace, 1835.

Proper, David B. "Joseph Smith and Salem." *Essex Institute Historical Collections* 100 (Apr. 1964): 88–98.

The Public Statutes at Large of the United States of America, from the Organization of the Government in 1789, to March 3, 1845. . . . Edited by Richard Peters. 8 vols. Boston: Charles C. Little and James Brown, 1846–1867.

Record of Seventies / First Council of the Seventy. "Book of Records," 1837–1843. Bk. A. In First Council of the Seventy, Records, 1837–1885. CHL.

A Record of the Revolutionary Soldiers Buried in Lake County, Ohio, with a Partial List of Those in Geauga County and a Membership Roll of New Connecticut Chapter Daughters of the American Revolution. Painesville, OH: Daughters of the American Revolution, New Connecticut Chapter, 1902.

Record of the Twelve / Quorum of the Twelve Apostles. "A Record of the Transactions of the Twelve Apostles of the Church of the Latter Day Saints from the Time of Their Call to the Apostleship Which Was on the 14th Day of Feby. AD 1835," Feb.–Aug. 1835. In Patriarchal Blessings, 1833–, vol. 2. CHL.

Records of the Bureau of Land Management, 1685–1993. National Archives and Records Administration. Washington DC.

Reeve, W. Paul. *Religion of a Different Color: Race and the Mormon Struggle for Whiteness.* New York: Oxford University Press, 2015.

Return. Davis City, IA. 1889–1891.

Re-union of the Sons and Daughters of the Old Town of Pompey, Held at Pompey Hill, June 29, 1871, Proceedings of the Meeting, Speeches, Toasts and Other Incidents of the Occasion. Also, a History of the Town, Reminiscences and Biographical Sketches of Early Inhabitants. Pompey, NY: By direction of the Re-union Meeting, 1875.

Revelations Collection, 1831–ca. 1844, 1847, 1861, ca. 1876. CHL.

The Revised Statutes of the State of Missouri, Revised and Digested by the Eighth General Assembly during the Years One Thousand Eight Hundred and Thirty-Four, and One Thousand Eight Hundred and Thirty-Five. . . . St. Louis: Argus Office, 1835.

Rhodes, Michael D. *The Hor Book of Breathings: A Translation and Commentary.* Studies in the Book of Abraham, edited by John Gee. Provo, UT: Foundation for Ancient Research and Mormon Studies, Brigham Young University, 2002.

Rich, Charles C. Collection, 1832–1908. CHL.

Richards, Willard. Journals, 1836–1853. Willard Richards, Journals and Papers, 1821–1854. CHL.

———. Journals and Papers, 1821–1854. CHL.

———. "Willard Richards Pocket Companion Written in England," ca. 1838. Willard Richards, Journals and Papers, 1821–1854. CHL.

Ricks, Stephen D. "The Appearance of Elijah and Moses in the Kirtland Temple and the Jewish Passover." *BYU Studies* 23, no. 4 (Fall 1983): 483–486.

Ritner, Robert K. *The Joseph Smith Egyptian Papyri: A Complete Edition, P. JS 1–4 and the Hypocephalus of Sheshonq.* Salt Lake City: Smith-Pettit Foundation, 2011.

Robinson, Andrew. *Cracking the Egyptian Code: The Revolutionary Life of Jean-Francois Champollion.* Oxford: Oxford University Press, 2012.

Robinson, George W. Letter, Kirtland, OH, to Thomas B. Marsh, Far West, MO, 10 Jan. 1838. CHL.

Robison, Elwin C. *The First Mormon Temple: Design, Construction, and Historic Context of the Kirtland Temple.* Provo, UT: Brigham Young University Press, 1997.

Rohrbough, Malcolm J. *The Land Office Business: The Settlement and Administration of American Public Lands, 1789–1837.* New York: Oxford University Press, 1968.

Rollmann, Hans. "The Early Baptist Career of Sidney Rigdon in Warren, Ohio." *BYU Studies* 21, no. 1 (Winter 1981): 37–50.

Rolnick, Arthur, and Warren E. Weber. "Free Banking, Wildcat Banking, and Shinplasters." *Federal Reserve Bank of Minneapolis Quarterly Review* 6 (Fall 1982): 10–19.

Rousseau, Peter L. "Jacksonian Monetary Policy, Specie Flows, and the Panic of 1837." *Journal of Economic History* 62 (June 2002): 457–488.

Russell, Isaac. Correspondence, 1837–1840. CHL.

Saints' Herald. Independence, MO. 1860–.

Salem Gazette. Salem, MA. 1833–1837.

Salem Observer. Salem, MA. 1828–1896.

Salem Register. Salem, MA. 1841–1903.

Salmon, Marylynn. *Women and the Law of Property in Early America*. Chapel Hill: University of North Carolina Press, 1986.

Salt Lake Tribune. Salt Lake City. 1871–.

Saltonstall, Leverett. *Address to the City Council, at the Organization of the City Government in Salem, May 9, 1836*. Salem, MA: Palfray and Chapman, 1836.

Satterfield, Bruce Kelly. "The History of Adult Education in Kirtland, Ohio, 1833–37." PhD diss., University of Idaho, 2002.

Scharf, J. Thomas, and Thompson Westcott. *History of Philadelphia, 1609–1884*. 3 vols. Philadelphia: L. H. Everts, 1884.

Scheiber, Harry N. "The Commercial Bank of Lake Erie, 1831–1843." *Business History Review* 40, no. 1 (Spring 1966): 47–65.

School of the Prophets Salt Lake City Minutes, Apr.–Dec. 1883. CHL.

Schweich, George. Letter, Richmond, MO, to O. R. Beardsley, 17 Jan. 1900. Miscellanea. Marie Eccles-Caine Archives of Intermountain Americana, Utah State University Special Collections, Logan.

Searle, Howard C. "Authorship of the History of Joseph Smith: A Review Essay." *BYU Studies* 21 (Winter 1981): 101–122.

Second Annual Report of the American Anti-Slavery Society; with the Speeches Delivered at the Anniversary Meeting, Held in the City of New-York, on the 12th May, 1835, and the Minutes of the Meetings of the Society for Business. New York: William S. Dorr, 1835.

Seixas, Joshua. Letter, Utica, NY, to John Shipherd, Oberlin, OH, 29 May 1835. Office of the Treasurer, Record Group 7, Series 7/1/5. Letters Received by Oberlin College, 1822–1907. Oberlin College Archives. Oberlin, OH.

———. *A Manual Hebrew Grammar for the Use of Beginners*. Andover, MA: Flagg, Gould, and Newman, 1833.

———. *Manual Hebrew Grammar for the Use of Beginners*. 2nd ed. Andover, MA: Gould and Newman, 1834.

———. *Supplement to J. Seixas' Manual Hebrew Grammar, for the Kirtland, Ohio, Theological Institution*. New York: West and Trow, 1836.

Sellers, Charles. *The Market Revolution: Jacksonian America, 1815–1846*. New York and Oxford: Oxford University Press, 1991.

Sewall, Samuel. *The Selling of Joseph: A Memorial*. Boston: Bartholomew Green and John Allen, 1700.

Shipps, Jan, and John W. Welch, eds. *The Journals of William E. McLellin, 1831–1836.* Provo, UT: BYU Studies; Urbana: University of Illinois Press, 1994.

"Signed on the Dotted Line: The Charles Aldrich Autograph Collection." *Iowa Historian,* Feb.–Mar. 2008, [6]–[7]. Newsletter of the State Historical Society of Iowa, Iowa City.

Singh, Simon. *The Code Book: The Science of Secrecy from Mary, Queen of Scots, to Quantum Cryptography.* New York: Doubleday, 1999.

Smith, Elias. Correspondence, 1834–1839. In Elias Smith, Papers, 1834–1846. CHL.

Smith, George Albert. "History of George Albert Smith," ca. 1857–1875. George Albert Smith Papers, 1834–1893. CHL.

———. "My Journal." *Instructor,* Nov. 1946, 514–517, 528.

———. Papers, 1834–1877. CHL.

Smith, George Albert, and Wilford Woodruff. Statement, 1859. CHL.

Smith, Heman C. Letter, Lamoni, IA, to George Schweich, 20 July 1896. CCLA.

Smith, Hyrum. Diary and Account Book, Nov. 1831–Feb. 1835. Hyrum Smith, Papers, ca. 1832–1844. BYU.

———. Papers, 1834–1843. CHL.

Smith, Hyrum, Reynolds Cahoon, and Jared Carter. Promissory Note, to Halsted, Haines and Co., Kirtland, OH, 1 Sept. 1837. Private possession. Copy at CHL.

Smith, Joseph. *General Smith's Views of the Powers and Policy of the Government of the United States.* Nauvoo, IL: John Taylor, 1844.

———. Letter, Salem, MA, to Emma Smith, [Kirtland Township], OH, 19 Aug. 1836. In Charles Aldrich Autograph Collection. State Historical Society of Iowa, Des Moines.

———. "Schedule of Debts," ca. 4–6 Oct. 1843. CCLA.

Smith, Joseph, and Others. Letter, Kirtland Township, OH, to Arial Hanson, [Kirtland Township], OH, 7 Nov. 1836. Lake County Historical Society, Painesville, OH.

———. Promissory Note to Mead, Stafford & Co., 11 July 1837. Copy. CHL.

Smith, Joseph, Sidney Rigdon, and Oliver Cowdery. Promissory Note, to Holbrook & Firme [Ferme], Kirtland, OH, 1 Sept. 1837. Ohio Historical Society, Columbus. Copy at CHL.

Smith, Lucy Mack. *Biographical Sketches of Joseph Smith the Prophet, and His Progenitors for Many Generations.* Liverpool: S. W. Richards, 1853.

———. History, 1844–1845. 18 books. CHL. Also available in Lavina Fielding Anderson, ed., *Lucy's Book: A Critical Edition of Lucy Mack Smith's Family Memoir* (Salt Lake City: Signature Books, 2001).

Smith, Mary Fielding. Collection, ca. 1832–1848. CHL.

Smith, Samuel Harrison. Diary, Feb. 1832–May 1833. CHL.

Smith, Walter W. Letter, Independence, MO, to S. A. Burgess, Independence, MO, 15 Apr. 1926. J. F. Curtis, Papers. CCLA.

———. Letter, Independence, MO, to the RLDS First Presidency, Independence, MO, 14 Sept. 1925. Whitmer Papers. CCLA.

Smith, William. *William Smith on Mormonism. . . .* Lamoni, IA: Herald Steam Book and Job Office, 1883.

Snow, Erastus. Journals, 1835–1851; 1856–1857. CHL.

Speth, Linda E. "The Married Women's Property Acts, 1839–1865." In *Women and the Law: A Social Historical Perspective*, edited by D. Kelly Weisberg, 69–91. Vol. 2. Cambridge, MA: Schenkman Publishing Company, 1982.

Staker, Mark L. *Hearken, O Ye People: The Historical Setting of Joseph Smith's Ohio Revelations*. Salt Lake City: Greg Kofford Books, 2009.

———. "'Thou Art the Man': Newel K. Whitney in Ohio." *BYU Studies* 42, no. 1 (2003): 75–138.

A Statement of the Reasons Which Induced the Students of Lane Seminary, to Dissolve Their Connection with That Institution. Cincinnati: No publisher, 1834.

The State of Ohio. General and . . . Local Acts Passed and Joint Resolutions Adopted by the Seventy-First General Assembly, at Its Regular Session, Begun and Held in the City of Columbus, January 1st, 1894. Norwalk: State of Ohio, 1894.

The Statutes at Large and Treaties of the United States of America. From December 1, 1845, to March 3, 1851. . . . Edited by George Minot. Vol. 9. Boston: Little, Brown, 1862.

The Statutes of Ohio and of the Northwestern Territory, Adopted or Enacted from 1788 to 1833 Inclusive: Together with the Ordinance of 1787; the Constitutions of Ohio and of the United States, and Various Public Instruments and Acts of Congress: Illustrated by a Preliminary Sketch of the History of Ohio; Numerous References and Notes, and Copious Indexes. 3 vols. Edited by Salmon P. Chase. Cincinnati: Corey and Fairbank, 1833–1835.

Statutes of the State of Ohio, of a General Nature, in Force, December 7, 1840; Also, the Statutes of a General Nature, Passed by the General Assembly at Their Thirty-Ninth Session, Commencing December 7, 1840. Columbus, OH: Samuel Medary, 1841.

Stauffer, David McNeely. *American Engravers upon Copper and Steel*. Part 1. New York: Grolier Club of the City of New York, 1907.

Stern, Malcom H., comp. *First American Jewish Families: 600 Genealogies, 1654–1977*. Cincinnati: American Jewish Archives, 1978.

Stevens, Edward W., Jr. "Science, Culture, and Morality: Educating Adults in the Early Nineteenth Century." In *". . . Schools and the Means of Education Shall Forever Be Encouraged": A History of Education in the Old Northwest, 1787–1880*, edited by Paul H. Mattingly and Edward W. Stevens Jr., 68–83. Athens: Ohio University Libraries, 1987.

Stevens, Harry R. "Bank Enterprisers in a Western Town, 1815–1822." *Business History Review* 29 (June 1955): 139–156.

Stevens, Walter B. *Centennial History of Missouri (The Center State), One Hundred Years in the Union, 1820–1921*. Vol. 2. St. Louis and Chicago: S. J. Clarke Publishing Company, 1921.

Stewart, I. D. *The History of the Freewill Baptists, for Half a Century, with an Introductory Chapter*. Vol. 1, *From the Year 1780 to 1830*. Dover, NH: Freewill Baptist Printing, 1862.

Stone, William L. *Matthias and His Impostures: Or, The Progress of Fanaticism. Illustrated in the Extraordinary Case of Robert Matthews, and Some of His Forerunners and Disciples*. New York: Harper and Brothers, 1835.

Stuart, Moses. Letter, Andover, MA, to Joshua Seixas, Charlestown, MA, 6 Sept. 1832. Nathan-Kraus Family Collection, 1738–1939. Jacob Rader Marcus Center of the American Jewish Archives, Cincinnati.

Summerfield, Arthur E., and Charles Hurd. *U.S. Mail: The Story of the United States Postal Service*. New York: Holt, Rinehart and Winston, 1960.

Susquehanna Register, and Northern Pennsylvanian. Montrose, PA. 1831–1836.

Swan, Joseph R., comp. *A Treatise on the Law Relating to the Powers and Duties of Justices of the Peace, and Constables, in the State of Ohio: With Practical Forms, &c. &c.* Columbus, OH: Isaac N. Whiting, 1837.

———, comp. *Statutes of the State of Ohio, of a General Nature, in Force January 1st, 1854: With References to Prior Repealed Laws*. Cincinnati: H. W. Derby, 1854.

Table of the Post Offices in the United States, on the Fifteenth July, 1837, Arranged in Alphabetical Order. . . . Washington DC: Langtree and O'Sullivan, 1837.

Tanner, Nathan. Address, no date. CHL.

Temple Records Index Bureau of the Church of Jesus Christ of Latter-day Saints. *Nauvoo Temple Endowment Register, 10 December 1845 to 8 February 1846*. Salt Lake City: The Church of Jesus Christ of Latter-day Saints, 1974.

Third Annual Report of the American Anti-Slavery Society; With the Speeches Delivered at the Anniversary Meeting, Held in the City of New-York, On the 10th May, 1836, and the Minutes of the Meetings of the Society for Business. New York: William S. Dorr, 1836.

Thorp, Joseph. *Early Days in the West: Along the Missouri One Hundred Years Ago*. Liberty, MO: Irving Gilmer, 1924.

Times and Seasons. Commerce/Nauvoo, IL. Nov. 1839–Feb. 1846.

Todd, Jay M. "Egyptian Papyri Rediscovered." *Improvement Era* 71, no. 1 (January 1968): 12–16.

To the Saints Scattered Abroad, the Bishop and His Counselors of Kirtland Send Greeting. [Kirtland, OH: 18 Sept. 1837]. CHL.

Tullidge, Edward W. *The Women of Mormondom*. New York: Tullidge and Crandall, 1877.

The Twelfth Annual Report of the American Society for Colonizing the Free People of Colour of the United States. Washington DC: No publisher, 1829.

The Twelve Apostles. Kirtland, OH: ca. Apr. 1836. Copy at CHL.

Tyldesley, Joyce. *Egypt: How a Lost Civilization Was Rediscovered*. London: BBC Books, 2005.

Tyler, Daniel. "Recollections of the Prophet Joseph Smith." *Juvenile Instructor* 27, no. 4 (15 Feb. 1892): 127–128.

Underwood, Amos L. Correspondence, 1831–1853. CHL.

Underwood, Grant. "Millenarianism and Popular Methodism in Early Nineteenth Century England and Canada." *Wesleyan Theological Journal* 29, nos. 1, 2 (Spring–Fall 1994): 81–91.

———. *The Millenarian World of Early Mormonism*. Urbana: University of Illinois Press, 1993.

Upton, Harriet Taylor. *History of the Western Reserve*. Vol. 2. Chicago: Lewis, 1910.

U.S. and Canada Record Collection. FHL.

U.S. Bureau of the Census. Population Schedules. Microfilm. FHL.

U.S. Customs Service. *Proof of Citizenship Used to Apply for Seamen's Certificates for the Port of Philadelphia, Pennsylvania, 1792–1875*. Record Group 36. Microfilm. National Archives and Records Administration, Washington DC.

Utah Genealogical and Historical Magazine. Salt Lake City. 1910–1940.

Vital Records of Salem Massachusetts, to the Year 1849. 6 vols. Salem, MA: Essex Institute, 1916–1925.

Vogel, Dan. *Indian Origins and the Book of Mormon: Religious Solutions from Columbus to Joseph Smith.* Salt Lake City: Signature Books, 1986.

———. "James Colin Brewster: The Boy Prophet Who Challenged Mormon Authority." In *Differing Visions: Dissenters in Mormon History,* edited by Roger D. Launius and Linda Thatcher, 120–139. Urbana: University of Illinois Press, 1994.

Vosburgh, Royden, ed. *Records of the Reformed Dutch Church of Stone Arabia, in the Town of Palatine, Montgomery County, N. Y.* 3 vols. New York: No publisher, 1916.

Waite, Frederick Clayton. *Western Reserve University, the Hudson Era: A History of Western Reserve College and Academy at Hudson, Ohio, from 1826 to 1882.* Cleveland: Western Reserve University Press, 1943.

Walker, Jeffrey N. "Looking Legally at the Kirtland Safety Society." In *Sustaining the Law: Joseph Smith's Legal Encounters,* edited by Gordon A. Madsen, Jeffrey N. Walker, and John W. Welch, 179–226. Provo, UT: BYU Studies, 2014.

———. "Mormon Land Rights in Caldwell and Daviess Counties and the Mormon Conflict of 1838: New Findings and New Understandings." *BYU Studies* 47, no. 1 (2008): 4–55.

———. "The Kirtland Safety Society and the Fraud of Grandison Newell: A Legal Examination." *BYU Studies* 54, no. 3 (2015): 32–148.

Walker, Kyle R. "Katherine Smith Salisbury: Sister to the Prophet." *Mormon Historical Studies* 3, no. 2 (Fall 2002): 5–34.

Watkin, David. *Sir John Soane: The Royal Academy Lectures.* Cambridge: Cambridge University Press, 2000.

Webb, Eliza Jane Churchill. Letter, Lockport, NY, to Mary Bond, 24 Apr. 1876. Myron H. Bond Folder. Biographical Folder Collection (P21, fd. 11). CCLA.

Webb, Philip R. "Mystery of the Mummies: An Update on the Joseph Smith Collection." *Religious Studies Center Newsletter* 20, no. 2 (2005): 1–5.

Weinstock, Joanna Smith. "Samuel Thomson's Botanic System: Alternative Medicine in Early Nineteenth Century Vermont." *Vermont History* 56, no. 1 (Winter 1988): 5–22.

Welch, John W. "Joseph Smith's Awareness of Greek and Latin." In *Approaching Antiquity: Joseph Smith and the Ancient World,* edited by Lincoln H. Blumell, Matthew J. Grey, and Andrew H. Hedges, 303–328. Provo, UT: Religious Studies Center, Brigham Young University; Salt Lake City: Deseret Book, 2015.

Wesley, John. *A Plain Account of Christian Perfection, as Believed and Taught by the Rev. John Wesley, from the Year 1725, to the Year 1777.* New York: Lane and Scott, 1850.

Western Reserve Chronicle. Warren, OH. 1816–1854.

Whitehill, Walter Muir. *The East India Marine Society and the Peabody Museum of Salem.* Salem, MA: Peabody Museum, 1949.

Whitman, T. Stephen. "Orphans in City and Countryside in Nineteenth-Century Maryland." In *Children Bound to Labor: The Pauper Apprentice System in Early America,* edited by Ruth Wallis Herndon and John E. Murray, 52–70. Ithaca, NY: Cornell University Press, 2009.

Whitmer, History / Whitmer, John. "The Book of John Whitmer Kept by Commandment," ca. 1838–1847. CCLA.

Whitmer, John. Daybook, 1832–1878. CHL.

———. Letter, Far West, MO, to Oliver Cowdery and David Whitmer, Kirtland Mills, OH, 29 Aug. 1837. Western Americana Collection, Beinecke Rare Book and Manuscript Library, Yale University.

———. "The Book of John Whitmer." Andrew Jenson manuscript copy, ca. Sept. 1893. In Andrew Jenson, Collection, ca. 1841–1942. CHL.

———. "The Book of John Whitmer." Microfilm, Oct. 1974. Research Library and Archives, Reorganized Church of Jesus Christ of Latter Day Saints, Independence, MO. Copy at CHL.

Whitney, Newel K. Papers, 1825–1906. BYU.

Whorton, James C. *Nature Cures: The History of Alternative Medicine in America*. New York: Oxford University Press, 2002.

Williams, Edwin. *The New-York Annual Register for the Year of Our Lord 1834. Containing an Almanac, Civil and Judicial List; with Political, Statistical and Other Information, respecting the State of New-York and the United States*. New York: By the author, 1834.

Williams, Frederick G. Account Book, 1837–1842. CHL.

———. Papers, 1834–1842. CHL.

———. *The Life of Dr. Frederick G. Williams: Counselor to the Prophet Joseph Smith*. Provo, UT: BYU Studies, 2012.

Wilson, Anderson, and Emelia Wilson. Letter, Clay Co., MO, to Samuel Turrentine, Orange Co., NC, 4 July 1836, Wilson Family Papers, Southern Historical Collection, Louis Round Wilson Special Collections Library, University of North Carolina, Chapel Hill. Also available in Durward T. Stokes, ed., "The Wilson Letters, 1835–1849," *Missouri Historical Review* 60, no. 4 (July 1966): 496–517.

Wilson Family Papers, 1835–1849. Southern Historical Collection, Louis Round Wilson Special Collections Library, University of North Carolina, Chapel Hill.

Winchester, Benjamin. *Plain Facts, Shewing the Origin of the Spaulding Story, concerning the Manuscript Found, and Its Being Transformed into the Book of Mormon; with a Short History of Dr. P. Hulbert, the Author of the Said Story . . . Re-published by George J. Adams, Minister of the Gospel, Bedford, England. To Which Is Added, a Letter from Elder S. Rigdon, Also, One from Elder O. Hyde, on the Above Subject*. Bedford, England: C. B. Merry, 1841.

Winegar, Alvin. Papers, 1841–1906. CHL.

Wolfe, S. J. With Robert Singerman. *Mummies in Nineteenth Century America: Ancient Egyptians as Artifacts*. Jefferson, NC: McFarland, 2009.

Woman's Exponent. Salt Lake City. 1872–1914.

Wood, Daniel. "A Letter to Daniel Wood's Brother Hosea Wood." No date. Typescript. Daniel Wood, Histories, ca. 1890. CHL.

Woodruff, Wilford. Journals, 1833–1898. Wilford Woodruff, Journals and Papers, 1828–1898. CHL. Also available as *Wilford Woodruff's Journals, 1833–1898*, edited by Scott G. Kenney, 9 vols. (Midvale, UT: Signature Books, 1983–1985).

———. Journals and Papers, 1828–1898. CHL.

———. *Leaves from My Journal, Third Book of the Faith-Promoting Series.* Salt Lake City: Juvenile Instructor Office, 1882.

Wyatt-Brown, Bertram. "The Abolitionists' Postal Campaign of 1835." *Journal of Negro History* 50, no. 4 (Oct. 1965): 227–238.

———. *Honor and Violence in the Old South.* New York: Oxford University Press, 1986.

Yorgason, Laurence Milton. "Some Demographic Aspects of One Hundred Early Mormon Converts, 1830–1837." Master's thesis, Brigham Young University, 1974.

Young, Brigham. Account Book, 1836–1837, 1841–1846. CHL.

———. Journal, 1837–1845. Brigham Young Office Files, 1832–1878. CHL.

Young, Emily Dow Partridge. "What I Remember," 1884. Typescript. CHL.

Young, Joseph. *History of the Organization of the Seventies. Names of the First and Second Quorums. Items in Relation to the First Presidency of the Seventies. Also, a Brief Glance at Enoch and His City. Embellished with a Likeness of Joseph Smith, the Prophet, and a View of the Kirtland Temple.* Salt Lake City: Deseret News Stream Printing Establishment, 1878.

———. Letter, Salt Lake City, to Lewis Harvey, 16–18 Nov. 1880. CHL.

Zion's Advocate. Portland, ME. 1828–1920.

Zion's Watchman. New York City. 1836–1838.

Zipf, Karin. "Labor of Innocents: Parents, Children, and Apprenticeship in Nineteenth-Century North Carolina." PhD diss., University of Georgia, 2000.

Corresponding Section Numbers
in Editions of the Doctrine and Covenants

The Book of Commandments, of which a number of partial copies were printed in 1833, was superseded by the Doctrine and Covenants. Because the numbering of comparable material in the Book of Commandments and different editions of the Doctrine and Covenants varies extensively, the following table is provided to help readers refer from the version of a canonized item cited in this volume to other published versions of that same item. This table includes revelations announced by JS—plus letters, records of visions, articles, minutes, and other items, some of which were authored by other individuals—that were published in the Book of Commandments or Doctrine and Covenants in or before 1844, the year of JS's death. The table also includes material originating with JS that was first published in the Doctrine and Covenants after 1844. Such later-canonized material includes, for example, extracts of JS's 20 March 1839 letter written from the jail in Liberty, Missouri. These extracts, first canonized in 1876, are currently found in sections 121 through 123 of the Latter-day Saint edition of the Doctrine and Covenants.

The 1835 and 1844 editions of the Doctrine and Covenants included a series of lectures on the subject of faith, which constituted part 1 of the volume. Only part 2, the compilation of revelations and other items, is represented in the table. Further, the table does not include materials originating with JS that were not canonized in his lifetime and that have never been canonized by The Church of Jesus Christ of Latter-day Saints or by the Community of Christ. As only one of many examples, JS's journal entry for 3 November 1835 contains a JS revelation concerning the Twelve. This revelation has never been canonized and therefore does not appear in the table. More information about documents not listed on the table below will be provided in other volumes of *The Joseph Smith Papers* and on the Joseph Smith Papers website, josephsmithpapers.org.

Some material was significantly revised after its initial publication in the canon. For instance, the revelation in chapter 28 of the Book of Commandments included twice as much material when it was republished in the Doctrine and Covenants in 1835. As another example, chapter 65 of the Book of Commandments stops abruptly before the end of the revelation because publication of the volume was disrupted; the revelation was not published in its entirety until 1835. These and other substantial changes of greater or lesser significance are not accounted for in the table, but they will be identified in the appropriate volumes of the Documents series.

The far left column of the table gives the standard date of each item, based on careful study of original sources. The "standard date" is the date a revelation was originally dictated or recorded. If that date is ambiguous or unknown, the standard date is the best approximation of the date, based on existing evidence. The standard date provides a way to identify each item and situate it chronologically with other documents, but it cannot be assumed that every date corresponds to the day an item was first dictated or recorded. In some cases, an item was recorded without a date notation. It is also possible that a few items were first dictated on a date other than the date surviving manuscripts bear. The dates found in this table were assigned based on all available evidence, including later attempts by JS and his contemporaries to recover date, place, and circumstances.

Where surviving sources provide conflicting information about dating, editorial judgment has been exercised to select the most likely date (occasionally only an approximate month), based on the most reliable sources. In cases in which two or more items bear the same date, they have been listed in the order in which they most likely originated, and a letter of the alphabet has been appended, providing each item a unique editorial title (for example, May 1829–A or May 1829–B). Information on dating issues will accompany publication of these items in the Documents series.

The remaining five columns on the table provide the number of the chapter (in the case of the Book of Commandments) or section (in the case of editions of the Doctrine and Covenants) in which the item was published in one or more of five different canonical editions, the first three of which were initiated by JS. Full bibliographic information about these five editions is given in the list of works cited. See also the Scriptural References section in the introduction to Works Cited for more information about the origins of the Doctrine and Covenants and other Mormon scriptures.

Key to column titles

1833: Book of Commandments
1835: Doctrine and Covenants, 1835 edition, part 2
1844: Doctrine and Covenants, 1844 edition, part 2[1]
2004: Doctrine and Covenants, 2004 edition, Community of Christ[2]
2013: Doctrine and Covenants, 2013 edition, The Church of Jesus Christ of
      Latter-day Saints[3]

| | JS-Era Canon | | | | |
Date	1833	1835	1844	2004	2013
21 Sept. 1823					2[4]
July 1828	2	30	30	2	3
Feb. 1829	3	31	31	4	4
Mar. 1829	4	32	32	5	5

1. The 1844 edition of the Doctrine and Covenants included one item written after the death of JS (section 111). That item is not included in this table.

2. The 2004 Community of Christ edition of the Doctrine and Covenants includes two extracts from JS's Bible revision (sections 22 and 36) and items written after the death of JS. Neither the extracts nor the later items are included in this table.

3. The 2013 Latter-day Saint edition of the Doctrine and Covenants includes some items written after the death of JS. Those items are not included in this table. Any item for which information appears only in the "2013" column and in the "Date" column is a later-canonized JS item, as discussed in the first paragraph of the preceding introduction.

4. This section, an extract from the history JS initiated in 1838, is here dated by the date of the event described in the section rather than the date of the document's creation.

	JS-Era Canon				
Date	**1833**	**1835**	**1844**	**2004**	**2013**
Apr. 1829–A	5	8	8	6	6
Spring 1829	9	36	36	3	10
Apr. 1829–B	7	34	34	8	8
Apr. 1829–C	6	33	33	7	7
Apr. 1829–D	8	35	35	9	9
15 May 1829					13[5]
May 1829–A	10	37	37	10	11
May 1829–B	11	38	38	11	12
June 1829–A	12	39	39	12	14
June 1829–B	15	43	43	16	18
June 1829–C	13	40	40	13	15
June 1829–D	14	41	41	14	16
June 1829–E		42	42	15	17
ca. Summer 1829	16	44	44	18	19
ca. Apr. 1830	24	2	2	17	20
6 Apr. 1830	22	46	46	19	21
Apr. 1830–A	17	45:1	45:1	21:1	23:1–2
Apr. 1830–B	18	45:2	45:2	21:2	23:3
Apr. 1830–C	19	45:3	45:3	21:3	23:4
Apr. 1830–D	20	45:4	45:4	21:4	23:5
Apr. 1830–E	21	45:5	45:5	21:5	23:6–7
16 Apr. 1830	23	47	47	20	22
July 1830–A	25	9	9	23	24
July 1830–B	27	49	49	25	26
July 1830–C	26	48	48	24	25
ca. Aug. 1830	28	50	50	26	27
Sept. 1830–A	29	10	10	28	29
Sept. 1830–B	30	51	51	27	28
Sept. 1830–C	31	52:1	52:1	29:1	30:1–4
Sept. 1830–D	32	52:2	52:2	29:2	30:5–8
Sept. 1830–E	33	52:3	52:3	29:3	30:9–11
Sept. 1830–F	34	53	53	30	31
Oct. 1830–A		54	54	31	32
Oct. 1830–B	35	55	55	32	33

---

5. This section, an extract from the history JS initiated in 1838, is here dated by the date of the event described in the section rather than the date of the document's creation.

	JS-Era Canon				
Date	1833	1835	1844	2004	2013
4 Nov. 1830	36	56	56	33	34
7 Dec. 1830	37	11	11	34	35
9 Dec. 1830	38	57	57	35	36
30 Dec. 1830	39	58	58	37	37
1830		73	74	74	74
2 Jan. 1831	40	12	12	38	38
5 Jan. 1831	41	59	59	39	39
6 Jan. 1831	42	60	60	40	40
4 Feb. 1831	43	61	61	41	41
9 Feb. 1831[6]	44	13:1–19	13:1–19	42:1–19	42:1–72
Feb. 1831–A	45	14	14	43	43
Feb. 1831–B	46	62	62	44	44
23 Feb. 1831	47	13:21–23, 20	13:21–23, 20	42:21–23, 20	42:78–93, 74–77
ca. 7 Mar. 1831	48	15	15	45	45
ca. 8 Mar. 1831–A	49	16	16	46	46
ca. 8 Mar. 1831–B	50	63	63	47	47
10 Mar. 1831	51	64	64	48	48
7 May 1831	52	65	65	49	49
9 May 1831	53	17	17	50	50
20 May 1831		23	23	51	51
6 June 1831	54	66	66	52	52
8 June 1831	55	66[7]	67	53	53
10 June 1831	56	67	68	54	54
14 June 1831	57	68	69	55	55
15 June 1831	58	69	70	56	56
20 July 1831		27	27	57	57
1 Aug. 1831	59	18	18	58	58
7 Aug. 1831	60	19	19	59	59
8 Aug. 1831	61	70	71	60	60
12 Aug. 1831	62	71	72	61	61
13 Aug. 1831	63	72	73	62	62
30 Aug. 1831	64	20	20	63	63

---

6. See also the following entry for 23 Feb. 1831. In the 1835 edition of the Doctrine and Covenants, the last sentence of verse 19 (corresponding to verse 73 in the 2013 edition) was added to the revelation.

7. The second of two sections numbered 66. Numbering remains one off for subsequent sections within the 1835 edition.

	JS-Era Canon				
Date	**1833**	**1835**	**1844**	**2004**	**2013**
11 Sept. 1831	65	21	21	64	64
29 Oct. 1831		74	75	66	66
30 Oct. 1831		24	24	65	65
1 Nov. 1831–A		22	22	68	68
1 Nov. 1831–B	1	1	1	1	1
ca. 2 Nov. 1831		25	25	67	67
3 Nov. 1831		100	108	108	133
11 Nov. 1831–A		28	28	69	69
11 Nov. 1831–B[8]		3 (partial[9])	3 (partial[10])	104 (partial[11])	107 (partial[12])
12 Nov. 1831		26	26	70	70
1 Dec. 1831		90	91	71	71
4 Dec. 1831–A		89:1–2	90:1–2	72:1–2	72:1–8
4 Dec. 1831–B		89:3–4	90:3–4	72:3–4	72:9–23
4 Dec. 1831–C		89:5	90:5	72:5	72:24–26
10 Jan. 1832		29	29	73	73
25 Jan. 1832–A		87:1–3	88:1–3	75:1–3	75:1–22
25 Jan. 1832–B		87:4–5	88:4–5	75:4–5	75:23–26
16 Feb. 1832		91	92	76	76
1 Mar. 1832		75	76	77	78
7 Mar. 1832		77	78	79	80
12 Mar. 1832		76	77	78	79
15 Mar. 1832		79	80	80	81
Between ca. 4 and ca. 20 Mar. 1832					77
26 Apr. 1832		86	87	81	82
30 Apr. 1832		88	89	82	83
29 Aug. 1832		78	79	96	99
22–23 Sept. 1832		4	4	83	84
27 Nov. 1832					85
6 Dec. 1832		6	6	84	86
25 Dec. 1832					87
27 and 28 Dec. 1832		7:1–38	7:1–38	85:1–38	88:1–126
3 Jan. 1833		7:39–46	7:39–46	85:39–46	88:127–137

8. See also the following entry for ca. Apr. 1835.

9. Verses 31–33, 35–42, 44.

10. Verses 31–33, 35–42, 44.

11. Verses 31–33, 35–42, 44.

12. Verses 59–69, 71–72, 74–75, 78–87, 91–92, 99–100.

		JS-Era Canon			
Date	**1833**	**1835**	**1844**	**2004**	**2013**
27 Feb. 1833		80	81	86	89
8 Mar. 1833		84	85	87	90
9 Mar. 1833		92	93	88	91
15 Mar. 1833		93	94	89	92
6 May 1833		82	83	90	93
1 June 1833		95	96	92	95
4 June 1833		96	97	93	96
2 Aug. 1833–A		81	82	94	97
2 Aug. 1833–B		83	84	91	94
6 Aug. 1833		85	86	95	98
12 Oct. 1833		94	95	97	100
16 and 17 Dec. 1833		97	98	98	101
18–19 Feb. 1834		5	5	99	102
24 Feb. 1834			101	100	103
23 Apr. 1834		98	99	101	104
22 June 1834			102	102	105
25 Nov. 1834		99	100	103	106
Between ca. 1 Mar. and ca. 4 May 1835[13]		3	3	104	107
ca. Aug. 1835 ("Marriage")		101	109	111	
ca. Aug. 1835 ("Of Governments and Laws in General")		102	110	112	134
26 Dec. 1835					108
21 Jan. 1836					137
27 Mar. 1836					109
3 Apr. 1836					110
6 Aug. 1836					111
23 July 1837			104	105	112
Mar. 1838					113
11 Apr. 1838					114
26 Apr. 1838					115
19 May 1838					116
8 July 1838–A					118

---

13. See also the preceding entry for 11 Nov. 1831–B.

	JS-ERA CANON				
DATE	1833	1835	1844	2004	2013
8 July 1838–C[14]			107	106	119
8 July 1838–D					120
8 July 1838–E					117
20 Mar. 1839					121–123
19 Jan. 1841			[103]	107[15]	124
ca. Mar. 1841					125
9 July 1841					126
1 Sept. 1842			105	109[16]	127
7 Sept. 1842			106	110[17]	128
9 Feb. 1843					129
2 Apr. 1843					130
16–17 May 1843					131
12 July 1843					132

14. This table skips from 8 July 1838–A to 8 July 1838–C because the revelation not shown here, 8 July 1838–B, has never been canonized.

15. The 2004 Community of Christ edition provides the following note regarding this section: "Placed in the Appendix by action of the 1970 World Conference: the Appendix was subsequently removed by the 1990 World Conference."

16. The 2004 Community of Christ edition provides the following note regarding this section: "Placed in the Appendix by action of the 1970 World Conference: the Appendix was subsequently removed by the 1990 World Conference."

17. The 2004 Community of Christ edition provides the following note regarding this section: "Placed in the Appendix by action of the 1970 World Conference: the Appendix was subsequently removed by the 1990 World Conference."

Acknowledgments

This volume is made possible by the help and generosity of numerous people and institutions. We are particularly grateful to the administrators and officials of The Church of Jesus Christ of Latter-day Saints, Salt Lake City, which sponsors the project. We also express deep appreciation to the Larry H. Miller and Gail Miller Family Foundation for its continued support of the project. The foundation's generosity and encouragement have enabled us to meet an ambitious production schedule while adhering to the highest scholarly standards. In particular, we express the sincerest gratitude to Gail Miller Wilson. Her continued devotion to this work has made this and all other volumes of *The Joseph Smith Papers* possible.

The Joseph Smith Papers Project relies on the skills and dedication of employees and volunteers in the Church History Department of The Church of Jesus Christ of Latter-day Saints; on faculty, researchers, and editors at Brigham Young University; and on independent scholars and editors. Those who have assisted us include Mark Ashurst-McGee, Quinten Barney, Ronald Barney, Suzy Bills, Jeffrey G. Cannon, LaJean Purcell Carruth, Gerrit J. Dirkmaat, Sherilyn Farnes, Melissa Garrison, Matthew J. Grey, David W. Grua, Brian Hauglid, Andrew H. Hedges, Richard L. Jensen, Robin S. Jensen, Shannon Kelly, Kelley Konzak, Melissa Rehon Kotter, Caroline Larsen, Michael Hubbard MacKay, Jeffrey Mahas, Scott D. Marianno, Spencer W. McBride, Adam McLain, Kerry Muhlestein, Andrea Kay Nelson, Sharon E. Nielsen, Rachel Osborne, Amanda Owens, Alison Palmer, Keaton Reed, Alex D. Smith, Mark L. Staker, Jed Woodworth, and Zachary Zundel. We especially thank Joseph F. Darowski and Kay Darowski, who assisted with early drafts of annotation in this volume. We are grateful to Jay R. Eastley and Naoma W. Eastley, volunteers at the Church History Library, who assisted with research and preliminary drafts for the Geographical Directory; Lee Ann Clanton and Eleanor Brainard, also volunteers, who helped with document transcription; and Noel R. Barton, Brian P. Barton, and Steven Motteshard, who provided professional genealogical research services in support of the Biographical Directory. Other research used in the Biographical Directory was provided by a volunteer team headed by Paddy Spilsbury and consisting of Marlene Breti, Patsy Hendrickson, James Jacobs, Beverly Jones, Paul Simpson, Laura Tropple, Judith Wight, Nola Wilkinson, and Kathleen Williams. We express thanks for their help. We are also very appreciative of Kate Mertes, who created the index for this volume, and Carolyn Call of the Joseph Smith Papers, who skillfully typeset the volume.

We express our thanks to Glenn N. Rowe and Brandon Metcalf, Church History Department, The Church of Jesus Christ of Latter-day Saints, for their diligent assistance with the documents; to Gordon A. Madsen and Jeffrey N. Walker for help in understanding legal issues touched on in this volume; and to Welden C. Andersen of the Publishing Services Department, The Church of Jesus Christ of Latter-day Saints, who shot textual photographs. We also thank Kiersten Olson for administrative assistance and Patrick Dunshee, Ben Ellis Godfrey, and Deb Xavier for their efforts in marketing the project and the volume.

In addition, we express special thanks to Kay Darowski, Joseph Smith Papers, who oversaw a talented team of student researchers at Brigham Young University from 2003 to 2012. They include Lisse L. Brox, Kendall Buchanan, Ethan J. Christensen, Jared P. Collette, Justin Collings, Lia Suttner Collings, Christopher K. Crockett, Eric Dowdle, Vanessa Ann Dominica Dowdle, James A. Goldberg, Angella M. Hamilton, Christopher C. Jones, Cort Kirksey, Mary-Celeste Lewis, Kara Nelson, Amy Norton, Jason M. Olson, Benjamin E. Park, Daren E. Ray, Ryan W. Saltzgiver, David Harrison Smith, Kelli M. Smith, Timothy D. Speirs, Virginia E. Stratford, M. Nathaniel Tanner, Kathryn Jensen Wall, and Stephen Whitaker.

Many libraries and repositories have provided essential assistance. We sincerely thank the management and staff of the Church History Library, The Church of Jesus Christ of Latter-day Saints, Salt Lake City, where the majority of Joseph Smith's papers are located; the Family History Library, The Church of Jesus Christ of Latter-day Saints, Salt Lake City; and the L. Tom Perry Special Collections, Harold B. Lee Library, Brigham Young University, Provo, Utah. We express special thanks to the Community of Christ Library-Archives, Independence, Missouri, and to the historians and site directors of the Community of Christ; in particular, we thank Mark Scherer, Ronald E. Romig, Barbara J. Bernauer, and Lachlan MacKay. We likewise extend gratitude to the Geauga County Archives and Records Center, Chardon, Ohio, and its staff; the Southern Historical Collection in the Louis Round Wilson Library Special Collections, University of North Carolina at Chapel Hill; the Oberlin College Archives, Oberlin, Ohio; Ann Sindelar and Vicki Catozza at the Western Reserve Historical Society, Cleveland, Ohio; the Henry E. Huntington Library; the Boston Public Library; Catherine Robertson at the Philips Library, Peabody Essex Museum, Salem, Massachusetts; Christine Kull at the Monroe County Historical Museum, Monroe, Michigan; and the National Archives and Records Administration, Washington DC. Finally, we are indebted to and extend our most sincere appreciation to Nan Lee, president of the North Haven Historical Society, North Haven, Maine, for opening up the archives there and pointing us to important sources used in researching this volume. Nan, along with Hope Richins Quicksage, generously took the time to show us around the island, giving us a tour of the places that Wilford Woodruff and Jonathan Hale visited on their trip to North Haven in 1837.

Many of the maps in this volume were developed by Geographic Information Services, The Church of Jesus Christ of Latter-day Saints, under the direction of David Peart, with cartography by Blake Baker. The maps are based on historical research; the names of those who performed the research are listed alongside the maps in this volume, and we thank these individuals for their contributions.

We also thank the management and staff at Deseret Book for the professional help and advice they provided regarding the design, printing, and distribution of this volume. We especially appreciate the contributions of Sheri L. Dew, Laurel Christensen Day, Lisa Roper, Amy Durham, Richard Erickson, David Kimball, and Derk Koldewyn.

We would be remiss if we did not express the utmost gratitude to our families for their love, support, and encouragement during the development and production of this volume. Thank you to all.

Index

In addition to the documents themselves, introductory essays, annotation, and most reference material have been indexed. Most maps are not indexed; map coordinates for specific locations are given in the Geographical Directory. Spelling, punctuation, and capitalization of quotations have been standardized. Personal names are listed by their correct spellings, not by variant spellings that may be found in the documents, unless the correct spelling is unknown. Entries for married women are generally listed under the names used during the period covered by the volume, with appropriate cross-references under maiden names or other married names. Unidentified individuals, such as "Mr. Childs," are included in this index. In subentry text, Joseph Smith (JS) and Emma Smith (ES) are referred to by their initials.

When found in an entry, "id." indicates an entry in the Biographical Directory or Geographical Directory or other text that summarizes the topic, "def." refers to a passage that defines the topic, "illus." indicates a photograph or other illustration, and "handwriting of" identifies documents that an individual inscribed.

Additional Resources

The Joseph Smith Papers website, josephsmithpapers.org, offers many resources that enrich the documents presented in this volume and can aid further research. These include the following:

- High-resolution color images and searchable transcripts of documents
- Additional primary sources that help contextualize this volume, including all Book of Abraham and Egyptian-related texts, documents related to the Kirtland Safety Society, and records of land transactions in Kirtland, Ohio
- A comprehensive calendar listing all known JS documents from the time period covered in this volume, including nonextant documents, forgeries, and a comprehensive collection of the licenses, deeds, mortgages, and promissory notes from this period.
- A glossary of terms that have particular meaning in Mormon usage, defined as they were used in JS's time
- More maps, photographs, charts, and other media that contextualize the documents and events discussed herein
- A detailed chronology of JS's life
- Complete documentation for the reference material found in the back of this volume
- Finding aids that link to JS documents related to selected topics
- Updated errata for this and other volumes of *The Joseph Smith Papers*